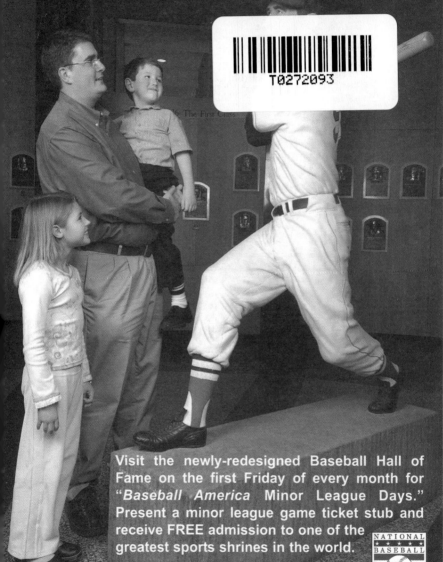

# TABLE OF
## CONTENTS

# 2006–2007
## CALENDAR

### 2006

#### March

| Sun | Mon | Tue | Wed | Thu | Fri | Sat |
|-----|-----|-----|-----|-----|-----|-----|
|     |     |     | 1   | 2   | 3   | 4   |
| 5   | 6   | 7   | 8   | 9   | 10  | 11  |
| 12  | 13  | 14  | 15  | 16  | 17  | 18  |
| 19  | 20  | 21  | 22  | 23  | 24  | 25  |
| 26  | 27  | 28  | 29  | 30  | 31  |     |

#### April

| Sun | Mon | Tue | Wed | Thu | Fri | Sat |
|-----|-----|-----|-----|-----|-----|-----|
|     |     |     |     |     |     | 1   |
| 2   | 3   | 4   | 5   | 6   | 7   | 8   |
| 9   | 10  | 11  | 12  | 13  | 14  | 15  |
| 16  | 17  | 18  | 19  | 20  | 21  | 22  |
| 23  | 24  | 25  | 26  | 27  | 28  | 29  |
| 30  |     |     |     |     |     |     |

#### May

| Sun | Mon | Tue | Wed | Thu | Fri | Sat |
|-----|-----|-----|-----|-----|-----|-----|
|     | 1   | 2   | 3   | 4   | 5   | 6   |
| 7   | 8   | 9   | 10  | 11  | 12  | 13  |
| 14  | 15  | 16  | 17  | 18  | 19  | 20  |
| 21  | 22  | 23  | 24  | 25  | 26  | 27  |
| 28  | 29  | 30  | 31  |     |     |     |

#### June

| Sun | Mon | Tue | Wed | Thu | Fri | Sat |
|-----|-----|-----|-----|-----|-----|-----|
|     |     |     |     | 1   | 2   | 3   |
| 4   | 5   | 6   | 7   | 8   | 9   | 10  |
| 11  | 12  | 13  | 14  | 15  | 16  | 17  |
| 18  | 19  | 20  | 21  | 22  | 23  | 24  |
| 25  | 26  | 27  | 28  | 29  | 30  |     |

#### July

| Sun | Mon | Tues | Wed | Thur | Fri | Sat |
|-----|-----|------|-----|------|-----|-----|
|     |     |      |     |      |     | 1   |
| 2   | 3   | 4    | 5   | 6    | 7   | 8   |
| 9   | 10  | 11   | 12  | 13   | 14  | 15  |
| 16  | 17  | 18   | 19  | 20   | 21  | 22  |
| 23  | 24  | 25   | 26  | 27   | 28  | 29  |
| 30  | 31  |      |     |      |     |     |

#### August

| Sun | Mon | Tue | Wed | Thu | Fri | Sat |
|-----|-----|-----|-----|-----|-----|-----|
|     |     | 1   | 2   | 3   | 4   | 5   |
| 6   | 7   | 8   | 9   | 10  | 11  | 12  |
| 13  | 14  | 15  | 16  | 17  | 18  | 19  |
| 20  | 21  | 22  | 23  | 24  | 25  | 26  |
| 27  | 28  | 29  | 30  | 31  |     |     |

#### September

| Sun | Mon | Tue | Wed | Thu | Fri | Sat |
|-----|-----|-----|-----|-----|-----|-----|
|     |     |     |     |     | 1   | 2   |
| 3   | 4   | 5   | 6   | 7   | 8   | 9   |
| 10  | 11  | 12  | 13  | 14  | 15  | 16  |
| 17  | 18  | 19  | 20  | 21  | 22  | 23  |
| 24  | 25  | 26  | 27  | 28  | 29  | 30  |

#### October

| Sun | Mon | Tue | Wed | Thu | Fri | Sat |
|-----|-----|-----|-----|-----|-----|-----|
| 1   | 2   | 3   | 4   | 5   | 6   | 7   |
| 8   | 9   | 10  | 11  | 12  | 13  | 14  |
| 15  | 16  | 17  | 18  | 19  | 20  | 21  |
| 22  | 23  | 24  | 25  | 26  | 27  | 28  |
| 29  | 30  | 31  |     |     |     |     |

#### November

| Sun | Mon | Tue | Wed | Thu | Fri | Sat |
|-----|-----|-----|-----|-----|-----|-----|
|     |     |     | 1   | 2   | 3   | 4   |
| 5   | 6   | 7   | 8   | 9   | 10  | 11  |
| 12  | 13  | 14  | 15  | 16  | 17  | 18  |
| 19  | 20  | 21  | 22  | 23  | 24  | 25  |
| 26  | 27  | 28  | 29  | 30  |     |     |

#### December

| Sun | Mon | Tue | Wed | Thu | Fri | Sat |
|-----|-----|-----|-----|-----|-----|-----|
|     |     |     |     |     | 1   | 2   |
| 3   | 4   | 5   | 6   | 7   | 8   | 9   |
| 10  | 11  | 12  | 13  | 14  | 15  | 16  |
| 17  | 18  | 19  | 20  | 21  | 22  | 23  |
| 24  | 25  | 26  | 27  | 28  | 29  | 30  |
| 31  |     |     |     |     |     |     |

### 2007

#### January

| Sun | Mon | Tue | Wed | Thu | Fri | Sat |
|-----|-----|-----|-----|-----|-----|-----|
|     | 1   | 2   | 3   | 4   | 5   | 6   |
| 7   | 8   | 9   | 10  | 11  | 12  | 13  |
| 14  | 15  | 16  | 17  | 18  | 19  | 20  |
| 21  | 22  | 23  | 24  | 25  | 26  | 27  |
| 28  | 29  | 30  | 31  |     |     |     |

#### February

| Sun | Mon | Tue | Wed | Thu | Fri | Sat |
|-----|-----|-----|-----|-----|-----|-----|
|     |     |     |     | 1   | 2   | 3   |
| 4   | 5   | 6   | 7   | 8   | 9   | 10  |
| 11  | 12  | 13  | 14  | 15  | 16  | 17  |
| 18  | 19  | 20  | 21  | 22  | 23  | 24  |
| 25  | 26  | 27  | 28  |     |     |     |

#### March

| Sun | Mon | Tue | Wed | Thu | Fri | Sat |
|-----|-----|-----|-----|-----|-----|-----|
|     |     |     |     | 1   | 2   | 3   |
| 4   | 5   | 6   | 7   | 8   | 9   | 10  |
| 11  | 12  | 13  | 14  | 15  | 16  | 17  |
| 18  | 19  | 20  | 21  | 22  | 23  | 24  |
| 25  | 26  | 27  | 28  | 29  | 30  | 31  |

#### April

| Sun | Mon | Tue | Wed | Thu | Fri | Sat |
|-----|-----|-----|-----|-----|-----|-----|
| 1   | 2   | 3   | 4   | 5   | 6   | 7   |
| 8   | 9   | 10  | 11  | 12  | 13  | 14  |
| 15  | 16  | 17  | 18  | 19  | 20  | 21  |
| 22  | 23  | 24  | 25  | 26  | 27  | 28  |
| 29  | 30  |     |     |     |     |     |

# Ripken Baseball Summer Camps

Each year, more than 2,000 youth baseball & softball campers from ages 7-18 will have an opportunity to learn "The Ripken Way" at our Youth Academy in Aberdeen, MD. Ripken Baseball camps provide youth players with the once-in-a-lifetime opportunity to learn the game exactly the way Cal and Bill learned from their father, Cal Ripken, Sr.

Both overnight & day camp formats are offered. Campers will improve their skills and play games on professional-quality fields modeled after famous ballparks such as Oriole Park at Camden Yards, Wrigley Field, Fenway Park & Memorial Stadium. Four skinned softball fields were added in 2005 when softball programming was introduced, and the Academy boasts a one-of-a-kind circular training infield, batting cages and a tee/soft-toss area. Bill Ripken is a frequent instructor at camps, and the Ripken Experience program features Cal, Bill & several of their former major league teammates.

# Tournaments - Aberdeen, MD and Myrtle Beach, SC

In 2003, Ripken Baseball created a series of youth tournaments; Hundreds of youth teams with thousands of players are able to play against other teams from around the country throughout the spring, summer and fall on the Academy's major league quality fields. Tournaments begin in March and run through October.

This year Ripken Baseball will have the chance to reach out to many more young baseball players with the opening of **The Ripken Experience - Myrtle Beach.** Located in one of the country's hottest vacation spots, this brand new tournament facility will combine summer vacations and tournament baseball for a one-of-a-kind family experience. Tournaments begin in June 2006 and run for 11 weeks this summer.

## Ripken Baseball also offers:
### Coaching Clinics
### Minor League Experience Fantasy Camp
### Spring & Winter Programming

## FOR MORE INFORMATION:
# www.RipkenCamps.com
# 800.486.0850

# EVENTS
## CALENDAR
### March 2006 – January 2007

## MARCH

**2**—Major league teams may renew contracts of unsigned players (through March 11).

**3**—World Baseball Classic at various sites (through March 20).

**12**—Opening Day: Korea Baseball Organization.

**21**—Opening Day: Mexican League.

**25**—Opening Day: Japan Pacific League.

**31**—Opening Day: Japan Central League.

## APRIL

**2**—Official Major League Opening Day: American League (Cleveland at Chicago); teams are required to cut rosters to 25 players by this date.

**3**—Opening Day: American League (Boston at Texas, Detroit at Kansas City, Los Angeles at Seattle, Minnesota at Toronto, New York at Oakland, Tampa Bay at Baltimore).

**3**—Opening Day: National League (Arizona at Colorado, Atlanta at Los Angeles, Chicago at Cincinnati, Florida at Houston, New York at Washington, Pittsburgh at Milwaukee, St. Louis at Philadelphia, San Diego at San Francisco).

**6**—Opening Day: International League, Pacific Coast League, Eastern League, Southern League, Texas League, California League, Carolina League, Florida State League, Midwest League, South Atlantic League.

**28**—Opening Day: Atlantic League.

## MAY

**1**—Earliest date major league clubs may re-sign free agents who were not offered arbitration.

**8**—Opening Day: Northern League.

**11**—Opening Day: American Association.

**15**—Hall of Fame Game at Cooperstown.

**16**—Opening Day: United League.

**19**—First interleague games.

**20**—Junior College Division III World Series at Glens Falls, N.Y. (through May 26).

**23**—Opening Day: Can-Am League.

**24**—Opening Day: Frontier League.

**25**—Northwest Athletic Association of Community Colleges championship tournament (through May 29)

**26**—NCAA Division III World Series at Appleton, Wis. (through May 30).

**26**—NAIA World Series at Lewiston, Idaho (through June 2).

**27**—NCAA Division II World Series at Montgomery, Ala. (through June 3).

**27**—Junior College World Series at Grand Junction, Colo. (through June 3).

**27**—Junior College Division II World Series at Millington, Tenn. (through June 2).

**27**—California Community College Commission state championship (through May 29).

**30**—Start of closed period for draft.

PNC Park, site of the 2006 All-Star Game in Pittsburgh

**30**—Opening Day: Southern Collegiate League.

**31**—Opening Day: Coastal Plain League.

## JUNE

**1**—Opening Day: Atlantic Collegiate League, California Collegiate League, Northwoods League, Pacific International League.

**1**—Opening Day: Golden League.

**2**—Opening Day: Clark Griffith Collegiate League, Mountain Collegiate League, Valley League.

**2**—NCAA Division I Regionals at campus sites (through June 5).

**3**—Opening Day: Dominican Summer League, Venezuela Summer League.

**6**—Opening Day: Texas Collegiate League.

**6**—Amateur draft (through June 7).

**8**—Opening Day: Cental Illinois Collegiate League, Florida Collegiate Summer League, New England Collegiate League.

**9**—Opening Day: Alaska League, Cal Ripken Collegiate League, New York Collegiate League.

**9**—NCAA Division I Super-Regionals at campus sites (through June 12).

**10**—Opening Day: Great Lakes League, Jayhawk League.

**11**—Opening Day: Florida Collegiate Instructional League.

**15**—Opening Day: Cape Cod League, West Coast Collegiate League.

**16**—60th College World Series at Omaha (through June 25/26).

**17**—Florida State League all-star game at Lakeland, Fla.

**19**—USA Baseball junior Tournament of Stars at Joplin, Mo. (through June 26).

**20**—Opening Day: New York-Penn League, Northwest League, Pioneer League, Gulf Coast League.

**20**—Texas League all-star game at Little Rock, Ark.; Midwest League all-star game at Davenport, Iowa; South

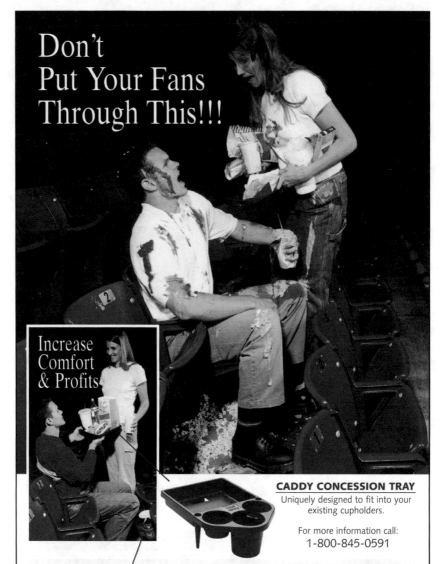

Atlantic League all-star game at Eastlake, Ohio.

**21**—Opening Day: Appalachian League.

**22**—Opening Day: Arizona League.

**23**—USA Baseball Junior Olympic Championships at Jupiter, Fla., and Peoria/Surprise, Ariz. (through July 1).

**27**—California League/Carolina League all-star game at Salem, Va.

## JULY

**9**—8th annual All-Star Futures Game at PNC Park, Pittsburgh.

**10**—Southern League all-star game at Montgomery, Ala.

**11**—77th Major League All-Star Game at PNC Park, Pittsburgh.

**12**—Triple-A all-star game at Toledo; Eastern League all-star game at Altoona, Pa.

**12**—Atlantic League all-star game at Bridgeport, Conn.; United League all-star game at Edinburg, Texas.

**17**—Golden League all-star game at Chico, Calif.

**18**—American Association/Can-Am League all-star game at El Paso, Texas; Northern League all-star game at Kansas City, Kan.

**21**—Japan All-Star Game I at Jingu Stadium, Tokyo.

**22**—Japan All-Star Game II at Sun Marine Stadium, Miyazaki.

**28**—National Baseball Congress World Series at Wichita (through Aug. 12).

**29**—Cape Cod League all-star game at South Yarmouth, Mass.

**30**—Hall of Fame induction ceremonies, Cooperstown.

**31**—Non-waiver trade deadline

## AUGUST

**1**—East Coast Professional Baseball Showcase at Wilmington, N.C. (through Aug. 4).

**4**—Connie Mack World Series at Farmington, N.M. (through Aug. 11).

**5**—Area Code Games at Long Beach (through Aug. 10).

**6**—World University Championship, Havana, Cuba (through Aug. 16).

**11**—Babe Ruth 16-18 World Series at Newark, Ohio (through Aug. 18).

**12**—Pony League World Series at Washington, Pa. (through Aug. 19).

**13**—AFLAC High School Classic at San Diego.

**17**—Canada Cup, Medicine Hat, Alberta (through Aug. 21).

**18**—Little League World Series at Williamsport, Pa. (through Aug. 27).

**18**—American Legion World Series at Cedar Rapids, Iowa. (through Aug. 22).

**18**—Babe Ruth 13-15 World Series at Clifton Park, N.Y. (through Aug. 25).

**21**—Americas Olympic Qualifier, Havana, Cuba (through Sept. 3).

**16**—New York-Penn League all-star game at Aberdeen, Md.

**31**—Postseason major league roster eligibility frozen.

## SEPTEMBER

**1**—Major league roster limits expanded from 25 to 40.

**17**—World Junior Championship, Sancti Spiritus, Cuba (through Sept. 27).

## OCTOBER

**1**—Major league season ends.

**2**—Beginning of major league trading period without waivers.

**3**—Major league Division Series begin.

**6**—Baseball America/Perfect Game 16 and under Wood Bat Championship at Fort Myers, Fla. (through Oct. 9).

**10**—League Championship Series begin.

**10**—Opening Day: Arizona Fall League.

**15**—Eligible players become minor league free agents.

**21**—Japan Series begins at home of Central League champion.

**22**—First day clubs can sign minor league free agents.

**21**—World Series begins.

**28**—Baseball America/Perfect Game World Wood Bat Championship at Jupiter, Fla. (through Oct. 31).

## NOVEMBER

**9**—Intercontinental Cup, Taiwan (through Nov. 19)

**20**—Filing date, 40-man major league winter rosters.

**30**—National High School Baseball Coaches Association convention at St. Louis. (through Dec. 3).

## DECEMBER

**4**—104th annual Winter Meetings at Orlando, Fla. (through Dec. 7).

**7**—Deadline for major league clubs to offer eligible players salary arbitration.

**7**—Rule 5 major league/minor league drafts.

**19**—Deadline for players offered arbitration to accept.

**20**—Last date for major league clubs to tender contracts.

## JANUARY 2007

**4**—American Baseball Coaches Association convention at Orlando, Fla. (through Jan. 7).

**5**—NCAA National Convention at Orlando, Fla. (through Jan. 8).

USA BASEBALL

National Training Center

Opening Spring 2007

www.usabaseball.com

TOWN OF CARY

Map illustrations by Paul Trap

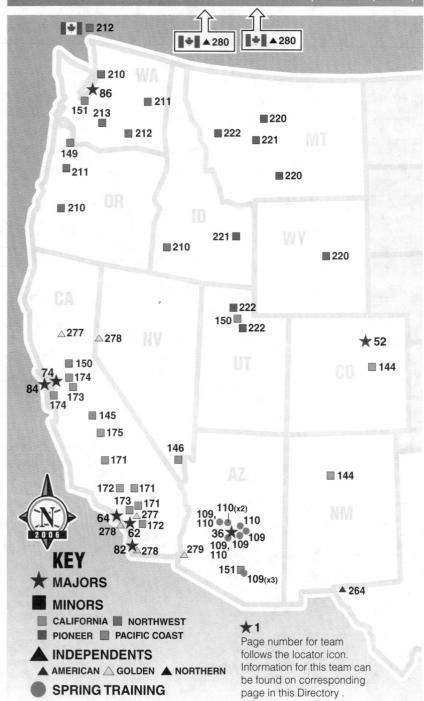

**KEY**

★ **MAJORS**

■ **MINORS**
- ■ CALIFORNIA  ■ NORTHWEST
- ■ PIONEER  ■ PACIFIC COAST

▲ **INDEPENDENTS**
- ▲ AMERICAN  △ GOLDEN  ▲ NORTHERN

● **SPRING TRAINING**

★1
Page number for team
follows the locator icon.
Information for this team can
be found on corresponding
page in this Directory .

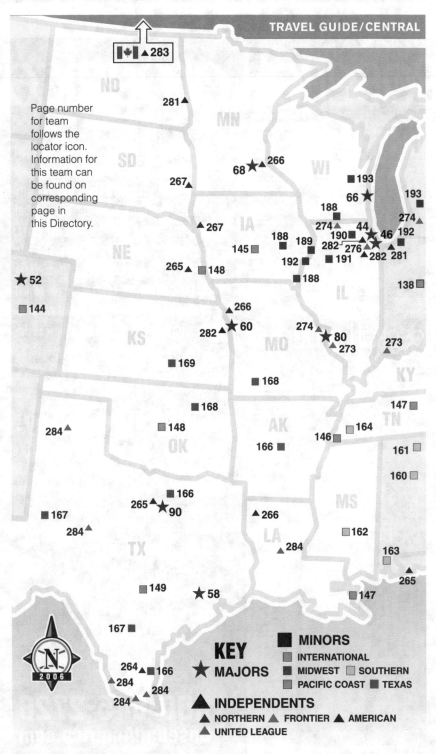

Page number for team follows the locator icon. Information for this team can be found on corresponding page in this Directory.

▲283

281▲

68 ★ ▲266

267▲

▲267

█193

66 ★

193

188

274▲

274

44 ★ 46 ▲

192

188

189

190

282

276

191

282 281

145

192

188

138

52 ★

265 ▲ █148

266 ▲

282 ▲ ★ 60

274 ▲ ★ 80

273

273 ▲

144

169 █

168 █

147 █

168 █

164

146

161

166 █

160

284 ▲

265 ▲ ★ 90

166 █

162

167 █

284 ▲

266 ▲

284 ▲

163

265 ▲

149 █

★ 58

167 █

264 ▲ █166

284 ▲

284 ▲

284 ▲

**KEY**

★ MAJORS

▲ INDEPENDENTS

- ▲ NORTHERN ▲ FRONTIER ▲ AMERICAN
- ▲ UNITED LEAGUE

█ MINORS

- █ INTERNATIONAL
- █ MIDWEST █ SOUTHERN
- █ PACIFIC COAST █ TEXAS

# 900 Player Reports

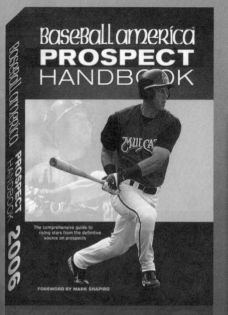

**D**iscover the 30 top prospects from each organization with the Baseball America Prospect Handbook. That's 900 player reports from the authority on prospect rating, Baseball America.

The Prospect Handbook is ideal for fantasy owners who want to win in 2006 and beyond. Remember, you'll get the scoop on established and emerging talent from all 30 teams.

The only volume of its kind, this 500-plus-page book features career statistics and analysis for each player profiled. And best of all, it can be yours for only $27.95 US (plus shipping).

# (800) 845-2726 or BaseballAmerica.com

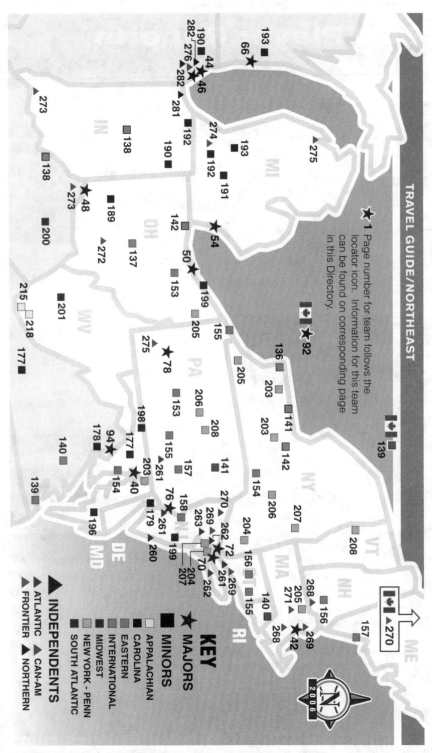

TRAVEL GUIDE/NORTHEAST

★ 1 Page number for team follows the locator icon. Information for this team can be found on corresponding page in this Directory.

**KEY**

**MAJORS**
★

**MINORS**
■ APPALACHIAN
■ CAROLINA
■ EASTERN
■ INTERNATIONAL
■ MIDWEST
■ NEW YORK - PENN
■ SOUTH ATLANTIC

**INDEPENDENTS**
▲ ATLANTIC
▲ CAN-AM
▲ FRONTIER
▲ NORTHERN

Rendering of Medlar Field at Lubrano Park in State College, Pa., a stadium that will be shared by the State College Spikes, the New York-Penn League Cardinals affiliate, and Penn State University's Big 10 team

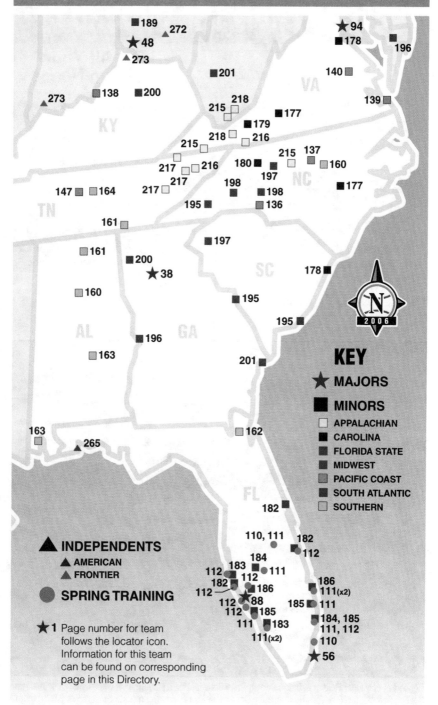

KEY

★ MAJORS

■ MINORS

☐ APPALACHIAN
■ CAROLINA
■ FLORIDA STATE
■ MIDWEST
■ PACIFIC COAST
■ SOUTH ATLANTIC
☐ SOUTHERN

▲ INDEPENDENTS
 ▲ AMERICAN
 ▲ FRONTIER

● SPRING TRAINING

★1 Page number for team
follows the locator icon.
Information for this team
can be found on corresponding
page in this Directory.

# DRIVING
## DIRECTIONS

## AMERICAN LEAGUE STADIUMS

### ANGEL STADIUM, ANAHEIM
Highway 57 (Orange Freeway) to Orangewood exit, west on Orangewood, stadium on west side of Orange Freeway.

### CAMDEN YARDS, BALTIMORE
From the north and east on I-95, take I-395 (exit 53), downtown to Russell Street; from the south or west on I-95, take exit 52 to Russell Street North.

### FENWAY PARK, BOSTON
Massachusetts Turnpike (I-90) to Prudential exit (stay left), right at first set of lights, right on Dalton Street, left on Boylston Street, right on Ipswich Street.

### U.S. CELLULAR FIELD, CHICAGO
Dan Ryan Expressway (I-90/94) to 35th Street exit.

### JACOBS FIELD, CLEVELAND
From south, I-77 North to East Ninth Street exit, to Ontario Street; From east, I-90/Route 2 west to downtown, remain on Route 2 to East Ninth Street, left to stadium.

### COMERICA PARK, DETROIT
I-75 to Grand River exit, follow service drive east to stadium, located off Woodward Avenue.

### KAUFFMAN STADIUM, KANSAS CITY
From north or south, take I-435 to stadium exits. From east or west, take I-70 to stadium exits.

### METRODOME, MINNESOTA
I-35W south to Washington Avenue exit or I-35W north to Third Street exit. I-94 East to I-35W north to Third Street exit or I-94 West to Fifth Street exit.

### YANKEE STADIUM, NEW YORK
From I-95 North, George Washington Bridge to Cross Bronx Expressway to exit 1C; Major Deegan South (I-87) to exit G (161st Street); I-87 North to 149th or 155th Streets; I-87 South to 161st Street.

### NETWORK ASSOCIATES COLISEUM, OAKLAND
From I-880, take either the 66th Avenue or Hegenberger Road exit.

### SAFECO FIELD, SEATTLE
I-5 or I-90 to Fourth Avenue South exit.

### TROPICANA FIELD, TAMPA BAY
I-275 South to St. Petersburg, exit 11, left onto Fifth Avenue, right onto 16th Street.

### AMERIQUEST FIELD IN ARLINGTON, TEXAS
From I-30, take Ballpark Way exit, south on Ballpark Way; From Route 360, take Randol Mill exit, west on Randol Mill.

### ROGERS CENTRE, TORONTO
From west, take QEW/Gardiner Expressway eastbound and exit at Spadina Avenue, north on Spadina one block, right on Bremner Boulevard. From east, take Gardiner Expressway westbound and exit at Spadina Avenue, north on Spadina one block, right on Bremner Boulevard.

## NATIONAL LEAGUE STADIUMS

### CHASE FIELD, ARIZONA
I-10 to Seventh Street exit, turn south; I-17 to Seventh Street, turn north.

### TURNER FIELD, ATLANTA
I-75/85 northbound/southbound, take exit 246 (Fulton Street); I-20 westbound, take exit 58A (Capitol Avenue); I-20 eastbound, take exit 56B (Windsor Street), right on Windsor Street, left on Fulton Street.

### WRIGLEY FIELD, CHICAGO
I-90/94 to Addison Street exit, follow Addison five miles to ballpark. One mile west of Lakeshore Drive, exit at Belmont going northbound, exit at Irving Park going southbound.

### GREAT AMERICAN BALL PARK, CINCINNATI
I-75 southbound, take Second Street exit. Ballpark is located off Second Street at Main Street. I-71 southbound, take Third Street exit, right on Broadway. I-75/I-71 northbound, take Second Street exit—far right lane on Brent Spence Bridge. Ballpark is located off Second Street at Main Street.

# The Definitive Annual

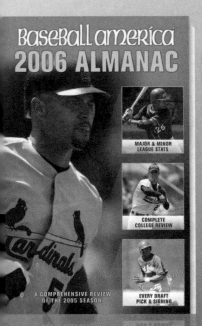

**Definitive year in review for majors, minors, college, high school, independent leagues, foreign leagues and draft**

The 2005 Almanac has all the major league news and statistics, plus so much more: complete minor league statistics, an overview of each organization's season, the minor league year in review, comprehensive college and high school coverage, a full recap of the 2004 draft and foreign and winter leagues as well as collegiate summer league coverage. You'll see lots of baseball annuals, but there's only one Baseball America Almanac. Only $18.95 regular or $21.95 spiral (plus shipping).

# (800) 845-2726 or BaseballAmerica.com

## COORS FIELD, COLORADO
I-70 to I-25 South to exit 213 (Park Avenue) or 212C (20th Street); I-25 to 20th Street, east to park.

## DOLPHINS STADIUM, FLORIDA
From south, Florida Turnpike extension to stadium exit; From north, I-95 to I-595 West to Florida Turnpike to stadium exit; From west, I-75 to I-595 to Florida Turnpike to stadium exit; From east, Highway 826 West to NW 27th Avenue, north to Dan Marino Blvd., right to stadium.

## MINUTE MAID PARK, HOUSTON
From I-10 East, take Smith Street (exit 769A), left at Texas Ave., 0.6 miles to park at corner of Texas Ave. and Crawford St.; from I-10 West, take San Jacinto St. (exit 769B), right on Fannin St., left on Texas Ave., 0.3 miles to park; From Hwy. 59 North: take Gray Ave./Pierce Ave. exit, 0.3 miles on Gray St. to Crawford St., one mile to park.

## DODGER STADIUM, LOS ANGELES
I-5 to Stadium Way exit, left on Stadium Way, right on Academy Road, left to Stadium Way to Elysian Park Avenue, left to stadium; I-110 to Dodger Stadium exit, left on Stadium Way, right on Elysian Park Avenue; US 101 to Alvarado exit, right on Sunset, left on Elysian Park Avenue.

## MILLER PARK, MILWAUKEE
From airport/south, I-94 West to Madison exit, to stadium.

## SHEA STADIUM, NEW YORK
From Bronx and Westchester, take Cross Bronx Expressway to Bronx-Whitestone Bridge, then take bridge to Whitestone Expressway to Northern Boulevard/Shea Stadium exit. From Brooklyn, take Eastbound BQE to Eastbound Grand Central Parkway. From Long Island, take either Northern State Parkway or LIE to Westbound Grand Central Parkway. From northern New Jersey, take George Washington Bridge to Cross Bronx Expressway. From Southern New Jersey, take any of bridge crossings to Verazzano Bridge, and then take either Belt Parkway or BQE to Grand Central Parkway.

## CITIZENS BANK PARK, PHILADELPHIA
From I-95 or I-76, take the Broad Street exit. The ballpark is on on the north side of Pattison Avenue, between 11th and Darien Streets.

## PNC PARK, PITTSBURGH
From south, I-279 through Fort Pitt Tunnel, make left off bridge to Fort Duquesne Bridge, cross Fort Duquesne Bridge, follow signs to PNC Park. From north, I-279 to PNC Park (exit 12, left lane), follow directions to parking.

## BUSCH STADIUM, ST. LOUIS
From Illinois, take I-55 South, I-64 West, I-70 West or US 40 West across the Mississippi River (Poplar Street Bridge) to Busch Stadium exit. In Missouri, take I-55 North, I-64 East, I-70 East, I-44 East or US 40 East to downtown St. Louis and Busch Stadium exit.

## PETCO PARK, SAN DIEGO
Four major thoroughfares feed into and out of downtown in all directions: Pacific Highway, I-5, State Route 163 and State Route 94/Martin Luther King Freeway. In addition, eight freeway on- and off-ramps service the area immediately around the ballpark.

## AT&T PARK, SAN FRANCISCO
From Peninsula/South Bay, I-280 north (or U.S. 101 north to I-280 north) to Mariposa Street exit, right on Mariposa, left on Third Street. From East Bay (Bay Bridge), I-80/Bay Bridge to Fifth Street exit, right on Fifth Street, right on Folsom Street, right on Fourth Street, continue on Fourth Street to parking lots (across bridge). From North Bay (Golden Gate Bridge), U.S. 101 south/Golden Gate Bridge to Downtown/Lombard Street exit, right on Van Ness Ave., left on Golden Gate Ave., right on Hyde Street and across Market Street to Eighth Street, left on Bryant Street, right on Fourth Street.

## RFK STADIUM, WASHINGTON
Follow I-95 South (merge with I-495 toward Virginia). Exit onto the Baltimore-Washington Parkway south toward D.C. On the B-W parkway, follow signs toward I-295. Take East Capitol St. Exit.

# TRAVEL INFO
## TOLL-FREE NUMBERS & WEBSITES

## AIRLINES

| | | |
|---|---|---|
| Aeromexico | aeromexico.com | 800-237-6639 |
| Air Canada | aircanada.com | 800-361-2159 |
| Airtran Airways | airtran.com | 800-247-8726 |
| Alaska Airlines | alaskaair.com | 800-426-0333 |
| Aloha Airlines | alohaairlines.com | 800-227-4900 |
| America West | americawest.com | 800-235-9292 |
| American Airlines | aa.com | 800-433-7300 |
| Continental Airlines | continental.com | 800-525-0280 |
| Delta Air Lines | delta.com | 800-221-1212 |
| Japan Air Lines | jal.co.jp/en/ | 800-525-3663 |
| Korean Air | koreanair.com | 800-438-5000 |
| Northwest Airlines | nwa.com | 800-225-2525 |
| Qantas Airways | qantas.com | 800-227-4500 |
| Southwest Airlines | southwest.com | 800-435-9792 |
| United Airlines | ual.com | 800-864-8331 |
| U.S. Airways | usairways.com | 800-428-4322 |

## CAR RENTALS

| | | |
|---|---|---|
| Alamo | goalamo.com | 800-732-3232 |
| Avis | avis.com | 800-331-1212 |
| Budget | budget.com | 800-527-0700 |
| Dollar | dollar.com | 800-800-4000 |
| Enterprise | enterprise.com | 800-325-8007 |
| Hertz | hertz.com | 800-654-3131 |
| National | nationalcar.com | 800-227-7368 |
| Thrifty | thrifty.com | 800-367-2277 |

## HOTELS/MOTELS

| | | |
|---|---|---|
| Best Western | bestwestern.com | 800-528-1234 |
| Choice Hotels | choicehotels.com | 800-424-6423 |
| Clarion | choicehotels.com | 800-221-2222 |
| Comfort Inn | choicehotels.com | 800-221-2222 |
| Courtyard by Marriott | marriott.com | 800-321-2211 |
| Days Inn | daysinn.com | 800-325-2525 |
| Doubletree Hotels | doubletree.com | 800-424-2900 |
| Econo Lodge | choicehotels.com | 800-424-4777 |
| Embassy Suites | embassy-suites.com | 800-362-2779 |
| Fairfield (Marriott) | fairfieldinn.com | 800-228-2800 |
| Hampton Inn | hampton-inn.com | 800-426-7866 |
| Hilton Hotels | hilton.com | 800-445-8667 |
| Holiday Inn/ | sixcontinentshotels.com | 800-465-4329 |
| Holiday Inn Express | | |
| Howard Johnson | hojo.com | 800-654-2000 |
| Hyatt Hotels | hyatt.com | 800-228-9000 |
| La Quinta | laquinta.com | 800-531-5900 |
| Marriott Hotels | marriott.com | 800-228-9290 |
| Omni Hotels | omnihotels.com | 800-843-6664 |
| Quality Inn | choicehotels.com | 800-221-2222 |
| Radisson Hotels | radisson.com | 800-333-3333 |
| Ramada Inns | ramada.com | 800-228-2828 |
| Red Lion | redlion.com | 800-547-8010 |
| Red Roof Inns | redroof.com | 800-843-7663 |
| Renaissance Hotels | renaissancehotels.com | 800-468-3571 |
| Residence Inn | marriott.com | 800-331-3131 |
| Rodeway Inn | choicehotels.com | 800-228-2000 |
| Sheraton Hotels | sheraton.com | 800-325-3535 |
| Sleep Inn | choicehotels.com | 800-221-2222 |
| Super 8 Motels | super8.com | 800-800-8000 |
| TraveLodge | travelodge.com | 800-578-7878 |
| Westin Hotels | starwood.com/westin | 800-228-3000 |
| Wyndham Hotels | wyndham.com | 800-996-3426 |

## RAIL

| | | |
|---|---|---|
| Amtrak | amtrak.com | 800-872-7245 |

# WHAT'S NEW
## IN 2006

## MAJOR LEAGUES

■ **BALLPARKS**
St. Louis: New Busch Stadium.
■ **BALLPARK NAMES**
Arizona: Bank One Ballpark becomes Chase Field.
San Francisco: SBC Park becomes AT&T Park.

## MINOR LEAGUES

### Triple-A
■ **NAME CHANGES**
Salt Lake Stingers (Pacific Coast) now known as Salt Lake Bees.

### Double-A
■ **NAME CHANGES**
Norwich Navigators (Eastern) now known as Connecticut Defenders.

### Class A
■ **NAME CHANGES**
Greenville Bombers (South Atlantic) now known as Greenville Drive.
■ **BALLPARKS**
Greenville, S.C.: Greenville Drive Stadium.

### Short-Season
■ **FRANCHISE MOVE**
New Jersey Cardinals (New York-Penn) move to become the State College Spikes.
■ **BALLPARKS**
State College, Pa.: Medlar Field at Lubrano Park.

## INDEPENDENT LEAGUES

American Association: New league forms with nine franchises formerly in Central and Northern leagues, plus new franchise in St. Joseph, Mo.

Atlantic League: Nashua franchise moves to Can-Am League; eighth franchise will operate as travel team in 2006.

Can-Am League: Nashua franchise moves from Atlantic League and new Sussex (N.J.) franchise begins play; two franchises replace league travel team and former Elmira franchise.

Central League: Ceases operations.

Frontier League: League shrinks from 12 to 10 teams, losing Mid-Missouri, Richmond and travel team and adding new Traverse City (Mich.) franchise.

Golden League: League shrinks from eight to six teams, losing Mesa, Surprise and Samurai Bears travel team and adding new franchise in Reno.

Northern League: League shrinks from 12 to eight teams with departure of Lincoln, St. Paul, Sioux City and Sioux Falls franchises to American Association.

United League begins play with six franchises in cities in Texas and Louisiana.

# BaseBall america.com

## Subscribers stay on top of their games with unique Baseball America content:

- Daily Dish
- Chats with BA editors
- Prospect Hot Sheet
- The Prospect Report delivered daily by e-mail
- Scores and stats from every minor league game
- Searchable stats for every minor league player
- Ask BA—your chance to pose questions to BA editors

## SUBSCRIBE TODAY!

**PRINT VERSION** Your print subscription includes access to premium content on BaseballAmerica.com

**WEB-ONLY VERSION** Choose the online version for all of Baseball America's content **One year Web-only $59.00**

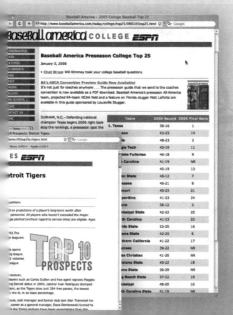

## UNPARALLELED COLLEGE COVERAGE

**Top 25 Rankings**
Every Monday

**College Weekend Preview**
Your guide to the top matchups and news from around the nation

**Defend the Rankings Chat**
Get your college questions answered

**Player & Coach Perspectives**
Features on the names shaping the college game

**College Weekend Recap**
Reviewing what happened over the weekend in the Top 25 and beyond

# BASEBALL AMERICA
## 2005 AWARD WINNERS

## MAJOR LEAGUES

**Organization of the Year**
Atlanta Braves
**Player of the Year**
Albert Pujols, 1b, Cardinals
**Executive of the Year**
Mark Shapiro, Indians
**Rookie of the Year**
Huston Street, rhp, Athletics
**Manager of the Year**
Ozzie Guillen, White Sox
**Coach of the Year**
Rudy Jaramillo, Rangers
**Roland Hemond Award (Contributions to Scouting and Player Development)**
Sandy Johnson, Mets
**Lifetime Achievement Award**
Jeff Bagwell/Craig Biggio, Astros
Tal Smith, Astros

## MINOR LEAGUES

**Player of the Year**
Delmon Young, of, Devil Rays (Montgomery/Southern, Durham/International)
**Manager of the Year**
Ken Oberkfell, Mets (Norfolk/International)
**Executive of the Year**
Jay Miller, Round Rock Express (Pacific Coast)
**Team of the Year**
Jacksonville Suns, Southern/Dodgers
**Bob Freitas Awards (Best Minor League Operations)**
Triple-A: Toledo Mud Hens (International)
Double-A: Tulsa Drillers (Texas)
Class A: Lakewood BlueClaws (South Atlantic)
Short-season: Brooklyn Cyclones (New York-Penn)
**Classification Players of the Year**
Triple-A: Francisco Liriano, lhp, Twins (Rochester/International)
Double-A: Delmon Young, of, Devil Rays (Montgomery/Southern)

**Baseball America's Minor League Player of the Year**
Devil Rays outfield prospect Delmon Young

**Baseball America's Player of the Year**
Cardinals first baseman Albert Pujols

High Class A: Brandon Wood, ss, Angels (Rancho Cucamonga/California)
Low Class A: Carlos Gonzales, of, Diamondbacks (South Bend/Midwest)
Short-season: Shane Lindsay, lhp, Rockies (Tri-City/Northwest)
Rookie: Eric Campbell, 3b, Braves (Danville/Appalachian)

## INDEPENDENT LEAGUES

**Player of the Year**
Eddie Lantigua, 3b, Quebec (Can-Am)

## WINTER LEAGUES

**2005-06 Player of the Year**
Yurendell De Caster, of, Oriente (Venezuela/Pirates)

## COLLEGES

**Player of the Year**
Alex Gordon, 3b, Nebraska
**Coach of the Year**
Rick Jones, Tulane
**Freshman of the Year**
Joe Savery, util, Rice

## AMATEUR/YOUTH LEAGUES

**Summer Player of the Year (College players)**
Andrew Miller, rhp, Chatham (Cape Cod/North Carolina)
**Youth Player of the Year (High school and younger)**
Robert Stock, rhp/c, Agoura, Calif.
**Ripken Baseball Youth Coach of the Year**
Tom Moran, Jefferson, La.

## HIGH SCHOOLS

**Player of the Year**
Justin Upton, ss, Chesapeake, Va.
**Baseball America/National High School Baseball Coaches Association Champion**
Russell County HS, Seale, Ala.

# Baseball America's
# 5th Annual Awards Gala

## Winter Meetings • Dallas • December 6, 2005

Another who's who of the baseball industry gathered as Baseball America honored 2005's winners including Lifetime Achievement Awards to long-time Astros players Jeff Bagwell and Craig Biggio and exec Tal Smith.

*Longtime executive Roland Hemond with the 2005 recipient of the Roland Hemond Award, Sandy Johnson of the Mets; Craig Biggio accepts his Lifetime Achievement Award*

*Another distinguished panel of baseball's best and brightest took home the hardware at the Baseball America Awards Gala. The Gala supported youth baseball initiatives in New Orleans.*

# BASEBALL
# INFORMATION

**■ Roster Limits**

Major league rosters may include 40 players until Opening Day, when the number must be reduced to 25. The number returns to 40 on Sept. 1. The minimum number of active players maintained by each club throughout the season is 24.

**■ Trading Regulations**

The trading deadline is July 31. Trades may be made with any other major league club in the period from the end of the season through July 31 (midnight) without waivers.

**■ Disabled Lists**

There are two disabled lists, 15-day and 60-day. Players may be disabled retroactively, up to a maximum of 10 days, beginning with the day after the last day they played. A player on the 15-day DL may be shifted to the 60-day DL at any time. Players may be assigned to a minor league club for injury rehabilitation for a maximum of 20 days (30 days for pitchers).

**15-day.** There is no limit on the number of players per club.

**60-day.** There is no limit on the number of players per club, but it may be used only when a club is at the maximum of 40 players. Players carried on this list do not count against a club's control limit of 40 players. If a player is transferred to this list after Aug. 1, he must remain through the end of the season and postseason.

**■ Options**

When a player is on a major league club's 40-man roster and in the minor leagues, he is on "optional assignment." Players have three options and may be sent up and down as many times as the club chooses within those seasons but will only be charged with one option per season. When a player is "out of options," it means he's been on a 40-man roster during at least three different seasons and in his fourth pro season or later, he will have to clear irrevocable waivers in order to be sent down.

**■ Waivers**

If a player placed on major league waivers is not claimed by another team within two business days after waivers have been requested, then the player has "cleared waivers," and the team has secured waivers for the remainder of the waiver period. The team then can do one of two things:

    1. Send him to the minors.

    2. Trade him to another team, even if the trading deadline has passed, or do nothing at all.

**Note**: Any trades involving a 40-man roster player from July 31 to the end of the season may only involve players who have cleared major league waivers. If a player does not clear waivers—he is claimed by another team or teams—the club requesting waivers may withdraw the waiver request. If the club does not withdraw the waiver request, the player's contract is assigned as follows:

    a. If only one claim is entered, the player's contract is assigned to the claiming club.

    b. If more than one club in the same league makes claims, the club currently lower in the standings gets the player.

    c. If clubs in both leagues claim the player, preference shall always go to the club in the same league as the club requesting waivers.

**■ Designated for Assignment**

This rule allows a club to open a roster spot for up to 10 days while waiting for a player to clear waivers.

**Recalled vs. Contract Purchased**

If a player is on the 40-man roster, he is "recalled." If not, then his contract is purchased from the minor league team. A player must be added to the 40-man roster when his contract is purchased.

**■ Free agency**

Six years of major league service are required to be eligible for free agency. A player has 15 days from the first day after the World Series to file for free agency.

By Dec. 7, a player's former club must offer to arbitrate or it becomes ineligible to sign the player. By Dec. 19, the player must accept the club's offer or on Jan. 9 the former club becomes ineligible to sign the player.

**Six-year free agent** (minor leagues). A player is eligible for free agency if he has played all or part of seven seasons in the major or minor leagues and is not placed on a major league team's 40-man roster as of Oct. 15.

**■ Salary Arbitration**

Three years of major league service are required for eligibility. A player with at least two years but less than three years of major league service will also be eligible if he ranks in the top 17 percent in total service in the class of players who have at least two but less than three years of major league service, however accumulated, but with at least 86 days of service accumulated during the immediately preceding season.

**■ Rule 5 Draft**

A player not on a major league 40-man roster as of Nov. 20 is eligible for the Rule 5 draft if:

    1. The player was 18 or younger when he first signed a pro contract and this is the fourth Rule 5 draft since he signed.

    2. The player was 19 or older when he first signed a pro contract and this is the third Rule 5 draft since he signed.

## ■ Consecutive Game Hitting Streak

A consecutive game hitting streak shall not be terminated if all the player's plate appearances (one or more) result in a base on balls, hit-by-pitch, defensive interference or a sacrifice bunt. The streak shall terminate if the player has a sacrifice fly and no hit.

## ■ Consecutive Games Played Streak

A consecutive games played streak shall be extended if the player plays one-half inning on defense, or if he completes a time at bat by reaching base or being put out.

## ■ Major League Service

A full year of service in the major leagues constitutes 172 days.

## ■ Rookie Qualifications

A player shall be considered a rookie if:

1. He does not have more than 130 at-bats or 50 innings pitched in the major leagues during a previous season or seasons and,

2. He has not accumulated more than 45 days on a major league roster during the 25-player limit, excluding time on the disabled list.

## ■ Save Rule

A pitcher shall be credited with a save when he meets the following three conditions:

1. He is the finishing pitcher in a game won by his club, and
2. He is not the winning pitcher, and
3. He qualifies under one of the following conditions:
   a. he enters the game with a lead of no more than three runs and pitches for at least one inning, or
   b. he enters the game with the potential tying run either on base, at bat or on deck, or
   c. he pitches effectively for at least three innings.

**Blown save.** When a relief pitcher enters a game in a save situation and departs with the save situation no longer in effect because he has given up the lead, he is charged with a blown save.

## ■ Qualifying Marks

**Batting Championship.** Major leagues—To qualify, a player must have a minimum of 502 plate appearances (3.1 plate appearances for each of the scheduled 162 games). Minor leagues—To qualify, a player must have accumulated 2.7 plate appearances for each scheduled game.

**Earned Run Average**. Major leagues—To qualify, a pitcher must have at least 162 innings pitched and have the lowest ERA. Minor leagues—To qualify, a pitcher must have pitched a number of innings at least .8 times the number of scheduled games.

**Fielding Average.** To qualify as a leader at the positions of first base, second base, third base, shortstop and outfield, a player must have appeared in a minimum of two-thirds of his team's games. For catcher, a player must have appeared in a minimum of one half of his team's games. For pitcher, the player with the highest average and the greatest number of total chances qualifies as the leader.

# HOW TO FIGURE

## ■ Batting Average

Divide the number of hits by the number of at-bats (H/AB).

## ■ Earned Run Average

Multiply the number of earned runs by nine; take that number and divide it by the number of innings pitched (ER x 9/IP).

## ■ Slugging Percentage

Divide the total bases of all safe hits by the total of times at bat. At-bats do not include walks, sacrifices, hit-by-pitches or times awarded first base because of interference or obstruction (TB/AB).

## ■ On-Base Percentage

Add the total number of hits, walks and number of times hit by pitches and divide by the total of at-bats, walks, hit-by-pitches and sacrifice flies (H+BB+HBP/AB+BB+HBP+SF).

## ■ Fielding Percentage

Divide the total number of putouts and assists by total chances—putouts, assists and errors (PO+A/PO+A+E).

## ■ Winning Percentage

Divide the number of games won by the total games won and lost (W/W+L).

## ■ Magic Number

Determine the number of games yet to be played, add one, and then subtract the number of games ahead in the loss column of the standings from the closest opponent.

# 2006 DRAFT ORDER

After having the highest draft pick in their history just a year ago, the Royals will have the first overall pick in the 2006 draft, scheduled for June 6-7. The Royals chose second last year but their .346 winning percentage—the worst in club history and the lowest mark among major league clubs by a wide margin—secured the top pick. Teams draft in the reverse order of their 2005 finish.

The order in the second half of the first round and in succeeding rounds has been adjusted for Type A and Type B free-agent signings, with the club that lost a ranked free agent gaining a draft pick as compensation. Teams that lost a Type A free agent have been further compensated with a supplemental pick between the first and second rounds.

The Nationals will reap two extra first-round picks for the loss of Type B free agents Hector Carrasco (Angels) and Esteban Loaiza (Athletics). The Braves, with two supplemental picks and two extra second-round picks, and Red Sox, with two supplemental picks and an extra third-rounder, will also come out ahead in this year's draft.

On the flip side, the Cubs will forfeit their second-, third- and fourth-round picks after signing free agents Bobby Howry, Scott Eyre and Jacque Jones. The Giants, after surrendering their first three picks a year ago, won't pick in the second or third rounds.

Here is the rotation with adjustments for this year's draft, though it is subject to change if free agent righthander Jeff Weaver signs with a club other than the Dodgers, his former team. If Weaver, a Type A free agent, signs elsewhere, the Dodgers would gain a pick from that team as well as a supplemental pick.

## FIRST ROUND

| Club | Pick From | For (Type) |
|---|---|---|
| 1. Royals | | |
| 2. Rockies | | |
| 3. Devil Rays | | |
| 4. Pirates | | |
| 5. Mariners | | |
| 6. Tigers | | |
| 7. Dodgers | | |
| 8. Reds | | |
| 9. Orioles | | |
| 10 Giants | | |
| 11. Diamondbacks | | |
| 12. Rangers | | |
| 13. Cubs | | |
| 14. Blue Jays | | |
| 15. Nationals | | |
| 16. Brewers | | |
| 17. Padres | | |
| 18. Phillies | Mets | Billy Wagner (A) |
| 19. Marlins | | |
| 20. Twins | | |
| 21. Yankees | Phillies | Tom Gordon (A) |
| 22. Nationals | Athletics | Esteban Loaiza (B) |
| 23. Astros | | |
| 24. Braves | | |
| 25. Angels | Indians | Paul Byrd (B) |
| 26. Nationals | Angels | Hector Carrasco (B) |
| 27. Red Sox | | |
| 28. Red Sox | Yankees | Johnny Damon (A) |
| 29. White Sox | | |
| 30. Cardinals | | |

## SUPPLEMENTAL FIRST ROUND

| Club | Pick From | For (Type) |
|---|---|---|
| 31. Orioles | | B.J. Ryan (A) |
| 32. Giants | | Scott Eyre (A) |
| 33. Diamondbacks | | Tim Worrell (A) |
| 34. Padres | | Ramon Hernandez (A) |
| 35. Marlins | | A.J. Burnett (A) |
| 36. Phillies | | Wagner |
| 37. Braves | | Kyle Farnsworth (A) |
| 38. Indians | | Bob Howry (A) |
| 39. Red Sox | | Damon |
| 40. Yankees | | Gordon |
| 41. Cardinals | | Matt Morris (A) |
| 42. Braves | | Rafael Furcal (A) |
| 43. Red Sox | | Bill Mueller (A) |

## SECOND-ROUND ADJUSTMENTS

| | Pick From | For |
|---|---|---|
| 50. Braves | Dodgers | Furcal |
| 52. Padres | Orioles | Hernandez |
| 53. Cardinals | Giants | Morris |
| 55. Indians | Rangers | Kevin Millwood (B) |
| 56. Indians | Cubs | Howry |
| 57. Orioles | Blue Jays | Ryan |
| 71. Braves | Yankees | Farnsworth |

## SUPPLEMENTAL SECOND ROUND

| | | |
|---|---|---|
| 74. Indians | | Scott Elarton (C) |
| 75. Cardinals | | Abraham Nunez (C) |

## THIRD-ROUND ADJUSTMENTS

| | Pick From | For |
|---|---|---|
| 82. Red Sox | Dodgers | Mueller |
| 85. Diamondbacks | Giants | Worrell |
| 88. Giants | Cubs | Eyre |
| 89. Marlins | Blue Jays | Burnett |

## FOURTH-ROUND ADJUSTMENT

| | Pick From | For |
|---|---|---|
| 118. Twins | Cubs | Jacque Jones (B) |

# The Leader in Baseball Information Management

by E Solutions Corporation

## Key Features

Bringing analysis and unrivaled access to your scouting and other player information, customized to meet your needs.

Discover what a third of MLB teams already know:

E Solutions' ScoutAdvisor™ system drastically improves the way baseball operations collect, organize and analyze critical data - downloaded securely and reliably to your PC, laptop or handheld (PDA) device.

Want to get the competitive edge other MLB teams already have?

Call 800-422-9892 or send an email to info@esnet.com.

Brought to you by

- Daily automated MLB transaction and stats updates

- Custom daily player listings, scouting reports, and game schedules

- "Super Search" that returns only relevant results

- Comprehensive medical module for trainer input and incident tracking

- Encrypted front office communications

- Major & Minor League game day reports

- Player development tracking with built-in statistical analysis

- Wireless-ready from laptop or PDA

# MAJOR
## LEAGUES

# MAJOR LEAGUE
## BASEBALL

**Mailing Address:** 245 Park Ave., New York, NY 10167.
**Telephone:** (212) 931-7800.
**Website:** www.mlb.com.
**Commissioner:** Allan H. "Bud" Selig.
**Senior Executive Assistant to Commissioner:** Kathy Dubinski. **Executive Protection Supervisor:** Earnell Lucas. **Administrative Assistant to Commissioner:** Sandy Ronback. **Supervisor, Investigations:** Tom Christopher. **Assistant to Commissioner:** Lori Keck.
**President/Chief Operating Officer:** Bob DuPuy.
**Executive VP, Administration:** John McHale. **Executive VP, Labor Relations/Human Resources:** Robert Manfred. **Executive VP, Business:** Tim Brosnan. **Executive VP, Finance:** Jonathan Mariner. **Executive Vice President, Baseball Operations:** Jimmie Lee Solomon.

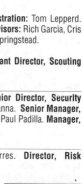

Bud Selig

## Baseball Operations

**Senior Vice President, Baseball Operations:** Joe Garagiola Jr. **VP, Baseball Operations/Administration:** Ed Burns. **Senior Director, Major League Operations:** Roy Krasik. **Manager, Baseball Operations:** Jeff Pfeifer.

**Manager, Waivers/Major League Records:** Brian Small. **Senior Manager, Minor League Operations:** Sylvia Lind. **Vice President, International Baseball Operations/Administration:** Lou Melendez. **Senior Manager, Dominican Operations:** Rafael Perez.

**VP, On-Field Operations:** Bob Watson.

**Vice President, Umpiring:** Mike Port. **Director, Umpire Administration:** Tom Lepperd. **Director, Umpire Medical Services:** Mark Letendre. **Umpiring Supervisors:** Rich Garcia, Cris Jones, Jim McKean, Steve Palermo, Frank Pulli, Rich Rieker, Marty Springstead.

**Executive Vice President, Arizona Fall League:** Steve Cobb.

**Director, Major League Scouting Bureau:** Frank Marcos. **Assistant Director, Scouting Bureau:** Rick Oliver.

## Security, Facilities

**Senior Vice President, Security/Facilities:** Kevin Hallinan. **Senior Director, Security Operations:** Dan Mullin. **Director, Security Investigations:** George Hanna. **Senior Manager, Facilities Operations:** Linda Pantell. **Manager, Security Operations:** Paul Padilla. **Manager, Investigations:** Leroy Hendricks.

Bob DuPuy

## General Administration

**Vice President, Accounting/Treasurer:** Bob Clark. **VP, Finance:** Kathleen Torres. **Director, Risk Management/Financial Reporting:** Anthony Avitable. **Manager, Payroll/Pension:** Rich Hunt.

**Senior VP/General Counsel:** Tom Ostertag. **Senior Manager, Records:** Mildred Delgado.

**Senior VP/General Counsel:** Ethan Orlinsky. **Deputy General Counsel:** Domna Candido, Jennifer Simms. **Director, Quality Control:** Peggy O'Neill-Janosik.

**VP, Information Technologies:** Julio Carbonell. **Director, Operations/Technical Support:** Peter Surhoff. **Manager, Software Development:** John Moran. **Senior Manager, Enterprise Systems:** Mike Morris.

**Executive Director, Baseball Assistance Team:** Jim Martin.

**Senior VP/General Counsel, Labor Relations:** Frank Coonelly. **Deputy General Counsel, Labor:** Jennifer Gefsky. **Director, Salary/Contract Administration:** John Abbamondi.

**VP, Strategic Planning for Recruitment/Diversity:** Wendy Lewis. **VP, Human Resources:** Ray Scott. **Director, Recruitment:** Francisco Estrada. **Senior Director, Office Services:** Donna Hoder. **Manager, Benefits/HRIS:** Diane Cuddy.

## Public Relations

Jimmie Solomon

**Telephone:** (212) 931-7878. **FAX:** (212) 949-5654.

**Senior Vice President, Public Relations:** Richard Levin. **Vice President, Public Relations Operations:** Patrick Courtney. **Senior Manager, Baseball Information:** Robert Doelger. **Manager, Marketing Communications:** Carmine Tiso. **Supervisor, Media Relations:** John Blundell. **Specialist, Media Relations:** Michael Teevan. **Specialist, Marketing Communications:** Matt Burton. **Specialist, Marketing Communications:** Paige Novack. **Coordinator, Media Relations:** Eric Schuster. **Coordinator, Marketing Communications:** Daniel Queen. **Senior Administrative Assistant:** Heather Flock. **Administrative Assistant:** Vincent Accardi. **Official Baseball Historian:** Jerome Holtzman.

## Licensing

**Senior Vice President, Licensing:** Howard Smith.

**VP, Adult Wearables/Authentics:** Steve Armus. **VP, Collectibles/Cooperstown:** Colin Hagen. **Director, Licensing/Minor Leagues:** Eliot Runyon. **Senior Manager, Apparel Retail:** Adam Blinderman. **Director, Authentics:** Dennis Nolan. **Director, Novelties/Gifts:** Maureen Mason. **Director, New Technology/New Business:** Mike Napolitano. **Director, Business Affairs:** Geary Sellers. **Director, Non-Authentics:** Greg Sim. **Senior Manager, Presence Marketing:** Robin Jaffe.

## Publishing and Photographs
**Vice President, Publishing/Photographs:** Don Hintze. **Editor, Publishing/Photographs:** Mike McCormick. **Art Director, Publications:** Faith Matorin. **Director, MLB Photographs:** Rich Pilling.

## Special Events
**Senior Vice President, Special Events:** Marla Miller. **Senior Director, Special Events:** Brian O'Gara. **Director, Special Events:** Morgan Littlefield. **Senior Manager, Special Events:** Eileen Buser. **Manager, Special Events:** Joe Fitzgerald.

## Broadcasting
**Senior Vice President, Broadcasting:** Chris Tully. **VP, Broadcast Administration/Operations:** Bernadette McDonald. **Senior Director, Distribution Development:** Susanne Hilgefort. **Manager, Broadcast Administration/Operations:** Chuck Torres.

## Community Affairs/Educational Programming
**Vice President, Community Affairs/Educational Programming:** Tom Brasuell. **Manager, Community Affairs/Educational Programs:** Jana Perry.

## Corporate Sales
**Senior VP, Corporate Sales:** John Brody. **Director, Local Sales:** Joe Grippo. **Director, Corporate Sales:** Jeremy Cohen.

## Advertising
**Senior VP, Advertising/Marketing:** Jacqueline Parkes. **Director, Marketing:** Mary Beck. **Senior Director, Marketing Research:** Dan Derian. **Manager, Marketing:** Greg Cesa. **Manager, Advertising:** Eric Cohen. **Research Manager, Advertising:** Marc Beck.
**Vice President, Design Services:** Anne Occi.

## Club Relations
**Senior VP, Scheduling/Club Relations:** Katy Feeney. **Coordinator, Scheduling/Club Relations:** Chris Tropeano. **Senior Administrative Assistant, Scheduling/Club Relations:** Raxel Concepcion.
**Senior VP, Club Relations:** Phyllis Merhige. **Coordinator, Club Relations:** David Murphy. **Senior Administrative Assistant, Club Relations:** Angelica Cintron.

## Major League Baseball Productions
**Office Address:** 75 Ninth Ave., New York, NY 10011. **Telephone:** (212) 931-7777. **FAX:** (212) 931-7788.
**Vice President/Executive Producer:** Dave Gavant.
**Senior Coordinating Producer:** David Check. **Managing Producer:** Adam Schlackman. **Director, Productions/Operations:** Shannon Valine. **Vice President, Productions Programming/Business Affairs:** Elizabeth Scott. **Manager, Videotape Library:** Frank Caputo.

## International Business Operations
**Mailing Address:** 245 Park Ave., 34th Floor, New York, NY 10167. **Telephone:** (212) 931-7500. **FAX:** (212) 949-5795.
**Senior Vice President, International Operations:** Paul Archey. **VP, International Licensing/Sponsorship:** Shawn Lawson-Cummings. **Vice President, International Broadcast Sales/U.S. Hispanic Marketing:** Italo Zanzi. **Managing Director, MLB Japan:** Jim Small. **Director, Australian Operations:** Thomas Nicholson. **Director, European Operations:** Clive Russell. **Director, Market Development/Events:** James Pearce. **Specialist, Business Development:** Dominick Balsamo. **Executive Producer, MLB International:** Russell Gabay.

## MLB Western Operations
**Office Address:** 2415 East Camelback Rd., Suite 850, Phoenix, AZ 85016.
**Telephone:** (602) 281-7300. **FAX:** (602) 281-7313.
**Vice President, Western Operations/Special Projects:** Laurel Prieb. **Office Coordinator:** Valerie Dietrich

## MLB Advanced Media (MLB.com)
**Office Address:** 75 Ninth Ave., 5th Floor, New York, NY 10011. **Telephone:** (212) 485-3444. **FAX:** (212) 485-3456.
**Chief Executive Officer:** Bob Bowman. **Vice President, Ticketing:** Heather Benz. **Senior VP, Chief Technology Officer:** Joe Choti. **Senior VP, Corporate Communications:** Jim Gallagher. **Executive VP, Commerce/Sponsorship:** Noah Garden. **Executive VP, Partnerships:** George Kliavkoff. **VP, Human Resources:** Leslie Knickerbocker. **Executive VP, Content:** Dinn Mann. **Senior VP, General Counsel:** Michael Mellis. **VP, Design:** Deck Rees. **VP, Sponsorship:** Betsy McCeney. **VP, Marketing:** Kristen Fergason.

## Umpires
Ted Barrett, Wally Bell, Joe Brinkman, C.B. Bucknor, Mark Carlson, Gary Cederstrom, Eric Cooper, Derryl Cousins, Terry Craft, Jerry Crawford, Fieldin Culbreth, Phil Cuzzi, Kerwin Danley, Gary Darling, Gerry Davis, Dana DeMuth, Laz Diaz, Mike DiMuro, Bruce Dreckman, Doug Eddings, Paul Emmel, Mike Everitt, Andy Fletcher, Marty Foster, Bruce Froemming, Greg Gibson, Brian Gorman, Angel Hernandez, John Hirschbeck, Bill Hohn, Sam Holbrook, Marvin Hudson, Dan Iassogna, Jim Joyce, Jeff Kellogg, Ron Kulpa, Jerry Layne, Alfonso Marquez, Randy Marsh, Tim McClelland, Jerry Meals, Chuck Meriwether, Bill Miller, Ed Montague, Paul Nauert, Jeff Nelson, Brian O'Nora, Larry Poncino, Tony Randazzo, Ed Rapuano, Rick Reed, Mike Reilly, Charlie Reliford, Jim Reynolds, Brian Runge, Paul Schrieber, Dale Scott, Tim Timmons, Tim Tschida, Larry Vanover, Mark Wegner, Bill Welke, Tim Welke, Hunter Wendelstedt, Joe West, Mike Winters, Jim Wolf, Larry Young.

## EVENTS
**2006 World Baseball Classic:** March 3-20.
**2006 Major League All-Star Game:** July 11 at PNC Park, Pittsburgh.
**2006 World Series:** Begins Oct. 21 at winning league in All-Star Game.

# AMERICAN LEAGUE

**Years League Active:** 1901-.
**2006 Opening Date:** April 2. **Closing Date:** Oct. 1.
**Regular Season:** 162 games.
**Division Structure: East**—Baltimore, Boston, New York, Tampa Bay, Toronto. **Central**—Chicago, Cleveland, Detroit, Kansas City, Minnesota. **West**—Anaheim, Oakland, Seattle, Texas.
   **Playoff Format:** Three division champions and second-place team with best record meet in best-of-5 Division Series. Winners meet in best-of-7 League Championship Series.
**All-Star Game:** July 11, PNC Park, Pittsburgh (American League vs. National League).
**Roster Limit:** 25, through Aug. 31 when rosters expand to 40.
**Brand of Baseball:** Rawlings.
**Statistician:** MLB Advanced Media, 75 Ninth Ave., 5th Floor, New York, NY 10011.

## STADIUM INFORMATION

| City | Stadium | Dimensions LF | CF | RF | Capacity | 2005 Att. |
|------|---------|-----|-----|-----|----------|-----------|
| Baltimore | Camden Yards | 333 | 410 | 318 | 48,876 | 2,624,804 |
| Boston | Fenway Park | 310 | 390 | 302 | 33,871 | 2,813,354 |
| Chicago | U.S. Cellular Field | 300 | 400 | 335 | 44,321 | 2,342,834 |
| Cleveland | Jacobs Field | 325 | 405 | 325 | 43,863 | 1,973,185 |
| Detroit | Comerica Park | 346 | 422 | 330 | 40,000 | 2,024,505 |
| Kansas City | Kauffman Stadium | 330 | 400 | 330 | 40,529 | 1,371,181 |
| Los Angeles | Angel Stadium | 365 | 406 | 365 | 45,050 | 3,404,686 |
| Minnesota | Humphrey Metrodome | 343 | 408 | 327 | 48,678 | 2,013,453 |
| New York | Yankee Stadium | 318 | 408 | 314 | 57,545 | 4,090,440 |
| Oakland | Network Associates Coliseum | 330 | 400 | 367 | 43,662 | 2,109,298 |
| Seattle | Safeco Field | 331 | 405 | 326 | 45,600 | 2,689,529 |
| Tampa Bay | Tropicana Field | 315 | 407 | 322 | 45,200 | 1,124,189 |
| Texas | Ameriquest Field in Arlington | 334 | 400 | 325 | 49,166 | 2,486,925 |
| Toronto | Rogers Centre | 328 | 400 | 328 | 50,516 | 1,977,949 |

# NATIONAL LEAGUE

**Years League Active:** 1876-.
**2006 Opening Date:** April 2. **Closing Date:** Oct. 1.
**Regular Season:** 162 games.
   **Division Structure: East**—Atlanta, Florida, Montreal, New York, Philadelphia. **Central**—Chicago, Cincinnati, Houston, Milwaukee, Pittsburgh, St. Louis. **West**—Arizona, Colorado, Los Angeles, San Diego, San Francisco.
   **Playoff Format:** Three division champions and second-place team with best record meet in best-of-5 Division Series. Winners meet in best-of-7 League Championship Series.
**All-Star Game:** July 11, PNC Park, Pittsburgh (American League vs. National League).
**Roster Limit:** 25, through Aug. 31 when rosters expand to 40.
**Brand of Baseball:** Rawlings.
**Statistician:** MLB Advanced Media, 75 Ninth Ave., 5th Floor, New York, NY 10011.

## STADIUM INFORMATION

| City | Stadium | Dimensions LF | CF | RF | Capacity | 2005 Att. |
|------|---------|-----|-----|-----|----------|-----------|
| Arizona | Chase Field | 330 | 407 | 334 | 48,500 | 2,059,331 |
| Atlanta | Turner Field | 335 | 401 | 330 | 50,528 | 2,521,534 |
| Chicago | Wrigley Field | 355 | 400 | 353 | 38,884 | 3,100,262 |
| Cincinnati | Great American Ball Park | 328 | 404 | 325 | 42,263 | 1,943,157 |
| Colorado | Coors Field | 347 | 415 | 350 | 50,200 | 1,915,586 |
| Florida | Dolphins Stadium | 335 | 410 | 345 | 40,585 | 1,823,388 |
| Houston | Minute Maid Park | 315 | 435 | 326 | 42,000 | 2,762,472 |
| Los Angeles | Dodger Stadium | 330 | 395 | 330 | 56,000 | 3,603,680 |
| Milwaukee | Miller Park | 315 | 402 | 315 | 53,192 | 2,211,023 |
| New York | Shea Stadium | 338 | 410 | 338 | 55,777 | 2,782,212 |
| Philadelphia | Citizens Bank Park | 329 | 401 | 330 | 43,500 | 2,665,301 |
| Pittsburgh | PNC Park | 335 | 400 | 335 | 48,044 | 1,794,237 |
| St. Louis | Busch Stadium | 336 | 400 | 335 | 46,000 | 3,491,837 |
| San Diego | PETCO Park | 334 | 398 | 322 | 42,000 | 2,832,039 |
| San Francisco | AT&T Park | 335 | 404 | 307 | 40,800 | 3,140,781 |
| Washington | RFK Stadium | 335 | 410 | 335 | 56,000 | 2,692,123 |

# ARIZONA DIAMONDBACKS

**Office Address:** Chase Field, 401 E. Jefferson St., Phoenix, AZ 85004.
**Mailing Address:** P.O. Box 2095, Phoenix, AZ 85001.
**Telephone:** (602) 462-6500. **FAX:** (602) 462-6599.
**Website:** www.diamondbacks.com.

## Ownership
**Operated by:** AZPB Limited Partnership.
**Managing General Partner:** Ken Kendrick.
**General Partners:** Mike Chipman, Dale Jensen, Jeff Moorad, Jeff Royer.

## BUSINESS OPERATIONS
**President:** Richard Dozer. **Assistant to President:** Michelle Libonati.
**Vice President and General Counsel:** Nona Lee.
**Vice President, Human Resources:** Peter Wong.

Ken Kendrick

## Finance
**Senior Vice President, Finance:** Tom Harris. **VP, Information Systems:** Bill Bolt.
**Controller:** Craig Bradley. **Executive Assistant to Senior VP, Finance/Office Manager:** Sandy Cox.

## Marketing, Sales
**Vice President, Marketing/Communications:** Derrick Hall. **VP, Broadcasting:** Scott Geyer.
**Director, Hispanic Marketing:** Richard Saenz. **Tucson Operations Manager:** Jack Donovan. **Senior Director, Marketing:** Mike Malo.

## Community Affairs
**Director, Community Affairs:** Karen Conway. **Senior Manager, Community Affairs:** Veronica Vaughn.

## Public Relations, Communications
**Telephone:** (602) 462-6519. **FAX:** (602) 462-6527.
**Director, Public Relations:** Mike Swanson. **Assistant Director, Public Relations:** Mike McNally. **Assistant to Director, Public Relations:** David Pape. **Senior Director, Publications:** Joel Horn.

## Stadium Operations
**Vice President, Chase Field Operations:** Russ Amaral. **Director, Security:** Sean Maguire. **Manager, Security:** Greg Green. **Director, Suite Services:** Diney Ransford. **Manager, Building Services:** Jim Hawkins. **Manager, Guest Services/Guest Relations:** Kurt Kleinknecht. **Director, Engineering:** Brian Wiley. **Event Coordinator:** Kevin Davis.
**Head Groundskeeper:** Grant Trenbeath.
**PA Announcer:** Unavailable. **Official Scorer:** Rodney Johnson.

## Ticketing
**Telephone:** (602) 514-8400. **FAX:** (602) 462-4141.
**Senior Vice President, Ticket Operations/Special Services:** Dianne Aguilar.
**Vice President, Sales/Group and Season Tickets:** Rob Kiese. **Director, Ticket Operations:** Darrin Mitch. **Director, Ballpark Attractions:** Charlene Vazquez-Inzunza.

## Travel, Clubhouse
**Director, Team Travel:** Roger Riley. **Visitors Clubhouse:** Bob Doty.

---

## GENERAL INFORMATION
**Stadium (year opened):** Chase Field (1998).
**Home Dugout:** Third base. **Playing Surface:** Grass.
**Team Colors:** Purple, copper and turquoise.
**Player Representative:** Craig Counsell.

Josh Byrnes

Bob Melvin

## BASEBALL OPERATIONS

**Telephone:** (602) 462-6500. **FAX:** (602) 462-6599.
**Senior Vice President, General Manager:** Josh Byrnes.
**Vice President, Special Assistant to GM:** Bob Gebhard.
**Assistant to GM:** Herta Bingham. **Assistant GM:** Peter Woodfork. **Assistant, Baseball Operations:** Shiraz Rehman.

### Major League Staff

**Manager:** Bob Melvin.
**Coaches:** Bench—Jay Bell; Pitching—Bryan Price; Batting—Mike Aldrete; First Base—Lee Tinsley; Third Base—Carlos Tosca; Bullpen—Glenn Sherlock.

### Medical, Training

**Club Physicians:** Dr. Michael Lee, Dr. Roger McCoy.
**Head Trainer:** Ken Crenshaw. **Assistant Trainer:** Dave Edwards. **Strength and Conditioning Coach:** Nate Shaw.

### Minor Leagues

**Telephone:** (602) 462-4400. **FAX:** (602) 462-6421.
**Manager, Minor League Operations:** A.J. Hinch. **Coordinator, Minor League Administration:** Susan Webner.
**Coordinators:** Dennis Lewallyn (pitching), Bob Didier (catching), Eric Fox (outfield), Rick Schu (hitting), Jack Howell (field), Tony Perezchica (infield).
**Head Trainer/Rehabilitation Coordinator:** Greg Latta. **Tucson Complex Coordinator:** Bob Bensinger. **Rehabilitation Coordinator:** Ed Vosberg. **Strength Coordinator:** Brett McCabe.

### Farm System

| Class | Farm Team | League | Manager | Coach | Pitching Coach |
|---|---|---|---|---|---|
| Triple-A | Tucson | Pacific Coast | Chip Hale | Lorenzo Bundy | Mike Parrott |
| Double-A | Tennessee | Southern | Bill Plummer | Tony Dello | Dan Carlson |
| High A | Lancaster | California | Brett Butler | Damon Mashore | Jeff Pico |
| Low A | South Bend | Midwest | Mark Haley | Todd Dunwoody | Wellington Cepeda |
| Short-season | Yakima | Northwest | Jay Gainer | Luis de los Santos | Erik Sabel |
| Rookie | Missoula | Pioneer | Hector de la Cruz | Jerry Stitt | Mel Stottlemyre Jr. |
| Rookie | Diamondbacks | Dominican | Audo Vicente | Juan Ballara | Jose Tapia |

### Scouting

**Telephone:** (602) 462-6518. **FAX:** (602) 462-6425.
**Vice President, Scouting Operations:** Mike Rizzo. **Director, Professional Scouting:** Jerry Dipoto. **Assistant Director, Scouting:** Chad MacDonald. **Scouting Assistant:** Jennifer Blatt.
**Major League Scouts:** Mack Babitt (Richmond, CA), Bill Earnhart (Point Clear, AL), Jim Marshall (Paradise Valley, AZ), Al Newman (Elko, MN), Mike Piatnik (Winter Haven, FL), Mike Sgobba (Scottsdale, AZ), Bill Singer (Osprey, FL), Paul Weaver (Phoenix).
**National Supervisor:** Kendall Carter (Scottsdale, AZ).
**Regional Supervisors:** East—Ed Durkin (Safety Harbor, FL), West—Kris Kline (Anthem, AZ), Central—Steve McAllister (Chillicothe, IL).
**Scouts:** Mark Baca (Temecula, CA), Ray Blanco (Miami, FL), Fred Costello (Livermore, CA), Trip Couch (Sugar Land, TX), Mike Daughtry (St. Charles, IL), Ed Gustafson (Spokane, WA), Matt Haas (Cincinnati), Scott Jaster (Midland, MI), Steve Kmetko (Phoenix), Hal Kurtzman (Van Nuys, CA), Greg Lonigro (Connellsville, PA), Howard McCullough (Greenville, NC), Matt Merullo (Madison, CT), Joe Robinson (St. Louis), Mike Valarezo (Cantonment, FL), Luke Wrenn (Lakeland, FL).
**Director, Latin American Operations:** Junior Noboa (Santo Domingo, Dominican Republic). **Coordinator, Mexico:** Mike Sgobba (Scottsdale, AZ). **Venezuela Supervisor:** Miguel Nava (Tampa).

Mike Rizzo

# ATLANTA BRAVES

**Office Address:** 755 Hank Aaron Dr., Atlanta, GA 30315.
**Mailing Address:** P.O. Box 4064, Atlanta, GA 30302.
**Telephone:** (404) 522-7630. **FAX:** (404) 614-1392.
**Website:** www.atlantabraves.com.

## Ownership
**Operated by:** Atlanta National Baseball Club, Inc.
**Owner:** Time Warner.
**Chairman Emeritus:** Bill Bartholomay.
**Chairman/President:** Terry McGuirk.
**Senior Vice President/Assistant to President:** Henry Aaron.

## BUSINESS OPERATIONS
**Executive Vice President, Business Operations:** Mike Plant. **Senior VP, Sales/Marketing:** Derek Schiller. **VP/Team Counsel:** John Cooper.

Terry McGuirk

## Finance
**Vice President, Controller:** Chip Moore.

## Marketing, Sales
**Director, Ticket Sales:** Paul Adams. **Director, Corporate Sales:** Jim Allen.

## Public Relations, Communications
**Telephone:** (404) 614-1556. **FAX:** (404) 614-1391.
**Senior Vice President, Public Relations/Communications:** Greg Hughes.
**Director, Public Relations:** Beth Marshall. **Director, Media Relations:** Brad Hainje. **Administrative Assistant, Media Relations:** Adrienne Midgley. **Publicists:** Adam Liberman, Meagan Swingle. **Publications Manager**: Andy Pressley. **Broadcasting/Photography Manager:** Sue Vandiver.

## Stadium Operations
**Director, Stadium Operations/Security:** Larry Bowman. **Field Director:** Ed Mangan.
**PA Announcer:** Bill Bowers. **Official Scorers:** Mark Frederickson, Mike Stamus.
**Director, Game Entertainment:** Scott Cunningham.

## Ticketing
**Telephone:** (800) 326-4000. **FAX:** (404) 614 -2480.
**Director, Ticket Operations:** Ed Newman.

## Travel, Clubhouse
**Director, Team Travel/Equipment Manager:** Bill Acree. **Visiting Clubhouse Manager:** John Holland.

---

## GENERAL INFORMATION
**Stadium (year opened):** Turner Field (1997).
**Home Dugout:** First Base. **Playing Surface:** Grass.
**Team Colors:** Red, white and blue.
**Player Representative:** Unavailable.

## BASEBALL OPERATIONS

Telephone: (404) 522-7630. **FAX:** (404) 614-3308.
**Executive Vice President, General Manager:** John Schuerholz.
**VP/Assistant GM, Player Personnel:** Frank Wren. **Assistant GM, Baseball Operations:** Dayton Moore. **Special Assistant to GM/Player Development:** Jose Martinez. **Executive Assistant:** Melissa Stone.

### Major League Staff
**Manager:** Bobby Cox.
**Coaches:** Dugout—Pat Corrales; Pitching—Roger McDowell; Batting—Terry Pendleton; First Base—Glenn Hubbard; Third Base—Fredi Gonzalez; Bullpen—Bobby Dews.

John Schuerholz

### Medical, Training
**Head Team Physician:** Dr. Norman Elliot
**Trainer:** Jeff Porter. **Assistant Trainer:** Jim Lovell. **Strength/Conditioning Coach:** Frank Fultz.

## Player Development
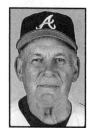

Telephone: (404) 522-7630. **FAX:** (404) 614-1350.
**Director, Baseball Operations:** Tyrone Brooks. **Director, Latin American Operations:** Marco Paddy.
**Director, Minor League Operations**: J.J. Picollo. **Administrative Assistants:** Lena Burney, Chris Rice.
**Assistant, Baseball Operations:** Matt Price.
**Field Coordinator, Instruction:** Chino Cadahia.
**Pitching Coordinator:** Bill Fischer. **Field Supervisor:** Jim Beauchamp. **Assistant Field Supervisor:** Tommy Shields. **Strength/Conditioning:** Phil Falco. **Physical Therapist:** Jeff Blum.
**Roving Instructors:** Mike Alvarez (pitching), Jack Maloof (hitting).

Bobby Cox

## Farm System

| Class | Farm Team | League | Manager | Coaches | Pitching Coach |
|---|---|---|---|---|---|
| AAA | Richmond | International | Brian Snitker | Rick Albert | Derek Botelho |
| AA | Mississippi | Southern | Jeff Blauser | Philip Wellman | Kent Willis |
| High A | Myrtle Beach | Carolina | Rocket Wheeler | Franklin Stubbs | Bruce Dal Canton |
| Low A | Rome | South Atlantic | Randy Ingle | Bobby Moore | Jim Czajkowski |
| Rookie | Danville | Appalachian | Paul Runge | Mel Roberts | Doug Henry |
| Rookie | Kissimmee | Gulf Coast | Luis Ortiz | Sixto Lezcano/Jim Saul | Derrick Lewis |
| Rookie | Braves I | Dominican | Argenis Salazar | Luis Rodriguez | Luis Alvarez |
| Rookie | Braves II | Dominican | Gabriel Luckert | Tommy Herrera | Juan Pablo Rojas |

## Scouting

Telephone: (404) 614-1359. **FAX:** (404) 614-1350.
**Director, Scouting:** Roy Clark. **Assistant, Scouting:** Dixie Keller.
**Advance Scout:** Bobby Wine (Norristown, PA).
**Special Assignment Scouts:** Dick Balderson (Englewood, CO), Tim Conroy (Monroeville, PA), Jim Fregosi (Tarpon Springs, FL), Duane Larson (Knoxville, TN), Chuck McMichael (Grapevine, TX), Bob Schaefer (Fort Myers, FL) Paul Snyder (Murphy, NC).
**Professional Scouts:** Sherard Clinkscales (Indianapolis, IN), Rod Gilbreath (Lilburn, GA), Pat Kelly (Sarasota, FL), John Stewart (Granville, NY), Bob Wadsworth (Westminster, CA).
**Crosscheckers:** Hep Cronin (Cincinnati, OH), Paul Faulk (Little River, SC), John Flannery (Austin, TX), Kurt Kemp (Vancouver, WA), Terry Tripp (Harrrisburg, IL).
**Area Supervisors:** Mike Baker (Santa Ana, CA), Daniel Bates (Phoenix, AZ), Tom Battista (Tustin, CA), Billy Best (Holly Springs, NC), Stu Cann (Bradley, IL,),) Ralph Garr (Missouri City, TX), Al Goetz (Suwanee, GA), Lonnie Goldberg (Canada), Nick Hostetler (Sacramento,

Dayton Moore

CA), Gregg Kilby (Jupiter, FL), Chris Knabenshue (Helton, TX), Robert Lucas (Atlanta, GA), Tim Moore (Elk Grove, CA), Bobby Myrick (Colonial Heights, VA), Don Thomas (Baton Rouge, LA), Terry Tripp (Carrier Mills, IL).
**Director, International Scouting:** Rene Francisco.
**International Supervisors:** Phil Dale (Victoria, Australia), Julian Perez (Dorado, PR)
**International Scouts:** Roberto Aquino (Dominican Republic), Neil Burke (Australia), Nehomar Caldera (Venezuela), Junior Carrion (Dominican Republic), Richard Castro (Venezuela), Jeremy Chou (Taiwan), Pedro Flores (Venezuela), Carlos Garcia (Colombia), Ruben Garcia (Venezuela), Duk Lee (Korea), Jose Leon (Venezuela), Luis Martinez (Venezuela), Luis Ortiz (Panama), Hiroyuki Oya (Japan), Rolando Petit (Venezuela), Manuel Samaniego (Mexico), Miguel Teran (Colombia), Marvin Throneberry (Nicaragua), Carlos Torres (Venezuela).

# BALTIMORE ORIOLES

Office Address: 333 W. Camden St., Baltimore, MD 21201.
Telephone: (410) 685-9800. FAX: (410) 547-6272.
E-Mail Address: birdmail@orioles.com. Website: www.orioles.com.

## Ownership

Operated by: The Baltimore Orioles Limited Partnership, Inc.
Chairman/Chief Executive Officer: Peter G. Angelos.

## BUSINESS OPERATIONS

Vice Chairman, Community Projects/Public Affairs: Thomas Clancy. Vice Chairman, Chief Operating Officer: Joe Foss.
Executive Vice President: John Angelos. VP/Special Liaison to Chairman: Lou Kousouris. General Legal Counsel: Russell Smouse.
Director, Human Resources: Lisa Tolson.
Director, Information Systems: James Kline.

## Finance

Vice President, Chief Financial Officer: Robert Ames. Controller: Edward Kabernagel.

Peter Angelos

## Marketing, Sales

Director, New Business Development: John Greeley. Director, Corporate Relations: Julie Wagner.

## Public Relations, Communications

Telephone: (410) 547-6150. FAX: (410) 547-6272.
Executive Director, Communications: Spiro Alafassos.
Director, Media Relations/Publications: Bill Stetka. Manager, Baseball Information: Kevin Behan. Manager, Communications: Monica Pence.
Director, Events/Programs: Kristen Schultz.

## Ballpark Operations

Director, Ballpark Operations: Roger Hayden. Manager, Event Operations: Doug Rosenberger.
Head Groundskeeper: Dave Nehila.
PA Announcer: Dave McGowan. Official Scorers: Jim Henneman, Marc Jacobsen.

## Fan, Ticket Services

Telephone: (410) 685-9800. FAX: (410) 547-6270.
Senior Director, Fan/Ticket Services: Don Grove. Assistant Director, Sales: Mark Hromalik. Ticket Manager: Audrey Brown. Systems Inventory Manager: Steve Kowalski.

## Travel, Clubhouse

Traveling Secretary: Phil Itzoe.
Equipment Manager (Home): Jim Tyler. Equipment Manager (Road): Fred Tyler. Umpires, Field Attendant: Ernie Tyler.

## GENERAL INFORMATION

Stadium (year opened): Oriole Park at Camden Yards (1992).
Home Dugout: First base. Playing Surface. Grass.
Team Colors: Orange, black and white.
Player Representative: Jay Gibbons.

## BASEBALL OPERATIONS

**Telephone:** (410) 547-6121. **FAX:** (410) 547-6271.
**Executive Vice President, Baseball Operations:** Mike Flanagan. **VP, Baseball Operations:** Jim Duquette. **Director, Baseball Administration:** Scott Proefrock. **Executive Assistant to VP, Baseball Operations:** Ann Lange.

### Major League Staff

**Manager:** Sam Perlozzo.
**Coaches:** Bench—Lee Elia; Pitching—Leo Mazzone; Batting—Terry Crowley; First Base—Dave Cash; Third Base—Tom Trebelhorn; Bullpen—Rick Dempsey.

Mike Flanagan

### Medical, Training

**Club Physician:** Dr. William Goldiner. **Club Physician, Orthopedics:** Dr. Andrew Cosgarea. **Head Athletic Trainer:** Richie Bancells. **Assistant Athletic Trainer:** Brian Ebel. **Strength/Conditioning Coach:** Tim Bishop.

### Minor Leagues

**Telephone:** (410) 547-6120. **FAX:** (410) 547-6298.
**Director, Minor League Operations:** David Stockstill. **Assistant Director, Minor League Operations:** Tripp Norton. **Assistant, Minor League Operations:** Kevin Ibach.
**Field/Hitting Coordinator:** Julio Vinas. **Pitching Coordinator:** Doc Watson. **Medical Coordinator:** Dave Walker. **Strength/Conditioning Coach:** Jay Shiner. **Facilities Coordinator:** Jaime Rodriguez. **Camp Coordinator:** Len Johnston.
**Roving Instructors:** Moe Drabowsky (rehab pitching), Andy Etchebarren (catching), Butch Davis (outfield/bunting), Tom Lawless (infield/baserunnng), Denny Walling (hitting).

Sam Perlozzo

### Farm System

| Class | Farm Team | League | Manager | Coach | Pitching Coach |
|---|---|---|---|---|---|
| Triple-A | Ottawa | International | Dave Trembley | Dallas Williams | Larry McCall |
| Double-A | Bowie | Eastern | Don Werner | Moe Hill | Scott McGregor |
| High A | Frederick | Carolina | Bien Figueroa | Alex Arias | Blaine Beatty |
| Low A | Delmarva | South Atlantic | Gary Kendall | Kimera Bartee | Kennie Steenstra |
| Short-season | Aberdeen | New York-Penn | Andy Etchebarren | Cesar Devarez | Dave Schmidt |
| Rookie | Bluefield | Appalachian | Unavailable | Unavailable | Larry Jaster |
| Rookie | Orioles | Dominican | Miguel Jabalera | Benny Adames | Robert Perez |
| Rookie | Orioles | Venezuelan | Russell Vasquez | Alcides Melendez | Carlos Leal |

### Professional Scouting

**Telephone:** (410) 547-6121. **FAX:** (410) 547-6298.
**Assistant General Manager, Professional, Major League and Instructional Scouting:** John Stockstill.
**Advance Scout:** Deacon Jones (Sugar Land, TX).
**Professional Scouts:** Dave Engle (San Diego), Todd Frohwirth (Waukesha, WI), Dave Hollins (Orchard Park, NY), Bruce Kison (Bradenton, FL), Ted Lekas (Worcester, MA), Randy Milligan (Baltimore), Gary Roenicke (Nevada City, CA), Fred Uhlman Sr. (Baltimore).

### Amateur Scouting

**Telephone:** (410) 547-6187. **FAX:** (410) 547-6298.
**Director, Amateur Scouting:** Joe Jordan.
**Scouting Administrator:** Marcy Zerhusen.
**National Crosschecker:** Alan Marr (Sarasota, FL).
**Regional Crosscheckers:** East—Jeff Taylor (Newark, DE), Central—Deron Rombach (Arlington, TX), West—Dave Blume (Elk Grove, CA).
**Full-Time Scouts:** Dean Albany (Baltimore), Dave Dangler (Camas, WA), Ralph Garr Jr. (Houston), John Gillette (Gilbert, AZ), Troy Hoerner (Gurnee, IL), Jim Howard (Clifton Park, NY), Dave Jennings (Daphne, AL), James Keller (Sacramento, CA), Gil Kubski (Huntington Beach, CA), Rich Morales (Indianapolis), Lamar North (Rossville, GA), Nick Presto (West Palm Beach, FL), Mark Ralston (San Diego), Jim Richardson (Marlow, OK), Mike Tullier (River Ridge, LA), Dominic Viola (Raleigh, NC).
**Director, Latin American Scouting:** Carlos Bernhardt (San Pedro de Macoris, Dominican Republic). **Supervisor, Central/South America, Lesser Antilles:** Jesus Halabi (Aruba).
**International Scouts:** Ubaldo Heredia (Venezuela), Salvador Ramirez (Dominican Republic), Arturo Sanchez (Venezuela).

Joe Jordan

# BOSTON RED SOX

**Office Address:** Fenway Park, 4 Yawkey Way, Boston, MA 02215.
**Telephone:** (617) 226-6000. **FAX:** (617) 226-6416.
**Website:** www.redsox.com.

## Ownership

**Principal Owner:** John Henry. **Chairman:** Tom Werner. **Vice Chairmen:** David Ginsberg, Phillip Morse, Leslie Otten.
**President/Chief Executive Officer:** Larry Lucchino.
**Director:** George Mitchell. **Chief Legal Officer, New England Sports Ventures:** Lucinda Treat.

## BUSINESS OPERATIONS

Larry Lucchino

**Chief Operating Officer:** Mike Dee. **Executive Vice President, Public Affairs:** Dr. Charles Steinberg. **Senior VP, Fenway Affairs:** Larry Cancro. **Senior VP, Corporate Relations:** Meg Vaillancourt. **Vice President:** Joe McDermott.
**VP, Business Operations:** Jonathan Gilula. **Financial/Business Analyst:** Tim Zue.
**Senior Adviser, Baseball Projects:** Jeremy Klapstein. **Senior Strategic Planning Adviser:** Michael Porter.
**VP, Club Counsel:** Elaine Steward. **Staff Counsel:** Jennifer Flynn. **Law Clerk:** Laura O'Neill.

## Finance

**Vice President, Chief Financial Officer:** Bob Furbush. **Director, Finance:** Ryan Oremus. **Central Purchasing Administrator:** Eileen Murphy-Tagrin. **Payroll Administrator:** Diane Sutty. **Assistant Controller:** Robin Willis. **Staff Accountant:** Cathy Fahy. **Accountants:** Kim Birn, Lou Stathis, Tina Young.
**VP, Finance/Human Resources:** Steve Fitch. **Director, Human Resources/Office Administration:** Michele Julian. **Director, Information Technology:** Steve Conley. **Senior Systems Analyst:** Randy George.

## Sales, Corporate Marketing

**Senior Vice President, Sales/Marketing:** Sam Kennedy. **Director, Corporate Partnerships:** Joe Januszewski. **Director, Client Services:** Troup Parkinson. **Senior Manager, Season/Group Sales:** Corey Bowdre. **Manager, .406 Club/VIP Services:** Carole Alkins. **Manager, Premium Seating Sales:** Stephanie Nelson.

## Media, Community Relations

**Vice President, Media Relations:** Glenn Geffner. **Manager, Media Relations:** Kerri Moore. **Media Relations Coordinator:** Peter Chase. **Coordinator, Credentials/Alumni/Archives:** Pam Ganley.
**VP, Publications/Archives:** Dick Bresciani. **Executive Consultant:** Lou Gorman. **Director, Publications:** Debbie Matson. **Manager, Publications/Archives:** Rod Oreste. **Staff Photographer:** Julie Cordeiro.
**Director, Community Relations:** Vanessa Leyvas. **Manager, Community Athletic Programs:** Ron Burton. **Manager, Community Relations:** Sarah Stevenson. **Director, Fan/Neighborhood Services:** Sarah McKenna.
**Director, Advertising/Television/Video Production:** Tom Catlin. **Manager, Television Production:** John Carter. **Manager, Video/Scoreboard Production:** Sarah Logan. **Advertising Coordinator:** Megan Kaiser.
**VP, Fenway Enterprises/Broadcast Services:** Chuck Steedman. **Manager, Fenway Park Enterprises:** Marcita Thompson. **Fenway Enterprises Assistants:** Colin Burch, Peter Pachios.

## Stadium Operations

**Senior Vice President, Planning/Development:** Janet Marie Smith. **Manager, Planning/Development:** Paul Hanlon. **Director, Security/Emergency Services:** Charles Cellucci. **Director, Facilities Management:** Tom Queenan.
**Director, Event Operations:** Jeff Goldenberg. **Manager, Event Operations:** Dan Lyons. **Director Emeritus, Grounds:** Joe Mooney. **Director, Grounds:** Dave Mellor.
**PA Announcer:** Carl Beane. **Official Scorers:** Charles Scoggins, Joe Guiliotti.

## Ticket Services, Operations

**Telephone:** (617) 482-4769, (877) REDSOX-9. **FAX:** (617) 226-6640.
**Director, Ticket Operations:** Richard Beaton. **Senior Manager, Season Ticket Services:** Joe Matthews. **Manager, Ticket Services:** Marcell Saporita. **Manager, Ticket Accounting/Administration:** Sean Carragher. **Senior Adviser, Ticketing:** Rob Bumgarner. **Ticket Service Coordinators:** Naomi Calder, Sandi Quinn.

## Travel, Clubhouse

**Traveling Secretary:** Jack McCormick. **Administrative Assistant:** Jean MacDougall. **Equipment Manager/Clubhouse Operations:** Joe Cochran. **Assistant Equipment Manager:** Pookie Jackson. **Visiting Clubhouse Manager:** Tom McLaughlin. **Video/Advance Scouting Coordinator:** Billy Broadbent.

---

## GENERAL INFORMATION

**Stadium (year opened):** Fenway Park (1912).
**Home Dugout:** First Base. **Playing Surface:** Grass.
**Team Colors:** Navy blue, red and white.
**Player Representative:** Unavailable.

Theo Epstein

## BASEBALL OPERATIONS
**Telephone:** (617) 226-6000. **FAX:** (617) 226-6695.
**Executive Vice President, General Manager:** Theo Epstein. **Assistant GM:** Jed Hoyer.
**Vice President, Player Personnel:** Ben Cherington. **VP, International Scouting/Special Assistant to GM:** Craig Shipley. **Special Adviser, Baseball Operations:** Bill Lajoie. **Senior Adviser, Baseball Operations:** Bill James. **Director, Baseball Operations:** Brian O'Halloran. **Assistant Director, Baseball Operations:** Zack Scott.

### Major League Staff
**Manager:** Terry Francona.
**Coaches:** Bench—Brad Mills; Pitching—Dave Wallace; Batting—Ron Jackson; First Base— Bill Haselman; Third Base—DeMarlo Hale; Bullpen—Al Nipper.

### Medical, Training
**Medical Director:** Dr. Th...
**Head Trai...
**Performance ...                                                    ...ach: Dave Page. **Director,

### Player Deve...
**Telephone:**
**Director, ...
Ferreira. **Assis...
**Player Dev...
Harper, Felix M...
**Coordinator...
Mike Stelmach...
**Field Coordi...
**Roving Inst...
Frazier (outfield,...
(Latin America f...
**Associate M...
**Athletic Trainin...
**Coordinator:** Jo...

*[handwritten notes:]*
Jon Dienstag
BoSox
617 226 6332
Special Projects
Coordinator

Terry Francona

### Farm System

| Class | F... | | | | Pitching Coach |
|---|---|---|---|---|---|
| Triple-A | P... | | | | Mike Griffin |
| Double-A | P... | | | | Ace Adams |
| High A | W... | | | | Mike Cather |
| Low A | Gree... | | | | Bob Kipper |
| Short-season | Lowell | | | | Walter Miranda |
| Rookie | Fort Myer... | | | U.L. Washington | Goose Gregson |
| Rookie | Red Sox | Dominican | Nelson Paulino | D. Reyes/ C. Hernandez | J. Gonzalez/C. Perez |

### Scouting
**Director, Scouting:** Jason McLeod.
**Assistant Scouting Director:** Amiel Sawdaye.
**Advance Scout:** Dana Levangie (Boston, MA). **Special Assignment Scout:** Marc DelPiano (Auburn, NY).
**Professional Scouts:** Galen Carr (Boston, MA), Murray Cook (Weston, FL), David Howard (Kansas City, KS), Bill Latham (Birmingham, AL), Dana Levangie (Boston, MA), Joe McDonald (Lakeland, FL), Rene Mons (Manchester, NH), Gus Quattlebaum (Long Beach, CA), Gary Rajsich (Temecula, CA), John Sanders (Atlanta, GA), Matt Sczesny (New York, NY), Jerry Stephenson (Fullerton, CA).
**National Crosschecker:** Dave Finley (San Diego, CA).
**Regional Crosscheckers:** East—Mike Rikard (Durham, NC), Midwest—Danny Haas (Louisville, KY), South—Mark Wasinger (El Paso, TX). West—Fred Peterson (Glendale, CA).

Jason McLeod

**Area Scouts:** John Booher (Vancouver, WA), Quincy Boyd (Plainfield, IL), Rob English (Duluth, GA), Ray Fagnant (East Granby, CT), Blair Henry (Roseville, CA), Ernie Jacobs (Wichita, KS), Wally Komatsubara (Aiea, HI), Brian Johnson (Tucson, AZ), Jon Lukens (Orlando, FL), Dan Madsen (Murrieta, CA), Darryl Milne (Denver, CO), Larry Owens (Louisville, KY), Jim Robinson (Arlington, TX), Anthony Turco (Tampa, FL), Danny Watkins (Tuscaloosa, AL), Jim Woodward (Claremont, CA), Jeff Zona (Mechanicsville, VA).
**Coordinator, Latin American Scouting:** John DiPuglia. **Coordinator, Pacific Rim Scouting:** Jon Deeble. **Director, Dominican Operations:** Jesus Alou. **Director, Baseball Operations, Dominican Republic:** Elvio Jimenez.

# CHICAGO CUBS

**Office Address:** Wrigley Field, 1060 W. Addison St., Chicago, IL 60613.
**Telephone:** (773) 404-2827. FAX: (773) 404-4129.
**E-Mail Address:** cubs@cubs.com.
**Website:** www.cubs.com.

## Ownership

**Operated by:** Chicago National League Ball Club, Inc. **Owner:** Tribune Company.
**Board of Directors:** Dennis Fitzsimmons, Andy MacPhail.
**President, Chief Executive Officer:** Andy MacPhail. **Special Assistant to President:** Billy Williams.

## BUSINESS OPERATIONS

**Executive Vice President, Business Operations:** Mark McGuire.
**Director, Information Systems/Special Projects:** Carl Rice. **PC Systems Analyst:** Sean True. **Information Systems Support Specialist:** Lucas Luecke. **Senior Legal Counsel/Corporate Secretary:** Crane Kenney. **Executive Secretary, Business Operations:** Gayle Finney. **Director, Human Resources:** Jenifer Surma. **Human Resources Representative:** Marisol Widmayer. **Human Resources Administrator:** Erin Harrington.

Andy MacPhail

## Finance

**Co-Controllers:** Jodi Reischl, Terri Fleischhacker. **Payroll Administrator:** Mary Jane Iorio. **Senior Accountants:** Theresa Bacholzky, Marion Greene

## Marketing, Broadcasting

**Senior Vice President, Marketing/Broadcasting:** John McDonough.
**Vice President, Community Relations/General Counsel:** Michael Lufrano.
**Director, Promotions/Advertising:** Jay Blunk. **Manager, Cubs Care/Community Relations:** Rebecca Polihronis. **Coordinator, Marketing/Community Affairs:** Mary Dosek. **Manager, Mezzanine Suites:** Louis Artiaga. **Manager, Special Events/Entertainment:** Joe Rios.

## Media Relations, Publications

**Telephone:** (773) 404-4191. **FAX:** (773) 404-4129.
**Director, Media Relations:** Sharon Pannozzo. **Manager, Media Relations:** Samantha Newby.
**Director, Publications:** Lena McDonagh. **Manager, Publications:** Jim McArdle. **Editorial Specialist, Publications:** Michael Huang. **Senior Graphic Designer:** Juan Alberto Castillo. **Graphic Design Specialist:** Joaquin Castillo. **Photographer:** Stephen Green.

## Stadium Operations

**Director, Stadium Operations:** Paul Rathje.
**Manager, Event Operations/Security:** Mike Hill. **Coordinator, Event Operations/Security:** Julius Farrell. **Head Groundskeeper:** Roger Baird. **Facility Supervisor:** Bill Scott. **Coordinator, Office Services:** Randy Skocz. **Coordinator, Stadium Operations:** Danielle Alexa. **Switchboard Operator:** Brenda Morgan.
**PA Announcers:** Paul Friedman, Wayne Messmer. **Official Scorers:** Bob Rosenberg, Don Friske.

## Ticketing

**Telephone:** (773) 404-2827. **FAX:** (773) 404-4014.
**Director, Ticket Operations:** Frank Maloney. **Assistant Director, Ticket Sales:** Brian Garza. **Assistant Director, Ticket Services:** Joe Kirchen. **Vault Room Supervisor:** Cherie Blake.

## Travel, Clubhouse

**Traveling Secretary:** Jimmy Bank.
**Home Clubhouse Manager:** Tom Hellmann. **Visiting Clubhouse Manager:** Michael Burkhart.

---

## GENERAL INFORMATION

**Stadium (year opened):** Wrigley Field (1914).
**Home Dugout:** Third base. **Playing Surface:** Grass.
**Team Colors:** Royal blue, red and white.
**Player Representative:** Mark Prior.

Jim Hendry

# BASEBALL OPERATIONS
**Telephone:** (773) 404-2827. **FAX:** (773) 404-4111.
**Vice President/General Manager:** Jim Hendry.
**Executive Assistant to President/GM:** Arlene Gill.
**Director, Baseball Operations:** Scott Nelson. **Manager, Baseball Information:** Chuck Wasserstrom.
**Special Assistants to GM:** Keith Champion (Ballwin, MO), Gary Hughes (Lantana, FL), Ken Kravec (Sarasota, FL), Ed Lynch (Scottsdale, AZ). **Scouting Consultant/Assistant to GM:** Randy Bush.

## Major League Staff
**Manager:** Dusty Baker.
**Coaches:** Dugout—Dick Pole; Pitching—Larry Rothschild; Batting—Gene Clines; First Base—Gary Matthews; Third Base—Chris Speier; Bullpen—Juan Lopez.

## Medical, Training
**Team Physicians:** Dr. Stephen Adams, Dr. Michael Schafer, Dr. Stephen Gryzlo.
**Head Trainer:** Mark O'Neal. **Assistant Trainer:** Ed Halbur. **Strength/Conditioning Coordinator:** Tim Buss.

## Player Development
**Telephone:** (773) 404-4035. **FAX:** (773) 404-4147.
**Director, Player Development/Latin American Operations:** Oneri Fleita. **Coordinator, Minor League Operations:** Patti Kargakis.
**Field Coordinator:** Dave Bialas. **Pitching Coordinator:** Lester Strode.
**Minor League Medical/Rehab Coordinator:** Justin Sharpe.
**Roving Instructors:** Vince Coleman (outfield/baserunning), Dave Keller (hitting), Buddy Bailey (catching), Nao Masamoto (strength/conditioning).

Dusty Baker

## Farm System

| Class | Farm Team | League | Manager | Coach | Pitching Coach |
|---|---|---|---|---|---|
| Triple-A | Iowa | Pacific Coast | Mike Quade | Von Joshua | Alan Dunn |
| Double-A | West Tenn | Southern | Pat Listach | Tom Beyers | Mike Anderson |
| High A | Daytona | Florida State | Don Buford | Richie Zisk | Tom Pratt |
| Low A | Peoria | Midwest | Jody Davis | Barbaro Garbey | Rich Bombard |
| Short season | Boise | Northwest | Steve McFarland | Ricardo Medina | David Rosario |
| Rookie | Mesa | Arizona | Carmelo Martinez | Antonio Grissom | Rick Tronerud |
| Rookie | Cubs | Dominican | Franklin Font | Ramon Carabello | Leo Hernandez |

## Scouting
**Telephone:** (773) 404-2827. **FAX:** (773) 404-4147.
**Director, Amateur and Professional Scouting:** Tim Wilken (Dunedin, FL). **Administrative Assistant:** Patricia Honzik.
**Advance Scout:** Brad Kelley (Phoenix).
**Major League Scout:** Bill Harford. **Professional Scouts:** Tom Bourque (Cambridge, MA), Jim Crawford (Madison, MS), Demie Manieri (South Bend, IN), Steve Hinton (Mather, CA), Joe Housey (Hollywood, FL), Mark Servais (LaCrosse, WI), Charlie Silvera (Millbrae, CA), Bob Lofrano (Woodland Hills, CA).
**Special Assignment Scouts:** Gene Handley (Huntington Beach, CA), Glen Van Proyen (Lisle, IL).
**Crosscheckers:** Mark Adair (Florissant, MO), Sam Hughes (Smyrna, GA), Scott Pleis (Tampa), Steve Riha (Houston).
**Full-Time Scouts:** John Bartsch (Rocklin, CA), Billy Blitzer (Brooklyn, NY), Trey Forkerway (Houston, TX), Steve Fuller (Brea, CA), Antonio Grissom (Red Oak, GA), Denny Henderson (Orange, CA), Steve McFarland (Scottsdale, AZ), Lukas McKnight (Westfield, NY), Brian Milner (Fort Worth, TX), Rolando Pino (Pembroke Pines, FL), Bob Rossi (Baton Rouge, LA), Tom Shafer (Olathe, KS), Keith Stohr (Viera, FL), Billy Swoope (Norfolk, VA), Stan Zielinski (Winfield, IL).
**International Scouts:** Hector Ortega (Venezuela), Jose Serra (Dominican Republic).

Tim Wilken

# CHICAGO WHITE SOX

Office Address: 333 W. 35th St., Chicago, IL 60616.
Telephone: (312) 674-1000. **FAX:** (312) 674-5116.
Website: www.whitesox.com.

## Ownership

Operated by: Chicago White Sox, Ltd.
**Chairman:** Jerry Reinsdorf. **Vice Chairman:** Eddie Einhorn.
**Board of Directors:** Fred Brzozowski, Robert Judelson, Judd Malkin, Robert Mazer, Allan Muchin, Jay Pinsky, Larry Pogofsky, Lee Stern, Sanford Takiff, Burton Ury, Charles Walsh.
**General Counsel:** Allan Muchin.
**Special Assistant to Chairman:** Dennis Gilbert. **Assistant to Chairman:** Anita Fasano.

## BUSINESS OPERATIONS

Executive Vice President: Howard Pizer.
**Senior Director, Information Services:** Don Brown.
**Senior Director, Human Resources:** Moira Foy. **Administrators, Human Resources:** Leslie Gaggiano, J.J. Krane.

Jerry Reinsdorf

### Finance

Senior Vice President, Administration/Finance: Tim Buzard. **Senior Director, Finance:** Bill Waters. **Accounting Manager:** Chris Taylor.

### Marketing, Sales

Vice President, Marketing: Brooks Boyer.
**Senior Director, Business Development/Broadcasting:** Bob Grim. **Manager, Scoreboard Operations:** Jeff Szynal. **Director, Game Operations:** Nichole Manning. **Coordinators, Game Operations:** Amy Sheridan, Dan Mielke.
**Senior Director, Corporate Partnerships:** Jim Muno. **Managers, Corporate Partnerships:** Ryan Gribble, Gail Tucker, Brad Dreher. **Coordinators, Corporate Partnerships Services:** Stephanie Johnson, Jorie Sax. **Director, Ticket Sales:** Tom Sheridan. **Manager, Premium Seating Service:** Debbie Theobald.
**Senior Director, Community Relations:** Christine O'Reilly. **Director, Mass Communications:** Amy Kress. **Manager, Design Services:** Nicole Crudo. **Senior Coordinator, Design Services:** Kyle White. **Senior Coordinator, Community Relations:** Danielle Disch. **Coordinators, Community Relations:** Andrea Voves, Dane Walkington.

### Public Relations

Telephone: (312) 674-5300. **FAX:** (312) 674-5116.
**Vice President, Communications:** Scott Reifert. **Director, Media Relations:** Bob Beghtol. **Director, Public Relations:** Katie Kirby. **Manager, Media Relations:** Pat O'Connell. **Coordinator, Public Relations:** Ryan Barry. **Coordinator, Media Services:** Vivian Jones.

### Stadium Operations

Senior Vice President, Stadium Operations: Terry Savarise. **Senior Director, Park Operations:** David Schaffer. **Senior Director, Guest Services/Diamond Suite Operations:** Julie Taylor.
**Head Groundskeeper:** Roger Bossard.
**PA Announcer:** Gene Honda. **Official Scorers:** Bob Rosenberg, Don Friske, Scott Reed.

### Ticketing

Telephone: (312) 674-1000. **FAX:** (312) 674-5102.
**Senior Director, Ticket Operations:** Bob Devoy. **Manager, Ticket Operations:** Mike Mazza. **Manager, Ticket Accounting Administration:** Ken Wisz.

### Travel, Clubhouse

Manager, Team Travel: Ed Cassin. **Home Clubhouse/Equipment Manager:** Vince Fresso. **Visiting Clubhouse:** Gabe Morell. **Umpires Clubhouse:** Joe McNamara.

---

## GENERAL INFORMATION

**Stadium (year opened):** U.S. Cellular Field (1991).
**Home Dugout:** Third base. **Playing Surface:** Grass.
**Team Colors:** Black, white and silver.
**Player Representative:** Mark Buehrle.

## BASEBALL OPERATIONS

**Senior Vice President/General Manager:** Ken Williams. **Assistant GM:** Rick Hahn. **Executive Adviser to GM:** Roland Hemond. **Special Assistants to GM:** Bill Scherrer, Dave Yoakum. **Executive Assistant to GM:** Nancy Nesnidal.
**Senior Director, Player Personnel:** Duane Shaffer. **Director, Baseball Operations Systems:** Dan Fabian. **Assistant Director, Scouting/Baseball Operations Systems:** Andrew Pinter. **Assistant, Baseball Operations:** J.J. Lally.

### Major League Staff

**Manager:** Ozzie Guillen.
**Coaches:** Bench—Harold Baines; Pitching—Don Cooper; Hitting—Greg Walker; First Base—Tim Raines; Third Base—Joey Cora; Bullpen—Art Kusnyer.

Ken Williams

### Medical, Training

**Senior Team Physician:** Dr. Charles Bush-Joseph. **Head Trainer:** Herm Schneider. **Assistant Trainer:** Brian Ball. **Director, Conditioning:** Allen Thomas.

### Player Development

**Telephone:** (312) 674-1000. **FAX:** (312) 674-5105.
**Director, Player Development:** David Wilder. **Assistant Director, Player Development:** Brian Porter.
**Director, Minor League Administration:** Grace Zwit. **Coordinator, Minor League Administration:** Kathy Potoski. **Manager, Clubhouse/Equipment:** Dan Flood.
**Roving Instructors/Coordinators:** Alan Regrer (field), Kirk Champion (pitching), Nick Capra (hitting), Daryl Boston (outfield), Manny Trillo (infield), John Orton (catching), Nate Oliver (bunting), Dale Torborg (conditioning coordinator). **Coordinator, Minor League Trainers/Rehabilitation:** Scott Takao.

Ozzie Guillen

### Farm System

| Class | Farm Team | League | Manager | Hitting Coach | Pitching Coach |
|---|---|---|---|---|---|
| Triple-A | Charlotte | International | Razor Shines | Tack Wilson | Juan Nieves |
| Double-A | Birmingham | Southern | Chris Cron | Andy Tomberlin | Richard Dotson |
| High A | Winston-Salem | Carolina | Rafael Santana | Ryan Long | J.R. Perdew |
| Low A | Kannapolis | South Atlantic | Omer Munoz | Joe Hall | Sean Snedeker |
| Rookie | Great Falls | Pioneer | Tommy Thompson | Jerry Hairston | Curt Hasler |
| Rookie | Bristol | Appalachian | Nick Leyva | Bobby Tolan | Roberto Espinoza |
| Rookie | White Sox | Dominican | Denny Gonzalez | Unavailable | Gustavo Martinez |

### Scouting

**Telephone:** (312) 674-1000. **FAX:** (312) 674-5105.
**Vice President, Free Agent/Major League Scouting:** Larry Monroe.
**Professional Scouts:** Doug Laumann (Florence, KY), Gary Pellant (Chandler, AZ), Paul Provas (Arlington, TX), Daraka Shaheed (Vallejo, CA), John Tumminia (Newburgh, NY), Derek Valenzuela (Temecula, CA), Bill Young (Long Beach, CA).
**National Crosschecker:** Ed Pebley (Brigham City, UT). **Regional Supervisors:** East Coast—Warren Hughes (Mobile, AL), West Coast—Joe Butler (Long Beach, CA), Midwest—Nathan Durst (Sycamore, IL).
**Full-Time Area Scouts:** Jayme Bane (Riverview, FL), Alex Cosmidis (Raleigh, NC), Dan Durst (Rockford, IL), Chuck Fox (Summit, NJ), Matt Hattabaugh (Westminster, CA), George Kachigian (Coronado, CA), John Kazanas (Chandler, AZ), Danny Ontiveros (Irvine, CA), Jose Ortega (Fort Lauderdale, FL), Clay Overcash (Oologan, OK), Mike Shirley (Anderson, IN), Alex Slattery (Smyrna, GA), Keith Staab (College Station, TX), Adam Virchis (Modesto, CA).

Duane Shaffer

**Part-Time Scouts:** Tom Butler (East Rancho Dominguez, CA), Javier Centeno (Guaynabo, Puerto Rico), John Doldoorian (Whitinsville, MA), Jason Morvant (Abbeville, LA), Phil Gulley (Morehead, KY), Jack Jolly (Murfreesboro, TN), Dario Lodigiani (Napa, CA), Bill Moran (Portsmouth, VA), Dave Mumpert (Highland Ranch, CO), Glen Murdock (Livonia, MI), Howard Nakagama (Salt Lake City), Al Otto (Schaumburg, IL), Mike Paris (Boone, IA), Scott Ramsey (Colbert, WA).
**International Scouts:** Mariano DeLeon (Dominican Republic), Amador Arias (Venezuela), Denny Gonzalez (Dominican Republic), Miguel Ibarra (Panama), Jorge Oquendo (Puerto Rico), Jhonny Pantoja (Colombia), Orlando Santana (Brazil).

# CINCINNATI REDS

**Office Address:** 100 Main St., Cincinnati, OH 45202.
**Telephone:** (513) 765-7000. **FAX:** (513) 765-7342.
**Website:** www.cincinnatireds.com.

## Ownership

**Operated by:** The Cincinnati Reds, LLC.
**Chief Executive Officer:** Robert Castellini.
**Chairman:** Joseph Williams Jr. **Vice Chairman/Treasurer:** Thomas Williams. **Chief Operating Officer:** John Allen. **Executive Assistant to COO:** Joyce Pfarr.

Robert Castellini

## BUSINESS OPERATIONS

**Senior Director, Business Operations:** Phil Castellini. **Senior Director, Finance Administration/Controller:** Anthony Ward.

### Finance/Administration

**Financial Analyst:** Robert Tore. **Accounting Manager:** Jason Randolph. **Payroll Manager:** Leanna Weiss. **Staff Accountant:** Jill Niemeyer. **Payroll Accountant:** Ayanna Goddard. **Accounts Payable Clerk:** Sarah Gullion. **Administrative Assistant:** Alice Wynn.

**Human Resources Manager:** Barbara Boles. **Human Resources Assistant:** Danielle Foust.

### Marketing, Sales

**Director, Business Development:** Brad Blettner. **Manager, Consumer Marketing:** Maya Wadleigh.

**Director, Corporate Sales/Marketing:** Bill Reinberger. **Director, Scoreboard Operations:** Russ Jenisch. **Managers, Corporate Sales:** Dave Collins, Tony Kountz. **Advertising/Promotions Manager:** Lori Watt. **Media Designer/Scoreboard Operations:** David Storm. **Marketing Operations Events Coordinator:** Zach Bonkowski.

**Director, Group Sales:** David Ziegler. **Manager, Group Tickets:** Brad Callahan. **Manager, Group Sales:** Ryan Niemeyer. **Group Ticket Representative:** Patrick Korosec. **Coordinator, Group Tickets:** Kim Knapp.

**Merchandise Manager:** Amy Hafer. **Manager, Game Day Retail:** Alicia King. **Coordinator, Merchandise Operations:** Drew Manley. **Merchandise Assistant/Buyer:** Brian Goggin. **Merchandise Inventory Control Clerk:** Paul Kidwell. **Store Manager, Reds Team Shop:** Brian Stoehr.

**Director, Premium Sales:** Jenny Gardner. **Manager, Special Events:** Jennifer Green. **Manager, Premium Services:** Jodi Czanik. **Director, Season Sales:** Pat McCaffrey. **Manager, Season Sales:** Chris Herrell. **Manager, Season Tickets:** Cyndi Strzynski.

### Public Relations, Communications

**Telephone:** (513) 765-7000. **FAX:** (513) 765-7180.

**Director, Media Relations:** Rob Butcher. **Assistant Director, Media Relations:** Michael Vassallo. **Coordinator, Media Relations:** Larry Herms. **Assistant, Media Relations:** Jamie Ramsey.

**Director, Creative Services:** Ralph Mitchell. **Manager, Creative Services:** Dann Stupp. **Coordinator, Creative Services:** Jarrod Rollins. **Production/Design Assistants:** Jansen Dell, Joe Zeinner.

**Manager, Community Relations:** Lorrie Platt. **Community Relations Assistant:** Mary Goebel. **Executive Director, Reds Community Fund:** Charley Frank. **Executive Director, Reds Hall of Fame:** Greg Rhodes. **Manager, Visitor Services:** Chris Eckes. **Education Manager:** Carrie Gravlee. **Project Coordinator:** Brittney Morris.

### Ballpark Operations

**Senior Director, Ballpark Operations:** Declan Mullin. **Director, Ballpark Operations:** Mike Maddox. **Superintendent, Ballpark Operations:** Bob Harrison. **Manager, Guest Relations:** Jan Koshover. **Chief Engineer:** Roger Smith. **Assistant Chief Engineer:** Eric Dearing.

**Director, Public Safety/Security:** Kerry Rowland.

**Head Groundskeeper:** Doug Gallant. **Assistant Groundskeeper:** Jon Phelps. **Grounds Supervisor:** Derrick Grubbs.

### Ticketing

**Telephone:** (513) 765-7000. **FAX:** (513) 765-7119.

**Director, Ticket Operations:** John O'Brien. **Assistant Director, Ticket Operations:** Ken Ayer. **Ticket Operations Administration Manager:** Hallie Kinney.

### Travel, Clubhouse

**Traveling Secretary:** Gary Wahoff.

**Senior Clubhouse/Equipment Manager:** Bernie Stowe. **Reds Clubhouse/Equipment Manager:** Rick Stowe. **Visiting Clubhouse Manager:** Mark Stowe. **Reds Clubhouse Assistant:** Josh Stewart.

---

## GENERAL INFORMATION

**Stadium (year opened):** The Great American Ball Park (2003).
**Home Dugout:** First base. **Playing Surface:** Grass.
**Team Colors:** Red, white and black.
**Player Representative:** Unavailable.

## BASEBALL OPERATIONS
**Telephone:** (513) 765-7000. **FAX:** (513) 765-7797.
**General Manager:** Wayne Krivsky. **Executive Assistant to GM:** Debbie Bent.
**Assistant GM:** Dean Taylor. **Special Assistant to GM/Player Personnel:** Scott Nethery. **Special Consultants to GM:** Johnny Bench, Ken Griffey Sr. **Special Assistants to GM:** Andres Reiner, Dick Williams. **Coordinator, Major League Scouting/Video Operations:** Nick Krall.
**Director, Baseball Administration:** Bob Miller.

### Major League Staff
**Manager:** Jerry Narron.

Wayne Krivsky

**Coaches:** Bench—Bucky Dent; Pitching—Vern Ruhle; Batting—Chris Chambliss; First Base—John Moses; Third Base—Mark Berry; Bullpen—Tom Hume; Bullpen Catcher—Mike Stefanski.

### Medical, Training
**Medical Director:** Dr. Tim Kremchek.
**Head Trainer:** Mark Mann. **Assistant Trainers:** Tim Elser, Steve Baumann. **Strength/Conditioning Coach:** Matt Krause.

### Player Development
**Telephone:** (513) 765-7000. **FAX:** (513) 765-7799.
**Director, Player Development/International Operations:** Johnny Almaraz. **Assistant Director, Player Development:** Grant Griesser. **Administrative Coordinator, Player Development:** Lois Hudson. **Manager, Florida Operations:** Jeff Maultsby. **Minor League Equipment Manager:** Tim Williamson.

**Minor League Field Coordinator:** Tim Naehring. **Roving Coordinators:** Freddie Benavides (infield), Joe Breeden (catching), Mack Jenkins (pitching), Lynn Jones (outfield/baserunning), Jorge Orta (hitting). **Coordinator, Rehabilitation:** John Walker. **Coordinator, Medical:** Mark Farnsworth. **Coordinator, Strength/Conditioning:** Sean Marohn.

Jerry Narron

### Farm System

| Class | Farm Team | League | Manager | Coach | Pitching Coach |
|-------|-----------|--------|---------|-------|----------------|
| Triple-A | Louisville | International | Rick Sweet | Alonzo Powell | Lee Tunnell |
| Double-A | Chattanooga | Southern | Jayhawk Owens | Jamie Dismuke | Bill Moloney |
| High A | Sarasota | Florida State | Donnie Scott | Joe Ayrault | Ed Hodge |
| Low A | Dayton | Midwest | Billy Gardner Jr. | Billy White | Larry Pierson |
| Rookie | Billings | Pioneer | Rick Burleson | Jeff Young | Butch Henry |
| Rookie | Sarasota | Gulf Coast | Luis Aguayo | Don Kruzel | Jamie Garcia |
| Rookie | Reds | Dominican | Frank Laureano | Victor Franco | Manuel Solano |
| Rookie | Reds | Venezuela | Jose Villa | Carlos Barrios | Jorge Lopez |

### Scouting
**Telephone:** (513) 765-7000. **FAX:** (513) 765-7799.
**Senior Director, Scouting:** Chris Buckley. **Assistant Director, Professional Scouting:** Matt Arnold. **Senior Special Assistant to GM/Advance Scout:** Gene Bennett. **Special Assistants to GM/Professional Scouts:** Larry Barton Jr., Leland Maddox, Bill Wood. **Professional Scouts:** Kelly Heath, Gene Kerns, Greg McClain, Tom Mooney, Les Parker, Jim Pransky, Ross Sapp.

**Director, Amateur Scouting:** Terry Reynolds. **Assistant Director, Amateur Scouting:** Paul Pierson. **Director, Scouting Administration:** Wilma Mann.
**National Crosschecker:** Butch Baccala (Weimar, CA). **Regional Crosscheckers:** East—Jim Thrift (Sarasota, FL); Midwest—Jim Gonzales (San Antonio); West—Jeff Barton (Higley, AZ).

Terry Reynolds

**Scouting Supervisors:** Jason Baker (Rome, NY), Jeff Brookens (Chambersburg, PA), Rex de la Nuez (Burbank, CA), Jerry Flowers (Baton Rouge, LA), Dan Huston (Bellevue, WA), Mike Keenan (Manhattan, KS), Steve Kring (Charlotte, NC), Mike Misuraca (Pomona, CA), Jeff Morris (Tucson, AZ), Rick Sellers (Remus, MI), Joe Siers (Wesley Chapel, FL), Perry Smith (Charlotte, NC), Tom Wheeler (Martinez, CA), Brian Wilson (Albany, TX), Tyler Wilt (Chicago), Greg Zunino (Cape Coral, FL).
**Coordinator, International Scouting:** Jhonathan Leyba. **Latin American Field Coordinator:** Marco Davalillo.
**International Scouts:** Oswaldo Alvarez (Mexico), Luis Baez (Dominican Republic), Luis Davalillo (Venezuela), Felix Delgado (Venezuela), John Gilmore (Pacific Rim), Robert Morillo (Venezuela), Victor Oramas (Venezuela), Miguel Pol (Dominican Republic), Luke Prokopec (Australia), Anibal Reluz (Panama), Maximo Rombley (Dominican Republic), Evereth Velasquez (Venezuela).

# CLEVELAND INDIANS

Office Address: Jacobs Field, 2401 Ontario St., Cleveland, OH 44115.
Telephone: (216) 420-4200. FAX: (216) 420-4396.
Website: www.indians.com.

## Ownership
Owner, Chief Executive Officer: Lawrence Dolan.
President: Paul Dolan.

## BUSINESS OPERATIONS
Executive Vice President, Business: Dennis Lehman. Executive Administrative
Assistant, Business: Dru Kosik.

### Corporate Marketing
Director, Corporate Sales: Matt Brown. Corporate Sales Account Executives: Karen
Bonsiewicz, Bryan Hoffart, Paul Corto.

### Finance/Administration
Senior Vice President, Finance/Chief Financial Officer: Ken Stefanov.

Larry Dolan

Controller: Sarah Taylor. Director, Planning/Analysis/Reporting: Rich Dorffer. Manager,
Accounting: Karen Menzing. Manager, Payroll Services: Jeanne Eligado. Senior Accountant: Mary Forkapa.
Senior Director, Human Resources: Sara Lehrke. Manager, Training/Recruitment: Susie Downey. Coordinator,
Human Resources/Benefits: Crystal Basile.
Senior Director, Information Systems: Dave Powell. Manager, End User Systems: Kelly Janda. Manager,
Application Development: Matt Tagliaferri. Systems Specialist: Nick Korosi. Network Manager: Whitney Kuszmaul.

### Marketing
Senior Vice President, Sales/Marketing: Vic Gregovits. Director, Marketing: Sanaa Julien. Manager, Promotions:
Jasod Kidik. Manager, Scoreboard Operations: Steve Warren. Manager, Broadcasting: Alex Slemc.
Vice President, Merchandising/Licensing: Jayne Churchmack. Director, Merchandise: Kurt Schloss.
Merchandise Manager: Karen Fox. Retail Controller: Marjorie Ruhl. Senior Staff Accountant: Diane Turner.
Warehouse Manager: Josh Cramer. Retail/Concession Manager: Nancy Schneider.

### Public Relations, Communications
Telephone: (216) 420-4350. FAX: (216) 420-4396.
Vice President, Public Relations: Bob DiBiasio. Coordinator, Public Relations: Angela Brdar.
Director, Media Relations: Bart Swain. Manager, Media Relations/Administration: Susie Giuliano. Coordinator,
Media Relations: Jeff Sibel. Press Box Supervisor: John Krepop.
Manager, Communications/Creative Services: Curtis Danburg. Coordinator, Communications/Creative Services:
Kate Buddenhagen. Manager, Community Relations: John Carter. Coordinator, Community Relations/Spring
Training: Monica Woodard. Coordinator, Charitable Programs: Stephanie Hierro.

### Stadium Operations
Vice President, Ballpark Operations: Jim Folk. Director, Ballpark Operations: Jerry Crabb. Director, Facility
Maintenance: Chris Donahoe. Head Groundskeeper: Brandon Koehnke.
Manager, Host and Greeters: Jim Goldwire. Manager, Game Day Staff: Brad Mohr.
Manager, Spring Training: Alex Slemc. Coordinator, Spring Training: Monica Woodard.

### Ticketing
Telephone: (216) 420-4487. FAX: (216) 420-4481.
Director, Ticket Services: Gene Connelly. Manager, Ticket Systems/Development: Marie Patten. Manager, Public
Sales: Michael Blackert. Manager, Vault/Processing: Kelly Kelly.
Director, Tickets and Premium Sales: Mike Mulhall. Manager, Customer Service/Sales: David Murray. Group
Sales Manager: Renee Boerner. Database Manager: Dan Foust. Manager, Premium Services: Cassy Baskin.
Manager, Season Ticket Sales: Nick Arndt.

### Travel, Clubhouse
Director, Team Travel: Mike Seghi.
Home Clubhouse/Equipment Manager: Tony Amato. Assistant Home Clubhouse/Equipment Manager: Tommy
Foster. Visiting Clubhouse Manager: Cy Buynak. Manager, Equipment Acquisition/Distribution: Jeff Sipos. Manager,
Video Operations: Bob Chester. Video Operations: Frank Velotta.

---

### GENERAL INFORMATION
Stadium (year opened): Jacobs Field (1994).
Home Dugout: Third base. Playing Surface: Grass.
Team Colors: Navy blue, red and silver.
Player Representative: Josh Bard.

Mark Shapiro

## BASEBALL OPERATIONS

**Telephone:** (216) 420-4200. **FAX:** (216) 420-4321.
**Executive Vice President, General Manager:** Mark Shapiro.
**Assistant GM:** Chris Antonetti. **Special Assistant to GM:** Neal Huntington.
**Director, Player Personnel:** Steve Lubratich. **Special Adviser, Baseball Operations:** Karl Kuehl. **Special Assistants, Baseball Operations:** Ellis Burks, Jason Bere, Tim Belcher, Robby Thompson.
**Director, Baseball Administration:** Wendy Hoppel. **Assistant Director, Baseball Operations:** Mike Chernoff. **Executive Administrative Assistant, Baseball Operations:** Marlene Lehky. **Administrative Assistant, Baseball Operations:** Barbara Lessman. **Senior Coordinator, Baseball Systems:** Dan Mendlik. **Sport Psychologist/Director, Psychological Services:** Dr. Charles Maher.

### Major League Staff
**Manager:** Eric Wedge.
**Coaches:** Bench—Joel Skinner; Pitching—Carl Willis; Batting—Derek Shelton; First Base—Luis Rivera; Third Base—Jeff Datz; Bullpen—Luis Isaac; Bullpen Catcher—Dan Williams.

### Medical, Training
**Team Physician:** Dr. Mark Schickendantz.
**Director, Medical Services/Head Athletic Trainer:** Lonnie Soloff. **Assistant Head Athletic Trainer:** Rick Jameyson. **Assistant Athletic Trainer:** Nick Kenney. **Strength/Conditioning Coach:** Tim Maxey. **Physical Therapy Consultant:** Jim Mehalik.

### Player Development
**Telephone:** (216) 420-4308. **FAX:** (216) 420-4321.
**Director, Player Development:** John Farrell. **Director, Latin American Operations:** Ross Atkins. **Assistant Director, Player Development:** Mike Hazen. **Adviser, Player Development:** Johnny Goryl. **Assistant Director, Player Development/Latin American Operations:** Llno Diaz. **Mental Skills Coordinator:** John Couture. **Nutrition Consultant:** Jackie Berning.
**Field Coordinator:** Tim Tolman. **Coordinators:** Brad Komminsk (outfield/baserunning), Ted Kubiak (defense), Lee Kuntz (rehab/medical), Jim Malone (strength/conditioning), Dave Miller (pitching), Dave Hudgens (hitting).
**Field Coordinator, Latin America:** Minnie Mendoza.

Eric Wedge

### Farm System

| Class | Farm Team | League | Manager | Coach(es) | Pitching Coach |
|---|---|---|---|---|---|
| Triple-A | Buffalo | International | Torey Lovullo | Bruce Fields | Greg Hibbard |
| Double-A | Akron | Eastern | Tim Bogar | Felix Fermin | Scott Radinsky |
| High A | Kinston | Carolina | Mike Sarbaugh | Unavailable | Steve Lyons |
| Low A | Lake County | South Atlantic | Lee May Jr. | Jack Mull | Ruben Niebla |
| Short season | Mahoning Valley | New York-Penn | Rouglas Odor | C. Tremie/J. Rickon | Ken Rowe |
| Rookie | Burlington | Appalachian | Kevin Higgins | Dennis Malave | Tony Arnold |
| Rookie | Indians | Dominican | Jose Stela | Luis Chavez | Juan Jimenez |

### Scouting
**Telephone:** (216) 420-4309. **FAX:** (216) 420-4321.
**Assistant General Manager/Scouting Operations:** John Mirabelli.
**Assistant Director, Scouting:** Brad Grant.
**Major League Scouts:** Don Poplin (Norwood, NC), Dave Malpass (Huntington Beach, CA), DeJon Watson (Phoenix).
**Professional Scouts:** Doug Carpenter (North Palm Beach, FL), Rob Guzik (Latrobe, PA), Pat Murtaugh (Lafayette, IN), Chuck Tanner (New Castle, PA), Bill Schudlich (Dearborn, MI).
**National Crosschecker:** Chuck Ricci (Greencastle, PA). **Free-Agent Supervisors:** East—Scott Meaney (Apex, NC), Midwest—Matt Ruebel (Oklahoma City),West Coast—Paul Cogan (Rocklin, CA).

**Full-Time Area Scouts:** Steve Abney (Lawrence, KS), Scott Barnsby (Brentwood, TN), Mike Daly (Dallas), Byron Ewing (Chicago), Joe Graham (Phoenix), Jerry Jordan (Kingsport,

John Mirabelli

TN), Don Lyle (Sacramento, CA), Bob Mayer (Somerset, PA), Les Pajari (Conroe, TX), Derrick Ross (Olmsted Township, OH), Vince Sagisi (Encino, CA), Jason Smith (Long Beach, CA), Mike Soper (Tampa, FL), Brent Urcheck (Philadelphia), Shawn Whalen (Vancouver, WA).
**Dominican Adviser:** Winston Llenas. **Latin American Supervisors:** Henry Centeno (Venezuela), Junior Betances (Dominican Republic).

# COLORADO ROCKIES

**Office Address:** 2001 Blake St., Denver, CO 80205.
**Telephone:** (303) 292-0200. **FAX:** (303) 312-2116.
**Website:** www.coloradorockies.com.

## Ownership

**Operated by:** Colorado Rockies Baseball Club, Ltd.
**Vice Chairman, Chief Executive Officer:** Charles Monfort. **Vice Chairman:** Richard Monfort. **Executive Assistant to Vice Chairmen:** Patricia Penfold.

## BUSINESS OPERATIONS

**President:** Keli McGregor. **Executive Assistant to President:** Terry Douglass.
**Senior Vice President, Business Operations:** Greg Feasel. **Assistant to Senior VP:** Donna Reed.
**Vice President, Human Resources:** Elizabeth Stecklein. **Director, Information Systems:** Bill Stephani.

Charles Monfort

## Finance

**Senior Vice President/Chief Financial Officer:** Hal Roth. **Assistant to Senior VP/CFO:** Tammy Vergara. **VP, Finance:** Michael Kent. **Senior Director, Accounting:** Gary Lawrence. **Payroll Administrator:** Phil Emerson. **Accountants:** Phil Delany, Laine Campbell.

## Marketing, Sales

**Senior Director, Corporate Sales:** Marcy English-Glasser. **Assistant to Senior Director, Corporate Sales:** Jenny Roope. **Senior Account Executive:** Kari Anderson. **Coordinator, Corporate Sales:** Amy Crawford.
**Senior Director, Promotions/Broadcasting:** Alan Bossart. **Assistant Director, Promotions:** Jason Fleming. **Manager, In-Game Entertainment,** Kent Krosbakken. **Coordinator, In-Game Entertainment:** Jeff Donehoo.
**Vice President, Community/Retail Operations:** Jim Kellogg. **Assistant to VP, Community/Retail Operations:** Kelly Hall. **Manager, Community Affairs:** Antigone Vigil. **Manager, Coors Field Receiving/Distribution Center:** Steve Tomlinson. **Assistant Director, Retail Operations:** Aaron Heinrich. **Rockies Dugout Store Managers:** Tina Kopp, Robin Rollins, Matt Smith, Kristi Baxter.

## Public Relations/Communications

**Telephone:** (303) 312-2325. **FAX:** (303) 312-2319.
**Vice President, Communications/Public Relations:** Jay Alves. **Assistant to VP, Communications/Public Relations:** Irma Thumim. **Manager, Communications/Public Relations:** Rich Rice. **Coordinator, Communications/Public Relations:** Matt Chisholm.

## Stadium Operations

**Vice President, Ballpark Operations:** Kevin Kahn.
**Director, Coors Field Administration/Development:** Dave Moore. **Manager, Ballpark Services:** Mary Beth Benner. **Director, Guest Services:** Steven Burke. **Supervisor, Guest Services:** Travis Howell. **Managers, Guest Services:** Brian Schneringer, Sandy Seta. **Director, Security:** Don Lyon. **Senior Director, Engineering/Facilities:** James Wiener. **Assistant Director, Engineering:** Randy Carlill. **Assistant Director, Facilities:** Oly Olsen.
**Head Groundskeeper:** Mark Razum. **Assistant Head Groundskeeper:** Jose Gonzalez.
**PA Announcer:** Kelly Burnham. **Official Scorers:** Dave Einspahr, Dave Plati.

## Ticketing

**Telephone:** (303) 762-5437, (800) 388-7625. **FAX:** (303) 312-2115.
**Vice President, Ticket Operations/Sales:** Sue Ann McClaren. **Senior Director, Ticket Operations/Development:** Kevin Fenton. **Director, Ticket Operations/Finances:** Kent Hakes. **Assistant Director, Vault:** Scott Donaldson.
**Senior Director, Advertising/Publications:** Jill Roberts. **Manager, Advertising:** Angela Keenan. **Manager, Publications:** Mike Kennedy. **Director, Ticket Services/Spring Training Business Operations:** Chuck Javernick. **Director, Group Sales:** Jeff Spector. **Director, Season Tickets/Outbound Sales:** Jeff Benner. **Assistant Director, Season Tickets/Outbound Sales:** Todd Thomas. **Manager, Outbound Sales/Services:** Doug Ruth. **Supervisor, Ticket Services:** Michael Bishop.

## Travel, Clubhouse

**Director, Major League Operations:** Paul Egins.
**Director, Clubhouse Operations:** Keith Schulz. **Assistant to Director, Clubhouse Operations:** Joe Diaz. **Visiting Clubhouse Manager:** Joe Tarnowski. **Video Coordinator:** Mike Hamilton.

---

### GENERAL INFORMATION

**Stadium (year opened):** Coors Field (1995).
**Home Dugout:** First base. **Playing Surface:** Grass.
**Team Colors:** Purple, black and silver.
**Player Representative:** Jason Jennings.

Dan O'Dowd

## BASEBALL OPERATIONS

**Telephone:** (303) 292-0200. **FAX:** (303) 312-2320.
**Executive Vice President/General Manager:** Dan O'Dowd. **Assistant to Executive VP/GM:** Adele Armagost. **VP/Assistant GM:** Bill Geivett. **Director, Baseball Operations:** Jeff Bridich. **Assistant, Baseball Operations:** Walter Sylvester.
**Special Assistants to GM:** Pat Daugherty (Aurora, CO), Marcel Lachemann (Penryn, CA), Kasey McKeon (Stoney Creek, NC). **Special Assistant to Baseball Operations:** Mark Wiley.

### Major League Staff

**Manager:** Clint Hurdle.
**Coaches:** Bench—Jamie Quirk; Pitching—Bob Apodaca; Batting—Duane Espy; First Base—Dave Collins; Third Base—Mike Gallego; Bullpen—Rick Mathews; Bullpen Catcher—Mark Strittmatter; Strength—Brad Andress; Video—Mike Hamilton.

## Medical, Training

**Director, Medical Operations:** Tom Probst. **Medical Director:** Dr. Thomas Noonan. **Senior Associate Orthopedist:** Dr. Richard Hawkins. **Club Physicians:** Dr. Allen Schreiber, Dr. Douglas Wyland.
**Head Athletic Trainer:** Keith Dugger. **Assistant Athletic Trainer:** Scott Gehret.
**Strength and Conditioning Coordinator:** Brian Jordan. **Rehabilitation Coordinator:** Scott Murayama.

## Player Development

**Telephone:** (303) 292-0200. **FAX:** (303) 312-2320.
**Director, Player Development:** Marc Gustafson. **Roving Instructors:** Ron Gideon (field coordinator). Jim Wright (pitching coordinator). Jim Johnson (hitting coordinator); Rich Dauer (infield coordinator). Marv Foley (catching coordinator).
**Video Coordinator:** Brian Jones. **Mental Skills Coach:** Ronn Svetich. **Equipment Manager:** Jerry Bass.

Clint Hurdle

## Farm System

| Class | Farm Team | League | Manager | Coach | Pitching Coach |
|---|---|---|---|---|---|
| Triple-A | Colorado Springs | Pacific Coast | Tom Runnells | Alan Cockrell | Chuck Kniffin |
| Double-A | Tulsa | Texas | Stu Cole | Orlando Merced | Bo McLaughlin |
| High A | Modesto | California | Chad Kreuter | Glenallen Hill | Butch Hughes |
| Low A | Asheville | South Atlantic | Joe Mikulik | Dave Hajek | Richard Palacios |
| Short-season | Tri-City | Northwest | Darron Cox | Freddie Ocasio | Doug Linton |
| Rookie | Casper | Pioneer | P.J. Carey | Tony Diaz | Mark Thompson |
| Rookie | Rockies | Dominican | Mauricio Gonzalez | Edison Lora | Pablo Paredes |
| Rookie | Rockies | Venezuela | Maurio Mendez | Unavailable | Unavailable |

## Scouting

**Telephone:** (303) 292-0200. **FAX:** (303) 312-2320.
**Senior Director, Scouting:** Bill Schmidt. **Assistant Director, Scouting:** Danny Montgomery. **Manager, Scouting:** Zach Wilson. **Manager, Professional Scouting:** Matt Vinnola.
**Major League Scouts:** Will George (Woolwich Township, NJ). Mike Paul (Tucson, AZ). **Professional Scouts:** Jack Gillis (Sarasota, FL), Art Pontarelli (Cranston, RI).
**Special Assignment Scout:** Terry Wetzel (Overland Park, KS).
**National Crosscheckers:** Ty Coslow (Louisville, KY), Dave Holliday (Coalgate, OK).
**Scouting Adviser:** Dave Snow (Seal Beach, CA).
**Full-Time Area Scouts:** Todd Blyleven (Fountain Valley, CA), John Cedarburg (Fort Myers, FL), Scott Corman (Lexington, KY), Dar Cox (Frisco, TX), Jeff Edwards (Houston), Mike Ericson (Glendale, AZ), Mike Garlatti (Edison, NJ), Mark Germann (Atkins, IA), Jeff Hipps (Long Beach, CA), Bert Holt (Visalia, CA), Damon Iannelli (Brandon, MS), Clarence Johns (Stockbridge, GA), Jay Matthews (Concord, NC), Jorge de Posada (Rio Piedras, PR), Ed Santa (Powell, OH), Gary Wilson (Sacramento, CA).

Bill Schmidt

**Scouts:** Steve Bernhardt (Perry Hall, MD), Norm DeBriyn (Fayetteville, AR), Casey Harvie (Lake Stevens, WA), Marc Johnson (Centennial, CO), Bobby Knopp (Phoenix), Greg Pullia (Quincy, MA), Dave McQueen (Bossier City, LA).
**Director, Latin America Operations:** Rolando Fernandez.
**International Scouts:** Phil Allen (Australia), Vladimir Bello (Dominican Republic), Francisco Cartaya (Venezuela), Felix Feliz (Dominican Republic), Carlos Gomez (Venezuela), Cristobal Giron (Panama), Orlando Medina (Venezuela), Frank Roa (Dominican Republic).

# DETROIT TIGERS

**Office Address:** 2100 Woodward Ave., Detroit, MI, 48201.
**Telephone:** (313) 471-2000. **FAX:** (313) 471-2138.
**Website:** www.detroittigers.com.

## Ownership

**Operated by:** Detroit Tigers, Inc.
**Owner:** Michael Ilitch.
**President, Chief Executive Officer:** David Dombrowski. **Special Assistants to President:** Al Kaline, Willie Horton. **Executive Assistant to President/CEO:** Patricia McConnell.
**Senior Vice President:** Jim Devellano.

## BUSINESS OPERATIONS

**Senior Vice President, Business Operations:** Duane McLean. **Executive Assistant to Senior VP, Business Operations:** Peggy Bacarella.

### Finance

**Vice President, Chief Financial Officer:** Steve Quinn.

Mike Ilitch

**Director, Finance:** Kelli Kollman. **Accounting Manager:** Sheila Robine. **Accounts Payable Coordinator:** Debbie Sword. **Accounts Receivable Coordinator:** Sharon Szkarlat. **Purchasing Manager:** DeAndre Berry. **Administrative/Accounting Assistant:** Tracy Billups.
**Director, Human Resources:** Karen Gruca. **Senior Manager, Payroll Administration:** Maureen Kraatz. **Payroll/Human Resources Coordinator:** Maria Delgado. **Financial Analyst:** Kristin Jorgensen. **Auditor:** Scott Calka.
**Director, Information Technology:** Scott Wruble.

### Marketing, Communications

**Vice President, Public Affairs/Strategic Planning:** Elaine Lewis. **Director, Community Affairs:** Celia Bobrowsky. **Manager, Public Affairs/Detroit Tigers Foundation:** Jordan Field. **Coordinator, Community Affairs:** Corey Bell.

### Sales, Marketing

**Vice President, Corporate Sales:** Steve Harms.
**Managers, Corporate Sales:** Greg Paddock, Zach Wagner, John Wolski. **Coordinator, Corporate Sales:** Jill Chamberlain.
**Director, Marketing:** Ellen Hill Zeringue. **Marketing Coordinator:** Ron Wade.
**Director, Promotions/In-Game Entertainment:** Joel Scott. **Coordinator, Promotions/Special Events:** Eli Bayless. **Promotions Assistant:** Jeff Clancy.
**Vice President, Corporate Suite Sales and Services/Hospitality:** Charles Jones. **Manager, Suite Sales/Service:** Scot Pett. **Coordinator, Suite Services:** Amy Howard.
**Director, Fantasy Camps:** Jerry Lewis.

### Media Relations, Communications

**Telephone:** (313) 471-2114. **FAX:** (313) 471-2138.
**Manager, Baseball Media Relations:** Brian Britten. **Assistant Manager, Baseball Media Relations:** Rick Thompson. **Media Relations/Broadcast Manager:** Molly Light.

### Park Operations

**Vice President, Park Operations:** Michael Healy. **Director, Park Operations:** Mike Churchill.
**Head Groundskeeper:** Heather Nabozny. **Senior Manager, Park Operations:** Ed Goward. **Park Operations Manager:** Allan Carisse. **Event Operations Manager:** Jill Baran. **Guest Services Manager:** Tessa Lawrence.
**Producer and Manager, Scoreboard Operations:** Scott Fearncombe.

### Ticketing

**Telephone:** (313) 471-2255.
**Vice President, Marketing/Ticket Sales:** Bob Raymond.
**Director, Ticket Sales:** Steve Fox. **Director, Group Sales:** Dwain Lewis.
**Director, Ticket Services:** Victor Gonzalez.

### Travel, Clubhouse

**Traveling Secretary:** Bill Brown
**Manager, Home Clubhouse:** Jim Schmakel. **Assistant Manager, Visiting Clubhouse:** John Nelson. **Clubhouse Assistant:** Tyson Steele.
**Baseball Video Operations:** Jeremy Kelch. **Assistant, Baseball Video Operations:** Andy Bjornstad

## GENERAL INFORMATION

**Stadium (year opened):** Comerica Park (2000).
**Home Dugout:** Third Base. **Playing Surface:** Grass.
**Team Colors:** Navy blue, orange and white.
**Player Representative:** Mike Maroth.

## BASEBALL OPERATIONS

**Telephone:** (313) 471-2059. **FAX:** (313) 471-2099.
**Prident, General Manager:** David Dombrowski.
**Vice President/Assistant GM:** Al Avila. **VP/Baseball Legal Counsel:** John Westhoff. **Administrative Assistant to VP/Assistant GM, Baseball Legal Counsel:** Eileen Surma. **Special Assistant to General Manager:** Ramon Pena.
**VP, Player Personnel:** Scott Reid. **Director, Baseball Operations:** Mike Smith.

### Major League Staff

**Manager:** Jim Leyland.
**Coaches:** Pitching—Chuck Hernandez; Hitting—Don Slaught; Infield—Rafael Belliard; First Base/Outfield/Base Running—Andy Van Slyke; Third Base—Gene Lamont; Bullpen—Lloyd McClendon.

Dave Dombrowski

### Medical, Training

**Team Physicians:** Dr. Louis Saco, Dr. Michael Workings.
**Director, Medical Services/Head Athletic Trainer:** Kevin Rand. **Assistant Athletic Trainers:** Steve Carter, Doug Teter. **Strength/Conditioning Coach:** Javiar Gillett.

### Player Development

**Telephone, Detroit:** (313) 471-2096. **FAX:** (313) 471-2099. **Telephone, Florida Operations:** (863) 686-8075. **FAX:** (863) 688-9589.
**Director, Minor League Operations:** Dan Lunetta. **Director, Minor League/Scouting Administration:** Cheryl Evans.
**Director, Player Development:** Glenn Ezell. **Director, Latin American Operations:** Manny Crespo.
**Roving Instructors:** Toby Harrah (hitting), Rafael Landestoy (infield), Jon Matlack (pitching), Brian Peterson (performance enhancement), Gene Roof (outfield/baserunning).

Jim Leyland

### Farm System

| Class | Farm Team | League | Manager | Coach | Pitching Coach |
|---|---|---|---|---|---|
| AAA | Toledo | International | Larry Parrish | Leon Durham | Jeff Jones |
| AA | Erie | Eastern | Duffy Dyer | Pete Incaviglia | Mike Caldwell |
| High A | Lakeland | Florida State | Mike Rojas | Larry Herndon | Britt Burns |
| Low A | West Michigan | Midwest | Matt Walbeck | Tony Jaramillo | A.J. Sager |
| Short season | Oneonta | New York-Penn | Tom Brookens | Basilio Cabrera | Ray Burris |
| Rookie | Lakeland | Gulf Coast | Kevin Bradshaw | Benny Distefano | Greg Sabat |
| Rookie | Tigers | Dominican | Andres Thomas | Francisco Cabrera | Marcos Aguasvivas |
| Rookie | Tigers | Venezuelan | Josman Robles | Jesus Laya | Unavailable |

### Scouting

**Telephone:** (863) 413-4112. **FAX:** (863) 413-1954.
**Vice President, Amateur Scouting:** David Chadd. **Assistant Director, Amateur Scouting:** James Orr.
**Assistant Director, International/Professional Scouting:** Tom Moore.
**Major League Scouts:** Scott Bream (Phoenix, AZ), Dick Egan (Phoenix, AZ), Al Hargesheimer (Arlington Heights, IL), Mike Russell (Gulf Breeze, FL), Greg Smith (Mount Juliet, TN)
**National Crosscheckers:** Ray Crone (Cedar Hill, TX), Jim Olander (Tucson, AZ).
**Regional Crosscheckers:** East—Steve Williams (Raleigh, NC), Central—Bob Cummings (Oak Lawn, IL), Midwest—Mike Hankins (Lee's Summit, MO), West—Joe Ferrone (Santa Clarita, CA).
**Area Scouts:** Grant Brittain (Hickory, NC), Bill Buck (Manassas, VA), Vaughn Calloway (Detroit, MI), Rolando Casanova (Miami, FL), Scott Cerny (Rocklin, CA), Mike Gambino (Chelsea, AL), German Geigel (Rio Piedras, PR), Tim Grieve (Katy, TX), Tim McWilliam (San Diego, CA), Marty Miller (Chicago, IL), Mark Monahan (Saline, MI), Steve Nichols (Mount Dora, FL), Tom Osowski (Dublin, OH), Brian Reid (Phoenix, AZ), Dennis Sheehan (Glasco, NY), Steve Taylor (Shawnee, OK), Clyde Weir (Portland, MI), Harold Zonder (Louisville, KY).
**Director of Venezuelan Operations/Central American Scouting:** Miguel Garcia.

David Chadd

# FLORIDA MARLINS

**Office Address:** Dolphins Stadium, 2267 Dan Marino Blvd. Miami, FL 33056.
**Telephone:** (305) 626-7400. **FAX:** (305) 626-7428.
**Website:** www.floridamarlins.com.

## Ownership

**Owner:** Jeffrey Loria. **Vice Chairman:** Joel Mael.
**President:** David Samson. **Special Assistants to President:** Andre Dawson, Tony Perez.
**Executive Assistant to Owner, Vice Chairman and President:** Beth McConville.

## BUSINESS OPERATIONS

**Senior Vice President/Chief Financial Officer:** Michel Bussiere. **Senior VP, Stadium Development:** Claude Delorme. **Executive Assistant to Senior VP/CFO:** Lisa Milk.
**Director, Human Resources:** Ana Hernandez. **Administrator, Benefits:** Ruby Mattei.
**Supervisor, Office Services:** Karl Heard. **Assistant, Office Services:** Donna Kirton. **Senior Receptionist:** Kathy Lanza. **Receptionist:** Christina Fredericks.

Jeffrey Loria

### Finance

**Vice President, Finance:** Susan Jaison. **Manager, Accounting:** Julio Garrido. **Administrator, Payroll:** Carolina Calderon. **Staff Accountant:** Martha Cao. **Coordinator, Accounts Payable:** Laura Martinez. **Coordinator, Finance:** Alina Quiros.
**Director, Information Technology:** Roger Sosa. **Manager, Technical Support:** David Kuan. **Network Engineer:** Matthew Larsh. **Telecommunications Manager:** Sam Mora.

### Marketing

**Vice President, Marketing:** Sean Flynn. **Manager, Retail Operations:** Robyn Fogel. **Manager, Hispanic Sales/Marketing:** Juan Martinez. **Manager, Promotions:** Matthew Britten. **Coordinator, Marketing:** Alice Estevez. **Coordinator, Promotions:** Jorge Suarez. **Coordinator, Mermaids:** Jose Guerrero. **Coordinator, Marlins en Miami:** Marisel Sordo. **Retail Associate, Marlins en Miami:** Joseph Santiago.

### Sales

**Vice President, New Business Development:** Dale Hendricks.
**Senior Director, Corporate Sales:** Brendan Cunningham. **Manager, Corporate Sales:** Tony Tome. **Corporate Sales Executives:** Ruben Cabrera, David Goldberg. **Coordinators, Corporate Sales:** Liz Chantz, Lorraine Yorke. **Assistant, Corporate Sales:** Judy Cavanagh.
**Director, Season/Group Sales:** Joseph Hovancak. **Director, Customer Service:** Spencer Linden. **Manager, Season/Group Sales:** Marty Mulford. **Account Executive, New Business Development:** Christopher Huff.

### Media Relations, Communications

**Telephone:** (305) 626-7429. **FAX:** (305) 626-7302.
**Vice President, Communications/Broadcasting:** P.J. Loyello.
**Director, Media Relations:** Matt Roebuck. **Manager, Media Relations:** Mike Gazda. **Administrative Assistant, Media Relations:** Maria Armella.
**Director, Broadcasting:** Suzanne Rayson. **Coordinator, Broadcasting/Media Relations:** Emmanuel Munoz. **Manager, Community Affairs:** Angela Smith. **Assistants, Community Affairs:** Paul Resnick, Ron Sklar. **Assistant, Player Relations:** Alex Morin. **Executive Director, Marlins Community Foundation:** Nancy Olson. **Assistants, Marlins Community Foundation:** Kelly Schnackenberg, Jeremy Stern.

### Stadium Operations

**Director, In-Game Entertainment:** Gary Levy. **Producer, Creative Services:** Eric Ramirez. **Coordinator, Game Presentation:** Edward Limia. **Producer, Creative Services:** Eric Ramirez. **Manager, Creative Services:** Alfred Hernandez. **Coordinator, Creative Services:** Robert Vigon. **Video Archivist:** Chris Myers. **Organist:** Lowery Ballew. **Mascot:** John DeCicco.
**PA Announcer:** Dick Sanford. **Official Scorer:** Ron Jernick.

### Travel, Clubhouse

**Director, Team Travel:** Bill Beck.
**Equipment Manager:** John Silverman. **Assistant Equipment Manager:** Mark Brown. **Visiting Clubhouse Manager:** Bryan Greenberg. **Assistant, Clubhouse/Umpire's Room:** Michael Hughes.

## GENERAL INFORMATION

**Stadium (year opened):** Dolphins Stadium (1993).
**Home Dugout:** First base. **Playing Surface:** Grass.
**Team Colors:** Teal, black and white.
**Player Representative:** Unavailable.

## BASEBALL OPERATIONS

**Telephone:** (305) 626-7400. **FAX:** (305) 626-7433.
**Senior Vice President/General Manager:** Larry Beinfest.
**Vice President, Player Personnel:** Dan Jennings. **Assistant GM:** Michael Hill. **Special Assistant to GM/Pro Scout:** Orrin Freeman. **General Counsel:** Derek Jackson. **Video Coordinator:** Cullen McRae. **Executive Assistant to Senior VP/GM:** Rita Filbert. **Assistant, Baseball Operations:** Jay Catalano.

### Major League Staff

**Manager:** Joe Girardi.

Larry Beinfest

**Coaches:** Bench—Gary Tuck; Pitching—Rick Kranitz; Batting—Jim Presley; First Base—Perry Hill; Third Base—Bobby Meacham; Bullpen—Mike Harkey; Bullpen Coordinator—Pierre Arsenault.

### Medical, Training

**Team Physician:** Dr. Daniel Kanell.
**Head Trainer:** Sean Cunningham. **Assistant Trainer:** Mike Kozak. **Director, Strength/ Conditioning:** Paul Fournier.

### Player Development

**Vice President, Player Development/Scouting:** Jim Fleming.
**Director, Player Development:** Brian Chattin. **Assistant Player Development:** Manny Colon.
**Field Coordinator:** John Pierson. **Coordinators:** Gene Basham (training/rehabilitation), Bo Porter (outfield), John Mallee (hitting), Ed Romero (infield), Wayne Rosenthal (pitching), Mike West (strength/conditioning).
**Minor League Equipment Manager:** Mark Brown. **Minor League Clubhouse Manager:** Dave Vonderhaar.

Joe Girardi

### Farm System

| Class | Farm Team | League | Manager | Coach | Pitching Coach |
|---|---|---|---|---|---|
| Triple-A | Albuquerque | Pacific Coast | Dean Treanor | Steve Phillips | Tom Brown |
| Double-A | Carolina | Southern | Luis Dorante | Paul Sanagorski | Scott Mitchell |
| High A | Jupiter | Florida State | Tim Cossins | Darin Everson | Reid Cornelius |
| Low A | Greensboro | South Atlantic | Brandon Hyde | Josue Espada | Steve Foster |
| Short-season | Jamestown | New York-Penn | Bo Porter | Anthony Iapoce | John Duffy |
| Rookie | Jupiter | Gulf Coast | Edwin Rodriguez | Johnny Rodriguez | Gary Buckels |
| Rookie | Marlins | Dominican | Jose Zapata | Basilio Alvarado | Edison Santana |
| Rookie | Marlins | Venezuelan | Romulo Oliveros | Unavailable | Rene Garcia |

### Scouting

**Telephone:** (305) 626-7400. **FAX:** (305) 626-7294.
**Director, Scouting:** Stan Meek. **Assistant Director, Scouting:** Gregg Leonard.
**Advance Scout:** Joe Moeller (Manhattan Beach, CA). **Pro Scouts:** Tommy Thompson (La Mesa, CA), Gene Watson.
**National Crosschecker:** David Crowson (College Station, TX). **Regional Supervisors:** East—Mike Cadahia (Miami Springs, FL); Central—Ray Hayward (Norman, OK); West—Scott Goldby (Yuba City, CA); Canada—Steve Payne (Barrington, RI).

**Area Scouts:** Matt Anderson (Williamsport, PA), Carlos Berroa (Caguas, PR), Brian Bridges (Canton, GA), Dennis Cardoza (College Station, TX), John Cole (Lake Forest, CA), Robby Corsaro (Victorville, CA), Scot Engler (Montgomery, IL), John Hughes (Walnut Creek, CA), John Martin (Tampa, FL), Joel Matthews (Concord, NC), Bob Oldis (Iowa City, IA), Steve Payne (Barrington, RI), David Post (Hillsboro, OR), Scott Stanley (Peoria, AZ), Ryan Wardinsky (Edmond, OK), Mark Willoughby (Hammond, LA).

Stan Meek

**Director, International Operations:** Albert Gonzalez.
**International Supervisors:** Venezuela—Carlos Acosta (Caracas); Dominican Republic—Jesus Campos (San Pedro de Macoris).
**International Scouts:** Wilmer Adrian (Venezuela), Aristides Bustamonte (Panama/Costa Rica), Nelson Castro (Venezuela), Enrique Constante (Dominican Republic), Todd Darvall (Australia), Luis Fermin (Venezuela), Rene Garcia (Venezuela), Ton Hofstede (Netherlands), A.B. Jesurun (Netherlands), Roberto Marquez (Venezuela), Willie Marrugo (Colombia), Pedro Martinez (Venezuela), Spencer Mills (Curacao), Romulo Oliveros (Venezuela), Rene Picota (Panama), Carlos Rivero (Venezuela), Craig Stoves (Australia), Orlando Tejeda (Venezuela).

# HOUSTON ASTROS

**Office Address:** Minute Maid Park, Union Station, 501 Crawford, Suite 400, Houston, TX 77002.
**Mailing Address:** P.O. Box 288, Houston, TX 77001.
**Telephone:** (713) 259-8000. **FAX:** (713) 259-8981.
**E-Mail Address:** fanfeedback@astros.mlb.com. **Website:** www.astros.com.

## Ownership
**Operated by:** McLane Group, LP.
**Chairman, Chief Executive Officer:** Drayton McLane.
**Board of Directors:** Drayton McLane, Bob McClaren, G.W. Sanford, Webb Stickney.

## BUSINESS OPERATIONS
**President, Business Operations:** Pam Gardner. **Executive Assistant:** Eileen Colgin.

### Finance/Administration
**Senior Vice President, Finance/Administration:** Jackie Traywick.
**Director, Treasury:** Damian Babin. **Controller:** Jonathan Germer. **Senior Accountant:** Abby Price. **Accounts Payable Clerk:** Irene Dumenil. **Accounting Coordinator:** Evelyn Tremaine. **Director, Ticket Services:** Brooke Ellenberger.
**Director, Human Resources:** Larry Stokes. **Human Resources Coordinator:** Jordon Kalina. **Director, Payroll/Employee Benefits:** Ruth Kelly. **Manager, Payroll/Benefits:** Jessica Horton.

Drayton McLane

### Marketing, Sales
**Vice President, Broadcasting/Advertising Sales/Promotions:** Jamie Hildreth.
**Director, Advertising Sales:** Alicia Nevins. **Manager, Advertising Sales:** Yvette Casares-Willis.
**VP, Market Development:** Rosi Hernandez. **Senior Director, Marketing:** Jennifer Randall. **Market Development Coordinator:** Caroline Montano.

### Public Relations, Communications
**Telephone:** (713) 259-8900. **FAX:** (713) 259-8981.
**Senior Vice President, Communications:** Jay Lucas.
**Director, Media Relations:** Jimmy Stanton. **Assistant Director, Media Relations:** Lisa Ramsperger.
**VP, Community Development:** Marian Harper. **Director, Business Communications:** Todd Fedewa.
**Director, Community Events:** Rita Suchma.
**Senior Director, Information Technology/Procurement:** Brad Bourland. **Information Technology Coordinator:** Arlene Hebert. **Assistant Director, Information Technology:** Rob Weaver.

### Stadium Operations
**Senior Vice President, Ballpark Operations/Customer Service:** Rob Matwick.
**VP, Special Events:** Kala Sorenson. **Senior Director, Engineering/Maintenance:** Bobby Forrest. **Assistant Director, Engineering:** David McKenzie. **Audio-Visual Supervisor:** Lowell Matheny. **Security Manager:** Kirk Benoit.
**Director, Ballpark Entertainment:** Kirby Kander. **Assistant Director, Ballpark Entertainment:** Brock Jessel. **Manager, Marketing/Promotions:** Clint Pasche. **Senior Broadcast Engineer/Affiliate Relations:** Mike Cannon. **Director, Telecommunications/Executive Assistant:** Tracy Faucette.
**Director, Customer Service:** Michael Kenny. **Manager, Special Events:** Leigh Ann Dawson. **Conference Center/Special Events Sales:** Christine O'Beirne. **Manager, Minute Maid Park Tours:** Marcos Ramos.
**Director, Major League Field Operations:** Dan Bergstrom. **Groundskeeper:** Willie Berry. **First Assistant Groundskeeper:** Chris Pearl. **Second Assistant Groundskeeper:** Geoffrey Humphrey.
**PA Announcer:** Bob Ford. **Official Scorers:** Rick Blount, Ivy McLemore, David Matheson, Trey Wilkinson.

### Ticketing
**Telephone:** (713) 259-8500. **FAX:** (713) 259-8326.
**Vice President, Business Development:** John Sorrentino.
**Director, Ticket Operations:** Marcia Coronado. **Director, Box Office Operations:** Bill Cannon. **Manager, Ticket Sales Support:** Rebecca Bond. **Manager, Premium Sales:** Andrea Levine-Spier. **Administrative Assistant, Ticket Services:** Joannie Cobb. **Senior Account Executive:** Brent Broussard. **Ticket Production Coordinator:** Sandy Luna.

### Travel, Clubhouse
**Director, Team Travel:** Barry Waters. **Equipment Manager:** Dennis Liborio. **Assistant Equipment Managers:** Carl Schneider, Butch New. **Visiting Clubhouse Manager:** Steve Perry. **Umpires/Clubhouse Assistant:** Chuck New.

---

## GENERAL INFORMATION
**Stadium (year opened):** Minute Maid Park (2000).
**Home Dugout:** First Base. **Playing Surface:** Grass.
**Team Colors:** Brick red, sand beige and black.
**Player Representative:** Morgan Ensberg.

Tim Purpura

## BASEBALL OPERATIONS

**Telephone:** (713) 259-8000. **FAX:** (713) 259-8600.
**President, Baseball Operations:** Tal Smith.
**General Manager:** Tim Purpura. **Senior Director, Baseball Operations:** David Gottfried. **Special Assistants to General Manager:** Enos Cabell, Al Pedrique, Nolan Ryan. **Consultant, Baseball Operations:** Matt Galante. **Executive Assistant, Major League Operations:** Traci Dearing. **Video Coordinator:** Jim Summers.

### Major League Staff

**Manager:** Phil Garner.
**Coaches:** Bench—Cecil Cooper; Pitching—Jim Hickey; Batting—Gary Gaetti; First Base—Jose Cruz Sr.; Third Base—Doug Mansolino; Bullpen—Mark Bailey.

### Medical, Training

**Medical Director:** Dr. David Lintner. **Team Physicians:** Dr. Tom Mehlhoff, Dr. Jim Muntz.
**Head Trainer:** Dave Labossiere. **Assistant Trainer:** Rex Jones. **Strength/Conditioning Coach:** Dr. Gene Coleman.

### Player Development

**Telephone:** (713) 259-8922. **FAX:** (713) 259-8600.
**Assistant General Manager/Director, Player Development:** Ricky Bennett. **Assistant Directors, Baseball Operations:** Jay Edmiston, Bryan Frazier, Carlos Perez, Charlie Norton
**Field Coordinator:** Tom Wiedenbauer. **Minor League Coordinators:** Sean Berry (hitting), Russ Nixon (defense), Dewey Robinson (pitching).
**Coordinator, Training/Rehabilitation:** Pete Fagan. **Coordinator, Strength/Conditioning:** Nate Lucero.

Phil Garner

### Farm System

| Class | Farm Team | League | Manager | Coach(es) | Pitching Coach |
|---|---|---|---|---|---|
| Triple A | Round Rock | Pacific Coast | Jackie Moore | Spike Owen/Harry Spilman | Burt Hooton |
| Double A | Corpus Christi | Texas | Dave Clark | John Tamargo Jr. | Joe Slusarski |
| High A | Salem | Carolina | Jim Pankovits | Chuck Carr | Stan Boroski |
| Low A | Lexington | South Atlantic | Jack Lind | Rodney Linares | Charley Taylor |
| Short-Season | Tri-City | New York-Penn | Gregg Langbehn | Joel Chimelis | Don Alexander |
| Rookie | Greeneville | Appalachian | Ivan DeJesus | Pete Rancont | Bill Ballou |
| Rookie | Astros | Dominican | Rafael Ramirez | A. DeFreitas/M. De laCruz | Rick Aponte |
| Rookie | Astros | Venezuela | Mario Gonzalez | Omar Lopez | Luis Yanez |

### Scouting

**Telephone:** (713) 259-8921. **FAX:** (713) 259-8600.
**Senior Director, Player Personnel:** Paul Ricciarini. **Assistant Director, Baseball Operations:** Charlie Norton.
**Coordinator, Major League Scouting:** Fred Nelson. **Major League Scouts:** Gordy MacKenzie (Fruitland Park, FL), Walt Matthews (Texarkana, TX), Tom Romenesko (Santee, CA), Bob Skinner (San Diego, CA).
**Coordinator, Professional Scouting:** J.D. Elliby (Orlando, FL). **Professional Scouts:** Glen Barker (Albany, NY), Ken Califano (Stafford, VA), Gene DeBoer (Brandon, WI), Scipio Spinks (Missouri City, TX).
**Coordinator, Amateur Scouting:** Tad Slowik (Arlington Heights, IL).
**National Supervisor:** Ralph Bratton (Dripping Springs, TX);
**Regional Supervisors:** East—Gerry Craft (St. Clairsville, OH); West—Dough Deutsch (Costa Mesa, CA).

Paul Ricciarini

**Area Scouts:** J.D. Alleva (Henderson, NV), Jon Bunnell (Tampa, FL), Ellis Dungan (Charlotte, NC), Ed Edwards (Landisburg, PA), James Farrar (Shreveport, LA), Paul Gale (Keizer, OR), Tim Harrington (Boston, MA), David Henderson (Edmond, OK), Brian Keegan (Matthews, NC), Bob King (La Mesa, CA), Mike Maggart (Penn Yan, NY), Tom McCormack (University City, MO), Rusty Pendergrass (Houston, TX), Bob Poole (Redwood City, CA), Mike Rosamond (Madison, MS), Mark Ross (Tucson, AZ), Joey Sola (Caguas, PR), Kevin Stein (Columbus, OH), Chuck Stone (Moreno Valley, CA), Dennis Twombley (Redondo Beach, CA), Nick Venuto (Massillon, OH), Gene Wellman (Danville, CA).
**Special Assistant to GM, Dominican Scouting/Development:** Julio Linares. **Coordinator, Venezuela:** Pablo Torrealba.

# KANSAS CITY ROYALS

**Office Address:** One Royal Way, Kansas City, MO 64129.
**Mailing Address:** P.O. Box 419969, Kansas City, MO 64141.
**Telephone:** (816) 921-8000. **FAX:** (816) 921-1366.
**Website:** www.royals.com.

## Ownership

**Operated by:** Kansas City Royals Baseball Club, Inc.
**Chairman/Chief Executive Officer:** David Glass. **President:** Dan Glass. **Board of Directors:** Ruth Glass, Don Glass, Dayna Martz, Julia Irene Kauffman, Herk Robinson.

## BUSINESS OPERATIONS

**Senior Vice President, Business Operations:** Mark Gorris. **Executive Administrative Assistant:** Cindy Hamilton.

### Finance

David Glass

**Vice President, Finance/Administration:** Dale Rohr. **Senior Administrative Assistant:** Janet Milone.
**Director, Finance:** Joe Kurtzman. **Manager, Accounting:** Sean Ritchie. **Manager, Ticket Operations/Concessions Accounting:** Lisa Kresha. **Coordinator, Accounts Payable:** Sarah Kosfeld. **Coordinator, Accounting:** Shelley Wilson.
**Senior Director, Payroll/Benefits/Human Resources:** Tom Pfannenstiel. **Manager, Human Resources:** Lynne Elder. **Payroll Administrator:** Margaret Willits.
**Senior Director, Information Systems:** Jim Edwards. **Manager, Programming/Systems Analyst:** Becky Randall. **Manager, Client Services Specialist:** Scott Novak. **Programmer/Analyst:** Bonnie Stalker.

### Communications, Marketing

**Vice President, Communications/Marketing:** David Witty.
**Director, Royals Charities:** Betty Kaegel.
**Director, Broadcast Services/Royals Alumni:** Fred White. **Manager, Radio Network Operations:** Don Free.
**Director, Community Relations:** Ben Aken. **Senior Director, Marketing:** Kim Hillix Burgess. **Manager, Marketing:** Curt Nelson. **Manager, Game Entertainment:** Chris DeRuyscher. **Graphic Designer:** Vic Royal. **Coordinator, Promotions:** Emily Rand. **Coordinator, Game Entertainment:** Ben Mertens.

### Media Relations

**Director, Media Relations:** Aaron Babcock. **Coordinator, Media Relations:** David Holtzman. **Director, Public Realtions:** Lora Grosshans. **Coordinator, Public/Community Relations:** Josh Diekmann. **Public Relations Administrative Assistant:** Precious Washington. **Mascot Coordinator:** Byron Shores.

### Ballpark Operations

**Vice President, Ballpark Operations/Development:** Bob Rice.
**Director, Event Operations/Guest Services:** Chris Richardson. **Managers, Event Operations/Guest Services:** Courtney Files, Renee VanLaningham. **Manager, Stadium Tours/Operations:** Morrie Carlson.
**Director, Groundskeeping/Landscaping:** Trevor Vance. **Manager, Groundskeeping:** Jerad Minnick. **Landscape Assistant:** Anthony Bruce.
**Director, Stadium Operations:** Rodney Lewallen. **Coordinators, Stadium Operations:** Jermaine Goodwin, Matthew Pellant. **Coordinator, Telephone Services:** Kathy Butler. **Coordinator, Mail Services:** Larry Garrett. **Manager, Stadium Services:** Johnny Williams. **Manager, Stadium Engineering:** Todd Burrow. **Supervisor, Stadium Operations Technicians:** Louis Noble. **Stadium Operations Technicians:** Byron Clark, Chris Frank, Terrence McKelvy, Mike Rader.

### Ticketing

**Senior Director, Ticket Sales/Operations:** Lance Buckley. **Director, Ticket Operations:** Chris Darr. **Director, Season Ticket Services:** Joe Grigoli. **Coordinator, Season Tickets:** Mary Lee Martino. **Coordinators, Ticket Operations:** Betty Bax, Jacque Tschirhart. **Ticket Operations Vault Manager:** Andew Coughlin. **Director, Group Sales/Call Center Operations:** Scott Wadsworth. **Account Executives:** Jen Hyland, Jeff Miller, Rachelle Smith. **Manager, Call Center:** Jim Evans. **Director, Season Ticket Sales/Royals Lancers:** Rick Amos. **Season Ticket Sales Administrative Assistant:** Janis Rowland.

### Business Development

**Vice President, Business Development:** Neil Harwell. **VP, Corporate/Group Sales:** Mike Phillips. **Director, Corporate Sponsorships:** Michele Kammerer. **Account Executives:** Carl Keenan, Brian Legenza.

---

### GENERAL INFORMATION

**Stadium (year opened):** Ewing M. Kauffman Stadium (1973).
**Home Dugout:** First base. **Playing Surface:** Grass.
**Team Colors:** Royal blue and white.
**Player Representative:** Jeremy Affeldt.

Allard Baird

## BASEBALL OPERATIONS

Telephone: (816) 921-8000. FAX: (816) 924-0347. *Daytona...*

Senior Vice President/General Manager: ~~Allard Baird~~.
VP/Assistant GM: Muzzy Jackson. Senior Adviser to GM: Art Stewart. Assistant to GM: Brian Murphy. Special Assistants to GM: Pat Jones, Luis Medina. Manager, Major League Operations: Karol Kyte.

Vice President, Baseball Operations: George Brett. Director, Baseball Operations: Jin Wong.

Senior Director, Player Personnel: Donny Rowland.

### Major League Staff

Manager: Buddy Bell

Coaches: Bench—Bill Doran; Pitching—Bob McClure; Batting—Andre David; First Base—Brian Poldberg; Third Base—Luis Silverio; Bullpen—Fred Kendall

## Medical, Training

Team Physician: Dr. Steven Joyce. Associate Physicians: Dr. Tim Badwey, Dr. Mark Bernhardt, Dr. Dan Gurba, Dr. Thomas Phillips, Dr. Charles Rhoades.

Athletic Trainer: Nick Swartz. Assistant Athletic Trainer: Frank Kyte. Strength/Conditioning Coordinator: Andy Kettler.

## Player Development

Telephone: (816) 921-8000. FAX: (816) 924-0347.

Senior Director, Player Development: Shaun McGinn. Manager, Minor League Operations: Amy Buckler.

Special Assignment, Player Development/Scouting: Joe Jones

Special Assistant, Baseball Operations: Guy Hansen.

Coordinator, Instruction: Jeff Garber. Roving Instructors: Ron Clark (infield), Mike Barnett (hitting), Ty Hill (strength/conditioning), Dale Gilbert (rehabilitation), Mike Mason (pitching), John Mizerock (catching); John Wathan (bunting/baserunning)

Minor League Equipment Coordinator: Johnny O'Donnell.

Buddy Bell

## Farm System

| Class | Farm Team | League | Manager | Coach(es) | Pitching Coach |
|---|---|---|---|---|---|
| AAA | Omaha | Pacific Coast | Mike Jirschele | Terry Bradshaw | Tom Burgmeier |
| AA | Wichita | Texas | Frank White | Al LeBeouf | Larry Carter |
| High A | High Desert | California | Jeff Carter | Boots Day | Steve Renko |
| Low A | Burlington | Midwest | Jim Gabella | Patrick Anderson | Steve Luebber |
| Short season | Idaho Falls | Pioneer | Brian Rupp | Theron Todd | Jose Bautista |
| Rookie | Surprise | Arizona | Lloyd Simmons | T. Poquette/N. Liriano | Mark Davis |
| Rookie | Royals | Dominican | Julio Bruno | M. Garcia/B. Liriano | Carlos Martinez |

## Scouting

Telephone: (816) 921-8000. FAX: (816) 924-0347.

Senior Director, Scouting: Deric Ladnier. Manager, Scouting Operations: Linda Smith.

Professional Scouts: Brannon Bonifay (Stuart, FL), Orlando Estevez (Pembroke Pines, FL), Dave Garcia (El Cajon, CA), Ben McLure (Hummelstown, PA), Earl Winn (Bowling Green, KY).

Advance Scout: Mike Pazik (Bethesda, MD).

Regional Supervisors: Junior Vizcaino (Raleigh, NC), Dennis Woody (Danville, AR).

Area Supervisors: Bob Bishop (San Dimas, CA), Mike Brown (Chandler, AZ), Jason Bryans (Windsor, Ontario), Steve Connelly (Wilson, NC), Spencer Graham (Kingsport, TN), Phil Huttman (Houston), Gary Johnson (Costa Mesa, CA), Jeff McKay (Springfield, OR), Cliff Pastornicky (Bradenton, FL), John Ramey (Wildomar, CA), Johnny Ramos (Carolina, PR), Brian Rhees (Little Rock, AR), Sean Rooney (Pompton Lakes, NJ), Toby Rumfield (Minooka, IL), Mark Ryal (Inola, OK), Max Semler (Lake City, FL), Greg Smith (Davenport, WA), Gerald Turner (Euless, TX).

Deric Ladnier

Part-Time Scouts: Frank Baez (Los Angeles), Steve Goodheart (Magnolia, AR), Buck O'Neil (Kansas City), Eric Tokunaga (Aiea, HI), Harry von Suskil (Coral Gables, FL).

Dominican Academy Administrator/Scouting Supervisor: Pedro Silverio.

Venezuelan Scouting Supervisor: Juan Indriago.

International Scouts: Wilmer Castillo (Venezuela), Luis Cordoba (Panama), Juan Lopez (Nicaragua), Ramon Martinez (Dominican Republic), Daurys Nin (Dominican Republic), Mike Randall (South Africa), Matthew Sheldon-Collins (Australia), Ra Vasquez (Dominican Republic).

# LOS ANGELES ANGELS

**Office Address:** Angel Stadium of Anaheim, 2000 Gene Autry Way, Anaheim, CA 92806.
**Mailing Address:** P.O. Box 2000, Anaheim, CA 92803.
**Telephone:** (714) 940-2000. **FAX:** (714) 940-2205.
**Website:** www.angelsbaseball.com.

## Ownership
**Operated by:** Angels Baseball LP.
**Chairman, Chief Executive Officer:** Arturo Moreno.

## BUSINESS OPERATIONS
**President:** Dennis Kuhl.

Arte Moreno

### Finance, Administration
**Chief Financial Officer:** Bill Beverage. **Vice President, Finance/Administration:** Molly Taylor. **Senior Financial Analyst:** Amy Langdale. **Assistant Controller:** Cris Fisher. **Accountants:** Lorelei Largey, Jean Ouyang. **Assistant, Accounting:** Linda Chubak.
**Director, Human Resources:** Jenny Price. **Human Resources Generalists:** Nathan Andres, Lidia Argomaniz. **Benefits Coordinator:** Tracie Key.

### Marketing, Corporate Sales
**Senior Vice President, Sales/Marketing:** John Carpino. **Director, Corporate Sales:** Richard McClemmy. **Corporate Sales Managers:** Pennie Contos, Joe Furmanski, Mike Gullo, Michael Means, Sabrina Warner.
**Sponsorship Services Manager:** Carrie Basham. **Administrative Assistant:** Maria Dinh.
**Director, Marketing/Ticket Sales:** Robert Alvarado. **Administrative Assistant, Marketing:** Monica Campanis. **Administrative Assistant, Sales:** Pat Lissy. **Marketing Coordinator/Designer:** Nancy Herrera. **Account Executives:** Dan Carnahan, Mike Kirby, Bryan Lawrence, Keith Rowe.
**Group Sales Account Executives:** Scott Booth, Carla Enriquez, Ernie Prukner, Ryan Redmond, Angel Rodriguez. **Telemarketing Supervisor:** Tom DeTemple.
**Manager, Entertainment:** Peter Bull. **Producer, Video/Scoreboard Operations:** Robert Castillo. **Associate Producer, Video/Scoreboard Operations:** David Tsuruda.

### Public/Media Relations, Communications
**Telephone:** (714) 940-2014. **FAX:** (714) 940-2205.
**Vice President, Communications:** Tim Mead. **Administrative Assistant:** Lindsay McHolm.
**Director, Communications:** Nancy Mazmanian. **Communications/Media Relations Manager:** Larry Babcock. **Media Relations Manager:** Eric Kay.
**Manager, Community Development:** Matt Bennett. **Coordinator, Community Relations:** Anne Blasius. **Publicity/Broadcasting Manager:** Aaron Tom. **Publications Manager:** Doug Ward. **Speakers' Bureau:** Bobby Grich, Clyde Wright. **Club Photographers:** Debora Robinson, John Cordes, Bob Binder.

### Ballpark Operations
**Director, Ballpark Operations:** Sam Maida. **Director, Facility Services:** Mike McKay. **Assistant Operations Manager:** Calvin Ching.
**Manager, Security:** Keith Cleary. **Manager, Field/Ground Maintenance:** Barney Lopas. **Purchasing Manager:** Ron Sparks. **Assisstant Manager, Facility Services:** Linda Fitzgerald. **Purchasing Assistant:** Suzanne Peters. **Office Support Assistant:** Calvin Ching. **Receptionists:** Sandy Sanford, Margie Walsh. **Manager, Information Services:** Al Castro. **Senior Network Engineer:** Neil Farris. **Senior Customer Support Analyst:** David Yun. **PA Announcer:** David Courtney.

### Ticketing
**Manager, Ticket Operations:** Sheila Brazelton. **Assistant Ticket Manager:** Susan Weiss. **Supervisor, Ticketing:** Amer Nadler. **Ticketing Representatives:** Clancy Holligan, Kim Weaver, Cyndi Nguyen.

### Travel, Clubhouse
**Traveling Secretary:** Tom Taylor.
**Clubhouse Manager:** Ken Higdon. **Assistant Clubhouse Manager:** Keith Tarter. **Visiting Clubhouse Manager:** Brian Harkins.
**Senior Video Coordinator:** Diego Lopez. **Video Coordinator:** Ruben Montano.

---

## GENERAL INFORMATION

**Stadium (year opened):** Angel Stadium of Anaheim (1998).
**Home Dugout:** Third Base. **Playing Surface:** Grass.
**Team Colors:** Red, dark red, blue and silver.
**Player Representative:** Unavailable.

## BASEBALL OPERATIONS
**Vice President, General Manager:** Bill Stoneman.
**Assistant GM:** Ken Forsch. **Special Assistant to GM:** Gary Sutherland.
**Administrative Assistant, Scouting/General Manager:** Laura Fazioli.

### Major League Staff
**Manager:** Mike Scioscia.
**Coaches:** Bench—Ron Roenicke; Pitching—Bud Black; Batting—Mickey Hatcher; First Base—Alfredo Griffin; Third Base—Dino Ebel; Bullpen—Orlando Mercado; Bullpen Catcher—Steve Soliz.

**Bill Stoneman**

### Medical, Training
**Medical Director:** Dr. Lewis Yocum. **Team Physician:** Dr. Craig Milhouse.
**Head Athletic Trainer:** Ned Bergert. **Athletic Trainer:** Rick Smith. **Assistant Athletic Trainer:** Adam Nevala. **Strength/Conditioning Coach:** Brian Grapes. **Administrative Assistant:** Chris Titchenal.

### Player Development
**Telephone:** (714) 940-2031. **FAX:** (714) 940-2203.
**Director, Player Development:** Tony Reagins. **Manager, Baseball Operations:** Abe Flores.
**Director, Arizona Operations:** Eric Blum.
**Field Coordinator:** Bruce Hines. **Roving Instructors:** Keith Comstock (pitching), T.J. Harrington (strength/conditioning), Geoff Hostetter (training coordinator), Bill Lachemann (catching/special assignment), Rob Picciolo (infield), Todd Takayoshi (catching), Ty Van Burkleo (hitting).

**Mike Scioscia**

### Farm System

| Class | Farm Team | League | Manager | Coach | Pitching Coach |
|-------|-----------|--------|---------|-------|----------------|
| AAA | Salt Lake | Pacific Coast | Brian Harper | Jim Eppard | Charles Nagy |
| AA | Arkansas | Texas | Tyrone Boykin | Keith Johnson | Ken Patterson |
| High A | Rancho Cucamonga | California | Bobby Mitchell | Craig Grebeck | Eric Bennett |
| Low A | Cedar Rapids | Midwest | Bobby Magallanes | Eric Owens | Kernan Ronan |
| Rookie | Orem | Pioneer | Tom Kotchman | Francisco Matos | Zeke Zimmerman |
| Rookie | Tempe | Arizona | Ever Magallanes | Rodney Davis | Dan Ricabal |
| Rookie | San Pedro de Macoris | Dominican | Charlie Romero | Edgal Rodriguez | Santos Alcala |

### Scouting
**Telephone:** (714) 940-2038. **FAX:** (714) 940-2203.
**Director, Amateur Scouting:** Eddie Bane.
**Director, Professional Scouting:** Gary Sutherland.
**Major League Scouts:** Rich Schlenker (Walnut Creek, CA), Jeff Schugel (Denver, CO), Brad Sloan (Brimfield, IL), Moose Stubing (Villa Park, CA), Dale Sutherland (La Crescenta, CA).
**National Crosscheckers:** Jeff Malinoff (Lopez, WA), Ric Wilson (Chandler, AZ). **Regional Supervisors:** East—Marc Russo (Clearwater, FL), Midwest—Ron Marigny (New Orleans, LA); West—Bo Hughes (Sherman Oaks, CA).
**Area Scouts:** Arnold Braithwaite (Steger, IL), Jim Bryant (Chattanooga, TN), John Burden (Fairfield, OH), Tim Corcoran (La Verne, CA), Bobby DeJardin (San Clemente, CA), John Gracio (Mesa, AZ), Kevin Ham (El Paso, TX), Tom Kotchman (Seminole, FL), Dan Lynch (Marlboro, MA), Chris McAlpin (Huntersville, NC), Joel Murrie (Bowling Green, KY), Dan

**Eddie Bane**

Radcliff (Green Belt, MD), Scott Richardson (Vacaville, CA), Jeff Scholzen (Hurricane, UT), Mike Silvestri (Davie, FL), Jack Uhey (Vancouver, WA), Rob Wilfong (San Dimas, CA).
**International Supervisor:** Clay Daniel (Jacksonville, FL).
**International Scouts:** Felipe Gutierrez (Mexico), Tak Kawamoto (Japan), Charlie Kim (Korea), Juan Melendez (Puerto Rico), Alex Messier (Canada), Leo Perez (Dominican Republic), Carlos Porte (Venezuela), Dennys Suarez (Venezuela), Ramon Valenzuela (Dominican Republic), Cesar Velasquez (Panama), Grant Weir (Australia).

# LOS ANGELES DODGERS

**Office Address:** 1000 Elysian Park Ave., Los Angeles, CA 90012.
**Telephone:** (323) 224-1500. **FAX:** (323) 224-1269.
**Website:** www.dodgers.com.

## Ownership
**Operated by:** Los Angeles Dodgers, LLC.
**Principal Owner/Chairman of the Board:** Frank McCourt. **President/Vice Chairman:** Jamie McCourt. **Special Adviser to Chairman:** Tommy Lasorda.

## BUSINESS OPERATIONS
**Executive Vice President, Chief Operating Officer:** Marty Greenspun. **Executive VP, Business:** Jeff Ingram. **Executive VP, Public Affairs:** Howard Sunkin.
**Senior VP, General Counsel:** Sam Fernandez.
**Chief Marketing Officer:** Tagg Romney. **Director, Marketing:** Drew McCourt. **Secretary, Legal:** Irma Duenas.

Frank McCourt

## Finance
**Senior Vice President, Chief Financial Officer:** Cris Hurley. **VP, Finance:** Amanda Shearer. **Controller:** Steven Anderson. **Senior Manager, Payroll:** Rebecca Aguilar.

## Sales, Advertising, Client Services
**Vice President, Sales:** Sergio del Prado. **VP, Ticket Sales:** Steve Shiffman. **Director, Sponsorship Sales:** Karen Marumoto. **Director, Premium Seat Sales:** David Siegel.

## Public Relations, Communications
**Senior Vice President, Communications:** Camille Johnston.
**Director, Public Relations:** Josh Rawitch. **Assistant Director, Public Relations:** Joe Jareck. **Director, Publications:** Jorge Martin. **Director, Community Relations:** Don Newcombe.

## Stadium Operations
**Vice President, Stadium Operations:** Lon Rosenberg.
**Director, Security:** Shahram Ariane. **Facilities Manager:** Mike Grove. **Assistant Director, Stadium Operations/Turf and Grounds:** Eric Hansen.
**PA Announcer:** Eric Smith. **Official Scorers:** Don Hartack, Ed Munson.-**Organist:** Nancy Bea Hefley.

## Ticketing
**Telephone:** (323) 224-1471. **FAX:** (323) 224-2609.
**Director, Ticket Operations:** Billy Hunter. **Assistant Director, Ticket Operations:** Seth Bluman.

## Travel, Clubhouse
**Manager, Team Travel:** Scott Akasaki. **Home Clubhouse Managers:** Dave Dickinson, Mitch Poole. **Visiting Clubhouse Manager:** Jerry Turner.

## GENERAL INFORMATION
**Stadium (year opened):** Dodger Stadium (1962).
**Home Dugout:** Third base. **Playing Surface:** Grass.
**Team Colors:** Dodger blue and white.
**Player Representative:** Jayson Werth.

Ned Colletti

## BASEBALL OPERATIONS

**Telephone:** (323) 224-1500. **FAX:** (323) 224-1463.
**General Manager:** Ned Colletti. **Vice President, Assistant GM:** Kim Ng.
**Vice President, Scouting/Player Development:** Roy Smith. **Vice President, Spring Training/Minor League Facilities:** Craig Callan.
**Special Assistant to GM/Advance Scout:** Mark Weidemaier (Tierre Verde, FL). **Coordinator, Baseball Operations:** Dan Feinstein. **Administrator, Baseball Operations:** Ellen Harrigan. **Executive Assistant, Baseball Operations:** Adriana Urzua.
**Director, Asian Operations:** Acey Kohrogi. **Manager, Asian Operations:** Curtis Jung.

## Major League Staff

**Manager:** Grady Little.
**Coaches:** Bench—Dave Jauss; Pitching—Rick Honeycutt; Hitting—Eddie Murray; First Base—Mariano Duncan; Third Base—Rich Donnelly; Bullpen—-Dan Warthen.

## Medical, Training

**Team Physicians:** Dr. Frank Jobe, Dr. Michael Mellman, Dr. Ralph Gambardella, Dr. Herndon Harding.
**Head Trainer:** Stan Johnston. **Assistant Trainer:** Matt Wilson. **Physical Therapist:** Pat Screnar. **Strength/Conditioning Coach:** Doug Jarrow.

## Player Development

Grady Little

**Telephone:** (323) 224-1431. **FAX:** (323) 224-1359.
**Director, Player Development:** Terry Collins. **Assistant Director, Player Development:** Luchy Guerra. **Coordinator, Minor League Operations:** Chris Haydock.
**Roving Coordinators:** Bill Robinson (hitting), Marty Reed (pitching), Jon Debus (catching), Dave Anderson (infield), Landon Brandes (strength/conditioning), David Rivera (physical therapist).
**Director, Campo Las Palmas/Dominican Republic:** Eleodoro Arias. **Coordinators, Dominican Republic Operations:** Victor Baez (field), Martin Berroa (training), Pedro Mega (infield), Jose Rosario (strength/conditioning).
**Supervisor, Venezuelan Operations:** Camilo Pascual.

## Farm System

| Class | Farm Team | League | Manager | Coach | Pitching Coach |
|-------|-----------|--------|---------|-------|----------------|
| Triple-A | Las Vegas | Pacific Coast | Jerry Royster | Steve Yeager | Ken Howell |
| Double-A | Jacksonville | Southern | John Shoemaker | Mike Easler | Danny Darwin |
| High A | Vero Beach | Florida State | Luis Salazar | Ramon Ortiz | Glenn Dishman |
| Low A | Columbus | South Atlantic | Travis Barbary | Garey Ingram | Richie Lewis |
| Rookie | Ogden | Pioneer | Lance Parrish | Rafael Rijo | Bob Welch |
| Rookie | Vero Beach | Gulf Coast | Juan Bustabad | M. Singleton/T.Brock | Hector Eduardo |
| Rookie | Dodgers | Dominican | Antonio Bautista | Jose Mejia | Kremlin Martinez |

## Scouting

Logan White

**Director, Amateur Scouting:** Logan White. **Special Adviser to Amateur Scouting Director/National Crosschecker:** Gib Bodet (San Clemente, CA). **Administrator, Scouting:** Jane Capobianco. **Coordinator, Scouting Operations:** Bill McLaughlin.
**Major League Scouts:** Carl Loewenstine (Hamilton, OH), Vance Lovelace (Tampa, FL), Matt Slater (Stevenson Ranch, CA)
**Professional Scouts:** Dan Freed (Lexington, IL), Ron Rizzi (Joppa, MD), Al LaMacchia (San Antonio).
**National Crosschecker:** Tim Hallgren (Clarkston, WA). **Regional Supervisors:** East—John Barr (Haddonfield, NJ); Midwest—Gary Nickels (Naperville, IL); West Coast—Tom Thomas (Phoenix).
**Area Scouts:** Bobby Darwin (Cerritos, CA), Manny Estrada (Brandon, FL), Paul Fryer (Calabasas, CA), Calvin Jones (Dallas), Hank Jones (Vancouver, WA), Lon Joyce (Spartanburg, SC), Tim Kelly (Carlsbad, CA), John Kosciak (Milford, MA), Marty Lamb (Nicholasville, KY), Dennis Moeller (Ridgeland, MS), Bill Pleis (Parrish, FL), Clair Rierson (Frederick, MD), Chris Smith (Montgomery, TX), Brian Stephenson (Phoenix), Gerric Waller (San Marcos, CA), Mitch Webster (Great Bend, KS).
**International Scout:** Mike Brito (Mexico).

# MILWAUKEE BREWERS

**Office Address:** Miller Park, One Brewers Way, Milwaukee, WI 53214.
**Telephone:** (414) 902-4400. **FAX:** (414) 902-4053.
**Website:** www.milwaukeebrewers.com.

## Ownership

**Chairman and Principal Owner:** Mark Attanasio.
**Operated by:** Milwaukee Brewers Baseball Club.

## BUSINESS OPERATIONS

**Executive Vice President:** Rick Schlesinger. **Senior Vice President, Chief Financial Officer:** Robert Quinn Jr. **General Counsel:** Marti Wronski. **Executive Assistant, Business Operations:** Adela Reeve. **Executive/Legal Assistant:** Mary Burns.

Mark Attanasio

### Finance, Accounting

**Controller:** Joe Zidanic. **Accounting Manager:** Dan Bradach. **Financial Analysts:** Wes Seidel, Vicki Wise. **Accounts Receivable, Cash Accounting:** Meredith Eland.
**Senior Director, Human Resources/Office Management:** Sally Andrist. **Manager, Human Resources:** Mariela Garcia-Danet.
**Director, Management Information Systems:** Dan Krautkramer. **Systems Analyst:** Corey Kmichik. **PC Support/Telecom Specialist:** Adam Bauer.

### Marketing, Corporate Sponsorships

**Vice President, Corporate Marketing:** Tom Hecht. **Senior Director, Corporate Marketing:** Greg Hilt. **Senior Director, Marketing:** Kathy Schwab. **Directors, Corporate Marketing:** Jason Hartlund, Dave Tamburrino. **Account Executive, Suites:** Andrew Pauls. **Manager, Corporate Suite Services:** Patty Harsch. **Coordinator, Promotions/Sales:** David Barnes. **Programs Administrator:** Carrie Strueder. **Marketing Coordinator:** Caitlin Suess.
**Senior Director, Broadcasting/Entertainment:** Aleta Mercer. **Manager, Audio/Video Productions:** Deron Anderson. **Broadcast Coordinator:** Andrew Olsen.

### Media Relations, Communications

**Telephone:** (414) 902-4500. **FAX:** (414) 902-4053.
**Vice President, Communications:** Tyler Barnes. **Assistant Director, Media Relations:** Nicole Saunches. **Media Relations Associate:** John Steinmiller. **Team Photographer:** Scott Paulus.
**Director, Community Relations:** Leonard Peace. **Coordinator, Community Relations:** Patricia Ramirez. **Manager, Youth Baseball Programs:** Larry Hisle.
**President, Brewers Charities:** Lynn Sprangers.

### Stadium Operations

**Senior Director, Guest Services:** Steve Ethier. **Director, Grounds:** Gary Vanden Berg. **Manager, Grounds:** Raechal Volkening. **Landscape Manager:** Miranda Lehman. **Supervisor, Warehouse:** Patrick Rogo. **Manager, Event Sales:** Amy Barnes. **Administrative Assistant/Miller Park Operations:** Jennacy Cruz. **Receptionist:** Willa Oden. **Mailroom/Receptionist:** Maria Saldana.
**PA Announcer:** Robb Edwards. **Official Scorers:** Tim O'Driscoll, Wayne Franke.

### Ticketing

**Telephone:** (414) 902-4000. **FAX:** (414) 902-4100.
**Senior Director, Ticket Sales:** Jim Bathey. **Senior Director, Ticket Services:** John Barnes.
**Manager, Group Sales:** Chris Barlow. **Manager, Season Ticket Sales:** Billy Friess. **Administrative Assistant:** Irene Bolton. **Assistant Director, Ticket Services:** Nancy Jorgensen. **Manager, Ticket Sales:** Glenn Kurylo. **Coordinator, Ticket Services:** Chad Olson. **Representative, Ticket Office Support Services:** Diane Schoenfeld. **Senior Account Executives:** Nathan Hardwick, Bill Junker, Kara Kabitzke, Chris Kimball, Jeff Hibicke, Jason Massopust. **Account Executive, Group Sales:** Shaunna Richardson. **Account Executives:** Ben Kaebisch, Jedidiah Justman.

### Travel, Clubhouse

**Director, Team Travel:** Dan Larrea.
**Director, Clubhouse Operations/Equipment Manager:** Tony Migliaccio. **Visiting Clubhouse Manager:** Phil Rozewicz. **Assistant, Home Clubhouse:** Mike Moulder.

## GENERAL INFORMATION

**Stadium (year opened):** Miller Park (2001).
**Home Dugout:** First base. **Playing Surface:** Grass.
**Team Colors:** Navy blue, gold and white.
**Player Representative:** Chris Capuano.

Doug Melvin

## BASEBALL OPERATIONS

**Telephone:** (414) 902-4400. **FAX:** (414) 902-4059.
**Executive Vice President, General Manager:**
Doug Melvin. **Assistant GM:** Gord Ash.
**Senior Special Assistant to GM:** Larry Haney (Barboursville, VA). **Director, Administration/Player Development and Scouting:** Tom Flanagan.
**Baseball Research Assistant:** Mike Schwartz. **Baseball Operations Assistant:** Zack Minasian. **Coaching Assistant/Digital Media Coordinator:** Joe Crawford. **Senior Administrator, Baseball Operations:** Barb Stark.

### Major League Staff

**Manager:** Ned Yost.
**Coaches:** Bench—Robin Yount; Pitching—Mike Maddux; Batting—Butch Wynegar; First Base—Dave Nelson; Third Base—Dale Sveum; Bullpen—Bill Castro.

### Medical, Training

Ned Yost

**Head Team Physician:** Dr. William Raasch. **Head Trainer:** Roger Caplinger. **Assistant Trainer:** Dan Wright. **Major League Conditioning Specialist:** Richard Spenner.

### Player Development

**Special Assistant to General Manager/Player Development:** Reid Nichols (Phoenix).
**Business Manager, Player Development:** Scott Martens. **Assistant Director, Player Development:** Tony Diggs. **Assistant, Player Development:** Mark Mueller.
**Field Coordinator:** Ed Sedar. **Coordinators:** Frank Neville (trainers), Jim Rooney (pitching), Jim Skaalen (hitting). **Roving Instructors:** Charlie Greene (catching), Norberto Martin (infield). **Director, Employee Assistance Program:** Tim Hewes.
**Equipment Manager:** J.R. Rinaldi. **Clubhouse Manager, Arizona:** Matt Bass.

### Farm System

| Class | Farm Team | League | Manager | Coach | Pitching Coach(es) |
|---|---|---|---|---|---|
| Triple-A | Nashville | Pacific Coast | Frank Kremblas | Gary Pettis | Stan Kyles |
| Double-A | Huntsville | Southern | Don Money | Sandy Guerrero | Rich Sauveur |
| High A | Brevard County | Florida State | Unavailable | Unavailable | Fred Dabney |
| Low A | West Virginia | South Atlantic | Ramon Aviles | Willie Morales | John Curtis |
| Rookie | Helena | Pioneer | Ed Sedar | Johnny Narron | Mark Littell |
| Rookie | Phoenix | Arizona | Mike Guerrero | Joel Youngblood | S. Cline/Y. Monzon |

### Scouting

Jack Zduriencik

**Telephone:** (414) 902-4400. **FAX:** (414) 902-4059.
**Special Assistant to GM/Director, Amateur Scouting:** Jack Zduriencik. **Special Assistant to GM/Director, Professional Scouting:** Dick Groch (Marysville, MI).
**Assistant Director, Amateur Scouting:** Tony Blengino. **Administrative Assistant:** Amanda Klecker. **Coordinator, Advance Scouting/Baseball Research:** Karl Mueller.
**Professional Scouts:** Lary Aaron (Atlanta), Hank Allen (Upper Marlboro, MD), Chris Bourjos (Scottsdale, AZ), J Harrison (Antelope, CA), Tom Hinkle (Atascadero, CA), Toney Howell (Gurnee, IL), Lee Thomas (Chesterfield, MO), Leon Wurth (Nashville, TN).
**Independent League Scout:** Brad Del Barba (Fort Mitchell, KY).
**Roving Crosschecker:** Jeff Cornell (Lee's Summit, MO). **Regional Supervisors:** West Coast—Tom Allison (Austin, TX); East Coast—Bobby Heck (Longwood, FL).
**Area Supervisors:** Charles Aliano (Land O'Lakes, FL), Kevin Clouser (Phoenix), Mike Farrell (Indianapolis), Manolo Hernandez (Moca, PR), Harvey Kuenn Jr. (New Berlin, WI), Jesse Levis (Elkin Park, PA), Joe Mason (Millbrook, AL), Justin McCray (Davis, CA), Tim McIlvaine (Richmond, VA), Ray Montgomery (Pearland, TX), Brandon Newell (Bellingham, WA), Doug Reynolds (Tallahassee, FL), Corey Rodriguez (Hermosa Beach, CA), Bruce Seid (Capistrano Beach, CA), Jim Stevenson (Tulsa, OK), Charles Sullivan (Miami).
**Scouts:** John Bushart (Sherman Oaks, CA), Edward Fastaia (Brooklyn, NY), Carmen Fusco (Mechanicsburg, PA), Joe Hodges (Rockwood, TN), Roger Janeway (Englewood, OH), John Logan (Milwaukee, WI), Brad Stoll (Lawrence, KS).
**Latin America Supervisor:** Fernando Arango (Davie, FL). **International Scouts:** Richard Clemons (Mississaugu, Ontario), John Haar (Burnaby, British Columbia), Mike LaBossiere (Brandon, Manitoba), Jay Lapp (London, Ontario), Marty Lehn (White Rock, British Columbia), Fausto Sosa Pena (Dominican Republic), Jean Roy (Saint Nicolas, Quebec), Freddy Torres (Venezuela).

# MINNESOTA TWINS

**Office Address:** 34 Kirby Puckett Place, Minneapolis, MN 55415.
**Telephone:** (612) 375-1366. **FAX:** (612) 375-7480.
**Website:** www.twinsbaseball.com.

## Ownership

**Operated by:** The Minnesota Twins.
**Owner:** Carl Pohlad. **Chairman, Executive Committee:** Howard Fox.
**Executive Board:** Jerry Bell, Carl Pohlad, James Pohlad, Robert Pohlad, William Pohlad, Dave St. Peter.

Carl Pohlad

## BUSINESS OPERATIONS

**President, Minnesota Twins:** Dave St. Peter. **President, Twins Sports Inc.:** Jerry Bell.
**Administrative Assistant to President/Office Manager:** Joan Boeser.

### Human Resources

**Vice President, Human Resources/Diversity:** Raenell Dorn. **Payroll Manager:** Lori Beasley. **Benefits Manager:** Leticia Silva. **Coordinator, Workers Compensation:** Tina Flowers.

### Finance

**Chief Financial Officer:** Kip Elliott. **Director, Finance:** Andy Weinstein. **Accounting Manager:** Brad Krutsch. **Manager, Ticket Accounting:** Jerry McLaughlin. **Accounts Payable:** Amy Fong-Christianson.
**Director, Information Systems:** Wade Navratil. **Director, Network/Baseball Information Systems:** John Avenson. **Manager, Technology Infrastructure:** Tony Persio. **Technical Services Specialist:** Brent Hildenbrandt.

### Marketing

**Vice President, Marketing:** Patrick Klinger. **Director, Advertising:** Nancy O'Brien. **Director, Corporate Communications:** Brad Ruiter. **Promotions Coordinator:** Chris Hodapp. **Director, Game Presentation:** Andy Price. **Executive Director, Twins Community Fund:** Peter Martin. **Manager, Community Relations:** Bryan Donaldson. **Manager, Community Programs:** Haivy Ngyuen. **Coordinator, Community Relations:** Gloria Westerdahl.

### Corporate Sales

**Vice President, Corporate Partnerships:** Eric Curry. **Corporate Partnerships Sales:** Dick Schultz. **Account Executives:** Kernal Buhler, Brock Maiser. **Manager, Client Services:** Bodie Forsling. **Corporate Partnerships Sales/Services Manager:** Jordan Woodcroft. **Coordinator, Client Services:** Katie Beaulieu.

### Ticket Sales

**Vice President, Ticket Sales/Service:** Steve Smith. **Director, Ticket Sales/Service:** Scott O'Connell.
**Manager, Customer Sales/Service:** Chris Malek. **Customer Sales/Service Account Executives:** Chris Carson, Lisa Rasmussen, Jason Stern. **Manager, Group Sales Development:** Rob Malec. **Manager, Ticket Sales/Service Support:** Beth Vail. **Ticket Sales/Service Coordinator:** Brandon Johnson.

### Communications

**Telephone:** (612) 375-7471. **FAX:** (612) 375-7473.
**Director, Team Travel/Baseball Communications:** Remzi Kiratli. **Manager, Baseball Communications:** Sean Harlin. **Manager, Media/Player Relations:** Mike Herman. **Coordinator, Publications/Baseball Communications:** Molly Gallatin. **Official Scorer:** Tom Mee.

### Stadium Operations

**Vice President, Operations:** Matt Hoy. **Director, Stadium Operations:** Dave Horsman. **Director, Special Events:** Heidi Sammon. **Manager, Stadium Operations:** Jeff Flom. **Manager, Security:** Dick Dugan. **Manager, Merchandise:** Matt Noll. **Manager, Roseville Pro Shop:** Joel Davis. **Manager, Minnetonka Pro Shop:** Courtney Pahlke. **Manager, Apple Valley Pro Shop:** Maria Flom.
**Coordinator, Office Services:** John McEvoy. **Office Services Assistant:** Mike Sather. **Receptionist:** Sharron Shannon.

### Ticket Operations

**Telephone:** (612) 338-9467, (800) 338-9467. **FAX:** (612) 375-7464.
**Director, Ticket Operations:** Paul Froehle. **Manager, Box Office:** Mike Stiles. **Supervisor, Ticket Office:** Karl Dedenbach. **Coordinator, Ticket Office:** Mike Johnson. **Manager, Telemarketing:** Patrick Forsland.

### Clubhouse

**Equipment Manager:** James Rosnau. **Visitors Clubhouse:** Troy Matchan.

## GENERAL INFORMATION

**Stadium (year opened):** Hubert H. Humphrey Metrodome (1982).
**Home Dugout:** Third base. **Playing Surface:** Field turf.
**Team Colors:** Burgundy, navy blue and white.
**Player Representative:** Kyle Lohse.

Terry Ryan

## BASEBALL OPERATIONS

**Telephone:** (612) 375-7484. **FAX:** (612) 375-7417.
**Vice President, General Manager:** Terry Ryan.
**VP, Assistant GM:** Bill Smith. **Special Assistants to GM:** Larry Corrigan, Joe McIlvaine, Tom Kelly.
**Director, Baseball Operations:** Rob Antony.
**Assistant Director, Baseball Operations:** Brad Steil. **Administrative Assistant to GM:** Jack Goin.

### Major League Staff

**Manager:** Ron Gardenhire.
**Coaches:** Bench—Steve Liddle; Pitching—Rick Anderson; Batting—Joe Vavra; First Base—Jerry White; Third Base—Scott Ulger; Bullpen—Rick Stelmaszek.

### Medical, Training

**Club Physicians:** Dr. Dan Buss, Dr. Vijay Eyunni, Dr. Tom Jetzer, Dr. John Steubs, Dr. Jon Hallberg, Dr. Alvaro Sanchez.
**Head Trainer:** Rick McWane. **Assistant Trainer:** Dave Pruemer. **Strength/Conditioning Coach:** Randy Popple.

### Player Development

**Telephone:** (612) 375-7488. **FAX:** (612) 375-7417.
**Director, Minor Leagues:** Jim Rantz. **Administrative Assistant, Minor Leagues:** Julie Rohloff.
**Minor League Field Coordinator:** Joel Lepel. **Minor League Infield and Batting Coordinator:** Paul Molitor.

Ron Gardenhire

### Farm System

| Class | Farm Team | League | Manager | Coach | Pitching Coach |
|-------|-----------|--------|---------|-------|----------------|
| Triple-A | Rochester | International | Stan Cliburn | Rich Miller | Stu Cliburn |
| Double-A | New Britain | Eastern | Riccardo Ingram | Floyd Rayford | Gary Lucas |
| High A | Fort Myers | Florida State | Kevin Boles | Jim Dwyer | Eric Rasmussen |
| Low A | Beloit | Midwest | Jeff Smith | Rudy Hernandez | Steve Mintz |
| Rookie | Elizabethton | Appalachian | Ray Smith | Jeff Reed | Jim Shellenback |
| Rookie | Fort Myers | Gulf Coast | Nelson Prada | Milt Cuyler | Unavailable |
| Rookie | Twins | Dominican | Nelson Norman | J. Paula/C. Almonte | Pablo Frias |
| Rookie | Twins | Venezuela | Asdrubal Estrada | Ramon Borrego | Ivan Arteaga |

### Scouting

**Telephone:** (612) 375-7525. **FAX:** (612) 375-7417.
**Director, Scouting:** Mike Radcliff (Overland Park, KS).
**Administrative Assistant, Scouting:** Kate Townley.
**Special Assignment Scouts:** Larry Corrigan (Fort Myers, FL), Cal Ermer (Chattanooga, TN), Joe McIlvaine (Newtown Square, PA).
**Major League Scout:** Bill Harford (Chicago). **Coordinator, Professional Scouting:** Vern Followell (Buena Park, CA). **Advance Scout:** Bob Hegman (Lee's Summit, MO).
**Scouting Supervisors:** East—Earl Frishman (Tampa, FL), West—Deron Johnson (Sacramento, CA), Midwest—Tim O'Neil (Lexington, KY), Mike Ruth (Lee's Summit, MO).
**Area Scouts:** Kevin Bootay (Sacramento, CA), Dan Cox (Santa Ana, CA), Marty Esposito (Robinson, TX), Sean Johnson (Chandler, AZ), John Leavitt (Garden Grove, CA), Bill Lohr (Centralia, WA), Gregg Miller (Chandler, OK), Billy Milos (Crown Point, IN), Billy Corrigan (Lexington, KY), Hector Otero (Miami), Mark Quimuyog (Lynn Haven, FL), Ricky Taylor (Hickory, NC), Brad Weitzel (Haines City, FL), Jay Weitzel (Salamanca, NY), John Wilson (Blairstown, NJ), Mark Wilson (Lindstrom, MN).
**Coordinator, International Scouting:** Howard Norsetter (Australia)
**International Scouts:** John Cortese (Italy), Gene Grimaldi (Europe), David Kim (South Korea), Jose Leon (Venezuela), Jim Ridley (Canada), Ken Su (Taiwan), Koji Takahashi (Japan), Fred Guerrero (Dominican Republic), Jose Marzan (Ft. Myers, FL).

Mike Radcliff

# NEW YORK METS

Office Address: 123-01 Roosevelt Ave., Flushing, NY 11368.
Telephone: (718) 507-6387. FAX: (718) 507-6395.
Website: www.mets.com.

## Ownership
Operated by: Sterling Mets, LP.
Board of Directors: Arthur Friedman, Steve Greenberg, David Katz, Michael Katz, Saul Katz, Tom Osterman, Stuart Sucherman, Marvin Tepper, Fred Wilpon, Jeff Wilpon, Richard Wilpon.
Chairman, Chief Executive Officer: Fred Wilpon. President: Saul Katz. Senior Executive Vice President, Chief Operating Officer: Jeff Wilpon.

## BUSINESS OPERATIONS
Executive Vice President, Business Operations: David Howard. Executive VP, General Counsel: David Cohen.

### Finance

Fred Wilpon

Chief Financial Officer: Mark Peskin. Vice President/Controller: Lenny Labita. Senior Director, Information Technology: Joe Milone. Assistant Controller: Rebecca Landau.

### Marketing, Sales
Senior Vice President, Marketing/Communications: David Newman. Senior VP, Corporate Sales/Services: Paul Danforth.
Senior Director, Marketing: Tina Bucciarelli. Senior Director, Marketing Productions: Tim Gunkel. Director, Broadcasting/Special Events: Lorraine Hamilton. Director, Corporate Services: Jim Plummer. Director, Corporate Sales/Services: Paul Asencio. Director, Marketing Communications: Jill Grabill. Director, Community Outreach: Jill Knee. Coordinator, Community Outreach: Chris Brown.

### Media Relations
Telephone: (718) 565-4330. FAX: (718) 639-3619.
Vice President, Media Relations: Jay Horwitz.
Director, Media Relations: Shannon Dalton. Media Relations Specialist: Ethan Wilson. Coordinators, Media Relations: Owen Bochner, Donald Muller.

### Stadium Operations
Vice President, Facilities: Karl Smolarz.
Manager, Stadium Operations: Sue Lucchi. Assistant Stadium Manager, Operations: Mark Spielvogel. Assistant Stadium Manager, Maintenance: Mike Dohnert. Manager, Field Operations: Unavailable.
PA Announcer: Alex Anthony. Official Scorers: Joe Donnelly, Howie Karpin, Bill Shannon, Jordan Sprechman.

### Ticketing
Telephone: (718) 507-7499. FAX: (718) 507-6396.
Vice President, Ticket Sales/Services: Bill Ianniciello.
Senior Director, Ticket Operations: Dan DeMato. Director, Ticket Sales Development: Jamie Ozure. Manager, Corporate Ticket Sales: Jeff Schindle. Director, Group Ticket Sales: Thomas Fersch. Manager, Group Ticket Sales: Mark Phillips.

### Travel, Clubhouse
Clubhouse Manager, Associate Travel Director: Charlie Samuels. Assistant Clubhouse Manager: Vinny Greco. Visiting Clubhouse Manager: Tony Carullo. Video Editor: Joe Scarola.

---

## GENERAL INFORMATION
Stadium (year opened): Shea Stadium (1964).
Home Dugout: First Base. Playing Surface: Grass.
Team Colors: Blue and orange.
Player Representative: Tom Glavine.

## BASEBALL OPERATIONS

**Telephone:** (718) 565-4315. **FAX:** (718) 507-6391.
**Executive Vice President/General Manager:** Omar Minaya.
**Assistant General Manager:** John Ricco. **Special Assistants to GM:** Tony Bernazard, Al Goldis, Sandy Johnson, Bryan Lambe, Bill Livesey. **Executive Assistant to GM:** Leonor Colon.

### Major League Staff

**Manager:** Willie Randolph.
**Coaches:** Bench—Jerry Manuel; Pitching—Rick Peterson; Batting—Rick Down; First Base—Sandy Alomar Sr.; Third Base—Manny Acta; Bullpen—Guy Conti; Catching—Tom Nieto.

Omar Minaya

### Medical, Training

**Medical Director:** Dr. David Altchek. **Team Physician:** Dr. Straun Coleman.
**Head Trainer:** Ray Ramirez. **Assistant Trainer:** Mike Herbst. **Coordinator, Strength/Conditioning:** Rick Slate. **Assistant Coordinator, Fitness/Conditioning:** Unavailable.

### Player Development

**Telephone:** (718) 565-4302. **FAX:** (718) 205-7920.
**Director, Minor League Operations:** Adam Wogan. **Assistant Director, Minor League Operations:** John Fantauzzi. **Assistant, Player Development:** Amy Neal.
**Advisor to Minor League Director:** Ray Rippelmeyer. **Infield Consultant:** Chico Fernandez.
**Field Coordinator:** Tony Tijerina. **Coordinator, Instruction:** Kevin Morgan. **Coordinators:** Edgar Alfonzo (infield), Lamar Johnson (hitting), Rick Patterson (base running/bunting), Bob Natal (catching), Rick Waits (pitching).
**Coordinator, Athletic Development:** Jason Craig. **Assistant Coordinator, Athletic Development:** Ken Coward. **Training Coordinator:** Mark Rogow. **Coordinator, Rehabilitation Pitching:** Randy Niemann. **Coordinator, Rehabilitation:** Mike Lopriore. **Equipment Manager:** Kevin Kierst. **Assistant Equipment Manager:** Jack Brenner.

Willie Randolph

### Farm System

| Class | Farm Team | League | Manager | Coach | Pitching Coach |
|---|---|---|---|---|---|
| Triple-A | Norfolk | International | Ken Oberkfell | Howard Johnson | Randy Niemann |
| Double-A | Binghamton | Eastern | Juan Samuel | John Valentin | Mark Brewer |
| High A | St. Lucie | Florida State | Gary Carter | Nelson Silverio | Ricky Bones |
| Low A | Hagerstown | South Atlantic | Frank Cacciatore | Luis Natera | Shawn Barton |
| Short-season | Brooklyn | New York-Penn | George Greer | Jack Voigt | Steve Merriman |
| Rookie | Kingsport | Appalachian | Donovan Mitchell | Juan Lopez | Dan Murray |
| Rookie | Mets | Gulf Coast | Bobby Floyd | Scott Hunter | Hector Berrios |
| Rookie | Mets | Dominican | Gilberto Reyes | Liliano Castro | Benjamin Marte |
| Rookie | Mets | Venezuelan | Jesus Tiamo | Leo Hernandez | Rafael Lazo |

### Scouting

**Telephone:** Amateur—(718) 565-4311; Professional—(718) 803-4013. **FAX:** (718) 205-7920.
**Director, Amateur Scouting:** Rudy Terrasas. **Assistant, Amateur Scouting:** Elizabeth Gadsden. **Coordinator, Amateur Scouting:** Adam Fisher.
**Vice President, Professional Scouting:** Gary LaRocque. **Assistant Professional/International Scouting:** Anne Fairbanks.
**Advance Scout:** Bruce Benedict.
**Professional Scouts:** Russ Bove (Longwood, FL), Howie Freiling (Apex, NC), Roland Johnson (Newington, CT), Jerry Krause (Highland Park, IL), Bob Minor (Garden Grove, CA), Harry Minor (Long Beach, CA), Scott Nethery (Houston, TX), Joe Nigro (Staten Island, NY).
**Regional Supervisors:** East—John Poloni (Tarpon Springs, FL); Midwest—David Lakey (Kingwood, TX); West—Tim Fortugno (Elk Grove, CA);

Rudy Terrasas

**Special Assignment Scouts:** Doug Gassaway (Blum, TX), Benny Latino, III (Hammond, LA).
**Area Supervisors:** Mike Baker (Cave Creek, AZ), Steve Bamingham (Dunedin, FL), Kevin Brand (Roseville, CA), Erwin Bryant (Lexington, KY), Larry Chase (Pearcy, AR), Ray Corbett (College Station, TX), Rodney Henderson (Lexington, KY), Scott Hunter (Mount Laurel, NJ), Larry Izzo (Deer Park, NY), Steve Leavitt (Huntington Beach, CA), Fred Mazuca (Tustin, CA), Marlin McPhail (Irmo, SC), Claude Pelletier (St. Lazare, Quebec), Jim Reeves (Camas, WA), Junior Roman (San Sebastian, PR), Rob Sidwell (Windermere, FL), Scott Trcka (Hobart, IN), Matt Wondolowski (Oakton, VA).
**Director, Pacific Rim Scouting:** Isao O'Jimi (Japan).
**International Scouts:** Eddy Toledo (Dominican Republic), Robert Alfonzo (Venezuela), Tony Harris (Australia).

# NEW YORK YANKEES

Office Address: Yankee Stadium, East 161st Street and River Avenue, Bronx, NY 10451.
Telephone: (718) 293-4300. FAX: (718) 293-8431.
Website: www.yankees.com.

## Ownership

Principal Owner: George Steinbrenner. General Partners: Hal Steinbrenner, Stephen Swindal.
Senior Executive: Hank Steinbrenner. Vice President: Felix Lopez.

## BUSINESS OPERATIONS

President: Randy Levine.
Chief Operating Officer: Lonn Trost. Vice President, Administration: Sonny Hight.

### Finance

Vice President, Chief Financial Officer: Steve Dauria. VP, Finance: Robert Brown.

### Business Development

George Steinbrenner

Senior Vice President, Marketing: Deborah Tymon. VP, Corporate/Community Relations: Brian Smith. VP, Sponsorship Sales/Services: Michael Tusiani.

### Media Relations, Publications

Telephone: (718) 579-4460. FAX: (718) 293-8414.
Senior Advisor: Arthur Richman. Senior Director, Media Relations/Publicity: Rick Cerrone. Assistant Director, Media Relations/Publicity: Jason Zillo. Manager, Media Relations/Publicity: Ben Tuliebitz. Director, Publications/Multimedia: Mark Mandrake.

### Stadium Operations

Director, Stadium Operations: Doug Behar. Assistant Director, Stadium Operations: Cliff Rowley. Stadium Superintendent: Pete Pullara.
Head Groundskeeper: Dan Cunningham. Scoreboard/Broadcasting Manager: Mike Bonner.
Director, Concessions: Joel White. Director, Hospitality: David Bernstein.
PA Announcer: Bob Sheppard. Official Scorers: Bill Shannon, Howie Karpin.

### Ticketing

Telephone: (718) 293-6000. FAX: (718) 293-4841.
Vice President, Ticket Operations: Frank Swaine. Senior Director, Ticket Operations: Irfan Kirimca.

### Travel, Clubhouse

Traveling Secretary: David Szen.
Equipment Manager: Rob Cucuzza. Visiting Clubhouse Manager: Lou Cucuzza Jr.

## GENERAL INFORMATION

Stadium (year opened): Yankee Stadium (1923).
Home Dugout: First Base. Playing Surface: Grass.
Team colors: Navy blue and white.
Player representative: Mike Mussina.

## BASEBALL OPERATIONS

**Telephone:** (718) 293-4300. **FAX:** (718) 293-0015.
**Senior Vice President/General Manager:** Brian Cashman.
**VP, Assistant GM:** Jean Afterman. **Senior VP, Player Personnel:** Gordon Blakeley. **Coordinator, Major League Operations:** Anthony Flynn. **VP/Senior Advisor:** Gene Michael. **Special Advisory Group:** Yogi Berra, Reggie Jackson, Clyde King.

### Major League Staff

**Manager:** Joe Torre.
**Coaches:** Bench/Outfield—Lee Mazzilli; Pitching—Ron Guidry; Batting—Don Mattingly; First Base—Tony Pena; Third Base—Larry Bowa; Bullpen—Joe Kerrigan.

Brian Cashman

### Medical, Training

**Team Physician, New York:** Dr. Stuart Hershon. **Team Physician, Tampa:** Dr. Andrew Boyer.
**Head Trainer:** Gene Monahan. **Assistant Trainer:** Steve Donohue.
**Strength/Conditioning Coach:** Jeff Mangold.

## Player Development

**Florida Complex:** 3102 N. Himes Ave., Tampa, FL 33607. **Telephone:** (813) 875-7569. **FAX:** (813) 873-2302.
**Senior Vice President, Baseball Operations:** Mark Newman.
**VP, Player Personnel:** Billy Connors. **Director, Player Development:** Pat Roessler. **Assistant Director, Player Development:** Troy Caradonna. **Player Development Coordinator, Latin America:** Oscar Acosta.
**Minor League Coordinators:** Nardi Contreras (pitching), Gary Denbo (hitting), Jack Hubbard (outfield).
**Head Trainer:** Mark Littlefield. **Coordinator, Strength/Conditioning:** E.J. Amo. **Equipment Manager:** David Hays. **Clubhouse Manager:** Jack Terry.

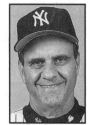

Joe Torre

### Farm System

| Class | Farm Club | League | Manager | Coaches | Pitching Coach |
|-------|-----------|--------|---------|---------|----------------|
| AAA | Columbus | International | Dave Miley | Kevin Long/Frank Howard | Neil Allen |
| AA | Trenton | Eastern | Billy Masse | Ralph Dickenson | Dave Eiland |
| High A | Tampa | Florida State | Luis Sojo | James Rowson | Greg Pavlick |
| Low A | Charleston | South Atlantic | Bill Mosiello | Torre Tyson | Scott Aldred |
| Short season | Staten Island | New York-Penn | Gaylen Pitts | Ty Hawkins | Mike Thurman |
| Rookie | Tampa | Gulf Coast | Oscar Acosta | Matt Martin/Hector Lopez | Carlos Reyes |
| Rookie | Yankees I | Dominican | Carlos Mota | Argenis Paulino/Julio Valdez | Wilfredo Cordova |
| Rookie | Yankees II | Dominican | Freddy Tiburcio | Sonder Encarnacion | Jose Duran |

### Scouting

**Telephone:** (813) 875-7569. **FAX:** (813) 873-2302.
**Vice President, Scouting:** Damon Oppenheimer. **Assistant Director, Amateur Scouting:** John Kremer.
**Director, Professional Scouting:** Billy Eppler. **Assistant Director, Professional Scouting:** John Coppolella.
**Advance Scouts:** Chuck Cottier (Tampa, FL), Wade Taylor (Orlando, FL).
**Professional Scouts:** Jim Benedict (Bradenton, FL), Ron Brand (Mesa, AZ), Joe Caro (Tampa, FL), Bill Emslie (Safety Harbor, FL), Greg Orr (Sacramento, CA), Jeff Wetherby (Wesley Chapel, FL).
**National Crosschecker:** Wayne Britton (Waynesboro, VA). **Regional Crosscheckers:** East—Joe Arnold (Lakeland, FL); Midwest—Tim Kelly (Pickerington, OH); West—Jeff Patterson (Yorba Linda, CA).

Mark Newman

**Area Scouts:** Brian Barber (Winter Garden, FL), Mark Batchko (Arlington, TX), Steve Boros (Kingwood, TX), Joe Caro (Tampa, FL), Mike Gibbons (Liberty Township, OH), Matt Hyde (East Boston, MA), Steve Lemke (Geneva, IL), Bill Mele (El Segundo, CA), Cesar Presbott (Bronx, NY), Trevor Schaffer (Tampa, FL), Andy Stankiewicz (Gilbert, AZ), D.J. Svihlik (Birmingham, AL), Steve Swail (Matthews, NC), Fay Thompson (Vallejo, CA), Mike Thurman (Corvallis, OR).
**Vice President, International Scouting:** Lin Garrett. **Vice President, International Operations:** Abel Guerra. **Assistant Director, International Operations:** Stephanie Carapazza.
**Coordinator, Latin American Scouting:** Carlos Rios (Santo Domingo, DR). **Coordinator, Pacific Rim Scouting:** John Cox (Redlands, CA). **Latin American Field Coordinator:** Humberto Trejo. **Latin American Administrator:** Richard Jimenez.
**International Scout:** Ramon Valdivia (Dominican Republic).

# OAKLAND ATHLETICS

**Office Address:** 7000 Coliseum Way, Oakland, CA 94621.
**Telephone:** (510) 638-4900. **FAX:** (510) 562-1633.
**Website:** www.oaklandathletics.com.

## Ownership
Co-Owner/Managing Partner: Lew Wolff. **Co-Owner/Partner:** Steve Schott.

## BUSINESS OPERATIONS
President: Michael Crowley. **Executive Assistant to President:** Carolyn Jones.
General Counsel: Steve Johnston. **Assistant General Counsel:** Rob Schantz.

Lew Wolff

## Finance, Administration
Vice President, Finance: Paul Wong.
Director, Finance: Linda Rease. **Payroll Manager:** Kathy Leviege. **Senior Accountant/Accounts Payable:** Isabelle Mahaffey. **Staff Accountant:** David Fucillo.
Accounts Receivable Specialist: David Bunnell.
Manager, Human Resources: Janet Aquino. **Assistant, Human Resources:** Kim Kubo.
Manager, Information Systems: Debbie Dean.

## Sales, Marketing
Vice President, Sales/Marketing: David Alioto.
Director, Corporate Sales: Franklin Lowe. **Corporate Account Managers:** Matthew Gallagher, Jill Golden, Susan Weiglein. **Coordinator, Marketing/Advertising:** Katie Kelly. **Assistant, Sales/Marketing:** Alexa Jontulovich. **Manager, Creative Services:** Mike Ono.
Director, Merchandising/Purchasing: Drew Bruno. **Coordinator, Merchandising:** Josh Vargo.

## Public Relations, Communications
Telephone: (510) 563-2207. **FAX:** (510) 562-1633.
Vice President, Broadcasting/Communications: Ken Pries.
Director, Public Relations: Jim Young. **Manager, Baseball Information:** Mike Selleck. **Manager, Media Relations:** Kristy Fick. **Coordinator, Media Services:** Debbie Gallas. **Team Photographer:** Michael Zagaris.
Manager, Community Relations: Detra Paige. **Manager, Broadcasting Services:** Warren Chu.

## Stadium Operations
Vice President, Stadium Operations: David Rinetti.
Director, Stadium Operations: David Avila. **Manager, Stadium Operations:** Paul La Veau. **Scheduler, Stadium Operations:** Keith Rudnick. **Manager, Stadium Services:** Randy Duran. **Events Manager, Stadium Operations:** Kristy Ledbetter. **Coordinator, Stadium Operations:** Tara O'Connor. **Assistant, Stadium Operations:** Meghan Mahrholz.
Director, In-Stadium Entertainment: Troy Smith. **Director, Multimedia Services:** David Don. **Coordinator, Multimedia Services:** Jonathan Martin. **Coordinator, In-Stadium Entertainment:** Jeff Gass. **Public Address Announcer:** Roy Steele.
Head Groundskeeper: Clay Wood. **Arizona Groundskeeper:** Chad Huss.

## Ticketing
Director, Ticket Operations: Steve Fanelli.
Senior Manager, Ticket Services: Josh Ziegenbusch. **Manager, Ticket Operations:** David Adame. **Box Office Manager:** Anthony Silva. **Coordinator, Ticket Operations:** Anthony Blue. **Spring Training Marketing/Operations Manager:** Mike Saverino. **Supervisor, Ticket Services:** Travis LoDolce.
Director, Premium Seating Services: Dayn Floyd. **Manager, Premium Seating Services:** Susie Weiss. **Special Events Manager:** Heather Rajeski. **Coordinator, Special Events:** Molly Sklut. **Assistants, Special Events:** Andy MacEwen, Patrick McBride.
Director, Ticket Sales: Todd Santino. **Senior Account Managers, Outside Sales:** Phil Chapman, Parker Newton. **Coordinator, Inside Sales:** Aaron Dragomir.

## Travel, Clubhouse
Director, Team Travel: Mickey Morabito.
Equipment Manager: Steve Vucinich. **Visitors Clubhouse:** Mike Thalblum. **Assistant Equipment Manager:** Brian Davis. **Clubhouse Assistant:** William Angel. **Umpires Clubhouse:** Matt Weiss. **Manager, Arizona Clubhouse:** Jesse Sotomayor. **Assistant Manager, Arizona Clubhouse:** James Gibson.

---

## GENERAL INFORMATION
Stadium (year opened): Network Associates Coliseum (1968).
Home Dugout: Third Base. **Playing Surface:** Grass.
Team Colors: Kelly green and gold.
Player Representative: Barry Zito.

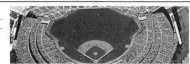

Billy Beane

## BASEBALL OPERATIONS

**Vice President, General Manager:** Billy Beane.
**Assistant GM/Coordinator, Professional Scouting:** David Forst. **Special Assistants to GM:** Randy Johnson, Matt Keough. **Executive Assistant:** Betty Shinoda.
**Director, Baseball Administration:** Pamela Pitts.
**Analyst, Baseball Operations:** Farhan Zaidi. **Video Coordinator:** Adam Rhoden.

### Major League Staff

**Manager:** Ken Macha.
**Coaches:** Dugout—Rene Lachemann; Pitching—Curt Young; Batting—Dave Hudgens; First Base—Brad Fischer; Third Base—Ron Washington; Bullpen—Bob Geren.

### Medical, Training

**Team Physician:** Dr. Allan Pont. **Team Orthopedist:** Dr. Jerrald Goldman. **Consulting Orthopedists:** Dr. John Frazier, Dr. Lewis Yocum. **Arizona Team Physician:** Dr. Fred Dicke.
**Head Trainer:** Larry Davis. **Assistant Trainer:** Steve Sayles. **Coordinator, Strength/ Conditioning:** Clarence Cockrell.

### Player Development

**Telephone, Oakland:** (510) 638-4900. **FAX:** (510) 563-2376.
**Arizona Complex:** Papago Park Baseball Complex, 1802 N. 64th St., Phoenix, AZ 85008. **Telephone:** (602) 949-5951. **FAX:** (602) 945-0557.
**Director, Player Development:** Keith Lieppman. **Director, Minor League Operations:** Ted Polakowski.
**Roving Instructors:** Juan Navarrete (infield), Ron Plaza, Ron Romanick (pitching), Greg Sparks (hitting).
**Medical Coordinator:** Jeff Collins. **Strength and Conditioning:** Judd Hawkins.

Ken Macha

### Farm System

| Class | Farm Team | League | Manager | Coach | Pitching Coach |
|-------|-----------|--------|---------|-------|----------------|
| Triple-A | Sacramento | Pacific Coast | Tony DeFrancesco | Brian McArn | Rick Rodriguez |
| Double-A | Midland | Texas | Von Hayes | Webster Garrison | Jim Coffman |
| High A | Stockton | California | Todd Steverson | Darren Bush | Scott Emerson |
| Low A | Kane County | Midwest | Aaron Nieckula | Tim Garland | Garvin Alston |
| Short-season | Vancouver | Northwest | Dennis Rogers | Unavailable | Craig Lefferts |
| Rookie | Phoenix | Arizona | Ruben Escalera | Juan Dilone | Mike Holmes |
| Rookie | Athletics I | Dominican | Unavailable | Unavailable | Unavailable |
| Rookie | Athletics II | Dominican | Unavailable | Unavailable | Unavailable |

### Scouting

**Telephone:** (510) 638-4900. **FAX:** (510) 563-2376.
**Director, Scouting:** Eric Kubota. **Coordinator, Scouting:** Bryn Alderson.
**Advance/Major League Scout:** Joe Sparks.
**National Field Coordinator:** Chris Pittaro (Robbinsville, NJ). **National Crosschecker:** Ron Vaughn (Corona, CA).
**Scouting Supervisors:** East Coast—Mike Holmes (Winston-Salem, NC); Midwest—Steve Bowden (Houston, TX).
**Area Scouts:** Neil Avent (Greensboro, NC), Jeff Bittiger (Saylorsburg, PA), Armann Brown (Smyrna, GA), Blake Davis (Dallas, TX), Ruben Escalera (San Juan, PR), Scott Kidd (San Jose, CA), Hank Lott (Sarasota, FL), Rick Magnante (Van Nuys, CA), Kevin Mello (Champaign, IL), Kelcey Mucker (Baton Rouge, LA), Jeremy Schied (Phoenix, AZ), Rich Sparks (Sterling Heights, MI), Craig Weissmann (Carlsbad, CA).
**Coordinator, Dominican Republic:** Raymond Abreu (Santo Domingo, DR).
**International Scouts:** Ruben Barradas (Venezuela), Juan Carlos De la Cruz (Dominican Republic), Angel Eusebio (Dominican Republic), Julio Franco (Venezuela), Juan Martinez (Dominican Republic), Bernardino Rosario (Dominican Republic), Oswaldo Troconis (Venezuela).

Eric Kubota

# PHILADELPHIA PHILLIES

**Office Address:** Citizens Bank Park, One Citizens Bank Way, Philadelphia, PA 19148.
**Telephone:** (215) 463-6000.
**Website:** www.phillies.com.

## Ownership
**Operated by:** The Phillies.
**President, Chief Executive Officer:** David Montgomery. **Chairman:** Bill Giles.

## BUSINESS OPERATIONS
**Vice President, General Counsel:** Bill Webb.
**Director, Ballpark Enterprises/Business Development:** Joe Giles. **Director, Human Resources:** Terry DeRugeriis.

### Finance
**Senior Vice President, Chief Financial Officer:** Jerry Clothier.
**Director, Finance/Accounting:** John Nickolas. **Manager, Payroll Services:** Karen Wright. **Director, Information Systems:** Brian Lamoreaux.

David Montgomery

### Marketing, Promotions
**Vice President, Advertising Sales:** David Buck.
**Manager, Client Services/Alumni Relations:** Debbie Nocito. **Manager, National Sales:** Rob MacPherson. **Manager, Advertising Sales:** Scott Nickle. **Managers, Corporate Sales:** Brian Mahoney, Tom Sullivan. **Director, Events:** Kurt Funk. **Director, Entertainment:** Chris Long. **Manager, Advertising/Internet Services:** Jo-Anne Levy-Lamoreaux.

### Public Relations, Communications
**Telephone:** (215) 463-6000. **FAX:** (215) 389-3050.
**Vice President, Public Relations:** Larry Shenk.
**Director, Media Relations:** Leigh Tobin. **Director, Print/Creative Services:** Tina Urban. **Manager, Publications:** Christine Negley. **Manager, Media Relations:** Greg Casterioto. **Media Relations Administrator:** Mary Ann Gettis. **Director, Community Relations:** Gene Dias.

### Ballpark Operations
**Vice President, Operations/Administration:** Michael Stiles.
**Director, Facility Management:** Mike DiMuzio. **Director, Event Operations:** Eric Tobin. **Head Groundskeeper:** Mike Boekholder.
**PA Announcer:** Dan Baker. **Official Scorers:** Jay Dunn, Bob Kenney, Mike Maconi.

### Ticketing
**Telephone:** (215) 463-1000. **FAX:** (215) 463-9878.
**Vice President, Ticket Operations:** Richard Deats.
**Director, Sales:** John Weber. **Director, Ticket Department:** Dan Goroff. **Director, Group Sales:** Kathy Killian. **Manager, Ticket Technology/Development:** Chris Pohl. **Manager, Suite Sales/Services:** Tom Mashek. **Manager, Phone Center:** Phil Feather. **Manager, Club Sales/Services:** Derek Schuster. **Manager, Season Ticket Services:** Mike Holdren.

### Travel, Clubhouse
**Manager, Equipment/Team Travel:** Frank Coppenbarger. **Assistant Equipment Manager:** Dan O'Rourke. **Manager, Visiting Clubhouse:** Kevin Steinhour. **Assistant, Home Clubhouse:** Phil Sheridan.

---

## GENERAL INFORMATION
**Stadium (year opened):** Citizens Bank Park (2004).
**Home Dugout:** First Base. **Playing Surface:** Natural grass.
**Team Colors:** Red, blue and white.
**Player Representative:** Jimmy Rollins.

Pat Gillick

## BASEBALL OPERATIONS
**Vice President, General Manager:** Pat Gillick. **Assistant GM:** Ruben Amaro Jr. **Director, Baseball Administration:** Susan Ingersoll. **Computer Analysis:** Jay McLaughlin. **Senior Advisor to GM:** Dallas Green. **Special Assistants to GM:** John Vukovich, Don Welke.

### Major League Staff
**Manager:** Charlie Manuel.
**Coaches:** Dugout—Gary Varsho; Pitching—Rich Dubee; Batting—Milt Thompson; First Base—Marc Bombard; Third Base—Bill Dancy; Bullpen—Ramon Henderson; Catching—Mick Billmeyer.

### Medical, Training
**Director, Medical Services:** Dr. Michael Ciccotti.
**Head Trainer:** Jeff Cooper. **Assistant Trainer:** Mark Andersen. **Conditioning Coordinator:** Scott Hoffman.

## Player Development

Charlie Manuel

**Telephone:** (215) 463-6000. **FAX:** (215) 755-9324.
**Assistant General Manager, Scouting/Player Development:** Mike Arbuckle.
**Director, Minor League Operations:** Steve Noworyta. **Assistant Director, Minor League Operations/Florida:** Lee McDaniel. **Administrative Assistant, Minor Leagues/Scouting:** Mike Ondo.
**Director, Latin American Operations:** Sal Artiaga. **Director, Florida Operations:** John Timberlake.
**Field Coordinator:** Mike Compton. **Coordinators:** Roly deArmas (catching), Dale Ellicott (conditioning), Gorman Heimueller (pitching), Don Long (hitting), Jerry Martin (outfield/base running), Dave Owen (infield), Scott Sheridan (trainers).

## Farm System

| Class | Farm Team | League | Manager | Coach | Pitching Coach |
|---|---|---|---|---|---|
| Triple-A | Scranton/W-B | International | John Russell | Sal Rende | Rod Nichols |
| Double-A | Reading | Eastern | P.J. Forbes | John Morris | Tom Filer |
| High A | Clearwater | Florida State | Greg Legg | Greg Gross | Scott Lovekamp |
| Low A | Lakewood | South Atlantic | Dave Huppert | Ken Dominguez | Steve Schrenk |
| Short-season | Batavia | New York-Penn | Steve Roadcap | Eric Richardson | Bill Bliss |
| Rookie | Clearwater | Gulf Coast | Jim Morrison | Luis Melendez | Carlos Arroyo |
| Rookie | Phillies | Dominican | Sammy Mejia | Domingo Brito | Cesar Mejia |
| Rookie | Phillies | Venezuelan | Rafael DeLima | Silverio Navas | Lester Straker |

## Scouting

Mike Arbuckle

**Telephone:** (215) 218-5204. **FAX:** (215) 755-9324.
**Director, Scouting:** Marti Wolever (Papillion, NE). **Assistant Director, Scouting:** Rob Holiday.
**Coordinators, Scouting:** Jim Fregosi Jr. (Murrieta, CA), Mike Ledna (Arlington Heights, IL).
**Director, Major League Scouts:** Gordon Lakey (Barker, TX). **Major League Scout:** Don Welke (Louisville, KY). **Advance Scout:** Hank King (Limerick, PA).
**Professional Scouts:** Sonny Bowers (Hewitt, TX), Ron Hansen (Baldwin, MD), Dean Jongewaard (Fountain Valley, CA), Larry Rojas (Clearwater, FL), Del Unser (Scottsdale, AZ).
**Scout/Instructor:** Ruben Amaro Sr. (Weston, FL).
**Regional Supervisors:** Central—Brian Kohlscheen (Norman, OK); East—John Castleberry (High Point, NC); West—Billy Moore (Alta Loma, CA).
**Area Scouts:** Sal Agostinelli (Kings Park, NY), Therron Brockish (Anthem, AZ), Steve Cohen (Spring, TX), Darrell Conner (Riverside, CA), Joey Davis (Rancho Murrieta, CA), Tim Kissner (Long Beach, CA), Jerry Lafferty (Kansas City, MO), Chip Lawrence (Somerfield, FL), Miguel Machado (Miami Lakes, FL), Paul Murphy (Wilmington, DE), Gene Schall (Harleysville, PA), Paul Scott (Frisco, TX), Stewart Smothers (Los Angeles, CA), Mike Stauffer (Ridgeland, MS), Bob Szymkowski (Chicago, IL), Roy Tanner (Charleston, SC).
**International Supervisor:** Sal Agostinelli (Kings Park, NY).
**International Scouts:** Tomas Herrera (Mexico), Kevin Hooker (Australia), Rick Jacques (Europe), Allan Lewis (Panama, Central America), Jesus Mendez (Venezuela), Angel Rivera (Korea), Wil Tejada (Dominican Republic), Steve Wilson (Taiwan).

# PITTSBURGH PIRATES

Office Address: PNC Park at North Shore, 115 Federal St., Pittsburgh, PA 15212.
Mailing Address: P.O. Box 7000, Pittsburgh, PA 15212.
Telephone: (412) 323-5000. FAX: (412) 325-4412.
Website: www.pittsburghpirates.com.

## Ownership

Operated by: Pittsburgh Pirates Acquisition, Inc.
Chief Executive Officer, Managing General Partner: Kevin McClatchy.
Board of Directors: Don Beaver, Frank Brenner, Kevin McClatchy, Ogden Nutting, Robert Nutting. Chairman: Robert Nutting..

Kevin McClatchy

## BUSINESS OPERATIONS

### Finance

Senior Vice President, Chief Financial Officer: Jim Plake.
Controller: David Bowman. Director, Office Services: Patti Mistick. Director, Information Technology: Terry Zeigler. Director, Human Resources: Pam Minteer.

### Marketing, Sales, Broadcasting

Vice President, Marketing/Sales/Broadcasting: Tim Schuldt.
Senior Director, Marketing: Brian Chiera. Senior Director, Ticket Sales/Business Development: Jim Alexander. Senior Director, Corporate Development: Bob Derda. Managing Director, Alumni Affairs, Licensing/Promotions: Joe Billetdeaux. Director, Corporate Partnerships: Mike Egan.
Director, Broadcasting: Mike Garda.
Manager, Special Events: Christine Serkoch. Manager, In-Game Entertainment: Eric Wolff. Manager, Creative Services: Alex Moser. Manager, Promotions: Megan Morris. Manager, Marketing: Kiley Cauvel.

### Communications

Telephone: (412) 325-4991. FAX: (412) 325-4413.
Vice President, Communications: Patty Paytas. Director, Media Relations: Jim Trdinich. Manager, Media Services: Dan Hart. Director, Community Development: Wende Torbert.
Alumni Liaison: Sally O'Leary.

### Stadium Operations

Vice President, PNC Park Operations/Facilities Management: Dennis DaPra.
Director, Operations: Chris Hunter. Director, Security/Contract Services: Jeff Podobnik. Manager, Security/Service Operations: Mark Weaver. Field Maintenance Manager: Steve Peeler.
PA Announcer: Tim DeBacco. Official Scorers: Bob Hertzel, Tony Krizmanich, Evan Pattak, Bob Webb.

### Ticketing

Telephone: (800) 289-2827. FAX: (412) 325-4404.
Manager, Ticket Services: Dave Wysocki. Manager, Guest Services: Charlene Cheroke. Manager, Client Relations: Jared Kramer.

### Travel, Clubhouse

Traveling Secretary: Greg Johnson.
Equipment Manager/Home Clubhouse Operations: Roger Wilson. Visitors Clubhouse Operations: Kevin Conrad.

---

## GENERAL INFORMATION

Stadium (year opened): PNC Stadium (2004).
Home Dugout: Third Base. Playing Surface: Grass.
Team Colors: Black, gold, red and white
Player Representative: Jason Bay.

David Littlefield

## BASEBALL OPERATIONS

**Telephone:** (412) 325-4743. **FAX:** (412) 325-4414.
**Senior Vice President, General Manager:** David Littlefield.
**Assistant GM:** Doug Strange. **Special Assistants to GM:** Jack Bowen, Louie Eljaua, Jesse Flores, Jax Robertson, Pete Vuckovich.
**Director, Baseball Operations:** Jon Mercurio. **Assistant, Baseball Operations:** Bryan Minniti. **Administrative Assistant, Baseball Operations:** Jeannie Donatelli.

### Major League Staff

**Manager:** Jim Tracy.
**Coaches:** Bench—Jim Lett; Pitching—Jim Colborn; Batting—Jeff Manto; First Base—John Shelby; Third Base—Jeff Cox; Bullpen—Bobby Cuellar.

### Medical, Training

**Medical Director:** Dr. Patrick DeMeo. **Team Physician:** Dr. Edward Snell.
**Head Athletic Trainer:** Brad Henderson. **Assistant Athletic Trainer:** Mike Sandoval. **Strength/Conditioning Coordinator:** Frank Velasquez. **Assistant Conditioning Coordinator:** Kiyoshi Momose.

### Minor Leagues

**Telephone:** (412) 325-4737. **FAX:** (412) 325-4414.
**Director, Player Development:** Brian Graham. **Administrator, Minor Leagues:** Diane DePasquale.
**Field Coordinator:** Jeff Banister. **Roving Instructors:** Alvaro Espinosa (infield), Gary Redus (outfield/base running), Gregg Ritchie (hitting), Gary Ruby (pitching).
**Latin American Field Coordinator:** Euclides Rojas. **Director, Dominican Republic Academy:** Esteban Beltre.

Jim Tracy

### Farm System

| Class | Farm Team | League | Manager | Coach | Pitching Coach |
|---|---|---|---|---|---|
| Triple-A | Indianapolis | International | Trent Jewett | Hensley Meulens | Jeff Andrews |
| Double-A | Altoona | Eastern | Tim Leiper | Brandon Moore | Ray Searage |
| High A | Lynchburg | Carolina | Gary Green | Ramon Sambo | Bob Milacki |
| Low A | Hickory | South Atlantic | Jeff Branson | Greg Briley | David Lundquist |
| Short-season | Williamsport | New York-Penn | Tom Prince | Ryan Newman | Bruce Banner |
| Rookie | Bradenton | Gulf Coast | Pete Mackanin | Woody Huyke | Miguel Bonilla |
| Rookie | Pirates | Dominican | Ramon Zapata | Ceciliio Beltre | Miguel Valdez |
| Rookie | Pirates | Venezuelan | Osmin Melendez | Ivan Colmenares | J. Prieto/D. Urbina |

### Scouting

**Telephone:** (412) 325-4738. **FAX:** (412) 325-4414.
**Director, Scouting:** Ed Creech. **Administrator, Scouting:** Sandy Deutsch.
**National Supervisor:** Jimmy Lester (Columbus, GA). **Regional Supervisors:** Joe Dellicarri (Longwood, FL), Tony DeMacio (Virginia Beach, VA). John Green (West Grove, PA), Bump Merriweather (Los Angeles, CA).
**Area Scouts:** Brad Cameron (Los Alamitos, CA), Sean Campbell (Fresno, CA), Steve Fleming (Louisa, VA), Duane Gustavson (Columbus, OH), Greg Hopkins (Beaverton, OR), Mike Leuzinger (Canton, TX), Darren Mazeroski (Panama City Beach, FL), Buddy Paine (Hartsdale, NY), Jim Rough (Wichita, KS), Everett Russell (Thibodaux, LA), Joe Salermo (Hallendale Beach, FL), Greg Schliz (Greenville, SC), Ted Williams (Peoria, AZ).
**Part-Time Scouts:** Tom Barnard (Arlington Heights, IL), Elmer Gray (Pittsburgh, PA), Homer Newlin (Tallahassee, FL), William Price (Austin, TX), Jose Rosario (Bayamon, PR), Bill Sizemore (Oxnard, CA), Troy Williams (Winder, GA).

Ed Creech

**Director, Latin American Scouting:** Rene Gayo. **Supervisor, Dominican Republic:** Josue Herrera. **Supervisor, Venezuela:** Rodolfo Petit. **Scouts, Dominican Republic:** Marcos Briseno, Ramon Perez, Carlos Santana. **Scouts, Venezuela:** Pablo Csorgi, Charles Curiel, Javier Magdelano. **International Scouts:** Daniel Garcia (Colombia), Jose Pineda (Panama), Jesus Valdez (Mexico), Marc Van Zanten (Netherland Antilles), Darryl Yrausquin (Aruba).

# ST. LOUIS CARDINALS

**Office Address:** 100 South 4th St., St. Louis, MO 63102.
**Telephone:** (314) 345-9600. **FAX:** (314) 345-9523.
**Website:** www.stlcardinals.com.

## Ownership

**Operated by:** St. Louis Cardinals, LLC.
**General Partner:** Bill DeWitt Jr. **Vice Chairman:** Fred Hanser. **Secretary/Treasurer:** Andrew Baur.
**President:** Mark Lamping.
**Senior Administrative Assistant to Chairman:** Grace Hale. **Senior Administrative Assistant to President:** Julie Laningham.

## BUSINESS OPERATIONS

**Senior Vice President, Business Development:** Bill DeWitt III.
**VP, Event Services:** Vicki Bryant. **Coordinator, Event Services:** Missy Tobey. **Director, Government Affairs/Special Projects:** Ron Watermon.
**VP, Public Affairs/Employee Relations:** Marian Rhodes. **Manager, Office Administration/Human Resources Specialist:** Karen Brown.

Mark Lamping

## Finance

**Senior Vice President, Controller:** Brad Wood.
**Director, Accounting:** Deborah Pfaff. **Director, Finance:** Rex Carter. **Supervisor, Ticket Accounting/Reporting:** Michelle Flach. **Senior Accountant:** Tracey Sessions.

## Marketing, Sales

**Senior Vice President, Sales/Marketing:** Dan Farrell. **Administrative Assistant, Corporate Sales:** Gail Ruhling.
**VP, Corporate Marketing/Stadium Entertainment:** Thane van Breusegen. **Director, Target Marketing:** Ted Savage. **Senior Account Executive:** Theron Morgan. **Manager, Scoreboard Operations:** Tony Simokaitis.

## Public Relations, Community Relations

**Telephone:** (314) 345-9600. **FAX:** (314) 345-9530.
**Director, Media Relations:** Brian Bartow. **Assistants to Director, Media Relations:** Jim Anderson, Melody Yount.
**Director, Publications:** Steve Zesch. **Publications Assistants:** Tom Raber, Larry State.
**Vice President, Community Relations:** Marty Hendin. **Community Relations Communications Specialist:** Gabrielle Martin.
**VP/Group Director, Community Outreach/Cardinals Care:** Tim Hanser. **Coordinator, Cardinals Care:** Lucretia Payne. **Youth Baseball Commissioner, Cardinals Care:** Keith Brooks.

## Stadium Operations

**Vice President, Stadium Operations:** Joe Abernathy. **Administrative Assistant:** Nan Bommarito.
**Director, Stadium Operations:** Mike Bertani. **Director, Security/Special Services:** Joe Walsh. **Administrative Assistant, Security:** Hope Baker.
**Director, Quality Assurance/Guest Services:** Mike Ball. **Manager, Stadium Operations:** Cindy Richards.
**Head Groundskeeper:** Bill Findley. **Assistant Head Groundskeeper:** Chad Casella.
**PA Announcer:** John Ulett. **Official Scorers:** Jeff Durbin, Gary Mueller, Mike Smith.

## Ticketing

**Telephone:** (314) 345-9600 **FAX:** (314) 345-9522.
**Vice President, Ticket Operations:** Josie Arnold.
**Vice President, Ticket Sales:** Joe Strohm.
**Manager, Ticket Operations:** Kim Kleeschulte. **Manager, Box Office:** Julie Baker. **Director, Season/Premium Ticket Sales:** Mark Murray. **Coordinator, Premium Seats:** Julia Kelley. **Coordinator, Prime Seat Club:** Jennifer Needham.
**Director, Group Sales:** Michael Hall. **Manager, Group Sales:** Mary Clare Bena. **Supervisor, Customer Service:** Marilyn Mathews.

## Travel, Clubhouse

**Traveling Secretary:** C.J. Cherre.
**Equipment Manager:** Rip Rowan. **Assistant Equipment Manager:** Ernie Moore. **Visiting Clubhouse Manager:** Jerry Risch. **Video Coordinator:** Chad Blair.

## GENERAL INFORMATION

**Stadium (year opened):** Busch Stadium (2006).
**Home Dugout:** First Base. **Playing Surface:** Grass.
**Team Colors:** Red and white.
**Player Representative:** Unavailable.

## BASEBALL OPERATIONS
**Telephone:** (314) 345-9600. **FAX:** (314) 345-9525.
**Senior Vice President, General Manager:** Walt Jocketty. **Assistant GM:** John Mozeliak. **Special Assistants to GM:** Mike Jorgensen, Red Schoendienst.
**VP, Player Personnel:** Jerry Walker. **Director, Major League Administration/Senior Executive Assistant to GM:** Judy Carpenter-Barada.

### Major League Staff
**Manager:** Tony La Russa.
**Coaches:** Bench—Joe Pettini; Pitching—Dave Duncan; Batting—Hal McRae; First Base—Dave McKay; Third Base—Jose Oquendo; Bullpen—Marty Mason.

Walt Jocketty

### Medical, Training
**Senior Medical Advisor:** Dr. Stan London. **Club Physician:** Dr. Rick Wright.
**Head Trainer:** Barry Weinberg. **Assistant Trainer:** Greg Hauck.

## Player Development
**Telephone:** (314) 345-9600. **FAX:** (314) 345-9525.
**Director, Player Development:** Bruce Manno. **Manager, Baseball Operations:** John Vuch. **Administrative Assistant:** Judy Francis.
**Senior Field Coordinator:** George Kissell.
**Field Coordinator:** Jim Riggleman. **Coordinators:** Mark Riggins (pitching), Gene Tenace (hitting), Tom Spencer (baserunning/outfield).
**Minor League Equipment Manager:** Buddy Bates.

Tony La Russa

## Farm System

| Class | Farm Team | League | Manager | Coach | Pitching Coach |
|---|---|---|---|---|---|
| Triple-A | Memphis | Pacific Coast | Danny Sheaffer | Tommy Gregg | Dyar Miller |
| Double-A | Springfield | Texas | Chris Maloney | Joe Cunningham | Blaise Ilsley |
| High A | Palm Beach | Florida State | Ron Warner | Derrick May | Derek Lilliquist |
| Low A | Quad Cities | Midwest | Keith Mitchell | Randy Whisler | Bryan Eversgerd |
| Short-season | State College | New York-Penn | Mark DeJohn | Mike Shildt | Sid Monge |
| Rookie | Johnson City | Appalachian | Dan Radison | Joe Almaraz | Al Holland |

## Scouting
**Telephone:** (314) 345-9445. **FAX:** (314) 345-9525.
**Vice President, Player Procurement:** Jeff Luhnow. **Assistant to Scouting Director:** Dan Kantrovitz. **Scouting Department Coordinator:** Mike Girsch. **Administrative Assistant:** Linda Brauer.
**Director, Professional Scouting:** Marteese Robinson.
**Major League/Special Assignment Scouts:** Bing Devine (St. Louis, MO), Mike Jorgensen (St. Louis, MO), Fred McAlister (Katy, TX).
**Professional Scouts:** Bill Harford (Chicago, IL), Marty Keough (Scottsdale, AZ), Mike Squires (Kalamazoo, MI), Ron Schueler (Paradise Valley, AZ).
**National/Regional Supervisors:** Chuck Fick (Newbury Park, CA), Marty Maier (St. Louis, MO), Joe Rigoli (Parsippany, NJ), Mike Roberts (Hot Springs, AR).
**Area Supervisors:** Joe Almaraz (San Antonio, TX), Clark Crist (Tucson, AZ), Steve Gossett (Broken Arrow, OK), Brian Hopkins (Cleveland, OH), Scott Melvin (Quincy, IL), Scott Nichols (Richland, MS), Jay North (Vacaville, CA), Joel Ronda (Puerto Rico), Mike Shildt (Charlotte, NC), Anup Sinha (Rancho Cucamonga, CA), Roger Smith (Eastman, GA), Steve Turco (Clearwater, FL), Dane Walker (Canby, OR).
**International Group Coordinator:** Maria Valentin. **Administrative Latin American Scouting Coordinator:** Enrique Brito (Venezuela). **International Scouts:** Wilmer Becerra (Venezuela), Neder Horta (Colombia), Rene Rojas (Dominican Republic).

Jeff Luhnow

# SAN DIEGO PADRES

**Office Address:** PETCO Park, 100 Park Blvd., San Diego, CA 92101.
**Mailing Address:** P.O. Box 122000, San Diego, CA 92112.
**Telephone:** (619) 795-5000.
**E-Mail Address:** comments@padres.com. **Website:** www.padres.com

## Ownership

**Operated by:** Padres, LP.
**Principal Owner, Chairman:** John Moores. **Co-Vice Chairmen:** Charlie Noell, Glen Doshay.
**Chief Executive Officer:** Sandy Alderson.
**President/Chief Operating Officer:** Dick Freeman.

Sandy Alderson

## BUSINESS OPERATIONS

**Executive Vice President/General Counsel:** Katie Pothier.
**VP, Senior Advisor:** Dave Winfield.

### Finance

**Executive Vice President/Chief Financial Officer:** Fred Gerson.
**VP/Controller:** Dan Fumai. **Director, Information Systems:** Joe Lewis. **VP, Corporate Sales:** Jim Ballweg. **Director, Corporate Sales:** Marty Gorsich.

### Public Relations, Community Relations

**Telephone:** (619) 795-5265. **FAX:** (619) 795-5266.
**Executive Vice President/Communications:** Jeff Overton.
**Director, Media Relations:** Luis Garcia. **Assistant Director, Media Relations:** Michael Uhlenkamp. **Coordinator, Baseball Information:** Dustin Morse. **VP, Community Relations:** Michele Anderson.
**Director, Padres Foundation:** Sue Botos. **Manager, Community Relations:** Nhu Tran.

### Stadium Operations

**Executive Vice President/Managing Director, Ballpark Management:** Richard Andersen. **VP, Ballpark Operations:** Mark Guglielmo.
**Director, Event Operations:** Ken Kawachi. **Director, Landscape/Field Maintenance:** Luke Yoder.
**PA Announcer:** Frank Anthony. **Official Scorers:** Dennis Smythe, Bill Zavestoski.

### Ticketing

**Telephone:** (619) 795-8025. **FAX:** (619) 795-5034.
**Vice President, Sales/Services:** Mark Tilson.

### Travel, Clubhouse

**Director, Team Travel/Equipment Manager:** Brian Prilaman.
**Home Clubhouse Operations:** Tony Petricca. **Visitors Clubhouse Operations:** David Bacharach.

---

## GENERAL INFORMATION

**Stadium (year opened):** PETCO Park (2004).
**Home Dugout:** First Base. **Playing Surface:** Grass.
**Team Colors:** Padres sand, navy blue, sky blue.
**Player Representative:** Unavailable.

Kevin Towers

## BASEBALL OPERATIONS

**Telephone:** (619) 795-5076. **FAX:** (619) 795-5036.
**Executive Vice President, General Manager:** Kevin Towers.
**Assistant GM:** Fred Uhlman Jr. **Special Assistant to GM/Field Coordinator:** Bill Bryk.
**Director, Baseball Operations:** Jeff Kingston. **Administrative Assistant:** Ryan Isaac.

### Major League Staff

**Manager:** Bruce Bochy.
**Coaches:** Bench—Tony Muser; Pitching—Darren Balsley; Batting—Dave Magadan; First Base—Tye Waller; Third Base—Glenn Hoffman; Bullpen—Darrel Akerfelds.

### Medical, Training

**Club Physician:** Scripps Clinic medical staff.
**Head Trainer:** Todd Hutcheson. **Assistant Trainer:** Paul Navarro. **Strength/Conditioning Coach:** Joe Hughes.

### Player Development

**Telephone:** (619) 795-5335. **FAX:** (619) 795-5036.
**Vice President, Scouting/Player Development:** Grady Fuson.
**Assistant to Vice President, Scouting/Player Development:** Mike Wickham. **Assistant, Player Development/International Operations:** Juan Lara.
**Roving Instructors:** Mike Couchee (pitching), Rob Deer (hitting), Tony Franklin (infield), Tom Gamboa (defensive coordinator/staff development), Carlos Hernandez (Latin America/catching), Danny Stinnett (strength/conditioning), John Maxwell (minor league medical coordinator).

Bruce Bochy

### Farm System

| Class | Farm Team | League | Manager | Hitting Coach | Pitching Coach |
|---|---|---|---|---|---|
| AAA | Portland | Pacific Coast | Craig Colbert | Jose Castro | Gary Lance |
| AA | Mobile | Southern | Gary Jones | Arnie Beyeler | Glenn Abbott |
| High A | Lake Elsinore | California | Rick Renteria | Tom Tornincasa | Steve Webber |
| Low A | Fort Wayne | Midwest | Randy Ready | Max Venable | Tom Bradley |
| Short season | Eugene | Northwest | Doug Dascenzo | Joe Ferguson | Wally Whitehurst |
| Rookie | Padres | Arizona | Carlos Lezcano | Manny Crespo | Dave Rajsich |
| Rookie | Padres | Dominican | Luis Quiñones | Jose Mateo | Efrain Valdez |

### Scouting

**Telephone:** (619) 795-5343. **FAX:** (619) 795-5036.
**Director, Scouting:** Bill Gayton. **Assistant Director, Scouting:** Jaron Madison.
**Director, Professional/International Scouting:** Randy Smith (Scottsdale, AZ)..
**Major League Scouts:** Ken Bracey (Morton, IL), Ray Crone (Waxahachie, TX), Ted Simmons (Wildwood, MO).
**Professional Scouts:** Tom McNamara (Lakewood Ranch, FL), Van Smith (Belleville, IL), Chris Gwynn (Rancho Cucamonga, CA).
**Regional Crosscheckers:** Jay Darnell (San Diego, CA), Scott Littlefield (Long Beach, CA).
**Scouting Supervisor, Independent Leagues:** Mal Fichman.
**Full-Time Scouts:** Joe Bochy (Plant City, FL), Rich Bordi (Rohnert Park, CA), Josh Boyd (Gig Harbor, WA), Jim Bretz (South Windsor, CT), Lane Decker (Piedmont, OK), Pete DeYoung (Atlanta, GA), Bob Filotei (Wilmer, AL), Brendan Hause (San Diego, CA), Tim Holt

Bill Gayton

(Allen, TX), Ashley Lawson (Cary, NC), Dave Lottsfeldt (Greenwood Village, CO), Jeff Stewart (Normal, IL), Jake Wilson (El Segundo, CA).
**Part-Time Scouts:** Dan Bleiwas (Thornhill, Ontario), Robert Gutierrez (Carol City, FL), Hank Krause (Akron, IA), Willie Ronda (Rio Piedras, PR), Cam Walker (Centerville, IA), Murray Zuk (Souris, Manitoba).
**International Scouts:** Rafael Belen (Dominican Republic), Jorge Carolus (Netherlands Antilles), Milton Croes (Caribbean), Marcial Del Valle (Colombia), Felix Francisco (Dominican Republic), Elvin Jarquin (Nicaragua), Yfrain Linares (Venezuela), Victor Magdaleno (Venezuela), Elis Mendoza (Venezuela), Ricardo Montenegro (Panama), Francis Mojica (Dominican Republic), Robert Rowley (Panama), Jose Salado (Dominican Republic), Trevor Schumm (Australia), Illich Salazar (Venezuela).

# SAN FRANCISCO GIANTS

**Office Address:** AT&T Park, 24 Willie Mays Plaza, San Francisco, CA 94107.
**Telephone:** (415) 972-2000. **FAX:** (415) 947-2800.
**Website:** sfgiants.com.

## Ownership
**Operated by:** San Francisco Baseball Associates, LP.
**President, Managing General Partner:** Peter Magowan.
**Senior General Partner:** Harmon Burns. **General Partner:** William Neukom. **Special Assistant:** Willie Mays. **Senior Advisor:** Willie McCovey.

## BUSINESS OPERATIONS
**Executive Vice President, Chief Operating Officer:** Larry Baer.
**Senior VP, General Counsel:** Jack Bair. **VP, Human Resources:** Joyce Thomas.

### Finance
**Senior Vice President, Chief Financial Officer:** John Yee. **VP, Chief Information Officer:** Bill Schlough. **Director, Management Information Systems:** John Winborn.
**VP, Administration:** Alfonso Felder.
**VP, Finance:** Lisa Pantages.

Peter Magowan

### Marketing, Sales
**Senior Vice President, Corporate Marketing:** Mario Alioto. **VP, Corporate Sponsorship:** Jason Pearl. **Director, Special Events:** Valerie McGuire.
**Senior VP, Consumer Marketing:** Tom McDonald. **Director, Marketing/Entertainment:** Bryan Srabian. **Director, Client Relations:** Annemarie Hastings. **Director, Sales:** Jeff Tucker. **Manager, Season Ticket Sales:** Craig Solomon. **VP/General Manager, Retail:** Connie Kullberg. **Director, Retail:** Derik Landry.

### Media Relations, Community Relations
**Telephone:** (415) 972-2448. **FAX:** (415) 947-2800.
**Manager, Media Relations:** Jim Moorehead. **Director, Broadcasting/Media Services:** Maria Jacinto. **Director, Media Relations:** Blake Rhodes. **Senior Coordinator, Media Relations:** Matt Hodson.
**VP, Print Publications/Creative Services:** Nancy Donati. **VP, Communications:** Staci Slaughter. **Director, Public Affairs:** Shana Daum. **Manager, Photography/Archives:** Missy Mikulecky.

### Ballpark Operations
**Senior Vice President, Ballpark Operations:** Jorge Costa.
**VP, Guest Services:** Rick Mears. **Senior Director, Ballpark Operations:** Gene Telucci. **Manager, Maintenance:** Frank Peinado. **Security Manager:** Tinie Roberson. **Head Groundskeeper:** Scott MacVicar.
**PA Announcer:** Renel Brooks-Moon. **Official Scorers:** Chuck Dybdal, Art Santo Domingo, Al Talboy.

### Ticketing
**Telephone:** (415) 972-2000. **FAX:** (415) 947-2500.
**Vice President, Ticket Services/Client Relations:** Russ Stanley. **Director, Ticket Services:** Devin Lutes. **Director, Luxury Suites:** Amy Luskotoff. **Manager, Ticket Services:** Bob Bisio. **Manager, Ticket Accounting:** Kem Easley. **Senior Manager, Ticket Operations:** Anita Sprinkles. **Special Events Ticket Manager:** Todd Pierce.

### Travel, Clubhouse
**Coordinator, Team Travel:** Michael King. **Equipment Manager:** Miguel Murphy. **Visitors Clubhouse:** Harvey Hodgerney. **Umpires Attendant:** Richard Cacace. **Coordinator, Organizational Travel:** Mike Scardino.

---

## GENERAL INFORMATION
**Stadium (year opened):** AT&T Park (2000).
**Home Dugout:** Third Base. **Playing Surface:** Grass.
**Team Colors:** Black, orange and cream.
**Player Representative:** Unavailable.

## BASEBALL OPERATIONS
**Telephone:** (415) 972-1922. **FAX:** (415) 947-2737.
**Senior Vice President, General Manager:** Brian Sabean.
**Vice President, Player Personnel:** Dick Tidrow.
**Special Assistants to GM:** Pat Dobson, Ron Perranoski. **Executive Assistant to GM:** Karen Sweeney. **Director, Baseball Operations:** Jeremy Shelley. **Coordinator, Baseball Operations:** Yeshayah Goldfarb.

### Major League Staff
**Manager:** Felipe Alou.
**Coaches:** Bench—Ron Wotus; Pitching—Dave Righetti; Batting—Joe Lefebvre; First Base—Luis Pujols; Third Base—Gene Glynn; Bullpen—Mark Gardner; Bullpen Catcher—Bill Hayes.

Brian Sabean

### Medical, Training
**Team Physicians:** Dr. Robert Murray, Dr. Ken Akizuki, Dr. Anthony Saglimbeni.
**Medical Director/Head Trainer:** Stan Conte. **Assistant Trainers:** Dave Groeschner, Ben Potenziano.

### Player Development
**Telephone:** (415) 972-1922. **FAX:** (415) 947-2929.
**Director, Player Personnel:** Bobby Evans. **Director, Player Development:** Jack Hiatt.
**Special Assistants, Player Personnel:** Jim Davenport, Ted Uhlaender.
**Coordinator, Instruction:** Fred Stanley. **Coordinator, Minor League Pitching:** Bert Bradley.
**Coordinator, Minor League Hitting:** Bob Mariano.
**Roving Instructors:** Joe Amalfitano (infield), Darren Lewis (baserunning/outfield), Kirt Manwaring (catching), Lee Smith (pitching).

Felipe Alou

### Farm System
| Class | Farm Team | League | Manager | Coach | Pitching Coach |
|---|---|---|---|---|---|
| AAA | Fresno | Pacific Coast | Shane Turner | Jim Bowie | Trevor Wilson |
| AA | Connecticut | Eastern | Dave Machemer | Gary Davenport | Bob Stanley |
| High A | San Jose | California | Lenn Sakata | Garrett Nago | Jim Bennett |
| Low A | Augusta | South Atlantic | Roberto Kelly | Andy Skeels | Ross Grimsley |
| Short season | Salem-Keizer | Northwest | Steve Decker | Ricky Ward | Jerry Cram |
| Rookie | Scottsdale | Arizona | Bert Hunter | Leo Garcia | Will Malerich |
| Rookie | Giants | Dominican | Manuel Jimenez | Hector Ortiz | Luis Prieto |

### Scouting
**Telephone:** (415) 972-1922. **FAX:** (415) 947-2737.
**Director, Scouting:** Matt Nerland.
**Major League Scouts:** Joe DiCarlo (Ringwood, NJ), Pat Dobson (San Diego, CA), Stan Saleski (Dayton, OH), Rudy Santin (Miami, FL), Paul Turco Sr. (Sarasota, FL), Ted Uhlaender (Parshall, CO), Tom Zimmer (St. Petersburg, FL).
**Special Assignment Scouts:** Dick Cole (Costa Mesa, CA), Larry Osborne (Woodstock, GA).
**National Crosschecker:** Doug Mapson (Chandler, AZ). **Regional Crosscheckers:** Canada—Steve Arnieri (Barrington, IL); Southwest—Lee Carballo (Westchester, CA); East Coast—Paul Turco Jr. (Tampa, FL); Midwest—Joe Strain (Englewood, CO), West Coast—Darren Wittcke (Gresham, OR).
**Area Scouts:** Dean Decillis (Weston, FL), John DiCarlo (Glenwood, NJ), Lee Elder (Martinez, GA), Tom Korenek (Houston, TX), Mike Kendall (Manhattan Beach, CA), Ray Krawczyk (Aliso Viejo, CA), Felix Negron (Bayamon, PR), Sean O'Connor (Westerville, OH), Pat Portugal (Raleigh, NC), John Shafer (Portland, OR), Keith Snider (Stockton, CA), Todd Thomas (Dallas, TX), Glenn Tufts (Bridgewater, MA), Harry Stavrenos (Soquel, CA), Matt Woodward (Vancouver, WA).
**Director, International Operations:** Rick Ragazzo (Leona Valley, CA).
**Director, Dominican Republic Operations:** Pablo Peguero (Santo Domingo, DR). **Special Assignment Scout:** Matty Alou (Santo Domingo, DR). **Venezuela Supervisor:** Ciro Villalobos (Zulia, VZ).
**International Scouts:** Jonathan Arraiz (Venezuela), Enrique Burgos (Panama), Philip Elhage (Curacao), Martin Hernandez (Venezuela), Daniel Mavarez (Columbia), Arthur Mari (Holland), Juan Marquez (Venezuela), Sebastian Martinez (Venezuela), Francisco Monet (Mexico), Fausto Pena (Dominican Republic), Luis Pena (Mexico), Jesus Stephens (Dominican Republic), Alex Torres (Nicaragua), Aguedo Vasquez (Dominican Republic).

Dick Tidrow

# SEATTLE MARINERS

Office Address: 1250 First Ave. S., Seattle, WA 98134.
Mailing Address: P.O. Box 4100, Seattle, WA 98194.
Telephone: (206) 346-4000. FAX: (206) 346-4400.
Website: www.seattlemariners.com.

## Ownership

Operated by: Baseball Club of Seattle, LP.
Board of Directors: Minoru Arakawa, John Ellis, Chris Larson, Howard Lincoln, Wayne Perry, Frank Shrontz, Craig Watjen.
Chairman, Chief Executive Officer: Howard Lincoln. President, Chief Operating Officer: Chuck Armstrong.

Chuck Armstrong

## BUSINESS OPERATIONS

### Finance

Executive Vice President, Finance/Ballpark Operations: Kevin Mather.
VP, Finance: Tim Kornegay. Controller: Greg Massey.
VP, Human Resources: Marianne Short.

### Marketing, Sales

Executive Vice President, Business/Operations: Bob Aylward.
VP, Corporate Business/Community Relations: Joe Chard. VP, Marketing: Kevin Martinez. Director, Marketing: Gregg Greene. Senior Director, Merchandise: Jim La Shell. Suite Sales: Moose Clausen.

### Baseball Information, Communications

Telephone: (206) 346-4000. FAX: (206) 346-4400.
Vice President, Communications: Randy Adamack.
Director, Baseball Information: Tim Hevly. Manager, Baseball Information: Warren Miller, Assistants, Baseball Information: Gillian Hagemen, Kelly Munro.
Director, Public Information: Rebecca Hale. Director, Graphic Design: Carl Morton.
Director, Community Relations: Gina Hasson. Manager, Community Programs: Sean Grindley.

### Ticketing

Telephone: (206) 346-4001. FAX: (206) 346-4100.
Director, Ticket Services: Kristin Fortier. Manager, Group/Suite Tickets Services: Steve Belling. Manager, Box Office: Malcolm Rogel. Director, Season Tickets/Group Sales: Bob Hellinger. Senior Director, Sales: Frances Traisman.

### Stadium Operations

Vice President, Ballpark Operations: Neil Campbell. Director, Safeco Field Operations: Tony Pereira.
Head Groundskeeper: Bob Christofferson.
PA Announcer: Tom Hutyler. Official Scorer: Eric Radovich.

### Travel, Clubhouse

Director, Team Travel: Ron Spellecy.
Clubhouse Manager: Ted Walsh. Visiting Clubhouse Manager: Henry Genzale.
Video Coordinator: Carl Hamilton.

## GENERAL INFORMATION

Stadium (year opened): Safeco Field (1999).
Home Dugout: First Base. Playing Surface: Grass.
Team Colors: Northwest green, silver and navy blue.
Player Representative: Joel Pineiro.

Bill Bavasi

## BASEBALL OPERATIONS

**Executive Vice President, General Manager:** Bill Bavasi.
**VP, Associate General Manager:** Lee Pelekoudas.
**Special Assistants to Executive VP, Player Personnel:** John Boles, Dan Evans.
**Director, Baseball Administration:** Jim Na.
**Administrator, Baseball Operations:** Debbie Larsen.

### Major League Staff

**Manager:** Mike Hargrove.
**Coaches:** Dugout—Ron Hassey; Pitching—Rafael Chavez; Batting—Jeff Pentland; First Base—Mike Goff; Third Base—Carlos Garcia; Bullpen—Jim Slaton.

### Medical, Training

**Medical Director:** Dr. Larry Pedegana. **Club Physician:** Dr. Mitchel Storey.
**Head Trainer:** Rick Griffin. **Assistant Trainer:** Tom Newberg, Takayoshi Morimoto.
**Strength/Conditioning Coach:** Allen Wirtala. **Physical Therapist:** Jason Steere

## Player Development

**Telephone:** (206) 346-4313. **FAX:** (206) 346-4300.
**Vice President, Player Development/Scouting:** Benny Looper.
**Director, Minor League Operations:** Greg Hunter. **Director, Player Development:** Frank Mattox. **Administrator, Player Development:** Jan Plein.
**Coordinator, Minor League Instruction:** Pedro Grifol. **Trainer Coordinator:** Mickey Clarizio.
**Roving Instructors:** Glenn Adams (hitting), James Clifford (strength/conditioning), Darrin Garner (infield), Roger Hansen (catching), Pat Rice (pitching). **Special Assignment Coaches:** Norm Charlton, Buzzy Keller.

Mike Hargrove

## Farm System

| Class | Farm Team | League | Manager | Coach | Pitching Coach |
|---|---|---|---|---|---|
| AAA | Tacoma | Pacific Coast | Dave Brundage | Terry Pollreisz | Dwight Bernard |
| AA | San Antonio | Texas | Daren Brown | Henry Cotto | Brad Holman |
| High A | Inland Empire | California | Gary Thurman | Rafael Santo Domingo | Scott Budner |
| Low A | Wisconsin | Midwest | Scott Steinmann | Tommy Cruz | Lance Painter |
| Short season | Everett | Northwest | James Horner | Dave Myers | Juan Alvarez |
| Rookie | Peoria | Arizona | Dana Williams | Andy Bottin | Gary Wheelock |
| Rookie | Mariners | Dominican | Raymond Mejia | Franklin Taveras | Manuel Marrero |
| Rookie | Mariners | Venezuela | Jose Moreno | Angel Escobar | Jesus Hernandez |

## Scouting

**Telephone:** (206) 346-4000. **FAX:** (206) 346-4300.
**Vice President, Scouting:** Bob Fontaine. **Scouting Assistant:** Jim Fitzgerald.
**Administrator, Scouting:** Hallie Larson.
**Special Assignments/Amateur Scouting:** Tom Davis.
**Advance Scout:** Steve Peck (Phoenix, AZ).
**Director, Professional Scouting:** Ken Compton (Cypress, CA).
**Major League Scouts:** John Boles (Melbourne, FL), Dan Evans (La Canada, CA), Al Gallagher (Kansas City, KS), Bob Harrison (Long Beach, CA), Bill Kearns (Milton, MA), Bob Miske (Amherst, NY), Wayne Morgan (Pebble Beach, CA), Chris Pelekoudas (Goodyear, AZ), Steve Pope (Asheville, NC), Tim Schmidt (San Bernardino, CA).
**National Coordinators:** Rick Ingalls (Long Beach, CA), Steve Jongewaard (Fountain Valley, CA).

Bob Fontaine

**Territorial Supervisors:** West—Ron Tostenson (El Dorado Hills, CA); East—John McMichen (Treasure Island, FL); Midwest—Ken Madeja (Novi, MI).
**Full-Time Scouts:** Craig Bell (Asheboro, NC), Joe Bohringer (DeKalb, IL), Phil Geisler (Bellevue, WA), Mark Leavitt (Maitland, FL), Mark Lummus (Cleburne, TX), David May (Bear, DE), Rob Mummau (Stephens City, VA), Stacey Pettis (Brentwood, CA), Tim Reynolds (Irvine, CA), Alvin Rittman (Memphis, TN), Rafael Santo Domingo (San Juan, PR), Mike Tosar (Miami, FL), Kyle Van Hook (Brenham, TX), Greg Whitworth (Canyon Country, CA), Brian Williams (Lakeside, MI).
**Director, International Operations:** Bob Engle (Tampa, FL).
**Assistant Director, International Operations:** Hide Sueyoshi (Bellevue, WA). **Director, Pacific Rim Operations:** Ted Heid (Glendale, AZ).
**Coordinator, Canada/Europe:** Wayne Norton (Port Moody, BC).
**Supervisors, International Scouting:** Pedro Avila (Venezuela), Emilio Carrasquel (Venezuela), Patrick Guerrero (Dominican Republic), Matt Stark (Mexico), Jamey Storvick (Taiwan), Curtis Wallace (Colombia), Yasushi Yamamoto (Japan).

# TAMPA BAY DEVIL RAYS

**Office Address:** Tropicana Field, One Tropicana Dr., St. Petersburg, FL 33705.
**Telephone:** (727) 825-3137. **FAX:** (727)-825-3111.
**Website:** www.devilrays.com.

## Ownership

**Operated by:** Tampa Bay Devil Rays, Ltd.
**Principal Owner:** Stuart Sternberg. **President:** Matthew Silverman. **Chairman:** Vince Naimoli.

## BUSINESS OPERATIONS

**Senior Vice President, Administration/General Counsel:** John Higgins.
**Chief of Staff:** Brian Auld. **VP, Branding/Fan Experience:** Darcy Raymond. **Senior Director, Procurement/Business Services:** Bill Weiner.

### Finance

Stuart Sternberg

**Controller:** Patrick Smith. **Executive Assistant:** Diane Villanova. **Human Resources Manager:** Jennifer Lyn Tran. **Benefits Coordinator:** Debbie Perry. **Supervisor, Accounting:** Sandra Faulkner. **Research Analyst:** Phil Wallace. **Payroll Supervisor:** Jill Baetz. **Coordinator, Accounts Payable:** Sam Reams. **Coordinator, Purchasing:** Mike Yodis. **Director, Information Technology:** Dave Hansen.

### Sales, Marketing

**Vice President, Sales/Marketing:** Kevin Terry.
**Senior Director, Marketing:** Tom Hoof. **Director, Marketing/Promotions:** Brian Killingsworth. **Director, Suite Sales/Premium Seating:** Clark Beacom. **Director, Ticket Sales:** Michael Bargagliotti. **Manager, Season Ticket Sales:** Bryan Ross. **Senior Account Executive:** Ryan Shirk. **Coordinator, Sales/Communication:** Carey Cox. **Manager, Group Sales:** Jude Tarris. **Senior Group Account Executives:** Kristin Aiello, Barry Jones.
**Director, Ticket Operations:** Robert Bennett. **Assistant Director, Ticket Operations:** Ken Mallory. **Manager, Account Services:** Craig Champagne. **Coordinator, Fan Development:** Kristi Capone.

### Corporate Sales, Broadcasting

**Vice President, Chief Sales Officer:** Mark Fernandez. **Senior Director, Corporate Partnerships/Broadcasting:** Larry McCabe. **Directors, Corporate Partnerships:** Aaron Cohn, Doug Holtzman. **Director, Radio Operations:** Rich Herrera. **Managers, Corporate Partnerships:** Beth Bohnsack, Erin Buscemi. **Manager, Corporate Partnerships/Television Operations:** Joe Ciaravino. **Manager, Corporate Partnerships/Radio Operations:** Jason Wilmoth. **Merchandise Manager:** Debbie Brooks. **Administrative Assistant:** Silvia Bynes.
**Senior Director, Creative Services/Entertainment:** John Franzone. **Manager, Video/Graphic Production:** Jason Rundle. **Manager, Print/Graphics:** Erik Ruiz. **Video Producer:** Doug Elsberry. **Multimedia Producer:** Scott Timmreck. **Event Producer:** Becky Shultz. **Matrix Producer:** Laura Cuozzo.

### Public Relations

**Telephone:** (727) 825-3242. **FAX:** (727) 825-3111.
**Vice President, Public Relations:** Rick Vaughn.
**Director, Media Relations:** Chris Costello. **Coordinator, Public Relations:** Carmen Molina. **Coordinator, Media Relations:** Jason Latimer.
**Vice President, Community Outreach:** Veronica Costello. **VP, Hispanic Outreach/Military Affairs:** Jose Tavarez. **Senior Adviser:** Dick Crippen. **Manager, Special Events:** Stephanie Renica.

### Stadium Operations

**Vice President, Operations/Facilities:** Rick Nafe. **Administrative Assistant:** Jaclyn Waechtel.
**Building Manager:** Scott Kelyman. **Event Manager:** Tom Karac. **Event Coordinator:** Todd Hardy. **Manager, Partner/VIP Relations:** Cass Halpin. **Booking Coordinator:** Caren Gramley. **Head Groundskeeper:** Dan Moeller. **Director, Audio/Visual Services:** Ron Golick. **PA Announcer:** Bill Couch.

### Travel, Clubhouse

**Director, Team Travel:** Jeff Ziegler.
**Equipment Manager, Home Clubhouse:** Chris Westmoreland. **Assistant Manager, Home Clubhouse:** Jose Fernandez. **Visitors Clubhouse:** Guy Gallagher.
**Video Coordinator:** Chris Fernandez.

## GENERAL INFORMATION

**Stadium (year opened):** Tropicana Field (1998).
**Home Dugout:** First Base. **Playing Surface:** FieldTurf.
**Team Colors:** Black, blue and green.
**Player Representative:** Rocco Baldelli.

Andrew Friedman

## BASEBALL OPERATIONS

**Executive Vice President, Baseball Operations:** Andrew Friedman. **Senior VP, Baseball Operations:** Gerry Hunsicker.

**Director, Major League Administration:** Sandy Dengler. **Assistant General Manager:** Bart Braun. **Special Assistant, Baseball Operations:** Rick Williams. **Senior Baseball Adviser:** Don Zimmer. **Assistant, Baseball Operations:** Chaim Bloom.

## Major League Staff

**Manager:** Joe Maddon.

**Coaches:** Bench—Bill Evers; Pitching—Mike Butcher; Batting—Steve Henderson; First Base—George Hendrick; Third Base—Tom Foley; Bullpen—Bobby Ramos.

## Medical, Training

**Medical Director:** Dr. James Andrews. **Medical Team Physician:** Dr. Michael Reilly. **Orthopedic Team Physician:** Dr. Koco Eaton.

**Head Athletic Trainer:** Ron Porterfield. **Assistant Athletic Trainer:** Paul Harker. **Strength/Conditioning Coach:** Kevin Barr.

## Minor Leagues

**Telephone:** (727) 825-3267. **FAX:** (727) 825-3493.

**Director, Minor League Operations:** Mitch Lukevics. **Administrative Assistant, Player Development:** Giovanna Rodriguez.

**Field Coordinator:** Jim Hoff. **Minor League Coordinators:** Trung Cao (strength/conditioning), Steve Livesey (hitting), Jerry Nyman (pitching), Nick Paparesta (medical/rehabilitation), Jimy Williams (special instructor). **Equipment Manager:** Tim McKechney.

Joe Maddon

## Farm System

| Class | Farm Team | League | Manager | Coach | Pitching Coach |
|---|---|---|---|---|---|
| Triple-A | Durham | International | John Tamargo Sr. | Richie Hebner | Joe Coleman |
| Double-A | Montgomery | Southern | Charlie Montoyo | Mako Oliveras | Xavier Hernandez |
| High A | Visalia | California | Steve Livesey | Omar Munoz | Marty DeMerritt |
| Low A | SW Michigan | Midwest | Dave Howard | Skeeter Barnes | R.C. Lichtenstein |
| Short-season | Hudson Valley | New York-Penn | Matt Quatraro | Hector Torres | Dick Bosman |
| Rookie | Princeton | Appalachian | Jamie Nelson | Rafael Deleon | Rafael Montalvo |

## Scouting

**Telephone:** (727) 825-3241. **FAX:** (727) 825-3493.

**Scouting Director:** R.J. Harrison (Phoenix, AZ). **Assistant to Scouting Director:** Nancy Berry.

**Major League Scouts:** Mike Cubbage (Keswick, VA), Bart Johnson  (Bridgeview, IL), Roger Jongewaard (Fallbrook, CA), Dave Roberts (Temecula, CA), Don Williams (Paragould, AR), Stan Williams (Lakewood, CA). **Major League Consultants:** Jerry Gardner (Los Alamitos, CA), George Zuraw (Englewood, FL).

**Regional Supervisors:** East—Mark McKnight (Matthews, NC); Midwest—Larry Doughty (Leawood, KS); West—Tim Huff (Cave Creek, AZ).

**Area Scouts:** Jonathan Bonifay (Austin, TX), Jim Bonnici (Davison, MI), Bill Byckowski (Georgetown, Ontario), John Ceprini (Massapequa, NY), Tom Couston (Chicago, IL), Carlos Delgado (San Francisco, CA), Dan Drake (Riverside, CA), Rickey Drexler (Jeanerette, LA), Kevin Elfering (Wesley Chapel, FL), Milt Hill (Cumming, GA), Paul Kirsch (Sherwood, OR), Brad Matthews (Concord, NC), Pat Murphy (The Woodlands, TX), Jack Powell (Sweetwater, TN), Fred Repke (Rancho Cucamonga, CA), Doug Witt (Brooklyn MD).

R.J. Harrison

**Part-Time Scouts:** Tom Delong (Ocala, FL), Jose Hernandez (Miami, FL), Larry Hill (Franklin, TN),  Mac Seibert (Cantonment, FL), Lee Seras (Flanders, NJ).

**Director, International Operations:** Carlos Alfonso (Naples, FL). **International Scout:** Junior Ramirez (Dominican Republic).

# TEXAS RANGERS

Office Address: 1000 Ballpark Way, Arlington, TX 76011.
Mailing Address: P.O. Box 90111, Arlington, TX 76004.
Telephone: (817) 273-5222. FAX: (817) 273-5110.
Website: www.texasrangers.com.

## Ownership
Owner: Hicks Holdings.
Chairman, Chief Executive Officer: Tom Hicks.
President: Jeff Cogen.
Executive Vice President, Hicks Holdings: Casey Shilts. Executive Director to President: Jim Sundberg. Executive Assistant to President: Jessica Anderson.

Tom Hicks

## BUSINESS OPERATIONS
Executive Vice President, Business Operations: Rick McLaughlin. Executive Assistant, Business Operations/Security: Judy Southworth.
Assistant VP, Human Resources: Terry Turner. Manager, Benefits/Compensation: Carla Clack. Supervisor, Staffing/Development: Shannon Cain. Associate Counsel: Kate Jett.
Director, Information Technology: Mike Bullock. Director, Application Systems: Russell Smutzer. Manager, Systems Administration: Karl Clark.

### Finance
Vice President, Finance: Kellie Fischer. Executive Assistant, Legal/Finance: Kay Turner.
Controller: Starr Pritchard. Manager, Payroll: Donna Blaylock. Manager, Accounting: Donna Kee.

### Corporate Sales, Marketing
Vice President, Sponsorship: Brad Alberts.
Directors, Sponsorship Sales: Jim Cochrane, Grady Raskin, Lillian Richey.
VP, Marketing/In-Park Entertainment: Chuck Morgan. Assistant VP, Marketing: Kelly Calvert. Senior Director, Graphic Design: Rainer Uhlir. Director, Publications: Kurt Daniels. Director, Promotions/Special Events: Sherry Flow. Director, Graphic Design: Michelle Hays. Director, Media: Heidi Leonards. Creative Director, Media: Rush Olson. Director, Broadcasting Sales Services: Angie Swint. Director, New Market Development: Karin Morris.

### Merchandising
Assistant Vice President, Merchandising: Todd Grizzle. Director, Merchandising: Diane Atkinson. Manager, Warehouse Operations: Gabriel Naggar. Manager, Ballpark Retail Operations: Stephen Moore.

### Communications
Telephone: (817) 273-5902. FAX: (817) 273-5110.
Senior Director, Baseball Media Relations: Gregg Elkin. Manager, Business Communications: Jessica Beard. Manager, Baseball Media Relations: Jeff Evans. Director, Player/Community Relations: Taunee Paur Taylor.
VP, Community Development/Government Relations: Norm Lyons.

### Stadium Operations
Vice President, Event Operations/Security: John Hardin. Senior Director, Customer Service: Donnie Pordash. Assistant Director, Security: Mickey McGovern. Coordinator, Seasonal Employment: Meredith Foster.
Assistant VP, Facilities Operations: Gib Searight. Director, Grounds: Tom Burns. Director, Maintenance: Mike Call.
PA Announcer: Chuck Morgan. Official Scorers: John Mocek, Steve Weller.

### Ticket Operations/Sales
Telephone: (817) 273-5100. FAX: (817) 273-5190.
Vice President, Ticket Sales: Andy Silverman. Assistant VP, Luxury Suite Sales: Paige Jackson Farragut. Director, Ticket Sales: Ken Troupe. Director, Baseball Programs/Youth Ballpark: Breon Dennis. Director, Inside Sales: Chip Kisabeth. Assistant Manager, Premium Services: Lacey Jones. Manager, Group Sales: Chris Faulkner.
Director, Ticket Services: Mike Lentz. Manager, Ticket Operations: David Larson.

### Travel, Clubhouse
Director, Travel: Chris Lyngos.
Equipment/Home Clubhouse Manager: Zack Minasian. Assistant Clubhouse Manager: Dave Bales. Visiting Clubhouse Manager: Kelly Terrell. Video Coordinator/Bullpen Catcher: Josh Frasier.

---

## GENERAL INFORMATION
Stadium (year opened): Ameriquest Field in Arlington (1994).
Home Dugout: First Base. Playing Surface: Grass.
Team Colors: Royal blue and red.
Player Representative: Mark Teixeira.

## BASEBALL OPERATIONS

**Telephone:** (817) 273-5222. **FAX:** (817) 273-5285.
**General Manager:** Jon Daniels. **Assistant GM:** Thad Levine. **Senior Adviser, Baseball Operations:** John Hart. **Special Assistants to GM:** Jay Robertson, Charley Kerfeld. **Senior Advisers to GM:** Tom Giordano, Mel Didier.
   **Director, Major League Administration:** Judy Johns. **Manager, Baseball Operations:** Jake Krug. **Administrative Assistant:** Barbara Pappenfus.

### Major League Staff

   **Manager:** Buck Showalter.
   **Coaches:** Bench—Don Wakamatsu; Pitching—Mark Connor; Batting—Rudy Jaramillo; First Base/Outfield—Bobby Jones; Third Base—Steve Smith; Bullpen—Dom Chiti.

Jon Daniels

### Medical, Training

**Team Physician:** Dr. Keith Meister. **Team Internist:** Dr. David Hunter.
**Head Athletic Trainer/Medical Director:** Jamie Reed. **Assistant Athletic Trainer:** Kevin Harmon. **Major League Strength/Conditioning Coach:** Jose Vazquez.

### Player Development

**Telephone:** (817) 273-5224. **FAX:** (817) 273-5285.
   **Director, Player Development:** Scott Servais. **Director, Minor League Operations:** Jon Lombardo. **Administrative Assistant, Player Development/Scouting:** Margaret Bales.
   **Field Coordinator:** Mike Brumley. **Roving Instructors:** Rick Adair (pitching), Damon Berryhill (catching), Wayne Kirby (baserunning/outfield), Brook Jacoby (hitting), Matthew Lucero (rehabilitation), Napoleon Pichardo (strength), Terry Shumpert (base running/bunting), Kyle Turner (medical).
   **Manager, Minor League Complex Operations:** Chris Guth. **Assistant Equipment Manager:** Russ Oliver. **Arizona Clubhouse Manager:** Troy Timney.

Buck Showalter

### Farm System

| Class | Farm Team | League | Manager | Coach | Pitching Coach |
|---|---|---|---|---|---|
| Triple-A | Oklahoma | Pacific Coast | Tim Ireland | Mike Boulanger | Andy Hawkins |
| Double-A | Frisco | Texas | Darryl Kennedy | Ronnie Ortegon | Terry Clark |
| High A | Bakersfield | California | Carlos Subero | Pedro Lopez | David Chavarria |
| Low A | Clinton | Midwest | Andy Fox | Brian Dayett | Stan Hilton |
| Short-season | Spokane | Northwest | Mike Micucci | Jim Nettles | Aris Tirado |
| Rookie | Surprise | Arizona | Bob Skube | Mark Whiten | Unavailable |
| Rookie | Rangers | Dominican | Josue Perez | Guillermo Mercedes | John Burgos |

### Scouting

**Telephone:** (817) 273-5277. **FAX:** (817) 273-5285.
   **Director, Scouting:** Ron Hopkins (Seattle, WA). **Director, Professional/International Scouting:** A.J. Preller.
   **Professional Scouts:** Keith Boeck (Chandler, AZ), Mel Didier (Phoenix, AZ), Bob Johnson (University Park, FL).
   **Regional Crosscheckers:** Kip Fagg (Gilbert, AZ), Dave Klipstein (Roanoke, TX), Doug Harris (Carlisle, PA).
   **Area Scouts:** Russ Ardolina (Baltimore, MD), Jim Cuthbert (Princeton Junction, NJ), Guy DeMutis (Windermere, FL), Jay Eddings (Sperry, OK), Steve Flores (Temecula, CA), Mark Giegler (Brighton, MI), Mike Grouse (Olathe, KS), Todd Guggiana (Long Beach, CA), Derek Lee (Homewood, IL), Gary McGraw (Gaston, OR), Butch Metzger (Sacramento, CA), Rick Schroeder (Phoenix, AZ), Scott Sharp (Charlotte, NC), Randy Taylor (Katy, TX), Frankie Thon (Guaynabo, PR), Jeff Wood (Birmingham, AL).

Ron Hopkins

   **Part-Time Scout:** Ron Toenjes (Georgetown, TX).
   **Latin Coordinator:** Manny Batista (Vega Alta, PR). **Coordinator, Dominican Program:** Danilo Troncoso (La Romana, DR) **Dominican Program/English Instructor:** Dennys Sanchez.
   **International Scouts:** Andres Espinoso (Venezuela), Jose Luis Montero (Venezuela), Jesus Ovalle (Dominican Republic), Rodolfo Rosario (Dominican Republic), Edgar Suarez (Venezuela), Eduardo Thomas (Panama).

# TORONTO BLUE JAYS

**Office/Mailing Address:** 1 Blue Jays Way, Suite 3200, Toronto, Ontario M5V 3M7.
**Telephone:** (416) 341-1000. **FAX:** (416) 341-1250.
**E-Mail Address:** bluejay@bluejays.ca **Website:** www.bluejays.com.

## Ownership

**Operated by:** Toronto Blue Jays Baseball Club.
**Principal Owner:** Rogers Communications, Inc.
**President, Chief Executive Officer:** Paul Godfrey. **Executive Assistant to President/CEO:** Julie Stoddart. **Vice President, Special Projects:** Howard Starkman. **VP, Business Performance, Rogers Communications, Inc.:** Richard Wong. **Executive Assistant to Senior VP, Communications/External Relations:** Jacey Chae.

Paul Godfrey

## BUSINESS OPERATIONS

**Senior Vice President, Operations/Corporate Development:** Lisa Power. **Director, Business Affairs:** Matthew Shuber.

### Finance

**Vice President, Finance/Administration:** Susan Brioux. **Executive Administrative Assistant:** Donna Kuzoff. **Controller:** Tony Loffreda. **Director, Payroll/Benefits:** Brenda Dimmer. **Director, Risk Management:** Suzanne Joncas. **Financial Business Managers:** Leslie Gallant-Gardiner, Tanya Proctor. **Manager, Ticket Receipts/Vault Services:** Joseph Roach. **Manager, Stadium Payroll:** Sharon Dykstra.
**Manager, Human Resources:** Michelle Carter. **Coordinator, Human Resources:** Tamara Edwards.
**Director, Information Technology:** Jacques Farand. **Information Technology Project Manager:** Anthony Miranda.

### Marketing, Community Relations

**Vice President, Consumer Marketing:** Laurel Lindsay. **Executive Director, Jays Care Foundation, Community, Player and Alumni Relations:** Jennifer Santamaria. **Executive Producer, Game Entertainment:** Deb Belinsky. **Manager, Game Entertainment/Productions:** Tim Sullivan. **Manager, Marketing:** Lisa Arai. **Manager, Promotions:** Jillian Stoltz. **Manager, Community/Player Relations:** Michael Volpatti. **Manager, Sports/Event Production:** Anastasia Stenhouse.
**Vice President, Corporate Partnerships/Business Development:** Mark Lemmon. **Director, Corporate Partnerships:** Robert Mackay. **Managers, Corporate Partnerships:** Honsing Leung, Paolo Pastore.
**Managing Director, Corporate Marketing:** Wilna Behr. **Director, Corporate Program Development:** Krista Semotiuk. **Executive Assistant, Corporate Marketing/Business Affairs:** Liza Daniels.

### Media Relations, Communications

**Telephone:** (416) 341-1301/1303. **FAX:** (416) 341-1250.
**Senior Vice President, Communications/External Relations:** Rob Godfrey. **Vice President, Communications:** Jay Stenhouse. **Director, Public Relations:** Will Hill.

### Stadium Operations

**Vice President, Stadium Operations/Security:** Mario Coutinho. **Executive Assistant, Stadium Operations:** June Sym. **Operations Assistant:** Marion Farrell. **Operations Intern:** Karyn Gottschalk.
**Head Groundskeeper:** Tom Farrell.

### Ticketing

**Telephone:** (416) 341-1234. **FAX:** (416) 341-1177.
**Vice President, Ticket Sales/Service:** Patrick Elster. **Senior Adviser, Director of Special Projects:** Sheila Stella. **Director, Ticket Sales/Service:** Jason Diplock. **Director, Ticket System/Box Office:** Doug Barr. **Director, Sales Channel Development:** Franc Rota. **Director, Premium Sales:** Nancy Spotton. **Executive Administrative Assistant:** Leigh-Ann Groombridge. **Manager, Direct Marketing:** Tanya Scholes. **Coordinator, Direct Marketing/Collateral:** Sherry Thurston. **Manager, Sales Channel Integration:** Craig Johnson. **Manager, Retail Development:** Scott Clark. **Coordinators, Special Projects:** Leeanne Jardine, Kellie O'Leary, Sonia Privato. **Manager, Premier Client Services:** Erik Bobson. **Account Executives, Premier Client Services:** Jonathan Collins, Steve Faveri, Matt Murdock, Nicola Prabhu. **Manager, Consumer Sales:** Paul Fruitman. **Supervisors, Consumer Sales:** Michael Hook, John Santana. **Manager, Group Development:** Shelby Nelson. **Manager, Database/System Administration:** Mark Nguyen.

### Travel, Clubhouse

**Manager, Team Travel:** Mike Shaw.
**Equipment Manager:** Jeff Ross. **Clubhouse Manager:** Kevin Malloy. **Visiting Clubhouse Manager:** Len Frejlich.
**Video Operations:** Robert Baumander.

---

## GENERAL INFORMATION

**Stadium (year opened):** Rogers Centre (1989).
**Home Dugout:** Third base. **Playing Surface:** Artificial turf.
**Team Colors:** Blue, metallic silver, metallic graphite, black and white.
**Player Representative:** Unavailable.

## BASEBALL OPERATIONS

**Senior Vice President, Baseball Operations/General Manager:** J.P. Ricciardi.
**Assistants to GM:** Alex Anthopoulos, Bart Given. **Special Assistants to GM:** Sal Butera, Keith Law. **Executive Assistant to GM:** Ainsley Doyle. **Executive Assistant, Major League Operations:** Heather Connolly.
**Director, Player Personnel:** Tony LaCava.
**Director, Florida Operations:** Ken Carson.

### Major League Staff

**Manager:** John Gibbons.
**Coaches:** Bench—Ernie Whitt; Pitching—Brad Arnsberg; Batting—Mickey Brantley; First Base—Marty Pevey; Third Base—Brian Butterfield; Bullpen—Bruce Walton.

J.P. Ricciardi

### Medical, Training

**Medical Advisor:** Dr. Bernie Gosevitz. **Team Physician:** Dr. Ron Taylor.
**Head Trainer:** George Poulis. **Assistant Trainer:** Dave Abraham. **Strength/Conditioning Coordinator:** Donovan Santas.
**Director, Team Safety:** Ron Sandelli.

### Player Development

**Telephone:** (727) 734-8007. **FAX:** (727) 734-8162.
**Director, Player Development:** Dick Scott. **Manager, Minor League Operations:** Charlie Wilson. **Baseball Assistant, Player Development:** Joanna Nelson. **Administrative Assistant:** Kim Marsh. **Director, Employee Assistance Program:** Ray Karesky. **Baseball Operations Assistant/Coordinator, Cultural Diversity:** Jeff Roemer.
**Roving Instructors:** Dane Johnson (pitching), Merv Rettenmund (hitting).
**Minor League Coordinators:** Mike Frostad (training), Chris Joyner (strength/conditioning), Billy Wardlow (equipment).

John Gibbons

### Farm System

| Class | Farm Team | League | Manager | Coach | Pitching Coach |
|---|---|---|---|---|---|
| Triple-A | Syracuse | International | Mike Basso | Dwayne Murphy | Rick Langford |
| Double-A | New Hampshire | Eastern | Doug Davis | Gary Cathcart | Dave LaRoche |
| High A | Dunedin | Florida State | Omar Malave | Paul Elliott | Darold Knowles |
| Low A | Lansing | Midwest | Ken Joyce | Charles Poe | Tom Signore |
| Short-season | Auburn | New York-Penn | Dennis Holmberg | Justin Mashore | Antonio Caceres |
| Rookie | Pulaski | Appalachian | Dave Pano | Unavailable | Unavailable |
| Rookie | Blue Jays | Dominican | Unavailable | None | Unavailable |
| Rookie | Blue Jays | Venezuelan | Domingo Carrasquel | H. Hurtado/J. Escobar | Enrique Vasquez |

### Scouting

**Telephone:** (416) 341-1115. **FAX:** (416) 341-1245.
**Director, Scouting:** Jon Lalonde.
**Professional Scouts:** Mike Berger (Oakmont, PA), Sal Butera (Lake Mary, FL), Kimball Crossley (Gilbert, AZ), Jim D'Aloia (Lakewood, NJ), Rob Ducey (Tarpon Springs, FL), Kevin O'Brien (Brockton, MA).
**National Crosscheckers:** Tom Clark (Shrewsbury, MA), Mike Mangan (Clermont, FL).
**Scouting Coordinators:** Ryan Mittleman, Andrew Tinnish.
**Area Scouts:** Tony Arias (Miami Lakes, FL), Andy Beene (Center Point, TX), Matt Briggs (Birmingham), Tom Burns (Harrisburg, PA), Dan Cholowsky (Queen Creek, AZ), Billy Gasparino (Venice, CA), Joel Grampietro (Tampa), Aaron Jersild (Chicago), Brandon Mozley (El Dorado Hills, CA), Ty Nichols (Broken Arrow, OK), Demerius Pittman (Corona, CA), Jorge Rivera (Puerto Nuevo, PR), Tom Tanous (Barrington, RI), Marc Tramuta (Matthews, NC).

Jon Lalonde

**Director, Canadian Scouting:** Kevin Briand (Etobicoke, Ontario). **Canadian Scouts:** Greg Brons (Saskatoon, Saskatchewan), Don Cowan (Delta, British Columbia), Jean Marc Mercier (Montreal, Quebec). **Associate Scout, Canada:** Sean McCann (Toronto, Ontario), John Milton (Bolton, Ontario).
**Director, Latin America Operations:** Tony Arias (Miami Lakes, FL).
**International Scouts:** Robinson Garces (Venezuela), Boris Miranda (Panama), Rafael Moncada (Venezuela), Juan Salavarria (Venezuela), Hilario Soriano (Dominican Republic), Greg Wade (Australia).

# WASHINGTON NATIONALS

Office Address: 2400 East Capitol St., SE Washington, DC 20003.
Telephone: (202) 675-5100. FAX: (202) 547-0025.
Website: www.nationals.com.

## Ownership
Operated by: Baseball Expos, LP.
President: Tony Tavares. Executive Assistant: Tanya Archie.

## BUSINESS OPERATIONS
Executive Vice President: Kevin Uhlich.

### Sales, Marketing
Vice President, Sales/Marketing: Unavailable.
Director, Ticket Sales: Joe Deoudes. Director, Marketing/Promotions: Carleen Martin.
Director, Corporate Sales: Joe Hickey. Manager, Corporate Sales: Craig Schulman.
Manager, Account Services: Amy Pennington.

### Media Relations, Communications
Vice President, Communications: Chartese Burnett.

Tony Tavares

Director, Baseball Information: John Dever. Manager, Media Relations: Mark Rogoff.
Director, Community Relations: Barbra Silva. Coordinator, Community Relations: Jennifer Skolochenko.
Assistant, Communications: Lisa Pagano.

### Stadium Operations
Vice President, Ballpark Operations: Unavailable. Manager, Guest Services: Aaron Chang. Director, Security: Emory Waters. Assistant, Ballpark Operations: Laura Allen.
Manager, Entertainment/Events: Josh Golden.
Producer, Scoreboard: Josh Rooney. Coordinator, Productions: Kellee Mickens.
Director, Management Information Systems: Jim Bernhardt. Computer Operations Specialist: Ken Ford.
PA Announcer: Unavailable. Official Scorers: David Vincent, Ben Trittipoe

### Ticketing
Director, Ticket Operations: Derek Younger. Assistant Manager, Ticketing: Peter Wallace.

### Travel, Clubhouse
Director, Team Travel: Rob McDonald.
Equipment Manager: Mike Wallace. Visiting Clubhouse: Matt Rosenthal.

## GENERAL INFORMATION
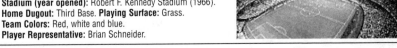

Stadium (year opened): Robert F. Kennedy Stadium (1966).
Home Dugout: Third Base. Playing Surface: Grass.
Team Colors: Red, white and blue.
Player Representative: Brian Schneider.

Jim Bowden

## BASEBALL OPERATIONS
**General Manager:** Jim Bowden. **Assistant GM:** Tony Siegle.
**Director, Major League Administration/Special Administration Scout:** Lee MacPhail.

### Major League Staff
**Manager:** Frank Robinson.
**Coaches:** Bench—Eddie Rodriguez; Pitching—Randy St. Claire; Hitting—Mitchell Page; First Base—Dave Lopes; Third Base—Tony Beasley.

### Medical, Training
**Medical Director:** Dr. Tom Graham. **Orthopedic Physicians:** Dr. Wiemi Douoguih, Dr. Dave Johnson. **Consultant:** Dr. Tim Kremchek. **Consultants:** Dr. James Andrews, Dr. Lewis Yocum.
**Head Trainer:** Tim Abraham. **Assistant Trainer:** Mike McGowan. **Strength/Conditioning Coach:** Kazuhiko Tomooka.

Frank Robinson

### Player Development
**Assistant General Manager/Senior Director, Player Development:** Bob Boone. **Assistant Director, Player Development:** Nick Manno.
**Farm Director:** Andy Dunn.
**Field Coordinator:** Scott Little. **Roving Coordinators:** Jose Alguacil (infield), Jose Cardenal (outfield/base running), Steve Gober (medical/rehabilitation), Abraham Gonzalez (strength/conditioning), Bobby Henley (catching), Brent Strom (pitching).
**Manager, Florida Operations:** Tyler Holmes. **Minor League Equipment Coordinator:** John Mullin.

### Farm System
| Class | Farm Team | League | Manager | Coach | Pitching Coach |
|---|---|---|---|---|---|
| AAA | New Orleans | Pacific Coast | Tim Foli | Rick Eckstein | Steve McCatty |
| AA | Harrisburg | Eastern | John Stearns | Mike Hart | Rick Tomlin |
| High A | Potomac | Carolina | Randy Knorr | Troy Gingrich | Charlie Corbell |
| Low A | Savannah | South Atlantic | Bobby Williams | Jerry Browne | Unavailable |
| Short season | Vermont | New York-Penn | Edgar Caceres | Tony Tarasco | Mark Grater |
| Rookie | Melbourne | Gulf Coast | Bobby Henley | Jason Camilli | Franklyn Bravo |
| Rookie | Nationals | Dominican | Sergio Mendez | Elvis Herrera | Manuel Santana |

### Scouting
**Director, Scouting:** Dana Brown. **Assistant Director, Scouting:** Brian Parker.
**Professional Scouts:** Jason Angel (Glen Allen, VA), Mike Toomey (Gaithersburg, MD), Fred Wright (Harrisburg, NC),
**Regional Crosscheckers:** East—Paul Tinnell (Bradenton, FL); West—Mike Williams (Valley Village, CA).
**Area Scouts:** Anthony Arango (Davie, FL), Denis Boucher (Montreal, Quebec), Ryan Fox (Broken Arrow, OK), Bob Hamelin (Concord, NC), Brian Hunter (Lake Elsinore, CA), Ray Jackson (Ocala, FL), Ben Jones (Fort Wayne, IN), Bob Laurie (Plano, TX), Guy Mader (Tewksbury, MA), Doug McMillan (Shingle Springs, CA), Eric Robinson (Hiram, GA), Alex Smith (Abingdon, MD), Delvy Santiago (Vega Alta, PR), Mitch Sokol (Phoenix, AZ), Ken Stauffer (Katy, TX).
**Coordinator, Latin American Operations:** Pablo Cruz. **Scout, Dominican Republic:** Sandi Rosario.

Dana Brown

# MAJOR LEAGUE
# SCHEDULES

## 2005 STANDINGS
## SPRING TRAINING

# AMERICAN
## LEAGUE

### 2005 STANDINGS

| EAST | W | L | Pct. | GB | Manager(s) | General Manager(s) |
|---|---|---|---|---|---|---|
| New York Yankees | 95 | 67 | .586 | — | Joe Torre | Brian Cashman |
| *Boston Red Sox | 95 | 67 | .586 | — | Terry Francona | Theo Epstein |
| Toronto Blue Jays | 80 | 82 | .494 | 15 | John Gibbons | J.P. Ricciardi |
| Baltimore Orioles | 74 | 88 | .457 | 21 | Lee Mazzilli/Sam Perlozzo | Jim Beattie/Mike Flanagan |
| Tampa Bay Devil Rays | 67 | 95 | .414 | 28 | Lou Piniella | Chuck LaMar |

| CENTRAL | W | L | Pct. | GB | Manager(s) | General Manager |
|---|---|---|---|---|---|---|
| Chicago White Sox | 99 | 63 | .611 | — | Ozzie Guillen | Ken Williams |
| Cleveland Indians | 93 | 69 | .574 | 6 | Eric Wedge | Mark Shapiro |
| Minnesota Twins | 83 | 79 | .512 | 16 | Ron Gardenhire | Terry Ryan |
| Detroit Tigers | 71 | 91 | .438 | 28 | Alan Trammell | Dave Dombrowski |
| Kansas City Royals | 56 | 106 | .346 | 43 | Tony Pena/Buddy Bell | Allard Baird |

| WEST | W | L | Pct. | GB | Manager | General Manager |
|---|---|---|---|---|---|---|
| Los Angeles Angels | 95 | 67 | .586 | — | Mike Scioscia | Bill Stoneman |
| Oakland Athletics | 88 | 74 | .543 | 7 | Ken Macha | Billy Beane |
| Texas Rangers | 79 | 83 | .488 | 16 | Buck Showalter | John Hart |
| Seattle Mariners | 69 | 93 | .426 | 26 | Mike Hargrove | Bill Bavasi |

*Won wild-card playoff berth

**PLAYOFFS: Division Series** (best-of-5)—Chicago defeated Boston 3-0; Los Angeles defeated New York 3-2. **League Championship Series** (best-of-7)—Chicago defeated Los Angeles 4-1.

# NATIONAL
## LEAGUE

### 2005 STANDINGS

| EAST | W | L | Pct. | GB | Manager | General Manager |
|---|---|---|---|---|---|---|
| Atlanta Braves | 90 | 72 | .556 | — | Bobby Cox | John Schuerholz |
| Philadelphia Phillies | 88 | 74 | .543 | 2 | Charlie Manuel | Ed Wade |
| Florida Marlins | 83 | 79 | .512 | 7 | Jack McKeon | Larry Beinfest |
| New York Mets | 83 | 79 | .512 | 7 | Willie Randolph | Omar Minaya |
| Washington Nationals | 81 | 81 | .500 | 9 | Frank Robinson | Jim Bowden |

| CENTRAL | W | L | Pct. | GB | Manager(s) | General Manager |
|---|---|---|---|---|---|---|
| St. Louis Cardinals | 100 | 62 | .617 | — | Tony La Russa | Walt Jocketty |
| *Houston Astros | 89 | 73 | .549 | 11 | Phil Garner | Tim Purpura |
| Milwaukee Brewers | 81 | 81 | .500 | 19 | Ned Yost | Doug Melvin |
| Chicago Cubs | 79 | 83 | .488 | 21 | Dusty Baker | Jim Hendry |
| Cincinnati Reds | 73 | 89 | .451 | 27 | Dave Miley/Jerry Narron | Dan O'Brien |
| Pittsburgh Pirates | 67 | 95 | .414 | 33 | Lloyd McClendon/Pete Mackanin | Dave Littlefield |

| WEST | W | L | Pct. | GB | Manager | General Manager(s) |
|---|---|---|---|---|---|---|
| San Diego Padres | 82 | 80 | .506 | — | Bruce Bochy | Kevin Towers |
| Arizona Diamondbacks | 77 | 85 | .475 | 5 | Bob Melvin | Joe Garagiola Jr./Bob Gebhard |
| San Francisco Giants | 75 | 87 | .463 | 7 | Felipe Alou | Brian Sabean |
| Los Angeles Dodgers | 71 | 91 | .438 | 11 | Jim Tracy | Paul DePodesta |
| Colorado Rockies | 67 | 95 | .414 | 15 | Clint Hurdle | Dan O'Dowd |

*Won wild-card playoff berth

**PLAYOFFS: Division Series** (best-of-5)—Houston defeated Atlanta 3-1; St. Louis defeated San Diego 3-0. **League Championship Series** (best-of-7)—Houston defeated St. Louis 4-2.

### 2005 WORLD SERIES
(Best-of-7)
Chicago (American) defeated Houston 4-0.

# AMERICAN
## LEAGUE

## BALTIMORE ORIOLES
### ORIOLE PARK AT CAMDEN YARDS
**Standard Game Times:** 7:05 p.m.; Sat. 4:35; Sun. 1:35.

| APRIL | |
|---|---|
| 3-5-6 | Tampa Bay |
| 7-**8**-**9** | Boston |
| 10-11-12-13 | at Tampa Bay |
| 14-**15**-**16**-17 | Angels |
| 18-19-20 | Cleveland |
| 21-**22**- **23** | at Yankees |
| 25-26-27 | at Toronto |
| 28-**29**-**30** | Seattle |

| MAY | |
|---|---|
| 1-2 | Toronto |
| 3-4 | at Texas |
| 5-6-7 | at Boston |
| 9-10-11 | Detroit |
| 12-**13**-**14** | Kansas City |
| 15-16-17 | Boston |
| 19-20-**21** | at Washington |
| 22-23-24-**25** | at Seattle |
| 26-27-**28** | at Angels |
| 30-31 | Tampa Bay |

| JUNE | |
|---|---|
| 1 | Tampa Bay |
| 2-**3**-**4** | Yankees |
| 5-6-7-8 | Toronto |
| 9-10-**11** | at Minnesota |
| 12-13-14-**15** | at Boston |
| 16-17-**18** | at Mets |
| 20-21-22 | Florida |
| 23-24-25 | Washington |
| 27-28-29 | Philadelphia |
| 30 | at Atlanta |

| JULY | |
|---|---|
| 1-**2** | at Atlanta |
| 3-**4**-5-**6** | at White Sox |
| 7-**8**-**9** | at Cleveland |
| 13-14-**15**-**16** | Texas |
| 17-18-**19** | Oakland |
| 21-22-23 | at Tampa Bay |
| 25-26-27 | at Kansas City |
| 28-**29**-30 | White Sox |
| 31 | Seattle |

| AUGUST | |
|---|---|
| 1-2 | Seattle |
| 4-**5**-**6** | Yankees |
| 7-**8**-**9** | at Toronto |
| 11-**12**-13 | at Boston |
| 15-16-**17** | at Yankees |
| 18-**19**-20 | Toronto |
| 22-23-24 | Minnesota |
| 25-**26**-**27** | Tampa Bay |
| 29-30-31 | at Texas |

| SEPTEMBER | |
|---|---|
| 1-**2**-3 | at Oakland |
| 4-**5**-**6** | at Angels |
| 8-**9**-**10**-11 | Yankees |
| 12-13-14 | Boston |
| 15-16-17 | at Detroit |
| 18-19-20 | at Tampa Bay |
| 22-**23**-**24** | Minnesota |
| 26-27-28 | Yankees |
| 29-30 | at Boston |

| OCTOBER | |
|---|---|
| 1 | at Boston |

## BOSTON RED SOX
### FENWAY PARK
**Standard Game Times:** Unavailable.

| APRIL | |
|---|---|
| 3-4-5 | at Texas |
| 7-**8**-**9** | at Baltimore |
| 11-12-13 | Toronto |
| 14-15-16-17 | Seattle |
| 18-19-20 | Tampa Bay |
| 21-**22**-**23** | at Toronto |
| 25-26-27 | at Cleveland |
| 28-29-30 | at Tampa Bay |

| MAY | |
|---|---|
| 1-2 | Yankees |
| 3-4 | Toronto |
| 5-6-7 | Baltimore |
| 9-10-11 | at Yankees |
| 12-13-14 | Texas |
| 15-16-17 | at Baltimore |
| 19-20-**21** | at Philadelphia |
| 22-23-24 | Yankees |
| 25-26-27-28 | Tampa Bay |
| 29-30-31 | at Toronto |

| JUNE | |
|---|---|
| 2-3-4 | at Detroit |
| 5-6-7-8 | at Yankees |
| 9-10-11 | Texas |
| 13-14-15 | at Minnesota |
| 16-**17**-**18** | at Atlanta |
| 19-20-21 | Washington |
| 23-**24**-25 | Philadelphia |
| 27-28-29 | Mets |
| 30 | at Florida |

| JULY | |
|---|---|
| 1-2 | at Florida |
| 3-4-5-6 | at Tampa Bay |
| 7-**8**-**9** | at White Sox |
| 13-14-15-16 | Oakland |
| 17-18-19 | Kansas City |
| 21-**22**-**23** | at Seattle |
| 24-25-**26** | at Oakland |
| 28-**29**-30 | Angels |
| 31 | Cleveland |

| AUGUST | |
|---|---|
| 1-2-3 | Cleveland |
| 4-5-6 | at Tampa Bay |
| 8-9-10 | at Kansas City |
| 11-**12**-13 | Baltimore |
| 14-15-16 | Detroit |

| 18-**19**-20-21 | Yankees |
|---|---|
| 22-23-24 | at Angels |
| 25-26-**27** | at Seattle |
| 28-29-**30** | at Oakland |
| 31 | Toronto |

| SEPTEMBER | |
|---|---|
| 1-2-3 | Toronto |
| 4-5-6 | White Sox |
| 8-9-10 | Kansas City |

## CHICAGO WHITE SOX
### U.S. CELLULAR FIELD
**Standard Game Times:** 7:05 p.m.; Sat. 6:05; Sun. 1:05.

| APRIL | |
|---|---|
| 2-**4**-**5** | Cleveland |
| 7-8-9 | at Kansas City |
| 10-12-13 | at Detroit |
| 14-**15**-**16** | Toronto |
| 17-18-19 | Kansas City |
| 21-22-**23** | Minnesota |
| 24-25-26 | at Seattle |
| 28-29-**30** | at Angels |

| MAY | |
|---|---|
| 1-2 | at Cleveland |
| 3-4 | Seattle |
| 5-6-**7** | Kansas City |
| 9-10-11 | Angels |
| 12-13-14-**15** | at Minnesota |
| 16-17-18 | at Tampa Bay |
| 19-**20**-21 | Cubs |
| 22-23-24 | Oakland |
| 26-**27**-**28** | at Toronto |
| **29**-30-31 | at Cleveland |

| JUNE | |
|---|---|
| 1 | at Cleveland |
| 2-3-**4** | Texas |
| 6-7-8 | Detroit |
| 9-**10**-**11** | Cleveland |
| 12-13-14-15 | at Texas |
| 16-17-**18** | at Cincinnati |
| 20-21-22 | St. Louis |
| 23-**24**-**25** | Houston |
| 27-28-**29** | at Pittsburgh |
| **30** | at Cubs |

| JULY | |
|---|---|
| 1-2 | at Cubs |
| 3-**4**-5-**6** | Baltimore |
| 7-**8**-**9** | Boston |
| 14-**15**-**16** | at Yankees |
| 18-19-20 | at Detroit |
| 21-22-**23** | Texas |
| 24-25-**26** | Minnesota |
| 28-**29**-30 | at Baltimore |
| 31 | at Kansas City |

| AUGUST | |
|---|---|
| 1-2 | at Kansas City |
| **4**-**5**-**6** | at Tampa Bay |
| 8-9-10 | Yankees |
| 11-12-**13** | Detroit |
| 14-15-16-**17** | Kansas City |
| 18-19-20 | at Minnesota |
| 21-22-23-24 | at Detroit |
| 25-26-**27** | Minnesota |
| 29-30-**31** | Tampa Bay |

| SEPTEMBER | |
|---|---|
| 1-2-3 | at Kansas City |
| 4-5-6 | at Boston |
| 7-**8**-**9**-**10** | Cleveland |
| 11-12-**13** | at Angels |
| 15-**16**-**17** | at Oakland |
| 18-19-20 | Detroit |
| 21-22-23-**24** | Seattle |
| 25-26-27 | at Cleveland |
| 29-**30** | at Minnesota |

| OCTOBER | |
|---|---|
| **1** | at Minnesota |

## CLEVELAND INDIANS
### JACOBS FIELD
**Standard Game Times:** 7:05 p.m.; Sun. 1:05.

| APRIL | |
|---|---|
| 2-**4**-**5** | at White Sox |
| **7**-**8**-**9** | Minnesota |
| 11-12-13 | Seattle |
| 14-15-16-17 | at Detroit |
| 18-19-20 | at Baltimore |
| 21-22-23 | at Kansas City |
| 25-26-27 | Boston |
| 28-29-30 | Texas |

| MAY | |
|---|---|
| 1-**2** | White Sox |
| 3-**4** | at Oakland |
| 5-6-**7** | at Seattle |
| 8-9-10 | at Kansas City |
| 12-13-**14** | Detroit |
| 15-16-17-**18** | Kansas City |
| 19-20-**21** | Pittsburgh |
| 23-**24** | at Minnesota |
| 26-27-28 | at Detroit |
| **29**-30-31 | White Sox |

| JUNE | |
|---|---|
| 1 | White Sox |
| 2-**3**-**4** | Angels |
| 6-7-**8** | Oakland |
| 9-**10**-**11** | at White Sox |
| 13-14-**15** | at Yankees |
| 16-17-**18** | at Milwaukee |
| 19-20-21 | Cubs |

23-24-**25** ............ Cincinnati
26-27-28 ......... at St. Louis
30 .................. at Cincinnati

**JULY**
1-**2** ................. at Cincinnati
3-4-5-**6** ................. Yankees
7-8-**9** ................. Baltimore
13-14-15-**16** .. at Minnesota
17-18-19 ........... at Angels
21-22-**23** .......... Minnesota
24-25-**26** ................. Detroit
28-29-**30** ................ Seattle
31 ..................... at Boston

**AUGUST**
1-2-3 ................... at Boston
4-5-6 .................. at Detroit
8-9-10 ................. Angels
11-12-**13** ........ Kansas City

15-16-**17** ....... at Minnesota
18-19-20 ........... Tampa Bay
22-23-24 ...... at Kansas City
25-26-**27** ................. Detroit
28-29-30 ............... Toronto

**SEPTEMBER**
1-2-**3** ................. at Texas
**4**-5-6 ................. at Toronto
7-8-9-**10** ....... at White Sox
12-13 ............... Kansas City
14-15-16-**17** ....... Minnesota
18-19-20-**21** ...... at Oakland
22-23-**24** ............. at Texas
25-26-27 ............ White Sox
28-29-30 .......... Tampa Bay

**OCTOBER**
1 ...................... Tampa Bay

# DETROIT TIGERS
COMERICA PARK
**Standard Game Times:** 7:05 p.m.; Sun. 1:05.

| APRIL | JULY |
|---|---|
| 3-5 ............. at Kansas City | 1-2 ................. at Pittsburgh |
| 6-7-8-**9** ............... at Texas | 3-**4**-**5** ................. at Oakland |
| 10-12-13 ............ White Sox | 7-8-**9** ................. at Seattle |
| 14-15-16-17....... Cleveland | 13-14-15-16 ..... Kansas City |
| 18-19-**20** ............ at Oakland | 18-19-20 ............ White Sox |
| 21-22-**23** ............ at Seattle | 21-22-23 ............. Oakland |
| 24-25-**26** ............. at Angels | 24-25-**26** ......... at Cleveland |
| 28-29-30............ Minnesota | 28-29-**30**....... at Kansas City |
| **MAY** | 31 ................ at Tampa Bay |
| 1-2 .................. Kansas City | **AUGUST** |
| 3-4 ....................... Angels | 1-2-3 ............. at Tampa Bay |
| 5-**6**-**7** ............ at Minnesota | 4-5-6 ................. Cleveland |
| 9-10-11 ........... at Baltimore | 7-8-9 ................ Minnesota |
| 12-13-**14**....... at Cleveland | 11-12-**13**....... at White Sox |
| 16-17-18........... Minnesota | 14-15-16 ............ at Boston |
| 19-20-21 ............. Cincinnati | 17-18-19-20 .......... Texas |
| 22-23-24-25 at Kansas City | 21-22-23-24...... White Sox |
| 26-27-28 ............ Cleveland | 25-26-**27** ......... at Cleveland |
| 29-30-31 ............... Yankees | 29-30-31 ............ at Yankees |
| **JUNE** | **SEPTEMBER** |
| 1 ......................... Yankees | 1-2-3 .................... Angels |
| 2-3-4 ..................... Boston | 4-5-6 .................... Seattle |
| 6-7-8 ............ at White Sox | 7-8-**9**-**10** ....... at Minnesota |
| 9-**10**-**11**.............. at Toronto | 12-13.................... Texas |
| 12-13-14-15 ..... Tampa Bay | 15-16-17 ............. Baltimore |
| **16**-17-18 ............... at Cubs | 18-19-20........ at White Sox |
| 19-20-**21** ...... at Milwaukee | 22-23-24...... at Kansas City |
| 23-24-25 ............. St. Louis | 26-27-28 ............... Toronto |
| 26-27-28 ............. Houston | 29-30 ............. Kansas City |
| 30 ................ at Pittsburgh | **OCTOBER** |
| | 1 ...................... Kansas City |

# KANSAS CITY ROYALS
KAUFFMAN STADIUM
**Standard Game Times:** 7:10 p.m.; Sat. 6:10; Sun. 1:10.

| APRIL | |
|---|---|
| 3-5 ...................... Detroit | 3-4 ................. at Minnesota |
| 7-8-9 ................. White Sox | 5-6-**7** ............ at White Sox |
| **11**-**12**-**13** .......... at Yankees | 8-9-10 ................ Cleveland |
| 14-15-16...... at Tampa Bay | 12-**13**-**14**......... at Baltimore |
| 17-18-**19** ...... at White Sox | 15-16-17-**18**...... at Cleveland |
| 21-22-23 ............ Cleveland | 19-20-21 ............. St. Louis |
| 25-26-27 .......... Minnesota | 22-23-24-25 ........... Detroit |
| 28-29-30 ............ Oakland | 26-**27**-**28** ........ at Yankees |
| **MAY** | 29-30-**31** ........... at Oakland |
| 1-2 ...................... at Detroit | **JUNE** |
| | 2-3-**4**-5 .............. at Seattle |

# LOS ANGELES ANGELS
ANGEL STADIUM OF ANAHEIM
**Standard Game Times:** 7:05 p.m.; Sun. 12:35.

| APRIL | |
|---|---|
| **3**-4-5 ................. at Seattle | **3**-4-5 ................. at Seattle |
| 7-8-**9** ................... Yankees | 6-7-8-**9** ............. at Oakland |
| 10-11-12 ................ Texas | 14-15-**16** .......... Tampa Bay |
| 14-**15**-**16**-17... at Baltimore | 17-18-19 ............. Cleveland |
| 18-19-**20** ...... at Minnesota | 20-21-22-23 at Kansas City |
| 21-**22**-**23** .......... at Oakland | 24-25-26....... at Tampa Bay |
| 24-25-**26** ............... Detroit | 28-29-30 ............ at Boston |
| 28-29-**30** ........... White Sox | 31 ...................... Oakland |
| **MAY** | **AUGUST** |
| 1-**2** ..................... Oakland | 1-2 ...................... Oakland |
| 3-4 ..................... at Detroit | 3-4-**5**-**6** ................... Texas |
| 5-**6**-**7**-8............. at Toronto | 8-9-10 ............. at Cleveland |
| 9-10-11 ........... at White Sox | 11-**12**-**13**-14...... at Yankees |
| 12-13-**14** ............. Seattle | 15-16................. at Texas |
| 16-17-18 ............... Toronto | 17-18-19-**20** ......... Seattle |
| 19-**20**-21............ at Dodgers | 22-23-24................ Boston |
| 22-23-**24** .............. at Texas | 25-**26**-**27** ............. Yankees |
| 26-27-**28** ........... Baltimore | 28-29-30 ........... at Seattle |
| 29-30-31 ........... Minnesota | **SEPTEMBER** |
| **JUNE** | 1-2-3 .................. at Detroit |
| 2-**3**-**4** ............. at Cleveland | 4-5-**6** ................. Baltimore |
| 5-6-7 ............ at Tampa Bay | 8-9-**10** ................. Toronto |
| 9-10-**11** ............... Seattle | 11-12-**13** ............ White Sox |
| 12-13-14-15 ..... Kansas City | 14-15-16-**17** ......... at Texas |
| 16-**17**-**18** ......... San Diego | 19-20 ........... at Kansas City |
| 19-20-**21** .. at San Francisco | 22-**23**-**24** ............ at Oakland |
| 23-24-**25** .......... at Arizona | 25-26-27 ................ Texas |
| 26-27-28 ............. Colorado | 28-29-30 ............... Oakland |
| 30 ..................... Dodgers | **OCTOBER** |
| **JULY** | 1 .......................... Oakland |
| 1-2 ...................... Dodgers | |

# MINNESOTA TWINS
HUBERT H. HUMPHREY METRODOME
**Standard Game Times:** 7:10 p.m.; Sat. 6:10; Sun 1:10.

| APRIL | MAY |
|---|---|
| 4-5-6 ................. at Toronto | 1-2............................ Seattle |
| **7**-8-**9** ............. at Cleveland | 3-4 .................. Kansas City |
| 11-12-**13** ............ Oakland | 5-6-**7** .................... Detroit |
| 14-15-**16** ............ Yankees | 8-9-**10** ................. at Texas |
| 18-19-20 ............... Angels | 12-13-14-**15**...... White Sox |
| 21-22-**23** ...... at White Sox | 16-17-18 ............... Detroit |
| 25-26-27...... at Kansas City | 19-20-21 ...... at Milwaukee |
| 28-29-30 ............ at Detroit | 23-**24** ................. Cleveland |

| | |
|---|---|
| 26-27-**28** | Seattle |
| 29-30-31 | at Angels |

**JUNE**

| | |
|---|---|
| 1-2-**3-4** | at Oakland |
| 6-7-**8** | at Seattle |
| 9-10-**11** | Baltimore |
| 13-14-15 | Boston |
| 16-17-**18** | at Pittsburgh |
| 20-21-22 | at Houston |
| 23-24-25 | Cubs |
| 26-27-**28** | Dodgers |
| 30 | Milwaukee |

**JULY**

| | |
|---|---|
| 1 **2** | Milwaukee |
| 3-4-5 | at Kansas City |
| 7-8-**9** | at Texas |
| 13-14-15-**16** | Cleveland |
| 17-18-19-**20** | Tampa Bay |
| 21-22-**23** | at Cleveland |
| 24-25-**26** | at White Sox |
| 28-29-**30** | Detroit |
| 31 | Texas |

**AUGUST**

| | |
|---|---|
| 1-**2** | Texas |
| 3-4-5-6 | at Kansas City |
| 7-8-9 | at Detroit |
| 10-11-12-**13** | Toronto |
| 15-16-**17** | Cleveland |
| 18-19-**20** | White Sox |
| 22-23-24 | at Baltimore |
| 25-26-**27** | at White Sox |
| 29-30-**31** | Kansas City |

**SEPTEMBER**

| | |
|---|---|
| 1-2-3 | at Yankees |
| 4-5-6 | at Tampa Bay |
| 7-8-**9-10** | Detroit |
| 11-12-**13** | Oakland |
| 14-15-16-**17** | at Cleveland |
| 19-20-21 | at Boston |
| 22-**23**-24 | at Baltimore |
| 25-26-27-28 | Kansas City |
| 29-30 | White Sox |

**OCTOBER**

| | |
|---|---|
| 1 | White Sox |

# NEW YORK YANKEES
### YANKEE STADIUM

Standard Game Times: 7:05 p.m.; Sat.-Sun. 1:05.

**APRIL**

| | |
|---|---|
| 3-4-5 | at Oakland |
| 7-8-**9** | at Angels |
| **11-12-13** | Kansas City |
| 14-**15-16** | at Minnesota |
| 18-**19** | at Toronto |
| 21-**22-23** | Baltimore |
| 25-26-27 | Tampa Bay |
| 28-**29-30** | Toronto |

**MAY**

| | |
|---|---|
| 1-2 | at Boston |
| 3-4 | at Tampa Bay |
| 5-6-7 | at Texas |
| 9-10-11 | Boston |
| 12-**13-14** | Oakland |
| 15-16-17-**18** | Cleveland |
| 19-**20**-21 | at Mets |
| 22-23-24 | at Boston |
| 26-27-**28** | Kansas City |
| 29-30-31 | at Detroit |

**JUNE**

| | |
|---|---|
| 1 | at Detroit |
| 2-**3-4** | at Baltimore |
| 5-6-7-8 | Boston |
| 9-**10-11** | Oakland |
| 13-14-**15** | Cleveland |
| 16-**17-18** | Washington |
| 19-20-**21** | at Philadelphia |
| 23-**24-25** | Florida |
| 26-27-**28** | Atlanta |
| 30 | Mets |

**JULY**

| | |
|---|---|
| **1**-2 | Mets |
| 3-4-5-**6** | at Cleveland |
| 7-8-9 | at Tampa Bay |
| 14-**15-16** | White Sox |
| 17-18-**19** | Seattle |
| 20-21-**22-23** | at Toronto |
| 24-25-26 | at Texas |
| 28-**29-30** | Tampa Bay |

**AUGUST**

| | |
|---|---|
| 1-2-**3** | Toronto |
| 4-**5-6** | at Baltimore |
| 8-9-10 | at White Sox |
| 11-**12-13**-14 | Angels |
| 15-16-**17** | Baltimore |
| 18-**19**-20-21 | at Boston |
| 22-23-24 | at Seattle |
| 25-**26-27** | at Angels |
| 29-30-**31** | Detroit |

**SEPTEMBER**

| | |
|---|---|
| 1-2-**3** | Minnesota |
| 4-5-6 | at Kansas City |
| 8-**9-10**-11 | at Baltimore |
| 12-13-14 | Tampa Bay |
| 15-**16**-17 | Boston |
| 18-19-20 | at Toronto |
| 22-23-24-25 | at Tampa Bay |
| 26-27-28 | Baltimore |
| 29-30 | Toronto |

**OCTOBER**

| | |
|---|---|
| 1 | Toronto |

# OAKLAND ATHLETICS
### MCAFEE COLISEUM

Standard Game Times: 7:05 p.m.; Sat.-Sun. 1:05.

**APRIL**

| | |
|---|---|
| 3-4-5 | Yankees |
| 6-7-8-**9** | at Seattle |
| 11-12-**13** | at Minnesota |
| 14-**15-16** | Texas |
| 18-19-20 | Detroit |
| 21-**22-23** | Angels |
| 24-25-**26** | at Texas |
| 28-29-30 | at Kansas City |

**MAY**

| | |
|---|---|
| 1-**2** | at Angels |
| 3-4 | Cleveland |
| 5-**6-7** | Tampa Bay |
| 9-10-**11** | at Toronto |
| 12-**13-14** | at Yankees |
| 16-17-**18** | Seattle |

| | |
|---|---|
| 19-**20-21** | San Francisco |
| 22-23-24 | at White Sox |
| 25-26-27-28 | at Texas |
| 29-30-**31** | Kansas City |

**JUNE**

| | |
|---|---|
| 1-2-**3-4** | Minnesota |
| 6-7-**8** | at Cleveland |
| 9-**10-11** | at Yankees |
| 13-14-**15** | Seattle |
| 16-17-**18** | Dodgers |
| 19-20-21 | at Colorado |
| 23-**24-25** | at San Francisco |
| 27-28-29 | at San Diego |
| 30 | Arizona |

**JULY**

| | |
|---|---|
| 1-2 | Arizona |
| **3-4** | Detroit |
| 6-7-8-**9** | Angels |
| 13-14-15-16 | at Boston |
| 17-18-**19** | at Baltimore |
| 21-22-23 | at Detroit |
| 24-25-**26** | Boston |
| 27-28-**29-30** | Toronto |

| | |
|---|---|
| 31 | at Angels |

**AUGUST**

| | |
|---|---|
| 1-**2** | at Angels |
| 4-**5-6** | at Seattle |
| 7-8-**9** | Texas |
| 11-12-**13** | Tampa Bay |
| 14-15-16 | Seattle |
| 18-19-20 | at Kansas City |
| 21-22-23 | at Toronto |
| 25-26-27 | at Texas |
| 28-29-**30** | Boston |

**SEPTEMBER**

| | |
|---|---|
| 1-2-**3** | Baltimore |
| **4**-5-6 | Texas |
| 8-9-10 | at Tampa Bay |
| 11-12-**13** | at Minnesota |
| 15-**16-17** | White Sox |
| 18-19-20-**21** | Cleveland |
| 22-**23-24** | Angels |
| 25-26-27 | at Seattle |
| 28-29-30 | at Angels |

**OCTOBER**

| | |
|---|---|
| 1 | at Angels |

# SEATTLE MARINERS
### SAFECO FIELD

Standard Game Times: 7:05 p.m.; Sun. 1:05.

**APRIL**

| | |
|---|---|
| **3-4-5** | Angels |
| 6-7-8-**9** | Oakland |
| 11-12-13 | at Cleveland |
| 14-15-16-17 | at Boston |
| 18-19-20 | Texas |
| 21-22-**23** | Detroit |
| 24-25-26 | White Sox |
| 28-**29-30** | at Baltimore |

**MAY**

| | |
|---|---|
| 1-2 | at Minnesota |
| **3-4** | at White Sox |
| 5-**6-7** | Cleveland |
| 8-9-**10** | Tampa Bay |
| 12-13-**14** | at Angels |
| 16-17-**18** | at Oakland |
| 19-20-**21** | San Diego |
| 22-23-24-**25** | Baltimore |
| 26-27-**28** | at Minnesota |
| 29-30-**31** | at Texas |

**JUNE**

| | |
|---|---|
| 2-3-**4-5** | Kansas City |
| 6-7-**8** | Minnesota |
| 9-10-**11** | at Angels |
| 13-14-**15** | at Oakland |
| 16-**17-18** | San Francisco |
| 20-21-22 | at Dodgers |
| 23-24-25 | at San Diego |
| 27-28-29 | at Arizona |
| 30 | Colorado |

**JULY**

| | |
|---|---|
| 1-2 | Colorado |

| | |
|---|---|
| 3-4-5 | Angels |
| 7-8-**9** | Detroit |
| 14-**15-16** | at Toronto |
| 17-18-**19** | at Yankees |
| 21-**22-23** | Boston |
| 24-25-26 | Toronto |
| 28-29-**30** | at Cleveland |
| 31 | at Baltimore |

**AUGUST**

| | |
|---|---|
| 1-2 | at Baltimore |
| 4-**5-6** | Oakland |
| 7-8-**9** | Tampa Bay |
| 10-11-12-13 | at Texas |
| 14-15-16 | at Oakland |
| 17-18-19-**20** | at Angels |
| 22-23-24 | Yankees |
| 25-26-**27** | Boston |
| 28-29-30 | Angels |

**SEPTEMBER**

| | |
|---|---|
| 1-2-3 | at Tampa Bay |
| 4-5-6 | at Detroit |
| 8-9-**10** | Texas |
| 11-12-**13** | Toronto |
| 14-15-16-17 | at Kansas City |
| 18-19-20 | at Texas |
| 21-22-23-**24** | at White Sox |
| 25-26-27 | Oakland |
| 29-30 | Texas |

**OCTOBER**

| | |
|---|---|
| 1 | Texas |

# TAMPA BAY DEVIL RAYS
### TROPICANA FIELD

Standard Game Times: Unavailable.

**APRIL**

| | |
|---|---|
| **3**-5-6 | at Baltimore |
| 7-**8-9** | at Toronto |
| 10-11-12-13 | Baltimore |
| 14-15-16 | Kansas City |
| 18-19-20 | at Boston |

| | |
|---|---|
| 21-22-**23** | at Texas |
| 25-26-27 | at Yankees |
| 28-29-30 | Boston |

**MAY**

| | |
|---|---|
| 1-2 | Texas |
| 3-4 | at Yankees |

5-**6**-**7** ................ at Oakland
8-9-**10** ................ at Seattle
12-13-14 .............. Toronto
16-17-18 .......... White Sox
19-20-21 ................ Florida
**22**-23-24 ........ at Toronto
25-26-27-28 ....... at Boston
30-31 ............. at Baltimore

### JUNE
1 ................. at Baltimore
2-3-4 ..................... Toronto
5-6-7 ....................... Angels
9-10-11 ....... at Kansas City
12-13-14-15 ....... at Detroit
16-17-**18** ..... at Philadelphia
20-21-22 .............. Arizona
23-24-25 ................ Atlanta
26-27-28 ............ at Florida
30 ................... Washington

### JULY
1-**2** ................. Washington
3-4-5-6 .................. Boston
7-8-9 ..................... Yankees
14-15-**16** ......... at Angels
17-18-19-**20** .. at Minnesota
21-22-23 ............. Baltimore

## TEXAS RANGERS
### AMERIQUEST FIELD IN ARLINGTON
Standard Game Times: 7:05 p.m.; Sun. 1:05.

### APRIL
**3**-4-5 ..................... Boston
6-7-8-**9** ................. Detroit
10-11-12 ........... at Angels
14-**15**-**16** .......... at Oakland
18-19-20 ............ at Seattle
21-22-**23** .......... Tampa Bay
24-25-**26** ............ Oakland
28-29-30 ......... at Cleveland

### MAY
1-2 ............... at Tampa Bay
3-4 ...................... Baltimore
5-6-**7** ..................... Yankees
8-9-**10** .............. Minnesota
12-13-14 ........... at Boston
15-16-17-**18** ..... at Yankees
19-20-**21** .......... at Houston
22-23-**24** ................ Angels

25-26-27-28 .......... Oakland
29-30-**31** ............... Seattle

### JUNE
2-3-**4** ............. at White Sox
6-7-**8** ........ at Kansas City
9-10-11 .............. at Boston
12-13-14-15 ....... White Sox
16-17-**18** .............. Arizona
20-21-**22** .......... San Diego
23-24-**25** ........ at Colorado
27-28-**29** .. at San Francisco
30 ...................... Houston

### JULY
1-**2** ...................... Houston
3-4-5 ..................... Toronto
7-8-**9** ................. Minnesota
13-14-**15**-**16** .... at Baltimore
17-18-19 ........... at Toronto

24-25-26 ................ Angels
28-**29**-**30** .......... at Yankees
31 ............................ Detroit

### AUGUST
1-2-3 ................... Detroit
4-5-6 ....................... Boston
7-8-**9** ................. at Seattle
11-12-**13** .......... at Oakland
15-16-17 ................ Toronto
18-19-20 ............ Cleveland
21-22-23-24 ............. Texas
25-**26**-**27** ....... at Baltimore
29-30-**31** ....... at White Sox

### SEPTEMBER
1-2-3 ..................... Seattle
4-5-6 .................. Minnesota
8-9-10 .................. Oakland
12-13-14 .......... at Yankees
15-**16**-**17** .......... at Toronto
18-19-20 ............. Baltimore
22-23-24-25 ........ Yankees
26-27 ............... at Boston
28-29-30 .......... at Cleveland

### OCTOBER
1 ..................... at Cleveland

## TORONTO BLUE JAYS
### ROGERS CENTRE
Standard Game Times: 7:07 p.m.; Sat. 4:07; Sun. 1:07.

21-22-**23** ....... at White Sox
24-25-26 .............. Yankees
28-29-30 ........... Kansas City
31 ................. at Minnesota

### AUGUST
1-**2** ............... at Minnesota
3-4-**5**-**6** ............... at Angels
7-8-**9** ................. at Oakland
10-11-12-13 .......... Seattle
15-16 ................... Angels
17-18-19-20 ....... at Detroit
21-22-23-24 . at Tampa Bay
25-26-27 .............. Oakland
29-30-31 ............ Baltimore

### SEPTEMBER
1-2-**3** ................. Cleveland
**4**-**5**-**6** ................. at Oakland
8-9-**10** ............... at Seattle
12-13 .................... at Detroit
14-15-16-**17** ........... Angels
18-19-20 ................ Seattle
22-23-**24** ............ Cleveland
25-26-27 ................ Angels
29-30 .................. at Seattle

### OCTOBER
1 ........................ at Seattle

### APRIL
4-5-6 ................. Minnesota
7-**8**-**9** ................. Tampa Bay
11-12-13 ............. at Boston
14-**15**-**16** ....... at White Sox
18-**19** .................... Yankees
21-**22**-23 ................. Boston
25-26-27 ............. Baltimore
28-**29**-**30** .......... at Yankees

### MAY
1-2 ................... at Baltimore
3-4 ...................... at Boston
5-**6**-**7**-8 ................... Angels
9-10-11 ................ Oakland
12-13-14 ...... at Tampa Bay
16-17-18 ............ at Angels
19-20-**21** ......... at Colorado
**22**-23-24 .......... Tampa Bay

26-**27**-**28** .......... White Sox
29-30-31 ................ Boston

### JUNE
2-3-4 ............. at Tampa Bay
5-6-7-**8** ......... at Baltimore
9-**10**-**11** ................. Detroit
12-13-14-**15** ..... Baltimore
16-17-18 ............ at Florida
20-21-22 ............ at Atlanta
23-**24**-**25** ..................... Mets
27-28-29 ........... Washington
30 ..................... Philadelphia

### JULY
**1**-**2** ................. Philadelphia
3-4-5 .................... at Texas
6-7-8-9 ...... at Kansas City
14-**15**-**16** ................. Seattle
17-18-19 .................. Texas
20-21-**22**-**23** ......... Yankees
24-25-26 ........... at Seattle
27-28-**29**-**30** ...... at Oakland

### AUGUST
1-2-**3** ................ at Yankees
4-**5**-**6** ................. White Sox
7-8-**9** .................. Baltimore
10-11-12-**13** .. at Minnesota
15-16-17 ....... at Tampa Bay
18-**19**-20 ......... at Baltimore
21-22-23 ................ at Texas
25-**26**-**27** ....... Kansas City
28-29-30 ......... at Cleveland
31 ........................ at Boston

### SEPTEMBER
1-2-3 ................. at Boston
**4**-5-6 .................. Cleveland
8-9-**10** ............... at Angels
11-12-**13** .......... at Seattle
15-**16**-**17** .......... Tampa Bay
18-19-20 .............. Yankees
22-**23**-**24**-25......... Boston
26-27-28 ............ at Detroit
29-30 ................ at Yankees

### OCTOBER
1 ........................ at Yankees

**NOTE:** Dates in **bold** indicate afternoon games. All game times are subject to change. Gaps in dates indicate scheduled off-days but may be affected by rainouts.

# NATIONAL
## LEAGUE

## ARIZONA DIAMONDBACKS
### CHASE FIELD
Standard Game Times: 6:40 p.m.; Sun. 1:40.

| APRIL | |
|---|---|
| 3-5-6 | at Colorado |
| 7-8-9 | at Milwaukee |
| 11-12-13 | Colorado |
| 14-15-16 | Houston |
| 17-18-19-20 | San Diego |
| 21-22-23 | at Dodgers |
| 24-25-26 | at San Diego |
| 28-29-30 | at San Francisco |

| MAY | |
|---|---|
| 1-2 | Dodgers |
| 3-4 | Cubs |
| 5-6-7 | Cincinnati |
| 9-10-11 | at Pittsburgh |
| 12-13-14 | at St. Louis |
| 15-16-17 | San Diego |
| 19-20-21 | Atlanta |
| 22-23-24 | Pittsburgh |
| 26-27-28 | at Cincinnati |
| 29-30-31 | at Mets |

| JUNE | |
|---|---|
| 1-2-3-4 | at Atlanta |
| 5-6-7 | Philadelphia |
| 9-10-11 | Mets |
| 13-14-15 | San Francisco |
| 16-17-18 | at Texas |
| 20-21-22 | at Tampa Bay |
| 23-24-25 | Angels |
| 27-28-29 | Seattle |
| 30 | at Oakland |

| JULY | |
|---|---|
| 1-2 | at Oakland |

| | |
|---|---|
| 3-4-5 | at Dodgers |
| 7-8-9 | at Colorado |
| 14-15-16 | Milwaukee |
| 17-18-19-20 | Dodgers |
| 21-22-23 | Colorado |
| 25-26-27 | at Philadelphia |
| 28-29-30 | at Houston |
| 31 | at Cubs |

| AUGUST | |
|---|---|
| 1-2-3 | at Cubs |
| 4-5-6 | Houston |
| 7-8-9 | San Francisco |
| 11-12-13 | Florida |
| 14-15-16-17 | at Colorado |
| 18-19-20 | at San Diego |
| 21-22-23 | at San Francisco |
| 25-26-27 | Dodgers |
| 28-29-30 | San Diego |

| SEPTEMBER | |
|---|---|
| 1-2-3 | at Washington |
| 4-5-6 | at Florida |
| 7-8-9-10 | St. Louis |
| 11-12-13 | Washington |
| 15-16-17 | Colorado |
| 19-20-21 | at San Diego |
| 22-23-24 | at Dodgers |
| 25-26-27 | at San Francisco |
| 28-29-30 | San Diego |

| OCTOBER | |
|---|---|
| 1 | San Diego |

## ATLANTA BRAVES
### TURNER FIELD
Standard Game Times: 7:35 p.m.; Mon./Sat. 7:05; Sun. 1:05.

| APRIL | |
|---|---|
| 3-4-5 | at Dodgers |
| 6-7-8-9 | at San Francisco |
| 10-12-13 | Philadelphia |
| 14-15-16 | San Diego |
| 17-18-19 | at Mets |
| 21-22-23 | at Washington |
| 24-25-26 | at Milwaukee |
| 28-29-30 | Mets |

| MAY | |
|---|---|
| 1-2 | Colorado |
| 3-4 | at Philadelphia |
| 5-6-7 | at Mets |
| 9-10-11 | at Florida |
| 12-13-14 | Washington |
| 15-16-17-18 | Florida |
| 19-20-21 | at Arizona |
| 22-23-24 | at San Diego |
| 26-27-28 | at Cubs |
| 29-30-31 | Dodgers |

| JUNE | |
|---|---|
| 1-2-3-4 | Arizona |
| 5-6-7 | Washington |

| | |
|---|---|
| 8-9-10-11 | at Houston |
| 13-14-15 | at Florida |
| 16-17-18 | Boston |
| 20-21-22 | Toronto |
| 23-24-25 | at Tampa Bay |
| 26-27-28 | at Yankees |
| 30 | Baltimore |

| JULY | |
|---|---|
| 1-2 | Baltimore |
| 3-4-5 | St. Louis |
| 6-7-8-9 | Cincinnati |
| 14-15-16 | at San Diego |
| 17-18-19 | at St. Louis |
| 21-22-23-24 | at Philadelphia |
| 25-26-27 | Florida |
| 28-29-30 | Mets |

| AUGUST | |
|---|---|
| 1-2-3 | at Pittsburgh |
| 4-5-6 | at Cincinnati |
| 7-8-9 | Philadelphia |
| 11-12-13 | Milwaukee |
| 14-15-16-17 | at Washington |
| 18-19-20 | at Florida |

## CHICAGO CUBS
### WRIGLEY FIELD
Standard Game Times: 1:20 p.m., 7:05.

| APRIL | |
|---|---|
| 3-5 | at Cincinnati |
| 7-8-9 | St. Louis |
| 11-12-13 | Cincinnati |
| 14-15-16 | at Pittsburgh |
| 17-18-19 | at Dodgers |
| 21-22-23 | at St. Louis |
| 24-25-26 | Florida |
| 28-29-30 | Milwaukee |

| MAY | |
|---|---|
| 1-2 | Pittsburgh |
| 3-4 | at Arizona |
| 5-6-7-8 | at San Diego |
| 9-10-11 | San Francisco |
| 12-13-14 | San Diego |
| 16-17-18 | Washington |
| 19-20-21 | at White Sox |
| 22-23-24 | at Florida |
| 26-27-28 | Atlanta |
| 29-30-31 | Cincinnati |

| JUNE | |
|---|---|
| 2-3-4 | at St. Louis |
| 5-6-7 | at Houston |
| 9-10-11 | at Cincinnati |
| 13-14-15 | Houston |
| 16-17-18 | Detroit |
| 19-20-21 | at Cleveland |
| 23-24-25 | at Minnesota |
| 26-27-28-29 | Milwaukee |
| 30 | White Sox |

| JULY | |
|---|---|
| 1-2 | White Sox |

| | |
|---|---|
| 3-4-5 | at Houston |
| 6-7-8-9 | at Milwaukee |
| 14-15-16 | Mets |
| 18-19-20 | Houston |
| 21-22-23 | at Washington |
| 24-25-26 | at Mets |
| 27-28-29-30 | St. Louis |
| 31 | Arizona |

| AUGUST | |
|---|---|
| 1-2-3 | Arizona |
| 4-5-6 | Pittsburgh |
| 8-9-10 | at Milwaukee |
| 11-12-13 | at Colorado |
| 14-15-16 | at Houston |
| 18-19-20 | St. Louis |
| 21-22-23-24 | Philadelphia |
| 25-26-27 | at St. Louis |
| 28-29-30 | at Pittsburgh |

| SEPTEMBER | |
|---|---|
| 1-2-3 | San Francisco |
| 4-5-6-7 | Pittsburgh |
| 8-9-10-11 | at Atlanta |
| 12-13-14 | Dodgers |
| 15-16-17 | Cincinnati |
| 18-19-20 | at Philadelphia |
| 22-23-24-25 | at Cincinnati |
| 26-27 | Milwaukee |
| 29-30 | Colorado |

| OCTOBER | |
|---|---|
| 1 | Colorado |

## CINCINNATI REDS
### GREAT AMERICAN BALL PARK
Standard Game Times: 7:10 p.m.; Sat. 6:10; Sun. 1:15.

| APRIL | |
|---|---|
| 3-5 | Cubs |
| 6-7-8-9 | Pittsburgh |
| 11-12-13 | at Cubs |
| 14-15-16 | at St. Louis |
| 17-18-19 | Florida |
| 20-21-22-23 | at Milwaukee |
| 24-25-26 | at Washington |
| 28-29-30 | Houston |

| MAY | |
|---|---|
| 1-2 | St. Louis |
| 3-4 | Colorado |
| 5-6-7 | at Arizona |
| 9-10-11 | Washington |
| 12-13-14 | Philadelphia |

| | |
|---|---|
| 16-17-18 | at Pittsburgh |
| 19-20-21 | at Detroit |
| 22-23-24 | Milwaukee |
| 26-27-28 | Arizona |
| 29-30-31 | at Cubs |

| JUNE | |
|---|---|
| 2-3-4 | at Houston |
| 5-6-7 | at St. Louis |
| 8-9-10-11 | Cubs |
| 12-13-14 | Milwaukee |
| 16-17-18 | White Sox |
| 19-20-21-22 | at Mets |
| 23-24-25 | at Cleveland |
| 27-28-29 | Kansas City |
| 30 | Cleveland |

The following top-margin right-column entries appear above CHICAGO CUBS:

| | |
|---|---|
| 21-22-23 | Pittsburgh |
| 25-26-27 | Washington |
| 29-30-31 | San Francisco |

| SEPTEMBER | |
|---|---|
| 1-2-3 | at Philadelphia |
| 4-5-6 | at Mets |
| 8-9-10-11 | Cubs |
| 12-13-14 | Philadelphia |

| | |
|---|---|
| 15-16-17 | Florida |
| 19-20 | at Washington |
| 21-22-23-24 | at Colorado |
| 26-27-28 | Mets |
| 29-30 | Houston |

| OCTOBER | |
|---|---|
| 1 | Houston |

<table>
</table>

**JULY**

| | |
|---|---|
| 1-2 | Cleveland |
| **3-4**-5 | at Milwaukee |
| 6-7-8-**9** | at Atlanta |
| 13-14-15-**16** | Colorado |
| 18-19-20 | Mets |
| 21-22-**23** | Milwaukee |
| 25-26-27 | at Houston |
| 28-29-**30** | at Milwaukee |

**AUGUST**

| | |
|---|---|
| 1-2-3 | Dodgers |
| 4-**5-6** | Atlanta |
| 7-8-9-**10** | St. Louis |
| 11-12-**13** | at Philadelphia |
| 15-16-**17** | at St. Louis |
| 18-19-**20** | Pittsburgh |

| | |
|---|---|
| 21-22-**23** | Houston |
| 24-25-26-**27** | at San Francisco |
| 28-29-30 | at Dodgers |

**SEPTEMBER**

| | |
|---|---|
| 1-2-3 | at San Diego |
| 4-5-**6** | San Francisco |
| 8-9-**10** | Pittsburgh |
| 12-13-**14** | San Diego |
| **15**-16-17 | at Cubs |
| 18-19-**20** | at Houston |
| 22-23-**24-25** | Cubs |
| 26-27-28 | at Florida |
| 29-30 | at Pittsburgh |

**OCTOBER**

| | |
|---|---|
| 1 | at Pittsburgh |

| | |
|---|---|
| 20-21-22 | at Baltimore |
| 23-**24-25** | at Yankees |
| 26-27-28 | Tampa Bay |
| 30 | Boston |

**JULY**

| | |
|---|---|
| 1-2 | Boston |
| 3-4-5-6 | at Washington |
| 7-**8-9** | at Mets |
| 13-14-15-16 | Houston |
| 17-18-19 | Washington |
| 20-21-22-23 | Pittsburgh |
| 25-26-**27** | at Atlanta |
| 28-29-**30-31** | at Philadelphia |

**AUGUST**

| | |
|---|---|
| 1-2-3 | Mets |
| 4-5-6 | Dodgers |
| 8-9-10 | at Washington |
| 11-12-**13** | at Arizona |

| | |
|---|---|
| 14-15-**16** | at Dodgers |
| 18-19-20 | Atlanta |
| 21-22-23 | Washington |
| 25-26-27-28 | Milwaukee |
| 29-30-31 | at St. Louis |

**SEPTEMBER**

| | |
|---|---|
| 1-2-**3** | at Milwaukee |
| 4-5-6 | Arizona |
| 7-8-9-10 | Philadelphia |
| 11-12-13 | Mets |
| **15**-**16-17** | at Atlanta |
| 18-19-20-21 | at Mets |
| 22-23-**24** | at Philadelphia |
| 26-27-28 | Cincinnati |
| 29-30 | Philadelphia |

**OCTOBER**

| | |
|---|---|
| 1 | Philadelphia |

# COLORADO ROCKIES
### COORS FIELD

Standard Game Times: 7:05 p.m.; Sat. 6:05; Sun. 1:05.

**APRIL**

| | |
|---|---|
| **3**-5-6 | Arizona |
| 7-8-**9** | at San Diego |
| 11-12-13 | at Arizona |
| 14-15-**16** | Philadelphia |
| 17-18-**19** | San Diego |
| 21-22-**23** | San Francisco |
| 24-25-26-**27** | at Philadelphia |
| 28-29-30 | at Florida |

**MAY**

| | |
|---|---|
| 1-2 | at Atlanta |
| 3-4 | Cincinnati |
| 5-6-7 | Houston |
| 8-9-**10** | at St. Louis |
| 12-13-**14** | at Houston |
| 15-16-**17** | Dodgers |
| 19-20-**21** | Toronto |
| 22-23-24 | at Arizona |
| 26-27-**28** | at San Francisco |
| 29-30-31 | at San Diego |

**JUNE**

| | |
|---|---|
| 2-3-**4** | Florida |
| 5-6-**7** | Pittsburgh |
| 9-10-**11** | Dodgers |
| 12-13-14-**15** | at Washington |
| 16-17-**18** | at St. Louis |
| 19-20-21 | Oakland |
| 23-24-**25** | Texas |
| 26-27-28 | at Angels |
| 30 | at Seattle |

**JULY**

| | |
|---|---|
| 1-**2** | at Seattle |

| | |
|---|---|
| 3-4-5 | San Francisco |
| 7-8-**9** | Arizona |
| 13-14-15-**16** | at Cincinnati |
| 17-18-**19** | at Pittsburgh |
| 21-22-**23** | at Arizona |
| 24-25-**26** | St. Louis |
| 27-28-29-**30** | Cubs |
| 31 | Milwaukee |

**AUGUST**

| | |
|---|---|
| 1-2 | Milwaukee |
| 4-5-**6** | at San Francisco |
| 7-8-9-10 | at Dodgers |
| 11-12-**13** | Cubs |
| 14-15-16-**17** | Arizona |
| 18-19-**20** | at Mets |
| 22-23-**24** | at Milwaukee |
| 25-26-**27** | San Diego |
| 29-30-31 | Mets |

**SEPTEMBER**

| | |
|---|---|
| 1-2-3 | at Dodgers |
| 4-5-6 | at Atlanta |
| 7-8-9-**10** | Washington |
| 12-13-**14** | at San Francisco |
| 15-16-**17** | at Arizona |
| 18-19-**20** | San Francisco |
| 21-22-23-**24** | Atlanta |
| 26-27-**28** | Dodgers |
| **29**-30 | at Cubs |

**OCTOBER**

| | |
|---|---|
| 1 | at Cubs |

# FLORIDA MARLINS
### DOLPHINS STADIUM

Standard Game Times: 7:05 p.m.; Fri. 7:05; Sat. 6:05; Sun. 1:05.

**APRIL**

| | |
|---|---|
| 3-5-6 | at Houston |
| 7-**8-9** | at Mets |
| 11-12-13 | San Diego |
| 14-15-16 | Washington |
| 17-18-**19** | at Cincinnati |
| 21-22-**23** | at Philadelphia |
| 24-25-**26** | at Cubs |
| 28-29-30 | Colorado |

**MAY**

| | |
|---|---|
| 1-2 | Philadelphia |
| 3-4 | at Washington |
| 5-6-7 | St. Louis |

| | |
|---|---|
| 9-10-11 | Atlanta |
| 12-13-**14** | at Pittsburgh |
| 15-16-17-**18** | at Atlanta |
| 19-20-21 | at Tampa Bay |
| 22-23-24 | Cubs |
| 26-**27**-28 | Mets |
| 29-30-31 | San Francisco |

**JUNE**

| | |
|---|---|
| 2-3-**4** | at Colorado |
| 5-6-7 | at San Francisco |
| 9-10-11 | at San Diego |
| 13-14-15 | Atlanta |
| 16-17-18 | Toronto |

# HOUSTON ASTROS
### MINUTE MAID PARK

Standard Game Times: 7:05 p.m.; Sat. 6:05; Sun. 1:05.

**APRIL**

| | |
|---|---|
| 3-4-5 | Florida |
| 7-8-**9-10** | Washington |
| 11-12-13 | at San Francisco |
| 14-15-**16** | at Arizona |
| 17-18-19 | Milwaukee |
| 21-22-**23** | Pittsburgh |
| 24-25-26 | Dodgers |
| 28-**29-30** | at Cincinnati |

**MAY**

| | |
|---|---|
| 1-2 | at Milwaukee |
| 3-4 | at Cubs |
| 5-6-7 | at Colorado |
| 9-10-**11** | at Dodgers |
| 12-13-**14** | Colorado |
| 15-16-17 | San Francisco |
| 19-20-**21** | Texas |
| 22-23-24-**25** | at Washington |
| 26-27-**28** | at Pittsburgh |
| **29**-30-31 | at St. Louis |

**JUNE**

| | |
|---|---|
| 2-3-**4** | Cincinnati |
| 5-6-**7** | Cubs |
| 8-9-**10-11** | Atlanta |
| 13-14-**15** | at Cubs |
| 16-17-**18** | Kansas City |
| 20-21-22 | Minnesota |
| 23-**24-25** | at White Sox |
| 26-27-28 | at Detroit |
| 30 | at Texas |

| | |
|---|---|
| **JULY** | |
| 1-2 | at Texas |
| 3-4-5 | Cubs |
| 6-7-**8-9** | St. Louis |
| 13-14-15-16 | at Florida |
| 18-19-**20** | at Cubs |
| 21-**22-23** | at Mets |
| 25-26-27 | Cincinnati |
| 28-29-**30** | Arizona |

**AUGUST**

| | |
|---|---|
| 1-2-3 | at San Diego |
| 4-5-6 | Pittsburgh |
| 8-9-10 | Pittsburgh |
| 11-12-**13** | San Diego |
| 14-15-**16** | Cubs |
| 17-18-19-**20** | at Milwaukee |
| 21-22-**23** | at Cincinnati |
| 25-26-**27** | at Pittsburgh |
| 29-30-31 | Milwaukee |

**SEPTEMBER**

| | |
|---|---|
| 1-2-**3** | Mets |
| **4**-5-6 | at Philadelphia |
| 8-9-**10** | at Milwaukee |
| 11-12-**13** | at St. Louis |
| 15-**16-17** | Philadelphia |
| 18-19-**20** | Cincinnati |
| 21-22-23-**24** | St. Louis |
| 26-27-**28** | at Pittsburgh |
| 29-30 | at Atlanta |

**OCTOBER**

| | |
|---|---|
| 1 | at Atlanta |

# LOS ANGELES DODGERS
### DODGER STADIUM

Standard Game Times: 7:10 p.m.; Fri. 7:40

**APRIL**

| | |
|---|---|
| **3**-4-5 | Atlanta |
| 7-**8-9** | at Philadelphia |
| **10**-11-12-**13** | at Pittsburgh |
| 14-15-16 | San Francisco |
| 17-18-19 | Cubs |
| 21-22-23 | Arizona |
| 24-25-26 | at Houston |
| 28-29-30 | at San Diego |

**MAY**

| | |
|---|---|
| 1-2 | at Arizona |
| 3-4 | San Diego |

| | |
|---|---|
| 5-6-7 | Milwaukee |
| 9-10-**11** | Houston |
| 12-**13-14** | at San Francisco |
| 15-16-**17** | at Colorado |
| 19-20-21 | Angels |
| 22-23-24 | Colorado |
| 26-**27-28** | at Washington |
| **29**-30-31 | at Atlanta |

**JUNE**

| | |
|---|---|
| 1-2-**3-4** | Philadelphia |
| 5-6-7 | Mets |
| 9-10-**11** | at Colorado |

13-14-15........ at San Diego
16-17-18.......... at Oakland
20-21-22............. Seattle
23-24-25........... Pittsburgh
26-27-**28**.... at Minnesota
30...................... at Angels

### JULY
**1-2**...................... at Angels
3-4-5...................... Arizona
6-7-**8-9**...... San Francisco
13-14-**15-16**.... at St. Louis
17-18-19-20..... at Arizona
21-22-23............ St. Louis
24-25-26........... San Diego
28-**29**-30........ Washington

### AUGUST
**1-2-3**............. at Cincinnati
4-5-6............... at Florida
7-8-9-10............. Colorado

11-**12**-13...... San Francisco
14-15-16................ Florida
18-19-**20**.. at San Francisco
21-22-23........ at San Diego
25-26-**27**....... at Arizona
28-29-30........... Cincinnati

### SEPTEMBER
1-2-3................... Colorado
**4**-5-6........... at Milwaukee
7-8-**9**-10........... at Mets
12-13-**14**............... at Cubs
15-16-17-18...... San Diego
19-20-21........... Pittsburgh
22-23-24............. Arizona
26-27-**28**......... at Colorado
29-30...... at San Francisco

### OCTOBER
**1**.............. at San Francisco

29 30-31 .............. Arizona

### JUNE
2-**3-4**........... San Francisco
5-6-7............... at Dodgers
8-9-10-**11**........... at Arizona
13-14-**15**.... at Philadelphia
16-17-**18**............ Baltimore
19-20-21-**22**....... Cincinnati
23-**24-25**............ at Toronto
27-28-29............ at Boston
30................... at Yankees

### JULY
**1-2**................... at Yankees
3-**4-5-6**............ Pittsburgh
7-**8-9**................... Florida
**14**-15-16............ at Cubs
18-19-**20**.... at Cincinnati
21-**22-23**............ Houston
24-25-**26**............... Cubs
28-**29-30**........ at Atlanta

### AUGUST
1-2-3............ at Florida

4-**5-6**.............. Philadelphia
8-9-10.............. San Diego
11-12-**13**..... at Washington
14-15-16-**17** at Philadelphia
18-19-**20**............ Colorado
22-23-24............ St. Louis
25-26-**27**......... Philadelphia
29-30-31........ at Colorado

### SEPTEMBER
1-2-**3**................ at Houston
4-5-6...................... Atlanta
7-8-**9**-10.............. Dodgers
11-12-13............ at Florida
15-**16-17**........ at Pittsburgh
18-19-20-21........... Florida
22-23-**24-25**.... Washington
26-27-28........... at Atlanta
29-30......... at Washington

### OCTOBER
**1**.................. at Washington

# MILWAUKEE BREWERS
## MILLER PARK
**Standard Game Times:** 7:05 p.m.; Sat. 6:05; Sun. 1:05.

### APRIL
3-4-5................ Pittsburgh
7-**8-9**...................... Arizona
**10**-12-13......... at St. Louis
14-**15-16**............. at Mets
17-18-19.......... at Houston
20-21-**22-23**.... Cincinnati
24-25-26................ Atlanta
**28-29-30**............ at Cubs

### MAY
1-2...................... Houston
3-4........... San Francisco
5-6-7............... at Dodgers
9-10-11........ at San Diego
12-13-**14**.................. Mets
16-17-**18**.......... Philadelphia
19-20-**21**........... Minnesota
22-23-24....... at Cincinnati
26-27-**28**..... at Philadelphia
29-30-31........ at Pittsburgh

### JUNE
1................. at Pittsburgh
2-3-**4**............. Washington
5-6-7-**8**.............. San Diego
9-10-**11**............. St. Louis
12-13-14..... at Cincinnati
16-17-**18**............ Cleveland
19-20-**21**.............. Detroit
23-24-25.... at Kansas City
26-27-**28-29**...... at Cubs
30............... at Minnesota

### JULY
**1-2**................ at Minnesota
**3**-4-5................. Cincinnati
6-7-**8-9**...................... Cubs
14-15-**16**............ at Arizona
17-18-**19**.. at San Francisco
21-22-**23**........... at Cincinnati
24-25-26............ Pittsburgh
28-29-**30**............. Cincinnati
31.................... at Colorado

### AUGUST
1-2...................... at Colorado
4-5-**6**.............. at St. Louis
8-9-**10**...................... Cubs
11-12-**13**............ at Atlanta
14-15-**16**........ at Pittsburgh
17-18-19-**20**........ Houston
22-23-**24**................ Colorado
25-26-27-28.... at Florida
29-30-31.......... at Houston

### SEPTEMBER
1-2-3...................... Florida
**4**-5-6.................... Dodgers
8-9-**10**................. Houston
11-12-**13**.......... at Pittsburgh
15-16-17...... at Washington
18-19-20............. St. Louis
21-22-23-**24**. San Francisco
26-27................... at Cubs
28-29-**30**........ at St. Louis

### OCTOBER
**1**........................ at St. Louis

# NEW YORK METS
## SHEA STADIUM
**Standard Game Times:** 7:10 p.m.; Sun. 1:10.

### APRIL
3-5-6............. Washington
7-**8-9**...................... Florida
**11**-12-13...... at Washington
14-**15-16**.......... Milwaukee
17-18-**19**............... Atlanta
20-21-22-23.. at San Diego
24-25-**26**.. at San Francisco
28-29-**30**............. at Atlanta

### MAY
1-2................... Washington
3-4...................... Pittsburgh
**5-6-7**...................... Atlanta
9-10-11....... at Philadelphia
12-13-**14**....... at Milwaukee
16-17-**18**....... at St. Louis
19-**20**-21............. Yankees
23-24-**25**......... Philadelphia
26-**27**-28............. at Florida

# PHILADELPHIA PHILLIES
## CITIZENS BANK PARK
**Standard Game Times:** 7:05 p.m.; Sun. 1:35.

### APRIL
3-5-**6**.................... St. Louis
7-**8-9**.................... Dodgers
10-12-13............ at Atlanta
14-15-**16**............ at Colorado
18-19-20......... Washington
21-22-**23**............... Florida
24-25-26-27....... Colorado
28-29-**30**........ at Pittsburgh

### MAY
1-2................... at Florida
3-4...................... Atlanta
5-6-7............ San Francisco
9-10-11..................... Mets
12-13-**14**.......... at Atlanta
16-17-**18**...... at Milwaukee
19-20-**21**............... Boston
23-24-**25**............. at Mets
26-27-**28**......... Milwaukee
29-30-**31**......... Washington

### JUNE
1-2-3-4............ at Dodgers
5-6-**7**............... at Arizona
8-9-**10-11**... at Washington
13-14-**15**.................. Mets
16-17-**18**........... Tampa Bay
19-20-21............. Yankees
23-**24**-25............. at Boston
27-28-29........ at Baltimore
30................... at Toronto

### JULY
**1-2**................... at Toronto
**4**-5-6.................. San Diego
7-**8-9**................ Pittsburgh
14-**15-16**.. at San Francisco
17-18-19....... at San Diego
21-**22-23**-24........... Atlanta
25-26-27............ Arizona
28-29-**30-31**........... Florida

### AUGUST
1-2-3.............. at St. Louis
**4-5-6**...................... at Mets
7-**8-9**................ at Atlanta
11-12-**13**........... Cincinnati
14-15-16-**17**.............. Mets
18-19-**20**......... Washington
21-22-23-**24**.......... at Cubs
25-26-**27**............. at Mets
29-30-31..... at Washington

### SEPTEMBER
1-2-**3**...................... Atlanta
4-5-6.................... Houston
7-8-**9**-10.............. at Florida
12-13-14.......... at Atlanta
15-**16-17**.......... at Houston
18-19-20................. Cubs
22-23-**24**................ Florida
26-27-28......... Washington
29-30................... at Florida

### OCTOBER
**1**......................... at Florida

# PITTSBURGH PIRATES
## PNC PARK
**Standard Game Times:** 7:05 p.m.; Sun. 1:35.

### APRIL
3-4-5............... at Milwaukee
6-7-**8-9**........... at Cincinnati
**10**-11-12-**13**......... Dodgers
14-**15-16**................... Cubs
17-18-**19**............. St. Louis
21-22-**23**......... at Houston
24-25-**26**......... at St. Louis

28-29-**30**........ Philadelphia

### MAY
**1-2**........................ at Cubs
3-4........................ at Mets
5-6-**7**........ at Washington
9-10-**11**................. Arizona
12-13-**14**................. Florida
16-17-**18**............ Cincinnati

19-20-21 ........ at Cleveland
22-23-24 ......... at Arizona
26-27-28 ............ Houston
29-30-31 .......... Milwaukee

### JUNE
1 ................... Milwaukee
2-3-4 ............... San Diego
5-6-7 .............. at Colorado
8-9-10-11. at San Francisco
13-14-15 ........... St. Louis
16-17-18 ........... Minnesota
20-21-22 ...... at Kansas City
23-24-25 ......... at Dodgers
27-28-29 .......... White Sox
30 ...................... Detroit

### JULY
1-2 .................... Detroit
3-4-5-6 ............... at Mets
7-8-9 .......... at Philadelphia
14-15-16 .......... Washington
17-18-19 ........... Colorado
20-21-22-23 ....... at Florida
24-25-26 ....... at Milwaukee

28-29-30 ...... San Francisco

### AUGUST
1-2-3 .................. Atlanta
4-5-6 ................. at Cubs
8-9-10 .............. at Houston
11-12-13 ............ St. Louis
14-15-16 .......... Milwaukee
18-19-20 ........ at Cincinnati
21-22-23 ........... at Atlanta
24-25-26-27 ......... Houston
28-29-30 ................. Cubs

### SEPTEMBER
1-2-3 ............. at St. Louis
4-5-6-7 .............. at Cubs
8-9-10 ........... at Cincinnati
11-12-13 ........... Milwaukee
15-16-17 ................. Mets
19-20-21 .......... at Dodgers
22-23-24 ....... at San Diego
26-27-28 ............ Houston
29-30 .............. Cincinnati

### OCTOBER
1 ...................... Cincinnati

12-13-14 .............. at Cubs
15-16-17 .......... at Arizona
19-20-21 ........... at Seattle
22-23-24 ............. Atlanta
26-27-28 .......... St. Louis
29-30-31 ............ Colorado

### JUNE
2-3-4 ............. at Pittsburgh
5-6-7-8 ........ at Milwaukee
9-10-11 ................ Florida
13-14-15 ............ Dodgers
16-17-18 ............ at Angels
20-21-22 ............. at Texas
23-24-25 ............. Seattle
27-28-29 ............. Oakland
30 ................. San Francisco

### JULY
1-2 ................ San Francisco
4-5-6 ........... at Philadelphia
7-8-9 ........... at Washington
14-15-16 ............. Atlanta
17-18-19 ........ Philadelphia
20-21-22-23 ............ at San Francisco

24-25-26 .......... at Dodgers
27-28-29-30.... at Colorado

### AUGUST
1-2-3 ................. Houston
4-5-6 ............. Washington
8-9-10 ................. at Mets
11-12-13 ......... at Houston
14-15-16-17. San Francisco
18-19-20 ............ Arizona
21-22-23 ............ Dodgers
25-26-27 ......... at Colorado
28-29-30 ........... at Arizona

### SEPTEMBER
1-2-3 ............... Cincinnati
4-5-6 ................ Colorado
8-9-10 ...... at San Francisco
12-13-14 ....... at Cincinnati
15-16-17-18 ..... at Dodgers
19-20-21 ............. Arizona
22-23-24 .......... Pittsburgh
25-26-27 ........ at St. Louis
28-29-30 .......... at Arizona

### OCTOBER
1 ...................... at Arizona

## ST. LOUIS CARDINALS
NEW BUSCH STADIUM

**Standard Game Times:** 7:10 p.m.; Sun. 1:15.

### APRIL
3-5-6 .......... at Philadelphia
7-8-9 ................. at Cubs
10-12-13 .......... Milwaukee
14-15-16 ........... Cincinnati
17-18-19 ....... at Pittsburgh
21-22-23 ................. Cubs
24-25-26 ........... Pittsburgh
27-28-29-30 .... Washington

### MAY
1-2 ................ at Cincinnati
3-4 ................. at Houston
5-6-7 ................. at Florida
8-9-10 ............... Colorado
12-13-14 ............ Arizona
16-17-18 ................. Mets
19-20-21 ...... at Kansas City
22-23-24 .... at San Francisco
26-27-28 ....... at San Diego
29-30-31 ............. Houston

### JUNE
2-3-4 .................... Cubs
5-6-7 ................ Cincinnati
9-10-11 ......... at Milwaukee
13-14-15 ....... at Pittsburgh
16-17-18 ............ Colorado
20-21-22 ...... at White Sox
23-24-25 ........... at Detroit
26-27-28 ............ Cleveland
30 .................. Kansas City

### JULY
1-2 ................. Kansas City
3-4-5 ................ at Atlanta
6-7-8-9 ........... at Houston
13-14-15-16 ........ Dodgers
17-18-19 ............. Atlanta
21-22-23 .......... at Dodgers
24-25-26 ......... at Colorado
27-28-29-30 .......... at Cubs

### AUGUST
1-2-3 ............. Philadelphia
4-5-6 .............. Milwaukee
7-8-9-10 ........ at Cincinnati
11-12-13 ........ at Pittsburgh
15-16-17 ............ Cincinnati
18-19-20 ............. at Cubs
22-23-24 ............. at Mets
25-26-27 ............ Colorado
29-30-31 .............. Florida

### SEPTEMBER
1-2-3 ................ Pittsburgh
4-5-6 .......... at Washington
7-8-9-10 .......... at Arizona
11-12-13 ............. Houston
15-16-17 ...... San Francisco
18-19-20 ....... at Milwaukee
21-22-23-24 ..... at Houston
25-26-27 ........... San Diego
28-29-30 .......... Milwaukee

### OCTOBER
1 ..................... Milwaukee

## SAN DIEGO PADRES
PETCO PARK

**Standard Game Times:** Unavailable.

### APRIL
3-4-5 ........... San Francisco
7-8-9 .................. Colorado
11-12-13 ............. at Florida
14-15-16 ........... at Atlanta
17-18-19 ......... at Colorado
20-21-22-23 ............. Mets

24-25-26 .............. Arizona
28-29-30 .............. Dodgers

### MAY
1-2 .......... at San Francisco
3-4 ................. at Dodgers
5-6-7-8 .................. Cubs
9-10-11 ............. Milwaukee

## SAN FRANCISCO GIANTS
SBC PARK

**Standard Game Times:** 7:05 p.m.; Sat.-Sun. 1:05.

### APRIL
3-4-5 ............. at San Diego
6-7-8-9 .............. Atlanta
11-12-13 ............. Houston
14-15-16 .......... at Dodgers
17-18-19-20 ...... at Arizona
21-22-23 ......... at Colorado
24-25-26 ................ Mets
28-29-30 ............. Arizona

### MAY
1-2 .................. San Diego
3-4 ............... at Milwaukee
5-6-7 .......... at Philadelphia
9-10-11 ................. Cubs
12-13-14 ............ Dodgers
15-16-17 .......... at Houston
19-20-21 .......... at Oakland
22-23-24 ........... St. Louis
26-27-28 ............ Colorado
29-30-31 .............. Florida

### JUNE
2-3-4 .................... Mets
5-6-7 ................... Florida
8-9-10-11 .......... Pittsburgh
13-14-15 .......... at Arizona
16-17-18 ............ at Seattle
19-20-21 ............. Angels
23-24-25 ............ Oakland
27-28-29 .............. Texas
30 ................. at San Diego

### JULY
1-2 ............... at San Diego

3-4-5 ................ at Colorado
7-8-9 ............. at Dodgers
14-15-16 ......... Philadelphia
17-18-19 .......... Milwaukee
20-21-22-23 ...... San Diego
25-26-27 ....... at Pittsburgh
28-29-30 ....... at Pittsburgh
31 .................. Washington

### AUGUST
1-2 ................ Washington
4-5-6 ................ Colorado
7-8-9 ................ at Arizona
11-12-13 ........ at San Diego
14-15-16-17... at San Diego
18-19-20 ............ Dodgers
21-22-23 ............. Arizona
24-25-26-27 ...... Cincinnati
29-30-31 ........... at Atlanta

### SEPTEMBER
1-2-3 .................. at Cubs
4-5-6 ............ at Cincinnati
8-9-10 .............. San Diego
12-13-14 ............. Colorado
15-16-17 .......... at St. Louis
18-19-20 .......... at Colorado
21-22-23-24 .. at Milwaukee
25-26-27 ............. Arizona
29-30 ................. Dodgers

### OCTOBER
1 ...................... Dodgers

## WASHINGTON NATIONALS
RFK STADIUM

**Standard Game Times:** 7:05 p.m.; Sun. 1:05.

### APRIL
3-5-6 ................... at Mets
7-8-9-10 ......... at Houston
11-12-13 ................ Mets
14-15-16 ............ at Florida

18-19-20 ...... at Philadelphia
21-22-23 ................ Atlanta
24-25-26 ........... Cincinnati
27-28-29-30..... at St. Louis

## MAY

1-2 ............................. at Mets
3-4 ................................. Florida
5-6-**7** ....................... Pittsburgh
9-10-11 ............ at Cincinnati
12-13-**14** ................ at Atlanta
16-17-**18** .................. at Cubs
19-20-**21** ............... Baltimore
22-23-24-**25** ......... Houston
26-**27-28** .............. Dodgers
29-30-**31** ..... at Philadelphia

## JUNE

2-3-**4** ............. at Milwaukee
5-6-7 ................... at Atlanta

8-9-**10-11** ....... Philadelphia
12-13-14-**15** ....... Colorado
16-**17-18** .............. Yankees
19-20-21 ............. at Boston
23-**24**-25 ......... at Baltimore
27-28-29 ........... at Toronto
30 .................... Tampa Bay

## JULY

1-2 .................. Tampa Bay
3-4-5-6 .................... Florida
7-8-**9** ................. San Diego
14-15-**16** ....... at Pittsburgh
17-18-19 ............. at Florida
21-**22-23** .................... Cubs

25-26-**27** ...... San Francisco
28-**29**-30 .......... at Dodgers
31 ............ at San Francisco

## AUGUST

1-**2** .......... at San Francisco
4-5-6 ............. at San Diego
8-9-10 .................... Florida
11-12-**13** ................... Mets
14-15-16-**17** ........... Atlanta
18-19-**20** ..... at Philadelphia
21-22-23 ............ at Florida
25-**26-27** ............ at Atlanta
29-30-31 ........ Philadelphia

## SEPTEMBER

1-2-**3** ..................... Arizona
**4**-5-**6** .................... St. Louis
7-8-9-**10** ......... at Colorado
11-12-13 ........... at Arizona
15-16-**17** .......... Milwaukee
19-20 ..................... Atlanta
22-23-**24**-25 .......... at Mets
26-27-28 ........ Philadelphia
29-30 .......................... Mets

## OCTOBER

**1** ................................ Mets

**NOTE**: Dates in **bold** indicate afternoon games. All game times are subject to change. Gaps in dates indicate scheduled off-days but may be affected by rainouts.

# INTERLEAGUE
## SCHEDULE

### May 19
Angels at Dodgers
Baltimore at Washington
Boston at Philadelphia
Cincinnati at Detroit
Cubs at White Sox
Florida at Tampa Bay
Kansas City at St. Louis
Minnesota at Milwaukee
Pittsburgh at Cleveland
San Francisco at Oakland
San Diego at Seattle
Texas at Houston
Toronto at Colorado
Yankees at Mets

### May 20
Angels at Dodgers
Baltimore at Washington
Boston at Philadelphia
Cincinnati at Detroit
Cubs at White Sox
Florida at Tampa Bay
Kansas City at St. Louis
Minnesota at Milwaukee
Pittsburgh at Cleveland
San Francisco at Oakland
San Diego at Seattle
Texas at Houston
Toronto at Colorado
Yankees at Mets

### May 21
Angels at Dodgers
Baltimore at Washington
Boston at Philadelphia
Cincinnati at Detroit
Cubs at White Sox
Florida at Tampa Bay
Kansas City at St. Louis
Minnesota at Milwaukee
Pittsburgh at Cleveland
San Francisco at Oakland
San Diego at Seattle
Texas at Houston
Toronto at Colorado
Yankees at Mets

### June 16
Arizona at Texas
Baltimore at Mets
Boston at Atlanta
Cleveland at Milwaukee
Detroit at Cubs
Dodgers at Oakland
Kansas City at Houston
Minnesota at Pittsburgh
San Diego at Angels
San Francisco at Seattle
Tampa Bay at Philadelphia
Toronto at Florida
Washington at Yankees

White Sox at Cincinnati

### June 17
Arizona at Texas
Baltimore at Mets
Boston at Atlanta
Cleveland at Milwaukee
Detroit at Cubs
Dodgers at Oakland
Kansas City at Houston
Minnesota at Pittsburgh
San Diego at Angels
San Francisco at Seattle
Tampa Bay at Philadelphia
Toronto at Florida
Washington at Yankees
White Sox at Cincinnati

### June 18
Arizona at Texas
Baltimore at Mets
Boston at Atlanta
Cleveland at Milwaukee
Detroit at Cubs
Dodgers at Oakland
Kansas City at Houston
Minnesota at Pittsburgh
San Diego at Angels
San Francisco at Seattle
Tampa Bay at Philadelphia
Toronto at Florida
Washington at Yankees
White Sox at Cincinnati

### June 19
Angels at San Francisco
Cubs at Cleveland
Detroit at Milwaukee
Oakland at Colorado
Yankees at Philadelphia
Washington at Boston

### June 20
Angels at San Francisco
Arizona at Tampa Bay
Baltimore at Florida
Cubs at Cleveland
Detroit at Milwaukee
Minnesota at Houston
Oakland at Colorado
Pittsburgh at Kansas City
St. Louis at White Sox
San Diego at Texas
Seattle at Dodgers
Toronto at Atlanta
Washington at Boston
Yankees at Philadelphia

### June 21
Angels at San Francisco
Arizona at Tampa Bay
Baltimore at Florida
Cubs at Cleveland

Detroit at Milwaukee
Minnesota at Houston
Oakland at Colorado
Pittsburgh at Kansas City
St. Louis at White Sox
San Diego at Texas
Seattle at Dodgers
Toronto at Atlanta
Washington at Boston
Yankees at Philadelphia

### June 22
Arizona at Tampa Bay
Baltimore at Florida
Minnesota at Houston
Pittsburgh at Kansas City
St. Louis at White Sox
San Diego at Texas
Seattle at Dodgers
Toronto at Atlanta

### June 23
Angels at Arizona
Atlanta at Tampa Bay
Cincinnati at Cleveland
Cubs at Minnesota
Houston at White Sox
Florida at Yankees
Mets at Toronto
Oakland at San Francisco
Milwaukee at Kansas City
Philadelphia at Boston
St. Louis at Detroit
Seattle at San Diego
Texas at Colorado
Washington at Baltimore

### June 24
Angels at Arizona
Atlanta at Tampa Bay
Cincinnati at Cleveland
Cubs at Minnesota
Florida at Yankees
Houston at White Sox
Mets at Toronto
Milwaukee at Kansas City
Oakland at San Francisco
Philadelphia at Boston
St. Louis at Detroit
Seattle at San Diego
Texas at Colorado
Washington at Baltimore

### June 25
Angels at Arizona
Atlanta at Tampa Bay
Cincinnati at Cleveland
Cubs at Minnesota
Florida at Yankees
Houston at White Sox
Mets at Toronto
Milwaukee at Kansas City
Oakland at San Francisco

Philadelphia at Boston
St. Louis at Detroit
Seattle at San Diego
Texas at Colorado
Washington at Baltimore

### June 26
Atlanta at Yankees
Cleveland at St. Louis
Colorado at Angels
Dodgers at Minnesota
Houston at Detroit
Tampa Bay at Florida

### June 27
Atlanta at Yankees
Cleveland at St. Louis
Colorado at Angels
Dodgers at Minnesota
Houston at Detroit
Kansas City at Cincinnati
Mets at Boston
Oakland at San Diego
Philadelphia at Baltimore
Seattle at Arizona
Tampa Bay at Florida
Texas at San Francisco
Washington at Toronto
White Sox at Pittsburgh

### June 28
Atlanta at Yankees
Cleveland at St. Louis
Colorado at Angels
Dodgers at Minnesota

Houston at Detroit
Kansas City at Cincinnati
Mets at Boston
Oakland at San Diego
Philadelphia at Baltimore
Seattle at Arizona
Tampa Bay at Florida
Texas at San Francisco
Washington at Toronto
White Sox at Pittsburgh

### June 29
Kansas City at Cincinnati
Mets at Boston
Oakland at San Diego
Philadelphia at Baltimore
Seattle at Arizona
Texas at San Francisco
Washington at Toronto
White Sox at Pittsburgh

### July 30
Arizona at Oakland
Baltimore at Atlanta
Boston at Florida
Cleveland at Cincinnati
Colorado at Seattle
Dodgers at Angels
Detroit at Pittsburgh
Houston at Texas
Kansas City at St. Louis
Mets at Yankees
Milwaukee at Minnesota
Philadelphia at Toronto

Washington at Tampa Bay
White Sox at Cubs

### July 1
Arizona at Oakland
Baltimore at Atlanta
Boston at Florida
Cleveland at Cincinnati
Colorado at Seattle
Dodgers at Angels
Detroit at Pittsburgh
Houston at Texas
Kansas City at St. Louis
Mets at Yankees
Milwaukee at Minnesota
Philadelphia at Toronto
Washington at Tampa Bay
White Sox at Cubs

### July 2
Arizona at Oakland
Baltimore at Atlanta
Boston at Florida
Cleveland at Cincinnati
Colorado at Seattle
Dodgers at Angels
Detroit at Pittsburgh
Houston at Texas
Kansas City at St. Louis
Mets at Yankees
Milwaukee at Minnesota
Philadelphia at Toronto
Washington at Tampa Bay
White Sox at Cubs

# SPRING TRAINING
## ARIZONA CACTUS LEAGUE

### ARIZONA DIAMONDBACKS
**Major League Club**
Complex Address (first year): Tucson Electric Park (1998), 2500 Ajo Way, Tucson, AZ 85713. Telephone: (520) 434-1400. FAX: (520) 434-1443. **Seating Capacity:** 11,000. **Location:** I-10 to exit 262 (Park Street) or 263 (Kino Street), south to Ajo Way, left (east) on Ajo Way to park.
Hotel Address: JW Marriott Starr Pass Resort, 3800 W. Starr Pass Blvd., Tucson, AZ 85745. Telephone: (520) 792-3500.

**Minor League Clubs**
Complex Address: Kino Veterans Memorial Sportspark, 3600 S. Country Club, Tucson, AZ 85713. Telephone: (520) 434-1400. FAX: (520) 434-1443. **Hotel Address:** The Hotel Arizona, 181 W. Broadway, Tucson, AZ 85701. Telephone: (520) 624-8711.

### CHICAGO CUBS
**Major League Club**
Complex Address (first year): HoHoKam Park (1979), 1235 N. Center St., Mesa, AZ 85201. Telephone: (480) 668-0500. FAX: (480) 668-4541. **Seating Capacity:** 12,575. **Location:** Main Street (U.S. Highway 60) to Center Street, north 1½ miles on Center Street.
Hotel Address: Best Western Dobson Ranch Inn, 1666 S. Dobson Rd., Mesa, AZ 85202. Telephone: (480) 831-7000.

**Minor League Clubs**
Complex Address: Fitch Park, 160 E. Sixth Place, Mesa, AZ 85201. Telephone: (480) 668-0500. FAX: (480) 668-4501. **Hotel Address:** Best Western Mezona, 250 W. Main St., Mesa, AZ 85201. Telephone: (480) 834-9233.

### CHICAGO WHITE SOX
**Major League Club**
Complex Address (first year): Tucson Electric Park (1998), 2500 E. Ajo Way, Tucson, AZ 85713. Telephone: (520) 434-1300. FAX: (520) 434-1151. **Seating Capacity:** 11,000. **Location:** I-10 to exit 262 (Park Street) or 263 (Kino Street), south to Ajo Way, left (east) on Ajo Way to park.
Hotel Address: Doubletree Guest Suites, 6555 E. Speedway Blvd., Tucson, AZ 85710. Telephone: (520) 721-7100.

**Minor League Clubs**
Complex Address: Same as major league club. **Hotel Address:** Ramada Palo Verde, 5251 S. Julian Dr., Tucson, AZ 85706. Telephone: (520) 294-5250.

### COLORADO ROCKIES
**Major League Club**
Complex Address (first year): Hi Corbett Field (1993), 3400 E. Camino Campestre, Tucson, AZ 85716. Telephone: (520) 322-4500. **Seating Capacity:** 8,655. **Location:** I-10 to Broadway exit, east on Broadway to Randolph Park.
Hotel Address: Hilton Tucson East, 7600 Broadway, Tucson, AZ 85710.

**Minor League Clubs**
Complex Address: Same as major league club. **Hotel**

Address: Clarion Hotel, 102 N. Alvernon, Tucson, AZ 85711. Telephone: (520) 795-0330.

### KANSAS CITY ROYALS
**Major League Club**
Complex Address (first year): Surprise Stadium (2003), 15946 N. Bullard Ave., Surprise, AZ 85374. **Telephone:** (623) 266-8800. **FAX:** (623) 266-8012. **Seating Capacity:** 10,700. **Location:** I-10 West to Route 101 North, 101 North to Bell Road, left on Bell for five miles, stadium on left.
Hotel Address: Wingate Inn & Suites, 1188 N. Dysart Rd., Avondale, AZ 85323. Telephone: (623) 547-1313.

**Minor League Clubs**
Complex: Same as Major League club. **Hotel Address:** Quality Inn, 16741 N. Greasewood St., Surprise, AZ 85374. Telephone: (623) 583-3500.

### LOS ANGELES ANGELS OF ANAHEIM
**Major League Club**
Complex Address (first year): Tempe Diablo Stadium (1993), 2200 W. Alameda, Tempe, AZ 85282. Telephone: (480) 858-7500. FAX: (480) 438-7583. **Seating Capacity:** 9,785. **Location:** I-10 to exit 153B (48th Street), south one mile on 48th Street to Alameda Drive, left on Alameda.

**Minor League Clubs**
Complex Address: Tempe Diablo Stadium, 2200 W. Alameda, Tempe, AZ 85282. Telephone: Unavailable.
Hotel Address: Extended Stay America, 3421 E. Elwood Street, Phoenix, AZ 85040. Telephone: (602) 438-2900.

### MILWAUKEE BREWERS
**Major League Club**
Complex Address (first year): Maryvale Baseball Park (1998), 3600 N. 51st Ave., Phoenix, AZ 85031. Telephone: (623) 245-5555. FAX: (623) 245-5580. **Seating Capacity:** 9,000. **Location:** I-10 to exit 139 (51st Ave.), north on 51st Ave.; I-17 to exit 202 (Indian School Road), west on Indian School Road.
Hotel Address: Holiday Inn Express-Tempe, 5300 S. Priest Dr., Tempe, AZ 85283. Telephone: (480) 820-7500.

**Minor League Clubs**
Complex Address: Maryvale Baseball Complex, 3805 N. 53rd Ave., Phoenix, AZ 85031. Telephone: (623) 245-5600. FAX: (623) 245-5607. **Hotel Address:** Same as major league club.

## OAKLAND ATHLETICS
### Major League Club
**Complex Address (first year):** Phoenix Municipal Stadium (1982), 5999 E. Van Buren, Phoenix, AZ 85008. Telephone: (602) 225-9400. FAX: (602) 225-9473. **Seating Capacity:** 8,500. **Location:** I-10 to exit 153 (48th Street), HoHoKam Expressway to Van Buren Street (U.S. Highway 60), right on Van Buren, park two miles on right.
**Hotel Address:** Doubletree Suites Hotel, 320 N. 44th St., Phoenix, AZ 85008. Telephone: (602) 225-0500.
### Minor League Clubs
**Complex Address:** Papago Park Baseball Complex, 1802 N. 64th St., Phoenix, AZ 85008. Telephone: (480) 949-5951. FAX: (480) 945-0557. **Hotel Address:** Fairfield Inn, 5101 N. Scottsdale Rd., Scottsdale, AZ 85251. Telephone: (480) 945-4392.

## SAN DIEGO PADRES
### Major League Club
**Complex Address (first year):** Peoria Sports Complex (1994), 8131 W. Paradise Lane, Peoria, AZ 85382. Telephone: (623) 486-7000. FAX: (623) 412-9382. **Seating Capacity:** 10,000. **Location:** I-17 to Bell Road exit, west on Bell to 83rd Ave.
**Hotel Address:** Comfort Suites, 8473 W. Paradise Lane, Peoria, AZ 85382. Telephone: (623) 334-3993.
### Minor League Clubs
**Complex Address:** Same as major league club.
**Hotel Address:** Sheraton Crescent, 2620 W. Dunlap Ave., Phoenix, AZ 85021. Telephone: (623) 943-8200.

## SAN FRANCISCO GIANTS
### Major League Club
**Complex Address (first year):** Scottsdale Stadium (1981), 7408 E. Osborn Rd., Scottsdale, AZ 85251. Telephone: (480) 990-7972. FAX: (480) 990-2643. **Seating Capacity:** 11,500. **Location:** Scottsdale Road to Osborne Road, east on Osborne ½ mile.
**Hotel Address:** Hilton Garden Inn Scottsdale Old Town, 7324 East Indian School Rd., Scottsdale, AZ 85251. Telephone: (480) 481-0400.

### Minor League Clubs
**Complex Address:** Indian School Park, 4415 N. Hayden Road at Camelback Road, Scottsdale, AZ 85251. Telephone: (480) 990-0052. FAX: (480) 990-2349.
**Hotel Address:** Days Inn, 4710 N. Scottsdale Rd., Scottsdale, AZ 85351. Telephone: (480) 947-5411.

## SEATTLE MARINERS
### Major League Club
**Complex Address (first year):** Peoria Sports Complex (1993), 15707 N. 83rd Ave., Peoria, AZ 85382. Telephone: (623) 776-4800. FAX: (623) 776-4829. **Seating Capacity:** 10,000. **Location:** I-17 to Bell Road exit, west on Bell to 83rd Ave.
**Hotel Address:** LaQuinta Inn & Suites, 16321 N. 83rd Ave., Peoria, AZ 85382. Telephone: (623) 487-1900.
### Minor League Clubs
**Complex Address:** Peoria Sports Complex (1993), 15707 N. 83rd Ave., Peoria, AZ 85382. Telephone: (602) 412-9000. FAX: (602) 412-9382. **Hotel Address:** Hampton Inn, 8408 W. Paradise Lane, Peoria, AZ 85382. Telephone: (623) 486-9918.

## TEXAS RANGERS
### Major League Club
**Complex Address (first year):** Surprise Stadium (2003), 15754 N. Bullard Ave., Surprise, AZ 85374. **Telephone:** (623) 266-8100. **FAX:** (623) 266-8120. **Seating Capacity:** 10,714. **Location:** I-10 West to Route 101 North, 101 North to Bell Road, left at Bell for seven miles, stadium on left.
**Hotel Address:** Windmill Suites at Sun City West, 12545 W. Bell Rd., Surprise, AZ 85374. Telephone: (623) 583-0133.
### Minor League Clubs
**Complex Address:** Same as major league club.
**Hotel Address:** Hampton Inn, 2000 N. Litchfield Rd., Goodyear, AZ 85338. Telephone: (623) 536-1313; Holiday Inn Express, 1313 N. Litchfield Rd., Goodyear, AZ 85338.

# FLORIDA GRAPEFRUIT LEAGUE

## ATLANTA BRAVES
### Major League Club
**Stadium Address (first year):** Disney's Wide World of Sports Complex (1998), The Ballpark at Disney's Wide World of Sports Complex, 700 S. Victory Way, Kissimmee, FL 34747. Telephone: (407) 939-2200. **Seating Capacity:** 9,500. **Location:** I-4 to exit 25B (Highway 192 West), follow signs to Magic Kingdom/Wide World of Sports Complex, right on Victory Way.
**Hotel Address:** World Center Marriott, World Center Drive, Orlando, FL 32821. Telephone: (407) 239-4200.
### Minor League Clubs
**Complex Address:** Same as major league club. Telephone: (407) 939-2232. FAX: (407) 939-2225. **Hotel Address:** Marriot Village at Lake Buena Vista, 8623 Vineland Ave., Orlando, FL 32821. Telephone: (407) 938-9001.

## BALTIMORE ORIOLES
### Major League Club
**Complex Address (first year):** Fort Lauderdale

Stadium (1996), 1301 NW 55th St., Fort Lauderdale, FL 33309. Telephone: (954) 776-1921. FAX: (954) 776-9116. **Seating Capacity:** 8,340. **Location:** I-95 to exit 32 (Commercial Blvd.), West on Commercial, right on Orioles Blvd. (NW 55th Street), stadium on left.
**Hotel Address:** Sheraton Suites, 555 NW 62nd St., Fort Lauderdale, FL 33309. Telephone: (954) 772-5400.

**Minor League Clubs**
**Complex Address:** Twin Lakes Park, 6700 Clark Rd., Sarasota, FL 34241. Telephone: (941) 923-1996. FAX: (941) 922-3751. **Hotel Address:** Ramada Inn Limited, 5774 Clark Rd., Sarasota, FL 34233. Telephone: (941) 921-7812; Americinn, 5931 Fruitville Rd., Sarasota, FL 34232. Telephone: (941) 342-8778.

## BOSTON RED SOX
**Major League Club**
**Complex Address (first year):** City of Palms Park (1993), 2201 Edison Ave., Fort Myers, FL 33901. Telephone: (239) 334-4799. FAX: (239) 334-6060. **Seating Capacity:** 8,200. **Location:** I-75 to exit 39, three miles west to Tuttle Ave., right on Tuttle to 12th Street, stadium on left.
**Hotel Address:** Homewood Suites Hotel, 5255 Big Pine Way, Fort Myers, FL 33907. Telephone: (239) 275-6000.
**Minor League Clubs**
**Complex Address:** Red Sox Minor League Complex, 4301 Edison Ave., Fort Myers, FL 33916. Telephone: (239) 461-4500. FAX: (239) 332-8107. **Hotel Address:** Ramada Inn, 2500 Edwards Dr., Fort Myers, FL 33901. Telephone: (239) 337-0300.

## CINCINNATI REDS
**Major League Club**
**Complex Address (first year):** Ed Smith Stadium (1998), 1090 N. Euclid Avenue, Sarasota, FL 34237. Telephone: (941) 955-6501. FAX: (941) 955-6365. **Seating Capacity:** 7,500. **Location:** I-75 to exit 39, west on Fruitville Road (Route 780) for four miles, right on Tuttle.
**Hotel Address—Staff:** Marriott Residence Inn, 1040 University Pkwy., Sarasota, FL 34234. Telephone: (941) 358-1468. FAX: (941) 358-0850. **Players:** Wellesley Inn, 1803 N. Tamiami Trail, Sarasota, FL 34234. Telephone: (941) 366-5128. FAX: (941) 953-4322.
**Minor League Clubs**
**Complex Address:** Same as major league club. **Hotel Address:** Holiday Inn, 7150 N. Tamiami Trail, Sarasota, FL 34243. Telephone: (941) 355-2781.

## CLEVELAND INDIANS
**Major League Club**
**Complex Address (fi:** Chain O' Lakes Park (1993), Cypress Gardens Blvd. at U.S. 17, Winter Haven, FL 33880. Telephone: (863) 293-5405. FAX: (863) 291-5772. **Seating Capacity:** 7,000. **Location:** U.S. 17 (3rd Street) south through Winter Haven to Cypress Gardens Boulevard.
**Hotel Address:** Holiday Inn, 1150 Third St. SW, Winter Haven, FL 33880. Telephone: (863) 294-4451.
**Minor League Clubs**
**Complex Address/Hotel:** Same as major league club.

## DETROIT TIGERS
**Major League Club**
**Complex Address (first year):** Joker Marchant Stadium (1946), 2301 Lakeland Hills Blvd., Lakeland, FL 33805. Telephone: (863) 686-8075. FAX: (863) 688-9589. **Seating Capacity:** 9,000. **Location:** I-4 to exit 19 (Lakeland Hills Boulevard), left 1½ miles.
**Hotel Address:** Wellesley Inn, 3520 Hwy. 98 N., Lakeland, FL 33805. Telephone: (863) 859-3399.
**Minor League Clubs**
**Complex/Hotel Address:** Tigertown, 2125 N. Lake Ave., Lakeland, FL 33805. Telephone: (863) 686-8075.

FAX: (863) 688-9589.

## FLORIDA MARLINS
**Major League Club**
**Complex Address (first year):** Roger Dean Stadium (1998), 4751 Main St., Jupiter, FL 33458. Telephone: (561) 775-1818. **Seating Capacity:** 7,000. **Location:** I-95 to exit 83, east on Donald Ross Road for one mile to Central Blvd, left at light, follow Central Boulevard to circle and take Main Street to Roger Dean Stadium.
**Hotel Address:** Hampton Inn, 401 RCA Blvd., Palm Beach Gardens, FL 33410. Telephone: (561) 625-8880. FAX: (561) 625-6766.
**Minor League Clubs**
**Complex Address:** Same as major league club. **Hotel Address:** Fairfield Inn, 6748 W. Indiantown Rd., Jupiter, FL 33458. Telephone: (561) 748-5252.

## HOUSTON ASTROS
**Major League Club**
**Complex Address (first year):** Osceola County Stadium (1985), 631 Heritage Park Way, Kissimmee, FL 34744. Telephone: (321) 697-3150. FAX: (321) 697-3199. **Seating Capacity:** 5,300. **Location:** From Florida Turnpike South, take exit 244, west on U.S. 192, right on Bill Beck Boulevard; From Florida Turnpike North, take exit 242, west on U.S. 192, right on Bill Beck Blvd.; From I-4, take exit onto 192 East for 12 miles, stadium on left; From 17-92 South, take U.S. 192, left for three miles.
**Hotel Address:** Renaissance Orlando Resort at Seaworld, 6677 Sea Harbor Dr., Orlando, FL 32821. Telephone: (407) 351-3555.
**Minor League Clubs**
**Complex Address:** 1000 Bill Beck Blvd., Kissimmee, FL 34744. Telephone: (321) 697-3100. FAX: (321) 697-3195. **Hotel Address:** Same as major league club.

## LOS ANGELES DODGERS
**Major League Club**
**Complex Address (first year):** Holman Stadium (1948). **Seating Capacity:** 6,500. **Location:** Exit I-95 to Route 60 East, left on 43rd Avenue, right on 26th Street.
**Hotel Address:** Dodgertown, 4001 26th St., Vero Beach, FL 32960. Telephone: (772) 569-4900. FAX: (772) 567-0819.
**Minor League Clubs**
**Complex/Hotel Address:** Same as major league club.

## MINNESOTA TWINS
**Major League Club**
**Complex Address (first year):** Lee County Sports Complex/Hammond Stadium (1991), 14100 Six Mile Cypress Pkwy., Fort Myers, FL 33912. Telephone: (239) 768-4282. FAX: (239) 768-4211. **Seating Capacity:** 7,500. **Location:** Exit 21 off I-75, west on Daniels Parkway, left on Six Mile Cypress Parkway.
**Hotel Address:** Radisson Inn, 12635 Cleveland Ave., Fort Myers, FL 33907. Telephone: (239) 936-4300.
**Minor League Clubs**
**Complex Address/Hotel:** Same as major league club.

## NEW YORK METS
**Major League Club**
**Complex Address (first year):** St. Lucie Sports Complex/Tradition Field (1987), 525 NW Peacock Blvd., Port St. Lucie, FL 34986. Telephone: (772) 871-2100. FAX: (772) 878-9802. **Seating Capacity:** 7,000.

**Location:** Exit 121C (St. Lucie West Boulevard) off I-95, east ¼ mile, left onto NW Peacock Boulevard.
**Hotel Address:** Spring Hill Suites, 2000 NW Courtyard Circle, Port St. Lucie, FL 34986. Telephone: (772) 871-2929.
**Minor League Clubs**
**Complex Address:** Same as major league club. **Hotel Address:** Holiday Inn, 10120 South Federal Hwy., Port St. Lucie, FL 34952. Telephone: (772) 337-2200.

## NEW YORK YANKEES
**Major League Club**
**Complex Address (first year):** Legends Field (1996), One Steinbrenner Dr., Tampa, FL 33614. Telephone: (813) 875-7753. FAX: (813) 673-3199. **Seating Capacity:** 10,000. **Location:** I-275 to Martin Luther King, west on Martin Luther King to Dale Mabry.
**Hotel Address:** Radisson Bay Harbor Inn, 770 Courtney Campbell Causeway, Tampa, FL 33607. Telephone: (813) 281-8900.
**Minor League Clubs**
**Complex Address:** Yankees Player Development/ Scouting Complex, 3102 N. Himes Ave., Tampa, FL 33607. Telephone: (813) 875-7569. FAX: (813) 873-2302. **Hotel Address:** Holiday Inn Express, 4732 N. Dale Mabry, Tampa, FL 33614.

## PHILADELPHIA PHILLIES
**Major League Club**
**Complex Address (first year):** Bright House Networks Field (2004), 601 N. Old Coachman Rd., Clearwater, FL 33765. Telephone: (727) 467-4457. FAX: (727) 712-4498. **Seating Capacity:** 7,300. **Location:** U.S. Highway 19 North, left on Drew Street, right on Old Coachman Road, ballpark on right.
**Hotel:** None.
**Minor League Clubs**
**Complex Address:** Carpenter Complex, 651 N. Old Coachman Rd., Clearwater, FL 33765. Telephone: (727) 799-0503. FAX: (727) 726-1793. **Hotel Addresses:** Hampton Inn, 21030 U.S. Highway 19 North, Clearwater, FL 34625. Telephone: (727) 797-8173; Econolodge, 21252 U.S. Hwy. 19, Clearwater, FL 34625. Telephone: (727) 799-1569.

## PITTSBURGH PIRATES
**Major League Club**
**Stadium Address (first year):** McKechnie Field (1969), 17th Ave. West and Ninth Street West, Bradenton, FL 34205. **Seating Capacity:** 6,562. **Location:** U.S. 41 to 17th Ave, west to 9th Street.
**Complex/Hotel Address:** Pirate City, 1701 27th St. E., Bradenton, FL 34208. Telephone: (941) 747-3031. FAX: (941) 747-9549.
**Minor League Clubs**
**Complex/Hotel Address:** Same as major league club.

## ST. LOUIS CARDINALS
**Major League Club**
**Complex Address (first year):** Roger Dean Stadium

(1998), 4795 University Dr., Jupiter, FL 33458. Telephone: (561) 775-1818. FAX: (561) 799-1380. **Seating Capacity:** 6,864. **Location:** I-95 to exit 58, east on Donald Ross Road for 1/4 mile.
**Hotel Address:** Embassy Suites, 4350 PGA Blvd., Palm Beach Gardens, FL 33410. Telephone: (561) 622-1000.
**Minor League Clubs**
**Complex:** Same as major league club. **Hotel:** Doubletree Hotel, 4431 PGA Blvd., Palm Beach Gardens, FL 33410. Telephone: (561) 622-2260.

## TAMPA BAY DEVIL RAYS
**Major League Club**
**Stadium Address (first year):** Progress Energy Park/Home of Al Lang Field (1998), 180 Second Ave. SE, St. Petersburg, FL 33701. Telephone: (727) 825-3137. FAX: (727) 825-3167. **Seating Capacity:** 6,438. **Location:** I-275 to exit 23A, left on First Street South to Second Avenue South, stadium on right.
**Complex/Hotel Address:** Raymond A. Naimoli Complex, 7901 30th Ave. N., St. Petersburg, FL 33710. Telephone: (727) 384-5517.
**Minor League Clubs**
**Complex/Hotel Address:** Same as major league club.

## TORONTO BLUE JAYS
**Major League Club**
**Stadium Address (first year):** Knology Park (1977), 373 Douglas Ave. #A, Dunedin, FL 34698. Telephone: (727) 733-9302. **Seating Capacity:** 5,509. **Location:** From I-275, north on Highway 19, left on Sunset Point Road for 4 miles, right on Douglas Avenue, stadium one mile on right.
**Minor League Clubs**
**Complex Address:** Bobby Mattick Training Center at Englebert Complex, 1700 Solon Ave., Dunedin, FL 34698. Telephone: (727) 743-8007. **Hotel Address:** Red Roof Inn, 3200 U.S. 19 N., Clearwater, FL 34684. Telephone: (727) 786-2529.

## WASHINGTON NATIONALS
**Major League Club**
**Complex Address (first year):** Space Coast Stadium (2003), 5800 Stadium Pkwy., Viera, FL 32940. Telephone: (321) 633-9200. **Seating Capacity:** 7,200. **Location:** I-95 southbound to Fiske Blvd. (exit 74), south on Fiske/Stadium Parkway to stadium; I-95 northbound to State Road #509/Wickham Road (exit 73), left off exit, right on Lake Andrew Drive; turn right on Stadium Parkway, stadium is 1/2 mile on left
**Hotel Address:** Courtyard by Marriott-Cocoa Beach, 3435 North Atlantic Ave, Cocoa Beach, FL, 32931 Telephone: (321) 784-4800.
**Minor League Clubs**
**Complex Address:** Carl Barger Complex, 5600 Stadium Pkwy., Viera, FL 32940. **Telephone:** (321) 633-8119. **Hotel Address:** Imperial Hotel & Conference Center, 8298 N. Wickman Rd., Viera, FL 32940. Telephone: (321) 255-0077.

# MEDIA
## INFO

# LOCAL MEDIA
## INFORMATION

**AMERICAN LEAGUE**

### BALTIMORE ORIOLES
**Radio Announcers:** Joe Angel, Jim Hunter, Fred Manfra. **Flagship Station:** Unavailable.
**TV Announcers:** Jim Hunter, Fred Manfra, Jim Palmer, Buck Martinez. **Flagship Station:** Mid-Atlantic Sports Network (MASN), Comcast SportsNet (regional cable).
**NEWSPAPERS, Daily Coverage (*national/beat writers):** Baltimore Sun (*Dan Connolly, Jeff Zerbiec), Washington Post (Jorge Arangure, *Dave Sheinin). **MLB.com:** Spencer Fordin.

### BOSTON RED SOX
**Radio Announcers:** Joe Castiglione, Jerry Trupiano. **Flagship Station:** WEEI 850-AM.
**TV Announcers:** Don Orsillo, Jerry Remy. **Flagship Stations:** WSBK 38, New England Sports Network (regional cable).
**NEWSPAPERS, Daily Coverage (*national/beat writers):** Boston Globe (Gordon Edes, Chris Snow, *Larry Whiteside), Boston Herald (Jeff Horrigan, Tony Massarotti, Michael Silverman), Providence Journal (Steve Krasner, Sean McAdam), Worcester Telegram & Gazette (Bill Ballou, Phil O'Neill), Hartford Courant (Paul Doyle, Dave Heuschkel). **MLB.com:** Ian Browne.

### CHICAGO WHITE SOX
**Radio Announcers:** John Rooney, Ed Farmer. **Flagship Station:** WMVP/ESPN Radio 1000-AM.
**TV Announcers:** Ken Harrelson, Darrin Jackson. **Flagship Stations:** WGN TV-9, WCIU-TV, Comcast Sports Net (regional cable).
**NEWSPAPERS, Daily Coverage (*national/beat writers):** Chicago Sun-Times (Doug Padilla), Chicago Tribune (Bob Foltman, *Phil Rogers), Arlington Heights Daily Herald (Scot Gregor), Daily Southtown (Joe Cowley). **MLB.com:** Scott Merkin, Damon Young.

### CLEVELAND INDIANS
**Radio Announcers:** Tom Hamilton, Mike Hegan, Matt Underwood. **Flagship Station:** WTAM 1100-AM.
**TV Announcers:** Rick Manning, John Sanders, Mike Hegan. **Flagship Station:** Fox Sports Net.
**NEWSPAPERS, Daily Coverage (beat writers):** Cleveland Plain Dealer (Paul Hoynes), Lake County News-Herald (Jim Ingraham), Akron Beacon-Journal (Sheldon Ocker), Canton Repository (Andy Call). **MLB.com:** Anthony Castrovince.

### DETROIT TIGERS
**Radio Announcers:** Dan Dickerson, Jim Price. **Flagship Station:** WXYT 1270-AM.
**TV Announcers:** Rod Allen, Mario Impemba. **Flagship Station:** Fox Sports Net Detroit (regional cable).
**NEWSPAPERS, Daily Coverage (beat writers):** Detroit Free Press (John Lowe), Detroit News (Tom Gage), Oakland Press (Crystal Evola, Pat Caputo), Booth Newspapers (Danny Knobler), Windsor Star (Jim Parker). **MLB.com:** Jason Beck.

### KANSAS CITY ROYALS
**Radio Announcers:** Ryan Lefebvre, Denny Matthews. **Flagship Station:** WHB 810-AM.
**TV Announcers:** Bob Davis, Paul Splittorff. **Flagship Stations:** Royals Television Network.
**NEWSPAPERS, Daily Coverage (beat writers):** Kansas City Star (Bob Dutton). **MLB.com:** Dick Kaegel.

### LOS ANGELES ANGELS OF ANAHEIM
**Radio Announcers:** Rory Markas, Terry Smith. Spanish—Ivan Lara, Jose Mota. **Flagship Station:** KSPN 710-AM, KTNQ 1090-AM (Spanish).
**TV Announcers:** Rex Hudler, Steve Physioc. **Flagship Stations:** FSN West (regional cable).
**NEWSPAPERS, Daily Coverage (*national/beat writers):** Long Beach Press Telegram, Los Angeles Times (Mike DiGiovanna, *Tim Brown), Orange County Register (Mark Saxon), Riverside Press Enterprise (Matt Hurst), San Gabriel Valley Tribune (Doug Padilla), Inland Valley Daily Bulletin. **MLB.com:** Mike Scarr.

### MINNESOTA TWINS
**Radio Announcers:** Herb Carneal, John Gordon, Dan Gladden. **Flagship Station:** WCCO 830-AM.
**TV Announcers:** Bert Blyleven, Dick Bremer. **Flagship Station:** Fox Sports Net North.
**NEWSPAPERS, Daily Coverage (beat writers):** St. Paul Pioneer Press (Jason Williams), Minneapolis Star Tribune (LaVelle Neal). **MLB.com:** Kelly Thesier.

### NEW YORK YANKEES
**Radio Announcers:** John Sterling, Suzyn Waldman. **Flagship Station:** WCBS 880-AM.
**TV Announcers:** Michael Kay, Jim Kaat, Ken Singleton, Paul O'Neill. **Flagship Stations:** YES Network.
**NEWSPAPERS, Daily Coverage (*national/beat writers):** New York Daily News (Sam Borden, *John Harper, *Bill Madden), New York Post (George King, *Joel Sherman), New York Times (*Murray Chass, *Jack Curry, Tyler Kepner), Newark Star-Ledger (Dan Graziano, Ed Price), The Bergen Record (Pete Caldera, *Bob Klapisch), Newsday (Jim Baumbach, Ken Davidoff, *Jon Heyman), Hartford Courant (Dom Amore), The Journal News (Pete Abraham). **MLB.com:** Mark Feinsand, Tom Singer.

### OAKLAND ATHLETICS
**Radio Announcers:** Vince Cotroneo, Ray Fosse, Ken Korach. **Flagship Station:** Unavailable.
**TV Announcers:** Ray Fosse, Tim Roye, Glen Kuiper. **Flagship Stations:** KICU, FOX Sports Net Bay Area (regional cable).
**NEWSPAPERS, Daily Coverage (*national/beat writers):** San Francisco Chronicle (*John Shea, Susan Slusser), Oakland Tribune (Josh Suchon), Contra Costa Times/San Jose Mercury News (Joe Roderick), Sacramento Bee (Paul

Gutierrez), Santa Rosa Press Democrat (Jeff Fletcher). **MLB.com:** Mychael Urban.

## SEATTLE MARINERS

**TV/Radio Announcers:** Ron Fairly, Dave Henderson, Dave Niehaus, Rick Rizzs, Dave Valle.
**Flagship Stations:** KOMO 1000-AM (radio), FOX Sports Net Northwest (TV).
**NEWSPAPERS, Daily Coverage (\*national/beat writers):** Seattle Times (Bob Finnigan, \*Larry Stone), Seattle Post-Intelligencer (\*John Hickey), Tacoma News Tribune (Larry LaRue), The Everett Herald (Kirby Arnold), Kyodo News (Keizo Konishi), Nikkan Sports (Mamoru Shikama). **MLB.com:** Doug Miller.

## TAMPA BAY DEVIL RAYS

**Radio Announcers:** Andy Freed, Dave Wills. **Flagship Station:** WHNZ 1250 AM.
**TV Announcers:** Dewayne Staats, Joe Magrane. **Flagship Stations:** PAX-TV, Fox SportsNet (regional cable).
**NEWSPAPERS, Daily Coverage (beat writers):** St. Petersburg Times (Marc Topkin), Tampa Tribune (Eduardo Encina), Bradenton Herald (Roger Mooney), Port Charlotte Sun-Herald (John Fineran), Lakeland Ledger (Dick Scanlon), Sarasota Herald-Tribune (Dennis Maffezoli). **MLB.com:** Bill Chastain.

## TEXAS RANGERS

**Radio Announcers:** Eric Nadel, Victor Rojas; Spanish—Eleno Ornelas, Jose Guzman. **Flagship Station:** KRLD 1080-AM, KESS 1270-AM (Spanish).
**TV Announcers:** Josh Lewin, Tom Grieve. **Flagship Stations:** KDFI, KDFW, Fox Sports Southwest (regional cable).
**NEWSPAPERS, Daily Coverage (beat writers):** Dallas Morning News (Evan Grant, Ben Shpigel), Fort Worth Star-Telegram (Kathleen O'Brien). **MLB.com:** T.R. Sullivan.

## TORONTO BLUE JAYS

**Radio Announcers:**, Jerry Howarth, Warren Sawkiw, Mike Wilner. **Flagship Station:** THE FAN 590-AM.
**TV Announcers:** Rogers SportsNet—Jamie Campbell, Pat Tabler, Rance Mulliniks, Darrin Fletcher. TSN—Rod Black, Pat Tabler. **Flagship Stations:** Rogers SportsNet, The Sports Network.
**NEWSPAPERS, Daily Coverage (\*national/beat writers):** Toronto Sun (Mike Rutsey, \*Bob Elliott, Mike Ganter), Toronto Star (Geoff Baker, \*Richard Griffin, Alan Ryan, Mark Zwolinski), Globe and Mail (Larry Millson, \*Jeff Blair), National Post (John Lott). **MLB.com:** Jordan Bastian.

# NATIONAL LEAGUE

## ARIZONA DIAMONDBACKS

**Radio Announcers:** Thom Brennaman, Tom Candiotti, Jeff Munn, Greg Schulte; Spanish—Miguel Quintana, Oscar Soria, Richard Saenz. **Flagship Stations:** KTAR 620-AM, KSUN 1400-AM (Spanish).
**TV Announcers:** Thom Brennaman, Mark Grace, Joe Garagiola, Greg Schulte. **Flagship Stations:** KTVK-TV 3, FSN Arizona (regional cable).
**NEWSPAPERS, Daily Coverage (beat writers):** Arizona Republic (Bob McManaman), East Valley Tribune (Jack Magruder), Arizona Daily Star, Tucson Citizen (Ken Brazzle). **MLB.com:** Steve Gilbert.

## ATLANTA BRAVES

**Radio Announcers:** Skip Caray, Chip Caray, Joe Simpson, Don Sutton, Pete Van Wieren. **Flagship Station:** WGST 640-AM.
**TV Announcers:** TBS—Skip Caray, Chip Caray, Joe Simpson, Don Sutton, Pete Van Wieren; Fox Sports Net—Bob Rathbun, Jeff Torborg. **Flagship Stations:** TBS (national cable); Fox Sports Net South, Turner South (regional cable).
**NEWSPAPERS, Daily Coverage (\*national/beat writers):** Atlanta Journal-Constitution (\*Guy Curtwright, Dave O'Brien), Morris News Service (\*Travis Haney). **MLB.com:** Mark Bowman.

## CHICAGO CUBS

**Radio Announcers:** Pat Hughes, Ron Santo. **Flagship Station:** WGN 720-AM.
**TV Announcers:** Len Kasper, Bob Brenly. **Flagship Stations:** WGN Channel 9 (national cable), Comcast Sports Net Chicago (regional cable), WCIU-TV Channel 26.
**NEWSPAPERS, Daily Coverage (\*national/beat writers):** Chicago Tribune (\*Phil Rogers, Paul Sullivan), Chicago Sun-Times (Mike Kiley), Arlington Heights Daily Herald (Bruce Miles), Daily Southtown (Jeff Vorva). **MLB.com:** Carrie Muskat.

## CINCINNATI REDS

**Radio Announcers:** Marty Brennaman, Steve Stewart, Joe Nuxhall. **Flagship Station:** WLW 700-AM.
**TV Announcers:** George Grande, Chris Welsh. **Flagship Station:** FSN Ohio (regional cable).
**NEWSPAPERS, Daily Coverage (beat writers):** Cincinnati Enquirer (John Fay), Cincinnati Post (Marc Lancaster), Dayton Daily News (Hal McCoy), Columbus Dispatch (Jim Massie). **MLB.com:** Mark Sheldon.

## COLORADO ROCKIES

**Radio Announcers:** Jack Corrigan, Jeff Kingery. **Flagship Station:** KOA 850-AM.
**TV Announcers:** Drew Goodman, George Frazier. **Flagship Stations:** KTVD Channel 20 (UPN), FSN Rocky Mountain (regional cable).
**NEWSPAPERS, Daily Coverage (beat writers):** Rocky Mountain News (\*Tracy Ringolsby, Jack Etkin), Denver Post (Troy Renck, Patrick Saunders). **MLB.com:** Thomas Harding.

## FLORIDA MARLINS

**Radio Announcers:** Dave Van Horne, Roxy Bernstein. **Spanish:** Felo Ramirez, Yiky Quintana. **Flagship Stations:** WQAM 560-AM, WQBA 1140-AM (Spanish).
**TV Announcers:** Tommy Hutton. Rich Waltz. **Flagship Stations:** FSN Florida, Sun Sports (regional cable).
**NEWSPAPERS, Daily Coverage (\*national/beat writers):** Miami Herald (\*Kevin Baxter, Clark Spencer), Fort Lauderdale Sun-Sentinel (\*Mike Berardino, Juan Rodriguez), Palm Beach Post (Joe Capozzi). Spanish—El Nuevo Herald (Jorge Ebro). **MLB.com:** Joe Frisaro.

## HOUSTON ASTROS

**Radio Announcers:** Brett Dolan, Milo Hamilton, Dave Raymond; Spanish—Francisco Ernesto Ruiz, Alex Trevino. **Flagship Stations:** KTRH 740-AM, KLAT 1010-AM (Spanish).

**TV Announcers:** Bill Brown, Jim Deshaies, Larry Dierker. **Flagship Station:** Fox Sports Net (regional cable).

**NEWSPAPERS, Daily Coverage (beat writers):** Houston Chronicle (Jesus Ortiz, Brian McTaggart), The Herald Coaster (Bill Hartman). **MLB.com:** Alyson Footer, Jim Molony.

## LOS ANGELES DODGERS

**Radio Announcers:** Vin Scully, Rick Monday, Charley Steiner; Spanish—Jaime Jarrin, Fernando Valenzuela, Pepe Yniguez. **Flagship Stations:** KFWB 980-AM, KWKW 1330-AM (Spanish).

**TV Announcers:** Vin Scully, Steve Lyons, Charley Steiner. **Flagship Stations:** KCAL 9, Fox Sports Net 2 (regional cable).

**NEWSPAPERS, Daily Coverage (*national/beat writers):** Los Angeles Times (*Tim Brown, Steve Henson), South Bay Daily Breeze (Bill Cizek), Los Angeles Daily News (Tony Jackson), Orange County Register (Bill Plunkett), Riverside Press-Enterprise (Allison Otto). Spanish—La Opinion (Carlos Alvarado). **MLB.com:** Ken Gurnick.

## MILWAUKEE BREWERS

**Radio Announcers:** Bob Uecker, Jim Powell. **Flagship Station:** WTMJ 620-AM.

**TV Announcers:** Bill Schroeder, Daron Sutton. **Flagship Station:** Fox Sports Net North.

**NEWSPAPERS, Daily Coverage (beat writers):** Milwaukee Journal Sentinel (Tom Haudricourt, Drew Olson), Wisconsin State Journal (Vic Feuerherd), Capital Times (Dennis Semrau). **MLB.com:** Adam McCalvy.

## NEW YORK METS

**Radio Announcers:** Howie Rose, Tom McCarthy, Ed Coleman. **Flagship Station:** WFAN 660-AM.

**TV Announcers:** Gary Cohen, Keith Hernandez, Ron Darling, Ralph Kiner, Siafa Lewis. **Flagship Stations:** WPIX-TV, Sports Net New York (regional cable).

**NEWSPAPERS, Daily Coverage (*national/beat writers):** New York Times (*Murray Chass, *Jack Curry, Ben Shpigel), New York Daily News (*Bill Madden, *John Harper, Adam Rubin), New York Post (*Joel Sherman, Mark Hale), Newsday (*Jon Heyman, *Ken Davidoff, Dave Lennon), Newark Star-Ledger (*Dan Graziano, Don Burke), The Bergen Record (*Bob Klapisch, Steve Popper), The News Journal (John Delcos). **MLB.com:** Marty Noble.

## PHILADELPHIA PHILLIES

**Radio Announcers:** Larry Andersen, Scott Graham, Harry Kalas, Chris Wheeler. **Flagship Stations:** WPHT 1210-AM, WIP 610-AM.

**TV Announcers:** Larry Andersen, Harry Kalas, Chris Wheeler. **Flagship Stations:** WPSG UPN-57, Comcast SportsNet (regional cable).

**NEWSPAPERS, Daily Coverage (*national/beat writers):** Philadelphia Inquirer (Todd Zolecki, *Jim Salisbury), Philadelphia Daily News (*Paul Hagen, Marcus Hayes), Bucks County Courier Times (Randy Miller), Delaware County Times (Dennis Deitch), Wilmington News-Journal (Scott Lauber). **MLB.com:** Ken Mandel.

## PITTSBURGH PIRATES

**Radio Announcers:** Steve Blass, Greg Brown, Lanny Frattare, Bob Walk, John Wehner. **Flagship Station:** KDKA 1020-AM.

**TV Announcers:** Steve Blass, Greg Brown, Lanny Frattare, Bob Walk, John Wehner. **Flagship Station:** Fox Sports Net Pittsburgh (regional cable).

**NEWSPAPERS, Daily Coverage (beat writers):** Pittsburgh Post-Gazette (Dejan Kovacevic), Pittsburgh Tribune-Review (Rob Rossi), Beaver County Times (John Perrotto). **MLB.com:** Ed Eagle.

## ST. LOUIS CARDINALS

**Radio Announcers:** Mike Shannon, John Rooney. **Flagship Station:** KTRS 550-AM.

**TV Announcers:** Joe Buck , Al Hrabosky, Dan McLaughlin, Rick Horton, Bob Carpenter. **Flagship Stations:** KPLR Channel 11, Fox Sports Midwest (regional cable).

**NEWSPAPER, Daily Coverage (beat writers):** St. Louis Post-Dispatch (Joe Strauss, Rick Hummel), Belleville, Ill., News-Democrat (Joe Ostermeier, David Wilhelm). **MLB.com:** Matthew Leach.

## SAN DIEGO PADRES

**Radio Announcers:** Ted Leitner, Jerry Coleman, Tim Flannery. **Flagship Station:** XPRS 1090-AM.

**TV Announcers:** Matt Vasgersian, Mark Grant, Tony Gwynn. **Flagship Station:** Channel 4 Padres (cable).

**NEWSPAPERS, Daily Coverage (beat writers):** San Diego Union-Tribune (Tom Krasovic, Bill Center), North County Times (Brian Hiro, John Maffei). **MLB.com:** Lyle Spencer.

## SAN FRANCISCO GIANTS

**Radio Announcers:** Mike Krukow, Duane Kuiper, Jon Miller, Greg Papa, Dave Flemming. **Flagship Station:** KNBR 680-AM (English); KLOK-1170 AM (Spanish).

**TV Announcers:** FSN Bay Area—Mike Krukow, Duane Kuiper; KTVU-FOX 2—Jon Miller, Mike Krukow, Duane Kuiper, Greg Papa. **Flagship Stations:** KTVU-FOX 2, FSN Bay Area (regional cable).

**NEWSPAPERS, Daily Coverage (*national/beat writers):** San Francisco Chronicle (Henry Schulman, *John Shea), San Jose Mercury News (Chris Haft), Sacramento Bee (Nick Peters), Oakland Tribune (Andrew Baggarly), Santa Rosa Press Democrat (Jeff Fletcher). **MLB.com:** Rich Draper.

## WASHINGTON NATIONALS

**Radio Announcers:** Charlie Slowes, Dave Jageler. **Flagship Station:** WTOP 1500-AM/107.7-FM.

**TV Announcers:** Unavailable. **Flagship Station:** Mid-Atlantic Sports Network (MASN).

**NEWSPAPERS, Daily Coverage (beat writers):** Baltimore Sun (Jeff Barker, Dan Connolly), The Free-Lance Star (Todd Jacobson), Washington Post (Barry Svrluga, Dave Sheinin), Washington Times (Mark Zuckerman, Ken Wright). **MLB.com:** Bill Ladson.

# NATIONAL MEDIA
## INFORMATION

## BASEBALL STATISTICS

### ELIAS SPORTS BUREAU INC.
Official Major League Statistician

**Mailing Address**: 500 Fifth Ave., Suite 2140, New York, NY 10110. **Telephone**: (212) 869-1530. **FAX**: (212) 354-0980. **Website**: www.esb.com.
**President**: Seymour Siwoff.
**Executive Vice President**: Steve Hirdt. **Vice President**: Peter Hirdt. **Data Processing Manager**: Chris Thorn.

### MAJOR LEAGUE BASEBALL ADVANCED MEDIA
Official Minor League Statistician

**Mailing Address**: 75 Ninth Ave., New York, NY 10011. **Telephone**: (212) 485-3444. FAX: (212) 485-3456. **Director, Minor League Baseball Advanced Media**: Misann Ellmaker. **Deputy Project Manager, Minor League Baseball Advanced Media**: Nathan Blackmon. **Senior Project Manager, Minor League Baseball Advanced Media**: Sammy Arena. **Assistant Managing Editor**: Matthew Gould. **Senior Manager, Statistics Operations**: Chris Lentine. **Senior Reporter**: Jonathan Mayo. **Reporter**: Kevin Czerwinski.

### STATS, Inc.
**Mailing Address**: 8130 Lehigh Ave., Morton Grove, IL 60053. **Telephone**: (847) 583-2100. **FAX**: (847) 470-9140. **Website**: biz.stats.com.
**Chief Executive Officer**: Gary Walrath. **Senior Vice Presidents**: Steve Byrd, Robert Schur. **Director, Sales**: Jim Capuano, Greg Kirkorsky. **Director, Marketing**: Walter Lis. **Director, Sports Operations**: Allan Spear. **Manager, Baseball Operations**: Jeff Chernow.

## TELEVISION NETWORKS

### ESPN/ESPN2

- Sunday Night Baseball
- Monday Night Baseball
- Wednesday Night Doubleheaders
- Opening Day, Holiday Games
- Spring Training Games
- Division Series, 2006
- ESPN DayGame, Baseball Tonight
- Home Run Derby, All-Star Game Programming

**Mailing Address, ESPN Connecticut**: ESPN Plaza, 935 Middle St., Bristol, CT 06010. **Telephone**: (860) 766-2000. **FAX**: (860) 766-2213.
**Mailing Address, ESPN New York Executive Offices**: 77 W. 66th St., New York, NY, 10023. **Telephone**: (212) 456-7777. **FAX**: (212) 456-2930.
**President, ESPN/ABC Sports**: George Bodenheimer.
**Executive Vice President, Administration**: Ed Durso.
**Executive VP, Content**: John Skipper. **Executive VP, Executive Editor**: John Walsh. **Executive VP, Studio/Remote Production**: Norby Williamson.
**Senior VP, Programming/Acquisitions**: Len DeLuca. **VP, Programming**: Mike Ryan.
**Senior VP, Remote Production**: Jed Drake. **Senior Coordinating Producer, Remote Production**: Tim Scanlan. **Coordinating Producer, Remote Production**: Patrick Cavanagh.
**Senior Coordinating Producer, Baseball Tonight**: Jay Levy.
**Senior VP, Corporate Communications/Outreach**: Rosa Gatti. **Senior VP, Consumer Communications**: Chris LaPlaca. **Senior Director, Media Relations**: Diane Lamb. **Senior Publicist**: Nate Smeltz.

### ESPN CLASSIC, ESPNEWS
**Vice President, Programming/Acquisitions**: Crowley Sullivan.

### ESPN INTERNATIONAL, ESPN DEPORTES
**Executive Vice President/Managing Director, ESPN International**: Russell Wolff.
**Senior VP, ESPN Radio and ESPN Deportes**: Traug Keller.
**General Manager, ESPN Deportes**: Lino Garcia.
**Senior VP, International Productions, ESPN Classic/ESPNEWS**: Jodi Markley. **Vice President, International Production/Operations**: Chris Calcinari.

### FOX SPORTS

- Saturday Game of the Week
- All-Star Game, 2006
- Division Series, 2006

■ American League Championship Series, 2006
■ National League Championship Series, 2006
■ World Series, 2006
**Mailing Address, Los Angeles:** Fox Network Center, Building 101, Fifth floor, 10201 West Pico Blvd., Los Angeles, CA 90035. **Telephone:** (310) 369-6000. **FAX:** (310) 969-6700.
**Mailing Address, New York:** 1211 Avenue of the Americas, 28th Floor, New York, NY 10036. **Telephone:** (212) 556-2500. **FAX:** (212) 354-6902. **Website:** www.foxsports.com.
**Chairman, Chief Executive Officer, Fox Sports Television Group:** David Hill. **President/Executive Producer:** Ed Goren. **Executive Vice President, Production/Coordinating Studio Producer:** Scott Ackerson. **Executive VP, Production/Senior Producer: Bill Brown. Senior VP, Production:** Jack Simmons. **Senior VP, Operations/MLB on Fox:** Jerry Steinberg. **Studio Producer, MLB on Fox:** Gary Lang. **Studio Director, MLB on Fox:** Bob Levy.
**Senior VP, Communcations:** Lou D'Ermilio. **VP, Communications:** Dan Bell. **Manager, Communications:** Tim Buckman. **Publicist:** Ileana Pena.
**Broadcasters:** Kenny Albert, Thom Brennaman, Joe Buck, Josh Lewin, Kevin Kennedy, Steve Lyons, Tim McCarver, Jeanne Zelasko.

## FOX SPORTS NET

■ Regional Coverage
**Mailing Address:** 10201 W. Pico Blvd., Building 101, Los Angeles, CA 90035. **Telephone:** (310) 369-1000. **FAX:** (310) 969-6049.
**President, Chief Executive Officer/Fox Sports Television Group:** David Hill. **President, Fox Sports Net/Fox Sports Cable Networks:** Bob Thompson. **Chief Operating Officer, Fox Sports Net:** Randy Freer. **President, Advertising Sales, Fox Cable Networks:** Lou LaTorre. **Executive VP, Programming/Production:** George Greenberg. **Executive Producer, Event Coverage:** Doug Sellers. **Manager, Communications:** Justin Simon. **Publicist:** Emily Corliss. **FSN News Manager:** Geoffrey Birchfield.

## Other Television Networks

### ABC SPORTS
**Mailing Address:** 47 W. 66th St., New York, NY 10023. **Telephone:** (212) 456-7777. **FAX:** (212) 456-4317.
**President, ABC Sports:** George Bodenheimer. **President:** George Bodenheimer. **Senior Vice President, Programming:** Loren Matthews.

### CBS SPORTS
**Mailing Address:** 51 W. 52nd St., New York, NY 10019. **Telephone:** (212) 975-5230. **FAX:** (212) 975-4063.
**President, CBS Sports:** Sean McManus. **Executive VP/Executive Producer:** Tony Petitti. **Senior Vice Presidents, Programming:** Mike Aresco, Rob Correa. **Vice President, Communications:** Leslie Anne Wade.

### CNN SPORTS
**Mailing Address:** One CNN Center, Atlanta, GA 30303. **Telephone:** (404) 878-1600. **FAX:** (404) 878-0011.
**Vice President, Production:** Jeffrey Green.

### HBO SPORTS
**Mailing Address:** 1100 Avenue of the Americas, New York, NY 10036. **Telephone:** (212) 512-1000. **FAX:** (212) 512-1751.
**President, HBO Sports:** Ross Greenburg.

### NBC SPORTS
**Mailing Address:** 30 Rockefeller Plaza, Suite 1558, New York, NY 10112. **Telephone:** (212) 664-2014. **FAX:** (212) 664-6365.
**Chairman, NBC Sports:** Dick Ebersol. **President, NBC Sports:** Ken Schanzer.
**Vice President, Sports Communications:** Mike McCarley.

## Superstations

### ROGERS SPORTSNET (Canada)
**Mailing Address:** 333 Bloor St. East, Toronto Ontario M4W 1G9. **Telephone:** (416) 332-5600. **FAX:** (416) 332-5629. **Website:** www.sportsnet.ca.
**President, Rogers Media:** Tony Viner. **President, Rogers Sportsnet:** Doug Beeforth. **Vice President, Communications:** Jan Innes. **Director, Communications/Promotions:** Dave Rashford.

### THE SPORTS NETWORK (Canada)
**Mailing Address:** Bell Globemedia Inc., 9 Channel Nine Court, Scarborough, Ontario M1S 4B5. **Telephone:** (416) 332-5000. **FAX:** (416) 332-4337. **Website:** www.tsn.ca
**Executive Producer, News:** Marc Milliere. **President, TSN:** Phil King. **Executive Producer:** Jim Marshall. **VP, Programming and Production:** Rick Chisholm, **VP, Marketing:** Adam Ashton. **Communications Director:** Andrea Goldstein. **Executive Producer, tsn.ca:** Mike Day.

### TURNER SPORTS
(Atlanta Braves)
**Mailing Address:** One CNN Center, P.O. Box 105366, Atlanta, GA 30348. **Telephone:** (404) 827-1700. **FAX:** (404) 827-1339. **Website:** www.tbs.com.
**Coordinating Producer:** Glenn Diamond. **Senior Director:** Garry Lehman. **Vice President, Production:** Jeff Behnke.

## WGN
(Chicago Cubs, Chicago White Sox)
**Mailing Address:** 2501 W Bradley Place, Chicago, IL 60618. **Telephone:** (773) 528-2311. **FAX:** (773) 528-6050. **Website:** www.wgntv.com.
**Director, Programming:** Bob Vorwald.

# RADIO NETWORKS

## ESPN RADIO
- Game of the Week
- Sunday Night Baseball
- All-Star Game, 2006
- Division Series, 2006
- League Championship Series, 2006
- World Series, 2006

**Address:** ESPN Plaza, 935 Middle St., Bristol, CT 06010. **Telephone:** (860) 766-2000, (800) 999-9985. **FAX:** (860) 589-5523. **Website:** espnradio.espn.go.com/espnradio/index.

**General Manager, ESPN Radio Network:** Bruce Gilbert. **Senior Director, Operations:** Keith Goralski. **Senior Director, Programming:** Peter Gianesini. **Senior Director, Marketing/Integration:** Freddy Rolon. **Executive Producer, Remote Broadcasts:** John Martin. **News Editor:** Peter Ciccone. **Program Directors:** Justin Craig, Louise Cornetta, Larry Gifford, David Zaslowsky. **Chief Engineer:** Tom Evans. **Administrative Coordinator:** Janet Alden. **VP/Sports, ABC Radio Network and VP/Affiliate Relations:** T.J. Lambert.

**Executive Producer, Major League Baseball on ESPN Radio:** John Martin.

**Commentators:** Dan Shulman, Dave Campbell, Jim Durham, Dave Barnett, Harold Reynolds, Jon Miller, Joe Morgan, Joe D'Ambrosio.

## MLB RADIO
**Mailing Address:** 75 Ninth Ave., New York, NY 10011. **Telephone:** (212) 485-3444. **FAX:** (212) 485-3456. **E-Mail Address:** radio@mlb.com. **Website:** www.mlb.com, www.mlbradio.net.
**Hosts:** Seth Everett, Billy Sample, Darryl Hamilton, Jim Leyritz, Vinny Micucci. **Contributor:** Brian McRae. **Coordinator:** Craig Chamides. **Senior Producer:** Mike Siano. **Producers:** Robby DeMarco, Mike Dillon, Dan Gentile.

## XM SATELLITE RADIO
- 24-hour MLB Home Plate channel (baseball talk)
- MLB live play-by-play for spring training, regular season, playoffs, World Series
- MLB En Espanol channel (Spanish language play-by-play and baseball talk)

**Mailing Address:** 1500 Eckington Place NE, Washington, DC 20002. **Telephone:** (202) 380-4000. **FAX:** 202-380-4500. **E-Mail Address:** mlb@xmradio.com. **Website:** www.xmradio.com.

**Executive Vice President, Programming:** Eric Logan. **Vice President, Talk Programming:** Kevin Straley. **Senior VP, Corporate Communications:** Nathaniel Brown. **VP, Corporate Affairs:** Chance Patterson. **Director, MLB Programming:** Chuck Dickemann. **Executive Producer, MLB Home Plate Channel:** Matt Fishman. **Commentators:** Joe Castellano, Rob Dibble, Kevin Kennedy, Ronnie Lane, Buck Martinez, Mark Patrick, Billy Ripken, Cal Ripken Jr., Charley Steiner, Chuck Wilson.

## SPORTING NEWS RADIO NETWORK
**Mailing Address:** 1935 Techny St., Suite 18, Northbrook IL 60062. **Telephone:** (847) 509-1661. **Producers Line:** (800) 224-2004. **FAX:** (847) 509-1677. **Website:** www.sportingnewsradio.com.
**President:** Clancy Woods. **Executive Vice President, Sales:** John Coulter. **Acting Director, Affiliate Relations:** Ryan Williams. **Program Director:** Matt Nahigian. **Sports Director:** Randy Merkin. **Executive Producer:** Jen Williams.

## SPORTS BYLINE USA
**Mailing Address:** 300 Broadway, Suite 8, San Francisco, CA 94133. **Telephone:** (415) 434-8300. **Guest Line:** (800) 358-4457. **Studio Line:** (800) 878-7529. **FAX:** (415) 391-2569. **E-Mail Address:** alex@sportsbyline.com. **Website:** www.sportsbyline.com.
**President:** Darren Peck. **Executive Producer:** Alex Murillo.

# NEWS ORGANIZATIONS

## ASSOCIATED PRESS
**Mailing Address:** 450 W. 33rd St., New York, NY 10010. **Telephone:** (212) 621-1630. **FAX:** (212) 621-1639. **Website:** www.ap.org.
**Sports Editor:** Terry Taylor. **Deputy Sports Editor:** Ben Walker. **Sports Photo Editor:** Mike Feldman. **Baseball Writers:** Ron Blum, Mike Fitzpatrick.

## BLOOMBERG SPORTS
**Address:** 731 Lexington Ave., New York, NY 10022. **Telephone:** (212) 617-2301. **FAX:** (917) 369-5633.
**Sports Editor:** Jay Beberman. **Deputy Sports Editor:** Mike Sillup. **Baseball Writer:** Danielle Sessa.

## CANADIAN PRESS
**Mailing Address, Toronto:** 36 King St. East, Toronto, Ontario M5C 2L9. **Mailing Address**, Montreal: 215 Saint-Jacques St., Suite 100, Montreal, Quebec H2Y 1M6. **Telephone:** (416) 507-2154 (Toronto), (514) 985-7240 (Montreal). **FAX:** (416) 507-2074 (Toronto), (514) 282-6915 (Montreal). **E-Mail Address:** sports@cp.org.
**Sports Editor:** Neil Davidson. **Baseball Writer, Toronto:** Shi Davidi. **Baseball Writer, Montreal:** Bill Beacon.

## CBS SPORTSLINE.com
**Mailing Address:** 2200 W. Cypress Creek, Fort Lauderdale, FL 33309. **Website:** cbs.sportsline.com.
**Senior Writer:** Scott Miller.

## ESPN.com
**Mailing Address:** ESPN Plaza, Bristol, CT 06010. **Telephone:** (860) 766-2000.
**Editor-In-Chief:** Neal Scarborough. **Executive Editor:** Len Lampugnale. **Deputy Editor:** David Kull.

## ESPN/SPORTSTICKER
**Mailing Address:** ESPN Plaza, Building B, Fourth Floor, Bristol, CT 06010. **Telephone:** (860) 766-1899. **FAX:** (800) 336-0383. **E-Mail Address:** newsroom@sportsticker.com.
**General Manager:** Jim Morganthaler. **News Director:** Chris Bernucca. **Baseball Editor:** Jim Keller. **Manager, Customer Marketing/Communications:** Lou Monaco.
**Senior Bureau Manager:** Michael Walczak. **Bureau Managers:** Tom Diorio. **Associate Bureau Manager:** Ian Anderson. **Programmer Analysts:** John Foley, Walter Kent. **Historical Consultant:** Bill Weiss.

## FOX SPORTS.com
**Mailing Address:** 1440 Sepulveda Blvd., Los Angeles, CA. **Telephone:** (310) 444-8000. **FAX:** (310) 444-8180. **Website:** www.msn.foxsports.com.
**Senior Vice President/General Manager:** Ross Levinsohn.

## MLB ADVANCED MEDIA (MLB.COM)
**Office Address:** 75 Ninth Ave., 5th Floor, New York, NY 10011. **Telephone:** (212) 485-3444. **FAX:** (212) 485-3456.
**Chief Executive Officer:** Bob Bowman.
**Vice President, Marketing:** Kristen Fergason. **VP, Ticketing:** Heather Benz. **VP, Human Resources:** Leslie Knickerbocker. **Senior VP/Chief Technical Officer:** Joe Choti. **Senior VP, Corporate Communications:** Jim Gallagher. **Executive VP, E-Commerce and Sponsorships:** Noah Garden. **Executive VP/Editor-In-Chief, mlb.com:** Dinn Mann. **VP, Design:** Deck Rees.
**Senior VP/General Counsel:** Michael Mellis, **Executive VP, Business:** George Kliavkoff.

## SI.com
**Mailing Address:** 1271 Avenue of the Americas, 32nd Floor, New York, NY 10020. **Telephone:** (212) 522-1212. **FAX:** (212) 467-0339.
**Managing Editor:** Paul Fichtenbaum.

## PRESS ASSOCIATIONS

### BASEBALL WRITERS' ASSOCIATION OF AMERICA
**Mailing Address:** P.O. Box 610611, Bayside, NY 11361. **Telephone:** (718) 767-2582. **FAX:** (718) 767-2583. **E-Mail Address:** bbwaa@aol.com.
**President:** Peter Schmuck (Baltimore Sun). **Vice President:** Paul Hoynes (Cleveland Plain Dealer). **Secretary/Treasurer:** Jack O'Connell (BBWAA). **Board of Directors:** Joel Sherman (New York Post), Joe Strauss (St. Louis Post Dispatch), T.R. Sullivan (honorary), Marc Topkin (St. Petersburg Times).

### NATIONAL COLLEGIATE BASEBALL WRITERS ASSOCIATION
**Mailing Address:** 2201 Stemmons Fwy., 28th Floor, Dallas, TX 75207. **Telephone:** (214) 753-0102. **FAX:** (214) 753-0145. **E-Mail Address:** bo@big12sports.com.
**Executive Director, Newsletter Editor:** Bo Carter (Big 12 Conference).

## NEWSPAPERS/PERIODICALS

### USA TODAY
**Mailing Address:** 7950 Jones Branch Dr., McLean, VA 22108. **Telephones/Baseball Desk:** (703) 854-5286, 854-5954, 854-3706, 854-3744, 854-3746. **FAX:** (703) 854-2072. **Website:** www.usatoday.com.
**Publishing Frequency:** Daily (Monday-Friday).
**Baseball Editors:** Peter Barzilai, Gabe Lacques, Matt Cimento, John Tkach. **Baseball Columnist:** Hal Bodley. **Baseball Writers:** Mel Antonen, Rod Beaton, Mike Dodd, Gary Graves, Jorge Ortiz.

### THE SPORTING NEWS
**Mailing Address:** 10176 Corporate Square Dr., Suite 200, St. Louis, MO 63132. **Telephone:** (314) 997-7111. **FAX:** (314) 993-7726. **Website:** www.sportingnews.com.
**Publishing Frequency:** Weekly.
**Senior Vice President/Editorial Director:** John Rawlings. **Executive Editor:** Bob Hille. **Managing Editor:** Stan McNeal. **Senior Writer:** Ken Rosenthal. **Senior Editor:** Tom Gatto. **Senior Photo Editor:** Paul Nisely.

### SPORTS ILLUSTRATED
**Mailing Address:** 1271 Avenue of the Americas, New York, NY 10020. **Telephone:** (212) 522-1212. **FAX, Editorial:** (212) 522-4543. **FAX, Public Relations:** (212) 522-0747. **Website:** www.si.com.
**Publishing Frequency:** Weekly.
**Managing Editor:** Terry McDonnell. **Senior Editor:** Larry Burke. **Associate Editor:** B.J. Schecter. **Senior Writer:** Tom Verducci. **Staff Writer:** Danny Habib. **Writers/Reporters:** Albert Chen, Melissa Segura
**Vice President, Communications:** Art Berke.

### USA TODAY SPORTS WEEKLY
**Mailing Address:** 7950 Jones Branch Dr., McLean, VA 22108. **Telephone:** (800) 872-1415, (703) 854-6319. **FAX:**

(703) 854-2034. **Website**: www.usatoday.com.
**Publishing Frequency:** Weekly.
**Managing Editor:** Monte Lorell. **Senior Editor:** Lee Ivory. **Senior Assignment Editor:** Tim McQuay, **Baseball Editors:** Peter Barzilai, Steve Borelli, Gabe Laques. **Baseball Writers:** Steve DiMeglio, Bob Nightengale, Paul White, Lisa Winston.

## STREET AND SMITH'S SPORTS BUSINESS JOURNAL
**Mailing Address**: 120 W. Morehead St., Suite 310, Charlotte, NC 28202. **Telephone**: (704) 973-1400. **FAX**: (704) 973-1401. **Website**: www.sportsbusinessjournal.com.
**Publishing Frequency:** Weekly.
**Publisher:** Richard Weiss. **Editor-in-chief:** Abraham Madkour. **Managing Editor:** Ross Nethery.

## ESPN THE MAGAZINE
**Mailing Address**: 19 E. 34th St., Seventh Floor, New York, NY 10016. **Telephone**: (212) 515-1000. **FAX**: (212) 515-1290. **Website**: www.espn.com.
**Publishing Frequency:** Bi-weekly.
**Executive Editor:** Steve Wulf. **Senior Editors:** Jon Scher, Ed McGregor. **Senior Writers:** Jeff Bradley, Peter Gammons, Tim Keown, Tim Kurkjian, Buster Olney. **Writer/Reporter:** Amy Nelson. **Photo Editor:** Catriona Ni Aolain. **Photo Operations Coordinator:** Tricia Reed. **Manager, Communications:** Ellie Seifert.

## BASEBALL AMERICA
**Address:** 201 West Main St., Suite 201, Durham, NC 27702. **Mailing Address**: P.O. Box 2089, Durham, NC 27702. **Telephone:** (919) 682-9635. **FAX:** (919) 682-2880.
**Publishing Frequency:** Bi-weekly.
**President:** Catherine Silver. **Publisher:** Lee Folger. **Founding Editor:** Allan Simpson. **Editors In Chief:** Will Lingo, John Manuel. **Executive Editor:** Jim Callis. **Senior Writer:** Alan Schwarz.

## BASEBALL DIGEST
**Mailing Address**: 990 Grove St., Evanston, IL 60201. **Telephone**: (847) 491-6440. **FAX**: (847) 491-6203. **E-Mail Address:** bkuenster@centurysports.net. **Website**: www.centurysports.net/baseball.
**Publishing Frequency:** Monthly, April through January.
**Publisher:** Norman Jacobs. **Editor:** John Kuenster. **Managing Editor:** Bob Kuenster.

## COLLEGIATE BASEBALL
**Mailing Address**: P.O. Box 50566, Tucson, AZ 85703. **Telephone**: (520) 623-4530. **FAX**: (520) 624-5501. **E-Mail Address:** editor@baseballnews.com. **Website**: www.baseballnews.com.
**Publishing Frequency:** Bi-weekly, January-June; September, October.
**Publisher:** Lou Pavlovich. **Editor:** Lou Pavlovich Jr.

## JUNIOR BASEBALL MAGAZINE
**Mailing Address**: P.O. Box 9099, Canoga Park, CA 91309. **Telephone**: (818) 710-1234. **Customer Service:** (888) 487-2448. **FAX:** (818) 710-1877. **E-Mail Address:** editor@juniorbaseball.com. **Website**: www.juniorbaseball.com.
**Publishing Frequency:** Bi-monthly.
**Publisher/Editor:** Dave Destler. **Publishing Director**: Dayna Destler.

## SPORTS ILLUSTRATED FOR KIDS
**Mailing Address**: 1271 Avenue of the Americas, Third Floor, New York, NY 10020. **Telephone**: (212) 522-1212. **FAX:** (212) 522-0120. **Website**: www.sikids.com.
**Publishing Frequency:** Monthly.
**Publisher:** Dave Watt. **Managing Editor:** Neil Cohen. **Deputy Managing Editor:** Bob Der. **Senior Editors:** Michael Northrop, Justin Tejada.

# BASEBALL ANNUALS

## ATHLON SPORTS BASEBALL
**Mailing Address**: 220 25th Ave. N., Suite 200, Nashville, TN 37203. **Telephone**: (615) 327-0747. **FAX**: (615) 327-1149. **E-Mail Address:** editor@athlonsports.com. **Website**: www.athlonsports.com.
**President/Chief Executive Officer:** Chuck Allen. **Managing Editor:** Charlie Miller. **Senior Editor:** Rob Doster. **Editor:** Mitch Light. **Website Editor:** Bill Trocchi

## SPORTING NEWS BASEBALL YEARBOOK
**Mailing Address**: 10176 Corporate Square Dr., Suite 200, St. Louis, MO 63132. **Telephone**: (314) 997-7111. **FAX**: (314) 993-7726. **Website**: www.sportingnews.com.
**Senior Vice President/Editorial Director**: John Rawlings. **Executive Editor:** Bob Hille. **Managing Editor:** Stan McNeal.

## SPRING TRAINING BASEBALL YEARBOOK
**Mailing Address**: Vanguard Publications, P.O. Box 667, Chapel Hill, NC 27514. **Telephone**: (919) 967-2420. **FAX:** (919) 967-6294. **E-Mail Address:** vanguard3@mindspring.com. **Website**: www.springtrainingmagazine.com, http://www.vanguardpublications.com.
**Publisher:** Merle Thorpe. **Editor:** Myles Friedman.

## STREET AND SMITH'S BASEBALL YEARBOOK
**Mailing Address**: 120 West Morehead St., Suite 230, Charlotte, NC 28202. **Telephone**: (704) 973-1575. **FAX:** (704) 973-1576. **E-Mail Address:** annuals@streetandsmiths.com. **Website**: www.streetandsmiths.com.

**Publisher:** Mike Kallay. **Editor:** Scott Smith.

## Baseball Encyclopedias

### THE ESPN BASEBALL ENCYCLOPEDIA
**Mailing Address:** Sterling Publishing, Co. Inc., 387 Park Ave. South, New York, NY 10016. **Telephone:** (212) 633-3516. **FAX:** (212) 633-3327. **E-Mail Address:** ggillette@247baseball.com. **Editors:** Pete Palmer, Gary Gillette.

### THE SPORTS ENCYCLOPEDIA: BASEBALL
**Mailing Address:** St. Martin's Press, 175 Fifth Ave., New York, NY 10010. **Telephone:** 646-307-5565. **E-Mail Address:** joseph.rinaldi@stmartins.com. **Website:** www.stmartins.com.
**Authors:** David Neft, Richard Cohen, Michael Neft. **Editor:** Marc Resnick.

### TOTAL BASEBALL
**Mailing Address:** SportClassic Books, Sport Media Publishing, 55 Mill St.-Building 5, Suite 240, Toronto, Ontario MSA 3C4. **Telephone:** (416) 466-0418. **FAX:** (416) 466-9530. **E-Mail Address:** info@sportclassicbooks.com. **Website:** www.sportclassicbooks.com.
**Editors:** John Thorn, Phil Birnbaum, Bill Deane.

## HOBBY PUBLICATIONS

### BECKETT MEDIA
Beckett Baseball Collector
**Mailing Address:** 15850 Dallas Pkwy., Dallas, TX 75248. **Telephone:** (972) 991-6657, (800) 840-3137. **FAX:** (972) 991-8930. **Website:** www.beckett.com.
**Chief Executive Officer:** Peter Gudmundsson. **Associate Publisher:** Tracy Hackler. **Editor:** Pepper Hastings. **Associate Editor:** Kevin Haake. **Senior Price Guide Editor:** Grant Sandground.

### KRAUSE PUBLICATIONS
**Mailing Address:** 700 E. State St., Iola, WI 54990. **Telephone:** (715) 445-2214. **FAX:** (715) 445-4087. **Website:** www.fantasysportsmag.com, www.sportscollectorsdigest.com, www.tuffstuff.com.
**Publisher:** Jeff Pozorski.
**Editor, Fantasy Sports:** Greg Ambrosius. **Editor, Sports Collectors Digest:** T.S. O'Connell. **Editor, Tuff Stuff:** Rocky Landsverk.

## TEAM PUBLICATIONS

### SCOUT PUBLISHING
Diehard (Boston Red Sox), Mets Inside Pitch (New York Mets), Indians Ink (Cleveland Indians)
**Mailing Address:** 1916 Pike Place, Suite 12-250, Seattle, WA 98101. **Telephone:** (888) 979-0979. **FAX:** (206) 267-4050.
**Managing Editor, Diehard:** Jerry Beach.
**Publisher/Editor In Chief, Indians Ink:** Frank Derry.
**Publisher/Managing Editor, Inside Pitch:** Bryan Hoch.

### VINE LINE
(Chicago Cubs)
**Mailing Address:** Chicago Cubs Publications, 1060 W. Addison St., Chicago, IL 60613. **Telephone:** (773) 404-2827. **FAX:** (773) 404-4758. **E-Mail Address:** vineline@cubs.com. **Managing Editor:** Lena McDonagh. **Editor:** Jim McArdle.

### YANKEES MAGAZINE
(New York Yankees)
**Mailing Address:** Yankee Stadium, Bronx, NY 10451. **Telephone:** (718) 293-4300. **Publisher/Director, Publications and Media:** Mark Mandrake. **Associate Director:** Alfred Santasiere. **Senior Editor:** Michael Margolis. **Photography Editor:** Ariele Goldman.

### OUTSIDE PITCH
(Baltimore Orioles)
**Mailing Address:** P.O. Box 27143, Baltimore, MD 21230. **Telephone:** (410) 234-8888, (800) 342-4737. **FAX:** (410) 234-1029. **Website:** www.outsidepitch.com. **Publisher:** David Simone. **Editor:** David Hill.

### REDS REPORT
(Cincinnati Reds)
**Mailing Address:** Columbus Sports Publications, P.O. Box 12453, Columbus, OH 43212. **Telephone:** (614) 486-2202. **FAX:** (614) 486-3650. **Publisher:** Frank Moskowitz. **Editor:** Mark Schmetzer. **Managing Editor:** Mark Rae.

# OTHER
## INFO

# GENERAL
## INFORMATION

## MAJOR LEAGUE BASEBALL PLAYERS ASSOCIATION
**Mailing Address:** 12 E. 49th St., 24th Floor, New York, NY 10017. **Telephone:** (212) 826-0808. **FAX:** (212) 752-4378. **E-Mail Address:** feedback@mlbpa.org. **Website:** www.mlbplayers.com.

**Year Founded:** 1966.

**Executive Director:** Donald Fehr.

**Chief Operating Officer:** Gene Orza. **General Counsel:** Michael Weiner. **Assistant General Counsel:** Doyle Pryor, Robert Lenaghan, Jeff Fannell.

**Special Assistants to Executive Director:** Bobby Bonilla, Phil Bradley, Steve Rogers, Allyne Price.

**Managing Officer:** Martha Child. **Manager, Financial Operations:** Marietta DiCamillo. **Contract Administrator:** Cindy Abercrombie. **Accounting Assistants:** Terri Hinkley, Yolanda Largo. **Administrative Assistants:** VIrginia Carballo, Aisha Hope, Melba Markowitz, Sharon O'Donnell, Lisa Pepin. **Receptionist:** Rebecca Rivera.

**Director, Business Affairs/Licensing:** Judy Heeter. **General Manager, Licensing:** Richard White. **Director, Communications:** Greg Bouris. **Assistant General Counsel, Licensing:** Evie Goldstein. **Category Director, Interactive Games:** John Olshan. **Communications Manager:** Chris Dahl. **Category Director, Trading Cards/Collectibles:** Evan Kaplan. **Category Manager, Apparel/Novelties:** Nancy Willis. **Manager, Player Trust:** Melissa Persaud. **Administrative Manager:** Heather Gould. **Program Coordinator:** Hillary Falk. **Licensing Assistant:** Eric Rivera. **Manager, Office Services:** Victor Lugo. **Executive Secretary/Licensing:** Sheila Peters.

**Executive Board:** Player representatives of the 30 major league clubs.

**MLBPA Representatives:** Tony Clark, Mark Loretta. **MLBPA Alternate Representatives:** Ray King, Craig Counsell.

## SCOUTING

### MAJOR LEAGUE BASEBALL SCOUTING BUREAU
**Mailing Address:** 3500 Porsche Way, Suite 100, Ontario, CA 91764. **Telephone:** (909) 980-1881. **FAX:** (909) 980-7794.

**Year Founded:** 1974.

**Director:** Frank Marcos. **Assistant Director:** Rick Oliver. **Office Coordinator:** Joanne Costanzo. **Administrative Assistant:** Debbie Keedy.

**Board of Directors:** Ed Burns (Major League Baseball), Dave Dombrowski (Tigers), Bob Gebhard (Diamondbacks), Roland Hemond (White Sox), Frank Marcos (MLBSB), Omar Minaya (Mets), Randy Smith (Padres), Art Stewart (Royals), Kevin Towers (Padres).

**Scouts:** Rick Arnold (Spring Mills, PA), Matt Barnicle (Huntington Beach, CA), Andy Campbell (Chandler, AZ), Mike Childers (Lexington, KY), Dick Colpaert (Utica, MI), Craig Conklin (Cayucos, CA), Dan Dixon (Temecula, CA), Jim Elliott (Winston-Salem, NC), Brad Fidler (Douglassville, PA), Art Gardner (Walnut Grove, MS), Rusty Gerhardt (New London, TX), Dennis Haren (San Diego, CA), Chris Heidt (Cherry Valley, IL), Don Jacoby (Winter Haven, FL), Don Kohler (Asbury, NJ), Mike Larson (Waseca, MN), Johnny Martinez (Overland Park, KS), Wayne Mathis (Cuero, TX), Jethro McIntyre (Pittsburg, CA), Paul Mirocke (Lutz, FL), Carl Moesche (Gresham, OR), Tim Osborne (Woodstock, GA), Gary Randall (Rock Hill, SC), Willie Romay (Miami Springs, FL), Kevin Saucier (Pensacola, FL), Harry Shelton (Ocoee, FL), Pat Shortt (South Hempstead, NY), Craig Smajstrla (Pearland, TX), Christie Stancil (Raleigh, NC), Ed Sukla (Irvine, CA), Marv Thompson (West Jordan, UT), Jim Walton (Shattuck, OK).

**Supervisor, Canada:** Walt Burrows (Brentwood Bay, B.C.). **Canadian Scouts:** Curtis Bailey (Red Deer, Alberta), Jason Chee-Aloy (Toronto, Ontario), Bill Green (Vancouver, B.C.), Sean Gulliver (St. John's, Newfoundland), Andrew Halpenny (Winnipeg, Manitoba), Ian Jordan (Kirkland, Quebec), Ken Lenihan (Bedford, Nova Scotia), Dave McConnell (Kelowna, B.C.), Dan Mendham (Dorchester, Ontario), Todd Plaxton (Saskatoon, Sask.), Jasmin Roy (Longueuil, Quebec), Tony Wylie (Anchorage, AK).

**Supervisor, Puerto Rico:** Pepito Centeno (Cidra, PR).

### PROFESSIONAL BASEBALL SCOUTS FOUNDATION
**Mailing Address:** 9665 Wilshire Blvd., Suite 801, Beverly Hills, CA 90212. **Telephone:** (310) 858 1935. **FAX:** (310) 246-4862. **E-Mail Address:** hitter19@aol.com. **Website:** www.professionalbaseballscoutsfoundation.com.

**Chairman:** Dennis Gilbert.

**Directors:** Bill Gayton, Pat Gillick, Derrick Hall, Roland Hemond, Gary Hughes, Lisa Jackson, Tommy Lasorda, Roberta Mazur, Harry Minor, Bob Nightengale, Tracy Ringolsby, Dale Sutherland, Dave Yoakum, John Young.

### SCOUT OF THE YEAR FOUNDATION
**Mailing Address:** P.O. Box 211585, West Palm Beach, FL 33421. **Telephone:** (561) 798-5897, (561) 818-4329. **FAX:** (561) 798-4644. **E-Mail Address:** bertmazur@aol.com.

**President:** Roberta Mazur. **Vice President:** Tracy Ringolsby. **Treasurer:** Ron Mazur II.

**Board of Advisers:** Joe L. Brown, Bob Fontaine, Pat Gillick, Roland Hemond, Gary Hughes, Tommy Lasorda, Allan Simpson, Ron Shapiro, Ted Spencer, Bob Watson.

## SCOUTING SERVICES

### INSIDE EDGE, INC.
**Mailing Address:** 5049 Emerson Ave. S., Minneapolis, MN 55419. **Telephone:** (800) 858-3343. **FAX:** (508) 526-

6145. **E-Mail Address:** insideedge@aol.com. **Website:** www.inside-edge.com.
**Partners:** Jay Donchetz, Randy Istre.

## PROSPECTS PLUS
(A Joint Venture of Baseball America and Perfect Game USA)
**Mailing Address:** Baseball America, P.O. Box 2089, Durham, NC 27702. **Telephone:** (800) 845-2726. **FAX:** (919) 682-2880. **E-Mail Addresses:** alanmatthews@baseballamerica.com; jerry@perfectgame.org. **Website:** www.baseball-america.com/prospectsplus; www.perfectgame.org.
**Editors, Baseball America:** Alan Matthews, Allan Simpson. **Director, Perfect Game USA:** Jerry Ford.

## SKILLSHOW, INC.
**Mailing Address:** 290 King of Prussia Rd., Suite 322, Radnor, PA 19087. **Telephone:** (610) 687-9072. **FAX:** (610) 687-9629. **E-Mail Address:** info@skillshow.com. **Website:** www.skillshow.com.
**Chief Executive Officer:** Tom Koerick Jr. **President/Director, Sales:** Tom Koerick Sr.

# UMPIRES

## Major Leagues
## WORLD UMPIRES ASSOCIATION
**Mailing Address:** P.O. Box 394, Neenah, WI 54957. **Telephone:** (920) 969-1580. **FAX:** (920) 969-1892. **E-Mail Address:** worldumpiresassn@aol.com.
**Year Founded:** 2000.
**President:** John Hirschbeck. **Vice President:** Joe Brinkman. **Secretary/Treasurer:** Jeff Nelson. **Labor Counsel:** Joel Smith. **Administrator:** Phil Janssen.

## Minor Leagues
## PROFESSIONAL BASEBALL UMPIRE CORPORATION
**Office Address:** 201 Bayshore Dr. SE, St. Petersburg, FL 33701. **Mailing Address:** P.O. Box A, St. Petersburg, FL 33731. **Telephone:** (727) 822-6937. **FAX:** (727) 821-5819.
**President:** Mike Moore. **Treasurer/Vice President, Administration:** Pat O'Conner. **Secretary/General Counsel:** Scott Poley. **Administrator:** Eric Krupa. **Assistant to Administrator:** Lillian Dixon.
**Executive Director, PBUC:** Mike Fitzpatrick (Kalamazoo, MI).
**Field Evaluators/Instructors:** Jorge Bauza, (San Juan, PR), Dennis Cregg (Webster, MA), Mike Felt (Lansing, MI), Justin Klemm (North Bethesda, MD), Larry Reveal (Chesapeake, VA).

# UMPIRE DEVELOPMENT SCHOOLS

## Harry Wendelstedt Umpire School
**Mailing Address:** 88 S. St. Andrews Dr., Ormond Beach, FL 32174. **Telephone:** (386) 672-4879. **FAX:** (386) 672-3212. **E-Mail Address:** admin@umpireschool.com. **Website:** www.umpireschool.com.
**Operators:** Harry Wendelstedt, Hunter Wendelstedt.

## Jim Evans Academy of Professional Umpiring
**Mailing Address:** 12741 Research Blvd., Suite 401, Austin, TX 78759. **Telephone:** (512) 335-5959. **FAX:** (512) 335-5411. **E-Mail Address:** jimsacademy@earthlink.net. **Website:** www.umpireacademy.com.
**Operator:** Jim Evans.

# TRAINERS

## PROFESSIONAL BASEBALL ATHLETIC TRAINERS SOCIETY
**Mailing Address:** 400 Colony Square, Suite 1750, 1201 Peachtree St., Atlanta, GA 30361. **Telephone:** (404) 875-4000. **FAX:** (404) 892-8560. **E-Mail Address:** rmallernee@mallernee-branch.com. **Website:** www.pbats.com.
**Year Founded:** 1983.
**President:** Jamie Reed (Texas Rangers). **Secretary:** Richie Bancells (Baltimore Orioles). **Treasurer:** Jeff Porter (Atlanta Braves). **American League Head Athletic Trainer Representative:** Kevin Rand (Detroit Tigers). **American League Assistant Athletic Trainer Representative:** Steve Carter (Detroit Tigers). **National League Head Athletic Trainer Representative:** Roger Caplinger (Milwaukee Brewers). **National League Assistant Athletic Trainer Representative:** Rex Jones (Houston Astros).
**General Counsel:** Rollin Mallernee.

# MUSEUMS

## BABE RUTH BIRTHPLACE
**Office Address:** 216 Emory St., Baltimore, MD 21230. **Telephone:** (410) 727-1539. **FAX:** (410) 727-1652. **E-Mail Address:** info@baberuthmuseum.com. **Website:** www.baberuthmuseum.com.
**Year Founded:** 1973.
**Executive Director:** Mike Gibbons. **Curator:** Shawn Herne.
**Museum Hours:** April-September, 10 a.m.-6 p.m (10 a.m.-7:30 p.m. for Baltimore Orioles home games); October-March, Tuesday-Sunday, 10 a.m.-5 p.m. (10a.m.-8 p.m. for Baltimore Ravens home games).

## CANADIAN BASEBALL HALL OF FAME AND MUSEUM
**Museum Address:** 386 Church St., St. Marys, Ontario N4X 1C2. **Mailing Address:** P.O. Box 1838, St. Marys, Ontario

N4X 1C2. **Telephone:** (519) 284-1838. **FAX:** (519) 284-1234. **E-Mail Address:** baseball@baseballhalloffame.ca.
**Website:** www.baseballhalloffame.ca.
**Year Founded:** 1983.
**President/Chief Executive Officer:** Tom Valcke. **Director, Operations:** Scott Crawford. **Curator:** Carl McCoomb.
**Museum Hours:** May—weekends only, June 1-Oct. 8—Daily, 10:30-4p.m.
**2006 Induction Ceremonies:** June 24.
**Boys/Girls Weeklong Camps:** July.

## FIELD OF DREAMS MOVIE SITE
**Address:** 28963 Lansing Rd., Dyersville, IA 52040. **Telephone:** (888) 875-8404. **FAX:** (319) 875-7253. **E-Mail Address:** shoelessjoe@fieldofdreamsmoviesite.com. **Website:** www.fieldofdreamsmoviesite.com.
**Year Founded:** 1989.
**Manager, Business/Marketing:** Betty Boeckenstedt.
**Hours:** April-November, 9 a.m.-6 p.m.

## LEGENDS OF THE GAME BASEBALL MUSEUM
**Address:** 1000 Ballpark Way, Suite 400, Arlington, TX 76011. **Telephone:** (817) 273-5600. **FAX:** (817) 273-5093. **E-Mail Address:** museum@texasrangers.com. **Website:** http://museum.texasrangers.com.
**Director:** Amy Polley.
**Hours:** April-September, game days/Texas Rangers, 9 a.m.-7:30 p.m.; non-game days, Mon.-Sat., 9 a.m.-4 p.m., Sunday 11 a.m.-4 p.m.; October-March, Tues.-Sat., 10 a.m.-4 p.m.

## LITTLE LEAGUE BASEBALL MUSEUM
**Office Address:** 525 Route 15 S., Williamsport, PA 17701. **Mailing Address:** P.O. Box 3485, Williamsport, PA 17701. **Telephone:** (570) 326-3607. **FAX:** (570) 326-2267. **E-Mail Address:** museum@littleleague.org. **Website:** www.littleleague.org/museum.
**Year Founded:** 1982.
**Director:** Janice Ogurcak. **Administrative Assistant:** Adam Thompson.
**Museum Hours:** Memorial Day-Labor Day, 10 a.m.-7 p.m. (Sun., noon-7 p.m.); Labor Day-Memorial Day, Mon., Thurs. and Fri., 10 a.m.-5 p.m., Sat. noon-5 p.m., Sun. noon-4 p.m.

## LOUISVILLE SLUGGER MUSEUM AND FACTORY
**Office Address:** 800 W. Main St., Louisville, KY 40202. **Telephone:** (502) 588-7228. **FAX:** (502) 585-1179. **Website:** www.sluggermuseum.org.
**Year Founded:** 1996.
**Executive Director:** Anne Jewell.
**Museum Hours:** Mon.-Sat., Jan. 2-Dec. 23, 9 a.m.-5 p.m,; Sunday (April-November), noon-5p.m.

## THE NATIONAL PASTIME: MUSEUM OF MINOR LEAGUE BASEBALL
(Under Development)
**Museum Address:** 175 Toyota Plaza, Suite 300, Memphis, TN 38103. **Telephone:** (901) 722-0207. **FAX:** (901) 527-1642. **E-Mail Address:** dchase@memphisredbirds.com. **Website:** www.memphisredbirds.com/autozone_park/museum.html.
**Founders:** Dean Jernigan, Kristi Jernigan.
**Executive Director:** Dave Chase.

## NATIONAL BASEBALL HALL OF FAME AND MUSEUM
**Address:** 25 Main St., Cooperstown, NY 13326. **Telephone:** (888) 425-5633, (607) 547-7200. **FAX:** (607) 547-2044. **E-Mail Address:** info@baseballhalloffame.org. **Website:** www.baseballhalloffame.org.
**Year Founded:** 1939.
**Chairman:** Jane Forbes Clark. **Vice Chairman:** Joe Morgan. **President:** Dale Petroskey. **VP, Marketing:** Sean Gahagan. **VP, Development,** Greg Harris. **VP, Communications/Education:** Jeff Idelson. **VP/Chief Curator:** Ted Spencer. **Curator, Collections:** Peter Clark. **Librarian:** Jim Gates. **Controller:** Fran Althiser. **Director, Communications:** Brad Horn.
**Museum Hours:** Memorial Day Weekend-Labor Day, 9 a.m.-9 p.m.; remainder of year, 9 a.m.-5 p.m. Open daily except Thanksgiving, Christmas, New Year's Day.
**2006 Hall of Fame Induction Ceremonies:** July 31, 1:30 p.m. **2006 Hall of Fame Game:** May 15, 2 p.m., Cincinnati Reds vs. Pittsburgh Pirates.

## NEGRO LEAGUES BASEBALL MUSEUM
**Mailing Address:** 1616 E. 18th St., Kansas City, MO 64108. **Telephone:** (816) 221-1920. **FAX:** (816) 221-8424. **E-Mail Address:** nlmuseum@hotmail.com. **Website:** www.nlbm.com.
**Year Founded:** 1990.
**Chairman:** Buck O'Neil. **President:** Mark Bryant.
**Executive Director:** Don Motley. **Marketing Director:** Bob Kendrick. **Curator:** Raymond Doswell.
**Museum Hours:** Tues.-Sat. 9 a.m.-6 p.m.; Sun. noon-6 p.m. Closed Monday.

## NOLAN RYAN FOUNDATION AND EXHIBIT CENTER
**Mailing Address:** 2925 S. Bypass 35, Alvin, TX 77511. **Telephone:** (281) 388-1134. **FAX:** (281) 388-1135. **Website:** www.nolanryanfoundation.org.
**Hours:** Mon.-Sat. 9 a.m.-4 p.m.

## TED WILLIAMS MUSEUM and HITTERS HALL OF FAME

**Mailing Address:** 2455 N. Citrus Hills Blvd., Hernando, FL 34442. **Telephone:** (352) 527-6566. **FAX:** (352) 527-4163. **E-Mail Address:** twm@tedwilliamsmuseum.com. **Website:** twmuseum.com.
**Executive Director:** Dave McCarthy. **Director, Operation:** Mike Colabelli.
**Museum Hours:** Tues.-Sun., 10 a.m.-4 p.m.

# RESEARCH

## SOCIETY FOR AMERICAN BASEBALL RESEARCH

**Mailing Address:** 812 Huron Rd. E., Suite 719, Cleveland, OH 44115. **Telephone:** (216) 575-0500. **FAX:** (216) 575-0502. **Website:** www.sabr.org.
**Year Founded:** 1971.
**President:** Dick Beverage. **Vice President:** Bill Nowlin. **Secretary:** Neil Traven. **Treasurer:** F.X. Flinn. **Directors:** Fred Ivor-Campbell, Tom Hufford, Norman Macht, Andy McCue.
**Executive Director:** John Zajc. **Membership Services Associate:** Ryan Chamberlain. **Director, Publications:** Jim Charlton.

# ALUMNI ASSOCIATIONS

## MAJOR LEAGUE BASEBALL PLAYERS ALUMNI ASSOCIATION

**Mailing Address:** 1631 Mesa Ave., Suite B, Colorado Springs, CO 80906. **Telephone:** (719) 477-1870. **FAX:** (719) 477-1875. **E-Mail Address:** postoffice@mlbpaa.com. **Website:** www.baseballalumni.com.
**President:** Brooks Robinson. **Chief Executive Officer:** Dan Foster. **Board of Directors:** Sandy Alderson, John Doherty, Denny Doyle, Brian Fisher, Jim "Mudcat" Grant, Rich Hand, Jim Hannan (chairman), Jim Poole, Steve Rogers, Will Royster, Jose Valdivielso, Fred Valentine (vice chairman).
**Legal Counsel:** Sam Moore. **Vice President, Player Appearances:** Chris Torgusen. **VP, Special Events:** Geoffrey Hixson. **Director, Administration:** Blaze Bautista. **Special Events Coordinator:** Mike Groll. **Youth Baseball Coordinator:** Derek Mayfield.

## ASSOCIATION OF PROFESSIONAL BALL PLAYERS OF AMERICA

**Mailing Address:** 1820 W. Orangewood Ave., Suite 206, Orange, CA 92868. **Telephone:** (714) 935-9993. **FAX:** (714) 935-0431. **E-Mail Address:** ballplayersassn@aol.com. **Website:** www.apbpa.org.
**Year Founded:** 1924.
**President:** Roland Hemond. **First Vice President:** Tal Smith. **Second VP:** Dick Wagner. **Secretary/Treasurer:** Dick Beverage. **Administrative Assistant:** Patty Helmsworth.
**Directors:** Sparky Anderson, Mark Grace, Tony Gwynn, Orel Hershiser, Whitey Herzog, Tony La Russa, Tom Lasorda, Brooks Robinson, Nolan Ryan, Tom Seaver.

## BASEBALL ASSISTANCE TEAM (BAT)

**Mailing Address:** 245 Park Ave., 31st Floor, New York, NY 10167. **Telephone:** (212) 931-7822, (212) 931-7823. **FAX:** (212) 949-5433.
**Year Founded:** 1986.
**President, Chief Executive Officer:** Ted Sizemore. **Vice Presidents:** Frank Torre, Greg Wilcox, Earl Wilson. **Chairman:** Bobby Murcer.
**Executive Director:** James Martin. **Secretary:** Thomas Ostertag. **Treasurer:** Jonathan Mariner. **Consultant:** Sam McDowell.

## MINOR LEAGUE BASEBALL ALUMNI ASSOCIATION

**Mailing Address:** P.O. Box A, St. Petersburg, FL 33731. **Telephone:** (727) 822-6937. **FAX:** (727) 821-5819. **E-Mail Address:** alumni@minorleaguebaseball.com. **Website:** www.milb.com.
**President:** Mike Moore. **Manager, Exhibiton Services/Alumni Association:** Noreen Brantner.

# MINISTRY

## BASEBALL CHAPEL

**Mailing Address:** P.O. Box 302, Springfield, PA 19064.**Telephone:** (610) 690-2474. **E-Mail Address:** office@baseballchapel.org. **Website:** www.baseballchapel.org.
**Year Founded:** 1973.
**President:** Vince Nauss.
**Staff:** Kyle Abbott, Wayne Beilgard, Rob Crose, Gio Llerena, Cali Magallanes, Steve Sisco, Rich Sparling. **Coordinator, Baseball Family:** Colleen Endres.
**Board of Directors:** Don Christenson, Dave Dravecky, Greg Gohr, Dave Howard, Chuck Murphy, Vince Nauss, Bill Sampen, Tye Waller, Walt Wiley (chairman).

# TRADE, EMPLOYMENT

## THE BASEBALL TRADE SHOW

**Mailing Address:** P.O. Box A, St. Petersburg, FL 33731. **Telephone:** (727) 822-6937, (727) 456-1718. **FAX:** (727) 825-3785.
**Manager, Exhibition Services/Alumni Association:** Noreen Brantner.
**2006 Convention:** Dec. 4-6 in Orlando, Fla. (Walt Disney World Swan and Dolphin Resort).

## PROFESSIONAL BASEBALL EMPLOYMENT OPPORTUNITIES

**Mailing Address:** P.O. Box A, St. Petersburg, FL 33731. **Telephone:** (866) 937-7236. **FAX:** (727) 821-5819. **E-Mail Address:** info@pbeo.com. **Website:** www.pbeo.com.
**Contact:** Scott Kravchuk.

## BASEBALL CARD MANUFACTURERS

### DONRUSS/PLAYOFF

**Mailing Address:** 2300 E. Randol Mill, Arlington, TX 76011. **Telephone:** (817) 983-0300. **FAX:** (817) 983-0400. **Website:** www.donruss.com.
**Marketing Manager:** Scott Prusha.

### GRANDSTAND CARDS

**Mailing Address:** 22647 Ventura Blvd., #192, Woodland Hills, CA 91364. **Telephone:** (818) 992-5642. **FAX:** (818) 348-9122. **E-Mail Address:** gscards1@pacbell.net. **Website:** www.grandstandcards.com.

### MULTIAD SPORTS

**Mailing Address:** 1720 W. Detweiller Dr., Peoria, IL 61615. **Telephone:** (800) 348-6485, ext. 5111. **FAX:** (309) 692-8378. **E-Mail Address:** bjeske@multiad.com. **Website:** www.multiad.com/sports.

### TOPPS

**Mailing Address:** One Whitehall St., New York, NY 10004. **Telephone:** (212) 376-0300. **FAX:** (212) 376-0573. **Website:** www.topps.com.

### UPPER DECK

**Mailing Address:** 5909 Sea Otter Place, Carlsbad, CA 92008. **Telephone:** (800) 873-7332. **FAX:** (760) 929-6548. **E-Mail Address:** customer_service@upperdeck.com. **Website:** www.upperdeck.com.

# MINOR
## LEAGUES

# MINOR LEAGUE
## BASEBALL

## NATIONAL ASSOCIATION
## OF PROFESSIONAL BASEBALL LEAGUES

**Office Address:** 201 Bayshore Dr. SE, St. Petersburg, FL 33701. **Mailing Address:** P.O. Box A, St. Petersburg, FL 33731. **Telephone:** (727) 822-6937. **FAX:** (727) 821-5819. **Website:** www.milb.com.

**Year Founded:** 1901.
**President, Chief Executive Officer:** Mike Moore.
**Vice President:** Stan Brand (Washington, D.C.).
**Treasurer, Chief Operating Officer/VP, Administration:** Pat O'Conner. **Assistant to VP, Administration:** Mary Wooters.
**Secretary/General Counsel:** Scott Poley. **Administrator, Legal Affairs:** Sandie Olmsted. **Special Counsel:** George Yund (Cincinnati, OH).

**MINOR LEAGUE BASEBALL** ™

Mike Moore

**Executive Director, Business Operations:** John Cook.
**Director, Baseball Operations:** Tim Brunswick.
**Director, Media Relations:** Jim Ferguson. **Associate Director, Media Relations:** Steve Densa.
**Director, Business/Finance:** Eric Krupa. **Manager, Accounting:** Jeff Carrier.
**Director, Information Technology:** Rob Colamarino.
**Official Statistician:** Major League Baseball Advanced Media, 75 Ninth Ave., New York, NY 10011. **Telephone:** (212) 485-3444.
**2006 Winter Meetings:** Dec. 4-7 at Lake Buena Vista, Fla. (Walt Disney World Swan & Dolphin).
**Affiliated Members/Council of League Presidents**

### Affiliated Members/Council of League Presidents

#### Class AAA

| League | President | Telephone | FAX Number |
|---|---|---|---|
| International | Randy Mobley | (614) 791-9300 | (614) 791-9009 |
| Mexican | Alejandro Hutt | 011-555-557-1007 | 011-555-395-2454 |
| Pacific Coast | Branch Rickey | (719) 636-3399 | (719) 636-1199 |

#### Class AA

| League | President | Telephone | FAX Number |
|---|---|---|---|
| Eastern | Joe McEacharn | (207) 761-2700 | (207) 761-7064 |
| Southern | Don Mincher | (770) 321-0400 | (770) 321-0037 |
| Texas | Tom Kayser | (210) 545-5297 | (210) 545-5298 |

#### High Class A

| League | President | Telephone | FAX Number |
|---|---|---|---|
| California | Joe Gagliardi | (408) 369-8038 | (408) 369-1409 |
| Carolina | John Hopkins | (336) 691-9030 | (336) 691-9070 |
| Florida State | Chuck Murphy | (386) 252-7479 | (386) 252-7495 |

#### Low Class A

| League | President | Telephone | FAX Number |
|---|---|---|---|
| Midwest | George Spelius | (608) 364-1188 | (608) 364-1913 |
| South Atlantic | John Moss | (704) 739-3466 | (704) 739-1974 |

#### Short-Season Class A

| League | President | Telephone | FAX Number |
|---|---|---|---|
| New York-Penn | Ben Hayes | (727) 576-6300 | (727) 576-6307 |
| Northwest | Bob Richmond | (208) 429-1511 | (208) 429-1525 |

#### Rookie Advanced

| League | President | Telephone | FAX Number |
|---|---|---|---|
| Appalachian | Lee Landers | (704) 873-5300 | (704) 873-4333 |
| Pioneer | Jim McCurdy | (509) 456-7615 | (509) 456-0136 |

#### Rookie

| League | President | Telephone | FAX Number |
|---|---|---|---|
| Arizona | Bob Richmond | (208) 429-1511 | (208) 429-1525 |
| Dominican Summer | Freddy Jana | (809) 532-3619 | (809) 532-3619 |
| Gulf Coast | Tom Saffell | (941) 966-6407 | (941) 966-6872 |
| Venezuela Summer | Saul Gonzalez | 011-58-41-24-0321 | 011-58-41-24-0705 |

## PROFESSIONAL BASEBALL
## PROMOTION CORPORATION

**Office Address:** 201 Bayshore Dr. SE, St. Petersburg, FL 33701. **Mailing Address:** P.O. Box A, St. Petersburg, FL 33731. **Telephone:** (727) 822-6937. **FAX/Marketing:** (727) 894-4227. **FAX/Licensing:** (727) 825-3785.

**President, Chief Executive Officer:** Mike Moore.

**Treasurer, Chief Operating Officer/VP, Administration:** Pat O'Conner.

**Executive Director, Business Operations:** John Cook. **Senior Assistant Director, Special Operations:** Kelly Ryan. **Assistant Director, Special Operations:** Scott Kravchuk.

**Director, Licensing:** Brian Earle. **Associate Director, Licensing:** Tina Gust. **Assistant, Licensing:** Bryan Sayre.

**Director, Marketing:** Rod Meadows. **Senior Manager, Marketing:** Jen Morris. **Senior Account Manager, Marketing:** Heather Raburn. **Account Manager, Marketing:** Melissa Keilen. **Club Coordinator Marketing:** Mary Marandi.

**Professional Baseball Employment Opportunities Contact:** Scott Kravchuk. **Manager, Exhibition Services/Alumni Association:** Noreen Brantner. **Manager, Special Operations/Charity Partners:** Jill Rusinko. **Manager, Trademarks/Contracts:** Susan Pinckney. **Administrative Assistant, Special Operations:** Jeannette Machicote.

## PROFESSIONAL BASEBALL
## UMPIRE CORPORATION

**Office Address:** 201 Bayshore Dr. SE, St. Petersburg, FL 33701. **Mailing Address:** P.O. Box A, St. Petersburg, FL 33731. **Telephone:** (727) 822-6937. **FAX:** (727) 821-5819.

**President:** Mike Moore.

**Treasurer/Vice President, Administration:** Pat O'Conner. **Secretary/General Counsel:** Scott Poley.

**Administrator:** Eric Krupa. **Assistant to Administrator:** Lillian Patterson

**Executive Director, PBUC:** Mike Fitzpatrick (Kalamazoo, MI).

**Field Evaluators/Instructors:** Dennis Cregg (Webster, MA), Mike Felt (Lansing, MI), Justin Klemm (Crofton, MD), Jorge Bauza (San Juan, PR), Larry Reveal (Chesapeake, VA).

# GENERAL
# INFORMATION

| | Teams | Games | Regular Season Open. Day | Clos. Day | All-Star Games Date | Site |
|---|---|---|---|---|---|---|
| International | 14 | 144 | April 6 | Sept. 4 | *July 12 | Toledo |
| Pacific Coast | 16 | 144 | April 6 | Sept. 4 | *July 12 | Toledo |
| Eastern | 12 | 142 | April 6 | Sept. 4 | July 12 | Altoona |
| Southern | 10 | 140 | April 6 | Sept. 4 | July 10 | Montgomery |
| Texas | 8 | 140 | April 6 | Sept. 3 | June 20 | Arkansas |
| California | 10 | 140 | April 6 | Sept. 4 | #June 27 | Salem |
| Carolina | 8 | 140 | April 6 | Sept. 4 | #June 27 | Salem |
| Florida State | 12 | 140 | April 6 | Sept. 3 | June 17 | Lakeland |
| Midwest | 14 | 140 | April 6 | Sept. 4 | June 20 | Quad Cities |
| South Atlantic | 16 | 140 | April 6 | Sept. 4 | June 20 | Lake County |
| New York-Penn | 14 | 76 | June 20 | Sept. 7 | Aug. 16 | Aberdeen |
| Northwest | 8 | 76 | June 20 | Sept. 6 | None | |
| Appalachian | 10 | 68 | June 21 | Aug. 30 | None | |
| Pioneer | 8 | 76 | June 20 | Sept. 7 | None | |
| Arizona | 9 | 56 | June 22 | Aug. 30 | None | |
| Gulf Coast | 12 | 54 | June 20 | Aug. 21 | None | |

*Triple-A All-Star Game
#California League vs. Carolina League

# MINOR LEAGUES

## 2005 STANDINGS

*Split-season champion. #Wild card.

### INTERNATIONAL LEAGUE                                                          AAA

| NORTH | W | L | Pct. | GB | Manager(s) |
|---|---|---|---|---|---|
| Buffalo Bisons (Indians) | 82 | 62 | .569 | — | Marty Brown |
| Pawtucket Red Sox (Red Sox) | 75 | 69 | .521 | 7 | Ron Johnson |
| Rochester Red Wings (Twins) | 75 | 69 | .521 | 7 | Phil Roof/Rich Miller |
| Syracuse SkyChiefs (Blue Jays) | 71 | 73 | .493 | 11 | Marty Pevey |
| Ottawa Lynx (Orioles) | 69 | 75 | .479 | 13 | Dave Trembley |
| Scranton/W-B Red Barons (Phillies) | 69 | 75 | .479 | 13 | Gene Lamont |
| **SOUTH** | **W** | **L** | **Pct.** | **GB** | **Manager(s)** |
| Norfolk Tides (Mets) | 79 | 65 | .549 | — | Ken Oberkfell |
| Durham Bulls (Devil Rays) | 65 | 79 | .451 | 14 | Bill Evers |
| Charlotte Knights (White Sox) | 57 | 87 | .396 | 22 | Nick Leyva/Manny Trillo |
| Richmond Braves (Braves) | 56 | 88 | .389 | 23 | Pat Kelly |
| **WEST** | **W** | **L** | **Pct.** | **GB** | **Manager** |
| Toledo Mud Hens (Tigers) | 89 | 55 | .618 | — | Larry Parrish |
| #Indianapolis Indians (Pirates) | 78 | 66 | .542 | 11 | Trent Jewett |
| Columbus Clippers (Yankees) | 77 | 67 | .535 | 12 | Bucky Dent |
| Louisville Bats (Reds) | 66 | 78 | .458 | 23 | Rick Sweet |

**GOVERNORS' CUP PLAYOFFS—Semifinals:** Toledo defeated Norfolk 3-2 and Indianapolis defeated Buffalo 3-2 in best-of-5 series. **Final:** Toledo defeated Indianapolis 3-0 in best-of-5 series.

### PACIFIC COAST LEAGUE                                                          AAA

| AMERICAN/NORTH | W | L | Pct. | GB | Manager |
|---|---|---|---|---|---|
| Nashville Sounds (Brewers) | 75 | 69 | .521 | — | Frank Kremblas |
| Omaha Royals (Royals) | 72 | 72 | .500 | 3 | Mike Jirschele |
| Memphis Redbirds (Cardinals) | 71 | 72 | .497 | 3½ | Danny Sheaffer |
| Iowa Cubs (Cubs) | 64 | 75 | .460 | 8½ | Mike Quade |
| **AMERICAN/SOUTH** | **W** | **L** | **Pct.** | **GB** | **Manager** |
| Oklahoma RedHawks (Rangers) | 80 | 63 | .559 | — | Bobby Jones |
| Albuquerque Isotopes (Marlins) | 78 | 66 | .542 | 2½ | Dean Treanor |
| Round Rock Express (Astros) | 74 | 70 | .514 | 6½ | Jackie Moore |
| New Orleans Zephyrs (Nationals) | 64 | 76 | .457 | 14½ | Tim Foli |
| **PACIFIC/NORTH** | **W** | **L** | **Pct.** | **GB** | **Manager** |
| Tacoma Rainiers (Mariners) | 80 | 64 | .556 | — | Dan Rohn |
| Salt Lake Stingers (Angels) | 79 | 65 | .549 | 1 | Dino Ebel |
| Portland Beavers (Padres) | 70 | 73 | .490 | 9½ | Craig Colbert |
| Colorado Springs Sky Sox (Rockies) | 65 | 78 | .455 | 14½ | Marv Foley |
| **PACIFIC/SOUTH** | **W** | **L** | **Pct.** | **GB** | **Manager** |
| Sacramento River Cats (Athletics) | 80 | 64 | .556 | — | Tony DeFrancesco |
| Fresno Grizzlies (Giants) | 68 | 76 | .472 | 12 | Shane Turner |
| Tucson Sidewinders (Diamondbacks) | 68 | 76 | .472 | 12 | Chip Hale |
| Las Vegas 51s (Dodgers) | 57 | 86 | .399 | 22½ | Jerry Royster |

**PLAYOFFS—Semifinals:** Tacoma defeated Sacramento 3-2 and Nashville defeated Oklahoma 3-2 in best-of-5 series. **Final:** Nashville defeated Tacoma 3-0 in best-of-5 series.

### EASTERN LEAGUE                                                          AA

| NORTH | W | L | Pct. | GB | Manager |
|---|---|---|---|---|---|
| Portland Sea Dogs (Red Sox) | 76 | 66 | .535 | — | Todd Claus |
| Trenton Thunder (Yankees) | 74 | 68 | .521 | 2 | Bill Masse |
| Norwich Navigators (Giants) | 71 | 71 | .500 | 5 | Dave Machemer |
| New Britain Rock Cats (Twins) | 70 | 72 | .493 | 6 | Stan Cliburn |
| New Hampshire Fisher Cats (Blue Jays) | 68 | 74 | .479 | 8 | Mike Basso |
| Binghamton Mets (Mets) | 63 | 79 | .444 | 13 | Jack Lind |
| **SOUTH** | **W** | **L** | **Pct.** | **GB** | **Manager** |
| Akron Aeros (Indians) | 84 | 58 | .592 | — | Torey Lovullo |
| Altoona Curve (Pirates) | 76 | 66 | .535 | 8 | Tony Beasley |
| Bowie Baysox (Orioles) | 74 | 68 | .521 | 10 | Don Werner |
| Reading Phillies (Phillies) | 69 | 73 | .486 | 15 | Steve Swisher |
| Harrisburg Senators (Nationals) | 64 | 78 | .451 | 20 | Keith Bodie |
| Erie SeaWolves (Tigers) | 63 | 79 | .444 | 21 | Duffy Dyer |

**PLAYOFFS—Semifinals:** Portland defeated Trenton 3-2 and Akron defeated Altoona 3-2 in best-of-5 series. **Final:** Akron defeated Portland 3-1 in best-of-5 series.

## SOUTHERN LEAGUE                                                    AA

| NORTH | W | L | Pct. | GB | Manager |
|---|---|---|---|---|---|
| *West Tenn Diamond Jaxx (Cubs) | 83 | 56 | .597 | — | Bobby Dickerson |
| #Carolina Mudcats (Marlins) | 77 | 57 | .575 | 3½ | Gary Allenson |
| Tennessee Smokies (Diamondbacks) | 64 | 76 | .457 | 19½ | Tony Perezchica |
| Huntsville Stars (Brewers) | 60 | 79 | .432 | 23 | Don Money |
| Chattanooga Lookouts (Reds) | 53 | 83 | .390 | 28½ | Jayhawk Owens |
| SOUTH | W | L | Pct. | GB | Manager |
| *Birmingham Barons (White Sox) | 82 | 57 | .590 | — | Razor Shines |
| *Jacksonville Suns (Dodgers) | 79 | 61 | .564 | 3½ | John Shoemaker |
| Montgomery Biscuits (Devil Rays) | 67 | 70 | .489 | 14 | Charlie Montoyo |
| Mississippi Braves (Braves) | 64 | 68 | .485 | 14½ | Brian Snitker |
| Mobile BayBears (Padres) | 58 | 80 | .420 | 23½ | Gary Jones |

**PLAYOFFS—Semifinals:** West Tenn defeated Carolina 3-0 and Jacksonville defeated Birmingham 3-0 in best-of-5 series. **Final:** Jacksonville defeated West Tenn 3-1 in best-of-5 series.

## TEXAS LEAGUE                                                       AA

| EAST | W | L | Pct. | GB | Manager |
|---|---|---|---|---|---|
| *Tulsa Drillers (Rockies) | 75 | 65 | .536 | — | Tom Runnells |
| *Arkansas Travelers (Angels) | 71 | 69 | .507 | 4 | Tom Gamboa |
| Springfield Cardinals (Cardinals) | 70 | 70 | .500 | 5 | Chris Maloney |
| Wichita Wranglers (Royals) | 68 | 72 | .486 | 7 | Frank White |
| WEST | W | L | Pct. | GB | Manager |
| **Midland RockHounds (Athletics) | 78 | 62 | .557 | — | Von Hayes |
| #San Antonio Missions (Mariners) | 76 | 64 | .543 | 2 | Dave Brundage |
| Corpus Christi Hooks (Astros) | 64 | 76 | .457 | 14 | Dave Clark |
| Frisco RoughRiders (Rangers) | 58 | 82 | .414 | 20 | Darryl Kennedy |

**PLAYOFFS—Semifinals:** Arkansas defeated Tulsa 3-0 and Midland defeated San Antonio 3-2 in best-of-5 series. **Final:** Midland defeated Arkansas 3-1 in best-of-5 series.

## CALIFORNIA LEAGUE                                                  HIGH A

| NORTH | W | L | Pct. | GB | Manager |
|---|---|---|---|---|---|
| *San Jose Giants (Giants) | 85 | 55 | .607 | — | Lenn Sakata |
| *Stockton Ports (Athletics) | 78 | 62 | .557 | 7 | Todd Steverson |
| #Modesto Nuts (Rockies) | 72 | 67 | .518 | 12½ | Stu Cole |
| Bakersfield Blaze (Rangers) | 68 | 72 | .486 | 17 | Arnie Beyeler |
| Visalia Oaks (Devil Rays) | 55 | 85 | .393 | 30 | Steve Livesey |
| SOUTH | W | L | Pct. | GB | Manager |
| *High Desert Mavericks (Royals) | 75 | 65 | .536 | — | Billy Gardner |
| #Lancaster JetHawks (Diamondbacks) | 75 | 65 | .536 | — | Bill Plummer |
| *Lake Elsinore Storm (Padres) | 70 | 68 | .507 | 4 | Rick Renteria |
| Rancho Cucamonga Quakes (Angels) | 62 | 77 | .446 | 12½ | Tyrone Boykin |
| Inland Empire 66ers (Mariners) | 58 | 82 | .414 | 17 | Daren Brown |

**PLAYOFFS—Division Series:** Modesto defeated Stockton 2-0 and Lancaster defeated High Desert 2-1 in best-of-3 series. **Semifinals:** San Jose defeated Modesto 3-0 and Lake Elsinore defeated Lancaster 3-0 in best-of-5 series. **Final:** San Jose defeated Lake Elsinore 3-2 in best-of-5 series.

## CAROLINA LEAGUE                                                    HIGH A

| NORTH | W | L | Pct. | GB | Manager(s) |
|---|---|---|---|---|---|
| *Frederick Keys (Orioles) | 79 | 61 | .564 | — | Bien Figueroa |
| *Lynchburg Hillcats (Pirates) | 78 | 62 | .557 | 1 | Tim Leiper |
| Potomac Nationals (Nationals) | 63 | 77 | .450 | 16 | Bob Henley |
| Wilmington Blue Rocks (Red Sox) | 60 | 80 | .429 | 19 | Dann Bilardello |
| SOUTH | W | L | Pct. | GB | Manager(s) |
| *Winston-Salem Warthogs (White Sox) | 77 | 64 | .546 | — | Chris Cron |
| *Kinston Indians (Indians) | 76 | 64 | .543 | ½ | Luis Rivera |
| Salem Avalanche (Astros) | 67 | 74 | .475 | 10 | Ivan DeJesus |
| Myrtle Beach Pelicans (Braves) | 61 | 79 | .436 | 15 | Randy Ingle |

**PLAYOFFS—Semifinals:** Frederick defeated Lynchburg 2-0 and Kinston defeated Winston-Salem 2-0 in best-of-3 series. **Final:** Frederick defeated Kinston 3-2 in best-of-5 series.

## FLORIDA STATE LEAGUE                                               HIGH A

| EAST | W | L | Pct. | GB | Manager |
|---|---|---|---|---|---|
| *Vero Beach Dodgers (Dodgers) | 77 | 56 | .579 | — | Scott Little |
| Daytona Cubs (Cubs) | 69 | 66 | .511 | 9½ | Richie Zisk |
| *Palm Beach Cardinals (Cardinals) | 69 | 71 | .493 | 11 | Ron Warner |
| St. Lucie Mets (Mets) | 66 | 68 | .493 | 12½ | Tim Teufel |
| Jupiter Hammerheads (Marlins) | 64 | 71 | .474 | 14½ | Tim Cossins |
| Brevard County Manatees (Brewers) | 63 | 73 | .463 | 16½ | John Tamargo |
| WEST | W | L | Pct. | GB | Manager |
| **Lakeland Tigers (Tigers) | 85 | 48 | .639 | — | Mike Rojas |

| | | | | | |
|---|---|---|---|---|---|
| #Dunedin Blue Jays (Blue Jays) | 81 | 57 | .587 | 6½ | Omar Malave |
| Fort Myers Miracle (Twins) | 74 | 59 | .556 | 11 | Riccardo Ingram |
| Sarasota Reds (Reds) | 65 | 67 | .492 | 19½ | Edgar Caceres |
| Tampa Yankees (Yankees) | 55 | 78 | .414 | 30 | Joe Breeden |
| Clearwater Threshers (Phillies) | 41 | 95 | .301 | 45½ | Greg Legg |

**PLAYOFFS—Semifinals:** Lakeland defeated Dunedin 2-0 and Palm Beach defeated Vero Beach 2-1 in best-of-3 series. **Final:** Palm Beach defeated Lakeland 3-2 in best-of-5 series.

## MIDWEST LEAGUE                                               LOW A

| EAST | W | L | Pct. | GB | Manager(s) |
|---|---|---|---|---|---|
| **South Bend Silver Hawks (Diamondbacks) | 84 | 56 | .600 | — | Mark Haley |
| #West Michigan Whitecaps (Tigers) | 73 | 67 | .521 | 11 | Matt Walbeck |
| #Southwest Michigan Devil Rays (Devil Rays) | 72 | 67 | .518 | 11½ | Joe Szekely |
| Lansing Lugnuts (Blue Jays) | 70 | 69 | .504 | 13½ | Ken Joyce |
| #Fort Wayne Wizards (Padres) | 65 | 75 | .464 | 19 | Randy Ready |
| Dayton Dragons (Reds) | 60 | 79 | .432 | 23½ | Alonzo Powell |
| WEST | W | L | Pct. | GB | Manager |
| **Wisconsin Timber Rattlers (Mariners) | 76 | 63 | .547 | — | Scott Steinmann |
| #Swing of the Quad Cities (Cardinals) | 72 | 67 | .518 | 4 | Joe Cunningham |
| #Clinton LumberKings (Rangers) | 71 | 69 | .507 | 5½ | Carlos Subero |
| #Beloit Snappers (Twins) | 69 | 71 | .493 | 8 | Kevin Boles |
| Peoria Chiefs (Cubs) | 68 | 72 | .486 | 9 | Julio Garcia |
| Kane County Cougars (Athletics) | 67 | 72 | .482 | 9½ | Dave Joppie |
| Burlington Bees (Royals) | 65 | 75 | .464 | 12 | Jim Gabella |
| Cedar Rapids Kernels (Angels) | 65 | 75 | .464 | 12 | Bobby Magallanes |

**PLAYOFFS—Division Series:** South Bend defeated Southwest Michigan 2-0, Clinton defeated Quad Cities 2-0, West Michigan defeated Fort Wayne 2-0 and Wisconsin defeated Beloit 2-1 in best-of-3 series. **Semifinals:** South Bend defeated West Michigan 2-0 and Wisconsin defeated Clinton 2-0 in best-of-3 series. **Final:** South Bend defeated Wisconsin 3-2 in best-of-5 series.

## SOUTH ATLANTIC LEAGUE                                        LOW A

| NORTH | W | L | Pct. | GB | Manager |
|---|---|---|---|---|---|
| Lexington Legends (Astros) | 81 | 58 | .583 | — | Tim Bogar |
| Lake County Captains (Indians) | 72 | 66 | .522 | 8½ | Mike Sarbaugh |
| *Delmarva Shorebirds (Orioles) | 72 | 67 | .518 | 9 | Gary Kendall |
| *Hagerstown Suns (Mets) | 71 | 66 | .518 | 9 | Gene Richards |
| Greensboro Grasshoppers (Marlins) | 67 | 71 | .486 | 13½ | Brandon Hyde |
| West Virginia Power (Brewers) | 60 | 78 | .435 | 20½ | Ramon Aviles |
| Hickory Crawdads (Pirates) | 54 | 80 | .403 | 24½ | Jeff Branson |
| Lakewood BlueClaws (Phillies) | 56 | 83 | .403 | 25 | P.J. Forbes |
| SOUTH | W | L | Pct. | GB | Manager |
| *Charleston RiverDogs (Yankees) | 80 | 58 | .580 | — | Bill Mosiello |
| Augusta GreenJackets (Giants) | 77 | 59 | .566 | 2 | Roberto Kelly |
| *Kannapolis Intimidators (White Sox) | 74 | 59 | .556 | 3½ | Nick Capra |
| Rome Braves (Braves) | 72 | 65 | .526 | 7½ | Rocket Wheeler |
| Greenville Bombers (Red Sox) | 72 | 66 | .522 | 8 | Chad Epperson |
| Asheville Tourists (Rockies) | 71 | 67 | .514 | 9 | Joe Mikulik |
| Savannah Sand Gnats (Nationals) | 62 | 76 | .449 | 18 | Randy Knorr |
| Columbus Catfish (Dodgers) | 57 | 79 | .419 | 22 | Travis Barbary |

**PLAYOFFS—Semifinals:** Kannapolis defeated Charleston 2-0 and Hagerstown defeated Delmarva 2-1 in best-of-3 series. **Final:** Kannapolis defeated Hagerstown 3-1, in best-of-5 series.

## NEW YORK-PENN LEAGUE                                  SHORT-SEASON A

| McNAMARA | W | L | Pct. | GB | Manager |
|---|---|---|---|---|---|
| Staten Island Yankees (Yankees) | 52 | 24 | .684 | — | Andy Stankiewicz |
| #Williamsport Crosscutters (Pirates) | 44 | 32 | .579 | 8 | Tom Prince |
| Brooklyn Cyclones (Mets) | 40 | 36 | .526 | 12 | Mookie Wilson |
| New Jersey Cardinals (Cardinals) | 37 | 39 | .487 | 15 | Mark DeJohn |
| Hudson Valley Renegades (Devil Rays) | 31 | 43 | .419 | 20 | Dave Howard |
| Aberdeen IronBirds (Orioles) | 27 | 48 | .360 | 24½ | Andy Etchebarren |
| PINCKNEY | W | L | Pct. | GB | Manager |
| Auburn Doubledays (Blue Jays) | 45 | 30 | .600 | — | Dennis Holmberg |
| Batavia Muckdogs (Phillies) | 36 | 39 | .480 | 9 | Manny Amador |
| Mahoning Valley Scrappers (Indians) | 33 | 43 | .434 | 12½ | Rouglas Odor |
| Jamestown Jammers (Marlins) | 31 | 44 | .413 | 14 | Mike Mordecai |
| STEDLER | W | L | Pct. | GB | Manager |
| Oneonta Tigers (Tigers) | 48 | 27 | .640 | — | Tom Brookens |
| Lowell Spinners (Red Sox) | 42 | 33 | .560 | 6 | Luis Alicea |
| Tri-City ValleyCats (Astros) | 34 | 42 | .447 | 14½ | Gregg Langbehn |
| Vermont Expos | 28 | 48 | .368 | 20½ | Bobby Williams |

**PLAYOFFS—Semifinals:** Auburn defeated Oneonta 2-0 and Staten Island defeated Williamsport 2-0, in best-of-3 series. **Final:** Staten Island defeated Auburn 2-0 in best-of-3 series.

## NORTHWEST LEAGUE — SHORT-SEASON A

| EAST | W | L | Pct. | GB | Manager |
|---|---|---|---|---|---|
| Spokane Indians (Rangers) | 37 | 39 | .487 | — | Greg Riddoch |
| Tri-City Dust Devils (Rockies) | 36 | 40 | .474 | 1 | Ron Gideon |
| Boise Hawks (Cubs) | 34 | 42 | .447 | 3 | Trey Forkerway |
| Yakima Bears (Diamondbacks) | 30 | 46 | .395 | 7 | Jay Gainer |
| **WEST** | **W** | **L** | **Pct.** | **GB** | **Manager** |
| Vancouver Canadians (Athletics) | 46 | 30 | .605 | — | Juan Navarrette |
| Salem-Keizer Volcanoes (Giants) | 45 | 31 | .592 | 1 | Steve Decker |
| Everett AquaSox (Mariners) | 42 | 34 | .553 | 4 | Pedro Grifol |
| Eugene Emeralds (Padres) | 34 | 42 | .447 | 12 | Roy Howell |

**PLAYOFFS**—Spokane defeated Vancouver 3-2 in best-of-5 series.

## APPALACHIAN LEAGUE — ROOKIE ADVANCED

| EAST | W | L | Pct. | GB | Manager(s) |
|---|---|---|---|---|---|
| Danville Braves | 47 | 20 | .701 | — | Paul Runge |
| Princeton Devil Rays | 34 | 31 | .523 | 12 | Jamie Nelson |
| Pulaski Blue Jays | 34 | 33 | .507 | 13 | Dave Pano |
| Bluefield Orioles | 31 | 36 | .463 | 16 | Jesus Alfaro |
| Burlington Indians | 25 | 43 | .368 | 22½ | Sean McNally/Lee May Jr. |
| **WEST** | **W** | **L** | **Pct.** | **GB** | **Manager** |
| Elizabethton Twins | 48 | 19 | .716 | — | Ray Smith |
| Bristol White Sox | 30 | 36 | .455 | 17½ | Jerry Hairston |
| Greeneville Astros | 29 | 37 | .439 | 18½ | Russ Nixon |
| Johnson City Cardinals | 28 | 39 | .418 | 20 | Tommy Kidwell |
| Kingsport Mets | 28 | 40 | .412 | 20½ | Jesse Levis |

**PLAYOFFS**—Elizabethton defeated Danville 2-1 in best-of-3 series.

## PIONEER LEAGUE — ROOKIE ADVANCED

| NORTH | W | L | Pct. | GB | Manager |
|---|---|---|---|---|---|
| **Helena Brewers (Brewers) | 46 | 30 | .605 | — | Eddie Sedar |
| #Billings Mustangs (Reds) | 43 | 33 | .566 | 3 | Rick Burleson |
| Missoula Osprey (Diamondbacks) | 34 | 42 | .447 | 12 | Jim Presley |
| Great Falls White Sox (White Sox) | 32 | 44 | .421 | 14 | John Orton |
| **SOUTH** | **W** | **L** | **Pct.** | **GB** | **Manager** |
| *Ogden Raptors (Dodgers) | 39 | 37 | .513 | 7 | Juan Bustabad |
| Casper Rockies (Rockies) | 38 | 38 | .500 | 8 | P.J. Carey |
| *Orem Owlz (Angels) | 38 | 38 | .500 | 8 | Tom Kotchman |
| Idaho Falls Chukars (Royals) | 34 | 42 | .447 | 12 | Brian Rupp |

**PLAYOFFS—Semifinals:** Helena defeated Billings 2-0 and Orem defeated Ogden 2-1 in best-of-3 series. **Final:** Orem defeated Helena 2-0 in best-of-3 series.

## ARIZONA LEAGUE — ROOKIE

| | W | L | Pct. | GB | Manager |
|---|---|---|---|---|---|
| **Giants | 39 | 17 | .696 | — | Bert Hunter |
| Royals | 34 | 22 | .607 | 5 | Lloyd Simmons |
| Athletics | 30 | 26 | .536 | 9 | Ruben Escalera |
| Padres | 29 | 27 | .518 | 10 | Carlos Lezcano |
| Mariners | 27 | 29 | .482 | 12 | Dana Williams |
| Rangers | 27 | 29 | .482 | 12 | Pedro Lopez |
| Angels | 25 | 31 | .446 | 14 | Brian Harper |
| Brewers | 22 | 34 | .393 | 17 | Mike Guerrero |
| Cubs | 19 | 37 | .339 | 20 | Steve McFarland |

**PLAYOFF**—Giants won both halves of the season to claim the league championship.

## GULF COAST LEAGUE — ROOKIE

| EAST | W | L | Pct. | GB | Manager |
|---|---|---|---|---|---|
| Mets | 37 | 16 | .698 | — | Gary Carter |
| Dodgers | 25 | 29 | .463 | 12½ | Luis Salazar |
| Marlins | 24 | 30 | .444 | 13½ | Edwin Rodriguez |
| Nationals | 21 | 32 | .396 | 16 | Wendell Kim |
| **SOUTH** | **W** | **L** | **Pct.** | **GB** | **Manager** |
| Red Sox | 30 | 24 | .556 | — | Ralph Treuel |
| Pirates | 28 | 26 | .519 | 2 | Jeff Livesey |
| Twins | 28 | 26 | .519 | 2 | Nelson Prada |
| Reds | 22 | 32 | .407 | 8 | Luis Aguayo |
| **NORTH** | **W** | **L** | **Pct.** | **GB** | **Manager** |
| Yankees | 33 | 20 | .623 | — | Oscar Acosta |
| Phillies | 24 | 27 | .471 | 8 | Jim Morrison |
| Braves | 24 | 28 | .462 | 8½ | Luis Ortiz |
| Tigers | 24 | 30 | .444 | 9½ | Kevin Bradshaw |

**PLAYOFFS—Semifinal:** Yankees defeated Red Sox 1-0 in one-game playoff. **Final:** Yankees defeated Mets 2-0 in best-of-3 series.

# INTERNATIONAL
## LEAGUE

### CLASS AAA

**Office Address:** 55 S. High St., Suite 202, Dublin, OH 43017. **Telephone:** (614) 791-9300. **FAX:** (614) 791-9009. **E-Mail Address:** office@ilbaseball.com. **Website:** www.ilbaseball.com.

**Years League Active:** 1884-2006.

**President/Treasurer:** Randy Mobley.

**Vice Presidents:** Harold Cooper, Dave Rosenfield (Norfolk), Tex Simone (Syracuse), George Sisler Jr. **Corporate Secretary:** Max Schumacher (Indianapolis).

**Directors:** Bruce Baldwin (Richmond), Don Beaver (Charlotte), George Habel (Durham), Joe Napoli (Toledo), Ray Pecor Jr. (Ottawa), Bob Rich Jr. (Buffalo), Dave Rosenfield (Norfolk), Jeremy Ruby (Scranton/Wilkes-Barre), Ken Schnacke (Columbus), Max Schumacher (Indianapolis), Naomi Silver (Rochester), John Simone (Syracuse), Mike Tamburro (Pawtucket), Gary Ulmer (Louisville).

**Administrative Assistant:** Chris Sprague. **Office Manager:** Gretchen Addison.

**Division Structure: North**—Buffalo, Ottawa, Pawtucket, Rochester, Scranton/Wilkes-Barre, Syracuse. **South**—Charlotte, Durham, Norfolk, Richmond. **West**—Columbus, Indianapolis, Louisville, Toledo.

**Randy Mobley**

**Regular Season:** 144 games. **2006 Opening Date:** April 6. **Closing Date:** Sept. 4.

**All-Star Game:** July 12 at Toledo, OH (IL vs. Pacific Coast League).

**Playoff Format:** West champion meets South champion in best-of-5 series; wild-card club (non-division winner with best record) meets North champion in best-of-5 series. Winners meet in best-of-5 series for Governors' Cup championship.

**Roster Limit:** 24. **Player Eligibility Rule:** No restrictions.

**Brand of Baseball:** Rawlings ROM-INT.

**Statistician:** Major League Baseball Advanced Media, 75 Ninth Ave., New York, NY 10011.

**Umpires:** Lance Barksdale (Terry, MS), Scott Barry (Quincy, MI), Damien Beal (Fultondale, AL), Tyler Bolick (Woodstock, GA), Kevin Causey (Maple Grove, MN), Brad Cole (Ormond Beach, FL), Brandon Cooper (Louisville, KY), Dan Cricks (Birmingham, AL), Dusty Dellinger (China Grove, NC), Adam Dowdy (Pontiac, IL), Mike Estabrook (Tampa, FL), Chad Fairchild (Sarasota, FL), Troy Fullwood (Hampton, VA), Chris Griffith (Fort Worth, TX), James Hoye (North Royalton, OH), Chris Hubler (Newtown, PA), Adrian Johnson (Houston, TX), Joe Judkowitz (Coral Springs, FL), Josh Miller (Parkland, FL), Pete Pederson (Orlando, FL), Brent Persinger (Lexington, KY), Andy Roberts (Birmingham, AL), Jamie Roebuck (Connelly Springs, NC), R.J. Thompson (Mt. Carmel, TN), David Uyl (Shorewood, IL).

### STADIUM INFORMATION

| Club | Stadium | Opened | LF | CF | RF | Capacity | 2005 Att. |
|------|---------|--------|----|----|----|----------|-----------|
| Buffalo | Dunn Tire Park | 1988 | 325 | 404 | 325 | 18,150 | 596,171 |
| Charlotte | Knights Stadium | 1990 | 325 | 400 | 325 | 10,002 | 289,409 |
| Columbus | Cooper Stadium | 1977 | 355 | 400 | 330 | 15,000 | 520,104 |
| Durham | Durham Bulls Athletic Park | 1995 | 305 | 400 | 327 | 10,000 | 520,371 |
| Indianapolis | Victory Field | 1996 | 320 | 402 | 320 | 15,500 | 558,901 |
| Louisville | Louisville Slugger Field | 2000 | 325 | 400 | 340 | 13,200 | 643,466 |
| Norfolk | Harbor Park | 1993 | 333 | 410 | 338 | 12,067 | 502,502 |
| Ottawa | Lynx Stadium | 1993 | 325 | 404 | 325 | 10,332 | 160,544 |
| Pawtucket | McCoy Stadium | 1946 | 325 | 400 | 325 | 10,031 | 688,421 |
| Richmond | The Diamond | 1985 | 330 | 402 | 330 | 12,134 | 414,959 |
| Rochester | Frontier Field | 1997 | 335 | 402 | 325 | 10,840 | 452,302 |
| Scranton/WB | Lackawanna County Stadium | 1989 | 330 | 408 | 330 | 10,982 | 400,726 |
| Syracuse | Alliance Bank Stadium | 1997 | 330 | 400 | 330 | 11,671 | 382,625 |
| Toledo | Fifth Third Field | 2002 | 320 | 412 | 315 | 8,943 | 556,995 |

# BUFFALO
## BISONS

**Office Address:** 275 Washington St., Buffalo, NY 14203.
**Telephone:** (716) 846-2000. **FAX:** (716) 852-6530.
**E-Mail Address:** info@bisons.com. **Website:** www.bisons.com.
**Affiliation (first year):** Cleveland Indians (1995). **Years in League:** 1886-90, 1912-70, 1998-.

### OWNERSHIP, MANAGEMENT
**Operated by:** Rich Products Corp.
**Chairman:** Robert Rich Sr. **Principal Owner, President:** Robert Rich Jr.
**President, Rich Entertainment Group:** Melinda Rich. **President, Rich Baseball Operations:** Jon Dandes. **Vice President/Treasurer:** David Rich. **VP/Secretary:** William Gisel.
**VP/General Manager:** Mike Buczkowski. **VP, Finance:** Joseph Segarra. **Corporate Counsel:** Jill Bond, William Grieshober. **Director, Sales:** Christopher Hill. **Director, Stadium Operations:** Tom Sciarrino. **Controller:** Kevin Parkinson. **Senior Accountants:** Rita Clark, Nicole Winiarski. **Accountant:** Amy Delaney. **Human Resource Specialist:** Pat De'Aeth. **Manager, Ticket Operations:** Mike Poreda. **Public Relations Coordinator:** Brad Bisbing. **Game Day Entertainment/Promotions Coordinator:** Matt LaSota. **Account Executives:** Kristen Burwell, Mark Gordon, Jim Harrington, Carrie Hontz, Brendan Kelly, Amanda Kolin, Geoff Lundquist, Burt Mirti, Frank Mooney, Anthony Sprague. **Sales/Marketing Coordinator:** Susan Kirk. **Manager, Merchandise:** Kathleen Wind. **Merchandising Assistant:** Kim Spoth. **Manager, Office Services:** Margaret Russo. **Executive Assistant:** Tina Sarcinelli. **Community Relations:** Gail Hodges. **Director, Food/Beverages:** John Rupp. **Assistant Concessions Manager:** Roger Buczek. **General Manager, Pettibones Grill:** Robert Free. **Head Groundskeeper:** Kari Allen. **Chief Engineer:** Pat Chella. **Home Clubhouse/Equipment Manager:** Scott Lesher. **Visiting Clubhouse Manager:** Dan Brick.

### FIELD STAFF
**Manager:** Torey Lovullo. **Coach:** Bruce Fields. **Pitching Coach:** Greg Hibbard. **Trainer:** Todd Tomczyk.

### GAME INFORMATION
**Radio Announcers:** Duke McGuire, Jim Rosenhaus. **No. of Games Broadcast:** Home-72, Away-72. **Flagship Station:** WECK 1230-AM.
**PA Announcer:** Jon Summers. **Official Scorers:** Mike Kelly, Kevin Lester.
**Stadium Name:** Dunn Tire Park. **Location:** From north, take I-190 to Elm Street exit, left onto Swan Street. From east, take I-90 West to exit 51 (Route 33) to end, exit at Oak Street, right onto Swan Street. From west, take I-90 East, exit 53 to I-190 North, exit at Elm Street, left onto Swan Street. **Standard Game Times:** 7:05 p.m., Sun 2:05. **Ticket Price Range:** $5-18.
**Visiting Club Hotels:** Adams Mark Hotel, 120 Church St., Buffalo, NY 14202. Telephone: (716) 845-5100. Hyatt Hotel, 2 Fountain Plaza, Buffalo, NY 14202. Telephone (716) 856-1234.

# CHARLOTTE
## KNIGHTS

**Office Address:** 2280 Deerfield Dr., Fort Mill, SC 29715.
**Telephone:** (704) 357-8071. **FAX:** (704) 329-2155.
**E-Mail Address:** knights@charlotteknights.com. **Website:** www.charlotteknights.com.
**Affiliation (first year):** Chicago White Sox (1999). **Years in League:** 1993-.

### OWNERSHIP, MANAGEMENT
**Operated by:** Knights Baseball, LLC.
**Principal Owners:** Bill Allen, Don Beaver. **President:** Don Beaver.
**Vice President/General Manager:** Dan Rajkowski. **Assistant GM:** Jon Percival. **Director, Group Sales:** Thomas Lee. **Director, Media/Community Relations:** Timothy O'Reilly. **Director, Creative Services:** Mike Riviello. **Director, Broadcasting/Team Travel:** Matt Swierad. **Director, Corporate Accounts:** Chris Semmens. **Business Manager:** Chris Moore. **Corporate Account Manager:** Matthew Finch. **Group Event Coordinators:** Heath Dillard, Justin Morelli, Matt Van Name, Ansley Robertson. **Director, Ticket Operations:** Zach Rutledge. **Director, Stadium Operations:** Tom Humrickhouse. **Office Manager/Merchandise:** Anne Kelley. **Administrative Assistant:** Stephanie Wilfong. **Receptionist:** Courtnie Carter. **Head Groundskeeper:** Eddie Busque. **Assistant Groundskeeper:** Mike Headd. **Clubhouse Manager:** John Bare.

### FIELD STAFF
**Manager:** Razor Shines. **Coach:** Tack Wilson. **Pitching Coach:** Juan Nieves. **Trainer:** Scott Johnson.

### GAME INFORMATION
**Radio Announcers:** Mike Pacheco, Matt Swierad. **No. of Games Broadcast:** Home-72, Away72. **Flagship Station:** WZRH 960-AM.
**PA Announcer:** Ken Conrad. **Official Scorers:** Sam Copeland, Jack Frost, Brent Stastny.

Stadium Name: Knights Stadium. Location: Exit 88 off I-77, east on Gold Hill Road. Standard Game Times: 7:15 p.m., Sun. 2:15. Ticket Price Range: $6-12.
Visiting Club Hotel: Quality Suites Pineville, 9840 Pineville Matthews Rd., Pineville, NC 28134. Telephone: (704) 889-7095

# COLUMBUS
## CLIPPERS

Office Address: 1155 W. Mound St., Columbus, OH 43223.
Telephone: (614) 462-5250. FAX: (614) 462-3271.
E-Mail Address: info@clippersbaseball.com. Website: www.clippersbaseball.com.
Affiliation (first year): New York Yankees (1979). Years in League: 1955-70, 1977-.

## OWNERSHIP, MANAGEMENT
Operated by: Columbus Baseball Team, Inc.
Principal Owner: Franklin County, Ohio.
Board of Directors: Donald Borror, Stephen Cheek, Wayne Harer, Thomas Katzenmeyer, David Leland, Cathy Lyttle, Richard Smith.
President, General Manager: Ken Schnacke. Assistant GM: Mark Warren. Director, Stadium Operations: Steve Dalin. Director, Ticket Operations: Scott Ziegler. Director, Marketing: Mark Galuska. Assistant Director, Marketing: Ty Debevoise. Director, Broadcasting: Scott Leo. Director, Communications/Media Relations: Joe Santry. Director, Merchandising: Krista Oberlander. Director, Finance: Bonnie Badgley. Director, Group Sales: Travis Hall. Assistant to GM: Judi Timmons. Administrative Assistants: Chris Anders, Eric Archibald, Kelly Ryther, Anthony Slosser.

## FIELD STAFF
Manager: Dave Miley. Coaches: Frank Howard, Kevin Long. Pitching Coach: Neil Allen. Trainer: Darren London.

## GAME INFORMATION
Radio Announcers: Scott Leo, Randy Rhinehart. No. of Games Broadcast: Home-72, Away-72. Flagship Station: WVKO 1580-AM.
PA Announcer: Rich Hanchette. Official Scorer: Dan Hill.
Stadium Name: Cooper Stadium. Location: From north/south, I-71 to I-70 West, exit at Mound Street. From west, I-70 East, exit at Broad Street, east to Glenwood, south to Mound Street. From east, I-70 West, exit at Mound Street. Standard Game Times: 7:05 p.m.; Fri. 7:05/7:25; Sat. 6:05/7:05; Sun. 1:05. Ticket Price Range: $6-10.
Visiting Club Hotels: Radisson Hotel, 7007 N. High St., Columbus, OH 43085. Telephone: (614) 436-0700. Sheraton Suites-Columbus, 201 Hutchinson Ave., Columbus, OH 43235. Telephone: (614) 781-7316. Holiday Inn, 175 Hutchinson Ave., Columbus, OH 43235. Telephone: (614) 431-4457.

# DURHAM
## BULLS

Office Address: 409 Blackwell St., Durham, NC 27701.
Mailing Address: P.O. Box 507, Durham, NC 27702.
Telephone: (919) 687-6500. FAX: (919) 687-6560.
Website: www.durhambulls.com.
Affiliation (first year): Tampa Bay Devil Rays (1998). Years in League: 1998-.

## OWNERSHIP, MANAGEMENT
Operated by: Capitol Broadcasting Co., Inc.
President, Chief Executive Officer: Jim Goodmon.
Vice President: George Habel. VP, Legal Counsel: Mike Hill.
General Manager: Mike Birling. Assistant GM: Jon Bishop. Account Executives, Sponsorship: Dusty Hickman, Chip Hutchinson, Chris Overby, Neil Solondz. Coordinator, Sponsorship Services: Suzi Paugh. Director, Media Relations/Promotions: Matt DeMargel. Coordinator, Marketing: Cicero Leak. Assistant, Media Relations: Drew Blake. Assistant, Promotions: Allison Phillips. Director, Ticketing: Tim Seaton. Supervisor, Ticket Operations: Ben DuGoff. Business Development Coordinators: Vince Logan, Jacob Powers, Mary Beth Warfford. Group Sales Assistant: Ben Sanderson. Coordinator, Ticket Services: Meredith Linden. Director, Stadium Operations: Shawn Kison. Supervisor, Operations: Derek Walsh. Manager, Merchandise: Yunhui Harris. General Manager, Concessions: Jamie Jenkins. Assistant GM, Concessions: Tammy Scott. Head Groundskeeper: Scott Strickland. Manager, Business: Rhonda Carlile. Supervisor, Accounting: Theresa Stocking. Accountant: Nicole Mazyck. Director, Security: Ed Sarvis. Box Office Sales: Jerry Mach. Manager, Home Clubhouse: Colin Saunders. Manager, Visiting/Umpires Clubhouse: Aaron Kuehner.

## FIELD STAFF
Manager: John Tamargo Sr. Coach: Richie Hebner. Pitching Coach: Joe Coleman. Trainer: Tom Tisdale.

## GAME INFORMATION
Radio Announcers: Steve Barnes, Neil Solondz, Ken Tanner. No. of Games Broadcast: Home-72, Away-72.

**Flagship Station:** WDNC 620-AM.
   **PA Announcer:** Bill Law. **Official Scorer:** Brent Belvin.
   **Stadium Name:** Durham Bulls Athletic Park. **Location:** From Raleigh, I-40 West to Highway 147 North, exit 12B to Willard, two blocks on Willard to stadium. From I-85, Gregson Street exit to downtown, left on Chapel Hill Street, right on Mangum Street. **Standard Game Times:** 7 p.m., Sun. 5. **Ticket Price Range:** $5-8.
   **Visiting Club Hotel:** Durham Marriott at the Civic Center, 201 Foster St., Durham, NC 27701. Telephone: (919) 768-6000.

# INDIANAPOLIS
## INDIANS

   **Office Address:** 501 W. Maryland St., Indianapolis, IN 46225.
   **Telephone:** (317) 269-3542. **FAX:** (317) 269-3541.
   **E-Mail Address:** indians@indyindians.com. **Website:** www.indyindians.com.
   **Affiliation (first year):** Pittsburgh Pirates (2005). **Years in League:** 1963, 1998-.

## OWNERSHIP, MANAGEMENT
   **Operated by:** Indians, Inc.
   **Chairman, President:** Max Schumacher.
   **Vice President, Treasurer:** Alan Kimbell. **Secretary:** Max Little.
   **General Manager:** Cal Burleson. **Assistant GM, Operations:** Randy Lewandowski. **Director, Facility Maintenance:** Tim Hughes. **Director, Business Operations:** Brad Morris. **Director, Baseball/Stadium Operations:** Scott Rubin. **Director, Facilities:** Bill Sampson. **Director, Marketing:** Chris Herndon. **Director, Broadcasting:** Howard Kellman. **Director, Corporate Development:** Bruce Schumacher. **Director, Merchandising:** Mark Schumacher. **Director, Ticket Sales:** Byron Stevens. **Director, Ticket Operations:** Matt Guay. **Assistant Director, Facility Maintenance:** Allan Danehy. **Graphic Designer:** Sherard Allen. **Ticket Sales Executives:** Chad Bohm, Greg Gilbertson, Desmond Hall, Jake Oakman, Tim Tiefenbach. **Video Producer:** David Harris. **Marketing Coordinator:** Beth Miller. **Box Office Manager:** Courtney Parker. **Account Executive:** Robert Portnoy. **Manager, Media Relations:** Matt Segal. **Manager, Community Relations:** Hillary Toivonen. **Manager, Premium Services:** Kerry Vick. **Office Manager:** Julie Fischer. **Head Groundskeeper:** Jamie Mehringer. **Assistant Groundskeeper:** Jeff Hermesch. **Administrative Assistant:** Stu Tobias. **Assistant, Business Operations:** Nicholas Giorgio. **Assistant, Community Relations:** Kelly Herner. **Assistants, Ticket Operations:** Kevin McCormick, Adam Morrissey, Tannis Terry. **Assistant, Media Relations:** Bill Potter. **Assistant, Stadium Operations:** Marco Price. **Assistant, Marketing:** Steven Tennies. **Home Clubhouse Manager:** Steve Humphrey. **Visiting Clubhouse Managers:** Bob Martin, Jeremy Martin.

## FIELD STAFF
   **Manager:** Trent Jewett. **Coach:** Hensley Meulens. **Pitching Coach:** Jeff Andrews. **Trainer:** Jason Palmer. **Strength/Conditioning:** Kevin Casula.

## GAME INFORMATION
   **Radio Announcers:** Howard Kellman, Robert Portnoy. **No. of Games Broadcast:** Home-72, Away-72. **Flagship Station:** ESPN 950-AM.
   **PA Announcer:** Bruce Schumacher. **Official Scorers:** Tom Akins, Gary Johnson, Kim Rogers.
   **Stadium Name:** Victory Field. **Location:** I-70 to West Street exit, north on West Street to ballpark; I-65 to Martin Luther King and West Street exit, south on West Street to ballpark. **Standard Game Times:** 7 p.m., Sun. 2/6. **Ticket Price Range:** $8-12.
   **Visiting Club Hotels:** Best Western City Centre, 410 South Missouri St., Indianapolis, IN 46225. Telephone: (317) 822-6400. Courtyard By Marriott Downtown, 510 W. Washington St., Indianapolis, IN 46204. Telephone: (317) 635-4443.

# LOUISVILLE
## BATS

   **Office Address:** 401 E. Main St., Louisville, KY 40202.
   **Telephone:** (502) 212-2287. **FAX:** (502) 515-2255.
   **E-Mail Address:** info@batsbaseball.com. **Website:** www.batsbaseball.com.
   **Affiliation (first year):** Cincinnati Reds (2000). **Years in League:** 1998-.

## OWNERSHIP, MANAGEMENT
   **Operated by:** Louisville Baseball Club, Inc.
   **Board of Directors:** Mike Brown, Ed Glasscock, Jack Hillerich, Kenny Huber, Bob Stallings, Steve Trager, Dan Ulmer, Gary Ulmer.
   **Chairman:** Dan Ulmer. **President:** Gary Ulmer.
   **Vice President/General Manager:** Dale Owens. **Assistant GM/Director, Marketing:** Greg Galiette. **Director, Baseball Operations:** Mary Barney. **Director, Stadium Operations:** Scott Shoemaker. **Director, Ticket Sales:** James Breeding. **Director, Broadcasting:** Jim Kelch. **Controller:** Michele Anderson. **Manager, Tickets:** George Veith. **Director, Public/Media Relations:** Svend Jansen. **Director, Suite Level Services:** Kyle Reh. **Manager, Ticket**

Accounting: Earl Stubblefield. **Coordinator, Group Sales:** Bryan McBride. **Senior Account Executives:** Jason Abraham, Nick Evans, Hal Norwood, Matt Wilmes. **Assistant Director, Public/Media Relations:** Megan Dimond. **Manager, Community Relations:** Karrie Harper. **Operations Assistant:** Doug Randol. **Senior Account Executive:** Matt Andrews. **Account Executives:** Joel Kammeyer, Evan Patrick. **Assistant Ticket Manager:** Josh Hargreaves. **Administrative Assistant:** Jodi Tischendorf. **Head Groundskeeper:** Tom Nielsen. **Assistant Groundskeeper:** Brad Smith.

### FIELD STAFF
**Manager:** Rick Sweet. **Coaches:** Adrian Garrett, Alonzo Powell. **Pitching Coach:** Lee Tunnell. **Trainer:** Chris Lapole.

### GAME INFORMATION
**Radio Announcers:** Matt Andrews, Jim Kelch. **No. of Games Broadcast:** Home-72, Away-72. **Flagship Station:** WGTK 970-AM.
**PA Announcer:** Charles Gazaway. **Official Scorer:** Ken Horn.
**Stadium Name:** Louisville Slugger Field. **Location:** I-64 and I-71 to I-65 South/North to Brook Street exit, right on Market Street, left on Jackson Street, stadium on Main Street between Jackson and Preston. **Standard Game Times:** 7:15 p.m.; Sat. 6:15, Sun. 1:15/6:15. **Ticket Price Range:** $4-9.
**Visiting Club Hotel:** Marriott Louisville Downtown, 280 W. Jefferson St., Louisville, KY 40202. Telephone: (502) 627-5044.

# NORFOLK
## TIDES

**Office Address:** 150 Park Ave., Norfolk, VA 23510.
**Telephone:** (757) 622-2222. **FAX:** (757) 624-9090.
**Website:** www.norfolktides.com. **E-Mail Address:** receptionist@norfolktides.com.
**Affiliation (first year):** New York Mets (1969). **Years in League:** 1969-.

### OWNERSHIP, MANAGEMENT
**Operated by:** Tides Baseball Club, LP.
**President:** Ken Young.
**General Manager:** Dave Rosenfield. **Assistant GM:** Ben Giancola. **Director, Media Relations:** Ian Locke. **Director, Community Relations:** Heather McKeating. **Director, Ticket Operations:** Glenn Riggs. **Business Manager:** Mike Giedlin. **Director, Group Sales:** Dave Harrah. **Director, Stadium Operations:** John Slagle. **Manager, Merchandising:** Mandy Cormier. **Local Sales Manager:** Jack Kotarides. **Assistant, Stadium Operations:** Mike Zeman. **Coordinator, Group Sales:** Stephanie Brammer. **Ticket Manager:** Linda Waisanen. **Administrative Assistant:** Jenn Moore. **Group Sales Representative:** Jonathan Slagle. **Group Sales Assistant:** Jonathan Mensink. **Sales Representative:** Anne Valihura. **Director, Video Operations:** Jody Cox. **Equipment/Clubhouse Manager:** Stan Hunter. **Head Groundskeeper:** Ken Magner. **Assistant Groundskeeper:** Keith Collins.

### FIELD STAFF
**Manager:** Ken Oberkfell. **Coach:** Howard Johnson. **Pitching Coach:** Randy Niemann. **Trainer:** Brian Chicklo.

### GAME INFORMATION
**Radio Announcers:** John Castleberry, Bob Socci. **No. of Games Broadcast:** Home-72, Away-72. **Flagship Station:** ESPN 1310-AM.
**PA Announcer:** John Lewis, Don Bolger. **Official Scorer:** Mike Holtzclaw.
**Stadium Name:** Harbor Park. **Location:** Exit 9, 11A or 11B off I-264, adjacent to the Elizabeth River in downtown Norfolk. **Standard Game Times:** 7:15 p.m.; Sun. (April-June) 1:15, (July-Sept.) 6:15. **Ticket Price Range:** $8.50-10.
**Visiting Club Hotels:** Sheraton Waterside, 777 Waterside Dr., Norfolk, VA 23510. Telephone: (757) 622-6664;

# OTTAWA
## LYNX

**Office Address:** Lynx Stadium, 300 Coventry Rd., Ottawa, Ontario K1K 4P5.
**Telephone:** (613) 747-5969. **FAX:** (613) 747-0003.
**E-Mail Address:** lynx@ottawalynx.com. **Website:** www.ottawalynx.com.
**Affiliation (first year):** Baltimore Orioles (2003). **Years in League:** 1951-54, 1993-.

### OWNERSHIP, MANAGEMENT
**Operated By:** Ottawa Lynx Company.
**Principal Owner:** Ray Pecor Jr.
**General Manager:** Kyle Bostwick. **Assistant GM:** Mark Sluban. **Office Administrator:** Lorraine Charrette. **Director, Media/Public Relations:** Brian Morris. **Director, Ticket Operations:** Melissa Rumble. **Promotions:** Angie Lynch. **Head Groundskeeper:** Steve Bennett. **Equipment Manager:** John Bryk. **Visiting Clubhouse Manager:** Jason Ross.

### FIELD STAFF
**Manager:** Dave Trembley. **Coach:** Dallas Williams. **Pitching Coach:** Larry McCall. **Athletic Trainer:** P.J. Mainville.

**Strength/Conditioning Coach**: Joe Hogarty.

## GAME INFORMATION

**Radio**: Unavailable.
**PA Announcer**: Jeff Lefebvre. **Official Scorer**: Frank Calamatas.
**Stadium Name**: Lynx Stadium. **Location**: Highway 417 to Vanier Parkway exit, Vanier Parkway north to Coventry Road to stadium. **Standard Game Times**: 7:05 p.m.; Sat. 6:05, Sun. 1:05. **Ticket Price Range**: $6.50-11.
**Visiting Club Hotel**: Chimo Hotel, 1199 Joseph Cyr Rd., Ottawa, Ontario K1K 3P5. Telephone: (613) 744-1060.

# PAWTUCKET
## RED SOX

**Office Address**: One Ben Mondor Way, Pawtucket, RI 02860.
**Mailing Address**: P.O. Box 2365, Pawtucket, RI 02861.
**Telephone**: (401) 724-7300. **FAX**: (401) 724-2140.
**E-Mail Address**: info@pawsox.com. **Website**: www.pawsox.com.
**Affiliation (first year)**: Boston Red Sox (1973). **Years in League**: 1973-.

## OWNERSHIP, MANAGEMENT

**Operated by**: Pawtucket Red Sox Baseball Club, Inc.
**Chairman**: Ben Mondor. **President**: Mike Tamburro.
**Vice President/General Manager**: Lou Schwechheimer. **VP, Chief Financial Officer**: Matt White. **VP, Sales/Marketing**: Michael Gwynn. **VP, Stadium Operations**: Mick Tedesco. **VP, Public Relations**: Bill Wanless. **Assistant to GM**: Daryl Jasper. **Director, Broadcasting/Community Affairs**: Unavailable. **Director, Ticket Operations**: Mike McAtee. **Manager, Finance**: Kathryn Tingley. **Director, Community Relations**: Jeff Bradley. **Director, Merchandising**: Eric Petterson. **Director, Media Services**: Jeff Ouimette. **Director, Warehouse Operations**: Dave Johnson. **Director, Concession Services**: Jim Hogan. **Director, Corporate Services**: Frank Quinn. **Director, Group Sales**: Bill Crawford. **Gameday Statistician/Account Executive**: Stephen Acciardo. **Secretary**: Kim Garcia. **Clubhouse Manager**: Unavailable. **Head Groundskeeper**: Casey Erven. **Assistant Groundskeeper**: Matt McKinnon. **Facility Operations**: Kevin Galligan. **Executive Chef**: Dom Rendine.

## FIELD STAFF

**Manager**: Ron Johnson. **Coach**: Mark Budaska. **Pitching Coach**: Mike Griffin. **Trainer**: Greg Barajas.

## GAME INFORMATION

**Radio Announcer**: Steve Hyder. **No. of Games Broadcast**: Home-72, Away-72. **Flagship Station**: WSKO 790-AM.
**PA Announcer**: Jim Martin. **Official Scorer**: Bruce Guindon.
**Stadium Name**: McCoy Stadium. **Location**: From north, Route 95 South to exit 2A in Massachusetts, follow Newport Ave. for 2 miles, right on Columbus Ave., follow Columbus Ave. for one mile, stadium on right. From south, Route 95 North to exit 28 (School Street), right at bottom of exit ramp, through two sets of lights, left onto Pond Street, right on Columbus Ave., stadium entrance on left. From west, Route 146 South to Route 295 North to Route 95 South and follow directions from north. From east, Route 195 West to Route 95 North and follow directions from south. **Standard Game Times**: 7 p.m.; Sat. 6, Sun. 1. **Ticket Price Range**: $6-9.
**Visiting Club Hotel**: Comfort Inn, 2 George St., Pawtucket, RI 02860. Telephone: (401) 723-6700.

# RICHMOND
## BRAVES

**Office Address**: 3001 North Blvd., Richmond, VA 23230.
**Mailing Address**: P.O. Box 6667, Richmond, VA 23230.
**Telephone**: (804) 359-4444. **FAX**: (804) 359-0731.
**E-Mail Address**: info@rbraves.com. **Website**: www.rbraves.com.
**Affiliation (first year)**: Atlanta Braves (1966). **Years in League**: 1884, 1915-17, 1954-64, 1966-.

## OWNERSHIP, MANAGEMENT

**Operated by**: Atlanta National League Baseball, Inc.
**General Manager**: Bruce Baldwin. **Assistant GM**: Toby Wyman. **Office Manager**: Joanne Curnutt. **Receptionist**: Janet Zimmerman. **Manager, Stadium Operations**: Jonathan Griffith. **Manager, Field Maintenance**: Gerry Huppman. **Manager, Public Relations**: John Emmett. **Assistant Manager, Community Relations**: Elizabeth Snavely. **Assistant Manager, Promotions/Entertainment**: Noir Fowler. **Manager, Corporate Sales**: Ben Terry. **Manager, Ticket Operations**: Meghan Lynch. **Assistant Manager, Ticket Operations**: Mike Castle. **Corporate Sales Representative**: Lisa Howell. **Clubhouse Manager**: Nick Dixon.

## FIELD STAFF

**Manager**: Brian Snitker. **Coach**: Rick Albert. **Pitching Coach**: Derek Botelho. **Trainer**: Jay Williams.

## GAME INFORMATION

**Radio Announcers**: Robert Fish, Steve Patras. **No. of Games Broadcast**: Home-72, Away-72. **Flagship Station**:

WXGI 950-AM.
**PA Announcer:** Mike Blacker. **Official Scorers:** Gary Criswell, Rusty Gold.
**Stadium Name:** The Diamond. **Location:** Exit 78 (Boulevard) at junction of I-64 and I-95, follow signs to park.
**Standard Game Times:** 7 p.m., Sun. 2. **Ticket Price Range:** $6-9.
**Visiting Club Hotel:** Quality Inn, 8008 W. Broad St., Richmond, VA 23230. Telephone: (804) 346-0000.

# ROCHESTER
## RED WINGS

**Office Address:** One Morrie Silver Way, Rochester, NY 14608.
**Telephone:** (585) 454-1001. **FAX:** (585) 454-1056, (585) 454-1057.
**E-Mail Address:** info@redwingsbaseball.com. **Website:** www.redwingsbaseball.com.
**Affiliation (first year):** Minnesota Twins (2003). **Years in League:** 1885-89, 1891-92, 1895-.

### OWNERSHIP, MANAGEMENT
**Operated by:** Rochester Community Baseball.
**Chairman, Chief Operating Officer:** Naomi Silver. **President, Chief Executive Officer:** Gary Larder.
**General Manager:** Dan Mason. **Assistant GM:** Will Rumbold. **Controller:** Darlene Giardina. **Head Groundskeeper:** Gene Buonomo. **Director, Media/Public Relations:** Chuck Hinkel. **Director, Corporate Development:** Nick Sciarratta. **Group/Picnic Director:** Parker Allen. **Director, Merchandising:** Mary Goldman. **Director, Human Resources:** Paula LoVerde. **Account Executive:** Rob Dermody. **Assistant Director, Groups/Picnics:** Zach Holmes. **APAR Manager:** Liz Ammons. **Executive Secretary:** Ginny Colbert. **Director, Food Services:** Jeff Dodge. **Manager, Suites/Catering:** Jennifer Pierce. **Catering Sales Manager:** Courtney Trawitz. **Manager, Concessions:** Jeff DeSantis. **Business Manager, Concessions:** Dave Bills. **Clubhouse Operations:** Terry Costello. **Night Secretary:** Cathie Costello.

### FIELD STAFF
**Manager:** Stan Cliburn. **Coach:** Rich Miller. **Pitching Coach:** Stu Cliburn. **Trainer:** Tony Leo.

### GAME INFORMATION
**Radio Announcers:** Joe Altobelli, Josh Whetzel. **No. of Games Broadcast:** Home-72, Away-72. **Flagship Stations:** WHTK 1280-AM, WYSL 1040-AM.
**PA Announcer:** Mike Pazdyk. **Official Scorer:** Warren Kozereski.
**Stadium Name:** Frontier Field. **Location:** I-490 East to exit 12 (Brown/Broad Street) and follow signs. I-490 West to exit 14 (Plymouth Ave.) and follow signs. **Standard Game Times:** 7:05 p.m., Sun 1:35. **Ticket Price Range:** $5.50-9.50
**Visiting Club Hotel:** Crown Plaza, 70 State St., Rochester, NY 14608. Telephone: (585) 546-3450.

# SCRANTON/WILKES-BARRE
## RED BARONS

**Office Address:** 235 Montage Mountain Rd., Moosic, PA 18507.
**Mailing Address:** P.O. Box 3449, Scranton, PA 18505.
**Telephone:** (570) 969-2255. **FAX:** (570) 963-6564.
**E-Mail Address:** barons@epix.net. **Website:** www.redbarons.com.
**Affiliation (first year):** Philadelphia Phillies (1989). **Years in League:** 1989-.

### OWNERSHIP, MANAGEMENT
**Operated by:** Lackawanna County Stadium Authority.
**Chairman:** Anthony Lomma.
**General Manager:** Jeremy Ruby. **Director, Media/Public Relations:** Mike Cummings. **Director, Accounts Payable:** Karen Healey. **Office Manager:** Donna Kunda. **Director, Baseball Operations:** Jon Stephenson. **Executive Assistant:** Kelly Byron. **Director, Corporate Sales:** Jason Tribbet. **Director, Ticketing:** Joe Shaughnessy. **Account Executives:** Kristina Knight, Andrew Marion, Mike Trudnak, Dave Walsh. **Box Office Manager:** Ann Marie Nocera. **Director, Stadium Operations:** Curt Camoni, **Director, Merchandising:** Ray Midura. **Controller:** Unavailable. **Head Groundskeeper:** Bill Casterline. **Clubhouse Operations:** Red Brower, Rich Revta.

### FIELD STAFF
**Manager:** John Russell. **Coach:** Sal Rende. **Pitching Coach:** Rod Nichols. **Trainer:** Brian Cammarota.

### GAME INFORMATION
**Radio Announcer:** Dean Corwin, Kent Westling. **No. of Games Broadcast:** Home-72, Away-72. **Flagship Station:** WWDL 104.9-FM.
**PA Announcer:** Johnny Davies. **Official Scorers:** Jeep Fanucci, Bob McGoff.
**Stadium Name:** Lackawanna County Stadium. **Location:** I-81 to exit 182 (Davis Street/Montage Mountain Road), take Montage Mountain Road one mile to stadium. **Standard Game Times:** 7 p.m.; Sun. 1:30. **Ticket Price Range:** $6.50-9.
**Visiting Club Hotel:** Radisson at Lackawanna Station, 700 Lackawanna Ave., Scranton, PA 18503. Telephone: (570) 342-8300.

# SYRACUSE
## SKYCHIEFS

**Office Address:** One Tex Simone Dr., Syracuse, NY 13208.
**Telephone:** (315) 474-7833. **FAX:** (315) 474-2658.
**E-Mail Address:** baseball@skychiefs.com. **Website:** www.skychiefs.com.
**Affiliation (first year):** Toronto Blue Jays (1978). **Years in League:** 1885-89, 1891-92, 1894-1901, 1918, 1920-27, 1934-55, 1961-.

### OWNERSHIP, MANAGEMENT
**Operated by:** Community Owned Baseball Club of Central New York, Inc.
**Chairman:** Charles Rich. **President:** Donald Waful. **Vice President/Treasurer:** Anton Kreuzer. **Vice President/Chief Operating Officer:** Anthony Simone.
**General Manager:** John Simone. **Assistant GM, Business:** Don Lehtonen. **Director, Group Sales:** Victor Gallucci. **Director, Operations:** H.J. Refici. **Director, Corporate Sales/Community Relations:** Andy Gee. **Associate Director, Group/Corporate Sales:** Mike Voutsinas. **Director, Merchandising:** Wendy Shoen. **Director, Ticket Office:** Jon Blumenthal. **Team Historian:** Ron Gersbacher. **Receptionist:** Priscilla Venditti. **Field Maintenance:** Jim Jacobson.

### FIELD STAFF
**Manager:** Mike Basso. **Coach:** Dwayne Murphy. **Pitching Coach:** Rick Langford. **Trainer:** Jon Woodworth.

### GAME INFORMATION
**Radio Announcer:** Bob McElligott. **No. of Games Broadcast:** Home-72, Away-72. **Flagship Station:** WNSS 1260-AM
**PA Announcer:** Jim Donovan. **Official Scorer:** Paul Fairbanks, Tom Leo, Dan Morgan.
**Stadium Name:** Alliance Bank Stadium. **Location:** New York State Thruway to exit 36 (I-81 South), to 7th North Street exit, left on 7th North, right on Hiawatha Boulevard. **Standard Game Times:** 7 p.m., Sun. 6. **Ticket Price Range:** $5-8.
**Visiting Club Hotel:** Ramada Inn, 1305 Buckley Rd., Syracuse, NY 13212. Telephone: (315) 457-8670.

# TOLEDO
## MUD HENS

**Office Address:** 406 Washington St., Toledo, OH 43604.
**Telephone:** (419) 725-4367. **FAX:** (419) 725-4368.
**E-Mail Address:** mudhens@mudhens.com. **Website:** www.mudhens.com.
**Affiliation (first year):** Detroit Tigers (1987). **Years in League:** 1889, 1965-.

### OWNERSHIP, MANAGEMENT
**Operated by:** Toledo Mud Hens Baseball Club, Inc.
**Chairman, President:** Michael Miller. **Vice President:** David Huey. **Secretary/Treasurer:** Charles Bracken.
**General Manager/Executive Vice President:** Joseph Napoli. **Assistant GM/Director, Marketing:** Scott Jeffer. **Assistant GM/Director, Corporate Partnerships:** Neil Neukam. **Assistant GM, Ticket Sales/Operations:** Erik Ibsen. **Chief Financial Officer:** Bob Eldridge. **Manager, Promotions:** Jamay Edwards. **Director, Public/Media Relations:** Jason Griffin. **Director, Ticket Sales/Services:** Thom Townley. **Manager, Group Sales/Services:** Brian Perkins. **Manager, Box Office Sales/Services:** Greg Setola. **Manager, Community Relations:** Cheri Pastula. **Corporate Sales Associate:** Neil Stein. **Season Ticket/Group Sales Associates:** Chris Hole, Teresa Kahle, John Mulka, Nathan Steinmetz, Eric Tomaszewski. **Manager, Video Board Operations:** Mike Ramirez. **Manager, Merchandising:** Craig Katz. **Assistant Manager, Merchandising:** Ed Sintic. **Manager, Stadium Operations:** Kirk Sausser. **Assistant Manager, Operations:** Melissa Ball. **Business Manager:** Dorothy Welniak. **Office Manager:** Carol Hamilton. **Executive Assistant:** Tracy Evans. **Maintenance Supervisor:** L.C. Bates. **Head Groundskeeper:** Jake Tyler. **Assistant Groundskeeper:** Matt Henn. **Clubhouse Manager:** Joe Sarkisian. **Team Historian:** John Husman.

### FIELD STAFF
**Manager:** Larry Parrish. **Coach:** Leon Durham. **Pitching Coach:** Jeff Jones. **Trainer:** Matt Rankin.

### GAME INFORMATION
**Radio Announcers:** Frank Gilhooley, Jason Griffin, Jim Weber. **No. of Games Broadcast:** Home-72, Away-72. **Flagship Station:** WLQR 1470-AM.
**PA Announcer:** Kevin Mullan. **Official Scorers:** Jeff Businger, Ron Kleinfelter, Guy Lammers.
**Stadium Name:** Fifth Third Field. **Location:** From Ohio Turnpike 80/90, exit 54 (4A) to I-75 North, follow I-75 North to exit 201-B, left onto Erie Street, right onto Washington Street. From Detroit, I-75 South to exit 202-A, right onto Washington Street. From Dayton, I-75 North to exit 201-B, left onto Erie Street, right onto Washington Street. From Ann Arbor, Route 23 South to I-475 East, I-475 East to I-75 South, I-75 South to exit 202-A, right onto Washington Street. **Standard Game Times:** 7 p.m.; Sun. 2. **Ticket Prices:** $8.
**Visiting Club Hotel:** Radisson, 101 North Summit, Toledo, OH 43604. Telephone: (419) 241-3000.

# PACIFIC COAST
## LEAGUE

**Mailing Address:** 1631 Mesa Ave., Suite A, Colorado Springs, CO 80906.
**Telephone:** (719) 636-3399. **FAX:** (719) 636-1199.
**E-Mail Address:** office@pclbaseball.com. **Website:** www.pclbaseball.com.

**President:** Branch B. Rickey.
**Vice President:** Don Logan (Las Vegas).
**Directors:** Don Beaver (New Orleans), Sam Bernabe (Iowa), **PACIFIC COAST LEAGUE**
Dave Chase (Memphis), Chris Cummings (Fresno), Tony Ensor
(Colorado Springs), George Foster (Tacoma), Don Logan (Las Vegas), Jay Miller (Round
Rock), Larry Miller (Salt Lake), Matt Minker (Omaha), Scott Pruitt (Oklahoma), Branch
Rickey (Portland), Art Savage (Sacramento), John Traub (Albuquerque), Glenn Yaeger
(Nashville), Jay Zucker (Tucson).
**Vice President, Business Operations:** George King. **Director, Adminstration:** Melanie
Fiore. **Operations Assistant:** Unavailable.
**Division Structure: American Conference—Northern:** Iowa, Memphis, Nashville,
Omaha. **Southern:** Albuquerque, New Orleans, Oklahoma, Round Rock. **Pacific
Conference—Northern:** Colorado Springs, Portland, Salt Lake, Tacoma. **Southern:** Fresno,
Las Vegas, Sacramento, Tucson.

**Branch Rickey**

**Regular Season:** 144 games. **2006 Opening Date:** April 6. **Closing Date:** Sept. 4.
**All-Star Game:** July 12 at Toledo (PCL vs. International League).
**Playoff Format:** Pacific Conference/Northern champion meets Southern champion, and American
Conference/Northern champion meets Southern champion in best-of-5 semifinal series. Winners meet in best-of-5
series for league championship.
**Roster Limit:** 24. **Player Eligibility Rule:** No restrictions.
**Brand of Baseball:** Rawlings ROM.
**Statistician:** Major League Baseball Advanced Media, 75 Ninth Ave., New York, NY 10011.
**Umpires:** Ramon Armendariz (Vista, CA), Lance Barksdale (Jackson, MS), Angel Campos (Ontario, CA), Scot
Chamberlain (Strawberry Plains, TN), Adam Dowdy (Pontiac, IL), Robert Drake (Mesa, AZ), Peter Durfee (Chico, CA),
Ray Gregson (LaPlace, LA), Chris Guccione (Brighton, CO), Darren Hyman (Sacramento, CA), Cameron Keller
(Colorado Springs, CO), Scott Kennedy (Louisville, KY), Jason Kiser (Columbia, MO), Brian Knight (Helena, MT), Mark
Mauro (San Mateo, CA), John McMasters (Tacoma, WA), Casey Moser (Iowa Park, TX), Michael Muchlinski (Ephrata,
WA), Shawn Rakos (Orting, WA), Travis Reininger (Brighton, CO), Joe Stegner (Boise, ID), Kevin Sweeney (Rio
Rancho, NM), Todd Tichenor (Holcomb, KS), A.J. Wendel (Arlington, TX).

## STADIUM INFORMATION

| Club | Stadium | Opened | Dimensions LF | CF | RF | Capacity | 2005 Att. |
|------|---------|--------|-----|-----|-----|----------|-----------|
| Albuquerque | Isotopes Park | 2003 | 360 | 410 | 340 | 10,510 | 582,839 |
| Colorado Springs | Sky Sox Stadium | 1988 | 350 | 400 | 350 | 9,000 | 235,502 |
| Fresno | Grizzlies Stadium | 2002 | 324 | 402 | 335 | 12,500 | 495,791 |
| Iowa | Principal Park | 1992 | 335 | 400 | 335 | 10,800 | 529,354 |
| Las Vegas | Cashman Field | 1983 | 328 | 433 | 323 | 9,334 | 334,485 |
| Memphis | AutoZone Park | 2000 | 319 | 400 | 322 | 14,200 | 696,083 |
| Nashville | Herschel Greer Stadium | 1978 | 327 | 400 | 327 | 10,700 | 419,412 |
| New Orleans | Zephyr Field | 1997 | 333 | 405 | 332 | 11,000 | 330,466 |
| Oklahoma | SBC Bricktown Ballpark | 1998 | 325 | 400 | 325 | 13,066 | 542,095 |
| Omaha | Johnny Rosenblatt Stadium | 1948 | 332 | 408 | 332 | 24,000 | 303,749 |
| Portland | PGE Park | 1926 | 319 | 405 | 321 | 19,810 | 360,772 |
| Round Rock | The Dell Diamond | 2000 | 330 | 400 | 325 | 10,000 | 700,277 |
| Sacramento | Raley Field | 2000 | 330 | 405 | 325 | 14,111 | 755,750 |
| Salt Lake | Franklin Covey Field | 1994 | 345 | 420 | 315 | 15,500 | 437,686 |
| Tacoma | Cheney Stadium | 1960 | 325 | 425 | 325 | 9,600 | 335,031 |
| Tucson | Tucson Electric Park | 1998 | 340 | 405 | 340 | 11,000 | 287,116 |

# ALBUQUERQUE
## ISOTOPES

**Office Address:** 1601 Avenida Cesar Chavez SE, Albuquerque, NM 87106. **Telephone:** (505) 924-2255. **FAX:** (505) 242-8899.
**E-Mail Address:** info@albuquerquebaseball.com. **Website:** www.albuquerque baseball.com.
**Affiliation (first year):** Florida Marlins (2003). **Years in League:** 1972-2000, 2003-.

### OWNERSHIP, MANAGEMENT
**Operated by:** Albuquerque Baseball Club, LLC.
**President:** Ken Young. **Secretary/Treasurer:** Emmett Hammond.
**General Manager:** John Traub. **Assistant GM, Sales/Marketing:** Nick LoBue. **Director, Accounting:** Barbara Campbell. **Director, Media Relations:** Steve Hurlbert. **Director, Community Relations:** Melissa Gomez. **Director, Group Sales/Season Tickets:** Adam Beggs. **Director, Retail Operations:** Chrissy Baines. **Box Office Manager:** Richard Lahr. **Manager, Corporate Sales/Promotions:** Chris Holland. **Manager, Suite Relations:** Paul Hartenberger. **Manager, Stadium Operations:** Cory Archibald. **Manager, Event Operations:** Bobby Atencio. **Executive, Corporate Sales:** Paul Warner. **Executives, Group/Ticket Sales:** Cheryl Hull, Justin Sommers, Andy Steavens. **Office Manager:** Amanda Martinez. **General Manager, Ovations Food Services:** Steve Bellacose. **Head Groundskeeper:** Jarad Alley. **Home Clubhouse Manager:** Jonathan Sanchez. **Visiting Clubhouse Manager:** Rick Pollack.

### FIELD STAFF
**Manager:** Dean Treanor. **Coach:** Steve Phillips. **Pitching Coach:** Tom Brown. **Trainer:** Steve Miller.

### GAME INFORMATION
**Radio Announcer:** Unavailable. **No. of Games Broadcast:** Home-72, Away-72. **Flagship Station:** KNML 610-AM. **PA Announcer:** Stu Walker. **Official Scorers:** Gary Herron, John Miller.
**Stadium Name:** Isotopes Park. **Location:** From 1-25, exit east on Avenida Cesar Chavez SE to University Boulevard; from I-40, exit south on University Boulevard SE to Avenida Cesar Chavez. **Standard Game Times:** 7:05 p.m.; Sun. (April-May) 1:35, (June-Sept.) 6:05. **Ticket Price Range:** $5-20.
**Visiting Club Hotel:** MCM Elegante, 2020 Menaul NE, Albuquerque, NM 87107. Telephone: (505) 884-2511.

# COLORADO SPRINGS
## SKY SOX

**Office Address:** 4385 Tutt Blvd., Colorado Springs, CO 80922.
**Telephone:** (719) 597-1449. **FAX:** (719) 597-2491.
**E-Mail Address:** info@skysox.com. **Website:** www.skysox.com.
**Affiliation (first year):** Colorado Rockies (1993). **Years in League:** 1988-.

### OWNERSHIP, MANAGEMENT
**Operated by:** Colorado Springs Sky Sox, Inc.
**Principal Owner:** David Elmore.
**President/General Manager:** Tony Ensor. **Senior Vice President, Operations:** Dwight Hall. **Senior VP, Marketing:** Rai Henniger. **Senior VP, Stadium Operations:** Mark Leasure. **GM, Diamond Creations:** Don Giuliano. **Director, Catering:** Tony Bujak. **Director, Sales:** Eric Day. **Coordinator, Special Events:** Brien Smith. **Director, Public Relations:** Mike Hobson. **Accountant:** Kelly Hanlon. **Director, Broadcast Operations:** Dan Karcher. **Assistant GM, Community Relations:** Corey Wynn. **Director, Corporate Events:** Adam Wasch. **Sponsorship Coordinator:** Jennifer Granado. **Group Sales/Ticket Operations:** Chip Dreamer. **Director, Season Ticket Sales:** Whitney Shellem. **Community Group Ticket Manager/Merchandise:** Erin Moroney. **Corporate Event Planner:** Keith Hodges. **Administrative Assistant:** Marianne Paine. **Home Clubhouse Manager:** Ricky Grima. **Visiting Clubhouse Manager:** Greg Grimaldo. **Marketing Representatives:** Kevin Bannan, Michael Claus.

### FIELD STAFF
**Manager:** Tom Runnells. **Coach:** Alan Cockrell. **Pitching Coach:** Chuck Kniffin. **Trainer:** Heath Townsend.

### GAME INFORMATION
**Radio Announcers:** Dick Chase, Dan Karcher. **No. of Games Broadcast:** Home-72, Away-72. **Flagship Station:** KRDO 1240-AM.
**PA Announcer:** Chip Dreamer. **Official Scorer:** Marty Grantz.
**Stadium Name:** Security Service Field. **Location:** I-25 South to Woodmen Road exit, east on Woodmen to Powers Boulevard, right on Powers to Barnes Road. **Standard Game Times:** 7:05 p.m., Sun. 1:05. **Ticket Price Range:** $5-9.
**Visiting Club Hotel:** Park Plaza Hotel, 505 Popes Bluff Trail, Colorado Springs, CO 80907. Telephone: (719) 598-7656.

# FRESNO GRIZZLIES

**Office Address:** 1800 Tulare St., Fresno, CA 93721.
**Telephone:** (559) 320-4487. **FAX:** (559) 264-0795.
**E-Mail Address:** info@fresnogrizzlies.com. **Website:** www.fresnogrizzlies.com.
**Affiliation (first year):** San Francisco Giants (1998). **Years in League:** 1998-.

## OWNERSHIP, MANAGEMENT

**Operated by:** Fresno Diamond Group, LLC.
**President, Chief Executive Officer:** Pat Filippone. **Vice President:** Gerard McKearney. **VP, Tickets:** Andrew Stuebner. **VP, Corporate Partnerships:** Mike Maiorana. **Director, Community Relations:** Sarah Marten. **Director, Media Relations:** Ryan Alexander. **Director, Entertainment:** Jessica Blada. **Director, Marketing:** Scott Carter. **Manager, Marketing:** Mike Palazzolo. **Director, Stadium Operations:** Garrett Fahrmann. **Director, Event Operations:** Matt Blankenheim. **Director, Special Events:** Andrew Bragman. **Special Events Account Executive:** Scott Bush. **Director, Tickets:** Tom Backemeyer. **Account Executive/Ticket Operations:** Joe Clasman. **Ticket Manager:** Karen Thomas. **Director, Business Development:** Stacie Johnson. **Director, Group Sales:** Luke Reiff. **Group Sales Manager:** Shaun Northup. **Account Executives:** Mike Amerikaner, Peter Marthedal, Matt McCandless, Joe Toler, John Watts. **Inside Sales Manager:** Ash Anunsen. **Director, Sponsorship Services:** Michelle Sanchez. **Corporate Partnerships Account Executive:** Evan Cole. **Director, Accounting:** Murray Shamp. **Finance Manager:** Jason Steffens. **Executive Administrative Assistant:** Annie Fagundes. **Receptionist:** Joann Lagomarsino. **Head Groundskeeper:** Peter Lockwood. **Assistant Groundskeeper:** David Jacinto. **Stadium Operations Manager:** Harvey Kawasaki. **Home Clubhouse Manager:** Matthew Cowger. **Visiting Clubhouse Manager:** Travis Hodges.

## FIELD STAFF

**Manager:** Shane Turner. **Coach:** Jim Bowie. **Pitching Coach:** Trevor Wilson. **Trainer:** Patrich Serbus.

## GAME INFORMATION

**Radio Announcers:** Doug Greenwald. **No. of Games Broadcast:** Home-72, Away-72. **Flagship Stations:** 1550-AM. **PA Announcer:** Unavailable. **Official Scorer:** Unavailable.
**Stadium Name:** Grizzlies Stadium. **Location:** From 99 North, take Fresno Street exit, left on Fresno Street, left on Inyo or Tulare to stadium; from 99 South, take Fresno Street exit, left on Fresno Street, right on Broadway to H Street; from 41 North, take Van Ness exit towards downtown Fresno, left on Van Ness, left on Inyo or Tulare, stadium is straight ahead; from 41 South, take Tulare exit, stadium is located at Tulare and H Streets, or take Van Ness exit, right on Van Ness, left on Inyo or Tulare, stadium is straight ahead. **Standard Game Times:** 7:05 p.m., Sun. (first half) 2:05. **Ticket Price Range:** $5-15.
**Visiting Club Hotel:** Radisson Hotel Fresno, 2233 Ventura St., Fresno, CA 93721. **Telephone:** (559) 441-2931.

# IOWA CUBS

**Office Address:** One Line Drive, Des Moines, IA 50309.
**Telephone:** (515) 243-6111. **FAX:** (515) 243-5152.
**E-Mail Address:** info@iowacubs.com. **Website:** www.iowacubs.com.
**Affiliation (first year):** Chicago Cubs (1981). **Years in League:** 1969-.

## OWNERSHIP, MANAGEMENT

**Operated by:** Raccoon Baseball Inc.
**Chairman, Principal Owner:** Michael Gartner. **Executive Vice President:** Michael Giudicessi.
**President, General Manager:** Sam Bernabe. **Vice President, Assistant GM:** Jim Nahas. **VP, Chief Financial Officer:** Sue Tollefson. **VP/Director, Stadium Operations:** Tom Greene. **VP/Director, Broadcast Operations:** Deene Ehlis. **Director, Media Relations:** Jeff Lantz. **Coordinator, Public Relations:** Matt Nordby. **Director, Logistics:** Scott Sailor. **Director, Community Relations:** Kenny Houser. **Coordinator, Group Sales:** Lindsay Cox. **Director, Sales:** Rich Gilman. **Director, Luxury Suites:** Brent Conkel. **Ticket Office Manager:** Katie Hogan. **Manager, Stadium Operations:** Jeff Tilley. **Assistant Manager, Stadium Operations:** Janelle Videgar. **Corporate Sales Executives:** Greg Ellis, Melanie Doser, Nate Teut. **Corporate Relations:** Red Hollis. **Head Groundskeeper:** Chris Schlosser. **Director, Merchandise:** T.J. Hucka. **Coordinator, Merchandise:** Rick Giudicessi. **Accountant:** Lori Auten. **Manager, Cub Club:** Bob Thormeier. **Office Manager:** Unavailable. **Director, Information Systems:** Larry Schunk. **Landscape Coordinator:** Shari Kramer.

## FIELD STAFF

**Manager:** Mike Quade. **Coach:** Von Joshua. **Pitching Coach:** Alan Dunn. **Trainer:** Bob Grimes.

## GAME INFORMATION

**Radio Announcer:** Deene Ehlis. **No. of Games Broadcast:** Home-72, Away-72. **Flagship Station:** KXNO 1460-AM. **PA Announcers:** Geoff Conn, Mark Pierce. **Official Scorers:** Dirk Brinkmeyer, Brian Gibson, Mike Mahon.
**Stadium Name:** Principal Park. **Location:** I-80 or I-35 to I-235, to Third Street exit, south on Third Street, left on

Line Drive. **Standard Game Times:** 7:05 p.m., Sun. 1:05. **Ticket Price Range:** $6-10.
   **Visiting Club Hotel:** Valley West Inn, 3535 Westown Pkwy., West Des Moines, IA 50266 . Telephone: (515) 225-2524.

# LAS VEGAS
## 51s

**Office Address:** 850 Las Vegas Blvd. N., Las Vegas, NV 89101.
**Telephone:** (702) 386-7200. **FAX:** (702) 386-7214.
**E-Mail Address:** info@lv51.com. **Website:** www.lv51.com.
**Affiliation (first year):** Los Angeles Dodgers (2001). **Years in League:** 1983-.

## OWNERSHIP, MANAGEMENT
   **Operated by:** Mandalay Baseball Properties.
   **President, General Manager:** Don Logan. **Vice President, Finance:** Allen Taylor. **VP, Operations/Security:** Nick Fitzenreider. **Director, Business Development:** Derek Eige. **Director, Ticket Operations:** Mike Rodriguez. **Director, Corporate Sponsorships:** Mike Hollister. **Director, Marketing:** Chuck Johnson. **Director, Merchandise:** Laurie Wanser. **Director, Broadcasting:** Russ Langer. **Managers, Corporate Marketing:** David Byrne, Melissa Harkavy, John Spoley, Greg Young. **Manager, Community Relations:** Larry Brown. **Manager, Baseball Administration:** Denise Korach. **Media Relations Director:** Jim Gemma. **Special Assistant to GM:** Bob Blum. **Administrative Assistants:** Pat Dressel, Michelle Taggart. **Interns:** Daniel Barnts, Kelli Edelbrock, Chase Rasmussen. **Operations Manager:** Chip Vespe.

## FIELD STAFF
   **Manager:** Jerry Royster. **Coach:** Steve Yeager. **Pitching Coach:** Ken Howell. **Trainer:** Jason Mahnke.

## GAME INFORMATION
   **Radio Announcer:** Russ Langer. **No. of Games Broadcast:** Home-72, Away-72. **Flagship Station:** KENO 1460-AM.
**PA Announcer:** Dan Bickmore. **Official Scorer:** Mark Wasik.
   **Stadium Name:** Cashman Field. **Location:** I-15 to U.S. 95 exit (Downtown), east to Las Vegas Boulevard North exit, one-half mile north to stadium. **Standard Game Times:** 7:05 p.m., Sun. 12:05. **Ticket Price Range:** $7-12.
   **Visiting Club Hotel:** Golden Nugget Hotel & Casino, 129 Fremont St., Las Vegas, NV 89101. Telephone: (702) 385-7111.

# MEMPHIS
## REDBIRDS

**Office Address:** 175 Toyota Plaza, Suite 300, Memphis, TN 38103.
**Telephone:** (901) 721-6000. **FAX:** 901-842-1222.
**Website:** www.memphisredbirds.com.
**Affiliation (first year):** St. Louis Cardinals (1998). **Years in League:** 1998-.

## OWNERSHIP, MANAGEMENT
   **Operated by:** Memphis Redbirds Baseball Foundation, Inc. **Founders:** Dean Jernigan, Kristi Jernigan.
   **President/General Manager:** Dave Chase. **Manager, Operations:** Tony Martin. **Controller:** Garry Condrey. **Accounting Specialist:** Leslie Wilkes. **Human Resources Specialist:** Pam Abney. **VP, Marketing:** Kerry Sewell. **Director, Game Entertainment:** Kim Jackson. **Media Relations Coordinator:** Kyle Parkinson. **Marketing Coordinator:** Tim Whang. **Graphic Designer:** Craig Patterson. **Retail Supervisor:** Starr Taiani. **Mascot Coordinator:** Chris Pegg. **Senior VP, Sales:** Pete Rizzo. **Executive Assistant:** Cindy Compton. **Senior Account Executive:** Rob Edgerton. **Account Executives:** Steve Giglio, Gary Saunders. **Sales Coordinator:** Sommer Collins. **VP, Community Relations:** Reggie Williams. **Community Relations Coordinator:** Emma Glover. **Programs Coordinator:** Jamison Morris. **Head Groundskeeper:** Ed Collins. **Manager, Ticket Sales:** Steve Berneman. **Manager, Season Tickets:** Cathy Allen. **Group Sales Executives:** Dan Schaefer, Ryan Thompson. **Ticket Sales Executives:** Dustin Holcumbrink, Ben Portis. **Chief Engineer:** Danny Abbott. **Maintenance:** Spencer Shields, Joe Webb. **Office Coordinator:** Linda Smith.

## FIELD STAFF
   **Manager:** Danny Sheaffer. **Coach:** Tommy Gregg. **Pitching Coach:** Dyar Miller. **Trainer:** Chris Conroy.

## GAME INFORMATION
   **Radio Announcers:** David Kelly, Steve Selby. **No. of Games Broadcast:** Home-72, Away-72. **Flagship Station:** WHBQ 560-AM.
**PA Announcer:** Tim Van Horn. **Official Scorer:** J.J. Guinozzo.
   **Stadium Name:** AutoZone Park. **Location:** North on I-240, exit at Union Avenue West, 1½ miles to park. **Standard Game Times:** 7:05 p.m., Sat. 6:05, Sun. 2:05. **Ticket Price Range:** $5-17.
   **Visiting Club Hotel:** Sleep Inn at Court Square, 40 N. Front, Memphis, TN 38103. Telephone: (901) 522-9700.

# NASHVILLE SOUNDS

**Office Address:** 534 Chestnut St., Nashville, TN 37203.
**Telephone:** (615) 242-4371. **FAX:** (615) 256-5684.
**E-Mail Address:** info@nashvillesounds.com. **Website:** www.nashvillesounds.com.
**Affiliation (first year):** Milwaukee Brewers (2005). **Years in League:** 1998-.

## OWNERSHIP, MANAGEMENT

**Operated by:** AmeriSports LLC.
**President/Owner:** Al Gordon.
**General Manager:** Glenn Yaeger. **Assistant GM:** Chris Snyder. **Director, Accounting:** Barb Walker. **Director, Sales:** Joe Hart. **Director, Ticketing:** Ricki Schlabach. **Director, Media Relations/Baseball Operations:** Doug Scopel. **Director, Marketing/Promotions:** Brandon Vonderharr. **Director, Food/Beverage:** Mark Lawrence. **Director, Corporate Sales:** Jason Bennett. **Account Executive:** Nick Barkley. **Director, Community Relations:** Sarah Barthol. **Managers, Stadium Operations/Sales:** P.J. Harrison, Kristi West. **Manager, Community Relations:** Amy Alder. **Manager, Mascot/Entertainment:** Buddy Yelton. **Coordinators, Corporate Events:** Andrew Chelton, Ben Goodman. **Office Manager:** Sharon Ridley. **Clubhouse Managers:** J.R. Rinaldi, Mike Valentine. **Groundskeeper:** John Farmer.

## FIELD STAFF

**Manager:** Frank Kremblas. **Coach:** Gary Pettis. **Pitching Coach:** Stan Kyles. **Trainer:** Jeff Paxson.

## GAME INFORMATION

**Radio Announcer:** Chuck Valenches. **No. of Games Broadcast:** Home-72, Away-72. **Flagship Station:** Unavailable.
**PA Announcer:** Eric Berner. **Official Scorers:** Andre Foushee, Eric Jones.
**Stadium Name:** Herschel Greer Stadium. **Location:** I-65 to Wedgewood exit, west to Eighth Avenue, right on Eighth to Chestnut Street, right on Chestnut. **Standard Game Times:** 7 p.m., Wed. 12, Sat. 6; Sun. (April-May) 2, (June-Aug.) 6. **Ticket Price Range:** $6-10.
**Visiting Club Hotel:** Select Hotel by Holiday Inn, 2613 West End Ave., Nashville, TN 37203. Telephone: (615) 327-4707.

# NEW ORLEANS ZEPHYRS

**Office Address:** 6000 Airline Dr., Metairie, LA 70003.
**Telephone:** (504) 734-5155. **FAX:** (504) 734-5118.
**E-Mail Address:** zephyrs@zephyrsbaseball.com. **Website:** www.zephyrsbaseball.com.
**Affiliation (first year):** Washington Nationals (2005). **Years in League:** 1998-.

## OWNERSHIP, MANAGEMENT

**Operated by:** New Orleans Zephyrs Baseball Club, LLC.
**Managing Partner/President:** Don Beaver.
**Executive Director:** Ron Maestri. **General Manager:** Mike Schline. **Director, Community Relations:** Marc Allen. **Director, Broadcasting:** Tim Grubbs. **Director, Operations:** Todd Wilson. **Director, Marketing/Special Events:** Jaime Burchfield. **Director, Ticket Operations:** Preston Gautrau. **Director, Finance:** Kim Topp. **Personal Assistant, GM:** Jessica DeOro. **Director, Media Relations:** Kevin Maney. **Media Manager/Speakers Bureau:** Ron Swoboda. **Group Sales Director:** Leah Rigby. **Group Sales Representatives:** Derek Dupepe, Lindsey Rall. **Accounting Assistant:** Doug Gill. **Director, Merchandising:** Dan Herndon. **Head Groundskeeper:** Thomas Marks. **Assistant Groundskeeper:** Craig Shaffer. **Maintenance Coordinator:** Bill Rowell. **Assistant Director, Operations:** Sonny Lee. **Media Intern:** Tory Mathias. **GM, Food Services:** George Messina. **Administrative Assistant, Food Services:** Priscilla Arbello.

## FIELD STAFF

**Manager:** Tim Foli. **Coach:** Rick Eckstein. **Pitching Coach:** Steve McCatty. **Trainer:** Mike Quinn.

## GAME INFORMATION

**Radio Announcers:** Tim Grubbs, Ron Swoboda (English), Herman Rodriguez (Spanish). **No. of Games Broadcast:** Home-72, Away-72 (English); Home-30 (Spanish). **Flagship Stations:** WIST 690-AM, WSLA 1560 -AM (Spanish).
**PA Announcer:** Doug Moreau. **Official Scorer:** J.L. Vangilder.
**Stadium Name:** Zephyr Field. **Location:** I-10 West toward Baton Rouge, exit at Clearview Parkway (exit 226) and continue south, right on Airline Drive (U.S. 61 North) for 1 mile, stadium on left; From airport, take Airline Drive (U.S. 61) east for 4 miles, stadium on right. **Standard Game Times:** 7 p.m.; Sat. 6, Sun. (April-May) 2, (June-Sept.) 6. **Ticket Price Range:** $5-9.50.
**Visiting Club Hotel:** Best Western-St. Christopher, 114 Magazine St., New Orleans, LA 70130. Telephone: (504) 648-0444.

# OKLAHOMA REDHAWKS

**Mailing Address:** 2 S. Mickey Mantle Dr., Oklahoma City, OK 73104.
**Telephone:** (405) 218-1000. **FAX:** (405) 218-1001.
**E-Mail Address:** info@oklahomaredhawks.com. **Website:** www.oklahoma redhawks.com.
**Affiliation (first year):** Texas Rangers (1983). **Years in League:** 1963-1968, 1998-.

## OWNERSHIP, MANAGEMENT
**Operated by:** Oklahoma Baseball Club, LLC
**Principal Owner:** Robert Funk. **Managing General Partner:** Scott Pruitt.
**Executive Director:** John Allgood. **Chief Financial Officer:** Steve McEwen. **Director, Public Relations/Assistant to Managing General Partner:** Laurie Gore. **Director, Facility Operations:** Harlan Budde. **Director, Guest Services:** Nancy Simmons. **Director, Operations:** Mike Prange. **Director, Sponsorships:** Mark Pritchard. **Director, Ticket Sales:** Mary Ramsey. **Director, Merchandise:** Chris Lucas. **Marketing Manager:** Jamie Cobb. **Senior Accountant:** Nicole Wise. **Accountant:** Patty Hoecker. **Promotions Manager:** Brandon Baker. **Ticket Sales Manager:** Johnny Walker. **Ticket Office Manager:** Jeff Kretchmar. **Account Executives:** Jason Black, Chad Humphrey, Kyle Newsom. **Group Sales Account Executives:** Adam Boxburger, Farah Woody. **Clubhouse Manager:** Russ Oliver. **Head Groundskeeper:** Monte McCoy.

## FIELD STAFF
**Manager:** Tim Ireland. **Coach:** Mike Boulanger. **Pitching Coach:** Andy Hawkins. **Trainer:** Chris DeLucia.

## GAME INFORMATION
**Radio Announcer:** Jim Byers. **No. of Games Broadcast:** Home-72, Away-72. **Flagship Station:** Unavailable.
**PA Announcer:** Randy Kemp. **Official Scorers:** Justin Tinder, Mike Treps.
**Stadium Name:** SBC Bricktown Ballpark. **Location:** At interchange of I-235 and I-40, take Reno exit, east on Reno. **Standard Game Times:** 7:05 p.m., Sun. (first half) 2:05. **Ticket Price Range:** $6-14.
**Visiting Club Hotel:** Sheraton, One N. Broadway, Oklahoma City, OK 73102. Telephone: (405) 235-2780.

# OMAHA ROYALS

**Office Address:** Rosenblatt Stadium, 1202 Bert Murphy Ave., Omaha, NE 68107.
**Telephone:** (402) 734-2550. **FAX:** (402) 734-7166.
**E-Mail Address:** info@oroyals.com. **Website:** www.oroyals.com.
**Affiliation (first year):** Kansas City Royals (1969). **Years in League:** 1998-.

## OWNERSHIP, MANAGEMENT
**Operated by:** Omaha Royals Limited Partnership.
**Principal Owners:** Matt Minker, Warren Buffett, Walter Scott.
**Managing General Partner/President:** Matt Minker. **Senior Vice President/General Manager:** Doug Stewart. **VP/Assistant GM:** Kyle Fisher. **Director, Marketing/Promotions:** Cassie Duncan. **Director, Broadcasting:** Mark Nasser. **Director, Media Relations:** Kevin McNabb. **Director, Ticket Operations/Group Sales:** Don Wilson. **Director, Community Relations:** Angela Mullen. **Director, Merchandise:** Pat Daly. **Sports Marketing Executive:** Mike Andreasen. **Ticket Office Manager:** Jeff Gogerty. **Ticket Sales Manager:** Gregg Jones. **Ticket Account Executive:** Jason Camp. **Group Sales Associate:** Jeremie Larkins. **Administrative Assistants:** Kay Besta, Lois Biggs. **Head Groundskeeper:** Jesse Cuevas. **GM, Concessions:** Ryan Slane.

## FIELD STAFF
**Manager:** Mike Jirschele. **Coach:** Terry Bradshaw. **Pitching Coach:** Tom Burgmeier. **Trainer:** Jeff Stevenson.

## GAME INFORMATION
**Radio Announcers:** Kevin McNabb, Mark Nasser. **No. of Games Broadcast:** Home-72, Away-72. **Flagship Station:** KOMJ 1490-AM.
**PA Announcer:** Paul Cohen, Bill Jensen, Ryan Schopperth. **Official Scorers:** Frank Adkisson, Ken Jones, Ryan White.
**Stadium Name:** Rosenblatt Stadium. **Location:** South off I-80 on 13th Street. **Standard Game Times:** 7:05 p.m., Sat. 6:05, Sun. 1:35.
**Visiting Club Hotel:** Holiday Inn at Ameristar, 2202 River Rd., Council Bluffs, IA 51501. Telephone: (712) 322-5050.

# PORTLAND
## BEAVERS

**Office Address:** 1844 SW Morrison, Portland, OR 97205.
**Telephone:** (503) 553-5400. **FAX:** (503) 553-5405.
**E-Mail Address:** info@pgepark.com. **Website:** www.portlandbeavers.com.
**Affiliation (first year):** San Diego Padres (2001). **Years in League:** 1903-1917, 1919-1972, 1978-1993, 2001-.

### OWNERSHIP, MANAGEMENT
**Operated by:** Beavers PCL Baseball, LLC.
**President/General Manager:** John Cunningham. **Senior Advisor:** Jack Cain. **Vice President, Corporate Partnerships/Suite Sales:** Ryan Brach. **VP, Ticket Sales/Marketing:** Ripper Hatch. **VP, Operations:** Ken Puckett. **Assistant GM/Director, Communications:** Chris Metz. **Director, Ticket Operations:** Bob Cain. **Director, Ticket Sales:** Ben Hoel. **Director, Finance:** Diane Rogers. **Managers, Corporate Sales:** Bobby Aguilera, Rick Barr. **Manager, Group Sales:** Ashley Bedford. **Manager, Marketing:** Danna Bubalo. **Managers, Partner Services:** Suzy Goss, Alex Ramberg. **Manager, Promotions:** Jadira Ruiz. **Manager, Community Outreach:** Keri Stoller. **Manager, Facility Maintenance:** Dave Tankersley. **Manager, Guest Services:** Andrea Tolonen. **Coordinator, Ticket Sales/Services:** Katrina Marshall. **Coordinator, Ticket Renewals:** Dan Zusman. **Account Executives, Group Tickets:** Amy Lilly, Jason Weatherley. **Account Executives, Corporate Ticket Sales:** Erik Bjornstad, Nate Liberman, Matt Peterson, Greg Stone. **Senior Accounting Clerk:** Penny Bishop. **Office Manager/Receptionist:** Jeanne Nichols. **Head Groundskeeper:** Jesse Smith. **Home Clubhouse Manager:** James Cameron. **Visiting Clubhouse Manager:** Mike Murray.

### FIELD STAFF
**Manager:** Craig Colbert. **Coach:** Jose Castro. **Pitching Coach:** Gary Lance. **Trainer:** Will Sinon.

### GAME INFORMATION
**Radio Announcers:** Rich Burk. **No. of Games Broadcast:** Home-72, Away-72. **Flagship Station:** Unavailable.
**PA Announcer:** Mike Stone. **Official Scorer:** Blair Cash.
**Stadium Name:** PGE Park. **Location:** I-405 to West Burnside exit, SW 20th Street to park. **Standard Game Times:** 7:05 p.m., Sat. 6:35, Sun. 2:05. **Ticket Price Range:** $8-13.
**Visiting Club Hotel:** Portland Marriott-Downtown, 1401 SW Naito Pkwy., Portland, OR 97201. Telephone: (503) 226-7600.

# ROUND ROCK
## EXPRESS

**Office Address:** 3400 East Palm Valley Blvd., Round Rock, TX 78664.
**Telephone:** (512) 255-2255. **FAX:** (512) 255-1558.
**E-Mail Address:** info@rrexpress.com. **Website:** www.roundrockexpress.com.
**Affiliation (first year):** Houston Astros (2000). **Years in League:** 2005.

### OWNERSHIP, MANAGEMENT
**Operated by:** Ryan-Sanders Baseball, LP.
**Principal Owners:** Eddie Maloney, Jay Miller, Nolan Ryan, Reese Ryan, Reid Ryan, Don Sanders, Brad Sanders, Bret Sanders.
**Chief Executive Officer:** Reid Ryan. **President:** Jay Miller. **Chief Financial Officer:** Reese Ryan.
**Vice President, General Manager:** Dave Fendrick. **VP, Communications:** John Blake. **Controller:** Debbie Coughlin. **Assistant GM, Promotions/Stadium Entertainment:** Derrick Grubbs. **Director, Media Relations:** Kirk Dressendorfer. **Director, Public Relations:** Heather Tantimonaco. **Director, Merchandising (Ryan-Sanders Baseball):** Brooke Milam. **Director, Ticket Operations:** Ross Scott. **Director, United Heritage Center:** Scott Allen. **Director, Special Events:** Laura Whatley. **Director, Group Sales:** Henry Green. **Director, Sales:** Gary Franke. **Director, Market Development:** Gregg Miller **Account Executives:** Brent Green, Richard Tapia. **Receptionist:** Wendy Gordon. **Field Superintendent:** Dennis Klein. **Director, Broadcasting:** Mike Capps. **Clubhouse Manager:** Kenny Bufton. **Visiting Clubhouse Manager:** Kevin Taylor. **Assistant Manager, The Railyard Retail Store:** Sherry Lato. **Director, Stadium Operations:** Mark Maloney. **Director, Stadium Maintenance:** Aurelio Martinez. **Stadium Operations:** Felipe Penaloza. **Housekeeping:** Ofelia Gonzalez.

### FIELD STAFF
**Manager:** Jackie Moore. **Coaches:** Spike Owen, Harry Spilman. **Pitching Coach:** Burt Hooton. **Trainer:** Mike Freer.

### GAME INFORMATION
**Radio Announcer:** Mike Capps. **No. of Games Broadcast:** Home-72, Away-72. **Flagship Station:** KWNX 1260-AM.
**PA Announcer:** Derrick Grubbs. **Official Scorer:** Tommy Tate.
**Stadium Name:** The Dell Diamond. **Location:** I-35 North to exit 253 (Highway 79 East/Taylor), stadium on left 3½ miles. **Standard Game Times:** 7:05 p.m.; Sun. (April-May) 2:05. **Ticket Price Range:** $5-10.
**Visiting Club Hotel:** Hilton Garden Inn, 2310 N. IH-35, Round Rock, TX 78681. Telephone: (512) 341-8200.

# SACRAMENTO
## RIVER CATS

**Office Address:** 400 Ballpark Dr., West Sacramento, CA 95691.
**Telephone:** (916) 376-4700. **FAX:** (916) 376-4710.
**E-Mail Address:** info@rivercats.com. **Website:** www.rivercats.com
**Affiliation (first year):** Oakland Athletics (2000). **Years in League:** 1903, 1909-11, 1918-60, 1974-76, 2000-

### OWNERSHIP, MANAGEMENT
**Owned by:** Sacramento River Cats Baseball Club, LLC.
**Principal Owner/Chief Executive Officer:** Art Savage.
**President/General Manager:** Alan Ledford. **Executive Vice Presidents:** Bob Hemond, Warren Smith. **General Counsel:** Matthew Re. **Senior VP/Chief Financial Officer:** Dan Vistica. **VP, Corporate Partnerships/Broadcasting:** Darrin Gross. **VP, Ticket Sales/Marketing:** Andy Fiske. **Senior Director, Guest Services/Employee Relations:** Mike Reichert. **Executive Assistant:** Shannon Diluccia. **Director, Marketing:** Joe Wagoner. **Director, Ticket Operations:** Steve Hill. **Senior Director, Community Relations:** Tony Asaro. **Manager, Merchandise:** Trish Dolan. **Manager, Accounting:** Stan Kelly. **Manager, Personnel:** Larisa Collins. **Executive Assistant:** Gay Caputo. **Assistant GM/Director, Media Relations:** Gabe Ross. **Coordinator, Media/Community Relations:** Rachel Rosen. **VP, Stadium Operations/Special Events:** Matt Larose. **Director, Stadium Operations/Team Travel:** Matt Thomas. **Manager, Grounds:** Chris Fahrner. **Manager, Special Events:** Mindy Jaime. **Coordinator, Stadium Operations:** Mario Constancio. **Coordinator, Grounds:** Justin Clarke. **Chief Engineer:** Warren Stahl. **Building Engineer:** Javier Navarro. **Senior Accounting Clerk/Information Technology:** Jess Olivares. **Accounting Clerk/IT:** Julie Dries. **Financial Consultant:** Jeff Savage. **Director, Corporate Sponsorships:** Scott Druskin. **Manager, Luxury Suites/Corporate Sales:** Josh Morin. **Manager, Corporate Services:** Jennifer Maiwald. **Coordinators, Corporate Services:** Heather Scherber, Kris Stringfellow. **Director, Ticket Sales:** Justin Piper. **Director, Ticket Services:** Cory Dolich. **Manager, Special Projects:** Jennifer Maxwell. **Senior Manager, Business Development:** Robert Dunham. **Manager, Business Development:** Kevin Hilton. **Managers, Season Tickets:** Scott Kemp, Jamie Von Sossan. **Manager, Group Sales:** Shasta Webster. **Manager, Inside Sales:** Chris Dreesman. **Senior Manager, Marketing:** Alexis Lee. **Manager, Game Entertainment:** Brooke Robinson. **Coordinator, Promotions:** Kim Ponce. **Coordinator, Website/Research:** Brent Savage. **Manager, Ticket Operations:** Larry Martinez. **Clubhouse Manager:** Rod Garcia.

### FIELD STAFF
**Manager:** Tony DeFrancesco. **Coach:** Brian McArn. **Pitching Coach:** Rick Rodriguez. **Trainer:** Walt Horn.

### GAME INFORMATION
**Radio Announcers:** Johnny Doskow (English), Jose Reynoso (Spanish). **No. of Games Broadcast:** Home-72, Away-72 (English); Home-72, Away-12 (Spanish). **Flagship Stations:** KTKZ 1380-AM (English), KCFA 106.1-FM (Spanish).
**PA Announcer:** Mark Standriff. **Official Scorers:** Brian Berger, Ryan Bjork, Mark Honbo.
**Stadium Name:** Raley Field. **Location:** I-5 to Business-80 West, exit at Jefferson Boulevard. **Standard Game Times:** 7:05 p.m. **Ticket Price Range:** $5-18.
**Visiting Club Hotel:** Holiday Inn, Capitol Plaza, 300 J St., Sacramento, CA 95814. Telephone: (916) 446-0100.

# SALT LAKE
## BEES

**Office Address:** 77 W. 1300 South, Salt Lake City, UT 84115.
**Mailing Address:** P.O. Box 4108, Salt Lake City, UT 84110.
**Telephone:** (801) 325-BEES. **FAX:** (801) 485-6818.
**E-Mail Address:** info@slbees.com. **Website:** www.slbees.com.
**Affiliation (first year):** Los Angeles Angels of Anaheim (2001). **Years in League:** 1915-25, 1958-65, 1970-84, 1994-.

### OWNERSHIP, MANAGEMENT
**Operated by:** Larry H. Miller Baseball, Inc.
**Principal Owner:** Larry Miller. **Chief Operating Officer:** Dennis Haslam.
**Senior Vice President, Business Operations/Chief Financial Officer:** Robert Hyde. **Senior VP, Broadcasting/Sales/Chief Marketing Officer:** Randy Rigby. **Senior VP, Facilities:** Scott Williams. **VP, General Manager:** Marc Amicone. **VP, Finance:** John Larson. **VP, Ticket Sales:** Jim Olson. **VP, Communications:** Linda Luchetti. **VP, Marketing:** Eric Schulz. **VP, Sponsorship Sales:** Mike Snarr. **Assistant GM/Director, Corporate Sales:** Brad Tammen. **Controller:** Travis Court. **Director, Ticket Sales:** Bobbie Walker. **Director, Broadcasting:** Steve Klauke. **Public/Community Relations:** Derek Garduño. **Box Office Manager:** Laura Russell. **Corporate Account Manager:** Jason Badell. **Ticket Sales Executive:** Rob Long, James Davis, Brian Prutch. **Team Photographer:** Brent Asay. **VP, Special Events:** Brent Allenbach. **VP, Security:** Jim Bell. **VP, Food Services:** Mark Stedman. **Concessions Manager:** Dave Dalton.

### FIELD STAFF
**Manager:** Brian Harper. **Coach:** Jim Eppard. **Pitching Coach:** Charles Nagy. **Trainer:** Armando Rivas.

## GAME INFORMATION

**Radio Announcer:** Steve Klauke. **No. of Games Broadcast:** Home-72, Away-72. **Flagship Station:** KFNZ 1320-AM. **PA Announcer:** Jeff Reeves. **Official Scorers:** Bruce Hilton, Howard Nakagama, Chuck Schell. **Stadium name:** Franklin Covey Field. **Location:** I-15 North/South to 1300 South exit, east to ballpark at West Temple. **Standard Game Times:** 7 p.m., 6:30 (April-May); Sun. 2. **Ticket Price Range:** $6-20. **Visiting Club Hotel:** Sheraton City Centre, 150 W. 500 South, Salt Lake City, UT 84101. Telephone: (801) 401-2000.

# TACOMA
## RAINIERS

**Office Address:** 2502 S. Tyler St., Tacoma, WA 98405.
**Telephone:** (253) 752-7707. **FAX:** (253) 752-7135.
**E-Mail Address:** rainiers@tacomarainiers.com. **Website:** www.tacomarainiers.com.
**Affiliation:** Seattle Mariners (1995). **Years in League:** 1904-1905, 1960-.

## OWNERSHIP, MANAGEMENT

**Operated by:** George's Pastime, Inc.
**President:** George Foster.
**Board of Directors:** George Foster, Jeff Foster, Jonathan Foster, Sue Foster, Mark Kanai, Jack Pless.
**General Manager:** Dave Lewis. **Assistant GM, Baseball Operations:** Kevin Kalal. **Controller:** Philip Cowan. **Director, Marketing:** Rachel Marecle. **Director, Sales:** Tim Sexton. **Director, Promotions:** Jocelyn Hill. **Account Executives:** Chris Aubertin, Michael Jermain, Leslie Mitchell, Shane Santman. **Director, Food/Beverage:** Corey Brandt. **Director, Merchandise:** Kathy Baxter. **Director, Ticket Operations:** Kurt Swanson. **Director, Publications:** Justin Glazier. **Staff Accountant:** Joyce Hardin. **Office Manager:** Patti Stacy. **Executive Director, Community Fund:** Margaret McCormick. **Head Groundskeeper:** Ryan Schutt. **Maintenance Supervisor:** Jim Smith. **Clubhouse Manager:** Jeff Bopp.

## FIELD STAFF

**Manager:** Dave Brundage. **Coach:** Terry Pollreisz. **Pitching Coach:** Dwight Bernard. **Trainer:** Rob Nodine.

## GAME INFORMATION

**Radio Broadcaster:** Mike Curto. **No. of Games Broadcast:** Home-72, Away-72. **Flagship Station:** KHHO 850-AM. **PA Announcer:** Unavailable. **Official Scorers:** Mark Kalal, Darin Padur. **Stadium Name:** Cheney Stadium. **Location:** From I-5, take exit 132 (Highway 16 West) for 1.2 miles to 19th Street East exit, right on Tyler Street for ⅓ mile. **Standard Game Times:** 7:05 p.m., 6:05 (April-May); Sun. 1:35. **Ticket Price Range:** $5-12. **Visiting Club Hotel:** La Quinta Inn, 1425 E. 27th St., Tacoma, WA 98421. Telephone: (253) 383-0146.

# TUCSON
## SIDEWINDERS

**Office Address:** 2500 E. Ajo Way, Tucson, AZ 85713.
**Mailing Address:** P.O. Box 27045, Tucson, AZ 85726.
**Telephone:** (520) 434-1021. **FAX:** (520) 889-9477.
**E-Mail Address:** mail@tucsonsidewinders.com. **Website:** www.tucsonsidewinders.com.
**Affiliation (first year):** Arizona Diamondbacks (1998). **Years in League:** 1969-.

## OWNERSHIP, MANAGEMENT

**Operated by:** Tucson Baseball LLC.
**Principal Owner/President:** Jay Zucker. **Chief Financial Officer/Owner:** Dave Smallhouse.
**Vice President/General Manager:** Rick Parr. **Assistant GM/Director, Sales:** Sean Smock. **Director, Broadcasting:** Ryan Radtke. **Director, Media Relations:** Landon Vincent. **Director, Stadium Operations:** Matthew Burke. **Director, Group Sales:** Brian Moss. **Director, Community Relations:** Sergio Pedroza. **Account Executive:** Jessica Withers. **Director, Ticket Operations:** Brad Hudecek. **Director, Inside Sales:** Sandy Davis. **Director, Merchandizing:** Kimberly Levin. **Group Sales Representative:** Whitney Evenchik. **Account Executive:** Teddi Fowler. **Office Manager:** Debbie Clark. **Home Clubhouse Manager:** Chris Rasnake. **Visiting Clubhouse Manager:** Brian Sprague. **Groundskeeper:** Chris Bartos.

## FIELD STAFF

**Manager:** Chip Hale. **Coach:** Lorenzo Bundy. **Pitching Coach:** Mike Parrott. **Trainer:** Greg Barber. **Strength/Conditioning:** Sean Renninger.

## GAME INFORMATION

**Radio Announcer:** Ryan Radtke. **No. of Games Broadcast:** Home-72, Away-72. **Flagship Station:** KTZR 1450-AM. **PA Announcer:** Dale Lopez. **Official Scorer:** Unavailable. **Stadium Name:** Tucson Electric Park. **Location:** From northwest, I-10 to Ajo exit, east on Ajo to stadium; from southeast, I-10 to Palo Verde exit, north to Ajo, west to stadium. **Standard Game Times:** 7 p.m., (April-May) 6:30; Sun. 6:30. **Ticket Price Range:** $6-9. **Visiting Club Hotel:** Doubletree Hotel Tucson, 455 S. Alvernon Way, Tucson, AZ 85711. Telephone: (520) 323-5200.

# EASTERN LEAGUE

## CLASS AA

**Office Address:** 30 Danforth St., Suite 208, Portland, ME 04101.
**Telephone:** (207) 761-2700. **FAX:** (207) 761-7064.
**E-Mail Address:** elpb@easternleague.com. **Website:** www.easternleague.com.
**Years League Active:** 1923-.
**President, Treasurer:** Joe McEacharn.

Joe McEacharn

**Vice President, Secretary:** Unavailable.
**Assistant to President:** Bill Rosario.
**Directors:** Greg Agganis (Akron), Lou DiBella (Connecticut), Bill Dowling (New Britain), Charles Eshbach (Portland), Joe Finley (Trenton), Chuck Greenberg (Altoona), Greg Martini (Harrisburg), Frank Miceli (Bowie), Arthur Solomon (New Hampshire), Craig Stein (Reading), Hank Stickney (Erie), Mike Urda (Binghamton).
**Division Structure: North**—Binghamton, Connecticut, New Britain, New Hampshire, Portland, Trenton. **South**—Akron, Altoona, Bowie, Erie, Harrisburg, Reading.
**Regular Season:** 142 games. **2006 Opening Date:** April 6. **Closing Date:** Sept. 4.
**All-Star Game:** July 12 at Altoona.
**Playoff Format:** Top two teams in each division meet in best-of-5 series. Winners meet in best-of-5 series for league championship.
**Roster Limit:** 23; 24 until 30th day of season and after Aug. 9. **Player Eligibility Rule:** No restrictions.
**Brand of Baseball:** Rawlings ROM-EL.
**Statistician:** Major League Baseball Advanced Media, 75 Ninth Ave., New York, NY 10011.
**Umpires:** Christopher Bakke (Alexandria, MN), Lance Barrett (Burleson, TX), Daniel Bellino (Carpentersville, IL), Cory Blaser (Westminster, CO), Francis Burke (Holly Springs, NC), Brandon Bushee (Tocsin, IN), Christopher Conroy (Williamstown, MA), John Coons (Streator, IL), Derek Crabill (Wonder Lake, IL), Timothy Donald (Mount Forest, Ontario), Robert Healey (Warwick, RI), Jason Klein (Orange, CT), Jonathan Merry (Dahlonega, GA), Alan Porter (Warminster, PA), Brian Reilly (Lansing, MI), Mark Ripperger (Carlsbad, CA), Jeffrey Spisak (Indianapolis, IN), Andrew Vincent (Simsbury, CT).

### STADIUM INFORMATION

| | | | Dimensions | | | | |
|---|---|---|---|---|---|---|---|
| **Club** | **Stadium** | **Opened** | **LF** | **CF** | **RF** | **Capacity** | **2005 Att.** |
| Akron | Canal Park | 1997 | 331 | 400 | 337 | 9,297 | 455,058 |
| Altoona | Blair County Ballpark | 1999 | 315 | 400 | 325 | 7,200 | 390,239 |
| Binghamton | NYSEG Stadium | 1992 | 330 | 400 | 330 | 6,012 | 222,243 |
| Bowie | Prince George's Stadium | 1994 | 309 | 405 | 309 | 10,000 | 314,277 |
| Connecticut | Thomas J. Dodd Memorial Stadium | 1995 | 309 | 401 | 309 | 6,275 | 170,686 |
| Erie | Jerry Uht Park | 1995 | 312 | 400 | 328 | 6,000 | 233,415 |
| Harrisburg | Commerce Bank Park | 1987 | 335 | 400 | 335 | 6,300 | 264,728 |
| New Britain | New Britain Stadium | 1996 | 330 | 400 | 330 | 6,146 | 337,687 |
| New Hampshire | Fisher Cats Ballpark | 2005 | 326 | 400 | 306 | 6,500 | 279,556 |
| Portland | Hadlock Field | 1994 | 315 | 400 | 330 | 6,975 | 396,277 |
| Reading | First Energy Stadium | 1950 | 330 | 400 | 330 | 9,000 | 469,105 |
| Trenton | Mercer County Waterfront Park | 1994 | 330 | 407 | 330 | 6,341 | 410,926 |

# AKRON
## AEROS

**Office Address:** 300 S. Main St., Akron, OH 44308.
**Telephone:** (330) 253-5151. **FAX:** (330) 253-3300.
**E-Mail Address:** info@akronaeros.com. **Website:** www.akronaeros.com.
**Affiliation (first year):** Cleveland Indians (1989). **Years in League:** 1989-.

### OWNERSHIP, MANAGEMENT

**Operated by:** Akron Professional Baseball, Inc.
**Principal Owners:** Mike Agganis, Greg Agganis.
**Chief Executive Officer:** Greg Agganis. **Executive Vice President/General Manager:** Jeff Auman. **Chief Financial Officer:** Bob Larkins. **Director, Public Relations:** James Carpenter. **Director, Corporate Sales:** Dan Burr. **Director, Ticket Operations:** Keith Solar. **Assistant Director, Ticket Operations:** Kevin Snyder. **Senior Account Representative, Group Sales:** Thomas Craven. **Account Representatives, Ticket Sales:** Mike Link, Ross Swaldo. **Director, Merchandising:** Unavailable. **Director, Field/Stadium Maintenance:** Matt Duncan. **Director, Player Facilities:** Fletcher Wilkes. **Office Manager:** Arlene Vidumanksy. **AeroFare General Manager:** Jeff Meehan.

### FIELD STAFF

**Manager:** Tim Bogar. **Coach:** Felix Fermin. **Pitching Coach:** Scott Radinsky. **Trainer:** Jeff Desjardins. **Strength/Conditioning Coach:** Brendon Huttmann.

### GAME INFORMATION

**Radio Announcer:** Jim Clark. **No. of Games Broadcast:** Home-71, Away-71. **Flagship Station:** FOX 1350-AM.
**PA Announcer:** Joe Jastrzemski/Joe Dunn. **Official Scorers:** Roger Grecni, Joe Jastrzemski.
**Stadium Name:** Canal Park. **Location:** From I-76 East or I-77 South, exit onto Route 59 East, exit at Exchange/Cedar, right onto Cedar, left at Main Street. From I-76 West or I-77 North, exit at Main Street/Downtown, follow exit onto Broadway Street, left onto Exchange Street, right at Main Street. **Standard Game Times:** 7:05 p.m.; Sat. (April) 2:05; Sun. 2:05. **Ticket Price Range:** $7-10.
**Visiting Club Hotel:** Radisson Hotel Akron City Centre, 20 W. Mill St., Akron, OH 44308. Telephone: (330) 384-1500.

# ALTOONA
## CURVE

**Office Address:** 1000 Park Ave., Altoona, PA 16602.
**Mailing Address:** P.O. Box 1029, Altoona, PA 16603.
**Telephone:** (814) 943-5400. **FAX:** (814) 942-9132, (814) 943-9050.
**E-Mail Address:** frontoffice@altoonacurve.com. **Website:** www.altoonacurve.com.
**Affiliation (first year):** Pittsburgh Pirates (1999). **Years in League:** 1999-.

### OWNERSHIP, MANAGEMENT

**Operated by:** Curve Baseball LP.
**President, Managing Partner:** Chuck Greenberg. **General Manager:** Todd Parnell. **Senior Director, Sales/Marketing:** Rick Janac. **Assistant GM, Senior Director of Ticketing:** Jeff Garner. **Director, Broadcasting/Communications:** Jason Dambach. **Director, Community Relations:** Elsie Zengel. **Director, Merchandising:** Ben Rothrock. **Director, Sports Turf Management:** Patrick Coakley. **Director, Ballpark Operations:** Kirk Stiffler. **Director, Finance:** Machelle Noel. **Director, Box Office Operations:** Jeff Adams. **Director, Information Services, Graphic/Web Design:** Bill Edevane. **Director, Promotions/New Business Development:** Chris Mundhenk. **Executive Producer, In-Game Entertainment:** Matt Zidik. **Director, Mascot Operations:** Charlton Jordan. **Assistant Directors, Ticket Sales:** Derek Martin, Chris Phillips. **Assistant Director, Promotions:** Matt Hoover. **Ticket Sales Associates:** Eric Fiscus, Bill Hallman, Corey Homan, Chris Keefer, Lane Kieffer, Jessica Nebel, Dennis Newberry, Dan Newhart, Kevin Steele, Denny Watson. **Sponsorship Sales Account Executives:** John Carey, Greg Parassio, Julie Price, Jessica Seretti. **Media Relations Manager:** Billy Harner. **Media Relations Assistant:** Joe Moore. **Producer, In-Game Entertainment:** John Foreman. **Sports Turf Manager:** Matt Neri. **Administrative Assistant:** Carol Schmittle. **Ballpark Operations Assistants:** Shawn Huber, Cindy Stephens. **Community Relations Manager:** Stefanie Brown. **Accounting Specialist:** Tara Figard. **Assistant Sports Turf Manager:** Lisa Guinivan.

### FIELD STAFF

**Manager:** Tim Leiper. **Coach:** Brandon Moore. **Pitching Coach:** Ray Searage. **Trainer:** Thomas Pribyl.

### GAME INFORMATION

**Radio Announcers:** Jason Dambach, Paul Steigerwald, Joe Moore. **No. of Games Broadcast:** Home-71, Away-71. **Flagship Station:** WHPA 95.3-FM.
**PA Announcer:** Rich DeLeo. **Official Scorer:** Ted Beam.
**Stadium Name:** Blair County Ballpark. **Location:** Frankstown Road exit off I-99. **Standard Game Times:** 7:05 p.m.,

6:35 (April-May); Sun. 6:05, 3:05 (April-May). **Ticket Price Range:** $4-12.
   **Visiting Club Hotel:** Ramada Inn of Altoona, Route 220 and Plank Road, Altoona, PA 16602. Telephone: (814) 946-1631.

# BINGHAMTON
## METS

**Office Address:** 211 Henry St., Binghamton, NY 13901.
**Mailing Address:** P.O. Box 598, Binghamton, NY 13902.
**Telephone:** (607) 723-6387. **FAX:** (607) 723-7779.
**E-Mail Address:** bmets@bmets.com. **Website:** www.bmets.com.
**Affiliation (first year):** New York Mets (1992). **Years in League:** 1923-37, 1940-63, 1966-68, 1992-.

## OWNERSHIP, MANAGEMENT
   **Operated by:** Binghamton Mets Baseball Club, Inc.
   **Principal Owners:** Bill Maines, David Maines, George Scherer, Michael Urda.
   **President:** Michael Urda. **Special Advisor to President:** Bill Terlecky.
   **General Manager:** Scott Brown. **Assistant GM:** Jim Weed. **Directors, Stadium Operations:** Richard Tylicki, Dan Abashian. **Director, Ticket Operations:** Jason Hall. **Special Event Coordinator:** Billy Grover. **Ticket Office Manager:** Casey Both. **Scholastic Programs Coordinator:** Lou Ferraro. **Community Relations Coordinator:** Nancy Wiseman. **Office Manager:** Rebecca Brown. **Merchandising Manager:** Lisa Shattuck. **Broadcasting Director:** Robert Ford. **Home Clubhouse Manager:** Matt Lane. **Visiting Clubhouse Manager:** Unavailable. **Sports Turf Manager:** Stephen Wiseman.

## FIELD STAFF
   **Manager:** Juan Samuel. **Coach:** John Valentin. **Pitching Coach:** Mark Brewer. **Trainer:** Unavailable.

## GAME INFORMATION
   **Radio Announcer:** Matt Park. **No. of Games Broadcast:** Home-71, Away-71. **Flagship Station:** WNBF 1290-AM.
   **PA Announcer:** Jeff Olin. **Official Scorer:** Steve Kraly.
   **Stadium Name:** NYSEG Stadium. **Location:** I-81 to exit 4S (Binghamton), Route 11 exit to Henry Street. **Standard Game Times:** 7 p.m., (April-May) 6; Sat. 6; Sun. 1:30. **Ticket Price Range:** $7-8.
   **Visiting Club Hotel:** Best Western, 569 Harry L Drive, Johnson City, NY 13790. Telephone: (607) 729-9194.

# BOWIE
## BAYSOX

**Office Address:** Prince George's Stadium, 4101 NE Crain Hwy., Bowie, MD 20716.
**Telephone:** (301) 805-6000. **FAX:** (301) 464-4911.
**E-Mail Address:** info@baysox.com. **Website:** www.baysox.com.
**Affiliation:** Baltimore Orioles (1993). **Years in League:** 1993-.

## OWNERSHIP, MANAGEMENT
   **Operated by:** Comcast-Spectacor.
   **President:** Peter Luukko. **Vice President:** Frank Miceli.
   **General Manager:** Brian Shallcross. **Director, Marketing:** Phil Wrye. **Assistant Director, Marketing:** Marlene Engberg. **Communications Manager:** Ryan Roberts. **Communications Assistant:** Nathan Coffey. **Marketing Assistant:** Jeffrey Gutt. **Director, Ticket Sales:** Addie Staebler. **Group Sales Manager:** Peter Sekulow. **Ticket Plan Sales Manager:** Clark Baker. **Fan Services/Box Office:** Charlene Fewer. **Group Events Managers:** Marsha Darbouze, Karida Jordan, Matt McLaughlin, Sean Ream. **Group Events Interns:** David Beekman, Brendan McClellan. **Senior Account Manager:** Kyle Droppers. **Sponsorship Account Managers:** Brian Bauer, Brad Tarr. **Sponsorship Intern:** Michael Wiggins. **Director, Facilities/Field Operations:** Matt Parrott. **Stadium Operations Manager:** Rick Wade. **Director, Game Day Personnel:** Darlene Mingioli. **Clubhouse Manager:** Milton Miles. **Office Manager:** Amber Sohl. **Bookkeeper:** Carol Terwilliger. **Controller:** Christy Hoos. **Assistant Controller:** Chris Fielding. **Accounts Receivable:** Kim Padgett. **Staff Accountant:** Jen Martenot.

## FIELD STAFF
   **Manager:** Don Werner. **Coach:** Moe Hill. **Pitching Coach:** Scott McGregor. **Trainer:** Mark Shires. **Strength/Conditioning Coach:** John Selzler.

## GAME INFORMATION
   **Radio Announcer:** Sam Farber. **No of Games Broadcast:** Home-71. **Flagship Station:** WRGW.
   **PA Announcer:** Unavailable. **Official Scorer:** Jeff Hertz.
   **Stadium Name:** Prince George's Stadium. **Location:** ¼ mile south of U.S. 50-U.S. 301 interchange in Bowie. **Standard Game Times:** 7:05 p.m.; Sun. (April-June) 1:05, (July-Aug.) 6:05. **Ticket Price Range:** $6-15.
   **Visiting Club Hotel:** Best Western Annapolis, 2520 Riva Rd., Annapolis, MD 21401. Telephone: (410) 224-2800.

# CONNECTICUT
## DEFENDERS

(Team previously known as Norwich Navigators)
**Office Address:** 14 Stott Ave., Norwich, CT 06360.
**Telephone:** (860) 887-7962. **FAX:** (860) 886-5996.
**E-Mail Address:** info@ctdefenders.com. **Website:** www.ctdefenders.com.
**Affiliation (first year):** San Francisco Giants (2003). **Years in League:** 1995-.

### OWNERSHIP, MANAGEMENT
**Operated by:** Navigators Baseball, LP.
**President/Managing Partner:** Lou DiBella. **Vice President:** Keith Hallal.
**General Manager:** Jim Beaudoin. **Director, Marketing:** Melissa Manfre. **Director, Finance:** Richard Darling. **Director, Corporate Sales:** Johnny Gill. **Director, Stadium Operations:** J.J. Reali. **Group Sales Managers:** John Muszkewycz, Brendon Porter, David Uden. **Director, Merchandise:** John Youngblood. **Ticket Manager:** Kaitlyn Tomasello. **Director, Media/Broadcasting:** Shawn Holliday. **Community Relations:** Meaghan Davis. **Office Manager:** Michelle Taylor. **Head Groundskeeper:** Chris Berube.

### FIELD STAFF
**Manager:** Dave Machemer. **Coach:** Gary Davenport. **Pitching Coach:** Bob Stanley. **Trainer:** Anthony Reyes.

### GAME INFORMATION
**Radio Announcers:** Shawn Holliday, Jeremy Lechan. **No. of Games Broadcast:** Home-71, Away-71. **Flagship Station:** WICH 1310-AM.
**PA Announcer:** Ed Weyant. **Official Scorer:** Chris Cote.
**Stadium Name:** Sen. Thomas J. Dodd Memorial Stadium. **Location:** I-395 to exit 82, follow signs to Norwich Industrial Park, stadium is in back of industrial park. **Standard Game Times:** 7:05 p.m.; Mon., Tues., Thur. (April-May) 6:35; Wed. (April-May) 12:35; Sat. (April-May) 2:05; Sun. 2:05. **Ticket Price Range:** $7-10.
**Visiting Club Hotel:** Comfort Inn Mystic, 48 Whitehall Avenue, Mystic, CT 06355. (860) 572-8531.

# ERIE
## SEAWOLVES

**Office Address:** 110 E. 10th St., Erie, PA 16501.
**Telephone:** (814) 456-1300. **FAX:** (814) 456-7520.
**E-Mail Address:** seawolves@seawolves.com. **Website:** www.seawolves.com.
**Affiliation (first year):** Detroit Tigers (2001). **Years in League:** 1999-.

### OWNERSHIP, MANAGEMENT
**Operated by:** Mandalay Baseball Properties.
**General Manager:** John Frey. **Head Groundskeeper:** Brandon Schanz. **Director, Marketing/Promotions:** Rob Magee. **Box Office Manager/ Merchandise:** Mark Pirrello. **Director, Ticket Sales:** Joe Etling. **Director, Operations:** Ragen Walker. **Operations Assistant:** Bob Jankowski. **Ticket Sales Representatives:** Becky Obradovic. **Accountant:** Bernie Mulvihill. **Office Manager:** Christine Gates. **Director, Sales:** Mike Uden. **Director, Entertainment:** Liz Braswell.

### FIELD STAFF
**Manager:** Duffy Dyer. **Coach:** Pete Incaviglia. **Pitching Coach:** Mike Caldwell. **Trainer:** Chris McDonald.

### GAME INFORMATION
**Radio Announcer:** Unavailable. **No. of Games Broadcast:** Home-71, Away-71. **Flagship Station:** WFNN 1330-AM.
**PA Announcer:** Dean Pepicello. **Official Scorer:** Les Caldwell.
**Stadium Name:** Jerry Uht Park. **Location:** U.S. 79 North to East 12th Street exit, left on State Street, right on 10th Street. **Standard Game Times:** 7:05 p.m., 6:35 p.m. (April-May); Sun. 1:05. **Ticket Price Range:** $5-8.
**Visiting Club Hotel:** Avalon Hotel, 16 W. 10th St., Erie, PA 16501. Telephone: (814) 459-2220.

# HARRISBURG
## SENATORS

**Office Address:** Commerce Bank Park, City Island, Harrisburg, PA 17101.
**Mailing Address:** P.O. Box 15757, Harrisburg, PA 17105.
**Telephone:** (717) 231-4444. **FAX:** (717) 231-4445.
**E-Mail Address:** hbgsenator@aol.com. **Website:** www.senatorsbaseball.com.
**Affiliation (first year):** Washington Nationals (2005). **Years in League:** 1924-35, 1987-.

## OWNERSHIP, MANAGEMENT

**Operated by:** Harrisburg Civic Baseball Club, Inc.
**Chairman:** Greg Martini.
**General Manager:** Todd Vander Woude. **Assistant GM, Baseball Operations:** Mark Mattern. **Assistant GM, Business Operations:** Mark Clarke. **Director, Facilities Operations:** Tim Foreman. **Director, Concessions Operations:** Steve Leininger. **Director, Ticket Sales:** Tom Wess. **Associate, Ticket Sales:** Mark Brindle. **Director, Group Sales:** Brian Egli. **Group Sales:** Melissa Altemose, Tony Duffy. **Associate, Ticket Sales:** Mark Brindle. **Director, Broadcasting/Media Relations:** Terry Byrom. **Interns:** Greg Brizek, Mark Cruttenden, Tony Colordo, Miranda Malkemes, Josh Mullins, Jonathan Naff, Shannon Wood, Karen Zoda.

## FIELD STAFF

**Manager:** John Stearns. **Coach:** Mike Hart. **Pitching Coach:** Rick Tomlin. **Trainer:** Beth Jarrett.

## GAME INFORMATION

**Radio Announcers:** Terry Byrom, Mark Mattern. **No. of Games Broadcast:** Home-71, Away-71. **Flagship Station:** WKBO 1230-AM.
**PA Announcer:** Chris Andree. **Official Scorer:** Dave Wright.
**Stadium Name:** Commerce Bank Park. **Location:** I-83, exit 23 (Second Street) to Market Street, bridge to City Island. **Standard Game Times:** 6:35 p.m.; Sat. 6:05; Sun. 1:05. **Ticket Price Range:** $3-9.
**Visiting Club Hotel:** Crowne Plaza, 23 S. Second St., Harrisburg, PA 17101. Telephone: (717) 234-5021.

**Office Address:** 230 John Karbonic Way, New Britain, CT 06051.
**Mailing Address:** P.O. Box 1718, New Britain, CT 06050.
**Telephone:** (860) 224-8383. **FAX:** (860) 225-6267.
**E-Mail Address:** rockcats@rockcats.com. **Website:** www.rockcats.com.
**Affiliation (first year):** Minnesota Twins (1995). **Years in League:** 1983-.

## OWNERSHIP, MANAGEMENT

**Operated by:** New Britain Baseball Club, Inc.
**Principal Owners:** Bill Dowling, Coleman Levy. **Chairman of Board:** Coleman Levy.
**President, General Manager:** Bill Dowling. **Assistant GMs:** Evan Levy, John Willi. **Director, Broadcasting:** Jeff Dooley. **Director, Ticket Operations:** Peter Colon. **Director, Corporate Sales:** Dennis Meehan. **Director, Media Relations:** Bob Dowling. **Senior Account Executives:** Ricky Ferrell, Frank Novak. **Director, Stadium Operations:** Mike Hyland. **Account Executive:** Kim Pizighelli. **Coordinator, Community Relations:** Courtney Lawson. **Corporate Sales Executive:** Logan Smith. **Controller:** Paula Perdelwitz. **Home Clubhouse Manager:** Tyler Greco. **Visiting Clubhouse Manager:** Anthony Desanto.

## FIELD STAFF

**Manager:** Riccardo Ingram. **Coach:** Floyd Rayford. **Pitching Coach:** Gary Lucas. **Trainer:** Chad Jackson.

## GAME INFORMATION

**Radio Announcers:** Jeff Dooley, Dan Lovallo. **No. of Games Broadcast:** Home-71, Away-71. **Flagship Station:** WDRC 1360-AM.
**PA Announcer:** Don Shamber. **Official Scorer:** Unavailable.
**Stadium Name:** New Britain Stadium. **Location:** From I-84, take Route 72 East (exit 35) or Route 9 South (exit 39A), left at Ellis Street (exit 25), left at South Main Street, stadium one mile on right. From Route 91 or Route 5, take Route 9 North to Route 71 (exit 24), first exit. **Standard Game Times:** 7:05 p.m., 6:35 (April-June); Sun. 1:35. **Ticket Price Range:** $5-12.
**Visiting Club Hotel:** Holiday Inn Express, 120 Laning St., Southington, CT 06489. Telephone: 860-276-0736.

**Office Address:** One Line Dr., Manchester, NH 03101.
**Telephone:** (603) 641-2005. **FAX:** (603) 641-2055.
**E-Mail Address:** baseballinfo@nhfishercats.com. **Website:** www.nhfishercats.com.
**Affiliation (first year):** Toronto Blue Jays (2004). **Years in League:** 2004-

## OWNERSHIP, MANAGEMENT

**Operated By:** Triple Play, LLC.
**Managing Partner:** Art Solomon. **Minority Partner:** Drew Weber.
**President, General Manager:** Shawn Smith. **Corporate Controller:** Karl Stone. **Assistant GM:** Jeff Tagliaferro. **Director, Merchandise:** John Egan. **Director, Corporate Sales:** Tim Dalton. **Director, Media Relations:** John Zahr. **Director, Food/Beverage:** Tim Restall. **Director, Group Sales:** Erik Lesniak. **Corporate Sales/Baseball Operations:**

Danielle Matteau. **Ticket Operations:** Amanda Baker, Mary Magoon. **Group Sales:** Randy Menken, Mike Murphy, Mike Tarleton, Brian Weigler. **Director, Stadium Operations:** Jim Davala. **Assistant Director, Stadium Operations:** Sam Boudle. **Head Turf Manager:** Eric Blanton. **Assistant Turf Manager:** Ken Harrington. **Director, Video Production:** Adam Jackson.

## FIELD STAFF
**Manager:** Doug Davis. **Coach:** Gary Cathcart. **Pitching Coach:** Dave LaRoche. **Trainer:** Voon Chong.

## GAME INFORMATION
**Radio Announcers:** Mike Murphy, Bob Lipman. **No. of Games Broadcast:** Home-71, Away-71. **Flagship Station:** Unavailable.

**PA Announcer:** John Zahr. **Official Scorer:** Kurt Svoboda, Tom Gauthier.

**Stadium Name:** Fisher Cats Ballpark. **Location:** From I-93 North, take I-293 North to exit 5 (Granite Street), right on Granite Street, right on South Commercial Street, right on Line Drive. **Standard Game Times:** 6:35 p.m.; Sat. (June-Sept.) 5:05, (April-May) 1:05; Sun. 1:05. **Ticket Price Range:** $4-$12.

**Visiting Club Hotel:** Comfort Inn, 298 Queen City Ave., Manchester, NH 03102. Telephone: (603) 668-2600.

# PORTLAND
## SEA DOGS

**Office Address:** 271 Park Ave., Portland, ME 04102.
**Mailing Address:** P.O. Box 636, Portland, ME 04104.
**Telephone:** (207) 874-9300. **FAX:** (207) 780-0317.
**E-Mail Address:** seadogs@portlandseadogs.com. **Website:** www.seadogs.com.
**Affiliation (first year):** Boston Red Sox (2003). **Years in League:** 1994-.

## OWNERSHIP, MANAGEMENT
**Operated By:** Portland, Maine Baseball, Inc.
**Principal Owner, Chairman:** Daniel Burke.
**President, General Manager:** Charles Eshbach. **Vice President/Assistant GM:** John Kameisha. **Assistant GM, Business Operations:** Jim Heffley. **Director, Public Relations:** Chris Cameron. **Director, Sales and Marketing/Promotions Coordinator:** Geoff Iacuessa. **Director, Group Sales:** Corey Thompson. **Director, Ticketing:** Dave Strong. **Assistant Director, Ticketing:** Tony Cameron. **Director, Broadcasting/Video Services:** Todd Jamison. **Director, Food Services:** Mike Scorza. **Special Projects:** Peter Drivas. **Office Manager:** Judy Bray. **Administrative Assistants:** Chad Bilodeau, Jason Brayman, Kate Dempsey, Dave Fazio, Tim Hammond, Sean Kimball, Jenessa Knowlton, Stephanie Livoli. **Clubhouse Managers:** Craig Candage Jr., Craig Candage Sr., Rick Goslin. **Head Groundskeeper:** Rick Anderson.

## FIELD STAFF
**Manager:** Todd Claus. **Coach:** Russ Morman. **Pitching Coach:** Ace Adams. **Trainer:** Masai Takahashi.

## GAME INFORMATION
**Radio Announcers:** Mike Antonellis, Todd Jamison. **No. of Games Broadcast:** Home-71, Away-71. **Flagship Station:** WBAE 1490-AM.

**PA Announcer:** Dean Rogers. **Official Scorer:** Thom Hinton.

**Stadium Name:** Hadlock Field. **Location:** From South, I-295 to exit 5, merge onto Congress Street, left at St. John Street, merge right onto Park Ave.; From North, I-295 to exit 6A, right onto Park Ave. **Standard Game Times:** 7 p.m., (April-May) 6; Sat. 6, (April-May) 1; Sun. 1. **Ticket Price Range:** $3-8.

**Visiting Club Hotel:** DoubleTree Hotel, 1230 Congress St., Portland, ME 04102. Telephone: (207) 774-5611.

# READING
## PHILLIES

**Office Address:** Route 61 South/1900 Centre Ave., Reading, PA 19601.
**Mailing Address:** P.O. Box 15050, Reading, PA 19612.
**Telephone:** (610) 375-8469. **FAX:** (610) 373-5868.
**E-Mail Address:** info@readingphillies.com. **Website:** www.readingphillies.com.
**Affiliation (first year):** Philadelphia Phillies (1967). **Years in League:** 1933-35, 1952-61, 1963-65, 1967-.

## OWNERSHIP, MANAGEMENT
**Operated By:** E&J Baseball Club, Inc.
**Principal Owner, President:** Craig Stein.
**General Manager:** Chuck Domino. **Assistant GM:** Scott Hunsicker. **Director, Stadium Operations/Concessions:** Andy Bortz. **Director, Game/Staff Operations:** Troy Pothoff. **Head Groundskeeper:** Dan Douglas. **Director, Merchandise:** Kevin Sklenarik. **Director, Ticket Operations:** Mike Becker. **Director, Group Sales/Game Presentation:** Ashley Forlini. **Manager, Group Sales/Customer Service:** Mike Robinson. **Ticket Assistant/Client Relationship Manager:** Josh Holly. **Group Sales Managers:** Brian Babik, Holly Frymyer. **Director, Communications:** Rob Hackash.

Communications Assistant: Andy Kauffman. Director, Sales: Joe Bialek. Corporate Sales, Graphic Artist/Game Entertainment: Matt Jackson. Client Relationship Managers: Lindsey Knupp, Chris McConney. Controller: Kristyne Haver. Office Manager: Deneen Giesen.

## FIELD STAFF
Manager: P.J. Forbes. Coach: John Morris. Pitching Coach: Tom Filer. Trainer: Shawn Fcasni.

## GAME INFORMATION
Radio Announcer: Steve Degler. No. of Games Broadcast: Home-71, Away-71. Flagship Station: ESPN 1240-AM. PA Announcer: Dave Bauman. Official Scorer: John Lemcke.
Stadium Name: FirstEnergy Stadium. Location: From east, take Pennsylvania Turnpike West to Morgantown exit, to 176 North, to 422 West, to Route 12 East, to Route 61 South exit. From west, take 422 East to Route 12 East, to Route 61 South exit. From north, take 222 South to Route 12 exit, to Route 61 South exit. From south, take 222 North to 422 West, to Route 12 East exit at Route 61 South.
Standard Game Times: 7:05 p.m., Mon.-Thurs. (April-May) 6:35; Sun. 1:05. Ticket Price Range: $4-9.
Visiting Club Hotel: Days Inn, 910 Woodland Ave., Wyomissing PA 19610. Telephone: (610) 375-1500.

# TRENTON
## THUNDER

Office Address: One Thunder Rd., Trenton, NJ 08611.
Telephone: (609) 394-3300. FAX: (609) 394-9666.
E-Mail Address: office@trentonthunder.com. Website: www.trentonthunder.com.
Affiliation (first year): New York Yankees (2003). Years in League: 1994-.

## OWNERSHIP, MANAGEMENT
Operated by: Garden State Baseball, LLP.
General Manager/Chief Operating Officer: Brad Taylor. Assistant GM: Greg Coleman. Vice President, Marketing: Eric Lipsman. Chief Financial Officer: Steve Ripa. Director, Merchandising: Joe Pappalardo. Director, Media Relations/Broadcasting: Dan Loney. Director, Ticket Operations: Matt Pentima. Director, Group Sales: Brian Cassidy. Director, Stadium Operations: Ryan Crammer. Director, Public Relations: Bill Cook. Assistant Directors, Group Sales: Jason Schubert, Brian Fox. Assistant Director, Ticket Sales: Patience Purdy. Coordinator of Fun: Gregg Tripp. Controller: Jeff Kluge. Manager, Community Relations/Baseball Operations: Jeff Hurley. Ticket Event Coordinators: Ross Mehalko, Adam Smedberg, Jackie Costa, Rob O'Rourke Assistant, Merchandise: Leora Kleist. Office Manager: Kathy Gallagher. Interns: Andy Bergbauer, Stephanie Bissell, Marc Bodinger, Steven Brokowsky, Ryan Carty, Alice Fodera, Tom Hipper, Britt Jerrom, Matt Krausse, Colin McBride, Brad Milausky, Chris O'Brien, Joe Rossi, Justin Sauer, Matt Schwartz, Jessica Smith, Andrew Sigal. Head Groundskeeper: Nicole Sherry. Home Clubhouse Manager: Tom Kackley. Visiting Clubhouse Manager: Daniel Rose

## FIELD STAFF
Manager: Billy Masse. Coach: Ralph Dickenson. Pitching Coach: Dave Eiland. Trainer: Zac Womack.

## GAME INFORMATION
Radio Announcers: Dan Loney, Steve Rudenstein. Flagship Station: WBUD 1260-AM. No. of Games Broadcast: Home-71, Away-71.
PA Announcer: Bill Bromberg. Official Scorers: Jay Dunn, Mike Maconi.
Stadium Name: Samuel J. Plumeri Sr. Field at Mercer County Waterfront Park. Location: From I-95, take Route 1 North to Route 29 South, stadium entrance just before tunnel. Standard Game Times: 7:05 p.m., Sat. (April-May) 1:35; Sun. 1:35. Ticket Price Range: $6-9.
Visiting Club Hotel: Howard Johnson Inn, 2995 Rte. 1 South, Lawrenceville, NJ 08648. Telephone: (609) 896-1100.

# SOUTHERN
## LEAGUE

**Mailing Address:** 2551 Roswell Rd., Suite 330, Marietta, GA 30062.
**Telephone:** (770) 321-0400. **FAX:** (770) 321-0037.
**E-Mail Address:** soleague@earthlink.net. **Website:** www.southernleague.com.
**Years League Active:** 1964-.

**President:** Don Mincher.
**Vice President:** Steve DeSalvo.
**Directors:** Peter Bragan Jr. (Jacksonville), Steve Bryant
(Carolina), Frank Burke (Chattanooga), Steve DeSalvo (Mississippi), Tom Dickson
(Montgomery), Doug Kirchhofer (Tennessee), Robert Lozinak (West Tenn.), Jonathan Nelson
(Birmingham), Miles Prentice (Huntsville), Bill Shanahan (Mobile).
**Vice President, Operations:** Lori Webb. **Coordinator, Media Relations:** Janelle
Kwietkauski.
**Division Structure: North**—Carolina, Chattanooga, Huntsville, Tennessee, West Tenn.
**South**—Birmingham, Jacksonville, Mississippi, Mobile, Montgomery.
**Regular Season:** 140 games (split-schedule). **2006 Opening Date:** April 6. **Closing Date:**
Sept. 4.
**All-Star Game:** July 10 at Montgomery.

**Don Mincher**

**Playoff Format:** First-half division champions meet second-half division champions in
best-of-5 series. Winners meet in best-of-5 series for league championship.
**Roster Limit:** 23; 24 until 30th day of season and after Aug. 9. **Player Eligibility Rule:** No restrictions.
**Brand of Baseball:** Rawlings.
**Statistician:** Major League Baseball Advanced Media, 75 Ninth Ave., New York, NY 10011.
**Umpires:** Shane Alexander (Smyrna, TN), Jason Bradley (Blackshear, GA), Josh Carlisle (New Philadelphia, OH),
Scott Childers (Martinez, GA), Steve Cummings (Satsuma, FL), Jason Dunn (Savannah, TN), Brian Kennedy (Charlotte,
NC), Buzz Laird (Norfolk, VA), Jeff Latter (Gresham, OR), Eric Loveless (Salt Lake, UT), Maria Papageorgiou (Rock
Island, IL), Todd Paskiet (Sarasota, FL), Will Robinson (Savannah, GA), Justin Vogel (Jacksonville, FL), Garrett Watson
(Las Vegas, NV).

## STADIUM INFORMATION

| Club | Stadium | Opened | Dimensions LF | CF | RF | Capacity | 2005 Att. |
|------|---------|--------|------|------|------|----------|-----------|
| Birmingham | Hoover Metropolitan Stadium | 1988 | 340 | 405 | 340 | 10,800 | 271,031 |
| Carolina | Five County Stadium | 1991 | 330 | 400 | 330 | 6,500 | 252,178 |
| Chattanooga | BellSouth Park | 2000 | 325 | 400 | 330 | 6,160 | 240,075 |
| Huntsville | Joe W. Davis Municipal Stadium | 1985 | 345 | 405 | 330 | 10,200 | 213,552 |
| Jacksonville | Baseball Grounds of Jacksonville | 2003 | 321 | 420 | 317 | 11,000 | 359,957 |
| Mississippi | Trustmark Park | 2005 | 337 | 332 | 400 | 6,000 | 242,423 |
| Mobile | Hank Aaron Stadium | 1997 | 325 | 400 | 310 | 6,000 | 187,505 |
| Montgomery | Montgomery Riverwalk Stadium | 2004 | 314 | 401 | 332 | 6,000 | 303,054 |
| Tennessee | Smokies Park | 2000 | 330 | 400 | 330 | 6,000 | 241,163 |
| West Tenn | Pringles Park | 1998 | 310 | 395 | 320 | 6,000 | 105,893 |

# BIRMINGHAM
## BARONS

**BIRMINGHAM**
**BASEBALL**

**Office Address:** 100 Ben Chapman Dr., Hoover, AL 35244.
**Mailing Address:** P.O. Box 360007, Birmingham, AL 35236.
**Telephone:** (205) 988-3200. **FAX:** (205) 988-9698.
**E-Mail Address:** barons@barons.com. **Website:** www.barons.com
**Affiliation (first year):** Chicago White Sox (1986). **Years in League:** 1964-65, 1967-75, 1981-.

## OWNERSHIP, MANAGEMENT

**Operated by:** Birmingham Barons, LLC.
**Principal Owners:** Don Logan, Jeff Logan, Stan Logan.
**General Manager:** Jonathan Nelson. **Assistant GM:** Michael Pepper. **Director, Stadium Operations:** James Young. **Director, Broadcasting:** Curt Bloom. **Director, Media Relations:** Jeff Duggan. **Director, Sales/Marketing:** Kevin Anderson. **Marketing Representative:** Patrick Pontarelli. **Group Ticket Assistant:** Alison McNulty. **Director, Promotions:** Jeremy Neisser. **Director, Season Tickets:** Jim Stennett. **GM, Grand Slam Food Service:** Eric Crook. **Director, Catering:** Robin Bellizzi. **Corporate Events Planners:** Paul Allen. **Group Ticket Manager:** Blair Holden. **Office Manager:** Kecia Braswell. **Receptionist:** Terri Calvert. **Head Groundskeeper:** Darren Seybold. **Assistant Groundskeeper:** Ryan Storey.

## FIELD STAFF

**Manager:** Chris Cron. **Coach:** Andy Tomberlin. **Pitching Coach:** Richard Dotson. **Trainer:** Joe Geck.

## GAME INFORMATION

**Radio Announcer:** Curt Bloom. **No. of Games Broadcast:** Home-70, Away-70. **Flagship Station:** WYDE 101.1-FM. **PA Announcer:** Justin Firesheets. **Official Scorer:** Mike Sullivan. **Stadium Name:** Hoover Metropolitan Stadium. **Location:** I-459 to Highway 150 (exit 10) in Hoover. **Standard Game Times:** 7:05 p.m.; Sun. 2:05, (July-Sept) 6:05. **Ticket Price Range:** $5-10.
**Visiting Club Hotel:** Best Western Riverchase Inn, 1800 Riverchase Dr., Birmingham, AL 35244. Telephone: (205) 985-7500.

# CAROLINA
## MUDCATS

CAROLINA

**Office Address:** 1501 N.C. Hwy. 39, Zebulon, NC 27597.
**Mailing Address:** P.O. Drawer 1218, Zebulon, NC 27597.
**Telephone:** (919) 269-2287. **FAX:** (919) 269-4910.
**E-Mail Address:** muddy@gomudcats.com. **Website:** www.gomudcats.com.
**Affiliation (first year):** Florida Marlins (2003). **Years in League:** 1991-.

## OWNERSHIP, MANAGEMENT

**Operated by:** Carolina Mudcats Professional Baseball Club, Inc.
**Principal Owner:** Steve Bryant.
**General Manager:** Joe Kremer. **Assistant GM:** Eric Gardner. **Director, Broadcasting:** Patrick Kinas. **Directors, Stadium Operations:** Alex Paul, Mike Snow. **Director, Marketing:** Brian DeWine. **Director, Special Events:** Nathan Priddy. **Office Manager:** Jackie DiPrimo. **Head Groundskeeper:** John Packer. **Director, Food/Beverage:** Zia Torabian. **Director, Group Sales:** Hampton Terry. **Director, Community Relations:** Jon Hill. **Merchandise Manager:** LuAnne Reynolds. **Director, Tickets:** David Kay. **Corporate Sales Representatives:** Kurt Kedzierzawski, Chris Opsomer. **Group Sales Associates:** Stacy Sheppard, Ward Warren, Lindsey Wiener. **Coordinator, Multi-Media Productions:** Aaron Bayles.

## FIELD STAFF

**Manager:** Luis Dorante. **Coach:** Paul Sanagorski. **Pitching Coach:** Scott Mitchell. **Trainer:** Steve Moreno.

## GAME INFORMATION

**Radio Announcer:** Patrick Kinas. **No. of Games Broadcast:** Home-70, Away-70. **Flagship Station:** WDNZ 570-AM, WKXU 102.5-FM.
**PA Announcer:** Dave Slade. **Official Scorer:** John Hobgood. **Stadium Name:** Five County Stadium. **Location:** From Raleigh, U.S. 64 East to 264 East, exit at Highway 39 in Zebulon. **Standard Game Times:** 7:15 p.m.; Sun. 4, (April-May, Sept) 2. **Ticket Price Range:** $4.50-8.50.
**Visiting Club Hotel:** Best Western Raleigh North, 2715 Capital Blvd., Raleigh, NC 27604. Telephone: (919) 872-5000.

# CHATTANOOGA
## LOOKOUTS

**Office Address:** 201 Power Alley, Chattanooga, TN 37402.
**Mailing Address:** P.O. Box 11002, Chattanooga, TN 37401.
**Telephone:** (423) 267-2208. **FAX:** (423) 267-4258.
**E-Mail Address:** lookouts@lookouts.com. **Website:** www.lookouts.com.
**Affiliation (first year):** Cincinnati Reds (1988). **Years in League:** 1964-65, 1976-.

### OWNERSHIP, MANAGEMENT
**Operated by:** Scenic City Baseball, LLC.
**Principal Owners:** Daniel Burke, Frank Burke, Charles Eshbach.
**President/General Manager:** Frank Burke. **Assistant GM:** John Maedel. **Assistant GM:** Debbie Triplett. **Director, Business Administration:** Trevor Reeves. **Director, Group Sales:** Bill Wheeler. **Director, Merchandising:** Karrie Ward. **Director, Media Relations:** Matt Ross. **Director, Game Day Presentation:** Christian Orth. **Director, Ticketing Operations:** Luis Gonzalez. **Director, Concessions:** Steve Sullivan. **Director, Broadcasting:** Larry Ward. **Assistant Broadcaster:** Mick Gillispie. **Head Groundskeeper:** Bo Henley. **Assistant Groundskeeper:** John Plumlee.

### FIELD STAFF
**Manager:** Jayhawk Owens. **Coach:** Jamie Dismuke. **Pitching Coach:** Bill Moloney. **Trainer:** Ryuji Araki.

### GAME INFORMATION
**Radio Announcers:** Mick Gillispie, Larry Ward. **No. of Games Broadcast:** Home-70, Away-70. **Flagship Station:** WDOD 1310-AM.
**PA Announcer:** John Maedel. **Official Scorers:** Wirt Gammon, Andy Paul.
**Stadium Name:** BellSouth Park. **Location:** From I-24, take U.S. 27 North to exit 1C (4th Street), first left onto Chestnut Street, left onto Third Street. **Standard Game Times:** 7:15 p.m.; Wed. 12:15; Sun. 2:15. **Ticket Price Range:** $4-8.
**Visiting Club Hotel:** Holiday Inn, 2345 Shallowford Rd., Chattanooga, TN 37412. Telephone: (423) 855-2898.

# HUNTSVILLE
## STARS

**Office Address:** 3125 Leeman Ferry Rd., Huntsville, AL 35801.
**Mailing Address:** P.O. Box 2769, Huntsville, AL 35804.
**Telephone:** (256) 882-2562. **FAX:** (256) 880-0801.
**E-Mail Address:** info@huntsvillestars.com. **Website:** www.huntsvillestars.com.
**Affiliation (first year):** Milwaukee Brewers (1999). **Years In League:** 1985-.

### OWNERSHIP, MANAGEMENT
**Operated by:** Huntsville Stars, LLC.
**President:** Miles Prentice.
**General Manager:** Tom Van Schaack. **Director, Broadcasting:** Brett Pollock. **Director, Media Relations:** Bryan Neece. **Marketing/Community Relations:** Unavailable. **Director, Ticketing:** Eric Laue. **Director, Field Maintenance:** Kyle Lewis. **Director, Stadium Operations:** Unavailable. **Group Sales Executives:** Eric Laue, Bryan Neece, Matt Price. **Office Manager/Assistant, Community Relations:** Earl Grilliot.

### FIELD STAFF
**Manager:** Don Money. **Coach:** Sandy Guerrero. **Pitching Coach:** Rich Sauveur. **Trainer:** Unavailable.

### GAME INFORMATION
**Radio Announcer:** Bryan Neece, Brett Pollock. **No. of Games Broadcast:** Home-70, Away-70. **Flagship Station:** WTKI 1450-AM.
**PA Announcers:** Todd Blass, J.J. Lewis **Official Scorer:** Don Rizzardi.
**Stadium Name:** Joe W. Davis Municipal Stadium. **Location:** I-65 to I-565 East, south on Memorial Parkway to Drake Avenue exit, right on Don Mincher Drive. **Standard Game Times:** 7:05 p.m., Sun. (first half) 2:05, (second half) 6:05. **Ticket Price Range:** $5-8.
**Visiting Club Hotel:** La Quinta Inn, 3141 University Dr., Huntsville, AL 35805. Telephone: (256) 533-0756.

# JACKSONVILLE
## SUNS

**Office Address:** 301 A. Philip Randolph Blvd, Jacksonville, FL 32202.
**Mailing Address:** P.O. Box 4756, Jacksonville, FL 32201.
**Telephone:** (904) 358-2846. **FAX:** (904) 358-2845.
**E-Mail Address:** jaxsuns@bellsouth.net. **Website:** www.jaxsuns.com.
**Affiliation (sixth year):** Los Angeles Dodgers (2001). **Years In League:** 1970-.

### OWNERSHIP, MANAGEMENT
**Operated by:** Baseball Jax, Inc.
**Principal Owner, Chairman of the Board:** Peter Bragan Sr. **Madame Chairman:** Mary Frances Bragan. **President:** Peter Bragan Jr.
**General Manager:** Kirk Goodman. **Assistant GM, Operations:** Brad Rodriguez. **Director, Ticket Operations:** Karlie Evatt. **Director, Community Relations:** Traci Barbour. **Director, Field Operations:** Ed Attalla. **Director, Group Sales:** Robyn Wassman. **Director, Food/Beverage:** David Leathers. **Director, Stadium Operations:** Geoff Freedman. **Office Manager:** Barbara O'Berry. **Director, Video Services:** David Scheldorf. **Assistant Director, Food/Beverage:** Mike Budd. **Manager, Box Office:** Jane Carole Bunting. **Manager, Human Resources:** Bunny Nelson. **Manager, Merchandise/Operations:** Andrew Grout. **Manager, Group Sales:** Eric Roth. **Manager, Fan Services:** Mark Hannah. **Manager, Inventory Control:** Mitch Buska. **Business Manager:** Craig Barnett. **Executive Assistant:** Darlene Short. **Groundskeeper:** Joe Soenksen. **Administrative Assistants:** Valerie Alter, Summer Gale, Jordan Patrick.

### FIELD STAFF
**Manager:** John Shoemaker. **Coach:** Mike Easler. **Pitching Coach:** Danny Darwin. **Trainer:** Tony Cordova.

### GAME INFORMATION
**Radio Announcer:** Unavailable. **No. of Games Broadcast:** Home-70, Away-70. **Flagship Station:** The Fox 930-AM. **PA Announcer:** John Leard. **Official Scorer:** Jason Eliopulos.
**Stadium Name:** The Baseball Grounds of Jacksonville. **Location:** I-95 South to Martin Luther King Parkway exit, follow Gator Bowl Blvd. around Alltel Stadium; I-95 North to Exit 347 (Emerson Street), go right to Hart Bridge Expressway, take Sports Complex exit, left at light to stop sign, take left and follow around Alltel Stadium; From Mathews Bridge, take A. Philip Randolph exit, right on A. Philip Randolph, straight to stadium. **Standard Game Times:** 7:05 p.m., Wed. 1:05, Sun. 3:05/5:05. **Ticket Price Range:** $5.50-19.50
**Visiting Club Hotel:** Hyatt Regency Jacksonville Riverfront, 225 Coastline Dr., Jacksonville, FL 32202. Telephone: (904) 633-9095.

# MISSISSIPPI
## BRAVES

**Office Address:** Trustmark Park, 1 Braves Way, Pearl, MS 39208.
**Mailing Address:** P.O. Box 97389, Pearl, MS 39288.
**Telephone:** (601) 932-8788. **FAX:** (601) 936-3567.
**Website:** www.mississippibraves.com.
**Affiliation (first year):** Atlanta Braves (2005). **Years in League:** 2005.

### OWNERSHIP, MANAGEMENT
**Operated by:** Atlanta National League Baseball Club, Inc.
**Principal Owner:** Time Warner.
**General Manager:** Steve DeSalvo. **Assistant GM:** Jim Bishop. **Promotions Director:** Brian Prochilo. **Community Relations Manager:** Lisa Dunn. **Public Relations Manager:** Nicholas Skinner. **Merchandise Director:** Sarah Banta. **Suites/Catering Manager:** Debbie Herrington. **Restaurant Manager:** Gene Slaughter. **Facility Maintenance Manager:** Greg Craddock. **Ticket Manager:** Bob Askin. **Director, Field/Facility Operations:** Matt Taylor. **Director, Food Services:** Jim Rawson. **Office Manager:** Christy Shaw. **Sales Associates:** Brian Emory, Sean Guillotte.

### FIELD STAFF
**Manager:** Jeff Blauser. **Coach:** Philip Wellman. **Pitching Coach:** Kent Willis. **Trainer:** Mike Graus.

### GAME INFORMATION
**Radio Announcer:** Bryan Eubank. **No. of Games Broadcast:** Home-70, Away-70. **Flagship Station:** WSFZ 930-AM. **PA Announcer:** Derrel Palmer. **Official Scorer:** Denny Hayles.
**Stadium Name:** Trustmark Park. **Location:** I-20 to exit 48/Pearl (Pearson Road). **Standard Game Times:** 7:05 p.m., Sun.1:05. **Ticket Price Range:** $5-12.
**Visiting Club Hotel:** Best Western Jackson North, 593 E. Beasley Rd., Jackson, MS 39206. Telephone: (601) 956-8686.

# MOBILE
## BAYBEARS

**Office Address:** Hank Aaron Stadium, 755 Bolling Bros. Blvd., Mobile, AL 36606.
**Telephone:** (251) 479.2327. **FAX:** (251) 476.1147.
**E-Mail Address:** baybears@mobilebaybears.com. **Website:** www.mobilebaybears.com.
**Affiliation (first year):** San Diego Padres (1997). **Years in League:** 1966, 1970, 1997-.

### OWNERSHIP, MANAGEMENT

**Operated by:** HWS Group.
**Principal Owner:** Mike Savit.
**President/Chief Operating Officer:** Bill Shanahan. **Vice President/General Manager:** Travis Toth. **Assistant GM, Finance:** Betty Adams. **Assistant GM, Ticket Operations:** Doug Stephens. **Director, Group Sales:** Jeff Long. **Director, Baseball Operations:** Jason Kirksey. **Director, Banquet Facilities:** Mike Callahan. **Office Manager:** LaLoni Taylor. **Director, Retail Operations:** John Hilliard. **Broadcaster:** Tim Hagerty. **Corporate Sales:** Tony Kaseta. **Head Groundskeeper:** Kyle Lewis. **Stadium Operations Manager:** Jonathan Nobles. **Sales/Youth Programs:** Lloyd Meyers. **Clubhouse Manager:** A.J. Niland. **Stadium Operations Assistant:** Wade Vadakin. **Internet Liaison/Team Chaplain:** Lorin Barr.

### FIELD STAFF

**Manager:** Gary Jones. **Coach:** Arnie Beyeler. **Pitching Coach:** Glenn Abbott. **Trainer:** Greg Harrell. **Strength Coach:** Greg Estep.

### GAME INFORMATION

**Radio Announcer:** Tim Hagerty. **No. of Games Broadcast:** Home-70, Away-70. **Flagship Station:** WABB 1480-AM.
**PA Announcers:** Jay Hasting, Matt McCoy. **Official Scorer:** Dave Knowles.
**Stadium Name:** Hank Aaron Stadium. **Location:** I-65 to exit 1 (Government Blvd. East), right at Satchel Paige Drive, right at Bolling Bros. Boulevard. **Standard Game Times:** 7:05 p.m.; Sun. 6:05, (April-May) 2:05. **Ticket Price Range:** $5-10.
**Visiting Club Hotel:** Riverview Plaza, 64 S. Water St., Mobile, AL 36602. Telephone: (251) 438-4000.

# MONTGOMERY
## BISCUITS

**Office Address:** 200 Coosa St., Montgomery, AL 36104.
**Telephone:** (334) 323-2255. **FAX:** (334) 323-2225.
**E-Mail Address:** info@biscuitsbaseball.com. **Website:** www.biscuitsbaseball.com.
**Affiliation (first year):** Tampa Bay Devil Rays (2004). **Years in League:** 1965-1980, 2004-.

### OWNERSHIP, MANAGEMENT

**Operated by:** Montgomery Professional Baseball, LLC.
**Principal Owners:** Tom Dickson, Sherrie Myers.
**General Manager:** Greg Rauch. **Assistant GM:** Patrick Day. **Marketing Assistants:** April Catarella, Jim Tocco, DeAndrae Watson. **Sponsorship Manager:** Marla Terranova. **Client Service Executive:** Hope Fussell. **Sponsorship Service Representative:** Brooke Neuhart. **Corporate Account Manager:** Travis Burkett. **Corporate Account Executive:** Brian Toy. **Box Office Manager:** Kerry Cranford. **Box Office Assistants:** Tyler Ericson, Patrick Walters. **Season Ticket Coordinator/Head Concierge:** Kent Rose. **Director, Operations:** Steve Blackwell. **Group Sales Manager:** Eric Clements. **Group Sales Representatives:** Jason Benton, Brandon Stevens. **Media/Marketing Coordinator:** Jesse Goldberg-Strassler. **Director, Food Service:** Nick Kavalauskas. **Concession Supervisor:** Ben Blankenship. **Director, Catering:** Jason Wilson. **Business Manager:** Linda Fast. **Assistant Business Manager:** Tranitra Avery. **Retail Manager:** Monte Meyers. **Office Manager:** Bill Sisk. **Warehouse Supervisor:** Edward Sole. **Head Groundskeeper:** Lane Oglesby.

### FIELD STAFF

**Manager:** Charlie Montoyo. **Coach:** Mako Oliveras. **Pitching Coach:** Xavier Hernandez. **Trainer:** Mark Vinson.

### GAME INFORMATION

**Radio Announcers:** Jesse Goldberg-Strassler, Jim Tocco. **No. of Games Broadcast:** Home-70, Away-70. **Flagship Stations:** WLWI 1440-AM, WMSP 740-AM.
**PA Announcer:** Rick Hendrick. **Official Scorer:** Travis Jarome.
**Stadium Name:** Montgomery Riverwalk Stadium. **Location:** I-65 to exit 172, east on Herron Street, left on Coosa Street. **Standard Game Times:** 7:05 p.m.; Sun. 5:05, (April-May) 2:05. **Ticket Price Range:** $6-10.
**Visiting Club Hotel:** La Quinta Inn, 128 Eastern Blvd., Montgomery, AL 36117. Telephone: (334) 271-1260.

# TENNESSEE
## SMOKIES

Office Address: 3540 Line Dr., Kodak, TN 37764.
Telephone: (865) 286-2300. FAX: (865) 523-9913.
E-Mail Address: info@smokiesbaseball.com. Website: www.smokiesbaseball.com.
Affiliation (first year): Arizona Diamondbacks (2005). Years in League: 1964-67, 1972-.

### OWNERSHIP, MANAGEMENT

Operated by: SPBC, LLC.
President: Doug Kirchhofer.
General Manager: Brian Cox. Assistant GM: Jeff Shoaf. Director, Broadcasting: Tom Hart. Director, Sales: Jon Kuka. Director, Marketing/Communications: Pete Ehmke. Director, Stadium Operations: Bryan Webster. Director, Ticket Sales: Jeff Stewart. Director, Ticket Operations: Kamryn Hollar. Director, Community Relations: Lauren Chesney. Director, Field Operations: Bob Shoemaker. Director, Food/Beverage: Tony DaSilveira. Group Sales Manager: Gabe Bowman. Group Sales Representatives: Dan Blue, Kyle Herschelman, Ryan Koehler, Andy Kroger. Business Manager: Suzanne French. Assistant, Broadcast/Media Relations: Chip Kain. Merchandise Assistant: Mark French. Operations Assistants: Justin Belsly, Ryan Cox, George Levandoski, Matt Tahja. Administrative Assistants: Carolyn Barbee, Tolena Trout.

### FIELD STAFF

Manager: Bill Plummer. Coach: Tony Dello. Pitching Coach: Dan Carlson. Trainer: Rodger Fleming. Strength Coach: Ed Yong.

### GAME INFORMATION

Radio Announcers: Tom Hart, Chip Kain. No. of Games Broadcast: Home-70, Away-70. Flagship Stations: WNML 99.1-FM, WNRX 99.3-FM.
PA Announcer: George Yardley. Official Scorers: Paul Barger, Randy Corrado, Jeff Muir.
Stadium Name: Smokies Park. Location: I-40 to exit 407, Highway 66 North. Standard Game Times: 7:15 p.m., Sun. 5. Ticket Price Range: $5-9.
Visiting Club Hotel: Days Inn-Exit 407, 3402 Winfield Dunn Pkwy., Kodak TN 37764. Telephone: (865) 933-4500.

# WEST TENN
## DIAMOND JAXX

Office Address: 4 Fun Place, Jackson, TN 38305.
Telephone: (731) 988-5299. FAX: (731) 988-5246.
E-Mail Address: fun@diamondjaxx.com. Website: www.diamondjaxx.com.
Affiliation (first year): Chicago Cubs (1998). Years in League: 1998-.

### OWNERSHIP, MANAGEMENT

Operated by: Lozinak Baseball Properties, LLC.
General Manager: Jeff Parker. Assistant GM: Dave Jojola. Director, Operations: Robert Jones. Director, Broadcasting/Media Relations: Ron Potesta. Director, Ticketing/Merchandise Sales: Jason Compton. Manager, Community Relations/Group Sales: Stephanie Pierce. Manager, Advertising Sales/Promotions: Mark Vanderhaar. Manager, Ticketing/Merchandising/Publications: Liz Malone. Head Groundskeeper: Justin Spillman. Manager, Catering/Concessions: Barbara Newsom. Clubhouse Manager: Bradley Arnold.

### FIELD STAFF

Manager: Pat Listach. Coach: Tom Beyers. Pitching Coach: Mike Anderson. Trainer: Matt Johnson.

### GAME INFORMATION

Radio Announcer: Ron Potesta. No. of Games Broadcast: Home-70, Away-70. Flagship Station: Unavailable.
PA Announcer: Dan Reaves. Official Scorer: Tracy Brewer.
Stadium Name: Pringles Park. Location: From I-40, take exit 85 South on F.E. Wright Drive, left onto Ridgecrest Road. Standard Game Times: 6:35 p.m.; Fri.-Sat. 7:05, Sun 1:05. Ticket Price Range: $4-9.
Visiting Club Hotel: Doubletree Hotel, 1770 Hwy. 45 Bypass, Jackson, TN 38305. Telephone: (731) 664-6900.

# TEXAS
# LEAGUE

## CLASS AA

**Mailing Address:** 2442 Facet Oak, San Antonio, TX 78232.
**Telephone:** (210) 545-5297. **FAX:** (210) 545-5298.
**E-Mail Address:** texasleague@sbcglobal.net. **Website:** www.texas-league.com.
**Years League Active:** 1888-1890, 1892, 1895-1899, 1902-1942, 1946-.

Tom Kayser

**President, Treasurer:** Tom Kayser.

**Vice President:** Burl Yarbrough. **Corporate Secretary:** Eric Edelstein. **Administrative Assistant:** Brian Durack.

**Directors:** Jon Dandes (Wichita), J.J. Gottsch (Corpus Christi), Mike Lamping (Springfield), Chuck Lamson (Tulsa), Mike McCall (Frisco), Miles Prentice (Midland), Bill Valentine (Arkansas), Burl Yarbrough (San Antonio).

**Division Structure: North**—Arkansas, Springfield, Tulsa, Wichita. **South**—Corpus Christi, Frisco, Midland, San Antonio.

**Regular Season:** 140 games (split schedule). **2006 Opening Date:** April 6. **Closing Date:** Sept. 3.

**All-Star Game:** June 20 at Little Rock.

**Playoff Format:** First-half division champions play second-half division champions in best-of-5 series. Winners meet in best-of-5 series for league championship.

**Roster Limit:** 23; 24 for first 30 days of season and after Aug. 9. **Player Eligibility Rule:** No restrictions.

**Brand of Baseball:** Rawlings.

**Statistician:** Major League Baseball Advanced Media, 75 Ninth Ave., New York, NY 10011.

**Umpires:** Aaron Banks (Olathe, KS), John Brammer (Fort Worth, TX), Delfin Colon (Houston, TX), Brandon Coony (San Antonio, TX), Rob Hansen (Corona, CA), Jason Nakaishi (Syracuse, UT), David Rackley (Seabrook, TX), Jeremy Sparling (Parker, CO), Jason Stein (Fort Worth, TX).

### STADIUM INFORMATION

| | | | Dimensions | | | | |
|---|---|---|---|---|---|---|---|
| **Club** | **Stadium** | **Opened** | **LF** | **CF** | **RF** | **Capacity** | **2005 Att.** |
| Arkansas | Ray Winder Field | 1932 | 330 | 390 | 345 | 6,083 | 196,366 |
| Corpus Christi | Whataburger Field | 2005 | 325 | 400 | 315 | 7,500 | 505,189 |
| Frisco | Dr. Pepper/Seven-Up Ballpark | 2003 | 330 | 410 | 322 | 10,000 | 581,074 |
| Midland | Citibank Ballpark | 2002 | 330 | 410 | 322 | 6,669 | 252,059 |
| San Antonio | Nelson Wolff Municipal Stadium | 1994 | 310 | 402 | 340 | 6,200 | 272,922 |
| Springfield | John Q. Hammonds Field | 2003 | 315 | 400 | 330 | 8,458 | 526,630 |
| Tulsa | Drillers Stadium | 1981 | 335 | 390 | 340 | 11,003 | 335,018 |
| Wichita | Lawrence-Dumont Stadium | 1934 | 344 | 401 | 312 | 6,055 | 165,077 |

# ARKANSAS
## TRAVELERS

**Office Address:** Ray Winder Field at War Memorial Park, Little Rock, AR 72205.
**Mailing Address:** P.O. Box 55066, Little Rock, AR 72215.
**Telephone:** (501) 664-1555. **FAX:** (501) 664-1834.
**E-Mail Address:** travs@travs.com. **Website:** www.travs.com.
**Affiliation (first year):** Los Angeles Angels of Anaheim (2001). **Years In League:** 1966-.

### OWNERSHIP, MANAGEMENT
**Operated by:** Arkansas Travelers Baseball Club, Inc.
**President:** Bert Parke.
**Executive Vice President, General Manager:** Bill Valentine. **Assistant GM:** Pete Laven. **Director, Media Relations/Broadcasting:** Phil Elson. **Director, Promotions:** Jamie Eatmon. **Director, Concessions:** Josh Dickey. **Director, Stadium Operations:** Fifty Green. **Park Superintendent:** Greg Johnston. **Assistant Park Superintendent:** Reggie Temple. **Bookkeeper:** Nena Valentine.

### FIELD STAFF
**Manager:** Tyrone Boykin. **Coach:** Keith Johnson. **Pitching Coach:** Ken Patterson. **Trainer:** Aaron Wells.

### GAME INFORMATION
**Radio Announcer:** Phil Elson. **No. of Games Broadcast:** Home-70, Away-70. **Flagship Station:** KASR 92.7-FM.
**PA Announcer:** Kevin Cruise. **Official Scorers:** Tim Cooper, Dan Floyd.
**Stadium Name:** Ray Winder Field. **Location:** I-630 to Fair Park Boulevard exit, north off exit, right after zoo.
**Standard Game Times:** 7:10 p.m., 6:30 DH; Sun. 2. **Ticket Price Range:** $5-8.
**Visiting Club Hotel:** Hilton Little Rock, 925 S. University, Little Rock, AR 72204. Telephone: (501) 664-5020.

# CORPUS CHRISTI
## HOOKS

**Office Address:** 734 East Port Ave., Corpus Christi, TX 78401.
**Telephone:** (361) 561-4665. **FAX:** (361) 561-4666.
**E-Mail Address:** info@cchooks.com. **Website:** www.cchooks.com.
**Affiliation (first year):** Houston Astros (2005). **Years in League:** 1958-59, 2005-.

### OWNERSHIP, MANAGEMENT
**Operated by:** Ryan-Sanders Baseball.
**Principal Owners:** Reese Ryan, Reid Ryan, Nolan Ryan, Brad Sanders, Bret Sanders, Don Sanders.
**Chief Executive Officer:** Reid Ryan. **Chief Financial Officer:** Reese Ryan. **Chief Operating Officer:** Jay Miller.
**President/General Manager:** J.J. Gottsch. **Vice President, Sales/Marketing:** Ken Schrom. **Vice President/Communications:** John Blake. **Assistant GM, Ticket Operations:** Michael Wood. **Director, Group Sales:** Matt Rogers. **Director, Broadcasting/Media Relations:** Matt Hicks. **Director, Community Relations:** Elisa Macias. **Director, Ballpark Entertainment:** Clint Musslewhite. **Director, Retail:** Brooke Milam. **Director, Game Day Operations:** Tina Athans. **Account Executive:** Adam Nuse. **Controller:** Christy Lockard. **Head Groundskeeper:** Brad Detmore. **Director, Stadium Operations:** Leslie Hitt. **Clubhouse Manager:** Unavailable.

### FIELD STAFF
**Manager:** Dave Clark. **Coach:** John Tamargo Jr. **Pitching Coach:** Joe Slusarski. **Trainer:** Jamey Snodgrass.

### GAME INFORMATION
**Radio Announcer (English):** Matt Hicks. **No. of Games Broadcast:** Home-70, Away-70. **Flagship Station:** KOUL 103.7-FM. **Radio Announcer (Spanish):** Eduardo Becerra. **No. of Games Broadcast:** Home-70. **Flagship Station:** KMJR 105.5-FM.
**PA Announcer:** Clint Musslewhite. **Official Scorer:** Rudy Rivera.
**Stadium Name:** Whataburger Field. **Location:** I-37 to end of interstate, left at Chaparral, left at Port Ave. **Standard Game Times:** 7:05 p.m.; Sun. (April-May) 2:05, (June-Sept.) 6:05. **Ticket Price Range:** $5-9.
**Visiting Club Hotel:** Omni Marina Hotel, 707 N. Shoreline Dr., Corpus Christi, TX 78401. Telephone: 361-887-1600.

# FRISCO
## ROUGHRIDERS

Office Address: 7300 RoughRiders Trail, Frisco, TX 75034.
Telephone: (972) 731-9200. FAX: (972) 731-5355.
E-Mail Address: info@ridersbaseball.com. Website: www.ridersbaseball.com.
Affiliation (first year): Texas Rangers (2003). Years in League: 2003-.

### OWNERSHIP, MANAGEMENT
Operated by: Mandalay Sports Entertainment.
President, General Manager: Mike McCall. Senior Vice President, Business Development: Scott Sonju. VP, Ticket Sales: Brent Stehlik. VP, Finance/Human Resources: Sally Morris. Assistant to VP, Finance/Human Resources: Cyndi Lopez. Director of Marketing: Rebecca King. Senior Director, Ticket Sales: Marcia Steinberg. Director, Media Development/Customer Service: Dick Harmon. Director, Corporate Partner Services: Michael Byrnes. Director, Corporate Partnerships: Michael Drake. Coordinator, Corporate Partner Promotions: Scott Burchett. Coordinator, Corporate Partner Services:  Lynsey Psimas. Creative Director: Justin McCord. Media Designer: Tony Canepa. Director, Ticket Operations: Sharon Aldridge. Coordinator, Ticket Operations: Shannon Muller. Manager, Suite Services: Casey Salley. Coordinator, Sales Administration: Gretchen Kiker. Senior Corporate Marketing Managers: Jason Cohen, Matt Goodman. Corporate Marketing Managers: Ryan Byrne, Michael Davidow, Chris Ghantous, Andrew Kahn, Ryan Limburg, Jay Lockett, Chip Maxson, Jake Repp. Customer Account Managers: Josh Loinette, Jon Gilbert. Group Sales Coordinators: Gina Beltrama, Tommie Harkness, Eric Hubbard, Justin Ramquist, Dustin Smalley, Jenna Snider. Director, Community Development: Cristal Rollins. Director Game Entertainment: Marianne Sexton. Manager, Event Services: Keri Butler. Stadium/Team Operations Manager: Mike Poole. Maintenance Manager: Alfonso Bailon. Head Groundskeeper: Billy Ball. Director, Game Entertainment: Unavailable. Administrative Assistant: Collette Robbins.

### FIELD STAFF
Manager: Darryl Kennedy. Coach: Ronnie Ortegon. Pitching Coach:  Terry Clark. Trainer: Brian Bobier.

### GAME INFORMATION
Radio Announcer: Scott Garner. No. of Games Broadcast: Home-70, Away-70. Radio Station: Unavailable.
PA Announcer: John Clemons. Official Scorer: Kenny King.
Stadium Name: Dr Pepper/Seven Up Ballpark. Location: Dallas North Tollway to State Highway 121. Standard Game Times: 7 p.m., Sun. 6. Ticket Price Range: $7-15.
Visiting Club Hotel: Embassy Suites, 7600 John Q. Hammons Dr., Frisco, TX 75034. Telephone: (972) 712-7200.

# MIDLAND
## ROCKHOUNDS

Office Address: 5514 Champions Dr., Midland, TX 79706.
Telephone: (432) 520-2255. FAX: (432) 520-8326.
Website: www.midlandrockhounds.org.
Affiliation (first year): Oakland Athletics (1999). Years in League: 1972-.

### OWNERSHIP, MANAGEMENT
Operated By: Midland Sports, Inc.
Principal Owners: Miles Prentice, Bob Richmond.
President: Miles Prentice. Executive Vice President: Bob Richmond.
General Manager: Monty Hoppel. Assistant GM: Jeff VonHolle. Assistant GM, Marketing/Tickets: Jamie Richardson. Assistant GM, Corporate Sales: Harold Fuller. Director, Broadcasting/Publications: Bob Hards. Executive Director, Midland Concessions: Dave Baur. Concessions Assistant: Edwin White. Assistant GM, Facilities Manager: Ray Fieldhouse. Director of Group Sales: Brent McFadden. Director, Business Operations: Eloisa Galvan. Head Groundskeeper: Eric Ferland. Media Relations/Advertising Director: Greg Bergman. Customer Service Manager:  Michael Richardson. Assistant Facilities Manager: Tony DeGrande. Sales Representative: Chuck Dunton. Administrative Assistant: Rich Del Soldato.

### FIELD STAFF
Manager: Von Hayes. Coach: Webster Garrison. Pitching Coach:  Jim Coffman. Trainer: Javier Alvidrez.

### GAME INFORMATION
Radio Announcer: Bob Hards. No. of Games Broadcast: Home-70, Away-70. Flagship Station: KCRS 550-AM.
PA Announcer: Ace O'Connell. Official Scorer: Paul Burnett.
Stadium Name: Citibank Ballpark. Location: From I-20, exit Loop 250 North to Highway 191 intersection. Standard Game Times: 7 p.m., 6:30 (April-May, August); Sun. 4, (June-Aug.) 6. Ticket Price Range: $5-9.
Visiting Club Hotel: Holiday Inn Hotel and Suites, 4300 W. Hwy. 80, Midland, TX 79703. Telephone: (432) 697-3181.

# SAN ANTONIO
## MISSIONS

**Office Address:** 5757 Hwy. 90 W., San Antonio, TX 78227.
**Telephone:** (210) 675-7275. **FAX:** (210) 670-0001.
**E-Mail Address:** sainfo@samissions.com. **Website:** www.samissions.com.
**Affiliation (first year):** Seattle Mariners (2001). **Years In League:** 1888, 1892, 1895-99, 1907-42, 1946-64, 1968-.

### OWNERSHIP, MANAGEMENT
**Operated by:** Elmore Sports Group.
**Principal Owner:** Dave Elmore. **President:** Burl Yarbrough.
**General Manager:** David Gasaway. **Assistant GMs:** Doug Campbell, Jeff Long, Jeff Windle. **Controller:** Dennis Mancias. **Stadium Manager:** Tom McAfee. **Director, Media Relations:** Mickey Holt. **Manager, Group Sales:** Bill Gerlt. **Director, Box Office:** Tiffany Johnson. **Director, Broadcasting:** Roy Acuff. **Account Executives:** Orlando Calderon, Brian Humphrey, Stu Paul, Mac Simmons. **Office Manager:** Delia Rodriguez. **Merchandising:** Karen Sada. **Clubhouse Operations:** Matt Martinez (home), Jim Vasaldua (visitors).

### FIELD STAFF
**Manager:** Daren Brown. **Coach:** Herny Cotto. **Pitching Coach:** Brad Holman. **Trainer:** Chris Gorosics.

### GAME INFORMATION
**Radio Announcers:** Roy Acuff, Stu Paul. **No. of Games Broadcast:** Home-70, Away-70. **Flagship Station:** KKYX 680-AM, KZDC 1250-AM (Spanish—Sunday home games only).
**PA Announcer:** Stan Kelly. **Official Scorer:** David Humphrey.
**Stadium Name:** Nelson W. Wolff Municipal Stadium. **Location:** From I-10, I-35 or I-37, take U.S. 90 West to Callaghan Road exit, stadium on right. **Standard Game Times:** 7:05 p.m., Sun. 6:05. **Ticket Price Range:** $4-9.
**Visiting Club Hotel:** Red Roof Inn, 1011 E. Houston St., San Antonio, TX 78205. Telephone: (210) 229-9973.

# SPRINGFIELD
## CARDINALS

**Office Address:** 955 East Trafficway, Springfield, MO 65802.
**Telephone:** (417) 863-2143. **FAX:** (417) 863-0388.
**E-Mail Address:** springfield@stlcardinals.com. **Website:** www.springfieldcardinals.com.
**Affiliation (first year):** St. Louis Cardinals (2005). **Years in League:** 2005-.

### OWNERSHIP, MANAGEMENT
**Operated by:** St. Louis Cardinals.
**Vice President/General Manager:** Matt Gifford. **VP, Sales/Marketing:** Kirk Elmquist. **VP, Baseball/Business Operations:** Scott Smulczenski. **VP, Facility Operations:** Bill Fischer. **Operations Manager:** Ron Henderson. **Box Office Manager:** Angela Deke. **Customer Relations Coordinator:** Nikki Love. **Public Relations Manager:** Mike Lindskog. **Media Relations Assistant:** Brittany Bremer. **Sales Manager:** Tom Ladd. **Account Executives:** Lindsey Bast, Heather Luetkemeyer, Kate Mata, Dan Reiter, Eric Tomb. **Office Services Coordinator:** Hope Hunt. **Head Groundskeeper:** Brock Phipps. **Assistant Groundskeeper:** Aaron Lowrey.

### FIELD STAFF
**Manager:** Chris Maloney. **Coach:** Joe Cunningham. **Pitching Coach:** Blake Ilsley. **Trainer:** Brad LaRosa.

### GAME INFORMATION
**Radio Announcers:** Rob Evans, Mike Lindskog. **No. of Games Broadcast:** Home-70, Away-70. **Flagship Station:** JOCK 98.7-FM.
**PA Announcer:** Kevin Howard. **Official Scorer:** Unavailable.
**Stadium Name:** Hammons Field. **Location:** Highway 65 to Chestnut Expressway exit, west to National, south on National, west on Trafficway. **Standard Game Time:** 7:10 p.m. **Ticket Price Range:** $5-22.50.
**Visiting Club Hotel:** University Plaza Hotel, 333 John Q. Hammons Parkway, Springfield, MO 65806. Phone: 417-864-7333.

# TULSA DRILLERS

**Office Address:** 4802 E. 15th St., Tulsa, OK 74112.
**Telephone:** (918) 744-5998. **FAX:** (918) 747-3267.
**E-Mail Address:** mail@tulsadrillers.com. **Website:** www.tulsadrillers.com.
**Affiliation (first year):** Colorado Rockies (2003). **Years in League:** 1933-42, 1946-65, 1977-.

## OWNERSHIP, MANAGEMENT

**Operated by:** Tulsa Baseball, Inc.
**Principal Owner, President:** Went Hubbard.
**Executive Vice President, General Manager:** Chuck Lamson. **Assistant GM:** Mike Melega. **Bookkeeper:** Cheryll Couey. **Office Manager:** D.D. Bristol. **Director, Promotions/Merchandise:** Jason George. **Manager, Ticket Sales:** Jeremy Lawson. **Director, Public/Media Relations:** Brian Carroll. **Director, Stadium Operations/Group Sales:** Mark Hilliard. **Operations Manager:** Peter McAdams. **Head Groundskeeper:** Gary Shepherd. **Corporate Sales Associate:** Josh Lovetere. **Group Ticket Sales Assistant:** Lindsay Gardner. **Promotions/Merchandise Assistant:** Maggie Hallgren. **Ticket Sales Assistant:** Amanda Kirk. **Assistant Groundskeeper:** Brian Hilliard.

## FIELD STAFF

**Manager:** Stu Cole. **Coach:** Orlando Merced. **Pitching Coach:** Bo McLaughlin. **Trainer:** Austin O'Shea.

## GAME INFORMATION

**Radio Announcer:** Mark Neely. **No. of Games Broadcast:** Home-70, Away-70. **Flagship Station:** KTBZ AM 1430.
**PA Announcer:** Kirk McAnany. **Official Scorers:** Unavailable.
**Stadium Name:** Drillers Stadium. **Location:** Three miles north of I-44 and 1½ miles south of I-244 at 15th Street and Yale Avenue. **Standard Game Times:** 7:05 p.m.; Sun. (April-June) 2:05, (July-Aug.) 6:05. **Ticket Price Range:** $5.00-9.50.
**Visiting Club Hotel:** Hampton Inn, 3209 S. 79th E. Ave., Tulsa, OK 74145. Telephone: (918) 663-1000.

# WICHITA WRANGLERS

**Office Address:** 300 S. Sycamore, Wichita, KS 67213.
**Mailing Address:** P.O. Box 1420, Wichita, KS 67201.
**Telephone:** (316)-267-3372. **FAX:** (316)-267-3382.
**E-Mail Address:** wranglers@wichitawranglers.com. **Website:** www.wichitawranglers.com.
**Affiliation (first year):** Kansas City Royals (1995). **Years in League:** 1987-.

## OWNERSHIP, MANAGEMENT

**Operated By:** Wichita Baseball, Inc.
**Principal Owner:** Rich Products Corp.
**Chairman:** Robert Rich Sr. **President:** Robert Rich Jr. **Executive Vice President:** Melinda Rich.
**General Manager:** Eric Edelstein. **Assistant GM, Director , Stadium/Baseball Operations:** Josh Robertson. **Director of Sales:** Justin Cole. **Business Manager:** Stephanie White. **Marketing Coordinator:** Abigail Cress. **Assistant, Stadium/Baseball Operations:** Jeff Kline. **Senior Sales Account Representative:** Robert Slaughter. **Sales Account Representative:** Becky Bowles. **Ticket Operations Coordinator:** Anna Whitham. **Game Day Operations Associate:** Megan Morgan. **Merchandise/Marketing Associate:** Chrysta Jorgensen. **Media Relations Associate:** Zack Kulesz.

## FIELD STAFF

**Manager:** Frank White. **Coach:** Al LeBoeuf. **Pitching Coach:** Larry Carter. **Trainer:** Charles Leddon.

## GAME INFORMATION

**Radio Announcers:** Rick Page. **No. of Games Broadcast:** Home-70, Away-70. **Flagship Station:** KGSO 1410-AM.
**PA Announcer:** Unavailable. **Official Scorer:** Bob Kirschner.
**Stadium Name:** Lawrence-Dumont Stadium. **Location:** I-35 to Kellogg Avenue West, North on Broadway, West on Lewis. **Standard Game Times:** 7 p.m.; Fri. 7:30; Sun. 6. **Ticket Price Range:** $5-10.
**Visiting Club Hotel:** La Quinta-Towne East, 7700 E. Kellogg, Wichita, KS 67207. Telephone: (316)-681-2881.

# CALIFORNIA
## LEAGUE

## CLASS A ADVANCED

**Office Address:** 2380 S. Bascom Ave., Suite 200, Campbell, CA 95008.
**Telephone:** (408) 369-8038. **FAX:** (408) 369-1409.
**E-Mail Address:** cabaseball@aol.com. **Website:** www.californialeague.com.
**Years League Active:** 1941-1942, 1946-.

**President/Treasurer:** Joe Gagliardi.
**Vice President:** David Elmore (Inland Empire). **Corporate Secretary:** John Oldham.
**Directors:** Bobby Brett (High Desert), Peter Carfagna (Lancaster), David Elmore (Inland Empire), D.G. Elmore (Bakersfield), Gary Jacobs (Lake Elsinore), Michael Savit (Modesto), Tom Seidler (Visalia), Hank Stickney (Rancho Cucamonga), Tom Volpe (Stockton), Jim Weyermann (San Jose).
**Director, Marketing:** Steve Fields. **League Administrator:** Kathleen Kelly. **Director, Umpire Development:** John Oldham.
**Division Structure: North**—Bakersfield, Modesto, San Jose, Stockton, Visalia. **South**—High Desert, Inland Empire, Lake Elsinore, Lancaster, Rancho Cucamonga.
**Regular Season:** 140 games (split-schedule). **2006 Opening Date:** April 6. **Closing Date:** Sept. 4.

**Joe Gagliardi**

**Playoff Format:** Six teams. First-half champions in each division earn first-round bye; second-half champions meet wild card with next best overall record in best-of-3 quarterfinals. Winners meet first-half champions in best-of-5 semifinals. Winners meet in best-of-5 series for league championship.
**All-Star Game:** June 27 at Salem, VA (California League vs. Carolina League).
**Roster Limit:** 25 active. **Player Eligibility Rule:** No more than two players and one player-coach on active list may have more than six years experience.
**Brand of Baseball:** Rawlings.
**Statistician:** Major League Baseball Advanced Media, 75 Ninth Ave., New York, NY 10011.
**Umpires:** Unavailable.

## STADIUM INFORMATION

| Club | Stadium | Opened | Dimensions | | | Capacity | 2005 Att. |
|------|---------|--------|-----|-----|-----|----------|-----------|
| | | | LF | CF | RF | | |
| Bakersfield | Sam Lynn Ballpark | 1941 | 328 | 354 | 328 | 4,200 | 76,738 |
| High Desert | Mavericks Stadium | 1991 | 340 | 401 | 340 | 3,808 | 118,387 |
| Inland Empire | Arrowhead Credit Union Park | 1996 | 330 | 410 | 330 | 5,000 | 211,117 |
| Lake Elsinore | The Diamond | 1994 | 330 | 400 | 310 | 7,866 | 222,624 |
| Lancaster | Clear Channel Stadium | 1996 | 350 | 410 | 350 | 4,500 | 123,601 |
| Modesto | John Thurman Field | 1952 | 312 | 400 | 319 | 4,000 | 136,612 |
| Rancho Cucamonga | The Epicenter | 1993 | 335 | 400 | 335 | 6,615 | 272,855 |
| San Jose | Municipal Stadium | 1942 | 340 | 390 | 340 | 4,000 | 150,338 |
| Stockton | Banner Island Ballpark | 2005 | 300 | 399 | 326 | 5,200 | 205,819 |
| Visalia | Recreation Park | 1946 | 320 | 405 | 320 | 1,647 | 63,475 |

# BAKERSFIELD
## BLAZE

**Office Address:** 4009 Chester Ave., Bakersfield, CA 93301.
**Mailing Address:** P.O. Box 10031, Bakersfield, CA 93389.
**Telephone:** (661) 716-4487. **FAX:** (661) 322-6199.
**E-Mail Address:** blaze@bakersfieldblaze.com. **Website:** www.bakersfieldblaze.com.
**Affiliation:** Texas Rangers (2005). **Years In League:** 1941-42, 1946-75, 1978-79, 1982-.

### OWNERSHIP, MANAGEMENT
**Principal Owner:** Bakersfield Baseball Club, LLC.
**Vice President, General Manager:** Chris Bitters. **Ticket Sales Manager:** Shawn Schoolcraft. **Group Sales/Community Relations Manager:** Tom Linehan. **Head Groundskeeper:** Chris Ralston.

### FIELD STAFF
**Manager:** Carlos Subero. **Coach:** Pedro Lopez. **Pitching Coach:** David Chavarria. **Trainer:** Lee Slagle.

### GAME INFORMATION
**Radio Announcer:** Unavailable. **No. of Games Broadcast:** Home-70, Away-70. **Flagship Station:** KGEO 1230-AM. **PA Announcer:** Unavailable. **Official Scorer:** Tim Wheeler.
**Stadium Name:** Sam Lynn Ballpark. **Location:** Highway 99 to California Avenue, east three miles to Chester Avenue, north two miles to stadium. **Standard Game Times:** 7:15 p.m. **Ticket Price Range:** $4-8.
**Visiting Club Hotel:** Unavailable.

# HIGH DESERT
## MAVERICKS

**Office Address:** 12000 Stadium Way, Adelanto, CA 92301.
**Telephone:** (760) 246-6287. **FAX:** (760) 246-3197.
**E-Mail Address:** mavsinfo@hdmavs.com. **Website:** www.hdmavs.com.
**Affiliation (first year):** Kansas City Royals (2005). **Years in League:** 1991-.

### OWNERSHIP, MANAGEMENT
**Operated by:** High Desert Mavericks, Inc.
**Principal Owner:** Bobby Brett. **President:** Andy Billig. **Vice President:** Brent Miles.
**General Manager:** Josh Roys. **Assistant GM, Tickets:** Monica Ortega. **Account Executives:** Tim Altier, Nate Hopkins. **Coordinator, Sponsorships:** Autumn Rose Saenz. **Controller:** Robin Buckles. **Head Groundskeeper:** Tino Gonzales. **Clubhouse Manager:** Eric Jenson.

### FIELD STAFF
**Manager:** Jeff Carter. **Coach:** Boots Day. **Pitching Coach:** Steve Renko. **Trainer:** Steve Guadalupe.

### GAME INFORMATION
**Radio Announcer:** Jon Rosen. **No. of Games Broadcast:** Home-70, Away-70. **Flagship Station:** KRAK 960-AM. **PA Announcer:** Ernie Escajieda. **Official Scorer:** Jack Tucker.
**Stadium Name:** Mavericks Stadium. **Location:** I-15 North to Highway 395 to Adelanto Road. **Standard Game Times:** 7:05 p.m.; Sun. 5:05, (April-May) 3:05. **Ticket Price Range:** $6-8.
**Visiting Club Hotel:** Ramada Inn, I-15 and Palmdale Road, Victorville, CA 92392. Telephone: (760) 245-6565.

# INLAND EMPIRE
## 66ERS

**Office Address:** 280 South E St., San Bernardino, CA 92401.
**Telephone:** (909) 888-9922. **FAX:** (909) 888-5251.
**Website:** www.ie66ers.
**Affiliation (first year):** Seattle Mariners (2001). **Years in League:** 1941, 1987-.

### OWNERSHIP, MANAGEMENT
**Operated by:** Inland Empire 66ers Baseball Club of San Bernardino.
**Principal Owners:** David Elmore, Donna Tuttle.
**President/General Manager:** Dave Oldham. **Vice President/Assistant GM:** Paul Stiritz. **Chief Financial Officer:** Peter Pham. **Director, Food and Beverage/Stadium Manager:** Joe Henderson. **Director, Corporate Communications:** Laura Tolbirt. **Director, Broadcasting:** Mike Saeger. **Director, Business Relations/Family Outreach:** Byron Marquez **Director, Merchandise:** Ryan English, Laura Tolbirt. **Manager, Stadium Operations:** Ryan English. **Director, Group**

**Sales:** Shawn Jeffers. **Account Executives:** Chris Apenbrink, Brandon De La Cruz, Raj Narayanan, Kyle Schoonover. **Administrative Assistant:** Ashley Rojas. **Head Groundskeeper:** Jesse Sandoval.

### FIELD STAFF
**Manager:** Gary Thurman. **Coach:** Rafael Santo Domingo. **Pitching Coach:** Scott Budner. **Trainer:** Matt Toth.

### GAME INFORMATION
**Radio Announcer:** Mike Saeger. **No. of Games Broadcast:** Mon.-Sat. only. **Flagship Station:** KVCR 91.9-FM. **PA Announcer:** J.J. Gould. **Official Scorer:** Unavailable.
**Stadium Name:** Arrowhead Credit Union Park. **Location:** From south, I-215 to 2nd Street exit, east on 2nd, right on G Street; from north, I-215 to 3rd Street exit, left on Rialto, right on G Street. **Standard Game Times:** 7:11 p.m.; Sun. 6:11, (April-May) 2:11. **Ticket Price Range:** $5-8.
**Visiting Club Hotel:** Unavailable.

# LAKE ELSINORE
## STORM

**Office Address:** 500 Diamond Dr., Lake Elsinore, CA 92530.
**Mailing Address:** P.O. Box 535, Lake Elsinore, CA 92531.
**Telephone:** (951) 245-4487. **FAX:** (951) 245-0305.
**E-Mail Address:** info@stormbaseball.com. **Website:** www.stormbaseball.com.
**Affiliation (first year):** San Diego Padres (2001). **Years in League:** 1994-.

### OWNERSHIP, MANAGEMENT
**Operated by:** Storm, LP.
**Principal Owner:** Gary Jacobs.
**President/General Manager:** Dave Oster. **Vice President/Assistant GM:** Chris Jones. **Assistant GM/Stadium Operations:** Bruce Kessman. **Assistant GM, Community Development:** Tracy Kessman. **Director, Corporate Sales:** Paul Engl. **Director, Media/Public Relations:** Casey Hauan. **Director, Graphic Communications:** Mark Beskid. **Director, Game Operations:** Sarah Heth. **Assistant Director, Game Operations:** Marie Maita. **Director, Broadcasting:** Sean McCall. **Director, Merchandising:** Donna Grunow. **Director, Concessions/Operations:** Arjun Suresh. **Assistant Director, Concessions/Operations:** Ryan Eifler. **Director, Group Sales:** Dave Endress. **Director, New Business Development:** Allan Benavides. **Assistant Directors, Sales:** Peter Bernstein, Matt Dompe. **Director, Business Administration:** Corrine Roberge. **Sales/Marketing Administrator:** Kristyn Andrews. **Director, Stadium Operations:** Matt Thompson. **Director, Ticket Operations:** Gretchen Todd. **Assistant Director, Ticket Operations:** Krystle Herold. **Director, Mascot Operations:** Alex Collins. **Director, Field Maintenance:** Francisco Castaneda. **Office Manager:** Jo Equila.

### FIELD STAFF
**Manager:** Rick Renteria. **Coach:** Tom Tornincasa. **Pitching Coach:** Steve Webber. **Trainer:** Jason Haeussinger.

### GAME INFORMATION
**Radio Announcer:** Sean McCall. **No. of Games Broadcast:** Home-70, Away-70. **Flagship Station:** KTMQ 103.3-FM. **PA Announcer:** Joe Martinez. **Official Scorer:** Lloyd Nixon.
**Stadium Name:** The Diamond. **Location:** From I-15, exit at Diamond Drive, west one mile to stadium. **Standard Game Times:** 7:05 p.m.; Wed. 6:05; Sun. (first half) 2:05, (second half) 6:05. **Ticket Price Range:** $6-10.
**Visiting Club Hotel:** Lake Elsinore Hotel and Casino, 20930 Malaga St., Lake Elsinore, CA 92530. Telephone: (951) 674-3101.

# LANCASTER
## JETHAWKS

**Office Address:** 45116 Valley Central Way, Lancaster, CA 93536.
**Telephone:** (661) 726-5400. **FAX:** (661) 726-5406.
**E-Mail Address:** info@jethawks.com. **Website:** www.jethawks.com.
**Affiliation (first year):** Arizona Diamondbacks (2001). **Years in League:** 1996-.

### OWNERSHIP, MANAGEMENT
**Operated By:** Hawks Nest, LLC.
**Chairman:** Peter Carfagna. **Senior Vice President:** Pete Carfagna.
**General Manager:** Brad Seymour. **Assistant GM:** Joe Reinsch. **Director, Stadium Operations:** John Laferney. **Director, Ticket Operations:** Craig Czubik. **Director, Special Projects:** Bill Levy. **Director, Merchandising/Community Relations:** Amy Schrecengost. **Assistant Director, Ticket Sales:** Gary Hunt. **Director, Food/Beverage:** Dustin Saunders. **Assistant Food/Beverage Manager:** Dana Torres. **Ticket Sales Account Executives:** Jeff Lasky, Andrew Painter. **Office Administrator:** Alisa Anderson. **Head Groundskeeper:** Dave Phatenhaur.

## FIELD STAFF

**Manager:** Brett Butler. **Coach:** Damon Mashore. **Pitching Coach:** Jeff Pico. **Trainer:** Rob Knepper.

## GAME INFORMATION

**Radio Announcer:** Jeff Lasky. **No. of Games Broadcast:** Home-70, Away-70. **Flagship Station:** KTPI 1340-AM. **PA Announcer:** Unavailable. **Official Scorer:** David Guenther.

**Stadium Name:** Clear Channel Stadium. **Location:** Highway 14 in Lancaster to Avenue I exit, west one block to stadium. **Standard Game Times:** 7 p.m., Mon-Fri. (April-May) 6:30; Sat. (April-May) 5; Sun. 6, (April–May) 2. **Ticket Price Range:** $5-8.

**Visiting Club Hotel:** Best Western Antelope Valley Inn, 44055 North Sierra Hwy., Lancaster, CA 93534 . Telephone: (661) 948-4651.

# MODESTO
## NUTS

**Office Address:** 601 Neece Dr., Modesto, CA 95351.
**Mailing Address:** P.O. Box 883, Modesto, CA 95353.
**Telephone:** (209) 572-4487. **FAX:** (209) 572-4490.
**E-Mail Address:** fun@modestonuts.com. **Website:** www.modestonuts.com.
**Affiliation (first year):** Colorado Rockies (2005). **Years in League:** 1946-64, 1966-.

## OWNERSHIP, MANAGEMENT

**Operated by:** HWS Group IV.
**Principal Owner:** Mike Savit.
**President:** Bill Shanahan. **General Manager:** Michael Gorrasi. **Assistant GM:** Alex Schwerin. **Director, Sales/Marketing:** Matt Person. **Director, Tickets**: Tyler Richardson. **Office/Accounting Manager:** Debra Baucom. **Director, Public Relations:** Will Murphy.

## FIELD STAFF

**Manager:** Chad Kreuter. **Coach:** Glenallen Hill. **Pitching Coach:** Butch Hughes. **Trainer:** Chris Strickland.

## GAME INFORMATION

**Radio Announcer:** Unavailable. **No. of Games Broadcast:** Home-50, Away-50. **Flagship Station:** KESP 970-AM. **PA Announcer:** Unavailable. **Official Scorer:** Unavailable.

**Stadium Name:** John Thurman Field. **Location:** Highway 99 in southwest Modesto to Tuolomne Boulevard exit, west on Tuolomne for one block to Neece Drive, left for 1/4 mile to stadium. **Standard Game Times:** 7:05 p.m.; Sun. (April-June) 1:05, (July-Aug.) 6:05. **Ticket Price Range:** $5-9.

**Visiting Club Hotel:** Ramada Inn, 2001 W. Orangeburg Ave., Modesto, CA 95350. Telephone: (209) 521-9000.

# RANCHO CUCAMONGA
## QUAKES

**Office Address:** 8408 Rochester Ave., Rancho Cucamonga, CA 91730.
**Mailing Address:** P.O. Box 4139, Rancho Cucamonga, CA 91729.
**Telephone:** (909) 481-5000. **FAX:** (909) 481-5005.
**E-Mail Address:** rcquakes@aol.com. **Website:** www.rcquakes.com.
**Affiliation (first year):** Los Angeles Angels of Anaheim (2001). **Years in League:** 1993-.

## OWNERSHIP, MANAGEMENT

**Operated by:** Valley Baseball Inc.
**Principal Owners:** Hank Stickney, Jack Cooley, Scott Ostlund.
**Chairman:** Hank Stickney.
**General Manager:** North Johnson. **Head Groundskeeper:** Rex Whitney. **Director, Entertainment:** Kristin Beernink. **Director, Guest Relations:** Linda Rathfon. **Director, Finance:** Heidi Acedo. **Director, Concessions:** Anita Johnson. **Director, Ticket Operations:** Kim Usselman-Fogel. **Director, Operations:** Ken Fogel. **Director, Broadcasting/Media Relations:** Rob Sinclair. **Director, Business Development:** Tim Renyi. **Manager, Community/Public Relations:** Meridith Zembal. **Manager, Sponsorship Services:** Brandon Tanner. **Manager, Ticket Office:** James Annos. **Manager, Food/Beverage:** Mike Liotta. **Ticket Sales Representatives:** Tom Beatty, Jim Fleming, Adam Hensleigh, Jan Selasky. **Corporate Sales Representative:** Kelly Bartlett. **Office Manager:** Stacie Lord. **Administrative Assistant:** Jessica De La Rosa.

## FIELD STAFF

**Manager:** Bobby Mitchell. **Coach:** Craig Grebeck. **Pitching Coach:** Eric Bennett. **Trainer:** Brian Reinker.

## GAME INFORMATION

**Radio Announcer:** Rob Sinclair. **No. of Games Broadcast:** Home-70, Away-70. **Flagship Station:** KWRM 1370-AM. **PA Announcer:** Unavailable.

Stadium Name: The Epicenter. Location: I-10 to I-15 North, exit at Foothill Boulevard, left on Foothill, left on Rochester to stadium. Standard Game Times: 7:15 p.m.; Sun. (first half) 2:15, (second half) 5:15. Ticket Price Range: $7-11.

Visiting Club Hotel: Best Western Heritage Inn, 8179 Spruce Ave., Rancho Cucamonga, CA 91730. Telephone: (909) 466-1111.

# SAN JOSE
## GIANTS

Office Address: 588 E. Alma Ave., San Jose, CA 95112.
Mailing Address: P.O. Box 21727, San Jose, CA 95151.
Telephone: (408) 297-1435. FAX: (408) 297-1453.
E-Mail Address: grouptickets@sjgiants.com Website: www.sjgiants.com.
Affiliation (first year): San Francisco Giants (1988). Years in League: 1942, 1947-58, 1962-76, 1979-.

## OWNERSHIP, MANAGEMENT
Operated by: Progress Sports Management.
Principal Owners: Heidi Cox, Richard Beahrs, Rich Kelley.
President, Chief Executive Officer: Jim Weyermann. Chief Operating Officer: Chris Lampe.
General Manager: Mark Wilson. Assistant GM: Zach Walter. Director, Player Relations: Linda Pereira. Ticket Director: Nick McAlpine. Director, Sales/Promotions: Matt Allen. Director, Public Affairs: Juliana Paoli. Manager, Stadium Operations: Leyton Lampe. Sales Manager: Ainslie Reynolds. Ticket Sales Account Executive: Laura Miller. Public Relations/Website Administrator: Greg Shelley.

## FIELD STAFF
Manager: Lenn Sakata. Coach: Garrett Nago. Pitching Coach: Jim Bennett. Trainer: Unavailable.

## GAME INFORMATION
Radio: None.
PA Announcer: Brian Burkett. Official Scorer: John Pletsch.
Stadium Name: Municipal Stadium. Location: From I-280, 10th Street exit to Alma, left on Alma, stadium on right; from U.S. 101, Tully Road exit to Senter, right on Senter, left on Alma, stadium on left. Standard Game Times: 7 p.m.; Sat. 5; Sun. 1. Ticket Price Range: $5-10.
Visiting Club Hotel: Pruneyard Inn, 1995 S. Bascom Ave., Campbell, CA 95008. Telephone: (408) 559-4300.

# STOCKTON
## PORTS

Mailing Address: 404 W. Fremont St., Stockton, CA 95203.
Telephone: (209) 644-1900. FAX: (209) 644-1931.
E-Mail Address: info@stocktonports.com. Website: www.stocktonports.com.
Affiliation (first year): Oakland Athletics (2005). Years in League: 1941, 1946-72, 1978-.

## OWNERSHIP, MANAGEMENT
Operated by: 7th Inning Stretch, LLC.
Chairman, Chief Executive Officer: Tom Volpe.
General Manager: Mike McCarroll. Assistant GM/Operations: Trevor Fawcett. Director, Ticket Operations: Nikki Pruett. Director, Broadcasting/Public Relations: Bo Fulginiti. Director, Stadium Operations: Josh Terrell. Director, Special Events: Mike Lopez. Director, Food/Beverage: Frank Pazzanese. Director, Merchandise: Kari McElwee. Director, Marketing/Promotions: Reza Wiriaatmadja. Corporate Sales Executive: Lynz Burrows. Box Office Manager: Tony Cohn. Broadcast/Community Relations Manager: Zach Bayrouty. Group Account Executives: Kevin Huisman, Jennifer Mayer, Derek Reyes. Office Manager: Dulcy Obrochta.

## FIELD STAFF
Manager: Todd Steverson. Coach: Darren Bush. Pitching Coach: Scott Emerson. Trainer: Brian Thorson.

## GAME INFORMATION
Radio Announcer: Bo Fulginiti. No. of Games Broadcast: Home-70, Away-70. Flagship Station: KSTN 1420-AM.
PA Announcer: A.J. Williams. Official Scorer: Paul Muyskens.
Stadium Name: Banner Island Ballpark. Location: From I-5/99, take Crosstown Freeway (Highway 4) exit to El Dorado Street, north on El Dorado to Freemont Street, left on Freemont. Standard Game Times: 7:05 p.m., Sat. 6:05; Sun. (first half) 1:05, (second half) 5:05. Ticket Price Range: $4-13.
Visiting Club Hotel: Unavailable.

# VISALIA OAKS

**Office Address:** 440 N. Giddings St., Visalia, CA 93291.
**Telephone:** (559) 625-0480. **FAX:** (559) 739-7732.
**E-Mail Address:** oaksbaseball@hotmail.com. **Website:** www.oaksbaseball.com.
**Affiliation (first year):** Tampa Bay Devil Rays (2005). **Years in League:** 1946-62, 1968-75, 1977-.

## OWNERSHIP, MANAGEMENT

**Operated by:** Top of the Third, Inc.
**Principal Owners:** Tom Seidler, Kevin O'Malley.
**General Manager:** Jon Peterson. **Director, Sales/Marketing:** Kevin Huffine. **Director, Broadcasting/Media Relations:** Ira Liebman. **Group Sales Executive:** Unavailable. **Head Groundskeeper:** Ken Peterson. **Clubhouse Manager:** Ivan Salinal.

## FIELD STAFF

**Manager:** Steve Livesey. **Coach:** Omer Muñoz. **Pitching Coach:** Marty DeMerritt. **Trainer:** Jimmy Southard.

## GAME INFORMATION

**Radio Announcer:** Ira Liebman. **No. of Games Broadcast:** Home-70, Away-70. **Flagship Station:** KJUG 1270-AM.
**PA Announcer:** Matt White. **Official Scorer:** Harry Kargenian.
**Stadium Name:** Recreation Park. **Location:** From Highway 99, take 198 East to Mooney Boulevard exit, left on Giddings Avenue. **Standard Game Times:** 6:35 p.m.; Fri.-Sat. 7:05; Sun. 1:35, (July-Aug) 5:05. **Ticket Price Range:** $5-7.
**Visiting Club Hotel:** Unavailable.

# CAROLINA
## LEAGUE

**Office Address:** 1806 Pembroke Rd., Greensboro, NC 27408.
**Mailing Address:** P.O. Box 9503, Greensboro, NC 27429.
**Telephone:** (336) 691-9030. **FAX:** (336) 691-9070.
**E-Mail Address:** office@carolinaleague.com. **Website:** www.carolinaleague.com.
**Years League Active:** 1945-.

John Hopkins

**President/Treasurer:** John Hopkins.
**Vice Presidents:** Kelvin Bowles (Salem), Calvin Falwell (Lynchburg). **Corporate Secretary:** Matt Minker (Wilmington).
**Directors:** Kelvin Bowles (Salem), Calvin Falwell (Lynchburg), George Habel (Myrtle Beach), Peter Luukko (Frederick), Cam McRae (Kinston), Matt Minker (Wilmington), Billy Prim (Winston-Salem), Art Silber (Potomac).
**Administrative Assistant:** Marnee Larkins.
**Division Structure: North**—Frederick, Lynchburg, Potomac, Wilmington. **South**—Kinston, Myrtle Beach, Salem, Winston-Salem.
**Regular Season:** 140 games (split schedule). **2006 Opening Date:** April 6. **Closing Date:** Sept. 4.
**All-Star Game:** June 27 at Salem (Carolina League vs. California League).
**Playoff Format:** First-half division champions play second-half division champions in best-of-3 series (team that wins both halves plays wild-card). Division champions meet in best-of-5 series for Mills Cup.

**Roster Limit:** 25 active. **Player Eligibility Rule:** No age limit. No more than two players and one player-coach on active list may have six or more years of prior minor league service.
**Brand of Baseball:** Rawlings.
**Statistician:** Major League Baseball Advanced Media, 75 Ninth Ave., New York, NY 10011.
**Umpires:** Mark Buchanan (Glendale, AZ), Ray Chamberlin (Lake City, FL), Tim Daub (Catonsville, MD), Clint Lawson (Rock Hill, SC), Grant Menke (North Bethesda, MD), Nick Nolde (Escanaba, MI), Roy Prauner (Madison, NE), David Warren (Celeste, TX).

## STADIUM INFORMATION

| Club | Stadium | Opened | Dimensions LF | CF | RF | Capacity | 2005 Att. |
|------|---------|--------|-----|-----|-----|----------|-----------|
| Frederick | Harry Grove Stadium | 1990 | 325 | 400 | 325 | 5,400 | 275,663 |
| Kinston | Grainger Stadium | 1949 | 335 | 390 | 335 | 4,100 | 103,069 |
| Lynchburg | City Stadium | 1940 | 325 | 390 | 325 | 4,000 | 150,139 |
| Myrtle Beach | Coastal Federal Field | 1999 | 325 | 405 | 328 | 4,324 | 197,626 |
| Potomac | Pfitzner Stadium | 1984 | 315 | 400 | 315 | 6,000 | 138,143 |
| Salem | Salem Memorial Stadium | 1995 | 325 | 401 | 325 | 6,300 | 255,225 |
| Wilmington | Frawley Stadium | 1993 | 325 | 400 | 325 | 6,532 | 322,287 |
| Winston-Salem | Ernie Shore Field | 1956 | 325 | 400 | 325 | 6,000 | 147,194 |

# FREDERICK
## KEYS

**Office Address:** 21 Stadium Dr., Frederick, MD 21703.
**Mailing Address:** P.O. Box 3169, Frederick, MD 21705.
**Telephone:** (301) 662-0013. **FAX:** (301) 662-0018.
**E-Mail Address:** info@frederickkeys.com. **Website:** www.frederickkeys.com.
**Affiliation (first year):** Baltimore Orioles (1989). **Years in League:** 1989-.

### OWNERSHIP, MANAGEMENT

**Operated by:** Comcast-Spectacor.
**Directors:** Peter Luukko, Frank Miceli.
**General Manager:** Dave Ziedelis. **Director, Marketing:** Keri Scrivani. **Assistant Director, Marketing:** Jennifer Smoral. **Director, Public Relations:** Ryan Sakamoto. **Public Relations Assistant:** Unavailable. **Director, Stadium Operations:** Dave Wisner. **Director, Sponsorship Sales:** Shaun O'Neal. **Senior Account Manager:** Mark Zeigler. **Account Manager:** Unavailable. **Ticket Sales Manager:** Deanna Davis. **Box Office Manager:** Rob Finn. **Box Office Assistant:** Mike Rosenow. **Events Coordinators:** Jason Grose, Darcie Hartwick, Brandan Kaiser, Doug Winter. **Administrative Assistant:** Barb Freund. **Bookkeeper:** Tami Hetrick. **Clubhouse Manager:** George Bell. **GM, Food Services:** Mike Jones. **Head Groundskeeper:** Jon Pawlik.

### FIELD STAFF

**Manager:** Bien Figueroa. **Coach:** Alex Arias. **Pitching Coach:** Blaine Beatty. **Trainer:** Trek Schuler.

### GAME INFORMATION

**Radio:** None.
**PA Announcer:** Victoria Gordon. **Official Scorers:** Dennis Hetrick, George Richardson.
**Stadium Name:** Harry Grove Stadium. **Location:** From I-70, take exit 54 (Market Street), left at light. From I-270, take exit 32 (I-70 Baltimore/Hagerstown) towards Baltimore (I-70 East), to exit 54, left at Market Street. **Standard Game Times:** 7 p.m., Sun. 2:05. **Ticket Price Range:** $8-11.
**Visiting Club Hotel:** Quality Inn, 420 Prospect Blvd., Frederick, MD 21701. Telephone: (301) 695-6200.

# KINSTON
## INDIANS

**Office Address:** 400 E. Grainger Ave., Kinston, NC 28501.
**Mailing Address:** P.O. Box 3542, Kinston, NC 28502.
**Telephone:** (252) 527-9111. **FAX:** (252) 527-0498.
**E-Mail Address:** info@kinstonindians.com. **Website:** www.kinstonindians.com.
**Affiliation (first year):** Cleveland Indians (1987). **Years in League:** 1956-57, 1962-74, 1978-.

### OWNERSHIP, MANAGEMENT

**Operated by:** Slugger Partners, LP.
**Principal Owners:** Cam McRae, North Johnson. **Chairman:** Cam McRae. **President:** North Johnson.
**General Manager:** Shari Massengill. **Assistant GM:** Jonathan Griffith. **Director, Broadcasting/Public Relations:** Chris Hemeyer. **Director, Sales:** Jessie Hays. **Director, Food/Beverage:** Unavailable. **Head Groundskeeper:** Tommy Walston. **Clubhouse Operations:** Robert Smeraldo. **Team Photographer:** Carl Kline.

### FIELD STAFF

**Manager:** Mike Sarbaugh. **Coach:** Unavailable. **Pitching Coach:** Steve Lyons. **Trainer:** Michael Salazar.

### GAME INFORMATION

**Radio Announcer:** Chris Hemeyer. **No. of Games Broadcast:** Home-70, Away-70. **Flagship Station:** WRNS 960-AM.
**PA Announcer:** Jeff Diamond. **Official Scorer:** Taplie Coile.
**Stadium Name:** Grainger Stadium. **Location:** From west, take U.S. 70 Business (Vernon Avenue), left on East Street; from east, take U.S. 70 West, right on Highway 58, right on Vernon Avenue, right on East Street. **Standard Game Times:** 7 p.m., Sun. 2. **Ticket Price Range:** $3-6.
**Visiting Club Hotel:** Hampton Inn, Highway 70 Bypass, Kinston NC 28504. Telephone: (252) 523-1400.

# LYNCHBURG
## HILLCATS

**Office Address:** Lynchburg City Stadium, 3180 Fort Ave., Lynchburg, VA 24501.
**Mailing Address:** P.O. Box 10213, Lynchburg, VA 24506.

Telephone: (434) 528-1144. **FAX**: (434) 846-0768.
**E-Mail Address**: info@lynchburg-hillcats.com. **Website**: www.lynchburg-hillcats.com.
**Affiliation (first year)**: Pittsburgh Pirates (1995). **Years in League**: 1966-.

## OWNERSHIP, MANAGEMENT

**Operated by**: Lynchburg Baseball Corp.
**President**: Calvin Falwell.
**General Manager**: Paul Sunwall. **Assistant GM**: Ronnie Roberts. **Group Sales/Promotions**: Kevin Donahue. **Head Groundskeeper/Sales**: Darren Johnson. **Director, Broadcasting/Publications**: Jon Schaeffer. **Stadium Operations/Concessions Director**: Chris Johnson. **Ticket Manager**: Brent Monticue. **Director, Information Technology**: Andrew Chesser. **Office Manager**: Diane Tucker.

## FIELD STAFF

**Manager**: Gary Green. **Coach**: Ramon Sambo. **Pitching Coach**: Bob Milacki. **Trainer**: Bryan Housand.

## GAME INFORMATION

**Radio Announcers**: Jon Schaeffer, Paul Kennedy. **No. of Games Broadcast**: Home-70, Away-70. **Flagship Station**: WKDE 105.5-FM.
**PA Announcer**: Chuck Young. **Official Scorers**: Malcolm Haley, Chuck Young.
**Stadium Name**: Calvin Falwell Field at Lynchburg City Stadium. **Location**: U.S. 29 Business South to Lynchburg City Stadium (exit 6); U.S. 29 Business North to Lynchburg City Stadium (exit 4). **Standard Game Times**: 7:05 p.m.; Sun. (April, May) 2:05, (June-Sept.) 6:05. **Ticket Price Range**: $4-8.
**Visiting Club Hotel**: Best Western, 2815 Candlers Mountain Rd., Lynchburg, VA 24502. Telephone: (434) 237-2986.

# MYRTLE BEACH
## PELICANS

**Office Address**: 1251 21st Ave. N., Myrtle Beach, SC 29577.
**Telephone**: (843) 918-6002. **FAX**: (843) 918-6001.
**E-Mail Address**: info@myrtlebeachpelicans.com. **Website**: www.myrtlebeachpelicans.com.
**Affiliation (first year)**: Atlanta Braves (1999). **Years in League**: 1999-.

## OWNERSHIP, MANAGEMENT

**Operated by**: Capitol Broadcasting Company.
**Principal Owner**: Jim Goodmon. **Vice President**: George Habel.
**VP, General Manager**: Matt O'Brien. **Accounting Manager**: Anne Frost. **Director, Corporate Sales**: Neil Fortier. **Director, Ticket/Retail Operations**: Richard Graves. **Director, Facility/Field Operations**: Chris Ball. **Manager, Group Sales**: Mike Junga. **Manager, Promotions**: Bradley Bell. **Manager, Ticket Sales**: Vince Nicoletti. **Administration/Community Relations**: Angela Barwick. **Manager, Marketing/Media**: Ryan Ibbotson. **Clubhouse Manager**: Unavailable.

## FIELD STAFF

**Manager**: Rocket Wheeler. **Coach**: Franklin Stubbs. **Pitching Coach**: Bruce Dal Canton. **Trainer**: Ricky Alcantara.

## GAME INFORMATION

**Radio Announcers**: Garry Griffith, Ryan Ibbotson. **No. of Games Broadcast**: Home-70, Away-70. **Flagship Station**: The TEAM 93.9-FM, 93.7-FM, 1050-AM.
**PA Announcer**: Mike Junga. **Official Scorer**: Unavailable.
**Stadium Name**: Coastal Federal Field. **Location**: U.S. Highway 17 Bypass to 21st Avenue North, 1/2 mile to stadium. **Standard Game Time**: 7:05 p.m. **Ticket Price Range**: $5.50-$9.
**Visiting Club Hotel**: Holiday Inn Express-Broadway at the Beach, U.S. Highway 17 Bypass & 29th Avenue North, Myrtle Beach, SC 29578. Telephone: (843) 916-4993.

# POTOMAC
## NATIONALS

**Office Address**: 7 County Complex Ct., Woodbridge, VA 22192.
**Mailing Address**: P.O. Box 2148, Woodbridge, VA 22195.
**Telephone**: (703) 590-2311. **FAX**: (703) 590-5716.
**E-Mail Address**: info@potomacnationals.com. **Website**: www.potomacnationals.com.
**Affiliation (first year)**: Washington Nationals (2005). **Years in League**: 1978-.

## OWNERSHIP, MANAGEMENT

**Operated by**: Prince William Professional Baseball Club, Inc.
**Principal Owner**: Art Silber. **President**: Lani Silber Weiss.
**General Manager**: Bobby Holland. **Assistant General Manager, Stadium Operations**: Eric Enders. **Assistant General Manager, Business Operations**: Jason Choi. **Director, Ticket Operations**: Brian Keller. **Director, Group Sales**:

Unavailable. **Director, Community Relations:** Maureen Connolly. **Director, Food Services:** Unavailable. **Promotions Coordinator:** Colin Smith. **Public Relations/Media Coordinator:** Jarrod Wronski. **Ticket Sales Manager:** Andrew Bashuk. **Director, Broadcasting:** Dan Laing. **Head Groundskeeper:** Mike Lundy.

## FIELD STAFF
**Manager:** Randy Knorr. **Coach:** Troy Gingrich. **Pitching Coach:** Charlie Corbell. **Trainer:** Steve Gober.

## GAME INFORMATION
**Radio:** None.
**PA Announcer:** Jarrod Wronski. **Official Scorer:** David Vincent.
**Stadium Name:** G. Richard Pfitzner Stadium. **Location:** From I-95, take exit 158B and continue on Prince William Parkway for 5 miles, right into County Complex Court. **Standard Game Times:** 7:05 p.m., Sun. 1:35. **Ticket Price Range:** $7-11.
**Visiting Club Hotel:** Best Western Potomac Mills, 14619 Potomac Mills Rd., Woodbridge, VA 22192. Telephone: (703) 494-4433.

# SALEM
## AVALANCHE

**Office Address:** 1004 Texas St., Salem, VA 24153.
**Mailing Address:** P.O. Box 842, Salem, VA 24153.
**Telephone:** (540) 389-3333. **FAX:** (540) 389-9710.
**E-Mail Address:** info@salemavalanche.com. **Website:** www.salemavalanche.com.
**Affiliation (first year):** Houston Astros (2003). **Years in League:** 1968-.

## OWNERSHIP, MANAGEMENT
**Operated by:** Salem Professional Baseball Club, Inc.
**Owner/President:** Kelvin Bowles.
**Vice President/General Manager:** John Katz. **VP, Finance:** Brian Bowles. **Assistant General Manager:** Allen Lawrence. **Director, Sales/Marketing:** Josh Eagan. **Director, Food/Beverage:** Scott Burton. **Director, Group Sales:** Jeremy Auker. **Director, Ticket Services:** Jeff Weinhold. **Director, Broadcasting:** Adam Pohl. **Head Groundskeeper:** Tracy Schneweis. **Special Events/Merchandising Manager:** Jessica Norden. **Ticket Manager:** Jeanne Boester. **Office Manager:** Jennifer Brady. **Account Executives:** Katherine Black, Chad Bouslog,

## FIELD STAFF
**Manager:** Jim Pankovits. **Coach:** Chuck Carr. **Pitching Coach:** Stan Boroski. **Trainer:** Eric Montague.

## GAME INFORMATION
**Radio Announcer:** Adam Pohl. **No. of Games Broadcast:** Home-70, Away-70. **Flagship Stations:** WGMN 1240-AM, WVGM 1320-AM.
**PA Announcer:** Adam Ranzer. **Official Scorer:** Billy Wells.
**Stadium Name:** Salem Memorial Baseball Stadium. **Location:** I-81 to exit 141 (Route 419), follow signs to Salem Civic Center Complex. **Standard Game Times:** 7:05 p.m.; Sun. (April-June) 2:05, (July-Aug) 6:05. **Ticket Price Range:** $6-8.
**Visiting Club Hotel:** Comfort Inn Airport, 5070 Valley View Blvd., Roanoke VA 24012. Telephone: (540) 527-2020.

# WILMINGTON
## BLUE ROCKS

**Office Address:** 801 S. Madison St., Wilmington, DE 19801.
**Telephone:** (302) 888-2015. **FAX:** (302) 888-2032.
**E-Mail Address:** info@bluerocks.com. **Website:** www.bluerocks.com.
**Affiliation (first year):** Boston Red Sox (2005). **Years in League:** 1993-.

## OWNERSHIP, MANAGEMENT
**Operated by:** Wilmington Blue Rocks, LP.
**President:** Matt Minker.
**General Manager:** Chris Kemple. **Assistant GM:** Andrew Layman. **Director, Marketing:** Tripp Baum. **Assistants, Marketing:** Dave Arthur, Rob Smith. **Director, Merchandise:** Jim Beck. **Merchandise Assistant:** Stefani DiChiara. **Director, Broadcasting/Media Relations:** Steve Lenox. **Assistant, Media Relations/Broadcasting:** Nick Barrale. **Director, Community Relations:** Dave Brown. **Assistant, Community Relations:** Tony Catalano. **Executive, Sales/Group Sales:** Kevin Linton. **Director, Ticket Operations/Group Sales:** Jared Forma. **Ticket Managers:** John Kramer, Steve Lovergine. **Ticket Interns:** Karen DiSantis, Bryan McGillick. **Group Sales Managers:** Joe Valenti, Shawn Vascellaro. **Director, Field Operations:** Steve Gold. **Office Manager:** Amy Hahn. **Centerplate General Manager:** Bobby Dichiaro. **Centerplate Assistant General Manager:** Beth Cullen.

**FIELD STAFF**

Manager: Chad Epperson. **Coach:** Dave Joppie. **Pitching Coach:** Mike Cather. **Athletic Trainer:** Brad Pearson.

**GAME INFORMATION**

Radio Announcers: Steve Lenox, Nick Barrale. **No. of Games Broadcast:** Home-70, Away-70. **Flagship Station:** WWTX 1290-AM.

PA Announcer: Kevin Linton. **Official Scorers:** E.J. Casey, Jay Dunn, Dick Shute.

Stadium Name: Judy Johnson Field at Daniel S. Frawley Stadium. **Location:** I-95 North to Maryland Ave. (exit 6), right onto Maryland Ave., right on Read Street, right on South Madison Street to ballpark; I-95 South to Maryland Ave. (exit 6), left at Martin Luther King Blvd., right on South Madison Street. **Standard Game Times:** 7:05 p.m., (April-May) 6:35; Sat. 6:05; Sun. 1:35. **Ticket Price Range:** $2-9.

Visiting Club Hotel: Quality Inn-Skyways, 147 N. DuPont Hwy., New Castle, DE 19720. Telephone: (302) 328-6666.

# WINSTON-SALEM
## WARTHOGS

Office Address: 401 Deacon Blvd., Winston-Salem, NC 27105.
Mailing Address: P.O. Box 4488, Winston-Salem, NC 27115.
Telephone: (336) 759-2233. **FAX:** (336) 759-2042.
E-Mail Address: warthogs@warthogs.com. **Website:** www.warthogs.com.
Affiliation (first year): Chicago White Sox (1997). **Years in League:** 1945-.

**OWNERSHIP, MANAGEMENT**

Operated by: Sports Menagerie, LLC.

Co-Owners: Billy Prim, Andrew Filipowski. **President:** Guy Schuman.

General Manager, Baseball Operations: Ryan Manuel. **Special Assistant to GM:** David Beal. **Chief Financial Officer:** Kurt Gehsmann. **Office Manager/Director, Tickets:** Amanda Elbert. **Director, Broadcasting/Media Relations:** Alan York. **Director, Community Relations:** Jacqi Jones. **Director, Merchandise:** Jim Gleitman. **Head Groundskeeper:** Unavailable. **Account Executives:** Steve Bartek, Sarcanda Bellisimo, Shaun McElhinny. **Interns:** Ed Collari, Lesley Crutcher, Ryan Ransom, Brian Shollenberger.

**FIELD STAFF**

Manager: Rafael Santana. **Coach:** Ryan Long. **Pitching Coach:** J.R. Perdew. **Trainer:** Josh Fallin.

**GAME INFORMATION**

Radio Announcer: Alan York. **No. of Games Broadcast:** Home-70, Away-70. **Flagship Station:** Unavailable.

PA Announcer: Larry Berry. **Official Scorer:** Unavailable.

Stadium Name: Ernie Shore Field. **Location:** I-40 Business to Cherry Street exit, north through downtown, right on Deacon Boulevard, park on left. **Standard Game Times:** 7 p.m.; Wed. 12; Sun. 5. **Ticket Price Range:** $6.50-$8.50.

Visiting Club Hotel: Holiday Inn, Hanes Mall, 2008 S. Hawthorne Rd., Winston-Salem, NC 27103. Telephone: (336) 765-6670.

# FLORIDA STATE LEAGUE

## CLASS A ADVANCED

**Street Address:** 115 E. Orange Ave., Daytona Beach, FL 32114.
**Mailing Address:** P.O. Box 349, Daytona Beach, FL 32115.
**Telephone:** (386) 252-7479. **FAX:** (386) 252-7495.
**E-Mail Address:** fslbaseball@cfl.rr.com. **Website:** www.floridastateleague.com.
**Years League Active:** 1919-1927, 1936-1941, 1946-.

Chuck Murphy

**President, Treasurer:** Chuck Murphy.

**Vice Presidents:** Ken Carson (Dunedin), Rob Rabenecker (Jupiter).

**Corporate Secretary:** David Hood.

**Directors:** Brian Barnes (Jupiter), Ken Carson (Dunedin), Emily Christy (Vero Beach), Chris Easom (Palm Beach), Marvin Goldklang (Fort Myers), Jeff Maultsby (Sarasota), Ron Myers (Lakeland), Andrew Rayburn (Daytona), Buck Rogers (Brevard County), Vance Smith (Tampa), Paul Taglieri (St. Lucie), John Timberlake (Clearwater).

**Office Secretary:** Peggy Catigano.

**Division Structure: East**—Brevard County, Daytona, Jupiter, Palm Beach, St. Lucie, Vero Beach. **West**—Clearwater, Dunedin, Fort Myers, Lakeland, Sarasota, Tampa.

**Regular Season:** 140 games (split schedule). **2006 Opening Date:** April 6. **Closing Date:** Sept. 3.

**All-Star Game:** June 17 at Clearwater.

**Playoff Format:** First-half division champions meet second-half champions in best-of-3 series. Winners meet in best-of-5 series for league championship.

**Roster Limit:** 25. **Player Eligibility Rule:** No age limit. No more than two players and one player-coach on active list may have six or more years of prior minor league service.

**Brand of Baseball:** Rawlings.

**Statistician:** Major League Baseball Advanced Media, 75 Ninth Ave., New York, NY 10011.

**Umpires:** Victor Carapazza (Palm Harbor, FL), Brent Cavins (Versailles, KY), Thomas Clarke (Andover, MA), Tyler Funnerman (Moweaqua, IL), John Gelatt (East Greenbush, NY), Manuel Gonzalez (Valencia-Carabobo, Venezuela), Mark Lollo (New Lexington, OH), Clinton Mahan (Taylorville, IL), Robert Price (Grand Rapids, MI), Arthur Thigpen (Lakeland, FL), John Tumpane (Oak Lawn, IL), Richard Young Cayce, SC).

## STADIUM INFORMATION

| | | | Dimensions | | | | |
|---|---|---|---|---|---|---|---|
| **Club** | **Stadium** | **Opened** | **LF** | **CF** | **RF** | **Capacity** | **2005 Att.** |
| Brevard County | Space Coast Stadium | 1994 | 340 | 404 | 340 | 7,500 | 101,847 |
| Clearwater | Bright House Networks Field | 2004 | 330 | 400 | 330 | 8,500 | 130,446 |
| Daytona | Jackie Robinson Ballpark | 1930 | 317 | 400 | 325 | 4,000 | 127,060 |
| Dunedin | Knology Park | 1977 | 335 | 400 | 315 | 6,106 | 40,479 |
| Fort Myers | William H. Hammond Stadium | 1991 | 330 | 405 | 330 | 7,500 | 112,272 |
| Jupiter | Roger Dean Stadium | 1998 | 330 | 400 | 325 | 6,871 | 88,580 |
| Lakeland | Joker Marchant Stadium | 1966 | 340 | 420 | 340 | 7,100 | 33,265 |
| Palm Beach | Roger Dean Stadium | 1998 | 330 | 400 | 325 | 6,871 | 98,841 |
| St. Lucie | Tradition Field | 1988 | 338 | 410 | 338 | 7,500 | 91,382 |
| Sarasota | Ed Smith Stadium | 1989 | 340 | 400 | 340 | 7,500 | 28,122 |
| Tampa | Legends Field | 1996 | 318 | 408 | 314 | 10,386 | 78,200 |
| Vero Beach | Holman Stadium | 1953 | 340 | 400 | 340 | 6,500 | 56,277 |

# BREVARD COUNTY
## MANATEES

**Office Address:** 5800 Stadium Pkwy. Suite 101, Viera, FL 32940.
**Telephone:** (321) 633-9200. **FAX:** (321) 633-4418.
**E-Mail Address:** info@spacecoaststadium.com. **Website:** www.manatees baseball.com.
**Affiliation (first year):** Milwaukee Brewers (2005). **Years in League:** 1994-.

### OWNERSHIP, MANAGEMENT
**Operated by:** Central Florida Baseball Group, LLC.
**General Manager:** Buck Rogers. **Assistant GM:** Babs Rogers. **Business Operations Manager:** Kelley Wheeler. **Director, Media/Group Sales:** Jenny Rennie. **Director, Ticket Operations:** Tyler Hubbard. **Facilities Engineer:** Chuck Bunch.

### FIELD STAFF
**Manager:** Ramon Aviles. **Coach:** Willie Aviles. **Pitching Coach:** Fred Dabney. **Trainer:** Masa Koyanagi.

### GAME INFORMATION
**Radio:** None.
**PA Announcer:** Unavailable. **Official Scorer:** Unavailable.
**Stadium Name:** Space Coast Stadium. **Location:** I-95 North to Wickham Road (exit 191), left onto Wickham, right at traffic circle onto Lake Andrew Drive for 1½ miles through the Brevard County government office complex to the four-way stop, right on Stadium Parkway. Space Coast Stadium ½ mile on left. I-95 South to Rockledge exit (exit 195), left onto Stadium Parkway. Space Coast Stadium is 3 miles on right. **Game Times:** 7 p.m., Sun. 4. **Ticket Prices:** $6.
**Visiting Club Hotel:** Imperial's Hotel & Conference Center, 8928 N. Wickham Rd., Viera, FL 32940. Telephone: (321) 255-0077.

# CLEARWATER
## THRESHERS

**Office Address:** 601 N. Old Coachman Rd, Clearwater, FL 33765.
**Telephone:** (727) 712-4300. **FAX:** (727) 712-4498.
**Website:** www.threshersbaseball.com.
**Affiliation (first year):** Philadelphia Phillies (1985). **Years in League:** 1985-.

### OWNERSHIP, MANAGEMENT
**Operated by:** The Philadelphia Phillies.
**Chairman:** Bill Giles. **President:** David Montgomery.
**Director, Florida Operations/General Manager:** John Timberlake. **Assistant Director, Florida Operations:** Lee McDaniel. **Business Manager:** Dianne Gonzalez. **Assistant GM/Director, Sales:** Dan McDonough. **Assistant GM/Ticketing:** Jason Adams. **Coordinator, Merchandising/Special Events:** Carrie Jenkins-Adams. **Group Sales:** Dan Madden, Bobby Mitchell. **Ballpark Operations:** Jay Warren. **Ticket Manager:** Kevin Brahm. **Maintenance Coordinator:** Cory Sipe. **Manager, Food/Beverage:** Tony Lenning. **Office Manager:** De De Angelillis. **Head Groundskeeper:** Opie Cheek. **Clubhouse Operations:** Cliff Armbruster.

### FIELD STAFF
**Manager:** Greg Legg. **Coach:** Greg Gross. **Pitching Coach:** Scott Lovekamp. **Trainer:** Jason Kirkman.

### GAME INFORMATION
**Radio:** None.
**PA Announcer:** Don Guckian. **Official Scorer:** Larry Wiederecht.
**Stadium Name:** Bright House Networks Field. **Location:** U.S. 19 North and Drew Street in Clearwater. **Standard Game Times:** 7:05 p.m., Sun. 1:05. **Ticket Price Range:** $3-8.
**Visiting Club Hotel:** Econo Lodge, 21252 U.S. 19 N., Clearwater, FL 33765. Telephone: (727) 796-3165.

# DAYTONA
## CUBS

**Office Address:** 105 E. Orange Ave., Daytona Beach, FL 32114.
**Telephone:** (386) 257-3172. **FAX:** (386) 257-3382.
**E-Mail Address:** info@daytonacubs.com. **Website:** www.daytonacubs.com.
**Affiliation (first year):** Chicago Cubs (1993). **Years in league:** 1920-24, 1928, 1936-41, 1946-73, 1977-87, 1993-.

## OWNERSHIP, MANAGEMENT

**Operated by:** Big Game Florida, LLC.
**Principal Owner/President:** Andrew Rayburn.
**General Manager:** Bill Papierniak. **Assistant GM:** Matthew Provence. **Director, Corporate Accounts:** Rick Polster. **Director, Stadium Operations:** J.R. Laub. **Director, Broadcasting/Media Relations:** Derek Ingram. **Director, Tickets:** Eric Freeman. **Director, Merchandise:** Brandon Greene. **Director, Food/Beverage:** Josh Lawther, **Director, Sales:** Brady Ballard. **Stadium Operations Assistants:** West Costa, Luke Foth, Atsushi Nagamata, Anthony Oppermann, Stephen Parr, Rishi Ragbir. **Office Manager:** Tammy Devine.

## FIELD STAFF

**Manager:** Don Buford. **Coach:** Richie Zisk. **Pitching Coach:** Tom Pratt. **Trainer:** Steve Melendez.

## GAME INFORMATION

**Radio Announcers:** Derek Ingram, Luke Foth, Anthony Oppermann. **No. of Games Broadcast:** Home-70, Away-70. **Flagship Station:** WELE 1380-AM.
**PA Announcer:** Tim Lecras. **Official Scorer:** Lyle Fox.
**Stadium Name:** Jackie Robinson Ballpark. **Location:** I-95 to International Speedway Blvd. exit (Route 92), east to Beach Street, south to Magnolia Ave., east to ballpark; A1A North/South to Orange Ave., west to ballpark. **Standard Game Times:** 7:05 p.m.; Sun. 6:05. **Ticket Price Range:** $6-9.
**Visiting Club Hotel:** Unavailable.

# DUNEDIN
## BLUE JAYS

**Office Address:** 373-A Douglas Ave., Dunedin, FL 34698.
**Telephone:** (727) 733-9302. **FAX:** (727) 734-7661.
**E-Mail Address:** feedback@dunedinbluejays.com. **Website:** www.dunedin bluejays.com.
**Affiliation (first year):** Toronto Blue Jays (1987). **Years in League:** 1978-79, 1987-.

## OWNERSHIP, MANAGEMENT

**Operated by:** Toronto Blue Jays.
**Director, Florida Operations/General Manager:** Ken Carson. **Assistant GM:** Carrie Johnson. **Manager, Ticket Sales:** Brandon McIntosh. **Manager, Group Sales:** Jerry Garland. **Office Manager:** Karen Howell **Sales Representatives:** Janette Donoghue. **Head Groundskeeper:** Budgie Clark. **Clubhouse Operations:** Unavailable.

## FIELD STAFF

**Manager:** Omar Malave. **Coach:** Paul Elliott. **Pitching Coach:** Darold Knowles. **Trainer:** Andrew Muccino.

## GAME INFORMATION

**Radio:** None.
**PA Announcers:** Dave Bell. **Official Scorer:** Bobby Porter.
**Stadium Name:** Dunedin Stadium. **Location:** From I-275, north on Highway 19, left on Sunset Point Road for 4 1/2 miles, right on Douglas Avenue, stadium is 1/2 mile on right. **Standard Game Times:** 7 p.m., Sun 1. **Ticket Price Range:** $5-7.
**Visiting Club Hotel:** Econo Lodge, 21252 U.S. 19 N., Clearwater, FL 34625. Telephone: (727) 799-1569.

# FORT MYERS
## MIRACLE

**Office Address:** 14400 Six Mile Cypress Pkwy., Fort Myers, FL 33912.
**Telephone:** (239) 768-4210. **FAX:** (239) 768-4211.
**E-Mail Address:** miracle@miraclebaseball.com. **Website:** www.miraclebaseball.com.
**Affiliation:** Minnesota Twins (1993). **Years in League:** 1926, 1978-87, 1991-.

## OWNERSHIP, MANAGEMENT

**Operated by:** Greater Miami Baseball Club, LP.
**Principal Owner/Chairman:** Marvin Goldklang. **Chief Executive Officer:** Mike Veeck. **President:** Linda McNabb.
**General Manager:** Steve Gliner. **Assistant GM:** Andrew Seymour. **Director, Business Operations:** Suzanne Reaves. **Manager, Sales/Marketing:** Terry Simon. **Head Groundskeeper:** Keith Blasingim. **Manager, Media Relations/Broadcasting:** Sean Aronson. **Sales Representatives:** Stephen Kaufman, Justin Stecz. **Manager, Food/Beverage:** John Acquavella. **Assistant Manager, Food/Beverage:** Kris Koch. **Special Events Manager:** Chris Ames. **Manager, Tickets/Community Relations:** Juli Greenleaf.

## FIELD STAFF

**Manager:** Kevin Boles. **Coach:** Jim Dwyer. **Pitching Coach:** Eric Rasmussen. **Trainer:** Larry Bennese.

## GAME INFORMATION

**Radio Announcer:** Sean Aronson. **No of Games Broadcast:** Home-70, Away-70. **Flagship Station:** ESPN 770-AM. **PA Announcer:** Sean Fox. **Official Scorer:** Benn Norton.

**Stadium Name:** William H. Hammond Stadium. **Location:** Exit 131 off I-75, west on Daniels Parkway, left on Six Mile Cypress Parkway. **Standard Game Times:** 7:05 p.m.; Sun. 1:05. **Ticket Price Range:** $4-6.

**Visiting Club Hotel:** Fairfield Inn by Marriott, 7090 Cypress Terrace, Fort Myers, FL 33907. **Telephone:** (239) 437-5600

# JUPITER
## HAMMERHEADS

**Office Address:** 4751 Main St., Jupiter, FL 33458.
**Telephone:** (561) 775-1818. **FAX:** (561) 691-6886.
**E-Mail Address:** info@rogerdeanstadium.com. **Website:** www.jupiterhammerheads.com.
**Affiliation (first year):** Florida Marlins (2002). **Years in League:** 1998-.

### OWNERSHIP, MANAGEMENT

**Owned by:** Florida Marlins. **Operated by:** Jupiter Stadium, Ltd.
**General Manager, JSL:** Rob Rabenecker. **Executive Assistant to GM, JSL:** Carol McAteer.
**GM, Jupiter Hammerheads:** Brian Barnes. **Associate GM:** Chris Easom. **Director, Marketing:** Jennifer Brown. **Manager, Merchandising:** Caitlin Bakum. **Manager, Stadium Building:** Jorge Toro. **Manager, Facility Operations:** Marshall Jennings. **Assistant Manager, Facility Operations:** Karsten Blackwelder, Johnny Simmons. **Office Manager:** Rene Waldrip. **Manager, Tickets:** Joe Schuler. **Marketing Manager:** Amanda Broadway. **Marketing Sales Representative:** Stephanie Francesco. **Ticket Sales Manager:** Scott Hodge. **Sales Representatives:** Bryan Knapp, Luke Worrell. **Interns:** Mike Boseak, Krista Boyd, Amelia Calulot, Kasey Carretto, Lisa Fegley, Mike Fowler, Jeff Grant, Doug Haake, Kathy Langenfeld, Brett Moldoff, Evan Paradis, Brandi Walls.

### FIELD STAFF

**Manager:** Tim Cossins. **Coach:** Darin Everson. **Pitching Coach:** Reid Cornelius. **Trainer:** Josh Seligman.

### GAME INFORMATION

**Radio:** None.
**PA Announcers:** John Frost, Lou Palmer, Dick Sanford. **Official Scorer:** Unavailable.
**Stadium Name (year opened):** Roger Dean Stadium (1998). **Location:** I-95 to exit 83, east on Donald Ross Road for ¼ mile. **Standard Game Times:** 7:05 p.m., Sun. 2:05, Sat. 6:05, Tues. 6:35.
**Visiting Club Hotel:** Comfort Inn & Suites Jupiter, 6752 West Indiantown Rd., Jupiter, FL 33458. Telephone: (561) 745-7997.

# LAKELAND
## TIGERS

**Office Address:** 2125 N. Lake Ave., Lakeland, FL 33805.
**Mailing Address:** P.O. Box 90187, Lakeland, FL 33804.
**Telephone:** (863) 686-8075. **FAX:** (863) 688-9589.
**E-Mail Address:** info@lakelandtigers.net.
**Affiliation (first year):** Detroit Tigers (1967). **Years in League:** 1919-26, 1953-55, 1960, 1962-64, 1967-.

### OWNERSHIP, MANAGEMENT

**Operated by:** Detroit Tigers.
**Principal Owner:** Mike Ilitch. **President:** David Dombrowski. **Director, Florida Operations:** Ron Myers.
**General Manager:** Zach Burek. **Assistant GM:** Shannon Follett. **Ticket Operations:** Erik Veenhuis. **Director, Merchandising/Concessions:** Kay LaLonde. **Media Relations:** Owen Rosen. **Clubhouse Operations:** Unavailable. **Head Groundskeeper:** Bryan French.

### FIELD STAFF

**Manager:** Mike Rojas. **Coach:** Larry Herndon. **Pitching Coach:** Britt Burns. **Trainer:** Dustin Campbell.

### GAME INFORMATION

**Radio:** None.
**PA Announcer:** Shari Szabo. **Official Scorer:** Sandy Shaw.
**Stadium Name:** Joker Marchant Stadium. **Location:** Exit 33 on I-4 to 33 South, 1½ miles on left. **Standard Game Times:** 7 p.m.; Sun. 1 (April-May), 6. **Ticket Price Range:** $4-5.
**Visiting Club Hotel:** Baymont Inn and Suites, 4315 Lakeland Park Dr., Lakeland, FL 33809. Telephone: (863) 815-0606.

# PALM BEACH
## CARDINALS

**Office Address:** 4751 Main St., Jupiter, FL 33458.
**Telephone:** (561) 775-1818. **FAX:** (561) 691-6886.
**E-Mail Address:** info@rogerdeanstadium.com. **Website:** www.palmbeachcardinals.com.
**Affiliation (first year):** St. Louis Cardinals (2003). **Years in League:** 2003-.

### OWNERSHIP, MANAGEMENT
**Owned by:** St. Louis Cardinals. **Operated by:** Jupiter Stadium, Ltd.
**General Manager, JSL:** Rob Rabenecker. **Executive Assistant to GM, JSL:** Carol McAteer.
**GM, Palm Beach Cardinals:** Chris Easom. **Associate GM:** Brian Barnes. **Director, Marketing:** Jennifer Brown. **Manager, Merchandising:** Caitlin Bakum. **Manager, Stadium Building:** Jorge Toro. **Manager, Facility Operations:** Marshall Jennings. **Assistant Manager, Facility Operations:** Karsten Blackwelder, Johnny Simmons. **Office Manager:** Rene Waldrip. **Manager, Tickets:** Joe Schuler. **Marketing Manager:** Amanda Broadway. **Marketing Sales Representative:** Stephanie Francesco. **Ticket Sales Manager:** Scott Hodge. **Sales Representatives:** Bryan Knapp, Luke Worrell.

### FIELD STAFF
**Manager:** Ron Warner. **Coach:** Derrick May. **Pitching Coach:** Derek Lilliquist. **Trainer:** Allen Thompson.

### GAME INFORMATION
**Radio:** None.
**PA Announcers:** John Frost, Lou Palmer, Dick Sanford. **Official Scorer:** Unavailable.
**Stadium Name (year opened):** Roger Dean Stadium (1998). **Location:** I-95 to exit 83, east on Donald Ross Road for ¼ mile. **Standard Game Times:** 7:05 p.m., Sun. 2:05, Sat. 6:05, Tues. 6:35.
**Visiting Club Hotel:** Comfort Inn & Suites Jupiter, 6752 W. Indiantown Rd., Jupiter, FL 33458. Telephone: (561) 745-7997.

# ST. LUCIE
## METS

**Office Address:** 525 NW Peacock Blvd., Port St. Lucie, FL 34986.
**Telephone:** (772) 871-2100. **FAX:** (772) 878-9802.
**Website:** www.stluciemets.com.
**Affiliation (first year):** New York Mets (1988). **Years in League:** 1988-.

### OWNERSHIP, MANAGEMENT
**Operated by:** Sterling Mets, LP.
**Chairman:** Fred Wilpon. **President:** Saul Katz. **Executive Vice President/Chief Operating Officer:** Jeff Wilpon.
**Director, Florida Operations/General Manager:** Paul Taglieri. **Manager, Stadium Operations:** Traer Van Allen. **Manager, St. Lucie Mets Operations:** Ari Skalet. **Manager, Food/Beverage Operations:** Brian Paupeck. **Ticketing/Merchandise Coordinator:** Erin Rescigno. **Office Assistant:** Cynthia Malaspino. **Sales Associate:** Ryan Strickland. **Head Groundskeeper:** Tommy Bowes. **Clubhouse Manager:** Jack Brenner.

### FIELD STAFF
**Manager:** Gary Carter. **Coach:** Nelson Silverio. **Pitching Coach:** Ricky Bones. **Trainer:** Ruben Barrera.

### GAME INFORMATION
**Radio:** None.
**PA Announcer:** Unavailable. **Official Scorer:** Bob Adams.
**Stadium Name:** Tradition Field. **Location:** Exit 121 (St. Lucie West Blvd.) off I-95, east ½ mile, left on NW Peacock Blvd. **Standard Game Times:** 7 p.m.; Sun 5. **Ticket Price Range:** $3-6.
**Visiting Club Hotel:** Holiday Inn, 10120 S. Federal Hwy., Port St. Lucie, FL 34952. Telephone: (772) 337-2200.

# SARASOTA
## REDS

**Office Address:** 2700 12th St., Sarasota, FL 34237.
**Mailing Address:** 1090 N. Euclid Ave., Sarasota, FL 34237.
**Telephone:** (941) 365-4460. **FAX:** (941) 365-4217.
**E-mail Address:** sarasotaredsinfo@reds.com. **Website:** www.sarasotareds.com.
**Affiliation (first year):** Cincinnati Reds (2005). **Years in League:** 1927, 1961-65, 1989-.

## OWNERSHIP, MANAGEMENT
**Operated by:** Cincinnati Reds, LLP.
**General Manager:** Dan Wolfert. **Assistant GM:** Blaine Smith. **Administrative Assistants:** Erin Ehnerd, Jay Puckett. **Ticket Manager:** Barbara Robinson. **Clubhouse Manager:** Russ Hoffman. **Equipment Manager:** Tim Williamson. **Florida Operations Assistant:** Eric Jordan. **Head Groundskeeper:** Gene Egan.

## FIELD STAFF
**Manager:** Donnie Scott. **Coach:** Joe Ayrault. **Pitching Coach:** Ed Hodge. **Athletic Trainer:** Trevor Carter. **Strength/Conditioning Coach:** Zach Gjestvang.

## GAME INFORMATION
**Radio:** None.
**PA Announcer:** Alex Topp. **Official Scorer:** Howard Spungen, Dave Taylor, Phil Denis.
**Stadium Name:** Ed Smith Stadium. **Location:** I-75 to exit 210, three miles west to Tuttle Avenue, right on Tuttle 1/2 mile to 12th Street, stadium on left. **Standard Game Times:** 7 p.m., Sun. 1. **Ticket Price Range:** $5-$6.
**Visiting Club Hotel:** AmericInn and Suites, 5931 Fruitville Rd., Sarasota, FL 34232. Telephone: (941) 342-8778.

# TAMPA
## YANKEES

**Office Address:** One Steinbrenner Dr., Tampa, FL 33614.
**Telephone:** (813) 875-7753. **FAX:** (813) 673-3174.
**E-Mail Address:** vsmith@yankees.com.
**Affiliation (first year):** New York Yankees (1994). **Years in League:** 1919-27, 1957-1988, 1994-.

## OWNERSHIP, MANAGEMENT
**Operated by:** New York Yankees, LP.
**Principal Owner:** George Steinbrenner.
**General Manager:** Vance Smith. **Assistant GM:** Julie Kremer. **Director, Stadium Operations:** Dean Holbert. **Director, Sales/Marketing:** Howard Grosswirth. **Director, Ticket Sales:** Brian Valdez. **Head Groundskeeper:** Ritchie Anderson.

## FIELD STAFF
**Manager:** Luis Sojo. **Coach:** James Rowson. **Pitching Coach:** Greg Pavlick. **Trainer:** Mike Wickland.

## GAME INFORMATION
**Radio:** None.
**PA Announcer:** Steve Hague. **Official Scorer:** Unavailable.
**Stadium Name:** Legends Field. **Location:** I-275 to Martin Luther King, west on Martin Luther King to Dale Mabry. **Standard Game Times:** 7 p.m.; Sun. 1. **Ticket Price Range:** $5-7.
**Visiting Club Hotel:** Holiday Inn Express, 4732 N. Dale Mabry Hwy., Tampa, FL 33614. Telephone: (813) 877-6061.

# VERO BEACH
## DODGERS

**Office Address:** 4101 26th St., Vero Beach, FL 32960.
**Mailing Address:** P.O. Box 2887, Vero Beach, FL 32961.
**Telephone:** (772) 569-4900. **FAX:** (772) 567-0819.
**E-Mail Address:** info@vbdodgers.com. **Website:** www.vbdodgers.com.
**Affiliation (first year):** Los Angeles Dodgers (1980). **Years in League:** 1980-.

## OWNERSHIP, MANAGEMENT
**Operated by:** Los Angeles Dodgers.
**President:** Martin Greenspun.
**General Manager:** Emily Christy. **Director, Sales/Promotions:** Shawn Marette. **Director, Community Relations/Ticket Sales:** Katie Siegfried. **Head Groundskeeper:** Steve Carlsward. **Director, Ticket Sales:** Louise Boissy. **Manager, Concessions/Souvenirs:** Roger Barzee. **Secretary:** Edith Marcelle. **Advertising Secretary:** Betty Rollins. **Administrative Assistants:** Scott Evans, Chris Madden, Katie Smith.

## FIELD STAFF
**Manager:** Luis Salazar. **Coach:** Ramon Ortiz. **Pitching Coach:** Glenn Dishman. **Trainer:** Carlos Olivas.

## GAME INFORMATION
**Radio Announcer:** Brian Petrotta. **No. of Games Broadcast:** Home-70, Away-70. **Flagship Station:** WTTB 1490-AM.
**PA Announcer:** Joe Sanchez. **Official Scorer:** Randy Phillips.
**Stadium Name:** Holman Stadium. **Location:** I-95 to Route 60 East, left on 43rd Avenue, right on Aviation Boulevard. **Standard Game Times:** 7 p.m.; Sun. 5. **Ticket Price Range:** $4-5.
**Visiting Club Hotel:** Unavailable.

# MIDWEST
## LEAGUE

**Office Address:** 1118 Cranston Rd., Beloit, WI 53511.
**Mailing Address:** P.O. Box 936, Beloit, WI 53512.
**Telephone:** (608) 364-1188. **FAX:** (608) 364-1913.
**E-Mail Address:** mwl@midwestleague.com. **Website:** www.midwestleague.com.
**Years League Active:** 1947-.

**President, Treasurer:** George Spelius.
**Vice President:** Ed Larson. **Legal Counsel/Secretary:** Richard Nussbaum.
**Directors:** Andrew Appleby (Fort Wayne), Tom Barbee (Cedar Rapids), Lew Chamberlin (West Michigan), Dennis Conerton (Beloit), Tom Dickson (Lansing), Kevin Krause (Quad Cities), Alan Levin (South Bend), Robert Murphy (Dayton), Paul Schnack (Clinton), William Shea (Southwest Michigan), Rocky Vonachen (Peoria), Dave Walker (Burlington), Mike Woleben (Kane County), Rob Zerjav (Wisconsin).
**League Administrator:** Holly Voss.
**Division Structure: East**—Dayton, Fort Wayne, Lansing, South Bend, Southwest Michigan, West Michigan. **West**—Beloit, Burlington, Cedar Rapids, Clinton, Kane County, Peoria, Quad Cities, Wisconsin.
**Regular Season:** 140 games (split-schedule). **2006 Opening Date:** April 6. **Closing Date:** Sept. 4.

**George Spelius**

**All-Star Game:** June 20 at Davenport, IA (Swing of the Quad Cities).
**Playoff Format:** Eight teams qualify. First-half and second-half division champions, and wild-card teams, meet in best-of-3 quarterfinal series. Winners meet in best-of-3 series for division championship. Division champions meet in best-of-5 final for league championship.
**Roster Limit:** 25 active. **Player Eligibility Rule:** No age limit. No more than two players and one player-coach on active list may have more than five years experience.
**Brand of Baseball:** Rawlings ROM-MID.
**Statistician:** Major League Baseball Advanced Media, 75 Ninth Ave., New York, NY 10011.
**Umpires:** Jason Creek (Manchester, TN), Joseph Dobo (Dunmore, PA), Clint Fagan (Tomball, TX), Shaun Francis (Cohoes, NY), Jeffrey La Scola (Garden Grove, CA), Bradley Lawhead (Kersey, CO), Douglas Levy (Sharon, MA), Michael Lusky (Baldwin Park, CA), Philip Mulroe (Portage, IN), Bradley Purdom (Corvallis, OR), Matthew Schaufert (St. Louis), Ryan Stockdale (Centralia, WA), Michael Weinstein (Chesterfield, MO), Garrett Wilson (Creswell, OR).

## STADIUM INFORMATION

| Club | Stadium | Opened | Dimensions LF | CF | RF | Capacity | 2005 Att. |
|------|---------|--------|-----|-----|-----|----------|-----------|
| Beloit | Pohlman Field | 1982 | 325 | 380 | 325 | 3,500 | 93,399 |
| Burlington | Community Field | 1947 | 338 | 403 | 318 | 3,200 | 70,807 |
| Cedar Rapids | Veterans Memorial Stadium | 2002 | 315 | 400 | 325 | 5,300 | 184,190 |
| Clinton | Alliant Energy Field | 1937 | 335 | 390 | 325 | 2,500 | 95,775 |
| Dayton | Fifth Third Field | 2000 | 338 | 402 | 338 | 7,230 | 572,003 |
| Fort Wayne | Memorial Stadium | 1993 | 330 | 400 | 330 | 6,516 | 278,641 |
| Kane County | Philip B. Elfstrom Stadium | 1991 | 335 | 400 | 335 | 7,400 | 518,394 |
| Lansing | Oldsmobile Park | 1996 | 305 | 412 | 305 | 11,000 | 354,855 |
| Peoria | O'Brien Field | 2002 | 310 | 400 | 310 | 7,500 | 256,612 |
| Quad Cities | John O'Donnell Stadium | 1931 | 343 | 400 | 318 | 4,024 | 165,124 |
| South Bend | Coveleski Regional Stadium | 1987 | 336 | 405 | 336 | 5,000 | 209,555 |
| Southwest Michigan | C.O. Brown Stadium | 1990 | 322 | 402 | 333 | 4,500 | 105,340 |
| West Michigan | Fifth Third Ballpark | 1994 | 317 | 402 | 327 | 10,900 | 370,153 |
| Wisconsin | Fox Cities Stadium | 1995 | 325 | 400 | 325 | 5,500 | 211,927 |

# BELOIT
## SNAPPERS

**Office Address:** 2301 Skyline Dr., Beloit, WI 53511.
**Mailing Address:** P.O. Box 855, Beloit, WI 53512.
**Telephone:** (608) 362-2272. **FAX:** (608) 362-0418.
**E-Mail Address:** snappy@snappersbaseball.com. **Website:** www.snappersbaseball.com.
**Affiliation (first year):** Minnesota Twins (2005). **Years in League:** 1982-.

### OWNERSHIP, MANAGEMENT
**Operated by:** Beloit Professional Baseball Association, Inc.
**Chairman:** Dennis Conerton. **President:** Marcy Olsen.
**General Manager:** Jeff Vohs. **Director, Community/Media Relations:** Jeremy Neuman. **Director, Operations:** Rick Valdez. **Director, Ticket Operations/Merchandise:** Brandon Smith. **Director, Corporate Sales:** Riley Gostisha.

### FIELD STAFF
**Manager:** Jeff Smith. **Coach:** Rudy Hernandez. **Pitching Coach:** Steve Mintz. **Trainer:** Alan Rail.

### GAME INFORMATION
**Radio Announcer:** Unavailable. **No. of Games Broadcast:** Unavailable. **Flagship Station:** WTJK 1380-AM.
**PA Announcer:** Bob Ace. **Official Scorer:** Jeremy Neuman.
**Stadium Name:** Pohlman Field. **Location:** I-90 to exit 185-A, right at Cranston Road for 1½ miles; I-43 to Wisconsin 81 to Cranston Road, right at Cranston for 1½ miles. **Standard Game Times:** 7 p.m., (April-May) 6:30; Sun. 2. **Ticket Price Range:** $6-8.
**Visiting Club Hotel:** Econo Lodge, 2956 Milwaukee Rd., Beloit, WI 53511. Telephone: (608) 364-4000.

# BURLINGTON
## BEES

**Office Address:** 2712 Mt. Pleasant St., Burlington, IA 52601.
**Mailing Address:** P.O. Box 824, Burlington, IA 52601.
**Telephone:** (319) 754-5705. **FAX:** (319) 754-5882.
**E-Mail Address:** staff@gobees.com. **Website:** www.gobees.com.
**Affiliation (first year):** Kansas City Royals (2001). **Years in League:** 1962-.

### OWNERSHIP, MANAGEMENT
**Operated by:** Burlington Baseball Association, Inc.
**President:** Dave Walker.
**General Manager:** Chuck Brockett. **Assistant GM, Baseball Operations:** Randy Wehofer. **Assistant GM, Sales/Marketing:** Adam Small. **Director, Group Outings:** Renae Roelfs. **Head Groundskeeper:** Elliott Josephson.

### FIELD STAFF
**Manager:** Jim Gabella. **Coach:** Patrick Anderson. **Pitching Coach:** Steve Luebber. **Trainer:** Mark Stubblefield. **Strength/Conditioning Coach:** Bryce Stone.

### GAME INFORMATION
**Radio Announcer:** Randy Wehofer. **No. of Games Broadcast:** Home-70, Away-70. **Flagship Stations:** KBUR 1490-AM, KBKB 1360-AM.
**PA Announcers:** Scott Mason, Brian Sines. **Official Scorer:** Scott Logas.
**Stadium Name:** Community Field. **Location:** From U.S. 34, take U.S. 61 North to Mt. Pleasant Street, east ⅛ mile. **Standard Game Times:** 7 p.m.; Sat. (April-May) 6; Sun. 2. **Ticket Price Range:** $4-7.
**Visiting Club Hotel:** Pzazz Best Western, 3001 Winegard Dr., Burlington, IA 52601. Telephone: (319) 753-2223.

# CEDAR RAPIDS
## KERNELS

**Office Address:** 950 Rockford Rd. SW, Cedar Rapids, IA 52404.
**Mailing Address:** P.O. Box 2001, Cedar Rapids, IA 52406.
**Telephone:** (319) 363-3887. **FAX:** (319) 363-5631.
**E-Mail Address:** kernels@kernels.com. **Website:** www.kernels.com.
**Affiliation (first year):** Los Angeles Angels of Anaheim (1993). **Years in League:** 1962-.

### OWNERSHIP, MANAGEMENT
**Operated by:** Cedar Rapids Baseball Club, Inc.
**President:** Tom Barbee.

**MIDWEST LEAGUE**

General Manager: Jack Roeder. Chief Operating Officer: Doug Nelson. Sports Information Director: Todd Brommelkamp. Sports Turf Manager: Jesse Roeder. Director, Tickets/Group Sales: Andrea Murphy. Director, Broadcasting: John Rodgers. Director, Finance: Charlie Patrick. Director, Graphics/Technology: Andrew Pantini. Director, Entertainment: Josh Boots. Stadium Operations Manager: Seth Dohrn. Customer Services/Suite Manager: Jessica Fergesen. Concessions Manager: Dave Soper. Sales Executive: Ken Franz. Clubhouse Operations: Ron Plein.

## FIELD STAFF
Manager: Bobby Magallanes. Coach: Eric Owens. Pitching Coach: Kernan Ronan. Trainer: Eric Munson.

## GAME INFORMATION
Radio Announcer: John Rodgers. No. of Games Broadcast: Home-70, Away-70. Flagship Stations: KCRG 1600-AM, KMRY 1450-AM.
PA Announcer: Dale Brodt. Official Scorer: Al Gruwell.
Stadium Name: Veterans Memorial Stadium. Location: I-380 to Wilson Ave. exit, west to Rockford Road, right one mile to corner of 8th Ave. and 15th Street SW. Standard Game Times: 7 p.m., (April-May, Sept.) 6:30; Sat. (April-May) 5; Sun. 2. Ticket Price Range: $6-9.
Visiting Club Hotel: Best Western Village Inn, 100 F Ave. NW, Cedar Rapids, IA 52405. Telephone: (319) 366-5323.

# CLINTON
## LUMBERKINGS

Office Address: Alliant Energy Field, Sixth Avenue and First Street, Clinton, IA 52732.
Mailing Address: P.O. Box 1295, Clinton, IA 52733.
Telephone: (563) 242-0727. FAX: (563) 242-1433.
E-Mail Address: lumberkings@lumberkings.com. Website: www.lumberkings.com.
Affiliation (first year): Texas Rangers (2003). Years in League: 1956-.

## OWNERSHIP, MANAGEMENT
Operated by: Clinton Baseball Club, Inc.
Chairman: Don Roode. President: Paul Schnack.
General Manager: Ted Tornow. Assistant GM: Nate Kreinbrink. Director, Operations: Derick Stoulil. Director, Promotions: Cary Dohman. Groundskeeper: Travis Stephen. Clubhouse Manager: Steve Martin.

## FIELD STAFF
Manager: Andy Fox. Coach: Brian Dayett. Pitching Coach: Stan Hilton. Trainer: Jeff Bodenhamer.

## GAME INFORMATION
Radio Announcers: Gary Determan, Cary Dohman. No. of Games Broadcast: Home-70, Away-70. Flagship Station: KROS 1340-AM.
PA Announcer: Brad Seward. Official Scorer: Tom Whaley.
Stadium Name: Alliant Energy Field. Location: Highway 67 North to Sixth Avenue North, right on Sixth, cross railroad tracks, stadium on right. Standard Game Times: 7 p.m., (April-May) 6; Sun. 2. Ticket Price Range: $5-7.
Visiting Club Hotel: Super 8 Motel, 1711 Lincoln Way, Clinton, IA 52732. Telephone: (563) 242-8870.

# DAYTON
## DRAGONS

Office Address: Fifth Third Field, 220 N. Patterson Blvd., Dayton, OH 45402.
Mailing Address: P.O. Box 2107, Dayton, OH 45401.
Telephone: (937) 228-2287. FAX: (937) 228-2284.
E-Mail Address: dragons@daytondragons.com. Website: www.daytondragons.com.
Affiliate (first year): Cincinnati Reds (2000). Years in League: 2000-.

## OWNERSHIP, MANAGEMENT
Operated by: Dayton Professional Baseball, LLC.
Owners: Hank Stickney, Ken Stickney, Peter Guber, Paul Schaeffer, Earvin Johnson, Archie Griffin.
President: Robert Murphy. Executive Vice President: Eric Deutsch. VP, Accounting/Finance: Mark Schlein. VP, Baseball/Stadium Operations: Gary Mayse. VP, Sponsorships: Jeff Webb. Director, Creative Services: Brad Eaton Director, Entertainment: Derek Dye. Director, Marketing: Jim Francis. Director, Media Relations/Broadcasting: Mike Vander Wood. Director, Ticket Sales: John Davis. Box Office Manager: Sally Ledford. Corporate Marketing Managers: Andrew Aldenderfer, Michael Blanton, Clint Taylor, Mike Vujea. Senior Marketing Manager: Emily Tincher. Marketing Managers: Brandy Abney, Kevin Johnson, Laura Rose. Operations Manager: Joe Eaglowski. Facilities Operations Manager: Joe Elking. Team Operations Manager: John Wallace. Head Groundskeeper: Dan Ochsner. Staff Accountant: Dorothy Day. Office Manager: Leslie Stuck.

## FIELD STAFF
Manager: Billy Gardner. Coach: Billy White. Pitching Coach: Larry Pierson. Trainer: Randy Brackney.

## GAME INFORMATION

**Radio Announcer:** Mike Vander Wood. **No. of Games Broadcast:** Home-70, Away-70. **Flagship Station:** WING 1410-AM.

**PA Announcer:** Unavailable. **Official Scorers:** Matt Lindsay, Jim Scott.

**Stadium Name:** Fifth Third Field. **Location:** I-75 South to downtown Dayton, left at First Street; I-75 North, right at First Street exit. **Standard Game Times:** 7 p.m.; Sun. 2. **Ticket Price Range:** $7-12.75.

**Visiting Club Hotel:** Fairfield Inn—Dayton North, 6960 Miller Lane, Dayton, OH 45414. Telephone: (937) 898-1120.

# FORT WAYNE
## WIZARDS

**Office Address:** 1616 E. Coliseum Blvd., Fort Wayne, IN 46805.
**Telephone:** (260) 482-6400. **FAX:** (260) 471-4678.
**E-Mail Address:** info@fortwaynewizards.com. **Website:** www.fortwaynewizards.com.
**Affiliation (first year):** San Diego Padres (1999). **Years in League:** 1993-.

## OWNERSHIP, MANAGEMENT

**Operated by:** General Sports and Entertainment, LLC.
**Owner:** Andrew Appleby.
**General Manager:** Mike Nutter. **Assistant GM, Business Operations:** Brian Schackow. **Senior Assistant GM:** David Lorenz. **Director, Community/Media Relations:** Jared Parcell. **Director, Marketing/Graphic Design:** Michael Limmer. **Director, Ticket Operations:** Patrick Ventura. **Director, Group Sales:** Brad Shank. **Director, Broadcasting:** Mike Maahs. **Group Sales Representatives:** Mark Fosnaugh, Chad Fuerbacher. **Group Sales Representative/Coordinator, Reading Program:** Jeff Bierly. **Group Sales Representative:** Tony Desplaines. **Office Manager:** Cathy Tinney.

## FIELD STAFF

**Manager:** Randy Ready. **Coach:** Max Venable. **Pitching Coach:** Tom Bradley. **Trainer:** Unavailable.

## GAME INFORMATION

**Radio Announcers:** Kent Hormann, Mike Maahs. **No. of Games Broadcast:** Home-70, Away-70. **Flagship Station:** WKJG 1380-AM.

**PA Announcers:** Jared Parcell, Jim Shovlin. **Official Scorers:** Jeff Bierly, Mike Jewell, Mike Maahs.

**Stadium Name:** Memorial Stadium. **Location:** Exit 112A (Coldwater Road South) off I-69 to Coliseum Blvd., left to stadium. **Standard Game Times:** 7 p.m., (April-May, Sept.) 6; Sun. 2. **Ticket Price Range:** $6.50-9.

**Visiting Club Hotel:** Best Western Luxbury, 5501 Coventry Lane, Fort Wayne, IN 46804. Telephone: (260) 436-0242.

# KANE COUNTY
## COUGARS

**Office Address:** 34W002 Cherry Lane, Geneva, IL 60134.
**Telephone:** (630) 232-8811. **FAX:** (630) 232-8815.
**E-Mail Address:** info@kccougars.com. **Website:** www.kccougars.com.
**Affiliation (first year):** Oakland Athletics (2003). **Years in League:** 1991-.

## OWNERSHIP, MANAGEMENT

**Operated by:** Cougars Baseball Partnership/American Sports Enterprises, Inc.
**President:** Mike Woleben. **Vice President:** Mike Murtaugh.
**VP/General Manager:** Jeff Sedivy. **Assistant GMs:** Curtis Haug, Jeff Ney. **Business Manager:** Mary Almlie. **Comptroller:** Doug Czurylo. **Concessions Controller:** Chris McGorry. **Director, Ticket Operations:** Amy Mason. **Account Executives:** David Edison, Steve McNelley, Michael Pieper, Patti Savage. **General Manager, K.C. Concessions:** Rich Essegian. **Director, Catering:** Mike Klafehn. **Catering Manager:** Mandy Murray. **Personnel Manager:** Megan Meyer. **Concessions Supervisor:** Bill Gentzler. **Warehouse Manager:** Alec Libby. **Graphic Designers:** Emmet Broderick, Todd Koenitz. **Manager, Advertising:** Bill Baker. **Community Relations Manager:** Amy Wilkinson. **Merchandise Manager:** Katie Doyle. **Facilities Management:** Jeff Snyder. **Director, Security:** Dan Klinkhamer.

## FIELD STAFF

**Manager:** Aaron Nieckula. **Coach:** Tim Garland. **Pitching Coach:** Garvin Alston. **Trainer:** Justin Whitehouse.

## GAME INFORMATION

**Radio Announcer:** Jeff Hem. **No. of Games Broadcast:** Home-70, Away-70. **Flagship Station:** WBIG 1280-AM.
**PA Announcer:** Kevin Sullivan. **Official Scorer:** Bill Baker.

**Stadium Name:** Philip B. Elfstrom Stadium. **Location:** From east or west, I-88 (East-West Tollway) to Farnsworth Avenue North exit, north five miles to Cherry Lane, left into stadium complex; from north, Route 59 south to Route 64 (North Ave.), west to Kirk Road, south past Route 38 to Cherry Lane, right into stadium complex; from northwest, I-90 to Randall Road South exit, south to Fabyan Parkway, east to Kirk Road, north to Cherry Lane, left into stadium complex. **Standard Game Times:** 6:30 p.m., (April-May 25) 6; Sat. 6, (April-May 6) 4; Sun. 2. **Ticket Price Range:** $8-10.

**Visiting Club Hotel:** Best Western Naperville Inn, 1617 Naperville Rd., Naperville, IL 60563. Telephone: (630) 505-0200.

# LANSING
## LUGNUTS

**Office Address:** 505 E. Michigan Ave., Lansing, MI 48912.
**Telephone:** (517) 485-4500. **FAX:** (517) 485-4518.
**E-Mail Address:** info@lansinglugnuts.com. **Website:** www.lansinglugnuts.com.
**Affiliation (first year):** Toronto Blue Jays (2005). **Years In League:** 1996-.

### OWNERSHIP, MANAGEMENT
**Operated by:** Take Me Out to the Ballgame, LLC.
**Principal Owners:** Tom Dickson, Sherrie Myers.
**General Manager:** Jeff Calhoun. **Director, Food Service:** Dave Parker. **Director, Sponsorship/Marketing:** Valerie Claus. **Director, Box Office/Retail:** Jeffrey Jaworski. **Assistant Manager, Ticket/Retail Operations:** Rachel McNeilly. **Director, Sales:** Nick Grueser. **Director, Operations:** Javier Arroyo. **Director, Broadcasting/Marketing Assistant:** Brad Tillery. **Marketing Assistant:** Justin Furr. **Head Groundskeeper:** Matt Anderson. **Group Sales Representatives:** Brian Keel, Matt LaMaster. **Corporate Account Executives:** Nick Brzenzinski, Jim LaPorte. **Sponsorship Service Representative:** Kelly Love. **Front Desk Administrator:** Sharon Jackson. **Sales Assistant:** Kevin Novack.

### FIELD STAFF
**Manager:** Ken Joyce. **Coach:** Charles Poe. **Pitching Coach:** Tom Signore. **Trainer:** Chris Vernon.

### GAME INFORMATION
**Radio Announcer:** Brad Tillery. **No. of Games Broadcast:** Home-70, Away-70. **Flagship Station:** The Ticket 92.1-FM. **PA Announcer:** J.J. Wright. **Official Scorer:** Mike Clark.
**Stadium Name:** Oldsmobile Park. **Location:** I-96 East/West to U.S. 496, exit at Larch Street, north of Larch, stadium on left. **Standard Game Times:** 7:05 p.m., (April-May) 6:05; Sun. 2:05. **Ticket Price Range:** $6.50-8.
**Visiting Club Hotel:** Holiday Inn South, 6820 South Cedar, Lansing, MI 48911. Telephone: (517) 694-8123.

# PEORIA
## CHIEFS

**Office Address:** 730 SW Jefferson, Peoria, IL 61602.
**Telephone:** (309) 680-4000. **FAX:** (309) 680-4080.
**Website:** www.peoriachiefs.com.
**Affiliation (first year):** Chicago Cubs (2005). **Years in League:** 1983-.

### OWNERSHIP, MANAGEMENT
**Operated by:** Peoria Chiefs Community Baseball Club, LLC.
**President:** Rocky Vonachen.
**General Manager:** Ralph Converse. **Director, Guest Services/Account Executive:** Howard Yates. **Manager, Box Office:** Ryan Sivori. **Manager, Broadcast/Media:** Nathan Baliva. **Manager, Events/Entertainment:** Piper Mead. **Director, Marketing:** Chip Dale. **Account Executives:** Holly Fisher, Joel Merill, Eric Obalil. **Head Groundskeeper:** Bryce Zeller.

### FIELD STAFF
**Manager:** Jody Davis. **Coach:** Barbaro Garbey. **Pitching Coach:** Rich Bombard. **Trainer:** Nick Frangella.

### GAME INFORMATION
**Radio Announcer:** Nathan Baliva. **No. of Games Broadcast:** Home-70, Away-70. **Flagship Station:** WOAM 1350-AM. **PA Announcer:** Unavailable. **Official Scorer:** Brandon Thome.
**Stadium Name:** O'Brien Field. **Location:** From South/East, I-74 to exit 93 (Jefferson Street), continue one mile, stadium is one block on left. From North/West, I-74 to exit 91 (Glendale Avenue), straight through stoplight and merge left on Glendale/Kumpf Boulevard, follow for five blocks and turn right on Jefferson Street, stadium on left. **Standard Game Times:** 7 p.m., 6:30 (April-May); Sat., 6; Sun. 2. **Ticket Price Range:** $6-10.
**Visiting Club Hotel:** Super 8—East Peoria, 725 Taylor, East Peoria, IL 61611. Telephone: (309) 698-8889.

# SWING OF THE
## QUAD CITIES

**Office Address:** 209 S. Gaines St., Davenport, IA 52802.
**Mailing Address:** P.O. Box 3496, Davenport, IA 52808.
**Telephone:** (563) 324-3000. **FAX:** (563) 324-3109.
**E-Mail Address:** jazzed@swingbaseball.com. **Website:** www.swingbaseball.com.
**Affiliation (first year):** St. Louis Cardinals (2005). **Years in League:** 1960-.

## OWNERSHIP, MANAGEMENT

**Operated by:** Seventh Inning Stretch, LC.
**President/General Manager:** Kevin Krause. **Vice President, Sales/Marketing:** Michael Weindruch. **Director, Promotions:** Greg Sprott. **Director, Food/Beverage:** James Johnson. **Premium Services Manager:** Brad Hurt. **Director, Broadcasting/Media Relations:** Ben Chiswick. **Office Manager/Merchandise Manager:** Lyndsey Yungen. **Director, Stadium Operations:** Bull Bubon. **Ticket Manager:** Tim Steege. **Group Sales Manager:** Megan Freer. **Finance Manager:** Greg Alcala.

## FIELD STAFF

**Manager:** Keith Mitchell. **Coach:** Randy Whisler. **Pitching Coach:** Bryan Eversgerd. **Trainer:** Brian Puchalski.

## GAME INFORMATION

**Radio Announcer:** Ben Chiswick. **No. of Games Broadcast:** Home-70, Away-70. **Flagship Station:** Unavailable. **PA Announcer:** Unavailable. **Official Scorer:** Unavailable.
**Stadium Name:** John O'Donnell Stadium. **Location:** From I-74, take Grant Street exit left, west onto River Drive, left on South Gaines Street; from I-80, take Brady Street exit south, right on River Drive, left on South Gaines Street. **Standard Game Times:** 7 p.m., (April) 6:30; Sun. 2. **Ticket Prices:** $6-12.
**Visiting Club Hotel:** Clarion Hotel, 5202 Brady St., Davenport, IA 52806. Telephone: (563) 391-1230

# SOUTH BEND
## SILVER HAWKS

**Office Address:** 501 W. South St., South Bend, IN 46601.
**Mailing Address:** P.O. Box 4218, South Bend, IN 46634.
**Telephone:** (574) 235-9988. **FAX:** (574) 235-9950. **E-Mail Address:** hawks@silverhawks.com. **Website:** www.silverhawks.com.
**Affiliation (first year):** Arizona Diamondbacks (1997). **Years in League:** 1988-.

## OWNERSHIP, MANAGEMENT

**Operated by:** Palisades Baseball, Ltd.
**Principal Owner:** Alan Levin. **Executive Vice President:** Erik Haag. **Director, Finance:** Cheryl Case.
**Assistant General Manager:** Tim Arseneau. **Director, Sales/Marketing:** Tony Wittrock. **Manager, Marketing:** Jeff Scholfield. **Manager, Box Office:** Kirk Lenderlic. **Director, Stadium Operations:** Mike Cook. **Manager, Stadium Operations:** Billy Peterman. **Director, Concessions:** Dennis Watson. **Account Executives:** Jon Lies, Billy Richards, Ian Zelenski. **Office Manager:** Kelly Devon. **Director, Media Relations:** Mike Lockert. **Head Groundskeeper:** Joel Reinebold.

## FIELD STAFF

**Manager:** Mark Haley. **Coach:** Todd Dunwoody. **Pitching Coach:** Wellington Cepeda. **Trainer:** Scott Jones.

## GAME INFORMATION

**Radio Announcer:** Mike Lockert. **No. of Games Broadcast:** Unavailable. **Flagship Station:** Unavailable. **PA Announcer:** Unavailable. **Official Scorer:** Unavailable.
**Stadium Name:** Stanley Coveleski Regional Stadium. **Location:** I-80/90 toll road to exit 77, take US 31/33 south to South Bend, to downtown (Main Street), to Western Avenue, right on Western, left on Taylor. **Standard Game Times:** 7 p.m., (April-May) 6:30; Sun. 1:30. **Ticket Price Range:** $5-7.
**Visiting Club Hotel:** Quality Inn, 515 Dixie Way North, South Bend, IN 46637. Telephone: (574) 272-6600.

# SOUTHWEST MICHIGAN
## DEVIL RAYS

**Office Address:** 189 Bridge St., Battle Creek, MI 49017.
**Telephone:** (269) 660-2287. **FAX:** (269) 660-2288.
**E-Mail Address:** info@southwestmichigandevilrays.com. **Website:** www.southwestmichigandevilrays.com.
**Affiliation:** Tampa Bay Devil Rays (2005). **Years in League:** 1995-.

## OWNERSHIP, MANAGEMENT

**Operated by:** Ivy Walls Management Company, LLC.
**President:** William Shea. **Chief Operating Officer:** Alan Stein. **General Manager:** Martie Cordaro. **Business Manager:** Brian Cheever. **Director, Group Sales:** Luke Kuboushek. **Corporate Sales Representative:** Rob Crain. **Group Sales Representative:** Greg Kruger. **Director, Stadium Operations:** Robin Santiago. **Head Groundskeeper:** Steve Kaylor.

## FIELD STAFF

**Manager:** Dave Howard. **Coach:** Skeeter Barnes. **Pitching Coach:** R.C. Lichtenstein. **Trainer:** Chris Russell.

## GAME INFORMATION

**Radio Announcer:** Unavailable. **No of Games Broadcast:** Home-70, Away-70. **Flagship Stations:** WBCK 930-AM, WRCC 1400-AM.
**PA Announcer:** Greg Morris. **Official Scorer:** Unavailable.

Stadium Name: C.O. Brown Stadium. Location: I-94 to exit 98B (downtown), to Capital Avenue and continue three miles to stadium. Standard Game Times: 7:05 p.m., (April-May) 6:35; Sunday 3:35. Ticket Price Range: $4-8. Visiting Club Hotel: Comfort Inn, 2590 Capital Ave. SW, Battle Creek, MI 49017. Telephone: (269) 965-3201

# WEST MICHIGAN
## WHITECAPS

Office Address: 4500 W. River Dr., Comstock Park, MI 49321.
Mailing Address: P.O. Box 428, Comstock Park, MI 49321.
Telephone: (616) 784-4131. FAX: (616) 784-4911.
E-Mail Address: playball@whitecaps-baseball.com. Website: www.whitecapsbaseball.com.
Affiliation (first year): Detroit Tigers (1997). Years in League: 1994-.

## OWNERSHIP, MANAGEMENT
Operated by: Whitecaps Professional Baseball Corp.
Principal Owners: Denny Baxter, Lew Chamberlin.
Chief Executive Officer, Managing Partner: Lew Chamberlin. Chief Financial Officer: Denny Baxter. President: Scott Lane. Vice President, Whitecaps Professional Baseball: Jim Jarecki. VP, Sales: Steve McCarthy. Director, Outside Events: Matt Costello. Managers, Human Resources: Ellen Chamberlin, Tina Porcelli. Director, Food/Beverage: Matt Timon. Director, New Business Development: Dan McCrath. Manager, Marketing/Promotions: Mickey Graham. Director, Ticket Sales: Kerri Troyer. Manager, Website/Merchandise: Lori Ashcroft. Manager, Public Relations: Jamie Farber. Coordinator, Media Relations: Brian Oropallo. Manager, Ticket Operations: Steve Klein. Head Groundskeeper: Terra Penninga. Manager, Facility Maintenance: John Passarelli. Corporate Sales: Eckelkamp, Dave Skoczen, Trevor Tkach. Sales Assistant: Katie Kroft. Manager, Group Sales Operations: Chad Sayen. Ticket Sales Consultants: Meghan Brennan, Dan Glowinski, Alanna Kuhn, Michael Kujawa, Alan Snodgrass, Drew Willard, Craig Yust. Assistant, Accounts Receivable: Barb Renteria. Assistant, Food/Beverage: Bill Moore. Administrative Assistant: Susie Former. Receptionist: Kim Banfill. Information Technology Coordinator: Scott Lutz.

## FIELD STAFF
Manager: Matt Walbeck. Coach: Tony Jaramillo. Pitching Coach: A.J. Sager. Trainer: Jay Pierson.

## GAME INFORMATION
Radio Announcer: Dave Skoczen. No. of Games Broadcast: Home-70, Away-70. Flagship Station: WBBL 1340-AM.
PA Announcers: Mike Newell, Bob Wells. Official Scorers: Mike Dean, Don Thomas.
Stadium Name: Fifth Third Ballpark. Location: U.S. 131 North from Grand Rapids to exit 91 (West River Drive). Standard Game Times: 7 p.m., (April-May) 6:35; Sat. (April-May) 2; Sun. 2. Ticket Price Range: $5-10.
Visiting Club Hotel: Days Inn-Downtown, 310 Pearl St. NW, Grand Rapids, MI 49504. Telephone: (616) 235-7611.

# WISCONSIN
## TIMBER RATTLERS

Office Address: 2400 N. Casaloma Dr., Appleton, WI 54913.
Mailing Address: P.O. Box 7464, Appleton, WI 54912.
Telephone: (920) 733-4152. FAX: (920) 733-8032.
E-Mail Address: info@timberrattlers.com. Website: www.timberrattlers.com.
Affiliation (first year): Seattle Mariners (1993). Years in League: 1962-.

## OWNERSHIP, MANAGEMENT
Operated by: Appleton Baseball Club, Inc.
Chairman: Steve Engmann.
President, General Manager: Rob Zerjav. Director, Operations: Tom Kulczewski. Controller: Cathy Spanbauer. Director, Community/Media Relations: Nikki Clipperton. Director, Promotions/Graphic Design: Angie Ceranski. Manager, Merchandise/Internet Specialist: Amanda Pickett. Director, Ticket Sales: Scott Moudry. Managers, Group Sales: Lindsay Kray, Lisa Nortman, Tiffany Timmerman. Director, Sales: Laurie Schill. Managers, Corporate Sales: Nicole Edge, Chris Mehring. Office Manager: Mary Robinson. Head Groundskeeper: Matt Gerhardt. Director of Food/Beverage: Ryan Grossman.

## FIELD STAFF
Manager: Scott Steinmann. Coach: Tommy Cruz. Pitching Coach: Lance Painter. Trainer: Jeremy Clipperton.

## GAME INFORMATION
Radio Announcer: Chris Mehring. No. of Games Broadcast: Home-70, Away-70. Flagship Station: WJMQ 92.3-FM.
PA Announcer: Joe Dotterweich. Official Scorer: Jay Grusznski.
Stadium Name: Fox Cities Stadium. Location: Highway 41 to Highway 15 (OO) exit, west to Casaloma Drive, left to stadium. Standard Game Times: 7:05 p.m., (April-May) 6:35; Sun. 1:05. Ticket Price Range: $5-8.50.
Visiting Club Hotel: Microtel Inn & Suites, 321 Metro Dr., Appleton, WI 54913. Telephone: (920) 997-3121.

# SOUTH ATLANTIC
## LEAGUE

### CLASS A

**Office Address:** 504 Crescent Hill, Kings Mountain, NC 28086.
**Mailing Address:** P.O. Box 38, Kings Mountain, NC 28086.
**Telephone:** (704) 739-3466. **FAX:** (704) 739-1974.
**E-Mail Address:** saleague@bellsouth.net. **Website:** www.southatlanticleague.com.
**Years League Active:** 1904-1964, 1979-.

**President/Secretary-Treasurer:** John Moss.
**Vice President:** Chip Moore (Rome). VP: John Simmons (Savannah).
**Directors:** Don Beaver (Hickory), Cooper Brantley (Greensboro), Greg Brown (Greenville), Peter Carfagna (Lake County), Joseph Finley (Lakewood), Marvin Goldklang (Charleston), David Heller (Columbus), Sean Henry (Asheville), Alan Levin (West Virginia), Frank Miceli (Delmarva), Chip Moore (Rome), Rich Neumann (Hagerstown), Michael Savit (Augusta), John Simmons (Savannah), Brad Smith (Kannapolis), Alan Stein (Lexington).
**Administrative Assistant:** Unavailable.
**Division Structure: North**—Delmarva, Greensboro, Hagerstown, Hickory, Lake County, Lakewood, Lexington, West Virginia. **South**—Asheville, Augusta, Charleston, Columbus, Greenville, Kannapolis, Rome, Savannah.
**Regular Season:** 140 games (split-schedule). **2006 Opening Date:** April 6. **Closing Date:** Sept. 4.

John Moss

**All-Star Game:** June 20 at Lake County.
**Playoff Format:** First-half and second-half division champions meet in best-of-3 semifinal series. Winners meet in best-of-5 series for league championship.
**Roster Limit:** 25 active. **Player Eligibility Rule:** No age limit. No more than two players and one player-coach on active list may have more than five years of experience.
**Brand of Baseball:** Rawlings.
**Statistician:** Major League Baseball Advanced Media, 75 Ninth Ave., New York, NY 10011.
**Umpires:** Unavailable.

### STADIUM INFORMATION

| Club | Stadium | Opened | LF | CF | RF | Capacity | 2005 Att. |
|------|---------|--------|-----|-----|-----|----------|-----------|
| Asheville | McCormick Field | 1992 | 328 | 402 | 300 | 4,000 | 155,129 |
| Augusta | Lake Olmstead Stadium | 1995 | 330 | 400 | 330 | 4,322 | 123,545 |
| Charleston | Joseph P. Riley Ballpark | 1997 | 306 | 386 | 336 | 5,800 | 249,374 |
| Columbus | Golden Park | 1951 | 330 | 415 | 330 | 5,000 | 62,547 |
| Delmarva | Arthur W. Perdue Stadium | 1996 | 309 | 402 | 309 | 5,200 | 219,361 |
| Greensboro | First Horizon Park | 2005 | 315 | 400 | 312 | 8,000 | 407,711 |
| Greenville | Greenville Drive Stadium | 2006 | 310 | 400 | 302 | 5,000 | 115,161 |
| Hagerstown | Municipal Stadium | 1931 | 335 | 400 | 330 | 4,600 | 153,675 |
| Hickory | L.P. Frans Stadium | 1993 | 330 | 401 | 330 | 5,062 | 163,863 |
| Kannapolis | Fieldcrest Cannon Stadium | 1995 | 330 | 400 | 310 | 4,700 | 104,781 |
| Lake County | Classic Park | 2003 | 320 | 400 | 320 | 7,273 | 394,208 |
| Lakewood | FirstEnergy Park | 2001 | 325 | 400 | 325 | 6,588 | 444,607 |
| Lexington | Applebee's Park | 2001 | 320 | 401 | 318 | 6,033 | 388,710 |
| Rome | State Mutual Stadium | 2003 | 335 | 400 | 330 | 5,100 | 232,187 |
| Savannah | Grayson Stadium | 1941 | 290 | 410 | 310 | 8,000 | 72,435 |
| West Virginia | Appalachian Power Park | 2005 | 330 | 400 | 320 | 4,300 | 233,143 |

# ASHEVILLE
## TOURISTS

**Office Address:** McCormick Field, 30 Buchanan Pl., Asheville, NC 28801.
**Telephone:** (828) 258-0428. **FAX:** (828) 258-0320.
**E-Mail Address:** info@theashevilletourists.com. **Website:** www.theasheville
tourists.com.
**Affiliation (first year):** Colorado Rockies (1994). **Years in League:** 1976-.

### OWNERSHIP, MANAGEMENT
**Operated by:** Palace Baseball.
**Principal Owners:** Palace Sports & Entertainment.
**Executive Director:** Mike Bauer.
**General Manager:** Larry Hawkins. **Assistant GM:** Chris Smith. **Director, Media Relations:** Bill Ballew. **Director, Tickets/Merchandise:** David King. **Head Groundskeeper:** Patrick Schrimplin. **Concessions Operator:** Center Plate. **Office Manager:** Rhett Blewett. **Manager, Corporate Sales:** Rawley Fox. **Director, Corporate Sales:** Matt Friedman.

### FIELD STAFF
**Manager:** Joe Mikulik. **Coach:** Dave Hajek. **Pitching Coach:** Richard Palacios. **Trainer:** Chris Dovey.

### GAME INFORMATION
**Radio:** None.
**PA Announcer:** Rick Diggler. **Official Scorer:** Mike Gore.
**Stadium Name:** McCormick Field. **Location:** I-240 to Charlotte Street South exit, south one mile on Charlotte, left on McCormick Place. **Standard Game Times:** 7:05 p.m., Sun. 2:05. **Ticket Price Range:** $6-10.
**Visiting Club Hotel:** Unavailable.

# AUGUSTA
## GREENJACKETS

**Office Address:** 78 Milledge Rd., Augusta, GA 30904.
**Mailing Address:** P.O. Box 3746, Augusta, GA 30904.
**Telephone:** (706) 736-7889. **FAX:** (706) 736-1122.
**E-Mail Address:** info@greenjacketsbaseball.com. **Website:** www.greenjacketsbaseball.com.
**Affiliation (first year):** San Francisco Giants (2005). **Years in League:** 1988-.

### OWNERSHIP, MANAGEMENT
**Operated by:** Ripken Baseball, LLC.
**President, Chief Executive Officer:** Cal Ripken Jr. **Co-Owner/Executive Vice President:** Bill Ripken. **VP:** Jeff Eiseman. **General Manager:** Nick Brown. **Director, Stadium Operations:** David Ryther. **Senior Director, Ticket Sales:** Tom D'Abruzzo. **Groundskeeper:** Andrew Wright.

### FIELD STAFF
**Manager:** Roberto Kelly. **Coach:** Andy Skeels. **Pitching Coach:** Ross Grimsley. **Trainer:** Oba Yukiya.

### GAME INFORMATION
**Radio:** None.
**PA Announcer:** Scott Skadan. **Official Scorer:** Unavailable.
**Stadium Name:** Lake Olmstead Stadium. **Location:** I-20 to exit 199 (Washington Road), east to Broad Street, left onto Milledge Road, stadium on right. **Standard Game Times:** 7:05 p.m., Sun. 5:35. **Ticket Price Range:** $6-10.
**Visiting Club Hotel:** Fairfield Inn by Marriott, 201 Boy Scout Rd., Augusta, GA 30909. Telephone: (706) 733-8200.

# CHARLESTON
## RIVERDOGS

**RIVERDOGS**

**Office Address:** 360 Fishburne St., Charleston, SC 29403.
**Mailing Address:** P.O. Box 20849, Charleston, SC 29413.
**Telephone:** (843) 723-7241. **FAX:** (843) 723-2641.
**E-Mail Address:** dogsrus@riverdogs.com. **Website:** www.riverdogs.com.
**Affiliation (first year):** New York Yankees (2005). **Years in League:** 1973-78, 1980-.

### OWNERSHIP, MANAGEMENT
**Operated by:** The Goldklang Group/South Carolina Baseball Club, LP.
**Principal Owners:** Marv Goldklang, Mike Veeck, Bill Murray.

General Manager: Dave Echols. **Assistant GM:** Andy Lange. **Director, Stadium Operations:** Ben Danosky. **Director, Promotions:** Jim Pfander. **Coordinators, Media Relations:** Noel Blaha, Andy Solomon. **Business Manager:** Aubra Carlton. **Directors, Special Events:** Melissa McCants, Mimi Walker. **Director, Food/Beverage:** Tim Savona. **Director, Technology Services:** Courtney Smith. **Office Manager:** Kristal Lessington. **Director, Community Relations:** Danielle Swigart. **Coordinator, Sales:** Harold Craw. **Director, Merchandise:** Scott Riley. **Manager, Food/Beverage:** Unavailable. **Manager, Tickets:** Jake Terrell. **Manager, Sales:** Unavailable. **Head Groundskeeper:** Mike Geiger.

## FIELD STAFF
**Manager:** Bill Mosiello. **Coach:** Torre Tyson. **Pitching Coach:** Scott Aldred. **Trainer:** Tim Lentych.

## GAME INFORMATION
**Radio Announcer:** Josh Mauer. **No. of Games Broadcast:** Home-70, Away-70. **Flagship Station:** WTMZ 910-AM. **PA Announcer:** Ken Carrington. **Official Scorer:** Chuck Manka. **Stadium Name:** Joseph P. Riley Jr. Ballpark. **Location:** From U.S. 17, take Lockwood Drive North, right on Fishburne Street. **Standard Game Times:** 7:05 p.m., Sun. 2:05. **Ticket Price Range:** $4-8.
**Visiting Club Hotel:** Howard Johnson Riverfront, 250 Spring St., Charleston, SC 29403. Telephone: (843) 722-4000.

# COLUMBUS
## CATFISH

**Office Address:** Golden Park, 100 Fourth St., Columbus, GA 31901.
**Telephone:** (706) 571-8866. **FAX:** (706) 571-9984.
**E-Mail Address:** info@columbuscatfish.com. **Website:** www.columbuscatfish.com.
**Affiliation (first year):** Los Angeles Dodgers (2002). **Years in League:** 1991-.

## OWNERSHIP, MANAGEMENT
**Operated by:** Main Street Baseball, LLC.
**Owner:** David Heller.
**General Manager:** Ken Clary. **Director, Ticketing/Merchandise:** Samantha Dunn. **Manager, Public Relations:** Jere Sisler. **Director, Stadium Operations:** Brad Hudson. **Head Groundskeeper:** Brock Van Faussien.

## FIELD STAFF
**Manager:** Travis Barbary. **Coach:** Garey Ingram. **Pitching Coach:** Richie Lewis. **Trainer:** Jason Roberts.

## GAME INFORMATION
**Radio:** None.
**Stadium Name:** Golden Park. **Location:** I-85 South to exit 7 (Manchester Expressway), right on Manchester Expressway for one mile, left on Veterans Parkway into South Commons complex. **Standard Game Times:** 7 p.m.; Sun. 2/6. **Ticket Price Range:** $4-7.
**Visiting Club Hotel:** Unavailable.

# DELMARVA
## SHOREBIRDS

**Office Address:** 6400 Hobbs Rd., Salisbury, MD 21804.
**Mailing Address:** P.O. Box 1557, Salisbury, MD 21802.
**Telephone:** (410) 219-3112. **FAX:** (410) 219-9164.
**E-Mail Address:** information@theshorebirds.com. **Website:** www.theshorebirds.com.
**Affiliation (first year):** Baltimore Orioles (1997). **Years in League:** 1996-.

## OWNERSHIP, MANAGEMENT
**Operated by:** Comcast-Spectacor.
**Directors:** Peter Luukko, Frank Miceli.
**General Manager:** Stephen Yaros. **Director, Ticket Operations:** Kris Rutledge. **Director, Stadium Operations:** DeAndre Ewell. **Head Groundskeeper:** Dave Super. **Director, Corporate Sales:** Jimmy Sweet. **Sponsorship Sales Executive:** Tom Denlinger. **Director, Community Relations/Customer Service:** Norb Sadilek. **Director, Marketing/Communications:** Nicholas Mirabello. **Marketing Manager/Media Relations:** Brian Patey. **Marketing Manager/Mascot Coordinator:** Unavailable. **Senior Group Account Manager:** Randy Atkinson. **Group/Ticket Sales Executives:** Kristina Neas, Bill O'Brien. **Box Office Manager:** Alex West. **Accounting:** Gail Potts. **Office Manager:** Dana Holyfield.

## FIELD STAFF
**Manager:** Gary Kendall. **Coach:** Kimera Bartee. **Pitching Coach:** Kennie Steenstra. **Trainer:** Joe Benge. **Strength Coach:** Steve Meccia.

## GAME INFORMATION
**Radio Announcer:** Randy Scott. **No. of Games Broadcast:** Home-70, Away-70. **Flagship Station:** WTGM 960-AM.

**PA Announcer:** Jim Whittemore. **Official Scorer:** Unavailable.
**Stadium Name:** Arthur W. Perdue Stadium. **Location:** From U.S. 50 East, right on Hobbs Road; From U.S. 50 West, left on Hobbs Road. **Standard Game Times:** 6:35 p.m. (first half), 7:05 (second half); Sun. 1:35. **Ticket Price Range:** $4-12.
**Visiting Club Hotel:** Best Value Inn, 2625 N. Salisbury Blvd., Salisbury, MD 21801. Telephone: (410) 742-7194.

# GREENSBORO
## GRASSHOPPERS

**Office Address:** 408 Bellemeade St., Greensboro, NC 27401.
**Telephone:** (336) 268-2255. **FAX:** (336) 273-7350.
**E-Mail Address:** info@gsohoppers.com. **Website:** www.gsohoppers.com.
**Affiliation (first year):** Florida Marlins (2003). **Years in League:** 1979-.

## OWNERSHIP, MANAGEMENT
**Operated by:** Greensboro Baseball, LLC.
**Principal Owners:** Cooper Brantley, Wes Elingburg, Len White.
**President, General Manager:** Donald Moore. **Vice President, Baseball Operations:** Katie Dannemiller. **Chief Financial Officer:** Jimmy Kesler. **Assistant GM/Head Groundskeeper:** Jake Holloway. **Assistant GM/Sales, Marketing:** Tim Vangel. **Director, Marketing/Community Relations:** Kerry Riley. **Director, Creative Services/Media Relations:** Amanda Williams. **Director, Ticketing:** Kate Barnhill. **Director, Merchandise:** Ashley Stephens. **Director, Group Sales:** Todd Olson. **Associate Group Sales:** Ben Kramer. **Executive Assistant:** Rosalee Brewer. **Assistant Groundskeeper:** Ian DiGiorgio. **Assistant Director, Stadium Operations:** A.T. Simmons.

## FIELD STAFF
**Manager:** Brandon Hyde. **Coach:** Josue Espada. **Pitching Coach:** Steve Foster. **Trainer:** Ben Heimos.

## GAME INFORMATION
**Radio Announcer:** Andy Durham. **No. of Games Broadcast:** Home-70. **Flagship Station:** WPET 950-AM.
**PA Announcer:** Jim Scott. **Official Scorer:** Paul Wirth.
**Stadium Name:** First Horizon Park. **Location:** From I-85, take Highway 220 South (exit 36) to Coliseum Blvd.; continue on Edgeworth Street, ballpark at corner of Edgeworth and Bellemeade Streets. **Standard Game Times:** 7 p.m.; Sun. 5. **Ticket Price Range:** $6-9.
**Visiting Club Hotel:** Ramada Inn Conference Center/Coliseum, 2003 Athena Ct., Greensboro, NC 27407. Telephone: (336) 294-9922.

# GREENVILLE
## DRIVE

**Office Address:** 945 South Main St., Greenville, SC 29601.
**Mailing Address:** P.O. Box 726, Greenville, SC 29602.
**Telephone:** (864) 422-1510. **FAX:** (864) 422-1435.
**E-Mail Address:** info@greenvilledrive.com. **Website:** www.greenvilledrive.com.
**Affiliation (first year):** Boston Red Sox (2005). **Years in League:** 2005-.

## OWNERSHIP, MANAGEMENT
**Operated by:** RB3, LLC.
**President:** Craig Brown. **General Manager:** Mike deMaine. **Vice President, Sales/Marketing:** Nate Lipscomb. **Director, Media Relations:** Eric Jarinko. **Director, Group Sales:** Andy Paul. **Director, Merchandise:** Renee Allen. **Director, Community Relations:** Brenda Yoder.

## FIELD STAFF
**Manager:** Luis Alicea. **Coach:** Randy Phillips. **Pitching Coach:** Bob Kipper. **Trainer:** Paul Buchheit.

## GAME INFORMATION
**Radio:** None.
**PA Announcer:** Unavailable. **Official Scorer:** Unavailable.
**Stadium Name:** Greenville Drive Stadium. **Location:** I-85 to exit 42 towards downtown Greenville, stadium 4 miles on left. **Standard Game Times:** 7:05 p.m., Sun., 2:05. **Ticket Price Range:** $5-8.
**Visiting Club Hotel:** Unavailable.

# HAGERSTOWN
## SUNS

**HAGERSTOWN
SUNS**

**Office Address:** 274 E. Memorial Blvd., Hagerstown, MD 21740.
**Telephone:** (301) 791-6266. **FAX:** (301) 791-6066.
**E-Mail Address:** info@hagerstownsuns.com. **Website:** www.hagerstownsuns.com.
**Affiliation (second year):** New York Mets (2005). **Years in League:** 1993-.

### OWNERSHIP, MANAGEMENT

**Operated by:** Mandalay Baseball Properties.
**Principal Owners:** Peter Guber, Paul Schaeffer, Hank Stickney, Ken Stickney.
**General Manager:** Kurt Landes. **Assistant GM:** Will Smith. **Director, Business Operations:** Carol Gehr. **Director, Stadium Operations:** Mike Showe. **Senior Director, Marketing:** C.J. Johnson. **Director, Group Sales:** Drew Himsworth. **Director, Food/Beverage:** Dave Fera. **Director, Promotions/Special Events:** Joel Pagliaro. **Director, Ticket Sales:** Jason Bucur. **Manager, Media Relations:** Jason Gordon. **Manager, Merchandise:** Mark Witmer. **Interns:** Nik Buckler, Ashley Gossert, Casey Lynn. **Clubhouse Manager:** Pete Stasio.

### FIELD STAFF

**Manager:** Frank Cacciatore. **Coach:** Luis Natera. **Pitching Coach:** Shawn Barton. **Trainer:** Matt Hunter.

### GAME INFORMATION

**Radio Announcers:** Jason Gordon, Casey Lynn. **No. of Games Broadcast:** Home-70, Away-70. **Flagship Station:** WHAG 1410-AM.
**PA Announcer:** Unavailable. **Official Scorer:** Chris Spaid.
**Stadium Name:** Municipal Stadium. **Location:** Exit 32B (U.S. 40 West) on I-70 West, left at Eastern Boulevard; Exit 6A (U.S. 40 East) on I-81, right at Eastern Boulevard. **Standard Game Times:** 7:05 p.m., (April-May) 6:35; Sun. 1:35, (July-Sept.) 5:35. **Ticket Price Range:** $5-9.
**Visiting Club Hotel:** Clarion Hotel & Conference Center, 901 Dual Hwy., Hagerstown, MD 21740. Telephone: (301) 733-5100.

# HICKORY
## CRAWDADS

**Office Address:** 2500 Clement Blvd. NW, Hickory, NC 28601.
**Mailing address:** P.O. Box 1268, Hickory, NC 28603.
**Telephone:** (828) 322-3000. **FAX:** (828) 322-6137.
**E-Mail Address:** crawdad@hickorycrawdads.com. **Website:** www.hickorycrawdads.com.
**Affiliation (first year):** Pittsburgh Pirates (1999). **Years in League:** 1952,1960,1993-.

### OWNERSHIP, MANAGEMENT

**Operated by:** Hickory Baseball, Inc.
**Principal Owners:** Don Beaver, Luther Beaver, Charles Young.
**President:** Don Beaver. **General Manager:** David Haas. **Assistant GM:** Brad Dail. **Group Sales Representative:** Mark Parker. **Director, Merchandise:** Barbara Beatty. **Office Manager/Special Events:** Jennifer Long. **Director, Broadcasting/Media Relations:** Dave Friedman. **Director, Community Relations:** Charlie Downs. **Account Executives:** Jeremy Brown, Jaime Koester, Jon Whitby.

### FIELD STAFF

**Manager:** Jeff Branson. **Coach:** Greg Briley. **Pitching Coach:** David Lundquist. **Trainer:** Mike Zalno.

### GAME INFORMATION

**Radio Announcer:** David Friedman. **No of Games Broadcast:** Home-70, Away-70. **Flagship Station:** WMNC 92.1-FM.
**PA Announcer:** Rocky Brooks, JuJu Phillips. **Official Scorer:** Gary Olinger.
**Stadium Name:** L.P. Frans Stadium. **Location:** I-40 to exit 123 (Lenoir North), 321 North to Clement Blvd., left for 1/2 mile. **Standard Game Times:** 7 p.m.; Sun. 6, (April-May) 2.
**Visiting Hotel:** Unavailable.

# KANNAPOLIS
## INTIMIDATORS

**Office Address:** 2888 Moose Rd., Kannapolis, NC 28083.
**Mailing Address:** P.O. Box 64, Kannapolis, NC 28082.
**Telephone:** (704) 932-3267. **FAX:** (704) 938-7040.
**E-Mail Address:** info@intimidatorsbaseball.com. **Website:** www.intimidatorsbaseball.com.

Affiliation (first year): Chicago White Sox (2001). **Years in League:** 1995-.

## OWNERSHIP, MANAGEMENT
Operated by: Smith Family Baseball, Inc.

President: Brad Smith. **General Manager:** Tim Mueller. **Associate GM:** Randy Long. **Assistant GM/Director, Stadium Operations:** Jaime Pruitt. **Director, Tickets/Merchandise:** Tracy Snelbaker. **Director, Corporate/Group Sales:** Chad Thomas. **Community Relations/Group Sales Associate:** Mellissa Wood. **Intern:** Candice Lesperance.

## FIELD STAFF
Manager: Omer Munoz. **Coach:** Joe Hall. **Pitching Coach:** Sean Snedeker. **Trainer:** Tomas Vera.

## GAME INFORMATION
Radio: Internet Only. **No of Games Broadcast:** Home-70, Away-70.
PA Announcer: Shea Griffin. **Official Scorer:** Tom Reilly.
Stadium Name: Fieldcrest Cannon Stadium. **Location:** Exit 63 on I-85, west on Lane Street to Stadium Drive. **Standard Game Times:** 7:05 p.m., Sun. 5:05. **Ticket Price Range:** $4-7.
Visiting Club Hotel: Fairfield Inn by Marriott, 3033 Cloverleaf Pkwy., Kannapolis, NC 28083. Telephone: (704) 795-4888.

# LAKE COUNTY
## CAPTAINS

Office Address: 35300 Vine St., Eastlake, OH 44095.
Mailing Address: 35300 Vine St., Eastlake, OH 44095.
Telephone: (440) 975-8085. **FAX:** (440) 975-8958.
E-Mail Address: info@captainsbaseball.com. **Website:** www.captainsbaseball.com.
Affiliation (first year): Cleveland Indians (2003). **Years in League:** 2003-.

## OWNERSHIP, MANAGEMENT
Operated by: Cascia, LLC.

Chairman, Secretary-Treasurer: Peter Carfagna. **Vice Chairman:** Rita Murphy Carfagna. **Vice President:** Ray Murphy. **Senior Vice President:** Pete Carfagna.

General Manager: Kevin Brodzinski. **Assistant GM, Operations:** Paul Siegwarth. **Assistant GM, Sales/Marketing:** Gary Thomas. **Executive Assistant to Chairman:** Sherry Carbeck. **Group Sales Ticket Coordinator:** Luke Cowgill. **Senior Corporate Account Manager:** Craig Deas. **Controller:** Jen Doan. **Sports Turf Manager:** Greg Elliott. **Receptionist:** Catherine Fleischhauer. **Director, Stadium Operations:** Bob Graham. **Group Sales Ticket Coordinator:** Greg Harrell. **Senior Account Executive, Group Sales:** Jeff Hull. **Director, Client Services:** Julia LaManna. **Group Sales Account Executive:** Eric Nelson. **Director, Community Relations:** Matt Phillips. **Director, Promotions:** Brock Richards. **Director, Ticket Sales/Merchandise:** Morey Seiden. **Director, Concessions/Catering:** Jeremy Verdi. **Director, Broadcasting:** Dave Wilson. **Group Sales Account Executive:** Celena Zevnik.

## FIELD STAFF
Manager: Lee May Jr. **Coach:** Jack Mull. **Pitching Coach:** Ruben Niebla. **Trainer:** Chad Wolfe.

## GAME INFORMATION
Radio Announcers: Dave Wilson, Craig Deas. **No. of Games Broadcast:** Home-70, Away-70. **Flagship Station:** WELW 1330-AM.
PA Announcer: Ray Milavec. **Official Scorer:** Fred Heyer.
Stadium Name: Classic Park. **Location:** From Route 2 East, exit at Ohio 91, stadium is ¼ mile north. **Standard Game Times:** 7:05 p.m.; Sat. (April-May) 2:05; Sun. 2:05. **Ticket Price Range:** $5-9.
Visiting Club Hotel: Radisson Hotel-Eastlake, 35000 Curtis Blvd., Eastlake, OH 44095. Telephone: (440) 953-8000.

# LAKEWOOD
## BLUECLAWS

Office Address: 2 Stadium Way, Lakewood, NJ 08701.
Telephone: (732) 901-7000. **FAX:** (732) 901-3967.
E-Mail Address: info@blueclaws.com. **Website:** www.blueclaws.com.
Affiliation: Philadelphia Phillies (2001). **Years In League:** 2001-.

## OWNERSHIP, MANAGEMENT
Operated by: American Baseball Company, LLC.
President: Joseph Finley. **Partners:** Joseph Caruso, Joseph Plumeri, Craig Stein.

General Manager: Geoff Brown. **Assistant GM:** John Clark. **Vice President, Marketing:** Eric Lipsman. **Director, Operations:** Brandon Marano. **Manager, Operations:** Unavailable. **Director, Marketing:** Mike Ryan. **Director, Promotions:** Hal Hansen. **Director, Media/Public Relations:** Ben Wagner. **Director, Community Relations:** Jim DeAngelis. **Special Events Manager:** Keri Conway. **Director, Ticket Sales:** Jeremy Fishman. **Director, Business

**Development:** Mike Leonard. **Ticket Sales Managers:** Dan DeYoung, Dan Kurland. **Director, Group Sales:** Nelson Constantino. **Group Sales Managers:** Erin Coyne, Jim McNamara, Adam Sciorsci, Mike Van Hise. **Manager, Merchandise:** Dan Kish. **Chief Financial Officer:** Steve Ripa. **Front Office Manager:** Robin Hill. **Head Groundskeeper:** Ryan Radcliffe. **Assistant Groundskeeper/Clubhouse Manager:** Russ Schaefer. **Concessions General Manager:** Chris Tafrow. **Executive Chef:** Sandy Cohen. **Office Manager, Concessions:** Joanna DiBella.

## FIELD STAFF

**Manager:** Dave Huppert. **Coach:** Ken Dominguez. **Pitching Coach:** Steve Schrenk. **Trainer:** Chris Mudd.

## GAME INFORMATION

**Radio Announcers:** Ben Wagner, Rich Lidstrom. **No. of Games Broadcast:** Home-70, Away-70. **Flagship Station:** WADB 1310-AM.
**PA Announcer:** Kevin Clark. **Official Scorer:** Joe Ballina.
**Stadium Name:** FirstEnergy Park. **Location:** Route 70 to New Hampshire Ave., north on New Hampshire for 2½ miles to ballpark. **Standard Game Times:** 7:05 p.m.; Mon.-Thur. (April-May) 6:35, Sat. (April) 1:05; Sun 1:05, (July-Aug.) 5:05. **Ticket Prices:** $6-9.
**Visiting Team Hotel:** Comfort Inn, 2016 Hwy. 37 W., West Manchester, NJ 08759. Telephone: (732) 657-7100.

# LEXINGTON
## LEGENDS

**Office Address:** 207 Legends Lane, Lexington, KY 40505.
**Mailing Address:** P.O. Box 11458, Lexington, KY 40575.
**Telephone:** (859) 252-4487. **FAX:** (859) 252-0747.
**E-Mail Address:** webmaster@lexingtonlegends.com. **Website:** www.lexingtonlegends.com.
**Affiliation (first year):** Houston Astros (2001). **Years in League:** 2001-.

## OWNERSHIP, MANAGEMENT

**Operated by:** Lexington Professional Baseball Company.
**President/Chief Operating Officer:** Alan Stein. **General Manager:** Kevin Kulp. **Chief Administrative Officer:** Sandy Canon. **Executive Assistant:** Monica Johnson. **Vice President, Facilities:** Gary Durbin. **Director, Stadium Operations/Human Resource Manager:** Shannon Kidd. **Director, Human Resources:** Connie Tarver. **Media/Creative Services Manager:** Lyndsay Conkin. **Administrative Services Manager:** Micci Murrell. **Director, Ticket Operations:** Renee Kulp. **Ticket Sales Representatives:** Daniel Griffith, Andy Shea. **Director, Broadcasting/Media Relations:** Larry Glover. **Community Relations Manager:** Tiffany King. **Director, Special Events:** Rick Bryant. **Head Groundskeeper:** Erin Sherrill. **Director, Group Sales:** Eric Leach. **Group Sales Representatives:** Justin Ball, David Barry, Brad Link. **Business Manager:** Jeff Black. **Finance Assistant:** Bill Wells. **Senior Corporate Account Executive:** Ron Borkowski. **Corporate Account Representative:** Sarah Frazier, Seth Poteat. **Elite Service Manager:** Beth Goldenberg. **Facility Specialist:** Steve Moore. **Receptionist:** Beverly Howard.

## FIELD STAFF

**Manager:** Jack Lind. **Coach:** Rodney Linares. **Pitching Coach:** Charley Taylor. **Trainer:** Mike Smith.

## GAME INFORMATION

**Radio Announcer:** Larry Glover. **No. of Games Broadcast:** Home-70, Away-70. **Flagship Station:** WLXG 1300-AM.
**PA Announcer:** Brad Link. **Official Scorer:** Larry Glover.
**Stadium Name:** Applebee's Park. **Location:** From I-64/75, take exit 113, right onto North Broadway toward downtown Lexington for 1.2 miles, past New Circle Road (Highway 4), right into stadium, located adjacent to Northland Shopping Center. **Standard Game Times:** 7:05 p.m.; Mon.-Thur. (April-May) 6:35; Sun. (April-May) 2:05, (June-Aug.) 6:05. **Ticket Price Range:** $4-16.50.
**Visiting Club Hotel:** Ramada Inn and Conference Center, 2143 N. Broadway, Lexington, KY 40505. Telephone: (859) 299-1261.

# ROME
## BRAVES

**Office Address:** State Mutual Stadium, 755 Braves Blvd., Rome, GA 30161.
**Mailing Address:** P.O. Box 5515, Rome, GA 30162.
**Telephone:** (706) 368-9388. **FAX:** (706) 368-6525.
**E-Mail Address:** rome.braves@turner.com. **Website:** www.romebraves.com.
**Affiliation (first year):** Atlanta Braves (2003). **Years in League:** 2003-.

## OWNERSHIP, MANAGEMENT

**Operated by:** Time Warner/Atlanta National League Baseball Club, Inc.
**General Manager:** Michael Dunn. **Assistant GM:** Jim Jones. **Director, Stadium Operations:** Eric Allman. **Director, Ticket Sales:** Erin White. **Director, Food/Beverage:** Dave Atwood. **Manager, Community Relations:** Rachel Rogers. **Administrative Manager:** Kristie Hancock. **Account Representatives:** Dave Butler, John Layng. **Head Groundskeeper:**

Mike Hurd. **Receptionist:** Starla Roden. **Retail Manager:** Seline McKoy. **Operations Manager:** Terry Morgan.

### FIELD STAFF

**Manager:** Randy Ingle. **Coach:** Bobby Moore. **Pitching Coach:** Jim Czajkowski. **Trainer:** Greg Hall.

### GAME INFORMATION

**Radio Announcer:** Randy Davis. **No. of Games Broadcast:** Home-70, Away-70. **Flagship Stations:** WLAQ 1410-AM, WATG 95.7-FM.

**PA Announcer:** Eddie Brock. **Official Scorer:** Ron Taylor.

**Stadium Name:** State Mutual Stadium. **Location:** I-75 North to exit 290 (Rome/Canton), left off exit and follow Highway 411/Highway 20 to Rome, right at intersection of Highway 411 and Highway 1 (Veterans Memorial Highway), stadium is at intersection of Veterans Memorial Highway and Riverside Parkway. **Standard Game Times:** 7 p.m., Sun. 2. **Ticket Price Range:** $4-10.

**Visiting Club Hotel:** Days Inn, 840 Turner McCall Blvd., Rome, GA 30161. Telephone: (706) 295-0400.

# SAVANNAH
## SAND GNATS

**Office Address:** 1401 E. Victory Dr., Savannah, GA 31404.
**Mailing Address:** P.O. Box 3783, Savannah, GA 31414.
**Telephone:** (912) 351-9150. **FAX:** (912) 352-9722.
**Website:** www.sandgnats.com.
**Affiliation (first year):** Washington Nationals (2003). **Years in League:** 1962, 1984 -.

### OWNERSHIP, MANAGEMENT

**Operated by:** Rickshaw Baseball.
**Co-General Managers:** Bradley Dodson, Brian Sheaffer. **Assistant GM/Director, Marketing:** Matt Barry. **Director, Community Relations:** Laura Turek. **Director, Media Relations/Creative Services:** Scott Gierman. **Director, Ticket Operations:** Greg Vojtanek. **Account Executives:** Q Hudson, Mike Perkins. **Director, Client Services:** Katie Stocz. **Groundskeeper:** Chuck Cannon.

### FIELD STAFF

**Manager:** Bobby Williams. **Coach:** Jerry Browne. **Pitching Coach:** Unavailable. **Trainer:** Sean Wayne.

### GAME INFORMATION

**Radio:** Internet Only (www.sportsjuice.com). **Radio announcer:** Scott Gierman.
**PA Announcer:** Jeff McDermott. **Official Scorer:** Marcus Holland.
**Stadium Name:** Grayson Stadium. **Location:** I-16 to 37th Street exit, left on 37th, right on Abercorn Street, left on Victory Drive; From I-95 to exit 16, east on 204, right on Victory Drive, stadium is on right in Daffin Park. **Standard Game Times:** 7:05 p.m.; Mon.-Wed. (April-May) 6:35 p.m.; Sun. 2:05. **Ticket Price Range:** $6-9.50.
**Visiting Club Hotel:** Days Inn, 114 Mall Blvd., Savannah, GA 31406. Telephone: (912)-352-4455.

# WEST VIRGINIA
## POWER

**Office Address:** 601 Morris St., Charleston, WV 25301.
**Telephone:** (304) 344-2287. **FAX:** (304) 344-0083.
**E-Mail Address:** team@wvpower.com. **Website:** www.wvpower.com.
**Affiliation (first year):** Milwaukee Brewers (2005). **Years in League:** 1987-.

### OWNERSHIP, MANAGEMENT

**Operated by:** Palisades Baseball.
**Principal Owner:** Alan Levin.
**General Manager:** Andy Milovich. **Director, Business Development:** Ryan Gates. **Director, Marketing:** Chad Hodson. **Accountant:** Jeremy Young. **Client Services:** Brian Harrigan. **Director, Concessions:** Ryan Montgomery. **Assistant Director, Concessions:** Jeremy Crookshanks. **Director, Broadcast/Media Relations:** Andy Barch. **Director, Stadium Operations:** Joe Payne. **Senior Sales Executive:** Marty Nash. **Groundskeeper:** Eric Bailey. **Box Office Manager:** Rebekah Hays. **Ticket Sales Executives:** Jon Jones, Jeremy Taylor, Matt Thompson.

### FIELD STAFF

**Manager:** Mike Guerrero. **Coach:** Mike Lum. **Pitching Coach:** John Curtis. **Trainer:** Alan Diamond.

### GAME INFORMATION

**Radio Announcer:** Andy Barch. **No. of Games Broadcast:** Home-70, Away-70. **Flagship Station:** WSWW 1490-AM.
**PA Announcer:** Donald Cook. **Official Scorer:** Lee France.
**Stadium Name:** Appalachian Power Park. **Location:** I-77 South to Capitol Street exit, left on Lee Street, left on Brooks Street. **Standard Game Times:** 7:05 p.m., Sun. 2:05. **Ticket Price Range:** $5-7.
**Visiting Club Hotel:** Ramada Plaza Hotel, 2nd Avenue and B Street, South Charleston, WV 25303. Telephone: (304) 744-4641.

# NEW YORK-PENN
## LEAGUE

**Mailing Address:** One Progress Plaza, 200 Central Ave., Suite 2300, St. Petersburg, FL 33701.
**Telephone:** (727) 576-6300. **FAX:** (727) 822-3768.
**Website:** www.nypennleague.com.

**Years League Active:** 1939-.
**President:** Ben Hayes.
**Presidents Emeritus:** Leo Pinckney, Bob Julian.
**Vice President:** Sam Nader (Oneonta). **Treasurer:** Jon Dandes (Jamestown). **Corporate Secretary:** Tony Torre (New Jersey).
**Directors:** Tim Bawmann (Lowell), David Burke (Hudson Valley), Steve Cohen (Brooklyn), Jon Dandes (Jamestown), Jeff Eiseman (Aberdeen), Josh Getzler (Staten Island), Bill Gladstone (Tri-City), Chuck Greenberg (State College), Alan Levin (Mahoning Valley), Paul Marriott (Batavia), Sam Nader (Oneonta), Ray Pecor (Vermont), Leo Pinckney (Auburn), Paul Velte (Williamsport).
**League Administrator:** Debbie Carlisle. **League Historian:** Charles Wride.
**Division Structure: McNamara**—Aberdeen, Brooklyn, Hudson Valley, New Jersey, Staten Island, Williamsport. **Pinckney**—Auburn, Batavia, Jamestown, Mahoning Valley. **Stedler**—Lowell, Oneonta, Tri-City, Vermont.

**Ben Hayes**

**Regular Season:** 76 games. **2006 Opening Date:** June 20. **Closing Date:** Sept. 7.
**All-Star Game:** Aug. 16 at Aberdeen. **Hall of Fame Game:** Tri-City vs. Oneonta, July 29 at Cooperstown, NY.
**Playoff Format:** Division champions and wild-card team meet in best-of-3 semi-finals. Winners meet in best-of-3 series for league championship.
**Roster Limit:** 30 active, but only 25 may be in uniform and eligible to play in any given game. **Player Eligibility Rule:** No more than four players 23 or older; no more than three players on active list may have four or more years of prior service.
**Brand of Baseball:** Rawlings.
**Statistician:** Major League Baseball Advanced Media, 75 Ninth Ave., New York, NY 10011.
**Umpires:** Unavailable.

## STADIUM INFORMATION

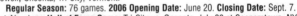

| Club | Stadium | Opened | LF | CF | RF | Capacity | 2005 Att. |
|------|---------|--------|----|----|----|----------|-----------|
| Aberdeen | Ripken Stadium | 2002 | 310 | 400 | 310 | 6,000 | 239,748 |
| Auburn | Falcon Park | 1995 | 330 | 400 | 330 | 2,800 | 69,716 |
| Batavia | Dwyer Stadium | 1996 | 325 | 400 | 325 | 2,600 | 40,557 |
| Brooklyn | KeySpan Park | 2001 | 315 | 412 | 325 | 7,500 | 285,818 |
| Hudson Valley | Dutchess Stadium | 1994 | 325 | 400 | 325 | 4,494 | 158,423 |
| Jamestown | Russell E. Diethrick Jr. Park | 1941 | 335 | 410 | 353 | 3,324 | 50,460 |
| Lowell | Edward LeLacheur Park | 1998 | 337 | 400 | 302 | 5,000 | 185,000 |
| Mahoning Valley | Eastwood Field | 1999 | 335 | 405 | 335 | 6,000 | 153,879 |
| Oneonta | Damaschke Field | 1906 | 350 | 406 | 350 | 4,200 | 45,349 |
| *State College | Medler Field at Lubrano Park | 2006 | 328 | 403 | 322 | 5,412 | 115,129 |
| Staten Island | Richmond County Bank Ballpark | 2001 | 325 | 400 | 325 | 6,500 | 155,541 |
| Tri-City | Joseph L. Bruno Stadium | 2002 | 325 | 400 | 325 | 5,000 | 116,674 |
| Vermont | Centennial Field | 1922 | 330 | 405 | 323 | 4,400 | 106,407 |
| Williamsport | Bowman Field | 1923 | 345 | 405 | 350 | 4,200 | 79,253 |

*Club operated in New Jersey in 2005.

# ABERDEEN
## IRONBIRDS

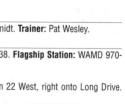

Office Address: 873 Long Dr., Aberdeen, MD 21001.
Telephone: (410) 297-9292. FAX: (410) 297-6653.
E-Mail Address: info@ironbirdsbaseball.com. Website: www.ironbirdsbaseball.com.
Affiliation (first year): Baltimore Orioles (2002). Years in League: 2002-.

### OWNERSHIP, MANAGEMENT
Operated by: Ripken Professional Baseball, LLC.
Principal Owner: Cal Ripken Jr.
General Manager: Aaron Moszer. Assistant GM: Unavailable. Director, Sales: Lev Shellenberger. Manager, Public Relations/Broadcasting: Jay Moskowitz.

### FIELD STAFF
Manager: Andy Etchebarren. Coach: Cesar Devarez. Pitching Coach: Dave Schmidt. Trainer: Pat Wesley.

### GAME INFORMATION
Radio Announcer: Steve Melewski. No. of Games Broadcast: Home-38, Away-38. Flagship Station: WAMD 970-AM.
PA Announcer: Andrew Holly. Official Scorer: Joe Stetka.
Stadium Name: Ripken Stadium. Location: I-95 to exit 85 (Route 22), west on 22 West, right onto Long Drive. Standard Game Times: 7:05 p.m. Ticket Price Range: $5-14.
Visiting Club Hotel: Wingate Inn, Riverside Parkway, Aberdeen, MD 21001. Telephone: (410) 272-2929.

# AUBURN
## DOUBLEDAYS

Office Address: 130 N. Division St., Auburn, NY 13021.
Telephone: (315) 255-2489. FAX: (315) 255-2675.
E-Mail Address: ddays@auburndoubledays.com. Website: www.auburndouble
days.com.
Affiliation (first year): Toronto Blue Jays (2001). Years in League: 1958-80, 1982-.

### OWNERSHIP, MANAGEMENT
Operated by: Auburn Community Non-Profit Baseball Association, Inc.
Chairman: Tom Ganey. President: Leo Pinckney.
General Manager: Carl Gutelius. Assistant GM: Kevin Breen. Head Groundskeeper: Rich Wild. Director, Media/Public Relations: Unavailable.

### FIELD STAFF
Manager: Dennis Holmberg. Coach: Justin Mashore. Pitching Coach: Antonio Caceres. Trainer: Shawn McDermott.

### GAME INFORMATION
Radio Announcer: Unavailable. No of Games Broadcast: Away-38. Flagship Station: WDWN 89.1-FM.
PA Announcer: Unavailable. Official Scorer: Unavailable.
Stadium Name: Falcon Park. Location: I-90 to exit 40, right on Route 34 for 8 miles to York Street, right on York, left on North Division Street. Standard Game Times: 7 p.m., Sat.-Sun. 6. Ticket Price Range: $4-5.50.
Visiting Club Hotel: Inn at the Fingerlakes, 12 Seminary Ave., Auburn, NY 13021. Telephone: (315) 253-5000.

# BATAVIA
## MUCKDOGS

Office Address: Dwyer Stadium, 299 Bank St., Batavia, NY 14020.
Telephone: (585) 343-5454. FAX: (585) 343-5620.
E-Mail Address: info@muckdogs.com. Website: www.muckdogs.com.
Affiliation (first year): Philadelphia Phillies (1988). Years in League: 1939-53, 1957-59, 1961-.

### OWNERSHIP, MANAGEMENT
Operated by: Genesee County Baseball Club.
President: Brian Paris.
General Manager: Derek Sharp. Assistant GM: Jennifer Pacino. Director, Media/Public Relations: Unavailable. Director, Community Relations: Linda Crook. Clubhouse Operations: Tony Pecora. Director, Stadium Operations: Don Rock.

## FIELD STAFF
**Manager:** Steve Roadcap. **Coaches:** Joe Alvarez, Eric Richardson. **Pitching Coach:** Bill Bliss. **Trainer:** Ichiro Kitano.

## GAME INFORMATION
**Radio Announcer:** Unavailable. **No. of Games Broadcast:** Away-38. **Flagship Station:** WBSU 89.1-FM. **PA Announcer/Official Scorer:** Wayne Fuller.
**Stadium Name:** Dwyer Stadium. **Location:** I-90 to exit 48, left on Route 98 South, left on Richmond Avenue, left on Bank Street. **Standard Game Times:** 7:05 p.m., Sun. 6:05. **Ticket Price Range:** $4-5.
**Visiting Club Hotel:** Days Inn of Batavia, 200 Oak St., Batavia, NY 14020. Telephone: (585) 343-1440.

# BROOKLYN
## CYCLONES

**Office/Mailing Address:** 1904 Surf Ave., Brooklyn, NY 11224.
**Telephone:** (718) 449-8497. **FAX:** (718) 449-6368. **E-Mail Address:** info@brooklyn cyclones.com. **Website:** www.brooklyncyclones.com.
**Affiliation (first year):** New York Mets (2001). **Years in League:** 2001-.

## OWNERSHIP, MANAGEMENT
**Operated by:** Brooklyn Baseball Co., LLC.
**Managing Member:** Fred Wilpon. **Senior Executive Vice President/Chief Operating Officer:** Jeff Wilpon.
**General Manager:** Steve Cohen. **Assistant GM:** Kevin Mahoney. **Manager, Media Relations:** Dave Campanaro. **Manager, Promotions and Entertainment/Community Relations:** Robert Field. **Manager, Audio/Video Production:** Ben Friedfeld. **Manager, Brooklyn Baseball Gallery/Community Relations:** Anna Isaacson. **Manager, Graphics:** Kevin Jimenez. **Manager, Operations:** Vladimir Lipsman. **Manager, Tickets:** Chris Parsons. **Administrative Assistant/Community Relations:** Sharon Lundy. **Account Executives:** Mark Cole, Will Gahagan, Elizabeth Lombardi, Kimberly Patterson, Greg Radin, Ricky Viola. **Bookkeeper:** Tatiana Kanevsky. **Head Groundskeeper:** Kevin Ponte. **Assistant Groundskeeper:** George Reeder. **Receptionist:** Brenda Regester.

## FIELD STAFF
**Manager:** George Greer. **Coaches:** Jack Voigt, Luis Jabalera. **Pitching Coach:** Steve Merriman. **Trainer:** Unavailable.

## GAME INFORMATION
**Radio Announcer:** Warner Fussell. **No. of Games Broadcast:** Home-38, Away-38. **Flagship Station:** WKRB 90.9-FM. **PA Announcer:** Dominick Alagia. **Official Scorer:** David Freeman.
**Stadium Name:** KeySpan Park. **Location:** Belt Parkway to Cropsey Avenue South, continue on Cropsey until it becomes West 17th Street, continue to Surf Avenue, stadium on south side of Surf Avenue. By subway, west/south to Stillwell Avenue/Coney Island station. **Standard Game Times:** 7 p.m., Sat. 6, Sun. 5:30. **Ticket Price Range:** $5-$14.
**Visiting Club Hotel:** Comfort Inn, 8315 Fourth Ave., Brooklyn, NY 11209. Telephone: (718) 238-3737.

# HUDSON VALLEY
## RENEGADES

**Office Address:** Dutchess Stadium, Route 9D, Wappingers Falls, NY 12590.
**Mailing Address:** P.O. Box 661, Fishkill, NY 12524.
**Telephone:** (845) 838-0094. **FAX:** (845) 838-0014.
**E-Mail Address:** info@hvrenegades.com. **Website:** www.hvrenegades.com.
**Affiliation (first year):** Tampa Bay Devil Rays (1996). **Years in League:** 1994-.

## OWNERSHIP, MANAGEMENT
**Operated by:** Keystone Professional Baseball Club, Inc.
**Principal Owner:** Marv Goldklang. **President:** Jeff Goldklang.
**General Manager:** David Burke. **Assistant GM:** Derek Sharp. **Director, Ticket Operations:** Mike Branda. **Director, Business Operations:** Jennifer Vitale. **Director, Food Services:** Joe Ausanio. **Director, Entertainment:** Jay Martyn. **Director, Communications:** Stacy Morgan. **Director, Special Events/Renegades Charitable Foundation:** Rick Zolzer. **Director, Client Services:** Bob Outer. **Director, Ticket Sales:** Justin Fowler. **Director, Promotions:** Corey Whitted. **Controller:** Wayne Engel. **Head Groundskeeper:** Tom Hubmaster. **Assistant Groundskeeper:** Evan Baruda. **Clubhouse Manager:** Joe Harry.

## FIELD STAFF
**Manager:** Dave Howard. **Coach:** Matt Quatraro. **Pitching Coach:** Dick Bosman. **Trainer:** Joel Smith.

## GAME INFORMATION
**Radio Announcer:** Sean Ford. **No. of Games Broadcast:** Home-38, Away-38. **Flagship Stations:** WBNR 1260-AM, WLNA 1420-AM.
**PA Announcer:** Rick Zolzer. **Official Scorer:** Rob Smalls.
**Stadium Name:** Dutchess Stadium. **Location:** I-84 to exit 11 (Route 9D North), north one mile to stadium. **Standard**

Game Times: 7:05 p.m., Sun. 5:05. **Ticket Price Range:** $4-9.
Visiting Club Hotel: Ramada Inn, 20 Schuyler Blvd. and Route 9, Fishkill, NY 12524. Telephone: (845) 896-4995.

# JAMESTOWN
## JAMMERS

Office Address: 485 Falconer St., Jamestown, NY 14701.
Mailing Address: P.O. Box 638, Jamestown, NY 14702.
Telephone: (716) 664-0915. **FAX:** (716) 664-4175.
E-Mail Address: email@jamestownjammers.com. **Website:** www.jamestownjammers.com.
Affiliation (first year): Florida Marlins (2002). **Years in League:** 1939-57, 1961-73, 1977-.

## OWNERSHIP, MANAGEMENT

Operated by: Rich Baseball Operations.
Principal Owner, President: Robert Rich Jr. **Chairman:** Robert Rich Sr. **President, Rich Baseball Operations:** Jonathon Dandes.
General Manager: Matthew Drayer. **Director, Sales/Marketing:** George Sisson. **Director, Baseball Operations:** Benjamin Burnett. **Head Groundskeeper:** Jamie Bloomquist. **Director, Food Services:** Robert Cross.

## FIELD STAFF

Manager: Bo Porter. **Coach:** Anthony Iapoce. **Pitching Coach:** John Duffy. **Trainer:** James Stone.

## GAME INFORMATION

Radio: None.
PA Announcer: Unavailable. **Official Scorer:** Jim Riggs.
Stadium Name: Russell E. Diethrick Jr. Park. **Location:** From I-90, south on Route 60, left on Buffalo Street, left on Falconer Street. **Standard Game Times:** 7:05 p.m., Sun. 6:05. **Ticket Price Range:** $4.50-$6.50.
Visiting Club Hotel: Red Roof Inn, 1980 E. Main St., Falconer, NY 14733. Telephone: (716) 665-3670.

# LOWELL
## SPINNERS

Office Address: 450 Aiken St., Lowell, MA 01854.
Telephone: (978) 459-2255. **FAX:** (978) 459-1674.
E-Mail Address: generalinfo@lowellspinners.com. **Website:** www.lowell
spinners.com.
Affiliation (first year): Boston Red Sox (1996). **Years in League:** 1996-.

## OWNERSHIP, MANAGEMENT

Operated by: Diamond Action, Inc.
Owners: Drew Weber, Joann Weber. **Chief Executive Officer:** Drew Weber.
General Manager: Tim Bawmann. **Vice President, Business Operations:** Brian Lindsay. **Controller:** Priscilla Harbour. **Director, Stadium Operations:** Dan Beaulieu. **Assistant Director, Stadium Operations:** Gareth Markey. **Director, Corporate Communications:** Jon Goode. **Director, Media Relations:** Jon Shestakofsky. **Director, Merchandising:** Joann Weber. **Merchandising Manager:** Melanie Hahn. **Director, Ticket Group Sales:** Jon Healy. **Ticket Manager:** Justin Williams. **Head Groundskeeper:** Rick Walker. **Clubhouse Manager:** Del Christman.

## FIELD STAFF

Manager: Bruce Crabbe. **Coach:** Alan Mauthe. **Pitching Coach:** Walter Miranda. **Trainer:** Chris McKenna.

## GAME INFORMATION

Radio Announcer: Unavailable. **No. of Games Broadcast:** Unavailable. **Flagship Station:** WCAP 980-AM.
PA Announcers: Peter Mundy, John Rafferty. **Official Scorers:** Bob Ellis, Dave Rourke.
Stadium Name: Edward LeLacheur Park. **Location:** From Routes 495 and 3, take exit 35C (Lowell Connector), follow connector to exit 5B (Thorndike Street) onto Dutton Street, left onto Father Morrissette Boulevard, right on Aiken Street. **Standard Game Times:** 7:05 p.m., Sat.-Sun. 5:05. **Ticket Price Range:** $3.50-7.50.
Visiting Club Hotel: Doubletree Inn, 50 Warren St., Lowell, MA 01852. Telephone: (978) 452-1200.

# MAHONING VALLEY
## SCRAPPERS

Office Address: 111 Eastwood Mall Blvd., Niles, OH 44446.
Mailing Address: P.O. Box 1357, Niles, OH 44446.
Telephone: (330) 505-0000. **FAX:** (330) 505-9696.

**E-Mail Address:** mvscrappers@onecom.com. **Website:** www.mvscrappers.com.
**Affiliation (first year):** Cleveland Indians (1999). **Years in League:** 1999-.

## OWNERSHIP, MANAGEMENT

**Operated by:** Palisades Baseball, Ltd.
**Managing General Partner:** Alan Levin. **Executive Vice President:** Erik Haag. **Director, Finance:** Cheryl Carlson.
**General Manager:** Dave Smith. **Director, Business Development:** Joe Gregory. **Director, Stadium Operations:** Chris Walsh. **Director, Ticket Operations:** Jordan Taylor. **Director, Box Office:** Heather Safarek. **Accountant:** Debbie Primmer. **Director, Client Services/Merchandise:** Mike Brent. **Director, Promotions/Marketing:** Jim Riley. **Ticket Sales Representatives:** Kevin Geiss, Andrea Zagger. **Director, Concessions:** Brad Hooser.

## FIELD STAFF

**Manager:** Rouglas Odor. **Coaches:** Jim Rickon, Chris Tremie. **Pitching Coach:** Ken Rowe. **Trainer:** Jeremy Heller.

## GAME INFORMATION

**Radio Announcer:** Unavailable. **No. of Games Broadcasts:** Home-38, Away-38. **Flagship Station:** WNIO 1390-AM.
**PA Announcer:** Ryan Pritt. **Official Scorer:** Al Thorne.
**Stadium Name:** Eastwood Field. **Location:** I-80 to 11 North to 82 West to 46 South, stadium located behind Eastwood Mall. **Standard Game Times:** 7 p.m., Sun. 1. **Ticket Price Range:** $6-8.
**Visiting Club Hotel:** Unavailable.

# ONEONTA
## TIGERS

**Office Address:** 95 River St., Oneonta, NY 13820.
**Telephone:** (607) 432-6326. **FAX:** (607) 432-1965.
**E-Mail Address:** naderas@telenet.net. **Website:** www.oneontatigers.com.
**Affiliation (first year):** Detroit Tigers (1999). **Years in League:** 1966-.

## OWNERSHIP, MANAGEMENT

**Operated by:** Oneonta Athletic Corp.
**President, General Manager:** Sam Nader. **Assistant GM/Director, Operations:** Bob Zeh. **Controller:** Sidney Levine.
**Director, Media/Public Relations:** Alice O'Conner. **Director, Marketing/Merchandising:** Suzanne Longo. **Director, Special Projects:** Mark Nader. **Director, Food Services:** Brad Zeh.

## FIELD STAFF

**Manager:** Tom Brookens. **Coach:** Basilio Cabrera. **Pitching Coach:** Ray Burris. **Trainer:** Unavailable.

## GAME INFORMATION

**Radio:** None.
**PA Announcer:** John Horne. **Official Scorer:** Tom Heitz.
**Stadium Name:** Damaschke Field. **Location:** Exit 15 off I-88. **Standard Game Times:** 7 p.m., Sun. 6. **Ticket Price Range:** $5-7.
**Visiting Club Hotel:** Oasis Motor Inn, 366 Chestnut St., Oneonta, NY 13820. **Telephone:** (607) 432-6041.

# STATE COLLEGE
## SPIKES

(Franchise operated in Augusta, N.J., in 2005)
**Office Address:** Medlar Field at Lubrano Park, University Park, PA 16802
**Telephone:** (814) 272-1711. **FAX:** (814) 272-1718.
**Website:** www.statecollegespikes.com.
**Affiliation (first year):** St. Louis Cardinals (2006). **Years in League:** 2006-.

## OWNERSHIP, MANAGEMENT

**Operated by:** Curve Baseball LP.
**President, Managing Partner:** Chuck Greenberg.
**General Manager:** Rick Janac. **Assistant GM/Senior Director, Ticketing:** Jeff Garner. **Director, Communications:** Jason Dambach. **Director, Community Relations:** Elsie Zengel. **Director, Merchandising:** Ben Rothrock. **Director, Sports Turf Management:** Patrick Coakley. **Director, Ballpark Operations:** Kirk Stiffler. **Director, Finance:** Machelle Noel. **Director, Box Office Operations:** Jeff Adams. **Director, Information Services, Graphic/Web Design:** Bill Edevane. **Director, Promotions/New Business Development:** Chris Mundhenk. **Executive Producer, In-Game Entertainment:** Matt Zidik. **Director, Mascot Operations:** Charlton Jordan. **Assistant Directors, Ticket Sales:** Derek Martin, Chris Phillips. **Assistant Director, Promotions:** Matt Hoover. **Ticket Sales Associates:** Eric Fiscus, Corey Homan, Bill Hallman, Chris Keefer, Lane Kieffer, Jessica Nebel, Dennis Newberry, Dan Newhart, Kevin Steele, Denny Watson. **Sponsorship Sales Account Executives:** John Carey, Greg Parassio, Julie Price, Jessica Seretti. **Media Relations Manager:** Billy Harner. **Media Relations Assistant:** Joe Moore. **Producer, In-Game Entertainment:** John

Foreman. **Sports Turf Manager:** Matt Neri. **Administrative Assistant:** Carol Schmittle. **Ballpark Operations Assistants:** Shawn Huber, Cindy Stephens. **Community Relations Manager:** Stefanie Brown. **Accounting Specialist:** Tara Figard. **Assistant Sports Turf Manager:** Lisa Guinivan.

### FIELD STAFF
**Manager:** Mark DeJohn. **Coaches:** Steve Balboni, Mike Shildt. **Pitching Coach:** Sid Monge. **Trainer:** Manabu Kawazuru.

### GAME INFORMATION
**Radio Announcers:** Steve Jones. **No. of Games Broadcast:** Home-38, Away-38. **Flagship Station:** WZWW 95.3-FM
**PA Announcer:** Dean Devore. **Official Scorer:** Unavailable.
**Stadium Name:** Medlar Field at Lubrano Park. **Location:** From west, U.S. 322 to Mount Nittany Expressway; I-80 to exit 158 (old exit 23/Milesburg), follow Route 150 South to Route 26 South. From east, I-80 to exit 161(old exit 24/Bellefonte) to Route 26 South or U.S. 220/I-99 South. **Standard Game Times:** 7:05 p.m., Sun. 6:05. **Ticket Price Range:** $6-14.
**Visiting Club Hotel:** Unavailable.

# STATEN ISLAND
## YANKEES

**Stadium Address:** 75 Richmond Terrace, Staten Island, NY 10301.
**Telephone:** (718) 720-9265. **FAX:** (718) 273-5763.
**E-Mail Address:** siyanks@siyanks.com. **Website:** www.siyanks.com.
**Affiliation (first year):** New York Yankees (1999). **Years in League:** 1999-.

### OWNERSHIP, MANAGEMENT
**Operated by:** Staten Island Minor League Holdings, LLC.
**Principal Owners:** Josh Getzler, Phyllis Getzler, Stan Getzler.
**Chairman:** Stan Getzler. **President:** Henry Steinbrenner. **Chief Operating Officer:** Josh Getzler.
**General Manager:** Jane Rogers. **Assistant GMs:** John Davison, Gary Perone. **Director, Tickets:** Dominic Constantino. **Director, Community Relations:** Polo Burgos. **Managers, Sales:** Taka Shirari, Matthew Slatus. **Sales Manager/Community Relations:** Christin Brincat. **Bookkeeper:** Louise Sabella. **Director, Stadium Operations:** Mario Azzapardi. **Mascot Coordinator:** Adam Cora. **Director, Concessions/Centerplate GM:** Al Austin. **Head Groundskeeper:** Unavailable.

### FIELD STAFF
**Manager:** Gaylen Pitts. **Coach:** Ty Hawkins. **Pitching Coach:** Mike Thurman. **Trainer:** Unavailable.

### GAME INFORMATION
**Radio Announcer:** Unavailable. **No. of Games Broadcast:** Home-38, Away-38. **Flagship Station:** Unavailable.
**PA Announcer:** Unavailable. **Official Scorer:** Unavailable.
**Stadium Name:** Richmond County Bank Ballpark at St. George. **Location:** From I-95, take exit 13E (1-278 and Staten Island), cross Goethals Bridge, stay on I-278 East and take last exit before Verrazano Narrows Bridge, north on Father Cappodanno Boulevard, which turns into Bay Street, which goes to ferry terminal; ballpark next to Staten Island Ferry Terminal. **Standard Game Times:** 7:05 p.m., Sun 5:05. **Ticket Price Range:** $9-11.
**Visiting Club Hotel:** The Navy Lodge, 408 North Path Rd., Staten Island, NY 10305. Telephone: (718) 442-0413.

# TRI-CITY
## VALLEYCATS

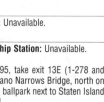

**Stadium Address:** 80 Vandenburgh Ave., Troy, NY 12180.
**Mailing Address:** P.O. Box 694, Troy, NY 12181.
**Telephone:** (518) 629-2287. **FAX:** (518) 629-2299.
**E-Mail Address:** info@tcvalleycats.com. **Website:** www.tcvalleycats.com.
**Affiliation:** Houston Astros (2001). **Years in League:** 2002-.

### OWNERSHIP, MANAGEMENT
**Operated by:** Tri-City ValleyCats, Inc.
**Principal Owners:** Martin Barr, John Burton, William Gladstone, Richard Murphy, Alfred Roberts, Stephen Siegel. **President:** William Gladstone.
**Vice President, General Manager:** R.C. Reuteman. **Assistant GM:** Vic Christopher. **Sales Manager:** Doug MacLeod. **Account Executives:** Brett Gilmore, Scott Obergefell, Kristan Pelletier. **Director, Corporate Communications:** Eileen McCarthy. **Administrative Assistant:** Liz Litsch.

### FIELD STAFF
**Manager:** Gregg Langbehn. **Coach:** Joel Chimelis. **Pitching Coach:** Don Alexander. **Trainer:** Unavailable.

### GAME INFORMATION
**Radio Announcer:** Dan Flanagan **No. of Games Broadcast:** Home-38, Away-38. **Flagship Station:** WABY 1160 AM.

**PA Announcer:** Tony Pettograsso. **Official Scorer:** Unavailable.

**Stadium Name:** Joseph L. Bruno Stadium. **Location:** From north, I-87 to exit 7 (Route 7), go east approximately 1½ miles to I-787 South, to Route 378 East, go over bridge to Route 4, right to Route 4 South, one mile to Hudson Valley Community College campus on left. From south, I-87 to exit 23 (I-787), I-787 north six miles to exit for Route 378 east, Route 378 over bridge to Route 4, go right to Route 4 South, one mile to Hudson Valley Community College campus on left. From east, Massachusetts Turnpike to exit B-1 (I-90), go nine miles to Exit 8 (Defreestville), left off ramp to Route 4 North, Route 4 North for five miles, Hudson Valley Community College on right. From West, I-90 to exit 24 (I-90 East), I-90 east for six miles to I-787 North (Troy), take I-787 North for 2.2 miles to exit for Route 378 East, take Route 378 over bridge to Route 4,, right to Route 4 south for one mile to Hudson Valley Community College campus on left. **Standard Game Times:** 7 p.m., Sun. 6. **Ticket Price Range:** $5-8.50.

**Visiting Club Hotel:** Red Roof Inn , 188 Wolf Rd., Albany, NY 12205. Telephone: (518) 459-1971.

# VERMONT
## LAKE MONSTERS

**Office Address:** 1 Main St., Suite 4, Winooski, VT 05404.
**Telephone:** (802) 655-4200. **FAX:** (802) 655-5660.
**E-Mail Address:** mail@vermontlakemonsters.com. **Website:** www.vermontlake monsters.com.
**Affiliation (first year):** Washington Nationals (2005). **Years in League:** 1994-.

## OWNERSHIP, MANAGEMENT

**Operated by:** Vermont Expos, Inc.
**Principal Owner, President:** Ray Pecor. **Vice President:** Kyle Bostwick.
**General Manager:** C.J. Knudsen. **Director, Stadium Operations:** Jim O'Brien. **Head Groundskeeper:** Unavailable. **Executive Operations Manager/Director, Promotions:** Adrienne Wilson. **Director, Media/Stadium Administration:** Paul Stanfield. **Director, Sales:** Shawn Quinn. **Director, Marketing/Ticket Operations:** Nate Cloutier. **Director, Food Services:** Steve Bernard. **Director, Special Projects:** Onnie Matthews. **Clubhouse Operations:** Phil Schelzo.

## FIELD STAFF

**Manager:** Edger Caceres. **Coach:** Tony Tarasco. **Pitching Coach:** Mark Grater. **Trainer:** Unavailable.

## GAME INFORMATION

**Radio Announcer:** George Commo. **No. of Games Broadcast:** Home-38, Away-38. **Flagship Station:** The Zone 96.7-FM, 960-AM.

**PA Announcer:** Rich Haskell. **Official Scorer:** Ev Smith.

**Stadium Name:** Centennial Field. **Location:** I-89 to exit 14W, right on East Avenue for one mile, right at Colchester Avenue. **Standard Game Times:** 7:05 p.m., Sun. 5:05. **Ticket Price Range:** $3-7.

**Visiting Club Hotel:** University Inn & Suites, 5 Dorset St., South Burlington, VT 05403. Telephone: (802) 863-5541.

# WILLIAMSPORT
## CROSSCUTTERS

**Office Address:** Bowman Field, 1700 W. Fourth St., Williamsport, PA 17701.
**Mailing Address:** P.O. Box 3173, Williamsport, PA 17701.
**Telephone:** (570) 326-3389. **FAX:** (570) 326-3494.
**E-Mail Address:** mail@crosscutters.com. **Website:** www.crosscutters.com.
**Affiliation (first year):** Pittsburgh Pirates (1999). **Years in League:** 1968-72, 1994-.

## OWNERSHIP, MANAGEMENT

**Operated by:** Geneva Cubs Baseball, Inc.
**Principal Owners:** Paul Velte, John Schreyer. **President:** Paul Velte. **Vice President:** John Schreyer.
**General Manager:** Doug Estes. **Director, Marketing/Public Relations:** Gabe Sinicropi. **Director, Food/Beverage:** Bill Gehron. **Director, Ticket Operations/Community Relations:** Sarah Budd. **Director, Client Services:** Ellie Davis. **Head Groundskeeper:** Melissa Slingerland. **Clubhouse Manager:** Mike Bates.

## FIELD STAFF

**Manager:** Tom Prince. **Coach:** Ryan Newman. **Pitching Coach:** Bruce Banner. **Trainer:** Jared Destro.

## GAME INFORMATION

**Radio Announcer:** Unavailable. **No. of Games Broadcast:** Unavailable. **Flagship Station:** WRLC 91.7-FM.

**PA Announcer:** Rob Thomas. **Official Scorer:** Ken Myers.

**Stadium Name:** Bowman Field. **Location:** From south, Route 15 to Maynard Street, right on Maynard, left on Fourth Street for one mile; From north, Route 15 to Fourth Street, left on Fourth. **Standard Game Time:** 7:05 p.m. **Ticket Price Range:** $3.75-6.

**Visiting Club Hotel:** Best Western, 1840 E. Third St., Williamsport, PA 17701. Telephone: (570) 326-1981.

# NORTHWEST
## LEAGUE

**NWL**
NORTHWEST LEAGUE OF PROFESSIONAL BASEBALL

**Office Address:** 910 Main St., Suite 351, Boise, ID 83702.
**Mailing Address:** P.O. Box 1645, Boise, ID 83701.
**Telephone:** (208) 429-1511. **FAX:** (208) 429-1525.
**E-Mail Address:** bobrichmond@worldnet.att.net.
**Years League Active:** 1954-.

**President, Treasurer:** Bob Richmond.
**Vice President:** Todd Rahr (Boise). **Corporate Secretary:** Jerry Walker (Salem-Keizer).
**Directors:** Bob Beban (Eugene), Bobby Brett (Spokane), Peter Carfagna (Everett), Fred Herrmann (Vancouver), Mike McMurray (Yakima), Brent Miles (Tri-City), Jerry Walker (Salem-Keizer), Thomas Wick (Boise).
**Administrative Assistant:** Rob Richmond.
**Division Structure: East**—Boise, Spokane, Tri-City, Yakima. **West**—Eugene, Everett, Salem-Keizer, Vancouver.
**Regular Season:** 76 games. **2006 Opening Date:** June 19. **Closing Date:** Sept. 6.
**Playoff Format:** Division winners meet in best-of-5 series for league championship.
**All-Star Game:** None.
**Roster Limit:** 30 active, 35 under control. **Player Eligibility Rule:** No more than four players 23 or older. No more than three players on active list may have four or more years of prior service.
**Brand of Baseball:** Rawlings.

**Bob Richmond**

**Statistician:** Major League Baseball Advanced Media, 75 Ninth Ave., New York, NY 10011.
**Umpires:** Unavailable.

## STADIUM INFORMATION

| Club | Stadium | Opened | LF | CF | RF | Capacity | 2005 Att. |
|------|---------|--------|-----|-----|-----|----------|-----------|
| Boise | Memorial Stadium | 1989 | 335 | 405 | 335 | 4,500 | 109,746 |
| Eugene | Civic Stadium | 1938 | 335 | 400 | 328 | 6,800 | 124,512 |
| Everett | Everett Memorial Stadium | 1984 | 330 | 395 | 330 | 3,682 | 108,884 |
| Salem-Keizer | Volcanoes Stadium | 1997 | 325 | 400 | 325 | 4,100 | 108,413 |
| Spokane | Avista Stadium | 1958 | 335 | 398 | 335 | 7,162 | 180,084 |
| Tri-City | Dust Devils Stadium | 1995 | 335 | 400 | 335 | 3,730 | 63,173 |
| Vancouver | Nat Bailey Stadium | 1951 | 335 | 395 | 335 | 6,500 | 124,708 |
| Yakima | Yakima County Stadium | 1993 | 295 | 406 | 295 | 3,000 | 60,150 |

# BOISE
## HAWKS

**Office Address:** 5600 N. Glenwood St., Boise, ID 83714.
**Telephone:** (208) 322-5000. **FAX:** (208) 322-6846.
**Website:** www.boisehawks.com.
**Affiliation (first year):** Chicago Cubs (2001). **Years in League:** 1975-76, 1978, 1987-.

### OWNERSHIP, MANAGEMENT

**Operated by:** Boise Hawks Baseball Club LLC.
**Board of Directors:** Jim Brown, Stan Carey, Joe Golando, Kevin Nagai, Tom Wick.
**President/General Manager:** Todd Rahr. **Assistant GM/Director, Business Operations:** Dina Duncan. **Assistant GM/Director, Ticket Sales:** Nat Reynolds. **Assistant GM/Director, Corporate Sales:** Roger Inwards. **Business Development Manager:** Ken Hyde. **Group Sales Manager:** Andy Simon. **Bookkeeper:** Joe Austin.

### FIELD STAFF

**Manager:** Steve McFarland. **Coach:** Ricardo Medina. **Pitching Coach:** David Rosario. **Trainer:** Unavailable.

### GAME INFORMATION

**Radio Announcer:** Mike Safford. **No. of Games Broadcast:** Home-38, Away-38. **Flagship Station:** KTIK 1350-AM.
**PA Announcer:** Unavailable. **Official Scorer:** Unavailable.
**Stadium Name:** Memorial Stadium. **Location:** I-84 to Cole Road, north to Western Idaho Fairgrounds at 5600 North Glenwood Street. **Standard Game Times:** 7:15 p.m., Sun. 6:15. **Ticket Price Range:** $5-9.
**Visiting Club Hotel:** Owyhee Plaza Hotel, 1109 Main St., Boise, ID 83702. Telephone: (208) 343-4611.

# EUGENE
## EMERALDS

**Office Address:** 2077 Willamette St., Eugene, OR 97405.
**Mailing Address:** P.O. Box 5566, Eugene, OR 97405.
**Telephone:** (541) 342-5367. **FAX:** (541) 342-6089.
**E-Mail Address:** ems@go-ems.com. **Website:** www.go-ems.com.
**Affiliation (first year):** San Diego Padres (2001). **Years in League:** 1955-68, 1974-.

### OWNERSHIP, MANAGEMENT

**Operated by:** Elmore Sports Group, Ltd.
**Principal Owner:** David Elmore.
**President, General Manager:** Bob Beban. **Assistant GMs:** Sergio Apodaca, Bryan Beban. **Director, Business Operations:** Eileen Beban. **Director, Food Services/Stadium Operations:** Jim Brelsford. **Director, Tickets/Special Events:** Nathan Skalsky. **Grounds Superintendent:** Joe Johannsen.

### FIELD STAFF

**Manager:** Doug Dascenzo. **Coach:** Joe Ferguson. **Pitching Coach:** Wally Whitehurst. **Trainer:** Jo Jo Tarantino.

### GAME INFORMATION

**Radio Announcer:** Ben Ingram. **No. of Games Broadcast:** Home-38, Away-38.
**Flagship Station:** KPNW 1120-AM.
**PA Announcer:** Unavailable. **Official Scorer:** George McPherson.
**Stadium Name:** Civic Stadium. **Location:** From I-5, take I-105 to Exit 2, stay left and follow to downtown, cross over Ferry Street Bridge to Eighth Avenue, left on Pearl Street, south to 20th Avenue. **Standard Game Times:** 7:05 p.m., Sun. 4:05. **Ticket Price Range:** $5.50-9.
**Visiting Club Hotel:** Valley River Inn, 1000 Valley River Way, Eugene, OR 97401. Telephone: (541) 687-0123.

# EVERETT
## AQUASOX

**Mailing Address:** 3802 Broadway, Everett, WA 98201.
**Telephone:** (425) 258-3673. **FAX:** (425) 258-3675.
**E-Mail Address:** aquasox@aquasox.com. **Website:** www.aquasox.com.
**Affiliation (first year):** Seattle Mariners (1995). **Years in League:** 1984-.

### OWNERSHIP, MANAGEMENT

**Operated by:** Famiglia II.
**President:** Peter Carfagna. **Vice President, Baseball Operations:** Pete Carfagna.

General Manager: Brian Sloan. Director, Broadcasting/Corporate Sales: Pat Dillon. Director, Ballpark Operations: Jason Jarett. Director, Ticket Services: Scott Gray. Director, Administration/Concessions: Cathy Bierman. Director, Merchandising: Alexis Welch. Director, Special Projects: Brad Baxter. Accountant: Teresa Sarsted. Group Sales Associates: Zach Mennie, Rick O'Connor, Nick Snyder.

## FIELD STAFF
Manager: James Horner. Coach: Dave Myers. Pitching Coach: Juan Alvarez. Trainer: Spyder Webb.

## GAME INFORMATION
Radio Announcer: Pat Dillon. No. of Games Broadcast: Home-38, Away-38. Flagship Station: KRKO 1380-AM. PA Announcer: Tom Lafferty. Official Scorer: Pat Castro.
Stadium Name: Everett Memorial Stadium. Location: I-5, exit 192. Standard Game Times: 7:05 p.m., Sun. 2:05. Ticket Price Range: $8-13.
Visiting Club Hotel: Best Western Cascadia Inn, 2800 Pacific Ave., Everett, WA 98201. Telephone: (425) 258-4141.

# SALEM-KEIZER
## VOLCANOES

Street Address: 6700 Field of Dreams Way NE, Keizer, OR 97307.
Mailing Address: P.O. Box 20936, Keizer, OR 97307.
Telephone: (503) 390-2225. FAX: (503) 390-2227.
E-Mail Address: probasebal@aol.com. Website: www.volcanoesbaseball.com.
Affiliation (first year): San Francisco Giants (1997). Years in League: 1997-.

## OWNERSHIP, MANAGEMENT
Operated By: Sports Enterprises, Inc.
Principal Owners: Jerry Walker, Bill Tucker.
President, General Manager: Jerry Walker. Vice President, Operations: Rick Nelson. Manager, Corporate Sales/Director, Promotions: Lisa Walker. Corporate Sponsorships: Sheryl Kelsh, Steve Wertz. Director, Sales/Media Relations: Pat Lafferty. Director, Community Relations: Unavailable. Corporate Ticket Sales: John Banks, Christine Campbell, Matt Palumbo. Director, Merchandising/Ticket Office Operations: Kate Hamm.

## FIELD STAFF
Manager: Steve Decker. Coach: Ricky Ward. Pitching Coach: Jerry Cram. Trainer: Larry Duensing.

## GAME INFORMATION
Radio Announcer: Pat Lafferty. No. of Games Broadcast: Home-38, Away-38. Flagship Station: KYKN 1430-AM. PA Announcer: Unavailable. Official Scorer: Dawn Hills.
Stadium Name: Volcanoes Stadium. Location: I-5 to exit 260 (Chemawa Road), west one block to Radiant Drive, north six blocks to stadium. Standard Game Times: 6:35 p.m.; Fri-Sat. 7:05, Sun. 5:05. Ticket Price Range: $6-10.
Visiting Club Hotel: Comfort Suites, 630 Hawthorne Ave. SE, Salem, OR 97301. Telephone: (503) 585-9705.

# SPOKANE
## INDIANS

Office Address: 602 N. Havana, Spokane, WA 99202.
Mailing Address: P.O. Box 4758, Spokane, WA 99220.
Telephone: (509) 535-2922. FAX: (509) 534-5368.
E-Mail Address: mail@spokaneindiansbaseball.com. Website: www.spokaneindiansbaseball.com.
Affiliation (first year): Texas Rangers (2003). Years in League: 1972, 1983-.

## OWNERSHIP, MANAGEMENT
Operated by: Longball, Inc.
Principal Owners: Bobby Brett, George Brett, J.B. Brett.
President: Andrew Billig.
Vice President, General Manager: Paul Barbeau. VP, Sponsorships: Otto Klein. Chief Financial Officer: Greg Sloan. Assistant GM, Ticket Sales: Paul Zilm. Assistant GM, Operations: Chris Duff. Assistant GM, Concessions: Lesley DeHart. Director, Sponsorships: Brad Poe. Director, Ticket Sales: Brian Burton. Director, Concessions: Leanne Kingston. Director, Public Relations: Brandon Hansen. Director, Accounting: Renee Stearnes. Account Executives: Kevin Stocker, Evan Wagner. Group Sales Managers: Randi Aud, Sarah Travis. Sales Support Manager: Jessica Henderson. Head Groundskeeper: Tony Lee. Assistant Director, Stadium Operations: Larry Blumer.

## FIELD STAFF
Manager: Mike Micucci. Coach: Jim Nettles. Pitching Coach: Aris Tirado. Trainer: Cesar Roman.

## GAME INFORMATION
Radio Announcer: Bob Robertson. No. of Games Broadcast: Home-38, Away-38. Flagship Station: KFAN 790-AM. PA Announcer: Brad Moon. Official Scorer: Unavailable.

**Stadium Name:** Avista Stadium at Spokane County Fair and Expo Center. **Location:** From west, I-90 to exit 283B (Thor/Freya), east on 3rd Avenue, left onto Havana; from east, I-90 to Broadway exit, right onto Broadway, left onto Havana. **Standard Game Time:** 6:30 p.m. **Ticket Price Range:** $4-9.

**Visiting Club Hotel:** Mirabeau Park Hotel & Convention Center, N. 1100 Sullivan Rd., Spokane, WA 99037. Telephone: (509) 924-9000.

# TRI-CITY
## DUST DEVILS

**Office Address:** 6200 Burden Rd., Pasco, WA 99301.
**Telephone:** (509) 544-8789. **FAX:** (509) 547-9570.
**E-Mail Address:** info@dustdevilsbaseball.com. **Website:** www.dustdevilsbaseball.com.
**Affiliation (first year):** Colorado Rockies (2001). **Years in League:** 1955-1974, 1983-1986, 2001-.

## OWNERSHIP, MANAGEMENT

**Operated by:** Northwest Baseball Ventures.
**Principal Owner:** George Brett. **President:** Brent Miles.
**Vice President/General Manager:** Derrel Ebert. **Assistant GM, Tickets:** Scott Litle. **Assistant GM, Business Operations:** Tim Gittel. **Director, Group Sales:** C.J. Loper. **Director, Season Tickets:** Matt Nash. **Director, Operations/Account Executive:** Joe Knippel. **Promotions Coordinator:** Kelli Walter. **Head Groundskeeper:** Michael Angel.

## FIELD STAFF

**Manager:** Darron Cox. **Coach:** Freddie Ocasio. **Pitching Coach:** Doug Linton. **Trainer:** Unavailable.

## GAME INFORMATION

**Radio Announcer:** Tom Barket. **No. of Games Broadcast:** Home-38, Away-38. **Flagship Station:** KJOX 970-AM.
**PA Announcer:** Patrick Harvey. **Official Scorer:** Tony Wise.
**Stadium Name:** Dust Devils Stadium. **Location:** I-182 to exit 9 (Road 68), north to Burden Road, right to stadium.
**Standard Game Times:** 7:15 p.m. **Ticket Price Range:** $4-9.
**Visiting Club Hotel:** Red Lion Hotel-Columbia Center, 1101 N. Columbia Center Blvd., Kennewick, WA 99336. Telephone: (509) 783-0611.

# VANCOUVER
## CANADIANS

**Office Address:** 4601 Ontario St., Vancouver, British Columbia V5V 3H4.
**Telephone:** (604) 872-5232. **FAX:** (604) 872-1714.
**E-Mail Address:** staff@canadiansbaseball.com. **Website:** www.canadiansbaseball.com.
**Affiliation (first year):** Oakland Athletics (2000). **Years in League:** 2000-.

## OWNERSHIP, MANAGEMENT

**Operated by:** National Sports Organization, Inc.
**Principal Owners:** Dwain Cross, Fred Herrmann, Bud Kaufman. **President:** Dan Kilgras.
**General Manager:** Delany Dunn. **Assistant GM:** Ben Ekren. **Special Assistant to Owner:** Bill Posthumus. **Ticket Manager:** Lori Bonang. **Director, Finance:** Nick Zakus. **Director, Media Relations:** Leanne Cass. **Clubhouse Manager:** Unavailable.

## FIELD STAFF

**Manager:** Dennis Rogers. **Coach:** Unavailable. **Pitching Coach:** Craig Lefferts. **Trainer:** Unavailable.

## GAME INFORMATION

**Radio Announcer:** Unavailable. **No. of Games Broadcast:** Unavailable. **Flagship Station:** The Team 1040-AM.
**PA Announcer:** Don Andrews. **Official Scorer:** Pat Karl.
**Stadium Name:** Nat Bailey Stadium. **Location:** From downtown, take Cambie Street Bridge, left on East 25th Avenue/King Edward Avenue, right on Main Street, right on 33rd Ave., right on Clancy Loranger Way to stadium; from south, take Highway 99 to Oak Street, right on 41st Avenue, left on Main Street to 33rd Ave., right on Clancy Loranger Way to stadium. **Standard Game Times:** 7:05 p.m., Sun. 1:05. **Ticket Price Range:** $8-20.
**Visiting Club Hotel:** Accent Inns, 10551 Edwards Dr., Richmond, B.C. V6X 3L8. Telephone: (604) 273-3311.

# YAKIMA
## BEARS

**Office Address:** 8 N. 2nd St., Yakima, WA 98901.
**Mailing Address:** P.O. Box 483, Yakima, WA 98907.
**Telephone:** (509) 457-5151. **FAX:** (509) 457-9909.
**E-Mail Address:** info@yakimabears.com. **Website:** www.yakimabears.com.
**Affiliation (first year):** Arizona Diamondbacks (2001). **Years in League:** 1955-66, 1990-.

## OWNERSHIP, MANAGEMENT

**Operated by:** Short Season, LLC.
**Managing Partners:** Mike McMurray, Mike Ellis, Josh Weinman, Myron Levin. **President:** Mike McMurray.
**General Manager:** K.L. Wombacher. **Director, Corporate Relations:** Aaron Arndt. **Director, Operations:** Broc Arndt. **Director, Ticket Operations:** Justin Glaser. **Director, Marketing/Promotions:** Tyler Eidson. **Office Manager:** Lauren Pietz. **Head Groundskeeper:** Unavailable. **Clubhouse Operations:** Unavailable. **Administrative Assistants:** Clark Smith, Tim Pickett.

## FIELD STAFF

**Manager:** Jay Gainer. **Coach:** Luis De los Santos. **Pitching Coach:** Erik Sabel. **Trainer:** Mark Ryan.

## GAME INFORMATION

**Radio Announcer:** Jon Laaser. **No. of Games Broadcast:** Home-38, Away-38. **Flagship Station:** KUTI 1460-AM.
**PA Announcer:** Todd Lyons. **Official Scorer:** Mike McMurray.
**Stadium Name:** Yakima County Stadium. **Location:** I-82 to exit 34 (Nob Hill Boulevard), west to Fair Avenue, right on Fair, right on Pacific Avenue. **Standard Game Times:** 7:05 p.m., Sun. 5:35. **Ticket Price Range:** $3.50-7.50.
**Visiting Club Hotel:** Best Western Ahtanum Inn, 2408 Rudkin Rd., Union Gap, WA 98903. Telephone: (509) 248-9700.

# APPALACHIAN
## LEAGUE

APPALACHIAN LEAGUE
of professional baseball clubs

**Mailing Address:** 283 Deerchase Circle, Statesville, NC 28625.
**Telephone:** (704) 873-5300. **FAX:** (704) 873-4333.
**E-Mail Address:** appylg@direcway.com.
**Years League Active:** 1921-25, 1937-55, 1957-.

**President, Treasurer:** Lee Landers. **Corporate Secretary:** Jim Holland (Princeton).

**Directors:** Ricky Bennett (Greeneville), Mitch Lukevics (Princeton), John Farrell (Burlington), Dave Wilder (Bristol), Len Johnston (Bluefield), Bruce Manno (Johnson City), Dayton Moore (Danville), Kevin Morgan (Kingsport), Jim Rantz (Elizabethton), Dick Scott (Pulaski).

**League Administrator:** Bobbi Landers.

**Division Structure: East**—Bluefield, Burlington, Danville, Princeton, Pulaski. **West**—Bristol, Elizabethton, Greeneville, Johnson City, Kingsport.

**Regular Season:** 68 games. **2006 Opening Date:** June 21. **Closing Date:** Aug. 30.

**All-Star Game:** None.

**Playoff Format:** Division winners meet in best-of-3 series for league championship.

**Roster Limit:** 35 active. **Player Eligibility Rule:** No more than two years of prior minor league service.

**Lee Landers**

**Brand of Baseball:** Rawlings.

**Statistician:** Major League Baseball Advanced Media, 75 Ninth Ave., New York, NY 10011.

**Umpires:** Unavailable.

## STADIUM INFORMATION

| Club | Stadium | Opened | LF | CF | RF | Capacity | 2005 Att. |
|------|---------|--------|----|----|----|----------|-----------|
| Bluefield | Bowen Field | 1939 | 335 | 365 | 335 | 2,250 | 27,420 |
| Bristol | DeVault Memorial Stadium | 1969 | 325 | 400 | 310 | 2,000 | 20,868 |
| Burlington | Burlington Athletic Stadium | 1960 | 335 | 410 | 335 | 3,000 | 37,673 |
| Danville | Dan Daniel Memorial Park | 1993 | 330 | 400 | 330 | 2,588 | 37,604 |
| Elizabethton | Joe O'Brien Field | 1974 | 335 | 414 | 326 | 1,500 | 25,949 |
| Greeneville | Pioneer Park | 2004 | 331 | 400 | 331 | 2,400 | 49,963 |
| Johnson City | Howard Johnson Field | 1956 | 320 | 410 | 320 | 2,500 | 24,338 |
| Kingsport | Hunter Wright Stadium | 1995 | 330 | 410 | 330 | 2,500 | 36,962 |
| Princeton | Hunnicutt Field | 1988 | 330 | 396 | 330 | 1,950 | 26,477 |
| Pulaski | Calfee Park | 1935 | 335 | 405 | 310 | 2,500 | 24,770 |

# BLUEFIELD
## ORIOLES

**Office Address:** Stadium Drive, Bluefield, WV 24701.
**Mailing Address:** P.O. Box 356, Bluefield, WV 24701.
**Telephone:** (276) 326-1326. **FAX:** (276) 326-1318.
**Affiliation (first year):** Baltimore Orioles (1958). **Years in League:** 1946-55, 1957-.

### OWNERSHIP, MANAGEMENT
**Operated by:** Bluefield Baseball Club, Inc.
**Director:** Len Johnston (Baltimore Orioles).
**Vice President:** Cecil Smith. **Secretary:** M.K. Burton. **Counsel:** David Kersey.
**President, General Manager:** George McGonagle. **Controller:** Charles Peters. **Director, Special Projects:** Tuillio Ramella.

### FIELD STAFF
**Manager:** Gary Allenson. **Coach:** Giomar Guevara, Len Johnston. **Pitching Coach:** Larry Jaster. **Trainer:** Aaron Scott.

### GAME INFORMATION
**Radio Announcer:** Buford Early. **No. of Games Broadcast:** Unavailable. **Flagship Station:** Unavailable.
**PA Announcer:** Buford Early. **Official Scorers:** Will Prewitt, Tim Richardson.
**Stadium Name:** Bowen Field. **Location:** I-77 to Bluefield exit, Route 290 to Route 460 West, right onto Leatherwood Lane, left at first light, past Chevron station and turn right, stadium ¼ mile on left. **Standard Game Times:** 7 p.m., Sun. 6. **Ticket Prices:** $3.50.
**Visiting Club Hotel:** The Upper-Classman, Bluefield State College.

# BRISTOL
## WHITE SOX

**Office Address:** 1501 Euclid Ave., Bristol, VA 24201.
**Mailing Address:** P.O. Box 1434, Bristol, VA 24203.
**Telephone:** (540) 645-7275. **FAX:** (540) 669-7686.
**E-Mail Address:** bwsox@3wave.com. **Website:** www.bristolsox.com.
**Affiliation (first year):** Chicago White Sox (1995). **Years in League:** 1921-25, 1940-55, 1969-.

### OWNERSHIP, MANAGEMENT
**Owned by:** Chicago White Sox.
**Operated by:** Bristol Baseball Inc.
**Director:** Dave Wilder (Chicago White Sox).
**President:** Mahlon Lutrell. **General Manager:** Boyce Cox.

### FIELD STAFF
**Manager:** Nick Leyva. **Coach:** Bobby Tolan. **Pitching Coach:** Roberto Espinoza. **Trainer:** Unavailable.

### GAME INFORMATION
**Radio:** None.
**PA Announcer:** Mahlon Lutrell. **Official Scorer:** Allen Shepherd.
**Stadium Name:** DeVault Memorial Stadium. **Location:** I-81 to exit 3 onto Commonwealth Ave., right on Euclid Ave. for ½ mile. **Standard Game Time:** 7 p.m. **Ticket Price Range:** $3-5.
**Visiting Club Hotel:** Ramada Inn, 2122 Euclid Ave., Bristol, VA 24201. Telephone: (540) 669-7171.

# BURLINGTON
## INDIANS

**Office Address:** 1450 Graham St., Burlington, NC 27217.
**Mailing Address:** P.O. Box 1143, Burlington, NC 27217.
**Telephone:** (336) 222-0223. **FAX:** (336) 226-2498.
**E-Mail Address:** info@burlingtonindians.net. **Website:** www.burlingtonindians.net.
**Affiliation (first year):** Cleveland Indians (1986). **Years in League:** 1986-.

### OWNERSHIP, MANAGEMENT
**Operated by:** Burlington Baseball Club, Inc.
**Director:** John Farrell (Cleveland Indians).
**President:** Miles Wolff. **Vice President:** Dan Moushon.

General Manager: Mark Cryan. **Assistant GM:** Ryan Snodgrass. **Director, Media Relations:** Jason Troop. **Director, Stadium Operations:** Josh Hall.

### FIELD STAFF
**Manager:** Kevin Higgins. **Coach:** Dennis Malave. **Pitching Coach:** Tony Arnold. **Trainer:** Teddy Blackwell.

### GAME INFORMATION
**Radio Announcer:** Jason Troop. **No. of Games Broadcast:** Home-34, Away-34. **Flagship Station:** WBAG 1150-AM. **PA Announcer:** Brad Hines. **Official Scorer:** Unavailable.
**Stadium Name:** Burlington Athletic Stadium. **Location:** I-40/85 to exit 145, north on Route 100 (Maple Avenue) for 1 1/2 miles, right on Mebane Street for 1½ miles, right on Beaumont, left on Graham. **Standard Game Time:** 7 p.m. **Ticket Price Range:** $4-6.
**Visiting Club Hotel:** Ramada Inn, I-85 at Exit 143, Burlington, NC 27217. Telephone: (336) 227-5541.

# DANVILLE
## BRAVES

**Office Address:** Dan Daniel Memorial Park, 302 River Park Dr., Danville, VA 24540.
**Mailing Address:** P.O. Box 378, Danville, VA 24543.
**Telephone:** (434) 797-3792. **FAX:** (434) 797-3799.
**E-Mail Address:** info@dbraves.com. **Website:** www.dbraves.com.
**Affiliation (first year):** Atlanta Braves (1993). **Years in League:** 1993-.

### OWNERSHIP, MANAGEMENT
**Operated by:** Atlanta National League Baseball Club, Inc.
**Director:** Dayton Moore (Atlanta Braves).
**General Manager:** David Cross. **Assistant GM:** Bob Kitzmiller. **Sales/Marketing Manager:** Calvin Funkhouser. **Office Manager:** Unavailable. **Head Groundskeeper:** Richard Gieselman.

### FIELD STAFF
**Manager:** Paul Runge. **Coach:** Mel Roberts. **Pitching Coach:** Doug Henry. **Trainer:** Charles Miller.

### GAME INFORMATION
**Radio:** None.
**PA Announcer:** Nick Pierce. **Official Scorer:** Unavailable.
**Stadium Name:** American Legion Field Post 325 Field at Dan Daniel Memorial Park. **Location:** U.S. 29 Bypass to River Park Drive/Dan Daniel Memorial Park exit; follow signs to park. **Standard Game Times:** 7 p.m., Sun. 4. **Ticket Price Range:** $3.50-6.50.
**Visiting Club Hotel:** Innkeeper-West, 3020 Riverside Dr., Danville, VA 24541. Telephone: (434) 799-1202.

# ELIZABETHTON
## TWINS

**Office Address:** 208 N. Holly Lane, Elizabethton, TN 37643.
**Mailing Address:** 136 S. Sycamore St., Elizabethton, TN 37643.
**Telephone:** (423) 547-6441. **FAX:** (423) 547-6442.
**E-Mail Address:** etwins@preferred.com. **Website:** www.elizabethtontwins.com.
**Affiliation (first year):** Minnesota Twins (1974). **Years in League:** 1937-42, 1945-51, 1974-.

### OWNERSHIP, MANAGEMENT
**Operated by:** City of Elizabethton.
**Director:** Jim Rantz (Minnesota Twins).
**President:** Harold Mains.
**General Manager:** Mike Mains. **Clubhouse Operations:** David McQueen. **Head Groundskeeper:** David Nanney. **Director, Ticket/Group Sales:** Kim Hodge. **Director, Merchandising:** Linda Church. **Director, Food Services:** Cindy Walker.

### FIELD STAFF
**Manager:** Ray Smith. **Coach:** Jeff Reed. **Pitching Coach:** Jim Shellenback. **Trainer:** Masauki Nakatsukasa.

### GAME INFORMATION
**Radio Announcer:** Unavailable. **No. of Games Broadcast:** Home-34, Away-6. **Flagship Station:** WBEJ 1240-AM. **PA Announcer:** Tom Banks. **Official Scorer:** Bill Crow.
**Stadium Name:** Joe O'Brien Field. **Location:** I-81 to Highway I-26, exit at Highway 321/67, left on Holly Lane. **Standard Game Times:** 7 p.m. **Ticket Price Range:** $3-5.
**Visiting Club Hotel:** Holiday Inn, 101 W. Springbrook Dr., Johnson City, TN 37601. Telephone: (423) 282-4611.

# GREENEVILLE
## ASTROS

\Office Address: 135 Shiloh Rd., Greeneville, TN 37743.
Mailing Address: P.O. Box 5192, Greeneville, TN 37743.
Telephone: (423) 638-0411. FAX: (423) 638-9450.
E-Mail Address: info@greenevilleastros.com. Website: www.greenevilleastros.com.
Affiliation (first year): Houston Astros (2004). Years in League: 2004-.

### OWNERSHIP, MANAGEMENT
Operated by: Houston Astros Baseball Club.
Director: Ricky Bennett (Houston Astros).
General Manager: Lynsi House. Assistant GM: David Lane. Assistant GM: Stephen Pugh. Director of Marketing/Media Relations: Hunter Reed. Head Groundskeeper: Unavailable. Clubhouse Operations: Larry Henderson.

### FIELD STAFF
Manager: Ivan DeJesus. Coach: Pete Rancont. Pitching Coach: Bill Ballou. Trainer: J.D. Shields.

### GAME INFORMATION
Radio Announcers: Bobby Rader, Brian Stayton. No. of Games Broadcast: Home-34. Flagship Station: WSMG 1450-AM.
PA Announcer: Jared Smith. Official Scorer: Johnny Painter.
Stadium Name: Pioneer Park. Location: Take I-81 to exit 23 toward Greeneville /Mosheim. Merge onto W. Andrew Johnson Highway (U.S. 11E North/Tennessee 34 East) and continue for 16.6 miles. Turn right at the Hardee's onto Tusculum Boulevard for 0.9 miles, Tusculum College campus on right. Turn right into the main entrance of college, go left onto Shiloh Road for 0.3 mile. Standard Game Times: 7 p.m., Sun. 6. Ticket Price Range: $3-6.
Visiting Club Hotel: The Jameson Inn, 3160 E. Andrew Johnson Hwy., Greeneville, TN 37743. Telephone: (423) 638-7511.

# JOHNSON CITY
## CARDINALS

Office Address: 111 Legion St., Johnson City, TN 37601.
Mailing Address: P.O. Box 179, Johnson City, TN 37605.
Telephone: (423) 461-4866. FAX: (423) 461-4864.
E-Mail Address: info@jccardinals.com. Website: www.jccardinals.com.
Affiliation (first year): St. Louis Cardinals (1975). Years in League: 1911-13, 1921-24, 1937-55, 1957-61, 1964-.

### OWNERSHIP, MANAGEMENT
Operated by: Johnson City Sports Foundation, Inc.
President: Dr. Jeff Banyas.
Director: Bruce Manno (St. Louis Cardinals).
General Manager: Chuck Arnold. Assistant GM: Benjamin Jones. Clubhouse Operations: Pat Kramer. Groundskeeper: Mike Whitson.

### FIELD STAFF
Manager: Dan Radison. Coach: Joe Almaraz. Pitching Coach: Al Holland. Trainer: Unavailable.

### GAME INFORMATION
Radio: None.
PA Announcer: Unavailable. Official Scorer: Unavailable.
Stadium Name: Howard Johnson Field at Cardinal Park. Location: I-181 to exit 32, left on East Main, through light onto Legion Street. Standard Game Times: 7 p.m. Ticket Price Range: $3-5.
Visiting Club Hotel: Holiday Inn, 101 W. Springbrook Dr., Johnson City, TN 37601. Telephone: (423) 282-4611.

# KINGSPORT
## METS

Office Address: 800 Granby Rd., Kingsport, TN 37660.
Mailing Address: P.O. Box 1128, Kingsport, TN 37662.
Telephone: (423) 378-3744. FAX: (423) 392-8538.
E-Mail Address: info@kmets.com. Website: www.kmets.com.
Affiliation (first year): New York Mets (1980). Years in League: 1921-25, 1938-52, 1957, 1960-63, 1969-82, 1984-.

## OWNERSHIP, MANAGEMENT
**Operated by:** S&H Baseball, LLC.
**Director:** Adam Wogan (New York Mets).
**President:** Rick Spivey. **Vice President:** Steve Harville.
**General Manager:** Roman Stout. **Assistant GM:** Tim Shelton. **Director, Housing:** Peggy Lozier. **Accountant:** Bob Dingus. **Head Groundskeeper:** Josh Warner. **Clubhouse Attendant:** Dustin Vaughn.

## FIELD STAFF
**Manager:** Donovan Mitchell. **Coach:** Juan Lopez. **Pitching Coach:** Dan Murray. **Trainer:** Matt Thayer. **Strength/Conditioning:** Steve Crosier.

## GAME INFORMATION
**Radio Announcer:** Mike Long. **No of Games Broadcast:** Home-34, Away-19. **Flagship Station:** Unavailable.
**PA Announcer:** Don Spivey. **Official Scorer:** Eddie Durham.
**Stadium Name:** Hunter Wright Stadium. **Location:** I-81 to I-181 North, exit 11E (Stone Drive), left on West Stone Drive (U.S. 11W), right on Granby Road. **Standard Game Times:** 7 p.m. **Ticket Price Range:** $3-5.
**Visiting Club Hotel:** Jameson Inn, 304 Bays Mountain Plaza, Kingsport, TN 37660. Telephone: (423) 230-0534.

# PRINCETON
## DEVIL RAYS

**Office Address:** Hunnicutt Field, Old Bluefield Road, Princeton, WV 24740.
**Mailing Address:** P.O. Box 5646, Princeton, WV 24740.
**Telephone:** (304) 487-2000. **FAX:** (304) 487-8762.
**E-Mail Address:** raysball@sunlitsurf.com. **Website:** www.princetondevilrays.com.
**Affiliation (first year):** Tampa Bay Devil Rays (1997). **Years in League:** 1988-.

## OWNERSHIP, MANAGEMENT
**Operated by:** Princeton Baseball Association, Inc.
**Director:** Mitch Lukevics (Tampa Bay Devil Rays).
**President:** Dewey Russell.
**General Manager:** Jim Holland. **Director, Stadium Operations:** Mick Bayle. **Head Groundskeeper:** Frankie Bailey. **Account Representative:** Andy Bradley. **Clubhouse Manager:** Unavailable.

## FIELD STAFF
**Manager:** Jamie Nelson. **Coach:** Rafael Deleon. **Pitching Coach:** Rafael Montalvo. **Trainer:** Unavailable.

## GAME INFORMATION
**Radio Announcer:** Unavailable. **No. of Games Broadcast:** Away-34. **Flagship Station:** WAEY 1490-AM.
**PA Announcer:** Unavailable. **Official Scorer:** Jarrod Hines.
**Stadium Name:** Hunnicutt Field. **Location:** Exit 9 off I-77, U.S. 460 West to downtown exit, left on Stafford Drive, stadium located behind Mercer County Technical Education Center. **Standard Game Times:** 7 p.m., Sun. 5:30. **Ticket Price Range:** $3-5.
**Visiting Club Hotel:** Days Inn, I-77 and Ambrose Lane, Princeton, WV 24740. Telephone: (304) 425-8100.

# PULASKI
## BLUE JAYS

**Mailing Address:** P.O. Box 676, Pulaski, VA 24301.
**Telephone:** (540) 980-1070. **FAX:** (540) 980-1850.
**E-Mail Address:** mail@pulaskibluejays.com. **Website:** www.pulaskibluejays.com.
**Affiliation (first year):** Toronto Blue Jays (2003). **Years in League:** 1946-50, 1952-55, 1957-58, 1969-77, 1982-92, 1997-.

## OWNERSHIP, MANAGEMENT
**Operated by:** Pulaski Baseball, Inc.
**President/General Manager:** Tom Compton. **Treasurer:** Wayne Compton. **Assistant GM:** Jaimee Marinke.

## FIELD STAFF
**Manager:** Dave Pano. **Coach:** Unavailable. **Pitching Coach:** Unavailable. **Trainer:** Bob Tarpey.

## GAME INFORMATION
**Radio:** None.
**PA Announcer:** Andy French. **Official Scorer:** Edgar Williams.
**Stadium Name:** Calfee Park. **Location:** I-81 to exit 89B (Route 11), north to Pulaski, right on Pierce Avenue. **Standard Game Time:** 7 p.m. **Ticket Price Range:** $4-6.
**Visiting Club Hotel:** Comfort Inn, 4424 Cleburne Blvd., Dublin, VA 24084. Telephone: (540) 674-1100.

# PIONEER
## LEAGUE

**Office Address:** 157 S. Lincoln Ave., Spokane, WA 99201.
**Mailing Address:** P.O. Box 2564, Spokane, WA 99220.
**Telephone:** (509) 456-7615. **FAX:** (509) 456-0136.
**E-Mail Address:** fanmail@pioneerleague.com. **Website:** www.pioneerleague.com.
**Years League Active:** 1939-42, 1946-.

**President/Secretary-Treasurer:** Jim McCurdy.
**Vice President:** Mike Ellis (Missoula).
**Directors:** Dave Baggott (Ogden), Mike Ellis (Missoula), D.G. Elmore (Helena), Kevin Greene (Idaho Falls), Kevin Haughian (Casper), Jeff Katofsky (Orem), Vinny Purpura (Great Falls), Bob Wilson (Billings).
**Administrative Assistant:** Teryl MacDonald.
**Division Structure: North**—Billings, Great Falls, Helena, Missoula. **South**—Casper, Idaho Falls, Ogden, Orem.
**Regular Season:** 76 games (split schedule). **2006 Opening Date:** June 20. **Closing Date:** Sept. 7.
**Playoff Format:** First-half division winners meet second-half division winners in best-of-3 series. Winners meet in best-of-3 series for league championship.
**All-Star Game:** None.

**Jim McCurdy**

**Roster Limit:** 35 active, 30 dressed for each game. **Player Eligibility Rule:** No more than 17 players 21 and older, provided that no more than two are 23 or older. No player on active list may have three or more years of prior minor league service.
**Brand of Baseball:** Rawlings.
**Statistician:** Major League Baseball Advanced Media, 75 Ninth Ave., New York, NY 10011.
**Umpires:** Unavailable.

## STADIUM INFORMATION

| Club | Stadium | Opened | LF | CF | RF | Capacity | 2005 Att. |
|------|---------|--------|-----|-----|-----|----------|-----------|
| Billings | Cobb Field | 1948 | 335 | 405 | 325 | 4,200 | 88,702 |
| Casper | Mike Lansing Field | 2002 | 355 | 400 | 345 | 2,500 | 50,087 |
| Great Falls | Legion Park | 1956 | 335 | 414 | 335 | 3,800 | 96,012 |
| Helena | Kindrick Field | 1939 | 335 | 400 | 325 | 1,700 | 40,141 |
| Idaho Falls | McDermott Field | 1976 | 340 | 400 | 350 | 2,928 | 65,313 |
| Missoula | Missoula Civic Stadium | 2004 | 309 | 398 | 287 | 2,600 | 67,922 |
| Ogden | Lindquist Field | 1997 | 335 | 396 | 334 | 5,000 | 131,371 |
| Orem | Home of the Owlz | 2005 | 305 | 408 | 312 | 4,000 | 76,784 |

# BILLINGS
## MUSTANGS

**Office Address:** Cobb Field, 901 N. 27th St., Billings, MT 59101.
**Mailing Address:** P.O. Box 1553, Billings, MT 59103.
**Telephone:** (406) 252-1241. **FAX:** (406) 252-2968.
**E-Mail Address:** mustangs@billingsmustangs.com. **Website:** www.billingsmustangs.com.
**Affiliation (first year):** Cincinnati Reds (1974). **Years in League:** 1948-63, 1969-.

### OWNERSHIP, MANAGEMENT
**Operated by:** Billings Pioneer Baseball Club, Inc.
**President:** Bob Wilson.
**General Manager:** Gary Roller. **Assistant GM:** Matt Bender. **Director, Field Maintenance:** John Barta. **Director, Broadcasting:** Andy Price. **Director, Clubhouse Operations:** Jeremy Haworth.

### FIELD STAFF
**Manager:** Rick Burleson. **Coach:** Jeff Young. **Pitching Coach:** Butch Henry. **Trainer:** Unavailable.

### GAME INFORMATION
**Radio Announcer:** Andy Price. **No. of Games Broadcast:** Home-38, Away-38. **Flagship Station:** KBUL 970-AM.
**PA Announcer:** Kyle Riley. **Official Scorer:** George Kimmet.
**Stadium Name:** Cobb Field. **Location:** I-90 to 27th Street North exit, north to Ninth Avenue North. **Standard Game Times:** 7:05 p.m., Sun. 4:05. **Ticket Price Range:** $4-7.50.
**Visiting Club Hotel:** Rimrock Inn, 1203 N. 27th St., Billings, MT 59101. Telephone: (406) 252-7107.

# CASPER
## ROCKIES

**Office Address:** 330 Kati Lane, Casper, WY 82601.
**Mailing Address:** P.O. Box 1293, Casper, WY 82602.
**Telephone:** (307) 232-1111. **FAX:** (307) 265-7867.
**E-Mail Address:** homerun@casperrockies.com. **Website:** www.casperrockies.com.
**Affiliation (first year):** Colorado Rockies (2001). **Years in League:** 2001-.

### OWNERSHIP, MANAGEMENT
**Operated by:** Casper Professional Baseball Club, LLC.
**Principal Owner, Chief Executive Officer:** Kevin Haughian.
**President, General Manager:** Danny Tetzlaff. **Assistant GM:** Unavailable. **Director of Operations:** Seth Mathews.

### FIELD STAFF
**Manager:** P.J. Carey. **Coach:** Tony Diaz. **Pitching Coach:** Mark Thompson. **Trainer:** Jeremy Spencer.

### GAME INFORMATION
**Radio Announcer:** Unavailable. **No. of Games Broadcast:** Home-38, Away-38. **Flagship Station:** KVOC 1230-AM.
**PA Announcer:** Unavailable. **Official Scorer:** Unavailable.
**Stadium Name:** Mike Lansing Field. **Location:** I-25 to Poplar Street exit, north on Poplar Street, right into Crossroads Park. **Standard Game Times:** 7:05 p.m., Sun. 4:05. **Ticket Price Range:** $7.50-9.
**Visiting Club Hotel:** Parkway Plaza, 123 W. "E" St., Casper, WY 82601. Telephone (307) 235-1777.

# GREAT FALLS
## WHITE SOX

**Office/Stadium Address:** 1015 25th St. N., Great Falls, MT 59401.
**Mailing Address:** P.O. Box 1621, Great Falls, MT 59403.
**Telephone:** (406) 452-5311. **FAX:** (406) 454-0811.
**E-Mail Address:** whitesox@greatfallswhitesox.com. **Website:** www.greatfallswhitesox.com.
**Affiliation (first year):** Chicago White Sox (2003). **Years in League:** 1948-1963, 1969-.

### OWNERSHIP, MANAGEMENT
**Operated by:** Great Falls Baseball Club, Inc.
**President:** Vinny Purpura.
**General Manager:** Jim Keough. **Assistant GM:** Ginger Burcham. **Head Groundskeeper:** Carl Christofferson. **Office Manager:** Christine Oxley. **Marketing Executive/Stadium Operations Manager:** Bob Pinski.

### FIELD STAFF
**Manager:** Tommy Thompson. **Coach:** Jerry Hairston. **Pitching Coach:** Curt Hasler. **Trainer:** Kevin Pillifant.
### GAME INFORMATION
**Radio Announcer:** Ray Alexander. **No. of Games Broadcast:** Home-38, Away-38. **Flagship Station:** KMON 560-AM. **PA Announcer:** Tim Paul. **Official Scorer:** Mike Lewis.
**Stadium Name:** Legion Park. **Location:** From I-15, take 10th Ave. South (exit 281) for four miles to 26th Street, left to 8th Ave. North, left to 25th Street North, right to ballpark. **Standard Game Times:** 7 p.m., Sun. 4. **Ticket Price Range:** $5-8.
**Visiting Club Hotel:** Midtown Hotel, 526 Second Ave. N., Great Falls, MT 59401. Telephone: (406) 453-2411.

# HELENA
## BREWERS

**Office Address:** 1300 N. Ewing, Helena, MT 59601.
**Mailing Address:** P.O. Box 6756, Helena, MT 59604.
**Telephone:** (406) 495-0500. **FAX:** (406) 495-0900.
**E-Mail Address:** info@helenabrewers.net. **Website:** www.helenabrewers.net.
**Affiliation (first year):** Milwaukee Brewers (2003). **Years in League:** 1978-2000, 2003-.
### OWNERSHIP, MANAGEMENT
**Operated by:** Helena Baseball Club LLC.
**Principal Owner:** D.G. Elmore.
**General Manager:** Paul Fetz. **Assistant GM:** Travis Brower. **Director, Tickets:** Unavailable. **Director, Broadcasting/Media Relations:** Unavailable.
### FIELD STAFF
**Manager:** Ed Sedar. **Coach:** Johnny Narron. **Pitching Coach:** Mark Littell. **Trainer:** Unavailable.
### GAME INFORMATION
**Radio Announcer:** Unavailable. **No. of Games Broadcast:** Home-38, Away-38. **Flagship Station:** KCAP 1340-AM. **PA Announcer:** Unavailable. **Official Scorer:** Unavailable.
**Stadium Name:** Kindrick Field. **Location:** Cedar Street exit off I-15, west to Main Street, left at Memorial Park. **Standard Game Time:** 7:05 p.m. **Ticket Price Range:** $5-7.
**Visiting Club Hotel:** Red Lion Colonial Hotel, 2301 Colonial Dr., Helena, MT 59601. Telephone: (406) 443-2100.

# IDAHO FALLS
## CHUKARS

**Office Address:** 568 W. Elva, Idaho Falls, ID 83402.
**Mailing Address:** P.O. Box 2183, Idaho Falls, ID 83403.
**Telephone:** (208) 522-8363. **FAX:** (208) 522-9858.
**E-Mail Address:** chukars@ifchukars.com. **Website:** www.ifchukars.com.
**Affiliation (first year):** Kansas City Royals (2004). **Years in League:** 1940-42, 1946-.
### OWNERSHIP, MANAGEMENT
**Operated by:** The Elmore Group.
**Principal Owner:** David Elmore.
**President, General Manager:** Kevin Greene. **Assistant GM, Merchandise:** Marcus Loyola. **Director, Concessions:** Nathan Peck. **Director, Public Relations:** Andrew Daugherty. **Head Groundskeeper:** Christopher Michaels.
### FIELD STAFF
**Manager:** Brian Rupp. **Coach:** Theron Todd. **Pitching Coach:** Jose Bautista. **Trainer:** Yoshi Kitaura.
### GAME INFORMATION
**Radio Announcers:** John Balginy, Jim Garshow. **No. of Games Broadcast:** Home-38, Away-38. **Flagship Station:** KUPI 980-AM.
**PA Announcer:** Steve Davis. **Official Scorer:** John Balginy.
**Stadium Name:** McDermott Field. **Location:** I-15 to West Broadway exit, left onto Memorial Drive, right on Mound Avenue, 1/4 mile to stadium. **Standard Game Times:** 7:15 p.m., Sun. 4. **Ticket Price Range:** $6-8.
**Visiting Club Hotel:** Guesthouse Inn & Suites, 850 Lindsay Blvd., Idaho Falls, ID 83402. Telephone: (208) 522-6260.

# MISSOULA
## OSPREY

**Office Address:** 412 W. Alder St, Missoula, MT 59802.
**Telephone:** (406) 543-3300. **FAX:** (406) 543-9463.
**E-Mail Address:** generalmgr@missoulaosprey.com. **Website:** www.missoula osprey.com.
**Affiliation (first year):** Arizona Diamondbacks (1999). **Years in League:** 1956-60, 1999-.

### OWNERSHIP, MANAGEMENT
**Operated by:** Mountain Baseball, LLC.
**President:** Mike Ellis. **Executive Vice President:** Judy Ellis.
**Vice President/General Manager:** Matt Ellis. **Assistant GMs:** Chris Hale, Jared Amoss. **VP, Finance/Purchasing:** Shelly Ellis. **Manager, Group Sales:** Jeff Griffin. **Director, Merchandise:** Lori Hale. **Office Manager:** Unavailable. **Clubhouse Manager:** Unavailable.

### FIELD STAFF
**Manager:** Hector De la Cruz. **Coach:** Jerry Stitt. **Pitching Coach:** Mel Stottlemyre Jr. **Trainer:** Tim Higgins.

### GAME INFORMATION
**Radio Announcer:** Tim Boulware. **No. of Games Broadcast:** Home-38, Away-38. **Flagship Station:** 1340-AM.
**PA Announcer:** Patrick Nikolay. **Official Scorer:** Unavailable.
**Stadium Name:** Play Ball Park. **Location:** Orange Street to Cregg Lane, west on Cregg Lane, stadium west of McCormick Park. **Standard Game Times:** 7:05 p.m., Sun. 5:05. **Ticket Price Range:** $4-10.
**Visiting Club Hotel:** Campus Inn, 744 E. Broadway, Missoula, MT 59802. Telephone: (406) 549-5134.

# OGDEN
## RAPTORS

**Office Address:** 2330 Lincoln Ave., Ogden, UT 84401.
**Telephone:** (801) 393-2400. **FAX:** (801) 393-2473.
**E-Mail Address:** homerun@ogden-raptors.com. **Website:** www.ogden-raptors.com.
**Affiliation (first year):** Los Angeles Dodgers (2003). **Years in League:** 1939-42, 1946-55, 1966-74, 1994-.

### OWNERSHIP, MANAGEMENT
**Operated by:** Ogden Professional Baseball, Inc.
**Principal Owners:** Dave Baggott, John Lindquist. **Chairman, President:** Dave Baggott.
**General Manager:** Joe Stein. **Director, Marketing:** John Stein. **Controller:** Carol Spickler. **Head Groundskeeper:** Ken Kopinski. **Director, Merchandising:** Geri Kopinski.

### FIELD STAFF
**Manager:** Lance Parrish. **Coach:** Rafael Rijo. **Pitching Coach:** Bob Welch. **Trainer:** Joe Fox.

### GAME INFORMATION
**Radio Announcer:** Eric Knighton. **No. of Games Broadcast:** Home-38, Away-38. **Flagship Station:** Unavailable.
**PA Announcer:** Pete Diamond. **Official Scorer:** Dennis Kunimura.
**Stadium Name:** Lindquist Field. **Location:** I-15 North to 21st Street exit, east to Lincoln Avenue, south three blocks to park. **Standard Game Times:** 7 p.m., Sun. 1. **Ticket Price Range:** $6-8.
**Visiting Club Hotel:** Marriott, 247 24th St., Odgen, UT 84401. Telephone: (801) 627-1190.

# OREM
## OWLZ

**Office Address:** Home of the OWLZ, 970 W. University Pkwy., Orem, UT 84058.
**Telephone:** (801) 377-2255. **FAX:** (801) 377-2345.
**E-Mail Address:** fan@oremowlz.com. **Website:** www.oremowlz.com.
**Affiliation:** Anaheim Angels (2001). **Years in League:** 2001-.

## OWNERSHIP, MANAGEMENT

**Operated by:** Bery Bery Gud To Me, LLC.
**Principal Owners:** Jeff Katofsky, Harvey Katofsky.
**Co-General Managers:** Ryan Pace, Zachary Fraser. **Assistant GM:** Sarah Hansen. **Director, Broadcasting/Media Relations:** Brandon Gaudin. **Director, Public Relations:** Nick Cottle. **Director, Sales:** Blake Stillman.

## FIELD STAFF

**Manager:** Tom Kotchman. **Coach:** Francisco Matos. **Pitching Coach:** Zeke Zimmerman. **Trainer:** Mike Metcalfe.

## GAME INFORMATION

**Radio Announcer:** Brandon Gaudin. **No. of Games Broadcast:** Home-38, Away-38. **Flagship Station:** The Zone 1280-AM/960-AM.
**PA Announcer:** Lincoln Fillmore. **Official Scorer:** Unavailable.
**Stadium Name:** Home of the OWLZ. **Location:** Exit 272 (University Parkway) off 1-15 at Utah Valley State College campus. **Standard Game Times:** 7:05 p.m., Sun. 4:05. **Ticket Price Range:** $3-8.
**Visiting Club Hotel:** Provo Days Inn, 1675 N. 200 West, Provo, UT 84604. Telephone: (801) 375-8600.

# ARIZONA LEAGUE

Office Address: 910 Main St., Suite 351, Boise, ID 83702.
Mailing Address: P.O. Box 1645, Boise, ID 83701.
Telephone: (208) 429-1511. FAX: (208) 429-1525. E-Mail Address: bobrichmond@worldnet.att.net.
Years League Active: 1988-.
President/Treasurer: Bob Richmond.
Vice President: Bobby Evans (Giants). Corporate Secretary: Ted Polakowski (Athletics).
Administrative Assistant: Rob Richmond.
Division Structure: None.
Regular Season: 56 games (split schedule). 2006 Opening Date: June 22. Closing Date: Aug. 30. Standard Game Times: 10:30 a.m.; night games—7 p.m.
Playoff Format: First-half winner meets second-half winner in one-game championship.
All-Star Game: None.
Roster Limit: 35 active. Player Eligibility Rule: No more than 12 players 20 or older, no more than four players 21 or older, and no more than four players of any age not selected in 2006 first-year draft. A maximum of four foreign players not subject to the draft playing in the United States for the first time are exempt from the age limits.
Brand of Baseball: Rawlings.
Statistician: Major League Baseball Advanced Media, 75 9th Ave., New York, NY 10011.

| Clubs | Playing Site | Manager | Coach | Pitching Coach |
|---|---|---|---|---|
| Angels | Tempe Diablo Stadium | Ever Magallanes | Rodney Davis | Dan Ricabal |
| Athletics | Papago Park Sports Complex, Phoenix | Ruben Escalera | Juan Dilone | Mike Holmes |
| Brewers | Maryvale Baseball Complex, Phoenix | Unavailable | Joel Youngblood | Steve Cline |
| Cubs | Fitch Park, Mesa | Carmelo Martinez | Antonio Grissom | Rick Tronerud |
| Giants | Giants minor league complex, Scottsdale | Bert Hunter | Leo Garcia | Will Malerich |
| Mariners | Peoria Sports Complex, Peoria | Dana Williams | Andy Bottin | Gary Wheelock |
| Padres | Peoria Sports Complex, Peoria | Carlos Lezcano | Manny Crespo | Dave Rajsich |
| Rangers | Surprise Recreation Campus | Bob Skube | Mark Whiten | Unavailable |
| Royals | Surprise Recreation Campus | Lloyd Simmons | Nelson Liriano | Mark Davis |

# GULF COAST LEAGUE

Office Address: 1503 Clower Creek Dr., Suite H-262, Sarasota, FL 34231.
Telephone: (941) 966-6407. FAX: (941) 966-6872.
Years League Active: 1964-.
President/Secretary-Treasurer: Tom Saffell.
First Vice President: Steve Noworyta (Phillies). Second Vice President: Jim Rantz (Twins).
Administrative Assistant: Bill Ventolo.
Division Structure: East—Dodgers, Marlins, Mets, Nationals. North—Braves, Phillies, Tigers, Yankees. South—Pirates, Reds, Red Sox, Twins.
Regular Season: 54 games. 2006 Opening Date: June 20. Closing Date: Aug. 21.
Playoff Format: Division winner with best regular season record meets winner of one-game playoff between other two division winners in best-of-3 series for championship.
Roster Limit: 35 active, but only 30 eligible for each game. Player Eligibility Rule: No age restrictions. No more than two years of prior service, excluding Rookie leagues outside the United States and Canada; a third year is allowed for players under 20.
Brand of Baseball: Rawlings.
Statistician: Major League Baseball Advanced Media, 75 9th Ave., New York, NY 10011.

| Clubs | Playing Site | Manager | Coach(es) | Pitching Coach |
|---|---|---|---|---|
| Braves | Disney's Wide World of Sports, Orlando | Luis Ortiz | S. Lezcano/J. Saul | Derrick Lewis |
| Dodgers | Dodgertown, Vero Beach | Juan Bustabad | M. Singleton/T. Brock | Hector Eduardo |
| Marlins | Roger Dean Stadium, Jupiter | Edwin Rodriguez | Johnny Rodriguez | Gary Buckels |
| Mets | St. Lucie Sports Complex, St. Lucie | Bobby Floyd | Scott Hunter | Hector Berrios |
| Nationals | Carl Barger Baseball Complex, Melbourne | Bobby Henley | Jason Camilli | Franklin Bravo |
| Phillies | Carpenter Complex, Clearwater | Jim Morrison | Luis Melendez | Carlos Arroyo |
| Pirates | Pirate City Complex, Bradenton | Pete Mackanin | Woody Huyke | Miguel Bonilla |
| Reds | Ed Smith Stadium, Sarasota | Luis Aguayo | Don Kruzel | Jamie Garcia |
| Red Sox | Red Sox Minor League Complex | Dave Tomlin | U.L. Washington | Goose Gregson |
| Tigers | Tigertown, Lakeland | Kevin Bradshaw | Benny Distefano | Greg Sabat |
| Twins | Lee County Stadium, Fort Myers | Nelson Prada | Milt Cuyler | Unavailable |
| Yankees | Yankee Complex, Tampa | Oscar Acosta | Matt Martin/Hector Lopez | Carlos Reyes |

# MINOR LEAGUE SCHEDULES

# TRIPLE-A
## INTERNATIONAL LEAGUE

### BUFFALO

**APRIL**
| | |
|---|---|
| 6-7-8-9 | at Richmond |
| 10-11-12-13 | at Norfolk |
| 14-15-16-17 | Columbus |
| 18-19-20-21 | Richmond |
| 22-23 | at Pawtucket |
| 24-25 | at Syracuse |
| 27-28 | Syracuse |
| 29-30 | Charlotte |

**MAY**
| | |
|---|---|
| 1-2 | Charlotte |
| 3-4-5 | at Scranton |
| 6-7-7-8 | Ottawa |
| 9-10 | at Rochester |
| 11-12 | Rochester |
| 13-14-15 | at Ottawa |
| 16-17-18-19 | Pawtucket |
| 20-21 | Syracuse |
| 23-24-25-26 | at Toledo |
| 27-28-29-30 | at Columbus |

**JUNE**
| | |
|---|---|
| 1-2-3-4 | Durham |
| 5-6-7-8 | Toledo |
| 9-10-11-12 | at Charlotte |
| 13-14-15-16 | at Durham |
| 17-18-19-20 | Indianapolis |
| 22-23-24-25 | Scranton |
| 26-27-28-29 | at Syracuse |
| 30 | at Rochester |

**JULY**
| | |
|---|---|
| 1 | at Rochester |
| 2-3 | Rochester |
| 4-5 | at Scranton |
| 6-7-8-9 | Pawtucket |
| 13-14-15-16 | at Ind. |
| 17-18-19-20 | at Louisville |
| 21-22-23-24 | Syracuse |
| 25-26-27-28 | Louisville |
| 29-30-31 | at Pawtucket |

**AUGUST**
| | |
|---|---|
| 1 | at Pawtucket |
| 3-4-5-6 | Norfolk |
| 7-8 | Ottawa |
| 10-11 | at Rochester |
| 12-13 | Rochester |
| 14-15 | at Pawtucket |
| 16-17-18 | at Ottawa |
| 19-20 | at Syracuse |
| 21-22-23-24 | Scranton |
| 25-26-27 | at Scranton |
| 28-29 | Ottawa |
| 30-31 | Rochester |

**SEPTEMBER**
| | |
|---|---|
| 1-2 | at Rochester |
| 3-4 | at Ottawa |

### CHARLOTTE

**APRIL**
| | |
|---|---|
| 6-7-8-9 | at Toledo |
| 10-11-12-13 | at Columbus |
| 14-15-16-17 | Pawtucket |
| 18-19-20-21 | Toledo |
| 22 | at Durham |
| 23-24 | Durham |
| 25-26-27-28 | at Ottawa |
| 29-30 | at Buffalo |

**MAY**
| | |
|---|---|
| 1-2 | at Buffalo |
| 4-5-6-7 | Louisville |
| 8-9-10-11 | Indianapolis |
| 12-13-14-15 | at Louisville |
| 16-17-18-19 | at Ind. |
| 20-21 | Durham |
| 23-24-25-26 | Ottawa |
| 27-28-29-30 | at Richmond |

**JUNE**
| | |
|---|---|
| 1-2-3-4 | at Norfolk |
| 5-6-7-8 | Richmond |
| 9-10-11-12 | Buffalo |
| 13-14-15-16 | at Scranton |
| 17-18 | Durham |
| 19-20 | at Durham |
| 22-23-24-25 | Norfolk |
| 26-27 | at Columbus |
| 28-29 | at Toledo |
| 30 | at Richmond |

**JULY**
| | |
|---|---|
| 1 | at Richmond |
| 2-3 | at Norfolk |
| 4-5 | Norfolk |
| 6-7-8-9 | Syracuse |
| 13-14-15-16 | at Pawtucket |
| 17-18-19-20 | Columbus |
| 21-22-23-24 | Scranton |
| 25-26-27-28 | at Rochester |
| 29-30-31 | at Syracuse |

**AUGUST**
| | |
|---|---|
| 1 | at Syracuse |
| 2 | at Durham |
| 3-4-5-6 | Rochester |
| 7-8 | Durham |
| 10 | at Durham |
| 11-12 | Louisville |
| 13-14 | Indianapolis |
| 15-16 | at Louisville |
| 17-18 | at Indianapolis |
| 19-20 | at Norfolk |
| 21-22 | Norfolk |
| 23-24 | at Richmond |
| 25-26-27 | at Durham |
| 28-29 | Columbus |
| 30-31 | Toledo |

**SEPTEMBER**
| | |
|---|---|
| 1-2-3-4 | Richmond |

### COLUMBUS

**APRIL**
| | |
|---|---|
| 6-7-8-9 | Scranton |
| 10-11-12-13 | Charlotte |
| 14-15-16-17 | at Buffalo |
| 18-19-20-21 | at Scranton |
| 22-23 | at Toledo |
| 24-25 | Indianapolis |
| 26-27 | Louisville |
| 28-29-30 | at Indianapolis |

**MAY**
| | |
|---|---|
| 1-2 | at Louisville |
| 4-5-6-7 | Norfolk |
| 8-9-10-11 | Richmond |
| 12-13-14-15 | at Norfolk |
| 16-17-18-19 | at Richmond |
| 20-21 | Toledo |
| 23-24-25-26 | Rochester |
| 27-28-29-30 | Buffalo |

**JUNE**
| | |
|---|---|
| 1-2-3-4 | at Rochester |
| 5-6-7-8 | at Ottawa |
| 9-10-11-12 | at Syracuse |
| 13-14-15-16 | Ottawa |
| 17-18-19-20 | Syracuse |
| 22-23-24-25 | at Pawtucket |
| 26-27 | Charlotte |
| 28-29 | Norfolk |
| 30 | Louisville |

**JULY**
| | |
|---|---|
| 1-2-3 | Louisville |
| 4-5-6 | at Indianapolis |
| 7-8-9 | at Louisville |
| 13-14-15-16 | at Durham |
| 17-18-19-20 | at Charlotte |
| 21-22-23-24 | Pawtucket |
| 25-26-27-28 | Durham |
| 29-30 | at Indianapolis |
| 31 | at Louisville |

**AUGUST**
| | |
|---|---|
| 1-2 | at Louisville |
| 4-5-6 | Indianapolis |
| 7-8 | Toledo |
| 9-10 | at Toledo |
| 11-12 | at Richmond |
| 13-14 | at Norfolk |
| 15-16 | Richmond |
| 17-18 | Durham |
| 19-20 | at Toledo |
| 21-22 | Toledo |
| 23-24 | Louisville |
| 25-26-27 | Indianapolis |
| 28-29 | at Charlotte |
| 30-31 | at Durham |

**SEPTEMBER**
| | |
|---|---|
| 1-2 | Toledo |
| 3-4 | at Toledo |

### DURHAM

**APRIL**
| | |
|---|---|
| 6-7-8-9 | at Norfolk |
| 10-11-12-13 | at Richmond |
| 14-15-16-17 | Toledo |
| 18-19-20-21 | Pawtucket |
| 22 | Charlotte |
| 23-24 | at Charlotte |
| 25-26-27-28 | at Pawtucket |
| 29-30 | at Syracuse |

**MAY**
| | |
|---|---|
| 1-2 | at Syracuse |
| 4-5-6-7 | Indianapolis |
| 8-9-10-11 | Louisville |
| 12-13-14-15 | at Ind. |
| 16-17-18-19 | at Louisville |
| 20-21 | at Charlotte |
| 23-24-25-26 | Richmond |
| 27-28-29-30 | Ottawa |

**JUNE**
| | |
|---|---|
| 1-2-3-4 | at Buffalo |
| 5-6-7-8 | at Rochester |
| 9-10-11-12 | Norfolk |
| 13-14-15-16 | Buffalo |
| 17-18 | at Charlotte |
| 19-20 | Charlotte |
| 22-23-24-25 | at Scranton |
| 26-27-28-29 | at Scranton |
| 30 | Norfolk |

**JULY**
| | |
|---|---|
| 1 | Norfolk |
| 2-3-4-5 | Syracuse |
| 6-7 | Richmond |
| 8-9 | at Richmond |
| 13-14-15-16 | Columbus |
| 17-18-19-20 | Scranton |
| 21-22-23-24 | at Toledo |
| 25-26-27-28 | at Columbus |
| 29-30-31 | Rochester |

**AUGUST**
| | |
|---|---|
| 1 | Rochester |
| 2 | Charlotte |
| 3-4 | at Richmond |
| 5-6 | Richmond |
| 7-8 | at Charlotte |
| 10 | Charlotte |
| 11-12 | Indianapolis |
| 13-14 | Louisville |
| 15-16 | at Toledo |
| 17-18 | at Columbus |
| 19-20 | at Louisville |
| 21-22 | at Indianapolis |
| 23-24 | Norfolk |
| 25-26-27 | Charlotte |
| 28-29 | Toledo |
| 30-31 | Columbus |

**SEPTEMBER**
| | |
|---|---|
| 1-2-3-4 | at Norfolk |

### INDIANAPOLIS

**APRIL**
| | |
|---|---|
| 6-7-8-9 | at Pawtucket |
| 10-11-12-13 | at Ottawa |
| 14-15-16-17 | Syracuse |
| 18-19-20-21 | Ottawa |
| 22-23 | at Louisville |
| 24-25 | at Columbus |
| 26-27 | at Toledo |
| 28-29-30 | Columbus |

**MAY**
| | |
|---|---|
| 1-2 | Toledo |
| 4-5-6-7 | at Durham |

| Date | Opponent |
|---|---|
| 8-9-10-11 | at Charlotte |
| 12-13-14-15 | Durham |
| 16-17-18-19 | Charlotte |
| 20-21 | Louisville |
| 23-24-25-26 | at Scranton |
| 27-28-29-30 | at Syracuse |
| **JUNE** | |
| 1-2-3-4 | Scranton |
| 5-6-7-8 | Pawtucket |
| 9-10 | at Louisville |
| 11-12 | Louisville |
| 13-14-15-16 | at Rochester |
| 17-18-19-20 | at Buffalo |
| 22-23-24-25 | Richmond |
| 26-27-28-29 | Rochester |
| 30 | at Toledo |
| **JULY** | |
| 1-2-3 | at Toledo |
| 4-5-6 | Columbus |
| 7-8-9 | Toledo |
| 13-14-15-16 | Buffalo |
| 17-18-19-20 | Norfolk |
| 21-22-23-24 | at Richmond |
| 25-26-27-28 | at Norfolk |
| 29-30 | Columbus |
| 31 | Toledo |
| **AUGUST** | |
| 1-2 | Toledo |
| 4-5-6 | at Columbus |
| 7-8 | at Louisville |
| 9-10 | Louisville |
| 11-12 | at Durham |
| 13-14 | at Charlotte |
| 15-16 | Norfolk |
| 17-18 | Charlotte |
| 19-20 | Richmond |
| 21-22 | Durham |
| 23-24 | at Toledo |
| 25-26-27 | at Columbus |
| 28-29 | at Richmond |
| 30-31 | at Norfolk |
| **SEPTEMBER** | |
| 1-2 | Louisville |
| 3-4 | at Louisville |

## LOUISVILLE

| Date | Opponent |
|---|---|
| **APRIL** | |
| 6-7-8-9 | at Ottawa |
| 10-11-12-13 | at Syracuse |
| 14-15-16-17 | Ottawa |
| 18-19-20-21 | Syracuse |
| 22-23 | Indianapolis |
| 24-25 | at Toledo |
| 26-27 | at Columbus |
| 28-29-30 | Toledo |
| **MAY** | |
| 1-2 | Columbus |
| 4-5-6-7 | at Charlotte |
| 8-9-10-11 | at Durham |
| 12-13-14-15 | Charlotte |
| 16-17-18-19 | Durham |
| 20-21 | at Indianapolis |
| 23-24-25-26 | at Pawtucket |
| 27-28-29-30 | at Scranton |
| **JUNE** | |
| 1-2-3-4 | Pawtucket |
| 5-6-7-8 | Scranton |
| 9-10 | Indianapolis |
| 11-12 | at Indianapolis |
| 13-14-15-16 | at Richmond |
| 17-18-19-20 | at Norfolk |
| 22-23-24-25 | Rochester |
| 26-27-28-29 | Richmond |
| 30 | at Columbus |
| **JULY** | |
| 1-2-3 | at Columbus |
| 4-5-6 | Toledo |
| 7-8-9 | Columbus |
| 13-14-15-16 | Norfolk |
| 17-18-19-20 | Buffalo |
| 21-22-23-24 | at Rochester |
| 25-26-27-28 | at Buffalo |
| 29-30 | Toledo |
| 31 | Columbus |
| **AUGUST** | |
| 1-2 | Columbus |
| 3-4-5 | at Toledo |
| 7-8 | Indianapolis |
| 9-10 | at Indianapolis |
| 11-12 | at Charlotte |
| 13-14 | at Durham |
| 15-16 | Charlotte |
| 17-18 | Norfolk |
| 19-20 | Durham |
| 21-22 | Richmond |
| 23-24 | at Columbus |
| 25-26-27 | at Toledo |
| 28-29 | at Norfolk |
| 30-31 | at Richmond |
| **SEPTEMBER** | |
| 1-2 | at Indianapolis |
| 3-4 | Indianapolis |

## NORFOLK

| Date | Opponent |
|---|---|
| **APRIL** | |
| 6-7-8-9 | Durham |
| 10-11-12-13 | Buffalo |
| 14-15-16-17 | at Scranton |
| 18-19-20-21 | at Rochester |
| 22-23 | at Richmond |
| 24 | Richmond |
| 25-26-27-28 | Scranton |
| 29-30 | Rochester |
| **MAY** | |
| 1-2 | Rochester |
| 4-5-6-7 | at Columbus |
| 8-9-10-11 | at Toledo |
| 12-13-14-15 | Columbus |
| 16-17-18-19 | Toledo |
| 20-21 | Richmond |
| 23-24-25-26 | at Syracuse |
| 27-28-29-30 | at Pawtucket |
| **JUNE** | |
| 1-2-3-4 | Charlotte |
| 5-6-7-8 | Syracuse |
| 9-10-11-12 | at Durham |
| 13-14-15-16 | Pawtucket |
| 17-18-19-20 | Louisville |
| 22-23-24-25 | at Charlotte |
| 26-27 | at Toledo |
| 28-29 | at Columbus |
| 30 | at Durham |
| **JULY** | |
| 1 | at Durham |
| 2-3 | Charlotte |
| 4-5 | at Charlotte |
| 6-7-8-9 | Ottawa |
| 13-14-15-16 | at Louisville |
| 17-18-19-20 | at Ind. |
| 21-22-23-24 | at Ottawa |
| 25-26-27-28 | Indianapolis |
| 29-30 | Richmond |
| 31 | at Richmond |
| **AUGUST** | |
| 1-2 | at Richmond |
| 3-4-5-6 | at Buffalo |
| 8-9 | Richmond |
| 10 | at Richmond |
| 11-12 | Toledo |
| 13-14 | Columbus |
| 15-16 | at Indianapolis |
| 17-18 | at Louisville |
| 19-20 | Charlotte |
| 21-22 | at Charlotte |
| 23-24 | at Durham |
| 25 | at Richmond |
| 26 | Richmond |
| 27 | at Richmond |
| 28-29 | Louisville |
| 30-31 | Indianapolis |
| **SEPTEMBER** | |
| 1-2-3-4 | Durham |

## OTTAWA

| Date | Opponent |
|---|---|
| **APRIL** | |
| 6-7-8-9 | Louisville |
| 10-11-12-13 | Indianapolis |
| 14-15-16-17 | at Louisville |
| 18-19-20-21 | at Ind. |
| 22-23 | Rochester |
| 25-26-27-28 | Charlotte |
| 29-30 | Pawtucket |
| **MAY** | |
| 1-2 | Pawtucket |
| 3-4-5 | at Buffalo |
| 6-7-7-8 | at Buffalo |
| 9-10-11-12 | at Scranton |
| 13-14-15 | Buffalo |
| 16-17-18-19 | Syracuse |
| 20-21 | Rochester |
| 23-24-25-26 | at Charlotte |
| 27-28-29-30 | at Durham |
| **JUNE** | |
| 1-2-3-4 | Toledo |
| 5-6-7-8 | Columbus |
| 9-10-11-12 | at Toledo |
| 13-14-15-16 | at Columbus |
| 17-18-19-20 | Scranton |
| 22-23-24-25 | Durham |
| 26-27-28-29 | at Pawtucket |
| 30 | Syracuse |
| **JULY** | |
| 1 | Syracuse |
| 2-3-4-5 | at Richmond |
| 6-7-8-9 | at Norfolk |
| 13-14 | Rochester |
| 15-16 | at Rochester |
| 17-18-19-20 | Richmond |
| 21-22-23-24 | Norfolk |
| 25-26-27-28 | at Syracuse |
| 29-30-31 | at Scranton |
| **AUGUST** | |
| 1 | at Scranton |
| 3-4-5-6 | Scranton |
| 7-8 | at Buffalo |
| 10-11-12-13 | at Syracuse |
| 14-15 | Rochester |
| 16-17-18 | Buffalo |
| 19-20-21-22 | Pawtucket |
| 23-24-25 | at Rochester |
| 26-27 | Syracuse |
| 28-29 | at Buffalo |
| 30-31 | at Pawtucket |
| **SEPTEMBER** | |
| 1-2 | at Pawtucket |
| 3-4 | Buffalo |

## PAWTUCKET

| Date | Opponent |
|---|---|
| **APRIL** | |
| 6-7-8-9 | Indianapolis |
| 10-11-12-13 | Rochester |
| 14-15-16-17 | at Charlotte |
| 18-19-20-21 | at Durham |
| 22-23 | Buffalo |
| 25-26-27-28 | Durham |
| 29-30 | at Ottawa |
| **MAY** | |
| 1-2 | at Ottawa |
| 3-4-5 | at Syracuse |
| 6-7-8 | at Rochester |
| 9-10-11-12 | Syracuse |
| 13-14-15 | Scranton |
| 16-17-18-19 | at Buffalo |
| 20-21 | at Scranton |
| 23-24-25-26 | Louisville |
| 27-28-29-30 | Norfolk |
| **JUNE** | |
| 1-2-3-4 | at Louisville |
| 5-6-7-8 | at Indianapolis |
| 9-10-11-12 | Richmond |
| 13-14-15-16 | at Norfolk |
| 17-18-19-20 | at Rochester |
| 22-23-24-25 | Columbus |
| 26-27-28-29 | Ottawa |
| 30 | at Scranton |
| **JULY** | |
| 1 | at Scranton |
| 2-3 | Scranton |
| 4-5 | at Rochester |
| 6-7-8-9 | at Buffalo |
| 13-14-15-16 | Charlotte |
| 17-18-19-20 | Toledo |
| 21-22-23-24 | at Columbus |
| 25-26-27-28 | at Toledo |
| 29-30-31 | Buffalo |
| **AUGUST** | |
| 1 | Buffalo |
| 3-4-5-6 | Syracuse |
| 7-8-9 | at Rochester |
| 10-11-12-13 | at Scranton |
| 14-15 | Buffalo |
| 16-17-18 | Scranton |
| 19-20-21-22 | at Ottawa |
| 23-24-25 | at Syracuse |
| 27-28-29 | Rochester |
| 30-31 | Ottawa |
| **SEPTEMBER** | |
| 1-2 | Ottawa |
| 3-4 | at Syracuse |

## RICHMOND

### APRIL
| | |
|---|---|
| 6-7-8-9 | Buffalo |
| 10-11-12-13 | Durham |
| 14-15-16-17 | at Rochester |
| 18-19-20-21 | at Buffalo |
| 22-23 | Norfolk |
| 24 | at Norfolk |
| 25-26-27-28 | Rochester |
| 29-30 | Scranton |

### MAY
| | |
|---|---|
| 1-2 | Scranton |
| 4-5-6-7 | at Toledo |
| 8-9-10-11 | at Columbus |
| 12-13-14-15 | Toledo |
| 16-17-18-19 | Columbus |
| 20-21 | at Norfolk |
| 23-24-25-26 | at Durham |
| 27-28-29-30 | Charlotte |

### JUNE
| | |
|---|---|
| 1-2-3-4 | Syracuse |
| 5-6-7-8 | at Charlotte |
| 9-10-11-12 | at Pawtucket |
| 13-14-15-16 | Louisville |
| 17-18-19-20 | Pawtucket |
| 22-23-24-25 | at Ind. |
| 26-27-28-29 | at Louisville |
| 30 | Charlotte |

### JULY
| | |
|---|---|
| 1 | Charlotte |
| 2-3-4-5 | Ottawa |
| 6-7 | at Durham |
| 8-9 | Durham |
| 13-14-15-16 | at Syracuse |
| 17-18-19-20 | at Ottawa |
| 21-22-23-24 | Indianapolis |
| 25-26-27-28 | at Scranton |
| 29-30 | at Norfolk |
| 31 | Norfolk |

### AUGUST
| | |
|---|---|
| 1-2 | Norfolk |
| 3-4 | Durham |
| 5-6 | at Durham |
| 8-9 | at Norfolk |
| 10 | Norfolk |
| 11-12 | Columbus |
| 13-14 | Toledo |
| 15-16 | at Columbus |
| 17-18 | at Toledo |
| 19-20 | at Indianapolis |
| 21-22 | at Louisville |
| 23-24 | Charlotte |
| 25 | Norfolk |
| 26 | at Norfolk |
| 27 | Norfolk |
| 28-29 | Indianapolis |
| 30-31 | Louisville |

### SEPTEMBER
| | |
|---|---|
| 1-2-3-4 | at Charlotte |

## ROCHESTER

### APRIL
| | |
|---|---|
| 6-7 | at Syracuse |
| 8-9 | Syracuse |
| 10-11-12-13 | at Pawtucket |
| 14-15-16-17 | Richmond |
| 18-19-20-21 | Norfolk |
| 22-23 | at Ottawa |
| 25-26-27-28 | at Richmond |
| 29-30 | at Norfolk |

### MAY
| | |
|---|---|
| 1-2 | at Norfolk |
| 3-4-5 | Ottawa |
| 6-7-8 | Pawtucket |
| 9-10 | Buffalo |
| 11-12 | at Buffalo |
| 13-14-15 | at Syracuse |
| 16-17-18-19 | Scranton |
| 20-21 | at Ottawa |
| 23-24-25-26 | at Columbus |
| 27-28-29-30 | at Toledo |
| 31 | Syracuse |

### JUNE
| | |
|---|---|
| 1-2-3-4 | Columbus |
| 5-6-7-8 | Durham |
| 9-10-11-12 | at Scranton |
| 13-14-15-16 | Indianapolis |
| 17-18-19-20 | Toledo |
| 22-23-24-25 | at Louisville |
| 26-27-28-29 | at Ind. |
| 30 | Buffalo |

### JULY
| | |
|---|---|
| 1 | Buffalo |
| 2-3 | at Buffalo |
| 4-5 | Pawtucket |
| 6-7 | Scranton |
| 8-9 | at Scranton |
| 13-14 | at Ottawa |
| 15-16 | Ottawa |
| 17-18 | Syracuse |
| 19-20 | at Syracuse |
| 21-22-23-24 | Louisville |
| 25-26-27-28 | Charlotte |
| 29-30-31 | at Durham |

### AUGUST
| | |
|---|---|
| 1 | at Durham |
| 3-4-5-6 | at Charlotte |
| 7-8-9 | Pawtucket |
| 10-11 | Buffalo |
| 12-13 | at Buffalo |
| 14-15 | at Ottawa |
| 16-17 | Syracuse |
| 18 | at Syracuse |
| 19-20 | at Scranton |
| 22 | Syracuse |
| 23-24-25 | Ottawa |
| 26-27-28-29 | at Pawtucket |
| 30-31 | at Buffalo |

### SEPTEMBER
| | |
|---|---|
| 1-2 | Buffalo |
| 3-4 | Scranton |

## SCRANTON

### APRIL
| | |
|---|---|
| 6-7-8-9 | at Columbus |
| 10-11-12-13 | at Toledo |
| 14-15-16-17 | Norfolk |
| 18-19-20-21 | Columbus |
| 22-23 | at Syracuse |
| 25-26-27-28 | at Norfolk |
| 29-30 | at Richmond |

### MAY
| | |
|---|---|
| 1-2 | at Richmond |
| 3-4-5 | Buffalo |
| 6-7-8 | Syracuse |
| 9-10-11-12 | Ottawa |
| 13-14-15 | at Pawtucket |
| 16-17-18-19 | at Rochester |
| 20-21 | Pawtucket |
| 23-24-25-26 | Indianapolis |
| 27-28-29-30 | Louisville |

### JUNE
| | |
|---|---|
| 1-2-3-4 | at Indianapolis |
| 5-6-7-8 | at Louisville |
| 9-10-11-12 | Rochester |
| 13-14-15-16 | Charlotte |
| 17-18-19-20 | at Ottawa |
| 22-23-24-25 | at Buffalo |
| 26-27-28-29 | Durham |
| 30 | Pawtucket |

### JULY
| | |
|---|---|
| 1 | Pawtucket |
| 2-3 | at Pawtucket |
| 4-5 | Buffalo |
| 6-7 | at Rochester |
| 8-9 | Rochester |
| 13-14-15-16 | Toledo |
| 17-18-19-20 | at Durham |
| 21-22-23-24 | at Charlotte |
| 25-26-27-28 | Richmond |
| 29-30-31 | Ottawa |

### AUGUST
| | |
|---|---|
| 1 | Ottawa |
| 3-4-5-6 | at Ottawa |
| 7-8-9 | at Syracuse |
| 10-11-12-13 | Pawtucket |
| 14-15 | Syracuse |
| 16-17-18 | at Pawtucket |
| 19-20 | Rochester |
| 21-22-23-24 | at Buffalo |
| 25-26-27 | Buffalo |
| 28-29-30 | Syracuse |
| 31 | at Syracuse |

### SEPTEMBER
| | |
|---|---|
| 1-2 | at Syracuse |
| 3-4 | at Rochester |

## SYRACUSE

### APRIL
| | |
|---|---|
| 6-7 | Rochester |
| 8-9 | at Rochester |
| 10-11-12-13 | Louisville |
| 14-15-16-17 | at Ind. |
| 18-19-20-21 | at Louisville |
| 22-23 | Scranton |
| 24-25 | Buffalo |
| 27-28 | at Buffalo |
| 29-30 | Durham |

### MAY
| | |
|---|---|
| 1-2 | Durham |
| 3-4-5 | Pawtucket |
| 6-7-8 | at Scranton |
| 9-10-11-12 | at Pawtucket |
| 13-14-15 | Rochester |
| 16-17-18-19 | at Ottawa |
| 20-21 | at Buffalo |
| 23-24-25-26 | Norfolk |
| 27-28-29-30 | Indianapolis |
| 31 | at Rochester |

### JUNE
| | |
|---|---|
| 1-2-3-4 | at Richmond |
| 5-6-7-8 | at Norfolk |
| 9-10-11-12 | Columbus |
| 13-14-15-16 | at Toledo |
| 17-18-19-20 | at Columbus |
| 22-23-24-25 | Toledo |
| 26-27-28-29 | Buffalo |
| 30 | at Ottawa |

### JULY
| | |
|---|---|
| 1 | at Ottawa |
| 2-3-4-5 | at Durham |
| 6-7-8-9 | at Charlotte |
| 13-14-15-16 | Richmond |
| 17-18 | at Rochester |
| 19-20 | Rochester |
| 21-22-23-24 | at Buffalo |
| 25-26-27-28 | Ottawa |
| 29-30-31 | Charlotte |

### AUGUST
| | |
|---|---|
| 1 | Charlotte |
| 3-4-5-6 | at Pawtucket |
| 7-8-9 | Scranton |
| 10-11-12-13 | Ottawa |
| 14-15 | at Scranton |
| 16-17 | at Rochester |
| 18 | Rochester |
| 19-20 | Buffalo |
| 22 | at Rochester |
| 23-24-25 | Pawtucket |
| 26-27 | at Ottawa |
| 28-29-30 | at Scranton |
| 31 | Scranton |

### SEPTEMBER
| | |
|---|---|
| 1-2 | Scranton |
| 3-4 | Pawtucket |

## TOLEDO

### APRIL
| | |
|---|---|
| 6-7-8-9 | Charlotte |
| 10-11-12-13 | Scranton |
| 14-15-16-17 | at Durham |
| 18-19-20-21 | at Charlotte |
| 22-23 | Columbus |
| 24-25 | Louisville |
| 26-27 | Indianapolis |
| 28-29-30 | at Louisville |

### MAY
| | |
|---|---|
| 1-2 | at Indianapolis |
| 4-5-6-7 | Richmond |
| 8-9-10-11 | Norfolk |
| 12-13-14-15 | at Richmond |
| 16-17-18-19 | at Norfolk |
| 20-21 | at Columbus |
| 23-24-25-26 | Buffalo |
| 27-28-29-30 | Rochester |

### JUNE
| | |
|---|---|
| 1-2-3-4 | at Ottawa |
| 5-6-7-8 | at Buffalo |
| 9-10-11-12 | Ottawa |
| 13-14-15-16 | Syracuse |
| 17-18-19-20 | at Rochester |
| 22-23-24-25 | at Syracuse |
| 26-27 | Norfolk |
| 28-29 | Charlotte |
| 30 | Indianapolis |

### JULY
| | |
|---|---|
| 1-2-3 | Indianapolis |
| 4-5-6 | at Louisville |
| 7-8-9 | at Indianapolis |
| 13-14-15-16 | at Scranton |
| 17-18-19-20 | at Pawtucket |
| 21-22-23-24 | Durham |

| 25-26-27-28 | Pawtucket |
| 29-30 | at Louisville |
| 31 | at Indianapolis |
| **AUGUST** | |
| 1-2 | at Indianapolis |
| 3-4-5 | Louisville |

| 7-8 | at Columbus |
| 9-10 | Columbus |
| 11-12 | at Norfolk |
| 13-14 | at Richmond |
| 15-16 | Durham |
| 17-18 | Richmond |

| 19-20 | Columbus |
| 21-22 | at Columbus |
| 23-24 | Indianapolis |
| 25-26-27 | Louisville |
| 28-29 | at Durham |
| 30-31 | at Charlotte |

| **SEPTEMBER** | |
| 1-2 | at Columbus |
| 3-4 | Columbus |

# PACIFIC COAST LEAGUE

## ALBUQUERQUE

**APRIL**
| 6-7-8-9 | at Iowa |
| 10-11-12-13 | at Omaha |
| 14-15-16-17 | New Orleans |
| 18-19-20-21 | Iowa |
| 22-23-24-25 | at N.O. |
| 27-28-29-30 | at Oklahoma |

**MAY**
| 1-2-3-4 | Omaha |
| 5-6-7-8 | Oklahoma |
| 9-10-11-12 | at Portland |
| 13-14-15-16 | at Tacoma |
| 18-19-20-21 | Las Vegas |
| 22-23-24-25 | Tucson |
| 26-27-28-29 | Round Rock |
| 30-31 | at Oklahoma |

**JUNE**
| 1-2 | at Oklahoma |
| 3-4-5-6 | at Nashville |
| 8-9-10-11 | Memphis |
| 12-13-14-15 | Round Rock |
| 16-17-18-19 | at Iowa |
| 21-22-23-24-25 | at Mem. |
| 26-27-28-29 | Omaha |
| 30 | Memphis |

**JULY**
| 1-2-3 | Memphis |
| 4-5-6 | at Round Rock |
| 7-8-9 | at Memphis |
| 13-14-15-16 | Iowa |
| 17-18-19-20 | New Orleans |
| 21-22-23-24 | at N.O. |
| 25-26-27-28 | Sacramento |
| 29-30-31 | Fresno |

**AUGUST**
| 1 | Fresno |
| 2-3-4-5 | at Salt Lake |
| 6-7-8-9 | at C.S. |
| 11-12-13-14 | Nashville |
| 15-16-17-18 | at Omaha |
| 19-20-21-22 | at Nashville |
| 23-24-25-26-27 | at R.R. |
| 28-29-30-31 | Nashville |

**SEPTEMBER**
| 1-2-3-4 | Oklahoma |

## COLORADO SPRINGS

**APRIL**
| 6-7-8-9 | at Tacoma |
| 10-11-12-13 | at Portland |
| 14-15-15-16 | Tucson |
| 18-19-20-21 | Portland |
| 22-23-24-25 | at Tucson |
| 27-28-29-30 | at Las Vegas |

**MAY**
| 1-2-3-4 | Tacoma |
| 5-6-7-8 | Las Vegas |
| 9-10-11-12 | at Iowa |
| 13-14-15-16 | at Omaha |
| 18-19-20-21 | New Orleans |
| 22-23-24-25 | Oklahoma |
| 26-27-28-29 | at Tacoma |
| 30-31 | at Portland |

**JUNE**
| 1-2 | at Portland |
| 3-4-5-6 | Tacoma |
| 8-9-10-11 | Fresno |
| 12-13-14-15 | at Las Vegas |
| 16-17-18-19 | Tucson |
| 21-22-23-24-25 | at Fresno |
| 26-27-28-29 | Salt Lake |
| 30 | Portland |

**JULY**
| 1-2-3 | Portland |
| 4-5-6 | at Salt Lake |
| 7-8-9 | at Fresno |
| 13-14-15-16 | Fresno |
| 17-18-19-20 | Sacramento |
| 21-22-23-24 | at Sac. |
| 25-26-27-28 | at Nashville |
| 29-30-31 | at Memphis |

**AUGUST**
| 1 | at Memphis |
| 2-3-4-5 | Round Rock |
| 6-7-8-9 | Albuquerque |
| 11-12-13-14 | Salt Lake |
| 15-16-17-18 | at Sac. |
| 19-20-21-22 | at Tucson |
| 23-24-25-26-27 | at S.L. |
| 28-29-30-31 | Las Vegas |

**SEPTEMBER**
| 1-2-3-4 | Sacramento |

## FRESNO

**APRIL**
| 6-7-8-9 | at Las Vegas |
| 10-11-12-13 | at Tucson |
| 14-15-16-17 | Tacoma |
| 18-19-20-21 | Las Vegas |
| 22-23-24-25 | at Tacoma |
| 27-28-29-30 | at Portland |

**MAY**
| 1-2-3-4 | Tucson |
| 5-6-7-8 | Portland |
| 9-10-11-12 | at N.O. |
| 13-14-15-16 | at Oklahoma |
| 18-19-20-21 | Iowa |
| 22-23-24-25 | Omaha |
| 26-27-28-29 | at Tucson |
| 30-31 | Tucson |

**JUNE**
| 1-2 | Tucson |
| 3-4-5-6 | Salt Lake |
| 8-9-10-11 | at C.S. |
| 12-13-14-15 | at Salt Lake |
| 16-17-18-19 | at Portland |
| 21-22-23-24-25 | C.S. |
| 26-27-28-29 | at Sac. |
| 30 | at Tacoma |

**JULY**
| 1-2-3 | at Tacoma |
| 4-5-6 | Sacramento |
| 7-8-9 | Colorado Springs |
| 13-14-15-16 | at C.S. |
| 17-18-19-20 | Salt Lake |
| 21-22-23-24 | Tacoma |
| 25-26-27-28 | at R.R. |
| 29-30-31 | at Albuquerque |

**AUGUST**
| 1 | at Albuquerque |
| 2-3-4-5 | Nashville |
| 6-7-8-10 | Memphis |
| 11-12-13-14 | Las Vegas |
| 15-16-17-18 | at Salt Lake |
| 19-20-21-22 | at Sac. |
| 23-24-25-26-27 | Sac. |
| 28-29-30-31 | Portland |

**SEPTEMBER**
| 1-2-3-4 | at Las Vegas |

## IOWA

**APRIL**
| 6-7-8-9 | Albuquerque |
| 10-11-12-13 | Nashville |
| 14-15-16-17 | at R.R. |
| 18-19-20-21 | at Alb. |
| 22-23-24-25 | Round Rock |
| 27-28-29-30 | Memphis |

**MAY**
| 1-2-3-4 | at Nashville |
| 5-6-7-8 | at Memphis |
| 9-10-11-12 | C.S. |
| 13-14-15-16 | Salt Lake |
| 18-19-20-21 | at Fresno |
| 22-23-24-25 | at Sac. |
| 26-27-28-29 | Nashville |
| 30-31 | at Nashville |

**JUNE**
| 1-2 | at Omaha |
| 3-4-5-6 | at Oklahoma |
| 8-9-10-11 | Round Rock |
| 12-13-14-15 | at N.O. |
| 16-17-18-19 | Albuquerque |
| 21-22-23-24-25 | Omaha |
| 26-27-28-29 | at N.O. |
| 30 | at Omaha |

**JULY**
| 1-2-3 | at Omaha |
| 4-5-6 | New Orleans |
| 7-8-9 | Omaha |
| 13-14-15-16 | at Alb. |
| 17-18-19-20 | Oklahoma |
| 21-22-23 | Memphis |
| 25-26-27-28 | at Tucson |
| 29-30-31 | at Las Vegas |

**AUGUST**
| 1 | at Las Vegas |
| 2-3-4-5 | Tacoma |
| 6-7-8-9 | Portland |
| 11-12-13-14 | at Memphis |
| 15-16-17-18 | at R.R. |
| 19-20-21-22 | Oklahoma |
| 23-24-25-26-27 | N.O. |
| 28-29-30-31 | at Oklahoma |

**SEPTEMBER**
| 1-2-3-4 | at Omaha |

## LAS VEGAS

**APRIL**
| 6-7-8-9 | Fresno |
| 10-11-12-13 | Salt Lake |
| 14-15-16-17 | at Sac. |
| 18-19-20-21 | at Fresno |
| 22-23-24-25 | Sacramento |
| 27-28-29-30 | C.S. |

**MAY**
| 1-2-3 | at Salt Lake |
| 5-6-7-8 | at C.S. |
| 9-10-11-12 | Memphis |
| 13-14-15-16 | Nashville |
| 18-19-20-21 | at Alb. |
| 22-23-24-25 | at R.R. |
| 26-27-28-29 | Salt Lake |
| 30-31 | Sacramento |

**JUNE**
| 1-2 | Sacramento |
| 3-4-5-6 | at Sacramento |
| 8-9-10-11 | Tacoma |
| 12-13-14-15 | C.S. |
| 16-17-18-19 | at Salt Lake |
| 21-22-23-24-25 | at Tucson |
| 26-27-28-29 | Tacoma |
| 30 | Tucson |

**JULY**
| 1-2-3 | Tucson |
| 4-5-6 | at Portland |
| 7-8-9 | at Tucson |
| 13-14-15-16 | Tucson |
| 17-18-19-20 | at Tacoma |
| 21-22-23-24 | Portland |
| 25-26-27-28 | Omaha |
| 29-30-31 | Iowa |

**AUGUST**
| 1 | Iowa |
| 2-3-4-5 | at Oklahoma |
| 6-7-9-10 | at New Orleans |
| 11-12-13-14 | at Fresno |
| 15-16-17-18 | Portland |
| 19-20-21-22 | at Tacoma |
| 23-24-25-26-27 | at Port. |

**SEPTEMBER**
1-2-3-4      Fresno

## MEMPHIS

**APRIL**
6-7-8-9      at Oklahoma
10-11-12-13      at N.O.
14-15-16-17      Omaha
18-19-20-21      Oklahoma
22-23-24-25      at Omaha
27-28-29-30      at Iowa
**MAY**
1-2-3-4      New Orleans
5-6-7-8      Iowa
9-10-11-12      at Las Vegas
13-14-15-16      at Tucson
18-19-20-21      Portland
22-23-24-25      Tacoma
26-27-28-29      at Omaha
30-31      at Round Rock
**JUNE**
1-2      at Round Rock
3-4-5-6      New Orleans
8-9-10-11      at Albuquerque
12-13-14-15      Oklahoma
16-17-18-19      Omaha
21-22-23-24-25      Alb.
26-27-28-29      at Nashville
30      at Albuquerque
**JULY**
1-2-3      at Albuquerque
4-5-6      Nashville
7-8-9      Albuquerque
13-14-15-16      at Nashville
17-18-19-20      Round Rock
21-22-23      at Iowa
25-26-27-28      Salt Lake
29-30-31      C.S.
**AUGUST**
1      Colorado Springs
2-3-4-5      at Sacramento
6-7-8-10      at Fresno
11-12-13-14      Iowa
15-16-17-18      at Oklahoma
19-20-21-22      Round Rock
23-24-25-26-27      Nashville
28-29-30-31      at R.R.
**SEPTEMBER**
1-2-3-4      at New Orleans

## NASHVILLE

**APRIL**
6-7-8-9      at Omaha
10-11-12-13      at Iowa
14-15-16-17      Oklahoma
18-19-20-21      Omaha
22-23-24-25      at Oklahoma
27-28-29-30      at N.O.
**MAY**
1-2-3-4      Iowa
5-6-7-8      New Orleans
9-10-11-12      at Tucson
13-14-15-16      at Las Vegas
18-19-20-21      Tacoma
22-23-24-25      Portland
26-27-28-29      at Iowa
30-31      Iowa
**JUNE**
1-2      Iowa
3-4-5-6      Albuquerque
8-9-10-11      at New Orleans
12-13-14-15      Omaha
16-17-17-18      Oklahoma
21-22-23-24-25      at R.R.
26-27-28-29      Memphis
30      Round Rock
**JULY**
1-2-3      Round Rock
4-5-6      at Memphis
7-8-9      at Round Rock
13-14-15-16      Nashville
17-18-19-20      at Omaha
21-22-23-24      at Oklahoma
25-26-27-28      C.S.
29-30-31      Salt Lake
**AUGUST**
1      Salt Lake
2-3-4-5      at Fresno
6-7-8-10      at Sacramento
11-12-13-14      at Alb.
15-16-17-18      New Orleans
19-20-21-22      Albuquerque
23-24-25-26-27      at Mem.
28-29-30-31      at Alb.
**SEPTEMBER**
1-2-3-4      Round Rock

## NEW ORLEANS

**APRIL**
6-7-8-9      Round Rock
10-11-12-13      Memphis
14-15-16-17      at Alb.
18-19-20-21      at R.R.
22-23-24-25      Albuquerque
27-28-29-30      Nashville
**MAY**
1-2-3-4      at Memphis
5-6-7-8      at Nashville
9-10-11-12      Fresno
13-14-15-16      Sacramento
18-19-20-21      at C.S.
22-23-24-25      at Salt Lake
26-27-28-29      Oklahoma
30-31      at Omaha
**JUNE**
1-2      at Omaha
3-4-5-6      at Memphis
8-9-10-11      Nashville
12-13-14-15      Iowa
16-17-18-19      at R.R.
21-22-23-24-25      at Okla.
26-27-28-29      Iowa
30      Oklahoma
**JULY**
1-2-3      Oklahoma
4-5-6      at Iowa
7-8-9      at Oklahoma
13-14-15-16      Round Rock
17-18-19-20      at Alb.
21-22-23-24      Albuquerque
25-26-27-28      at Tacoma
29-30-31      at Portland
**AUGUST**
1      at Portland
2-3-4-5      Tucson
6-7-9-10      Las Vegas
11-12-13-14      Omaha
15-16-17-18      at Nashville
19-20-21-22      at Omaha
23-24-25-26-27      at Iowa
28-29-30-31      Omaha
**SEPTEMBER**
1-2-3-4      Memphis

## OKLAHOMA

**APRIL**
6-7-8-9      Memphis
10-11-12-13      Round Rock
14-15-16-17      at Nashville
18-19-20-21      at Memphis
22-23-24-25      Nashville
27-28-29-30      Albuquerque
**MAY**
1-2-3-4      at Round Rock
5-6-7-8      at Albuquerque
9-10-11-12      Sacramento
13-14-15-16      Fresno
18-19-20-21      at Salt Lake
22-23-24-25      at C.S.
26-27-28-29      at N.O.
30-31      Albuquerque
**JUNE**
1-2      Albuquerque
3-4-5-6      Iowa
8-9-10-11      at Omaha
12-13-14-15      at Nashville
16-17-18-19      at Nashville
21-22-23-24-25      N.O.
26-27-28-29      Round Rock
30      at New Orleans
**JULY**
1-2-3      at New Orleans
4-5-6      Omaha
7-8-9      New Orleans
13-14-15-16      at Omaha
17-18-19-20      at Iowa
21-22-23-24      Nashville
25-26-27-28      at Portland
29-30-31      at Tacoma
**AUGUST**
1      at Tacoma
2-3-4-5      Las Vegas
6-7-8-10      Tucson
11-12-13-14      at R.R.
15-16-17-18      Memphis
19-20-21-22      at Iowa
23-24-25-26-27      Omaha
28-29-30-31      Iowa
**SEPTEMBER**
1-2-3-4      at Albuquerque

## OMAHA

**APRIL**
6-7-8-9      Nashville
10-11-12-13      Albuquerque
14-15-16-17      at Memphis
18-19-20-21      at Nashville
22-23-24-25      Memphis
27-28-29-30      Round Rock
**MAY**
1-2-3-4      at Albuquerque
5-6-7-8      at Round Rock
9-10-11-12      Salt Lake
13-14-15-16      C.S.
18-19-20-21      at Sac.
22-23-24-25      at Fresno
26-27-28-29      Memphis
30-31      New Orleans
**JUNE**
1-2      New Orleans
3-4-5-6      at Round Rock
8-9-10-11      Oklahoma
12-13-14-15      at Nashville
16-17-18-19      at Memphis
21-22-23-24-25      at Iowa
26-27-28-29      at Alb.
30      Iowa
**JULY**
1-2-3      Iowa
4-5-6      at Oklahoma
7-8-9      at Iowa
13-14-15-16      Oklahoma
17-18-19-20      Nashville
21-22-23-24      Round Rock
25-26-27-28      at Las Vegas
29-30-31      at Tucson
**AUGUST**
1      at Tucson
2-3-4-5      Portland
6-7-8-9      Tacoma
11-12-13-14      at N.O.
15-16-17-18      Albuquerque
19-20-21-22      New Orleans
23-24-25-26-27      at Okla.
28-29-30-31      at N.O.
**SEPTEMBER**
1-2-3-4      Iowa

## PORTLAND

**APRIL**
6-7-8-9      Sacramento
10-11-12-13      C.S.
14-15-16-17      at Salt Lake
18-19-20-21      at C.S.
22-23-24-25      Salt Lake
27-28-29-30      Fresno
**MAY**
1-2-3-4      at Sacramento
5-6-7-8      at Fresno
9-10-11-12      Albuquerque
13-14-15-16      Round Rock
18-19-20-21      at Memphis
22-23-24-25      at Nashville
26-27-28-29      Sacramento
30-31      Colorado Springs
**JUNE**
1-2      Colorado Springs
3-4-5-6      at Tucson
8-9-10-11      at Sacramento
12-13-14-15      Tucson
16-17-18-19      Fresno
21-22-23-24-25      at Tac.
26-27-28-29      Tucson
30      at Colorado Springs
**JULY**
1-2-3      at Colorado Springs
4-5-6      Las Vegas
7-8-9      at Tacoma
13-14-15-16      Tacoma
17-18-19-20      at Tucson
21-22-23-24      at Las Vegas

25-26-27-28 Oklahoma
29-30-31 New Orleans
**AUGUST**
1 New Orleans
2-3-4-5 at Omaha
6-7-8-9 at Iowa
11-12-13-14 Tacoma
15-16-17-18 at Las Vegas
19-20-21-22 Salt Lake
23-24-25-26-27 L.V.
28-29-30-31 at Fresno
**SEPTEMBER**
1-2-3-4 at Salt Lake

## ROUND ROCK
**APRIL**
6-7-8-9 at New Orleans
10-11-12-13 at Oklahoma
14-15-16-17 Iowa
18-19-20-21 New Orleans
22-23-24-25 at Iowa
27-28-29-30 at Omaha
**MAY**
1-2-3-4 Oklahoma
5-6-7-8 Omaha
9-10-11-12 at Tacoma
13-14-15-16 at Portland
18-19-20-21 Tucson
22-23-24-25 Las Vegas
26-27-28-29 at Alb.
30-31 Memphis
**JUNE**
1-2 Memphis
3-4-5-6 Omaha
8-9-10-11 at Iowa
12-13-14-15 at Alb.
16-17-18-19 New Orleans
21-22-23-24-25 Nashville
26-27-28-29 at Oklahoma
30 at Nashville
**JULY**
1-2-3 at Nashville
4-5-6 Albuquerque
7-8-9 Nashville
13-14-15-16 at N.O.
17-18-19-20 at Memphis
21-22-23-24 at Omaha
25-26-27-28 Fresno
29-30-31 Sacramento
**AUGUST**
1 Sacramento
2-3-4-5 at C.S.
7-8-9 at Salt Lake
11-12-13-14 Oklahoma
15-16-17-18 Iowa
19-20-21-22 at Memphis
23-24-25-26-27 Alb.
28-29-30-31 Memphis
**SEPTEMBER**
1-2-3-4 Oklahoma

## SACRAMENTO
**APRIL**
6-7-8-9 at Portland
10-11-12-13 at Tacoma
14-15-16-17 Las Vegas
18-19-20-21 Tacoma
22-23-24-25 at Las Vegas
27-28-29-30 at Tucson
**MAY**
1-2-3-4 Portland
5-6-7-8 Tucson
9-10-11-12 at Oklahoma
13-14-15-16 at N.O.
18-19-20-21 Omaha
22-23-24-25 Iowa
26-27-28-29 at Portland
30-31 at Las Vegas
**JUNE**
1-2 at Las Vegas
3-4-5-6 Las Vegas
8-9-10-11 Portland
12-13-14-15 at Tacoma
16-17-18-19 Tacoma
21-22-23-24-25 at S.L.
26-27-28-29 Fresno
30 Salt Lake
**JULY**
1-2-3 Salt Lake
4-5-6 at Fresno
7-8-9 at Salt Lake
13-14-15-16 Salt Lake
17-18-19-20 at C.S.
21-22-23-24 C.S.
25-26-27-28 at Alb.
29-30-31 at Round Rock
**AUGUST**
1 at Round Rock
2-3-4-5 Memphis
6-7-8-10 Nashville
11-12-13-14 at Tucson
15-16-17-18 C.S.
19-20-21-22 Fresno
23-24-25-26-27 at Fresno
28-29-30-31 Tucson
**SEPTEMBER**
1-2-3-4 at C.S.

## SALT LAKE
**APRIL**
6-7-8-9 at Tucson
10-11-12-13 at Las Vegas
14-15-16-17 Portland
18-19-20-21 Tucson
22-23-24-25 at Portland
27-28-29-30 at Tacoma
**MAY**
1-2-3-4 Las Vegas
5-6-7-8 Tacoma
9-10-11-12 at Omaha
13-14-15-16 at Iowa
18-19-20-21 Oklahoma
22-23-24-25 New Orleans
26-27-28-29 at Las Vegas

30-31 Tacoma
**JUNE**
1-2 Tacoma
3-4-5-6 at Fresno
8-9-10-11 at Tucson
12-13-14-15 Fresno
16-17-18-19 Las Vegas
21-22-23-24-25 Sac.
26-27-28-29 at C.S.
30 at Sacramento
**JULY**
1-2-3 at Sacramento
4-5-6 Colorado Springs
7-8-9 Sacramento
13-14-15-16 at Sac.
17-18-19-20 at Fresno
21-22-23-24 Tucson
25-26-27-28 at Memphis
29-30-31 at Nashville
**AUGUST**
1 at Nashville
2-3-4-5 Albuquerque
7-8-9-10 Round Rock
11-12-13-14 at C.S.
15-16-17-18 Fresno
19-20-21-22 at Portland
23-24-25-26-27 C.S.
28-29-30-31 at Tacoma
**SEPTEMBER**
1-2-3-4 Portland

## TACOMA
**APRIL**
6-7-8-9 Colorado Springs
10-11-12-13 Sacramento
14-15-16-17 at Fresno
18-19-20-21 at Sac.
22-23-24-25 Fresno
27-28-29-30 Salt Lake
**MAY**
1-2-3-4 at C.S.
5-6-7-8 at Salt Lake
9-10-11-12 Round Rock
13-14-15-16 Albuquerque
18-19-20-21 at Nashville
22-23-24-25 at Memphis
26-27-28-29 C.S.
30-31 at Salt Lake
**JUNE**
1-2 at Salt Lake
3-4-5-6 at C.S.
8-9-10-11 at Las Vegas
12-13-14-15 Sacramento
16-17-18-19 at Sac.
21-22-23-24-25 Portland
26-27-28-29 at Las Vegas
30 Fresno
**JULY**
1-2-3 Fresno
4-5-6 at Tucson
7-8-9 Portland
13-14-15-16 at Portland
17-18-19-20 Las Vegas

21-22-23-24 at Fresno
25-26-27-28 New Orleans
29-30-31 Oklahoma
**AUGUST**
1 Oklahoma
2-3-4-5 at Iowa
6-7-8-9 at Omaha
11-12-13-14 at Portland
15-16-17-18 Tucson
19-20-21-22 Las Vegas
23-24-25-26-27 at Tucson
28-29-30-31 Salt Lake
**SEPTEMBER**
1-2-3-4 Tucson

## TUCSON
**APRIL**
6-7-8-9 Salt Lake
10-11-12-13 Fresno
14-15-15-16 at C.S.
18-19-20-21 at Salt Lake
22-23-24-25 C.S.
27-28-29-30 Sacramento
**MAY**
1-2-3-4 at Fresno
5-6-7-8 at Sacramento
9-10-11-12 Nashville
13-14-15-16 Memphis
18-19-20-21 at R.R.
22-23-24-25 at Alb.
26-27-28-29 Fresno
30-31 at Fresno
**JUNE**
1-2 at Fresno
3-4-5-6 Portland
8-9-10-11 Salt Lake
12-13-14-15 at Portland
16-17-18-19 at C.S.
21-22-23-24-25 L.V.
26-27-28-29 at Portland
30 at Las Vegas
**JULY**
1-2-3 at Las Vegas
4-5-6 Tacoma
7-8-9 Las Vegas
13-14-15-16 at Las Vegas
17-18-19-20 Portland
21-22-23-24 at Salt Lake
25-26-27-28 Iowa
29-30-31 Omaha
**AUGUST**
1 Omaha
2-3-4-5 at New Orleans
6-7-8-10 at Oklahoma
11-12-13-14 Sacramento
15-16-17-18 at Tacoma
19-20-21-22 C.S.
23-24-25-26-27 Tacoma
28-29-30-31 at Sac.
**SEPTEMBER**
1-2-3-4 at Tacoma

# DOUBLE A
## EASTERN LEAGUE

*at Citizens Bank Park, Philadelphia

### AKRON

**APRIL**
| | |
|---|---|
| 6-7-8-9 | at Binghamton |
| 10-11-12 | at Bowie |
| 13-14-15-16 | Harrisburg |
| 17-18-19 | Bowie |
| 20-21-22-23 | at Altoona |
| 24-25-26 | at Binghamton |
| 28-29-30 | Altoona |

**MAY**
| | |
|---|---|
| 1-2-3-4 | Binghamton |
| 5-6-7 | at Bowie |
| 8-9-10 | at Erie |
| 11-12-13-14 | Harrisburg |
| 15-16-17 | Erie |
| 19-20-21 | at Harrisburg |
| 22-23-24-25 | at Reading |
| 26-27-28-29 | Bowie |
| 30-31 | Altoona |

**JUNE**
| | |
|---|---|
| 1 | Altoona |
| 2-3-4 | at Erie |
| 6-7-8 | New Britain |
| 9-10-11 | Connecticut |
| 13-14-15 | at Connecticut |
| 16-17-18 | at New Britain |
| 20-21-22-23 | Binghamton |
| 24-25-26 | Altoona |
| 27-28-29 | at Erie |
| 30 | at Altoona |

**JULY**
| | |
|---|---|
| 1-2-3 | at Altoona |
| 4-5-6 | at Erie |
| 7-8-9-10 | Reading |
| 13-14-15-16 | Trenton |
| 17-18-19 | Altoona |
| 20-21-22-23 | at Harris. |
| 24-25-26 | Erie |
| 27-28-29-30 | at Trenton |

**AUGUST**
| | |
|---|---|
| 1-2-3 | New Hampshire |
| 4-5-6 | Portland |
| 8-9-10 | at New Hamp. |
| 11-12-13 | at Portland |
| 15-16-17 | Reading |
| 18-19-20 | Bowie |
| 21-22-23 | at Harrisburg |
| 24-25-26-27 | Trenton |
| 28-29-30-31 | at Altoona |

**SEPTEMBER**
| | |
|---|---|
| 1-2-3-4 | at Erie |

### ALTOONA

**APRIL**
| | |
|---|---|
| 6-7-8-9 | Trenton |
| 10-11-12 | Erie |
| 13-14-15 | at Reading |
| 17-18-19 | at Trenton |
| 20-21-22-23 | Akron |
| 24-25-26 | Portland |
| 28-29-30 | at Akron |

**MAY**
| | |
|---|---|
| 1-2-3-4 | at Erie |
| 5-6-7 | Reading |
| 8-9-10 | at Harrisburg |
| 11-12-13-14 | Binghamton |
| 15-16-17 | Reading |
| 19-20-21 | at Binghamton |
| 22-23-24-25 | Bowie |
| 26-27-28-29 | at Erie |
| 30-31 | at Akron |

**JUNE**
| | |
|---|---|
| 1 | at Akron |
| 2-3-4 | New Hampshire |
| 6-7-8 | at Portland |
| 9-10-11 | at New Hamp. |
| 12 | at Reading* |
| 13-14-15 | Harrisburg |
| 16-17-18 | Reading |
| 20-21-22-23 | at Harris. |
| 24-25-26 | at Akron |
| 27-28-29 | Bowie |
| 30 | Akron |

**JULY**
| | |
|---|---|
| 1-2-3 | Akron |
| 4-5-6 | at Reading |
| 7-8-9-10 | at Erie |
| 13-14-15-16 | Erie |
| 17-18-19 | at Akron |
| 20-21-22-23 | at Bowie |
| 24-25-26 | Harrisburg |
| 27-28-29-30 | at Conn. |

**AUGUST**
| | |
|---|---|
| 1-2-3 | at Harrisburg |
| 4-5-6 | New Britain |
| 7-8-9 | Connecticut |
| 11-12-13 | at New Britain |
| 14-15-16 | at Connecticut |
| 18-19-20 | Harrisburg |
| 21-22-23 | Bowie |
| 24-25-26-27 | at Harris. |
| 28-29-30-31 | Akron |

**SEPTEMBER**
| | |
|---|---|
| 1-2-3-4 | Bowie |

### BINGHAMTON

**APRIL**
| | |
|---|---|
| 6-7-8-9 | Akron |
| 10-11-12 | Reading |
| 13-14-15-16 | at Portland |
| 17-18-19 | at New Hamp. |
| 20-21-22-23 | Erie |
| 24-25-26 | Akron |
| 28-29-30 | at Erie |

**MAY**
| | |
|---|---|
| 1-2-3-4 | at Akron |
| 5-6-7 | New Hampshire |
| 8-9-10 | Connecticut |
| 11-12-13-14 | at Altoona |
| 16-17-18 | at Connecticut |
| 19-20-21 | Altoona |
| 22-23-24-25 | Portland |
| 26-27-28-29 | at Trenton |

---

| 30-31 | Reading |
|---|---|

**JUNE**
| | |
|---|---|
| 1 | Reading |
| 2-3-4 | Harrisburg |
| 6-7-8 | at Reading |
| 9-10-11 | at Bowie |
| 13-14-15 | New Britain |
| 16-17-18 | Trenton |
| 20-21-22-23 | at Akron |
| 24-25-26 | at Harrisburg |
| 27-28-29 | Reading |
| 30 | New Hampshire |

**JULY**
| | |
|---|---|
| 1-2-3 | New Hampshire |
| 4-5-6 | at Bowie |
| 7-8-9-10 | at Trenton |
| 13-14-15-16 | Bowie |
| 17-18-19 | at Trenton |
| 20-21-22-23 | at Portland |
| 24-25-26 | New Hamp. |
| 27-28-29-30 | Harrisburg |

**AUGUST**
| | |
|---|---|
| 1-2-3 | at New Britain |
| 4-5-6 | Connecticut |
| 8-9-10 | at Trenton |
| 11-12-13 | at Bowie |
| 15-16-17 | Bowie |
| 18-19-20 | at New Hamp. |
| 21-22-23 | at Portland |
| 24-25-26-27 | Erie |
| 28-29-30-31 | Portland |

**SEPTEMBER**
| | |
|---|---|
| 1-2-3-4 | at Connecticut |

### BOWIE

**APRIL**
| | |
|---|---|
| 6-7-8-9 | Reading |
| 10-11-12 | Akron |
| 13-14-15-16 | at Erie |
| 17-18-19 | at Akron |
| 20-21-22-23 | New Hamp. |
| 24-25-26 | Erie |
| 28-29-30 | at Portland |

**MAY**
| | |
|---|---|
| 1-2-3-4 | at New Hamp. |
| 5-6-7 | Akron |
| 8-9-10 | New Britain |
| 11-12-13-14 | at Trenton |
| 16-17-18 | Harrisburg |
| 19-20-21 | Trenton |
| 22-23-24-25 | at Altoona |
| 26-27-28-29 | at Akron |
| 30-31 | Erie |

**JUNE**
| | |
|---|---|
| 1 | Erie |
| 2-3-4 | at New Britain |
| 6-7-8 | at Trenton |
| 9-10-11 | Binghamton |
| 13-14-15 | Portland |
| 16-17-18 | at Connecticut |
| 20-21-22-23 | New Britain |
| 24-25-26 | Erie |

---

**JUNE**
| | |
|---|---|
| 1 | Reading |
| 2-3-4 | Harrisburg |
| 6-7-8 | at Reading |
| 9-10-11 | at Bowie |
| 13-14-15 | New Britain |
| 16-17-18 | Trenton |
| 20-21-22-23 | at Akron |
| 24-25-26 | at Harrisburg |
| 27-28-29 | Reading |
| 30 | New Hampshire |

**JULY**
| | |
|---|---|
| 1-2-3 | New Hampshire |
| 4-5-6 | at Bowie |
| 7-8-9-10 | at Trenton |
| 13-14-15-16 | Bowie |
| 17-18-19 | at Trenton |
| 20-21-22-23 | at Portland |
| 24-25-26 | New Hamp. |
| 27-28-29-30 | Harrisburg |

**AUGUST**
| | |
|---|---|
| 1-2-3 | at New Britain |
| 4-5-6 | Connecticut |
| 8-9-10 | at Trenton |
| 11-12-13 | at Bowie |
| 15-16-17 | Bowie |
| 18-19-20 | at New Hamp. |
| 21-22-23 | at Portland |
| 24-25-26-27 | Erie |
| 28-29-30-31 | Portland |

**SEPTEMBER**
| | |
|---|---|
| 1-2-3-4 | at Connecticut |

### CONNECTICUT

**APRIL**
| | |
|---|---|
| 6-7-8-9 | Portland |
| 10-11-12 | New Hamp. |
| 13-14-15 | at Trenton |
| 17-18-19 | at Reading |
| 20-21-22-23 | Trenton |
| 24-25-26 | Reading |
| 28-29-30 | at New Hamp. |

**MAY**
| | |
|---|---|
| 1-2-3-4 | at Portland |
| 5-6-7 | Trenton |
| 8-9-10 | at Binghamton |
| 11-12-13-14 | New Britain |
| 16-17-18 | Binghamton |
| 19-20-21 | at New Britain |
| 22-23-24-25 | New Hamp. |
| 26-27-28-29 | at Reading |
| 30-31 | New Hampshire |

**JUNE**
| | |
|---|---|
| 1 | New Hampshire |
| 2-3-4 | Portland |
| 6-7-8 | at Harrisburg |
| 9-10-11 | at Akron |
| 13-14-15 | Akron |
| 16-17-18 | Bowie |
| 19-20-21-22 | at Portland |
| 23-24-25-26 | at Trenton |
| 27-28-29 | Harrisburg |
| 30 | at New Britain |

**JULY**
| | |
|---|---|
| 1-2-3 | at New Britain |
| 4-5-6 | Portland |
| 7-8-9-10 | New Britain |
| 13-14-15-16 | at Portland |
| 17-18-19 | at Harrisburg |
| 20-21-22-23 | at Reading |
| 24-25-26 | Bowie |

---

| | |
|---|---|
| 27-28-29-30 | Altoona |
| **AUGUST** | |
| 1-2-3 | at Bowie |
| 4-5-6 | at Binghamton |
| 7-8-9 | at Altoona |
| **11-12-13** | **Erie** |
| **14-15-16** | **Altoona** |
| 18-19-20 | at Erie |
| 21-22-23 | at New Hamp. |
| **24-25-26-27** | **Reading** |
| 28-29-30-31 | at New Hamp. |
| **SEPTEMBER** | |
| **1-2-3-4** | **Binghamton** |

## ERIE

| | |
|---|---|
| **APRIL** | |
| 6-7-8-9 | at Harrisburg |
| 10-11-12 | at Altoona |
| **13-14-15-16** | **Bowie** |
| **17-18-19** | **Harrisburg** |
| 20-21-22-23 | at Bing. |
| 24-25-26 | at Bowie |
| **28-29-30** | **Binghamton** |
| **MAY** | |
| **1-2-3-4** | **Altoona** |
| 5-6-7 | at Harrisburg |
| **8-9-10** | **Akron** |
| 12-13-14 | at Reading |
| 15-16-17 | at Akron |
| **18-19-20-21** | **Reading** |
| 22-23-24-25 | at Harrisburg |
| **26-27-28-29** | **Altoona** |
| 30-31 | at Bowie |
| **JUNE** | |
| 1 | at Bowie |
| **2-3-4** | **Akron** |
| 6-7-8 | at New Hampshire |
| 9-10-11 | at Portland |
| **13-14-15** | **Reading** |
| **16-17-18** | **Harrisburg** |
| 20-21-22-23 | at Reading |
| 24-25-26 | at Bowie |
| **27-28-29** | **Akron** |
| 30 | at Reading |
| **JULY** | |
| 1-2-3 | at Reading |
| **4-5-6** | **Akron** |
| **7-8-9-10** | **Altoona** |
| 13-14-15-16 | at Altoona |
| **17-18-19** | **Bowie** |
| **20-21-22-23** | **New Britain** |
| 24-25-26 | at Akron |
| 27-28-29-30 | at Bowie |
| **AUGUST** | |
| **1-2-3** | **Portland** |
| **4-5-6** | **New Hampshire** |
| 8-9-10 | at New Britain |
| 11-12-13 | at Connecticut |
| **15-16-17** | **New Britain** |
| **18-19-20** | **Connecticut** |
| 21-22-23 | at Trenton |
| 24-25-26-27 | at Bing. |
| **28-29-30-31** | **Trenton** |
| **SEPTEMBER** | |
| **1-2-3-4** | **Akron** |

## HARRISBURG

| | |
|---|---|
| **APRIL** | |
| **6-7-8-9** | **Erie** |
| **10-11-12** | **Trenton** |
| 13-14-15-16 | at Akron |
| 17-18-19 | at Erie |
| **20-21-22-23** | **Portland** |
| **24-25-26** | **New Hamp.** |
| 28-29-30 | at Reading |
| **MAY** | |
| 1-2-3-4 | at New Britain |
| **5-6-7** | **Erie** |
| **8-9-10** | **Altoona** |
| 11-12-13-14 | at Akron |
| 16-17-18 | at Bowie |
| **19-20-21** | **Akron** |
| **22-23-24-25** | **Erie** |
| 26-27-28-29 | at New Hamp. |
| 30-31 | at New Britain |
| **JUNE** | |
| 1 | at New Britain |
| 2-3-4 | at Binghamton |
| **6-7-8** | **Connecticut** |
| **9-10-11** | **New Britain** |
| 13-14-15 | at Altoona |
| 16-17-18 | at Erie |
| **20-21-22-23** | **Altoona** |
| **24-25-26** | **Binghamton** |
| 27-28-29 | at Connecticut |
| **30** | **Bowie** |
| **JULY** | |
| **1-2-3** | **Bowie** |
| 4-5-6 | at Trenton |
| 7-8-9-10 | at Bowie |
| **13-14-15-16** | **Reading** |
| **17-18-19** | **Connecticut** |
| **20-21-22-23** | **Akron** |
| 24-25-26 | at Altoona |
| 27-28-29-30 | at Bing. |
| **AUGUST** | |
| **1-2-3** | **Altoona** |
| **4-5-6** | **Reading** |
| 8-9-10 | at Portland |
| 11-12-13 | at Reading |
| **15-16-17** | **Trenton** |
| 18-19-20 | at Altoona |
| **21-22-23** | **Akron** |
| **24-25-26-27** | **Altoona** |
| 28-29-30-31 | at Bowie |
| **SEPTEMBER** | |
| 1-2-3-4 | at Portland |

## NEW BRITAIN

| | |
|---|---|
| **APRIL** | |
| **6-7-8-9** | **New Hampshire** |
| **10-11-12** | **Portland** |
| 13-14-15-15 | at New Hamp. |
| 17-18-19 | at Portland |
| **20-21-22-23** | **Reading** |
| **24-25-26** | **Trenton** |
| 28-29-30 | at Trenton |
| **MAY** | |
| **1-2-3-4** | **Harrisburg** |
| **5-6-7** | **Portland** |
| 8-9-10 | at Bowie |
| 11-12-13-14 | at Conn. |
| 16-17-18 | at New Hamp. |

| | |
|---|---|
| **19-20-21** | **Connecticut** |
| **22-23-24-25** | **Trenton** |
| 26-27-28-29 | at Portland |
| **30-31** | **Harrisburg** |
| **JUNE** | |
| **1** | **Harrisburg** |
| **2-3-4** | **Bowie** |
| 6-7-8 | at Akron |
| 9-10-11 | at Harrisburg |
| 13-14-15 | at Binghamton |
| **16-17-18** | **Akron** |
| 20-21-22-23 | at Bowie |
| 24-25-26 | at Reading |
| **27-28-29** | **Portland** |
| **30** | **Connecticut** |
| **JULY** | |
| **1-2-3** | **Connecticut** |
| 4-5-6 | at New Hampshire |
| 7-8-9-10 | at Connecticut |
| **13-14-15-16** | **New Hamp.** |
| 17-18-19 | at Reading |
| 20-21-22-23 | at Erie |
| **24-25-26** | **Trenton** |
| 27-28-29-30 | at New Hamp. |
| **AUGUST** | |
| **1-2-3** | **Binghamton** |
| 4-5-6 | at Altoona |
| **8-9-10** | **Erie** |
| **11-12-13** | **Altoona** |
| 15-16-17 | at Erie |
| 18-19-20 | at Reading |
| **21-22-23** | **Connecticut** |
| **24-25-26-27** | **Portland** |
| 28-29-30-31 | at Reading |
| **SEPTEMBER** | |
| **1-2-3-4** | **Harrisburg** |

## NEW HAMPSHIRE

| | |
|---|---|
| **APRIL** | |
| 6-7-8-9 | at New Britain |
| 10-11-12 | at Connecticut |
| **13-14-15-15** | **New Britain** |
| **17-18-19** | **Binghamton** |
| 20-21-22-23 | at Bowie |
| 24-25-26 | at Harrisburg |
| **28-29-30** | **Connecticut** |
| **MAY** | |
| **1-2-3-4** | **Bowie** |
| 5-6-7 | at Binghamton |
| 8-9-10 | at Reading |
| **11-12-13-14** | **Portland** |
| **16-17-18** | **New Britain** |
| 19-20-21 | at Portland |
| 22-23-24-25 | at Conn. |
| **26-27-28-29** | **Harrisburg** |
| 30-31 | at Connecticut |
| **JUNE** | |
| 1 | at Connecticut |
| 2-3-4 | at Altoona |
| **6-7-8** | **Erie** |
| **9-10-11** | **Altoona** |
| 13-14-15 | at Trenton |
| **16-17-18** | **Portland** |
| 19-20-21-22 | at Trenton |
| 23-24-25 | at Portland |
| **27-28-29** | **Trenton** |
| 30 | at Binghamton |

| | |
|---|---|
| **JULY** | |
| 1-2-3 | at Binghamton |
| **4-5-6** | **New Britain** |
| **7-8-9-10** | **Portland** |
| 13-14-15-16 | at New Brit. |
| **17-18-19** | **Portland** |
| **20-21-22-23** | **Trenton** |
| 24-25-26 | at Binghamton |
| **27-28-29-30** | **New Britain** |
| **AUGUST** | |
| 1-2-3 | at Akron |
| 4-5-6 | at Erie |
| **8-9-10** | **Akron** |
| **11-12-13** | **Trenton** |
| 15-16-17 | at Portland |
| **18-19-20** | **Binghamton** |
| **21-22-23** | **Reading** |
| 24-25-26-27 | at Bowie |
| **28-29-30-31** | **Connecticut** |
| **SEPTEMBER** | |
| 1-2-3-4 | at Portland |

## PORTLAND

| | |
|---|---|
| **APRIL** | |
| 6-7-8-9 | at Connecticut |
| 10-11-12 | at New Britain |
| **13-14-15-16** | **Binghamton** |
| **17-18-19** | **New Britain** |
| 20-21-22-23 | at Harris. |
| 24-25-26 | at Altoona |
| **28-29-30** | **Bowie** |
| **MAY** | |
| **1-2-3-4** | **Connecticut** |
| 5-6-7 | at New Britain |
| **8-9-10** | **Trenton** |
| 11-12-13-14 | at New Hamp. |
| 15-16-17 | at Trenton |
| **19-20-21** | **New Hamp.** |
| 22-23-24-25 | at Bing. |
| **26-27-28-29** | **New Britain** |
| **30-31** | **Trenton** |
| **JUNE** | |
| **1** | **Trenton** |
| 2-3-4 | at Connecticut |
| **6-7-8** | **Altoona** |
| **9-10-11** | **Erie** |
| 13-14-15 | at Bowie |
| 16-17-18 | at New Hamp. |
| **19-20-21-22** | **Connecticut** |
| **23-24-25** | **New Hamp.** |
| 27-28-29 | at New Britain |
| **30** | **Trenton** |
| **JULY** | |
| **1-2-3** | **Trenton** |
| 4-5-6 | at Connecticut |
| 7-8-9-10 | at New Hamp. |
| **13-14-15-16** | **Connecticut** |
| 17-18-19 | at New Hamp. |
| **20-21-22-23** | **Binghamton** |
| **24-25-26** | **Reading** |
| 28-29-30-31 | at Reading |
| **AUGUST** | |
| 1-2-3 | at Erie |
| 4-5-6 | at Akron |
| **8-9-10** | **Harrisburg** |
| **11-12-13** | **Akron** |
| **15-16-17** | **New Hamp.** |
| 18-19-20 | at Trenton |

**DOUBLE-A SCHEDULES**

## Eastern League (continued)

**(Binghamton, continued)**
- 21-22-23 Binghamton
- 24-25-26-27 at New Brit.
- 28-29-30-31 at Bing.
- **SEPTEMBER**
- 1-2-3-4 New Hampshire

### READING
**APRIL**
- 6-7-8-9 at Bowie
- 10-11-12 at Binghamton
- **13-14-15 Altoona**
- **17-18-19 Connecticut**
- 20-21-22-23 at New Brit.
- 24-25-26 at Connecticut
- **28-29-30 Harrisburg**

**MAY**
- 1-2-3-4 at Trenton
- 5-6-7 at Altoona
- **8-9-10 New Hampshire**
- **12-13-14 Erie**
- 15-16-17 at Altoona
- 18-19-20-21 at Erie
- **22-23-24-25 Akron**
- **26-27-28-29 Connecticut**
- 30-31 at Binghamton

**JUNE**
- 1 at Binghamton
- 2-3-4 at Trenton
- 6-7-8 Binghamton
- **9-10-11 Trenton**
- 12 *Altoona
- 13-14-15 at Erie
- 16-17-18 at Altoona
- **20-21-22-23 Erie**
- **24-25-26 New Britain**
- 27-28-29 at Binghamton
- **30 Erie**

**JULY**
- 1-2-3 Erie
- 4-5-6 Altoona
- 7-8-9-10 at Akron
- 13-14-15-16 at Harris.
- **17-18-19 New Britain**
- **20-21-22-23 Connecticut**
- 24-25-26 at Portland
- **28-29-30-31 Portland**

**AUGUST**
- 1-2-3 Trenton
- 4-5-6 at Harrisburg
- **8-9-10 Bowie**
- **11-12-13 Harrisburg**
- 15-16-17 at Akron
- **18-19-20 New Britain**
- 21-22-23 at New Hamp.
- 24-25-26-27 at Conn.
- **28-29-30-31 New Britain**

**SEPTEMBER**
- 1-2-3-4 at Trenton

### TRENTON
**APRIL**
- 6-7-8-9 at Altoona
- 10-11-12 at Harrisburg
- **13-14-15 Connecticut**
- **17-18-19 Altoona**
- 20-21-22-23 at Conn.
- 24-25-26 at New Britain
- **28-29-30 New Britain**

**MAY**
- **1-2-3-4 Reading**
- 5-6-7 at Connecticut
- 8-9-10 at Portland
- **11-12-13-14 Bowie**
- **15-16-17 Portland**
- 19-20-21 at Bowie
- 22-23-24-25 at New Brit.
- **26-27-28-29 Binghamton**
- 30-31 at Portland

**JUNE**
- 1 at Portland
- 2-3-4 at Connecticut
- **6-7-8 Bowie**
- 9-10-11 at Reading
- **13-14-15 New Hamp.**
- 16-17-18 at Binghamton
- **19-20-21-22 New Hamp.**
- **23-24-25-26 Connecticut**
- 27-28-29 at New Hamp.
- 30 at Portland

**JULY**
- 1-2-3 at Portland
- **4-5-6 Harrisburg**
- **7-8-9-10 Binghamton**
- 13-14-15-16 at Akron
- **17-18-19 Binghamton**
- 20-21-22-23 at New Hamp.
- 24-25-26 at New Britain
- **27-28-29-30 Akron**

**AUGUST**
- 1-2-3 at Reading
- **4-5-6 Bowie**
- **8-9-10 Binghamton**
- 11-12-13 at New Hamp.
- 15-16-17 at Harrisburg
- **18-19-20 Portland**
- **21-22-23 Erie**
- 24-25-26-27 at Akron
- 28-29-30-31 at Erie

**SEPTEMBER**
- **1-2-3-4 Reading**

# SOUTHERN LEAGUE

### BIRMINGHAM
**APRIL**
- 6-7-8-9-10 West Tenn
- 11-12-13-14-15 at Hunt.
- **16-17-18-19-20 Tenn.**
- 21-22-23-24-25 at Jack.
- 26-27-28-29-30 at Mont.

**MAY**
- **2-3-4-5-6 Jacksonville**
- 7-8-9-10-11 at Tennessee
- **12-13-14-15-16 Miss.**
- **17-18-19-20-21 Mont.**
- 23-24-25-26-27 at Miss.
- 28-29-30-31 at Mobile

**JUNE**
- 1 at Mobile
- **2-3-4-5-6 Huntsville**
- 7-8-9-10-11 at Tennessee
- **13-14-15-16-17 Carolina**
- **19-20-21-22-23 Tenn.**
- 24-25-26-27-28 at Miss.
- 29-30 at Mobile

**JULY**
- 1-2-3 at Mobile
- **4-5-6-7-8 Hunstville**
- 12-13-14-15-16 at Chat.
- **18-19-20-21-22 Mobile**
- 24-25-26-27-28 at Hunt.
- **29-30-31 Montgomery**

**AUGUST**
- **1-2 Montgomery**
- 4-5-6-7-8 at Tennessee
- 9-10-11-12-13 at Carolina
- **15-16-17-18-19 Jack.**
- **20-21-22-23-24 Chat.**
- 25-26-27-28-29 at Mont.
- **30 Huntsville**

**SEPTEMBER**
- 1-2-3-4 Huntsville

### CAROLINA
**APRIL**
- 6-7-8-9-10 at Mobile
- 11-12-13-14-15 at Chat.
- **16-17-18-19-20 Jack.**
- 21-22-23-24-25 at Tenn.
- **26-27-28-29-30 Chat.**

**MAY**
- **2-3-4-5-6 Mobile**
- 7-8-9-10-11 at Jack.
- **12-13-14-15-16 Chat.**
- **17-18-19-20-21 Tenn.**
- 23-24-25-26-27 at W. Tenn
- 28-29-30-31 at Tennessee

**JUNE**
- 1 at Tennessee
- **2-3-4-5-6 Mississippi**
- **7-8-9-10-11 Montgomery**
- 13-14-15-16-17 at Birm.
- 19-20-21-22-23 at Chat.
- **24-25-26-27-28 Jack.**
- **29-30 Tennessee**

**JULY**
- **1-2-3 Tennessee**
- 4-5-6-7-8 at Jacksonville
- 12-13-14-15-16 at Mont.
- **18-19-20-21-22 Hunt.**
- 24-25-26-27-28 at Tenn.
- 29-30-31 at Mississippi

**AUGUST**
- 1-2 at Mississippi
- **4-5-6-7-8 West Tenn**
- **9-10-11-12-13 Birm.**
- 15-16-17-18-19 at Hunt.
- **20-21-22-23-24 Tenn.**
- 25-26-27-28-29 at Chat.
- **31 Jacksonville**

**SEPTEMBER**
- **1-2-3-4 Jacksonville**

### CHATTANOOGA
**APRIL**
- 6-7-8-9 at Jack.
- **11-12-13-14-15 Carolina**
- 16-27-18-19-20 at Mobile
- **21-22-23-24-25 W. Tenn**
- 26-27-28-29 at Car.

**MAY**
- **2-3-4-5-6 Tennessee**
- **7-8-9-10-11 Mobile**
- 12-13-14-15-16 at Car.
- **17-18-19-20-21 Hunt.**
- 23-24-25-26-27 at Tenn.
- 28-29-30-31 Mississippi

**JUNE**
- 1 Mississippi
- **2-3-4-5-6 Montgomery**
- 8-9-10-11-12 at Miss.
- 14-15-16-17-18 at Tenn.
- **19-20-21-22-23 Carolina**
- 24-25-26-27-28 at Hunt.
- **29-30 Jacksonville**

**JULY**
- **1-2-3 Jacksonville**
- 4-5-6-7-8 at West Tenn
- **12-13-14-15-16 Birm.**
- 18-19-20-21-22 at Jack.
- **24-25-26-27-28 W. Tenn**
- 29-30-31 at Huntsville

**AUGUST**
- 1-2 at Huntsville
- **4-5-6-7-8 Jacksonville**
- **9-10-11-12-13 Tennessee**
- 15-16-17-18-19 at Mont.
- **20-21-22-23-24 Carolina**
- **25-26-27-28-29 Carolina**
- 30 at West Tenn

**SEPTEMBER**
- 1-2-3-4 at West Tenn

### HUNTSVILLE
**APRIL**
- 6-7-8-9-10 at Mississippi
- **11-12-13-14-15 Birm.**
- 16-17-18-19-20 at Mont.
- **21-22-23-24-25 Mobile**
- **27-28-29-30 Tennessee**

**MAY**
- **1 Tennessee**
- 2-3-4-5-6 at West Tenn
- **7-8-9-10-11 Montgomery**
- 12-13-14-15 at Chat.
- **23-24-25-26-27 Jack.**
- **28-29-30-31 West Tenn**

**JUNE**
- **1 West Tenn**
- 2-3-4-5-6 at Birmingham
- 7-8-9-10-11 at Jack.
- **13-14-15-16-17 W. Tenn**
- 19-20-21-22-23 at Mobile
- **24-25-26-27-28 Chat.**
- **29-30 West Tenn**

## JULY
1-2-3 West Tenn
4-5-6-7-8 at Birmingham
12-13-14-15-16 Miss.
18-19-20-21-22 at Car.
24-25-26-27-28 Birm.
29-30-31 Chattanooga
## AUGUST
1-2 Chattanooga
4-5-6-7-8 at Mobile
9-10-11-12-13 at Miss.
15-16-17-18-19 Carolina
20-21-22-23-24 at W. Tenn
25-26-27-28-29 Miss.
30 at Birmingham
## SEPTEMBER
1-2-3-4 at Birmingham

## JACKSONVILLE
### APRIL
6-7-8-9-10 Chattanooga
11-12-13-14-15 Mont.
16-17-18-19-20 at Car.
21-22-23-24-25 Birm.
27-28-29-30 at W. Tenn
### MAY
1 at West Tenn
2-3-4-5-6 at Birmingham
7-8-9-10-11 Carolina
12-13-14-15-16 at Mobile
17-18-19-20-21 Miss.
23-24-25-26-27 at Mont.
28-29-30-31 at Mont.
### JUNE
1 at Montgomery
2-3-4-5-6 Mobile
7-8-9-10-11 Huntsville
13-14-15-16-17 at Miss.
19-20-21-22-23 Mont.
24-25-26-27-28 at Car.
29-30 at Chattanooga
### JULY
1-2-3 at Chattanooga
4-5-6-7-8 Carolina
12-13-14-15-16 at Tenn.
18-19-20-21-22 Chat.
24-25-26-27-28 at Mont.
29-30-31 Mobile
### AUGUST
1-2 Mobile
4-5-6-7-8 at Chattanooga
9-10-11-12-13 W. Tenn
15-16-17-18-19 at Birm.
20-21-22-23-24 Mont.
25-26-27-28-29 Tenn.
30 at Carolina
### SEPTEMBER
1-2-3-4 at Carolina

## MISSISSIPPI
### APRIL
6-7-8-9-10 Huntsville
11-12-13-14-15 Mobile
16-17-18-19-20 at W. Tenn
21-22-23-24-25 Mont.
26-27-28-29-30 at Mobile

### MAY
2-3-4-5-6 at Montgomery
7-8-9-10-11 West Tenn
12-13-14-15-16 at Birm.
17-18-19-20-21 at Jack.
23-24-25-26-27 Birm.
28-29-30-31 at Chat.
### JUNE
1 at Chattanooga
2-3-4-5-6 at Carolina
8-9-10-11-12 Chat.
13-14-15-16-17 Jack.
19-20-21-22-23 at W. Tenn
24-25-26-27-28 Birm.
29-30 at Montgomery
### JULY
1-2-3 at Montgomery
4-5-6-7-8 Mobile
12-13-14-15-16 at Hunt.
18-19-20-21-22 Tenn.
24-25-26-27-28 at Mobile
29-30-31 Carolina
### AUGUST
1-2 Carolina
4-5-6-7-8 at Montgomery
9-10-11-12-13 Huntsville
15-16-17-18-19 at Tenn.
20-21-22-23-24 Mobile
25-26-27-28-29 at Hunt.
30 Montgomery
### SEPTEMBER
1-2-3-4 Montgomery

## MOBILE
### APRIL
6-7-8-9-10 Carolina
11-12-13-14-15 at Miss.
16-17-18-19-20 Chat.
21-22-23-24-25 at Hunt.
26-27-28-29-30 Miss.
### MAY
2-3-4-5-6 at Carolina
7-8-9-10-11 at Chat.
12-13-14-15-16 Jack.
17-18-19-20-21 at W. Tenn
23-24-25-26-27 Mont.
28-29-30-31 Birmingham
### JUNE
1 Birmingham
2-3-4-5-6 at Jacksonville
7-8-9-10-11 Tennessee
13-14-15-16-17 at Mont.
19-20-21-22-23 Hunt.
24-25-26-27-28 at Mont.
29-30 Birmingham
### JULY
1-2-3 Birmingham
4-5-6-7-8 at Mississippi
12-13-14-15-16 W. Tenn
18-19-20-21-22 at Birm.
24-25-26-27-28 Miss.
29-30-31 at Jacksonville
### AUGUST
1-2 at Jacksonville
4-5-6-7-8 Huntsville
9-10-11-12-13 Mont.

15-16-17-18-19 at W. Tenn
20-21-22-23-24 at Miss.
25-26-27-28-29 W. Tenn
30 at Tennessee
### SEPTEMBER
1-2-3-4 at Tennessee

## MONTGOMERY
### APRIL
6-7-8-9-10 Tennessee
11-12-13-14-15 at Jack.
16-17-18-19-20 Hunt.
21-22-23-24-25 at Miss.
26-27-28-29-30 Birm.
### MAY
2-3-4-5-6 Mississippi
7-8-9-10-11 at Huntsville
12-13-14-15-16 W. Tenn
17-18-19-20-21 at Birm.
23-24-25-26-27 at Mobile
28-29-30-31 Jacksonville
### JUNE
1 Jacksonville
2-3-4-5-6 at Chattanooga
7-8-9-10-11 at Carolina
13-14-15-16-17 Mobile
19-20-21-22-23 at Jack.
24-25-26-27-28 Mobile
29-30 Mississippi
### JULY
1-2-3 Mississippi
4-5-6-7-8 at Tennessee
12-13-14-15-16 Carolina
18-19-20-21-22 at W. Tenn
24-25-26-27-28 Jack.
29-30-31 at Birmingham
### AUGUST
1-2 at Birmingham
4-5-6-7-8 Mississippi
9-10-11-12-13 at Mobile
15-16-17-18-19 Chat.
20-21-22-23-24 at Jack.
25-26-27-28-29 Birm.
31 at Mississippi
### SEPTEMBER
1-2-3-4 at Mississippi

## TENNESSEE
### APRIL
6-7-8-9-10 at Mont.
11-12-13-14-15 W. Tenn
16-17-18-19-20 at Birm.
21-22-23-24-25 Carolina
27-28-29-30 at Huntsville
### MAY
1 at Huntsville
2-3-4-5-6 at Chattanooga
7-8-9-10-11 Birmingham
12-13-14-15-16 Hunt.
17-18-19-20-21 at Car.
23-24-25-26-27 Chat.
28-29-30-31 Carolina
### JUNE
1 Carolina
2-3-4-5-6 at West Tenn
7-8-9-10-11 at Mobile

13-14-15-16-17 Chat.
19-20-21-22-23 at Birm.
24-25-26-27-28 W. Tenn
29-30 at Carolina
### JULY
1-2-3 at Carolina
4-5-6-7-8 Montgomery
12-13-14-15-16 Jack.
18-19-20-21-22 at Miss.
24-25-26-27-28 Carolina
29-30-31 at West Tenn
### AUGUST
1-2 at West Tenn
4-5-6-7-8 Birmingham
9-10-11-12-13 at Chat.
15-16-17-18-19 Miss.
20-21-22-23-24 at Car.
25-26-27-28-29 at Jack.
30 Mobile
### SEPTEMBER
1-2-3-4 Mobile

## WEST TENN
### APRIL
6-7-8-9-10 at Birm.
11-12-13-14-15 at Tenn.
16-17-18-19-20 Miss.
21-22-23-24-25 at Chat.
27-28-29-30 Jacksonville
### MAY
1 Jacksonville
2-3-4-5-6 Huntsville
7-8-9-10-11 at Miss.
12-13-14-15-16 at Mont.
17-18-19-20-21 Mobile
23-24-25-26-27 Carolina
28-29-30-31 at Huntsville
### JUNE
1 at Huntsville
2-3-4-5-6 Tennessee
7-8-9-10-11 Birmingham
13-14-15-16-17 at Hunt.
19-20-21-22-23 Miss.
24-25-26-27-28 at Tenn.
29-30 at Huntsville
### JULY
1-2-3 at Huntsville
4-5-6-7-8 Chattanooga
12-13-14-15-16 at Mobile
18-19-20-21-22 Mont.
24-25-26-27-28 at Chat.
29-30-31 Tennessee
### AUGUST
1-2 Tennessee
4-5-6-7-8 at Carolina
9-10-11-12-13 at Jack.
15-16-17-18-19 Mobile
20-21-22-23-24 Hunt.
25-26-27-28-29 at Mobile
30 Chattanooga
### SEPTEMBER
1-2-3-4 Chattanooga

# TEXAS LEAGUE

## ARKANSAS

### APRIL
6-7-8-9 at Springfield
11-12-13-14-15 at Wich.
**16-17-18-19-20 Tulsa**
**21-22-23-24-25 Wichita**
26-27-28-29 at S.A.
30 at Corpus Christi

### MAY
1-2 at Corpus Christi
**4-5-6 San Antonio**
**7-8-9-10 Corpus Christi**
13-13-14-15-16 at Tulsa
**17-18-19-20-21 Spring.**
22-23-24 at Frisco
25-26-27-28 at Midland
**30-30-31 Frisco**

### JUNE
**1 Frisco**
**2-3-4 Midland**
6-7-8-9 at Tulsa
10-11-12-13-14 at Spring.
**15-16-17-18 Wichita**
22-23-24-25 at C.C.
26-27-28 at San Antonio
**30 Tulsa**

### JULY
**1-1-3-4 Tulsa**
5-6-7-8-9 at Wichita
**10-11-12-13 San Antonio**
**14-15-15 Corpus Christi**
18-19-20-21-22 at Tulsa
23-24-25-26-27 at Spring.
**28-29-29-31 Wichita**

### AUGUST
**1 Wichita**
**2-3-4-5 Springfield**
**7-8-9 Frisco**
10-11-12 at Midland
13-14-15-16 at Frisco
**17-18-19-20 Midland**
22-23-24-25 at Wichita
**26-27-28-29 Tulsa**
**30-31 Springfield**

### SEPTEMBER
**1-2-3 Springfield**

## CORPUS CHRISTI

### APRIL
**6-7-8-9 San Antonio**
**11-12-13-14-15 Frisco**
16-17-18-19-20 at Mid.
21-22-23-24-25 at Frisco
**26-27-28-29 Springfield**
**30 Arkansas**

### MAY
**1-2 Arkansas**
4-5-6 at Springfield
7-8-9-10 at Arkansas
**12-13-14-15-16 Midland**
17-18-19-20-21 at S.A.
**22-23-24 Wichita**
25-26-27-28 at Tulsa
29-30-31 at Wichita

### JUNE
1 at Wichita
**2-3-4 Tulsa**
**6-7-8-9 Midland**
**10-11-12-13-14 S.A.**
15-16-17-18 at Frisco
**22-23-24-25 Arkansas**
**26-27-28 Springfield**
30 at Midland

### JULY
1-2-3-4 at Midland
**5-6-7-8-9 Frisco**
10-11-12-13 at Spring.
14-15-15 at Arkansas
**18-19-20-21-22 Midland**
23-24-25-26 at S.A.
27-28-29-30-31 at Frisco

### AUGUST
**2-3-4-5-6 San Antonio**
7-8-9 at Tulsa
**10-11-12-13 Wichita**
**14-15-16-17 Tulsa**
18-19-20 at Wichita
**22-23-24-25 Frisco**
26-27-28-29 at Midland
30-31 at San Antonio

### SEPTEMBER
1-2-3 at San Antonio

## FRISCO

### APRIL
**6-7-8-9 Midland**
11-12-13-14-15 at C.C.
**16-17-18-19-20 S.A.**
**21-22-23-24-25 C.C.**
27-28-29-30 at Tulsa

### MAY
1-2-3 at Wichita
**4-5-6 Tulsa**
**7-8-9-10 Wichita**
12-13-14-15-16 at S.A.
17-18-19-20-21 at Mid.
**22-23-24 Arkansas**
25-26-27-28 at Spring.
30-30-31 at Arkansas

### JUNE
1 at Arkansas
**2-3-4 Springfield**
6-7-8-9 at San Antonio
**10-11-12-13-14 Midland**
**15-16-17-18 C.C.**
22-23-24-25 at Wichita
26-27-28 at Tulsa
**30 San Antonio**

### JULY
**1-2-3-4 San Antonio**
5-6-7-8-9 at C.C.
**10-11-12-13 Tulsa**
**14-15-16 Wichita**
18-19-20-21-22 at S.A.
23-24-25-26 at Midland
**27-28-29-30-31 C.C.**

### AUGUST
**2-3-4-5-6 Midland**
7-8-9 at Arkansas
10-11-12 at Springfield
**13-14-15-16 Arkansas**
**17-18-19-20 Springfield**
22-23-24-25 at C.C.
**26-27-28-29 San Antonio**
30-31 at Midland

### SEPTEMBER
1-2-3 at Midland

## MIDLAND

### APRIL
6-7-8-9 at Frisco
10-12-13-14-15 at S.A.
**16-17-18-19-20 C.C.**
**21-22-23-24-25 S.A.**
27-28-29-30 at Wichita

### MAY
1-2-3 at Tulsa
**4-5-6 Wichita**
**7-8-9-10 Tulsa**
12-13-14-15-16 at C.C.
**17-18-19-20-21 Frisco**
22-23-24 at Springfield
**25-26-27-28 Arkansas**
**29-30-31 Springfield**

### JUNE
**1 Springfield**
2-3-4 at Arkansas
6-7-8-9 at Corpus Christi
10-11-12-13-14 at Frisco
**15-16-17-18 San Antonio**
22-23-24-25 at Tulsa
26-27-28 at Wichita
**30 Corpus Christi**

### JULY
**1-2-3-4 Corpus Christi**
5-6-7-8-9 at San Antonio
**10-11-12-13 Wichita**
**14-15-16 Tulsa**
18-19-20-21-22 at C.C.
**23-24-25-26 Frisco**
**27-28-29-30-31 S.A.**

### AUGUST
2-3-4-5-6 at Frisco
**7-8-9 Springfield**
**10-11-12 Arkansas**
13-14-15-16 at Spring.
17-18-19-20 at Arkansas
22-23-24-25 at S.A.
**26-27-28-29 C.C.**
**30-31 Frisco**

### SEPTEMBER
**1-2-3 Frisco**

## SAN ANTONIO

### APRIL
6-7-8-9 at Corpus Christi
**10-12-13-14-15 Midland**
16-17-18-19-20 at Frisco
21-22-23-24-25 at Mid.
**26-27-28-29 Arkansas**
**30 Springfield**

### MAY
**1-2 Springfield**
4-5-6 at Arkansas
7-8-9-10 at Springfield
**12-13-14-15-16 Frisco**
**17-18-19-20-21 C.C.**
22-23-24 at San Antonio
**25-26-27-28 Wichita**
**29-30-31 Tulsa**

### JUNE
**1 Tulsa**
2-3-4 at Wichita
**6-7-8-9 Frisco**
10-11-12-13-14 at C.C.
15-16-17-18 at Midland
**22-23-24-25 Springfield**
**26-27-28 Arkansas**
30 at Frisco

### JULY
1-2-3-4 at Frisco
**5-6-7-8-9 Midland**
10-11-12-13 at Arkansas
14-15-16 at Springfield
**18-19-20-21-22 Frisco**
**23-24-25-26 C.C.**
27-28-29-30-31 at Mid.

### AUGUST
2-3-4-5-6 at C.C.
**7-8-9 Wichita**
**11-12-13 Tulsa**
14-15-16-17 at Wichita
18-19-20-21 at Tulsa
**22-23-24-25 Midland**
26-27-28-29 at Frisco
**30-31 Corpus Christi**

### SEPTEMBER
**1-2-3 Corpus Christi**

## SPRINGFIELD

### APRIL
**6-7-8-9 Arkansas**
11-12-13-14-15 at Tulsa
**16-17-18-19-20 Wichita**
**21-22-23-24-25 Tulsa**
26-27-28-29 at C.C.
30 at San Antonio

### MAY
1-2 at San Antonio
**4-5-6 Corpus Christi**
**7-8-9-10 San Antonio**
12-13-14-15-16 at Wich.
17-18-19-20-21 at Ark.
**22-23-24 Midland**
**25-26-27-28 Frisco**
29-30-31 at Midland

### JUNE
1 at Midland
2-3-4 at Frisco
6-7-8-9 at Wichita
**10-11-12-13-14 Ark.**
**15-16-17-18 Tulsa**
22-23-24-25 at S.A.
26-27-28 at C.C.
**30 Wichita**

### JULY
**1-2-3-4 Wichita**
5-6-7-8-9 at Tulsa
**10-11-12-13 C.C.**

14-15-16 San Antonio
18-19-20-21-22 at Wich.
**23-24-25-26-27 Arkansas**
**28-29-30-31 Tulsa**
### AUGUST
**1 Tulsa**
2-3-4-5 at Arkansas
7-8-9 at Midland
**10-11-12 Frisco**
**13-14-15-16 Midland**
17-18-19-20 at Frisco
22-23-24-25 at Tulsa
**26-27-28-29 Wichita**
30-31 at Arkansas
### SEPTEMBER
1-2-3 at Arkansas

## TULSA
### APRIL
**6-7-8-9 Wichita**
**11-12-13-14-15 Spring.**
16-17-18-19-20 at Ark.
21-22-23-24-25 at Spring.
**27-28-29-30 Frisco**
### MAY
**1-2-3 Midland**
4-5-6 at Frisco

7-8-9-10 at Midland
**13-13-14-15-16 Ark.**
17-18-19-20 at Wich.
**22-23-24 San Antonio**
**25-26-27-28 C.C.**
29-30-31 at San Antonio
### JUNE
1 at San Antonio
2-3-4 at Corpus Christi
**6-7-8-9 Arkansas**
**10-11-12-13-14 Tulsa**
15-16-17-18 at Spring.
**22-23-24-25 Midland**
**26-27-28 Frisco**
30 at Arkansas
### JULY
1-1-3-4 at Arkansas
**5-6-7-8-9 Springfield**
10-11-12-13 at Frisco
14-15-16 at Midland
**18-19-20-21-22 Arkansas**
23-24-25-26 at Wichita
28-29-30-31 at Spring.
### AUGUST
1 at Springfield
**2-3-4-5-6 Wichita**
**7-8-9 Corpus Christi**

11-12-13 at San Antonio
14-15-16-17 at C.C.
**18-19-20-21 San Antonio**
**22-23-24-25 Springfield**
26-27-28-29 at Arkansas
30-31 at Wichita
### SEPTEMBER
1-2-3 at Wichita

## WICHITA
### APRIL
6-7-8-9 at Tulsa
**11-12-13-14-15 Arkansas**
16-17-18-19-20 at Spring.
21-22-23-24-25 at Ark.
**27-28-29-30 Midland**
### MAY
**1-2-3 Frisco**
4-5-6 at Midland
7-8-9-10 at Frisco
**12-13-14-15-16 Spring.**
**17-18-19-20 Tulsa**
22-23-24 at C.C.
25-26-27-28 at S.A.
**29-30-31 Corpus Christi**
### JUNE
1 Corpus Christi

**2-3-4 San Antonio**
**6-7-8-9 Springfield**
10-11-12-13-14 at Tulsa
15-16-17-18 at Arkansas
**22-23-24-25 Frisco**
**26-27-28 Midland**
30 at Springfield
### JULY
1-2-3-4 at Springfield
**5-6-7-8-9 Arkansas**
10-11-12-13 at Midland
14-15-16 at Frisco
**18-19-20-21-22 Spring.**
**23-24-25-26 Tulsa**
28-29-29-31 at Arkansas
### AUGUST
1 at Arkansas
2-3-4-5-6 at Tulsa
7-8-9 at San Antonio
10-11-12-13 at C.C.
**14-15-16-17 San Antonio**
**18-19-20 Corpus Christi**
**22-23-24-25 Arkansas**
26-27-28-29 at Spring.
30-31 Tulsa
### SEPTEMBER
**1-2-3 Tulsa**

# HIGH CLASS A
## CALIFORNIA LEAGUE

### BAKERSFIELD

**APRIL**
- 7-8-9 at R.C.
- **10-11-12-13 Visalia**
- **14-15-16 Stockton**
- 17-18-19-20 at Visalia
- **21-22-23 Inland Empire**
- **24 San Jose**
- 25-26-27 at Inland Empire
- 28-29-30 at Lake Elsinore

**MAY**
- 1-2-3 at High Desert
- **5-6-7 R.C.**
- **8-9-10 High Desert**
- 12-13-14 at Modesto
- 15-16-17-18 at Stockton
- **19-20-21 Visalia**
- **22-23-24-25 Modesto**
- 26-27-28-29 at Visalia
- 30-31 at Modesto

**JUNE**
- 1 at Modesto
- **2-3-4-5 San Jose**
- 6-7 at Lancaster
- **9-10-11-12 Modesto**
- **13-14-15 Stockton**
- 16-17-18 at San Jose
- 19-20-21 at Stockton
- 22-23-24 at Lake Elsinore
- **29 Stockton**
- 30 at Lancaster

**JULY**
- 1-2-3 at Lancaster
- **4-5-6 Visalia**
- **7-8-9 Modesto**
- 10-11-12-13 at San Jose
- **14-15-16 Visalia**
- **18-19-20 San Jose**
- 21-22-23 at Modesto
- 25-26 at Visalia
- **28-29-30-31 Stockton**

**AUGUST**
- **1-2-3 Lake Elsinore**
- 4-5-6 at San Jose
- 7-8-9-10 at Modesto
- **11-12-13 Stockton**
- **15-16-17 San Jose**
- 18-29-20-21 at Stockton
- **22-23-24 R.C.**
- 25-26-27 at Inland Empire
- **29-30-31 Lancaster**

**SEPTEMBER**
- **1-2-3 High Desert**
- 3 at Visalia

### HIGH DESERT

**APRIL**
- **6 Inland Empire**
- 7 at Inland Empire
- **8-9 Inland Empire**
- 10-11-12-13 at R.C.
- **14 Inland Empire**
- 15 at Inland Empire
- 17 at Inland Empire
- **18-19-20 San Jose**
- **21-22-23-24 Lancaster**
- 25-26-27 at Stockton
- 28-29-30 at San Jose

**MAY**
- **1-2-3 Bakersfield**
- **5-6-7 Modesto**
- 8-9-10 at Bakersfield
- 12-13-14 at R.C.
- 15-16-17-18 at Lancaster
- **19-20-21 Lake Elsinore**
- **22-23-24-25 R.C.**
- **26-27-28 Inland Empire**
- 29-30-31 at Lake Elsinore

**JUNE**
- 1 at Lake Elsinore
- **2-3-4 Visalia**
- **5-6-7 Inland Empire**
- 9-10-11 at Lake Elsinore
- **12-13-14-15 R.C.**
- 16-17-18 at R.C.
- 19-20-21 at Inland Empire
- **22-23-24 R.C.**
- 29-30 at Lake Elsinore

**JULY**
- 1-2-3 at Lake Elsinore
- **4-5-6 Lancaster**
- **7-8-9 Lake Elsinore**
- 11-12-13 at Stockton
- 14-15-16 at Modesto
- 17-18-19-20 at Lancaster
- **21-22-23 Stockton**
- **25-26-27 Modesto**
- 28-29-30-31 at I.E.

**AUGUST**
- 1-2-3 at San Jose
- 4-5-6 at Visalia
- **7-8-9-10 Lancaster**
- **11-12-13 R.C.**
- **15-16-17 Visalia**
- 18-19-20 at Lancaster
- 21-22 at Inland Empire
- **23 Inland Empire**
- **24-25-26-27 L.E.**
- **28-29 Inland Empire**
- 30 at Inland Empire
- **31 Inland Empire**

**SEPTEMBER**
- 1-2-3 at Bakersfield

### INLAND EMPIRE

**APRIL**
- 6 at High Desert
- **7 High Desert**
- 8-9 at High Desert
- **10-11-12-13 Lancaster**
- 14 at High Desert
- **15 High Desert**
- **17 High Desert**
- 18-19-20 at Stockton
- 21-22-23 at Bakersfield
- **25-26-27 Modesto**
- **28-29-30 Visalia**

**MAY**
- 1-2-3-4 at Lake Elsinore
- **5-6-7 San Jose**
- 9-10-11 at Modesto
- 12-13-14 at Stockton
- 15-16-17 at Lake Elsinore
- **18-19-20-21 R.C.**
- **22-23-24-25 L.E.**
- 26-27-28 at High Desert
- **30-31 Visalia**

**JUNE**
- **1 Visalia**
- 2-3-4 at R.C.
- 5-6-7 at High Desert
- **8-9-10-11 Lancaster**
- 13-14-15 at San Jose
- 16-17-18 at Visalia
- **19-20-21 High Desert**
- **22-23-24 Modesto**
- 29-30 at R.C.

**JULY**
- 1-2-3 at R.C.
- **4-5-6 Lake Elsinore**
- **7-8-9 Lancaster**
- **10-11-12 R.C.**
- **14-15-16 Lancaster**
- **18-19-20 Lake Elsinore**
- **21-22-23 R.C.**
- 24-25-26-27 at Lancaster
- **28-29-30-31 High Desert**

**AUGUST**
- **1-2-3 Stockton**
- 4-5-6 at Modesto
- **8-9-10 San Jose**
- 11-12-13-14 at Lancaster
- 15-16-17 at Lake Elsinore
- 18-19-20 at R.C.
- **21-22 High Desert**
- 23 at High Desert
- **24 Lancaster**
- **25-26-27 Bakersfield**
- 28-29 at High Desert
- **30 High Desert**
- 31 at High Desert

**SEPTEMBER**
- **1-2-3-4 Lake Elsinore**

### LAKE ELSINORE

**APRIL**
- **6-7-8-9 Lancaster**
- 11-12-13 at Modesto
- 14-15-16 at Visalia
- **18-19-20 R.C.**
- **21-22-23 San Jose**
- 24-25-26-27 at R.C.
- **28-29-30 Bakersfield**

**MAY**
- **1-2-3-4 Inland Empire**
- **5-6-7 Lancaster**
- 9-10-11 at Stockton
- 12-13-14 at San Jose
- **15-16-17 Inland Empire**
- 19-20-21 at High Desert
- 22-23-24-25 at I.E.
- **26-27-28 Lancaster**
- **29-30-31 High Desert**

**JUNE**
- **1 High Desert**
- 2-3-4-5 at Lancaster
- **6-7-8 Stockton**
- **9-10-11 High Desert**
- 13-14-15 at Visalia
- 16-17-18 at Modesto
- 19-20-21 at R.C.
- **22-23-24 Bakersfield**
- **29-30 High Desert**

**JULY**
- **1-2-3 High Desert**
- 4-5-6 at Inland Empire
- 7-8-9 at High Desert
- **10-11-12 Lancaster**
- 13-14-15-16 at R.C.
- **18-19-20 Inland Empire**
- 21-22-23 at Lancaster
- **24-25-26-27 R.C.**
- **28-29-30 Modesto**

**AUGUST**
- 1-2-3 at Bakersfield
- 4-5-6 at Lancaster
- 7-8-9-10 at R.C.
- **11-12-13 San Jose**
- **15-16-17 Inland Empire**
- **18-19 Visalia**
- 21-22-23 at Lancaster
- 24-25-26-27 at H.D.
- **28-20-30-31 R.C.**

**SEPTEMBER**
- 1-2-3-4 at Inland Empire

### LANCASTER

**APRIL**
- 6-7-8-9 at Lake Elsinore
- 10-11-12-13 at I.E.
- **14-15-16 R.C.**
- **18-19-20 Modesto**
- 21-22-23-24 at H.D.
- **25-26-27 Visalia**
- **28-29-30 R.C.**

**MAY**
- **1 R.C.**
- **2-3-4 Stockton**
- 5-6-7 at Lake Elsinore
- 9-10-11 at San Jose
- 12-13-14 at Visalia
- **15-16-17-18 High Desert**
- **19-20-21 San Jose**
- **23-24-25 Stockton**
- 26-27-28 at Lake Elsinore
- 29-30-31 at R.C.

## JUNE
| | |
|---|---|
| 1 | at R.C. |
| 2-3-4-5 | Lake Elsinore |
| 6-7 | Bakersfield |
| 8-9-10-11 | at I.E. |
| 13-14-15 | at Modesto |
| 16-17-18 | at Stockton |
| 19-20-21 | Modesto |
| 22-23-24 | at San Jose |
| 30 | Bakersfield |

## JULY
| | |
|---|---|
| 1-2-3 | Bakersfield |
| 4-5-6 | at High Desert |
| 7-8-9 | Inland Empire |
| 10-11-12 | at Lake Elsinore |
| 14-15-16 | at Inland Empire |
| 17-18-19-20 | High Desert |
| 21-22-23 | Lake Elsinore |
| 24-25-26-27 | I.E. |
| 28-29-30 | at R.C. |

## AUGUST
| | |
|---|---|
| 1-2-3 | at Visalia |
| 4-5-6 | Lake Elsinore |
| 7-8-9-10 | at High Desert |
| 11-12-13-14 | I.E. |
| 15-16-17 | at R.C. |
| 18-19-20 | High Desert |
| 21-22-23 | Lake Elsinore |
| 24 | at Inland Empire |
| 25-26-27 | at R.C. |
| 29-30-31 | at Bakersfield |

## SEPTEMBER
| | |
|---|---|
| 1-2-3-4 | R.C. |

## MODESTO
### APRIL
| | |
|---|---|
| 6-7-8-9 | at Stockton |
| 11-12-13 | Lake Elsinore |
| 14-15-16 | San Jose |
| 17 | at Stockton |
| 18-19-20 | at Lancaster |
| 21-22-23 | at R.C. |
| 25-26-27 | at San Jose |
| 28-29-29-30 | Stockton |

### MAY
| | |
|---|---|
| 1 | Stockton |
| 3-3-4 | at R.C. |
| 5-6-7 | at High Desert |
| 9-10-11 | Inland Empire |
| 12-13-14 | Bakersfield |
| 16-17-18 | at Visalia |
| 19-20-21 | Stockton |
| 22-23-24-25 | at Bak. |
| 26 | at San Jose |
| 27 | San Jose |
| 28-29 | at San Jose |
| 30-31 | Bakersfield |

### JUNE
| | |
|---|---|
| 1 | Bakersfield |
| 2-3-4 | Stockton |
| 6 | San Jose |
| 7 | at San Jose |
| 8 | San Jose |
| 9-10-11-12 | at Bakersfield |
| 13-14-15 | Lancaster |
| 16-17-18 | Lake Elsinore |
| 19-20-21 | at Lancaster |
| 22-23-24 | at Inland Empire |
| 29-30 | San Jose |

### JULY
| | |
|---|---|
| 1 | at San Jose |
| 2-3 | San Jose |
| 4-5-6 | at Stockton |
| 7-8-9 | at Bakersfield |
| 10-11-12-13 | at Visalia |
| 14-15-16 | High Desert |
| 18-19-20 | Visalia |
| 21-22-23 | Bakersfield |
| 25-26-27 | at High Desert |
| 28-29-30 | at Lake Elsinore |

### AUGUST
| | |
|---|---|
| 1-2-3 | R.C. |
| 4-5-6 | Inland Empire |
| 7-8-9-10 | Bakersfield |
| 11-12-13 | at Visalia |
| 15-16-17 | Stockton |
| 18 | at San Jose |
| 19 | San Jose |
| 20 | at San Jose |
| 21-22-23-24 | Visalia |
| 25-26-27 | at Stockton |
| 28-29-30-31 | at San Jose |

### SEPTEMBER
| | |
|---|---|
| 1-2-3 | Visalia |

## RANCHO CUCAMONGA
### APRIL
| | |
|---|---|
| 7-8-9 | Bakersfield |
| 10-11-12-13 | High Desert |
| 14-15-16 | at Lancaster |
| 18-19-20 | at Lake Elsinore |
| 21-22-23-24 | at H.D. |
| 25-26-27 | Lake Elsinore |
| 28-29-30 | at Lancaster |

### MAY
| | |
|---|---|
| 1 | at Lancaster |
| 2-3-4 | Modesto |
| 5-6-7 | at Bakersfield |
| 9-10-11 | Visalia |
| 12-13-14 | High Desert |
| 15-16-17 | San Jose |
| 18-19-20-21 | at I.E. |
| 22-23-24-25 | at H.D. |
| 26-27-28 | Stockton |
| 29-30-31 | Lancaster |

### JUNE
| | |
|---|---|
| 1 | Lancaster |
| 2-3-4 | Inland Empire |
| 6-7-8 | at Visalia |
| 9-10-11 | at San Jose |
| 12-13-14-15 | at H.D. |
| 16-17-18 | High Desert |
| 19-20-21 | Lake Elsinore |
| 22-23-24 | at High Desert |
| 29-30 | Inland Empire |

### JULY
| | |
|---|---|
| 1-2-3 | Inland Empire |
| 4-5-6 | at San Jose |
| 7-8-9 | at Visalia |
| 10-11-12 | at Inland Empire |
| 13-14-15-16 | L.E. |
| 18-19-20 | Stockton |
| 21-22-23 | at Inland Empire |
| 24-25-26-27 | at L.E. |
| 28-29-30 | Lancaster |

### AUGUST
| | |
|---|---|
| 1-2-3 | at Modesto |
| 4-5-6 | at Stockton |
| 7-8-9-10 | Lake Elsinore |
| 11-12-13 | at High Desert |
| 15-16-17 | Lancaster |
| 18-19-20 | Inland Empire |
| 22-23-24 | at Bakersfield |
| 25-26-27 | Lancaster |
| 28-29-30-31 | at L.E. |

### SEPTEMBER
| | |
|---|---|
| 1-2-3-4 | at Lancaster |

## SAN JOSE
### APRIL
| | |
|---|---|
| 6-7-8-9 | Visalia |
| 10-11-12-13 | Stockton |
| 14-15-16 | at Modesto |
| 18-19-20 | at High Desert |
| 21-22-23 | at Bakersfield |
| 25-26-27 | Modesto |
| 28-29-30 | High Desert |

### MAY
| | |
|---|---|
| 1-2-3-4 | Visalia |
| 5-6-7 | at Inland Empire |
| 9-10-11 | Lancaster |
| 12-13-14 | Lake Elsinore |
| 15-16-17 | at R.C. |
| 19-20-21 | at Lancaster |
| 22-23-24-25 | at Visalia |
| 26 | Modesto |
| 27 | at Modesto |
| 28-29 | Modesto |
| 30-31 | at Stockton |

### JUNE
| | |
|---|---|
| 1 | at Stockton |
| 2-3-4-5 | at Bakersfield |
| 6 | at Modesto |
| 7 | Modesto |
| 8 | at Modesto |
| 9-10-11 | R.C. |
| 13-14-15 | Inland Empire |
| 16-17-18 | Bakersfield |
| 19-20-21 | at Visalia |
| 22-23-24 | Lancaster |
| 29-30 | at Modesto |

### JULY
| | |
|---|---|
| 1 | Modesto |
| 2-3 | at Modesto |
| 4-5-6 | R.C. |
| 7-8-9 | at Stockton |
| 10-11-12-13 | Bakersfield |
| 14-15-16 | Stockton |
| 18-19-20 | at Bakersfield |
| 21-22-23-24 | at Visalia |
| 25-26-27 | at Stockton |
| 28-29-30-31 | Visalia |

### AUGUST
| | |
|---|---|
| 1-2-3 | High Desert |
| 4-5-6 | Bakersfield |
| 8-9-10 | at Inland Empire |
| 11-12-13 | at Lake Elsinore |
| 15-16-17 | at Bakersfield |
| 18 | Modesto |
| 19 | at Modesto |
| 20 | Modesto |
| 22-23 | Stockton |
| 24 | at Stockton |
| 25-26-27 | at Visalia |
| 28-29-30-31 | Modesto |

### SEPTEMBER
| | |
|---|---|
| 1-2-3 | at Stockton |
| 4 | Stockton |

## STOCKTON
### APRIL
| | |
|---|---|
| 6-7-8-9 | Modesto |
| 10-11-12-13 | at Bakersfield |
| 14-15-16 | at Bakersfield |
| 17 | Modesto |
| 18-19-20 | Inland Empire |
| 21-22-23 | Visalia |
| 25-26-27 | High Desert |
| 28-29-29-30 | at Modesto |

### MAY
| | |
|---|---|
| 1 | at Modesto |
| 2-3-4 | at Lancaster |
| 5-6-7 | at Visalia |
| 9-10-11 | Lake Elsinore |
| 12-13-14 | Inland Empire |
| 15-16-17-18 | Bakersfield |
| 19-20-21 | at Modesto |
| 23-24-25 | at Lancaster |
| 26-27-28 | at R.C. |
| 30-31 | San Jose |

### JUNE
| | |
|---|---|
| 1 | San Jose |
| 2-3-4 | at Modesto |
| 6-7-8 | at Lake Elsinore |
| 9-10-11-12 | Visalia |
| 13-14-15 | at Bakersfield |
| 16-17-18 | Lancaster |
| 19-20-21 | Bakersfield |
| 22-23-24 | Visalia |
| 29 | at Bakersfield |
| 30 | at Visalia |

### JULY
| | |
|---|---|
| 1-2-3 | at Visalia |
| 4-5-6 | Modesto |
| 7-8-9 | San Jose |
| 11-12-13 | High Desert |
| 14-15-16 | at San Jose |
| 18-19-20 | at R.C. |
| 21-22-23 | at High Desert |
| 25-26-27 | San Jose |
| 28-29-30-31 | at Bak. |

### AUGUST
| | |
|---|---|
| 1-2-3 | at Inland Empire |
| 4-5-6 | R.C. |
| 7-8-9-10 | Visalia |
| 11-12-13 | at Bakersfield |
| 15-16-17 | at Modesto |
| 18-19-20-21 | Bakersfield |
| 22-23 | at San Jose |
| 24 | San Jose |
| 25-26-27 | Modesto |
| 28-29-30-31 | at Visalia |

### SEPTEMBER
| | |
|---|---|
| 1-2-3 | San Jose |
| 4 | at San Jose |

## VISALIA
### APRIL
| | |
|---|---|
| 6-7-8-9 | at San Jose |
| 10-11-12-13 | at Bak. |
| 14-15-16 | Lake Elsinore |

**CLASS A SCHEDULES**

| 17-18-19-20 | Bakersfield |
|---|---|
| 21-22-23 | at Stockton |
| 25-26-27 | at Lancaster |
| 28-29-30 | at Inland Empire |
| **MAY** | |
| 1-2-3-4 | at San Jose |
| 5-6-7 | Stockton |
| 9-10-11 | at R.C. |
| 12-13-14 | Lancaster |
| 16-17-18 | Modesto |
| 19-20-21 | at Bakersfield |
| 22-23-24-25 | San Jose |

| 26-27-28-29 | Bakersfield |
|---|---|
| 30-31 | at Inland Empire |
| **JUNE** | |
| 1-2-3-4 | at Inland Empire |
| 6-7-8 | R.C. |
| 9-10-11-12 | at Stockton |
| 13-14-15 | Lake Elsinore |
| 16-17-18 | Inland Empire |
| 29-20-21 | San Jose |
| 22-23-24 | at San Jose |
| 30 | Stockton |

| **JULY** | |
|---|---|
| 1-2-3 | Stockton |
| 4-5-6 | at Bakersfield |
| 7-8-9 | R.C. |
| 10-11-12-13 | Modesto |
| 14-15-16 | at Bakersfield |
| 18-29-20 | at Modesto |
| 21-22-23-24 | San Jose |
| 25-26 | Bakersfield |
| 28-29-30-31 | at San Jose |
| **AUGUST** | |
| 1-2-3 | Lancaster |

| 4-5-6 | High Desert |
|---|---|
| 7-8-9-10 | at Stockton |
| 11-12-13 | Modesto |
| 15-16-17 | at High Desert |
| 18-19-20 | at Lake Elsinore |
| 21-22-23-24 | at Modesto |
| 25-26-27 | San Jose |
| 28-29-30-31 | Stockton |
| **SEPTEMBER** | |
| 1-2-3 | at Modesto |
| 4 | Bakersfield |

# CAROLINA LEAGUE

## FREDERICK

| **APRIL** | |
|---|---|
| 6-7-8 | Lynchburg |
| 10-11-12-13 | Salem |
| 14-15-16 | at Lynchburg |
| 17-18-19 | at Salem |
| 21-22-23 | Potomac |
| 24-25-26-27 | at W-S |
| 28-29-30 | at Potomac |
| **MAY** | |
| 1-2-3-4 | Winston-Salem |
| 5-6-7 | Wilmington |
| 8-9-10-11 | at Myrtle Beach |
| 12-13-14 | at Kinston |
| 15-16-17 | Myrtle Beach |
| 19-20-21 | Kinston |
| 22-23-24 | at Wilmington |
| 25-26-27-28 | at Lynchburg |
| 29-30-31 | Salem |
| **JUNE** | |
| 1-2-3-4 | Kinston |
| 5-6-7 | at Salem |
| 8-9-10-11 | Potomac |
| 13-14-15 | at W-S |
| 16-17-18 | at Potomac |
| 19-20-21 | Winston-Salem |
| 23-24-25 | Potomac |
| 29-30 | at Myrtle Beach |
| **JULY** | |
| 1 | at Myrtle Beach |
| 2-3-4 | at Lynchburg |
| 5-6-7 | Myrtle Beach |
| 8-9-10 | Lynchburg |
| 12-13-14-15 | at Wilm. |
| 17-18-19-20 | at Kinston |
| 21-22-23 | Salem |
| 24-25-26 | Kinston |
| 27-28-29-30 | at Salem |
| 31 | Wilmington |
| **AUGUST** | |
| 1-2 | Wilmington |
| 3-4-5 | at Winston-Salem |
| 6-7-8-9 | at Potomac |
| 11-12-13 | Winston-Salem |
| 14-15-16-17 | Wilmington |
| 18-19-20 | at Myrtle Beach |
| 21-22-23 | at Kinston |
| 25-26-27-28 | M.B. |
| 29-30-31 | Lynchburg |
| **SEPTEMBER** | |
| 1 | Lynchburg |
| 2-3-4 | at Wilmington |

## KINSTON

| **APRIL** | |
|---|---|
| 6-7-8 | at Winston-Salem |
| 10-11-12-13 | Wilmington |
| 14-15-16 | Winston-Salem |
| 17-18-19 | at Wilmington |
| 20-21-22 | Myrtle Beach |
| 24-25-26-27 | Lynchburg |
| 28-29-30 | at Salem |
| **MAY** | |
| 1-2-3-4 | at Lynchburg |
| 5-6-7 | Salem |
| 8-9-10-11 | at Potomac |
| 12-13-14 | Frederick |
| 15-16-17 | Potomac |
| 19-20-21 | at Frederick |
| 22-23-24 | at Salem |
| 25-26-27-28 | W-S |
| 29-30-31 | Wilmington |
| **JUNE** | |
| 1-2-3-4 | at Frederick |
| 5-6-7 | at Salem |
| 8-9-10-11 | Myrtle Beach |
| 13-14-15 | Lynchburg |
| 16-17-18 | at Myrtle Beach |
| 20-21-22 | at Lynchburg |
| 23-24-25 | Salem |
| 29-30 | at Potomac |
| **JULY** | |
| 1 | at Potomac |
| 2-3-4 | at Winston-Salem |
| 5-6-7 | Wilmington |
| 8-9-10 | Winston-Salem |
| 12-13-14-15 | at Salem |
| 17-18-19-20 | Frederick |
| 21-22-23 | Potomac |
| 24-25-26 | at Frederick |
| 27-28-29-30 | at Wilm. |
| 31 | Myrtle Beach |
| **AUGUST** | |
| 1-2 | Myrtle Beach |
| 3-4-5 | Lynchburg |
| 7-8-9-10 | at Myrtle Beach |
| 11-12-13 | at Lynchburg |
| 14-15-16-17 | Salem |
| 18-19-20 | at Potomac |
| 21-22-23 | Frederick |
| 25-26-27-28 | Potomac |
| 29-30-31 | at W-S |

| **SEPTEMBER** | |
|---|---|
| 1 | at Winston-Salem |
| 2-3-4 | at Myrtle Beach |

## LYNCHBURG

| **APRIL** | |
|---|---|
| 6-7-8 | at Frederick |
| 9-10-11-12 | Potomac |
| 14-15-16 | Frederick |
| 17-18-19 | at Potomac |
| 21-22-23 | Salem |
| 24-25-26-27 | at Kinston |
| 28-29-30 | at Myrtle Beach |
| **MAY** | |
| 1-2-3-4 | Kinston |
| 5-6-7 | Myrtle Beach |
| 8-9-10-11 | at Wilmington |
| 12-13-14 | Winston-Salem |
| 15-16-17 | Wilmington |
| 19-20-21 | at W-S |
| 22-23-24 | at Potomac |
| 25-26-27-28 | Frederick |
| 29-30-31 | Potomac |
| **JUNE** | |
| 1-2-3-4 | at Winston-Salem |
| 5-6-7 | at Myrtle Beach |
| 8-9-10-11 | Salem |
| 13-14-15 | at Kinston |
| 16-17-18 | at Salem |
| 20-21-22 | Kinston |
| 23-24-25 | Myrtle Beach |
| 29-30 | at Wilmington |
| **JULY** | |
| 1 | at Wilmington |
| 2-3-4 | Frederick |
| 5-6-7 | Salem |
| 8-9-10 | at Frederick |
| 13-14-15-16 | at Potomac |
| 17-18-19-20 | W-S |
| 21-22-23 | Wilmington |
| 24-25-26 | at W-S |
| 27-28-29-30 | at Myrtle Beach |
| 31 | Potomac |
| **AUGUST** | |
| 1-2 | Potomac |
| 3-4-5 | at Kinston |
| 7-8-9-10 | at Salem |
| 11-12-13 | Kinston |
| 14-15-16-17 | M.B. |
| 18-19-20 | at Wilmington |
| 22-23-24 | Winston-Salem |

| 25-26-27-28 | Wilmington |
|---|---|
| 29-30-31 | at Frederick |
| **SEPTEMBER** | |
| 1 | at Frederick |
| 2-3-4 | at Salem |

## MYRTLE BEACH

| **APRIL** | |
|---|---|
| 6-7-8-9 | Wilmington |
| 10-11-12-13 | at W-S |
| 14-15-16 | Potomac |
| 17-18-19 | Winston-Salem |
| 20-21-22 | at Kinston |
| 24-25-26-27 | Salem |
| 28-29-30 | Lynchburg |
| **MAY** | |
| 1-2-3-4 | at Salem |
| 5-6-7 | at Lynchburg |
| 8-9-10-11 | Frederick |
| 12-13-14 | at Potomac |
| 15-16-17 | at Frederick |
| 18-19-20 | at Wilmington |
| 22-23-24 | Winston-Salem |
| 26-27-28 | Wilmington |
| 29-30-31 | Winston-Salem |
| **JUNE** | |
| 1-2-3-4 | at Potomac |
| 5-6-7 | Lynchburg |
| 8-9-10-11 | at Kinston |
| 13-14-15 | Salem |
| 16-17-18 | Kinston |
| 20-21-22 | at Salem |
| 23-24-25 | at Lynchburg |
| 29-30 | Frederick |
| **JULY** | |
| 1 | Frederick |
| 2-3-4 | at Potomac |
| 5-6-7 | at Frederick |
| 8-9-10 | Wilmington |
| 12-13-14-15 | W-S |
| 17-18-19-20 | at Wilm. |
| 21-22-23 | at W-S |
| 24-25-26 | Potomac |
| 27-28-29-30 | Lynchburg |
| 31 | at Kinston |
| **AUGUST** | |
| 1-2 | at Kinston |
| 3-4-5 | Salem |
| 7-8-9-10 | Kinston |
| 11-12-13 | at Salem |
| 14-15-16-17 | at Lynchburg |
| 18-19-20 | Frederick |

22-23-24 at Wilmington
25-26-27-28 at Frederick
**29-30-31 Potomac**
**SEPTEMBER**
**1 Potomac**
**2-3-4 Kinston**

## POTOMAC
**APRIL**
**6-7-8** at Salem
9-10-11-12 at Lynchburg
14-15-16 at Myrtle Beach
**17-18-19 Lynchburg**
21-22-23 at Frederick
**24-25-26-27 Wilmington**
**28-29-30 Frederick**
**MAY**
1-2-3-4 at Wilmington
5-6-7 at Winston-Salem
**8-9-10-11 Kinston**
**12-13-14 Myrtle Beach**
15-16-17 at Kinston
**19-20-21 Salem**
**22-23-24 Lynchburg**
25-26-27-28 at Salem
29-30-31 at Lynchburg
**JUNE**
**1-2-3-4 Myrtle Beach**
**5-6-7 Winston-Salem**
8-9-10-11 at Frederick
**13-14-15 Wilmington**
**16-17-18 Frederick**
20-21-22 at Wilmington
23-24-25 at Frederick
**29-30 Kinston**
**JULY**
**1 Kinston**
**2-3-4 Myrtle Beach**
5-6-7 at Winston-Salem
8-9-10 at Salem
**13-14-15-16 Lynchburg**
**17-18-19-20 Salem**
21-22-23 at Kinston
24-25-26 at Myrtle Beach
**27-28-29-30 W-S**
31 at Lynchburg
**AUGUST**
1-2 at Lynchburg
3-4-5 at Wilmington
**6-7-8-9 Frederick**
**11-12-13 Wilmington**
14-15-16-17 at W-S
**18-19-20 Kinston**
**22-23-24 Salem**
25-26-27-28 at Kinston

29-30-31 at Myrtle Beach
**SEPTEMBER**
1 at Myrtle Beach
**2-3-4 Winston-Salem**

## SALEM
**APRIL**
**6-7-8 Potomac**
10-11-12-13 at Frederick
14-15-16 at Wilmington
**17-18-19 Frederick**
21-22-23 at Lynchburg
24-25-26-27 at M.B.
**28-29-30 Kinston**
**MAY**
**1-2-3-4 Myrtle Beach**
5-6-7 at Kinston
**8-9-10-11 Winston-Salem**
**12-13-14 Wilmington**
16-17-18 at W-S
19-20-21 at Potomac
**22-23-24 Kinston**
**25-26-27-28 Potomac**
29-30-31 at Frederick
**JUNE**
1-2-3-4 at Wilmington
**5-6-7 Frederick**
8-9-10-11 at Lynchburg
13-14-15 at Myrtle Beach
**16-17-18 Lynchburg**
**20-21-22 Myrtle Beach**
23-24-25 at Kinston
**29-30 Winston-Salem**
**JULY**
**1 Winston-Salem**
2-3-4 at Wilmington
5-6-7 at Lynchburg
**8-9-10 Potomac**
**12-13-14-15 Kinston**
17-18-19-20 at Potomac
21-22-23 at Frederick
**24-25-26 Wilmington**
**27-28-29-30 Frederick**
31 at Winston-Salem
**AUGUST**
1-2 at Winston-Salem
3-4-5 at Myrtle Beach
**7-8-9-10 Lynchburg**
**11-12-13 Myrtle Beach**
14-15-16-17 at Kinston
**18-19-20 Winston-Salem**
22-23-24 at Potomac
25-26-27-28 at W-S
**29-30-31 Wilmington**

**SEPTEMBER**
**1 Wilmington**
**2-3-4 Lynchburg**

## WILMINGTON
**APRIL**
6-7-8-9 at Myrtle Beach
10-11-12-13 at Kinston
**14-15-16 Salem**
**17-18-19 Kinston**
21-22-23 at W-S
24-25-26-27 at Potomac
**28-29-30 Winston-Salem**
**MAY**
**1-2-3-4 Potomac**
5-6-7 at Frederick
**8-9-10-11 Lynchburg**
12-13-14 at Salem
15-16-17 at Lynchburg
**18-19-20 Myrtle Beach**
**22-23-24 Frederick**
26-27-28 at Myrtle Beach
29-30-31 at Kinston
**JUNE**
**1-2-3-4 Salem**
**5-6-7 Kinston**
8-9-10-11 at W-S
13-14-15 at Potomac
**16-17-18 Winston-Salem**
**20-21-22 Potomac**
23-24-25 at W-S
**29-30 Lynchburg**
**JULY**
**1 Lynchburg**
**2-3-4 Salem**
5-6-7 at Kinston
8-9-10 at Myrtle Beach
**12-13-14-15 Frederick**
**17-18-19-20 M.B.**
21-22-23 at Lynchburg
24-25-26 at Salem
**27-28-29-30 Kinston**
31 at Frederick
**AUGUST**
1-2 at Frederick
**3-4-5 Potomac**
**7-8-9-10 Winston-Salem**
11-12-13 at Potomac
14-15-16-17 at Frederick
**18-19-20 Lynchburg**
**22-23-24 Myrtle Beach**
25-26-27-28 at Lynchburg
29-30-31 at Salem
**SEPTEMBER**
1 at Salem

**2-3-4 Frederick**

## WINSTON-SALEM
**APRIL**
**6-7-8 Kinston**
**10-11-12-13 M.B.**
14-15-16 at Kinston
17-18-19 at Myrtle Beach
**21-22-23 Wilmington**
**24-25-26-27 Frederick**
28-29-30 at Wilmington
**MAY**
1-2-3-4 at Frederick
**5-6-7 Potomac**
8-9-10-11 at Salem
12-13-14 at Lynchburg
**16-17-18 Salem**
**19-20-21 Lynchburg**
22-23-24 at Myrtle Beach
25-26-27-28 at Kinston
**29-30-31 Myrtle Beach**
**JUNE**
**1-2-3-4 Lynchburg**
5-6-7 at Potomac
**8-9-10-11 Wilmington**
**13-14-15 Frederick**
16-17-18 at Wilmington
19-20-21 at Frederick
**23-24-25 Wilmington**
29-30 at Salem
**JULY**
1 at Salem
**2-3-4 Kinston**
**5-6-7 Potomac**
8-9-10 at Kinston
12-13-14-15 at M.B.
17-18-19-20 at Lynchburg
**21-22-23 Myrtle Beach**
**24-25-26 Lynchburg**
27-28-29-30 at Potomac
**31 Salem**
**AUGUST**
**1-2 Salem**
**3-4-5 Frederick**
7-8-9-10 at Wilmington
11-12-13 at Frederick
**14-15-16-17 Potomac**
18-19-20 at Salem
22-23-24 at Lynchburg
**25-26-27-28 Salem**
**29-30-31 Kinston**
**SEPTEMBER**
**1 Kinston**
2-3-4 at Potomac

## BREVARD COUNTY

**APRIL**

| Date | Opponent |
|---|---|
| 6-7-8-9 | at Daytona |
| 10-11-12 | Palm Beach |
| 13-14-15 | Vero Beach |
| 17-18-19 | at Palm Beach |
| 20-21-22 | at Jupiter |
| 23-24-25 | St. Lucie |
| 26-27-28 | at Vero Beach |
| 29-30 | at St. Lucie |

**MAY**

| Date | Opponent |
|---|---|
| 1 | at St. Lucie |
| 3-4-5 | Jupiter |
| 6-7-8-9 | at Tampa |
| 10-11-12-13 | Clearwater |
| 15-16-17-18 | at Lakeland |
| 19-20-21-22 | Sarasota |
| 23-24-25-26 | at Fort Myers |
| 27-28-30-31 | Daytona |

**JUNE**

| Date | Opponent |
|---|---|
| 1-2-3-4 | Lakeland |
| 5-6-7 | at Vero Beach |
| 8-9-10 | Jupiter |
| 11-12-13 | Vero Beach |
| 14-15 | Daytona |
| 19-20 | at St Lucie |
| 21 | St. Lucie |
| 22-23-24 | Palm Beach |
| 25-26-27 | St. Lucie |
| 28-29-30 | at Palm Beach |

**JULY**

| Date | Opponent |
|---|---|
| 1-2 | Daytona |
| 3-4 | at Daytona |
| 5-6-7 | at Jupiter |
| 8-9-10 | at Palm Beach |
| 12 | St. Lucie |
| 13-14 | at St. Lucie |
| 15-16-17 | at Vero Beach |
| 18-19-20-21 | Dunedin |
| 22-23-24-25 | at Clearwater |
| 26-27-28-29 | at Dunedin |
| 31 | Jupiter |

**AUGUST**

| Date | Opponent |
|---|---|
| 1-2 | Jupiter |
| 3-4-5-6 | Fort Myers |
| 7-8-9-10 | at Sarasota |
| 11-12 | at Daytona |
| 14-15-16-17 | Tampa |
| 18 | St. Lucie |
| 19-20 | at St. Lucie |
| 21-22-23 | Vero Beach |
| 24-25-26 | Palm Beach |
| 28-29-30 | at Jupiter |
| 31 | at Daytona |

**SEPTEMBER**

| Date | Opponent |
|---|---|
| 1 | at Daytona |
| 2-3 | Daytona |

## CLEARWATER

**APRIL**

| Date | Opponent |
|---|---|
| 6 | Dunedin |
| 7 | at Dunedin |
| 8 | Dunedin |
| 9 | at Dunedin |
| 10-11-12 | at Sarasota |
| 13-14-15 | at Fort Myers |
| 17-18-19 | Sarasota |
| 20-21-22 | at Tampa |
| 23-24-25 | Lakeland |
| 26-27-28 | Fort Myers |
| 29-30 | at Lakeland |

**MAY**

| Date | Opponent |
|---|---|
| 1 | at Lakeland |
| 3-4-5 | Tampa |
| 6-7-8-9 | Palm Beach |
| 10-11-12-13 | at Brevard |
| 15-16-17-18 | Jupiter |
| 19-20-21-22 | at V.B. |
| 23-24-25-26 | at Jupiter |
| 27-28 | Dunedin |
| 30-31 | at Dunedin |

**JUNE**

| Date | Opponent |
|---|---|
| 1-2-3-4 | Vero Beach |
| 5-6-7 | at Lakeland |
| 8 | Sarasota |
| 9-10 | at Sarasota |
| 11-12-13 | Fort Myers |
| 14-15 | at Dunedin |
| 19 | at Sarasota |
| 20-21 | Sarasota |
| 22-23-24 | at Fort Myers |
| 25-26-27 | at Tampa |
| 28-29-30 | Lakeland |

**JULY**

| Date | Opponent |
|---|---|
| 1 | at Tampa |
| 2-3 | Tampa |
| 4 | at Lakeland |
| 5 | Lakeland |
| 6 | at Lakeland |
| 7-8 | Dunedin |
| 9 | at Dunedin |
| 10 | Dunedin |
| 12 | at Lakeland |
| 13-14 | Lakeland |
| 15 | Tampa |
| 16-17 | at Tampa |
| 18-19-20-21 | Daytona |
| 22-23-24-25 | Brevard |
| 26-27-28-29 | at Daytona |
| 31 | Tampa |

**AUGUST**

| Date | Opponent |
|---|---|
| 1-2 | Tampa |
| 3-4-5-6 | St. Lucie |
| 7-8-9-10 | at Palm Beach |
| 11 | Dunedin |
| 12 | at Dunedin |
| 14-15-16-17 | at St. Lucie |
| 18-19-20 | at Fort Myers |
| 21-22-23 | at Fort Myers |
| 24-25-26 | at Sarasota |
| 28-29-30 | Fort Myers |
| 31 | at Dunedin |

**SEPTEMBER**

| Date | Opponent |
|---|---|
| 1 | at Dunedin |
| 2-3 | Dunedin |

## DAYTONA

**APRIL**

| Date | Opponent |
|---|---|
| 6-7-8-9 | Brevard |
| 10-11-12 | at St. Lucie |
| 13-14-15 | Palm Beach |
| 17-18-19 | St. Lucie |
| 20-21-22 | at Vero Beach |
| 23-24-25 | Jupiter |
| 26-27-28 | at Palm Beach |
| 29-30 | at Jupiter |

**MAY**

| Date | Opponent |
|---|---|
| 1 | at Jupiter |
| 3-4-5 | Vero Beach |
| 6-7-8-9 | at Lakeland |
| 10-11-12-13 | at Fort Myers |
| 15-16-17-18 | Sarasota |
| 19-20-21-22 | Tampa |
| 23-24-25-26 | at Dunedin |
| 27-28-30-31 | at Brevard |

**JUNE**

| Date | Opponent |
|---|---|
| 1-2-3-4 | Fort Myers |
| 5-6-7 | at Jupiter |
| 8-9-10 | at St. Lucie |
| 11-12-13 | Jupiter |
| 14-15 | at Brevard |
| 19-20-21 | at Palm Beach |
| 22-23-24 | Vero Beach |
| 25-26-27 | Palm Beach |
| 28-29-30 | at Vero Beach |

**JULY**

| Date | Opponent |
|---|---|
| 1-2 | at Brevard |
| 3-4 | Brevard |
| 5-6-7 | St. Lucie |
| 8-9-10 | Vero Beach |
| 12-13-14 | at Jupiter |
| 15-16-17 | Palm Beach |
| 18-19-20-21 | at Clearwater |
| 22-23-24-25 | Dunedin |
| 26-27-28-29 | Clearwater |
| 31 | at St. Lucie |

**AUGUST**

| Date | Opponent |
|---|---|
| 1-2 | at St. Lucie |
| 3-4-5-6 | Lakeland |
| 7-8-9-10 | at Tampa |
| 11-12 | Brevard |
| 14-15-16-17 | at Sarasota |
| 18-19-20 | at Palm Beach |
| 21-22-23 | Jupiter |
| 24-25-26 | St. Lucie |
| 28-29-30 | at Vero Beach |
| 31 | Brevard |

**SEPTEMBER**

| Date | Opponent |
|---|---|
| 1 | Brevard |
| 2-3 | at Brevard |

## DUNEDIN

**APRIL**

| Date | Opponent |
|---|---|
| 6 | at Clearwater |
| 7 | Clearwater |
| 8 | at Clearwater |
| 9 | Clearwater |
| 10-11 | Lakeland |
| 12 | at Lakeland |
| 13-14-15 | Tampa |
| 17 | at Lakeland |
| 18 | Lakeland |
| 19 | at Lakeland |
| 20-21-22 | Sarasota |
| 23-24 | Fort Myers |
| 26-27-28 | at Tampa |
| 29 | Fort Myers |
| 30 | at Fort Myers |

**MAY**

| Date | Opponent |
|---|---|
| 1-2 | at Fort Myers |
| 3 | at Sarasota |
| 4 | Sarasota |
| 5 | at Sarasota |
| 6-7-8-9 | at Vero Beach |
| 10-11-12-13 | Palm Beach |
| 15-16-17-18 | at St. Lucie |
| 19-20-21-22 | Jupiter |
| 23-24-25-26 | Daytona |
| 27-28 | at Clearwater |
| 30-31 | Clearwater |

**JUNE**

| Date | Opponent |
|---|---|
| 1-2-3-4 | at Palm Beach |
| 5 | at Sarasota |
| 6-7 | Sarasota |
| 8-9 | at Tampa |
| 10 | Tampa |
| 11-12-13 | Lakeland |
| 14-15 | Clearwater |
| 19-20 | Tampa |
| 21 | at Tampa |
| 22-23-24 | at Lakeland |
| 25-26-27 | Fort Myers |
| 28-29-30 | at Sarasota |

**JULY**

| Date | Opponent |
|---|---|
| 1-2-3 | at Fort Myers |
| 4 | Sarasota |
| 5 | at Sarasota |
| 6 | Sarasota |
| 7-8 | at Clearwater |
| 9 | Clearwater |
| 10 | at Clearwater |
| 12-13 | at Sarasota |
| 14 | Sarasota |
| 15-16-17 | Fort Myers |
| 18-19-20-21 | at Brevard |
| 22-23-24-25 | at Daytona |
| 26-27-28-29 | Brevard |
| 31 | at Fort Myers |

**AUGUST**

| Date | Opponent |
|---|---|
| 1-2 | at Fort Myers |
| 3-4-5-6 | at Jupiter |
| 7-8-9-10 | St. Lucie |
| 11 | at Clearwater |
| 12 | Clearwater |
| 14-15-16-17 | Vero Beach |
| 18-19-20 | at Tampa |
| 21-22 | Lakeland |
| 23 | at Lakeland |
| 24-25-26 | Tampa |
| 28-29 | at Lakeland |
| 30 | Lakeland |
| 31 | Clearwater |

**SEPTEMBER**

| Date | Opponent |
|---|---|
| 1 | Clearwater |
| 2-3 | at Clearwater |

## FORT MYERS

**APRIL**

| Date | Opponent |
|---|---|
| 6-7 | at Sarasota |

## (Continued team, Column 1)

| | |
|---|---|
| 8-9 | Sarasota |
| 10-11-12 | at Tampa |
| 13-14-15 | Clearwater |
| 17-18-19 | Tampa |
| 20-21-22 | at Lakeland |
| 23-24 | at Dunedin |
| 26-27-28 | at Clearwater |
| 29 | at Dunedin |
| 30 | Dunedin |

**MAY**

| | |
|---|---|
| 1-2 | Dunedin |
| 3-4-5 | Lakeland |
| 6-7-8-9 | at St. Lucie |
| 10-11-12-13 | Daytona |
| 15-16-17-18 | at P.B. |
| 19-20-21-22 | St. Lucie |
| 23-24-25-26 | Brevard |
| 27-28 | at Sarasota |
| 30-31 | Sarasota |

**JUNE**

| | |
|---|---|
| 1-2-3-4 | at Daytona |
| 5-6-7 | Tampa |
| 8-9-10 | at Lakeland |
| 11-12-13 | at Clearwater |
| 14-15 | at Sarasota |
| 19-20-21 | Lakeland |
| 22-23-24 | Clearwater |
| 25-26-27 | at Dunedin |
| 28-29-30 | at Tampa |

**JULY**

| | |
|---|---|
| 1-2-3 | Dunedin |
| 4-5-6 | at Tampa |
| 7 | at Sarasota |
| 8 | Sarasota |
| 9 | at Sarasota |
| 10 | Sarasota |
| 12-13-14 | Tampa |
| 15-16-17 | at Dunedin |
| 18-19-20-21 | Jupiter |
| 22-23-24-25 | Palm Beach |
| 26-27-28-29 | at V.B. |
| 31 | Dunedin |

**AUGUST**

| | |
|---|---|
| 1-2 | Dunedin |
| 3-4-5-6 | at Brevard |
| 7-8-9-10 | Vero Beach |
| 11-12 | Sarasota |
| 14-15-16-17 | at Jupiter |
| 18-19-20 | Lakeland |
| 21-22-23 | Clearwater |
| 25-26-27 | at Lakeland |
| 28-29-30 | at Clearwater |
| 31 | Sarasota |

**SEPTEMBER**

| | |
|---|---|
| 1 | Sarasota |
| 2-3 | at Sarasota |

## JUPITER

**APRIL**

| | |
|---|---|
| 6-7 | Palm Beach |
| 8-9 | at Palm Beach |
| 10-11-12 | Vero Beach |
| 13-14-15 | St. Lucie |
| 17-18-19 | at Vero Beach |
| 20-21-22 | Brevard |
| 23-24-25 | at Daytona |
| 26-27-28 | at St. Lucie |
| 29-30 | Daytona |

**MAY**

| | |
|---|---|
| 1 | Daytona |
| 3-4-5 | at Brevard |
| 6-7-8-9 | Sarasota |
| 10-11-12-13 | Tampa |
| 15-16-17-18 | at Clearwater |
| 19-20-21-22 | at Dunedin |
| 23-24-25-26 | Clearwater |
| 27-28 | at Palm Beach |
| 30-31 | Palm Beach |

**JUNE**

| | |
|---|---|
| 1-2-3-4 | at Sarasota |
| 5-6-7 | Daytona |
| 8-9-10 | at Brevard |
| 11-12-13 | at Daytona |
| 14-15 | Palm Beach |
| 19-20-21 | at Vero Beach |
| 22-23-24 | St. Lucie |
| 25-26-27 | Vero Beach |
| 28-29-30 | at St. Lucie |

**JULY**

| | |
|---|---|
| 1 | at Palm Beach |
| 2-3 | Palm Beach |
| 4 | at Palm Beach |
| 5-6-7 | Brevard |
| 8-9-10 | at St. Lucie |
| 12-13-14 | Daytona |
| 15-16-17 | St. Lucie |
| 18-19-20-21 | at Fort Myers |
| 22-23-24-25 | Lakeland |
| 27-28-29-30 | at Tampa |
| 31 | at Brevard |

**AUGUST**

| | |
|---|---|
| 1-2 | at Brevard |
| 3-4-5-6 | Dunedin |
| 7-8-9-10 | at Lakeland |
| 11-12 | at Palm Beach |
| 14-15-16-17 | Fort Myers |
| 18-19-20 | at Vero Beach |
| 21-22-23 | at Daytona |
| 24-25-26 | Vero Beach |
| 28-29-30 | Brevard |
| 31 | at Palm Beach |

**SEPTEMBER**

| | |
|---|---|
| 1 | at Palm Beach |
| 2-3 | Palm Beach |

## LAKELAND

**APRIL**

| | |
|---|---|
| 6 | Tampa |
| 7 | at Tampa |
| 8 | Tampa |
| 9 | at Tampa |
| 10-11 | at Dunedin |
| 12 | Dunedin |
| 13-14 | at Sarasota |
| 15 | Sarasota |
| 17 | Dunedin |
| 18 | at Dunedin |
| 19 | Dunedin |
| 20-21-22 | Fort Myers |
| 23-24-25 | at Clearwater |
| 26 | at Sarasota |
| 27-28 | Sarasota |
| 29-30 | Clearwater |

**MAY**

| | |
|---|---|
| 1 | Clearwater |
| 3-4-5 | at Fort Myers |
| 6-7-8-9 | Daytona |
| 10-11-12-13 | at V.B. |
| 15-16-17-18 | Brevard |
| 19-20-21-22 | at P.B. |
| 23-24-25-26 | Vero Beach |
| 27 | at Tampa |
| 28-30-31 | Tampa |

**JUNE**

| | |
|---|---|
| 1-2-3-4 | at Brevard |
| 5-6-7 | Clearwater |
| 8-9-10 | Fort Myers |
| 11-12-13 | at Dunedin |
| 14-15 | at Tampa |
| 19-20-21 | at Fort Myers |
| 22-23-24 | Dunedin |
| 25-26 | Sarasota |
| 27 | at Sarasota |
| 28-29-30 | at Clearwater |

**JULY**

| | |
|---|---|
| 1 | Sarasota |
| 2-3 | at Sarasota |
| 4 | Clearwater |
| 5 | at Clearwater |
| 6 | Clearwater |
| 7 | Tampa |
| 8 | at Tampa |
| 9 | Tampa |
| 10 | at Tampa |
| 12 | Clearwater |
| 13-14 | at Clearwater |
| 15 | at Sarasota |
| 16-17 | Sarasota |
| 18-19-20-21 | at St. Lucie |
| 22-23-24-25 | at Jupiter |
| 26-27-28-29 | St. Lucie |
| 31 | Sarasota |

**AUGUST**

| | |
|---|---|
| 1-2 | at Sarasota |
| 3-4-5-6 | at Daytona |
| 7-8-9-10 | Jupiter |
| 11 | Tampa |
| 12 | at Tampa |
| 14-15-16-17 | Palm Beach |
| 18-19-20 | at Fort Myers |
| 21-22 | at Dunedin |
| 23 | Dunedin |
| 25-26-27 | Fort Myers |
| 28-29 | Dunedin |
| 30 | at Dunedin |
| 31 | at Tampa |

**SEPTEMBER**

| | |
|---|---|
| 1 | at Tampa |
| 2-3 | Tampa |

## PALM BEACH

**APRIL**

| | |
|---|---|
| 6-7 | at Jupiter |
| 8-9 | Jupiter |
| 10-11-12 | at Brevard |
| 13-14-15 | at Daytona |
| 17-18-19 | Brevard |
| 20-21-22 | at St. Lucie |
| 23-24-25 | Vero Beach |
| 26-27-28 | Daytona |
| 29-30 | at Vero Beach |

**MAY**

| | |
|---|---|
| 1 | at Vero Beach |
| 2-4-5 | St. Lucie |
| 6-7-8-9 | at Clearwater |
| 10-11-12-13 | at Dunedin |
| 15-16-17-18 | Fort Myers |
| 19-20-21-22 | Lakeland |
| 23-24-25-26 | at Sarasota |
| 27-28 | Jupiter |
| 30-31 | at Jupiter |

**JUNE**

| | |
|---|---|
| 1-2-3-4 | Dunedin |
| 5-6-7 | at St. Lucie |
| 8-9-10 | Vero Beach |
| 11-12-13 | St. Lucie |
| 14-15 | at Jupiter |
| 19-20-21 | Daytona |
| 22-23-24 | at Brevard |
| 25-26-27 | at Daytona |
| 28-29-30 | Brevard |

**JULY**

| | |
|---|---|
| 1 | Jupiter |
| 2-3 | at Jupiter |
| 4 | Jupiter |
| 5-6-7 | at Vero Beach |
| 8-9-10 | Brevard |
| 12-13-14 | at Vero Beach |
| 15-16-17 | at Daytona |
| 18-19-20-21 | Tampa |
| 22-23-24-25 | at Fort Myers |
| 26-27-28-29 | Sarasota |
| 31 | Vero Beach |

**AUGUST**

| | |
|---|---|
| 1-2 | Vero Beach |
| 3-4-5-6 | at Brevard |
| 7-8-9-10 | Clearwater |
| 11-12 | Jupiter |
| 14-15-16-17 | at Lakeland |
| 18-19-20 | Daytona |
| 21-22-23 | St. Lucie |
| 24-25-26 | at Brevard |
| 28-29-30 | at St. Lucie |
| 31 | Jupiter |

**SEPTEMBER**

| | |
|---|---|
| 1 | Jupiter |
| 2-3 | at Jupiter |

## ST. LUCIE

**APRIL**

| | |
|---|---|
| 6 | Vero Beach |
| 7 | at Vero Beach |
| 8 | Vero Beach |
| 9 | at Vero Beach |
| 10-11-12 | Daytona |
| 13-14-15 | at Jupiter |
| 17-18-19 | at Daytona |
| 20-21-22 | Palm Beach |
| 23-24-25 | at Brevard |
| 26-27-28 | Jupiter |
| 29-30 | Brevard |

**MAY**

| | |
|---|---|
| 1 | Brevard |
| 2-4-5 | at Palm Beach |
| 6-7-8-9 | Fort Myers |
| 10-11-12-13 | at Sarasota |
| 15-16-17-18 | Dunedin |
| 19-20-21-22 | at Fort Myers |
| 23-24-25-26 | Tampa |
| 27-28 | Vero Beach |
| 30-31 | at Vero Beach |

## (continued)

| JUNE | |
|---|---|
| 1-2-3-4 | at Tampa |
| 5-6-7 | **Palm Beach** |
| 8-9-10 | **Daytona** |
| 11-12-13 | at Palm Beach |
| 14-15 | at Vero Beach |
| 19-20 | **Brevard** |
| 21 | at Brevard |
| 22-23-24 | at Jupiter |
| 25-26-27 | at Brevard |
| 28-29-30 | **Jupiter** |

| JULY | |
|---|---|
| 1-2 | **Vero Beach** |
| 3 | at Vero Beach |
| 4 | **Vero Beach** |
| 5-6-7 | at Daytona |
| 8-9-10 | **Jupiter** |
| 12 | at Brevard |
| 13-14 | **Brevard** |
| 15-16-17 | at Jupiter |
| 18-19-20-21 | **Lakeland** |
| 22-23-24-25 | **Sarasota** |
| 26-27-28-29 | at Lakeland |
| 31 | **Daytona** |

| AUGUST | |
|---|---|
| 1-2 | **Daytona** |
| 3-4-5-6 | at Clearwater |
| 7-8-9-10 | at Dunedin |
| 11 | **Vero Beach** |
| 12 | at Vero Beach |
| 14-15-16-17 | **Clearwater** |
| 18 | at Brevard |
| 19-20 | **Brevard** |
| 21-22-23 | at Palm Beach |
| 24-25-26 | at Daytona |
| 28-29-30 | **Palm Beach** |
| 31 | at Vero Beach |

| SEPTEMBER | |
|---|---|
| 1-2 | **Vero Beach** |
| 3 | at Vero Beach |

## SARASOTA

| APRIL | |
|---|---|
| 6-7 | **Fort Myers** |
| 8-9 | at Fort Myers |
| 10-11-12 | **Clearwater** |
| 13-14 | **Lakeland** |
| 15 | at Lakeland |
| 17-18-19 | at Clearwater |
| 20-21-22 | at Dunedin |
| 23 | at Tampa |
| 24-25 | **Tampa** |
| 26 | **Lakeland** |
| 27-28 | at Lakeland |
| 29 | at Tampa |
| 30 | **Tampa** |

| MAY | |
|---|---|
| 1 | at Tampa |
| 3 | **Dunedin** |
| 4 | at Dunedin |
| 5 | **Dunedin** |

| 6-7-8-9 | at Jupiter |
|---|---|
| 10-11-12-13 | **St. Lucie** |
| 15-16-17-18 | at Daytona |
| 19-20-21-22 | at Brevard |
| 23-24-25-26 | **Palm Beach** |
| 27-28 | **Fort Myers** |
| 30-31 | at Fort Myers |

| JUNE | |
|---|---|
| 1-2-3-4 | **Jupiter** |
| 5 | **Dunedin** |
| 6-7 | at Dunedin |
| 8 | at Clearwater |
| 9-10 | **Clearwater** |
| 11-12-13 | at Tampa |
| 14-15 | **Fort Myers** |
| 19 | **Clearwater** |
| 20-21 | at Clearwater |
| 22-23-24 | **Tampa** |
| 25-26 | at Lakeland |
| 27 | **Lakeland** |
| 28-29-30 | **Dunedin** |

| JULY | |
|---|---|
| 1 | at Lakeland |
| 2-3 | **Lakeland** |
| 4 | at Dunedin |
| 5 | **Dunedin** |
| 6 | at Dunedin |
| 7 | **Fort Myers** |
| 8 | at Fort Myers |
| 9 | **Fort Myers** |
| 10 | at Fort Myers |
| 12-13 | **Dunedin** |
| 14 | at Dunedin |
| 15 | **Lakeland** |
| 16-17 | at Lakeland |
| 18-19-20-21 | **Vero Beach** |
| 22-23-24-25 | at St. Lucie |
| 26-27-28-29 | at P.B. |
| 31 | at Lakeland |

| AUGUST | |
|---|---|
| 1-2 | **Lakeland** |
| 3-4-5-6 | at Vero Beach |
| 7-8-9-10 | **Brevard** |
| 11-12 | at Fort Myers |
| 14-15-16-17 | **Daytona** |
| 18-19-20 | at Clearwater |
| 21-22-23 | **Tampa** |
| 24-25-26 | **Clearwater** |
| 28-29-30 | at Tampa |
| 31 | at Fort Myers |

| SEPTEMBER | |
|---|---|
| 1 | at Fort Myers |
| 2-3 | **Fort Myers** |

## TAMPA

| APRIL | |
|---|---|
| 6 | at Lakeland |
| 7 | **Lakeland** |
| 8 | at Lakeland |
| 9 | **Lakeland** |
| 10-11-12 | **Fort Myers** |

| 13-14-15 | at Dunedin |
|---|---|
| 17-18-19 | at Fort Myers |
| 20-21-22 | **Clearwater** |
| 23 | **Sarasota** |
| 24-25 | at Sarasota |
| 26-27-28 | **Dunedin** |
| 29 | **Sarasota** |
| 30 | at Sarasota |

| MAY | |
|---|---|
| 1 | **Sarasota** |
| 3-4-5 | at Clearwater |
| 6-7-8-9 | **Brevard** |
| 10-11-12-13 | at Jupiter |
| 15-16-17-18 | **Vero Beach** |
| 19-20-21-22 | at Daytona |
| 23-24-25-26 | at St. Lucie |
| 27 | **Lakeland** |
| 28-30-31 | at Lakeland |

| JUNE | |
|---|---|
| 1-2-3-4 | **St. Lucie** |
| 5-6-7 | at Fort Myers |
| 8-9 | **Dunedin** |
| 10 | at Dunedin |
| 11-12-13 | **Sarasota** |
| 14-15 | **Lakeland** |
| 19-20 | at Dunedin |
| 21 | **Dunedin** |
| 22-23-24 | at Sarasota |
| 25-26-27 | **Clearwater** |
| 28-29-30 | **Fort Myers** |

| JULY | |
|---|---|
| 1 | **Clearwater** |
| 2-3 | at Clearwater |
| 4-5-6 | **Fort Myers** |
| 7 | at Lakeland |
| 8 | **Lakeland** |
| 9 | at Lakeland |
| 10 | **Lakeland** |
| 12-13-14 | at Fort Myers |
| 15 | at Clearwater |
| 16-17 | **Clearwater** |
| 18-19-20-21 | at P.B. |
| 22-23-24-25 | at V.B. |
| 27-28-29-30 | **Jupiter** |
| 31 | at Clearwater |

| AUGUST | |
|---|---|
| 1-2 | at Clearwater |
| 3-4-5-6 | **Palm Beach** |
| 7-8-9-10 | **Daytona** |
| 11 | at Lakeland |
| 12 | **Lakeland** |
| 14-15-16-17 | at Brevard |
| 18-19-20 | **Dunedin** |
| 21-22-23 | at Sarasota |
| 24-25-26 | at Dunedin |
| 28-29-30 | **Sarasota** |
| 31 | **Lakeland** |

| SEPTEMBER | |
|---|---|
| 1 | **Lakeland** |
| 2-3 | at Lakeland |

## VERO BEACH

| APRIL | |
|---|---|
| 6 | at St. Lucie |
| 7 | **St. Lucie** |
| 8 | at St. Lucie |
| 9 | **St. Lucie** |
| 10-11-12 | at Jupiter |
| 13-14-15 | at Brevard |
| 17-18-19 | **Jupiter** |
| 20-21-22 | **Daytona** |
| 23-24-25 | at Palm Beach |
| 26-27-28 | **Brevard** |
| 29-30 | **Palm Beach** |

| MAY | |
|---|---|
| 1 | **Palm Beach** |
| 3-4-5 | at Daytona |
| 6-7-8-9 | **Dunedin** |
| 10-11-12-13 | **Lakeland** |
| 15-16-17-18 | at Tampa |
| 19-20-21-22 | **Clearwater** |
| 23-24-25-26 | at Lakeland |
| 27-28 | at St. Lucie |
| 30-31 | **St. Lucie** |

| JUNE | |
|---|---|
| 1-2-3-4 | at Clearwater |
| 5-6-7 | **Brevard** |
| 8-9-10 | at Palm Beach |
| 11-12-13 | at Brevard |
| 14-15 | **St. Lucie** |
| 19-20-21 | **Jupiter** |
| 22-23-24 | at Daytona |
| 25-26-27 | at Jupiter |
| 28-29-30 | **Daytona** |

| JULY | |
|---|---|
| 1-2 | at St. Lucie |
| 3 | **St. Lucie** |
| 4 | at St. Lucie |
| 5-6-7 | **Palm Beach** |
| 8-9-10 | at Daytona |
| 12-13-14 | **Palm Beach** |
| 15-16-17 | **Brevard** |
| 18-19-20-21 | at Sarasota |
| 22-23-24-25 | **Tampa** |
| 26-27-28-29 | **Fort Myers** |
| 31 | at Palm Beach |

| AUGUST | |
|---|---|
| 1-2 | at Palm Beach |
| 3-4-5-6 | **Sarasota** |
| 7-8-9-10 | at Fort Myers |
| 11 | at St. Lucie |
| 12 | **St. Lucie** |
| 14-15-16-17 | at Dunedin |
| 18-19-20 | **Jupiter** |
| 21-22-23 | at Brevard |
| 24-25-26 | at Jupiter |
| 28-29-30 | **Daytona** |
| 31 | **St. Lucie** |

| SEPTEMBER | |
|---|---|
| 1-2 | at St. Lucie |
| 3 | **St. Lucie** |

# LOW CLASS A
## MIDWEST LEAGUE

### BELOIT

**APRIL**
6-7-8-9    Cedar Rapids
10-11-12    Wisconsin
13-14-15    at Burlington
17-18-19-20    Peoria
21-22-23-24    at Lansing
25-26-27-28    at Q.C.
29-30    Fort Worth
**MAY**
1-2    Fort Worth
4-5-6-7    SW Michigan
8-9-10-11    at W. Michigan
12-13-14-15    Kane County
16-17-18-19    at Clinton
20-21-22-23    at Peoria
25-26-27-28    Burlington
29-30-31    Quad Cities
**JUNE**
1    Quad Cities
2-3-4-5    at Dayton
6-7-8-9    at Clinton
10-11-12-13    South Bend
15-16-17-18    at C.R.
22-23-24-25    Lansing
26-27-28    Kane County
29-30    at Kane County
**JULY**
1-2    Kane County
3-4-5-6    at South Bend
7-8    Peoria
9-10    at Peoria
12-13-14    at Quad Cities
15-16-17-18    W. Michigan
20-21-22-23    at Clinton
24-25-26-27    at Burlington
28-29-30-31    Wisconsin
**AUGUST**
1-2-3-4    Dayton
5-6-7-8    at Wisconsin
10-11-12-13    at Fort Worth
14-15-16-17    Quad Cities
18-19-20-21    Clinton
24-25-26-27    at C.R.
28-29-30-31    at SW Mich.
**SEPTEMBER**
1-2-3-4    Peoria

### BURLINGTON

**APRIL**
6-7-8-9    Clinton
10-11-12    at Kane County
13-14-15    Beloit
17-18-19-20    Fort Worth
21-22-23-24    at Peoria
25-26-27-28    at SW Mich.
29-30    Dayton
**MAY**
1-2    Dayton
4-5-6-7    at W. Michigan
8-9-10-11    at South Bend

### CEDAR RAPIDS

**APRIL**
6-7-8-9    at Beloit
10-11-12    Peoria
13-14-15    at Wisconsin
17-18-19-20    W. Michigan
21-22-23-24    at SW Mich.
25-26-27-28    at Lansing
29-30    South Bend
**MAY**
1-2    South Bend
4-5-6-7    Wisconsin
8-9-10-11    at Dayton
12-13-14-15    at Clinton
16-17-18-19    Quad Cities
20-21-22-23    Kane County
25-26-27-28    at Q.C.
29-30-31    at Clinton
**JUNE**
1    at Clinton
2-3-4-5    Burlington
6-7-8-9    at Quad Cities
10-11-12-13    Fort Worth
15-16-17-18    Beloit
22-23-24-25    at Fort Worth

12-13-14-15    Quad Cities
16-17-18-19    Lansing
20-21-22-23    at Wisconsin
25-26-27-28    at Beloit
29-30-31    Wisconsin
**JUNE**
1    Wisconsin
2-3-4    at Cedar Rapids
6-7-8-9    Peoria
10-11-12-13    Kane County
15-16-17-18    at Clinton
22-23-24-25    W. Michigan
26-27-28    Cedar Rapids
29-30    at Peoria
**JULY**
1-2    Peoria
3-4-5-6    at Cedar Rapids
7-8-9-10    SW Michigan
12-13-14    at Kane County
15-16-17-18    at Fort Worth
20-21-22-23    Wisconsin
24-25-26-27    Beloit
28-29-30-31    at Lansing
**AUGUST**
1-2-3-4    Clinton
5-6-7-8    at Dayton
10-11-12-13    at Peoria
14-15-16-17    South Bend
18-19    at Quad Cities
20-21    Quad Cities
24-25    at Kane County
26-27    Kane County
28-29-30-31    at C.R.
**SEPTEMBER**
1-2    Quad Cities
3-4    at Quad Cities

26-27-28    at Burlington
29-30    Dayton
**JULY**
1-2    Dayton
3-4-5-6    Burlington
7-8-9-10    at W. Michigan
12-13-14    Clinton
15-16-17-18    SW Mich.
20-21-22-23    at Q.C.
24-25-26-27    Kane County
28-29-30-31    at S.B.
**AUGUST**
1-2-3-4    at Peoria
5-6-7-8    Lansing
10-11-12-13    Wisconsin
14-15-16-17    at Clinton
18-19-20-21    at Kane Co.
24-25-26-27    Beloit
28-29-30-31    Burlington
**SEPTEMBER**
1-2-3-4    at Kane County

### CLINTON

**APRIL**
6-7-8-9    at Burlington
10-11-12    at Quad Cities
13-14-15    Kane County
17-18-19-20    Lansing
21-22-23-24    at W. Mich.
25-26-27-28    at S.B.
29-30    at Kane County
**MAY**
1-2    at Kane County
4-5-6-7    Dayton
8-9-10-11    at SW Michigan
12-13-14-15    C.R.
16-17-18-19    Beloit
20-21-22-23    at Q.C.
25-26-27-28    Peoria
29-30-31    Cedar Rapids
**JUNE**
1    Cedar Rapids
2-3-4-5    at Wisconsin
6-7-8-9    Beloit
10-11-12-13    at Peoria
15-16-17-18    Burlington
22-23-24-25    SW Mich.
26-27-28    Quad Cities
29-30    at Lansing
**JULY**
1-2    at Lansing
3-4-5-6    at Peoria
7-8-9-10    South Bend
12-13-14    at Cedar Rapids
15-16-17-18    at Dayton
20-21-22-23    Beloit
24-25-26-27    at F.W.
28-29-30-31    W. Michigan
**AUGUST**
1-2-3-4    at Burlington
5-6-7-8    at Quad Cities
10-11-12-13    Kane County

14-15-16-17    C.R.
18-19-20-21    at Beloit
24-25-26-27    at Wisconsin
28-29-30-31    Fort Wayne
**SEPTEMBER**
1-2-3-4    Wisconsin

### DAYTON

**APRIL**
6-7-8-9    South Bend
10-11-12    Lansing
13-14-15    at Fort Wayne
17-18-19-20    at Q.C.
21-22-23-24    Kane County
25-26-27-28    Peoria
29-30    at Burlington
**MAY**
1-2    at Burlington
4-5-6-7    at Clinton
8-9-10-11    Cedar Rapids
12-13-14-15    at Wisconsin
16-17-18-19    Fort Wayne
20-21-22-23    at SW Mich.
25-26-27-28    at S.B.
29-30-31    at W. Michigan
**JUNE**
1    at W. Michigan
2-3-4-5    Beloit
6-7-8-9    at Lansing
10-11-12-13    W. Michigan
15-16-17-18    SW Mich.
22-23-24-25    at S.B.
26-27-28    SW Michigan
29-30    at Cedar Rapids
**JULY**
1-2    at Cedar Rapids
3-4-5-6    at Kane County
7-8-9-10    Quad Cities
12-13-14    at South Bend
15-16-17-18    Clinton
20-21-22-23    at W. Mich.
24-25-26-27    Lansing
28-29-30-31    at Peoria
**AUGUST**
1-2-3-4    at Beloit
5-6-7-8    Burlington
10-11-12-13    SW Mich.
14-15-16-17    at F.W.
18-19-20-21    Wisconsin
24-25-26-27    at SW Mich.
28-29-30-31    at S.B.
**SEPTEMBER**
1-2-3-4    W. Michigan

### FORT WAYNE

**APRIL**
6-7    at W. Michigan
8-9    W. Michigan
10-11-12    at SW Michigan
13-14-15    Dayton
17-18-19-20    at Burlington
21-22-23-24    Quad Cities

**25-26-27-28** Wisconsin
29-30 at Beloit

**MAY**
1-2 at Beloit
4-5-6-7 at Kane County
**8-9-10-11** Peoria
**12-13-14-15** SW Mich.
16-17-18-19 at Dayton
20-21-22-23 at Lansing
**25-26-27-28** Lansing
**29-30-31** South Bend

**JUNE**
**1** South Bend
2-3-4-5 at Peoria
**6-7-8-9** W. Michigan
10-11-12-13 at C.R.
**15-16-17-18** W. Michigan
**22-23-24-25** C.R.
**26-27-28** Lansing
29-30 at SW Michigan

**JULY**
1-2 at SW Michigan
3-4-5-6 at Quad Cities
**7-8-9-10** Kane County
12-13-14 at Lansing
**15-16-17-18** Burlington
20-21-22-23 at SW Mich.
**24-25-26-27** Clinton
**28-29-30-31** SW Mich.

**AUGUST**
1-2-3-4 at Wisconsin
5-6-7-8 at W. Michigan
**10-11-12-13** Burlington
**14-15-16-17** Dayton
**18-19** South Bend
20-21 at South Bend
24-25-26-27 at W. Mich.
28-29-30-31 at Clinton

**SEPTEMBER**
**1-2** South Bend
3-4 at South Bend

## KANE COUNTY

**APRIL**
**6-7-8-9** Quad Cities
**10-11-12** Burlington
13-14-15 at Clinton
**17-18-19-20** South Bend
21-22-23-24 at Dayton
25-26-27-28 at W. Mich.
**29-30** Clinton

**MAY**
**1-2** Clinton
**4-5-6-7** Fort Wayne
8-9-10-11 at Lansing
12-13-14-15 at Peoria
**16-17-18-19** Wisconsin
20-21-22-23 at C.R.
**25-26-27-28** Wisconsin
29-30-31 at Peoria

**JUNE**
1 at Peoria
**2-3-4-5** SW Michigan
6-7-8-9 at Wisconsin
10-11-12-13 at Burlington
**15-16-17-18** Peoria
22-23-24-25 at Wisconsin
26-27-28 at Beloit

---

29-30 **Beloit**

**JULY**
1-2 at Beloit
**3-4-5-6** Dayton
7-8-9-10 at Fort Wayne
**12-13-14** Burlington
**15-16-17-18** Lansing
20-21-22-23 at S.B.
24-25-26-27 at C.R.
**28-29-30-31** Quad Cities

**AUGUST**
1-2-3-4 at SW Michigan
**5-6-7-8** Peoria
10-11-12-13 at Clinton
**14-15-16-17** W. Michigan
**18-19-20-21** C.R.
**24-25** Burlington
26-27 at Burlington
28-29-30-31 at Q.C.

**SEPTEMBER**
**1-2-3-4** Cedar Rapids

## LANSING

**APRIL**
**6-7** SW Michigan
8-9 at SW Michigan
10-11-12 at Beloit
**13-14-15** South Bend
17-18-19-20 at Clinton
**21-22-23-24** Beloit
**25-26-27-28** C.R.
29-30 at Quad Cities

**MAY**
1-2 at Quad Cities
4-5-6-7 at Peoria
**8-9-10-11** Kane County
**12-13-14-15** W. Michigan
16-17-18-19 at Burlington
**20-21-22-23** Fort Wayne
25-26-27-28 at F.W.
29-30 at SW Michigan
**31** SW Michigan

**JUNE**
**1** SW Michigan
2-3-4-5 at South Bend
**6-7-8-9** Dayton
**10-11-12-13** Wisconsin
15-16-17 at S.B.
22-23-24-25 at Beloit
**26-27-28** Fort Wayne
**29-30** Clinton

**JULY**
**1-2** Clinton
**3-4-5-6** W. Michigan
7-8-9-10 at Wisconsin
**12-13-14** Fort Wayne
15-16-17-18 at Kane Co.
**20-21-22-23** Peoria
24-25-26-27 at Dayton
**28-29-30-31** Burlington

**AUGUST**
**1-2-3-4** Quad Cities
5-6-7-8 at Cedar Rapids
10-11-12-13 at S.B.
**14-15-16-17** SW Mich.
18-19-20-21 at W. Mich.
**24-25-26-27** South Bend
28-29-30-31 at W. Mich.

---

**SEPTEMBER**
**1-2-3-4** SW Michigan

## PEORIA

**APRIL**
6-7-8-9 at Wisconsin
10-11-12 at Cedar Rapids
**13-14-15** Quad Cities
17-18-19-20 at Beloit
**21-22-23-24** Burlington
25-26-27-28 at Dayton
**29-30** SW Michigan

**MAY**
**1-2** SW Michigan
**4-5-6-7** Lansing
8-9-10-11 at Fort Worth
12-13-14-15 at S.B.
**16-17-18-19** W. Michigan
**20-21-22-23** at Clinton
25-26-27-28 at Clinton
**29-30-31** Kane County

**JUNE**
**1** Kane County
**2-3-4-5** Fort Wayne
6-7-8-9 at Burlington
**10-11-12-13** Clinton
15-16-17-18 at Kane Co.
**22-23** Quad Cities
24-25 at Quad Cities
26-27-28 at Wisconsin
**29-30** Burlington

**JULY**
1-2 at Burlington
**3-4-5-6** Clinton
7-8 at Beloit
**9-10** Beloit
**12-13-14** Wisconsin
**15-16-17-18** South Bend
20-21-22-23 at Lansing
24-25-26-27 at W. Mich.
**28-29-30-31** Dayton

**AUGUST**
**1-2-3-4** Cedar Rapids
5-6-7-8 at Kane County
**10-11-12-13** Clinton
14-15-16-17 at Wisconsin
18-19-20-21 at SW Mich.
**24-25** Quad Cities
26-27 at Quad Cities
**28-29-30-31** Wisconsin

**SEPTEMBER**
1-2-3-4 at Beloit

## QUAD CITIES

**APRIL**
6-7-8-9 at Kane County
**10-11-12** Clinton
13-14-15 at Peoria
**17-18-19-20** Dayton
21-22-23-24 at F.W.
**25-26-27-28** Beloit
29-30 **Lansing**

**MAY**
**1-2** Lansing
**4-5-6-7** South Bend
8-9-10-11 at Wisconsin
12-13-14-15 at Burlington
16-17-18-19 at C.R.

---

**20-21-22-23** Clinton
**25-26-27-28** C.R.
29-30-31 at Beloit

**JUNE**
1 at Beloit
2-3-4-5 at W. Michigan
**6-7-8-9** Cedar Rapids
10-11-12-13 at SW Mich.
**15-16-17-18** Wisconsin
22-23 at Peoria
**24-25** Peoria
26-27-28 at Clinton
29-30 at South Bend

**JULY**
1-2 at South Bend
**3-4-5-6** Fort Wayne
7-8-9-10 at Dayton
**12-13-14** Beloit
15-16-17-18 at Wisconsin
**20-21-22-23** C.R.
**24-25-26-27** SW Mich.
28-29-30-31 at Kane Co.

**AUGUST**
1-2-3-4 at Lansing
**5-6-7-8** Clinton
**10-11-12-13** W. Michigan
14-15-16-17 at Beloit
**18-19-20-21** Burlington
24-25 at Peoria
**26-27** Peoria
**28-29-30-31** Kane County

**SEPTEMBER**
1-2 at Burlington
**3-4** Burlington

## SOUTH BEND

**APRIL**
6-7-8-9 at Dayton
**10-11-12** W. Michigan
13-14-15 at Lansing
17-18-19-20 at Kane Co.
**21-22-23-24** Wisconsin
**25-26-27-28** Clinton
29-30 at Cedar Rapids

**MAY**
1-2 at Cedar Rapids
4-5-6-7 at Quad Cities
**8-9-10-11** Burlington
**12-13-14-15** Peoria
16-17-18-19 at SW Mich.
20-21-22-23 at W. Mich.
**25-26-27-28** Dayton
29-30-31 at Fort Wayne

**JUNE**
1 at Fort Wayne
**2-3-4-5** Lansing
**6-7-8-9** SW Michigan
10-11-12-13 at Beloit
**15-16-17-18** Lansing
22-23-24-25 at Dayton
26-27-28 at W. Michigan
**29-30** Quad Cities

**JULY**
**1-2** Quad Cities
**3-4-5-6** Beloit
7-8-9-10 at Clinton
**12-13-14** Dayton
15-16-17-18 at Peoria

20-21-22-23 **Kane County**
24-25-26-27 at Wisconsin
28-29-30-31 **C.R.**
## AUGUST
1-2-3-4 **W. Michigan**
5-6-7-8 at SW Michigan
10-11-12-13 **Lansing**
14-15-16-17 at Burlington
18-19 at Fort Wayne
20-21 **Fort Wayne**
24-25-26-27 at Lansing
28-29-30-31 **Dayton**
## SEPTEMBER
1-2 at Fort Wayne
3-4 **Fort Wayne**

### SW MICHIGAN
## APRIL
6-7 at Lansing
8-9 **Lansing**
10-11-12 **Fort Wayne**
13-14-15 at W. Michigan
17-18-19-20 at Wisconsin
21-22-23-24 **C.R.**
25-26-27-28 **Burlington**
29-30 at Peoria
## MAY
1-2 at Peoria
4-5-6-7 at Beloit
8-9-10-11 **Clinton**
12-13-14-15 at F.W.
16-17-18-19 **South Bend**
20-21-22-23 **Dayton**
25-26-27-28 **W. Michigan**
29-30 **Lansing**
31 at Lansing
## JUNE
1 at Lansing
2-3-4-5 at Kane County
6-7-8-9 at South Bend

10-11-12-13 **Quad Cities**
15-16-17-18 at Dayton
22-23-24-25 at Clinton
26-27-28 at Dayton
29-30 **Fort Wayne**
## JULY
1-2 **Fort Wayne**
3-4-5-6 **Wisconsin**
7-8-9-10 at Burlington
12-13-14 **W. Michigan**
15-16-17-18 at C.R.
20-21-22-23 **Fort Wayne**
24-25-26-27 at Q.C.
28-29-30-31 at F.W.
## AUGUST
1-2-3-4 **Kane County**
5-6-7-8 **South Bend**
10-11-12-13 at Dayton
14-15-16-17 at Lansing
18-19-20-21 **Peoria**
24-25-26-27 **Dayton**
28-29-30-31 **Beloit**
## SEPTEMBER
1-2-3-4 at Lansing

### WEST MICHIGAN
## APRIL
6-7 **Fort Wayne**
8-9 at Fort Wayne
10-11-12 at South Bend
13-14-15 **SW Michigan**
17-18-19-20 at C.R.
21-22-23-24 **Clinton**
25-26-27-28 **Kane County**
29-30 at Wisconsin
## MAY
1-2 at Wisconsin
4-5-6-7 **Burlington**
8-9-10-11 **Beloit**
12-13-14-15 at Lansing

16-17-18-19 at Peoria
20-21-22-23 **South Bend**
25-26-27-28 at SW Mich.
29-30-31 **Dayton**
## JUNE
1 **Dayton**
2-3-4-5 **Quad Cities**
6-7-8-9 at Fort Wayne
10-11-12-13 at Dayton
15-16 **Fort Wayne**
17-18 at Fort Wayne
22-23-24-25 at Burlington
26-27-28 **South Bend**
29-30 **Wisconsin**
## JULY
1-2 **Wisconsin**
3-4-5-6 at Lansing
7-8-9-10 **Cedar Rapids**
12-13-14 at SW Michigan
15-16-17-18 at Beloit
20-21-22-23 **Dayton**
24-25-26-27 **Peoria**
28-29-30-31 at Clinton
## AUGUST
1-2-3-4 at South Bend
5-6-7-8 **Fort Wayne**
10-11-12-13 at Q.C.
14-15-16-17 at Kane Co.
18-19-20-21 **Lansing**
24-25-26-27 **Fort Wayne**
28-29-30-31 **Lansing**
## SEPTEMBER
1-2-3-4 at Dayton

### WISCONSIN
## APRIL
6-7-8-9 **Peoria**
10-11-12 at Beloit
13-14-15 **Cedar Rapids**
17-18-19-20 **SW Mich.**

21-22-23-24 at S.B.
25-26-27-28 at F.W.
29-30 **W. Michigan**
## MAY
1-2 **W. Michigan**
4-5-6-7 at Cedar Rapids
8-9-10-11 **Quad Cities**
12-13-14-15 **Dayton**
16-17-18-19 at Kane Co.
20-21-22-23 **Burlington**
25-26-27-28 at Kane Co.
29-30-31 **Burlington**
## JUNE
1 **Burlington**
2-3-4-5 **Clinton**
6-7-8-9 **Kane County**
10-11-12-13 at Kane Co.
15-16-17-18 at Q.C.
22-23-24-25 **Kane County**
26-27-28 **Peoria**
29-30 at W. Michigan
## JULY
1-2 at W. Michigan
3-4-5-6 at SW Michigan
7-8-9-10 **Kane County**
12-13-14 at Peoria
15-16-17-18 **Quad Cities**
20-21-22-23 at Burlington
24-25-26-27 **South Bend**
28-29-30-31 at Beloit
## AUGUST
1-2-3-4 **Fort Wayne**
5-6-7-8 **Beloit**
10-11-12-13 at C.R.
14-15-16-17 **Peoria**
18-19-20-21 at Dayton
24-25-26-27 **Clinton**
28-29-30-31 at Peoria
## SEPTEMBER
1-2-3-4 at Clinton

# SOUTH ATLANTIC LEAGUE
*at Citizens Bank Park, Philadelphia

### ASHEVILLE
## APRIL
6-7-8-9 **Savannah**
11-12-13-14 at Kan.
15-16-17-18 at Savannah
20-21-22-23 **Columbus**
24-25-26-27 **Augusta**
28-29-30 at Columbus
## MAY
1 at Columbus
2-3-4-5 at Rome
6-7-8-9 **Charleston**
10-11-12-13 **West Va.**
15-16-17-18 at G'boro
19-20-21-22 at Hickory
23-24-25-26 **Lexington**
27-28-29-30 **Kannapolis**
## JUNE
1-2-3-4 at Augusta
5-6-7-8 at Kannapolis
9-10-11 **Greenville**
12-13-14-15 **Greensboro**

16-17-18 at Greenville
22-23-24-25 at Lexington
26-27-28-29 at G'boro
29 **Hickory**
## JULY
1-2-3 **Hickory**
4-5-6-7 at West Virginia
8-9-10 **Augusta**
12-13-14 at Greenville
15-16-17-18 at Charleston
19-20-21-22 **Columbus**
24-25-26-27 at Lake Co.
28-29-30-31 at Hag.
## AUGUST
2-3-4-5 **Delmarva**
6-7-8-9 **Lakewood**
10-11-12-13 at Savannah
15-16-17-18 **Rome**
18-19-20 **Kannapolis**
21-22 at Kannapolis
24-25-26-27 **Greenville**
28-29 at Kannapolis
30-31 **Kannapolis**

## SEPTEMBER
1-2-3-4 at Augusta

### AUGUSTA
## APRIL
6-7-8-9 at Charleston
11-12-13-14 **Greenville**
15-16-17-18 **Charleston**
20-21-22-23 at Rome
24-25-26-27 at Asheville
28-29-30 **Rome**
## MAY
1 **Rome**
2-3-4-5 **Columbus**
6-7-8-9 at Savannah
11-12-13-14 **Greensboro**
15-16-17-18 at West Va.
19-20-21-22 at Lexington
23-24-25-26 **Hickory**
27-28-29-30 at Greenville
## JUNE
1-2-3-4 **Asheville**
5-6-7-8 at Rome

9-10-11 **Kannapolis**
12-13-14-15 **Rome**
16-17-18 at Kannapolis
22-23-24-25 at G'boro
26-27-28-29 **West Va.**
30 **Lexington**
## JULY
1-2-3 **Lexington**
4-5-6-7 at Hickory
8-9-10 at Asheville
12-13-14 **Kannapolis**
15-16-17-18 at Columbus
19-20-21-22 **Charleston**
24-25-26-27 at Lakewood
28-29-30-31 at Delmarva
## AUGUST
2-3-4-5 **Hagerstown**
6-7-8-9 **Lake County**
10-11-12-13 at Rome
15-16-17-18 **Savannah**
19-20-21-22 at Greenville
23-24-25-26 at Kan.
28-29-30-31 **Greenville**

1-2-3-4   Asheville

## CHARLESTON
### APRIL
| | |
|---|---|
| 6-7-8-9 | Augusta |
| 11-12-13-14 | at Columbus |
| 15-16-17-18 | at Augusta |
| 20-21-22-23 | Kannapolis |
| 24-25-26-27 | Savannah |
| 28-29-30 | at Kannapolis |

### MAY
| | |
|---|---|
| 1 | at Kannapolis |
| 2-3-4-5 | Greenville |
| 6-7-8-9 | at Asheville |
| 10-11-12-13 | at Rome |
| 15-16-17-18 | Savannah |
| 19-20-21-22 | Rome |
| 23-24-25-26 | at Columbus |
| 27-28-29-30 | at Savannah |
| 31 | Columbus |

### JUNE
| | |
|---|---|
| 1-2-3 | Columbus |
| 5-6-7-8 | at Greenville |
| 9-10-11 | Savannah |
| 12-13-14-15 | Greenville |
| 16-17-18 | at Savannah |
| 22-23-24-25 | at Rome |
| 26-27-28-29 | Columbus |
| 30 | Rome |

### JULY
| | |
|---|---|
| 1-2-3 | Rome |
| 4-5-6-7 | at Columbus |
| 8-9-10 | Savannah |
| 12-13-14 | at Rome |
| 15-16-17-18 | Asheville |
| 19-20-21-22 | at Augusta |
| 24-25-26-27 | West Va. |
| 28-29-30-31 | Lexington |

### AUGUST
| | |
|---|---|
| 2-3-4-5 | at Hickory |
| 6-7-8-9 | at Greensboro |
| 10-11-12-13 | Kannapolis |
| 15-16-17-18 | at Greenville |
| 19-20-21-22 | Savannah |
| 24-25-26-27 | at Columbus |
| 28-29-30-31 | at Savannah |

### SEPTEMBER
| | |
|---|---|
| 1-2-3-4 | Columbus |

## COLUMBUS
### APRIL
| | |
|---|---|
| 6-7-8-9 | at Greenville |
| 11-12-13-14 | Charleston |
| 15-16-17-18 | Greenville |
| 20-21-22-23 | at Asheville |
| 24-25-26-27 | at Rome |
| 28-29-30 | Asheville |

### MAY
| | |
|---|---|
| 1 | Asheville |
| 2-3-4-5 | at Augusta |
| 6-7-8-9 | at Kannapolis |
| 11-12-13-14 | Savannah |
| 15-16-17-18 | Rome |
| 19-20-21-22 | at Savannah |
| 23-24-25-26 | Charleston |
| 27-28-29-30 | at Rome |
| 31 | at Charleston |

### JUNE
| | |
|---|---|
| 1-2-3 | at Charleston |
| 5-6-7-8 | Savannah |
| 9-10-11 | Rome |
| 12-13-14-15 | at Savannah |
| 16-17-18 | at Rome |
| 22-23-24-25 | Savannah |
| 26-27-28-29 | at Charleston |
| 30 | at Savannah |

### JULY
| | |
|---|---|
| 1-2-3 | at Savannah |
| 4-5-6-7 | Charleston |
| 8-9-10 | Rome |
| 12-13-14 | at Savannah |
| 15-16-17-18 | Augusta |
| 19-20-21-22 | at Asheville |
| 24-25-26-27 | Hickory |
| 28-29-30-31 | Greensboro |

### AUGUST
| | |
|---|---|
| 2-3-4-5 | at West Virginia |
| 6-7-8-9 | at Lexington |
| 10-11-12-13 | Greenville |
| 15-16-17-18 | Kannapolis |
| 19-20-21-22 | at Rome |
| 24-25-26-27 | Charleston |
| 28-29-30-31 | Rome |

### SEPTEMBER
| | |
|---|---|
| 1-2-3-4 | at Charleston |

## DELMARVA
### APRIL
| | |
|---|---|
| 6-7-8-9 | at West Virginia |
| 10-11-12 | Lake County |
| 13-14-15-16 | at Lakewood |
| 18-19-20-21 | Hickory |
| 22-23-24-25 | Lakewood |
| 26-27-28 | at Lake County |
| 29-30 | at Hagerstown |

### MAY
| | |
|---|---|
| 1 | at Hagerstown |
| 3-4-5 | Lakewood |
| 6-7-8 | at Lake County |
| 9-10-11 | Lakewood |
| 12-13-14 | Lake County |
| 16-17-18 | at Lakewood |
| 19-20-21-22 | Lake County |
| 23-24 | Hagerstown |
| 25-26 | at Hagerstown |
| 27-28-29-30 | at Lexington |

### JUNE
| | |
|---|---|
| 1-2-3-4 | Greensboro |
| 5-6-7-8 | at Lakewood |
| 9-10-11 | Hagerstown |
| 12-13-14-15 | Lakewood |
| 16-17-18 | at Hagerstown |
| 22-23-24-25 | at Lake Co. |
| 26-27 | Hagerstown |
| 28-29 | at Hagerstown |
| 30 | Lake County |

### JULY
| | |
|---|---|
| 1-2 | Lake County |
| 3-4-5 | at Lakewood |
| 6-7-8-9 | Lake County |
| 11-12-13-14 | Lexington |
| 15-16-17-18 | at Hickory |
| 19-20-21-22 | at G'boro |
| 24-25-26-27 | Greenville |
| 28-29-30-31 | Augusta |

## AUGUST
| | |
|---|---|
| 2-3-4-5 | at Asheville |
| 6-7-8-9 | at Kannapolis |
| 10-11-12-13 | West Va. |
| 15-16-17-18 | at Lake Co. |
| 19-20-21-22 | at Lakewood |
| 24-25-26-27 | Lakewood |
| 28-29-30-31 | Lakewood |

### SEPTEMBER
| | |
|---|---|
| 1-2-3-4 | at Hagerstown |

## GREENSBORO
### APRIL
| | |
|---|---|
| 6-7-8-9 | Hagerstown |
| 10-11-12-13 | West Va. |
| 14-15-16 | at Hickory |
| 18-19-20-21 | at Lakewood |
| 22-23-24 | Hickory |
| 25-26-27 | at West Virginia |
| 28-29-30 | West Virginia |

### MAY
| | |
|---|---|
| 2 | at Hickory |
| 3-4 | Hickory |
| 5 | at Hickory |
| 6-7 | Hickory |
| 8-9 | at Lexington |
| 11-12-13-14 | at Augusta |
| 15-16-17-18 | Asheville |
| 19-20-21-22 | Kannapolis |
| 23-24-25-26 | at Greenville |
| 27-28-29-30 | Lake County |

### JUNE
| | |
|---|---|
| 1-2-3-4 | at Delmarva |
| 5 | Hickory |
| 6-7 | at Hickory |
| 8 | Hickory |
| 9-10-11 | at Lexington |
| 12-13-14-15 | at Asheville |
| 16-17-18 | Lexington |
| 22-23-24-25 | Augusta |
| 26-27-28-29 | at Delmarva |
| 30 | at Kannapolis |

### JULY
| | |
|---|---|
| 1-2-3 | at Kannapolis |
| 4-5-6-7 | Greenville |
| 8-9 | Hickory |
| 11-12-13-14 | at Lake Co. |
| 15-16-17-18 | Lakewood |
| 19-20-21-22 | Delmarva |
| 24-25-26-27 | at Rome |
| 28-29-30-31 | at Columbus |

### AUGUST
| | |
|---|---|
| 2-3-4-5 | Savannah |
| 6-7-8-9 | Charleston |
| 10-11-12-13 | at Hag. |
| 15-16-17-18 | Lexington |
| 19-20-21-22 | at Hickory |
| 23-24-25 | West Virgina |
| 26-27 | Hickory |
| 28-29-30-31 | at West Va. |

### SEPTEMBER
| | |
|---|---|
| 1-2-3-4 | at Lexington |

## GREENVILLE
### APRIL
| | |
|---|---|
| 6-7-8-9 | Columbus |
| 11-12-13-14 | at Augusta |
| 15-16-17-18 | at Columbus |

### (continued)
| | |
|---|---|
| 20-21-22-23 | Savannah |
| 24-25-26-27 | Kannapolis |
| 28-29-30 | at Savannah |

### MAY
| | |
|---|---|
| 1 | at Savannah |
| 2-3-4-5 | at Charleston |
| 6-7-8-9 | Rome |
| 11-12-13-14 | Hickory |
| 15-16-17-18 | at Lexington |
| 19-20-21-22 | at West Va. |
| 23-24-25-26 | Greensboro |
| 27-28-29-30 | Augusta |

### JUNE
| | |
|---|---|
| 1-2-3-4 | at Kannapolis |
| 5-6-7-8 | Charleston |
| 9-10-11 | at Asheville |
| 12-13-14-15 | at Charleston |
| 16-17-18 | Asheville |
| 22-23-24-25 | at Hickory |
| 26-27-28-29 | Lexington |
| 30 | West Virginia |

### JULY
| | |
|---|---|
| 1-2-3 | West Virginia |
| 4-5-6-7 | at Greensboro |
| 8-9-10 | at Kannapolis |
| 11-12-13 | Asheville |
| 15-16-17-18 | at Rome |
| 19-20-21-22 | Savannah |
| 24-25-26-27 | at Delmarva |
| 28-29-30-31 | at Lakewood |

### AUGUST
| | |
|---|---|
| 2-3-4-5 | Lake County |
| 6-7-8-9 | Hagerstown |
| 10-11-12-13 | at Columbus |
| 15-16-17-18 | Charleston |
| 19-20-21-22 | Augusta |
| 24-25-26-27 | at Asheville |
| 28-29-30-31 | at Augusta |

### SEPTEMBER
| | |
|---|---|
| 1-2-3-4 | Kannapolis |

## HAGERSTOWN
### APRIL
| | |
|---|---|
| 6-7-8-9 | at Greensboro |
| 10-11-12 | Lakewood |
| 13-14-15-16 | at Lake Co. |
| 18-19-20-21 | West Va. |
| 22-23-24-25 | Lake County |
| 26-27-28 | at Lakewood |
| 29-30 | Delmarva |

### MAY
| | |
|---|---|
| 1 | Delmarva |
| 3-4-5 | at Lake County |
| 6-7-8 | at Lakewood |
| 9-10-11 | Lake County |
| 12-13-14 | Lakewood |
| 16-17-18 | at Lake County |
| 19-20-21-22 | at Delmarva |
| 23-24-25-26 | at Delmarva |
| 27-28-29-30 | at Hickory |

### JUNE
| | |
|---|---|
| 1-2-3-4 | Lexington |
| 5-6 | at West Virginia |
| 7-8 | West Virginia |
| 9-10-11 | at Delmarva |
| 12-13 | at West Virginia |
| 14-15 | West Virginia |
| 16-17-18 | Delmarva |

| | |
|---|---|
| 22-23-24-25 | Lakewood |
| 26-27 | at Delmarva |
| 28-29 | Delmarva |
| 30 | Lakewood |

**JULY**

| | |
|---|---|
| 1-2 | Lakewood |
| 3-4-5 | at Lake County |
| 6-7-8-9 | Lakewood |
| 11-12-13-14 | Hickory |
| 15-16-17-18 | at Lake Co. |
| 19-20-21-22 | at Lexington |
| 24-25-26-27 | Kannapolis |
| 28-29-30-31 | Asheville |

**AUGUST**

| | |
|---|---|
| 2-3-4-5 | at Augusta |
| 6-7-8-9 | at Greenville |
| 10-11-12-13 | Greensboro |
| 15-16-17-18 | at Lakewood |
| 19-20-21-22 | at West Va. |
| 24-25-26-27 | at Delmarva |
| 28-29-30-31 | Lake County |

**SEPTEMBER**

| | |
|---|---|
| 1-2-3-4 | Delmarva |

## HICKORY

**APRIL**

| | |
|---|---|
| 6-7-8-9 | Lake County |
| 10-11-12-13 | at Lexington |
| 14-15-16 | Greensboro |
| 18-19-20-21 | at Delmarva |
| 22-23-24 | at Greensboro |
| 25-26-27 | Lexington |
| 28-29-30 | at Lexington |

**MAY**

| | |
|---|---|
| 2 | Greensboro |
| 3-4 | at Greensboro |
| 4 | Greensboro |
| 6-7 | at Greensboro |
| 8-9 | West Virginia |
| 11-12-13-14 | at G'boro |
| 15-16 | Kannapolis |
| 17-18 | at Kannapolis |
| 19-20-21-22 | Asheville |
| 23-24-25-26 | at Augusta |
| 27-28-29-30 | Hagerstown |

**JUNE**

| | |
|---|---|
| 1-2-3-4 | at Lakewood |
| 5 | at Greensboro |
| 6-7 | Greensboro |
| 7 | Greensboro |
| 9-10-11 | West Virginia |
| 12-13-14-15 | Kannapolis |
| 16-17 at West Virginia |
| 22-23-24-25 | Greensboro |
| 26-27 | at Kannapolis |
| 28-29 | Kannapolis |
| 29 | at Asheville |

**JULY**

| | |
|---|---|
| 1-2-3 | at Asheville |
| 4-5-6-7 | Augusta |
| 8-9 | at Greensboro |
| 11-12-13-14 | at Hag. |
| 15-16-17-18 | Delmarva |
| 19-20-21-22 | Lakewood |
| 24-25-26-27 | at Columbus |
| 28-29-30-31 | at Rome |

**AUGUST**

| | |
|---|---|
| 2-3-4-5 | Charleston |

| | |
|---|---|
| 6-7-8-9 | Savannah |
| 11-12-13-14 | at Lake Co. |
| 15-16-17-18 | at West Va. |
| 19-20-21-22 | Greensboro |
| 23-24-25 | at Lexington |
| 26-27 | at Greensboro |
| 29-30-31 | Lexington |

**SEPTEMBER**

| | |
|---|---|
| 1-2-3-4 | West Virginia |

## KANNAPOLIS

**APRIL**

| | |
|---|---|
| 6-7-8-9 | at Rome |
| 11-12-13-14 | Asheville |
| 15-16-17-18 | Rome |
| 20-21-22-23 | at Charleston |
| 24-25-26-27 | at Greenville |
| 28-29-30 | Charleston |

**MAY**

| | |
|---|---|
| 1 | Charleston |
| 2-3-4-6 | at Savannah |
| 6-7-8-9 | Columbus |
| 10-11-12-13 | Lexington |
| 15-16 | at Hickory |
| 17-18 | Hickory |
| 19-20-21-22 | at G'boro |
| 23-24-25-26 | West Va. |
| 27-28-29-30 | at Asheville |

**JUNE**

| | |
|---|---|
| 1-2-3-4 | Greenville |
| 5-6-7-8 | Asheville |
| 9-10-11 | at Augusta |
| 12-13-14-15 | at Hickory |
| 16-17-18 | Augusta |
| 22-23-24-25 | at West Va. |
| 26-27 | Hickory |
| 28-29 | at Hickory |
| 30 | Greensboro |

**JULY**

| | |
|---|---|
| 1-2-3 | Greensboro |
| 4-5-6-7 | at Lexington |
| 8-9-10 | Greenville |
| 12-13-14 | at Augusta |
| 15-16-17-18 | Savannah |
| 20-21-22-23 | Rome |
| 24-25-26-27 | at Hag. |
| 28-29-30-31 | at Lake Co. |

**AUGUST**

| | |
|---|---|
| 2-3-4-5 | Lakewood |
| 6-7-8-9 | Delmarva |
| 10-11-12-13 | at Charleston |
| 15-16-17-18 | at Columbus |
| 19-20 | at Asheville |
| 21-22 | Asheville |
| 23-24-25-26 | Augusta |
| 28-29 | Asheville |
| 30-31 | at Asheville |

**SEPTEMBER**

| | |
|---|---|
| 1-2-3-4 | at Greenville |

## LAKE COUNTY

**APRIL**

| | |
|---|---|
| 6-7-8-9 | at Hickory |
| 10-11-12 | at Delmarva |
| 13-14-15-16 | Hagerstown |
| 18-19-20-21 | Lexington |
| 22-23-24-25 | Hagerstown |
| 26-27-28 | Delmarva |

| | |
|---|---|
| 29-30 | at Lakewood |

**MAY**

| | |
|---|---|
| 1 | at Lakewood |
| 3-4-5 | Hagerstown |
| 6-7-8 | Delmarva |
| 9-10-11 | at Hagerstown |
| 12-13-14 | at Delmarva |
| 16-17-18 | Hagerstown |
| 19-20-21-22 | at Delmarva |
| 23-24-25-26 | Lakewood |
| 27-28-29-30 | at G'boro |

**JUNE**

| | |
|---|---|
| 1-2-3-4 | West Virginia |
| 5-6-7-8 | at Lexington |
| 9-10-11 | Lakewood |
| 12-13-14-15 | Lexington |
| 16-17-18 | at Lakewood |
| 22-23-24 | Delmarva |
| 26-27-28-29 | at Lakewood |
| 30 | at Delmarva |

**JULY**

| | |
|---|---|
| 1-2 | at Delmarva |
| 3-4-5 | Hagerstown |
| 6-7-8-9 | at Delmarva |
| 11-12-13-14 | Greensboro |
| 15-16-17-18 | Hagerstown |
| 20-21-22-23 | West Va. |
| 24-25-26-27 | Asheville |
| 28-29-30-31 | Kannapolis |

**AUGUST**

| | |
|---|---|
| 2-3-4-5 | at Greenville |
| 6-7-8-9 | at Augusta |
| 11-12-13-14 | Hickory |
| 15-16-17-18 | Delmarva |
| 19-20-21-22 | at Lexington |
| 24-25-26-27 | Lakewood |
| 28-29-30-31 | at Hag. |

**SEPTEMBER**

| | |
|---|---|
| 1-2-3-4 | at Lakewood |

## LAKEWOOD

**APRIL**

| | |
|---|---|
| 6-7-8-9 | at Lexington |
| 10-11-12 | at Hagerstown |
| 13-14-15 | Delmarva |
| 18-19-20-21 | Greensboro |
| 22-23-24-25 | at Delmarva |
| 26-27-28 | Hagerstown |
| 29-30 | Lake County |

**MAY**

| | |
|---|---|
| 1 | Lake County |
| 3-4-5 | at Delmarva |
| 6-7-8 | Hagerstown |
| 8-10-11 | at Delmarva |
| 12-13-14 | at Hagerstown |
| 15 | *Delmarva |
| 15-17-18 | Delmarva |
| 19-20-21-22 | Hagerstown |
| 23-24-25-26 | at Lake Co. |
| 27-28-29-30 | West Va. |

**JUNE**

| | |
|---|---|
| 1-2-3-4 | Hickory |
| 5-6-7-8 | Delmarva |
| 9-10-11 | at Lake County |
| 12-13-14-15 | at Delmarva |
| 16-17-18 | Lake County |
| 22-23-24-25 | at Hag. |
| 26-27-28-29 | Lake County |

| | |
|---|---|
| 30 | at Hagerstown |

**JULY**

| | |
|---|---|
| 1-2 | at Hagerstown |
| 3-4-5 | Delmarva |
| 6-7-8-9 | at Hagerstown |
| 11-12-13-14 | West Va. |
| 15-16-17-18 | at Savannah |
| 19-20-21-22 | at Hickory |
| 24-25-26-27 | Augusta |
| 28-29-30-31 | Greenville |

**AUGUST**

| | |
|---|---|
| 2-3-4-5 | at Kannapolis |
| 6-7-8-9 | at Asheville |
| 11-12-13-14 | Lexington |
| 15-16-17-18 | Hagerstown |
| 19-20-21-22 | Delmarva |
| 24-25-26-27 | at Lake Co. |
| 28-29-30-31 | a Delmarva |

**SEPTEMBER**

| | |
|---|---|
| 1-2-3-4 | Lake County |

## LEXINGTON

**APRIL**

| | |
|---|---|
| 6-7-8-9 | Lakewood |
| 10-11-12-13 | Hickory |
| 14-15-16 | at West Virginia |
| 18-19-20-21 | at Lake Co. |
| 22-23-24 | West Virginia |
| 25-25-27 | at Hickory |
| 28-29-30 | Hickory |

**MAY**

| | |
|---|---|
| 2-3-4-5-6-7 | at West Va. |
| 8-9 | Greensboro |
| 10-11-12-13 | at Kan. |
| 15-16-17-18 | Greenville |
| 19-20-21-22 | Augusta |
| 23-24-25-26 | at Asheville |
| 27-28-29-30 | Delmarva |

**JUNE**

| | |
|---|---|
| 1-2-3-4 | at Hagerstown |
| 5-6-7-8 | Lake County |
| 9-10-11 | Greensboro |
| 12-13-14-15 | at Lake Co. |
| 16-17-18 | at Greensboro |
| 22-23-24-25 | Asheville |
| 26-27-28-29 | at Greenville |
| 30 | at Augusta |

**JULY**

| | |
|---|---|
| 1-2-3 | at Augusta |
| 4-5-6-7 | Kannapolis |
| 8-9 | West Virginia |
| 11-12-13-14 | at Delmarva |
| 15-16 | at West Virginia |
| 17-18 | West Virginia |
| 19-20-21-22 | Hagerstown |
| 24-25-26-27 | at Charleston |
| 28-29-30-31 | at Charleston |

**AUGUST**

| | |
|---|---|
| 2-3-4-5 | Rome |
| 6-7-8-9 | Columbus |
| 11-12-13-14 | at Lakewood |
| 15-16-17-18 | at G'boro |
| 19-20-21-22 | Lake County |
| 23-24-25 | Hickory |
| 26-27 | at West Virginia |
| 29-30-31 | at Hickory |

**SEPTEMBER**

| | |
|---|---|
| 1-2-3-4 | Greensboro |

## ROME

### APRIL
| | |
|---|---|
| **6-7-8-9** | **Kannapolis** |
| 11-12-13-14 | at Savannah |
| 15-16-17-18 | at Kan. |
| **20-21-22-23** | **Augusta** |
| **24-25-26-27** | **Columbus** |
| 28-29-30 | at Augusta |

### MAY
| | |
|---|---|
| 1 | at Augusta |
| **2-3-4-5** | **Asheville** |
| 6-7-8-9 | at Greenville |
| **10-11-12-13** | **Charleston** |
| 15-16-17-18 | at Columbus |
| 19-20-21-22 | at Charleston |
| **23-24-25-26** | **Savannah** |
| **27-28-29-30** | **Columbus** |

### JUNE
| | |
|---|---|
| 1-2-3-4 | at Savannah |
| **5-6-7-8** | **Augusta** |
| 9-10-11 | at Columbus |
| 12-13-14-15 | at Augusta |
| **16-17-18** | **Columbus** |
| **22-23-24-25** | **Charleston** |
| 26-27-28-29 | at Savannah |
| 30 | at Charleston |

### JULY
| | |
|---|---|
| 1-2-3 | at Charleston |
| **4-5-6-7** | **Savannah** |
| 8-9-10 | at Columbus |
| **12-13-14** | **Charleston** |
| **15-16-17-18** | **Greenville** |
| 20-21-22-23 | at Kan. |
| **24-25-26-27** | **Greensboro** |
| **28-29-30-31** | **Hickory** |

### AUGUST
| | |
|---|---|
| 2-3-4-5 | at Lexington |
| 6-7-8-9 | at West Virginia |
| **10-11-12-13** | **Augusta** |
| 15-16-17-18 | at Asheville |
| **19-20-21-22** | **Columbus** |
| 24-25-26-27 | at Savannah |
| 28-29-30-31 | at Columbus |

### SEPTEMBER
| | |
|---|---|
| **1-2-3-4** | **Savannah** |

## SAVANNAH

### APRIL
| | |
|---|---|
| 6-7-8-9 | at Asheville |
| **11-12-13-14** | **Rome** |
| **15-16-17-18** | **Asheville** |
| 20-21-22-23 | at Greenville |
| 24-25-26-27 | at Charleston |
| **28-29-30** | **Greenville** |

### MAY
| | |
|---|---|
| 1 | **Greenville** |
| **2-3-4-5** | **Kannapolis** |
| **6-7-8-9** | **Augusta** |
| 11-12-13-14 | at Columbus |
| 15-16-17-18 | at Charleston |
| **19-20-21-22** | **Columbus** |
| 23-24-25-26 | at Rome |
| **27-28-29-30** | **Charleston** |

### JUNE
| | |
|---|---|
| **1-2-3-4** | **Rome** |
| 5-6-7-8 | at Columbus |
| 9-10-11 | at Charleston |
| **12-13-14-15** | **Columbus** |
| **16-17-18** | **Charleston** |
| 22-23-24-25 | at Columbus |
| **26-27-28-29** | **Rome** |

### JULY
| | |
|---|---|
| 30 | **Columbus** |

### JULY
| | |
|---|---|
| **1-2-3** | **Columbus** |
| 4-5-6-7 | at Rome |
| 8-9-10 | at Charleston |
| **12-13-14** | **Columbus** |
| 15-16-17-18 | at Kan. |
| 19-20-21-22 | at Greenville |
| **24-25-26-27** | **Lexington** |
| **28-29-30-31** | **West Va.** |

### AUGUST
| | |
|---|---|
| 2-3-4-5 | at Greensboro |
| 6-7-8-9 | at Hickory |
| **10-11-12-13** | **Asheville** |
| 15-16-17-18 | at Augusta |
| 19-20-21-22 | at Charleston |
| **24-25-26-27** | **Rome** |
| **28-29-30-31** | **Charleston** |

### SEPTEMBER
| | |
|---|---|
| 1-2-3-4 | at Hickory |

## WEST VIRGINIA

### APRIL
| | |
|---|---|
| **6-7-8-9** | **Delmarva** |
| 10-11-12-13 | at G'boro |
| **14-15-16** | **Lexington** |
| 18-19-20-21 | at Hag. |
| 22-23-24 | at Lexington |
| **25-26-27** | **Greensboro** |
| 28-29-30 | at Greensboro |

### MAY
| | |
|---|---|
| **2-3-4-5-6-7** | **Lexington** |
| 8-9 | at Hickory |
| 10-11-12-13 | at Asheville |
| **15-16-17-19** | **Augusta** |
| **19-20-21-22** | **Greenville** |

### (June)
| | |
|---|---|
| 23-24-25-26 | at Kan. |
| **27-28-29-30** | **Lakewood** |

### JUNE
| | |
|---|---|
| 1-2-3-4 | at Lake County |
| **5-6** | **Hagerstown** |
| 7-8 | at Hagerstown |
| 9-10-11 | at Hickory |
| **12-13** | **Hagerstown** |
| 14-15 | at Hagerstown |
| **16-17-18** | **Hickory** |
| **22-23-24-25** | **Kannapolis** |
| 26-27-28-29 | at Augusta |
| 30 | at Greenville |

### JULY
| | |
|---|---|
| 1-2-3 | at Greenville |
| **4-5-6-7** | **Asheville** |
| 8-9 | at Lexington |
| 11-12-13-15 | at Lakewood |
| **15-16** | **Lexington** |
| 17-18 | at Lexington |
| **20-21-22-23** | **Lake County** |
| 24-25-26-27 | at Charleston |
| 28-29-30-31 | at Savannah |

### AUGUST
| | |
|---|---|
| **2-3-4-5** | **Columbus** |
| **6-7-8-9** | **Rome** |
| 10-11-12-13 | at Delmarva |
| **15-16-17-18** | **Hickory** |
| **19-20-21-22** | **Hagerstown** |
| 23-24-25 | at Greensboro |
| **26-27** | **Lexington** |
| **29-30-31** | **Greensboro** |

### SEPTEMBER
| | |
|---|---|
| 1-2-3-4 | at Hickory |

*Game at Fenway Park, Boston

## ABERDEEN

**JUNE**
| | |
|---|---|
| 20-21-22 | at Hud. Valley |
| 23-24-25 | Brooklyn |
| 26-27-28 | at Staten Island |
| 29-30 | at Brooklyn |

**JULY**
| | |
|---|---|
| 1 | at Brooklyn |
| 2-3-4 | Staten Island |
| 5-6-7 | Hudson Valley |
| 8-9-10 | at Mahoning Valley |
| 12-13-14 | Auburn |
| 15-16-17 | Jamestown |
| 18-19-20 | at Batavia |
| 21-22-23 | Tri-City |
| 25-26-27 | at Lowell |
| 28-29 | at Hudson Valley |
| 30-31 | Brooklyn |

**AUGUST**
| | |
|---|---|
| 1-2-3 | at Tri-City |
| 4-5-6 | Oneonta |
| 7-8 | Hudson Valley |
| 9-10-11 | at Vermont |
| 12-13-14 | at Williamsport |
| 17-18-19 | State College |
| 20-21 | at Hudson Valley |
| 22-23 | Staten Island |
| 24-25 | at Brooklyn |
| 26-27 | at Staten Island |
| 28-29 | Hudson Valley |
| 30-31 | at Oneonta |

**SEPTEMBER**
| | |
|---|---|
| 1 | at Oneonta |
| 2-3-4 | Vermont |
| 5-6-7 | Lowell |

## AUBURN

**JUNE**
| | |
|---|---|
| 20 | at Batavia |
| 21 | Batavia |
| 23-24-25 | Jamestown |
| 26-27-28 | at Williamsport |
| 29-30 | at Jamestown |

**JULY**
| | |
|---|---|
| 1 | at Jamestown |
| 2-3-4 | Mahoning Valley |
| 5-6-7 | at Mahoning Valley |
| 8-9-10 | Lowell |
| 12-13-14 | at Aberdeen |
| 15-16-17 | at H.V. |
| 18-19-20 | Tri-City |
| 21-22-23 | Staten Island |
| 25-26-27 | at Vermont |
| 28-29-30 | at State College |
| 31 | State College |

**AUGUST**
| | |
|---|---|
| 1-2 | State College |
| 3 | Batavia |
| 4 | at Batavia |
| 5 | Batavia |
| 6-7-8 | Williamsport |
| 9 | at Batavia |
| 10 | Batavia |
| 11 | at Batavia |
| 12-13-14 | at Oneonta |
| 17-18-19 | Brooklyn |
| 20-21 | State College |
| 22 | Batavia |
| 23 | at Batavia |
| 24 | Batavia |
| 25-26 | at State College |
| 27-28 | at Mahoning Valley |
| 29-30 | at Williamsport |
| 31 | Jamestown |

**SEPTEMBER**
| | |
|---|---|
| 1 | Jamestown |
| 2-3 | Williamsport |
| 4-5 | at Jamestown |
| 6-7 | Mahoning Valley |

## BATAVIA

**JUNE**
| | |
|---|---|
| 20 | Auburn |
| 21 | at Auburn |
| 22 | Auburn |
| 23-24-25 | at State College |
| 26 | at Jamestown |
| 27 | Jamestown |
| 28 | at Jamestown |
| 29-30 | State College |

**JULY**
| | |
|---|---|
| 1 | State College |
| 2-3-4 | Williamsport |
| 5-6-7 | at Williamsport |
| 8-9-10 | Hudson Valley |
| 12-13-14 | at Vermont |
| 15-16-17 | at Tri-City |
| 18-19-20 | Aberdeen |
| 21-22-23 | Lowell |
| 25-26-27 | at Staten Island |
| 28-29-30 | M.V. |
| 31 | at Mahoning Valley |

**AUGUST**
| | |
|---|---|
| 1-2 | at Mahoning Valley |
| 3 | at Auburn |
| 4 | Auburn |
| 5 | at Auburn |
| 6 | Jamestown |
| 7 | at Jamestown |
| 8 | Jamestown |
| 9 | Auburn |
| 10 | at Auburn |
| 11 | Auburn |
| 12-13-14 | at Brooklyn |
| 17-18-19 | Oneonta |
| 20-21 | at Mahoning Valley |
| 22 | at Auburn |
| 23 | Auburn |
| 24 | at Auburn |
| 25-26 | Mahoning Valley |
| 27-28 | Williamsport |
| 29 | at Jamestown |
| 30 | Jamestown |
| 31 | at State College |

**SEPTEMBER**
| | |
|---|---|
| 1 | at State College |
| 2 | at Jamestown |
| 3 | Jamestown |
| 4-5 | State College |
| 6-7 | at Williamsport |

## BROOKLYN

**JUNE**
| | |
|---|---|
| 20 | Staten Island |
| 21 | at Staten Island |
| 22 | Staten Island |
| 23-24-25 | at Aberdeen |
| 26 | Hudson Valley |
| 27 | at Hudson Valley |
| 28 | Hudson Valley |
| 29-30 | Aberdeen |

**JULY**
| | |
|---|---|
| 1 | Aberdeen |
| 2 | at Hudson Valley |
| 3 | Hudson Valley |
| 4 | at Hudson Valley |
| 5 | at Staten Island |
| 6 | Staten Island |
| 7 | at Staten Island |
| 8-9-10 | State College |
| 12-13-14 | at Williamsport |
| 15-16-17 | at Vermont |
| 18-19-20 | Oneonta |
| 21-22-23 | at Jamestown |
| 25-26-27 | M.V. |
| 28 | at Staten Island |
| 29 | Staten Island |
| 30-31 | at Aberdeen |

**AUGUST**
| | |
|---|---|
| 1-2-3 | at Oneonta |
| 4-5-6 | Tri-City |
| 7 | Staten Island |
| 8 | at Staten Island |
| 9-10 | at Lowell |
| 12-13-14 | Batavia |
| 17-18-19 | at Auburn |
| 20 | at Staten Island |
| 21 | Staten Island |
| 22 | Hudson Valley |
| 23 | at Hudson Valley |
| 24-25 | Aberdeen |
| 26 | Hudson Valley |
| 27 | at Hudson Valley |
| 28 | at Staten Island |
| 29 | Staten Island |
| 30-31 | at Tri-City |

**SEPTEMBER**
| | |
|---|---|
| 1 | at Tri-City |
| 2-3-4 | Lowell |
| 5-6-7 | Vermont |

## HUDSON VALLEY

**JUNE**
| | |
|---|---|
| 20-21-22 | Aberdeen |
| 23 | at Staten Island |
| 24 | Staten Island |
| 25 | at Staten Island |
| 26 | at Brooklyn |
| 27 | Brooklyn |
| 28 | at Brooklyn |
| 29 | Staten Island |
| 30 | at Staten Island |

**JULY**
| | |
|---|---|
| 1 | Staten Island |
| 2 | Brooklyn |
| 3 | at Brooklyn |
| 4 | Brooklyn |
| 5-6-7 | at Aberdeen |
| 8-9-10 | Batavia |
| 12-13-14 | Jamestown |
| 15-16-17 | Auburn |
| 18-19-20 | at M.V. |
| 21-22-23 | Williamsport |
| 25-26-27 | at State College |
| 28-29 | Aberdeen |
| 30 | at Staten Island |
| 31 | Staten Island |

**AUGUST**
| | |
|---|---|
| 1-2-3 | at Lowell |
| 4-5-6 | Vermont |
| 7-8 | at Aberdeen |
| 9-10-11 | at Oneonta |
| 12-13-14 | Lowell |
| 17-18-19 | at Tri-City |
| 20-21 | Aberdeen |
| 22 | at Brooklyn |
| 23 | Brooklyn |
| 24 | Staten Island |
| 25 | at Staten Island |
| 26 | at Brooklyn |
| 27 | Brooklyn |
| 28-29 | at Aberdeen |
| 30-31 | at Vermont |

**SEPTEMBER**
| | |
|---|---|
| 1 | at Vermont |
| 2-3-4 | Tri-City |
| 5-6-7 | Oneonta |

## JAMESTOWN

**JUNE**
| | |
|---|---|
| 20-21-22 | M.V. |
| 23-24-25 | at Auburn |
| 26 | Batavia |
| 27 | at Batavia |
| 28 | Batavia |
| 29-30 | Auburn |

**JULY**
| | |
|---|---|
| 1 | Auburn |
| 2-3-4 | at State College |
| 5-6-7 | State College |
| 8-9-10 | Oneonta |
| 12-13-14 | at H.V. |
| 15-16-17 | at Aberdeen |
| 18-19-20 | Vermont |
| 21-22-23 | Brooklyn |
| 25-26-27 | at Tri-City |
| 28-29-30 | at Williamsport |
| 31 | Williamsport |

**AUGUST**
| | |
|---|---|
| 1-2 | Williamsport |

| Date | Opponent |
|---|---|
| 3-4-5 | at Mahoning Valley |
| 6 | at Batavia |
| 7 | Batavia |
| 8 | at Batavia |
| 9-10-11 | Mahoning Valley |
| 12-13-14 | Staten Island |
| 17-18-19 | at Vermont |
| 20-21 | at Williamsport |
| 22-23-24 | at M.V. |
| 25-26 | Williamsport |
| 27-28 | State College |
| 29 | Batavia |
| 30 | at Batavia |
| 31 | at Auburn |
| **SEPTEMBER** | |
| 1 | at Auburn |
| 2 | Batavia |
| 3 | at Batavia |
| 4-5 | Auburn |
| 6-7 | at State College |

## LOWELL

| Date | Opponent |
|---|---|
| **JUNE** | |
| 20-21-22 | Vermont |
| 23-24-25 | at Oneonta |
| 26-27-28 | Tri-City |
| 29-30 | Oneonta |
| **JULY** | |
| 1 | Oneonta |
| 2-3-4 | at Tri-City |
| 5-6-7 | at Vermont |
| 8-9-10 | at Auburn |
| 12-13-14 | M.V. |
| 15-16-17 | at Williamsport |
| 18-19-20 | State College |
| 21-22-23 | at Batavia |
| 25-26-27 | Aberdeen |
| 28-29 | Vermont |
| 30-31 | at Vermont |
| **AUGUST** | |
| 1-2-3 | Hudson Valley |
| 4-5-6 | at Staten Island |
| 7-8 | Vermont |
| 9-10-11 | Brooklyn |
| 12-13-14 | at H.V. |
| 17-18-19 | Jamestown |
| 20-21 | Tri-City |
| 22-23 | at Oneonta |
| 24-25 | at Tri-City |
| 26 | *Oneonta |
| 27 | Oneonta |
| 28-29 | at Vermont |
| 30-31 | Staten Island |
| **SEPTEMBER** | |
| 1 | Staten Island |
| 2-3-4 | at Brooklyn |
| 5-6 | at Aberdeen |

## MAHONING VALLEY

| Date | Opponent |
|---|---|
| **JUNE** | |
| 20-21-22 | at Jamestown |
| 23-24-25 | Williamsport |
| 26-27-28 | State College |
| 29-30 | at Williamsport |
| **JULY** | |
| 1 | at Williamsport |
| 2-3-4 | at Auburn |
| 5-6-7 | Auburn |
| 8-9-10 | Aberdeen |
| 12-13-14 | at Lowell |
| 15-16-17 | at Oneonta |
| 18-19-20 | Hudson Valley |
| 21-22-23 | Vermont |
| 25-26-27 | at Brooklyn |
| 28-29-30 | at Batavia |
| 31 | Batavia |
| **AUGUST** | |
| 1-2 | Batavia |
| 3-4-5 | Jamestown |
| 6-7-8 | at State College |
| 9-10-11 | at Jamestown |
| 12-13-14 | Tri-City |
| 17-18-19 | at Staten Island |
| 20-21 | Batavia |
| 22-23-24 | Jamestown |
| 25-26 | at Batavia |
| 27-28 | Auburn |
| 29-30 | at State College |
| 31 | Williamsport |
| **SEPTEMBER** | |
| 1 | Williamsport |
| 2-3 | State College |
| 4-5 | at Williamsport |
| 6-7 | at Auburn |

## ONEONTA

| Date | Opponent |
|---|---|
| **JUNE** | |
| 20 | at Tri-Cities |
| 21 | Tri-Cities |
| 22 | at Tri-Cities |
| 23-24-25 | Lowell |
| 26-27-28 | at Vermont |
| 29-30 | at Lowell |
| **JULY** | |
| 1 | at Lowell |
| 2-3-4 | Vermont |
| 5 | at Tri-City |
| 6 | Tri-City |
| 7 | at Tri-City |
| 8-9-10 | at Jamestown |
| 12-13-14 | Staten Island |
| 15-16-17 | M.V. |
| 18-19-20 | at Brooklyn |
| 21-22-23 | State College |
| 25-26-27 | at Williamsport |
| 28-29-30 | Tri-City |
| 31 | at Tri-City |
| **AUGUST** | |
| 1-2-3 | Brooklyn |
| 4-5-6 | at Aberdeen |
| 7 | Tri-City |
| 8 | at Tri-City |
| 9-10-11 | Hudson Valley |
| 12-13-14 | Auburn |
| 17-18-19 | at Batavia |
| 20-21 | Vermont |
| 22-23 | Lowell |
| 24-25 | at Vermont |
| 26-27 | at Lowell |
| 28 | at Tri-City |
| 29 | Tri-City |
| 30-31 | Aberdeen |
| **SEPTEMBER** | |
| 1 | Aberdeen |
| 2-3-4 | at Staten Island |
| 5-6-7 | at Hudson Valley |

## STATE COLLEGE

| Date | Opponent |
|---|---|
| **JUNE** | |
| 20 | at Williamsport |
| 21 | Williamsport |
| 22 | at Williamsport |
| 23-24-25 | Batavia |
| 26-27-28 | at M.V. |
| 29-30 | at Batavia |
| **JULY** | |
| 1 | at Batavia |
| 2-3-4 | Jamestown |
| 5-6-7 | at Jamestown |
| 8-9-10 | at Brooklyn |
| 12-13-14 | Tri-City |
| 15-16-17 | Staten Island |
| 18-19-20 | at Lowell |
| 21-22-23 | at Oneonta |
| 25-26-27 | Hudson Valley |
| 28-29-30 | Auburn |
| 31 | at Auburn |
| **AUGUST** | |
| 1-2 | at Auburn |
| 3 | Williamsport |
| 4 | at Williamsport |
| 5 | Williamsport |
| 6-7-8 | Mahoning Valley |
| 9 | at Williamsport |
| 10 | Williamsport |
| 11 | at Williamsport |
| 12-13-14 | Vermont |
| 17-18-19 | at Aberdeen |
| 20-21 | at Auburn |
| 22 | Williamsport |
| 23 | at Williamsport |
| 24 | Williamsport |
| 25-26 | Auburn |
| 27-28 | at Jamestown |
| 29-30 | Mahoning Valley |
| 31 | Batavia |
| **SEPTEMBER** | |
| 1 | Batavia |
| 2-3 | at Mahoning Valley |
| 4-5 | at Batavia |
| 6-7 | Jamestown |

## STATEN ISLAND

| Date | Opponent |
|---|---|
| **JUNE** | |
| 20 | at Brooklyn |
| 21 | Brooklyn |
| 22 | at Brooklyn |
| 23 | Hudson Valley |
| 24 | at Hudson Valley |
| 25 | Hudson Valley |
| 26-27-28 | Aberdeen |
| 29 | at Hudson Valley |
| 30 | Hudson Valley |
| **JULY** | |
| 1 | at Hudson Valley |
| 2-3-4 | at Aberdeen |
| 5 | Brooklyn |
| 6 | at Brooklyn |
| 7 | Brooklyn |
| 8-9-10 | Vermont |
| 12-13-14 | at Oneonta |
| 15-16-17 | at State College |
| 18-19-20 | Williamsport |
| 21-22-23 | at Auburn |
| 25-26-27 | Batavia |
| 28 | Brooklyn |
| 29 | at Brooklyn |
| 30 | Hudson Valley |
| 31 | at Hudson Valley |
| **AUGUST** | |
| 1-2-3 | at Vermont |
| 4-5-6 | Lowell |
| 7 | at Brooklyn |
| 8 | Brooklyn |
| 9-10-11 | at Tri-City |
| 12-13-14 | at Jamestown |
| 17-18-19 | M.V. |
| 20 | Brooklyn |
| 21 | at Brooklyn |
| 22-23 | at Aberdeen |
| 24 | at Hudson Valley |
| 25 | Hudson Valley |
| 26-27 | Aberdeen |
| 28 | Brooklyn |
| 29 | at Brooklyn |
| 30-31 | at Lowell |
| **SEPTEMBER** | |
| 1 | at Lowell |
| 2-3-4 | Oneonta |
| 5-6-7 | Tri-City |

## TRI-CITY

| Date | Opponent |
|---|---|
| **JUNE** | |
| 20 | Oneonta |
| 21 | at Oneonta |
| 22 | Oneonta |
| 23-24-25 | at Vermont |
| 26-27-28 | at Lowell |
| 29-30 | Vermont |
| **JULY** | |
| 1 | Vermont |
| 2-3-4 | Lowell |
| 5 | Oneonta |
| 6 | at Oneonta |
| 7 | Oneonta |
| 8-9-10 | Williamsport |
| 12-13-14 | at State College |
| 15-16-17 | Batavia |
| 18-19-20 | at Auburn |
| 21-22-23 | at Aberdeen |
| 25-26-27 | Jamestown |
| 28-29-30 | at Oneonta |
| 31 | Oneonta |
| **AUGUST** | |
| 1-2-3 | Aberdeen |
| 4-5-6 | at Brooklyn |
| 7 | at Oneonta |
| 8 | Oneonta |
| 9-10-11 | Staten Island |
| 12-13-14 | at M.V. |
| 17-18-19 | Hudson Valley |
| 20-21 | at Lowell |
| 22-23 | at Vermont |
| 24-25 | Lowell |
| 26-27 | Vermont |
| 28 | Oneonta |
| 29 | at Oneonta |
| 30-31 | Brooklyn |
| **SEPTEMBER** | |
| 1 | Brooklyn |
| 2-3-4 | at Hudson Valley |
| 5-6-7 | at Staten Island |

## VERMONT
### JUNE
| | |
|---|---|
| 20-21-23 | at Lowell |
| **23-24-25** | **Tri-City** |
| **26-27-28** | **Oneonta** |
| 29-30 | at Tri-City |
### JULY
| | |
|---|---|
| 1 | at Tri-City |
| 2-3-4 | at Oneonta |
| **5-6-7** | **Lowell** |
| 8-9-10 | at Staten Island |
| **12-13-14** | **Batavia** |
| **15-16-17** | **Brooklyn** |
| 18-19-20 | at Jamestown |
| 21-22-23 | at M.V. |
| **25-26-27** | **Auburn** |
| 28-29 | at Lowell |
| **30-31** | **Lowell** |
### AUGUST
| | |
|---|---|
| **1-2-3** | **Staten Island** |

| | |
|---|---|
| 4-5-6 | at Hudson Valley |
| 7-8 | at Lowell |
| **9-10-11** | **Aberdeen** |
| 12-13-14 | at State College |
| **17-18-19** | **Williamsport** |
| 20-21 | at Oneonta |
| **22-23** | **Tri-City** |
| **24-25** | **Oneonta** |
| 26-27 | at Tri-City |
| **28-29** | **Lowell** |
| **30-31** | **Hudson Valley** |
### SEPTEMBER
| | |
|---|---|
| **1** | **Hudson Valley** |
| 2-3-4 | at Aberdeen |
| 5-6-7 | at Brooklyn |

## WILLIAMSPORT
### JUNE
| | |
|---|---|
| **20** | **State College** |
| 21 | at State College |

| | |
|---|---|
| **22** | **State College** |
| 23-24-25 | at M.V. |
| **26-27-28** | **Auburn** |
| **29-30** | **Mahoning Valley** |
### JULY
| | |
|---|---|
| **1** | **Mahoning Valley** |
| 2-3-4 | at Batavia |
| **5-6-7** | **Batavia** |
| 8-9-10 | at Tri-City |
| **12-13-14** | **Brooklyn** |
| **15-16-17** | **Lowell** |
| 18-19-20 | at Staten Island |
| 21-22-23 | at H.V. |
| **25-26-27** | **Oneonta** |
| **28-29-30** | **Jamestown** |
| 31 | at Jamestown |
### AUGUST
| | |
|---|---|
| 1-2 | at Jamestown |
| 3 | at State College |
| **4** | **State College** |

| | |
|---|---|
| 5 | at State College |
| 6-7-8 | at Auburn |
| **9** | **State College** |
| 10 | at State College |
| **11** | **State College** |
| **12-13-14** | **Aberdeen** |
| 17-18-19 | at Vermont |
| **20-21** | **Jamestown** |
| 22 | at State College |
| **23** | **State College** |
| 24 | at State College |
| 25-26 | at Jamestown |
| 27-28 | at Batavia |
| **29-30** | **Auburn** |
| 31 | at Mahoning Valley |
### SEPTEMBER
| | |
|---|---|
| **1** | **Mahoning Valley** |
| 2-3 | at Auburn |
| **4-5** | **Mahoning Valley** |
| **6-7** | **Batavia** |

# NORTHWEST LEAGUE

## BOISE
### JUNE
| | |
|---|---|
| **19-20-21-22-23** | **Eugene** |
| 24-25-26-27-28 | at S-K |
| 29-30 | at Tri-City |
### JULY
| | |
|---|---|
| 1 | at Tri-City |
| **2-3-4** | **Yakima** |
| **5-6-7** | **Tri-City** |
| 8-9-10 | at Yakima |
| **12-13-14-15-16** | **Van.** |
| 17-18-19-20-21 | at Everett |
| **22-23-24** | **Yakima** |
| 25-26-27 | at Spokane |
| **28-29-30-31** | **S-K** |
### AUGUST
| | |
|---|---|
| **1** | **Salem-Keizer** |
| 3-4-5-6-7 | at Eugene |
| **8-9-10** | **Spokane** |
| **11-12-13-14-15** | **Everett** |
| 17-18-19-20-21 | at Van. |
| 22-23-24 | at Spokane |
| 26-26-27 | at Yakima |
| **29-30-31** | **Spokane** |
### SEPTEMBER
| | |
|---|---|
| **1-2-3** | **Tri-City** |
| 4-5-6 | at Tri-City |

## EUGENE
### JUNE
| | |
|---|---|
| 19-20-21-22-23 | at Boise |
| **24-25-26-27-28** | **Spokane** |
| 29-30 | at Vancouver |
### JULY
| | |
|---|---|
| 1 | at Vancouver |
| **2-3** | **Salem-Keizer** |
| 4-5-6 | at Salem-Keizer |
| **7** | **Salem-Keizer** |
| 8-9-10 | at Everett |
| **12-13-14-15-16** | **Yakima** |
| 17-18-19-20-21 | at Tri-City |
| **22-23-24** | **Vancouver** |
| **25-26-27** | **Everett** |
| 28-29-30-31 | at Yakima |

## SALEM-KEIZER
### JUNE
| | |
|---|---|
| 19-20-21-22-23 | at Spok. |

### AUGUST
| | |
|---|---|
| 1 | at Yakima |
| **3-4-5-6-7** | **Boise** |
| 8-9-10 | at Vancouver |
| **11-12-13-14-15** | **Tri-City** |
| 17-18-19-20-21 | at Spok. |
| **22-23-24** | **Vancouver** |
| **25-26-27** | **Everett** |
| 29-30-31 | at Everett |
### SEPTEMBER
| | |
|---|---|
| 1-2-3 | at Salem-Keizer |
| **4-5-6** | **Salem-Keizer** |

## EVERETT
### JUNE
| | |
|---|---|
| **19-20-21-22-23** | **Tri-City** |
| 24-25-26-27-28 | at Yakima |
| **29-30** | **Salem-Keizer** |
### JULY
| | |
|---|---|
| **1** | **Salem-Keizer** |
| **2-3-4** | **Vancouver** |
| 5-6-7 | at Vancouver |
| **8-9-10** | **Eugene** |
| 12-13-14-15-16 | at Spok. |
| **17-18-19-20-21** | **Boise** |
| 22-23-24 | at Salem-Keizer |
| 25-26-27 | at Eugene |
| **28-29-30-31** | **Spokane** |
### AUGUST
| | |
|---|---|
| **1** | **Spokane** |
| 3-4-5-6-7 | at Tri-City |
| **8-9-10** | **Salem-Keizer** |
| 11-12-13-14-15 | at Boise |
| **17-18-19-20-21** | **Yakima** |
| 22-23-24 | at Salem-Keizer |
| 25-26-27 | at Eugene |
| **29-30-31** | **Eugene** |
### SEPTEMBER
| | |
|---|---|
| **1-2-3** | **Vancouver** |
| 4-5-6 | at Vancouver |

| | |
|---|---|
| **24-25-26-27-28** | **Boise** |
| 29-30 | at Everett |
### JULY
| | |
|---|---|
| 1 | at Everett |
| 2-3 | at Eugene |
| **4-5-6** | **Eugene** |
| 7 | at Eugene |
| 8-9-10 | at Vancouver |
| **12-13-14-15-16** | **Tri-City** |
| 17-18-19-20-21 | at Yakima |
| **22-23-24** | **Everett** |
| **25-26-27** | **Vancouver** |
| 28-29-30-31 | at Boise |
### AUGUST
| | |
|---|---|
| 1 | at Boise |
| **3-4-5-6-7** | **Yakima** |
| 8-9-10 | at Everett |
| **11-12-13-14-15** | **Spokane** |
| 17-18-19-20-21 | at Tri-City |
| **22-23-24** | **Everett** |
| **25-26-27** | **Vancouver** |
| 29-30-31 | at Vancouver |
### SEPTEMBER
| | |
|---|---|
| **1-2-3** | **Eugene** |
| 4-5-6 | at Eugene |

## SPOKANE
### JUNE
| | |
|---|---|
| **19-20-21-22-23** | **S-K** |
| 24-25-26-27-28 | at Eugene |
| 29-30 | at Yakima |
### JULY
| | |
|---|---|
| 1 | at Yakima |
| **2-3-4** | **Tri-City** |
| **5-6-7** | **Yakima** |
| 8-9-10 | at Tri-City |
| **12-13-14-15-16** | **Everett** |
| 17-18-19-20-21 | at Van. |
| **22-23-24** | **Tri-City** |
| **25-26-27** | **Boise** |
| 28-29-30-31 | at Everett |
### AUGUST
| | |
|---|---|
| 1 | at Everett |
| **3-4-5-6-7** | **Vancouver** |

| | |
|---|---|
| 8-9-10 | at Boise |
| 11-12-13-14-15 | at S-K |
| **17-18-19-20-21** | **Eugene** |
| **22-23-24** | **Boise** |
| 25-26-27 | at Tri-City |
| 29-30-31 | at Boise |
### SEPTEMBER
| | |
|---|---|
| **1-2-3** | **Yakima** |
| 4-5-6 | at Yakima |

## TRI-CITY
### JUNE
| | |
|---|---|
| 19-20-21-22-23 | at Everett |
| **24-25-26-27-28** | **Van.** |
| **29-30** | **Boise** |
### JULY
| | |
|---|---|
| **1** | **Boise** |
| 2-3-4 | at Spokane |
| **5-6-7** | **Boise** |
| **8-9-10** | **Spokane** |
| 12-13-14-15-16 | at S-K |
| **17-18-19-20-21** | **Eugene** |
| 22-23-24 | at Spokane |
| **25-26-27** | **Yakima** |
| 28-29-30-31 | at Vancouver |
### AUGUST
| | |
|---|---|
| 1 | at Vancouver |
| **3-4-5-6-7** | **Everett** |
| **8-9-10** | **Yakima** |
| 11-12-13-14-15 | at Eugene |
| **17-18-19-20-21** | **S-K** |
| 22-23-24 | at Yakima |
| **25-26-27** | **Spokane** |
| 29-30-31 | at Yakima |
### SEPTEMBER
| | |
|---|---|
| 1-2-3 | at Boise |
| **4-5-6** | **Boise** |

## VANCOUVER
### JUNE
| | |
|---|---|
| **19-20-21-22-23** | **Yakima** |
| 24-25-26-27-28 | at Tri-City |
| **29-30** | **Eugene** |

| JULY | |
|---|---|
| 1 | Eugene |
| 2-3-4 | at Everett |
| 5-6-7 | Everett |
| 8-9-10 | Salem-Keizer |
| 12-13-14-15-16 | at Boise |
| 17-18-19-20-21 | Spokane |
| 22-23-24 | at Eugene |
| 25-26-27 | at Salem-Keizer |
| 28-29-30-31 | Tri-City |
| **AUGUST** | |
| 1 | Tri-City |
| 3-4-5-6-7 | at Spokane |

| | |
|---|---|
| 8-9-10 | Eugene |
| 11-12-13-14-15 | at Yakima |
| 17-18-19-20-21 | Boise |
| 22-23-24 | at Eugene |
| 25-26-27 | at Salem-Keizer |
| 29-30-31 | Salem-Keizer |
| **SEPTEMBER** | |
| 1-2-3 | at Everett |
| 4-5-6 | Everett |

### YAKIMA

| JUNE | |
|---|---|
| 19-20-21-22-23 | at Van. |

| | |
|---|---|
| 24-25-26-27-28 | Everett |
| 29-30 | Spokane |
| **JULY** | |
| 1 | Spokane |
| 2-3-4 | at Boise |
| 5-6-7 | at Spokane |
| 8-9-10 | Boise |
| 12-13-14-15-16 | at Eugene |
| 17-18-19-20-21 | S-K |
| 22-23-24 | at Boise |
| 25-26-27 | at Tri-City |
| 28-29-30-31 | Eugene |

| AUGUST | |
|---|---|
| 1 | Eugene |
| 3-4-5-6-7 | at Salem-Keizer |
| 8-9-10 | at Tri-City |
| 11-12-13-14-15 | Van. |
| 17-18-19-20-21 | at Everett |
| 22-23-24 | Tri-City |
| 25-26-27 | Boise |
| 29-30-31 | Tri-City |
| **SEPTEMBER** | |
| 1-2-3 | at Spokane |
| 4-5-6 | Spokane |

# ROOKIE
## APPALACHIAN LEAGUE

### BLUEFIELD

| JUNE | |
|---|---|
| 21-22-23 | at Elizabethton |
| 24-25-26 | Princeton |
| 27-28-29 | Elizabethton |
| 30 | at Bristol |
| **JULY** | |
| 1-2 | at Bristol |
| 3 | at Princeton |
| 4 | Princeton |
| 5-6-7 | Kingsport |
| 8-9-10 | Greeneville |
| 12-13-14 | at Danville |
| 15-16-17 | at Princeton |
| 18-19-20 | Pulaski |
| 21-22-23 | at Greeneville |
| 24-25-26 | Burlington |
| 27-28-29 | Danville |
| 30-31 | at Burlington |
| **AUGUST** | |
| 1 | at Burlington |
| 3-4-5 | at Kingsport |
| 6-7-8 | at Princeton |
| 9-10-11 | Danville |
| 12-13-14 | Pulaski |
| 15-16-17 | at Pulaski |
| 18-19-20 | at Burlington |
| 22-23-24 | Johnson City |
| 25-26-27 | Bristol |
| 28-29-30 | at Johnson City |

### BRISTOL

| JUNE | |
|---|---|
| 21-22-23 | Johnson City |
| 24-25-26 | at Burlington |
| 27-28-29 | Kingsport |
| 30 | Bluefield |
| **JULY** | |
| 1-2 | Bluefield |
| 3 | Pulaski |
| 4-5-6-7 | at Pulaski |
| 8-9-10 | Elizabethton |
| 12-13-14 | at Princeton |
| 15-16-17 | Greeneville |
| 18-19-20 | Danville |
| 21-22-23 | Johnson City |
| 24-25-26 | at Kingsport |
| 27-28-29 | at Princeton |
| 30 | Greeneville |
| 31 | at Greeneville |
| **AUGUST** | |
| 1 | at Greeneville |
| 3-4-5 | Burlington |
| 6-7-8 | at Burlington |
| 9-10-11 | at Elizabethton |
| 12-13-14 | at Kingsport |
| 15-16-17 | Elizabethton |
| 18-19-20 | Princeton |
| 22-23-24 | at Danville |
| 25-26-27 | at Bluefield |
| 28-29-30 | Pulaski |

### BURLINGTON

| JUNE | |
|---|---|
| 21-22-23 | at Danville |
| 24-25-26 | Bristol |
| 27-28-29 | at Pulaski |
| 30 | at Princeton |
| **JULY** | |
| 1-2 | at Princeton |
| 3 | at Danville |
| 4 | Danville |
| 5-6-7 | Elizabethton |
| 8-9-10 | Johnson City |
| 12-13-14 | at Greeneville |
| 15-16-17 | at Danville |
| 18-19-20 | Princeton |
| 21-22-23 | Kingsport |
| 24-25-26 | at Bluefield |
| 27-28-29 | Pulaski |
| 30-31 | Bluefield |
| **AUGUST** | |
| 1 | Bluefield |
| 3-4-5 | at Bristol |
| 6-7-8 | at Johnson City |
| 9-10-11 | Greeneville |
| 12-13-14 | at Elizabethton |
| 15-16-17 | Princeton |
| 18-19-20 | Bluefield |
| 22-23-24 | at Kingsport |
| 25-26-27 | at Pulaski |
| 28-29-30 | Danville |

### DANVILLE

| JUNE | |
|---|---|
| 21-22-23 | Burlington |
| 24-25-26 | at Greeneville |
| 27-28-29 | at Princeton |
| 30 | Greeneville |
| **JULY** | |
| 1-2 | Greeneville |
| 3 | Burlington |
| 4 | at Burlington |
| 5-6-7 | at Johnson City |
| 8-9-10 | at Kingsport |
| 12-13-14 | Bluefield |
| 15-16-17 | Burlington |
| 18-19-20 | at Bristol |
| 21-22-23 | at Princeton |
| 24-25-26 | Pulaski |
| 27-28-29 | at Bluefield |
| 30-31 | Johnson City |
| **AUGUST** | |
| 1 | Johnson City |
| 3-4-5 | Pulaski |
| 6-7-8 | at Pulaski |
| 9-10-11 | at Bluefield |
| 12-13-14 | Princeton |
| 15-16-17 | Kingsport |
| 18-19-20 | at Greeneville |
| 22-23-24 | Bristol |
| 25-26-27 | Elizabethton |
| 28-29-30 | at Burlington |

### ELIZABETHTON

| JUNE | |
|---|---|
| 21-22-23 | Bluefield |
| 24-25-26 | at Pulaski |
| 27-28-29 | at Bluefield |
| 30 | Johnson City |
| **JULY** | |
| 1-2 | Johnson City |
| 3 | Greeneville |
| 4 | at Kingsport |
| 5-6-7 | at Burlington |
| 8-9-10 | at Bristol |
| 12-13-14 | Kingsport |
| 15-16-17 | at Johnson City |
| 18-19-20 | Greeneville |
| 21-22-23 | Pulaski |
| 24-25-26 | at Johnson City |
| 27-28-29 | Greeneville |
| 30-31 | Kingsport |
| **AUGUST** | |
| 1 | Kingsport |
| 3-4-5 | at Greeneville |
| 6-7-8 | at Kingsport |
| 9-10-11 | Bristol |
| 12-13-14 | Burlington |
| 15-16-17 | at Bristol |
| 18-19-20 | Danville |
| 22-23-24 | at Princeton |
| 25-26-27 | at Danville |
| 28-29-30 | Princeton |

### GREENEVILLE

| JUNE | |
|---|---|
| 21-22-23 | at Kingsport |
| 24-25-26 | Danville |
| 27-28-29 | Johnson City |
| 30 | at Danville |
| **JULY** | |
| 1-2 | at Danville |
| 3 | at Elizabethton |
| 4 | Elizabethton |
| 5-6-7 | Princeton |
| 8-9-10 | at Bluefield |
| 12-13-14 | Burlington |
| 15-16-17 | Bristol |
| 18-19-20 | at Elizabethton |
| 21-22-23 | Bluefield |
| 24-25-26 | at Princeton |
| 27-28-29 | at Elizabethton |
| 30 | at Bristol |
| 31 | Bristol |
| **AUGUST** | |
| 1 | Bristol |
| 3-4-5 | Elizabethton |
| 6 | Bristol |
| 7-8 | at Bristol |
| 9-10-11 | at Burlington |
| 12-13-14 | at Johnson City |
| 15-16-17 | Johnson City |
| 18-19-20 | Pulaski |
| 22-23-24 | at Pulaski |
| 25-26-27 | at Kingsport |
| 28-29-30 | Kingsport |

### JOHNSON CITY

| JUNE | |
|---|---|
| | at Bristol |
| 24-25-26 | Kingsport |
| 27-28-29 | at Greeneville |
| 30 | at Elizabethton |
| **JULY** | |
| 1-2 | at Elizabethton |

| | |
|---|---|
| 3 | at Kingsport |
| 4 | **Kingsport** |
| 5-6-7 | **Danville** |
| 8-9-10 | at Burlington |
| 12-13-14 | **Pulaski** |
| 15-16-17 | **Elizabethton** |
| 18-19-20 | at Kingsport |
| 21-22-23 | at Bristol |
| 24-25-26 | **Elizabethton** |
| 27-28-29 | **Bristol** |
| 30-31 | at Danville |

**AUGUST**

| | |
|---|---|
| 1 | at Danville |
| 3-4-5 | **Princeton** |
| 6-7-8 | **Burlington** |
| 9-10-11 | at Pulaski |
| 12-13-14 | **Greeneville** |
| 15-16-17 | at Greeneville |
| 18-19-20 | **Kingsport** |
| 22-23-24 | at Bluefield |
| 25-26-27 | at Princeton |
| 28-29-30 | **Bluefield** |

## PRINCETON

**JUNE**

| | |
|---|---|
| 21-22-23 | **Pulaski** |
| 24-25-26 | at Bluefield |
| 27-28-29 | **Danville** |
| 30 | **Burlington** |

**JULY**

| | |
|---|---|
| 1-2 | **Burlington** |
| 3 | **Bluefield** |
| 4 | at Bluefield |
| 5-6-7 | at Greeneville |
| 8-9-10 | at Pulaski |
| 12-13-14 | **Bristol** |
| 15-16-17 | **Bluefield** |
| 18-19-20 | at Burlington |
| 21-22-23 | **Danville** |
| 24-25-26 | **Greeneville** |
| 27-28-29 | at Kingsport |
| 30-31 | at Pulaski |

**AUGUST**

| | |
|---|---|
| 1 | at Pulaski |
| 3-4-5 | at Johnson City |
| 6-7-8 | **Bluefield** |
| 9-10-11 | **Kingsport** |
| 12-13-14 | at Danville |
| 15-16-17 | at Burlington |
| 18-19-20 | at Bristol |
| 22-23-24 | **Elizabethton** |
| 25-26-27 | **Johnson City** |
| 28-29-30 | at Elizabethton |

## PULASKI

**JUNE**

| | |
|---|---|
| 21-22-23 | at Princeton |
| 24-25-26 | **Elizabethton** |
| 27-28-29 | **Burlington** |
| 30 | at Kingsport |

**JULY**

| | |
|---|---|
| 1-2 | at Kingsport |
| 3 | at Bristol |
| 4-5-6-7 | **Bristol** |
| 8-9-10 | **Princeton** |
| 12-13-14 | at Johnson City |
| 15-16-17 | **Kingsport** |
| 18-19-20 | at Bluefield |
| 21-22-23 | at Greeneville |
| 24-25-26 | at Danville |
| 27-28-29 | at Burlington |
| 30-31 | **Princeton** |

**AUGUST**

| | |
|---|---|
| 1 | **Princeton** |
| 3-4-5 | **Danville** |
| 6-7-8 | **Danville** |
| 9-10-11 | **Johnson City** |
| 12-13-14 | at Bluefield |
| 15-16-17 | **Bluefield** |
| 18-19-20 | at Greeneville |
| 22-23-24 | **Greeneville** |
| 25-26-27 | **Burlington** |
| 28-29-30 | at Elizabethton |

# PIONEER LEAGUE

## BILLINGS

**JUNE**

| | |
|---|---|
| 20-21-22-23 | **Great Falls** |
| 24-25 | **Helena** |
| 26-27-28 | at Missoula |
| 29-30 | at Great Falls |

**JULY**

| | |
|---|---|
| 1-2 | at Great Falls |
| 3-4-5 | **Missoula** |
| 6-7-8 | at Helena |
| 10-11-12 | **Idaho Falls** |
| 13-14-15-16 | **Casper** |
| 17-18-19-20 | at Idaho Falls |
| 21-22-23 | at Casper |
| 24-25-26 | **Helena** |
| 27-28-29 | at Missoula |
| 30-31 | at Helena |

**AUGUST**

| | |
|---|---|
| 1 | at Helena |
| 3-4-5 | **Missoula** |
| 6-7 | at Great Falls |
| 8-9-10-11 | **Great Falls** |
| 12-13 | at Missoula |
| 14-15 | at Helena |
| 16-17-18-19 | **Orem** |
| 20-21-22 | **Ogden** |
| 24-25-26 | at Orem |
| 27-28-29-30 | at Ogden |

**SEPTEMBER**

| | |
|---|---|
| 1-2-3 | **Helena** |
| 4-5 | **Missoula** |
| 6-7 | at Great Falls |

## CASPER

**JUNE**

| | |
|---|---|
| 20-21-22-23 | **Idaho Falls** |
| 24-25-26 | **Orem** |
| 27-28-29-30 | at Idaho Falls |

**JULY**

| | |
|---|---|
| 1-2-3 | at Ogden |
| 4-5-6-7-8 | **Orem** |
| 10-11-12 | at Great Falls |
| 13-14-15-16 | at Billings |
| 17-18-19-20 | **Great Falls** |
| 21-22-23 | **Billings** |
| 24-25-26 | at Orem |
| 27-28-29 | at Ogden |

**AUGUST**

| | |
|---|---|
| 1-2-3-4 | **Orem** |
| 5-6 | **Idaho Falls** |
| 7-8-9-10 | at Idaho Falls |
| 11-12-13-14 | at Ogden |
| 16-17-18 | **Helena** |
| 19-20-21-22 | **Missoula** |
| 24-25-26 | at Missoula |
| 27-28-29-30 | at Helena |
| 31 | **Ogden** |

**SEPTEMBER**

| | |
|---|---|
| 1-2 | **Ogden** |
| 3-4 | **Idaho Falls** |
| 5-6-7 | at Orem |

## GREAT FALLS

**JUNE**

| | |
|---|---|
| 20-21-22-23 | at Billings |
| 24-25 | **Missoula** |
| 26-27-28 | at Helena |
| 29-30 | **Billings** |

**JULY**

| | |
|---|---|
| 1-2 | **Billings** |
| 3-4 | **Helena** |
| 5 | at Helena |
| 6-7-8 | at Missoula |
| 10-11-12 | **Casper** |
| 13-14-15-16 | **Idaho Falls** |
| 17-18-19-20 | at Casper |
| 21-22-23 | at Idaho Falls |
| 24-25-26 | **Missoula** |
| 27 | **Helena** |
| 28-29 | at Helena |
| 30-31 | at Missoula |

**AUGUST**

| | |
|---|---|
| 1 | at Missoula |
| 3-4-5 | **Helena** |
| 6-7 | **Billings** |
| 8-9-10-11 | at Billings |
| 12-13 | **Helena** |
| 14-15 | at Missoula |
| 16-17-18-19 | **Ogden** |
| 20-21-22 | **Orem** |
| 24-25-26 | at Ogden |
| 27-28-29-30 | at Orem |

**SEPTEMBER**

| | |
|---|---|
| 1-2-3 | **Missoula** |
| 4-5 | at Helena |
| 6-7 | **Billings** |

## HELENA

**JUNE**

| | |
|---|---|
| 20-21-22-23 | **Missoula** |
| 24-25 | at Billings |
| 26-27-28 | **Great Falls** |
| 29-30 | at Missoula |

**JULY**

| | |
|---|---|
| 1-2 | at Missoula |
| 3-4 | at Great Falls |
| 5 | **Great Falls** |
| 6-7-8 | **Billings** |
| 10-11-12-13 | at Ogden |
| 14-15-16 | at Orem |
| 17-18-19-20 | at Idaho Falls |
| 21-22-23 | **Orem** |
| 24-25-26 | at Billings |
| 27 | at Great Falls |
| 28-29 | **Great Falls** |
| 30-31 | **Billings** |

**AUGUST**

| | |
|---|---|
| 1 | **Billings** |
| 3-4-5 | at Great Falls |
| 6-7 | at Missoula |
| 8-9-10-11 | **Missoula** |
| 12-13 | at Great Falls |
| 14-15 | **Billings** |
| 16-17-18 | at Casper |
| 19-20-21-22 | at Idaho Falls |
| 24-25-26 | **Idaho Falls** |
| 27-28-29-30 | **Casper** |

**SEPTEMBER**

| | |
|---|---|
| 1-2-3 | at Billings |
| 4-5 | **Great Falls** |
| 6-7 | at Missoula |

## IDAHO FALLS

**JUNE**

| | |
|---|---|
| 20-21-22-23 | at Casper |
| 24-25-26 | **Ogden** |
| 27-28-29-30 | **Casper** |

**JULY**

| | |
|---|---|
| 1-2-3 | at Orem |
| 4-5-6 | **Orem** |
| 7-8 | **Ogden** |
| 10-11-12 | at Billings |
| 13-14-15-16 | at Great Falls |
| 17-18-19-20 | **Billings** |
| 21-22-23 | **Great Falls** |
| 24-25-26 | at Ogden |
| 27-28-29 | at Orem |
| 31 | **Orem** |

**AUGUST**

| | |
|---|---|
| 1 | **Orem** |
| 2-3-4 | **Ogden** |
| 5-6 | at Casper |
| 7-8-9-10 | **Casper** |
| 11-12-13-14 | at Orem |
| 16-17-18 | **Missoula** |
| 19-20-21-22 | **Helena** |
| 24-25-26 | at Helena |
| 27-28-29-30 | at Missoula |
| 31 | **Orem** |

**SEPTEMBER**

| | |
|---|---|
| 1-2 | **Orem** |
| 3-4 | at Casper |
| 5-6-7 | at Ogden |

## MISSOULA

**JUNE**

| | |
|---|---|
| 20-21-22-23 | at Helena |
| 24-25 | at Great Falls |
| 26-27-28 | **Billings** |
| 29-30 | **Helena** |

**JULY**

| | |
|---|---|
| 1-2 | **Helena** |
| 3-4-5 | at Billings |
| 6-7-8 | **Great Falls** |
| 10-11-12-13 | at Orem |

| | |
|---|---|
| 14-15-16 | at Ogden |
| **17-18-19** | **Orem** |
| **20-21-22-23** | **Ogden** |
| 24-25-26 | at Great Falls |
| **27-28-29** | **Billings** |
| **30-31** | **Great Falls** |

### AUGUST

| | |
|---|---|
| **1** | **Great Falls** |
| 3-4-5 | at Billings |
| **6-7** | **Helena** |
| 8-9-10-11 | at Helena |
| **12-13** | **Billings** |
| **14-15** | **Great Falls** |
| 16-17-18 | at Idaho Falls |
| 19-20-21-22 | at Casper |
| **24-25-26** | **Casper** |
| **27-28-29-30** | **Idaho Falls** |

### SEPTEMBER

| | |
|---|---|
| 1-2-3 | at Great Falls |
| 4-5 | at Billings |
| **6-7** | **Helena** |

## OGDEN

### JUNE

| | |
|---|---|
| **20-21** | **Orem** |
| 22-23 | at Orem |
| 24-25-26 | at Idaho Falls |
| 27-28 | at Orem |
| **29-30** | **Orem** |

### JULY

| | |
|---|---|
| **1-2-3** | **Casper** |
| 4-5-6 | at Casper |
| 7-8 | at Idaho Falls |
| **10-11-12-13** | **Helena** |
| **14-15-16** | **Missoula** |
| 17-18-19 | at Helena |
| 20-21-22-23 | at Missoula |
| **24-25-26** | **Idaho Falls** |
| **27-28-29** | **Casper** |
| 31 | at Casper |

### AUGUST

| | |
|---|---|
| 1 | at Casper |
| 2-3-4 | at Idaho Falls |
| **5-6-7-8** | **Orem** |
| 9-10 | at Orem |
| **11-12-13-14** | **Casper** |
| 16-17-18-19 | at Great Falls |
| 20-21-22 | at Billings |
| **24-2-26** | **Great Falls** |
| **27-28-29-30** | **Billings** |
| 31 | at Casper |

### SEPTEMBER

| | |
|---|---|
| 1-2 | at Casper |
| 3-4 | at Orem |
| **5-6-7** | **Idaho Falls** |

## OREM

### JUNE

| | |
|---|---|
| 20-21 | at Ogden |
| **22-23** | **Ogden** |
| 24-25-26 | at Casper |
| **27-28** | **Ogden** |
| 29-30 | at Ogden |

### JULY

| | |
|---|---|
| **1-2-3** | **Idaho Falls** |
| 4-5-6 | at Idaho Falls |
| **7-8** | **Casper** |
| **10-11-12-13** | **Missoula** |
| **14-15-16** | **Helena** |
| 17-18-19-20 | at Helena |
| 21-22-23 | at Missoula |
| **24-25-26** | **Casper** |
| **27-28-29** | **Idaho Falls** |
| 31 | at Idaho Falls |

### AUGUST

| | |
|---|---|
| 1 | at Idaho Falls |
| 2-3-4 | at Casper |
| 5-6-7-8 | at Ogden |
| **9-10** | **Ogden** |
| **11-12-13-14** | **Idaho Falls** |
| 16-17-18-19 | at Billings |
| 20-21-22 | at Great Falls |
| **24-25-26** | **Billings** |
| **27-28-29-30** | **Great Falls** |
| **31** | **Idaho Falls** |

### SEPTEMBER

| | |
|---|---|
| 1-2 | at Idaho Falls |
| **3-4** | **Ogden** |
| **5-6-7** | **Casper** |

# ARIZONA LEAGUE

## ANGELS

### JUNE

| | |
|---|---|
| 22 | at Cubs |
| **23** | **Mariners** |
| 25 | at Giants |
| **26** | **Rangers** |
| **27** | **Athletics** |
| **28** | **Cubs** |
| 30 | at Mariners |

### JULY

| | |
|---|---|
| **1-21** | **Athletics** |
| **2-6-16** | **Rangers** |
| 3-23 | at Brewers |
| **5-25** | **Giants** |
| **7-10** | **Royals** |
| 8-26 | at Rangers |
| **11-22** | **Padres** |
| **12-18** | **Cubs** |
| **13** | **Mariners** |
| 15 | at Giants |
| 17 | at Athletics |
| 20 | at Mariners |
| 27-30 | at Royals |
| **28** | **Brewers** |
| 31 | at Padres |

### AUGUST

| | |
|---|---|
| 1-7-21 | at Cubs |
| **2-22** | **Mariners** |
| 4-24 | at Giants |
| 5-15 | at Rangers |
| 6-10-26 | at Athletics |
| 9 | at Mariners |
| 11-20-30 | at Padres |
| 12 | at Brewers |
| **14** | **Giants** |
| 16-27 | at Royals |
| **17-29** | **Brewers** |
| **19** | **Royals** |
| **25** | **Rangers** |

## ATHLETICS

### JUNE

| | |
|---|---|
| **22** | **Giants** |
| 23 | at Brewers |
| **24** | **Royals** |
| 26 | at Padres |
| 27 | at Angels |
| 28 | at Giants |
| **29** | **Mariners** |

### JULY

| | |
|---|---|
| 1-21 | at Angels |
| **2-22** | **Rangers** |
| 3-23 | at Royals |
| 4-24 | at Cubs |
| **6-26** | **Padres** |
| 7-27 | at Mariners |
| 8-28 | at Rangers |
| **9-29** | **Cubs** |
| **11-31** | **Brewers** |
| **12** | **Giants** |
| 13 | at Brewers |
| **14** | **Royals** |
| 16 | at Padres |
| **17** | **Angels** |
| 18 | at Giants |
| **19** | **Mariners** |

### AUGUST

| | |
|---|---|
| **1-21** | **Giants** |
| 2-22 | at Brewers |
| **3-23** | **Royals** |
| 5-25 | at Padres |
| **6-10-26** | **Angels** |
| 7 | at Giants |
| **8** | **Mariners** |
| **11** | **Rangers** |
| **12** | **Royals** |
| 13 | at Cubs |
| **15** | **Padres** |
| 16-27 | at Mariners |
| 17-28 | at Rangers |
| **18-30** | **Cubs** |
| **20** | **Brewers** |

## BREWERS

### JUNE

| | |
|---|---|
| **23** | **Athletics** |
| 24 | at Padres |
| 25 | at Mariners |
| **26** | **Cubs** |
| **28** | **Mariners** |
| 29 | at Rangers |
| 30 | at Royals |

### JULY

| | |
|---|---|
| **1-21** | **Rangers** |
| **3-23** | **Angels** |
| 4-24 | at Giants |
| **5-25** | **Royals** |
| 6-26 | at Cubs |
| 8-28 | at Angels |
| **9-29** | **Giants** |
| **10-30** | **Padres** |
| 11-31 | at Athletics |
| **13** | **Athletics** |
| 14 | at Padres |
| 15 | at Mariners |
| **16** | **Cubs** |
| **18** | **Mariners** |
| 19 | at Rangers |
| 20 | at Royals |

### AUGUST

| | |
|---|---|
| **2-22** | **Athletics** |
| 3-23 | at Padres |
| 4-24 | at Mariners |
| **5-25** | **Cubs** |
| **7** | **Mariners** |
| 8 | at Rangers |
| 9-28 | at Royals |
| **10-30** | **Rangers** |
| **12** | **Angels** |
| 13 | at Giants |
| **14** | **Royals** |
| 15 | at Cubs |
| 17-29 | at Angels |
| **18-27** | **Giants** |
| **19** | **Padres** |
| 20 | at Athletics |

## CUBS

### JUNE

| | |
|---|---|
| **22** | **Angels** |
| 23 | at Royals |
| **24** | **Giants** |
| 26 | at Brewers |
| **27** | **Padres** |
| 28 | at Angels |
| **29** | **Royals** |

### JULY

| | |
|---|---|
| 1-21 | at Padres |
| **2-22** | **Mariners** |
| 3-23 | at Rangers |
| **4-24** | **Athletics** |
| **6-26** | **Brewers** |
| 7-27 | at Giants |
| 8-28 | at Mariners |
| 9-29 | at Athletics |
| **11-31** | **Rangers** |
| 12-18 | at Angels |
| 13 | at Royals |
| **14** | **Giants** |
| 16 | at Brewers |
| **17** | **Padres** |
| **19** | **Royals** |

### AUGUST

| | |
|---|---|
| **1-7-21** | **Angels** |
| 2-22 | at Royals |
| **3-23** | **Giants** |
| 5-25 | at Brewers |
| **6-28** | **Padres** |
| **8** | **Royals** |
| 10 | at Padres |
| **11-26** | **Mariners** |
| 12-27 | at Rangers |
| **13** | **Athletics** |
| **15** | **Brewers** |
| 16 | at Giants |

| | | | |
|---|---|---|---|
| 17 | at Mariners | | |
| 18-30 | at Athletics | | |
| 20 | Rangers | | |

## GIANTS
### JUNE
| | |
|---|---|
| 22 | at Athletics |
| 23 | Rangers |
| 24 | at Cubs |
| 25 | Angels |
| 27 | at Rangers |
| 28 | Athletics |
| 29 | at Padres |
| 30 | Padres |

### JULY
| | |
|---|---|
| 2-22 | at Royals |
| 3-23 | Mariners |
| 4-24 | Brewers |
| 5-25 | at Angels |
| 7-27 | Cubs |
| 8-28 | Royals |
| 9-29 | at Brewers |
| 10-30 | at Mariners |
| 12 | at Athletics |
| 13 | Rangers |
| 14 | at Cubs |
| 15 | Angels |
| 17 | at Rangers |
| 18 | Athletics |
| 19 | at Padres |
| 20 | Padres |

### AUGUST
| | |
|---|---|
| 1-21 | at Athletics |
| 2-22 | Rangers |
| 3-23 | at Cubs |
| 4-24 | Angels |
| 6 | at Rangers |
| 7 | Athletics |
| 8-29 | at Padres |
| 9 | Padres |
| 11 | at Royals |
| 12-28 | Mariners |
| 13 | Brewers |
| 14 | at Angels |
| 16 | Cubs |
| 17-26 | Royals |
| 18-27 | at Brewers |
| 19 | at Mariners |

## MARINERS
### JUNE
| | |
|---|---|
| 22 | Padres |
| 23 | at Angels |
| 24 | at Rangers |
| 25 | Brewers |
| 27 | Royals |
| 28 | at Brewers |
| 29 | at Athletics |
| 30 | Angels |

### JULY
| | |
|---|---|
| 2-22 | at Cubs |
| 3-23 | at Giants |
| 4-24 | Rangers |
| 5-25 | at Padres |
| 7-27 | Athletics |
| 8-28 | Cubs |
| 9-29 | at Royals |
| 10-30 | Giants |
| 12 | Padres |
| 13 | at Angels |
| 14 | at Rangers |
| 15 | Brewers |
| 17 | Royals |
| 18 | at Brewers |
| 19 | at Athletics |
| 20 | Angels |

### AUGUST
| | |
|---|---|
| 1-21 | Padres |
| 2-22 | at Angels |
| 3-23 | at Rangers |
| 4-24 | Brewers |
| 6-29 | Royals |
| 7 | at Brewers |
| 8 | at Athletics |
| 9 | Angels |
| 11-26 | at Cubs |
| 12-28 | at Giants |
| 13 | Rangers |
| 14 | at Padres |
| 16-27 | Athletics |
| 17 | Cubs |
| 18 | at Royals |
| 19 | Giants |

## PADRES
### JUNE
| | |
|---|---|
| 22 | at Mariners |
| 24 | Brewers |
| 25 | at Royals |
| 26 | Athletics |
| 27 | at Cubs |
| 29 | Giants |
| 30 | at Giants |

### JULY
| | |
|---|---|
| 1-21 | Cubs |
| 2-22 | at Angels |
| 4-24 | Royals |
| 5-25 | Mariners |
| 6-26 | at Athletics |
| 7-27 | Rangers |
| 9-29 | at Rangers |
| 10-30 | at Brewers |
| 11 | at Angels |
| 12 | at Mariners |
| 14 | Brewers |
| 15 | at Royals |
| 16 | Athletics |
| 17 | at Cubs |
| 19 | Giants |
| 20 | at Giants |
| 31 | Angels |

### AUGUST
| | |
|---|---|
| 1-21 | at Mariners |
| 3-23 | Brewers |
| 4-24 | at Royals |
| 5-25 | Athletics |
| 6-28 | at Cubs |
| 8-29 | Giants |
| 9 | at Giants |
| 10 | Cubs |
| 11-20 | Angels |
| 13 | Royals |
| 14 | Mariners |
| 15 | at Athletics |
| 16-26 | Rangers |
| 18 | at Rangers |
| 19 | at Brewers |
| 25 | Athletics |
| 30 | at Angels |

## RANGERS
### JUNE
| | |
|---|---|
| 22 | Royals |
| 23 | at Giants |
| 24 | Mariners |
| 26 | at Angels |
| 27 | Giants |
| 28 | at Rangers |
| 29 | Brewers |

### JULY
| | |
|---|---|
| 1-21 | at Brewers |
| 2-22 | at Athletics |
| 3-23 | Cubs |
| 4-24 | at Mariners |
| 6-16 | at Angels |
| 7-27 | at Padres |
| 8-28 | Athletics |
| 9-29 | Padres |
| 11-31 | at Cubs |
| 12 | Royals |
| 13 | at Giants |
| 14 | Mariners |
| 17 | Giants |
| 18 | at Royals |
| 19 | Brewers |
| 26 | Angels |

### AUGUST
| | |
|---|---|
| 1-21 | Royals |
| 2-22 | at Giants |
| 3-23 | Mariners |
| 5-15 | Angels |

## (continued)
| | |
|---|---|
| 6 | Giants |
| 7 | at Royals |
| 8 | Brewers |
| 10-30 | at Brewers |
| 11 | at Athletics |
| 12-27 | Cubs |
| 13 | at Mariners |
| 16-26 | at Padres |
| 17-28 | Athletics |
| 18 | Padres |
| 20 | at Cubs |
| 25 | at Angels |

## ROYALS
### JUNE
| | |
|---|---|
| 22 | at Rangers |
| 23 | Cubs |
| 24 | at Athletics |
| 25 | Padres |
| 27 | at Mariners |
| 28 | Rangers |
| 29 | at Cubs |
| 30 | Brewers |

### JULY
| | |
|---|---|
| 2-22 | Giants |
| 3-23 | Athletics |
| 4-24 | at Padres |
| 5-25 | at Brewers |
| 7-27 | at Angels |
| 8-28 | at Giants |
| 9-29 | Mariners |
| 10 | at Angels |
| 12-18 | Rangers |
| 13 | Cubs |
| 14 | at Athletics |
| 15 | Padres |
| 17 | at Mariners |
| 19 | at Cubs |
| 20 | Brewers |
| 30 | Angels |

### AUGUST
| | |
|---|---|
| 1-21 | at Rangers |
| 2-22 | Cubs |
| 3-23 | at Athletics |
| 4-24 | Padres |
| 6-29 | at Mariners |
| 7 | Rangers |
| 8 | at Cubs |
| 9-28 | Brewers |
| 11 | Giants |
| 12 | Athletics |
| 13 | at Padres |
| 14 | at Brewers |
| 16-27 | Angels |
| 17-26 | at Giants |
| 18 | Mariners |
| 19 | at Angels |

# GULF COAST LEAGUE

## BRAVES
### JUNE
| | |
|---|---|
| 20-27 | at Yankees |
| 21-28 | Yankees |
| 22-30 | Phillies |
| 23-29 | at Phillies |
| 24 | at Tigers |
| 26 | Tigers |

### JULY
| | |
|---|---|
| 1-10-15-24-29 | Tigers |
| 3-8-17-22-31 | at Tigers |
| 4-12-18-25 | Yankees |
| 5-11-19-26 | at Yankees |
| 6-14-20-28 | Phillies |
| 7-13-21-27 | at Phillies |

### AUGUST
| | |
|---|---|
| 1-8-16 | at Yankees |
| 2-9-15 | Yankees |
| 3-11-17 | Phillies |
| 4-10-18 | at Phillies |
| 5-12-20 | at Tigers |
| 7-14-19 | Tigers |

## DODGERS
### JUNE
| | |
|---|---|
| 20-27 | Mets |
| 21-28 | at Mets |
| 22-30 | at Marlins |

## (continued)

| Date | Opponent |
|---|---|
| 23-29 | Marlins |
| 24 | Nationals |
| 26 | at Nationals |
| **JULY** | |
| 1-10-15-24-29 | at Nats |
| 3-8-17-22-31 | Nationals |
| 4-12-19-25 | at Mets |
| 5-11-18-26 | Mets |
| 6-14-20-28 | at Marlins |
| 7-13-21-27 | Marlins |
| **AUGUST** | |
| 1-8-16 | Mets |
| 2-9-15 | at Mets |
| 3-11-17 | at Marlins |
| 4-10-18 | Marlins |
| 5-12-21 | Nationals |
| 7-14-19 | at Nationals |

## MARLINS

| Date | Opponent |
|---|---|
| **JUNE** | |
| 20-27 | Nationals |
| 21-28 | at Nationals |
| 22-29 | Dodgers |
| 23-30 | at Dodgers |
| 24 | Mets |
| 26 | at Mets |
| **JULY** | |
| 1-10-15-24-29 | at Mets |
| 3-8-17-22-31 | Mets |
| 4-11-19-25 | Nationals |
| 5-12-18-26 | at Nationals |
| 6-14-20-28 | Dodgers |
| 7-13-21-27 | at Dodgers |
| **AUGUST** | |
| 1-9-15 | at Nationals |
| 2-8-16 | Nationals |
| 3-11-17 | Dodgers |
| 4-10-18 | at Dodgers |
| 5-12-20 | Mets |
| 7-14-19 | at Mets |

## METS

| Date | Opponent |
|---|---|
| **JUNE** | |
| 20-27 | at Dodgers |
| 21-28 | Dodgers |
| 22-30 | Nationals |
| 23-29 | at Nationals |
| 24 | at Marlins |
| 26 | Marlins |
| **JULY** | |
| 1-10-15-24-29 | Marlins |
| 3-8-17-22-31 | at Marlins |
| 4-12-18-25 | Dodgers |
| 5-11-19-26 | at Dodgers |
| 6-14-20-28 | Nationals |
| 7-13-21-27 | at Nationals |
| **AUGUST** | |
| 1-8-16 | at Dodgers |
| 2-9-15 | Dodgers |
| 3-11-17 | Nationals |
| 4-10-18 | at Nationals |
| 5-12-20 | at Marlins |
| 7-14-19 | Marlins |

## NATIONALS

| Date | Opponent |
|---|---|
| **JUNE** | |
| 20-27 | at Marlins |
| 21-28 | Marlins |
| 22-30 | at Mets |
| 23-29 | Mets |
| 24 | at Dodgers |
| 26 | Dodgers |
| **JULY** | |
| 1-10-15-24-29 | Dodgers |
| 3-8-17-22-31 | at Dodgers |
| 4-12-18-26 | Marlins |
| 5-11-19-25 | at Marlins |
| 6-14-20-28 | at Mets |
| 7-13-21-27 | Mets |
| **AUGUST** | |
| 1-9-16 | Marlins |
| 2-8-15 | at Marlins |
| 3-11-17 | at Mets |
| 4-10-18 | Mets |
| 5-12-20 | at Dodgers |
| 7-14-19 | Dodgers |

## PHILLIES

| Date | Opponent |
|---|---|
| **JUNE** | |
| 20-27 | at Tigers |
| 21-28 | Tigers |
| 22-30 | at Braves |
| 23-29 | Braves |
| 24 | at Yankees |
| 26 | Yankees |
| **JULY** | |
| 1-10-15-24-29 | Yankees |
| 3-8-17-22-31 | at Yankees |
| 4-12-18-26 | Tigers |
| 5-11-19-25 | at Tigers |
| 6-14-20-28 | at Braves |
| 7-13-21-27 | Braves |
| **AUGUST** | |
| 1-9-15 | Tigers |
| 2-8-16 | at Tigers |
| 3-11-17 | at Braves |
| 4-10-18 | Braves |
| 5-12-21 | at Yankees |
| 7-14-19 | Yankees |

## PIRATES

| Date | Opponent |
|---|---|
| **JUNE** | |
| 20-27 | Red Sox |
| 21-28 | at Red Sox |
| 22-30 | Twins |
| 23-29 | at Twins |
| 24 | Reds |
| 26 | at Reds |
| **JULY** | |
| 1-10-17-29-30 | at Reds |
| 3-8-15-22-24 | Reds |
| 4-12-18-26 | at Red Sox |
| 5-11-19-25 | Red Sox |
| 6-14-20-28 | Twins |
| 7-13-21-27 | at Twins |
| **AUGUST** | |
| 1-9-15 | at Red Sox |
| 2-8-16 | Red Sox |
| 3-11-18 | Twins |
| 4-10-17 | at Twins |
| 5-12-21 | Reds |
| 7-14 | at Reds |

## RED SOX

| Date | Opponent |
|---|---|
| **JUNE** | |
| 20-27 | at Pirates |
| 21-28 | Pirates |
| 22-30 | at Reds |
| 23-29 | Reds |
| 24 | at Twins |
| 26 | Twins |
| **JULY** | |
| 1-10-15-24-29 | Twins |
| 3-8-17-22-31 | at Twins |
| 4-12-18-26 | Pirates |
| 5-11-19-25 | at Pirates |
| 6-13-20 | at Reds |
| 7-14-21-27-28 | Reds |
| **AUGUST** | |
| 1-7-14-21 | Twins |
| 2-8-16 | at Pirates |
| 3-4-11-18 | at Reds |
| 5-12-19 | at Twins |
| 9-15 | Pirates |
| 10-17 | Reds |

## REDS

| Date | Opponent |
|---|---|
| **JUNE** | |
| 20-27 | at Twins |
| 21-28 | Twins |
| 22-30 | Red Sox |
| 23-29 | at Red Sox |
| 24 | at Pirates |
| 26 | Pirates |
| **JULY** | |
| 1-17-29-31 | Pirates |
| 3-15-22-24 | at Pirates |
| 4-11-19 | Twins |
| 5-12-18-25-26 | at Twins |
| 6-13-20 | Red Sox |
| 7-14-21-27-28 | at Red Sox |
| **AUGUST** | |
| 1-2-9-15 | Twins |
| 3-4-11-18 | Red Sox |
| 5-12-21 | at Pirates |
| 7-14-19 | Pirates |
| 8-16 | at Twins |
| 10-17 | at Red Sox |

## TIGERS

| Date | Opponent |
|---|---|
| **JUNE** | |
| 20-27 | Phillies |
| 21-28 | at Phillies |
| 22-30 | Yankees |
| 23-29 | at Yankees |
| 24 | Braves |
| 26 | at Braves |
| **JULY** | |
| 1-10-15-24-29 | at Braves |
| 3-8-17-22-31 | Braves |
| 4-12-18-26 | at Phillies |
| 5-11-19-25 | Phillies |
| 6-14-20-28 | Yankees |
| 7-13-21-27 | at Yankees |
| **AUGUST** | |
| 1-9-15 | at Phillies |
| 2-8-16 | Phillies |
| 3-11-17 | Yankees |
| 4-10-18 | at Yankees |
| 5-12-21 | Braves |
| 7-14-19 | at Braves |

## TWINS

| Date | Opponent |
|---|---|
| **JUNE** | |
| 20-27 | Reds |
| 21-28 | at Reds |
| 22-30 | at Pirates |
| 23-29 | Pirates |
| 24 | Red Sox |
| 26 | at Red Sox |
| **JULY** | |
| 1-10-15-24-29 | at Red Sox |
| 3-8-17-22-31 | Red Sox |
| 4-11-19 | at Reds |
| 5-12-18-25-26 | Reds |
| 6-14-20-28 | at Pirates |
| 7-13-21-27 | Pirates |
| **AUGUST** | |
| 1-2-9-15 | at Reds |
| 3-11-18 | at Pirates |
| 4-10-17 | Pirates |
| 5-12-19 | Red Sox |
| 7-14-21 | at Red Sox |
| 8-16 | Reds |

## YANKEES

| Date | Opponent |
|---|---|
| **JUNE** | |
| 20-27 | Braves |
| 21-28 | at Braves |
| 22-30 | at Tigers |
| 23-29 | Tigers |
| 24 | Phillies |
| 26 | at Phillies |
| **JULY** | |
| 1-2-9-15-24-29 | at Phillies |
| 3-8-17-22-31 | Phillies |
| 4-12-18-25 | at Braves |
| 5-11-19-26 | Braves |
| 6-14-20-28 | at Tigers |
| 7-13-21-27 | Tigers |
| **AUGUST** | |
| 1-8-16 | Braves |
| 2-9-15 | at Braves |
| 3-11-17 | at Tigers |
| 4-10-18 | Tigers |
| 5-12-21 | Phillies |
| 7-14-19 | at Phillies |

# INDEPENDENT
## LEAGUES

# INDEPENDENT
## LEAGUES

## ATLANTIC LEAGUE

| NORTH | W | L | PCT | GB |
|---|---|---|---|---|
| *Nashua Pride | 78 | 62 | .557 | — |
| *Long Island Ducks | 67 | 73 | .479 | 11 |
| Newark Bears | 58 | 82 | .414 | 20 |
| Bridgeport Bluefish | 55 | 85 | .393 | 23 |
| **SOUTH** | **W** | **L** | **PCT** | **GB** |
| *Atlantic City Surf | 80 | 60 | .571 | — |
| Camden Riversharks | 79 | 61 | .564 | 1 |
| *Somerset Patriots | 78 | 61 | .561 | 1½ |
| Lancaster Barnstomers | 64 | 76 | .457 | 16 |

**PLAYOFFS: Semifinals**—Nashua defeated Long Island 2-1 and Somerset defeated Atlantic City 2-1 in best-of-three series. **Finals**—Somerset defeated Nashua 3-0 in best-of-five series.

## CAN-AM LEAGUE

| NORTH | W | L | PCT | GB |
|---|---|---|---|---|
| *Quebec Capitales | 59 | 33 | .641 | — |
| North Shore Spirit | 55 | 36 | .604 | 3½ |
| *Brockton Rox | 50 | 42 | .543 | 9 |
| Grays | 33 | 59 | .359 | 26 |
| **SOUTH** | **W** | **L** | **PCT** | **GB** |
| *Worcester Tornadoes | 50 | 42 | .543 | — |
| New Jersey Jackals | 48 | 44 | .522 | 2 |
| *New Haven County Cutters | 46 | 46 | .500 | 4 |
| Elmira Pioneers | 28 | 64 | .304 | 22 |

**PLAYOFFS: Semifinals**—Quebec defeated Brockton 3-0 and Worcester defeated New Haven County 3-1 in best-of-five series. **Finals**—Worcester defeated Quebec 3-0 in best-of-five series.

## CENTRAL LEAGUE

| | W | L | PCT | GB |
|---|---|---|---|---|
| **Fort Worth Cats | 60 | 34 | .638 | — |
| Pensacola Pelicans | 53 | 39 | .576 | 6 |
| Edinburg Roadrunners | 49 | 45 | .521 | 11 |
| San Angelo Colts | 46 | 47 | .495 | 13½ |
| Shreveport Sports | 46 | 48 | .489 | 14 |
| El Paso Diablos | 44 | 50 | .468 | 16 |
| Coastal Bend Aviators | 41 | 53 | .436 | 19 |
| Jackson Senators | 35 | 58 | .376 | 24½ |

**PLAYOFFS: Semifinals**—Fort Worth defeated Pensacola 3-2 and San Angelo defeated Edinburg 3-2 in best-of-five series. **Finals**—Fort Worth defeated San Angelo 3-2 in best-of-five series.

## FRONTIER LEAGUE

| EAST | W | L | PCT | GB |
|---|---|---|---|---|
| Washington Wild Things | 63 | 32 | .663 | — |
| Chillicothe Paints | 53 | 42 | .558 | 10 |
| Florence Freedom | 53 | 42 | .558 | 10 |
| Evansville Otters | 52 | 43 | .547 | 11 |
| Ohio Valley Redcoats | 46 | 49 | .484 | 17 |
| Richmond Roosters | 39 | 56 | .411 | 24 |
| **WEST** | **W** | **L** | **PCT** | **GB** |
| Kalamazoo Kings | 53 | 43 | .552 | — |
| Rockford Riverhawks | 51 | 45 | .531 | 2 |
| Gateway Grizzlies | 48 | 47 | .505 | 4½ |
| River City Rascals | 42 | 51 | .452 | 9½ |
| Windy City Thunderbolts | 39 | 57 | .406 | 14 |
| Mid-Missouri Mavericks | 31 | 63 | .330 | 21 |

**PLAYOFFS: Semifinals**—Kalamazoo defeated Rockford 3-1 and Chillicothe defeated Washington 3-2 in best-of-five series. **Finals**—Kalamazoo defeated Chillicothe 3-2 in best-of-five series.

## GOLDEN LEAGUE

| ARIZONA | W | L | PCT | GB |
|---|---|---|---|---|
| Mesa Miners | 53 | 40 | .570 | — |
| Yuma Scorpions | 47 | 43 | .522 | 4½ |
| Surprise Fighting Falcons | 45 | 45 | .500 | 6½ |
| Samurai Bears | 33 | 57 | .367 | 18½ |
| **CALIFORNIA** | **W** | **L** | **PCT** | **GB** |
| San Diego Surf Dawgs | 55 | 39 | .585 | — |
| Chico Outlaws | 50 | 43 | .538 | 4½ |
| Long Beach Armada | 49 | 43 | .533 | 5 |
| Fullerton Flyers | 34 | 56 | .378 | 19 |

**PLAYOFFS:** San Diego defeated Mesa to win four-team, double elimination tournament.

## NORTHERN LEAGUE

| NORTH | W | L | PCT | GB |
|---|---|---|---|---|
| Fargo-Moorhead RedHawks | 68 | 27 | .716 | — |
| Calgary Vipers | 51 | 44 | .537 | 17 |
| Winnipeg Goldeyes | 47 | 48 | .495 | 21 |
| Edmonton Cracker-Cats | 47 | 48 | .495 | 21 |
| Sioux City Explorers | 44 | 52 | .458 | 24½ |
| Sioux Falls Canaries | 35 | 60 | .368 | 33 |
| **NORTH** | **W** | **L** | **PCT** | **GB** |
| St. Paul Saints | 55 | 40 | .579 | |
| Kansas City T-Bones | 45 | 49 | .479 | |
| Gary SouthShore RailCats | 54 | 42 | .563 | |
| Lincoln Saltdogs | 52 | 44 | .542 | |
| Joliet Jackhammers | 36 | 60 | .375 | |
| Schaumburg Flyers | 38 | 58 | .396 | |

**PLAYOFFS: Semifinals**—Fargo-Moorhead defeated Lincoln 3-1 and Gary defeated St. Paul 3-2 in best-of-five series. **Finals**—Gary defeated Fargo-Moorhead 3-2 in best-of-five series.

# AMERICAN
## ASSOCIATION

**Office Address:** 1415 Hwy. 54 West, Suite 210, Durham, NC 27707.
**Telephone:** (919) 401-8150. **FAX:** (919) 401-8152.
**Website:** www.americanassociationbaseball.com.
**Year Founded:** 2006.

**Commissioner:** Miles Wolff. **President:** Dan Moushon. **Administrative Assistant:** Jason Deans. **Director of Umpires:** Kevin Winn.
**Division Structure: North**—Lincoln, St. Joseph, St. Paul, Sioux City, Sioux Falls. **South**—Coastal Bend, El Paso, Fort Worth, Pensacola, Shreveport.
**Regular Season:** 96 games (split schedule). **2006 Opening Date:** May 11. **Closing Date:** Aug. 26.
**All-Star Game:** July 18 at El Paso (American Association vs. Can-Am League).
**Playoff Format:** First-half division winners and second-half division winners in best-of-5 series. Winners meet in best-of-5 series for league championship.
**Roster Limit:** 22. **Player Eligibility Rule:** Minimum of five first-year players, maximum of four veterans with at least four years of professional experience.
**Brand of Baseball:** Rawlings.
**Statistician:** SportsTicker, ESPN Plaza—Building B, Bristol, CT 06010.

## STADIUM INFORMATION

| Club | Stadium | Opened | LF | CF | RF | Capacity | 2005 Att. |
|------|---------|--------|----|----|----|----------|-----------|
| *Coastal Bend | Fairgrounds Field | 2003 | 330 | 400 | 330 | 4,000 | 79,826 |
| *El Paso | Cohen Stadium | 1990 | 340 | 410 | 340 | 9,725 | 190,429 |
| *Fort Worth | LaGrave Field | 2002 | 325 | 400 | 335 | 5,100 | 173,946 |
| #Lincoln | Haymarket Park | 2001 | 335 | 395 | 325 | 4,500 | 207,744 |
| *Pensacola | Pelican Park | 1991 | 320 | 390 | 320 | 2,500 | 70,855 |
| St. Joseph | Phil Welch Stadium | 1939 | 320 | 420 | 320 | 3,600 | N/A |
| #St. Paul | Midway Stadium | 1982 | 320 | 400 | 320 | 6,069 | 283,886 |
| *Shreveport | Fair Grounds Field | 1986 | 330 | 400 | 330 | 4,500 | 55,207 |
| #Sioux City | Lewis and Clark Park | 1993 | 330 | 400 | 330 | 3,630 | 113,590 |
| #Sioux Falls | Sioux Falls Stadium | 1964 | 312 | 410 | 312 | 4,029 | 118,611 |

*Member of Central League in 2005
#Member of Northern League in 2005

# COASTAL BEND
## AVIATORS

**Office Address:** 1151 E. Main Ave., Robstown, TX 78380.
**Telephone:** (361) 387-8585. **FAX:** (361) 387-3535.
**E-Mail Address:** teaminfo@aviators.com. **Website:** www.aviatorsbaseball.com.

**General Manager:** Rudy Rodriguez. **Senior Sales Executive:** Javier Limon. **Food/Beverage Manager:** Evelyn Charles. **Director, Community Relations:** Melissa Munoz. **Director, Operations:** Esteban Lopez. **Account Executive:** Christy Montano. **Office Manager:** Brandi Ramon. **Bookkeeper:** Lalita Hughes.
**Director, Baseball Operations:** Chad Treadway. **Manager:** John Harris.

## GAME INFORMATION

**Radio Announcer:** Unavailable. **No. of Games Broadcast:** Home-48, Away-48. **Flagship Station:** ESPN 1230-AM.
**Stadium Name:** Fairgrounds Field. **Location:** 12 miles west of downtown Corpus Christi at junction of Highway 77 and Highway 44. **Standard Game Times:** 7:05 p.m., Sun. 6:05.
**Visiting Club Hotel:** Best Western Marina Grand, 300 North Shore Lane, Corpus Christi, TX 78401.

# EL PASO
## DIABLOS

**Office Address:** 9700 Gateway North Blvd., El Paso, Texas, 79924.
**Telephone:** (915) 755-2000. **FAX:** (915) 757-0671.
**E-mail Address:** info@diablos.com. **Website:** www.diablos.com.

**General Manager:** Jeff Stewart. **Corporate Marketing Manager:** Bernie Ricono. **Manager, Marketing/Promotions:**

Kelly Rogers. **Manager, Communications:** Valerie Venegas. **Group/Ticket Sales:** Joe Scacco, Jeff Hoover. **Controller:** Angela Truett. **Maintenance Manager:** Richard Bellah. **General Manager, Rocky Mountain Concessions:** Neftali Torres.

**Manager:** Mike Marshall.

### GAME INFORMATION

**Radio Announcers:** Unavailable. **No. of Games Broadcast:** Home-48, Away-48; Home-48 (Spanish). **Flagship Stations:** KHEY 1380-AM.

**Stadium Name:** Cohen Stadium. **Location:** I-10 to U.S. 54 (Patriot Freeway), east to Diana exit to Gateway North Boulevard. **Standard Game Time:** 7:05 p.m.

**Visiting Club Hotel:** Best Western Airport Inn, 7144 Gateway Blvd. E., El Paso, TX 79915. Telephone: (915) 779-7700.

# FORT WORTH
## CATS

**Office Address:** 301 NE Sixth St., Fort Worth, TX 76106.
**Telephone:** (817) 226-2287. **FAX:** (817) 534-4620.
**E-Mail Address:** info@fwcats.com. **Website:** www.fwcats.com.

**Operated By:** Texas Independent Baseball.
**Principal Owner:** Carl Bell.
**President, Chief Operating Officer:** John Dittrich. **Senior Vice President, General Manager:** Monty Clegg. **Senior VP, Business Development:** Mark Presswood. **VP, Assistant GM:** John Bilbow. **VP, Special Projects:** Maury Wills. **Director, Communications:** David Hatchett. **Assistant Communications Director/Website:** Emil Moffatt. **Business Manager:** Lois Dittrich. **Group Sales Manager:** Joby Raymond. **Corporate Sales Manager:** Mike Forrester. **VP, Stadium Manager:** Dick Smith. **Merchandise Manager:** Kristie Voss. **Interns:** Caroline James, Ross Utley, DeAnna Beseda, Brittney Smith.

**Director, Player Development:** Barry Moss. **Manager:** Stan Hough. **Coach:** Wayne Terwilliger. **Pitching Coach:** Dan Smith. **Trainer:** Alan Reid.

### GAME INFORMATION

**Radio Announcers:** David Hatchett, Emil Moffatt. **No. of Games Broadcast:** Home-48, Away-48. **Flagship Station:** KHFX 1460-AM.

**Stadium Name:** LaGrave Field. **Location:** From 1-30, take 1-35 North to North Side Drive exit, left (west) off exit to Main Street, left (south) on Main, left (east) onto NE Sixth Street. **Standard Game Times:** 7:05 p.m.; Sun. 1:05.

**Visiting Club Hotel:** Unavailable.

# LINCOLN
## SALTDOGS

**Office Address:** 403 Line Dr., Suite A, Lincoln, NE 68508.
**Telephone:** (402) 474-2255. **FAX:** (402) 474-2254.
**E-Mail Address:** info@saltdogs.com. **Website:** www.saltdogs.com.

**Owner:** Jim Abel. **President:** Charlie Meyer.
**Vice President, General Manager:** Tim Utrup. **Assistant GM/Director, Marketing:** Bret Beer. **Director, Merchandising/Promotions:** Anne Duchek. **Director, Ticketing:** Tim Petersen. **Director, Stadium Operations:** Ryan Lockhart. **Assistant Director, Stadium Operations:** Josh Jorgensen. **Ticket Account Executive:** Nick Donahue. **Office Manager:** Jeanette Eagleton. **Athletic Turf Manager:** Josh Klute.

**Manager:** Tim Johnson. **Coaches:** Mike Workman, Jim Allen. **Trainers:** Corey Courtney, Joel Jasa.

### GAME INFORMATION

**Radio Announcers:** Unavailable. **No. of Games Broadcast:** Home-48, Away-48. **Flagship Station:** KFOR 1240-AM.

**Stadium Name:** Haymarket Park. **Location:** I-80 to Cornhusker Highway West, left on First Street, right on Sun Valley Boulevard, left on Line Drive. **Standard Game Times:** 7:05 p.m., Sun. 5:05.

**Visiting Club Hotel:** Holiday Inn Downtown, 141 N. Ninth St., Lincoln, NE 68508. Telephone: (402) 475-4011.

# PENSACOLA
## PELICANS

**Office Address:** 913 Gulf Breeze Pkwy., Suite 36, Gulf Breeze, FL 32561.
**Telephone:** (850) 934-8444. **FAX:** (850) 934-8744.

**E-Mail Address**: info@pensacolapelicans.com. **Website**: www.pensacolapelicans.com.

**Owners**: Quint Studer, Rishy Studer. **President**: Rishy Studer. **Chief Executive Officer**: Quint Studer.
**General Manager**: George Stavrenos. **Senior Sales Executive**: Talmadge Nunnari. **Sales Executive**: Mike Coziahr.
**Director, Media Relations**: Jason Libbert. **Manager, Front Office/Ticket Operations**: Casey Flanagan. **Director, Community Relations**: Jessica Morris. **Director, Promotions/Merchandise**: Michael Ann Riley. **Director, Stadium Operations**: Sebastian Pantano.
**Director, Player Procurement**: James Gamble. **Manager**: Unavailable.

### GAME INFORMATION
**Radio Announcer**: Jay Burnham. **No. of Games Broadcast**: Home-48, Away-48. **Flagship Station**: WNRP 1620-AM.
**Stadium Name**: Pelican Park. **Location**: On the campus of University of West Florida. From I-10 West, north on Davis Highway (SR 291) to exit 13, left on University Parkway, right on Campus Drive, stadium 1/2 mile on right. **Standard Game Times**: 6:35 p.m., Sat./Sun. 6:05.

# ST. JOSEPH
## BLACKSNAKES

**Office Address**: 520 Francis St., St. Joseph, MO 64501.
**Telephone**: (816) 279-6777. **FAX**: (816) 279-9025.
**Website**: www.stjoebaseball.com.

**Principal Owner**: Van Schley. **President**: Mark Schuster.
**General Manager**: Duane Miller. **Head, Baseball Operations**: Chris Carminucci. **Account Executive**: Eric McGrath.
**Manager**: Chris Carminucci. **Coach**: Mark Nussbeck.

### GAME INFORMATION
**Stadium Name**: Phil Welch Stadium. **Location**: From I-29, take Highway 36 West exit to 28th Street exit, left onto 28th Street, stadium 1½ miles on right. **Standard Game Times**: Unavailable.

# ST. PAUL
## SAINTS

**Office Address**: 1771 Energy Park Dr., St. Paul, MN 55108.
**Telephone**: (651) 644-3517. **FAX**: (651) 644-1627.
**E-Mail Address**: funsgood@saintsbaseball.com. **Website**: www.saintsbaseball.com.

**Operated By**: St. Paul Saints Baseball Club, Inc.
**Principal Owners**: Marv Goldklang, Mike Veeck, Bill Murray.
**Chairman**: Marv Goldklang. **President**: Mike Veeck.
**Executive Vice President, General Manager**: Derek Sharrer. **VP, Business Development**: Tom Whaley. **Assistant GM**: Eben Yager. **Community Relations/Customer Service Director**: Annie Huidekoper. **Sales/Marketing Director**: Dan Lehv. **Promotions Director**: Jack Weatherman. **Director, Ticket Sales**: Matt Bomberg. **Ticket Sales Manager**: Matt Teske. **Ticket Manager/IT Coordinator**: Ryan Wiese. **Special Events Manager**: Amy Heimer. **Media Relations Director**: Dave Wright. **Promotions Director**: Mike Nachreiner. **Group Sales Director**: Jeremy Loosbrock. **Merchandise Director**: Amy Alt. **Concessions Director**: Curtis Nachtsheim. **Controller**: Wayne Engel. **Business Manager**: Leesa Anderson. **Interns**: Jill Young, Karen Turok, Laura Yager, Will Esser, Amy Dox, Angie Stein, Shedrick Taylor. **Stadium Operations Director**: Bob Klepperich. **Groundskeeper**: Connie Rudolph.
**Manager**: George Tsamis. **Coaches**: Jason Verdugo, Jackie Hernandez, Lamarr Rogers, T.J. Wiesner. **Trainer**: Justin Plecko.

### GAME INFORMATION
**Radio Announcer**: Kris Atteberry. **No. of Games Broadcast**: Home-48, Away-48. **Flagship Station**: Unavailable.
**Stadium Name**: Midway Stadium. **Location**: From I-94, take Snelling Avenue North exit, west onto Energy Park Drive. **Standard Game Times**: 7:05 p.m., Sun. 1:05/4:05.
**Visiting Club Hotel**: AmericInn of Mounds View, 1100 Highway 10, Mounds View, MN 55112. Telephone: (763) 786-2000.

# SHREVEPORT
## SPORTS

**Office Address**: 2901 Pershing Blvd, Shreveport, LA 71109.
**Telephone**: (318) 636-5555. **FAX**: (318) 636-5670.
**Website**: www.shreveportsports.com.

**Owners:** Gary Elliston, Carl Bell.
**General Manager:** Terry Sipes. **Assistant GM/Market Development:** Jerry Bagwell. **Director, Stadium/Ticket Operations:** George Reynolds. **Director, Community/Media Relations:** Dave Nitz.
**Manager:** Bob Flori. **Coaches:** Angel Aragon, Eddie Gerald.

## GAME INFORMATION

**Radio Announcer:** Dave Nitz. **No. of Games Broadcast:** Home-48, Away-48. **Flagship Station:** KRMD 1340-AM.
**Stadium Name:** Fair Grounds Field. **Location:** Hearne Avenue (U.S. 171) exit off I-20 at Louisiana State Fairgrounds.
**Standard Game Times:** 7:05 p.m.; Sun. 2:05 (May-June), 6:05 (July-Aug.).
**Visiting Club Hotel:** Unavailable.

# SIOUX CITY
## EXPLORERS

**Office Address:** 3400 Line Dr., Sioux City, IA 51106.
**Telephone:** (712) 277-9467. **FAX:** (712) 277-9406.
**E-Mail Address:** siouxcityxs@yahoo.com. **Website:** www.xsbaseball.com.

**Operated by:** Sioux City Explorers Baseball Club, LLC.
**General Manager:** Shane Tritz. **Assistant GM:** Luke Nielsen. **Assistant GM, Sales/Marketing:** Mike Gorsett.
**Director, Broadcasting:** Chris Varney. **Office Manager:** Karla Hertz.
**Manager:** Ed Nottle.

## GAME INFORMATION

**Radio Announcer:** Chris Varney. **No. of Games Broadcast:** Home-48, Away-48. **Flagship Station:** Unavailable.
**Stadium Name:** Lewis and Clark Park. **Location:** I-29 to Singing Hills Blvd. North, right on Line Drive. **Standard Game Times:** 7:05 p.m., Sun. 5:05.
**Visiting Club Hotel:** Best Western City Centre, 130 Nebraska St., Sioux City, IA 51106. Telephone: (712) 277-1550.

# SIOUX FALLS
## CANARIES

**Office Address:** 1001 N. West Ave., Sioux Falls, SD 57104.
**Telephone:** (605) 333-0179. **FAX:** (605) 333-0139.
**E-Mail Address:** info@canariesbaseball.com. **Website:** www.canariesbaseball.com.

**Operated by:** Sioux Falls Canaries Professional Baseball Club, LLC.
**Principal Owner, Chairman:** Ben Zuraw. **President:** John Kuhn.
**General Manager:** Matt Hansen. **Assistant GM/Groundskeeper:** Larry McKenney. **Assistant GM/Director, Corporate Sales:** Ned Gavlick. **VP, Group/Ticket Sales:** Chris Schwab. **Director, Media/Public Relations:** Matt Meola. **Client Relations, Sales/Marketing:** Tamara Nelson. **Director, Fun:** Dan Christopherson.
**Manager:** Mike Pinto. **Coaches:** Bart Zeller, Rich Hyde. **Trainer:** Curt Jackson.

## GAME INFORMATION

**Radio Announcer:** Matt Meola. **No. of Games Broadcast:** Home-48, Away-48. **Flagship Station:** KWSN 1230-AM.
**Stadium Name:** Sioux Falls Stadium. **Location:** I-29 to Russell Street, south one mile, right on West Avenue.
**Standard Game Times:** 7:05 p.m., Sun. 2:05.
**Visiting Club Hotel:** Unavailable.

# ATLANTIC
## LEAGUE

**Mailing Address:** 401 N. Delaware Ave., Camden, NJ 08102.
**Telephone:** (856) 541-9400. **FAX:** (856) 541-9410.
**E-Mail Address:** atllge@aol.com. **Website:** www.atlanticleague.com.
**Year Founded:** 1998.

**Chief Executive Officer/Founder:** Frank Boulton.
**Executive Director:** Joe Klein.
**Vice President:** Mickey Herbert (Bridgeport).
**Directors:** Mark Berson (Newark), Frank Boulton (Long Island), Mary Jane Foster (Bridgeport), Steve Kalafer (Somerset), Peter Kirk (Camden/Lancaster), Tony Rosenthal (Atlantic City).
**League Operations Latin Coordinator:** Ellie Rodriguez.
**League Office Administration:** Patty MacLuckie.
**Division Structure: North**—Bridgeport, Lancaster, Long Island, Road Warriors. **South**—Atlantic City, Camden, Newark, Somerset.
**Regular Season:** 126 games (split schedule). **2006 Opening Date:** April 28. **Closing Date:** Sept. 17.
**All-Star Game:** July 12 at Bridgeport.
**Playoff Format:** First-half division winners meet second-half winners in best-of-3 series. Winners meet in best-of-5 final for league championship.
**Roster Limit:** 25. **Eligibility Rule:** No restrictions.
**Brand of Baseball:** Rawlings.
**Statistician:** SportsTicker, ESPN Plaza—Building B, Bristol, CT 06010.

## STADIUM INFORMATION

| Club | Stadium | Opened | LF | CF | RF | Capacity | 2005 Att. |
|------|---------|--------|----|----|-----|----------|-----------|
| Atlantic City | The Sandcastle | 1998 | 307 | 408 | 307 | 6,000 | 129,158 |
| Bridgeport | The Ballpark at Harbor Yard | 1998 | 325 | 405 | 325 | 5,300 | 197,337 |
| Camden | Campbell's Field | 2001 | 325 | 405 | 325 | 6,425 | 266,794 |
| Lancaster | Clipper Magazine Stadium | 2005 | 372 | 400 | 300 | 6,000 | 378,310 |
| Long Island | Citibank Park | 2000 | 325 | 400 | 325 | 6,002 | 429,218 |
| Newark | Bears & Eagles Riverfront Stadium | 1999 | 302 | 394 | 323 | 6,200 | 178,818 |
| *Road Warriors | | | | | | | |
| Somerset | Commerce Bank Ballpark | 1999 | 317 | 402 | 315 | 6,100 | 365,146 |

*League's former Nashua franchise moved to Can-Am League; eighth franchise will operate at travel team in 2006.

# ATLANTIC CITY
## SURF

**Office Address:** 545 N. Albany Ave., Atlantic City, NJ 08401.
**Telephone:** (609) 344-8873. **FAX:** (609) 344-7010.
**E-Mail Address:** surf@acsurf.com. **Website:** www.acsurf.com.

**Operated by:** Atlantic City Surf Professional Baseball LLC. **President:** Mark Schuster.
**General Manager:** Mario Perrucci. **Director, Ticket Sales:** John Kiphorn. **Assistant Director, Ticket Sales:** Frank Dougherty. **Director, Media Relations/Marketing:** Chuck Betson. **Director, Advertising:** Greg Lynch. **Director, Merchandising/Stadium Operations:** Danny Petrazzolo. **Director, Promotions/Community Relations:** Carl Grider. **Director, Finance:** Tom Clark.
**Manager/Director, Baseball Operations:** Jeff Ball. **Coaches:** Unavailable.

### GAME INFORMATION

**Radio Announcer:** Unavailable. **No. of Games Broadcast:** Home-72, Away-54. **Flagship Station:** WUSS 1490-AM.
**PA Announcer:** Unavailable. **Official Scorer:** Jeff Bohrer.
**Stadium Name:** The Sandcastle. **Location:** Atlantic City Expressway to exit 2, east on Routes 40/322. **Standard Game Times:** 6:35 p.m.; Sun. 1:35, (May-June, Sept.) 5:05.
**Visiting Club Hotel:** Fairfield Inn, 405 White Horse Pike, Absecon, NJ. Telephone: (609) 646-5000.

# BRIDGEPORT
## BLUEFISH

**Office Address:** 500 Main St., Bridgeport, CT 06604.
**Telephone:** (203) 345-4800. **FAX:** (203) 345-4830.
**Website:** www.bridgeportbluefish.com.

**Operated by:** Get Hooked, LLC. **Management Board:** Michael Kramer, Jack McGregor, Thomas D'Addario, Thomas Kushner, Thomas Schneider, Mary-Jane Foster.
**Chairmen:** Michael Kramer, Jack McGregor. **Chief Executive Officer:** Mary-Jane Foster.
**General Manager:** Charlie Dowd. **Assistant GM:** John Cunningham. **Sales Manager:** Ralph Gangi. **Senior Account Executive:** John Harris. **Account Executives:** Tammi Lynn Morse, Dave Usdan. **Promotions Manager:** Shannon Walsh. **Director, Marketing:** Kathy Geiling. **Box Office:** Jacqui Lopez. **Group Sales:** Sue Livingston, Judie Fixler. **Assistant, Finance:** Barbara Prato. **Administration:** Nicole Winn. **Head Groundskeeper:** Jon Festa.
**Manager:** David LaPoint. **Coach:** Terry McGriff. **Pitching Coach:** Brian Warren. **Trainer:** Unavailable.

### GAME INFORMATION

**Radio Announcer:** Jeff Holtz. **No. of Games Broadcast:** Unavailable. **Flagship Station:** WVOF 88.5-FM.
**PA Announcer:** Bill Jensen. **Official Scorer:** Joel Pleban.
**Stadium Name:** The Ballpark at Harbor Yard. **Location:** I-95 to exit 27, Route 8/25 to exit 1. **Standard Game Times:** 7:05 p.m., Sun. 1:35.
**Visiting Club Hotel:** Holiday Inn Bridgeport, 1070 Main St., Bridgeport, CT 06604. Telephone: (203) 334-1234.

# CAMDEN
## RIVERSHARKS

**Office Address:** 401 N. Delaware Ave., Camden, NJ 08102.
**Telephone:** (856) 963-2600. **FAX:** (856) 963-8534.
**E-Mail Address:** riversharks@riversharks.com. **Website:** www.riversharks.com.

**Operated by:** BKK Sports, LLC.
**Principal Owners:** Frank Boulton, Steve Kalafer, Peter Kirk. **President:** Jon Danos. **Vice President:** Brad Simms.
**General Manager:** Adam Lorber. **Assistant GM:** Kristen Daffin. **Director, Ticket Services:** Randy Newsome. **Director, Group Events:** Robert Nehring. **Director, Operations:** Matthew Tirrell. **Community Partnerships Manager:** Natalie Filomeno. **Corporate Partnerships Managers:** Andy Shultz, Joel Seiden, Brad Strauss, Brian Randle. **Group Account Managers:** Ryan Arnold, Marissa Perri, Michelle Metzgar. **Finance Manager:** Jenny Hitzelberger. **Director, Baseball Operations:** Patty MacLuckie. **Receptionist:** Dolores Rozier. **Groundskeeper:** Unavailable.
**Manager:** Wayne Krenchicki. **Coach:** Brad Strauss. **Pitching Coach:** Steve Foucault. **Trainer:** Unavailable.

### GAME INFORMATION

**Radio:** Unavailable.
**PA Announcer:** Kevin Casey. **Official Scorer:** Dick Shute.
**Stadium Name:** Campbell's Field. **Location:** From Philadelphia, right on Sixth Street, right after Ben Franklin Bridge

toll booth, right on Cooper Street until it ends at Delaware Ave. From Camden, I-676 to exit 5B, follow signs to field. **Standard Game Times:** 7:05 p.m., Sun. 1:05.

**Visiting Club Hotel:** Holiday Inn, Route 70 and Sayer Avenue, Cherry Hill, NJ 08002. Telephone. (856) 663-5300.

# LANCASTER
## BARNSTORMERS

**Office Address:** 650 North Prince St., Lancaster, PA 17603.
**Telephone:** (717) 509-4487. **FAX:** (717) 509-4456.
**E-Mail Address:** info@lancasterbarnstormers.com. **Website:** www.lancasterbarnstormers.com.

**Operated by:** Keystone Baseball, LLC.
**Principal Owners:** Peter Kirk, Keystone Baseball, LLC. **President:** Jon Danos.
**Senior Vice President:** Brad Sims. **Executive VP, Baseball Operations:** Keith Lupton. **General Manager:** Joe Pinto. **Assistant GM:** Gina Stepoulos. **Director, Public Affairs:** Andy Frankel. **Directors, Corporate Partnerships:** Vince Bulik, Jeff Bertoni, Pete Tsirigotis. **Corporate Partnerships Representative:** Dave Cochran. **Group Event Managers:** Shawn Gelnett, Meagan Hample. **Group Event Coordinators:** Scott Stephen, Mike Minney. **Ticket Operations Manager:** Joan Dubord. **Marketing Manager:** Jason Jesberger. **Customer Service Specialist:** Kaye Willis. **Executive Assistant:** Kim Draude. **Bookkeeper:** Jackie Zanghi. **Receptionist:** Amanda Kowalski. **Controller:** Emily Merrill. **Director, Stadium Operations:** Don Pryer. **Food Service Manager, Centerplate:** Josh Leatherman. **Merchandise Manager, Centerplate:** John Farrell.
**Manager:** Tom Herr. **Coach:** Frank Klebe. **Pitching Coach:** Rick Wise. **Trainer:** Mark Francis.

### GAME INFORMATION
**Radio Announcer:** Dave Collins. **No. of Games Broadcast:** Home-72, Away-54. **Flagship Station:** WLPA 1490-AM.
**PA Announcer:** John Witwer. **Official Scorer:** Joel Schreiner.
**Stadium Name:** Clipper Magazine Stadium. **Location:** From Route 30, take Fruitville Pike or Harrisburg Pike toward downtown Lancaster, stadium at intersection of Prince Street and Harrisburg Pike. **Standard Game Times:** 7:05 p.m., Sun. 1:35.
**Visiting Club Hotel:** Westfield Inn and Suites, 2929 Hempland Road, Lancaster, PA 17601. Telephone: (800) 547-1395.

# LONG ISLAND
## DUCKS

**Mailing Address:** 3 Court House Dr., Central Islip, NY 11722.
**Telephone:** (631) 940-3825. **FAX:** (631) 940-3800.
**E-Mail Address:** info@liducks.com. **Website:** www.liducks.com.

**Operated by:** Long Island Ducks Professional Baseball, LLC.
**Principal Owner, Chief Executive Officer:** Frank Boulton. **Owner/Senior Vice President, Baseball Operations:** Bud Harrelson.
**General Manager:** Michael Hirsch. **Assistant GMs:** Michael Pfaff, Alex Scanella. **Business Manager:** Gerry Anderson. **Manager, Ticket Sales:** Ben Harper. **Manager, Media Relations:** Jeff Esposito. **Manager, Group Sales:** Bill Harney. **Manager, Operations:** Russ Blatt. **Manager, Promotions:** Morgan Tranquist. **Manager, Community Relations:** Paul DeGrocco. **Manager, Merchandise:** Kate DeMio. **Manager, Clubhouse Operations:** Jimmy Russell. **Assistant Manager, Facilities:** Chris Gee. **Assistant Manager, Tickets:** Brad Kallman. **Coordinator, Administration:** Stephanie Valentinetti.
**Manager:** Don McCormack. **Coach:** Bud Harrelson. **Trainers:** Tony Amin, Adam Lewis, Dorothy Pitchford.

### GAME INFORMATION
**Radio Announcers:** Chris King, David Weiss. **No. of Games Broadcast:** 66. **Flagship Station:** WLIE 540-AM.
**PA Announcer:** Unavailable. **Official Scorers:** Joe Donnelly, Red Foley.
**Stadium Name:** Citibank Park. **Location:** Southern State Parkway east to Carleton Avenue North (exit 43 A), right onto Courthouse Drive, stadium behind federal courthouse complex. **Standard Game Times:** 7:05 p.m., Sun. 1:35.
**Visiting Club Hotels:** Holiday Inn Express-Stony Brook, 3131 Nesconset Hwy., Stony Brook, NY 11720. Telephone: (631) 471-8000. Holiday Inn Express-Hauppauge, 2050 Express Dr. South, Hauppauge, NY 11788. Telephone: (631) 348-1400.

# NEWARK
## BEARS

**Office Address:** 450 Broad St., Newark, NJ 07102.
**Telephone:** (973) 848-1000. **FAX:** (973) 621-0095.
**Website:** www.newarkbears.com.

**Operated by:** Newark Bears Professional Baseball Club, Inc.
**Owners:** Marc Berson, Steven Kalafer.
**General Manager:** John Brandt. **Assistant GMs:** Jim Cerny, Mark Gallego. **Controller:** Ken Bossart. **Director, Operations:** Dave Falco. **Ticket Sales Managers:** Mike Luteran, Robert Riccardi. **Manager, Fan Development:** Fred Ewig. **Director, Media Relations:** Joe Montefusco. **Head Groundskeeper:** Carlos Arocho.
**Manager:** Chris Jones. **Coach:** Victor Torres. **Pitching Coach:** Pete Filson.

### GAME INFORMATION

**Radio Announcer:** Jim Cerny. **No. of Games Broadcast:** Home-72, Away-54. **Flagship Station:** Unavailable.
**PA Announcer:** Steve Boland. **Official Scorers:** Kim DeRitter, Jim Hague.
**Stadium Name:** Bears & Eagles Riverfront Stadium. **Location:** Garden State Parkway North/South to exit 145 (280 East), to exit 15; New Jersey Turnpike North/South to 280 West, to exit 15A. **Standard Game Times:** 7:05 p.m., Sat. 6:05, Sun. 1:35.
**Visiting Club Hotel:** Wellesley Inn & Suites, 265 Route 3 East, Clifton, NJ 07014. Telephone: (973) 778-6500.

# ROAD WARRIORS

The franchise will operate as a travel team in 2006 and will be managed through the league office in Camden.
**Manager:** Unavailable. **Coaches:** Unavailable.

# SOMERSET
## PATRIOTS

**Office Address:** One Patriots Park, Bridgewater, NJ 08807.
**Telephone:** (908) 252-0700. **FAX:** (908) 252-0776.
**Website:** www.somersetpatriots.com.

**Operated by:** Somerset Patriots Baseball Club, LLC.
**Principal Owners:** Steven Kalafer, Jack Cust, Byron Brisby, Don Miller. **Chairman:** Steven Kalafer.
**President, General Manager:** Patrick McVerry. **Vice President, Ticketing:** Brendan Fairfield. **VP, Marketing:** Dave Marek. **VP, New Business Development:** Chris Bryan. **Controller:** Wayne Seguin. **Head Groundskeeper:** Ray Cipperly. **Director, Public Relations:** Marc Russinoff. **Assistant GM:** Rob Lukachyk. **Account Representatives:** John Gibson, Dan Neville. **Manager, Community Relations:** Matt Rothenberg. **Director, Ticket Sales:** Bryan Iwicki. **Group Sales:** Matthew Kopas, Tim Ur. **Executive Assistant to GM:** Michele DaCosta. **Accountants:** Stephanie Diez, Wendy Miervaldis. **Receptionist:** Lorraine Ott. **GM, Centerplate:** Mike McDermott. **Assistant Groundskeeper:** Joe Zavodnick.
**Director, Player Procurement:** Unavailable. **Manager:** Sparky Lyle. **Pitching Coach:** Unavailable. **Trainer:** Ryan McMahon.

### GAME INFORMATION

**Radio Announcer:** Brian Bender. **No. of Games Broadcast:** Home-72, Away-54. **Flagship Station:** WCTC 1450-AM.
**PA Announcer:** Paul Spychala. **Official Scorer:** John Nolan.
**Stadium Name:** Commerce Bank Ballpark. **Location:** Route 287 North to exit 13B/Route 287 South to exit 13 (Somerville Route 28 West); follow signs to ballpark. **Standard Game Times:** 7:05 p.m., Sun. 1:35.
**Visiting Club Hotel:** Somerset Ramada, 60 Cottontail Lane, Somerset, NJ 08873. Telephone: (732) 560-9880.

# CAN-AM
## LEAGUE

**Office Address:** 1415 Hwy. 54 West, Suite 210, Durham, NC 27707.
**Telephone:** (919) 401-8150. **FAX:** (919) 401-8152.
**Website:** www.canamleague.com.
**Year Founded:** 2005.

**Commissioner:** Miles Wolff. **President:** Dan Moushon. **Administrative Assistant:** Jason Deans. **Director, Umpires:** Kevin Winn.
**Division Structure:** None.
**Regular Season:** 92 games (split schedule). **2006 Opening Date:** May 23. **Closing Date:** Sept. 4.
**All-Star Game:** July 18 at El Paso, Texas (Can-Am League vs. American Association).
**Playoff Format:** First- and second-half winners meet two teams with best overall records in best-of-5 series. Winners meet in best-of-5 series for league championship.
**Roster Limit:** 22. **Eligibility Rule:** Minimum of five first-year players; maximum of four veterans with at least four years of professional experience.
**Brand of Baseball:** Rawlings.
**Statistician:** SportsTicker, ESPN Plaza-Building B, Bristol, CT 06010.

## STADIUM INFORMATION

| Club | Stadium | Opened | Dimensions LF | CF | RF | Capacity | 2005 Att. |
|------|---------|--------|------|------|------|----------|-----------|
| Brockton | Campanelli Stadium | 2002 | 340 | 404 | 320 | 4,750 | 203,094 |
| # Nashua | Holman Stadium | 1937 | 307 | 401 | 315 | 4,375 | 87,645 |
| New Haven County | Yale Field | 1927 | 330 | 405 | 315 | 5,000 | 67,607 |
| New Jersey | Yogi Berra Stadium | 1998 | 308 | 398 | 308 | 3,784 | 122,092 |
| North Shore | Fraser Field | 1940 | 320 | 400 | 320 | 3,804 | 110,663 |
| Quebec | Stade Municipal de Quebec | 1938 | 315 | 385 | 315 | 4,800 | 156,663 |
| * Sussex | Skylands Park | 1994 | 330 | 392 | 330 | 4,300 | N/A |
| Worcester | Hanover Insurance Park at Fitton Field | 1905 | 361 | 417 | 307 | 3,000 | 124,745 |

# Franchise operated as Grays in 2005
*Franchise operated in Elmira in 2005

# BROCKTON
ROX

**Office Address:** 1 Lexington Ave, Brockton, MA 02301.
**Telephone:** (508) 559-7000. **FAX:** (508) 587-2802.
**Website:** www.brocktonrox.com.

**Principal Owner:** Van Schley. **President:** Jim Lucas.
**General Manager:** Andy Crossley. **Assistant GM:** Brian Voelkel. **Director, Business Operations:** Mary Scarlett. **Director, Promotions:** Bailey Frye. **Director, Community Relations/Merchandise:** Andrea Thrubis. **Director, Special Events:** Danni Barrall. **Media Relations:** Bill Chuck. **Food/Beverage:** Michael Canina, Steve Bowker. **Box Office Manager:** Cory Englehardt. **Ticket Sales Representatives:** Aaron Seifer, Matt Strasburg, Rachel Sherman. **Corporate Sales:** Gary MacKinnon, Ryan Kane. **Receptionist:** Me'Shay Hurt.
**Manager:** Chris Miyake. **Coach:** Ryan Kane. **Pitching Coach:** Shad Williams. **Trainer:** Unavailable.

## GAME INFORMATION
**Radio Announcer:** Unavailable. **No. of Games Broadcast:** Home-46, Away-46. **Flagship Station:** WBET 1460-AM.
**Stadium Name:** Campanelli Stadium. **Directions:** Route 24 North/South to Route 123 east, stadium is two miles on right. **Standard Game Times:** 7:05 p.m.; Sun. (May-June) 1:05, (July-Sept.) 5:05.
**Visiting Club Hotel:** Country Inn & Suites, 50 Christy's Drive, Brockton, MA 02301. Telephone: (508) 559-0099.

# NASHUA
PRIDE

**Office Address:** 67 Amherst St., Nashua, NH 03064.
**Telephone:** (603) 883-2255. **FAX:** (603) 883-0880.
**E-Mail Address:** info@nashuapride.com. **Website:** www.nashuapride.com.

**Operated by:** Nashua Pride Baseball, LLC.
**Principal Owner:** John Stabile.
**General Manager:** Marty Wheeler. **Community Relations Manager:** Anna Turbe. **Merchandising Operations Manager:** Chris Moran. **Media Relations Manager:** Joe Chamas. **Office Manager:** Beverly Taylor.
**Manager:** Butch Hobson. **Coach:** Jay Yennaco.

## GAME INFORMATION
**Radio:** Unavailable.
**PA Announcer:** Ken Kail. **Official Scorer:** Roger Pepin.
**Stadium Name:** Historic Holman Stadium. **Location:** Route 3 to exit 7E (Amherst Street), stadium one mile on left. **Standard Game Times:** 7:05 p.m., Sun. 2:05.
**Visiting Club Hotel:** Unavailable.

# NEW HAVEN COUNTY
CUTTERS

**Office Address:** 252 Derby Ave., West Haven, CT 06516.
**Telephone:** (203) 777-5636. **FAX:** (203) 777-4369.
**Website:** www.cuttersbaseball.com.

**Operated by:** Flying Bats and Balls, LLC.
**Principal Owner:** Jonathan Fleisig. **President:** Rick Handelman.
**General Manager:** Marie Heikkinen Webb. **Assistant GM:** Ryan Conley. **Director, Food/Beverage:** Mike McQuillan. **Director, Promotions/Special Events:** Stephen Colvin. **Ticket Sales Representatives:** Blair Tugman, Stephen Given. **Community Relations:** Jennifer Roccanti. **Box Office Manager:** David Caprio. **Head Groundskeeper:** Peter Webb. **Director, Player Personnel:** Bob Wirz. **Manager:** Mike Church. **Coach:** Unavailable. **Trainer:** Unavailable.

## GAME INFORMATION
**Radio Announcer:** Brian Irizarry. **No. of Games Broadcast:** Home-46, Away-46. **Flagship Station:** cuttersbaseball.com.
**Stadium Name:** Yale Field. **Directions:** From I-95, take eastbound exit 44 or westbound exit 45 to Route 10 and follow the Yale Bowl signs. From Merritt Parkway, take exit 57, follow to 34 east. **Standard Game Times:** 7:05 p.m., Sun. 2:05.
**Visiting Club Hotel:** Candlewood Suites, 1151 E. Main St., Meriden, CT 06450. Telephone: (203) 379-5048.

# NEW JERSEY
## JACKALS

**Office Address:** One Hall Dr., Little Falls, NJ 07424.
**Telephone:** (973) 746-7434. **FAX:** (973) 655-8021.
**E-Mail Address:** info@jackals.com. **Website:** www.jackals.com.

**Operated by:** Floyd Hall Enterprises, LLC.
**Principal Owner, Chairman:** Floyd Hall. **President:** Greg Lockard.
**General Manager:** Unavailable. **Business Manager:** Jennifer Fertig. **Director, Ticket Operations:** Pierson Van Raalte.
**Corporate Sales Representative:** Jim Rodriguez. **Group Sales Representatives:** Brooke Kenna, Trish Vignola. **Media Relations:** Joe Ameruoso. **Facilities Manager:** Aldo Licitra. **Concessions Manager:** Michele Guarino. **Clubhouse Manager:** Wally Brackett.
**Manager:** Joe Calfapietra. **Coaches:** Kevin Dattola, Ani Ramos. **Pitching Coach:** Brian Drahman. **Trainer:** Unavailable.

### GAME INFORMATION
**Radio Announcer:** Unavailable. **No. of Games Broadcast:** Home-46, Away-46. **Flagship Station:** jackals.com.
**Stadium Name:** Yogi Berra Stadium. **Location:** Route 80 or Garden State Parkway to Route 46, take Valley Road exit to Montclair State University. **Standard Game Times:** 7:05 p.m.; Sun. 2:05.
**Visiting Club Hotel:** Unavailable.

# NORTH SHORE
## SPIRIT

**Office Address:** 365 Western Ave., Lynn, MA 01904.
**Mailing Address:** P.O. Box 8120, Lynn, MA 01904.
**Telephone:** (781) 592-0007. **FAX:** (781) 592-0004.
**E-Mail Address:** info@northshorespirit.com. **Website:** www.northshorespirit.com.

**Operated by:** Spirit of New England Baseball Club, LLC.
**Principal Owner:** Nicholas Lopardo.
**Senior VP/General Manager:** Brent Connolly. **VP, Sales/Marketing:** Kevin Kelly. **Assistant GM:** Anne Ronan. **Promotions/Media Coordinator:** Courtney Deveau. **Advertising/Marketing Assistant:** Meredith Wentworth. **Account Executive, Operations Director:** Marty Ginivan. **Account Executives:** Chris Ellison, Frank James. **Group Sales Coordinator:** Nick Majocha.
**Director, Player Procurement:** Jeff Kunion. **Manager:** John Kennedy. **Coaches:** Frank Carey, Vic Davilla, Tom Donahue, Jim Tgettis, Jeff Ware. **Strength/Conditioning Coach:** Paul Melanson.

### GAME INFORMATION
**Radio Announcer:** John Leahy. **No. of Games Broadcast:** Home-46, Away-46. **Flagship Station:** WESX 1230-AM.
**Stadium Name:** Fraser Field. **Location:** Route 129 (Lynn exit) into Lynn on Lynnfield Street, left at Chestnut Street; right at Western Avenue (Route 107), stadium on right. **Standard Game Times:** 7:05 p.m., Sun. 2:05.
**Visiting Club Hotel:** Sheraton Ferncroft, 50 Ferncroft Rd., Danvers, MA 01923. Telephone: (978) 777-2500.

# QUEBEC
## LES CAPITALES

**Office Address:** 100 Rue du Cardinal Maurice-Roy, Quebec City, Quebec G1K 8Z1.
**Telephone:** (418) 521-2255. **FAX:** (418) 521-2266.
**E-Mail Address:** baseball@capitalesdequebec.com. **Website:** www.capitales dequebec.com.
**President/General Manager:** Miles Wolff. **Director, Business Operations:** Rémi Bolduc. **Director, Media/Public Relations:** Alex Harvey. **Sales/Marketing:** Ed Sweeney. **Director, Ticket Sales:** Nathalie Gauthier.
**Manager:** Michel Laplante. **Coaches:** J.P. Roy, Stephane Dionne.

### GAME INFORMATION
**Radio Announcer:** Stephane Levesque. **No. of Games Broadcast:** Unavailable. **Flagship Station:** CHRC 800-AM.
**Stadium Name:** Stade Municipal de Québec. **Location:** Highway 40 to Highway 173 (Centre-Ville) exit 2 to Parc Victoria. **Standard Game Times:** 7:05 p.m., Sun. 1:05.
**Visiting Club Hotel:** Hotel du Nord, 640 St. Vallier W., Quebec City, Quebec G1N 1C5. Telephone: (418) 522-1554.

# SUSSEX
## SKYHAWKS

**Office Address:** 94 Championship Place, Suite 11, Augusta, NJ 07822.
**Telephone:** (973) 300-1000. **FAX:** (508) 300-9000.
**E-Mail Address:** info@sussexprofessionalbaseball.com. **Website:** www.sussex
skyhawks.com.

**Operated By:** Sussex Professional Baseball, LLC.
**President:** Larry Hall.
**General Manager:** Ben Wittkowski. **Director, Corporate Sales:** Herm Sorcher. **Director, Corporate Partnerships:** Matt Millet. **Group Sales Representatives:** Greg Kubala. **Director, Ticket Sales/Operations:** Seth Bettan.
**Director, Player Personnel:** Pete Caliendo. **Manager:** Unavailable.

### GAME INFORMATION

**Stadium Name:** Skylands Park. **Location:** From New Jersey, I-80 to exit 34B (Rt. 15 N) to Route 565; From Pennsylvania, I-84 to Route 6 to Route 206 north to Route 565 east. **Standard Game Times:** 7:05 p.m., Sat. 5:05, Sun. 2:05.
**Visiting Club Hotel:** Unavailable.

# WORCESTER
## TORNADOES

**Office Address:** 303 Main St., Worcester, MA 01613.
**Telephone:** (508) 792-2288. **FAX:** (781) 592-0004.
**E-Mail Address:** info@worcestertornadoes.com. **Website:** www.worcester
tornadoes.com.

**President/Chief Executive Officer:** Alan Stone.
**General Manager:** Todd Marlin. **Assistant GM/Ballpark Operations:** Jorg Bassiacos. **Assistant GM/Sales and Marketing:** Joe Izzo. **Director, Sales/Marketing:** Cheryl Rivers. **Ticket Manager:** James Wong. **Account Managers:** Christina Tashjian, Dave Gwozdz, Sandie Rousseau.
**Director, Player Personnel:** Brad Michals. **Manager:** Rich Gedman. **Coaches:** Bob Ojeda, Ed Gallagher, Barry Glinski, Chip Plante, Dave Smith.

### GAME INFORMATION

**Stadium Name:** Hanover Insurance Park at Fitton Field. **Location:** I-290 to exit 11 College Square, right on College Street, left on Fitton Avenue. **Standard Game Times:** 7:05 p.m., Sun. 2:05.
**Visiting Club Hotel:** Holiday Inn, 500 Lincoln St., Worcester, MA 01613.

# FRONTIER
## LEAGUE

**Office Address:** 408 W. U.S. Hwy 40, Suite 100, Troy, IL 62294.
**Mailing Address:** P.O. Box 62, Troy, IL 62294.
**Telephone:** (618) 667-8000. **FAX:** (618) 667-8524.
**E-Mail Address:** office@frontierleague.com. **Website:** www.frontierleague.com.
**Year Founded:** 1993.

**Commissioner:** Bill Lee. **Chairman:** Chris Hanners (Chillicothe).
**President:** Rich Sauget (Gateway). **Vice President:** John Swiatek (Washington). **Corporate Secretary/Treasurer:** Bob Wolfe. **Legal Counsel/Deputy Commissioner:** Kevin Rouch. **Director, Development:** Leo Trich.
**Directors:** Dan Brennan (Windy City), Clint Brown (Florence), Harold Burkemper (River City), Bill Bussing (Evansville), Dave Ciarrachi (Rockford), Chris Hanners (Chillicothe), Joe Rosenhagen (Kalamazoo), Rich Sauget (Gateway), John Swiatek (Washington), Leslye Wuerfel (Traverse City).
**Division Structure: East**—Chillicothe, Florence, Kalamazoo, Traverse City, Washington. **West**—Evansville, Gateway, River City, Rockford, Windy City.
**Regular Season:** 96 games. **2006 Opening Date:** May 24. **Closing Date:** Sept. 4.
**All-Star Game:** July 12 at Evansville.
**Playoff Format:** Top two teams in each division meet in best-of-5 semifinal series. Winners meet in best-of-5 series for league championship.
**Roster Limit:** 24. **Eligibility Rule:** Minimum of 10 first-year players; maximum of seven players with one year of professional experience, maximum of two players with two years of experience and maximum of three players with three or more years of experience. No player may be 27 prior to Jan. 1 of current season.
**Brand of Baseball:** Wilson.
**Statistician:** SportsTicker, ESPN Plaza—Building B, Bristol, CT 06010 .

## STADIUM INFORMATION

| Club | Stadium | Opened | LF | Dimensions CF | RF | Capacity | 2005 Att. |
|------|---------|--------|-----|-----|-----|----------|-----------|
| Chillicothe | V.A. Memorial Stadium | 1954 | 328 | 400 | 325 | 4,000 | 85,667 |
| Evansville | Bosse Field | 1915 | 315 | 415 | 315 | 5,181 | 136,941 |
| Florence | Champion Window Field | 2004 | 325 | 395 | 325 | 4,200 | 94,191 |
| Gateway | GMC Stadium | 2002 | 318 | 385 | 301 | 6,500 | 177,353 |
| Kalamazoo | Homer Stryker Field | 1995 | 306 | 400 | 330 | 4,806 | 132,909 |
| River City | T.R. Hughes Ballpark | 1999 | 320 | 382 | 299 | 4,989 | 107,072 |
| Rockford | RiverHawks Stadium | 2006 | 315 | 380 | 312 | 4,056 | 103,248 |
| Traverse City | Wuerfel Park | 2006 | | | | | N/A |
| Washington | Falconi Field | 2002 | 325 | 400 | 325 | 3,200 | 159,857 |
| Windy City | Hawkinson Ford Field | 1999 | 335 | 390 | 335 | 4,000 | 78,011 |

# CHILLICOTHE
## PAINTS

**Office Address:** 59 N. Paint St., Chillicothe, OH 45601.
**Telephone:** (740) 773-8326. **FAX:** (740) 773-8338.
**E-Mail Address:** paints@bright.net. **Website:** www.chillicothepaints.com.

**Operated by:** Chillicothe Paints Professional Baseball Association, Inc.
**Principal Owner:** Chris Hanners. **President:** Shirley Bandy.
**Vice President, General Manager:** Bryan Wickline. **Stadium Superintendent:** Jim Miner. **Director, Finance:** Maleine Davis. **Director, Sales/Marketing:** John Wend. **Administrative Assistant:** Lori Watson. **Director, Group Sales:** Julie Hess. **Regional Sales Directors:** Greg Bigam, J.J. Hale. **Head Groundskeeper:** Jim Miner.
**Manager:** Glenn Wilson. **Coaches:** Marty Dunn, James Frisbie. **Trainer:** Scott Street.

### GAME INFORMATION
**Radio Announcer:** Ryan Mitchell. **No. of Games Broadcast:** Home-48, Away-48. **Flagship Station:** WXIZ 100.9-FM. **PA Announcer:** John Wend. **Official Scorer:** Aaron Lemaster.
**Stadium Name:** V.A. Memorial Stadium. **Location:** Route 23 to Bridge Street, west on Route 35, north on Route 104. **Standard Game Times:** 7:05 p.m., Sun. 6:05.
**Visiting Club Hotel:** Comfort Inn, 20 N. Plaza Blvd., Chillicothe, OH 45601. Telephone: (740) 775-3500.

# EVANSVILLE
## OTTERS

**Office Address:** 1701 N. Main St., Evansville, IN 47711.
**Mailing Address:** P.O. Box 3565, Evansville, IN 47734.
**Telephone:** (812) 435-8686. **FAX:** (812) 435-8688.
**E-Mail Address:** ottersbb@evansville.net. **Website:** www.evansvilleotters.com.

**Operated by:** Evansville Baseball, LLC.
**President:** Bill Bussing. **Senior Vice President:** Pat Rayburn.
**Vice President, General Manager:** Steve Tahsler. **Assistant GM:** Liam Miller. **Director, Sales:** Joel Padfield. **Party Planner:** Deana Johnson. **Director, Baseball Operations:** Jeff Pohl. **Facilities Manager:** Mike Duckworth. **Assistant, Operations:** Tammy Berg. **Flag Chairman:** Marvin Gray.
**Manager:** Greg Jelks. **Coaches:** Brett Myers, J.R. Seymour. **Pitching Coach:** Jeff Pohl. **Trainer:** Unavailable.

### GAME INFORMATION
**Radio Announcers:** Mark Moesner. **No. of Games Broadcast:** Home-48, Away-48. **Flagship Station:** WUEV 91.5-FM. **PA Announcer:** Brett Devault. **Official Scorer:** Unavailable.
**Stadium Name:** Bosse Field. **Location:** U.S. 41 to Diamond Ave. West, left at Heidelbach Ave. **Standard Game Times:** 7:05 p.m., Sun. 6:05.
**Visiting Club Hotel:** Baymont Inn & Suites West, 5737 Pearl Dr., Evansville, IN 47712. Telephone: 812-475-1700.

# FLORENCE
## FREEDOM

**Office Address:** 7950 Freedom Way, Florence, KY 41042.
**Telephone:** (859) 594-4487. **FAX:** (859) 594-3194.
**E-Mail Address:** info@florencefreedom.com. **Website:** www.florencefreedom.com.

**Operated by:** Canterbury Baseball, LLC.
**President, Managing Partner:** Clint Brown.
**Assistant General Manager:** Morgan West. **Director, Game Day Operations:** Yumi Blackburn. **Director, Corporate Sales:** Tom Tessar. **Ticket/Merchandise Manager:** Amy Seipp. **Group Sales Manager:** Kevin Schwab. **Controller:** Dave Flischel. **Sales Executive:** Shelley Helton. **Groundskeeper:** Lyle Travis.
**Director, Baseball Operations/Manager:** Jamie Keefe. **Coach:** Jason Graham. **Pitching Coach:** Chris Hook. **Trainer:** Dominic Favia.

### GAME INFORMATION
**Radio:** Unavailable.
**PA Announcer:** Unavailable. **Official Scorer:** Unavailable.
**Stadium:** Champion Window Field. **Location:** I-71/75 South to exit 180, left onto U.S. 42, right on Freedom Way; I-71/75 North to exit 180. **Standard Game Times:** 7:05 p.m., Sun. 6:05.
**Visiting Club Hotel:** Unavailable.

# GATEWAY
## GRIZZLIES

Mailing Address: 2301 Grizzlie Bear Blvd., Sauget, IL 62206.
Telephone: (618) 337-3000. **FAX:** (618) 332-3625.
E-Mail Address: grizzlies@accessus.net. **Website:** www.gatewaygrizzlies.com.

Operated by: Gateway Baseball, LLC.
Managing Officer: Richard Sauget.
General Manager: Tony Funderburg. **Assistant GM:** Steven Gomric. **Administrative Assistant to GM:** Jevon Heany. Director, Group Sales: Evan Bolesta. **Office Operations:** Brent Pownall. **Media Relations Director:** Jeff O'Neill. Director, Corporate Sales: C.J. Hendrickson. **Director, Stadium Operations:** Heath Kassing. **Director, Mechandise/Ticket Sales Associate:** Gina Perschbacher. **Head Groundskeeper/Corporate Sales Associate:** Craig Kuhl. **Interns:** Christine Dieckmann, Jarrod Mains, Carrie Snyder, Patrick May, Michael Reuther, Jason Fluchel, Tony Glosser, Kylie Sullivan, Brien Rea.
Manager: Danny Cox. **Coaches:** Jack Clark, Neil Fiala, Donnie Hillerman. **Trainer:** Geof Manzo.

### GAME INFORMATION

Radio Announcer: Joe Pott. **No of Games Broadcast:** Home-48, Away-48. **Flagship Station:** ESPN 1380-AM.
PA Announcer: Tom Calhoun. **Official Scorer:** Bree Haas.
Stadium Name: GMC Stadium. **Location:** I-255 at exit 15 (Mousette Lane). **Standard Game Times:** 7:05 p.m., Sun. 6:05.
Visiting Club Hotel: Ramada Inn, 6900 N. Illinois St., Fairview Heights, IL 62208. Telephone: (618) 632-4747.

# KALAMAZOO
## KINGS

Mailing Address: 251 Mills St., Kalamazoo, MI 49048.
Telephone: (269) 388-8326. **FAX:** (269) 388-8333.
Website: www.kalamazookings.com.

Operated by: Team Kalamazoo, LLC.
Owners: Bill Wright, Mike Seelye, Pat Seelye, Joe Rosenhagen, Ed Bernard, Scott Hocevar.
General Manager/Managing Partner: Linda Diehl. **Fundraising Coordinator/Community Relations:** Chris Peake. Vice President, Sales/Baseball Operations: Joe Rosenhagen. **Director, Marketing:** Kim Sherry.
Director, Baseball Operations/Field Manager: Fran Riordan. **Pitching Coach:** Joseph Thomas.

### GAME INFORMATION

Radio Announcers: Mike Levine. **No. of Games Broadcast:** Home-48, Away-48. **Flagship Station:** WQSN 1660-AM.
PA Announcers: Jim Lefler. **Official Scorer:** Jason Zerban.
Stadium Name: Homer Stryker Field. **Location:** I-94 to Sprinkle Road (exit 80), north on Sprinkle Road, left on Business Loop I-94, left on Kings Highway, right on Mills Street. **Standard Game Times:** 6:35 p.m., Sun. 2:05.
Visiting Club Hotel: Days Inn Airport Hotel, 3522 Sprinkle Rd., Kalamazoo, MI 49002. Telephone: (269) 381-7070.

# RIVER CITY
## RASCALS

Office Address: 900 Ozzie Smith Dr., O'Fallon, MO 63366.
Mailing Address: P.O. Box 662, O'Fallon, MO 63366.
Telephone: (636) 240-2287. **FAX:** (636) 240-7313.
E-Mail Address: info@rivercityrascals.com. **Website:** www.rivercityrascals.com.

Operated by: Missouri River Baseball, LLC.
Managing Partner: Harold Burkemper. **Executive Director:** Bob Wente. **Assistant General Manager:** Aaron McCreight. **Director, Ticket Sales:** Peyton Curlee. **Director, Group Sales:** Zach Ziler. **Director, Food/Beverage:** Rick Bronwell. **Director, Broadcasting:** Ned Bowdern. **Director, Marketing:** Marlena Huenefeld. **Head Groundskeeper:** Chris Young.
Manager: Randy Martz. **Coach:** Brian Lewis.

### GAME INFORMATION

Radio Announcer: Mike Morgan. **No. of Games Broadcast:** Home-48, Away-48. **Flagship Station:** KSLQ 104.5-FM.
Stadium Name: T.R. Hughes Ballpark. **Location:** I-70 to exit 219, north on T.R. Hughes Road, follow signs to ballpark. **Standard Game Times:** 7:05 p.m., Sun. 6:05.
Visiting Club Hotel: Hilton Garden Inn, 2310 Technology Dr., O'Fallon, MO 63366. Telephone: (636) 625-2700.

# ROCKFORD
## RIVERHAWKS

**Office Address:** 4503 Interstate Blvd., Loves Park, IL 61111.
**Telephone:** (815) 885-2255. **FAX:** (815) 964-2462.
**E-Mail Address:** playball@rockfordriverhawks.com. **Website:** www.rockfordriverhawks.com.

**Owners:** Dave Ciarrachi, Jim Ciarrachi, Nick Belleson, Brian McClure, Kurt Carlson. **Managing Partner:** Dave Ciarrachi.
**General Manager:** Josh Olerud. **Assistant GM:** Todd Fulk. **Director, Broadcasting:** Bill Czaja. **Account Executive:** Marshall Mackinder. **Head Groundskeeper:** Mark McCarty.
**Manager:** J.D. Arndt. **Coaches:** Jason Ciarrachi, Bob Koopman, Sam Knaack, Brian Isoz. **Trainer:** Alan Chase.

## GAME INFORMATION
**Radio Announcer:** Bill Czaja. **No. of Games Broadcast:** Home-48, Away-48. **Flagship Station:** WRHL 102.3-FM.
**PA Announcer:** Unavailable. **Official Scorer:** Aaron Nester.
**Stadium Name:** RiverHawks Stadium. **Location:** I-90 to Riverside Boulevard exit, east to Interstate Drive, left on Interstate Drive. **Standard Game Times:** 7:05 p.m., Sun 6:05.
**Visiting Club Hotel:** Sleep Inn, 725 Clark Rd., Rockford, IL 61107. Telephone: (815) 398-8900.

# TRAVERSE CITY
## BEACH BUMS

**Office Address:** 333 Stadium Dr., Traverse City, MI 49684.
**Telephone:** (231) 943-0100. **FAX:** (231) 943-0900.
**E-Mail Address:** info@tcbeachbums.com. **Website:** www.traversecitybeach bums.com.

**Operated by:** Traverse City Beach Bums, LLC. **Managing Partners:** John Wuerfel, Leslye Wuerfel, Jason Wuerfel.
**President:** John Wuerfel. **General Manager:** Lesley Wuerfel. **Vice President:** Jason Wuerfel. **Director, Media/Broadcasting:** Chad Cooper. **Director, Ticketing:** Aaron Studebaker. **Director, Merchandise:** Jeremy Hinde. **Director, Concessions:** Randy Brown. **Account Executives:** Michele Orloski, Nicolle Meyer, Jessica Coleman, Alex Coleman. **Head Groundskeeper:** Mark Picucci. **Director, Stadium Maintenance:** Ken Garvin.
**Manager/Director, Baseball Operations:** Jeff Isom. **Coach:** John Cahill. **Trainer:** Unavailable.

## GAME INFORMATION
**Radio Announcer:** Chad Cooper. **No. of Games Broadcast:** Home-48, Away-48. **Flagship Stations:** WFCX 94.3-FM; WFDX 92.5-FM.
**PA Announcer:** Unavailable. **Official Scorer:** Unavailable.
**Stadium Name:** Wuerfel Park. **Location:** North of U.S. 31 and Michigan 37 Chums Corner intersection, west on Chums Village Drive, north on Village Park Drive, right on Stadium Drive. **Standard Game Times:** 7:05 p.m., Sun 6:05.
**Visiting Club Hotel:** Unavailable.

# WASHINGTON
## WILD THINGS

**Office Address:** Falconi Field, One Washington Federal Way, Washington, PA 15301.
**Telephone:** (724) 250-9555. **FAX:** (724) 250-2333.
**E-Mail Address:** info@washingtonwildthings.com. **Website:** www.washington wildthings.com.

**Owned by:** Sports Facility, LLC. **Operated by:** Washington Frontier League Baseball, LLC.
**Managing Partner:** John Swiatek.
**President/Chief Executive Officer:** John Swiatek. **General Manager:** Ross Vecchio. **Director, Marketing:** Christine Blaine. **Director, Merchandise:** Scott Eafrati. **Director, Sales/Services:** Jeff Ptak. **Director, Corporate Sales:** Michael Dixon. **Director, Stadium Operations:** Steve Zavacky. **Group/Season Ticket Manager:** Shawn Gough.
**Manager:** John Massarelli. **Coach:** Ryan Ellis. **Pitching Coach:** Mark Mason. **Trainer:** Unavailable.

## GAME INFORMATION
**Radio Announcer:** Bob Gregg. **No. of Games Broadcast:** Home-48, Away-48. **Flagship Station:** WJPA 95.3-FM.
**PA Announcer:** Bill DiFabio. **Official Scorer:** Scott McGuinness.
**Stadium Name:** Falconi Field. **Location:** I-70 to exit 15 (Chesnut Street), right on Chesnut Street to Washington Crown Center Mall, right at mall entrance, right on to Mall Drive to stadium. **Standard Game Times:** 7:05 p.m., Sun. 6:35.

# WINDY CITY
## THUNDERBOLTS

**Office Address:** 14011 South Kenton Ave., Crestwood, IL 60445.
**Telephone:** (708) 489-2255. **FAX:** (708) 489-2999.
**E-Mail Address:** info@wcthunderbolts.com. **Website:** www.wcthunderbolts.com.

**Owned by:** Crestwood Professional Baseball, LLC.
**General Manager:** Tom O'Reilly. **Director, Baseball Operations:** Mike Lucas. **Director, Group Sales:** Pete Kelly. **Director, Media/Community Relations:** Dan Wachowski. **Office Manager:** Robbin Zaffino. **Director, Ticket Operations:** Dan Rinder. **Director, Merchandise/Marketing:** Mike Smolka.
**Manager:** Brent Bowers. **Coach:** Mike Kashirsky. **Trainer:** Unavailable.

### GAME INFORMATION
**Radio Announcer:** Jason Benetti. **No. of Games Broadcast:** Unavailable. **Flagship Station:** Unavailable.
**PA Announcer:** Unavailable. **Official Scorer:** Unavailable.
**Stadium Name:** Hawkinson Ford Field. **Location:** I-294 to Cicero Ave. exit (Route 50), south for 1½ miles, left at Midlothian Turnpike, right on Kenton Ave.; I-57 to 147th Street, west on 147th to Cicero, north on Cicero, right on Midlothian Turnpike, right on Kenton. **Standard Game Times:** 7:05 p.m., Sat. 6:05, Sun. 1:05/5:05.
**Visiting Club Hotel:** Georgio's Comfort Inn, 8800 W. 159th St., Orland Park, IL 60462. Telephone: (708) 403-1100.

# GOLDEN LEAGUE

**Office Address:** 6140 Stoneridge Mall Rd., Suite 550, Pleasanton, CA 94588
**Telephone:** (925) 226-2889. **FAX:** (925) 226-2891.
**E-mail Address:** info@goldenbaseball.com. **Website:** www.goldenbaseball.com.
**Founded:** 2005.

**Chief Executive Officer:** David Kaval. **President:** Amit Patel. **Commissioner:** Kevin Outcalt. **Chief Operating Officer:** Jim Peters. **Director, Marketing:** Kimberlee Kelso.
**League Historian/Secretary:** Bill Weiss.
**Supervisor, Officials:** Dan Perugini. **Director, Player Development/Scouting:** Kash Beauchamp. **Controller:** Mike Munson. **Executive Assistant:** Joyce Prescott.
**Division Structure:** None.
**Regular Season:** 80 games. **2006 Opening Date:** June 1. **Closing Date:** Aug. 28.
**All-Star Game:** July 17 at Chico.
**Playoff Format:** First- and second-half winners meet in best-of-5 series for league championship.
**Roster Limit:** 23. **Eligibility Rules:** Minimum five rookies; maximum four players 27 or older.
**Brand of Baseball:** Spalding TF PRO.
**Statistician:** SportsTicker, ESPN Plaza—Building B, Bristol, CT 06010.

## STADIUM INFORMATION

| | | | Dimensions | | | | |
|---|---|---|---|---|---|---|---|
| Club | Stadium | Opened | LF | CF | RF | Capacity | 2005 Att. |
| Chico | Nettleton Stadium | 1997 | 330 | 405 | 330 | 4,400 | 87,208 |
| Yuma | Desert Sun Stadium | 1969 | 335 | 410 | 335 | 7,100 | 90,730 |
| Long Beach | Blair Field | 1958 | 348 | 400 | 348 | 3,500 | 47,881 |
| San Diego | Tony Gwynn Stadium | 1997 | 340 | 412 | 340 | 3,000 | 74,522 |
| Fullerton | Goodwin Field | 1992 | 330 | 400 | 330 | 3,500 | 52,464 |
| *Reno | Peccole Park | 1994 | 340 | 401 | 340 | 3,000 | N/A |

*Expansion franchise

# CHICO
## OUTLAWS

**Office Address:** 555 Main St., Suite 200, Chico, CA 95928.
**Telephone:** (530) 345-3210.
**E-Mail Address:** bob@goldenbaseball.com. **Website:** www.chicooutlaws
baseball.com.

**General Manager:** Bob Linscheid. **Assistant GM, Sales/Marketing:** Chris Holen. **Director, Operations:** Becca Hofer. **Director, Tickets Sales:** Brian Ceccon. **Director, Public Relations/Broadcasting:** Rory Miller. **Office Manager:** Tracey Perotti.
**Manager:** Mark Parent. **Coach:** John Macalutas.

### GAME INFORMATION
**Radio Announcer:** Unavailable. **No. of Games Broadcast:** Home-40, Away-40. **Flagship Station:** KPAY 1290-AM. **PA Announcer:** Rory Miller. **Official Scorer:** Unavailable.
**Stadium Name:** Nettleton Stadium. **Location:** California 99 North to California 32 West/East Eighth Street, right on Main Street, left on West First Street; stadium at 400 West First Street. **Standard Game Times:** 7:05 p.m., Sun. 1:05.
**Visiting Club Hotel:** Holiday Inn Chico, 685 Manzanita Ct., Chico, CA 95926. Telephone: (530) 345-2491.

# FULLERTON
## FLYERS

**Office Address:** 2461 E. Orangethorpe, Suite 102, Fullerton, CA 92831.
**Telephone:** (714) 526-8326.
**E-Mail Address:** ehart@goldenbaseball.com. **Website:** www.fullertonflyers.com.

**General Manager:** Ed Hart. **Assistant GM, Sales/Marketing:** Unavailable. **Director, Operations:** Unavailable. **Director, Tickets Sales:** Unavailable. **Director, Public Relations/Broadcasting:** Unavailable. **Office Manager:** Unavailable
**Manager:** Garry Templeton. **Coach:** Jerry Turner. **Pitching Coach:** Charlie Hough.

### GAME INFORMATION
**Radio:** Unavailable.
**PA Announcer:** Unavailable. **Official Scorer:** Unavailable.
**Stadium Name:** Goodwin Field. **Location:** From Orange Freeway, take Yorba Linda Blvd. Exit, west on Yorba Linda, left on Associated Road to parking lot G. **Standard Game Times:** 7:05 p.m., Sun. 1:05.
**Visiting Club Hotel:** Four Points by Sheraton, 1500 S. Raymond Ave., Fullerton, CA 92831. Telephone: (714) 635-9000.

# LONG BEACH
## ARMADA

**Office Address:** 4510 E. Pacific Coast Hwy., Suite 505, Long Beach, CA 90804
**Telephone:** (562) 597-9787
**E-Mail Address:** gsampras@goldenbaseball.com. **Website:** www.longbeach
armada.com.

**General Manager:** Gus Sampras. **Director, Corporate Sales:** Jared Florin. **Director, Operations:** Darren Zinser. **Director, Tickets Sales:** Jason Delp. **Director, Public Relations/Broadcasting:** Unavailable. **Office Manager:** Unavailable
**Manager:** Darrell Evans. **Coach:** Dan DiPace. **Pitching Coach:** Jon Warden.

### GAME INFORMATION
**Radio:** Unavailable
**PA Announcer:** Unavailable. **Official Scorer:** Unavailable.
**Stadium Name:** Blair Field. **Location:** From Orange County, take 405 North to Seventh Street/22 West, right at Park Avenue. From Los Angeles, take 405 South to Lakewood Boulevard South, go to traffic circle and get on Pacific Coast Highway South, right on Ximeno, left on 10th Street; park at intersection of 10th Street and Park Avenue. **Standard Game Times:** 7:05 p.m., Sun. 1:05.
**Visiting Club Hotel:** Unavailable.

# RENO
## SILVER SOX

**Office Address:** 1010 Caughlin Crossing, Reno NV 89509.
**Telephone:** (775) 348-7769.
**E-Mail Address:** renoinfo@goldenbaseball.com. **Website:** www.renosilversox.com.

**General Manager:** Dwight Dortch. **Director, Sales/Marketing:** Curt Jacey. **Director, Operations:** Unavailable. **Director, Tickets Sales:** Unavailable. **Director, Public Relations/Broadcasting:** Unavailable. **Office Manager:** Unavailable.
**Manager:** Les Lancaster. **Coach:** Rafael Melchione. **Pitching Coach:** Mike Hartley.

### GAME INFORMATION
**Radio:** Unavailable
**PA Announcer:** Unavailable. **Official Scorer:** Unavailable.
**Stadium Name:** Peccole Park. **Location:** Take 395 North, exit at I-80 West, exit at Virginia Street, right (north) on Virginia, right on Ninth Street/Evans Avenue, park on left. **Standard Game Times:** 7:05 p.m., Sun. 1:05.
**Visiting Club Hotel:** Unavailable.

# SAN DIEGO
## SURF DAWGS

**Office Address:** 6160 Mission Gorge Rd., Suite 120, San Diego, CA 92120.
**Telephone:** (619) 282-4487.
**E-Mail Address:** jgrow@goldenbaseball.com. **Website:** www.sandiegosurf dawgs.com.

**General Manager:** Jeffrey Grow. **Director, Sales/Marketing:** Corey McManimen. **Director, Operations:** Unavailable. **Director, Tickets Sales:** Unavailable. **Director, Public Relations/Broadcasting:** Unavailable. **Office Manager:** Unavailable.
**Manager:** Terry Kennedy. **Coach:** Steve Ontiveros. **Pitching Coach:** Tim Blackwell.

### GAME INFORMATION
**Radio:** Unavailable.
**PA Announcer:** Unavailable. **Official Scorer:** Unavailable.
**Stadium Name:** Tony Gwynn Stadium. **Location:** From I-8, take College Avenue exit and go south, right at Montezuma, right at 55th Street, left at first stoplight into parking structure. **Standard Game Times:** 7:05 p.m., Sun. 1:05.
**Visiting Club Hotel:** Unavailable.

# YUMA
## SCORPIONS

**Address:** 1280 W. Desert Sun Dr., Yuma, AZ 85366.
**Telephone:** (928) 257-4700.
**E-Mail Address:** jmatlock@goldenbaseball.com. **Website:** www.yumascorpions.com.

**General Manager:** Jason Matlock. **Director, Sales/Marketing:** Damien Beasley. **Director, Operations:** Blake Englert. **Director, Tickets Sales:** Chris Carlson. **Director, Public Relations/Broadcasting:** Unavailable. **Office Manager:** Maureen Lee.
**Manager:** Benny Castillo. **Coach:** Pete Whisler. **Pitching Coach:** Rusty Meacham.

### GAME INFORMATION
**Radio Announcer:** Unavailable. **No. of Games Broadcast:** Home-40, Away-5. **Flagship Station:** KBLU 560-AM.
**PA Announcer:** Damien Beasley. **Official Scorer:** Unavailable.
**Stadium Name:** Desert Sun Stadium. **Location:** From I-8, take Fourth Avenue or 16th Street exit to Avenue A. **Standard Game Times:** 7:05 p.m., Sun. 1:05.
**Visiting Club Hotel:** Ramada Inn, 300 E. 32nd St., Yuma, AZ 85364. Telephone: (928) 344-1050.

# NORTHERN
## LEAGUE

**Office Address:** 320 Waterstone Way, Suite 600, Joliet, IL 60431.
**Telephone:** (817) 378-9898. **FAX:** (815) 744-4515.
**E-Mail Address:** info@northernleague.com. **Website:** www.northernleague.com.
**Founded:** 1993.

**Commissioner:** Jim Weigel. **Supervisor, Umpires:** Randy Hoback.
**Directors:** John Ehlert (Kansas City), Rich Ehrenreich (Schaumburg), Jeff Gidney (Calgary), Mike Hansen (Joliet), Sam Katz (Winnipeg), Dan Orlich (Edmonton), Mike Tatoian (Gary), Bruce Thom (Fargo-Moorhead).
**Division Structure: North**—Calgary, Edmonton, Fargo-Moorhead, Winnipeg. **South**—Gary, Joliet, Kansas City, Schaumburg.
**Regular Season:** 96 games (split schedule). **2006 Opening Date:** May 8. **Closing Date:** Sept. 3.
**All-Star Game:** July 18 at Kansas City.
**Playoff Format:** First-half division winner meets second half division winner in best-of-5 semifinal series. Winners meet in best-of-5 series for league championship.
**Roster Limit:** 22. **Eligibility Rule:** Minimum of five first-year players; maximum of four players with at least five years of professional experience.
**Brand of Baseball:** Rawlings.
**Statistician:** SportsTicker, ESPN Plaza-Building B, Bristol, CT 06010.

## STADIUM INFORMATION

| Club | Stadium | Opened | Dimensions | | | Capacity | 2005 Att. |
|------|---------|--------|----|-----|-----|----------|-----------|
| | | | LF | CF | RF | | |
| Calgary | Foothills Stadium | 1966 | 345 | 400 | 345 | 8,000 | 55,066 |
| Edmonton | TELUS Field | 1995 | 340 | 420 | 320 | 9,200 | 107,987 |
| Fargo-Moorhead | Newman Outdoor Field | 1996 | 318 | 400 | 314 | 4,513 | 181,829 |
| Gary | U.S. Steel Yard | 2003 | 320 | 400 | 335 | 6,139 | 151,850 |
| Joliet | Silver Cross Field | 2002 | 330 | 400 | 327 | 4,616 | 201,149 |
| Kansas City | Community America Ballpark | 2003 | 300 | 396 | 328 | 4,365 | 244,414 |
| Schaumburg | Alexian Field | 1999 | 355 | 400 | 353 | 7,048 | 200,267 |
| Winnipeg | CanWest Global Park | 1999 | 325 | 400 | 325 | 7,481 | 322,758 |

# CALGARY
## VIPERS

**Office Address:** 2255 Crowchild Trail NW, Calgary, Alberta T2N 3R5.
**Telephone:** (403) 277-2255.
**E-Mail Address:** info@calgaryvipers.com. **Website:** www.calgaryvipers.com.

**Owner:** Jeffrey Gidney. **President, Chief Operating Officer:** Peter Young.
**Merchandise Manager:** Branden Young. **Director, Ticket Operations:** Brenda Routly. **Facility Director:** Kent Saunders. **Executive Assistant:** Jody Wheeler. **Director, Sales/Marketing:** Perry McGeough. **Groundskeeper:** Phil Schumacher.
**Manager:** Mike Busch. **Coaches:** Wes Crawford, Brad Doss, Juan Thomas. **Athletic Therapist:** Schad Richea.

### GAME INFORMATION
**Radio:** The Fan 960-AM.
**PA Announcer:** Peter Watts. **Official Scorer:** Gord Simonin.
**Stadium Name:** Foothills Stadium. **Location:** Crowchild Trail NW to 24th Avenue. **Standard Game Times:** 7:05 p.m., Wed. 12:35, Sat./Sun. 1:35.
**Visiting Club Hotel:** Unavailable.

# EDMONTON
## CRACKER-CATS

**Office Address:** 10233 96th Ave., Edmonton, Alberta T5K 0A5.
**Telephone:** (780) 423-2255. **FAX:** (780) 423-3112.
**E-Mail address:** info@crackercats.ca. **Website:** www.crackercats.ca.

**Operated by:** Northern League in Edmonton Inc. **Owner/President:** Dan Orlich. Vice President: Ericka Cruise.
**General Manager/Director, League Relations:** Dean Hengel. **Assistant GM/Director, Media and Team Relations:** Al Coates. **Director, Sales/Marketing:** Dale Roy. **Director, Stadium Operations:** Don Benson. **Group Sales Manager:** Ken McKinstry. **Key Account Manager:** Terry Nistor. **Sales/Promotions Manager:** Melanie Gehmlich. **Accountant:** Heather Pick. **Office Manager:** Lindsay Weizenbach. **Ticket Manager:** Kendra Morton. **Assistant Office Manager:** Kim Schneider. **Field Operations Manager:** Tom Archibald. **Assistant Field Operations Manager:** Brett Jones. **Clubhouse Operations:** Jared King.
**Manager/Director, Baseball:** Terry Bevington. **Coach:** John Barlow. **Trainer:** Unavailable.

### GAME INFORMATION
**Radio Announcer:** Al Coates. **No. of Games Broadcast:** Home-48. **Flagship Station:** The Team 1260-AM.
**PA Announcer:** Unavailable. **Official Scorer:** Al Coates.
**Stadium Name:** TELUS Field. **Location:** From north, 101st Street to 96th Avenue, left on 96th, one block east; from south, Calgary Trail North to Queen Elizabeth Hill, right across Walterdale Bridge, right on 96th Avenue. **Standard Game Times:** 7:05 p.m., Sun. 1:35.
**Visiting Club Hotel:** The Sutton Place Hotel, 10235 101st St., Edmonton, Alberta T5J 3E9. Telephone: (780) 428-7111.

# FARGO-MOORHEAD
## REDHAWKS

**Office Address:** 1515 15th Ave. N., Fargo, ND 58102.
**Telephone:** (701) 235-6161. **FAX:** (701) 297-9247.
**E-Mail Address:** redhawks@fmredhawks.com. **Website:** www.fmredhawks.com.

**Operated by:** Fargo Baseball, LLC.
**President:** Bruce Thom. **Vice President:** Brad Thom.
**General Manager:** Josh Buchholz. **Senior Accountant:** Sue Wild. **Stadium Superintendent/Head Groundskeeper:** Matt Wallace. **Director, Promotions:** Megan Salic. **Director, Merchandise/Special Events:** Sara Garaas. **Director, Ticket Sales:** Nicole Ellis. **Media Relations Manager:** Justin Stottlemyre. **Clubhouse Operations:** Brent Tehven.
**Manager/Director, Player Procurement:** Doug Simunic. **Assistant Director, Player Procurement/Consultant:** Jeff Bittiger. **Pitching Coach:** Steve Montgomery. **Coaches:** Bucky Burgau, Robbie Lopez. **Trainer:** Don Bruenjes.

### GAME INFORMATION
**Radio Announcers:** Scott Miller, Maury Wills. **No. of Games Broadcast:** Home-48, Away-48. **Flagship Station:** WDAY 970-AM.
**PA Announcer:** Merrill Piepkorn. **Official Scorer:** Rob Olson.

**Stadium Name:** Newman Outdoor Field. **Location:** I-29 North to exit 67, right on 19th Ave. North, right on Albrecht Boulevard. **Standard Game Times:** 7:05 p.m., Sun. 2:05.
**Visiting Club Hotel:** Comfort Inn West, 3825 9th Ave. SW, Fargo, ND 58103. Telephone: (701) 282-9596.

# GARY SOUTHSHORE
## RAILCATS

**Office Address:** One Stadium Plaza, Gary, IN 46402.
**Telephone:** (219) 882-2255. **FAX:** (219) 882-2259.
**E-Mail Address:** info@railcatsbaseball.com **Website:** www.railcatsbaseball.com.

**Operated by:** SouthShore Baseball, LLC. **Principal Owners:** Victory Sports Group, LLC.
**Chairman:** George Huber. **President, Chief Executive Officer:** Mike Tatoian.
**Vice President, General Manager:** Roger Wexelberg. **Assistant GM:** Unavailable. **Director, Broadcasting:** Tom Nichols. **Director, Facility:** Mike Figg. **Group Sales Manager:** Mike Smith. **Corporate Sales Managers:** Milton Thaxton. **Merchandise Manager:** Raeann Suggs. **Community Relations:** Jamie Kurpiel. **Manager, Field Maintenance:** Tom Preslar. **Director, Ticket Operations:** Becky Kremer. **Marketing/Promotions Coordinator:** Jahi Garrett. **Group Sales Assistant:** Peter Argueta. **Executive Assistant:** Tiffany Gaston.
**Manager:** Greg Tagert. **Coaches:** Unavailable.

## GAME INFORMATION
**Radio Announcer:** Tom Nichols. **No. of Games Broadcast:** Home-48, Away-48. **Flagship Station:** WEFM 95.5-FM.
**Stadium Name:** U.S. Steel Yard. **Location:** I-65 to I-90 West (toll), one mile to Broadway South, left on Fifth Street. **Standard Game Times:** 7 p.m., Sat. 6, Sun. 2.
**Visiting Club Hotel:** Trump Hotel, 21 Buffington Harbor Dr., Gary, IN 46406. Telephone: (219) 977-9999.

# JOLIET
## JACKHAMMERS

**Office Address:** 1 Mayor Art Schultz Dr., Joliet, IL 60432.
**Telephone:** (815) 726-2255. **FAX:** (815) 726-9223.
**E-Mail Address:** info@jackhammerbaseball.com. **Website:** www.jackhammer baseball.com.

**Operated by:** Joliet Professional Baseball Club, LLC.
**Chairman:** Peter Ferro. **Vice Chairman:** Charles Hammersmith. **Chief Executive Officer/General Counsel:** Michael Hansen. **Chief Financial Officer/President:** John Costello.
**Executive Vice President/General Manager:** Steve Malliet. **Assistant GM:** Kelly Sufka. **Director, Ticket Sales:** Rich Kuchar. **Box Office Manager:** Ryan Harris. **Corporate Sales Manager:** Kyle Kreger. **Ticket Sales Representatives:** Chris Franklin, Amanda Willing, Drew Heinker. **Director, Broadcasting/Media Relations:** Bryan Dolgin. **Director, Community Relations:** Chad Therrien. **Director, Corporate Sales:** Kari Rumfield. **Head Groundskeeper:** Nick Hill. **Director, Accounting/Human Resources:** Tammy Harvey. **Administrative Assistant:** Sonia Little.
**Manager:** Hal Lanier. **Coaches:** Ira Smith, Bubba Smith. **Pitching Coach:** Jim Boynewicz.

## GAME INFORMATION
**Radio Announcers:** Bryan Dolgin. **No. of Games Broadcast:** Home-48, Away-48. **Flagship Stations:** WJOL 1340-AM.
**PA Announcer:** Unavailable. **Official Scorer:** Dave Laketa.
**Stadium Name:** Silver Cross Field. **Location:** I-80 to Chicago Street/Route 53 North exit, go 1/2 mile on Chicago Street, right on Washington Street to Jefferson Street/U.S. 52, right on Jefferson, ballpark on left. **Standard Game Times:** 7:05 p.m., Tues. 6:05, Sun. 2:05/5:05.
**Visiting Club Hotel:** Hampton Inn, 3555 Mall Loop Dr., Joliet, IL 60431. Telephone: (815) 439-9500.

# KANSAS CITY
## T-BONES

**Office Address:** 1800 Village West Pkwy., Kansas City, KS 66111.
**Telephone:** (913) 328-2255. **FAX:** (913) 328-5652.
**E-Mail Address:** batterup@tbonesbaseball.com. **Website:** www.tbonesbaseball.com.

**Operated By:** T-Bones Baseball Club, LLC; Ehlert Development.
**Owner, President:** John Ehlert. **Vice President:** Adam Ehlert.
**Vice President/General Manager:** Rick Muntean. **Assistant GM:** Chris Browne. **Director, Merchandising:** Kacy

Roe. **Director, Media Relations:** Loren Foxx. **Director, Promotions:** Bryan Williams. **Director, Group Sales:** Brandon Smith. **Head Groundskeeper:** Don Frantz. **Bookkeeper:** Nikki White.

**Manager:** Al Gallagher. **Coach:** Tim Doherty. **Pitching Coach:** Greg Bicknell. **Trainer:** Unavailable.

### GAME INFORMATION

**Radio Announcer:** Loren Foxx. **No. of Games Broadcast:** Home-48, Away-48. **Flagship Station:** Unavailable.

**PA Announcer:** Randy Birch. **Official Scorer:** Louis Spry.

**Stadium Name:** Community America Ballpark. **Location:** State Avenue West off I-435, corner of 110th and State Avenue. **Standard Game Times:** 7:05 p.m., Sun. 5:05.

**Visiting Club Hotel:** Unavailable.

# SCHAUMBURG
## FLYERS

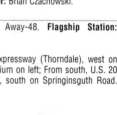

**Office Address:** 1999 S. Springinsguth Rd., Schaumburg, IL 60193.
**Telephone:** (847) 891-2255. **FAX:** (847) 891-6441.
**E-Mail Address:** info@flyersbaseball.com. **Website:** www.flyersbaseball.com.

**Principal Owners:** Richard Ehrenreich, John Hughes, Gregory Smith. **Managing Partner/President:** Richard Ehrenreich.

**General Manager:** Rick Rungaitis. **Director, Media Relations/Broadcasting:** Matt McLaughlin. **Director, Corporate Sales/Marketing:** Ben Burke. **Director, Group Sales:** Shaun Kelly. **Ticket Manager:** Scott Boor. **Director, Graphics/Publications:** Sarah Wienman. **Group Sales Assistant/Merchandise:** Tracey Power. **Head Groundskeeper:** Ryan Pfeiffer. **Director, Operations:** Matt Benning. **Clubhouse Manager:** Joe Correy. **Director, Security:** Dean Norman.

**Manager:** Andy McCauley. **Coach:** Bobby Bell. **Pitching Coach:** Brett Gray. **Trainer:** Brian Czachowski.

### GAME INFORMATION

**Radio Announcer:** Unavailable. **No. of Games Broadcast:** Home-48, Away-48. **Flagship Station:** flyersbaseball.com.

**PA Announcer:** Steve Brandy. **Official Scorer:** Mark Madorin.

**Stadium Name:** Alexian Field. **Location:** From north, I-290 to Elgin-O'Hare Expressway (Thorndale), west on expressway to Irving Park Road exit, left on Springinsguth under expressway, stadium on left; From south, U.S. 20 West (Lake Street) to Elgin-O'Hare Expressway (Thorndale), east on expressway, south on Springinsguth Road. **Standard Game Times:** 7:05 p.m., Sat. 6:20, Sun. 12:05.

**Visiting Club Hotel:** Unavailable.

# WINNIPEG
## GOLDEYES

**Office Address:** One Portage Ave. E., Winnipeg, Manitoba R3B 3N3.
**Telephone:** (204) 982-2273. **FAX:** (204) 982-2274.
**E-Mail Address:** goldeyes@goldeyes.com. **Website:** www.goldeyes.com.

**Operated by:** Winnipeg Goldeyes Baseball Club, Inc.

**Principal Owner, President:** Sam Katz.

**General Manager:** Andrew Collier. **Director, Marketing:** Dan Chase. **Director, Communications:** Jonathan Green. **Director, Promotions:** Barb McTavish. **Director, Sales:** Lorraine Maciboric. **Director, Group Sales:** Regan Katz. **Account Representatives:** Paul Duque, Paul Edmonds, Dave Loat, Darren McCabe, Dennis McLean, Scott Taylor. **Director, Merchandising:** Carol Orchard. **Controller:** Judy Jones. **Facility Manager:** Scott Horn. **Administrative Assistants:** Heather Mann-O'Hara, Angela Sanche. **Head Groundskeeper:** Don Ferguson.

**Manager/Director, Player Procurement:** Rick Forney. **Coaches:** Steve Maddock, Tom Vaeth. **Pitching Coach:** Steve Shirley. **Trainer:** Brad Shaw.

### GAME INFORMATION

**Radio Announcer:** Paul Edmonds. **No. of Games Broadcast:** Home-48, Road-48. **Flagship Station:** CFRW 1290-AM.

**PA Announcer:** Ron Arnst. **Official Scorer:** Steve Eitzen.

**Stadium Name:** CanWest Global Park. **Location:** Pembina Highway (Route 75), east on River Ave., north on Main Street, east on Water Ave. **Standard Game Times:** 7:05 p.m., Sun. 1:35.

**Visiting Club Hotel:** Ramada Marlborough, 331 Smith St., Winnipeg, Manitoba R3B 2G9. Telephone: (204) 942-6411.

# UNITED
## LEAGUE

**Office Address:** One Galleria Tower, 22nd Floor, Dallas, TX 75240.
**Telephone:** (877) 803-0555. **FAX:** (214) 257-0841
**E-mail Address:** info@unitedleague.org. **Website:** www.unitedleague.org.
**Founded:** 2006.

**Chief Executive Officer:** John Bryant. **President:** Brad Wendt. **Chief Operating Officer:** Byron Pierce. **Director, Business Development:** Gary Wendt. **Chief Financial Officer:** Amie Nappi. **Director, Communications:** Eileen Wright.

**Member Clubs:** Alexandria, La.; Amarillo, Texas; Edinburg, Texas; Harlingen, Texas; Laredo, Texas; San Angelo, Texas (central ownership of clubs by league).

**Regular Season:** 90 games. **2006 Opening Date:** May 16. **Closing Date:** August 28.

**All-Star Game:** July 12 at Edinburg, Texas.

**Playoff Format:** Top four teams meet in best-of-3 series. Winners meet in best-of-5 series for league championship.

**Roster Limit:** 22. **Eligibility Rules:** Must be at least 18 years old; no restrictions on rookies or veterans.

**Brand of Baseball:** D-Bat.

**Statistician:** SportsTicker, ESPN Plaza—Building B, Bristol, CT 06010.

# INTERNATIONAL
## LEAGUES

# FOREIGN LEAGUES

## 2005 STANDINGS

### AMERICAS

#### MEXICAN LEAGUE

FIRST HALF

| NORTH | W | L | PCT | GB |
|---|---|---|---|---|
| Saltillo Sarape Makers | 32 | 24 | .571 | — |
| Monterrey Sultans | 32 | 24 | .571 | — |
| Tijuana Colts | 29 | 27 | .518 | 3 |
| Mexico Red Devils | 29 | 27 | .518 | 3 |
| Aguascalientes Railroadmen | 28 | 28 | .500 | 4 |
| Monclova Steelers | 28 | 28 | .500 | 4 |
| Laguna Cowboys | 22 | 34 | .393 | 10 |
| San Luis Potosi Cactus Pear Growers | 20 | 36 | .357 | 12 |

| SOUTH | W | L | PCT | GB |
|---|---|---|---|---|
| Campeche Pirates | 38 | 18 | .679 | — |
| Angelopolis Tigers | 34 | 22 | .607 | 4 |
| Yucatan Lions | 31 | 25 | .554 | 7 |
| Veracruz Reds | 28 | 28 | .500 | 10 |
| Oaxaca Warriors | 26 | 30 | .464 | 12 |
| Puebla Parrots | 25 | 31 | .446 | 13 |
| Tabasco Olmecas | 24 | 32 | .429 | 14 |
| Cancun Lobstermen | 22 | 34 | .393 | 16 |

SECOND HALF

| NORTH | W | L | PCT | GB |
|---|---|---|---|---|
| Tijuana Colts | 35 | 19 | .648 | — |
| Saltillo Sarape Makers | 31 | 23 | .574 | 4 |
| Mexico Red Devils | 27 | 24 | .529 | 6½ |
| Aguascalientes Railroadmen | 27 | 25 | .519 | 7 |
| Monclova Steelers | 25 | 27 | .481 | 9 |
| San Luis Potosi Cactus Pear Growers | 25 | 27 | .481 | 9 |
| Monterrey Sultans | 24 | 26 | .480 | 9 |
| Laguna Cowboys | 16 | 37 | .302 | 18½ |

| SOUTH | W | L | PCT | GB |
|---|---|---|---|---|
| Angelopolis Tigers | 32 | 19 | .627 | — |
| Oaxaca Warriors | 31 | 20 | .608 | 1 |
| Tabasco Olmecas | 29 | 23 | .558 | 3½ |
| Yucatan Lions | 26 | 25 | .510 | 6 |
| Puebla Parrots | 26 | 27 | .491 | 7 |
| Campeche Pirates | 24 | 25 | .490 | 7 |
| Veracruz Reds | 23 | 30 | .434 | 10 |
| Cancun Lobstermen | 15 | 39 | .278 | 18½ |

· **PLAYOFFS: First Round**—Monterrey defeated Mexico 4-2, Saltillo defeated Aguascalientes 4-2, Yucatan defeated Oaxaca 4-3 and Tabasco defeated Campeche 4-3, in best-of-7 series. **Division Series**—Tijuana defeated Mexico 4-2, Saltillo defeated Monterrey 4-2, Angelopolis defeated Oaxaca 4-2 and Yucatan defeated Tabasco 4-3, in best-of-7 series. **Semifinals**—Angelopolis defeated Yucatan 4-2 and Saltillo defeated Tijuana 4-3, in best-of-7 series. **Final**—Angelopolis defeated Saltillo 4-2, in best-of-7 series.

#### DOMINICAN SUMMER LEAGUE

| BOCA CHICA/American | W | L | PCT | GB |
|---|---|---|---|---|
| Indians I | 38 | 31 | .551 | — |
| Twins | 36 | 33 | .522 | 2 |
| Red Sox | 26 | 42 | .382 | 11½ |
| Indians II | 25 | 42 | .373 | 12 |

| BOCA CHICA/National | W | L | PCT | GB |
|---|---|---|---|---|
| Giants | 43 | 24 | .642 | — |

| | W | L | PCT | GB |
|---|---|---|---|---|
| Rockies | 42 | 27 | .609 | 2 |
| Diamondbacks | 38 | 30 | .559 | 5½ |
| Reds | 32 | 38 | .457 | 12½ |
| Cubs | 27 | 40 | .403 | 16 |

| SANTO DOMINGO NORTH | W | L | PCT | GB |
|---|---|---|---|---|
| Athletics II | 43 | 26 | .623 | — |
| Mariners | 39 | 30 | .565 | 4 |
| Dodgers | 37 | 29 | .561 | 4½ |
| Cardinals | 36 | 35 | .507 | 8 |
| Phillies | 34 | 36 | .486 | 19½ |
| Athletics I | 18 | 51 | .261 | 25 |

| SANTO DOMINGO WEST | W | L | PCT | GB |
|---|---|---|---|---|
| Yankees I | 44 | 26 | .629 | — |
| Tigers | 40 | 30 | .571 | 4 |
| Padres | 37 | 34 | .521 | 7½ |
| Nationals | 37 | 35 | .514 | 8 |
| Yankees II | 28 | 43 | .394 | 16½ |
| Mets | 27 | 45 | .375 | 18 |

| SAN PEDRO de MACORIS | W | L | PCT | GB |
|---|---|---|---|---|
| Angels | 44 | 26 | .629 | — |
| Orioles | 42 | 29 | .592 | 2½ |
| Pirates | 38 | 34 | .528 | 7 |
| Rangers | 33 | 37 | .471 | 11 |
| Blue Jays | 31 | 39 | .443 | 13 |
| Astros | 23 | 46 | .333 | 20½ |

| CIBAO | W | L | PCT | GB |
|---|---|---|---|---|
| Royals | 45 | 13 | .776 | — |
| Braves I | 29 | 29 | .500 | 16 |
| Marlins | 28 | 31 | .467 | 17½ |
| White Sox | 26 | 32 | .441 | 19 |
| Braves II | 19 | 42 | .311 | 27½ |

**PLAYOFFS: Quarterfinals**—Yankees I defeated Indians 2-1 and Angels defeated Athletics II 2-0 in best-of-3 series. **Semifinals**—Royals defeated Angels 2-0 and Yankees I defeated Giants 2-0 in best-of-3 series. **Final**—Yankees I defeated Royals 3-0 in best-of-5 series.

#### VENEZUELAN SUMMER LEAGUE

| | W | L | PCT | GB |
|---|---|---|---|---|
| Mariners | 37 | 23 | .617 | — |
| Astros | 37 | 25 | .597 | 1 |
| Phillies | 37 | 27 | .578 | 2 |
| Red Sox/Padres | 36 | 28 | .563 | 3 |
| Orioles | 34 | 27 | .557 | 3½ |
| Mets | 33 | 30 | .524 | 5½ |
| Pirates | 29 | 33 | .468 | 9 |
| Reds | 25 | 37 | .403 | 13 |
| Marlins/Nationals | 13 | 51 | .203 | 26 |

**PLAYOFFS:** Astros defeated Mariners 2-0 in best-of-3 series.

#### CUBA

WEST

| GROUP A | W | L | PCT | GB |
|---|---|---|---|---|
| Pinar del Río | 55 | 34 | .618 | — |
| Isla de la Juventud | 42 | 48 | .467 | 13½ |
| Metropolitanos | 33 | 57 | .367 | 22½ |
| Matanzas | 28 | 61 | .633 | 27 |

| GROUP B | W | L | PCT | GB |
|---|---|---|---|---|
| Industriales | 59 | 30 | .656 | — |
| Habana Province | 54 | 35 | .600 | 5 |
| Sancti Spíritus | 54 | 36 | .600 | 5 ½ |
| Cienfuegos | 31 | 59 | .344 | 28 ½ |

| EAST | | | | |
|---|---|---|---|---|
| GROUP C | W | L | PCT | GB |
| Ciego de Ávila | 54 | 36 | .600 | — |
| Villa Clara | 51 | 39 | .567 | 3 |
| Las Tunas | 47 | 43 | .522 | 7 |
| Camagüey | 35 | 55 | .389 | 19 |

| GROUP D | W | L | PCT | GB |
|---|---|---|---|---|
| Santiago de Cuba | 55 | 35 | .611 | — |
| Granma | 50 | 40 | .556 | 5 |
| Holguín | 37 | 53 | .411 | 18 |
| Guantánamo | 33 | 57 | .367 | 22 |

**Playoffs—Quarterfinals:** Santiago defeated Granma 3-0; Villa Clara defeated Ciego de Ávila 3-0; Habana Province defeated Pinar del Río 3-1; Sancti Spíritus defeated Industriales 3-1 in best-of-5 series. **Semifinals:** Santiago defeated Villa Clara 4-0 and Habana Province defeated Sancti Spíritus 4-2 in best-of-7 series. **Final:** Santiago defeated Habana Province 4-2 in best-of-7 series.

# ASIA

## JAPAN

| CENTRAL LEAGUE | W | L | T | PCT | GB |
|---|---|---|---|---|---|
| Hanshin Tigers | 87 | 54 | 5 | .617 | — |
| Chunichi Dragons | 79 | 66 | 1 | .545 | 10 |
| Yokohama BayStars | 69 | 70 | 7 | .496 | 17 |
| Yakult Swallows | 71 | 73 | 2 | .493 | 17 ½ |
| Yomiuri Giants | 62 | 80 | 4 | .437 | 25 ½ |
| Hiroshima Carp | 58 | 84 | 4 | .408 | 29 ½ |

| PACIFIC LEAGUE | W | L | T | PCT | GB |
|---|---|---|---|---|---|
| Fukuoka SoftBank Hawks | 89 | 45 | 2 | .664 | — |
| Chiba Lotte Marines | 84 | 49 | 3 | .632 | 4 ½ |
| Seibu Lions | 67 | 69 | 0 | .493 | 23 |
| Orix Buffaloes | 62 | 70 | 4 | .470 | 26 |
| Hokkaido Nippon Ham Fighters | 62 | 71 | 3 | .466 | 26 ½ |
| Tohoku Rakuten Golden Eagles | 38 | 97 | 1 | .281 | 51 ½ |

**PLAYOFFS—Semifinals**—Chiba Lotte defeated Seibu 2-0 in best-of-3 series. **Final**—Chiba Lotte defeated Fukuoka SoftBank 3-2 in best-of-5 series for league championship.

## KOREA

| | W | L | T | PCT | GB |
|---|---|---|---|---|---|
| Samsung Lions | 74 | 48 | 4 | .607 | — |
| Doosan Bears | 72 | 51 | 3 | .585 | 2 ½ |
| SK Wyverns | 70 | 50 | 6 | .583 | 3 |
| Hanwha Eagles | 64 | 61 | 1 | .512 | 11 ½ |
| Lotte Giants | 58 | 67 | 1 | .464 | 17 ½ |
| LG Twins | 54 | 71 | 1 | .432 | 21 ½ |
| Hyundai Unicorns | 53 | 70 | 3 | .431 | 21 ½ |
| Kia Tigers | 49 | 76 | 1 | .392 | 26 ½ |

**PLAYOFFS: First Round**—Hanwha defeated SK 3-2 in best-of-5 series. **Semifinals**—Doosan defeated Hanwha 3-0 in best-of-5 series. **Finals**—Samsung defeated Doosan 4-0 in best-of-7 series.

## TAIWAN

| FIRST HALF | W | L | T | PCT | GB |
|---|---|---|---|---|---|
| Macoto Cobras | 29 | 20 | 2 | .592 | — |
| Sinon Bulls | 28 | 21 | 2 | .571 | 1 |
| Brother Elephants | 25 | 23 | 2 | .521 | 3 ½ |
| China Trust Whales | 24 | 24 | 2 | .500 | 4 |
| President Lions | 24 | 26 | 0 | .480 | 5 ½ |
| La New Bears | 16 | 32 | 2 | .333 | 12 ½ |

| SECOND HALF | W | L | T | PCT | GB |
|---|---|---|---|---|---|
| Sinon Bulls | 25 | 21 | 4 | .543 | — |
| La New Bears | 26 | 23 | 1 | .531 | ½ |
| President Lions | 24 | 23 | 1 | .511 | 1 ½ |
| China Trust Whales | 23 | 25 | 2 | .479 | 3 |
| Macoto Cobras | 21 | 23 | 6 | .477 | 3 |
| Brother Elephants | 22 | 26 | 2 | .458 | 4 |

**PLAYOFFS**—Sinon defeated Macoto 4-0 in best-of-7 series.

## CHINA

| | W | L | PCT | GB |
|---|---|---|---|---|
| Beijing Tigers | 22 | 7 | .759 | — |
| Tianjin Lions | 20 | 10 | .667 | 2 ½ |
| Guandong Leopards | 19 | 11 | .633 | 3 ½ |
| Shanghai Eagles | 16 | 13 | .552 | 6 |
| Sichuan Dragons | 8 | 22 | .267 | 15 ½ |
| Hopestars | 4 | 26 | .133 | 18 ½ |

**PLAYOFFS**—China defeated Tianjin 2-0 in best-of-3 series.

# EUROPE

## ITALY

| | W | L | PCT | GB |
|---|---|---|---|---|
| Bologna | 35 | 19 | .648 | — |
| San Marino | 35 | 19 | .648 | — |
| Nettuno | 34 | 20 | .630 | 1 |
| Rimini | 33 | 21 | .611 | 2 |
| Parma | 33 | 21 | .611 | 2 |
| Grosseto | 30 | 24 | .556 | 5 |
| Modena | 24 | 30 | .444 | 11 |
| Reggio Emilia | 19 | 35 | .352 | 16 |
| Trieste | 16 | 38 | .296 | 19 |
| Paterno | 11 | 43 | .204 | 24 |

**PLAYOFFS—Semifinals:** Bologna defeated Rimini 4-1 and San Marino defeated Nettuno 4-2 in best-of-7 series. **Final:** Bologna defeated San Marino 4-3 in best-of-7 series.

## NETHERLANDS

| | W | L | T | PCT | GB |
|---|---|---|---|---|---|
| Neptunus | 31 | 10 | 1 | .750 | — |
| Hoofddorp Pioniers | 28 | 12 | 2 | .690 | 2 |
| HCAW | 26 | 14 | 2 | .643 | 4 ½ |
| Sparta/Feyenoord | 21 | 21 | 0 | .500 | 10 ½ |
| Kinheim | 20 | 22 | 0 | .476 | 11 ½ |
| Hague Tornado's | 14 | 27 | 1 | .345 | 17 |
| Amsterdam Pirates | 14 | 27 | 1 | .345 | 17 |
| Almere '90 | 10 | 31 | 1 | .250 | 21 |

**Playoffs—Semifinals:** Neptunus defeated Sparta/Feyenoord 3-0 and HCAW defeated Hoofddorp 3-2 in best-of-5 series. **Final:** Neptunus defeated HCAW 3-1 in best-of-5 series.

# AMERICAS

## *MEXICO*

### MEXICAN LEAGUE

Member, National Association
**Class AAA**

*NOTE: The Mexican League is a member of the National Association of Professional Baseball Leagues and has a Triple-A classification. However, its member clubs operate largely independent of the 30 major league teams, and for that reason the league is listed in the international section.*

**Mailing Address:** Angel Pola No. 16, Col. Periodista, CP 11220, Mexico, D.F. **Telephone:** (011-52) 555-557-1007. **FAX:** (011-52) 555-395-2454. **E-Mail Address:** mbl@prodigy.net.mx. **Website:** www.lmb.com.mx.

**Years League Active:** 1955-.
**President:** Alejandro Hutt. **Operations Manager:** Nestor Alba Brito.

**Division Structure: North**—Aguascalientes, Laguna, Monclova, Monterrey, Puebla, San Luis Potosi, Saltillo, Tijuana. **South**—Angelopolis, Campeche, Cancún, Mexico City, Oaxaca, Tabasco, Veracruz, Yucatan.

**Regular Season:** 110 games (split-schedule). **2006 Opening Date:** March 21. **Closing Date:** July 30.

**All-Star Game:** May 27, site unavailable..

**Playoff Format:** Top six teams in each division qualify; first- and second-place teams in each division receive first-round byes. First, second and semifinal rounds are best-of-7 series; division champions meet in best-of-7 series for league championship.

**Roster Limit:** 28. **Roster Limit, Imports:** 6.

### AGUASCALIENTES RAILROADMEN

**Office Address:** Calle Manuel Madrigal y Juan de la Barrera, Colonia Heroes, Aguascalientes, Aguascalientes, CP 20250. **Telephone:** (011-52) 449-970-4585. **E-Mail Address:** rieleros@lmb.com.mx. **Website:** www.rieleros-deaguascalientes.com.mx.

**President:** Jean Paul Mansur Beltran. **General Manager:** Antelmo Hernandez.

**Manager:** Edurado Diaz.

### ANGELOPOLIS TIGERS

**Office Address:** Calle Paseo de las Fuentes, #13 Col. Arbodedas de Guadalupe, CP 72210, Puebla, Puebla. **Telephone:** (011-52) 222-236-4909. **FAX:** (011-52) 222-234-0192. **E-Mail Address:** tigres@tigresdemexico.com.mx. **Website:** www.tigresdemexico.com.mx.

**President:** Cuauhtémoc Rodriguez. **General Manager:** Iram Campos Lara.

**Manager:** Lee Sigman.

### CAMPECHE PIRATES

**Office Address:** Unidad Deportiva 20 de Noviembre, Local 4, CP 24000, Campeche, Campeche. **Telephone:** (011-52) 981-816-2116. **FAX:** (011-52) 981-816-3807. **E-Mail Address:** piratasc@prodigy.net.mx.

**President:** Gabriel Escalante Castillo. **General Manager:** Maria del Socorro Morales.

**Manager:** Manual Cazarin.

### CANCUN LOBSTERMEN

**Office Address:** Blvd. Kukulkan Km. 16.5, Zona Hotelera 2a. Seccion, Cancun, Quintana Roo, Mexico 77609. **Telephone:** (011-52) 998-885-2390. **FAX:** (011-52) 998-885-0516. **E-Mail Address:** fvillanueva@royal-resorts.com. **Website:** www.langosteros.com.mx.

**President:** Chara Mansur Beltran. **General Manager:** Carlos Aristi.

**Manager:** Javier Martinez.

### LAGUNA COWBOYS

**Office Address:** Juan Gutenberg s/n, Col. Centro, CP 27000, Torreon, Coahuila. **Telephone:** (011-52) 871-718-5515. **FAX:** (011-52) 871-717-4335. **E-Mail Address:** unionlag@prodigy.net.mx. **Website:** www.vaqueros laguna.com.

**President:** Jose Antonio Mansur Beltran. **General Manager:** Felipe Rodriguez.

**Manager:** Unavailable.

### MEXICO CITY RED DEVILS

**Office Address:** Av. Cuauhtemoc #451-101, Col. Narvarte, CP 03020, Mexico DF **Telephone:** (011-52) 555-639-8722. **FAX:** (011-52) 555-639-9722. **E-Mail Address:** diablos@sportsya.com. **Website:** www.diablos.com.mx.

**President:** Roberto Mansur Galán. **General Manager:** Eduardo de la Cerda.

**Manager:** Bernie Tatis.

### MONCLOVA STEELERS

**Office Address:** Cuauhtemoc #299, Col. Ciudad Deportiva, CP 25750, Monclova, Coahuila. **Telephone:** (011-52) 866-636-2334. **FAX:** (011-52) 866-636-2688. **E-Mail Address:** acererosdelnorte@prodigy.net.mx. **Website:** www.acereros.com.mx.

**President:** Donaciano Garza Gutierrez. **General Manager:** Victor Favela Lopez.

**Manager:** Lino Rivera.

### MONTERREY SULTANS

**Office Address:** Av. Manuel Barragan s/n, Estadio Monterrey, Apartado Postal 870, Monterrey, Nuevo Leon, CP 66460. **Telephone:** (011-52) 818-351-8022. **FAX:** (011-52) 818-351-8634. **E-Mail Address:** sultanes@sultanes.com.mx. **Website:** www.sultanes.com.mx.

**President:** José Maiz García. **General Manager:** Roberto Magdaleno Ramírez.

**Manager:** Dan Finova.

### OAXACA WARRIORS

**Office Address:** Privada del Chopo #105, Fraccionamiento El Chopo, CP 68050, Oaxaca, Oaxaca. **Telephone:** (011-52) 951-515-5522. **FAX:** (011-52) 951-515-4966. **E-Mail Address:** guerreros@infosel.net.mx. **Website:** www.guerrerosdeoaxaca.com.

**President:** Vicente Pérez Avellá Villa. **General Manager:** Guillermo Rodriguez Velazquez.

**Manager:** Nelson Barrera.

### PUEBLA PARROTS

**Office Address:** Calle Paseo de las Fuentes, #13 Col Arboledas de Guadalupe, CP 72210, Puebla, Puebla. **Telephone:** (011-52) 222-236-3313. **FAX:** (011-52) 222-236-2906. **E-Mail Address:** oficina@pericosdepuebla.com.mx. **Website:** www.pericosdepuebla.com.mx.

**President:** Samuel Lozano Molina. **General Manager:** Francisco Minjarez Garcia.

**Manager:** Unavailable.

### SALTILLO SARAPE MAKERS

**Office Address:** Blvd. Nazario Ortiz Esquina con Blvd.

Jesus Sanchez, CP 25280, Saltillo, Coahuila. **Telephone:** (011-52) 844-416-9455. **FAX:** (011-52) 844-439-1330. **E-Mail Address:** aley@grupoley.com. **Website:** www.saraperos.com.mx.
**President:** Juan Manuel Ley. **General Manager:** Carlos de la Garza.
**Manager:** Raul Cano.

### SAN LUIS POTOSI TUNEROS
**Office Address:** Av. Himno Nacional #400, Col. Himno Nacional, San Luis Postosi, CP 78280. **Telephone:** (011-52) 444-812-4940. **FAX:** (011-52) 444-812-4939.
**President:** Marcello De los Santos. **General Manager:** Leo Clayton.
**Manager:** Unavailable.

### TABASCO CATTLEMEN
**Office Address:** Explanada de la Ciudad Deportiva, Parque de Beisbol Centenario del 27 de Febrero, Col. Atasta de Serra, CP 86100, Villahermosa, Tabasco. **Telephone:** (011-52) 993-352-2787. **FAX:** (011-52) 993-352-2788. **E-Mail Address:** olmecastab@prodigy.net.mx.
**President:** Maximo Evia Ramirez. **General Manager:** Juan Antonio Balmaceda.
**Manager:** Sergio Borges.

### TIJUANA COLTS
**Office Address:** Blvd. Insurgentes 17017-21, Colonia Los Alamos, Tijuana, Baja California, Mexico 22320. **Telephone:**(011-52) 664-621-3787. **FAX:** (011-52) 664-621-3883. **E-Mail Address:** potros@potrosdetijuana.com. **Website:** www.potrosdetijuana.com.
**President:** Belisario Cabrera. **General Manager:** David Gonzalez.
**Manager:** Unavailable.

### VERACRUZ REDS
**Office Address:** Av. Jacarandas s/n, Esquina España, Fraccionamiento Virginia, CP 94294, Boca del Rio, Veracruz. **Telephone:** (011-52) 229-935-5004. **FAX:** (229) 935-5008. **E-Mail Address:** rojosdelaguila@terra.com.mx. **Website:** www.rojosdelaguila.com.mx.
**President/General Manager:** Carlos Nahun Hernandez.
**Manager:** Andres Mora.

### YUCATAN LIONS
**Office Address:** Calle 50 #406-B, Entre 35 y 37, Col. Jesus Carranza, CP 97109, Merida, Yucatán. **Telephone:** (011-52) 999-926-3022. **FAX:** (011-52) 999-926-3631. **E-Mail Addresses:** leonesy@sureste.com. **Website:** www.leonesdeyucatan.com.mx.
**President:** Gustavo Ricalde Durán. **General Manager:** Jose Rivero.
**Manager:** Francisco Estrada.

### MEXICAN ACADEMY
#### Rookie Classification
**Mailing Address:** Angel Pola No. 16, Col. Periodista, CP 11220, Mexico, D.F. **Telephone:** (011-52) 555-557-1007. **FAX:** (011-52) 555-395-2454. **E-Mail Address:** mbl@prodigy.net.mx. **Website:** www.lmb.com.mx.
**Member Clubs:** Celaya, Guanajuato, Queretaro, Salamanca.
**Regular Season:** 50 games. **2006 Opening Date:** Oct. 6. **Closing Date:** Dec. 18.

# DOMINICAN REPUBLIC
## DOMINICAN SUMMER LEAGUE
Member, National Association
#### Rookie Classification
**Mailing Address:** Calle Segunda No. 64, Reparto Antilla, Santo Domingo, Dominican Republic. **Telephone/FAX:** (809) 532-3619. **Website:** www.dominicansummerleague.com. **E-Mail Address:** ligadeverano@codetel.net.do.
**Years League Active:** 1985-.
**President:** Freddy Jana. **Administrative Assistant:** Orlando Diaz.
**2006 Member Clubs/Participating Organizations:** Angels, Astros, Athletics I, Athletics II, Blue Jays, Braves I, Braves II, Cardinals, Cubs, Diamondbacks, Dodgers I, Dodgers II, Giants, Indians I, Indians II, Mariners, Marlins, Mets, Nationals, Orioles, Padres, Phillies, Pirates, Rangers, Reds, Red Sox, Rockies, Royals, Tigers, Twins, White Sox, Yankees I, Yankees II.
**Regular Season:** 70-72 games, depending on divisions. **2006 Opening Date:** June 3. **Closing Date:** Aug. 25.
**Playoff Format:** Six divisions; two division champions with best winning percentages receive first-round byes. Four teams meet in best-of-3 quarterfinals; winners and division champions with first-round byes meet in best-of-3 semifinals; winners meet in best-of-5 series for league championship.
**Roster Limit:** 35; 30 active. **Player Eligibility Rule:** No more than eight players 20 or older and no more than two players 21 or older. At least 10 players must be pitchers. No more than four years of prior service, excluding Rookie leagues outside the U.S. and Canada.

# VENEZUELA
## VENEZUELAN SUMMER LEAGUE
Member, National Association
#### Rookie Classification
**Mailing Address:** C.C. Caribbean Plaza Modulo 8, P.A. Local 173-174, Valencia, Carabobo, Venezuela. **Telephone:** (011-58) 241-824-0321, (011) 58-241-824-0980. **FAX:** (011-58) 241-824-0705. **Website:** www.vsl.com.ve.
**Years League Active:** 1997-.
**Administrator:** Saul Gonzalez Acevedo. **Coordinator:** Ramon Feriera.
**2006 Member Clubs:** Aguirre, Cagua, Ciudad Alienza, San Joaquin, Troconero 1, Tronconero 2, Universidad, Venoco 1, Venoco 2. **Participating Organizations:** Astros, Blue Jays, Mariners, Marlins, Mets, Orioles, Phillies, Pirates, Reds, Red Sox, Rockies, Twins.
**Regular Season:** 60 games. **2006 Opening Date:** June 3. **Closing Date:** Aug. 25.
**Playoffs:** Best-of-3 series between top two teams in regular season.
**Roster Limit:** 35; 30 active. **Player Eligibility Rule:** No player on active list may have more than three years of minor league service. Open to players from all Latin American Spanish-speaking countries except the Dominican Republic and Puerto Rico.

# ASIA

## *CHINA*

### CHINA BASEBALL ASSOCIATION

**Mailing Address:** 5, Tiyuguan Road, Beijing 100763, Peoples Republic of China. **Telephone:** (011-86) 10-85826002. **FAX:** (011-86) 10-85825994. **E-Mail Address:** chinabaseball2008@yahoo.com.cn.

**Years League Active:** 2002-.

**Chairman:** Hu Jian Guo. **Vice Chairmen:** Tom McCarthy, Shen Wei. **Executive Director:** Yang Jie. **General Manager, Marketing/Promotion:** Lin Xiao Wu.

**Member Clubs:** Beijing Tigers, China Hopestars, Guangdong Leopards, Shanghai Eagles, Sichuan Dragons, Tianjin Lions.

**Regular Season:** 30 games.

**Playoff Format:** Top two teams meet in best-of-5 series for league championship.

**Import Rule:** Three players on active roster.

## *JAPAN*

**Mailing Address:** Imperial Tower, 14F, 1-1-1 Uchisaiwai-cho, Chiyoda-ku, Tokyo 100-0011. **Telephone:** 03-3502-0022. **FAX:** 03-3502-0140.

**Commissioner:** Yasuchika Negoro.

**Executive Secretary:** Kazuo Hasegawa. **Executive Director:** Kunio Shimoda. **Director, Baseball Operations:** Nobby Ito. **Assistant Directors, International Affairs:** Tack Nakajima, Tex Nakamura.

**Japan Series:** Best-of-7 series between Central and Pacific League champions, begins Oct. 21 at home of Central League club.

**All-Star Series:** July 21 at Jingu Stadium, Tokyo; July 22 at Sun Marine Stadium, Miyazaki.

**Roster Limit:** 70 per organization (one major league club, one minor league club). Major league club is permitted to register 28 players at a time, though just 25 may be available for each game.

**Roster Limit, Imports:** 4 (2 position players and 2 pitchers; 3 position players and 1 pitcher or 3 pitchers and 1 position player) in majors; unlimited in minors.

### CENTRAL LEAGUE

**Mailing Address:** Asahi Bldg. 3F, 6-6-7 Ginza, Chuo-ku, Tokyo 104-0061. **Telephone:** 03-3572-1673. **FAX:** 03-3571-4545.

**President:** Hajime Toyokura.

**Secretary General:** Hideo Okoshi. **Planning Department:** Masaaki Nagino. **Public Relations:** Kazu Ogaki.

**Regular Season:** 146 games. **2006 Opening Date:** March 31. **Closing Date:** Oct. 5.

**Playoff Format:** None.

### CHUNICHI DRAGONS

**Mailing Address:** Chunichi Bldg. 6F, 4-1-1 Sakae, Naka-ku, Nagoya 460-0008. **Telephone:** 052-252-5226. **FAX:** 052-263-7696.

**Chairman:** Bungo Shirai. **President:** Junnosuke Nishikawa. **General Manager:** Kazumasa Ito. **Field Manager:** Hiromitsu Ochiai.

**2006 Foreign Players:** Domingo Guzman, Luis Martinez, Alex Ochoa, Tyrone Woods, Chen Wei Yin (Taiwan).

### HANSHIN TIGERS

**Mailing Address:** 1-47 Koshien-cho, Nishinomiya-shi, Hyogo-ken 663-8152.

**Telephone:** 0798-46-1515. **FAX:** 0798-46-3555.

**Chairman:** Masatoshi Tezuka. **President:** Yoshihiro Makita. **Field Manager:** Akinobu Okada.

**2006 Foreign Players:** Darwin Cubillan, Chris Oxspring, Andy Sheets, Shane Spencer, Jeff Williams.

### HIROSHIMA TOYO CARP

**Mailing Address:** 5-25 Motomachi, Naka-ku, Hiroshima 730-8508.

**Telephone:** 082-221-2040. **FAX:** 082-228-5013.

**President:** Hajime Matsuda. **General Manager:** Kiyoaki Suzuki. **Field Manager:** Marty Brown.

**2006 Foreign Players:** John Bale, Sean Douglass, Juan Feliciano, Mike Romano. **Coach:** Jeff Livesey.

### TOKYO YAKULT SWALLOWS

**Mailing Address:** Shimbashi MCV Bldg. 5F, 5-13-5 Shimbashi, Minato-ku, Tokyo 105-0004. **Telephone:** 03-5470-8915. **FAX:** 03-5470-8916.

**Chairman:** Sumiya Hori. **President:** Yoshikazu Tagiku. **General Manager:** Kesanori Kurashima. **Field Manager:** Atsuya Furuta.

**2006 Foreign Players:** Dicky Gonzalez, Rick Guttormson, Greg LaRocca, Alex Ramirez, Alex Ramirez Jr., Adam Riggs.

### YOKOHAMA BAYSTARS

**Mailing Address:** Kannai Arai Bldg, 7F, 1-8 Onoe-cho, Naka-ku, Yokohama 231-0015. **Telephone:** 045-681-0811. **FAX:** 045-661-2500.

**Chairman:** Kiyoshi Wakabayashi. **President:** Susumu Minegishi. **Field Manager:** Kazuhiko Ushijima.

**2006 Foreign Players:** Jason Beverlin, Marc Kroon. **Coach:** John Turney.

### YOMIURI GIANTS

**Mailing Address:** Otemachi Nomura Bldg., 7F, 2-1-1 Otemachi, Chiyoda-ku, Tokyo 100-8151. **Telephone:** 03-3246-7733. **FAX:** 03-3246-2726.

**Chairman:** Takuo Takihana. **President:** Tsunekazu Momoi. **General Manager:** Hidetoshi Kiyotake. **Field Manager:** Tatsunori Hara.

**2006 Foreign Players:** Chiang Chien-ming (Taiwan), Joe Dillon, Gary Glover, Jeremy Powell, Lee Seung-Yeop (Korea).

### PACIFIC LEAGUE

**Mailing Address:** Asahi Bldg. 9F, 6-6-7 Ginza, Chuo-ku, Tokyo 104-0061. **Telephone:** 03-3573-1551. **FAX:** 03-3572-5843.

**President:** Tadao Koike. **Secretary General:** Shigeru Murata. **Administration Department:** Katsuhisa Matsuzaki. **Regular Season:** 136 games. **2006 Opening Date:** March 25. **Closing Date:** Sept. 27.

**Playoff Format—**Stage 1: second-place team meets third-place team in best-of-3 series. Stage 2: Winner of Stage 1 meets first-place team in best-of-5 series for league championship.

### CHIBA LOTTE MARINES

**Mailing Address:** WBG Marive West 26F, 2-6 Nakase, Mihama-ku, Chiba-shi, Chiba-ken 261-8587. **Telephone:** 043-297-2101. **FAX:** 043-297-2181.

**Chairman:** Takeo Shigemitsu. **President:** Eisuke Hamamoto. **Field Manager:** Bobby Valentine.

**2006 Foreign Players:** Benny Agbayani, Kevin Beirne, Matt Franco, Val Pascucci. **Coaches:** Frank Ramppen, Tom Robson.

## FUKUOKA SOFTBANK HAWKS

**Mailing Address:** Fukuoka Yahoo! Japan Dome, Hawks Town, Chuo-ku, Fukuoka 810-0065. **Telephone:** 092-844-1189. **FAX:** 092-844-4600.

**Chairman:** Masayoshi Son. **General Manager:** Sadaharu Oh. **Field Manager:** Sadaharu Oh.

**2006 Foreign Players:** Jolbert Cabrera, D.J. Carrasco, Yang Yao-hsun (Taiwan), Julio Zuleta.

## HOKKAIDO NIPPON HAM FIGHTERS

**Mailing Address:** 1 Hitsujigaoka, Toyohira-ku, Sapporo 062-8655. **Telephone:** 011-857-3939. **FAX:** 011-857-3900.

**Chairman:** Hiroji Okoso. **Acting Owner:** Takeshi Kojima. **President:** Junji Imamura. **General Manager:** Shigeru Takada. **Field Manager:** Trey Hillman.

**2006 Foreign Players:** Felix Diaz, Corey Lee, Jose Macias, Fernando Seguignol, Brad Thomas. **Coach:** Mike Brown.

## ORIX BUFFALOES

**Mailing Address:** Skymark Stadium, Midoridai, Suma-ku, Kobe 654-0163. **Telephone:** 078-795-1203. **FAX:** 078-795-1205.

**Chairman:** Yoshihiko Miyauchi. **President:** Takashi Koizumi. **Field Manager:** Katsuhiro Nakamura.

**2006 Foreign Players:** Cliff Brumbaugh, Tom Davey, Karim Garcia, Jason Grabowski, Dan Serafini.

## SEIBU LIONS

**Mailing Address:** 2135 Kami-Yamaguchi, Tokorozawa-shi, Saitama-ken 359-1189. **Telephone:** 04-2924-1155. **FAX:** 04-2928-1919.

**Team President:** Hidekazu Ota. **General Manager:** Akira Kuroiwa. **Field Manager:** Tsutomu Ito.

**2006 Foreign Players:** Alex Cabrera, Chang Chi-Chie (Taiwan), Alex Graman, Chris Gissell, Jeff Liefer, Hsu Ming-chieh (Taiwan).

## TOHOKU RAKUTEN GOLDEN EAGLES

**Mailing Address:** NAViS Building, 5-12-55 Tsutsujigaoka, Miyagino-ku, Sendai 983-0852. **Telephone:** 022-298-5300. FAX: 022-298-5360.

**Chairman:** Hiroshi Mikitani. **President:** Toru Shimada. **Field Manager:** Katsuya Nomura.

**2006 Foreign Players:** Cedrick Bowers, Jose Fernandez, Rick Short, Lin Ying-chieh (Taiwan).

# *KOREA*

## KOREA BASEBALL ORGANIZATION

**Mailing Address:** 946-16 Dokokdong, Kangnam-gu, Seoul, Korea. **Telephone:** (02) 3460-4643. **FAX:** (02) 3460-4649.

**Years League Active:** 1982-.

**Commissioner:** Park Yong-oh. **Secretary General:** Lee Sang-kook. **Deputy Secretary General:** Lee Sang-il.

**Division Structure:** None.

**Regular Season:** 132. **2006 Opening Date:** March 12. **Closing Date:** Aug. 30.

**Korean Series:** Regular-season champion automatically qualifies for Korean Series. Third- and fourth-place teams meet in best-of-3 series; winner advances to meet second-place team in best-of-5 series; winner meets first-place team in best-of-7 series for league championship.

**Roster Limit:** 27 active through Sept. 1, when rosters expand to 32. **Imports:** 2 active.

## DOOSAN BEARS

**Mailing Address:** Chamsil Baseball Stadium, 10 Chamsil-1 dong, Songpa-ku, Seoul, Korea 138-221. **Telephone:** (02) 2240-1777. **FAX:** (02) 2240-1788. **Website:** www.doosanbears.com.

**President:** Kyung Chang-Ho. **Manager:** Kim Kyung-Moon.

## HANHWA EAGLES

**Mailing Address:** 22-1 Youngjeon-dong, Dong-ku, Daejeon, Korea 300-200. **Telephone:** (042) 637-6001. **FAX:** (042) 632-2929. **Website:** www.hanwhaeagles.co.kr.

**General Manager:** Song Kyu-Soo. **Manager:** Yoo Seung-an.

## HYUNDAI UNICORNS

**Mailing Address:** Hyundai Haesang Bldg., 9th Floor, 1014 Kwonseon-dong, Kwonseon-ku, Suwon, Kyungki-do, Korea 441-390. **Telephone:** (031) 226-9000. **FAX:** (031) 224-9107. **Website:** www.hd-unicorns.co.kr.

**General Manager:** Jeong Jae-ho. **Manager:** Kim Jae-park.

## KIA TIGERS

**Mailing Address:** 266 Naebang-dong, Seo-ku, Gwangju, Korea 502-807. **Telephone:** (062) 370-1895. **FAX:** (062) 525-5350. **Website:** www.kiatigers.co.kr.

**General Manager:** Jeong Jae-kong. **Manager:** Kim Sung-han.

## LG TWINS

**Mailing Address:** Chamshil Baseball Stadium, 10 Chamshil 1-dong, Songpa-ku, Seoul, Korea 138-221. **Telephone:** (02) 2005-5760-5. **FAX** (02) 2005-5801. **Website:** www.lgtwins.com.

**General Manager:** You Sung-min. **Manager:** Lee Soon-Chul.

## LOTTE GIANTS

**Mailing Address:** 930 Sajik-dong Dongrae-Ku, Pusan, Korea, 607-120. **Telephone:** (051) 505-7422. **FAX:** 51-506-0090. **Website:** www.lotte-giants.co.kr.

**General Manager:** Lee Sang-koo. **Manager:** Kang Byng-chul.

## SAMSUNG LIONS

**Mailing Address:** 184-3, Sunhwari-jinrliangyun, Kyungsan, Kyungsan, Kyungsangbuk-do, Korea 712-830. **Telephone:** (053) 859-3114. **FAX:** (053) 859-3117. **Website:** www.samsunglions.com.

**General Manager:** Kim Eung-yong. **Manager:** Sun Dong-yeol.

## SK WYVERNS

**Mailing Address:** 8 San, Moonhak-dong, Nam-ku, Inchon, Korea 402-070. **Telephone:** (032) 422-7949. **FAX:** (032) 429-4565. **Website:** www.skwyvers.com.

**General Manager:** Choi Jong-joon. **Manager:** Cho Bum-hyun.

# *TAIWAN*

## CHINESE PROFESSIONAL BASEBALL LEAGUE

**Mailing Address:** 2F, No. 32, Pateh Road, Sec. 3, Taipei, Taiwan. **Telephone:** 886-2-2577-6992. **FAX:** 886-2-2577-2606. **Website:** www.cpbl.com.tw.

**Years League Active:** 1990-.

**Commissioner:** Harvey Chen. **Secretary General:** Wayne Lee.

**Member Clubs:** Brother Elephants (Taipei), China

Trust Whales (Chiayi City), President Lions (Tainan), Sinon Bulls (Taichung), La New Bears (Kaohsiung), Makoto Cobras (Taipei).

**Regular Season:** 100 games (split schedule). **2005 Opening Date:** March 6. **Closing Date:** Oct. 1.

**Championship Series:** Split-season champions meet in best-of-7 series for league championship.

**Import Rule:** Only three import players may be active, and only two may be on the field at the same time.

# EUROPE

## *HOLLAND*

### DUTCH MAJOR LEAGUE

**Mailing Address:** Koninklijke Nederlandse Baseball en Softball Bond (Royal Dutch Baseball and Softball Association), "Twinstate II", Perkinsbaan 15, 3439 ND Nieuwegein, Holland. **Telephone:** 31-(0) 30-607-6070. **FAX:** 31-30-294-3043. **Website:** www.knbsb.nl.
**President:** Hans Meijer.

### ADO TORNADOS

**Mailing Address:** Postbus 47994, 2504 CG Den Haag. **Telephone:** +31 (0) 70-366 97 22. **Website:** www.svado.nl.

### ALMERE '90

**Mailing Address:** B.S.C. Almere '90, Estafettelaan 2, 1318 EG Almere. **Telephone:** +31 (0) 36-536 4576. **Website:** www.almere90.nl.

### AMSTERDAM PIRATES

**Mailing Address:** Postbus 8862, 1006 JB Amsterdam. **Telephone:** +31 (0) 20-6126969.

### HCAW

**Mailing Address:** Mr. Cocker HCAW, Postbus 1321, 1400 BH Bussum. **Telephone:** +31 (0) 35-693- 14 30. **Website:** www.hcaw.nl.

### HOOFDDORP PIONIERS

**Mailing Address:** Postbus 475, 2130 AL Hoofddorp. **Telephone:** +31 (0) 23-561 35 57. **Website:** www.hoofddorp-pioniers.nl.

### KINHEIM

**Mailing Address:** Gemeentelijk Sportpark, Badmintonpad, 2023 BT Haarlem. **Telephone:** +31 (0) 23-525 13 39. **Website:** www.kinheim.net.

### NEPTUNUS

**Mailing Address:** Sportclub Neptunus, Postbus 35064, 3005 DB Rotterdam. **Telephone:** +31 (0) 180-412 722. **Website:** www.neptunussport.com.

### SPARTA/FEYENOORD

**Mailing Address:** Postbus 9211, 3007 AE Rotterdam. **Telephone:** +31 (0) 181-326-194. **Website:** www.spartafeyenoord.com.

## *ITALY*

### SERIE A

**Mailing Address:** Federazione Italiana Baseball Softball, Viale Tiziano 74, 00196 Roma, Italy. **Telephone:** 39-06-36858376. **FAX:** 39-06-36858201. **Website:** www.baseball-softball.it.
**President:** Riccardo Fraccari. **General Secretary:** Marcello Standoli.

### BOLOGNA

**Mailing Address:** Piazzale Atleti Azzurri d'Italia, 40122 Bologna. **Telephone:** 39-051-479618. **FAX:** 39-051-554000. **E-Mail Address:** fortitudobaseball@tin.it. **Website:** www.fortitudobaseball.com.

**President:** Alfredo Pacini. **Manager:** Marco Nanni.

### GROSSETO

**Mailing Address:** Via Papa Giovanni XXIII, 8, 58100 Grosseto. **Telephone:** 39-0564-494149. **FAX:** 39-0564-476750. **E-Mail Address:** info@bbcgrosseto.it. **Website:** www.bbcgrosseto.it.
**President:** Claudio Banchi. **Manager:** Mauro Mazzotti.

### MODENA

**Mailing Address:** Via Minutara 24, 41100 Modena. **Telephone:** 39-059-371655. **FAX:** 39-059-365300. **E-Mail Address:** info@modenabaseball.com. **Website:** www.modenabaseball.com.
**President:** Giovanni Tinti. **Manager:** Mario Labastidas.

### NETTUNO

**Mailing Address:** Via Borghese Scipione, 00048 Nettuno (Roma). **Telephone/FAX:** 39-06-9854966. **E-Mail Address:** web@nettunobaseball.net. **Website:** www.nettunobaseball.net.
**President:** Augusto Spigoni. **Manager:** Ruggero Bagialemani.

### PARMA

**Mailing Address:** Via Donatore 4, Collecchio, 43044 Parma. **Telephone/FAX:** 39-0521-774-301. **E-Mail Address:** info@parmabaseball.it. **Website:** www.parmabaseball.it.
**President:** Rossano Rinaldi. **Manager:** Chris Catanoso.

### PATERNO

**Mailing Address:** Viale dei Platani 15 , 95047 Paterno. **Telephone/FAX:** 39-095 843152. **E-Mail Address:** team@warriorspaterno.com. **Website:** www.warriorspaterno.com.
**President:** Mario Raciti. **Manager:** Alejandro Duret.

### REGGIO EMILIA

**Mailing Address:** Via Petit Bon 1, 42100 Reggio Emilia. **Telephone/FAX:** 39-0522 558156. **E-Mail Address:** info@reggiobaseball.it. **Website:** www.reggiobaseball.it.
**President:** Graziella Casali. **Manager:** Gilberto Gerali.

### RIMINI

**Mailing Address:** Via Monaco 2, 47900 Rimini. **Telephone/FAX:** 39-0541-741761. **E-Mail Address:** pirati@baseballrimini.com. **Website:** www.baseballrimini.com. **President:** Cesare Zangheri. **Manager:** Michele Romano.

### SAN MARINO

**Mailing Address:** Via Piana 37, 47031 Republic of San Marino. **Telephone:** 39-0549-991170. **FAX:** 39-0549-991247.
**President:** Giorgio Pancotti. **Manager:** Doriano Bindi.

### TRIESTE

**Mailing Address:** Via degli Alpini 15, 34100 Trieste. **Telephone/FAX:** 39-040-213585. **E-Mail Address:** segreteria@alpinabaseball.it. **Website:** www.alpinabaseball.it.
**President:** Igor Dolenc. **Manager:** Unavailable.

# WINTER
## LEAGUES

# 2005-2006
## STANDINGS

### CARIBBEAN SERIES

|  | W | L | PCT | GB |
|---|---|---|---|---|
| Venezuela | 6 | 0 | 1.000 |  |
| Dominican Republic | 4 | 2 | .667 |  |
| Puerto Rico | 2 | 4 | .333 |  |
| Mexico | 0 | 6 | .000 |  |

### DOMINICAN LEAGUE

| REGULAR SEASON | W | L | PCT | GB |
|---|---|---|---|---|
| Licey | 32 | 18 | .640 | — |
| Aguilas | 27 | 23 | .540 | 5 |
| Escogido | 26 | 23 | .531 | 5 ½ |
| Azucareros | 25 | 24 | .510 | 6 ½ |
| Estrellas | 22 | 28 | .440 | 10 |
| Gigantes | 17 | 33 | .340 | 15 |

| ROUND-ROBIN | W | L | PCT | GB |
|---|---|---|---|---|
| Aguilas | 12 | 5 | .706 | — |
| Licey | 10 | 8 | .556 | 2 ½ |
| Escogido | 7 | 10 | .412 | 5 |
| Azucareros | 6 | 12 | .333 | 6 ½ |

**CHAMPIONSHIP SERIES:** Licey defeated Aguilas 5-2 in best-of-7 series for league championship.

### MEXICAN PACIFIC LEAGUE

|  | W | L | PCT | GB |
|---|---|---|---|---|
| *Navojoa | 39 | 29 | .574 | — |
| Guasave | 36 | 32 | .529 | 3 |
| #Mazatlan | 35 | 32 | .522 | 3 ½ |
| Hermosillo | 34 | 33 | .507 | 4 ½ |
| Mochis | 34 | 34 | .500 | 5 |
| Obregon | 33 | 35 | .485 | 6 |
| Culiacan | 31 | 36 | .463 | 7 ½ |
| Mexicali | 28 | 39 | .418 | 10 ? |

(* first half champion, # second half champion)

**PLAYOFFS: Quarterfinals**—Navojoa defeated Culiacan 4-1; Guasave defeated Mochis 4-2 and Hermosillo defeated Mazatlan 4-2 in best-of-7 series. **Semifinals**—Mazatlan defeated Navojoa 4-2 and Guasave defeated Hermosillo 4-3 in best-of-7 series. **Final**—Mazatlan defeated Gusave 4-1 in best-of-7 series.

### PUERTO RICAN LEAGUE

|  | W | L | PCT | GB |
|---|---|---|---|---|
| Manati | 24 | 17 | .585 | — |

|  | W | L | PCT | GB |
|---|---|---|---|---|
| Carolina | 23 | 18 | .561 | 1 |
| Ponce | 21 | 22 | .488 | 4 |
| Caguas | 20 | 21 | .488 | 4 |
| Mayaguez | 19 | 23 | .452 | 5 ½ |
| Arecibo | 17 | 23 | .425 | 6 ½ |

**PLAYOFFS: Semifinals**—Ponce defeated Manati 4-0 and Carolina defeated Caguas 4-1 in best-of-7 series. **Final**—Carolina defeated Ponce 5-3 in best-of-9 series for league championship.

### VENEZUELAN LEAGUE

| OCCIDENTE | W | L | PCT | GB |
|---|---|---|---|---|
| Aragua | 38 | 24 | .613 | — |
| Lara | 27 | 35 | .435 | 11 |
| Occidente | 23 | 38 | .377 | 14 ½ |
| Zulia | 23 | 39 | .371 | 15 |

| ORIENTE | W | L | PCT | GB |
|---|---|---|---|---|
| Magallanes | 39 | 23 | .629 | — |
| Caracas | 34 | 27 | .557 | 4 ½ |
| Oriente | 32 | 30 | .516 | 7 |
| La Guaira | 31 | 31 | .500 | 8 |

| ROUND-ROBIN | W | L | PCT | GB |
|---|---|---|---|---|
| Aragua | 10 | 6 | .625 | — |
| Caracas | 10 | 6 | .625 | — |
| Magallanes | 9 | 7 | .563 | 1 |
| Lara | 7 | 9 | .467 | 3 |
| Oriente | 4 | 12 | .250 | 6 |

**CHAMPIONSHIP SERIES:** Caracas defeated Aragua 4-1 in best-of-7 series for league championship.

### ARIZONA FALL LEAGUE

| AMERICAN | W | L | PCT | GB |
|---|---|---|---|---|
| Scottsdale Scorpions | 17 | 15 | .531 | — |
| Mesa Solar Sox | 15 | 16 | .484 | 1 ½ |
| Peoria Saguaros | 8 | 23 | .258 | 8 ½ |

| NATIONAL | W | L | PCT | GB |
|---|---|---|---|---|
| Phoenix Desert Dogs | 22 | 10 | .688 | — |
| Peoria Javelinas | 17 | 14 | .548 | 4 ½ |
| Grand Canyon Rafters | 15 | 16 | .484 | 6 ½ |

**PLAYOFF:** Phoenix Desert Dogs defeated Scottsdale Scorpions 1-0 for league championship.

# WINTER
## BASEBALL

## CARIBBEAN BASEBALL CONFEDERATION

**Mailing Address:** Frank Feliz Miranda No. 1 Naco, Santo Domingo, Dominican Republic. **Telephone:** (809) 562-4737, 562-4715. **FAX:** (809) 565-4654.

**Commissioner:** Juan Fco. Puello Herrera. **Secretary:** Benny Agosto.

**Member Countries:** Dominican Republic, Mexico, Puerto Rico, Venezuela.

**2007 Caribbean Series:** Dates/site unavailable.

## DOMINICAN LEAGUE

**Office Address:** Estadio Quisqueya, 2da. Planta, Ens. La Fe, Santo Domingo, D.N., Dominican Republic. **Mailing Address:** Apartado Postal 1246, Santo Domingo, D.N., Dominican Republic. **Telephone:** (809) 567-6371, (809) 563-5085. **FAX:** (809) 567-5720. **E-Mail Address:** info@besiboldominicano.com. **Website:** www.lidom.com.

**Years League Active:** 1951-.

**President:** Dr. Leonardo Matos Berrido. **Administrator:** Marcos Rodríguez. **Public Relations Director:** Jorge Torres.

**Regular Season:** 50 games. **2006 Opening Date:** Oct. 22. **Closing Date:** Dec 22.

**Playoff Format:** Top four teams meet in 18-game round-robin. Top two teams advance to best-of-9 series for league championship. Winner advances to Caribbean Series.

**Roster Limit:** 30. **Roster Limit, Imports:** 7.

### AGUILAS CIBAENAS

**Office Address:** Estadio Cibao, Apartado 111, Santiago, Dom. Rep. **Mailing Address:** Calle 3, No. 16, Reparto Oquet, Santiago, Dom. Rep.. **Telephone:** (809) 575-1810. **FAX:** (809) 575-0865. **E-Mail Address:** info@lasaguilas.com **Website:** www.lasaguilas.com.

**President:** Winston Llenas. **General Manager:** Reynaldo Bisono.

**2005-2006 Manager:** Felix Fermin.

### AZUCAREROS DEL ESTE

**Mailing Address:** Estadio Francisco Micheli, La Romana, Dom. Rep. **Telephone:** (809) 556-6189. **FAX:** (809) 550-1550. **E-Mail Address:** torosdeleste@codetel.net.do. **Website:** www.azucarerosdeleste.com.

**President:** Francisco Micheli. **General Manager:** Pablo Peguero.

**2005-2006 Manager:** Luis Silverio.

### LEONES DEL ESCOGIDO

**Office Address:** Estadio Quisqueya, Ens. la Fe, Apartado Postal 1287, Santo Domingo, Dom. Rep. **Telephone:** (809) 565-1910. **FAX:** (809) 567-7643. **E-Mail Address:** info@escogido.com. **Website:** www.escogido.com.do.

**President:** Julio Hazim Risk. **General Manager:** Raymond Abreu.

**2005-2006 Managers:** Bob Geren/Mike Guerrero.

### ESTRELLAS ORIENTALES

**Office Address:** Estadio Tetelo Vargas, San Pedro de Macoris, Dom. Rep. **Telephone:** (809) 529-3618. **FAX:** (809) 526-7658. **E-Mail Address:** info@estrellasdeoriente.com . **Website:** www.estrellasdeoriente.com.

**President:** Manuel Antim Battle. **General Manager:** Manuel Antun.

**2005-2006 Manager:** Luis Natera.

### TIGRES DE LICEY

**Office Address:** Estadio Quisqueya, Apartado Postal 1321, Santo Domingo, Dom. Rep. **Telephone:** (809) 567-3090. **FAX:** (809) 542-7714. **E-Mail Address:** fernando.ravelo@codetel.net.do. **Website:** www.licey.com.

**President:** Emigolo Garrido. **General Manager:** Fernando Ravelo Jana.

**2005-2006 Manager:** Manny Acta.

### GIGANTES DEL CIBAO

**Office Address:** Estadio Julian Javier, San Francisco de Macoris, Dom. Rep. **Telephone:** (809) 482-0741. **FAX:** (809) 588-8733. **Website:** www.gigantesdelcibao.com.

**President:** Alberto Genao. **General Manager:** Martin Almanzar.

**2005-2006 Manager:** Arturo de Freites.

## MEXICAN PACIFIC LEAGUE

**Mailing Address:** Av. Insurgentes No. 847 Sur, Interior 402, Edificio San Carlos, Col. Centro, CP 80120, Culiacan, Sinaloa. **Telephone/FAX:** (011-52) 667-761-25-70, (011-52) 667-761-25-71. **E-Mail Address:** ligadelpacifico@ligadelpacifico.com.mx. **Website:** www.ligadelpacifico.com.mx.

**Years League Active:** 1958-.

**President:** Renato Vega Alvarado. **General Manager:** Oviel Dennis Gonzalez.

**Regular Season:** 68 games. **2005-2006 Opening Date:** Oct. 9. **Closing Date:** Dec. 28.

**Playoff Format:** Six teams advance to best-of-7 quarterfinals. Three winners and losing team with best record advance to best-of-7 semifinals. Winners meet in best-of-7 series for league championship. Winner advances to Caribbean World Series.

**Roster Limit:** 30. **Roster Limit, Imports:** 5.

### TOMATEROS DE CULIACAN

**Street Address:** Av. Alvaro Obregon 348 Sur, CP 8000, Culiacan, Sinaloa, Mexico. **Telephone:** (011-52) 667-712-2446. **FAX:** (011-52) 667-715-6828. **E-Mail Address:** tomateros@infosel.com.mx. **Website:** www.tomateros.com.mx.

**President:** Juan Manuel Ley Lopez. **General Managers:** Eduardo Valenzuela.

**2005-2006 Manager:** Francisco Estrada.

### ALGODONEROS DE GUASAVE

**Mailing Address:** Obregon No. 43, CP 81000, Guasave, Sinaloa, Mexico. **Telephone:** (011-52) 687-872-29-98. **FAX:** (011-52) 687-872-14-31. **E-Mail Address:** algodon@prodigy.net.mx. **Website:** www.clubalgodoneros.org.

**President:** Fausto Perez. **General Manager:** Jaime Blancarte.

**2005-2006 Manager:** Unavailable.

### NARANJEROS DE HERMOSILLO

**Mailing Address:** Blvd. Solidaridad s/n, Estadio Hector Espino, E/Jose S. Healey Y Blvd., Luis Encinas, CP 83188,

Hermosillo, Sonora, Mexico. **Telephone:** (011-52) 662-260-69-32. **FAX:** (011-52) 662-260-69-31. **E-Mail Address:** webmaster@naranjeros.com.mx. **Website:** www.naranjeros.com.
**President:** Enrique Mazon Rubio. **General Manager:** Marco Antonio Manzo.
**2005-2006 Manager:** Lorenzo Bundy.

### CANEROS DE LOS MOCHIS
**Mailing Address:** Francisco I. Madero No. 116 Oriente, CP 81200, Los Mochis, Sinaloa, Mexico. **Telephone:** (011-52) 668-812-86-02. **FAX:** (011-52) 668-812-67-40. **E-Mail Address:** www.verdes.com.mx. **Website:** verdes@prodigy.net.mx.
**President:** Mario Lopez Valdez. **General Manager:** Antonio Castro Chavez.
**2005-2006 Manager:** Juan Navarrete.

### VENADOS DE MAZATLAN
**Mailing Address:** Gutierrez Najera No. 821, CP 82000, Mazatlan, Sinaloa, Mexico. **Telephone:** (011-52) 669-981-17-10. **FAX:** (011-52) 669-981-17-11. **E-Mail Address:** club@venadosdemazatlan.com.mx. **Website:** www.venadosdemazatlan.com.mx.
**President:** José Luis Martínez Moreno. **General Manager:** Alejandro Lizarraga.
**2005-2006 Manager:** Unavailable.

### AGUILAS DE MEXICALI
**Mailing Address:** Estadio De Beisbol De La Cd. Deportiva, Calz. Cuautemoc s/n, Las Fuentes Mexicali, Baja, CA, Mexico. **Telephone:** (011-52) 686-567-0040. **FAX:** (011-52) 686-567-0095. **E-Mail Address:** aguilas2@telnor.net. **Website:** www.aguilasdemexicali.com.mx.
**President:** Dio Alberto Murillo. **General Manager:** Jesus Sommers.
**2005-2006 Manager:** Tim Johnson.

### MAYOS DE NAVOJOA
**Mailing Address:** Antonio Rosales No. 102, E/Pesqueira Y no Reeleccion, CP 85830, Navojoa, Sonora, Mexico. **Telephone:** (011-52) 642-422-14-33. **FAX:** (011-52) 642-422-89-97. **E-Mail Address:** mayosbeisbol@mayosbeisbol.com. **Website:** www.mayosbeisbol.com.
**President:** Victor Cuevas Garibay. **General Manager:** Lauro Villalobos.
**2005-2006 Manager:** Mario Mendoza.

### YAQUIS DE OBREGON
**Mailing Address:** Guerrero y Michoacan, Estadio de Beisbol Tomas Oroz Gaytan, CP 85130, Ciudad Obregon, Sonora, Mexico. **Telephone:** (011-52) 644-413-77-66. **FAX:** (011-52) 644-414-11-56. **E-Mail Address:** clubyaquisdeobregon@yaquisdeobregon.com.mx. **Website:** www.yaquisdeobregon.com.mx.
**President:** Luis Alfonso Lugo Platt. **General Manager:** Roberto Diaz Gonzalez.
**2005-2006 Manager:** Homar Rojas.

## PUERTO RICAN LEAGUE
**Office Address:** Avenida Munoz Rivera 1056, Edificio First Federal, Suite 501, Rio Piedras, PR 00925. **Mailing Address:** P.O. Box 191852, San Juan, PR 00019. **Telephone:** (787) 765-6285, 765-7285. **FAX:** (787) 767-3028. **Website:** hitboricua.com.
**Years League Active:** 1938-.
**President:** Joaquin Monserrate Matienzo. **Executive Director:** Benny Agosto.
**Regular Season:** 42 games. **2005-2006 Opening Date:** Nov. 10. **Closing Date:** Jan. 4.

**Playoff Format:** Top four teams meet in best-of-7 semifinal series. Winners meet in best-of-9 series for league championship. Winner advances to Caribbean Series.
**Roster Limit:** 30. **Roster Limit, Imports:** 5.

### ARECIBO
**Mailing Address:** Unavailable. **Telephone:** (787) 765-6285, 765-7285. **FAX:** (787) 767-3028.

### CAGUAS CRIOLLOS
**Mailing Address:** P.O. Box 1415, Caguas, PR 00726. **Telephone:** (787) 258-2222. **FAX:** (787) 743-0545.
**President, General Manager:** Filiberto Berrios.

### CAROLINA GIANTS
**Mailing Address:** Roberto Clemente Stadium, P.O. Box 366246, San Juan, PR 00936. **Telephone:** (787) 643-4351. **FAX:** (787) 834-7480.
**President:** Benjamin Rivera. **General Manager/Manager:** Ramon Aviles.

### MANATI ATHENIANS
**Mailing Address:** Direccion Postal Box 1155, Manati, PR 00674. **Telephone:** (787) 854-5757. **FAX:** (787) 854-6767.
**President:** Tony Valentin.

### MAYAGUEZ INDIANS
**Mailing Address:** 3089 Marina Station, Mayaguez, PR 00681. **Telephone:** (787) 834-6111, 834-5211. **FAX:** (787) 834-7480.
**President, General Manager:** Daniel Aquino.

### PONCE LIONS
**Mailing Address:** P.O. Box 363148, San Juan, PR 00936. **Telephone:** (787) 848-8884. **FAX:** (787) 848-0050.
**President:** Antonio Munoz Jr.

## VENEZUELAN LEAGUE
**Mailing Address:** Avenida Casanova, Centro Comercial "El Recreo," Torre Sur, Piso 3, Oficinas 6 y 7, Sabana Grande, Caracas, Venezuela. **Telephone:** (011-58) 212-761-4932. **FAX:** (011-58) 212-761-7661. **Website:** www.lvbp.com.
**Years League Active:** 1946-.
**President:** Ramon Guillermo Aveledo. **General Manager:** Jose Domingo Alvarez.
**Division Structure: East**—Caracas, La Guaira, Magallanes, Oriente. **West**—Aragua, Lara, Pastora, Zulia.
**Regular Season:** 62 games. **2005-2006 Opening Date:** Oct. 15. **Closing Date:** Dec. 29.
**Playoff Format:** Top two teams in each division, plus a wild-card team, meet in 16-game round-robin series. Top two finishers meet in best-of-7 series for league championship. Winner advances to Caribbean Series.
**Roster Limit:** 26. **Roster Limit, Imports:** 7.

### ARAGUA TIGERS
**Mailing Address:** Estadio Jose Perez Colmenares, Calle Campo Elias, Barrio Democratico, Maracay, Aragua, Venezuela. **Telephone:** (011-58) 243-554-4134. **FAX:** (011-58) 243-553-8655. **E-Mail Address:** tigres@telcel.net.ve. **Website:** www.tigresdearagua.net.
**President, General Manager:** Rafael Rodriguez.
**2005-2006 Manager:** Buddy Bailey.

### CARACAS LIONS
**Mailing Address:** Av. Francisco de Miranda, Centro Seguros la Paz, Piso 4, ofc. 42-C, La California Norte. **Telephone:** (011-58) 212-238-7733. **FAX:** (011-58) 212-238-0691. **E-Mail Address:** contacto@leones.com.

**Website:** www.leones.com.
**President:** Ariel Prat. **General Manager:** Oscar Prieto.
**2005-2006 Manager:** Omar Malave.

## LA GUAIRA SHARKS

**Mailing Address:** Primera Transversal, Urbanizacion Miramar Pariata, Maiquetia, Vargas, Venezuela. **Telephone:** (011-58) 212-332-5579. **FAX:** (011-58) 212-332-3116. **E-Mail Addres:** tiburones@cantv.net. **Website:** www.tiburonesdelaguaira.com.ve.
**President:** Dr. Francisco Arocha Hernández. **Vice President, General Manager:** Dr. Antonio José Herrera.
**2005-2006 Manager:** Joey Cora.

## LARA CARDINALS

**Mailing Address:** Av. Rotaria, Estadio Antonio Herrera Gutiérrez, Barquisimeto, Lara, Venezuela. **Telephone:** (011-58) 251-442- 4543. **FAX:** (011-58) 251-442-1921. **E-Mail Address:** contacto@cardenalesdelara.com. **Website:** www.cardenalesdelara.com.
**President, General Manager:** Humberto Oropeza.
**2005-2006 Manager:** Unavailable.

## MAGALLANES NAVIGATORS

**Mailing Address:** Centro Comercial Caribbean Plaza, Modulo 8, Local 173, Valencia, Carabobo, Venezuela. **Telephone:** (011-58) 241-824-0980. **FAX:** (011-58) 241-824-0705. **E-Mail Address:** Magallanes@telcel.net.ve. **Website:** www.magallanesbbc.com.ve.
**President:** Edgar Rincones Cedeño. **Vice President,**

**General Manager:** José Alberto Ettedgui.
**2005-2006 Manager:** Unavailable.

## ORIENTE CARIBBEANS

**Mailing Address:** Avenida Estadio Alfonso Carrasquel, Oficina Caribes de Oriente, Centro Comercial Novocentro, Piso 2, Local 2-4, Puerto la Cruz, Anzoategui, Venezuela. **Telephone:** (011-58) 281-266-2536. **FAX:** (011-58) 281-266-7054. **Website:** caribesdeanzoategui.terra.com.ve.
**President:** Aurelio Fernandez-Concheso. **Vice President:** Pablo Ruggeri.
**2005-2006 Manager:** Unavailable.

## PASTORA DE LOS LLANOS

**Mailing Address:** Estadio Bachiller Julio Hernandez Molina, Avenida Romulo Gallegos, Aruare, Portuguesa, Venezuela. **Telephone:** (011-58) 255-622-2945. **FAX:** (011-58) 255-621-8595.
**President, General Manager:** Enrique Finol.
**2005-2006 Manager:** Luis Dorante.

## ZULIA EAGLES

**Mailing Address:** Avenida 8 con Calle 81, Urb. Santa Rita, Edificio Las Carolinas, Mezzanine Local M-3, Maracaibo, Zulia, Venezuela. **Telephone:** (011-58) 261-797-9834, (011-58) 261-798-0541. **FAX:** (011-58) 261-798-0579. **Website:** www.aguilas.terra.com.ve.
**President:** Lucas Rincon Colmenares. **General Manager:** Luis Rodolfo Machado Silva.
**2005-2006 Manager:** Unavailable.

# ARIZONA FALL LEAGUE

**Mailing Address:** 2415 E. Camelback Road, Suite 850, Phoenix, AZ 85016. **Telephone:** (602)281-7250. **FAX:** (602) 281-7313. **E-Mail Address:** afl@mlb.com **Website:** www.mlb.com.
**Years League Active:** 1992-.
**Operated by:** Major League Baseball.
**Executive Vice President:** Steve Cobb. **Executive Assistant:** Joan McGrath.
**Division Structure: American**—Mesa, Peoria Saguaros, Scottsdale; **West**—Grand Canyon, Peoria Javelinas, Phoenix.
**Regular Season:** 32 games. **2006 Opening Date:** Oct. 10. **Closing Date:** Nov. 18.
**Playoff Format:** Division champions meet in one-game championship.
**Roster Limit:** 30. Players with less than two years of major league service are eligible.

## GRAND CANYON RAFTERS

**Mailing Address:** Scottsdale Stadium, 7408 East Osborn Rd., Scottsdale, AZ 85251.
**Working Agreements:** Florida Marlins, Minnesota Twins, New York Mets, New York Yankees, Texas Rangers.
**2005 Manager:** Ken Oberkfell (Mets). **Coach:** David Chavarria (Rangers). **Pitching Coach:** John Mallee (Marlins).

## MESA SOLAR SOX

**Mailing Address:** Mesa HoHoKam Park, 1235 N. Center, Mesa, AZ 85201.
**Working Agreements:** Chicago Cubs, Cincinnati Reds, Cleveland Indians, Detroit Tigers, San Francisco Giants.
**2005 Manager:** Luis Rivera (Indians). **Coach:** Von Joshua (Cubs). **Pitching Coach:** Mike Caldwell (Tigers).

## PEORIA JAVELINAS

**Mailing Address:** Peoria Sports Complex, 16101 N. 83rd Ave., Peoria, AZ 85382.

**Working Agreements:** Baltimore Orioles, Colorado Rockies, Milwaukee Brewers, San Diego Padres, Seattle Mariners.
**2005 Manager:** Gary Pettis (Brewers). **Coach:** Larry McCall (Orioles). **Pitching Coach:** Stu Cole (Rockies).

## PEORIA SAGUAROS

**Mailing Address:** Peoria Sports Complex, 16101 N. 83rd Ave., Peoria, AZ 85382.
**Working Agreements:** Boston Red Sox, Chicago White Sox, Pittsburgh Pirates, Toronto Blue Jays, Washington Nationals.
**2005 Manager:** Eddie Rodriguez (Nationals). **Coach:** Ralph Treuel (Red Sox). **Pitching Coach:** Hensley Meulens (Pirates).

## PHOENIX DESERT DOGS

**Mailing Address:** Phoenix Municipal Stadium, 5999 E. Van Buren St., Phoenix, AZ 85007.
**Working Agreements:** Arizona Diamondbacks, Atlanta Braves, Los Angeles Dodgers, Oakland Athletics, Tampa Bay Devil Rays.
**2005 Manager:** Scott Little (Dodgers). **Coach:** Steve Livesey (Devil Rays). **Pitching Coach:** Scott Emerson (Athletics).

## SCOTTSDALE SCORPIONS

**Mailing Address:** Scottsdale Stadium, 7408 East Osborn Rd., Scottsdale, AZ 85251.
**Working Agreements:** Houston Astros, Kansas City Royals, Los Angeles Angels, Philadelphia Phillies, St. Louis Cardinals.
**2005 Manager:** Ron Warner (Cardinals). **Coach:** Kernan Ronan (Angels). **Pitching Coach:** P.J. Forbes (Phillies).

# COLLEGES

# COLLEGE BASEBALL

## NATIONAL COLLEGIATE ATHLETIC ASSOCIATION

**Mailing Address:** P.O. Box 6222, Indianapolis, IN 46206. **Telephone:** (317) 917-6222. **FAX:** (317) 917-6826 (championships), 917-6857 (baseball). **E-Mail Addresses:** dpoppe@ncaa.org (Dennis Poppe), rbuhr@ncaa.org (Randy Buhr), dleech@ncaa.org (Damani Leech), jhamilton@ncaa.org (J.D. Hamilton), wburrow@ncaa.org (Wayne Burrow). **Websites:** www.ncaa.org, www.ncaasports.com.

**President:** Myles Brand. **Managing Director, Baseball:** Dennis Poppe. **Associate Director, Baseball:** Damani Leech. **Director, Championships:** Wayne Burrow. **Assistant Director, Championships:** Randy Buhr. **Media Contact, College World Series:** J.D. Hamilton. **Contact, Statistics:** Sean Straziscar.

**Chairman, Division I Baseball Committee:** Larry Templeton (athletic director, Mississippi State). **Division I Baseball Committee:** Michael Cross (senior associate athletic director, Princeton), John D'Argenio (athletic director, Siena), Rick Dickson (athletic director, Tulane), Mike Gaski (baseball coach, UNC Greensboro), Mike Hamrick (athletic director, Nevada-Las Vegas), Paul Krebs (athletic director, Bowling Green State), Brian Quinn (athletic director, Cal State Fullerton), Bob Steitz (senior associate athletic director, Villanova), Tim Weiser (athletic director, Kansas State).

**Chairman, Division II Baseball Committee:** Britt Bonneau (baseball coach, Abilene Christian). **Chairman, Division III Baseball Committee:** John Casey (baseball coach, Tufts).

**2007 National Convention:** Jan. 5-8 at Orlando.

## 2006 Championship Tournaments
### NCAA Division I

| | |
|---|---|
| 60th College World Series | Omaha, Neb., June 16-25/26 |
| Super Regionals (8) | Campus sites, June 9-12 |
| Regionals (16) | Campus sites, June 2-5 |

### NCAA Division II

| | |
|---|---|
| 39th World Series | Montgomery, Ala., May 27-June 3 |
| Regionals (8) | Campus sites, May 18-21 |

### NCAA Division III

| | |
|---|---|
| 30th World Series | Appleton, Wis., May 26-30 |
| Regionals (8) | Campus sites, May 17-21 |

## NATIONAL ASSOCIATION OF INTERCOLLEGIATE ATHLETICS

**Mailing Address:** 23500 W. 105th St., P.O. Box 1325, Olathe, KS 66051. **Telephone:** (913) 791-0044. **FAX:** (913) 791-9555. **Website:** www.naia.org.

**President, Chief Executive Officer:** Steve Baker. **Director, Championships:** Lori Thomas. **Administrators, Championship Events:** Ruth Feldblum, Scott McClure. **Sports Information Director:** Dawn Harmon.

### 2006 Championship Tournament

| | |
|---|---|
| NAIA World Series | Lewiston, Idaho, May 26-June 2 |

## NATIONAL JUNIOR COLLEGE ATHLETIC ASSOCIATION

**Mailing Address:** 1755 Telstar Dr., Suite 103, Colorado Springs, CO 80920. **Telephone:** (719) 590-9788. **FAX:** (719) 590-7324. **Website:** www.njcaa.org.

**Executive Director:** Wayne Baker. **Director, Division I Baseball Tournament:** Jamie Hamilton. **Director, Division II Baseball Tournament:** John Daigle. **Director, Division III Baseball Tournament:** Charles Adams. **Director, Media Relations:** Amy Tagliareni.

### 2006 Championship Tournaments
#### Division I

| | |
|---|---|
| World Series | Grand Junction, Colo., May 27-June 3 |

#### Division II

| | |
|---|---|
| World Series | Millington, Tenn., May 27-June 2 |

#### Division III

| | |
|---|---|
| World Series | Glens Falls, N.Y., May 20-26 |

## CALIFORNIA COMMUNITY COLLEGE COMMISSION ON ATHLETICS

**Mailing Address:** 2017 O St., Sacramento, CA 95814. **Telephone:** (916) 444-1600. **FAX:** (916) 444-2616. **E-Mail Address:** deadie@coasports.org. **Website:** www.coasports.org.

**Executive Director:** Carlyle Carter. **Director, Sports Information:** David Eadie.

### 2006 Championship Tournament

| | |
|---|---|
| State Championship | Fresno, Calif., May 27-29 |

## NORTHWEST ATHLETIC ASSOCIATION OF COMMUNITY COLLEGES

**Mailing Address:** 1800 E. McLoughlin Blvd., Vancouver, WA 98663-3598. **Telephone:** (360) 992-2833. **FAX:** (360) 696-6210. **Website:** www.nwaacc.org. **E-Mail Address:** rkelly@clark.edu.

**Executive Director:** Dick McClain. **Sports Information Director:** Rob Kelly.

## 2006 Championship Tournament

NWAACC Championship ........................................................................................ Longview, Wash., May 25-29

## AMERICAN BASEBALL COACHES ASSOCIATION

**Office Address:** 108 S. University Ave., Suite 3, Mount Pleasant, MI 48858. **Telephone:** (989) 775-3300. **FAX:** (989) 775-3600. **E-Mail Address:** abca@abca.org. **Website:** www.abca.org.

**Executive Director:** Dave Keilitz. **Assistant to Executive Director:** Betty Rulong. **Membership/Convention Coordinator:** Nick Phillips. **Assistant Coordinator:** Juahn Clark.

**Chairman:** Glen Tuckett (Brigham Young University). **President:** Bill Holowaty (Eastern Connecticut State).

**2007 National Convention:** Jan. 4-7 at Orlando (Orlando Marriott World Center).

# NCAA DIVISION I CONFERENCES

### AMERICA EAST CONFERENCE

**Mailing Address:** 10 High St., Suite 860, Boston, MA 02110. **Telephone:** (617) 695-6369. **FAX:** (617) 695-6385. **E-Mail Address:** cardinal@americaeast.com. **Website:** www.americaeast.com.

**Baseball Members (First Year):** Albany (2002), Binghamton (2002), Hartford (1990), Maine (1990), Maryland-Baltimore County (2004), Stony Brook (2002), Vermont (1990).

**Director, Communications:** K.J. Cardinal.

**2006 Tournament:** Four teams, double-elimination. May 24-27 at highest-seeded team with lights.

### ATLANTIC COAST CONFERENCE

**Office Address:** 4512 Weybridge Lane, Greensboro, NC 27407. **Mailing Address:** P.O. Drawer ACC, Greensboro, NC 27417. **Telephone:** (336) 851-6062. **FAX:** (336) 854-8797. **E-Mail Address:** sbrown@theacc.org. **Website:** www.theacc.com.

**Baseball Members (First Year):** Boston College (2006), Clemson (1953), Duke (1953), Florida State (1992), Georgia Tech (1980), Maryland (1953), Miami (2005), North Carolina (1953), North Carolina State (1953), Virginia (1953), Virginia Tech (2005), Wake Forest (1953).

**Assistant Director, Public Relations:** Amy Yakola.

**2006 Tournament:** Eight teams, double-elimination. May 24-28 at Jacksonville, Fla. (The Baseball Grounds of Jacksonville).

### ATLANTIC SUN CONFERENCE

**Mailing Address:** 3370 Vineville Ave., Suite 108-B, Macon, GA 31204. **Telephone:** (478) 474-3394. **FAX:** (478) 474-4272. **E-Mail Address:** mwilson@atlanticsun.org. **Website:** www.atlanticsun.org.

**Baseball Members (First Year):** Belmont (2002), Campbell (1994), East Tennessee State (2006), Florida Atlantic (1993), Gardner-Webb (2003), Jacksonville (1999), Kennesaw State (2006), Lipscomb (1994), Mercer (1978), North Florida (2006), Stetson (1985).

**Assistant Commissioner, Championships/Communications:** Matt Wilson.

**2006 Tournament:** Six teams, double-elimination. May 24-27 at DeLand, Fla. (Stetson University).

### ATLANTIC 10 CONFERENCE

**Mailing Address:** 230 S. Broad St., Suite 1700, Philadelphia, PA 19102. **Telephone:** (215) 545-6678. **FAX:** (215) 545-3342. **E-Mail Address:** shaug@atlantic10.org. **Website:** www.atlantic10.org.

**Baseball Members (First Year):** Charlotte (2006), Dayton (1996), Duquesne (1977), Fordham (1996), George Washington (1977), LaSalle (1996), Massachusetts (1977), Rhode Island (1981), Richmond (2002), St. Bonaventure (1980), Saint Joseph's (1983), Saint Louis (2006), Temple (1983), Xavier (1996).

**Director, Baseball Communications:** Stephen Haug.

**2006 Tournament:** Six teams, double-elimination. May 24-27 at Bronx, N.Y. (Fordham University).

### BIG EAST CONFERENCE

**Mailing Address:** 222 Richmond St., Suite 110, Providence, RI 02903. **Telephone:** (401) 453-0660. **FAX:** (401) 751-8540. **E-Mail Address:** jgust@bigeast.org. **Website:** www.bigeast.org.

**Baseball Members (First Year):** Cincinnati (2006), Connecticut (1985), Georgetown (1985), Louisville (2006), Notre Dame (1996), Pittsburgh (1985), Rutgers (1996), St. John's (1985), Seton Hall (1985), South Florida (2006), Villanova (1985), West Virginia (1996).

**Director, Communications:** John Gust.

**2006 Championship:** Eight teams, double-elimination. May 23-28 at Clearwater, Fla. (Brighthouse Networks Field).

### BIG SOUTH CONFERENCE

**Mailing Address:** 7233 Pineville-Matthews Rd., Suite 100, Charlotte, NC 28226. **Telephone:** (704) 341-7990. **FAX:** (704) 341-7991. **E-Mail Address:** marks@bigsouth.org. **Website:** www.bigsouthsports.com.

**Baseball Members (First Year):** Birmingham-Southern (2002), Charleston Southern (1983), Coastal Carolina (1983), High Point (1999), Liberty (1991), UNC Asheville (1985), Radford (1983), Virginia Military Institute (2004), Winthrop (1983).

**Director, Public Relations:** Mark Simpson.

**2006 Tournament:** Six teams, double-elimination. May 24-27 at Conway, S.C. (Coastal Carolina).

### BIG 10 CONFERENCE

**Mailing Address:** 1500 W. Higgins Rd., Park Ridge, IL 60068. **Telephone:** (847) 696-1010. **FAX:** (847) 696-1110.

**E-Mail Addresses:** schipman@bigten.org; jsmith@bigten.org. **Website:** www.bigten.org.
   **Baseball Members (First Year):** Illinois (1896), Indiana (1906), Iowa (1906), Michigan (1896), Michigan State (1950), Minnesota (1906), Northwestern (1898), Ohio State (1913), Penn State (1992), Purdue (1906).
   **Assistant Commissioner, Communications:** Scott Chipman. **Assistant Director, Communications:** Jeff Smith.
   **2006 Tournament:** Six teams, double-elimination. May 24-27 at regular-season champion.

## BIG 12 CONFERENCE
   **Mailing Address:** 2201 Stemmons Freeway, 28th Floor, Dallas, TX 75207. **Telephone:** (214) 753-0102. **FAX:** (214) 753-0145. **E-Mail Address:** bo@big12sports.com. **Website:** www.big12sports.com.
   **Baseball Members (First Year):** Baylor (1997), Kansas (1997), Kansas State (1997), Missouri (1997), Nebraska (1997), Oklahoma (1997), Oklahoma State (1997), Texas (1997), Texas A&M (1997), Texas Tech (1997).
   **Sports Information Director:** Bo Carter.
   **2006 Tournament:** Eight teams, modified double elimination. May 24-28 at Oklahoma City, Okla. (AT&T Bricktown Park).

## BIG WEST CONFERENCE
   **Mailing Address:** 2 Corporate Park, Suite 206, Irvine, CA 92606. **Telephone:** (949) 261-2525. **FAX:** (949) 261-2528. **E-Mail Address:** dcouch@bigwest.org. **Website:** www.bigwest.org.
   **Baseball Members (First Year):** Cal Poly (1997), UC Davis (2004), UC Irvine (2002), UC Riverside (2002), UC Santa Barbara (1970), Cal State Fullerton (1975), Cal State Northridge (2001), Long Beach State (1970), Pacific (1972).
   **Assistant Director, Information:** Darcy Couch.
   **2006 Tournament:** None.

## COLONIAL ATHLETIC ASSOCIATION
   **Mailing Address:** 8625 Patterson Ave., Richmond, VA 23229. **Telephone:** (804) 754-1616. **FAX:** (804) 754-1830. **E-Mail Address:** rwashburn@caasports.com. **Website:** www.caasports.com.
   **Baseball Members (First Year):** Delaware (2002), George Mason (1986), Georgia State (2006), Hofstra (2002), James Madison (1986), UNC Wilmington (1986), Northeastern (2006), Old Dominion (1992), Towson (2002), Virginia Commonwealth (1996), William & Mary (1986).
   **Sports Information Director:** Rob Washburn.
   **2006 Tournament:** Six teams, double-elimination. May 24-27 at Wilmington, N.C. (UNC Wilmington).

## CONFERENCE USA
   **Mailing Address:** 5201 N. O'Connor Blvd., Suite 300, Irving, TX 75039. **Telephone:** (214) 774-1300. **FAX:** (214) 496-0055. **E-Mail Address:** rdanderson@c-usa.org. **Website:** www.c-usasports.com.
   **Baseball Members (First Year):** Alabama-Birmingham (1996), Central Florida (2006), East Carolina (2002), Houston (1997), Marshall (2006), Memphis (1996), Rice (2006), Southern Mississippi (1996), Tulane (1996).
   **Assistant Commissioner, Media Relations:** Russell Anderson.
   **2006 Tournament:** Eight teams, double-elimination. May 24-28 at Houston (Rice University).

## HORIZON LEAGUE
   **Mailing Address:** 201 S. Capitol Ave., Suite 500, Indianapolis, IN 46225. **Telephone:** (317) 237-5622. **FAX:** (317) 237-5620. **E-Mail Address:** rhester@horizonleague.org. **Website:** www.horizonleague.org.
   **Baseball Members (First Year):** Butler (1979), Cleveland State (1994), Illinois-Chicago (1994), Wisconsin-Milwaukee (1994), Wright State (1994), Youngstown State (2002).
   **Director, Communications:** Robert Hester.
   **2006 Tournament:** Six teams, double-elimination. May 24-28 at Dayton, Ohio (Wright State University).

## IVY LEAGUE
   **Mailing Address:** 228 Alexander Rd., Second Floor, Princeton, NJ 08544. **Telephone:** (609) 258-6426. **FAX:** (609) 258-1690. **E-Mail Address:**info@ivyleaguesports.com. **Website:** www.ivyleaguesports.com.
   **Baseball Members** (First Year): **Rolfe**—Brown (1948), Dartmouth (1930), Harvard (1948), Yale (1930). **Gehrig**—Columbia (1930), Cornell (1930), Pennsylvania (1930), Princeton (1930).
   **Assistant, Public Information:** E.J. Crawford.
   **2006 Tournament:** Best-of-3 series between division champions. May 6-7 at team with best overall record.

## METRO ATLANTIC ATHLETIC CONFERENCE
   **Mailing Address:** 712 Amboy Ave., Edison, NJ 08837. **Telephone:** (732) 738-5455. **FAX:** (732) 738-8366. **E-Mail Address:** jill.skotarczak@maac.org. **Website:** www.maacsports.com.
   **Baseball Members (First Year):** Canisius (1990), Fairfield (1982), Iona (1982), LeMoyne (1990), Manhattan (1982), Marist (1998), Niagara (1990), Rider (1998), St. Peter's (1982), Siena (1990).
   **Director, Media Relations:** Jill Skotarczak.
   **2006 Tournament:** Four teams, double-elimination. May 25-27 at Fishkill, N.Y. (Dutchess Stadium).

## MID-AMERICAN CONFERENCE
   **Mailing Address:** 24 Public Square, 15th Floor, Cleveland, OH 44113. **Telephone:** (216) 566-4622. **FAX:** (216) 858-9622. **E-Mail Address:** jguy@mac-sports.com. **Website:** www.mac-sports.com.
   **Baseball Members (First Year):** Akron (1992), Ball State (1973), Bowling Green State (1952), Buffalo (2001), Central Michigan (1971), Eastern Michigan (1971), Kent State (1951), Miami (1947), Northern Illinois (1997), Ohio (1946). Toledo (1950), Western Michigan (1947).

**Associate Director, Media Relations:** Jeremy Guy.

**2006 Tournament:** Six teams (top two in each division, two wild-card teams with next-best conference winning percentage), double-elimination. May 24-27 at team with best conference winning percentage.

## MID-CONTINENT CONFERENCE

**Mailing Address:** 340 W. Butterfield Rd., Suite 3-D, Elmhurst, IL 60126. **Telephone:** (630) 516-0661. **FAX:** (630) 516-0673. **E-Mail Address:** petersen@mid-con.com. **Website:** www.mid-con.com.

**Baseball Members (First Year):** Centenary (2004), Chicago State (1994), Oakland (2000), Oral Roberts (1998), Southern Utah (2000), Valparaiso (1984), Western Illinois (1984).

**Director, Media Relations:** Kristina Petersen.

**2006 Tournament:** Four teams, double-elimination. May 25-27 at Tulsa, Okla. (Oral Roberts University).

## MID-EASTERN ATHLETIC CONFERENCE

**Mailing Address:** 222 Central Park Ave., Suite 1150, Virginia Beach, VA 23462. **Telephone:** (757) 416-7100. **FAX:** (757) 416-7109. **E-Mail Address:** jinksm@themeac.com; allemanm@themeac.com. **Website:** www.meacsports.com.

**Baseball Members (First Year):** Bethune-Cookman (1979), Coppin State (1985), Delaware State (1970), Florida A&M (1979), Maryland-Eastern Shore (1970), Norfolk State (1998), North Carolina A&T (1970).

**Director, Media Relations:** Michelle Jinks. **Baseball Contact:** Megan Alleman.

**2006 Tournament:** Seven teams, double-elimination. May 18-21 at Norfolk, Va. (Norfolk State University).

## MISSOURI VALLEY CONFERENCE

**Mailing Address:** 1818 Chouteau Ave., St. Louis, MO 63103. **Telephone:** (314) 421-0339. **FAX:** (314) 421-3505. **E-Mail Address:** fricke@mvc.org. **Website:** www.mvc.org.

**Baseball Members (First Year):** Bradley (1955), Creighton (1976), Evansville (1994), Illinois State (1980), Indiana State (1976), Missouri State (1990), Northern Iowa (1991), Southern Illinois (1974), Wichita State (1945).

**Director, Communications:** Erica Fricke.

**2006 Tournament:** Six teams, double-elimination. May 24-27 at Wichita, Kan. (Wichita State University).

## MOUNTAIN WEST CONFERENCE

**Mailing Address:** 15455 Gleneagle Dr., Suite 200B, Colorado Springs, CO 80921. **Telephone:** (719) 488-4040. **FAX:** (719) 487-7241. **E-Mail Address:** medge@TheMWC.com. **Website:** www.TheMWC.com.

**Baseball Members (First Year):** Air Force (2000), Brigham Young (2000), Nevada-Las Vegas (2000), New Mexico (2000), San Diego State (2000), Texas Christian (2006), Utah (2000).

**Assistant Director, Communications:** Marlon Edge.

**2006 Tournament:** Seven teams, double-elimination. May 23-27 at Las Vegas, Nev. (University of Nevada-Las Vegas).

## NORTHEAST CONFERENCE

**Mailing Address:** 200 Cottontail Lane, Vantage Court North, Somerset, NJ 08873. **Telephone:** (732) 469-0440. **FAX:** (732) 469-0744. **E-Mail Address:** rratner@northeastconference.org. **Website:** www.northeastconference.org.

**Baseball Members (First Year):** Central Connecticut State (1999), Fairleigh Dickinson (1981), Long Island (1981), Monmouth (1985), Mount St. Mary's (1989), Quinnipiac (1999), Sacred Heart (2000), St. Francis, N.Y. (1981), Wagner (1981).

**Associate Commissioner:** Ron Ratner.

**2006 Tournament:** Four teams, double-elimination. May 25-27 at Lakewood, N.J. (First Energy Park).

## OHIO VALLEY CONFERENCE

**Mailing Address:** 215 Centerview Dr., Suite 115, Brentwood, TN 37027. **Telephone:** (615) 371-1698. **FAX:** (615) 371-1788. **E-Mail Address:** kmelcher@ovc.org. **Website:** www.ovcsports.com.

**Baseball Members (First Year):** Austin Peay State (1962), Eastern Illinois (1996), Eastern Kentucky (1948), Jacksonville State (2003), Morehead State (1948), Murray State (1948), Samford (2003), Southeast Missouri State (1991), Tennessee-Martin (1992), Tennessee Tech (1949).

**Assistant Commissioner:** Kim Melcher.

**2006 Tournament:** Six teams, double-elimination. May 23-27 at Paducah, Ky. (Brooks Stadium).

## PACIFIC-10 CONFERENCE

**Mailing Address:** 800 S. Broadway, Suite 400, Walnut Creek, CA 94596. **Telephone:** (925) 932-4411. **FAX:** (925) 932-4601. **E-Mail Address:** kcavender@pac-10.org. **Website:** www.pac-10.org.

**Baseball Members (First Year):** Arizona (1979), Arizona State (1979), California (1916), UCLA (1928), Oregon State (1916), Southern California (1923), Stanford (1918), Washington (1916), Washington State (1919).

**Public Relations Intern:** Katie Cavender.

**2006 Tournament:** None.

## PATRIOT LEAGUE

**Mailing Address:** 3773 Corporate Pkwy., Suite 190, Center Valley, PA 18034. **Telephone:** (610) 289-1950. **FAX:** (610) 289-1952. **E-Mail Address:** jsiegel@patriotleague.com. **Website:** www.patriotleague.com.

**Baseball Members (First Year):** Army (1993), Bucknell (1991), Holy Cross (1991), Lafayette (1991), Lehigh (1991), Navy (1993).

**Assistant Director, Media Relations:** Jessica Siegel.

**2006 Tournament:** Top three teams; No. 2 plays No. 3 in one-game playoff. Winner faces No. 1 team in best-of-3 series at No. 1 seed, May 13-14.

## SOUTHEASTERN CONFERENCE

**Mailing Address:** 2201 Richard Arrington Blvd. N., Birmingham, AL 35203. **Telephone:** (205) 458-3000. **FAX:** (205)

458-3030. **E-Mail Address:** cdunlap@sec.org. **Website:** www.secsports.com.
  **Baseball Members (First Year): East**—Florida (1933), Georgia (1933), Kentucky (1933), South Carolina (1992), Tennessee (1933), Vanderbilt (1933). **West**—Alabama (1933), Arkansas (1992), Auburn (1933), Louisiana State (1933), Mississippi (1933), Mississippi State (1933).
  **Assistant Director, Media Relations:** Chuck Dunlap.
  **2006 Tournament:** Eight teams, modified double-elimination. May 23-28 at Birmingham, Ala. (Hoover Metropolitan Stadium).

## SOUTHERN CONFERENCE
  **Mailing Address:** 702 N. Pine St., Spartanburg, SC 29303. **Telephone:** (864) 591-5100. **FAX:** (864) 591-4282. **E-Mail Address:** bmcgowan@socon.org. **Website:** www.soconsports.com.
  **Baseball Members (First Year):** Appalachian State (1971), Charleston (1998), The Citadel (1936), Davidson (1991), Elon (2004), Furman (1936), Georgia Southern (1991), UNC Greensboro (1997), Western Carolina (1976), Wofford (1997).
  **Assistant Commissioner, Public Affairs:** Bryan McGowan.
  **2006 Tournament:** Ten teams, double-elimination. May 23-27 at Charleston, S.C. (The Citadel).

## SOUTHLAND CONFERENCE
  **Mailing Address:** 1700 Alma Dr., Suite 550, Plano, TX 75075. **Telephone:** (972) 422-9500. **FAX:** (972) 422-9225. **E-Mail Address:** bludlow@southland.org. **Website:** www.southland.org.
  **Baseball Members (First Year):** Lamar (1999), Louisiana-Monroe (1983), McNeese State (1973), Nicholls State (1992), Northwestern State (1988), Sam Houston State (1988), Southeastern Louisiana (1998), Stephen F. Austin (2006), Texas State (1988), Texas-Arlington (1964), Texas-San Antonio (1992).
  **Baseball Contact/Associate Commissioner:** Bruce Ludlow.
  **2006 Tournament:** Six teams, double-elimination. May 24-27 at Beaumont, Texas (Lamar University).

## SOUTHWESTERN ATHLETIC CONFERENCE
  **Mailing Address:** A.G. Gaston Building, 1527 Fifth Ave. N., Birmingham, AL 35203. **Telephone:** (205) 252-7573, ext. 111. **FAX:** (205) 252-9997. **E-Mail Address:** w.dooley@swac.org. **Website:** www.swac.org.
  **Baseball Members (First Year): East**—Alabama A&M (2000), Alabama State (1982), Alcorn State (1962), Jackson State (1958), Mississippi Valley State (1968). **West**—Arkansas-Pine Bluff (1999), Grambling State (1958), Prairie View A&M (1920), Southern (1934), Texas Southern (1954).
  **Assistant Commissioner, Media Relations:** Wallace Dooley.
  **2006 Tournament:** Six teams, double-elimination. May 17-21 at Pearl, Miss. (Trustmark Park).

## SUN BELT CONFERENCE
  **Mailing Address:** 601 Poydras St., Suite 2355, New Orleans, LA 70130. **Telephone:** (504) 299-9066. **FAX:** (504) 299-9068. **E-Mail Address:** broussard@sunbeltsports.org. **Website:** www.sunbeltsports.org.
  **Baseball Members (First Year):** Arkansas-Little Rock (1991), Arkansas State (1991), Florida International (1999), Louisiana-Lafayette (1991), Middle Tennessee (2001), New Orleans (1976/1991), South Alabama (1976), Troy (2006), Western Kentucky (1982).
  **Director, Media Relations:** Rob Broussard.
  **2006 Tournament:** Eight teams, double-elimination. May 24-27 at Bowling Green, Ky. (Western Kentucky University).

## WEST COAST CONFERENCE
  **Mailing Address:** 1250 Bayhill Dr., Suite 101, San Bruno, CA 94066. **Telephone:** (650) 873-8622. **FAX:** (650) 873-7846. **E-Mail Addresses:** jwilson@westcoast.org; wkiss@westcoast.org. **Website:** www.wccsports.com.
  **Baseball Members (First Year):** Gonzaga (1996), Loyola Marymount (1968), Pepperdine (1968), Portland (1996), Saint Mary's (1968), San Diego (1979), San Francisco (1968), Santa Clara (1968).
  **Director, Communications:** Jae Wilson. **Assistant Director, Communications:** Will Kiss.
  **2006 Tournament:** Top two teams meet in best-of-3 series at home of regular-season winner, May 26-28.

## WESTERN ATHLETIC CONFERENCE
  **Mailing Address:** 9250 East Costilla Ave., Suite 300, Englewood, CO 80112. **Telephone:** (303) 799-9221. **FAX:** (303) 799-3888. **E-Mail Address:** wac@wac.org. **Website:** www.wacsports.com.
  **Baseball Members (First Year):** Fresno State (1993), Hawaii (1980), Louisiana Tech (2002), Nevada (2001), New Mexico State (2006), Sacramento State (2006), San Jose State (1997).
  **Commissioner:** Karl Benson. **Senior Associate Commissioner:** Jeff Hurd. **Director, Sports Information:** Dave Chaffin.
  **2006 Tournament:** Six teams, double elimination. May 25-28 at Fresno, Calif. (Fresno State University).

# NCAA DIVISION II CONFERENCES

## CALIFORNIA COLLEGIATE ATHLETIC ASSOCIATION
  **Mailing Address:** 800 S. Broadway, Suite 309, Walnut Creek, CA 94596. **Telephone:** (925) 472-8299. **FAX:** (925) 472-8887. **Website:** www.goccaa.org.
  **Baseball Members:** UC San Diego, Cal Poly Pomona, Cal State Dominguez Hills, Cal State Los Angeles, Cal State San Bernardino, Cal State Stanislaus, Chico State, San Francisco State, Sonoma State.

## CAROLINAS-VIRGINIA ATHLETIC CONFERENCE
  **Mailing Address:** 26 Cub Dr., Thomasville, NC 27360. **Telephone:** (336) 884-0482. **FAX:** (336) 499-6031. **E-Mail**

**Address:** CVAC@triad.rr.com. **Website:** www.cvac.net.

**Baseball Members:** Anderson (S.C.), Barton, Belmont Abbey, Coker, Erskine, Limestone, Mount Olive, Pfeiffer, St. Andrews Presbyterian.

## CENTRAL ATLANTIC COLLEGIATE CONFERENCE

**Mailing Address:** NJIT Sports Information, University Heights, Newark, NJ 07102. **Telephone:** (973) 596-8324. **FAX:** (973) 596-8440. **E-Mail Address:** mentone@adm.njit.edu. **Website:** www.caccathletics.org.

**Baseball Members:** Bloomfield, Caldwell, Dominican (N.Y.), Felician, New Jersey Institute of Technology, Nyack, University of the Sciences/Philadelphia, Teikyo Post, Wilmington (Del.).

## CENTRAL INTERCOLLEGIATE ATHLETIC ASSOCIATION

**Mailing Address:** 303 Butler Farm Rd., Suite 102, Hampton, VA 23666. **Telephone:** (757) 865-0071. **FAX:** (757) 865-8436. **E-Mail Address:** TheCiaa@aol.com. **Website:** www.theciaa.com.

**Baseball Members:** Elizabeth City State, Saint Augustine's, Saint Paul's, Shaw, Virginia State.

## GREAT LAKES INTERCOLLEGIATE ATHLETIC CONFERENCE

**Mailing Address:** 1110 Washington Ave., Bay City, MI 48708. **Telephone:** (989) 894-2529. **FAX:** (989) 894-2825. **E-Mail Address:** tomjb@gliac.org. **Website:** www.gliac.org.

**Baseball Members:** Ashland, Findlay, Gannon, Grand Valley State, Hillsdale, Mercyhurst, Northwood (Mich.), Saginaw Valley State, Wayne State (Mich.).

## GREAT LAKES VALLEY CONFERENCE

**Mailing Address:** Pan Am Plaza, Suite 560, 201 S. Capitol Ave., Indianapolis, IN 46225. **Telephone:** (317) 237-5633. **FAX:** (317) 237-5632. **E-Mail Address:** jim@glvc-sports.org. **Website:** www.glvcsports.com.

**Baseball Members:** Bellarmine, Indianapolis, Kentucky Wesleyan, Lewis, Missouri-Rolla, Missouri-Saint Louis, Northern Kentucky, Quincy, Rockhurst, Saint Joseph's (Ind.), Southern Illinois-Edwardsville, Southern Indiana, Wisconsin-Parkside.

## GULF SOUTH CONFERENCE

**Mailing Address:** 2101 Providence Park, Suite 200, Birmingham, AL 35242. **Telephone:** (205) 991-9880. **FAX:** (205) 437-0505. **E-Mail Address:** gscsid@mindspring.com. **Website:** www.gulfsouthconference.org.

**Baseball Members:** Alabama-Huntsville, Arkansas-Monticello, Arkansas Tech, Central Arkansas, Christian Brothers, Delta State, Harding, Henderson State, Lincoln Memorial, Montevallo, North Alabama, Ouachita Baptist, Southern Arkansas, Valdosta State, West Alabama, West Florida, West Georgia.

## HEARTLAND CONFERENCE

**Mailing Address:** P.O. Box 131569, Tyler, TX 75713. **Telephone:** (210) 313-7053. **FAX:** (877) 258-9077. **E-Mail Address:** gerard@heartlandsports.org. **Website:** www.heartlandsports.org.

**Baseball Members:** Incarnate Word, Lincoln (Mo.), Montana State-Billings, Oklahoma Panhandle State, St. Edward's, St. Mary's (Texas).

## LONE STAR CONFERENCE

**Mailing Address:** 1221 W. Campbell Rd., No. 245, Richardson, TX 75080. **Telephone:** (972) 234-0033. **FAX:** (972) 234-4110. **E-Mail Address:** wagnons@lonestarconference.org. **Website:** www.lonestarconference.org.

**Baseball Members:** Abilene Christian, Angelo State, Cameron, Central Oklahoma, East Central, Eastern New Mexico, Northeastern State, Southeastern Oklahoma State, Southwestern Oklahoma State, Tarleton State, Texas A&M-Kingsville, West Texas A&M.

## MID-AMERICA INTERCOLLEGIATE ATHLETICS ASSOCIATION

**Mailing Address:** 10551 Barkley, Suite 401, Overland Park, KS 66212. **Telephone:** (913) 341-3839/3080. **FAX:** (913) 341-5887/2995. **E-Mail Address:** rmcfillen@themiaa.com. **Website:** www.themiaa.com.

**Baseball Members:** Central Missouri State, Emporia State, Missouri Southern State, Missouri Western State, Northwest Missouri State, Pittsburg State, Southwest Baptist, Truman State, Washburn.

## NEW YORK COLLEGIATE ATHLETIC CONFERENCE

**Mailing Address:** 733 3rd Ave., Suite 1910, New York, NY 10017. **Telephone:** (212) 682-6318. **FAX:** (212) 286-1243. **E-Mail Address:** gonycac@hotmail.com. **Website:** www.nycac.net.

**Baseball Members:** Adelphi, Bridgeport, Concordia (N.Y.), C.W. Post-Long Island, Dowling, Mercy, Molloy, New Haven, Queens, St. Thomas Aquinas.

## NORTH CENTRAL INTERCOLLEGIATE ATHLETIC ASSOCIATION

**Mailing Address:** Ramkota Hotel, 3200 W. Maple St., Sioux Falls, SD 57107. **Telephone:** (605) 338-0907. **FAX:** (605) 338-1889. **E-Mail Address:** info@northcentralconference.org. **Website:** www.northcentralconference.org.

**Baseball Members:** Augustana (S.D.), Minnesota-Duluth, Minnesota State-Mankato, Nebraska-Omaha, North Dakota, St. Cloud State.

## NORTHEAST-10 CONFERENCE

**Mailing Address:** 16 Belmont St., South Easton, MA 02375. **Telephone:** (508) 230-9844. **FAX:** (508) 230-9845. **E-Mail:** kbelbin@northeast10.org. **Website:** www.northeast10.org.

**Baseball Members:** American International, Assumption, Bentley, Bryant, Franklin Pierce, Massachusetts-Lowell, Merrimack, Pace, Saint Anselm, Saint Rose, Southern Connecticut State, Southern New Hampshire, Stonehill.

## NORTHERN SUN INTERCOLLEGIATE CONFERENCE

**Mailing Address:** 161 Anthony Ave., Suite 920, St. Paul, MN 55103. **Telephone:** (651) 288-4017. **FAX:** (651) 224-

8583. **E-Mail**: dossantos@northernsun.org. **Website**: www.northernsun.org.
   **Baseball Members**: Bemidji State, Concordia-St. Paul, Minnesota-Crookston, Minnesota State-Moorhead, Northern State, Southwest Minnesota State, Wayne State (Neb.), Winona State.

## PEACH BELT CONFERENCE
   **Mailing Address**: P.O. Box 204290, Augusta, GA 30917. **Telephone**: (706) 860-8499. **FAX**: (706) 650-8113. **E-Mail Address**: sports@peachbelt.com. **Website**: www.peachbelt.com.
   **Baseball Members**: Armstrong Atlantic State, Augusta State, Columbus State, Francis Marion, Georgia College & State, Lander, UNC Pembroke, North Georgia College and State, South Carolina-Aiken, South Carolina-Upstate.

## PENNSYLVANIA STATE ATHLETIC CONFERENCE
   **Mailing Address**: 204 Annex Building, Susquehanna Ave., Lock Haven, PA 17745. **Telephone**: (570) 893-2780. **FAX**: (570) 893-2206. **E-Mail Address**: wadair@lhup.edu. **Website**: www.psacsports.org.
   **Baseball Members**: Bloomsburg, California (Pa.), Clarion, East Stroudsburg, Indiana (Pa.), Kutztown, Lock Haven, Mansfield, Millersville, Shippensburg, Slippery Rock, West Chester.

## ROCKY MOUNTAIN ATHLETIC CONFERENCE
   **Mailing Address**: 1867 Austin Bluffs Pkwy., Suite 101, Colorado Springs, CO 80918. **Telephone**: (719) 471-4530. **FAX**: (719) 471-0088. **E-Mail Address**: edanner@rmacsports.org. **Website**: www.rmacsports.org.
   **Baseball Members**: Colorado Christian, Colorado School of Mines, Colorado State-Pueblo, Fort Hays State, Mesa State, Metro State, Nebraska-Kearney, New Mexico Highlands, Regis.

## SOUTH ATLANTIC CONFERENCE
   **Mailing Address**: Gateway Plaza, Suite 130, 226 N. Park Dr., Rock Hill, SC 29730. **Telephone**: (803) 981-5240. **FAX**: (803) 981-9444. **E-Mail Address**: thesac@comporium.net. **Website**: www.thesac.com.
   **Baseball Members**: Carson-Newman, Catawba, Lenoir-Rhyne, Mars Hill, Newberry, Presbyterian, Tusculum, Wingate.

## SOUTHERN INTERCOLLEGIATE ATHLETIC CONFERENCE
   **Mailing Address**: 3469 Lawrenceville Hwy., Suite 207, Tucker, GA 30084. **Telephone**: (770) 908-0482. **FAX**: (770) 908-2772. **Website**: www.thesiac.com.
   **Baseball Members**: Albany State (Ga.), Benedict (S.C.), Clark Atlanta, Kentucky State, Lane, LeMoyne-Owen, Miles, Morehouse, Paine, Tuskegee.

## SUNSHINE STATE CONFERENCE
   **Mailing Address**: 7061 Grand National Dr., Suite 140, Orlando, FL 32819. **Telephone**: (407) 248-8460. **FAX**: (407) 248-8325. **E-Mail Address**: info@ sunshinestateconference.org. **Website**: www.sunshinestateconference.org.
   **Baseball Members**: Barry, Eckerd, Florida Southern, Florida Tech, Lynn, Nova Southeastern, Rollins, Saint Leo, Tampa.

## WEST VIRGINIA INTERCOLLEGIATE ATHLETIC CONFERENCE
   **Mailing Address**: 1422 Main St., Princeton, WV 24740. **Telephone**: (304) 487-6298. **FAX**: (304) 487-6299. **E-Mail Address**: will@wviac.org. **Website**: www.wviac.org.
   **Baseball Members**: Alderson-Broaddus, Bluefield State, Charleston (W.Va.), Concord, Davis & Elkins, Fairmont State, Ohio Valley, Salem International, Shepherd, West Liberty State, West Virginia State, West Virginia Wesleyan, Wheeling Jesuit.

\* Recruiting coordinator
\# Provisional Division I status

## AIR FORCE ACADEMY Falcons
**Conference:** Mountain West.
**Mailing Address:** 2168 Field House Dr., USAF Academy, CO 80840. **Website:** www.airforcesports.com.
**Head Coach:** Mike Hutcheon. **Assistant Coaches:** Scott Marchand, Marty Nelson, \*Ryan Thompson. **Telephone:** (719) 333-7914. • **Baseball SID:** Nick Arseniak. **Telephone:** (719) 333-9251. **FAX:** (719) 333-3798.

## AKRON Zips
**Conference:** Mid-American (East).
**Mailing Address:** Rhodes Arena, 373 Carroll St., Suite 76, Akron, OH 44325. **Website:** www.gozips.com.
**Head Coach:** Pat Bangtson. **Assistant Coaches:** Chris Arvay, Brian Donohew. **Telephone:** (330) 972-7290. • **Baseball SID:** Kevin Alcox. **Telephone:** (330) 972-2677. **FAX:** (330) 374-8844.

## ALABAMA Crimson Tide
**Conference:** Southeastern (West).
**Mailing Address:** P.O. Box 87031, Tuscaloosa, AL 35487. **Website:** www.rolltide.com.
**Head Coach:** Jim Wells. **Assistant Coaches:** Jim Gatewood, B.J. Green, \*Joe Raccuia. **Telephone:** (205) 348-4029. • **Baseball SID:** Barry Allen. **Telephone:** (205) 348-6084. **FAX:** (205) 348-8841.
**Home Field:** Sewell-Thomas Stadium. **Seating Capacity:** 6,118. **Outfield Dimensions:** LF—325, CF—400, RF—325. **Press Box Telephone:** (205) 348-4927.

## ALABAMA-BIRMINGHAM Blazers
**Conference:** Conference USA.
**Mailing Address:** 1530 Third Ave. South, Birmingham, AL 35294. **Website:** www.uabsports.com.
**Head Coach:** Larry Giangrosso. **Assistant Coaches:** Nick Dumas, \*Frank Walton. **Telephone:** (205) 934-5181. • **Baseball SID:** Jeremy Hoffman. **Telephone:** (205) 976-2576. **FAX:** (205) 934-7505.
**Home Field:** Jerry D. Young Memorial Field. **Seating Capacity:** 1,000. **Outfield Dimensions:** LF—330, CF—400, RF—330. **Press Box Telephone:** (205) 934-0200.

## ALABAMA A&M Bulldogs
**Conference:** Southwestern Athletic.
**Mailing Address:** P.O. Box 1597, Normal, AL 35762. **Website:** www.aamusports.com.
**Head Coach:** Thomas Wesley. **Telephone:** (256) 372-4005. • **Baseball SID:** Thomas Galbraith. **Telephone:** (256) 372-4550. **FAX:** (256) 372-5919.

## ALABAMA STATE Hornets
**Conference:** Southwestern Athletic.
**Mailing Address:** 915 S. Jackson St., Montgomery, AL 36101. **Website:** www.bamastatesports.com.
**Head Coach:** Larry Watkins. **Telephone:** (334) 229-4228. • **Baseball SID:** A.A. Moore. **Telephone:** (334) 229-4511. **FAX:** (334) 262-2971.

## ALBANY Great Danes
**Conference:** America East.
**Mailing Address:** 1400 Washington Ave., Albany, NY 12222. **Website:** www.albany.edu/sports.
**Head Coach:** Jon Mueller. **Assistant Coaches:** Garett Baron, Greg Keagle, Matt Quatraro. **Telephone:** (518) 442-3014. • **Baseball SID:** Sean Tainsh. **Telephone:** (518) 442-5733. **FAX:** (518) 442-3139.

## ALCORN STATE Braves
**Conference:** Southwestern Athletic.
**Mailing Address:** 1000 ASU Drive, Box 510, Alcorn State, MS 39096. **Website:** www.alcornsport.com.
**Head Coach:** Willie McGowan. **Assistant Coaches:** \*Marqus Johnson, Luis Marquez, Rockeil Thompson. **Telephone:** (601) 877-6279. • **Baseball SID:** Josh Bean. **Telephone:** (601) 877-6466. **FAX:** (601) 877-3821.

## APPALACHIAN STATE Mountaineers
**Conference:** Southern.
**Mailing Address:** Owens Fieldhouse, Boone, NC 28608. **Website:** www.goasu.com.
**Head Coach:** Chris Pollard. **Assistant Coaches:** Mike Boykin, Andrew See. **Telephone:** (828) 262-6097. • **Baseball SID:** Mike Flynn. **Telephone:** (828) 262-2845. **FAX:** (828) 262-6106.

## ARIZONA Wildcats
**Conference:** Pacific-10.
**Mailing Address:** Room 106, McKale Center, Tucson, AZ 85716. **Website:** www.arizonaathletics.com.
**Head Coach:** Andy Lopez. **Assistant Coaches:** Andy Diver, Josh Bendik, \*Mark Wasikowski. **Telephone:** (520) 621-4102. • **Baseball SID:** Matt Rector. **Telephone:** (520) 621-0914. **FAX:** (520) 621-2681.
**Home Field:** Jerry Kindall Field at Frank Sancet Stadium. **Seating Capacity:** 6,500. **Outfield Dimensions:** LF—360, CF—400, RF—360. **Press Box Telephone:** (520) 621-4440.

## ARIZONA STATE Sun Devils
**Conference:** Pacific-10.
**Mailing Address:** Carson Student-Athlete Center, P.O. Box 872505, Tempe, AZ 85287. **Website:** www.thesundevils.com.
**Head Coach:** Pat Murphy. **Assistant Coaches:** Tim Esmay, Jeff Mousser, Graham Rossini, \*Jay Sferra. **Telephone:** (480) 965-3677. • **Baseball SID:** Randy Policar. **Telephone:** (480) 965-6594. **FAX:** (480) 965-5408.
**Home Field:** Packard Stadium. **Seating Capacity:** 3,879. **Outfield Dimensions:** LF—338, CF—395, RF—338. **Press Box Telephone:** (480) 727-7253.

## ARKANSAS Razorbacks
**Conference:** Southeastern (West).
**Mailing Address:** Broyles Athletic Center, Maple and Razorback Roads, Fayetteville, AR 72701. **Website:** www.hogwired.com.
**Head Coach:** Dave Van Horn. **Assistant Coaches:** \*Todd Butler, Clay Goodwin, Dave Jorn, Bubba Merrill. **Telephone:** (479) 575-3655. • **Baseball SID:** Josh Maxson. **Telephone:** (479) 575-6862. **FAX:** (479) 575-7181.
**Home Field:** Baum Stadium. **Seating Capacity:** 9,133. **Outfield Dimensions:** LF—320, CF—400, RF—320. **Press Box Telephone:** (479) 575-4141.

## ARKANSAS-LITTLE ROCK Trojans
**Conference:** Sun Belt.
**Mailing Address:** 2801 S. University Ave., Little Rock, AR 72204. **Website:** www.ualrtrojans.com.
**Head Coach:** Jim Lawler. **Assistant Coaches:** Brent Heaberlin, \*Scott Lawler, Bobby Pierce. **Telephone:** (501) 663-8095. • **Baseball SID:** Joe Angiola. **Telephone:** (501) 569-3449. **FAX:** (501) 683-7002.

## ARKANSAS-PINE BLUFF Golden Lions
**Conference:** Southwestern Athletic.

Mailing Address: 1200 N. University Dr., Mail Slot 4805, Pine Bluff, AR 71601. Website: www.uapb.edu/athletics.

Head Coach: Elbert Bennett. Assistant Coach: Michael Bumpers. Telephone: (870) 575-8938. • Baseball SID: Tamara Williams. Telephone: (870) 575-7174. FAX: (870) 543-8114.

## ARKANSAS STATE Indians

Conference: Sun Belt.

Mailing Address: P.O. Box 1000, State University, AR 72467. Website: www.asuindians.com.

Head Coach: Keith Kessinger. Assistant Coaches: Brad Henderson, *Christian Ostrander, Joe Wingate. Telephone: (870) 972-2700. • Baseball SID: Matt McCollester. Telephone: (870) 972-2541. FAX: (870) 972-3367.

## ARMY Cadets

Conference: Patriot.

Mailing Address: 639 Howard Rd., West Point, NY 10996. Website: www.goarmysports.com.

Head Coach: Joe Sottolano. Assistant Coaches: Fritz Hamburg, Nick Schnabel. Telephone: (845) 938-3712. • Baseball SID: Bob Beretta. Telephone: (845) 938-3303. FAX: (845) 446-2556.

## AUBURN Tigers

Conference: Southeastern (West).

Mailing Address: P.O. Box 351, Auburn, AL 36830. Website: www.auburntigers.com.

Head Coach: Tom Slater. Assistant Coaches: Matt Myers, *Butch Thompson. Telephone: (334) 844-4975. • Baseball SID: Dan Froehlich. Telephone: (334) 844-9803. FAX: (334) 844-9807.

Home Field: Plainsman Park. Seating Capacity: 4,096. Outfield Dimensions: LF—315, CF—385, RF—331. Press Box Telephone: (334) 844-4138.

## AUSTIN PEAY STATE Governors

Conference: Ohio Valley.

Mailing Address: P.O. Box 4515, Clarksville, TN 37044. Website: www.apsu.edu/letsgopeay.

Head Coach: Gary McClure. Assistant Coaches: Chris Cook, Ryan Edwards, *Brian Hetland. Telephone: (931) 221-6266. • Baseball SID: Cody Bush. Telephone: (931) 221-7561. FAX: (931) 221-7562.

## BALL STATE Cardinals

Conference: Mid-American (West).

Mailing Address: HP 120, Muncie, IN 47306. Website: www.ballstatesports.com.

Head Coach: Greg Beals. Assistant Coaches: Scott French, Alex Marconi, *Mike Stafford. Telephone: (765) 285-8226. • Baseball SID: Mike Potter. Telephone: (765) 285-8242. FAX: (765) 285-8929.

Home Field: Ball Diamond. Seating Capacity: 1,700. Outfield Dimensions: LF—330, CF—400, RF—330. Press Box Telephone: (765) 285-8932.

## BAYLOR Bears

Conference: Big 12.

Mailing Address: 150 Bear Run, Waco, TX 76712. Website: www.BaylorBears.com.

Head Coach: Steve Smith. Assistant Coaches: Chris Berry, Steve Johnigan, *Mitch Thompson. Telephone: (254) 710-3029. • Baseball SID: Larry Little. Telephone: (254) 710-4389. FAX: (254) 710-1369.

Home Field: Baylor Ballpark at Ferrell Field. Seating Capacity: 5,000. Outfield Dimensions: LF—330, CF—400, RF—330. Press Box Telephone: (254) 754-5546.

## BELMONT Bruins

Conference: Atlantic Sun.

Mailing Address: 1900 Belmont Blvd., Nashville, TN 37212. Website: www.belmont.edu/athletics.

Head Coach: Dave Jarvis. Assistant Coaches: Matt Barnett, *Jason Stein. Telephone: (615) 460-6166. • Baseball SID: Charles Cochrum. Telephone: (615) 460-8023. FAX: (615) 460-5584.

## BETHUNE-COOKMAN Wildcats

Conference: Mid-Eastern Athletic.

Mailing Address: 640 Dr. Mary McLeod Bethune Blvd., Daytona Beach, FL 32114. Website: www.cookman.edu/athletics.

Head Coach: Mervyl Melendez. Assistant Coaches: *Joel Sanchez, Micah Simmons, Jose Vazquez. Telephone: (386) 481-2224. • Baseball SID: Bryan Harvey. Telephone: (386) 481-2206. FAX: (386) 481-2238.

## BINGHAMTON Bearcats

Conference: America East.

Mailing Address: Vestal Parkway East, P.O. Box 6000, Binghamton, NY 13902. Website: athletics.binghamton.edu.

Head Coach: Tim Sinicki. Assistant Coach: Ryan Hurba. Telephone: (607) 777-2525. • Baseball SID: John Hartrick. Telephone: (607) 777-6800. FAX: (607) 777-4597.

## BIRMINGHAM-SOUTHERN Panthers

Conference: Big South.

Mailing Address: 900 Arkadelphia Rd., Birmingham, AL 35254. Website: www.bscsports.net.

Head Coach: Brian Shoop. Assistant Coaches: *Doug Kovash, Perry Roth, Jard Walker. Telephone: (205) 226-4797. • Baseball SID: Fred Sington. Telephone: (205) 226-7736. FAX: (205) 226-3049.

## BOSTON COLLEGE Eagles

Conference: Atlantic Coast (Atlantic).

Mailing Address: 140 Commonwealth Ave., Chestnut Hill, MA 02467. Website: www.bceagles.com.

Head Coach: Pete Hughes. Assistant Coaches: Mikio Aoki, Steve Englert. Telephone: (617) 552-1131. • Baseball SID: Brian Caruso. Telephone: (617) 552-4508. FAX: (617) 552-4903.

Home Field: Commander Shea Field. Seating Capacity: 1,000. Outfield Dimensions: LF—330, CF—400, RF—320. Press Box Telephone: (617) 552-0119.

## BOWLING GREEN STATE Falcons

Conference: Mid-American (East).

Mailing Address: 201 Perry Stadium East, Bowling Green, OH 43403. Website: www.bgsufalcons.com.

Head Coach: Danny Schmitz. Assistant Coaches: *Tod Brown, Dave Whitmire. Telephone: (419) 372-2401. • Baseball SID: Kyle Kuhlman. Telephone: (419) 372-7077. FAX: (419) 372-6015.

Home Field: Warren Steller Field. Seating Capacity: 1,100. Outfield Dimensions: LF—340, CF—400, RF—340. Press Box Telephone: (419) 372-1234.

## BRADLEY Braves

Conference: Missouri Valley.

Mailing Address: 1501 W. Bradley Ave., Peoria, IL 61625. Website: www.bubraves.com.

Head Coach: Dewey Kalmer. Assistant Coaches: Mike Dunne, *Marc Wagner. Telephone: (309) 677-2684. • Baseball SID: Bobby Parker. Telephone: (309) 677-2624. FAX: (309) 677-2626.

Home Field: O'Brien Field. Seating Capacity: 7,500.

Outfield Dimensions: LF—310, CF—400, RF—310. Press Box Telephone: (309) 680-4045.

## BRIGHAM YOUNG Cougars
Conference: Mountain West.
Mailing Address: 30 SFH, Brigham Young University, Provo, UT 84602. Website: www.byucougars.com.
Head Coach: Vance Law. Assistant Coaches: Bobby Applegate, Brad Eagar, *Ryan Roberts. Telephone: (801) 422-5049. • Baseball SID: Ralph Zobell. Telephone: (801) 422-9769. FAX: (801) 422-0633.
Home Field: Larry Miller Field. Seating Capacity: 2,204. Outfield Dimensions: LF—345, CF—400, RF—345. Press Box Telephone: (801) 422-4041.

## BROWN Bears
Conference: Ivy League (Rolfe).
Mailing Address: 235 Hope St., Providence, RI 02912. Website: www.BrownBears.com.
Head Coach: Marek Drabinski. Assistant Coach: *Matt Kirby. Telephone: (401) 863-3090. • Baseball SID: Kristen DiChiaro. Telephone: (401) 863-7014. FAX: (401) 863-1436.

## BUCKNELL Bison
Conference: Patriot.
Mailing Address: Department of Athletics, Bucknell University, Lewisburg, PA 17837. Website: www.buck-nellbison.com.
Head Coach: Gene Depew. Assistant Coaches: Scott Heather, Brian Hoyt. Telephone: (570) 577-3593. • Baseball SID: Jillian Jakuba. Telephone: (570) 577-1835. FAX: (570) 577-1660.

## BUFFALO Bulls
Conference: Mid-American (East).
Mailing Address: 175 Alumni Arena, Buffalo, NY 14260. Website: www.buffalobulls.com.
Head Coach: Bill Breene. Assistant Coaches: Ed Marko, *Ron Torgalski, Neal Turvey. Telephone: (716) 645-6808. • Baseball SID: Joe Guistina. Telephone: (716) 645-5523. FAX: (716) 645-6840.

## BUTLER Bulldogs
Conference: Horizon.
Mailing Address: 510 W. 49th St., Indianapolis, IN 46208. Website: www.butlersports.com.
Head Coach: Steve Farley. Assistant Coaches: Dennis Kas, Bob Keeney, Jason Taulman. Telephone: (317) 940-9721. • Baseball SID: Jim McGrath. Telephone: (317) 940-9414. FAX: (317) 940-9808.

## CALIFORNIA Golden Bears
Conference: Pacific-10.
Mailing Address: 210 Memorial Stadium, Berkeley, CA 94720. Website: www.calbears.com.
Head Coach: David Esquer. Assistant Coaches: *Dan Hubbs, Kevin Pritchard, Jon Zuber. Telephone: (510) 642-9026. • Baseball SID: Scott Ball. Telephone: (510) 643-1741. FAX: (510) 643-7778.
Home Field: Evans Diamond. Seating Capacity: 2,500. Outfield Dimensions: LF—320, CF—395, RF—320. Press Box Telephone: (510) 642-3098.

## #UC DAVIS Aggies
Conference: Big West.
Mailing Address: One Shields Ave., Davis, CA 95616. Website: www.ucdavisaggies.com.
Head Coach: Rex Peters. Assistant Coaches: *Lloyd Acosta, Bobby Calderon, Matt Vaughn. Telephone: (530) 752-7513. • Baseball SID: Mike Robles. Telephone: (530) 754-3680. FAX: (530) 754-5674.
Home Field: Dobbins Stadium. Seating Capacity:

2,500. Outfield Dimensions: LF—310, CF—400, RF—310.

## UC IRVINE Anteaters
Conference: Big West.
Mailing Address: 1394 Crawford Hall, Irvine, CA 92697. Website: www.athletics.uci.edu.
Head Coach: Dave Serrano. Assistant Coaches: Chad Baum, Greg Bergeron, *Sergio Brown. Telephone: (949) 824-4292. • Baseball SID: Fumi Kimura. Telephone: (949) 824-9474. FAX: (949) 824-5260.
Home Field: Anteater Ballpark. Seating Capacity: 3,200. Outfield Dimensions: LF—335, CF—405, RF—335. Press Box Telephone: (949) 824-9905.

## UCLA Bruins
Conference: Pacific-10.
Mailing Address: P.O. Box 24044, Los Angeles, CA 90024. Website: www.uclabruins.com.
Head Coach: John Savage. Assistant Coaches: Brian Green, Matt Jones, *Pat Shine. Telephone: (310) 794-2470. • Baseball SID: Julian Temblador. Telephone: (310) 206-4008. FAX: (310) 825-8664.
Home Field: Jackie Robinson Stadium. Seating Capacity: 1,250. Outfield Dimensions: LF—330, CF—390, RF—330. Press Box Telephone: (310) 794-8213.

## UC RIVERSIDE Highlanders
Conference: Big West.
Mailing Address: 900 University Ave., Riverside, CA 92521. Website: www.athletics.ucr.edu.
Head Coach: Doug Smith. Assistant Coaches: Randy Betten, *Andrew Checketts, Kevin Ellis. Telephone: (951) 827-5441. • Baseball SID: Mark Dodson. Telephone: (951) 827-4571. FAX: (951) 827-5889.
Home Field: Riverside Sports Complex. Seating Capacity: 2,500. Outfield Dimensions: LF—330, CF—400, RF—330. Press Box Telephone: (951) 827-6415.

## UC SANTA BARBARA Gauchos
Conference: Big West.
Mailing Address: Intercollegiate Athletics Building, UCSB, Santa Barbara, CA 93106. Website: www.ucsb-gauchos.com.
Head Coach: Bob Brontsema. Assistant Coaches: John Kirkgard, *Tom Myers. Telephone: (805) 893-3690. • Baseball SID: Tyler Geivett. Telephone: (805) 893-8603. FAX: (805) 893-4537.
Home Field: Caesar Uyesaka Stadium. Seating Capacity: 1,000. Outfield Dimensions: LF—335, CF—400, RF—335. Press Box Telephone: (805) 893-4671.

## CAL POLY Mustangs
Conference: Big West.
Mailing Address: One Grand Ave., San Luis Obispo, CA 93407. Website: www.gopoly.com.
Head Coach: Larry Lee. Assistant Coaches: Drew Gillmore, Brian Gosney, Jerry Weinstein, *Jesse Zepeda. Telephone: (805) 756-6367. • Baseball SID: Eric Burdick. Telephone: (805) 756-6550. FAX: (805) 756-2650.
Home Field: Baggett Stadium. Seating Capacity: 1,734. Outfield Dimensions: LF—335, CF—405, RF—335. Press Box Telephone: (805) 756-7456.

## CAL STATE FULLERTON Titans
Conference: Big West.
Mailing Address: 800 North State College Blvd., Fullerton, CA 92834. Website: fullertontitans.collegesports.com.
Head Coach: George Horton. Assistant Coaches: *Jason Gill, Ted Silva, Rick Vanderhook. Telephone:

(714) 278-3780. • **Baseball SID:** Michael Greenlee. **Telephone:** (714) 278-3081. **FAX:** (714) 278-3141.
**Home Field:** Goodwin Field. **Seating Capacity:** 3,500. **Outfield Dimensions:** LF—330, CF—400, RF—330. **Press Box Telephone:** (714) 278-5327.

### CAL STATE NORTHRIDGE Matadors
**Conference:** Big West.
**Mailing Address:** 18111 Nordhoff St., Northridge, CA 91330. **Website:** www.gomatadors.com.
**Head Coach:** Steve Rousey. **Assistant Coaches:** Grant Hohman, Mark Kertenian, *Rob McKinley. **Telephone:** (818) 677-7055. • **Baseball SID:** Stacie Hunter. **Telephone:** (818) 677-3243. **FAX:** (818) 677-4950.
**Home Field:** Matador Field. **Seating Capacity:** 1,200. **Outfield Dimensions:** LF—325, CF—400, RF—330. **Press Box Telephone:** Unavailable.

### CAMPBELL Fighting Camels
**Conference:** Atlantic Sun.
**Mailing Address:** P.O. Box 10, Buies Creek, NC 27506. **Website:** www.gocamels.com.
**Head Coach:** Chip Smith. **Assistant Coaches:** *Kent Cox, Sean Fleming, Brad Schrock. **Telephone:** (910) 893-1354. • **Baseball SID:** Scott Dunford. **Telephone:** (910) 814-4367. **FAX:** (910) 893-1330.

### CANISIUS Golden Griffins
**Conference:** Metro Atlantic.
**Mailing Address:** 2001 Main St., Buffalo, NY 14208. **Website:** www.gogriffs.com.
**Head Coach:** Mike McRae. **Assistant Coaches:** Chris Barry, Marc Kunigonis. **Telephone:** (716) 888-3207. • **Baseball SID:** Marc Gignac. **Telephone:** (716) 888-2978. **FAX:** (716) 888-3178.

### CENTENARY Gents
**Conference:** Mid-Continent.
**Mailing Address:** 2911 Centenary Blvd., Shreveport, LA 71134. **Website:** www.gocentenary.com.
**Head Coach:** Ed McCann. **Assistant Coaches:** Mike Diaz, Jeff Poulin. **Telephone:** (318) 869-5298. • **Baseball SID:** David Pratt. **Telephone:** (318) 869-5092. **FAX:** (318) 869-5128.

### CENTRAL CONNECTICUT STATE Blue Devils
**Conference:** Northeast.
**Mailing Address:** 1615 Stanley St., New Britain, CT 06050. **Website:** www.ccsubluedevils.com.
**Head Coach:** Charlie Hickey. **Assistant Coaches:** *Paul LaBella, Jim Ziogas. **Telephone:** (860) 832-3074. • **Baseball SID:** Tom Pincince. **Telephone:** (860) 832-3089. **FAX:** (860) 832-3084.

### CENTRAL FLORIDA Golden Knights
**Conference:** Conference USA.
**Mailing Address:** 4000 Central Florida Blvd., Orlando, FL 32816. **Website:** www.ucfathletics.com.
**Head Coach:** Jay Bergman. **Assistant Coaches:** *Craig Cozart, Rich Wallace, Derek Wolfe. **Telephone:** (407) 823-0140. • **Baseball SID:** Jason Baum. **Telephone:** (407) 823-0994. **FAX:** (407) 823-5266.
**Home Field:** Jay Bergman Field. **Seating Capacity:** 1,980. **Outfield Dimensions:** LF—325, CF—400, RF—325. **Press Box Telephone:** (407) 823-4487.

### CENTRAL MICHIGAN Chippewas
**Conference:** Mid-American (West).
**Mailing Address:** 106 West Hall, Mount Pleasant, MI 48859. **Website:** www.cmuchippewas.com.
**Head Coach:** Steve Jaksa. **Assistant Coaches:** Jeremy Crum, Jeff Opalewski, Brad Stromdahl, *Mike Villano, Kurtis Wells. **Telephone:** (989) 774-4392. • **Baseball SID:**

Scott Rex. **Telephone/FAX:** (989) 774-7323.

### CHARLESTON Cougars
**Conference:** Southern.
**Mailing Address:** 30 George St., Charleston, SC 29424. **Website:** www.cofcsports.com.
**Head Coach:** John Pawlowski. **Assistant Coaches:** *Scott Foxhall, David Scoggin, Seth Von Behren. **Telephone:** (843) 953-5556. • **Baseball SID:** Tony Ciuffo. **Telephone:** (843) 953-5465. **FAX:** (843) 953-6534.
**Home Field:** Patriots Point Stadium. **Seating Capacity:** 2,000. **Outfield Dimensions:** LF—300, CF—400, RF—330. **Press Box Telephone:** (843) 953-9141.

### CHARLESTON SOUTHERN Buccaneers
**Conference:** Big South.
**Mailing Address:** P.O. Box 118087, 9200 University Blvd., Charleston, SC 29423. **Website:** www.csu sports.com.
**Head Coach:** Jason Murray. **Assistant Coaches:** *Brian Hoop, Matt Ishee, Josh Walker. **Telephone:** (843) 863-7591. • **Baseball SID:** David Shelton. **Telephone:** (843) 863-7688. **FAX:** (843) 863-7676.

### CHARLOTTE 49ers
**Conference:** Atlantic 10.
**Mailing Address:** 9201 University City Blvd., Charlotte, NC 28223. **Website:** www.charlotte49ers.com.
**Head Coach:** *Loren Hibbs. **Assistant Coaches:** Bo Durkac, *Brandon Hall, Adam Willard. **Telephone:** (704) 687-3935. • **Baseball SID:** Matt McCullough. **Telephone:** (704) 687-6312. **FAX:** (704) 687-4918.
**Home Field:** Tom and Lib Phillips Field. **Seating Capacity:** 2,000. **Outfield Dimensions:** LF—335, CF—390, RF—335. **Press Box Telephone:** (704) 687-3148.

### CHICAGO STATE Cougars
**Conference:** Mid-Continent.
**Mailing Address:** 9501 S. King Dr. JDC 100E, Chicago, IL 60628. **Website:** www.csu.edu/athletics.
**Head Coach:** Vern Hasty. **Assistant Coaches:** Jim Sammons, Emanuel Wheeler. **Telephone:** (773) 995-3659. • **Baseball SID:** Quenjana Adams. **Telephone:** (773) 995-2217. **FAX:** (773) 995-3656.

### CINCINNATI Bearcats
**Conference:** Big East.
**Mailing Address:** One Edwards Center, Suite 4150 ML 0021, Cincinnati, OH 45221. **Website:** www.ucbear cats.com.
**Head Coach:** Brian Cleary. **Assistant Coaches:** *Brad Meador, Joe Regruth. **Telephone:** (513) 556-1577. • **Baseball SID:** Shawn Sell. **Telephone:** (513) 556-0618. **FAX:** (513) 556-0619.
**Home Field:** UC Baseball Stadium. **Seating Capacity:** 3,200. **Outfield Dimensions:** LF—325, CF—400, RF—325. **Press Box Telephone:** (513) 556-9645.

### THE CITADEL Bulldogs
**Conference:** Southern.
**Mailing Address:** 171 Moultrie St., Charleston, SC 29409. **Website:** www.citadelsports.com.
**Head Coach:** Fred Jordan. **Assistant Coaches:** David Beckley, Randy Carlson, *Chris Lemonis. **Telephone:** (843) 953-5285. • **Baseball SID:** Melanie Long. **Telephone:** (843) 953-5120. **FAX:** (843) 953-5058.
**Home Field:** Joseph P. Riley Jr. Park. **Seating Capacity:** 6,000. **Outfield Dimensions:** LF—305, CF—398, RF—337. **Press Box Telephone:** (843) 965-4151.

### CLEMSON Tigers
**Conference:** Atlantic Coast (Atlantic).
**Mailing Address:** 100 Perimeter Rd., P.O. Box 31,

Clemson, SC 29634. **Website:** www.clemsontigers.com.
**Head Coach:** Jack Leggett. **Assistant Coaches:** *Kevin O'Sullivan, Tom Riginos, Russell Triplett. **Telephone:** (864) 656-1947. • **Baseball SID:** Brian Hennessy. **Telephone:** (864) 656-1921. **FAX:** (864) 656-0299.
**Home Field:** Doug Kingsmore Stadium. **Seating Capacity:** 5,000. **Outfield Dimensions:** LF—320, CF—400, RF—330. **Press Box Telephone:** (864) 656-7731.

### CLEVELAND STATE Vikings
**Conference:** Horizon.
**Mailing Address:** 2000 Prospect Ave., Cleveland, OH 44115. **Website:** www.csuvikings.com.
**Head Coach:** Jay Murphy. **Assistant Coaches:** Carmen DeChristofaro, Ernest Simpson, Dave Sprochi. **Telephone:** (216) 687-4822. • **Baseball SID:** Chris Urban. **Telephone:** (216) 687-4818. **FAX:** (216) 523-7257.

### COASTAL CAROLINA Chanticleers
**Conference:** Big South.
**Mailing Address:** P.O. Box 261954, Conway, SC 29528. **Website:** www.goccusports.com.
**Head Coach:** Gary Gilmore. **Assistant Coaches:** Clint Ayers, Brendan Dougherty, *Kevin Schnall. **Telephone:** (843) 349-2816. • **Baseball SID:** Kent Reichert. **Telephone:** (843) 349-2840. **FAX:** (843) 349-2819.
**Home Field:** Watson Stadium/Vrooman Field. **Seating Capacity:** 2,000. **Outfield Dimensions:** LF—320, CF—390, RF—325. **Press Box Telephone:** (843) 421-8244.

### COLUMBIA Lions
**Conference:** Ivy League (Gehrig).
**Mailing Address:** Dodge Physical Fitness Center, 3030 Broadway, New York, NY 10027. **Website:** www.gocolumbialions.com.
**Head Coach:** Brett Boretti. **Assistant Coaches:** *Bryan Haley, Jim Walsh. **Telephone:** (212) 854-8448. • **Baseball SID:** Darlene Camacho. **Telephone:** (212) 854-2535. **FAX:** (212) 854-8168.

### CONNECTICUT Huskies
**Conference:** Big East.
**Mailing Address:** 2095 Hillside Rd., Storrs, CT 06269. **Website:** www.uconnhuskies.com.
**Head Coach:** Jim Penders. **Assistant Coaches:** *Justin Blood, Bruce Elliott, Chris Podeszwa. **Telephone:** (860) 486-4089. • **Baseball SID:** Lydia Panayotidis. **Telephone:** (860) 486-4707. **FAX:** (860) 486-5085.
**Home Field:** J.O. Christian Field. **Seating Capacity:** 2,000. **Outfield Dimensions:** LF—340, CF—405, RF—340. **Press Box Telephone:** Unavailable.

### COPPIN STATE Eagles
**Conference:** Mid-Eastern Athletic.
**Mailing Address:** 2500 W. North Ave., Baltimore, MD 21216. **Website:** www.coppin.edu/athletics.
**Head Coach:** Guy Robertson. **Assistant Coaches:** Ruffin Bell, Tim Brown, Nick Wenger. **Telephone:** (410) 951-3740. • **Baseball SID:** John Kneisly. **Telephone:** (410) 951-3744. **FAX:** (410) 951-3718.

### CORNELL Big Red
**Conference:** Ivy League (Rolfe).
**Mailing Address:** Teagle Hall, Campus Rd., Ithaca, NY 14853. **Website:** www.cornellbigred.com.
**Head Coach:** Tom Ford. **Assistant Coach:** Scott Marsh. **Telephone:** (607) 255-6604. • **Baseball SID:** Eric Lawrence. **Telephone:** (607) 255-5627. **FAX:** (607) 255-9791.

### CREIGHTON Blue Jays
**Conference:** Missouri Valley.
**Mailing Address:** 2500 California Ave., Omaha, NE

68178. **Website:** www.gocreighton.com.
**Head Coach:** Ed Servais. **Assistant Coaches:** Spencer Allen, Travis Wyckoff. **Telephone:** (402) 280-2483. • **Baseball SID:** Ben Adamson. **Telephone:** (402) 280-5801. **FAX:** (402) 280-2495.
**Home Field:** Creighton Sports Complex. **Seating Capacity:** 1,000. **Outfield Dimensions:** LF—330, CF—402, RF—330. **Press Box Telephone:** (402) 280-2787.

### DALLAS BAPTIST Patriots
**Conference:** Independent.
**Mailing Address:** 3000 Mt. Creek Pkwy., Dallas, TX 75104. **Website:** www.dbu.edu/athletics.
**Head Coach:** Eric Newman. **Assistant Coaches:** Nate Frieling, *Dan Heefner, Jamie Kennedy. **Telephone:** (214) 333-6951. • **Baseball SID:** Ryan Erwin. **Telephone:** (214) 333-5436. **FAX:** (214) 333-5306.

### DARTMOUTH Big Green
**Conference:** Ivy League (Rolfe).
**Mailing Address:** 6083 Alumni Gym, Hanover, NH 03755. **Website:** athletics.dartmouth.edu.
**Head Coach:** Bob Whalen. **Assistant Coaches:** Nicholas Enriquez, *Robin Harriss. **Telephone:** (603) 646-2477. • **Baseball SID:** Ben Flickinger. **Telephone:** (603) 646-2468. **FAX:** (603) 646-1286.

### DAVIDSON Wildcats
**Conference:** Southern.
**Mailing Address:** P.O. Box 7158, 200 Baker Dr., Davidson, NC 28035. **Website:** www.davidson.edu/athletics.
**Head Coach:** Dick Cooke. **Assistant Coaches:** Matt Hanson, Craig Hanson, Eli Benefield. **Telephone:** (704) 894-2368. • **Baseball SID:** Rick Bender. **Telephone:** (704) 894-2123. **FAX:** (704) 894-2636.

### DAYTON Flyers
**Conference:** Atlantic 10.
**Mailing Address:** 300 College Park, Dayton, OH 45469. **Website:** www.daytonflyers.com.
**Head Coach:** Tony Vittorio. **Assistant Coaches:** Cory Allen, Terry Bell, *Todd Linklater. **Telephone:** (937) 229-4456. • **Baseball SID:** Bill Thomas. **Telephone:** (937) 229-4419. **FAX:** (937) 272-4461.

### DELAWARE Fightin' Blue Hens
**Conference:** Colonial Athletic.
**Mailing Address:** 112 Delaware Field House, Newark, DE 19716. **Website:** www.udel.edu/sportsinfo
**Head Coach:** Jim Sherman. **Assistant Coaches:** Jim Fallers, Dan Hammer, *Greg Mamula. **Telephone:** (302) 831-8596. • **Baseball SID:** Andy Sturgill. **Telephone:** (302) 831-2186. **FAX:** (302) 831-8653.
**Home Field:** Bob Hannah Stadium. **Seating Capacity:** 1,300. **Outfield Dimensions:** LF—330, CF—400, RF—330. **Press Box Telephone:** (302) 831-4122.

### DELAWARE STATE Hornets
**Conference:** Mid-Eastern Athletic.
**Mailing Address:** 1200 N. DuPont Hwy., Dover, DE 19901. **Website:** www.desu.edu/athletics.
**Head Coach:** J.P. Blandin. **Assistant Coaches:** Mike August, Will Gardner, Tim Valliancourt. **Telephone:** (302) 857-6035. • **Baseball SID:** Dennis Jones. **Telephone:** (302) 857-6068. **FAX:** (302) 857-6069.

### DUKE Blue Devils
**Conference:** Atlantic Coast (Coastal).
**Mailing Address:** Cameron Indoor Stadium, P.O. Box 90555, Durham, NC 27708. **Website:** www.GoDuke.com.
**Head Coach:** Sean McNally. **Assistant Coaches:** Matthew Boggs, *Dave Turgeon. **Telephone:** (919) 668-

0255. • **Baseball SID:** Lee Aldridge. **Telephone:** (919) 684-8708. **FAX:** (919) 684-2489.

**Home Field:** Jack Coombs Field. **Seating Capacity:** 2,000. **Outfield Dimensions:** LF—330, CF—400, RF—330. **Press Box Telephone:** Unavailable.

## DUQUESNE Dukes
**Conference:** Atlantic 10.
**Mailing Address:** A.J. Palumbo Center, 600 Forbes Ave., Pittsburgh, PA 15282. **Website:** www.goduquesne.com.
**Head Coach:** *Mike Wilson. **Assistant Coaches:** Brock Bollinger, Todd Schiffhauer, Dan Schwartzbauer. **Telephone:** (412) 396-5245. • **Baseball SID:** George Nieman. **Telephone:** (412) 396-5376. **FAX:** (412) 396-6210.

## EAST CAROLINA Pirates
**Conference:** Conference USA.
**Mailing Address:** 320 Ward Sports Medicine Building, Greenville, NC 27858. **Website:** www.ecupirates.com.
**Head Coach:** Billy Godwin. **Assistant Coaches:** *Link Jarrett, Ryan Riley, George Whitfield. **Telephone:** (252) 737-1985. • **Baseball SID:** Malcolm Gray. **Telephone:** (252) 328-4523. **FAX:** (252) 328-4528.
**Home Field:** Clark-LeClair Stadium. **Seating Capacity:** 3,000. **Outfield Dimensions:** LF—320, CF—390, RF—320. **Press Box Telephone:** (252) 328-0068.

## EAST TENNESSEE STATE Buccaneers
**Conference:** Atlantic Sun.
**Mailing Address:** P.O. Box 70041, Johnson City, TN 37614. **Website:** www.ETSUBucs.com.
**Head Coach:** Tony Skole. **Assistant Coaches:** Clay Greene, *Maynard McClarrinon. **Telephone:** (423) 439-4496. • **Baseball SID:** John Roberts. **Telephone:** (423) 439-5263. **FAX:** (423) 439-6138.

## EASTERN ILLINOIS Panthers
**Conference:** Ohio Valley.
**Mailing Address:** 600 Lincoln Ave., Charleston, IL 61920. **Website:** www.eiu.edu/panthers.
**Head Coach:** Jim Schmitz. **Assistant Coaches:** *Sean Lyons, Mike Rolih. **Telephone:** (217) 581-2522. • **Baseball SID:** Ben Turner. **Telephone:** (217) 581-7020. **FAX:** (217) 581-6434.

## EASTERN KENTUCKY Colonels
**Conference:** Ohio Valley.
**Mailing Address:** 115 Alumni Coliseum, Richmond, KY 40475. **Website:** www.ekusports.com.
**Head Coach:** Elvis Dominguez. **Assistant Coaches:** *John Corbin, Scott Pickens. **Telephone:** (859) 622-2128. • **Baseball SID:** Jeremy Cohen. **Telephone:** (859) 622-1253. **FAX:** (859) 622-1230.

## EASTERN MICHIGAN Eagles
**Conference:** Mid-American (West).
**Mailing Address:** 799 Hewitt Rd., Convocation Center, Room 307, Ypsilanti, MI 48197. **Website:** www.emich.edu/goeagles.
**Head Coach:** *Roger Coryell. **Assistant Coach:** Chris Hoiles. **Telephone:** (734) 487-0315. • **Baseball SIDs:** Mekye Phelps, Jay Sofen. **Telephone:** (734) 487-0317. **FAX:** (734) 485-3840.
**Home Field:** Oestrike Stadium. **Seating Capacity:** 2,000. **Outfield Dimensions:** LF—330, CF—390, RF—330. **Press Box Telephone:** (734) 487-2835.

## ELON Phoenix
**Conference:** Southern.
**Mailing Address:** 100 Campus Dr., 2500 Campus Box, Elon College, NC 27244. **Website:** www.elon.edu/athletics.

**Head Coach:** Mike Kennedy. **Assistant Coaches:** Jason Simmons, Robbie Huffstettler, *Greg Starbuck. **Telephone:** (336) 278-6741. • **Baseball SID:** Chris Rash. **Telephone:** (336) 278-6712. **FAX:** (336) 278-6768.
**Home Field:** Latham Park. **Seating Capacity:** 2,000. **Outfield Dimensions:** LF—317, CF—385, RF—327. **Press Box Telephone:** (336) 278-6788.

## EVANSVILLE Purple Aces
**Conference:** Missouri Valley.
**Mailing Address:** 1800 Lincoln Ave., Evansville, IN 47722. **Website:** www.gopurpleaces.com.
**Head Coach:** Dave Schrage. **Assistant Coaches:** Jacob Gill, Kevin Koch, *David Seifert. **Telephone:** (812) 488-2059. • **Baseball SID:** Tom Benson. **Telephone:** (812) 488-1152. **FAX:** (812) 488-2090.
**Home Field:** Braun Stadium. **Seating Capacity:** 1,200. **Outfield Dimensions:** LF—330, CF—400, RF—330. **Press Box Telephone:** (812) 488-2587.

## FAIRFIELD Stags
**Conference:** Metro Atlantic.
**Mailing Address:** 1073 N. Benson Rd., Fairfield, CT 06430. **Website:** www.fairfieldstags.com.
**Head Coach:** John Slosar. **Assistant Coaches:** Patrick Hall, Kevin Huber, Dennis Whalen. **Telephone:** (203) 254-4000, ext. 2605. • **Baseball SID:** Patrick Moran. **Telephone:** (203) 254-4000, ext. 2877. **FAX:** (203) 254-4117.

## FAIRLEIGH DICKINSON Knights
**Conference:** Northeast.
**Mailing Address:** 1000 River Rd., Teaneck, NJ 07666. **Website:** www.fduknights.com.
**Head Coach:** *Jerry DeFabbia. **Assistant Coaches:** Chris Bagley, Dan Grey, Daryl Morhardt. **Telephone:** (201) 692-2245. • **Baseball SID:** Wes Heinel. **Telephone:** (201) 692-2204. **FAX:** (201) 692-9361.

## FLORIDA Gators
**Conference:** Southeastern (East).
**Mailing Address:** P.O. Box 14485, Gainesville, FL 32604. **Website:** www.gatorzone.com.
**Head Coach:** Pat McMahon. **Assistant Coaches:** Brian Fleetwood, *Ross Jones, Tim Parenton. **Telephone:** (352) 375-4683, ext. 4457. • **Baseball SID:** John Hines. **Telephone:** (352) 375-4683, ext. 6100. **FAX:** (352) 375-4809.
**Home Field:** McKethan Stadium at Perry Field. **Seating Capacity:** 5,000. **Outfield Dimensions:** LF—329, CF—400, RF—325. **Press Box Telephone:** (352) 375-4683, ext. 4355.

## FLORIDA A&M Rattlers
**Conference:** Mid-Eastern Athletic.
**Mailing Address:** 1500 Wahnish Way, Tallahassee, FL 32307. **Website:** www.thefamurattlers.com.
**Head Coach:** Joe Durant. **Assistant Coaches:** K.C. Carter, *Brett Richardson. **Telephone:** (850) 599-3202. • **Baseball SID:** Ronnie Thompson. **Telephone:** (850) 599-2701. **FAX:** (850) 599-3206.

## FLORIDA ATLANTIC Blue Wave
**Conference:** Atlantic Sun.
**Mailing Address:** 777 Glades Rd., Boca Raton, FL 33431. **Website:** www.fausports.com.
**Head Coach:** Kevin Cooney. **Assistant Coaches:** Tony Fossas, *John McCormack, George Roig. **Telephone:** (561) 297-3956. • **Baseball SID:** Dawn Elston. **Telephone:** (561) 297-3513. **FAX:** (561) 297-3499.
**Home Field:** FAU Stadium. **Seating Capacity:** 2,500. **Dimensions:** LF—330, CF—400, RF—330. **Press Box**

Telephone: (561) 297-3455.

### FLORIDA INTERNATIONAL Golden Panthers
Conference: Sun Belt.
Mailing Address: 11200 SW 8th St., Pharmed Arena, Room 265, Miami, FL 33199. Website: www.fiusports.com.
Head Coach: Danny Price. Assistant Coaches: *Tony Casas, Chris Holick, Lou Sanchez. Telephone: (305) 348-3166. • Baseball SID: Danny Kambel. Telephone: (305) 348-2084. FAX: (305) 348-2963.
Home Field: University Park. Seating Capacity: 2,000. Outfield Dimensions: LF—325, CF—400, RF—325. Press Box Telephone: Unavailable.

### FLORIDA STATE Seminoles
Conference: Atlantic Coast (Atlantic).
Mailing Address: University Center D 107, Tallahassee, FL 32306. Website: www.seminoles.com.
Head Coach: Mike Martin. Assistant Coaches: Pete Jenkins, Mike Martin Jr., *Jamey Shouppe. Telephone: (850) 644-1073. • Baseball SID: Elliott Finebloom. Telephone: (850) 644-5656. FAX: (850) 644-3820.
Home Field: Mike Martin Field at Dick Howser Stadium. Seating Capacity: 6,700. Outfield Dimensions: LF—340, CF—400, RF—320. Press Box Telephone: (850) 644-1553.

### FORDHAM Rams
Conference: Atlantic 10.
Mailing Address: 441 E. Fordham Rd., Bronx, NY 10458. Website: www.fordhamsports.com.
Head Coach: Nick Restaino. Assistant Coaches: Gene Calamari, Jeff Cohen, *Kiko Reyes. Telephone: (718) 817-4292. • Baseball SID: Scott Kwiatkowski. Telephone: (718) 817-4219. FAX: (718) 817-4244.

### FRESNO STATE Bulldogs
Conference: Western Athletic.
Mailing Address: 5305 N. Campus Dr., Room 153, Fresno, CA 93740. Website: www.gobulldogs.com.
Head Coach: Mike Batesole. Assistant Coaches: *Matt Curtis, Chad Edwards, Bobby Jones, Pat Waer. Telephone: (559) 278-2178. • Baseball SID: Roger Kirk. Telephone: (559) 278-2509. FAX: (559) 278-4689.
Home Field: Beiden Field. Seating Capacity: 5,575. Outfield Dimensions: LF—330, CF—400, RF—330. Press Box Telephone: (559) 278-7678.

### FURMAN Paladins
Conference: Southern.
Mailing Address: 3300 Poinsett Hwy., Greenville, SC 29613. Website: www.furmanpaladins.com.
Head Coach: Ron Smith. Assistant Coaches: Jon Placko, Brent Shade. Telephone: (864) 294-2146. • Baseball SID: Hunter Reid. Telephone: (864) 294-2061. FAX: (864) 294-3061.

### GARDNER-WEBB Runnin' Bulldogs
Conference: Atlantic Sun.
Mailing Address: P.O. Box 877, 112 E. Main St., Boiling Springs, NC 28017. Website: www.gwusports.com.
Head Coach: Rusty Stroupe. Assistant Coaches: Morgan Frazier, Ryan Quirello, *Dan Roszel. Telephone: (704) 406-4421. • Baseball SID: Marc Rabb. Telephone: (704) 406-4355. FAX: (704) 406-4739.

### GEORGE MASON Patriots
Conference: Colonial Athletic.
Mailing Address: 4400 University Dr., Fairfax, VA 22030. Website: www.gomason.com.
Head Coach: Bill Brown. Assistant Coach: Shawn

Stiffler. Telephone: (703) 993-3282. • Baseball SID: Richard Coco. Telephone: (703) 993-3264. FAX: (703) 993-3259.
Home Field: Hap Spuhler Field. Seating Capacity: 900. Outfield Dimensions: LF—320, CF—400, RF—320. Press Box Telephone: Unavailable.

### GEORGE WASHINGTON Colonials
Conference: Atlantic 10.
Mailing Address: 600 22nd St. NW, Washington, DC 20052. Website: gwsports.collegesports.com.
Head Coach: Steve Mrowka. Assistant Coaches: Dan Hodgson, *Jim Mason, Don Norris. Telephone: (202) 994-7399. • Baseball SID: Ted Leshinski. Telephone: (202) 994-0339. FAX: (202) 994-2713.

### GEORGETOWN Hoyas
Conference: Big East.
Mailing Address: McDonough Arena, 37th & O Streets NW, Washington, DC 20057. Website: www.guhoyas.com.
Head Coach: Pete Wilk. Assistant Coaches: Matt Bok, Rodney Brock, *Mark Van Ameyde. Telephone: (202) 687-2462. • Baseball SID: Ben Shove. Telephone: (202) 687-7155. FAX: (202) 687-2491.
Home Field: Shirley Povich Field. Seating Capacity: 1,500. Outfield Dimensions: LF—330, CF—375, RF—330. Press Box Telephone: (202) 359-2266.

### GEORGIA Bulldogs
Conference: Southeastern (East).
Mailing Address: P.O. Box 1472, Athens, GA 30603. Website: www.georgiadogs.com.
Head Coach: David Perno. Assistant Coaches: Jason Eller, *Doug Sisson, Roger Williams. Telephone: (706) 542-7971. • Baseball SID: Christopher Lakos. Telephone: (706) 542-1621. FAX: (706) 542-7993.
Home Field: Foley Field. Seating Capacity: 3,291. Outfield Dimensions: LF—345, CF—404, RF—314. Press Box Telephone: (706) 542-6161.

### GEORGIA SOUTHERN Eagles
Conference: Southern.
Mailing Address: P.O. Box 8095, Statesboro, GA 30460. Website: www.georgiasoutherneagles.com.
Head Coach: Rodney Hennon. Assistant Coaches: Brett Lewis, *Mike Tidick. Telephone: (912) 871-1350. • Baseball SID: Patrick Osterman. Telephone: (912) 681-0352. FAX: (912) 681-0046.
Home Field: J.I. Clements Stadium/Jack Stallings Field. Seating Capacity: 3,000. Outfield Dimensions: LF—330, CF—385, RF—330. Press Box Telephone: (912) 681-2508.

### GEORGIA STATE Panthers
Conference: Colonial Athletic.
Mailing Address: 125 Decatur St., Suite 201, Atlanta, GA 30303. Website: www.georgiastatesports.com.
Head Coach: Mike Hurst. Assistant Coaches: Greg Frady, Michael Nelson, Ronnie Robinson. Telephone: (404) 651-1198. • Baseball SID: Jason Hanes. Telephone: (404) 651-4629. FAX: (404) 651-3204.
Home Field: Panthersville Field. Seating Capacity: 1,000. Outfield Dimensions: LF—334, CF—385, RF—338. Press Box Telephone: 404-244-5801.

### GEORGIA TECH Yellow Jackets
Conference: Atlantic Coast (Coastal).
Mailing Address: 150 Bobby Dodd Way, Atlanta, GA 30332. Website: www.ramblinwreck.com.
Head Coach: Danny Hall. Assistant Coaches: *Josh Holliday, Bobby Moranda, Bryan Prince. Telephone:

(404) 894-5471. • **Baseball SID:** Chris Capo. **Telephone:** (404) 894-5445. **FAX:** (404) 894-1248.

**Home Field:** Russ Chandler Stadium. **Seating Capacity:** 4,157. **Outfield Dimensions:** LF—328, CF—400, RF—334. **Press Box Telephone:** (404) 894-3167.

## GONZAGA Bulldogs
**Conference:** West Coast.

**Mailing Address:** 502 E. Boone Ave., Spokane, WA 99202. **Website:** www.gozags.com.

**Head Coach:** Mark Machtolf. **Assistant Coaches:** Steve Bennett, *Danny Evans, Gary Van Tol. **Telephone:** (509) 323-4209. • **Baseball SID:** Chris Loucks. **Telephone:** (509) 323-4227. **FAX:** (509) 323-5730.

**Home Field:** Avista Stadium. **Seating Capacity:** 7,800. **Outfield Dimensions:** LF—330, CF—400, RF—330. **Press Box Telephone:** (509) 279-1005.

## GRAMBLING STATE Tigers
**Conference:** Southwestern Athletic.

**Mailing Address:** P.O. Box 868, Grambling, LA 71245. **Website:** www.gram.edu/sports.

**Head Coach:** James "Sapp" Randall. **Telephone:** (318) 274-6566. • **Baseball SID:** Unavailable. **Telephone:** (318) 274-6281. **FAX:** (318) 274-2761.

**Home Field:** Tiger Field. **Seating Capacity:** 3,000. **Outfield Dimensions:** LF—330, CF—400, RF—335. **Press Box Telephone:** Unavailable.

## HARTFORD Hawks
**Conference:** America East.

**Mailing Address:** 200 Bloomfield Ave., West Hartford, CT 06117. **Website:** www.HartfordHawks.com.

**Head Coach:** Jeff Calcaterra. **Assistant Coaches:** Mike Susi. John Turner. **Telephone:** (860) 768-5760. • **Baseball SID:** Dan Ruede. **Telephone:** (860) 768-4501. **FAX:** (860) 768-4068.

## HARVARD Crimson
**Conference:** Ivy League (Rolfe).

**Mailing Address:** 65 N. Harvard St., Boston, MA 02163. **Website:** www.gocrimson.com.

**Head Coach:** Joe Walsh. **Assistant Coaches:** Gary Donovan, *Tom Lo Ricco. **Telephone:** (617) 495-2629. • **Baseball SID:** Kurt Svoboda. **Telephone:** (617) 495-2206. **FAX:** (617) 495-2130.

## HAWAII Rainbows
**Conference:** Western Athletic.

**Mailing Address:** 1337 Lower Campus Rd., Honolulu, HI 96822. **Website:** www.hawaiiathletics.com.

**Head Coach:** Mike Trapasso. **Assistant Coaches:** Greg Kish, Keith Komeiji, *Chad Konishi. **Telephone:** (808) 956-6247. • **Baseball SID:** Pakalani Bello. **Telephone:** (808) 956-7506. **FAX:** (808) 956-4470.

**Home Field:** Les Murakami Stadium. **Seating Capacity:** 4,312. **Outfield Dimensions:** LF—325, CF—385, RF—325. **Press Box Telephone:** (808) 956-6253.

## HAWAII-HILO Vulcans
**Conference:** Independent.

**Mailing Address:** 200 W. Kawili St., Hilo, HI 96720. **Website:** vulcans.uhh.hawaii.edu.

**Head Coach:** Joey Estrella. **Assistant Coaches:** Kallen Miyataki, Kevin Yee. **Telephone:** (808) 974-7700. • **Baseball SID:** Kelly Leong. **Telephone:** (808) 974-7606. **FAX:** (808) 974-7711.

## HIGH POINT Panthers
**Conference:** Big South.

**Mailing Address:** 833 Montlieu Ave., High Point, NC 27262. **Website:** www.highpointpanthers.com.

**Head Coach:** *Sal Bando Jr. **Assistant Coaches:** Phil

Maier, Travis Motsigner, Rey Rojas. **Telephone:** (336) 841-9190. • **Baseball SID:** Brian Morgan. **Telephone:** (336) 841-4605. **FAX:** (336) 841-9276.

## HOFSTRA Pride
**Conference:** Colonial Athletic.

**Mailing Address:** 230 Hofstra University PFC 230, Hempstead, NY 11549. **Website:** www.hofstra.edu/athletics.

**Head Coach:** Chris Dotolo. **Assistant Coaches:** *Asa Grunenwald, Josh Stewart. **Telephone:** (516) 463-5065. • **Baseball SID:** Tim Casale. **Telephone:** (516) 463-2907. **FAX:** (516) 463-5033.

## HOLY CROSS Crusaders
**Conference:** Patriot.

**Mailing Address:** One College St., Worcester, MA 01610. **Website:** goholycross.com.

**Head Coach:** *Craig Najarian. **Assistant Coaches:** Wayne Mazzoni, Jeff Miller, Steve Simoes. **Telephone:** (508) 793-2753. • **Baseball SID:** Brianne Mallaghan. **Telephone:** (508) 793-2583. **FAX:** (508) 793-2309.

## HOUSTON Cougars
**Conference:** Conference USA.

**Mailing Address:** 3100 Cullen Blvd., Houston, TX 77204. **Website:** www.uhcougars.com.

**Head Coach:** Rayner Noble. **Assistant Coaches:** Sean Allen, *Kirk Blount, Jorge Garza. **Telephone:** (713) 743-9396. • **Baseball SID:** Jeff Conrad. **Telephone:** (713) 743-9410. **FAX:** (713) 743-9411.

**Home Field:** Cougar Field. **Seating Capacity:** 3,500. **Outfield Dimensions:** LF—330, CF—390, RF—330. **Press Box Telephone:** (713) 743-0840.

## ILLINOIS Fighting Illini
**Conference:** Big Ten.

**Mailing Address:** 1700 S. Fourth St., Champaign, IL 61820. **Website:** www.fightingillini.com.

**Head Coach:** Dan Hartleb. **Assistant Coaches:** *Eric Snider, Ken Westray. **Telephone:** (217) 244-8144. • **Baseball SID:** Ben Taylor. **Telephone:** (217) 244-4982. **FAX:** (217) 244-5540.

**Home Field:** Illinois Field. **Seating Capacity:** 1,500. **Outfield Dimensions:** LF—330, CF—390, RF—330. **Press Box Telephone:** (217) 333-1227.

## ILLINOIS-CHICAGO Flames
**Conference:** Horizon.

**Mailing Address:** 839 W. Roosevelt Rd., Chicago, IL 60608. **Website:** www.uicflames.com.

**Head Coach:** Mike Dee. **Assistant Coaches:** Craig Bruce, *Sean McDermott, Mike Nall. **Telephone:** (312) 996-8645. • **Baseball SID:** John Jaramillo. **Telephone:** (312) 996-5880. **FAX:** (312) 996-8349.

## ILLINOIS STATE Redbirds
**Conference:** Missouri Valley.

**Mailing Address:** Campus Box 7130, Normal, IL 61790. **Website:** www.goredbirds.com.

**Head Coach:** Jim Brownlee. **Assistant Coaches:** Mike Current, *Tim Brownlee. **Telephone:** (309) 438-5151. • **Baseball SID:** Mike Williams. **Telephone:** (309) 438-3598. **FAX:** (309) 438-5643.

**Home Field:** Redbird Field. **Seating Capacity:** 1,500. **Outfield Dimensions:** LF—330, CF—400, RF—330. **Press Box Telephone:** (309) 438-3504.

## INDIANA Hoosiers
**Conference:** Big Ten.

**Mailing Address:** 1001 E. 17th St., Bloomington, IN 47408. **Website:** www.iuhoosiers.com.

**Head Coach:** Tracy Smith. **Assistant Coaches:** Ty Neal,

Micah Nori, Ted Torn. **Telephone:** (812) 855-1680. • **Baseball SID:** Jeff Keag. **Telephone:** (812) 855-6209. **FAX:** (812) 855-9401.

**Home Field:** Sembower Field. **Seating Capacity:** 2,000. **Outfield Dimensions:** LF—333, CF—400, RF—333. **Press Box Telephone:** (812) 855-4787.

### INDIANA-PURDUE UNIVERSITY-FORT WAYNE Mastodons
**Conference:** Independent.
**Mailing Address:** 2101 E. Coliseum Blvd., Fort Wayne, IN 46805. **Website:** www.ipfw.edu/athletics.
**Head Coach:** Billy Gernon. **Assistant Coach:** Chad Newhard. **Telephone:** (260) 481-5480. • **Baseball SID:** Rudy Yovich. **Telephone:** (260) 481-6646. **FAX:** (260) 481-6002.

### INDIANA STATE Sycamores
**Conference:** Missouri Valley.
**Mailing Address:** Baseball Office, Indiana State University, Terre Haute, IN 47809. **Website:** web.indstate.edu/athletic/baseball.
**Head Coach:** Bob Warn. **Assistant Coaches:** *C.J. Keating, Matt Kennedy, Josh Prickett. **Telephone:** (812) 237-4051. • **Baseball SID:** Dan Gisel. **Telephone:** (812) 237-4073. **FAX:** (812) 237-4157.
**Home Field:** Sycamore Field. **Seating Capacity:** 2,500. **Outfield Dimensions:** LF—340, CF—402, RF—340. **Press Box Telephone:** (812) 237-3654.

### IONA Gaels
**Conference:** Metro Atlantic.
**Mailing Address:** 715 North Ave., New Rochelle, NY 10801. **Website:** www.iona.edu/gaels.
**Head Coach:** Pat Carey. **Assistant Coaches:** Allan Christenson, Darren Gurney. **Telephone:** (914) 633-2319. • **Baseball SID:** Daniel Kuberka. **Telephone:** (914) 633-2310. **FAX:** (914) 633-2072.

### IOWA Hawkeyes
**Conference:** Big Ten.
**Mailing Address:** 232 Carver-Hawkeye Arena, Iowa City, IA 52242. **Website:** www.hawkeyesports.com.
**Head Coach:** Jack Dahm. **Assistant Coaches:** *Ryan Brownlee, Chris Maliszewski, Nick Zumsande. **Telephone:** (319) 335-9329. • **Baseball SID:** Tony Wirt. **Telephone:** (319) 335-9411. **FAX:** (319) 335-9417.

### JACKSON STATE Tigers
**Conference:** Southwestern Athletic.
**Mailing Address:** 1400 John R. Lynch St., Jackson, MS 39217. **Website:** www.jsums.edu.
**Head Coach:** Mark Salter. **Assistant Coach:** Omar Johnson. **Telephone:** (601) 979-3928. • **Baseball SID:** Henry Goolsby. **Telephone:** (601) 979-5899. **FAX:** (601) 979-2000.

### JACKSONVILLE Dolphins
**Conference:** Atlantic Sun.
**Mailing Address:** 2800 University Blvd. N., Jacksonville, FL 32211. **Website:** www.judolphins.com.
**Head Coach:** Terry Alexander. **Assistant Coaches:** *Chris Hayes, Tim Montez, Les Wright. **Telephone:** (904) 256-7412. • **Baseball SID:** Josh Ellis. **Telephone:** (904) 256-7402. **FAX:** (904) 256-7424.
**Home Field:** Alexander Brest Stadium. **Seating Capacity:** 2,300. **Outfield Dimensions:** LF—340, CF—405, RF—340. **Press Box Telephone:** (904) 256-7588.

### JACKSONVILLE STATE Gamecocks
**Conference:** Ohio Valley.
**Mailing Address:** 201 Kennamer Hall, 700 Pelham Road N., Jacksonville, AL 36265. **Website:** www.jsugamecocksports.com.

**Head Coach:** Jim Case. **Assistant Coaches:** Steve Gillispie, Travis Janssen. **Telephone:** (256) 782-5367. • **Baseball SID:** Greg Seitz. **Telephone:** (256) 782-5279. **FAX:** (256) 782-5958.

### JAMES MADISON Dukes
**Conference:** Colonial Athletic.
**Mailing Address:** MSC 2303 Godwin Hall, Harrisonburg, VA 22807. **Website:** www.jmusports.com.
**Head Coach:** Spanky McFarland. **Assistant Coaches:** Travis Ebaugh, Rob McCoy, *Jay Sullenger. **Telephone:** (540) 568-3932. • **Baseball SID:** Curt Dudley. **Telephone:** (540) 568-6154. **FAX:** (540) 568-3932.
**Home Field:** Long Field/Mauck Stadium. **Seating Capacity:** 1,200. **Outfield Dimensions:** LF—340, CF—400, RF—320. **Press Box Telephone:** (540) 568-6545.

### KANSAS Jayhawks
**Conference:** Big 12.
**Mailing Address:** 1651 Naismith Dr., Lawrence, KS 66045. **Website:** www.kuathletics.com.
**Head Coach:** Ritch Price. **Assistant Coaches:** Ryan Graves, *Rick Sabath, Kevin Tucker. **Telephone:** (785) 864-7907. • **Baseball SID:** Brandon Holtz. **Telephone:** (785) 864-7314. **FAX:** (785) 864-7944.
**Home Field:** Hoglund Ballpark. **Seating Capacity:** 2,500. **Outfield Dimensions:** LF—330, CF—392, RF—330. **Press Box Telephone:** (785) 864-4037.

### KANSAS STATE Wildcats
**Conference:** Big 12.
**Mailing Address:** 1800 College Ave., Manhattan, KS 66502. **Website:** www.k-statesports.com.
**Head Coach:** Brad Hill. **Assistant Coaches:** *Sean McCann, Tom Myers, Josh Reynolds. **Telephone:** (785) 532-3926. • **Baseball SID:** Kenny Lannou. **Telephone:** (785) 532-7708. **FAX:** (785) 532-6093.
**Home Field:** Tointon Stadium. **Seating Capacity:** 2,331. **Outfield Dimensions:** LF—340, CF—400, RF—325. **Press Box Telephone:** (785) 532-5801.

### #KENNESAW STATE Owls
**Conference:** Atlantic Sun.
**Mailing Address:**. **Website:** www.ksuowls.com.
**Head Coach:** Mike Sansing. **Assistant Coaches:** William Brennan, Ryan Coe, Bob Roman. **Telephone:** (904) 620-1556. • **Baseball SID:** Andy Brown. **Telephone:** (904) 620-4029. **FAX:** (904) 620-2821.

### KENT STATE Golden Flashes
**Conference:** Mid-American (East).
**Mailing Address:** PO Box 5190, Kent, OH 44242. **Website:** www.kentstatesports.com.
**Head Coach:** Scott Stricklin. **Assistant Coaches:** *Mike Birkbeck, Scott Daeley, Tim Donnelly. **Telephone:** (330) 672-8432. • **Baseball SID:** Aaron Chimenti. **Telephone:** (330) 672-8468. **FAX:** (330) 672-2112.

### KENTUCKY Wildcats
**Conference:** Southeastern (East).
**Mailing Address:** Memorial Coliseum, Room 23, Lexington, KY 40506. **Website:** www.ukathletics.com.
**Head Coach:** John Cohen. **Assistant Coaches:** Brad Bohannon, *Gary Henderson. **Telephone:** (859) 257-8052. • **Baseball SID:** Scott Dean. **Telephone:** (859) 257-3838. **FAX:** (859) 323-4310.
**Home Field:** Cliff Hagan Stadium. **Seating Capacity:** 3,000. **Outfield Dimensions:** LF—340, CF—390, RF—310. **Press Box Telephone:** (859) 257-9311.

### LAFAYETTE Leopards
**Conference:** Patriot.
**Mailing Address:** Kirby Sports Center, Easton, PA

18042. **Website:** www.goleopards.com.
**Head Coach:** Joe Kinney. **Assistant Coaches:** Gregg Durrah, Paul Englehardt, Scott Stewart. **Telephone:** (610) 330-5476. • **Baseball SIDs:** Philip LaBella. **Telephone:** (610) 330-5123. **FAX:** (610) 330-5519.

## LAMAR Cardinals
**Conference:** Southland.
**Mailing Address:** 211 Redbird Lane, Beaumont, TX 77710. **Website:** www.lamarcardinals.com.
**Head Coach:** Jim Gilligan. **Assistant Coaches:** Scott Hatten, *Jim Ricklefsen. **Telephone:** (409) 880-8135. • **Baseball SID:** Daucy Crizer. **Telephone:** (409) 880-8329. **FAX:** (409) 880-2338.
**Home Field:** Vincent-Beck Stadium. **Seating Capacity:** 3,500. **Outfield Dimensions:** LF—330, CF—380, RF—330. **Press Box Telephone:** (409) 880-8327.

## LA SALLE Explorers
**Conference:** Atlantic 10.
**Mailing Address:** 1900 W. Olney Ave., Box 805, Philadelphia, PA 19141. **Website:** www.goexplorers.com.
**Head Coach:** Lee Saverio. **Assistant Coaches:** John Duffy, Mike Lake. **Telephone:** (215) 951-1995. • **Baseball SID:** Marc Mullen. **Telephone:** (215) 951-1633. **FAX:** (215) 951-1694.

## LEHIGH Mountain Hawks
**Conference:** Patriot.
**Mailing Address:** 641 Taylor St., Bethlehem, PA 18015. **Website:** www.lehighsports.com.
**Head Coach:** *Sean Leary. **Assistant Coaches:** Dennis Morgan, Josh Perich. **Telephone:** (610) 758-4315. • **Baseball SID:** Jeff Tourial. **Telephone:** (610) 758-3158. **FAX:** (610) 758-6629.

## LE MOYNE Dolphins
**Conference:** Metro Atlantic.
**Mailing Address:** 1419 Salt Springs Rd., Syracuse, NY 13214. **Website:** www.lemoynedolphins.com.
**Head Coach:** Steve Owens. **Assistant Coaches:** *Pete Hoy, Scott Landers, Bob Nandin. **Telephone:** (315) 445-4415. • **Baseball SID:** Mike Donlin. **Telephone:** (315) 445-4412. **FAX:** (315) 445-4678.

## LIBERTY Flames
**Conference:** Big South.
**Mailing Address:** 1971 University Blvd., Lynchburg, VA 24502. **Website:** www.libertyflames.com.
**Head Coach:** Matt Royer. **Assistant Coaches:** Reggie Reynolds, Randy Tomlin, *Terry Weaver. **Telephone:** (434) 582-2103. • **Baseball SID:** Ryan Bomberger. **Telephone:** (434) 582-2292. **FAX:** (434) 582-2076.
**Home Field:** Worthington Stadium. **Seating Capacity:** 1,000. **Outfield Dimensions:** LF—325, CF—390, RF—325. **Press Box Telephone:** (434) 582-2914.

## LIPSCOMB Bisons
**Conference:** Atlantic Sun.
**Mailing Address:** 3901 Granny White Pike, Nashville, TN 37204. **Website:** www.lipscombsports.com.
**Head Coach:** Wynn Fletcher. **Assistant Coaches:** John Massey, *Cliff Terracuso. **Telephone:** (615) 279-5716. • **Baseball SID:** Mark McGee. **Telephone:** (615) 279-5862. **FAX:** (615) 269-1806.

## LONG BEACH STATE 49ers (Dirtbags)
**Conference:** Big West.
**Mailing Address:** 1250 Bellflower Blvd., Long Beach, CA 90840. **Website:** www.longbeachstate.com.
**Head Coach:** Mike Weathers. **Assistant Coaches:** *Troy Buckley, Cole Jacobsen, Tim McConnell, Jon Strauss. **Telephone:** (562) 985-7548. • **Baseball SID:**

Niall Adler. **Telephone:** (562) 985-7565. **FAX:** (562) 985-1549.
**Home Field:** Blair Field. **Seating Capacity:** 3,000. **Outfield Dimensions:** LF—330, CF—400, RF—330. **Press Box Telephone:** (562) 433-8605.

## LONG ISLAND Blackbirds
**Conference:** Northeast.
**Mailing Address:** One University Plaza, Brooklyn, NY 11201. **Website:** www.liu.edu/blackbirds.
**Head Coach:** Don Maines. **Assistant Coaches:** Derek Hurley, Craig Noto, Chris Reyes. **Telephone:** (718) 488-1538. • **Baseball SID:** Dan Lobacz. **Telephone:** (718) 488-1420. **FAX:** (718) 488-3302.

## #LONGWOOD Lancers
**Conference:** Independent.
**Mailing Address:** 201 High St., Athletics Complex T2 M, Farmville, VA 23909. **Website:** www.longwood-lancers.com.
**Head Coach:** Buddy Bolding. **Assistant Coaches:** *Rick Blanc, Brett Mooney. **Telephone:** (434) 395-2352. • **Baseball SID:** Greg Prouty. **Telephone:** (434) 395-2097. **FAX:** (434) 395-2568.

## LOUISIANA-LAFAYETTE Ragin' Cajuns
**Conference:** Sun Belt.
**Mailing Address:** 201 Reinhardt Dr., Lafayette, LA 70506. **Website:** www.ragincajuns.com.
**Head Coach:** Tony Robichaux. **Assistant Coaches:** Anthony Babineaux, Chris Domingue, *John Szefc. **Telephone:** (337) 482-6189. • **Baseball SID:** Chris Yandle. **Telephone:** (337) 851-6332. **FAX:** (337) 482-6649.
**Home Field:** Moore Field. **Seating Capacity:** 3,755. **Outfield Dimensions:** LF—330, CF—400, RF—330. **Press Box Telephone:** (337) 482-2255.

## LOUISIANA-MONROE Indians
**Conference:** Southland.
**Mailing Address:** 308 Stadium Dr., Monroe, LA 71209. **Website:** www.ulmathletics.com.
**Head Coach:** Brad Holland. **Assistant Coaches:** Chuck Finley, Britten Oubre, *Jeff Schexnaider. **Telephone:** (318) 342-3591. • **Baseball SID:** Judy Willson. **Telephone:** (318) 342-5463. **FAX:** (318) 342-5464.
**Home Field:** Indian Field. **Seating Capacity:** 3,000. **Outfield Dimensions:** LF—330, CF—400, RF—330. **Press Box Telephone:** (318) 342-5476.

## LOUISIANA STATE Tigers
**Conference:** Southeastern (West).
**Mailing Address:** P.O. Box 25095, Baton Rouge, LA 70894. **Website:** www.LSUsports.net
**Head Coach:** Smoke Laval. **Assistant Coaches:** Justin Hill, *Turtle Thomas, Brady Wiederhold. **Telephone:** (225) 578-4148. • **Baseball SID:** Bill Franques. **Telephone:** (225) 578-2527. **FAX:** (225) 578-1861.
**Home Field:** Alex Box Stadium. **Seating Capacity:** 7,760. **Outfield Dimensions:** LF—330, CF—405, RF—330. **Press Box Telephone:** (225) 578-4149.

## LOUISIANA TECH Bulldogs
**Conference:** Western Athletic.
**Mailing Address:** Thomas Assembly Center, Ruston, LA 71270. **Website:** www.latechsports.com.
**Head Coach:** Wade Simoneaux. **Assistant Coaches:** Fran Andermann, *Brian Rountree, Toby White. **Telephone:** (318) 257-4111. • **Baseball SID:** Kyle Roberts. **Telephone:** (318) 257-3144. **FAX:** (318) 257-3757.
**Home Field:** J.C. Love Field. **Seating Capacity:** 3,200.

Outfield Dimensions: LF—315, CF—380, RF—325. Press Box Telephone: (318) 257-3144.

## LOUISVILLE Cardinals
Conference: Big East.
Mailing Address: Athletics Department, University of Louisville, Louisville, KY 40292. Website: www.UofLsports.com.
Head Coach: Lelo Prado. Assistant Coaches: Lazaro Collazo, James McAuley, *Brian Mundorf. Telephone: (502) 852-0103. • Baseball SID: Sean Moth. Telephone: (502) 852-2159. FAX: (502) 852-7401.
Home Field: Jim Patterson Stadium. Seating Capacity: 2,500. Outfield Dimensions: LF—330, CF—402, RF—330. Press Box Telephone: (502) 852-3700.

## LOYOLA MARYMOUNT Lions
Conference: West Coast.
Mailing Address: One LMU Drive, Gersten Pavilion, Los Angeles, CA 90045. Website: www.lmulions.com.
Head Coach: Frank Cruz. Assistant Coaches: *Vince Beringhele, Tim Leary, Robbie Moen. Telephone: (310) 338-5466. • Baseball SID: Alissa Zito. Telephone: (310) 338-7638. FAX: (310) 338-2703.
Home Field: Page Stadium. Seating Capacity: 600. Outfield Dimensions: LF—326, CF—413, RF—330. Press Box Telephone: (310) 338-3046.

## MAINE Black Bears
Conference: America East.
Mailing Address: 5747 Memorial Gym, Orono, ME 04469. Website: www.goblackbears.com.
Head Coach: Steve Trimper. Assistant Coaches: *Cory Domel, Jared Holowaty, Aaron Izaryk. Telephone: (207) 581-1097. • Baseball SID: Laura Reed. Telephone: (207) 581-3646. FAX: (207) 581-3297.
Home Field: Mahaney Diamond. Seating Capacity: 4,400. Outfield Dimensions: LF—330, CF—400, RF—330. Press Box Telephone: (207) 581-1049.

## MANHATTAN Jaspers
Conference: Metro Atlantic.
Mailing Address: 4513 Manhattan College Pkwy., Riverdale, NY 10471. Website: www.gojaspers.com.
Head Coach: Kevin Leighton. Assistant Coaches: *Mike Cole, Ryan Darcy. Telephone: (718) 862-7396. • Baseball SID: Mike Antonaccio. Telephone: (718) 862-7228. FAX: (718) 862-8020.

## MARIST Red Foxes
Conference: Metro Atlantic.
Mailing Address: 3399 North Rd., Poughkeepsie, NY 12601. Website: www.GoRedFoxes.com.
Head Coach: Dennis Healy. Assistant Coaches: Tag Montague, Chris Tracz. Telephone: (845) 575-2570. • Baseball SID: Jason Corriher. Telephone: (845) 575-3321. FAX: (845) 471-3322.

## MARSHALL Thundering Herd
Conference: Conference USA.
Mailing Address: P.O. Box 1360, Huntington, WV 25715. Website: www.herdzone.com.
Head Coach: Dave Piepenbrink. Assistant Coaches: *Jim Koerner, Rick Reed, Tim Rice. Telephone: (304) 696-5277. • Baseball SID: Andy Fledderjohan. Telephone: (304) 696-4662. FAX: (304) 696-2325.

## MARYLAND Terrapins
Conference: Atlantic Coast (Atlantic).
Mailing Address: Comcast Center, 1 Terrapin Trail, College Park, MD 20742. Website: www.umterps.com.
Head Coach: Terry Rupp. Assistant Coaches: Carmen Carcone, *Jim Farr. Telephone: (301) 314-7122. •

Baseball SID: Mike Gerton. Telephone: (301) 314-8093. FAX: (301) 314-9094.
Home Field: Shipley Field. Seating Capacity: 2,500. Outfield Dimensions: LF—320, CF—380, RF—325. Press Box Telephone: (301) 314-0379.

## MARYLAND-BALTIMORE COUNTY Retrievers
Conference: America East.
Mailing Address: 1000 Hilltop Circle, Baltimore, MD 21250. Website: www.umbcretrievers.com.
Head Coach: *John Jancuska. Assistant Coach: Bob Mumma, Kyle Wildason. Telephone: (410) 455-2239. • Baseball SID: Andy Warner. Telephone: (410) 455-2639. FAX: (410) 455-3994.

## MARYLAND-EASTERN SHORE Fighting Hawks
Conference: Mid-Eastern Athletic.
Mailing Address: William P. Hytche Athletic Center, Backbone Road, Princess Anne, MD 21853. Website: www.umeshawks.com.
Head Coach: Bobby Rodriguez. Assistant Coaches: Ed Erisman, Bob Janeski, Brandon McCabe. Telephone: (410) 651-8908. • Baseball SID: Stan Bradley. Telephone: (410) 651-6499. FAX: (410) 651-7514.

## MASSACHUSETTS Minutemen
Conference: Atlantic 10.
Mailing Address: Baseball Office, 248 Boyden Building, Amherst, MA 01003. Website: www.umassathletics.com.
Head Coach: Mike Stone. Assistant Coaches: Ernie May, Matt Reynolds, Michael Sweeney. Telephone: (413) 545-3120. • Baseball SID: Kimberly Gardner. Telephone: (413) 545-5292. FAX: (413) 545-1556.

## McNEESE STATE Cowboys
Conference: Southland.
Mailing Address: Box 92735, McNeese State University, Lake Charles, LA 70609. Website: www.mcneesesports.com.
Head Coach: Chad Clement. Assistant Coaches: Chris Fackler, Blair Barbier. Telephone: (337) 475-5484. • Baseball SID: Louis Bonnette. Telephone: (337) 475-5207. FAX: (337) 475-5202.
Home Field: Cowboy Diamond. Seating Capacity: 2,000. Outfield Dimensions: LF—330, CF—400, RF—330. Press Box Telephone: (337) 475-8007.

## MEMPHIS Tigers
Conference: Conference USA.
Mailing Address: 570 Normal, Memphis, TN 38152. Website: www.gotigersgo.com.
Head Coach: Daron Schoenrock. Assistant Coaches: *Mike Federico, Corey Kines, Jerry Zulli. Telephone: (901) 678-2452. • Baseball SID: Jason Redd. Telephone: (901) 678-4640. FAX: (901) 678-4134.
Home Field: Nat Buring Stadium. Seating Capacity: 2,000. Outfield Dimensions: LF—320, CF—380, RF—320. Press Box Telephone: (901) 678-1301.

## MERCER Bears
Conference: Atlantic Sun.
Mailing Address: 1400 Coleman Ave., Macon, GA 31207. Website: www.mercerbears.com.
Head Coach: Craig Gibson. Assistant Coaches: Tim Boeth, Jason Jackson, Ty McGehee. Telephone: (478) 301-2396. • Baseball SID: Brett Jarrett. Telephone: (478) 301-5217. FAX: (478) 301-5350.

## MIAMI Hurricanes
Conference: Atlantic Coast (Coastal).
Mailing Address: 5821 San Amaro Dr., Coral Gables, FL 33146. Website: www.hurricanesports.com.

**Head Coach:** Jim Morris. **Assistant Coaches:** J.D. Arteaga, *Gino DiMare, Joe Mercadante. **Telephone:** (305) 284-4171. • **Baseball SID:** Evan Koch. **Telephone:** (305) 284-3241. **FAX:** (305) 284-2807.

**Home Field:** Mark Light Field. **Seating Capacity:** 5,000. **Outfield Dimensions:** LF—330, CF—400, RF—330. **Press Box Telephone:** Unavailable.

## MIAMI RedHawks

**Conference:** Mid-American (East).

**Mailing Address:** 230 Milett Hall, Oxford, OH 45056. **Website:** www.MURedHawks.com.

**Head Coach:** Dan Simonds. **Assistant Coaches:** *Ben Bachmann, Kevin Erminio. **Telephone:** (513) 529-6631. • **Baseball SID:** Jess Bechard. **Telephone:** (513) 529-1601. **FAX:** (513) 529-6729.

**Home Field:** McKie Field at Hayden Park. **Seating Capacity:** 2,000. **Outfield Dimensions:** LF—332, CF—400, RF—343. **Press Box Telephone:** (513) 529-4331.

## MICHIGAN Wolverines

**Conference:** Big Ten.

**Mailing Address:** 1000 S. State St., Ann Arbor, MI 48109. **Website:** www.mgoblue.com.

**Head Coach:** Rich Maloney. **Assistant Coaches**: *Jake Boss, Bob Keller, Blaine McFerrin. **Telephone:** (734) 647-4550. • **Baseball SID:** Jim Schneider. **Telephone:** (734) 763-4423. **FAX:** (734) 647-1188.

**Home Field:** Ray Fisher Stadium. **Seating Capacity:** 2,500. **Outfield Dimensions:** LF—330, CF—400, RF—330. **Press Box Telephone:** (734) 647-1283.

## MICHIGAN STATE Spartans

**Conference:** Big Ten.

**Mailing Address:** 304 Jenison Field House, East Lansing, MI 48824. **Website:** msuspartans.collegesports.com.

**Head Coach:** David Grewe. **Assistant Coaches:** *Tony Baldwin, Danny Lopaze, Mike Steele. **Telephone:** (517) 355-4899. • **Baseball SID:** Kristin Keirns. **Telephone:** (517) 355-2271. **FAX:** (517) 353-9636.

**Home Fields** Kobs Field. **Seating Capacity:** 2,000. **Outfield Dimensions:** LF—340, CF—400, RF—301. **Press Box Telephone:** Unavailable.

## MIDDLE TENNESSEE STATE Blue Raiders

**Conference:** Sun Belt.

**Mailing Address:** 1301 E. Main St., Murfreesboro, TN 37132. **Website:** www.goblueraiders.com.

**Head Coach:** Steve Peterson. **Assistant Coaches:** *Jim McGuire, Mike McLaury, Luis Rodriguez. **Telephone:** (615) 898-2984. • **Baseball SID:** Jo Jo Freeman. **Telephone:** (615) 898-5270. **FAX:** (615) 898-5626.

**Home Field:** Reese Smith Field. **Seating Capacity:** 2,600. **Outfield Dimensions:** LF—330, CF—390, RF—330. **Press Box Telephone:** (615) 898-2117.

## MINNESOTA Golden Gophers

**Conference:** Big Ten.

**Mailing Address:** 600 15th Ave. SE, Minneapolis, MN 55455. **Website:** www.gophersports.com.

**Head Coach:** John Anderson. **Assistant Coaches:** *Rob Fornasiere, Todd Oakes, Lee Swenson. **Telephone:** (612) 625-0869. • **Baseball SID:** Steve Geller. **Telephone:** (612) 624-9396. **FAX:** (612) 625-0359.

**Home Fields (Seating Capacity):** Siebert Field (1,100), Metrodome (48,678). **Outfield Dimensions:** Siebert Field/LF—330, CF—380, RF—330; Metrodome/LF—343, CF—408, RF—327. **Press Box Telephones:** Siebert Field/(612) 625-4031; Metrodome/(612) 627-4400.

## MISSISSIPPI Rebels

**Conference:** Southeastern (West).

**Mailing Address:** P.O. Box 217, University, MS 38677. **Website:** www.OleMissSports.com.

**Head Coach:** Mike Bianco. **Assistant Coaches:** Kyle Bunn, Stuart Lake, *Dan McDonnell. **Telephone:** (662) 915-6643. • **Baseball SID:** Bill Bunting. **Telephone:** (662) 915-1083. **FAX:** (662) 915-7006.

**Home Field:** Oxford-University Stadium/Swayze Field. **Seating Capacity:** 3,500. **Outfield Dimensions:** LF—330, CF—390, RF—330. **Press Box Telephone:** (662) 915-7851.

## MISSISSIPPI STATE Bulldogs

**Conference:** Southeastern (West).

**Mailing Address:** P.O. Box 5327, Starkville, MS 39762. **Website:** www.mstateathletics.com.

**Head Coach:** Ron Polk. **Assistant Coaches:** Wade Hedges, Russ McNickle, Tommy Raffo. **Telephone:** (662) 325-3597. • **Baseball SID:** Joe Dier. **Telephone:** (662) 325-8040. **FAX:** (662) 325-3600.

**Home Field:** Dudy Noble Field/Polk-DeMent Stadium. **Seating Capacity:** 15,000. **Outfield Dimensions:** LF—330, CF—390, RF—326. **Press Box Telephone:** (662) 325-3776.

## MISSISSIPPI VALLEY STATE Delta Devils

**Conference:** Southwestern Athletic.

**Mailing Address:** 14000 Hwy. 82 W., No. 7246, Itta Bena, MS 38941. **Website:** www.mvsu.edu/athletics.html.

**Head Coach:** Doug Shanks. **Assistant Coach:** Aaron Stevens. **Telephone:** (662) 254-3834. • **Baseball SID:** Rodrick Moseley. **Telephone:** (662) 254-3011. **FAX:** (662) 254-3639.

## MISSOURI Tigers

**Conference:** Big 12.

**Mailing Address:** 370 Hearnes Center, Columbia, MO 65211. **Website:** www.mutigers.com.

**Head Coach:** Tim Jamieson. **Assistant Coaches:** Kevin Cullen, Evan Pratte, *Tony Vitello. **Telephone:** (573) 882-0731. • **Baseball SID:** Josh Murray. **Telephone:** (573) 884-0711. **FAX:** (573) 882-4720.

**Home Field:** Taylor Stadium at Simmons Field. **Seating Capacity:** 3,000. **Outfield Dimensions:** LF—340, CF—400, RF—340. **Press Box Telephone:** (573) 884-8912.

## MISSOURI STATE Bears

**Conference:** Missouri Valley.

**Mailing Address:** 901 S. National Ave., Springfield, MO 65804. **Website:** www.missouristatebears.com.

**Head Coach:** Keith Guttin. **Assistant Coaches:** *Paul Evans, Brent Thomas. **Telephone:** (417) 836-5242. • **Baseball SID:** Celya McCullah. **Telephone:** (417) 836-5402. **FAX:** (417) 836-4868.

**Home Field:** Hammons Field. **Seating Capacity:** 8,000. **Outfield Dimensions:** LF—315, CF—400, RF—330. **Press Box Telephone:** (417) 863-0395, ext. 3070.

## MONMOUTH Hawks

**Conference:** Northeast.

**Mailing Address:** 400 Cedar Ave., West Long Branch, NJ 07764. **Website:** www.monmouth.edu/athletics.

**Head Coach:** Dean Ehehalt. **Assistant Coaches:** Cip Apicelly, *Jeff Barbalinardo, Chuck Ristano. **Telephone:** (732) 263-5186. • **Baseball SID:** Chris Tobin. **Telephone:** (732) 263-5180. **FAX:** (732) 571-3535.

## MOREHEAD STATE Eagles

**Conference:** Ohio Valley.
**Mailing Address:** Allen Field, Morehead State University, Morehead, KY 40351. **Website:** www.msueagles.com.
**Head Coach:** John Jarnagin. **Assistant Coaches:** *Rob Taylor. **Telephone:** (606) 783-2882. • **Baseball SID:** Randy Stacy. **Telephone:** (606) 783-2500. **FAX:** (606) 783-2500.

## MOUNT ST. MARY'S Mountaineers

**Conference:** Northeast.
**Mailing Address:** 16300 Old Emmitsburg Rd., Emmitsburg, MD 21727. **Website:** www.mountathletics.com.
**Head Coach:** Scott Thomson. **Assistant Coaches:** Steve Thomson, Jason Weszka. **Telephone:** (301) 447-3806. • **Baseball SID:** Mark Vandergrift. **Telephone:** (301) 447-5384. **FAX:** (301) 447-5300.

## MURRAY STATE Thoroughbreds

**Conference:** Ohio Valley.
**Mailing Address:** 218 Stewart Stadium, Murray, KY 42071. **Website:** www.goracers.com.
**Head Coach:** Rob McDonald. **Assistant Coaches:** Brian Hicks, Paul Wyczawski. **Telephone:** (270) 762-4892. • **Baseball SID:** David Snow. **Telephone:** (270) 762-3351. **FAX:** (270) 762-6814.

## NAVY Midshipmen

**Conference:** Patriot.
**Mailing Address:** 566 Brownson Rd., Annapolis, MD 21402. **Website:** www.navysports.com.
**Head Coach:** Pete Kostacopoulos. **Assistant Coaches:** Scott Friedholm, Dan Nellum, Jason Ronai. **Telephone:** (410) 293-5571. • **Baseball SID:** Jonathan Maggart. **Telephone:** (410) 293-8771. **FAX:** (410) 293-8954.

## NEBRASKA Cornhuskers

**Conference:** Big 12.
**Mailing Address:** 403 Lind Drive Circle, Lincoln, NE 68588. **Website:** www.huskers.com.
**Head Coach:** Mike Anderson. **Assistant Coaches:** Dave Bingham, *Andy Sawyers. **Telephone:** (402) 472-9166. • **Baseball SID:** Shamus McKnight. **Telephone:** (402) 472-7772. **FAX:** (402) 472-2005.
**Home Field:** Hawks Field at Haymarket Park. **Seating Capacity:** 8,486. **Outfield Dimensions:** LF—335, CF—395, RF—325. **Press Box Telephone:** (402) 434-6861.

## NEVADA Wolf Pack

**Conference:** Western Athletic.
**Mailing Address:** 1664 N. Virginia St., M/S 232, Reno, NV 89557. **Website:** www.nevadawolfpack.com.
**Head Coach:** Gary Powers. **Assistant Coaches:** Brian Gazerro, *Stan Stolte, Jay Uhlman. **Telephone:** (775) 784-6900, ext. 252. • **Baseball SID:** Jack Kuestermeyer. **Telephone:** (775) 784-6900, ext. 244. **FAX:** (775) 784-4386.
**Home Field:** Peccole Park. **Seating Capacity:** 3,000. **Outfield Dimensions:** LF—340, CF—401, RF—340. **Press Box Telephone:** (775) 784-5815.

## NEVADA-LAS VEGAS Rebels

**Conference:** Mountain West.
**Mailing Address:** 4505 Maryland Pkwy., Las Vegas, NV 89154. **Website:** www.unlvrebels.com.
**Head Coach:** Buddy Gouldsmith. **Assistant Coaches:** Matt Fonteno, *Scott Malone, Nate Yeskie. **Telephone:** (702) 895-3499. • **Baseball SID:** Bryan Haines. **Telephone:** (702) 895-3764. **FAX:** (702) 895-0989.
**Home Field:** Wilson Stadium at Barnson Field.

**Seating Capacity:** 3,000. **Outfield Dimensions:** LF—335, CF—400, RF—335. **Press Box Telephone:** (702) 895-1595.

## NEW MEXICO Lobos

**Conference:** Mountain West.
**Mailing Address:** South Athletic Complex, MSCO 42590, 1 University of New Mexico, Albuquerque, NM 87131. **Website:** www.GoLobos.com.
**Head Coach:** Rich Alday. **Assistant Coaches:** Ken Jacome, Trent Petrie, Josh Simpson. **Telephone:** (505) 925-5720. • **Baseball SID:** RaeAnn Feenaughty. **Telephone:** (505) 925-5851. **FAX:** (505) 925-5529.
**Home Field:** Isotopes Park. **Seating Capacity:** 11,124. **Outfield Dimensions:** LF—340, CF—400, RF—340. **Press Box Telephone:** (505) 222-4093.

## NEW MEXICO STATE Aggies

**Conference:** Western Athletic.
**Mailing Address:** P.O. Box 30001, Las Cruces, NM 88003. **Website:** www.nmstatesports.com.
**Head Coach:** Rocky Ward. **Assistant Coaches:** *Brad Dolejsi, John Michael Herrera, Chad Wolff. **Telephone:** (505) 646-5813. • **Baseball SID:** Matt Stephens. **Telephone:** (505) 646-1805. **FAX:** (505) 646-2425.
**Home Field:** Presley Askew Field. **Seating Capacity:** 1,000. **Outfield Dimensions:** LF—340, CF—400, RF—340. **Press Box Telephone:** (505) 646-5700.

## NEW ORLEANS Privateers

**Conference:** Sun Belt.
**Mailing Address:** Lakefront Arena-Baseball Office, 2000 Lakeshore Dr., New Orleans, LA 70148. **Website:** www.unoprivateers.com.
**Head Coach:** Tom Walter. **Assistant Coaches:** *Chuck Bartlett, Bill Cilento, Ross Kott. **Telephone:** (504) 280-7021. • **Baseball SID:** Jack Duggan. **Telephone:** (504) 280-7027. **FAX:** (504) 280-7240.
**Home Field:** Maestri Field. **Seating Capacity:** 4,500. **Outfield Dimensions:** LF—330, CF—410, RF—330. **Press Box Telephone:** Unavailable.

## NEW YORK TECH Bears

**Conference:** Independent.
**Mailing Address:** P.O. Box 8000, Old Westbury, NY 11568. **Website:** www.nyit.edu/athletics/baseball.
**Head Coach:** Bob Hirschfield. **Assistant Coaches:** *Mike Caulfield, Ray Giannelli, Ron McKay. **Telephone:** (516) 686-7513. • **Baseball SID:** Ben Acuri. **Telephone:** (516) 686-7504. **FAX:** (516) 686-1219.

## NIAGARA Purple Eagles

**Conference:** Metro Atlantic.
**Mailing Address:** P.O. Box 2009, Upper Gallagher Center, Niagara University, NY 14109. **Website:** www.purpleeagles.com.
**Head Coach:** Chris Chernisky. **Assistant Coach:** *Kyle Swiatocha, Joe Winkelsas. **Telephone:** (716) 286-8624. • **Baseball SID:** Brian Ormiston. **Telephone:** (716) 286-8586. **FAX:** (716) 286-8582.

## NICHOLLS STATE Colonels

**Conference:** Southland.
**Mailing Address:** P.O. Box 2032, 906 East First St., Thibodaux, LA 70310. **Website:** www.colonelsports.com.
**Head Coach:** Chip Durham. **Assistant Coaches:** Dustin Breaux, *Kerrick Jackson, Clint Stoy. **Telephone:** (985) 448-4808. • **Baseball SID:** Michelle Fakier. **Telephone:** (985) 448-4281. **FAX:** (985) 448-4924.
**Home Field:** Ray Didier Field. **Seating Capacity:** 1,000. **Outfield Dimensions:** LF—330, CF—410, RF—330. **Press Box Telephone:** (985) 448-4834.

## NORFOLK STATE Spartans
**Conference:** Mid-Eastern Athletic.
**Mailing Address:** 700 Park Ave., Norfolk, VA 23504. **Website:** www.nsu.edu/athletics.
**Head Coach:** Claudell Clark. **Assistant Coaches:** A.J. Corbin, Byron Talton. **Telephone:** (757) 823-8196. • **Baseball SID:** Matt Michalec. **Telephone:** (757) 823-2628. **FAX:** (757) 823-8218.

## NORTH CAROLINA Tar Heels
**Conference:** Atlantic Coast (Coastal).
**Mailing Address:** P.O. Box 2126, Chapel Hill, NC 27515. **Website:** www.tarheelblue.com.
**Head Coach:** Mike Fox. **Assistant Coaches:** Scott Forbes, *Chad Holbrook, Jason Howell. **Telephone:** (919) 962-2351. • **Baseball SID:** John Martin. **Telephone:** (919) 962-0084. **FAX:** (919) 962-0612.
**Home Field:** Boshamer Stadium. **Seating Capacity:** 2,500. **Outfield Dimensions:** LF—335, CF—395, RF—335. **Press Box Telephone:** (919) 962-3509.

## UNC ASHEVILLE Bulldogs
**Conference:** Big South.
**Mailing Address:** One University Heights, CPO 2600, Asheville, NC 28804. **Website:** www.uncabulldogs.com.
**Head Coach:** Willie Stewart. **Assistant Coaches:** Bob Fenn, Matt Reid, *Tim Perry. **Telephone:** (828) 251-6920. • **Baseball SID:** Everett Hutto. **Telephone:** (828) 251-6931. **FAX:** (828) 251-6386.

## UNC GREENSBORO Spartans
**Conference:** Southern.
**Mailing Address:** P.O. Box 26168, Greensboro, NC 27402. **Website:** www.uncgspartans.com.
**Head Coach:** Mike Gaski. **Assistant Coaches:** *Sammy Serrano, *Shane Schumaker. **Telephone:** (336) 334-3247. • **Baseball SID:** Jay D'Abramo. **Telephone:** (336) 334-5615. **FAX:** (336) 334-8182.
**Home Field:** UNCG Baseball Stadium. **Seating Capacity:** 4,000. **Outfield Dimensions:** LF—340, CF—405, RF—340. **Press Box Telephone:** (336) 334-5625.

## UNC WILMINGTON Seahawks
**Conference:** Colonial Athletic.
**Mailing Address:** 601 S. College Rd., Wilmington, NC 29804. **Website:** www.uncwsports.com.
**Head Coach:** Mark Scalf. **Assistant Coaches:** *Randy Hood, Scott Jackson, Chad Oxendine. **Telephone:** (910) 962-3570. • **Baseball SID:** Tom Riordan. **Telephone:** (910) 962-4099. **FAX:** (910) 962-3686.
**Home Field:** Brooks Field. **Seating Capacity:** 3,500. **Outfield Dimensions:** LF—340, CF—380, RF—340. **Press Box Telephone:** (910) 395-5141.

## NORTH CAROLINA A&T Aggies
**Conference:** Mid-Eastern Athletic.
**Mailing Address:** 1601 E. Market St., Moore Gym, Greensboro, NC 27411. **Website:** www.ncataggies.edu.
**Head Coach:** *Keith Shumate. **Assistant Coaches:** Austin Love, Tim Wilson. **Telephone:** (336) 334-7371. • **Baseball SID:** Brian Holloway. **Telephone:** (336) 334-7141. **FAX:** (336) 334-7181.

## NORTH CAROLINA STATE Wolfpack
**Conference:** Atlantic Coast (Atlantic).
**Mailing Address:** P.O. Box 8505, Raleigh, NC 27695. **Website:** www.gopack.com.
**Head Coach:** Elliott Avent. **Assistant Coaches:** Tony Guzzo, Chris Roberts, Jeff Waggoner. **Telephone:** (919) 515-3613. • **Baseball SID:** Bruce Winkworth. **Telephone:** (919) 515-1182. **FAX:** (919) 515-2898.
**Home Field:** Doak Field at Dail Park. **Seating Capacity:** 2,500. **Outfield Dimensions:** LF—325, CF—400, RF—330. **Press Box Telephone:** (919) 513-0653.

## #NORTH DAKOTA STATE Bison
**Conference:** Independent.
**Mailing Address:** P.O. Box 5600, University Station, Fargo, ND 58105. **Website:** www.gobison.com.
**Head Coach:** Mitch McLeod. **Assistant Coaches:** B.J. Griffith, Steve Montgomery, Mike Skogen. **Telephone:** (701) 231-8853. • **Baseball SID:** Ryan Perreault. **Telephone:** (701) 231-8331. **FAX:** (701) 866-8022.

## #NORTH FLORIDA Ospreys
**Conference:** Atlantic Sun.
**Mailing Address:** 4567 St. John's Bluff Rd. South, Jacksonville, FL, 32224. **Website:** www.unfospreys.com.
**Head Coach:** Dusty Rhodes. **Assistant Coaches:** Mike Fryrear, Greg Labbe, Judd Loveland, Bob Shepherd. **Telephone:** (904) 620-1556. • **Baseball SID:** Andy Brown. **Telephone:** (904) 620-4029. **FAX:** (904) 620-2821.

## NORTHEASTERN Huskies
**Conference:** Colonial Athletic.
**Mailing Address:** 360 Huntington Ave., Boston, MA 02115. **Website:** www.gonu.com/baseball.
**Head Coach:** Neil McPhee. **Assistant Coaches:** *Greg DiCenzo, Patrick Mason, Tim Troville. **Telephone:** (617) 373-3657. • **Baseball SID:** Thomas Chen. **Telephone:** (617) 373-3643. **FAX:** (617) 373-3152.

## #NORTHERN COLORADO Bears
**Conference:** Independent.
**Mailing Address:** 208 Butler-Hancock Athletic Center, Greeley, CO 80639. **Website:** www.uncbears.com.
**Head Coach:** Kevin Smallcomb. **Assistant Coaches:** *Chris Forbes, Ben Lewis, Bruce Vaughn. **Telephone:** (970) 351-1714. • **Baseball SID:** Kyle Schwartz. **Telephone:** (970) 351-2522. **FAX:** (970) 351-1995.

## NORTHERN ILLINOIS Huskies
**Conference:** Mid-American (West).
**Mailing Address:** 1525 W. Lincoln Hwy., Suite 224, DeKalb, IL 60115. **Website:** www.niuhuskies.com.
**Head Coach:** Ed Mathey. **Assistant Coaches:** Steve Joslyn, *Tim McDonough, Luke Sabers. **Telephone:** (815) 753-2225. • **Baseball SID:** Dave Retier. **Telephone:** (815) 753-1706. **FAX:** (815) 753-9540.

## NORTHERN IOWA Panthers
**Conference:** Missouri Valley.
**Mailing Address:** UNI-Dome NW Upper, Cedar Falls, IA 50613. **Website:** www.unipanthers.com.
**Head Coach:** Rick Heller. **Assistant Coaches:** *Dan Davis, Brock Sabers, Marty Sutherland. **Telephone:** (319) 273-6323. • **Baseball SID:** Brandie Glasnapp. **Telephone:** (319) 273-5455. **FAX:** (319) 273-3602.
**Home Field:** Riverfront Stadium. **Seating Capacity:** 4,277. **Outfield Dimensions:** LF—335, CF—380, RF—335. **Press Box Telephone:** (319) 232-5633.

## NORTHWESTERN Wildcats
**Conference:** Big Ten.
**Mailing Address:** 1501 Central St., Evanston, IL 60208. **Website:** www.nusports.com.
**Head Coach:** Paul Stevens. **Assistant Coaches:** Joe Keenan, Ron Klein, *Tim Stoddard. **Telephone:** (847) 491-4652. • **Baseball SID:** Aaron Bongle. **Telephone:** (847) 491-7503. **FAX:** (847) 491-8818.
**Home Field:** Rocky Miller Park. **Seating Capacity:** 1,000. **Outfield Dimensions:** LF—330, CF—400, RF—330. **Press Box Telephone:** (847) 491-4200.

## NORTHWESTERN STATE Demons
**Conference:** Southland.
**Mailing Address:** Athletic Fieldhouse, Natchitoches, LA 71497. **Website:** www.nsudemons.com.
**Head Coach:** Mitch Gaspard. **Assistant Coaches:** *J.P. Davis, Jeff McCannon. **Telephone:** (318) 357-4139. • **Baseball SID:** Matt Bonnette. **Telephone:** (318) 357-6467. **FAX:** (318) 357-4515.

## NOTRE DAME Fighting Irish
**Conference:** Big East.
**Mailing Address:** 112 Joyce Center, Notre Dame, IN 46556. **Website:** www.und.com.
**Head Coach:** Paul Mainieri. **Assistant Coaches:** Cliff Godwin, *Terry Rooney. **Telephone:** (574) 631-8466. • **Baseball SID:** Pete LaFleur. **Telephone:** (574) 631-7516. **FAX:** (574) 631-7941.
**Home Field:** Frank Eck Stadium. **Seating Capacity:** 2,500. **Outfield Dimensions:** LF—331, CF—401, RF—331. **Press Box Telephone:** (574) 631-9018.

## OAKLAND Golden Grizzlies
**Conference:** Mid-Continent.
**Mailing Address:** 2200 N. Squirrel Rd., Rochester, MI 48309. **Website:** www.ougrizzlies.com.
**Head Coach:** Dylan Putnam. **Assistant Coaches:** Ty Herriott, John Musachio. **Telephone:** (248) 370-4059. • **Baseball SID:** Rebecca Vick. **Telephone:** (248) 370-3123. **FAX:** (248) 370-4056.

## OHIO Bobcats
**Conference:** Mid-American (East).
**Mailing Address:** N117 Convocation Center, Richland Ave., Athens, OH 45701. **Website:** www.ohiobobcats.com.
**Head Coach:** *Joe Carbone. **Assistant Coaches:** Scott Malinowski, Bill Toadvine. **Telephone:** (740) 593-1180. • **Baseball SID:** Jason Cunningham. **Telephone:** (740) 593-1828. **FAX:** (740) 597-1838.
**Home Field:** Bob Wren Stadium. **Seating Capacity:** 4,000. **Outfield Dimensions:** LF—340, CF—405, RF—340. **Press Box Telephone:** (740) 593-0526.

## OHIO STATE Buckeyes
**Conference:** Big Ten.
**Mailing Address:** Room 124, St. John Arena, 410 Woody Hayes Dr., Columbus, OH 43210. **Website:** www.ohiostatebuckeyes.com.
**Head Coach:** Bob Todd. **Assistant Coaches:** *Greg Cypret, Harry Gurley, Eric Parker. **Telephone:** (614) 292-1075. • **Baseball SID:** Todd Lamb. **Telephone:** (614) 688-0343. **FAX:** (614) 292-8547.
**Home Field:** Bill Davis Stadium. **Seating Capacity:** 4,450. **Outfield Dimensions:** LF—330, CF—400, RF—330. **Press Box Telephone:** (614) 292-0021.

## OKLAHOMA Sooners
**Conference:** Big 12.
**Mailing Address:** 180 W. Brooks St., Norman, OK 73019. **Website:** www.soonersports.com.
**Head Coach:** Sunny Golloway. **Assistant Coaches:** Fred Corral, *Tim Tadlock. **Telephone:** (405) 325-8358. • **Baseball SID:** Craig Moran. **Telephone:** (405) 325-6449. **FAX:** (405) 325-7623.
**Home Field:** L. Dale Mitchell Park. **Seating Capacity:** 2,700. **Outfield Dimensions:** LF—335, CF—411, RF—335. **Press Box Telephone:** (405) 325-8363.

## OKLAHOMA STATE Cowboys
**Conference:** Big 12.
**Mailing Address:** 220 OSU Athletics Center, Stillwater, OK 74078. **Website:** www.okstate.com.

**Head Coach:** Frank Anderson. **Assistant Coaches:** *Greg Evans, Billy Jones. **Telephone:** (405) 744-5849. • **Baseball SID:** Wade McWhorter. **Telephone:** (405) 744-7853. **FAX:** (405) 744-7754.
**Home Field:** Allie P. Reynolds Stadium. **Seating Capacity:** 4,000. **Outfield Dimensions:** LF—330, CF—400, RF—330. **Press Box Telephone:** Unavailable.

## OLD DOMINION Monarchs
**Conference:** Colonial Athletic.
**Mailing Address:** Athletic Department, Norfolk, VA 23529. **Website:** www.odusports.com.
**Head Coach:** Jerry Meyers. **Assistant Coaches:** Nate Goulet, *Ryan Morris, Thomas Seay. **Telephone:** (757) 683-4230. • **Baseball SID:** Carol Hudson. **Telephone:** (757) 683-3372. **FAX:** (757) 683-3119.
**Home Field:** Bud Metheny Stadium. **Seating Capacity:** 2,500. **Outfield Dimensions:** LF—325, CF—395, RF—325. **Press Box Telephone:** (757) 683-5036.

## ORAL ROBERTS Golden Eagles
**Conference:** Mid-Continent.
**Mailing Address:** 7777 S. Lewis Ave., Tulsa, OK 74171. **Website:** www.orugoldeneagles.com.
**Head Coach:** Rob Walton. **Assistant Coaches:** Ryan Folmar, Ryan Neill, Todd Shelton. **Telephone:** (918) 495-7205. • **Baseball SID:** Cris Belvin. **Telephone:** (918) 495-7181. **FAX:** (918) 495-7142.
**Home Field:** J.L. Johnson Stadium. **Seating Capacity:** 2,418. **Outfield Dimensions:** LF—330, CF—400, RF—330. **Press Box Telephone:** (918) 495-7165.

## OREGON STATE Beavers
**Conference:** Pacific-10.
**Mailing Address:** Gill Coliseum, Room 127, Corvallis, OR 97331. **Website:** www.osubeavers.com.
**Head Coach:** Pat Casey. **Assistant Coaches:** Marty Lees, *Dan Spencer. **Telephone:** (541) 737-2825. • **Baseball SID:** Kip Carlson. **Telephone:** (541) 737-7472. **FAX:** (541) 737-3720.
**Home Field:** Goss Stadium at Coleman Field. **Seating Capacity:** 2,000. **Outfield Dimensions:** LF—330, CF—400, RF—330. **Press Box Telephone:** (541) 737-7475.

## PACIFIC Tigers
**Conference:** Big West.
**Mailing Address:** 3601 Pacific Ave., Stockton, CA 95211. **Website Address:** www.pacifictigers.com.
**Head Coach:** Ed Sprague. **Assistant Coaches:** Jim Brink, *Steve Pearse, Rob Selna. **Telephone:** (209) 946-2709. • **Baseball SID:** Glen Sisk. **Telephone:** (209) 946-2289. **FAX:** (209) 946-2757.
**Home Field:** Klein Family Field. **Seating Capacity:** Unavailablr. **Outfield Dimensions:** Unavailable. **Press Box Telephone:** (209) 244-5153.

## PENNSYLVANIA Quakers
**Conference:** Ivy League (Gehrig).
**Mailing Address:** 235 S. 33rd St., Philadelphia, PA 19104. **Website:** www.pennathletics.com.
**Head Coach:** John Cole. **Assistant Coaches:** Nolan Neiman, *Ryan Wheeler. **Telephone:** (215) 898-6282. • **Baseball SID:** Brady Smith. **Telephone:** (215) 573-4125. **FAX:** (215) 898-1747.

## PENN STATE Nittany Lions
**Conference:** Big Ten.
**Mailing Address:** 112 Bryce Jordan Center, University Park, PA 16802. **Website:** www.GoPSUsports.com.
**Head Coach:** Robbie Wine. **Assistant Coaches:** Jason Bell, Eric Folmar. **Telephone:** (814) 863-0230. • **Baseball SID:** Bob Volkert. **Telephone:** (814) 865-1757. **FAX:** (814)

863-3165.
**Home Field:** Beaver Field. **Seating Capacity:** 1,000. **Outfield Dimensions:** LF—350, CF—405, RF—350. **Press Box Telephone:** (814) 865-2552.

## PEPPERDINE Waves
**Conference:** West Coast.
**Mailing Address:** 24255 Pacific Coast Hwy., Malibu, CA 90263. **Website:** www.pepperdinesports.com.
**Head Coach:** Steve Rodriguez. **Assistant Coaches:** Chuck Hazzard, *Rick Hirtensteiner, Sean Kenny. **Telephone:** (310) 506-4371. • **Baseball SID:** Al Barba. **Telephone:** (310) 506-4455. **FAX:** (310) 506-4322.
**Home Field:** Eddy D. Field Stadium. **Seating Capacity:** 1,800. **Outfield Dimensions:** LF—330, CF—400, RF—330. **Press Box Telephone:** (310) 506-4598.

## PITTSBURGH Panthers
**Conference:** Big East.
**Mailing Address:** PO Box 7436, Pittsburgh, PA 15213. **Website:** www.pittsburghpanthers.com.
**Head Coach:** Joe Jordano. **Assistant Coaches:** Joel Dombkowski, *Sean Moran. **Telephone:** (412) 648-8202. • **Baseball SID:** Brad Cuprik. **Telephone:** (412) 648-8240. **FAX:** (412) 648-8248.
**Home Field:** Trees Field. **Seating Capacity:** 500. **Outfield Dimensions:** LF—302, CF—400, RF—330. **Press Box Telephone:** Unavailable.

## PORTLAND Pilots
**Conference:** West Coast.
**Mailing Address:** 5000 N. Willamette Blvd., Portland, OR 97203. **Website:** www.portlandpilots.com.
**Head Coach:** Chris Sperry. **Assistant Coach:** Matt Hollod. **Telephone:** (503) 943-7707. • **Baseball SID:** Adam Linnman. **Telephone:** (503) 943-7731. **FAX:** (503) 943-7242.
**Home Field:** Joe Etzel Stadium. **Seating Capacity:** 1,500. **Outfield Dimensions:** LF—350, CF—390, RF—340. **Press Box Telephone:** (503) 943-7253.

## PRAIRIE VIEW A&M Panthers
**Conference:** Southwestern Athletic.
**Mailing Address:** P.O. Box 97, Prairie View, TX 77446. **Website:** www.pvamu.edu/sports.
**Head Coach:** Michael Robertson. **Telephone:** (936) 857-4290. • **Baseball SID:** Stephan Robinson. **Telephone:** (936) 857-2114. **FAX:** (936) 857-2408.

## PRINCETON Tigers
**Conference:** Ivy League (Gehrig).
**Mailing Address:** Jadwin Gym, Princeton, NJ 08544. **Website:** www.goprincetontigers.com.
**Head Coach:** Scott Bradley. **Assistant Coaches:** Lloyd Brewer, Kevin Leighton, Jeremy Meccage. **Telephone:** (609) 258-5059. • **Baseball SID:** Yariv Amir. **Telephone:** (609) 258-5701. **FAX:** (609) 258-2399.

## PURDUE Boilermakers
**Conference:** Big Ten.
**Mailing Address:** Mollenkopf Athletic Center, 1225 Northwestern Ave., West Lafayette, IN 47907. **Website:** www.purduesports.com.
**Head Coach:** Doug Schreiber. **Assistant Coaches:** *Todd Murphy, Ryan Sawyers, Rob Smith. **Telephone:** (765) 494-3998. • **Baseball SID:** Mark Leddy. **Telephone:** (765) 494-3281. **FAX:** (765) 494-5447.
**Home Field:** Lambert Field. **Seating Capacity:** 1,100. **Outfield Dimensions:** LF—340, CF—408, RF—340. **Press Box Telephone:** Unavailable.

## QUINNIPIAC Bobcats
**Conference:** Northeast.

**Mailing Address:** 275 Mount Carmel Ave., Hamden, CT 06518. **Website:** www.quinnipiacbobcats.com.
**Head Coach:** Dan Gooley. **Assistant Coaches:** Dan Scarpa, Marc Stonaha, Joe Tonelli. **Telephone:** (203) 582-8966. • **Baseball SID:** Tom Wilkins. **Telephone:** (203) 582-5387. **FAX:** (203) 582-5385.

## RADFORD Highlanders
**Conference:** Big South.
**Mailing Address:** P.O. Box 6913, Radford, VA 24142. **Website:** www.ruhighlanders.com.
**Head Coach:** Lew Kent. **Assistant Coaches:** *Ryan Brittle, Chip Schaffner. **Telephone:** (540) 831-5881. • **Baseball SID:** Drew Dickerson. **Telephone:** (540) 831-5726. **FAX:** (540) 831-5556.

## RHODE ISLAND Rams
**Conference:** Atlantic 10.
**Mailing Address:** 3 Keaney Rd., Suite One, Kingston, RI 02881. **Website:** www.gorhody.com.
**Head Coach:** Jim Foster. **Assistant Coaches:** Tyler Alfred, Stephen Breitbach. **Telephone:** (401) 874-4550. • **Baseball SID:** Tim Volkmann. **Telephone:** (401) 874-2409. **FAX:** (401) 874-5354.

## RICE Owls
**Conference:** Conference USA.
**Mailing Address:** 6100 Main St., Houston, TX 77006. **Website:** www.RiceOwls.com.
**Head Coach:** Wayne Graham. **Assistant Coaches:** Patrick Hallmark, *David Pierce, *Mike Taylor. **Telephone:** (713) 348-8864. • **Baseball SID:** John Sullivan. **Telephone:** (713) 348-5636. **FAX:** (713) 348-6019.
**Home Field:** Reckling Park. **Seating Capacity:** 4,500. **Outfield Dimensions:** LF—330, CF—400, RF—330. **Press Box Telephone:** (713) 348-4931.

## RICHMOND Spiders
**Conference:** Atlantic 10.
**Mailing Address:** Baseball Office, Robins Center, Richmond, VA 23173. **Website:** www.richmondspiders.com.
**Head Coach:** Ron Atkins. **Assistant Coaches:** Joe Frostik, *Jason Johnson, Keith Little. **Telephone:** (804) 289-8391. • **Baseball SID:** Scott Meyer. **Telephone:** (804) 289-6313. **FAX:** (804) 289-8820.
**Home Field:** Pitt Field. **Seating Capacity:** 600. **Outfield Dimensions:** LF—328, CF—390, RF—328. **Press Box Telephone:** (804) 289-8714.

## RIDER Broncs
**Conference:** Metro Atlantic.
**Mailing Address:** 2083 Lawrenceville Rd., Lawrenceville, NJ 08648. **Website:** www.gobroncs.com.
**Head Coach:** Barry Davis. **Assistant Coaches:** Thomas Carr, Josh Copskey, *Benny Davis. **Telephone:** (609) 896-5055. • **Baseball SID:** Bud Focht. **Telephone:** (609) 896-5138. **FAX:** (609) 896-0341.

## RUTGERS Scarlet Knights
**Conference:** Big East.
**Mailing Address:** 83 Rockefeller Rd., Piscataway, NJ 08854. **Website:** www.scarletknights.com.
**Head Coach:** Fred Hill. **Assistant Coaches:** Jay Blackwell, Rick Freeman, *Glen Gardner. **Telephone:** (732) 445-7833. • **Baseball SID:** Doug Drabik. **Telephone:** (732) 445-4200. **FAX:** (732) 445-3063.
**Home Field:** Class of '53 Baseball Complex. **Seating Capacity:** 1,500. **Outfield Dimensions:** LF—330, CF—410, RF—325. **Press Box Telephone:** (732) 445-2776.

## SACRAMENTO STATE Hornets
**Conference:** Western Athletic.

**Mailing Address:** 6000 J St., Sacramento, CA 95819. **Website:** www.hornetsports.com.

**Head Coach:** John Smith. **Assistant Coaches:** Dan Barbara, Jim Barr, John Callahan, Matt Wilson. **Telephone:** (916) 278-7225. • **Baseball SID:** Andria Wenzel. **Telephone:** (916) 278-6896. **FAX:** (916) 278-5429.

## SACRED HEART Pioneers
**Conference:** Northeast.
**Mailing Address:** 5151 Park Ave., Fairfield, CT 06825. **Website:** www.sacredheartpioneers.com.
**Head Coach:** Nick Giaquinto. **Assistant Coaches:** Bob Andrews, *Seth Kaplan. **Telephone:** (203) 365-7632. • **Baseball SID:** Gene Gumbus. **Telephone:** (203) 396-8127. **FAX:** (203) 365-7696.

## ST. BONAVENTURE Bonnies
**Conference:** Atlantic 10.
**Mailing Address:** Reilly Center, St. Bonaventure, NY 14778. **Website:** www.gobonnies.com.
**Head Coach:** Larry Sudbrook. **Assistant Coach:** Jon Myler. **Telephone:** (716) 375-2641. • **Baseball SID:** Steve Mest. **Telephone:** (716) 375-2319. **FAX:** (716) 375-2383.

## ST. FRANCIS Terriers
**Conference:** Northeast.
**Mailing Address:** 180 Remsen St., Brooklyn, NY 11201. **Website:** athletics.stfranciscollege.edu.
**Head Coach:** Frank Del George. **Assistant Coach:** *Bobby Cruz. **Telephone:** (718) 489-5490. • **Baseball SID:** Gus Figeroa. **Telephone:** (718) 489-5490. **FAX:** (718) 797-2140.

## ST. JOHN'S Red Storm
**Conference:** Big East.
**Mailing Address:** 8000 Utopia Pkwy., Queens, NY 11439. **Website:** www.redstormsports.com.
**Head Coach:** Ed Blankmeyer. **Assistant Coaches:** Scott Brown, Bill Consiglio, *Mike Hampton. **Telephone:** (718) 990-6148. • **Baseball SID:** Dustin Hockensmith. **Telephone:** (718) 990-1521. **FAX:** (718) 969-8468.
**Home Field:** The Ballpark at St. John's. **Seating Capacity:** 3,500. **Outfield Dimensions:** LF—325, CF—400, RF—325. **Press Box Telephone:** (718) 990-2724.

## ST. JOSEPH'S Hawks
**Conference:** Atlantic 10.
**Mailing Address:** 5600 City Ave., Philadelphia, PA 19131. **Website:** www.sjuhawks.com.
**Head Coach:** Shawn Pender. **Assistant Coaches:** Rich Coletta, Tim Gunn, *Greg Manco. **Telephone:** (610) 660-1718. • **Baseball SID:** Phil Denne. **Telephone:** (610) 660-1738. **FAX:** (610) 660-1724.

## SAINT LOUIS Billikens
**Conference:** Atlantic 10.
**Mailing Address:** 3672 W. Pine Blvd., St. Louis, MO 63108. **Website:** www.slubillikens.com.
**Head Coach:** Bob Hughes. **Assistant Coaches:** Dan Nicholson, *Wes Sells. **Telephone:** (314) 977-3172. • **Baseball SID:** Diana Koval. **Telephone:** (314) 977-3463. **FAX:** (314) 977-7193.
**Home Field:** Billiken Sports Center. **Seating Capacity:** 500. **Outfield Dimensions:** LF—330, CF—395, RF—330. **Press Box Telephone:** (314) 402-8655.

## ST. MARY'S Gaels
**Conference:** West Coast.
**Mailing Address:** 1928 St. Mary's Rd., Moraga, CA 94575. **Website:** www.smcgaels.com.
**Head Coach:** Jedd Soto. **Assistant Coaches:** Steve Roberts, Jordan Twohig, *Gabe Zappin. **Telephone:** (925)

631-4637. • **Baseball SID:** Skip Powers. **Telephone:** (925) 631-8562. **FAX:** (925) 631-4405.
**Home Field:** Louis Guisto Field. **Seating Capacity:** 500. **Outfield Dimensions:** LF—340, CF—390, RF—340. **Press Box Telephone:** (925) 376-3906.

## ST. PETER'S Peacocks
**Conference:** Metro Atlantic.
**Mailing Address:** 2641 John F. Kennedy Blvd., Jersey City, NJ 07306. **Website:** www.spc.edu/athletics.
**Head Coach:** Derek England. **Assistant Coaches:** Marty Craft, Tim Nagurka, *Charles Rozzi. **Telephone:** (201) 915-9459. • **Baseball SID:** Jared Fowler. **Telephone:** (201) 915-9122. **FAX:** (201) 915-9102.

## SAM HOUSTON STATE Bearkats
**Conference:** Southland.
**Mailing Address:** P.O. Box 2268, Huntsville, TX 77341. **Website:** www.gobearkats.com.
**Head Coach:** Chris Rupp. **Assistant Coach:** Chris Todd. **Telephone:** (936) 294-1731. • **Baseball SID:** Paul Ridings. **Telephone:** (936) 294-1764. **FAX:** (936) 294-3538.

## SAMFORD Bulldogs
**Conference:** Ohio Valley.
**Mailing Address:** 800 Lakeshore Dr., Birmingham, AL 35229. **Website:** www.samfordsports.com.
**Head Coach:** Casey Dunn. **Assistant Coaches:** *Tony David, Mick Fieldbinder, Shane Kelley, Gerald Tuck. **Telephone:** (205) 726-2134. • **Baseball SID:** Joey Mullins. **Telephone:** (205) 726-2799. **FAX:** (205) 726-2545.

## SAN DIEGO Toreros
**Conference:** West Coast.
**Mailing Address:** 5998 Alcala Park, San Diego, CA 92110. **Website:** usdtoreros.com.
**Head Coach:** Rich Hill. **Assistant Coaches:** Jay Johnson, Eric Valenzuela. **Telephone:** (619) 260-5953. • **Baseball SID:** Chris Loucks. **Telephone:** (619) 260-7930. **FAX:** (619) 260-2990.
**Home Field:** Cunningham Stadium. **Seating Capacity:** 1,500. **Outfield Dimensions:** LF—309, CF—395, RF—329. **Press Box Telephone:** (619) 260-8829.

## SAN DIEGO STATE Aztecs
**Conference:** Mountain West.
**Mailing Address:** Department of Athletics, San Diego, CA 92182. **Website:** www.goaztecs.com.
**Head Coach:** Tony Gwynn. **Assistant Coaches:** Rusty Filter, Anthony Johnson, *Mark Martinez. **Telephone:** (619) 594-6889. • **Baseball SID:** Dave Kuhn. **Telephone:** (619) 594-5242. **FAX:** (619) 582-6541.
**Home Field:** Tony Gwynn Stadium. **Seating Capacity:** 3,000. **Outfield Dimensions:** LF—340, CF—410, RF—340. **Press Box Telephone:** (619) 594-4103.

## SAN FRANCISCO Dons
**Conference:** West Coast.
**Mailing Address:** 2130 Fulton St., San Francisco, CA 94118. **Website:** www.usfdons.com.
**Head Coach:** Nino Giarratano. **Assistant Coaches:** Rigo Lopez, *Greg Moore, Troy Nakamura. **Telephone:** (415) 422-2393. • **Baseball SID:** Ryan McCrary. **Telephone:** (415) 422-6162. **FAX:** (415) 422-2510.
**Home Field:** Benedetti Diamond. **Seating Capacity:** 3,000. **Outfield Dimensions:** LF—321, CF—415, RF—321. **Press Box Telephone:** (415) 422-5395.

## SAN JOSE STATE Spartans
**Conference:** Western Athletic.
**Mailing Address:** One Washington Square, San Jose,

CA 95192. **Website:** www.sjsuspartans.com.
**Head Coach:** Sam Piraro. **Assistant Coaches:** Jason Bugg, Dean Madsen, *Doug Thurman. **Telephone:** (408) 924-1255. • **Baseball SID:** Doga Gur. **Telephone:** (408) 924-1211. **FAX:** (408) 924-1291.
**Home Field:** Municipal Stadium. **Seating Capacity:** 5,000. **Outfield Dimensions:** LF—330, CF—400, RF—330. **Press Box Telephone:** (408) 924-7276.

### SANTA CLARA Broncos
**Conference:** West Coast.
**Mailing Address:** 500 El Camino Real, Santa Clara, CA 95053. **Website:** www.santaclarabroncos.com.
**Head Coach:** Mark O'Brien. **Assistant Coaches:** Matt Mueller, *Mike Oakland, Mike Zirelli. **Telephone:** (408) 554-4680. • **Baseball SID:** Aaron Juarez. **Telephone:** (408) 554-4659. **FAX:** (408) 554-6942.
**Home Field:** Stephen Schott Stadium. **Seating Capacity:** 1,500. **Outfield Dimensions:** LF—340, CF—400, RF—335. **Press Box Telephone:** Unavailable.

### SAVANNAH STATE Tigers
**Conference:** Independent.
**Mailing Address:** 3219 College St., Savannah, GA 31404. **Website:** www.savstate.edu/athletics.
**Head Coach:** Carlton Hardy. **Telephone:** (912) 356-2801. • **Baseball SID:** Opio Mashariki. **Telephone:** (912) 356-2446. **FAX:** (912) 353-5287.

### SETON HALL Pirates
**Conference:** Big East.
**Mailing Address:** 400 S. Orange Ave., South Orange, NJ 07079. **Website:** www.shupirates.com.
**Head Coach:** Rob Sheppard. **Assistant Coaches:** Phil Cundari, Jim Duffy, Charlie Killeen. **Telephone:** (973) 761-9557. • **Baseball SID:** Danya Johnson. **Telephone:** (973) 761-9493. **FAX:** (973) 761-9061.
**Home Field:** Owen T. Carroll Field. **Seating Capacity:** 1,000. **Outfield Dimensions:** LF—320, CF—400, RF—320. **Press Box Telephone:** Unavailable.

### SIENA Saints
**Conference:** Metro Atlantic.
**Mailing Address:** 515 Loudon Rd., Loudonville, NY 12211. **Website:** www.sienasaints.com.
**Head Coach:** Tony Rossi. **Assistant Coaches:** Tim Brown, *Casey Fahy, Paul Thomson. **Telephone:** (518) 786-5044. • **Baseball SID:** Jason Rich. **Telephone:** (518) 783-2411. **FAX:** (518) 783-2992.

### SOUTH ALABAMA Jaguars
**Conference:** Sun Belt.
**Mailing Address:** 1209 Mitchell Center, Mobile, AL 36608. **Website:** www.usajaguars.com.
**Head Coach:** Steve Kittrell. **Assistant Coaches:** Brian Hastings, Ronnie Powell, *Rob Reinstetle. **Telephone:** (251) 460-6876. • **Baseball SID:** Kit Strief. **Telephone:** (251) 414-8032. **FAX:** (251) 460-7297.
**Home Field:** Eddie Stanky Field. **Seating Capacity:** 3,500. **Outfield Dimensions:** LF—330, CF—400, RF—330. **Press Box Telephone:** (251) 461-1842.

### SOUTH CAROLINA Gamecocks
**Conference:** Southeastern (East).
**Mailing Address:** 1300 Rosewood Dr., Columbia, SC 29208. **Website:** www.uscsports.com.
**Head Coach:** Ray Tanner. **Assistant Coaches:** Mark Calvi, Monte Lee, *Jim Toman. **Telephone:** (803) 777-0116. • **Baseball SID:** Andrew Kitick. **Telephone:** (803) 777-5257. **FAX:** (803) 777-2967.
**Home Field:** Sarge Frye Field. **Seating Capacity:** 6,000. **Outfield Dimensions:** LF—320, CF—390, RF—

320. **Press Box Telephone:** (803) 777-6648.

### #SOUTH DAKOTA STATE Jackrabbits
**Conference:** Independent.
**Mailing Address:** Stanley J. Marshall HPER Center, Brookings, SD 57007. **Website:** www.gojacks.com.
**Head Coach:** Reggie Christiansen. **Assistant Coaches:** Pat Holmes, Chris Smart. **Telephone:** (605) 688-5027. • **Baseball SID:** Ron Lenz. **Telephone:** (605) 688-4623. **FAX:** (605) 688-5999.

### SOUTH FLORIDA Bulls
**Conference:** Big East.
**Mailing Address:** 4202 E. Fowler Ave., ATH 100, Tampa, FL 33620. **Website:** www.GoUSFBulls.com.
**Head Coach:** Eddie Cardieri. **Assistant Coaches:** Reggie Jefferson, *Nelson North, Greg Parris. **Telephone:** (813) 974-4023. • **Baseball SID:** Paul Dodson. **Telephone:** (813) 974-4029. **FAX:** (813) 974-5328.
**Home Field:** Red McEwen Field. **Seating Capacity:** 1,500. **Outfield Dimensions:** LF—340, CF—400, RF—340. **Press Box Telephone:** (813) 974-3604.

### SOUTHEAST MISSOURI STATE Indians
**Conference:** Ohio Valley.
**Mailing Address:** One University Plaza, Cape Girardeau, MO 63701. **Website:** www.gosoutheast.com.
**Head Coach:** Mark Hogan. **Assistant Coaches:** *Jeff Dodson, Scott Southard. **Telephone:** (573) 651-2645. • **Baseball SID:** Patrick Clark. **Telephone:** (573) 651-2937. **FAX:** (573) 651-2810.

### SOUTHEASTERN LOUISIANA Lions
**Conference:** Southland.
**Mailing Address:** SLU Station 10309, Hammond, LA 70402. **Website:** www.LionSports.net.
**Head Coach:** Jay Artigues. **Assistant Coaches:** Chad Caillet, Jered Salazar, Seth Thibodeaux. **Telephone:** (985) 549-3566. • **Baseball SID:** Matt Sullivan. **Telephone:** (985) 549-3774. **FAX:** (985) 549-3773.

### SOUTHERN Jaguars
**Conference:** Southwestern Athletic.
**Mailing Address:** P.O. Box 10850, Baton Rouge, LA 70813. **Website:** www.subr.edu/baseball.
**Head Coach:** Roger Cador. **Assistant Coaches:** Calvin Beal, Fernando Puebla, *Barret Rey. **Telephone:** (225) 771-2513. • **Baseball SID:** Kevin Manns. **Telephone:** (225) 771-4142. **FAX:** (225) 771-5671.

### SOUTHERN CALIFORNIA Trojans
**Conference:** Pacific-10.
**Mailing Address:** 3501 Watt Way, Los Angeles, CA 90089. **Website:** www.usctrojans.com.
**Head Coach:** Mike Gillespie. **Assistant Coaches:** Rob Klein, *Dave Lawn, Andy Nieto. **Telephone:** (213) 740-5762. • **Baseball SID:** Jason Pommier. **Telephone:** (213) 740-3807. **FAX:** (213) 740-7584.
**Home Field:** Dedeaux Field. **Seating Capacity:** 2,500. **Outfield Dimensions:** LF—335, CF—395, RF—335. **Press Box Telephone:** (213) 748-3449.

### SOUTHERN ILLINOIS Salukis
**Conference:** Missouri Valley.
**Mailing Address:** 130B Lingle Hall-SIU Arena, Carbondale, IL 62901. **Website:** www.siusalukis.com.
**Head Coach:** Dan Callahan. **Assistant Coaches:** Greg Andrews, Tony Etiner, *Ken Henderson, Bryan Wolff. **Telephone:** (618) 453-2802. • **Baseball SID:** Jeff Honza. **Telephone:** (618) 453-5470. **FAX:** (618) 453-2648.
**Home Field:** Abe Martin Field. **Seating Capacity:** 2,000. **Outfield Dimensions:** LF—340, CF—390, RF—340. **Press Box Telephone:** (618) 453-3794.

## SOUTHERN MISSISSIPPI Golden Eagles
**Conference:** Conference USA.
**Mailing Address:** 118 College Dr. #5017, Hattiesburg, MS 39406. **Website:** www.southernmiss.com.
**Head Coach:** Corky Palmer. **Assistant Coaches:** Scott Berry, *Lane Burroughs, Josh Hoffpauir. **Telephone:** (601) 266-5017. • **Baseball SID:** Mike Montoro. **Telephone:** (601) 266-5947. **FAX:** (601) 266-4507.
**Home Field:** Pete Taylor Park at Hill Denson Field. **Seating Capacity:** 3,678. **Outfield Dimensions:** LF—340, CF—400, RF—340. **Press Box Telephone:** (601) 266-5684.

## SOUTHERN UTAH Thunderbirds
**Conference:** Mid-Continent.
**Mailing Address:** 351 W. University Blvd., Cedar City, UT 84720. **Website:** www.suu.edu/athletics/baseball.
**Head Coach:** David Eldredge. **Assistant Coaches:** Jason Ruiz, Robert Stephens. **Telephone:** (435) 586-7932. • **Baseball SID:** Steve Johnson. **Telephone:** (435) 586-7752. **FAX:** (435) 865-8037.

## STANFORD Cardinal
**Conference:** Pacific-10.
**Mailing Address:** Arrillaga Family Sports Center, Stanford, CA 94305. **Website:** www.gostanford.com.
**Head Coach:** Mark Marquess. **Assistant Coaches:** Tom Kunis, David Nakama, *Dean Stotz. **Telephone:** (650) 723-4528. • **Baseball SID:** Kyle McRae. **Telephone:** (650) 725-2959. **FAX:** (650) 725-2957.
**Home Field:** Sunken Diamond. **Seating Capacity:** 4,000. **Outfield Dimensions:** LF—335, CF—400, RF—335. **Press Box Telephone:** (650) 723-4629.

## STEPHEN F. AUSTIN Lumberjacks
**Conference:** Southland.
**Mailing Address:** P.O. Box 13010, SFA Station, Nacogdoches, TX 75962. **Website:** www.sfajacks.com.
**Head Coach:** Donnie Watson. **Assistant Coaches:** *Johnny Cardenas, Chris Connally, Stuart Musick. **Telephone:** (936) 468-4599. • **Baseball SID:** James Dixon. **Telephone:** (936) 468-2606. **FAX:** (936) 468-4593.

## STETSON Hatters
**Conference:** Atlantic Sun.
**Mailing Address:** 421 N. Woodland Blvd., Box 8359, DeLand, FL 32723. **Website:** www.stetson.edu/athletics.
**Head Coach:** Pete Dunn. **Assistant Coaches:** Mitch Markham, Bryan Peters, *Garrett Quinn. **Telephone:** (386) 822-8730. • **Baseball SID:** Jamie Bataille. **Telephone:** (386) 822-8130. **FAX:** (386) 822-7486.
**Home Field:** Melching Field at Conrad Park. **Seating Capacity:** 2,500. **Outfield Dimensions:** LF—335, CF—403, RF—335. **Press Box Telephone:** (386) 736-7360.

## STONY BROOK Seawolves
**Conference:** America East.
**Mailing Address:** Indoor Sports Complex, Stony Brook, NY 11794. **Website:** www.goseawolves.org.
**Head Coach:** Matt Senk. **Assistant Coach:** Gerry Sputo. **Telephone:** (631) 632-9226. • **Baseball SID:** Mike Newhouse-Bailey. **Telephone:** (631) 632-7289. **FAX:** (631) 632-8841.

## TEMPLE Owls
**Conference:** Atlantic 10.
**Mailing Address:** 1700 N. Broad St., Fourth Floor, Philadelphia, PA 19122. **Website:** www.owlsports.com.
**Head Coach:** Rob Valli. **Assistant Coaches:** Greg Chew, Casey Fahy, John Tredinnick. **Telephone:** (215) 204-3146. • **Baseball SID:** Kevin Bonner. **Telephone:**

(215) 204-9149. **FAX:** (215) 204-7499.

## TENNESSEE Volunteers
**Conference:** Southeastern (East).
**Mailing Address:** 1720 Volunteer Blvd., Knoxville, TN 37996. **Website:** www.utsports.com.
**Head Coach:** Rod Delmonico. **Assistant Coaches:** Mike Bell, Larry Simcox. **Telephone:** (865) 974-2057. • **Baseball SID:** Tom Satkowiak. **Telephone:** (865) 974-4947. **FAX:** (865) 974-1269.
**Home Field:** Lindsey Nelson Stadium. **Seating Capacity:** 4,000. **Outfield Dimensions:** LF—320, CF—404, RF—330. **Press Box Telephone:** (865) 974-3376.

## TENNESSEE-MARTIN Skyhawks
**Conference:** Ohio Valley.
**Mailing Address:** 1037 Elam Center, Martin, TN 38238. **Website:** www.utmsports.com.
**Head Coach:** Bubba Cates. **Assistant Coaches:** Brad Goss, Mark Meinhart. **Telephone:** (731) 881-7337. • **Baseball SID:** Joe Lofaro. **Telephone:** (731) 881-7632. **FAX:** (731) 881-7624.

## TENNESSEE TECH Golden Eagles
**Conference:** Ohio Valley.
**Mailing Address:** 1100 McGee Blvd., Box 5057, Cookeville, TN 38505. **Website:** www.ttusports.com.
**Head Coach:** Matt Bragga. **Assistant Coach:** *Craig Moore. **Telephone:** (931) 372-3925. • **Baseball SID:** Rob Schabert. **Telephone:** (931) 372-3088. **FAX:** (931) 372-6139.

## TEXAS Longhorns
**Conference:** Big 12.
**Mailing Address:** P.O. Box 7399, Austin, TX 78713. **Website:** www.TexasSports.com.
**Head Coach:** Augie Garrido. **Assistant Coaches:** *Tommy Harmon, Tom Holliday. **Telephone:** (512) 471-5732. • **Baseball SID:** Mike Forcucci. **Telephone:** (512) 471-6039. **FAX:** (512) 471-6040.
**Home Field:** Disch-Falk Field. **Seating Capacity:** 6,649. **Outfield Dimensions:** LF—340, CF—400, RF—325. **Press Box Telephone:** (512) 471-1146.

## TEXAS-ARLINGTON Mavericks
**Conference:** Southland.
**Mailing Address:** P.O. Box 19079, Arlington, TX 76019. **Website:** www.utamavs.edu.
**Head Coach:** Jeff Curtis. **Assistant Coaches:** Jay Sirrianni, *Darin Thomas. **Telephone:** (817) 272-2542. • **Baseball SID:** John Brush. **Telephone:** (817) 272-5706. **FAX:** (817) 272-2254.
**Home Field:** Clay Gould Ballpark. **Seating Capacity:** 1,600. **Outfield Dimensions:** LF—330, CF—400, RF—330. **Press Box Telephone:** (817) 272-2213.

## TEXAS-PAN AMERICAN Broncs
**Conference:** Independent.
**Mailing Address:** 1201 W. University Dr., Edinburg, TX 78541. **Website:** www.utpabroncs.com.
**Head Coach:** *Willie Gawlik. **Assistant Coaches:** Jason Alamo, *Justin Meccage, Terry Tuck. **Telephone:** (956) 381-2235. • **Baseball SID:** Jeff Sutton. **Telephone:** (956) 380-8799. **FAX:** (956) 381-2261.

## TEXAS-SAN ANTONIO Roadrunners
**Conference:** Southland.
**Mailing Address:** 6900 N. Loop 1604 West, San Antonio, TX 78249. **Website:** www.goutsa.com.
**Head Coach:** Sherman Corbett. **Assistant Coaches:** Jim Blair, Mike Clement, *Jason Marshall. **Telephone:** (210) 458-4805. • **Baseball SID:** Carlos Valdez. **Telephone:** (210) 458-4930. **FAX:** (210) 458-4569.

## TEXAS A&M Aggies

**Conference:** Big 12.
**Mailing Address:** P.O. Box 30017, College Station, TX 77842. **Website:** www.aggieathletics.com.
**Head Coach:** Rob Childress. **Assistant Coaches:** Will Bolt, *Matt Deggs, Jason Hutchins, Jeremy Talbot. **Telephone:** (979) 845-5556. • **Baseball SID:** Chuck Glenewinkel. **Telephone:** (979) 845-3239. **FAX:** (979) 845-1618.
**Home Field:** Olsen Field. **Seating Capacity:** 7,500. **Outfield Dimensions:** LF—330, CF—400, RF—330. **Press Box Telephone:** (979) 458-3604.

## TEXAS A&M-CORPUS CHRISTI Islanders

**Conference:** Independent.
**Mailing Address:** 6300 Ocean Dr., Corpus Christi, TX 78412. **Website:** www.goislanders.com.
**Head Coach:** Hector Salinas. **Assistant Coach:** *Gene Salazar. **Telephone:** (361) 825-3252. **Baseball SID:** Aaron Ames. **Telephone:** (361) 825-3411. **FAX:** (361) 825-3218.

## TEXAS CHRISTIAN Horned Frogs

**Conference:** Mountain West.
**Mailing Address:** TCU Box 297600, Fort Worth, TX 76129. **Website:** www.gofrogs.com.
**Head Coach:** Jim Schlossnagle. **Assistant Coaches:** Derek Matlock, Matt Siegel, *Todd Whitting. **Telephone:** (817) 257-5354. • **Baseball SID:** Brandie Davidson. **Telephone:** (817) 257-7479. **FAX:** (817) 257-7964.
**Home Field:** Lupton Stadium. **Seating Capacity:** 3,500. **Outfield Dimensions:** LF—330, CF—400, RF—330. **Press Box Telephone:** (817) 257-7966.

## TEXAS SOUTHERN Tigers

**Conference:** Southwestern Athletic.
**Mailing Address:** 3100 Cleburne St., Houston, TX 77004. **Website:** www.msbn.tv/tsuvision/index.aspx.
**Head Coach:** Candy Robinson. **Assistant Coach:** Brian White. **Telephone:** (713) 313-7993. • **Baseball SID:** Rodney Bush. **Telephone:** (713) 313-6829. **FAX:** (713) 313-1045.

## TEXAS STATE Bobcats

**Conference:** Southland.
**Mailing Address:** 601 University Dr., San Marcos, TX 78666. **Website:** www.txstatebobcats.com.
**Head Coach:** Ty Harrington. **Assistant Coaches:** *Howard Bushong, John Maley. **Telephone:** (512) 245-8395. • **Baseball SID:** Ron Mears. **Telephone:** (512) 245-2966. **FAX:** (512) 245-2967.
**Home Field:** Bobcat Field. **Seating Capacity:** 1,500. **Outfield Dimensions:** LF—325, CF—404, RF—325. **Press Box Telephone:** Unavailable.

## TEXAS TECH Red Raiders

**Conference:** Big 12.
**Mailing Address:** P.O. Box 43021, Lubbock, TX 79409. **Website:** www.texastech.com.
**Head Coach:** Larry Hays. **Assistant Coaches:** Lance Brown, *Daren Hays, Bobby Sherrard. **Telephone:** (806) 742-3355. • **Baseball SID:** Blayne Beal. **Telephone:** (806) 742-2770. **FAX:** (806) 742-1970.
**Home Field:** Dan Law Field. **Seating Capacity:** 5,050. **Outfield Dimensions:** LF—330, CF—405, RF—330. **Press Box Telephone:** (806) 742-3688.

## TOLEDO Rockets

**Conference:** Mid-American (West).
**Mailing Address:** 2801 W. Bancroft St., Toledo, OH 43606. **Website:** www.utrockets.com.
**Head Coach:** Cory Mee. **Assistant Coaches:** J.J.

Brock, Matt Husted. **Telephone:** (419) 530-6264. • **Baseball SID:** Brian DeBenedictis. **Telephone:** (419) 530-4919. **FAX:** (419) 530-4930.

## TOWSON Tigers

**Conference:** Colonial Athletic.
**Mailing Address:** 8000 York Rd., Towson, MD 21252. **Website:** www.towsontigers.com.
**Head Coach:** Mike Gottlieb. **Assistant Coaches:** Mel Bacon, Anthony Quaranta, *Scott Roane. **Telephone:** (410) 704-3775. • **Baseball SID:** Dan O'Connell. **Telephone:** (410) 704-3102. **FAX:** (410) 704-3861.
**Home Field:** John Schuerholz Park. **Seating Capacity:** 1,500. **Outfield Dimensions:** LF—312, CF—424, RF—302. **Press Box Telephone:** (410) 704-5810.

## TROY Trojans

**Conference:** Sun Belt.
**Mailing Address:** 5000 Veterans Stadium Dr., Troy, AL 36082. **Website:** www.troytrojans.com.
**Head Coach:** Bobby Pierce. **Assistant Coaches:** Todd Lamberth, Michael Murphee, *Mark Smartt. **Telephone:** (334) 670-3489. • **Baseball SID:** Ricky Hazel. **Telephone:** (334) 670-3832. **FAX:** (334) 670-5665.
**Home Field:** Riddle-Pace Field. **Seating Capacity:** 2,000. **Outfield Dimensions:** LF—322, CF—390, RF—308. **Press Box Telephone:** (334) 670-5701.

## TULANE Green Wave

**Conference:** Conference USA.
**Mailing Address:** Wilson Center, New Orleans, LA 70018. **Website:** www.tulanegreenwave.com.
**Head Coach:** Rick Jones. **Assistant Coaches:** *Mark Kingston, Chad Sutter, Luke Weatherford. **Telephone:** (504) 862-8239. • **Baseball SID:** Richie Weaver. **Telephone:** (504) 314-7232. **FAX:** (504) 865-5512.
**Home Field:** Turchin Stadium. **Seating Capacity:** 3,600. **Outfield Dimensions:** LF—325, CF—400, RF—325. **Press Box Telephone:** (504) 862-8224.

## UTAH Utes

**Conference:** Mountain West.
**Mailing Address:** 1825 E. South Campus Dr., Salt Lake City, UT 84112. **Website:** utahutes.collegesports.com.
**Head Coach:** Bill Kinneberg. **Assistant Coaches:** *Bryan Conger, Todd Delnose. **Telephone:** (801) 581-3526. • **Baseball SID:** Andy Seeley. **Telephone:** (801) 581-3771. **FAX:** (801) 581-4358.
**Home Field:** Franklin Covey Field. **Seating Capacity:** 15,000. **Outfield Dimensions:** LF—345, CF—400, RF—315. **Press Box Telephone:** Unavailable.

## #UTAH VALLEY STATE Wolverines

**Conference:** Independent.
**Mailing Address:** 800 W. University Parkway, Orem, UT 84058. **Website:** www.wolverinegreen.com.
**Head Coach:** Steve Gardner. **Assistant Coaches:** *Eric Madsen, Nate Mathis. **Telephone:** (801) 863-8647. • **Baseball SID:** Clint Burgi. **Telephone:** (801) 863-8644. **FAX:** (801) 863-8813.

## VALPARAISO Crusaders

**Conference:** Mid-Continent.
**Mailing Address:** 1009 Union St., Valparaiso, IN 46383. **Website:** www.valpo.edu/athletics.
**Head Coach:** Paul Twenge. **Assistant Coaches:** Cliff Brown, Ken Klawitter, John Olson. **Telephone:** (219) 464-5239. • **Baseball SID:** Ryan Wronkowicz. **Telephone:** (219) 464-5232. **FAX:** (219) 464-5762.

## VANDERBILT Commodores

**Conference:** Southeastern (East).
**Mailing Address:** 2619 Jess Neely Dr., Nashville, TN

37219. **Website:** www.vucommodores.com.
**Head Coach:** Tim Corbin. **Assistant Coaches:** Blake Allen, *Erik Bakich, Derek Johnson. **Telephone:** (615) 322-7725. • **Baseball SID:** Thomas Samuel. **Telephone:** (615) 343-0020. **FAX:** (615) 343-7064.
**Home Field:** Hawkins Field. **Seating Capacity:** 2,000. **Outfield Dimensions:** LF—310, CF—400, RF—330. **Press Box Telephone:** (615) 320-0436.

## VERMONT Catamounts
**Conference:** America East.
**Mailing Address:** Patrick Gym, Burlington, VT 05405. **Website:** www.uvmathletics.com.
**Head Coach:** Bill Currier. **Assistant Coaches:** Jim Carter, Mark Choiniere, *Anthony DeCicco. **Telephone:** (802) 656-7701. • **Baseball SID:** Bruce Bosley. **Telephone:** (802) 656-1109. **FAX:** (802) 656-8328.
**Home Field:** Centennial Field. **Seating Capacity:** 4,400. **Outfield Dimensions:** LF—324, CF—405, RF—320. **Press Box Telephone:** Unavailable.

## VILLANOVA Wildcats
**Conference:** Big East.
**Mailing Address:** 800 Lancaster Ave., Jake Nevin Field House, Villanova, PA 19085. **Website:** villanova.collegesports.com.
**Head Coach:** Joe Godri. **Assistant Coaches:** *Rick Clagett, Rod Johnson, Doc Kennedy. **Telephone:** (610) 519-4529. • **Baseball SID:** David Berman. **Telephone:** (610) 519-4122. **FAX:** (610) 519-7323.
**Home Field:** Villanova Ballpark at Plymouth. **Seating Capacity:** 750. **Outfield Dimensions:** LF—320, CF—405, RF—320. **Press Box Telephone:** (860) 490-6398.

## VIRGINIA Cavaliers
**Conference:** Atlantic Coast (Coastal).
**Mailing Address:** 300 Massie Rd., P.O. Box 400853, Charlottesville, VA 22904. **Website:** www.virginiasports.com.
**Head Coach:** Brian O'Connor. **Assistant Coaches:** Brian Anderson, Karl Kuhn, *Kevin McMullan. **Telephone:** (434) 982-5092. • **Baseball SID:** Kerwin Lonzo. **Telephone:** (434) 982-5131. **FAX:** (434) 982-5525.
**Home Field:** Davenport Field at UVa Baseball Stadium. **Seating Capacity:** 2,016. **Outfield Dimensions:** LF—335, CF—408, RF—352. **Press Box Telephone:** (434) 244-4071.

## VIRGINIA COMMONWEALTH Rams
**Conference:** Colonial Athletic.
**Mailing Address:** 1300 W. Broad St., Richmond, VA 23284. **Website:** www.vcurams.vcu.edu.
**Head Coach:** Paul Keyes. **Assistant Coaches:** Justin Clift, Tim Haynes, *Mark McQueen. **Telephone:** (804) 828-4820. • **Baseball SID:** Phil Stanton. **Telephone:** (804) 828-3440. **FAX:** (804) 828-9428.
**Home Field:** The Diamond. **Seating Capacity:** 12,134. **Outfield Dimensions:** LF—330, CF—402, RF—330. **Press Box Telephone:** (804) 359-1565.

## VIRGINIA MILITARY INSTITUTE Keydets
**Conference:** Big South.
**Mailing Address:** Baseball Office, Cameron Hall, Lexington, VA 24450. **Website:** www.vmikeydets.com.
**Head Coach:** Marlin Ikenberry. **Assistant Coaches:** Joe Hastings, Ryan Mau. **Telephone:** (540) 464-7609. • **Baseball SID:** Christian Hoffman. **Telephone:** (540) 464-7514. **FAX:** (540) 464-7583.

## VIRGINIA TECH Hokies
**Conference:** Atlantic Coast (Coastal).
**Mailing Address:** 460 Jamerson Athletic Center,

Blacksburg, VA 24061. **Website:** www.hokiesports.com.
**Head Coach:** Chuck Hartman. **Assistant Coaches:** Anthony Everman, Jon Hartness, *Jay Phillips. **Telephone:** (540) 231-9974. • **Baseball SID:** Dave Smith. **Telephone:** (540) 231-9965. **FAX:** (540) 231-6984.
**Home Field:** English Field. **Seating Capacity:** 1,500. **Outfield Dimensions:** LF—330, CF—400, RF—330. **Press Box Telephone:** (540) 231-4013.

## WAGNER Seahawks
**Conference:** Northeast.
**Mailing Address:** One Campus Rd., Staten Island, NY 10301. **Website:** www.wagnerathletics.com.
**Head Coach:** *Joe Litterio. **Assistant Coaches:** *Jim Carone, Jason Jurgens. **Telephone:** (718) 390-3154. • **Baseball SID:** Kevin Ross. **Telephone:** (718) 390-3215. **FAX:** (718) 390-3347.

## WAKE FOREST Demon Deacons
**Conference:** Atlantic Coast (Atlantic).
**Mailing Address:** P.O. Box 7426, Winston-Salem, NC 27109. **Website:** www.wakeforestsports.com.
**Head Coach:** Rick Rembielak. **Assistant Coaches:** Marshall Canosa, *Jon Palmieri, Chris Sinacori. **Telephone:** (336) 758-5570. • **Baseball SID:** Michael Bertsch. **Telephone:** (336) 758-5640. **FAX:** (336) 758-5140.
**Home Field:** Hooks Stadium. **Seating Capacity:** 2,500. **Outfield Dimensions:** LF—340, CF—400, RF—315. **Press Box Telephone:** (336) 759-9711.

## WASHINGTON Huskies
**Conference:** Pacific-10.
**Mailing Address:** Graves Building, Box 354070, Seattle, WA 98195. **Website:** www.gohuskies.com.
**Head Coach:** Ken Knutson. **Assistant Coaches:** Tighe Dickinson, Donny Harrel, *Joe Ross. **Telephone:** (206) 616-4335. • **Baseball SID:** Jeff Bechthold. **Telephone:** (206) 685-7910. **FAX:** (206) 543-5000.
**Home Field:** Husky Ballpark. **Seating Capacity:** 1,500. **Outfield Dimensions:** LF—327, CF—390, RF—317. **Press Box Telephone:** (206) 685-1994.

## WASHINGTON STATE Cougars
**Conference:** Pacific-10.
**Mailing Address:** PO Box, 641602, Pullman, WA 99164. **Website:** www.wsucougars.com.
**Head Coach:** Donnie Marbut. **Assistant Coaches:** Matt Dorey, Travis Jewett, Gregg Swenson. **Telephone:** (509) 335-0332. • **Baseball SID:** Bill Stevens. **Telephone:** (509) 335-4294. **FAX:** (509) 335-0267.
**Home Field:** Bailey-Brayton Field. **Seating Capacity:** 3,500. **Outfield Dimensions:** LF—330, CF—400, RF—335. **Press Box Telephone:** (509) 335-8291.

## WEST VIRGINIA Mountaineers
**Conference:** Big East.
**Mailing Address:** P.O. Box 0877, Morgantown, WV 26507. **Website:** www.MSNSportsnet.com.
**Head Coach:** Greg Van Zant. **Assistant Coaches:** *Bruce Cameron, Pat Sherald, Andrew Wright. **Telephone:** (304) 293-2308. • **Baseball SID:** Scott Castleman. **Telephone:** (304) 293-2821. **FAX:** (304) 293-4105.
**Home Field:** Hawley Field. **Seating Capacity:** 1,500. **Outfield Dimensions:** LF—325, CF—390, RF—325. **Press Box Telephone:** (304) 293-5988.

## WESTERN CAROLINA Catamounts
**Conference:** Southern.
**Mailing Address:** Ramsey Center, Cullowhee, NC 28723. **Website:** www.catamountsports.com.

Head Coach: Todd Raleigh. Assistant Coaches: Alan Beck, *Eric Filipek, Bradley LeCroy. Telephone: (828) 227-2011. • Baseball SID: Mike Cawood. Telephone: (828) 227-2339. FAX: (828) 227-7688.
Home Field: Childress Field at Hennon Stadium. Seating Capacity: 1,500. Outfield Dimensions: LF—325, CF—390, RF—325. Press Box Telephone: (828) 227-7020.

## WESTERN ILLINOIS Leathernecks
Conference: Mid-Continent.
Mailing Address: 1 University Circle, Macomb, IL 61455. Website: www.wiuathletics.com.
Head Coach: Stan Hyman. Assistant Coaches: *Justin Gordon, Cory Hall, Greg Schaub. Telephone: (309) 298-1521. • Baseball SID: Greg Mette. Telephone: (309) 298-1133. FAX: (309) 298-3366.
Home Field: Boyer Stadium. Seating Capacity: 4,000. Outfield Dimensions: LF—372, CF—400, RF—372. Press Box Telephone: Unavailable.

## WESTERN KENTUCKY Hilltoppers
Conference: Sun Belt.
Mailing Address: 1605 Ave. of Champions, Bowling Green, KY 42101. Website: www.wkusports.com.
Head Coach: Chris Finwood. Assistant Coaches: Ryan Halla, *Andrew Slater. Telephone: (270) 745-2277. • Baseball SID: Chris Glowacki. Telephone: (270) 745-5388. FAX: (270) 745-3444.
Home Field: Nick Denes Field. Seating Capacity: 1,050. Outfield Dimensions: LF—330, CF—400, RF—330. Press Box Telephone: (270) 745-4281.

## WESTERN MICHIGAN Broncos
Conference: Mid-American (West).
Mailing Address: 1903 W. Michigan Ave., Kalamazoo, MI 49008. Website: www.wmubroncos.com.
Head Coach: Randy Ford. Assistant Coach: *Scott Demetral. Telephone: (269) 387-8160. • Baseball SID: Paula Haughn. Telephone: (269) 387-4123. FAX: (269) 387-4139.

## WICHITA STATE Shockers
Conference: Missouri Valley.
Mailing Address: 1845 Fairmount St., Campus Box 18, Wichita, KS 67260. Website: www.goshockers.com.
Head Coach: Gene Stephenson. Assistant Coaches: *Brent Kemnitz, Mike Stover, Jim Thomas. Telephone: (316) 978-3636. • Baseball SID: Tami Cutler. Telephone: (316) 978-5559. FAX: (316) 978-3336.
Home Field: Tyler Field-Eck Stadium. Seating Capacity: 7,851. Outfield Dimensions: LF—330, CF—390, RF—330. Press Box Telephone: (316) 978-3390.

## WILLIAM & MARY Tribe
Conference: Colonial Athletic.
Mailing Address: P.O. Box 399, Williamsburg, VA 23187. Website: www.tribeathletics.com.
Head Coach: Frank Leoni. Assistant Coaches: Jad Prachniak, *Adam Taylor. Telephone: (757) 221-3399. • Baseball SID: Chris Poore. Telephone: (757) 221-3370. FAX: (757) 221-3412.
Home Field: Plumeri Park. Seating Capacity: 1,000. Outfield Dimensions: LF—315, CF—400, RF—315. Press Box Telephone: (757) 221-3562.

## WINTHROP Eagles
Conference: Big South.
Mailing Address: Winthrop Coliseum, Rock Hill, SC 29733. Website: www.winthropeagles.com.
Head Coach: Joe Hudak. Assistant Coaches: Kyle DiEduardo, *Mike McGuire, Stas Swerdzewski. Telephone: (803) 323-6235. • Baseball SID: Lauren Biggers. Telephone: (803) 323-6067. FAX: (803) 323-2433.
Home Field: Winthrop Ballpark. Seating Capacity: 1,989. Outfield Dimensions: LF—325, CF—390, RF—325. Press Box Telephone: (803) 323-2155.

## WISCONSIN-MILWAUKEE Panthers
Conference: Horizon.
Mailing Address: P.O. Box 413, Milwaukee, WI 53201. Website: www.uwmpanthers.com.
Head Coach: Jerry Augustine. Assistant Coaches: Cory Bigler, *Scott Doffek. Telephone: (414) 229-5670. • Baseball SID: Chris Zills. Telephone: (414) 229-4593. FAX: (414) 229-6759.

## WOFFORD Terriers
Conference: Southern.
Mailing Address: 429 N. Church St., Spartanburg, SC 29301. Website: www.wofford.edu/athletics.
Head Coach: Steve Traylor. Assistant Coaches: Scott Brickman, *Todd Interdonato, Jason Burke. Telephone: (864) 597-4126. • Baseball SID: Steve Shutt. Telephone: (864) 597-4093. FAX: (864) 597-4129.

## WRIGHT STATE Raiders
Conference: Horizon.
Mailing Address: 3640 Col. John Glenn Hwy., Dayton, OH 45435. Website: www.wsuraiders.com.
Head Coach: Rob Cooper. Assistant Coaches: Nate Griffin, *Greg Lovelady. Telephone: (937) 775-2771. • Baseball SID: Greg Campbell. Telephone: (937) 775-4687. FAX: (937) 775-2818.

## XAVIER Musketeers
Conference: Atlantic 10.
Mailing Address: 3800 Victory Pkwy., Cincinnati, OH 45207. Website: www.goxavier.com.
Head Coach: Scott Googins. Assistant Coaches: Bob Biger, *J.D. Heilmann, Zach Schmidt. Telephone: (513) 745-2891. • Baseball SID: Jake Linder. Telephone: (513) 745-3388. FAX: (513) 745-2825.

## YALE Bulldogs
Conference: Ivy League (Rolfe).
Mailing Address: P.O. Box 208216, New Haven, CT 06520. Website: www.yalebulldogs.com.
Head Coach: John Stuper. Assistant Coaches: Bill Asermely, John Dorman, Glenn Lungarini. Telephone: (203) 432-1466. • Baseball SID: Hank Gargiulo. Telephone: (203) 432-1448. FAX: (203) 432-1454.

## YOUNGSTOWN STATE Penguins
Conference: Horizon.
Mailing Address: One University Plaza, Youngstown, OH 44555. Website: www.ysusports.com.
Head Coach: Mike Florak. Assistant Coaches: Craig Antush, Jim Lipinski, Kyle Sobecki. Telephone: (330) 941-3485. • Baseball SID: John Vogel. Telephone: (330) 941-3192. FAX: (330) 941-3191.

# SMALL COLLEGES

## NCAA DIVISION II (II) / NCAA DIVISION III (III) / NAIA (A)
## NATIONAL CHRISTIAN COLLEGE (C) / UNITED STATES COLLEGIATE ATHLETIC ASSOCIATION (U)

| School | Class | Mailing Address | Head Coach | Telephone |
|---|---|---|---|---|
| Abilene Christian U. | II | ACU Station, Box 27916, Abilene, TX 79699 | Britt Bonneau | (325) 674-2325 |
| Adelphi U. | II | One South Ave., Garden City, NY 11530 | Dom Scala | (516) 877-4240 |
| Adrian College | III | 110 S. Madison St., Adrian, MI 49221 | Craig Rainey | (517) 264-3977 |
| Alabama-Huntsville, U. of | II | 205 Spragins Hall, Huntsville, AL 35899 | Lowell Mooneyham | (256) 824-2197 |
| Albany State U. | II | 504 College Dr., Albany, GA 31705 | Edward Taylor | (229) 430-1829 |
| Albertson College | A | 2112 Cleveland Blvd., Caldwell, ID 83605 | Shawn Humberger | (208) 459-5861 |
| Albertus Magnus College | III | 700 Prospect St., New Haven, CT 06511 | Brian Leighton | (203) 773-8586 |
| Albion College | III | 611 E. Porter St., Albion, MI 49224 | Scott Carden | (517) 629-0517 |
| Albright College | III | PO Box 15234, Reading, PA 19612 | Jeff Feiler | (610) 921-7678 |
| Alderson-Broaddus | II | 500 College Hill Rd., Philippi, WV 26416 | Milan Rasic | (304) 457-6265 |
| Alice Lloyd College | A | 100 Purpose Rd., Pippa Passes, KY 41844 | Scott Cornett | (606) 368-6119 |
| Allegheny College | III | 520 N. Main St., Meadville, PA 16335 | Mike Ferris | (814) 332-2830 |
| Alma College | III | 614 W. Superior St., Alma, MI 48801 | John Leister | (989) 463-7265 |
| Alvernia College | III | 400 Saint Bernardine St., Reading, PA 19607 | Yogi Lutz | (610) 796-8476 |
| American Int'l Coll. | II | 1000 State St., Springfield, MA 01109 | Nick Callini | (413) 205-3574 |
| Amherst College | III | PO Box 5000, Amherst, MA 01002 | Bill Thurston | (413) 542-2284 |
| Anderson College | II | 316 Boulevard St., Anderson, SC 29621 | Joe Miller | (864) 231-2013 |
| Anderson U. | III | 1100 E. 5th St., Anderson, IN 46012 | Don Brandon | (765) 641-4488 |
| Angelo State U. | II | 2601 West Ave. N., San Angelo, TX 76909 | Kevin Brooks | (325) 942-2091 |
| Anna Maria College | III | 50 Sunset Lane, Paxton, MA 01612 | Mike Wilson | (508) 849-3446 |
| Apprentice School, The | U | 4101 Washington Ave., Bldg. 14, Newport News, VA 23607 | Bryan Cave | (757) 380-3525 |
| Aquinas College | A | 1607 Robinson Rd., Grand Rapids, MI 49506 | Doug Greenslate | (616) 632-2935 |
| Arcadia University | III | 450 S. Easton Rd., Glenside, PA 19038 | Stan Exeter | (215) 572-2976 |
| Arkansas Tech | II | 1604 Coliseum Dr., Russellville, AR 72801 | Billy Goss | (479) 968-0648 |
| Arkansas-Monticello, U. of | II | UAM Box 3066, Monticello, AR 71656 | Kevin Downing | (870) 460-1257 |
| Armstrong Atlantic State U. | II | 11935 Abercorn St., Savannah, GA 31419 | Joe Roberts | (912) 921-5686 |
| Ashford U. | A | PO Box 2967, Clinton, IA 52732 | Bob Koopmann | (563) 242-4140 |
| Ashland U. | II | 916 King Rd., Ashland, OH 44805 | John Schaly | (419) 289-5444 |
| Assumption College | II | 500 Salisbury St., Worcester, MA 01609 | Jamie Pinzino | (508) 767-7232 |
| Atlanta Christian College | C | 2605 Ben Hill Rd., East Point, GA 30344 | Alan Wilson | (404) 669-2059 |
| Auburn U.-Montgomery | A | PO Box 244023, Montgomery, AL 36124 | Q.V. Lowe | (334) 244-3237 |
| Augsburg College | III | 2211 Riverside Ave., Minneapolis, MN 55454 | Keith Bateman | (612) 330-1395 |
| Augusta State U. | II | 2500 Walton Way #10, Augusta, GA 30904 | Stanley Fite | (706) 731-7917 |
| Augustana College | III | 3500 5th Ave., Rock Island, IL 61201 | Greg Wallace | (309) 794-7521 |
| Augustana College | II | 2001 S. Summit Ave, Sioux Falls, SD 57197 | Jeff Holm | (605) 274-5541 |
| Aurora U. | III | 347 S. Gladstone Ave, Aurora, IL 60506 | Shaun Neitzel | (630) 844-6515 |
| Austin College | III | 900 N. Grand Ave, Suite 6A, Sherman, TX 75090 | Carl Iwasaki | (903) 813-2516 |
| Averett University | III | 420 W. Main St., Danville, VA 24541 | Ed Fulton | (434) 791-5030 |
| Avila U. | A | 11901 Wornall Rd., Kansas City, MO 64145 | Ryan Howard | (816) 501-3739 |
| Azusa Pacific U. | A | PO Box 7000, Azusa, CA 91702 | Paul Svagdis | (626) 815-6000 |
| Babson College | III | Webster Center, Babson Park, MA 02457 | Matt Noone | (781) 239-5823 |
| Bacone College | A | 2299 Old Bacone Rd., Muskogee, OK 74403 | Dan Bowers | (918) 781-7237 |
| Baker U. | A | PO Box 65, Baldwin City, KS 66006 | Phil Hannon | (785) 594-8493 |
| Baldwin-Wallace College | III | 275 Eastland Rd., Berea, OH 44017 | Bob Fisher | (440) 826-2182 |
| Baptist Bible College | C | 538 Venard Rd., Clarks Summit, PA 18411 | Don Sintic | (570) 585-9322 |
| Barry U. | II | 11300 NE 2nd Ave., Miami Shores, FL 33161 | Unavailable | (305) 899-3558 |
| Barton College | II | 401 Rountree St., Wilson, NC 27893 | Todd Wilkinson | (252) 399-6552 |
| Baruch College | III | 55 Lexington Ave., New York, NY 10010 | Miguel Iglesias | (646) 312-5052 |
| Bates College | III | 130 Central Ave., Lewiston, ME 04240 | Craig Vandersea | (207) 786-6063 |
| Becker College | III | 964 Main St., Leicester, MA 01524 | Walter Beede | (508) 791-9241 |
| Belhaven College | A | 1500 Peachtree St., Jackson, MS 39202 | Hill Denson | (601) 968-8898 |
| Bellarmine College | II | 2001 Newburg Rd., Louisville, KY 40205 | Deron Spink | (502) 452-8278 |
| Bellevue U. | A | 1000 Galvin Rd. S., Bellevue, NE 68005 | Mike Evans | (402) 293-3782 |
| Belmont Abbey College | II | 100 Belmont-Mount Holly Rd., Belmont, NC 28012 | Kermit Smith | (704) 825-6804 |
| Beloit College | III | 700 College St., Beloit, WI 53511 | Dave DeGeorge | (608) 363-2039 |
| Bemidji State U. | II | 1500 Birchmont Dr. NE, Bemidji, MN 56601 | Unavailable | (218) 755-4620 |
| Benedict College | II | 1600 Harden St., Columbia, SC 29204 | Derrick Johnson | (803) 733-7421 |
| Benedictine College | A | 1020 N. 2nd St., Atchison, KS 66002 | Dan Griggs | (913) 360-5376 |
| Benedictine U. | III | 5700 College Rd., Lisle, IL 60532 | John Ostrowski | (630) 829-6147 |
| Bentley College | II | 175 Forest St., Waltham, MA 02452 | Bob DeFelice | (781) 891-2332 |
| Berea College | A | CPO 2187, Berea, KY 40404 | Ryan Hess | (859) 985-3429 |
| Berry College | A | PO Box 495015, Mount Berry, GA 30149 | David Beasley | (706) 236-1743 |
| Bethany College | III | Hummel Fieldhouse, Bethany, WV 26032 | Rick Carver | (304) 829-7246 |
| Bethany College | A | 800 Bethany Dr., Scotts Valley, CA 95066 | Dennis Patton | (831) 438-3800 |
| Bethany College | A | 421 N. First, Lindsborg, KS 67456 | Matt Tramel | (785) 227-3380 |
| Bethany Lutheran College | III | 700 Luther Dr., Mankato, MN 56001 | Ryan Kragh | (507) 344-7868 |

| Bethel College | A | 1001 W. McKinley Ave, Mishawaka, IN 46545 | Seth Zartman | (574) 257-3287 |
|---|---|---|---|---|
| Bethel College | A | 325 E. Cherry Ave., McKenzie, TN 38201 | Glenn Hayes | (731) 352-4206 |
| Bethel U. | III | 3900 Bethel Dr., St. Paul, MN 55112 | Greg Indlecoffer | (651) 638-6143 |
| Biola U. | A | 13800 Biola Ave, La Mirada, CA 90639 | John Verhoeven | (562) 944-0351 |
| Blackburn College | III | 700 College Ave., Carlinville, IL 62626 | Mike Neal | (217) 854-3231 |
| Bloomfield College | II | 467 Franklin St., Bloomfield, NJ 07003 | Matt Belford | (973) 748-9000 |
| Bloomsburg U. | II | 400 E. 2nd St., Bloomsburg, PA 17815 | Mike Collins | (570) 389-4375 |
| Bluefield College | A | Box 38, Bluefield, VA 24605 | Mike Scolinos | (276) 322-5071 |
| Bluefield State College | II | 219 Rock St., Bluefield, WV 24701 | Geoff Hunter | (304) 327-4084 |
| Bluffton U. | III | 1 University Dr., Bluffton, OH 45817 | James Grandey | (419) 358-3292 |
| Bowdoin College | III | 9000 College Station, Brunswick, ME 04011 | Michael Connolly | (207) 725-3734 |
| Brandeis U. | III | Gosman Sports Center, MS 007, Waltham, MA 02454 | Pete Varney | (781) 736-3639 |
| Brescia U. | A | 717 Frederica St., Owensboro, KY 42301 | Jason Vittone | (270) 686-4207 |
| Brevard College | A | 400 N. Broad St., Brevard, NC 28712 | Gill Payne | (828) 884-8273 |
| Brewton Parker College | A | Hwy. 280, Mt. Vernon, GA 30445 | Chad Parker | (912) 583-3177 |
| Briar Cliff U. | A | PO Box 2100, Sioux City, IA 51104 | Boyd Pitkin | (712) 279-5553 |
| Briarcliffe College | U | 1055 Stewart Ave., Bethpage, NY 11714 | Gary Puccio | (516) 918-3730 |
| Bridgeport, U. of | II | 120 Waldemere Ave., Bridgeport, CT 06601 | John Anquillare | (203) 576-4229 |
| Bridgewater College | III | 402 E. College St., Bridgewater, VA 22812 | Curt Kendall | (540) 828-5407 |
| Bridgewater State College | III | 200-325 Plymouth St., Bridgewater, MA 02325 | Rick Smith | (508) 531-2898 |
| British Columbia, U. of | A | 272-6081 University Blvd., Vancouver, B.C. V6T 1Z1 | Terry McKaig | (604) 822-4270 |
| Bryan College | A | PO Box 7000, Dayton, TN 37321 | Joel Johnson | (423) 775-7569 |
| Bryant U. | II | 1150 Douglas Pike, Smithfield, RI 02917 | Jon Sjogren | (401) 232-6397 |
| Buena Vista U. | III | 610 West 4th St., Storm Lake, IA 50588 | Steve Eddie | (712) 749-2298 |
| C.W. Post/Long Island U. | II | 720 Northern Blvd., Brookville, NY 11548 | Pete Timmes | (516) 299-2287 |
| Caldwell College | II | 9 Ryerson Ave., Caldwell, NJ 07006 | Chris Reardon | (973) 618-3462 |
| UC San Diego | III | 9500 Gilman Dr., La Jolla, CA 92093 | Dan O'Brien | (858) 534-4211 |
| Cal Poly Pomona | II | 3801 West Temple Ave., Pomona, CA 91768 | Mike Ashman | (909) 869-2829 |
| Cal State Dominguez Hills | II | 1000 E. Victoria St., Carson, CA 90747 | George Wing | (310) 243-3765 |
| Cal State East Bay | III | 25800 Carlos Bee Blvd., Hayward, CA 94542 | Dirk Morrison | (510) 885-3046 |
| Cal State Los Angeles | II | 5151 State University Dr., Los Angeles, CA 90032 | Dave Taylor | (323) 343-3093 |
| Cal State Monterey Bay | II | 100 Campus Ctr., Seaside, CA 93955 | Rich Aldrete | (831) 582-3015 |
| Cal State San Bernardino | II | 5500 University Pwy., San Bernardino, CA 92407 | Don Parnell | (909) 880-5021 |
| Cal State Stanislaus | II | 801 W. Monte Vista Ave., Turlock, CA 95382 | Kenny Leonesio | (209) 667-3272 |
| Cal Tech | III | 1200 E. California Blvd., Pasadena, CA 91125 | John D'Auria | (626) 395-3263 |
| California Baptist U. | A | 8432 Magnolia Ave., Riverside, CA 92504 | Gary Adcock | (951) 343-4382 |
| California Lutheran U. | III | 60 W. Olsen Rd., Thousand Oaks, CA 91360 | Marty Slimak | (805) 493-3398 |
| California U. (Pa.) | II | 250 University Ave., California, PA 15419 | Mike Conte | (724) 938-4388 |
| Calumet College | A | 2400 New York Ave., Whiting, IN 46394 | Dan Soria | (219) 473-4241 |
| Calvin College | III | 3195 Knight Way SE, Grand Rapids, MI 49546 | Jim Timmer | (616) 526-6037 |
| Cameron U. | II | 2800 West Gore Blvd., Lawton, OK 73505 | Todd Holland | (580) 581-2479 |
| Campbellsville U. | A | PO Box 1316, Campbellsville, KY 42718 | Beauford Sanders | (270) 789-5056 |
| Capital U. | III | 2199 E. Main St., Columbus, OH 43209 | Greg Weyrich | (614) 236-6203 |
| Cardinal Stritch U. | A | 6801 N. Yates Rd., Milwaukee, WI 53217 | Michael Zolecki | (414) 410-4519 |
| Carleton College | III | One N. College St., Northfield, MN 55057 | Aaron Rushing | (507) 646-4051 |
| Carroll College | III | 100 N. East Ave, Waukesha, WI 53186 | Steve Dannhoff | (262) 524-7105 |
| Carson-Newman College | II | 2130 Branner Ave., Jefferson City, TN 37760 | Tom Griffin | (865) 471-3465 |
| Carthage College | III | 2001 Alford Park Dr., Kenosha, WI 53140 | Augie Schmidt | (262) 551-5935 |
| Case Western Reserve U. | III | 10900 Euclid Ave., Cleveland, OH 44106 | Jerry Seimon | (216) 368-5379 |
| Castleton State College | III | One Glennbrook Rd., Castleton, VT 05735 | Ted Shipley | (802) 468-1491 |
| Catawba College | II | 2300 W. Innes St., Salisbury, NC 28144 | Jim Gantt | (704) 637-4469 |
| Catholic U. | III | 3606 McCormack Rd. NE, Washington, DC 20064 | Ross Natoli | (202) 319-6092 |
| Cazenovia College | III | Liberty Street, Cazenovia, NY 13035 | Peter Liddell | (315) 655-7141 |
| Cedarville U. | A | 251 N. Main St., Cedarville, OH 45314 | Greg Hughes | (937) 766-3246 |
| Centenary College | III | 400 Jefferson St., Hackettstown, NJ 07840 | Dave Sawicki | (908) 852-1400 |
| Central Arkansas, U. of | II | PO Box 5004, Conway, AR 72032 | Doug Clark | (501) 450-3407 |
| Central Baptist College | C | 1501 College Ave., Conway, AR, 72032 | Jason McGinty | (501) 329-6872 |
| Central Christian College | A | PO Box 1403, McPherson, KS 67460 | Jared Hamilton | (620) 241-0723 |
| Central College | III | 812 University St., Pella, IA 50219 | Adam Stevens | (641) 628-5396 |
| Central Methodist U. | A | 411 Central Methodist Square, Fayette, MO 65248 | Van Vanatta | (660) 248-6352 |
| Central Missouri State U. | II | 500 Washington St., Warrensburg, MO 64093 | Darin Hendrickson | (660) 543-4800 |
| Central Oklahoma, U. of | II | 100 N. University Dr., Edmond, OK 73034 | Wendell Simmons | (405) 974-2506 |
| Central Washington U. | II | 400 E. University Way, Ellensburg, WA 98926 | Desi Storey | (509) 963-3018 |
| Centre College | III | 600 W. Walnut St., Danville, KY 40422 | Mike Pritchard | (859) 238-5489 |
| Chapman U. | III | One University Dr., Orange, CA 92866 | Tom Tereschuk | (714) 997-6662 |
| Charleston, U. of | II | 2300 MacCorkle Ave. SE, Charleston, WV 25304 | Tom Nozica | (304) 357-4823 |
| Chicago, U. of | III | 5530 S. Ellis Ave., Chicago, IL 60637 | Brian Baldea | (773) 702-4643 |
| Chico State U. | II | 1st & Orange Sts., Chico, CA 95929 | Lindsay Meggs | (530) 898-4374 |
| Chowan College | III | 200 Jones Dr., Murfreesboro, NC 27855 | Aaron Carroll | (252) 398-6287 |
| Christian Brothers U. | II | 650 E. Parkway South, Memphis, TN 38104 | Phil Goodwin | (901) 321-3375 |
| Christopher Newport U. | III | 1 University Place, Newport News, VA 23606 | John Harvell | (757) 594-7054 |
| Circleville Bible Coll. | C | 1476 Lancaster Pike, Circleville, OH 43113 | Larry Olson | (740) 477-7761 |
| Claflin U. | II | 400 Magnolia St., Orangeburg, SC 29115 | Brian Newsome | (803) 535-5295 |

| Claremont-Mudd-Scripps Col | III | 500 E. 9th St., Claremont, CA 91711 | Randy Town | (909) 607-3796 |
|---|---|---|---|---|
| Clarion U. | II | Wood St., Tippin Gym, Room 112 Clarion, PA 16214 | Scott Feldman | (814) 393-1651 |
| Clark Atlanta U. | II | 223 Brawley Dr. SW, Atlanta, GA 30314 | Chris Atwell | (404) 880-8215 |
| Clark U. | III | 950 Main St., Worcester, MA 01610 | Jason Falcon | (508) 421-3832 |
| Clarke College | III | 1550 Clarke Dr., Dubuque, IA 52001 | Eric Frese | (563) 588-6601 |
| Clarkson U. | III | 8 Clarkson Ave., CU Box 5830, Potsdam, NY 13669 | Jim Kane | (315) 268-3759 |
| Clearwater Christian | C | 2400 Gulf-to-Bay Blvd., Clearwater, FL 33759 | Steve Milton | (727) 726-1153 |
| Coe College | III | 1220 First Ave. NE, Cedar Rapids, IA 52402 | Steve Cook | (319) 399-8849 |
| Coker College | II | 300 E. College Ave., Hartsville, SC 29550 | Dave Schmotzer | (843) 383-8105 |
| Colby College | III | 4900 Mayflower Hill, Waterville, ME 04901 | Tom Dexter | (207) 859-4917 |
| Colby-Sawyer College | III | 541 Main St., New London, NH 03257 | Jim Broughton | (603) 526-3607 |
| Colorado Christian U. | II | 180 S. Garrison St., Lakewood, CO 80226 | Robb Pegg | (303) 963-3180 |
| Colorado School of Mines | II | 1500 Illinois St., Volk Gym, Golden, CO 80401 | Mike Mulvaney | (303) 273-3367 |
| Colorado State U.-Pueblo | II | 2200 N. Bonforte Blvd., Pueblo, CO 81001 | Stan Sanchez | (719) 549-2065 |
| Columbia Union College | II | 7600 Flower Ave., Takoma Park, MD 20912 | Michael Ricucci | (301) 891-4026 |
| Columbus State U. | II | 4225 University Ave., Columbus, GA 31907 | Greg Appleton | (706) 568-2444 |
| Concord U. | II | Campus Box 77, Athens, WV 24712 | Kevin Garrett | (304) 384-5340 |
| Concordia College (Ala.) | U | 1804 Green St., Selma, AL 36701 | Raymond Brown | (334) 874-5700 |
| Concordia College (Minn.) | III | 901 8th Street S., Moorhead, MN 56562 | Don Burgau | (218) 299-3209 |
| Concordia College (N.Y.) | II | 171 White Plains Rd., Bronxville, NY 10708 | Bob Greiner | (914) 337-9300 |
| Concordia U. (Calif.) | A | 1530 Concordia West, Irvine, CA 92612 | Tony Barbone | (949) 584-8002 |
| Concordia U. (Ill.) | III | 7400 Augusta St., River Forest, IL 60305 | Spiro Lempesis | (708) 209-3125 |
| Concordia U. (Mich.) | A | 4090 Geddes Rd., Ann Arbor, MI 48105 | Karl Kling | (734) 995-7343 |
| Concordia U. (Minn.) | II | 275 Syndicate St. N., St. Paul, MN 55104 | Mark McKenzie | (651) 603-6208 |
| Concordia U. (Neb.) | A | 800 N. Columbia Ave., Seward, NE 68434 | Jeremy Geidel | (402) 643-7347 |
| Concordia U. (Ore.) | A | 2811 NE Holman St., Portland, OR 97211 | Rob Vance | (503) 280-8691 |
| Concordia U. (Texas) | III | 3400 I-35 North, Austin, TX 78705 | Mike Gardner | (512) 486-1160 |
| Concordia U. (Wis.) | III | 12800 N. LakeShore Dr., Mequon, WI 53097 | Val Keiper | (262) 243-4266 |
| Corban College | A | 5000 Deer Park Dr. SE, Salem, OR 97301 | Larry Casian | (503) 589-8183 |
| Cornell College | III | 600 1st St. W., Mount Vernon, IA 52314 | Frank Fisher | (319) 895-4150 |
| Covenant College | A | 14049 Scenic Hwy., Lookout Mountain, GA 30750 | Doug Simons | (706) 419-1507 |
| Crichton College | A | 255 N. Highland, Memphis, TN 38111 | Junior Weaver | (901) 320-1706 |
| Crown College | III | 8700 College View Dr., St. Bonafacius, MN 55375 | Kelly Spann | (952) 446-4146 |
| Culver-Stockton College | A | One College Hill, Canton, MO 63435 | Doug Bletcher | (573) 288-6374 |
| Cumberlands, U. of the | A | 7526 College Station Dr., Williamsburg, KY 40769 | Brad Shelton | (606) 539-4387 |
| Cumberland U. | A | One Cumberland Sq., Lebanon, TN 37087 | Woody Hunt | (615) 444-2562 |
| Curry College | III | 1071 Blue Hill Ave., Miller Gym, Milton, MA 02186 | Dave Perdios | (617) 333-2055 |
| D'Youville College | III | 320 Porter Ave., Buffalo, NY 14201 | Jeff Helmbrecht | (716) 829-7789 |
| Dakota State U. | A | 820 N. Washington Ave, Madison, SD 57042 | Pat Dolan | (605) 256-5235 |
| Dakota Wesleyan U. | A | 1200 W. University Ave, Mitchell, SD 57301 | Adam Neisius | (605) 995-2853 |
| Dallas, U. of | III | 1845 E. Northgate Dr., Irving, TX 75062 | Chris Strockbine | (972) 265-5778 |
| Dana College | A | 2848 College Dr., Blair, NE 68008 | Chad Gorman | (402) 426-7913 |
| Daniel Webster College | III | 20 University Dr., Nashua, NH 03063 | Jim Cardello | (603) 577-6497 |
| David N. Myers U. | A | 3813 Euclid Ave., Cleveland, OH 44115 | Charles Cangeosi | (216) 432-8950 |
| Davis & Elkins College | II | 100 Campus Dr., Elkins, WV 26241 | Ryan Brisbin | (304) 637-1342 |
| Defiance College | III | 701 N. Clinton St., Defiance, OH 43512 | Chad Donsbach | (419) 783-2341 |
| Delaware Valley College | III | 700 E. Butler Ave., Doylestown, PA 18901 | Bob Altieri | (215) 489-2379 |
| Delta State U. | II | DSU BOX A3, Cleveland, MS 38733 | Mike Kinnison | (662) 846-4291 |
| Denison U. | III | PO Box 111, Granville, OH 43023 | Barry Craddock | (740) 587-6714 |
| DePauw U. | III | Lilly Center, Greencastle, IN 46135 | Matt Walker | (765) 658-4939 |
| DeSales U. | III | 2755 Station Ave., Center Valley, PA 18034 | Tim Nieman | (610) 282-1100 |
| Dickinson College | III | PO Box 1773, Carlisle, PA 17013 | Russell Wrenn | (717) 245-1320 |
| Dickinson State U. | A | 291 Campus Dr., Dickinson, ND 58601 | Duane Monlux | (701) 483-2716 |
| Doane College | A | 1014 Boswell Ave., Crete, NE 68333 | Jack Hudkins | (402) 826-8646 |
| Dominican College | II | 470 Western Hwy., Orangeburg, NY 10962 | Rick Giannetti | (845) 398-3008 |
| Dominican U. | III | 7900 W. Division St., River Forest, IL 60305 | Terry Casey | (708) 524-6542 |
| Dordt College | A | 498 4th Ave. NE, Sioux Center, IA 51250 | Jeff Schouten | (712) 722-6232 |
| Dowling College | II | 150 Idle Hour Blvd., Oakdale, NY 11769 | Chris Celano | (631) 244-3229 |
| Drew U. | III | 36 Madison Ave., Madison, NJ 07940 | Vince Masco | (973) 408-3443 |
| Dubuque, U. of | III | 2000 University Ave., Dubuque, IA 52001 | Shane Schmellsmidt | (563) 589-3124 |
| Earlham College | III | 801 National Rd. W., Richmond, IN 47374 | Tom Parkevich | (765) 983-1237 |
| East Central U. | II | 1100 East 14th St., Ada, OK 74820 | Ron Hill | (580) 436-4940 |
| East Stroudsburg U. | II | Smith & Normal St., East Stroudsburg, PA 18301 | Roger Barren | (570) 422-3263 |
| East Texas Baptist U. | III | 1209 N. Grove St., Marshall TX 75670 | Robert Riggs | (903) 923-2228 |
| Eastern U. | III | 1300 Eagle Rd., St. Davids, PA 19087 | Brian Burke | (610) 341-1582 |
| Eastern Connecticut State U. | III | 83 Windham St., Willimantic, CT 06226 | Bill Holowaty | (860) 465-5185 |
| Eastern Mennonite U. | III | 1200 Park Rd., Harrisonburg, VA 22802 | Rob Roeschley | (540) 432-4333 |
| Eastern Nazarene College | III | 23 East Elm Ave., Quincy, MA 02170 | Todd Reid | (617) 745-3648 |
| Eastern New Mexico U. | II | Greyhound Arena, Station 17, Portales, NM 88130 | Phil Clabaugh | (505) 562-2889 |
| Eastern Oregon U. | A | One University Blvd., La Grande, OR 97850 | Wes McAllaster | (541) 962-3110 |
| Eckerd College | II | 4200 54th Ave. S., St. Petersburg, FL 33711 | Bill Mathews | (727) 864-8253 |
| Edgewood College | III | 1000 Edgewood College Dr., Madison, WI 53711 | Al Brisack | (608) 663-3289 |

| College | Div | Address | Coach | Phone |
|---|---|---|---|---|
| Edward Waters College | A | 1658 Kings Rd., Jacksonville, FL 32209 | Carl Burden | (904) 470-8276 |
| Elizabeth City State U. | II | Campus Box 900, Elizabeth City, NC 27909 | Terrance Whittle | (252) 335-3392 |
| Elizabethtown College | III | One Alpha Dr., Elizabethtown, PA 17022 | Matt Jones | (717) 361-1463 |
| Elmhurst College | III | 190 Prospect Ave., Elmhurst, IL 60126 | Clark Jones | (630) 617-3143 |
| Elms College | III | 291 Springfield St., Chicopee, MA 01013 | Don LaValley | (413) 265-2433 |
| Embry-Riddle U. | A | 600 S. Clyde Morris Blvd., Daytona Beach, FL 32114 | Greg Guilliams | (386) 323-5010 |
| Emmanuel College | A | PO Box 129, Franklin Springs, GA 30639 | Aaron Brister | (706) 245-2859 |
| Emory & Henry College | III | King Athletic Center, 1 Garnand Dr., Emory, VA 24327 | Trey McCall | (276) 944-6860 |
| Emory U. | III | 600 Asbury Circle, Atlanta, GA 30322 | Mike Twardoski | (404) 727-0877 |
| Emporia State U. | II | 12th & Commercial St., Emporia, KS 66801 | Bob Fornelli | (620) 341-5930 |
| Endicott College | III | 376 Hale St., Beverly, MA 01915 | Larry Hiser | (978) 232-2304 |
| Erskine College | II | PO Box 338, Due West, SC 29639 | Kevin Nichols | (864) 379-8777 |
| Eureka College | III | 300 E. College Ave., Eureka, IL 61530 | Robert Doty | (309) 467-6372 |
| Evangel U. | A | 1111 N. Glenstone Ave, Springfield, MO 65802 | Al Poland | (417) 865-2815 |
| Fairleigh Dickinson U.-Florham | III | 285 Madison Ave., Madison, NJ 07940 | Doug Radziewicz | (973) 443-8826 |
| Fairmont State College | II | 1201 Locust Ave., Fairmont, WV 26554 | Ray Bonnett | (304) 367-4220 |
| Faulkner U. | A | 5345 Atlanta Hwy., Montgomery, AL 36109 | Andy Priola | (334) 386-7318 |
| Felician College | II | 262 S. Main St., Lodi, NJ 07644 | Chris Langan | (201) 559-3509 |
| Ferrum College | III | 435 Ferrum Mtn. Rd., Ferrum, VA 24088 | Abe Naff | (540) 365-4488 |
| Findlay, U. of | II | 1000 N. Main St., Findlay, OH 45840 | Troy Berry | (419) 434-6684 |
| Finlandia U. | III | 601 W. Quincy St., Hancock, MI 49930 | Matt Farrell | (906) 487-7212 |
| Fisher College | A | 118 Beacon St., Boston, MA 02116 | Scott Dulin | (617) 236-8877 |
| Fisk U. | III | 17 Avenue N., Nashville, TN 37208 | McKinley Young | (615) 329-1109 |
| Fitchburg State College | III | 160 Pearl St., Fitchburg, MA 01420 | Pete Egbert | (978) 665-3726 |
| Flagler College | A | PO Box 1027, St. Augustine, FL 32085 | David Barnett | (904) 819-6252 |
| Florida College | U | 119 N. Glen Arven Ave., Temple Terrace, FL 33617 | Rich Leggatt | (813) 899-6789 |
| Florida Gulf Coast U. | II | 10501 FGCU Blvd. S., Fort Myers, FL 33965 | Dave Tollett | (239) 590-7051 |
| Florida Memorial U. | A | 15800 NW 42nd Ave., Miami, FL 33054 | Robert Smith | (305) 626-3168 |
| Florida Southern College | II | 111 Lake Hollingsworth Dr., Lakeland, FL 33801 | Pete Meyer | (863) 680-4264 |
| Florida Tech | II | 150 W. University Blvd., Melbourne, FL 32901 | Paul Knight | (321) 674-8193 |
| Fontbonne U. | III | 6800 Wydown St., St. Louis, MO 63105 | Michael Domenick | (314) 719-8064 |
| Fort Hays State U. | II | 600 Park St., Hays, KS 67601 | Matt Ranson | (785) 628-4357 |
| Framingham State College | III | 100 State St., Framingham, MA 01701 | Mike Sarno | (508) 626-4566 |
| Francis Marion U. | II | PO Box 100547, Florence, SC 29501 | Art Inabinet | (843) 661-1242 |
| Franklin & Marshall College | III | PO Box 3003, Lancaster, PA 17604 | Brett Boretti | (717) 358-4530 |
| Franklin College | III | 101 Branigin Blvd., Franklin, IN 46131 | Lance Marshall | (317) 738-8136 |
| Franklin Pierce College | II | 20 College Rd., Rindge, NH 03461 | Jayson King | (603) 899-4084 |
| Fredonia State U. | III | Dods Hall, Fredonia, NY 14063 | Matt Palisin | (716) 673-3743 |
| Free Will Baptist College | C | 3606 West End Ave., Nashville, TN 37205 | Mick Donahue | (615) 485-2510 |
| Freed-Hardeman U. | A | 158 E. Main St., Henderson, TN 38340 | Patrick McCarthy | (731) 989-6994 |
| Fresno Pacific U. | A | 1717 S. Chestnut Ave., Fresno, CA 93702 | Oscar Hirschkorn | (559) 453-2050 |
| Friends U. | A | 2100 W. University St., Wichita, KS 67213 | Mark Carvalho | (316) 295-5769 |
| Frostburg State U. | III | 101 Braddock Rd, Frostburg, MD 21532 | Chris McKnight | (301) 687-4273 |
| Gallaudet U. | III | 800 Florida Ave. NE, Washington, DC 20002 | Kris Gould | (202) 651-5603 |
| Gannon U. | II | 109 University Square, Erie, PA 16541 | Rick Iacobucci | (814) 871-5846 |
| Geneva College | A | 3200 College Ave., Beaver Falls, PA 15010 | Alan Sumner | (724) 847-6647 |
| George Fox U. | III | 414 N. Meridian St., Newberg, OR 97132 | Pat Bailey | (503) 554-2914 |
| Georgetown College | A | 400 E. College St., Georgetown, KY 40324 | Erik Hagen | (502) 863-8207 |
| Georgia College & State U. | II | Campus Box 65, Milledgeville, GA 31061 | Chris Calciano | (478) 445-5319 |
| Georgia Southwestern | A | 800 Wheatley St., Americus, GA 31709 | Bryan McLain | (229) 931-2843 |
| Gettysburg College | III | 300 N. Washington St, Gettysburg, PA 17325 | John Campo | (717) 337-6413 |
| Gordon College | III | 255 Grapevine Rd., Wenham, MA 01984 | Joe Scarano | (978) 867-4116 |
| Goshen College | A | 1700 S. Main St., Goshen, IN 46526 | Josh Keister | (574) 535-7748 |
| Grace College | A | 200 Seminary Dr., Winona Lake, IN 46590 | Glenn Goldsmith | (574) 372-5100 |
| Graceland U. | A | 1 University Pl., Lamoni, IA 50140 | Brady McKillip | (641) 784-5351 |
| Grand Canyon U. | II | PO Box 11097, Phoenix, AZ 85061 | Dave Stapleton | (602) 589-2817 |
| Grand Valley State U. | II | 192 Fieldhouse, 1 Campus Dr., Allendale, MI 49401 | Steve Lyon | (616) 331-3584 |
| Grand View College | A | 1200 Grandview Ave., Des Moines, IA 50316 | Lou Yacinich | (515) 263-2965 |
| Greensboro College | III | 815 W. Market St., Greensboro, NC 27401 | Ken Carlyle | (336) 272-7102 |
| Greenville College | III | 315 E. College Ave., Greenville, IL 62246 | Lynn Carlson | (618) 664-6623 |
| Grinnell College | III | 1118 10th Ave., Grinnell, IA 50112 | Tim Hollibaugh | (641) 269-3822 |
| Grove City College | III | 100 Campus Dr., Grove City, PA 16127 | Rob Skaricich | (724) 458-3836 |
| Guilford College | III | 5800 W. Friendly Ave., Greensboro, NC 27410 | Unavailable | (336) 316-2161 |
| Gustavus Adolphus College | III | 800 W. College Ave., St. Peter, MN 56082 | Mike Carroll | (507) 933-6297 |
| Gwynedd-Mercy College | III | 1325 Sumneytown Pike, Gwynedd Valley, PA 19437 | Paul Murphy | (215) 646-7300 |
| Hamilton College | III | 198 College Hill Rd., Clinton, NY 13323 | Rocco Bouse | (315) 859-4589 |
| Hamline U. | III | 1536 Hewitt Ave., St. Paul, MN 55104 | Jason Verdugo | (651) 523-2035 |
| Hampden-Sydney College | III | 1 Kirby Field House Lane, Hampden-Sydney, VA 23943 | Jeff Kinne | (434) 223-6981 |
| Hannibal-LaGrange College | A | 2800 Palmyra Rd., Hannibal, MO 63401 | Brad Lingafelter | (573) 221-3675 |
| Hanover College | III | PO Box 108, Hanover, IN 47243 | Shayne Stock | (812) 866-7374 |
| Hardin-Simmons U. | III | PO Box 16185, Abilene, TX 79698 | Steve Coleman | (325) 670-1493 |
| Harding U. | II | Box 12281, Searcy, AR 72149 | Patrick McGaha | (501) 279-4344 |

| College | | Address | Contact | Phone |
|---|---|---|---|---|
| Harris-Stowe State College | A | 3026 Laclede Ave., St. Louis, MO 63103 | Darren Munns | (314) 340-3530 |
| Hartwick College | III | Binder Phys. Ed. Ctr., Oneonta, NY 13820 | Doug Kimbler | (607) 431-4706 |
| Hastings College | A | PO Box 269, Hastings, NE 68901 | Jim Boeve | (402) 461-7468 |
| Haverford College | III | 370 Lancaster Ave., Haverford, PA 19041 | Dave Beccaria | (610) 896-1172 |
| Hawaii Pacific U. | II | 1060 Bishop St., Honolulu, HI 96813 | Garrett Yukumoto | (808) 543-8021 |
| Heidelberg College | III | 310 E. Market St., Tiffin, OH 44883 | Matt Palm | (419) 448-2009 |
| Henderson State U. | II | PO Box 7630, Arkadelphia, AR 71999 | John Harvey | (870) 230-5071 |
| Hendrix College | III | 1600 Washington Ave., Conway, AR 72032 | Lane Stahl | (501) 450-3898 |
| Hesser College | U | 3 Sundial Ave., Manchester, NH 03103 | Eric Woods | (603) 668-6660 |
| Hilbert College | III | 5200 S. Park Ave, Hamburg, NY 14075 | Randy Cialone | (716) 649-7900 |
| Hillsdale College | II | 201 Oak St., Hillsdale, MI 49242 | Paul Noce | (517) 607-3146 |
| Hillsdale Free Will Baptist | C | PO Box 7208, Moore, OK 73153 | James Coil | (405) 912-9094 |
| Hiram College | III | PO Box 1777, Hiram, OH 44234 | Howard Jenter | (330) 569-5348 |
| Hope College | III | PO Box 9000, Holland, MI 49422 | Stu Fritz | (616) 395-7692 |
| Houston Baptist U. | A | 7502 Fondren Rd., Houston, TX 77074 | Brian Huddleston | (281) 649-3332 |
| Howard Payne U. | III | 508 2nd St., Brownwood, TX 76801 | Stephen Lynn | (325) 649-8117 |
| Huntingdon College | III | 1500 E. Fairview Ave, Montgomery, AL 36106 | D.J. Conville | (334) 833-4252 |
| Huntington U. | A | 2303 College Ave., Huntington, IN 46750 | Mike Frame | (260) 359-4082 |
| Husson College | III | 1 College Circle, Husson, ME 04401 | John Winkin | (207) 941-7096 |
| Huston-Tillotson College | A | 900 Chicon St., Austin, TX 78702 | Alvin Moore | (512) 505-3151 |
| Illinois College | III | 1101 W. College Ave., Jacksonville, IL 62650 | Jay Eckhouse | (217) 245-3387 |
| Illinois Tech | A | 3300 S. Federal St., Chicago, IL 60616 | John Fitzgerald | (312) 567-7128 |
| Illinois Wesleyan U. | III | PO Box 2900, Bloomington, IL 61702 | Dennis Martel | (309) 556-3335 |
| Incarnate Word, U. of the | II | 4301 Broadway St., San Antonio, TX 78209 | Danny Heep | (210) 829-3830 |
| Indiana Tech | A | 1600 E. Washington Blvd., Fort Wayne, IN 46803 | Randy Stegall | (260) 422-5561 |
| Indiana U. (Pa.) | II | 660 S. 11th St., Indiana, PA 15705 | Jeffrey Ditch | (724) 357-7830 |
| Indiana U.-Northwest | A | 3400 Broadway, Gary, IN 46408 | Tom Bainbridge | (219) 980-6746 |
| Indiana U.-Southeast | A | 4201 Grantline Rd., New Albany, IN 47150 | Joe Decker | (812) 941-2435 |
| Indiana Wesleyan U. | A | 4201 S. Washington St., Marion, IN 46953 | Mark DeMichael | (765) 677-2324 |
| Indianapolis, U. of | II | 1400 E. Hanna Ave., Indianapolis, IN 46227 | Gary Vaught | (317) 788-3414 |
| Iowa Wesleyan College | A | 601 N. Main St., Mount Pleasant, IA 52641 | Matt Cloud | (319) 385-6349 |
| Ithaca College | III | Ceracche Athletics Ctr., Ithaca, NY 14850 | George Valesente | (607) 274-3749 |
| Jamestown College | A | 6000 College Lane, Jamestown, ND 58405 | Tom Hager | (701) 252-3467 |
| Jarvis Christian College | A | PO Box 1470, Hawkins, TX 75765 | Robert Thomas | (903) 769-5763 |
| John Carroll U. | III | 20700 N. Park Blvd., University Heights, OH 44118 | Marc Thibeault | (216) 397-4660 |
| John Jay College | III | 899 10th Ave., New York, NY 10019 | Dan Palumbo | (212) 237-8639 |
| Johns Hopkins U. | III | Newton H. White Jr. Athletic Ctr., Baltimore, MD 21218 | Bob Babb | (410) 516-7485 |
| Johnson & Wales U. | III | 8 Abbott Park Pl., Providence, RI 02903 | John LaRose | (401) 598-1609 |
| Johnson Bible College | C | 7900 Johnson Dr., Knoxville, TN 37998 | Jack Barr | (865) 251-2210 |
| Judson College | A | 1151 N. State St., Elgin, IL 60123 | Loren Torres | (847) 628-1579 |
| Juniata College | III | 1700 Moore St., Huntingdon, PA 16652 | George Zanic | (814) 641-3515 |
| Kalamazoo College | III | 1200 Academy St., Kalamazoo, MI 49006 | Steve Wideen | (269) 337-7287 |
| Kansas Wesleyan U. | A | 100 E. Claflin Ave, Salina, KS 67401 | Tim Bellew | (785) 827-5541 |
| Kean U. | III | 1000 Morris Ave., Union, NJ 07083 | Neil Ioviero | (908) 737-0614 |
| Keene State College | III | 229 Main St., Keene, NH 03435 | Ken Howe | (603) 357-2809 |
| Kentucky State U. | II | 400 E. Main St., Frankfort, KY 40601 | Elwood Johnson | (502) 597-6018 |
| Kentucky Wesleyan College | A | PO Box 1039, Owensboro, KY 42301 | Todd Lillpop | (270) 852-3342 |
| Kenyon College | III | Athletic Dept., Duff Street, Gambier, OH 43022 | Matt Burdette | (740) 427-5810 |
| Keuka College | III | 141 Central Ave., Keuka Park, NY 14478 | Chris Arnold | (315) 279-5687 |
| Keystone College | III | One College Green, La Plume, PA 18440 | Jamie Shevchik | (570) 945-8234 |
| King College | A | 1350 King College Rd., Bristol, TN 37620 | Larry Lipker | (423) 652-6017 |
| King's College | III | 133 N. River St., Wilkes-Barre, PA 18711 | Jerry Greeley | (570) 208-5855 |
| Knox College | III | 2 E. South St., Galesburg, IL 61401 | Jami Isaacson | (309) 341-7456 |
| Kutztown U. | II | Keystone Hall, Kutztown, PA 19530 | Chris Blum | (610) 683-4063 |
| La Roche College | III | 9000 Babcock Blvd., Pittsburgh, PA 15237 | Rich Pasquale | (412) 536-1046 |
| La Verne, U. of | III | 1950 3rd St., La Verne, CA 91750 | Scott Winterburn | (909) 593-3511 |
| LaGrange College | III | 601 Broad St., La Grange, GA 30240 | Kevin Howard | (706) 880-8295 |
| Lake Erie College | III | 391 W. Washington St., Painesville, OH 44077 | Ken Krsolovic | (440) 375-7470 |
| Lakeland College | III | PO Box 359, Sheboygan, WI 53082 | John Govek | (920) 565-1411 |
| Lambuth U. | A | 705 Lambuth Blvd., Jackson, TN 38301 | John Massey | (731) 425-3385 |
| Lancaster Bible College | C | 901 Eden Rd., Lancaster, PA 17608 | Unavailable | (717) 560-8267 |
| Lander U. | II | CPO 6016, Greenwood, SC 29649 | Unavailable | (864) 388-8961 |
| Lane College | II | 545 Lane Ave., Jackson, TN 38301 | John Gore | (731) 426-7571 |
| Lawrence U. | III | PO Box 599, Appleton, WI 54912 | Korey Krueger | (920) 832-7346 |
| Lebanon Valley College | III | 101 N. College Ave., Annville, PA 17003 | Keith Evans | (717) 867-6271 |
| Lee U. | A | PO Box 3450, Cleveland, TN 37320 | Dave Altopp | (423) 614-8445 |
| Lehman College | III | 250 Bedford Park Blvd. W., Bronx, NY 10468 | John Mehling | (718) 960-7746 |
| LeMoyne-Owen College | II | 807 Walker Ave., Memphis, TN 38126 | Eric Lee | (901) 942-6237 |
| Lenoir-Rhyne College | II | PO Box 7356, Hickory, NC 28603 | Frank Pait | (828) 328-7136 |
| LeTourneau U. | III | PO Box 7001, Longview, TX 75602 | Bernie Martinez | (903) 233-3771 |
| Lewis & Clark College | III | 0615 SW Palatine Hill Rd., Portland, OR 97219 | Justin Baughman | (503) 768-7059 |
| Lewis U. | II | One University Pkwy, Romeoville, IL 60446 | Irish O'Reilly | (815) 836-5255 |

| Name | Div | Address | Coach | Phone |
|---|---|---|---|---|
| Lewis-Clark State College | A | 500 8th Ave., Lewiston, ID 83501 | Ed Cheff | (208) 792-2272 |
| Limestone College | II | 1115 College Dr., Gaffney, SC 29340 | Chico Lombardo | (864) 488-4565 |
| Lincoln Christian College | C | 100 Campus View Dr., Lincoln, IL 62656 | Greg Lowes | (217) 732-3168 |
| Lincoln Memorial U. | II | PO Box 2028, Harrogate, TN 37752 | Jeff Sziksai | (423) 869-6345 |
| Lincoln U. | II | 820 Chestnut St., Jefferson City, MO 65102 | Jim Dapkus | (573) 681-5334 |
| Lincoln U. | III | PO Box 179, Lincoln University, PA 19352 | Douglas Thompson | (610) 932-8300 |
| Lindenwood U. | A | 209 S. Kings Highway, St. Charles, MO 63301 | Brian Behrens | (636) 949-4185 |
| Lindsey Wilson College | A | 210 Lindsey Wilson St., Columbia, KY 42728 | Mike Talley | (270) 384-8074 |
| Linfield College | III | 900 SE Baker St., McMinnville, OR 97128 | Scott Carnahan | (503) 883-2229 |
| Lock Haven U. | II | Thomas Fieldhouse, Lock Haven, PA 17745 | Smokey Stover | (570) 893-2245 |
| Longwood U. | II | 201 High St., Farmville, VA 23909 | Buddy Bolding | (434) 395-2352 |
| Loras College | III | 1450 Alta Vista St., Dubuque, IA 52004 | Carl Tebon | (563) 588-7732 |
| Louisiana College | III | 1140 College Dr., Pineville, LA 71359 | Mike Byrnes | (318) 487-7322 |
| Loyola U. | A | PO Box 53, New Orleans, LA 70118 | Michael Beeman | (504) 864-7392 |
| LSU-Shreveport | A | One University Place, Shreveport, LA 71115 | Rocke Musgraves | (318) 798-4106 |
| Lubbock Christian U. | A | 5601 19th St., Lubbock, TX 79407 | Nathan Blackwood | (806) 720-7853 |
| Luther College | III | 700 College Dr., Decorah, IA 52101 | Brian Gillogly | (563) 387-1590 |
| Lynchburg College | III | 1501 Lakeside Dr., Lynchburg, VA 24501 | Percy Abell | (434) 544-8496 |
| Lyndon State College | A | PO Box 919, Lyndonville, VT 05851 | Ryan Farley | (802) 626-6224 |
| Lynn U. | II | DeHoernle Sports & Cult. Ctr., Boca Raton, FL 33431 | Rudy Garbalosa | (561) 237-7242 |
| Lyon College | A | PO Box 2317, Batesville, AR 72503 | Kirk Kelley | (870) 698-4337 |
| Macalester College | III | 1600 Grand Ave., St. Paul, MN 55105 | Matt Parrington | (651) 696-6770 |
| MacMurray College | III | 447 E. College Ave, Jacksonville, IL 62650 | Kevin Vest | (217) 479-7153 |
| Madonna U. | A | 36600 Schoolcraft Rd., Livonia, MI 48150 | Greg Haeger | (734) 432-5609 |
| Maine-Farmington, U. of | III | 111 South St., Farmington, ME 04938 | Richard Meader | (207) 778-7148 |
| Maine-Presque Isle, U. of | III | 181 Main St., Presque Isle, ME 04769 | Doug Coldwell | (207) 768-9506 |
| Malone College | A | 515 25th St. NW, Canton, OH 44709 | Tom Crank | (330) 471-8286 |
| Manchester College | III | 604 E. College Ave., North Manchester, IN 46962 | Rick Espeset | (260) 982-5034 |
| Manhattan Christian College | C | 1415 Anderson Ave., Manhattan KS 66502 | Matt Barnett | (785) 539-3571 |
| Manhattanville College | III | 2900 Purchase St., Purchase, NY 10577 | Jeff Caulfield | (914) 323-7284 |
| Mansfield U. | II | Decker Gym, Mansfield, PA 16933 | Harry Hillson | (570) 662-4457 |
| Maranatha Baptist College | III | 745 W. Main St., Watertown, WI 53094 | Phil Price | (920) 206-2362 |
| Marian College | II | 45 S. National Ave., Fond du Lac, WI 54935 | Jason Bartelt | (920) 923-8090 |
| Marian College | A | 3200 Cold Spring Rd., Indianapolis, IN 46222 | Kurt Guldner | (317) 955-6310 |
| Marietta College | III | 215 5th St., Marietta, OH 45750 | Brian Brewer | (740) 376-4517 |
| Mars Hill College | II | 100 Athletic St., Mars Hill, NC 28754 | Daniel Taylor | (828) 689-1173 |
| Martin Luther College | III | 1995 Luther Court, New Ulm, MN 56073 | Drew Buck | (507) 354-8221 |
| Martin Methodist College | A | 433 W. Madison St., Pulaski, TN 38478 | George Ogilvie | (931) 363-9827 |
| Mary, U. of | II | 7500 University Dr., Bismarck, ND 58504 | Brad Walsh | (701) 355-8232 |
| Mary Hardin-Baylor U. | III | UMHB Box 8010, Belton, TX 76513 | Micah Wells | (254) 295-4619 |
| Mary Washington, U. of | III | 1301 College Ave., Fredericksburg, VA 22401 | Tom Sheridan | (540) 654-1882 |
| Maryville College | III | 502 E. Lamar Alexander Pkwy., Maryville, TN 37804 | Eric Etchison | (865) 981-8283 |
| Maryville U. | III | 13550 Conway Rd., St. Louis, MO 63141 | Mike Sigler | (314) 529-9355 |
| Marywood U. | III | 2300 Adams Ave., Scranton, PA 18509 | Joe Ross | (570) 961-4724 |
| Mass. College of Liberal Arts | III | 375 Church St., North Adams, MA 01247 | Jeff Puleri | (413) 662-5403 |
| Mass. Institute of Technology | III | MIT Box 397404, Cambridge, MA  02139 | Andy Barlow | (617) 258-7310 |
| Mass. Maritime Academy | III | 101 Academy Dr., Buzzards Bay, MA 02532 | Bob Corradi | (508) 830-5055 |
| Mass.-Boston, U. of | III | 100 Morrissey Blvd., Boston, MA 02125 | Brendan Eygabroat | (617) 287-7817 |
| Mass.-Dartmouth, U. of | III | 285 Old Wesport Rd., North Dartmouth, MA 02747 | Robert Curran | (508) 999-8721 |
| Mass-Lowell, U. of | II | 1 University Ave, Costello Gym, Lowell, MA 01854 | Ken Harring | (978) 934-2344 |
| Master's College, The | A | 21726 Placerita Canyon Rd., Santa Clarita, CA 91321 | Monte Brooks | (661) 259-3540 |
| Mayville State U. | A | 330 3rd St. NE, Mayville, ND 58257 | Scott Berry | (701) 788-4771 |
| McDaniel College | III | 2 College Hill, Westminster, MD 21157 | David Seibert | (410) 857-2583 |
| McKendree College | A | 701 College Rd., Lebanon, IL 62254 | Jim Boehne | (618) 537-6906 |
| McMurry U. | III | McM Box 188, Abilene, TX 79697 | Lee Driggers | (325) 793-4650 |
| Medaille College | III | 18 Agassiz Cir., Buffalo, NY 14214 | Ron Nero | (716) 884-3281 |
| Menlo College | A | 1000 El Camino Real, Atherton, CA 94027 | Ken Bowman | (650) 543-3932 |
| Mercy College | II | 555 Broadway, Dobbs Ferry, NY 10522 | Billy Sullivan | (914) 674-7566 |
| Mercyhurst College | II | 501 E. 38th St., Erie, PA 16546 | Joe Spano | (814) 824-2441 |
| Merrimack College | II | 315 Turnpike St., North Andover, MA 01845 | Joe Sarno | (978) 837-5000 |
| Mesa State College | II | 1100 North Ave., Grand Junction, CO 81501 | Chris Hanks | (970) 248-1891 |
| Messiah College | III | One College Ave., Grantham, PA 17027 | Frank Montgomery | (717) 766-2511 |
| Methodist College | III | 5400 Ramsey St., Fayetteville, NC 28311 | Tom Austin | (910) 630-7176 |
| Metropolitan State College | II | PO Box 173362, Campus Box 9, Denver, CO 80217 | Vince Porreco | (303) 556-3301 |
| Mid-America Christian U. | C | 3500 SW 119th St., Oklahoma City, OK 73170 | Jason Blackwell | (405) 692-3138 |
| Mid-Continent U. | A | 99 Powell Rd. E., Mayfield, KY 42066 | William Russell | (270) 247-8521 |
| MidAmerica Nazarene | A | 2030 E. College Way, Olathe, KS 66062 | Todd Garrett | (913) 791-3462 |
| Middlebury College | III | Memorial Fieldhouse, Middlebury, VT 05753 | Bob Smith | (802) 443-5264 |
| Midland Lutheran College | A | 900 N. Clarkson St., Fremont, NE 68025 | Jef Field | (402) 941-6371 |
| Miles College | II | 5500 Myron Massey Blvd., Birmingham, AL 35208 | Ken Hatcher | (205) 929-1617 |
| Millersville U. | II | PO Box 1002, Millersville, PA 17551 | Glenn Gallagher | (717) 871-2411 |
| Milligan College | A | PO Box 500, Milligan College, TN 37682 | Danny Clark | (423) 461-8722 |
| Millikin U. | III | 1184 W. Main St., Decatur, IL 62522 | Josh Manning | (217) 424-3608 |

| College | Div | Address | Contact | Phone |
|---|---|---|---|---|
| Millsaps College | III | 1701 N. State St., Jackson, MS 39210 | Jim Page | (601) 974-1196 |
| Milwaukee Engineering | III | 1025 N. Broadway, Milwaukee, WI 53202 | Unavailable | (414) 277-4552 |
| Minnesota-Crookston, U. of | II | 2900 University Ave., Crookston, MN 56716 | Steve Olson | (218) 281-8419 |
| Minnesota-Duluth, U. of | II | 1216 Ordean Ct., Duluth, MN 55812 | Unavailable | (218) 726-7967 |
| Minnesota-Morris, U. of | II | E. 2nd St., Morris, MN 56267 | Mark Fohl | (320) 589-6421 |
| Minnesota State U.-Mankato | II | 135 Myers Fieldhouse, Mankato, MN 56001 | Dean Bowyer | (507) 389-2689 |
| Minot State U. | A | 500 University Ave. W., Minot, ND 58707 | Randy Nelson | (701) 858-3833 |
| Misericordia College | III | 301 Lake St., Dallas, PA 18612 | Josh Tehonica | (570) 674-6374 |
| Mississippi College | III | PO Box 4049, Clinton, MS 39058 | Lee Kuyrkendall | (601) 925-3346 |
| Missouri Baptist U. | A | 1 College Park Dr., St. Louis, MO 63141 | Eddie Uschold | (314) 392-2384 |
| Missouri Southern State U. | II | 3950 E. Newman Rd, Joplin, MO 64801 | Warren Turner | (417) 625-9312 |
| Missouri-Rolla, U. of | II | 705 W. 10th St., Rolla, MO 65401 | Todd DeGraffenreid | (573) 341-4191 |
| Missouri-St. Louis, U. of | II | 8001 Natural Bridge Rd., St. Louis, MO 63121 | Jim Brady | (314) 516-5647 |
| Missouri Valley College | A | 500 E. College St., Marshall, MO 65340 | Scott Kelly | (660) 831-4113 |
| Missouri Western State U. | II | 4525 Downs Dr., St. Joseph, MO 64507 | Buzz Verduzco | (816) 271-4484 |
| Mitchell College | III | 437 Pequot Ave., New London, CT 06320 | Len Farquhar | (860) 701-5043 |
| Mobile, U. of | A | PO Box 13220, Mobile, AL 36663 | Mike Jacobs | (251) 442-2228 |
| Molloy College | II | PO Box 5002, Rockville Centre, NY 11570 | Joe Fucarino | (516) 256-2207 |
| Monmouth College | II | 700 E. Broadway, Monmouth, IL 61462 | Roger Sander | (309) 457-2169 |
| Montana State U.-Billings | II | 1500 University Dr., Billings, MT 59101 | Chris Brown | (406) 657-2394 |
| Montclair State U. | III | One Normal Ave., Montclair, NJ 07043 | Norm Schoenig | (973) 655-5281 |
| Montevallo, U. of | II | Station 6600, Montevallo, AL 35115 | Greg Goff | (205) 665-6761 |
| Montreat College | A | PO Box 1267, Montreat, NC 28757 | Travis Little | (828) 669-8011 |
| Moravian College | III | 1200 Main St., Bethlehem, PA 18018 | Ed Little | (610) 861-1536 |
| Morehouse College | II | 830 Westview Dr. SW, Atlanta, GA 30314 | Andre Pattillo | (404) 215-2752 |
| Morningside College | A | 1501 Morningside Ave., Sioux City, IA 51106 | Jim Scholten | (712) 274-5258 |
| Morris College | A | 100 W. College St., Sumter, SC 29150 | Clarence Houck | (803) 934-3235 |
| Mount Aloysius College | III | 7373 Admiral Peary Hwy., Cresson, PA 16630 | Garrett Sidor | (814) 886-6339 |
| Mount Marty College | A | 1105 West 8th St., Yankton, SD 57078 | Andy Bernatow | (605) 668-1601 |
| Mount Mercy College | A | 1330 Elmhurst Drive NE, Cedar Rapids, IA 52402 | Justin Schulte | (319) 363-1323 |
| Mount Olive College | II | 634 Henderson St., Mount Olive, NC 28365 | Carl Lancaster | (919) 658-7806 |
| Mount St. Joseph, College of | III | 5701 Delhi Rd., Cincinnati, OH 45233 | Chuck Murray | (513) 244-4402 |
| Mount St. Mary College | III | 330 Powell Ave., Newburgh, NY 12550 | Matt Dembinsky | (845) 569-3593 |
| Mount St. Vincent, College of | III | 6301 Riverdale Ave., Riverdale, NY 10471 | Andy McNamara | (718) 405-3417 |
| Mount Union College | III | 1972 Clark Ave., Alliance, OH 44601 | Paul Hesse | (330) 823-4878 |
| Mount Vernon Nazarene Coll. | A | 800 Martinsburg Rd., Mt. Vernon, OH 43050 | Keith Veale | (740) 392-6868 |
| Muhlenberg College | III | 2400 W. Chew St., Allentown, PA 18104 | Bob Macaluso | (484) 664-3684 |
| Muskingum College | III | 163 Stormont St., New Concord, OH 43762 | Gregg Thompson | (740) 826-8318 |
| Nebraska-Kearney, U. of | II | Health & Sports Ctr., 2501 15th Ave., Kearney, NE 68849 | Damon Day | (308) 865-8022 |
| Nebraska-Omaha, U. of | II | 6001 Dodge St., Omaha, NE 68182 | Bob Herold | (402) 554-3388 |
| Nebraska Wesleyan U. | A | 5000 St. Paul Ave., Lincoln, NE 68504 | Bill Fagler | (402) 465-2171 |
| Neumann College | III | One Neumann Dr., Aston, PA 19014 | Len Schuler | (610) 558-5625 |
| New England College | III | Clement Arena, 24 Bridge St., Henniker, NH 03242 | Dave DeCew | (603) 428-2447 |
| New Haven, U. of | II | 300 Boston Post Rd., West Haven, CT 06516 | Frank Vieira | (203) 932-7018 |
| New Jersey City U. | III | 2039 Kennedy Blvd., Jersey City, NJ 07305 | Ken Heaton | (201) 200-3079 |
| New Jersey Tech | II | 323 Dr. MLK Jr. Blvd., Newark, NJ 07102 | Brian Callahan | (973) 596-5827 |
| New Jersey, College of | III | PO Box 7718, Ewing, NJ 08628 | Rick Dell | (609) 771-2374 |
| New Mexico Highlands U. | II | Athletic Dept. Field House, Las Vegas, NM 87701 | Steve Jones | (505) 454-3587 |
| New York, City College of | III | 138th St. & Convent Ave., J-20, New York, NY 10031 | Scott Losche | (212) 650-8228 |
| Newberry College | II | 2100 College St., Newberry, SC 29108 | Bob Rikeman | (803) 321-5162 |
| Newman U. | A | 3100 McCormick Ave., Wichita, KS 67213 | Leonard Rau | (316) 942-4291 |
| Nichols College | III | PO Box 5000, Dudley, MA 01571 | Mike Wilson | (508) 213-2184 |
| North Alabama, U. of | II | Box 5072, Florence, AL 35632 | Mike Lane | (256) 765-4615 |
| North Carolina Wesleyan | III | 3400 N. Wesleyan Blvd., Rocky Mount, NC 27804 | Charlie Long | (252) 985-5219 |
| North Carolina-Pembroke, U. of | II | PO Box 1510, Pembroke, NC 28372 | Paul O'Neil | (910) 521-6810 |
| North Central College | III | 30 N. Brainard St., Naperville, IL 60540 | Brian Michalak | (630) 637-5512 |
| North Central U. | C | 910 Elliot Ave., Minneapolis, MN 55404 | Mike Carrell | (612) 343-4145 |
| North Dakota, U. of | II | PO Box 9013, Grand Forks, ND 58202 | Kelvin Ziegler | (701) 777-4038 |
| North Georgia Col & State U. | II | 82 College Cir., Dahlonega, GA 30597 | Tom Cantrell | (706) 867-2754 |
| North Greenville College | II | PO Box 1892, Tigerville, SC 29688 | Tim Nihart | (864) 977-7156 |
| North Park U. | III | 3225 W. Foster Ave, Chicago, IL 60625 | Luke Johnson | (773) 244-5675 |
| Northeastern State U. | II | 603 N. Grand Ave., Tahlequah, OK 74464 | Sergio Espinal | (918) 456-5511 |
| Northern Colorado, U. of | II | Butler-Hancock Athletic Ctr., Greeley, CO 80639 | Kevin Smallcomb | (970) 351-1714 |
| Northern Kentucky U. | II | 250 Albright Health Ctr., Highland Heights, KY 41099 | Todd Asalon | (859) 572-6474 |
| Northern State U. | II | 1200 South Jay St., Aberdeen, SD 57401 | Curt Fredrickson | (605) 626-7735 |
| Northland College | A | 1411 Ellis Ave., Ashland, WI 54806 | Joel Barta | (715) 682-1387 |
| Northwest Missouri State | II | 800 University Dr., Maryville, MO 64468 | Darin Loe | (660) 562-1352 |
| Northwest Nazarene U. | II | 623 Holly St., Nampa, ID 83686 | Tim Onofrei | (208) 467-8351 |
| Northwestern College | A | 101 7th St. SW, Orange City, IA 51041 | Dave Nonnemacher | (712) 707-7366 |
| Northwestern College | III | 3003 Snelling Ave. N., St. Paul, MN 55113 | Dave Hieb | (651) 631-5345 |
| Northwestern Okla. State U. | A | 709 Oklahoma Blvd., Alva, OK 73717 | Joe Phillips | (580) 327-8635 |
| Northwood U. | A | 2600 N. Military Tr., West Palm Beach, FL 33409 | Rick Smoliak | (561) 478-5552 |
| Northwood U. | II | 4000 Whiting Drive, Midland, MI 48640 | Joe DiBenedetto | (989) 837-4427 |

| | | | | |
|---|---|---|---|---|
| Northwood U. | A | 1114 West FM 1382, Cedar Hill, TX 75104 | Todd Johnson | (972) 293-5484 |
| Norwich U. | III | 158 Harmon Dr., Northfield, VT 05663 | John Rhodes | (802) 485-2246 |
| Notre Dame College | A | 4545 College Rd., Cleveland, OH 44121 | Craig Moro | (216) 373-5426 |
| Nova Southeastern U. | II | 3301 College Ave., Fort Lauderdale, FL 33314 | Michael Mominey | (954) 262-8252 |
| Nyack College | II | 1 South Blvd., Nyack, NY 10960 | Josh Norton | (845) 358-1710 |
| Oakland City U. | II | 138 N. Lucretia St., Oakland City, IN 47660 | T. Ray Fletcher | (812) 749-1576 |
| Oberlin College | III | 200 Woodland St., Oberlin, OH 44074 | Eric Lahetta | (440) 775-8502 |
| Occidental College | III | 1600 Campus Rd., Los Angeles, CA 90041 | Elliot Strankman | (323) 259-2683 |
| Oglethorpe U. | III | 4484 Peachtree Rd. NE, Atlanta, GA 30319 | Dan Giordano | (404) 364-8487 |
| Ohio Dominican U. | A | 1216 Sunbury Rd., Columbus, OH 43219 | Paul Page | (614) 251-4535 |
| Ohio Northern U. | III | 525 S. Main, Ada, OH 45810 | Unavailable | (419) 772-2442 |
| Ohio Valley U. | II | 1 Campus View Dr., Vienna, WV 26105 | Chad Porter | (304) 865-6209 |
| Ohio Wesleyan U. | III | 61 S. Sandusky St., Delaware, OH 43015 | Roger Ingles | (740) 368-3738 |
| Oklahoma Baptist U. | A | 500 W. University St., Shawnee, OK 74801 | Bobby Cox | (405) 878-2139 |
| Oklahoma City U. | A | 2501 N. Blackwelder, Oklahoma City, OK 73106 | Denny Crabaugh | (405) 521-5156 |
| Oklahoma Panhandle State U. | II | PO Box 430, Goodwell, OK 73939 | Jason Kueffler | (580) 349-1327 |
| Oklahoma Wesleyan Coll. | A | 2201 Silver Lake Rd., Bartlesville, OK 74006 | Bill Barr | (918) 335-6848 |
| Oklahoma, U. of Science/Arts | A | 1727 W. Alabama Ave., Chickasha, OK 73018 | L.J. Powell | (405) 574-1228 |
| Olivet College | III | 320 S. Main St., Olivet, MI 49076 | Carlton Hardy | (269) 749-4184 |
| Olivet Nazarene U. | A | One University Ave., Bourbonnais, IL 60914 | Elliot Johnson | (815) 939-5119 |
| Oneonta State U. | III | Ravine Pkwy., Oneonta, NY 13820 | Rick Ferchen | (607) 436-2661 |
| Oregon Tech | A | 3201 Campus Dr., Klamath Falls, OR 97601 | Pete Whisler | (541) 885-1722 |
| Ottawa U. | A | 1001 South Cedar St., Ottawa, KS 66067 | Jarrod Titus | (785) 242-5200 |
| Otterbein College | III | One Otterbein College, Westerville, OH 43081 | George Powell | (614) 823-3521 |
| Ouachita Baptist U. | II | Box 3788, 410 Ouachita St., Arkadelphia, AR 71998 | Scott Norwood | (870) 245-4255 |
| Ozarks, College of the | A | PO Box 17, Point Lookout, MO 65726 | Chris Pfatenhauer | (417) 334-6411 |
| Ozarks, U. of the | III | 415 N. College Ave., Clarksville, AR 72830 | Jimmy Clark | (479) 979-1409 |
| Pace U. | II | 861 Bedford Rd., Pleasantville, NY 10570 | Hank Manning | (914) 773-3413 |
| Pacific Lutheran U. | III | 12180 Park Ave. S., Tacoma, WA 98447 | Geoff Loomis | (253) 535-8789 |
| Pacific U. | III | 2043 College Way, Forest Grove, OR 97116 | Greg Bradley | (503) 359-2142 |
| Paine College | II | 1235 15th St., Augusta, GA 30901 | Pete Cardenas | (706) 821-8228 |
| Palm Beach Atlantic U. | II | 901 S. Flagler Dr., West Palm Beach, FL 33416 | Rob Avila | (561) 803-2523 |
| Park U. | A | PO Box 66, Parkville, MO 64152 | Cary Lundy | (816) 584-6746 |
| Patten U. | A | 2433 Coolidge Ave., Oakland, CA 94601 | Darin Wright | (925) 260-6900 |
| Paul Quinn College | A | 3837 Simpson Stuart Rd., Dallas, TX 75241 | Don Cofer | (214) 801-1168 |
| Penn State Behrend College | III | 5091 Station Rd., Erie, PA 16563 | Paul Benim | (814) 898-6322 |
| Penn State-Altoona | III | 3000 Ivyside Park, Altoona, PA 16601 | Joe Piotti | (814) 949-5226 |
| Penn-State-Berks College | III | PO Box 7009, Reading, PA 19610 | Joe Smull | (610) 396-6151 |
| Penn State-Beaver | | 100 University Dr., Monaca, PA 15601 | John Bellaver | (724) 773-3826 |
| Penn State-Hazelton | | 76 University Dr., Hazelton, PA 18202 | Tim Thompson | (570) 459-1869 |
| Penn State-McKeesport | | 4000 University Dr., McKeesport, PA 15132 | Mike Cherepko | (412) 675-9487 |
| Peru State College | A | PO Box 10, Peru, NE 68421 | Jason Cronin | (402) 872-2443 |
| Pfeiffer U. | II | PO Box 960, Misenheimer, NC 28109 | Mark Hayes | (704) 463-1360 |
| Philadelphia, U. of Sciences | II | 600 S. 43rd St., Philadelphia, PA 19104 | Frank Angeloni | (215) 596-8782 |
| Philadelphia U. | II | 4201 Henry Ave., Philadelphia, PA 19144 | Mark Heineman | (215) 951-2630 |
| Philadelphia Biblical U. | III | 200 Manor Ave., Langhorne, PA 19047 | Rich Sparling | (215) 702-4405 |
| Piedmont College | III | PO Box 10, Demorest, GA 30535 | Jim Peeples | (706) 776-0147 |
| Pikeville College | A | 147 Sycamore St., Pikeville, KY 41501 | Johnnie LeMaster | (606) 218-5370 |
| Pillsbury Baptist College | C | 315 S. Grove Ave., Owatonna, MN 55060 | Brian Boldt | (507) 451-2710 |
| Pittsburg State U. | II | 1701 S. Broadway, Pittsburg, KS 66762 | Steve Bever | (620) 232-7951 |
| Pittsburgh-Bradford, U. of | III | 300 Campus Dr., Bradford, PA 16701 | Bret Butler | (814) 362-5271 |
| Pittsburgh-Greensburg, U. of | III | 1150 Mt. Pleasant Rd., Greensburg, PA 15601 | Joe Hill | (724) 836-7185 |
| Pittsburgh-Johnstown, U. of | II | Sports Ctr., Johnstown, PA 15904 | Todd Williams | (814) 269-7170 |
| Plymouth State U. | III | PE Center, MSC 32, Plymouth, NH 03264 | Dennis McManus | (603) 535-2756 |
| Point Loma Nazarene U. | A | 3900 Lomaland Dr., San Diego, CA 92106 | Jack Northam | (619) 749-2765 |
| Point Park College | A | 201 Wood St., Pittsburgh, PA 15222 | Albert Liberi | (412) 392-3845 |
| Polytechnic U. | III | 6 Metro Tech Ctr., Brooklyn, NY 11201 | Arty Williams | (718) 242-1143 |
| Pomona-Pitzer College | III | 220 E. 6th St., Claremont, CA 91711 | Frank Pericolosi | (909) 621-8422 |
| Post U. | II | 800 Country Club Rd., Waterbury, CT 06723 | Rico Biogna | (203) 596-4690 |
| Presbyterian College | II | 105 Ashland Ave., Clinton, SC 29325 | Elton Pollock | (864) 833-8236 |
| Presentation College | III | 1500 N. Main, Aberdeen, SD 57401 | Brian Gruber | (605) 229-8634 |
| Principia College | III | 100 Maybeck Place, Elsah, IL 62028 | Steve Stock | (618) 374-5680 |
| Puget Sound, U. of | III | 1500 N. Warner St., CMB 1044, Tacoma, WA 98416 | Brian Billings | (253) 879-3418 |
| Purdue U.-North Central | A | 1401 S. U.S. Hwy. 421, Westville, IN 46391 | John Weber | (219) 785-5273 |
| Queens College | III | 65-30 Kissena Blvd., Flushing, NY 11367 | Frank Battaglia | (718) 997-2781 |
| Quincy U. | II | 1800 College Ave., Quincy, IL 62301 | Greg McVey | (217) 228-5268 |
| Ramapo College | III | 505 Ramapo Valley Rd., Mahwah, NJ 07430 | Rich Martin | (201) 684-7066 |
| Randolph-Macon College | III | PO Box 5005, Ashland, VA 23005 | Ray Hedrick | (804) 752-7303 |
| Redlands, U. of | III | 1200 E. Colton Ave., Redlands, CA 92373 | Scott Laverty | (909) 793-2121 |
| Reinhardt College | A | 7300 Reinhardt College Cir., Waleska, GA 30183 | Bill Popp | (770) 720-5568 |
| Regis U. | II | 3333 Regis Blvd., Box F-20, Denver, CO 80221 | Dan McDermott | (303) 458-3519 |
| Rensselaer Poly Institute | III | 110 8th St., Troy, NY 12180 | Karl Steffen | (518) 276-6185 |

| | | | | |
|---|---|---|---|---|
| Rhode Island College | III | 600 Mt. Pleasant Ave., Providence, RI 02908 | Jay Grenier | (401) 456-8258 |
| Rhodes College | III | 2000 N. Parkway, Memphis, TN 38112 | Jeff Cleathes | (901) 843-3456 |
| Richard Stockton College | III | PO Box 195, Pomona, NJ 08240 | Marty Kavanagh | (609) 652-4217 |
| Rio Grande, U. of | A | Box 500, Rio Grande, OH 45674 | Brad Warnimont | (740) 245-7486 |
| Ripon College | III | PO Box 248, Ripon, WI 54971 | Bob Gillespie | (920) 748-8774 |
| Rivier College | III | 420 Main St., Nashua, NH 03060 | Bill Maniotis | (603) 897-8257 |
| Roanoke College | III | 221 College Lane, Salem, VA 24153 | Larry Wood | (540) 378-5147 |
| Robert Morris College | A | 401 S. State St., Chicago, IL 60605 | Woody Urchak | (312) 935-6801 |
| Robert Morris Col-Springfield | U | 3101 Montvale Dr., Springfield, IL 62704 | Mark Rabideau | (217) 899-6569 |
| Rochester, U. of | III | Goergen Athletic Center, Rochester, NY 14627 | Joe Reina | (585) 275-6027 |
| Rochester College | U | 800 W. Avon Rd., Rochester Hills, MI 48307 | Virgil Smith | (248) 218-2135 |
| Rochester Tech | III | 51 Lomb Memorial Dr., Rochester, NY 14623 | Rob Grow | (585) 475-2615 |
| Rockford College | III | 5050 E. State St., Rockford, IL 61108 | Brian Nelson | (815) 394-5062 |
| Rockhurst U. | III | 1100 Rockhurst Rd., Kansas City, MO 64110 | Gary Burns | (816) 501-4130 |
| Roger Williams U. | III | 1 Old Ferry Rd., Bristol, RI 02809 | Derek Carlson | (401) 254-3163 |
| Rogers State U. | A | 1701 W. Will Rogers Blvd., Claremore, OK 74017 | Ron Bradley | (918) 343-7787 |
| Rollins College | II | 1000 Holt Ave., Box 2730, Winter Park, FL 32789 | Unavailable | (407) 646-2328 |
| Rose-Hulman Tech | III | 5500 Wabash Ave., Terre Haute, IN 47803 | Jeff Jenkins | (812) 877-8209 |
| Rowan U. | III | 201 Mullica Hill Rd., Glassboro, NJ 08028 | Juan Ranero | (856) 256-4687 |
| Rust College | III | 150 Rust Ave., Holly Springs, MS 38635 | Avery Mason | (662) 252-4661 |
| Rutgers U.-Camden | III | 3rd & Linden Streets, Camden, NJ 08102 | Keith Williams | (856) 225-2746 |
| Rutgers U.-Newark | III | 42 Warren St., Newark, NJ 07102 | Mark Rizzi | (973) 353-1473 |
| Saginaw Valley State | II | 7400 Bay Rd., University Center, MI 48710 | Walt Head | (989) 964-7334 |
| St. Ambrose U. | A | 518 W. Locust St., Davenport, IA 52803 | Jim Callahan | (563) 333-6237 |
| St. Andrews Presbyterian Col | II | 1700 Dogwood Mile St., Laurinburg, NC 28352 | Unavailable | (910) 277-5426 |
| St. Anselm College | II | 100 St. Anselm Dr., Box 1727, Manchester, NH 03102 | Jon Pyne | (603) 656-6016 |
| St. Augustine's College | II | 1315 Oakwood Ave., Raleigh, NC 27610 | Andy Wood | (919) 516-4711 |
| St. Cloud State U. | II | 720 4th Ave. S., HaH 329, St. Cloud, MN 56301 | Denny Lorsung | (320) 308-3208 |
| St. Edward's U. | II | 3001 S. Congress Ave., Austin, TX 78704 | Jerry Farber | (512) 448-8497 |
| St. Francis, U. of | A | 500 Wilcox St., Joliet, IL 60435 | Gordie Gillespie | (815) 740-3406 |
| St. Francis, U. of | A | 2701 Spring St., Fort Wayne, IN 46808 | Greg Roberts | (260) 434-7414 |
| St. Gregory's U. | A | 1900 W. MacArthur St., Shawnee, OK 74804 | Chris Pingry | (405) 878-5151 |
| St. John Fisher College | III | 3690 East Ave., Rochester, NY 14618 | Dan Pepicelli | (585) 385-8419 |
| St. John's U. | III | PO Box 7277, Collegeville, MN 56321 | Jerry Haugen | (320) 363-2756 |
| St. Joseph, College of | A | 71 Clement Rd., Rutland, VT 05701 | Kevin Knauer | (802) 776-5247 |
| St. Joseph's College | II | PO Box 875, Rensselaer, IN 47978 | Rick O'Dette | (219) 866-6399 |
| St. Joseph's College | III | 278 Whites Bridge Rd., Standish, ME 04084 | Will Sanborn | (207) 893-6675 |
| St. Joseph's College | III | 155 W. Roe Blvd., Patchogue, NY 11772 | Randy Caden | (631) 447-3349 |
| St. Lawrence U. | III | Park Street, Canton, NY 13617 | Tom Fay | (315) 229-5882 |
| St. Leo U. | II | MC 2038, Box 6665, St. Leo, FL 33574 | Ricky Ware | (352) 588-8227 |
| St. Louis Christian College | C | 1360 Grandview Dr., Florissant, MO 63033 | Derrick Johnston | (314) 837-6777 |
| St. Martin's U. | II | 5300 Pacific Ave. SE, Lacey, WA 98503 | Joe Dominiak | (360) 438-4531 |
| St. Mary, U. of | A | 4100 S. 4 Trafficway, Leavenworth, KS 66048 | Rob Miller | (913) 758-6160 |
| St. Mary's College | III | Athletic & Rec. Ctr., St. Mary's City, MD 20686 | Lew Jenkins | (240) 895-4312 |
| St. Mary's U. | III | 700 Terrace Heights #62, Winona, MN 55987 | Nick Whaley | (507) 457-1577 |
| St. Mary's U. | II | 1 Camino Santa Maria St., Box 8, San Antonio, TX 78228 | Charlie Migl | (210) 436-3034 |
| St. Michael's College | II | One Winooski Park, Colchester, VT 05439 | Perry Bove | (802) 654-2725 |
| St. Norbert College | III | 100 Grant St., De Pere, WI 54115 | Tom Winske | (920) 403-3545 |
| St. Olaf College | III | 1520 St. Olaf Ave., Northfield, MN 55057 | Matt McDonald | (507) 646-3638 |
| St. Paul's College | II | 115 College Dr., Lawrenceville, VA 23868 | Damon Frenchers | (434) 848-6401 |
| St. Rose, College of | II | 432 Western Ave., Albany, NY 12203 | Bob Bellizzi | (518) 454-2041 |
| St. Scholastica, College of | A | 1200 Kenwood Ave., Duluth, MN 55811 | John Baggs | (218) 723-6298 |
| St. Thomas Aquinas | II | 125 Route 340, Sparkill, NY 10976 | T. Scott Muscat | (845) 398-4027 |
| St. Thomas U. | A | 16400 NW 32nd Ave., Miami Gardens, FL 33054 | Manny Mantrana | (305) 628-6730 |
| St. Thomas, U. of | III | Mail #5003, 2115 Summit Ave., St. Paul, MN 55105 | Dennis Denning | (651) 962-5924 |
| St. Vincent College | A | 300 Fraser Purchase Rd., Latrobe, PA 15650 | Michael Janosko | (724) 805-2396 |
| St. Xavier U. | A | 3700 W. 103rd St., Chicago, IL 60655 | Mike Dooley | (773) 298-3103 |
| Salem International U. | II | 223 W. Main St., Salem, WV 26426 | Rich Leitch | (304) 782-5632 |
| Salem State College | III | 352 Lafayette St., Salem, MA 01970 | Ken Perrone | (978) 542-7260 |
| Salisbury U. | III | 1101 Camden Ave., Salisbury, MD 21801 | Doug Fleetwood | (410) 543-6034 |
| Salve Regina U. | III | 100 Ochre Point Ave., Newport, RI 02840 | Steve Cirella | (401) 341-2267 |
| San Francisco State U. | II | 1600 Holloway Ave., San Francisco, CA 94132 | Matt Markovich | (415) 338-1226 |
| Savannah Art & Design | A | PO Box 3146, Savannah, GA 31402 | Doug Wollenburg | (912) 525-4782 |
| Schreiner U. | III | 2100 Memorial Blvd., CMB 5905, Kerrville, TX 78028 | Joe Castillo | (830) 792-7292 |
| Scranton, U. of | III | John J. Long S.J. Ctr., Scranton, PA 18510 | Mike Bertoletti | (570) 451-0339 |
| Seton Hill U. | A | PO Box 287, Greensburg, PA 15601 | Marc Marizzaldi | (724) 830-1169 |
| Shaw U. | II | 118 E. South St., Raleigh, NC 27601 | Bobby Sanders | (919) 546-8278 |
| Shawnee State U. | A | 940 2nd St., Portsmouth, OH 45662 | Tom Bergan | (740) 351-3537 |
| Shenandoah U. | III | 1460 University Dr., Winchester, VA 22601 | Kevin Anderson | (540) 665-4531 |
| Shepherd U. | II | P.O. Box 3210, Shepherdstown, WV 25443 | Wayne Riser | (304) 876-5472 |
| Shippensburg U. | II | 1871 Old Main Dr., Shippensburg, PA 17257 | Bruce Peddie | (717) 477-1508 |
| Shorter College | A | 315 Shorter Ave., Rome, GA 30165 | Matt Larry | (706) 233-7510 |
| Siena Heights U. | A | 1247 E. Siena Heights Dr., Adrian, MI 49221 | John Kolasinski | (517) 264-7872 |

| College | Class | Address | Contact | Phone |
|---|---|---|---|---|
| Simpson U. | A | 2211 College View Dr., Redding, CA 96003 | Josh Gleason | (530) 226-4731 |
| Simpson College | III | 701 North C St., Indianola, IA 50125 | John Sirianni | (515) 961-1620 |
| Sioux Falls, U. of | A | 1101 W. 22nd St., Sioux Falls, SD 57105 | Luke Langenfeld | (605) 331-6638 |
| Skidmore College | III | 815 N. Broadway, Saratoga Springs, NY 12866 | Ron Plourde | (518) 580-5380 |
| Slippery Rock U. | II | 102 Morrow Field House, Slippery Rock, PA 19383 | Jeff Messer | (724) 738-2813 |
| Sonoma State U. | II | 1801 E. Cotati Ave., Rohnert Park, CA 94928 | John Goelz | (707) 664-2524 |
| South Carolina-Aiken, U. of | II | 471 University Pkwy., Aiken, SC 29801 | Kenny Thomas | (803) 641-3410 |
| South Carolina-Upstate, U. of | II | 800 University Way, Spartanburg, SC 29303 | Matt Fincher | (864) 503-5135 |
| South, U. of the | III | 735 University Ave., Sewanee, TN 37383 | Scott Baker | (931) 598-1545 |
| Southeastern U. | C | 1000 Longfellow Blvd, Lakeland, FL 33801 | Jason Beck | (863) 667-5046 |
| Southeastern Oklahoma State | II | 1405 N. 4th Ave., Durant, OK 74701 | Mike Metheny | (580) 745-2478 |
| Southern Arkansas U. | II | 100 E. University St., Magnolia, AR 71753 | Allen Gum | (870) 235-4127 |
| Southern Connecticut State | II | 125 Wintergreen Ave., New Haven, CT 06515 | Tim Shea | (203) 392-6021 |
| Southern Illinois U.-Edwardsville | II | SIUE Box 1027, Edwardsville, IL 62026 | Gary Collins | (618) 650-2872 |
| Southern Indiana, U. of | II | 8600 University Blvd, Evansville, IN 47712 | Mike Goedde | (812) 464-1943 |
| Southern Maine, U. of | III | 37 College Ave., Gorham, ME 04038 | Ed Flaherty | (207) 780-5474 |
| Southern Nazarene U. | A | 6729 NW 39th Expy., Bethany, OK 73008 | Scott Selby | (405) 491-6630 |
| Southern New Hampshire U. | II | 2500 N. River Rd., Manchester, NH 03106 | Bruce Joyce | (603) 645-9637 |
| Southern Tech | A | 1100 S. Marietta Pkwy., Marietta, GA 30060 | Matt Griffin | (678) 915-5445 |
| Southern Vermont College | III | 982 Mansion Dr., Bennington, VT 05201 | Charlie Barfelz | (802) 447-4670 |
| Southern Virginia U. | A | 1 College Hill Dr., Buena Vista, VA 24416 | Jerry Schlegelmilch | (540) 261-8400 |
| Southern Wesleyan U. | A | PO Box 1020, SWU 498, Central, SC 29630 | Mike Gillespie | (864) 644-5035 |
| Southwest, College of the | A | 6610 N. Lovington Hwy., Hobbs, NM 88240 | Mike Galvan | (505) 392-6561 |
| Southwest Baptist U. | II | 1600 University Ave., Bolivar, MO 65613 | Sam Berg | (417) 328-1794 |
| Southwest Minnesota State U. | II | 1501 State St., Marshall, MN 56258 | Paul Blanchard | (507) 537-7268 |
| Southwestern Assemblies of God U. | A | 1200 Sycamore, Waxahachie, TX 75165 | Greg Hayes | (972) 825-4809 |
| Southwestern Oklahoma State | II | 100 Campus Dr., Weatherford, OK 73096 | Charles Teasley | (580) 774-3263 |
| Southwestern U. | III | Maple at University, Box 770, Georgetown, TX 78626 | Jim Shelton | (512) 863-1386 |
| Spalding U. | A | 851 S. 4th St., Louisville, KY 40203 | Kevin Kocks | (502) 452-2580 |
| Spring Arbor U. | A | PO Box 219, Spring Arbor, MI 49283 | Sam Riggleman | (517) 750-6713 |
| Spring Hill College | A | 4000 Dauphin St., Mobile, AL 36608 | Frank Sims | (251) 380-3486 |
| Springfield College | III | 263 Alden St., Springfield, MA 01109 | Mark Simeone | (413) 748-3274 |
| Staten Island, College of | III | 2800 Victory Blvd., Staten Island, NY 10314 | Bill Cali | (718) 982-3171 |
| Sterling College | A | PO Box 98, Sterling, KS 67579 | Matt Elliot | (620) 278-4227 |
| Stevens Tech | III | 1 Castle Point on Hudson, Hoboken, NJ 07030 | John Crane | (201) 216-8033 |
| Stillman College | III | 3600 Stillman Blvd., Tuscaloosa, AL 35401 | Donny Crawford | (205) 366-8891 |
| Stonehill College | II | 320 Washington St., Easton, MA 02357 | Patrick Boen | (508) 565-1351 |
| Suffolk U. | III | 41 Temple St., Boston, MA 02114 | Cary McConnell | (617) 573-8379 |
| Sul Ross State U. | III | Box C-17, Alpine, TX 79832 | Mike Pallanez | (432) 837-8231 |
| SUNY Brockport | III | 350 New Campus Dr., Brockport, NY 14420 | Mark Rowland | (585) 395-5329 |
| SUNY Cortland | III | Pashley Dr., Cortland, NY 13045 | Joe Brown | (607) 753-4950 |
| SUNY Farmingdale | III | 2350 Broadhollow Rd., Farmingdale, NY 11735 | Keith Osik | (631) 420-2153 |
| SUNY Maritime College | III | 6 Pennyfield Ave., Bronx, NY 10465 | Frank Menna | (718) 409-7331 |
| SUNY New Paltz | III | 75 S. Manheim Blvd., New Paltz, NY 12561 | Mike Juhl | (845) 257-3915 |
| SUNY Old Westbury | III | PO Box 210, Old Westbury, NY 11568 | Hector Aristy | (516) 876-3461 |
| SUNY Oswego | III | 202 Laker Hall, Oswego, NY 13126 | Frank Paino | (315) 312-2405 |
| SUNY Purchase | III | 735 Anderson Hill Rd., Purchase, NY 10577 | Bill Guerrero | (914) 251-7855 |
| SUNY Plattsburg | III | 101 Broad St., Plattsburg, NY 12901 | Kris Doorey | (518) 564-4136 |
| SUNY Tech | III | PO Box 3050, Utica, NY 13504 | Kevin Edick | (315) 792-7523 |
| Susquehanna U. | III | 514 University Ave., Selinsgrove, PA 17870 | Denny Bowers | (570) 372-4417 |
| Swarthmore College | III | 500 College Ave., Swarthmore, PA 19081 | Frank Agovino | (610) 328-8216 |
| Tabor College | A | 400 S. Jefferson St., Hillsboro, KS 67063 | John Sparks | (620) 947-3121 |
| Tampa, U. of | II | 401 W. Kennedy Blvd., Box I, Tampa, FL 33610 | Joe Urso | (813) 253-6240 |
| Tarleton State U. | II | Box T-80, Stephenville, TX 76402 | Trey Felan | (254) 968-9528 |
| Taylor U. | A | 236 W. Reade Ave, Upland, IN 46989 | Kyle Gould | (765) 998-4635 |
| Tennessee Temple U. | C | 1815 Union Ave., Chattanooga, TN 37404 | Bob Hall | (423) 493-4234 |
| Tennessee Wesleyan College | A | PO Box 40, Athens, TN 37371 | Billy Berry | (423) 746-5277 |
| Texas A&M-Kingsville | II | MSC 202, Kingsville, TX 78363 | Russell Stockton | (361) 593-3487 |
| Texas College | A | PO Box 4500, Tyler, TX 75702 | Daniel Stuckey | (903) 593-8311 |
| Texas Wesleyan U. | A | 1201 Wesleyan St., Fort Worth, TX 76105 | Mike Jeffcoat | (817) 531-7547 |
| Texas-Brownsville, U. of | A | 80 Fort Brown, Brownsville, TX 78520 | Eliseo Herrera | (956) 882-8293 |
| Texas-Dallas, U. of | III | Box 830688 AB 10, Richardson, TX 75083 | Shane Shewmake | (972) 883-2392 |
| Texas-Tyler, U. of | III | 3900 University Blvd., Tyler, TX 75799 | James Vilade | (903) 565-5640 |
| Texas Lutheran U. | III | 1000 W. Court St., Seguin, TX 78155 | Bill Miller | (830) 372-8124 |
| Texas-Permian Basin, U. of | A | 4901 E. University Blvd., Odessa, TX 79762 | Brian Reinke | (432) 552-4677 |
| Thiel College | III | 75 College Ave., Greenville, PA 16125 | Joe Schaly | (724) 589-2139 |
| Thomas College | III | 180 W. River Rd., Waterville, ME 04901 | Greg King | (207) 859-1208 |
| Thomas U. | A | 1501 Millpond Rd., Thomasville, GA 31792 | Mike Lee | (229) 226-1621 |
| Thomas More College | III | 333 Thomas More Pkwy., Crestview Hills, KY 41017 | Jeff Hetzer | (859) 344-3332 |
| Tiffin U. | A | 155 Miami St., Tiffin, OH 44883 | Lonny Allen | (419) 448-3359 |
| Toccoa Falls College | C | PO Box 800818, Toccoa Falls, GA 30598 | Justin Pollock | (706) 886-6831 |
| Tougaloo College | A | 500 W. County Line Rd., Tougaloo, MS 39174 | Earl Sanders | (601) 977-6186 |
| Transylvania U. | III | 300 N. Broadway, Lexington, KY 40508 | Shayne Stock | (859) 233-8699 |

| | | | | |
|---|---|---|---|---|
| Trevecca Nazarene U. | A | 333 Murfreesboro Rd., Nashville, TN 37210 | Jeff Forehand | (615) 248-1276 |
| Tri-State U. | III | 1 University Ave., Angola, IN 46703 | Greg Perschke | (260) 665-4135 |
| Trinity Bible College | C | 50 S. 6th Ave., Ellendale, ND 58436 | Eric Slivoskey | (701) 249-5754 |
| Trinity Christian College | A | 6601 W. College Dr., Palos Heights, IL 60463 | Matt Schans | (708) 239-4780 |
| Trinity College | III | 380 Summit St., Hartford, CT 06106 | Bill Decker | (860) 297-2066 |
| Trinity International U. | A | 2065 Half Day Rd., Deerfield, IL 60015 | Mike Manes | (847) 317-7093 |
| Trinity U. | III | 1 Trinity Place, San Antonio, TX 78212 | Tim Scannell | (210) 999-8287 |
| Truman State U. | II | 100 E. Normal St., Kirksville, MO 63501 | Larry Scully | (660) 785-6003 |
| Tufts U. | III | 161 College Ave., Medford, MA 02155 | John Casey | (617) 627-5218 |
| Tusculum College | II | PO Box 5090, Greenville, TN 37743 | Doug Jones | (423) 636-7322 |
| Tuskegee U. | II | 321 James Ctr., Tuskegee, AL 36088 | Gregory Ruffin | (334) 727-8856 |
| Union College | A | CPO 22, Barbourville, KY 40906 | Bart Osborne | (606) 546-1355 |
| Union College | III | Alumni Gym, 807 Union St.., Schenectady, NY 12308 | Jeremy Rivenburg | (518) 388-8025 |
| Union U. | A | 1050 Union University Dr., Jackson, TN 38305 | Andy Rushing | (731) 661-5333 |
| U.S. Coast Guard Academy | III | 33 Mohegan Ave., New London, CT 06320 | Pete Barry | (860) 701-6132 |
| U.S. Merchant Marine Acad. | III | 300 Steamboat Rd., Kings Point, NY 11024 | Dennis Gagnon | (516) 773-5727 |
| Upper Iowa U. | II | PO Box 1857, Fayette, IA 52142 | Mark Danker | (563) 425-5290 |
| Urbana U. | A | 579 College Way, Urbana, OH 43078 | Scott Spriggs | (937) 454-1377 |
| Ursinus College | III | 601 Main St., Collegeville, PA 19426 | Brian Thomas | (610) 409-3606 |
| Utica College | III | 1600 Burrstone Rd., Utica, NY 13502 | Don Guido | (315) 752-3378 |
| Valdosta State U. | II | 1500 N. Patterson St., Valdosta, GA 31698 | Tommy Thomas | (229) 259-5562 |
| Valley City State U. | A | 101 College St. SW, Valley City, ND 58072 | Cory Anderson | (701) 845-7413 |
| Valley Forge Christian Col | C | 1401 Charlestown Rd., Phoenixville, PA 19460 | Don Hoover | (610) 917-1479 |
| Vanguard U. | A | 55 Fair Dr., Costa Mesa, CA 92626 | Scott Mallernee | (714) 556-3610 |
| Vassar College | III | 124 Raymond Ave., Poughkeepsie, NY 12604 | Chris Campassi | (845) 437-5344 |
| Vermont Tech | | Randolph Center, VT 05061 | Charles Bradley | (802) 728-1381 |
| Villa Julie College | III | 1525 Greenspring Valley Rd., Stevenson, MD 21153 | Jason Tawney | (443) 334-2334 |
| Virginia Intermont | A | Vi Box S-812, Bristol, VA 24201 | Chris Holt | (276) 466-7945 |
| Virginia State U. | II | PO Box 9058, Petersburg, VA 23806 | Merrill Morgan | (804) 524-5816 |
| Virginia Wesleyan College | III | 1584 Wesleyan Dr., Norfolk, VA 23502 | Nick Boothe | (757) 455-3348 |
| Virginia-Wise, U. of | A | 1 College Ave., Wise, VA 24293 | Hank Banner | (276) 376-4504 |
| Viterbo College | A | 900 Viterbo Dr., La Crosse, WI 54601 | Chad Miller | (608) 796-3824 |
| Voorhees College | A | PO Box 678, Denmark, SC 29042 | Adrian West | (803) 703-7142 |
| Wabash College | III | PO Box 352, Crawfordsville, IN 47933 | Tom Flynn | (765) 361-6209 |
| Waldorf College | A | 106 S. 6th St., Forest City, IA 50436 | Brian Grunzke | (641) 585-8263 |
| Walsh U. | A | 2020 E. Maple St., North Canton, OH 44720 | Tim Mead | (330) 490-7013 |
| Warner Southern College | A | 13895 Hwy. 27, Lake Wales, FL 33859 | Jeff Sikes | (863) 638-7259 |
| Wartburg College | III | 100 Wartburg Blvd., Waverly, IA 50677 | Joel Holst | (319) 352-8532 |
| Washburn U. | II | 1700 SW College Ave., Topeka, KS 66621 | Steve Anson | (785) 231-1134 |
| Washington & Jefferson College | III | 60 S. Lincoln St., Washington, PA 15301 | Jeff Mountain | (724) 250-3306 |
| Washington & Lee U. | III | P.O. Drawer 928, Lexington, VA 24450 | Jeff Stickley | (540) 458-8680 |
| Washington College | III | 300 Washington Ave., Chestertown, MD 21620 | Al Streelman | (410) 778-7239 |
| Washington U. | III | Campus Box 1067, St. Louis, MO 63130 | Ric Lessmann | (314) 935-5200 |
| Wayland Baptist U. | A | 1900 W. 7th St., Plainview, TX 79072 | Brad Bass | (806) 291-1132 |
| Wayne State College | II | 1111 Main St., Wayne, NE 68787 | John Manganaro | (402) 375-7012 |
| Wayne State U. | II | 5101 Lodge Dr., Detroit, MI 48202 | Jay Alexander | (313) 577-2749 |
| Waynesburg College | III | 51 W. College St., Waynesburg, PA 15370 | Mike Humiston | (724) 852-3390 |
| Webber International U. | A | PO Box 96, Babson Park, FL 33827 | Brad Niethammer | (863) 638-2951 |
| Webster U. | III | 470 E. Lockwood Ave, St. Louis, MO 63119 | Marty Hunsucker | (314) 961-2660 |
| Wentworth Tech | III | 550 Huntington Ave., Boston, MA 02115 | Steve Studley | (617) 989-4824 |
| Wesley College | III | 120 N. State St., Dover, DE 19901 | Tripp Keister | (302) 735-5939 |
| Wesleyan U. | III | Dept. of Phys. Ed., Middletown, CT 06459 | Mark Woodworth | (860) 685-2924 |
| West Alabama, U. of | II | UWA Station 5, Livingston, AL 35470 | Gary Rundles | (205) 652-3870 |
| West Chester U. | II | Sturzebecker Center, West Chester, PA 19383 | Matt Brainard | (610) 436-2152 |
| West Florida, U. of | II | 11000 University Pkwy., Pensacola, FL 32514 | Unavailable | (850) 474-2488 |
| West Georgia, U. of | II | 1600 Maple St., Carrollton, GA 30118 | Doc Fowlkes | (770) 836-3956 |
| West Liberty State College | II | Bartell Fieldhouse, West Liberty, WV 26074 | Bo McConnaughy | (304) 336-8235 |
| West Texas A&M U. | II | WTAMU Box 60049, Canyon, TX 79016 | Mark Jones | (806) 651-2676 |
| West Virginia State U. | II | PO Box 1000, FH 210, Institute, WV 25112 | Cal Bailey | (304) 766-3208 |
| West Virginia Tech | II | 405 Fayette Pike, Montgomery, WV 25136 | Tim Epling | (304) 442-3831 |
| West Virginia Wesleyan | II | 59 College Ave., Buckhannon, WV 26201 | Randy Tenney | (304) 473-8054 |
| Western Connecticut State | III | 181 White St., Danbury, CT 06810 | John Susi | (203) 837-8608 |
| Western New England College | III | 1215 Wilbraham Rd., Springfield, MA 01119 | Matt LaBranche | (413) 782-1792 |
| Western Oregon U. | II | 345 Monmouth Ave N., Monmouth, OR 97361 | Terry Baumgartner | (503) 838-8448 |
| Westfield State College | III | 577 Western Ave., Westfield, MA 01086 | Ray Arra | (413) 572-5633 |
| Westminster College | III | 501 Westminster Ave, Fulton, MO 65251 | Scott Pritchard | (573) 592-5333 |
| Westminster College | III | 319 Market St., New Wilmington, PA 16172 | Carmen Nocera | (724) 658-7334 |
| Westmont College | A | 955 La Paz Rd., Santa Barbara, CA 93108 | Robert Crawford | (805) 565-6012 |
| Wheaton College | III | 501 East College Ave, Wheaton, IL 60187 | Bobby Elder | (630) 752-7164 |
| Wheaton College | III | 26 E. Main St., Norton, MA 02766 | Eric Podbelski | (508) 286-3394 |
| Wheeling Jesuit U. | II | 13406 Washington Ave., Wheeling, WV 26003 | Terry Edwards | (304) 243-2212 |
| Whitman College | III | 345 Boyer Ave., Walla Walla, WA 99362 | Casey Powell | (509) 527-4931 |

| Whittier College | III | 13406 E. Philadelphia St., Whittier, CA 90608 | Mike Rizzo | (562) 907-4967 |
|---|---|---|---|---|
| Whitworth College | III | 300 W. Hawthorne Rd., Spokane, WA 99251 | Keith Ward | (509) 777-4394 |
| Widener U. | III | 1 University Place, Chester, PA 19013 | Steve Carcarey | (610) 499-4446 |
| Wiley College | A | 711 Wiley Ave., Marshall, TX 75670 | Eddie Watson | (903) 927-3292 |
| Wilkes U. | III | 84 W. South St., Wilkes-Barre, PA 18766 | Joe Folek | (570) 408-4024 |
| Willamette U. | III | 900 State St., Salem, OR 97301 | Matt Allison | (503) 370-6011 |
| William Carey College | A | 498 Tuscan Ave., Hattiesburg, MS 39401 | Bobby Halford | (601) 318-6110 |
| William Jewell Col | A | 500 College Hill, Liberty, MO 64068 | Mike Stockton | (816) 415-5962 |
| William Paterson U. | III | 300 Pompton Rd., Wayne, NJ 07470 | Jeff Albies | (973) 720-2210 |
| William Penn U. | A | 201 Trueblood Ave., Oskaloosa, IA 52577 | Mike Laird | (641) 673-1023 |
| William Woods U. | A | 1 University Ave., Fulton, MO 65251 | Ryan Bay | (573) 592-1187 |
| Williams Baptist College | A | PO Box 3387, College City, AR 72476 | John Katrosh | (870) 759-4192 |
| Williams College | III | 22 Spring St., Williamstown, MA 01267 | Dave Barnard | (413) 597-3326 |
| Wilmington College | II | 320 N. DuPont Hwy., New Castle, DE 19720 | Brian August | (302) 328-9435 |
| Wilmington College | III | 251 Ludovic St., Pyle Ctr. 1246, Wilmington, OH 45177 | Tony Haley | (937) 382-6661 |
| Wingate U. | II | 230 N. Camden Rd., Wingate, NC 28174 | Bill Nash | (704) 233-8381 |
| Winona State U. | II | PO Box 5838, Winona, MN 55987 | Kyle Poock | (507) 457-2332 |
| Wisconsin Lutheran College | III | 8800 W. Bluemound Rd., Milwaukee, WI 53226 | Brook Smith | (414) 443-8990 |
| Wisconsin-La Crosse, U. of | III | 126 Mitchell Hall, La Crosse, WI 54601 | Chris Schwarz | (608) 785-6540 |
| Wisconsin-Oshkosh, U. of | III | 800 Algoma Blvd., Oshkosh, WI 54901 | Tom Lechnir | (920) 424-0374 |
| Wisconsin-Parkside, U. of | II | PO Box 2000, Kenosha, WI 53141 | Tracy Archuleta | (262) 595-2317 |
| Wisconsin-Platteville, U. of | III | 1 University Plaza, Platteville, WI 53818 | Jamie Sailors | (608) 342-1572 |
| Wisconsin-Stevens Point, U. of | III | 205 4th Ave., Stevens Point, WI 54481 | Pat Bloom | (715) 346-4412 |
| Wisconsin-Stout, U. of | III | 241 Sports & Fitness Center, Menomonie, WI 54751 | Craig Walter | (715) 232-1459 |
| Wisconsin-Superior, U. of | III | PO Box 2000, Superior, WI 54880 | Chris Vito | (715) 395-4671 |
| Wisconsin-Whitewater, U. of | III | 800 W. Main St., Whitewater, WI 53190 | John Vodenlich | (262) 472-1420 |
| Wittenberg U. | III | PO Box 720, Springfield, OH 45501 | Jay Lewis | (937) 327-6494 |
| Wooster, College of | III | 1189 Beall Ave., Wooster, OH 44691 | Tim Pettorini | (330) 263-2180 |
| Worcester Polytechnic Institute | III | 100 Institute Rd., Worcester, MA 01609 | Chris Robertson | (508) 831-5624 |
| Worcester State College | III | 486 Chandler St., Worcester, MA 01602 | Dirk Baker | (508) 929-8852 |
| Yeshiva U. | III | 500 W. 185th St., New York, NY 10033 | Norman Ringel | (212) 960-5211 |
| York College | A | 1125 E. 8th St., York, NE 68467 | Nick Harlan | (402) 363-5736 |
| York College | III | 441 Country Club Rd., York, PA 17405 | Paul Saikia | (717) 815-1245 |

# JUNIOR COLLEGES

| School | Address | Coach | Telephone |
|---|---|---|---|
| Abraham Baldwin College | ABAC 41, 2802 Moore Hwy, Tifton, GA 31793 | Steve Janousek | (229) 386-3931 |
| Adirondack CC | 640 Bay Rd., Queensbury, NY 12804 | John Hayes | (518) 743-2269 |
| Alabama Southern CC | PO Box 2000, Monroeville, AL 36461 | Scott Sealy | (251) 575-3156 |
| Alfred State Col | Department of Athletics, Alfred, NY 14802 | Tom Keeney | (607) 587-4361 |
| Allan Hancock College | 800 S. College Dr., Santa Maria, CA 93454 | Chris Stevens | (805) 922-6966 |
| Allegany College | 12401 Willowbrook Rd., Cumberland, MD 21502 | Steve Bazarnic | (301) 784-5265 |
| Allegheny County-Allegheny, CC of | 808 Ridge Ave., Pittsburgh, PA 15212 | Scott Downer | (412) 237-2563 |
| Allegheny County-Boyce, CC of | 595 Beatty Rd., Monroeville, PA 15146 | Bill Holmes | (724) 325-6621 |
| Allegheny County-South, CC of | 1750 Clairton Rd., West Mifflin, PA 15122 | Ron Rocco | (412) 469-6245 |
| Allen County CC | 1801 N. Cottonwood St., Iola, KS 66749 | Val McLean | (620) 365-5116 |
| Alvin CC | 3110 Mustang Rd., Alvin, TX 77511 | Bryan Alexander | (281) 756-3696 |
| American River CC | 4700 College Oak Dr., Sacramento, CA 95841 | Doug Jumelet | (916) 484-8294 |
| Ancilla College | 9601 Union Rd., Donaldson, IN 46513 | Joe Yonto | (574) 936-8898 |
| Andrew College | 413 College St., Cuthbert, GA 31740 | Scot Hemmings | (912) 732-5953 |
| Angelina College | PO Box 1768, Lufkin, TX 75902 | Jeff Livin | (936) 633-5282 |
| Anne Arundel CC | 101 College Pkwy., Arnold, MD 21012 | Mark Palmerino | (410) 777-2300 |
| Anoka-Ramsey CC | 11200 Mississippi Blvd. NW, Coon Rapids, MN 55433 | Tom Yelle | (763) 422-3431 |
| Antelope Valley Col | 3041 W. Avenue K, Lancaster, CA 93536 | John Livermont | (661) 722-6300 |
| Arizona Western College | PO Box 929, Yuma, AZ 85366 | John Stratton | (928) 344-7535 |
| Arkansas-Fort Smith | PO Box 3649, Fort Smith, AR 72913 | Dale Harpenau | (479) 788-7590 |
| Bakersfield College | 1801 Panorama Dr., Bakersfield, CA 93305 | Tim Painton | (661) 871-6891 |
| Baltimore City CC | 2901 Liberty Heights Ave, Baltimore, MD 21215 | Lance Mauck | (410) 462-8325 |
| Barstow CC | 2700 Barstow Rd., Barstow, CA 92311 | Mike Shipley | (760) 252-2411 |
| Barton County CC | 245 NE 30th Rd., Great Bend, KS 67530 | Mike Warren | (620) 792-9378 |
| Baton Rouge CC | 5310 Florida Blvd., Baton Rouge, LA 70806 | L.J. Dupuy | (225) 216-8200 |
| Bellevue CC | 3000 Landerholm Circle SE, Bellevue, WA 98007 | Mark Yoshino | (425) 564-2356 |
| Bergen CC | 400 Paramus Rd., Paramus, NJ 07652 | Unavailable | (201) 447-7183 |
| Bevill State CC-Fayette | 2631 Temple Ave N., Fayette, AL 35555 | Joey May | (205) 387-0511 |
| Bevill State CC-Sumiton | PO Box 800, Sumiton, AL 35148 | Ed Langham | (205) 932-3221 |
| Big Bend CC | 7662 Chanute St., Moses Lake, WA 98837 | Don Lindgren | (509) 793-2230 |
| Bishop State CC | 351 N. Broad St., Mobile, AL 36603 | Greg Conner | (251) 690-6436 |
| Bismarck State CC | PO Box 5587, Bismarck, ND 58506 | Len Stanley | (701) 224-5512 |
| Black Hawk College | 6600 34th Ave., Moline, IL 61265 | Arnie Chauera | (309) 796-5602 |
| Blinn College | 902 College Ave., Brenham, TX 77833 | Brian Roper | (979) 830-4170 |
| Blue Mountain CC | 2411 NW Carden Ave., Pendleton, OR 97801 | Brett Bryan | (541) 278-5900 |

| | | | |
|---|---|---|---|
| Blue Ridge CC | 180 Campus Dr., Flat Rock, NC 28731 | Damon Towe | (828) 694-1778 |
| Borough of Manhattan CC | 199 Chambers St., New York, NY 10007 | John Torres | (212) 220-8261 |
| Bossier Parish CC | 2719 Airline Dr., Bossier City, LA 71111 | Aaron Vorachek | (318) 746-9851 |
| Brevard CC | 1519 Clearlake Rd., Cocoa, FL 32922 | Ernie Rosseau | (321) 433-5600 |
| Bronx CC | W. 181 St. & University Ave., Bronx, NY 10453 | Adolfo DeJesus | (718) 289-5276 |
| Brookdale CC | 765 Newman Springs Rd., Lincroft, NJ 07738 | Johnny Johnson | (732) 224-2044 |
| Brookhaven College | 3939 Valley View Lane, Farmers Branch, TX 75244 | Corey Thornton | (972) 860-4121 |
| Broome CC | PO Box 1017, Binghamton, NY 13902 | Brett Carter | (607) 778-5003 |
| Broward CC | 3501 SW Davie Rd., Central Campus #10, Davie, FL 33314 | Rob Deutschman | (945) 201-6997 |
| Brown Mackie CC | 2106 S. Ninth, Salina, KS 67401 | Steve Bartow | (785) 825-5422 |
| Bucks County CC | 275 Swamp Rd, Newton, PA 18940 | Craig Scioscia | (215) 968-8450 |
| Bunker Hill CC | 250 New Rutherford Ave, Boston, MA 02129 | Charles Coughlin | (617) 228-2088 |
| Burlington County College | 601 Pemberton-Browns Mill Rd., Pemberton, NJ 08068 | John Holt | (609) 894-9311 |
| Butler CC | 901 S. Haverhill Rd., El Dorado, KS 67042 | Steve Johnson | (316) 322-3201 |
| Butler County CC | PO Box 1203, Butler, PA 16003 | Steve Boyd | (724) 287-8711 |
| Butte College | 3536 Butte Campus Dr., Oroville, CA 95965 | Anthony Ferro | (530) 895-2475 |
| | | | |
| Cabrillo College | 6500 Soquel Dr., Aptos, CA 95003 | Andy Messersmith | (831) 479-6409 |
| Calhoun CC | PO Box 2216, Decatur, AL 35609 | Jim Morrill | (256) 306-2856 |
| Camden County College | PO Box 200, Blackwood, NJ 08012 | Ken Bouillon | (856) 227-7200 |
| Canada College | 4200 Farmhill Rd., Redwood City, CA 94061 | Tonny Lucca | (650) 306-3269 |
| Canyons, College of the | 26455 N. Rockwell Canyon Rd., Valencia, CA 91355 | Chris Cota | (661) 259-7800 |
| Carl Albert State College | 1507 S. McKenna St., Poteau, OK 74953 | Mark Pollard | (918) 647-1376 |
| Carl Sandburg College | 2400 Tom L. Wilson Blvd., Galesburg, IL 61401 | Justin Inskeep | (309) 341-5276 |
| CCBC-Catonsville | 800 S. Rolling Rd., Catonsville, MD 21228 | Dan Blue | (410) 455-4102 |
| CCBC-Dundalk | 7200 Sollers Point Rd., Dundalk, MD 21222 | Jason King | (410) 285-9741 |
| CCBC-Essex | 7201 Rossville Blvd., Baltimore, MD 21237 | George Henderson | (410) 780-6859 |
| Cecil CC | One Seahawk Dr., North East, MD 21901 | Charlie O'Brien | (410) 287-1080 |
| Cedar Valley College | 3030 N. Dallas Ave., Lancaster, TX 75134 | Kyle Koehler | (972) 860-8177 |
| Central Alabama CC | PO Box 699, Alexander City, AL 35010 | Don Ingram | (256) 215-4320 |
| Central Arizona College | 8470 N. Overfield Rd., Coolidge, AZ 85228 | Jon Wente | (520) 426-4300 |
| Central Florida CC | 3001 SW College Rd., Ocala, FL 34474 | Marty Smith | (352) 854-2322 |
| Central Lakes College | 501 W. College Dr., Brainerd, MN 56401 | Warren Mertens | (218) 855-8210 |
| Centralia College | 600 W. Locust St., Centralia, WA 98531 | Bruce Pocklington | (360) 736-9391 |
| Cerritos College | 11110 East Alondra Blvd., Norwalk, CA 90650 | Ken Gaylord | (562) 860-2451 |
| Cerro Coso CC | 3000 College Heights Blvd., Ridgecrest, CA 93555 | Dick Adams | (760) 384-6386 |
| Chabot College | 25555 Hesperian Blvd., Hayward, CA 94545 | Steve Friend | (510) 723-6935 |
| Chaffey College | 5885 Haven Ave., Rancho Cucamonga, CA 91737 | Jeff Harlow | (909) 941-2328 |
| Chandler-Gilbert CC | 2626 E. Pecos Rd., Chandler, AZ 85225 | Doyle Wilson | (480) 732-7177 |
| Chattahoochee Valley CC | 2602 College Dr., Phenix City, AL 36869 | Adam Thomas | (334) 214-4880 |
| Chattanooga State Tech CC | 4501 Amnicola Hwy., Chattanooga, TN 37406 | Greg Dennis | (423) 697-3397 |
| Chemeketa CC | 4000 Lancaster Dr. NE, Salem, OR 97309 | Tucker Brack | (503) 399-7953 |
| Chesapeake College | PO Box 8, Wye Mills, MD 21679 | Frank Szymanski | (410) 822-5400 |
| Chipola JC | 3094 Indian Circle, Marianna, FL 32446 | Jeff Johnson | (850) 718-2302 |
| Cisco JC | 101 College Heights, Cisco, TX 76437 | David White | (254) 442-5000 |
| Citrus College | 1000 W. Foothill Blvd., Glendora, CA 91741 | Steve Gomez | (626) 914-8800 |
| Clackamas CC | 19600 S. Molalla Ave., Oregon City, OR 97045 | Robin Robinson | (503) 657-6958 |
| Clarendon College | PO Box 968, Clarendon, TX 79226 | Cory Hall | (806) 874-3571 |
| Clark State CC | PO Box 570, Springfield, OH 45501 | Al Fulk | (937) 328-7819 |
| Cleveland State CC | PO Box 3570, Cleveland, TN 37320 | Mike Policastro | (423) 478-6219 |
| Clinton CC | 136 Clinton Point Dr., Plattsburgh, NY 12901 | Tom Neale | (518) 562-4220 |
| Cloud County CC | 2221 Campus Dr., Box 1002, Concordia, KS 66901 | Greg Brummett | (785) 243-1435 |
| Coahoma JC | 3240 Friars Point Rd., Clarksdale, MS 38614 | Billy Fields | (662) 627-4231 |
| Cochise College | 4190 W. Hwy. 80, Douglas, AZ 85607 | Todd Inglehart | (520) 417-4095 |
| Coffeyville CC | 400 W. 11th St., Coffeyville, KS 67337 | Ryan McCune | (620) 252-7095 |
| Colby CC | 1255 S. Range Ave, Colby, KS 67701 | Ryan Carter | (785) 462-3984 |
| Colorado Northwestern CC | 500 Kennedy Dr., Rangely, CO 81648 | Dustin Colborn | (970) 675-3314 |
| Columbia Basin CC | 2600 N. 20th Ave., Pasco, WA 99301 | Scott Rogers | (509) 547-0511 |
| Columbia State CC | PO Box 1315, Columbia, TN 38402 | James Painter | (931) 540-2632 |
| Columbia-Greene CC | 4400 Route 23, Hudson, NY 12534 | Unavailable | (518) 828-4181 |
| Columbus State CC | 550 E. Spring St., Columbus, OH 43215 | Harry Caruso | (614) 287-2674 |
| Compton CC | 11111 Artesia Blvd., Compton, CA 90221 | Shannon Williams | (310) 900-1600 |
| Connecticut-Avery Point, U. of | 1084 Shennescossett Rd., Groton, CT 06340 | Roger Bidwell | (860) 405-9183 |
| Connors State College | Rt. 1, Box 1000, Warner, OK 74469 | Perry Keith | (918) 463-6231 |
| Contra Costa College | 2600 Mission Bell Dr., San Pablo, CA 94806 | Marvin Webb | (510) 235-7800 |
| Copiah-Lincoln JC | PO Box 649, Wesson, MS 39191 | Keith Case | (601) 643-8381 |
| Corning CC | 1 Academic Dr., Corning, NY 14830 | Brian Hill | (607) 962-9383 |
| Cosumnes River CC | 8401 Center Pkwy., Sacramento CA 95823 | Tony Bloomfield | (916) 691-7397 |
| Cowley County CC | 125 S. 2nd St., Arkansas City, KS 67005 | Dave Burroughs | (620) 441-5246 |
| Crowder College | 601 Laclede Ave., Neosho, MO 64850 | Travis Lallemand | (417) 451-3223 |
| Crowley's Ridge College | 100 College Dr., Paragould, AR 72450 | James Scott | (870) 236-6901 |
| Cuesta College | PO Box 8106, San Luis Obispo, CA 93403 | Bob Miller | (805) 546-3100 |
| Cumberland County College | PO Box 1500, Vineland, NJ 08362 | Lou Camilli | (856) 691-8600 |

| | | | |
|---|---|---|---|
| Cuyahoga CC | 11000 Pleasant Valley Rd., Parma, OH 44130 | Jerry Chase | (216) 987-5459 |
| Cypress College | 9200 Valley View St., Cypress, CA 90630 | Scott Pickler | (714) 826-7870 |
| | | | |
| Dakota County Tech College | 1300 145th St. E, Rosemount, MN 55068 | Tim Huber | (651) 423-8462 |
| Danville Area CC | 2000 E. Main St., Danville, IL 61832 | Tim Bunton | (217) 443-8807 |
| Darton College | 2400 Gillionville Rd., Albany, GA 31707 | Glenn Eames | (229) 430-6788 |
| Dawson CC | PO Box 421, Glendive, MT 59330 | Brent Diegel | (406) 377-9450 |
| Daytona Beach CC | 1200 Int'l Speedway Blvd., Daytona Beach, FL 32114 | Tim Touma | (386) 506-4486 |
| Dean College | 99 Main St., Franklin, MA 02038 | John Flanders | (508) 541-1814 |
| De Anza College | 21250 Stevens Creek Blvd., Cupertino, CA 95014 | Scott Hertler | (408) 864-8741 |
| Delaware County CC | 901 S. Media Line Rd., Media, PA 19063 | Paul Motta | (610) 353-5354 |
| Delaware Tech & CC | PO Box 610, Georgetown, DE 19947 | Curtis Brock | (302) 855-1636 |
| Delgado CC | 615 City Park Ave., New Orleans, LA 70119 | Joe Scheuermann | (504) 483-4383 |
| Des Moines Area CC | 1125 Hancock Dr., Boone, IA 50036 | John Smith | (515) 433-5050 |
| Desert, College of the | 43-500 Monterey Ave., Palm Desert, CA 92260 | Dave Buttles | (760) 775-2585 |
| Diablo Valley College | 321 Golf Club Rd., Pleasant Hill, CA 94523 | Carl Fraticelli | (925) 685-1230 |
| Dixie State College of Utah | 225 S. 700 E., St. George, UT 84770 | Mike Littlewood | (435) 652-7525 |
| Dodge City CC | 2501 N. 14th Ave., Dodge City, KS 67801 | Phil Stephenson | (620) 227-9347 |
| DuPage, College of | 425 Fawell Blvd., Glen Ellyn, IL 60137 | Dan Kusinski | (630) 942-2365 |
| Dutchess CC | Falcon Hall, Poughkeepsie, NY 12601 | Jay Curtis Jr. | (845) 431-8468 |
| Dyersburg State CC | 1510 Lake Rd., Dyersburg, TN 38024 | Robert White | (901) 286-3259 |
| | | | |
| East Central CC | PO Box 129, Decatur, MS 39327 | Jake Yarborough | (601) 635-2111 |
| East Los Angeles College | 1301 Cesar Chavez Ave., Monterey Park, CA 91754 | James Hines | (323) 265-8914 |
| East Mississippi CC | PO Box 158, Scooba, MS 39358 | Bill Baldner | (662) 476-5128 |
| Eastern Arizona JC | 615 N. Stadium Ave., Thatcher, AZ 85552 | Jim Bagnall | (520) 428-8414 |
| Eastern Oklahoma State College | 1301 W. Main St., Wilburton, OK 74578 | Aric Thomas | (918) 465-1734 |
| Eastern Utah, College of | 451 E. 400 N., Price, UT 84501 | Scott Madsen | (435) 613-5357 |
| Eastfield College | 3737 Motley Dr., Mesquite, TX 75150 | Michael Martin | (972) 860-7140 |
| Edmonds CC | 20000 68th Ave. W., Lynnwood, WA 98036 | Hal DeBerry | (425) 640-1507 |
| El Camino College | 16007 Crenshaw Blvd., Torrance, CA 90506 | Chad Nammack | (310) 660-3679 |
| El Paso CC | PO Box 20500, El Paso, TX 79998 | Shannon Hunt | (915) 831-2623 |
| Elgin CC | 1700 Spartan Dr., Elgin, IL 60123 | Bill Angelo | (847) 214-7552 |
| Ellsworth CC | 1100 College Ave., Iowa Falls, IA 50126 | Joel Lueken | (800) 322-9235 |
| Enterprise-Ozark CC | 600 Plaza Dr., Enterprise, AL 36630 | Tim Hulsey | (334) 347-2623 |
| Erie CC | 21 Oak St., Buffalo, NY 14203 | Joe Bauth | (716) 851-1294 |
| Everett CC | 2000 Tower St., Everett, WA 98201 | Levi Lacey | (425) 388-9322 |
| | | | |
| Faulkner State CC | 1900 Hwy. 31 S., Bay Minette, AL 36507 | Wayne Larker | (251) 580-2160 |
| Feather River College | 570 Golden Eagle Ave., Quincy, CA 95971 | Reed Peters | (530) 283-0202 |
| Finger Lakes CC | 4355 Lakeshore Dr., Canandaigua, NY 14424 | Patrick Greer | (585) 394-3500 |
| Florence-Darlington Tech College | PO Box 100548, Florence, SC 29501 | Curtis Hudson | (800) 228-5745 |
| Florida CC | 11901 Beach Blvd., Jacksonville, FL 32246 | Chris Blaquierre | (904) 646-2205 |
| Fort Scott CC | 2108 S. Horton St., Fort Scott, KS 66701 | Chris Moddelmog | (620) 223-2700 |
| Frank Phillips College | PO Box 5118, Borger, TX 79008 | Guy Simmons | (806) 457-4200 |
| Frederick CC | 7932 Opossumtown Pike, Frederick, MD 21702 | Rodney Bennett | (301) 846-2501 |
| Fresno City College | 1101 University Ave., Fresno, CA 93741 | Ron Scott | (559) 237-8974 |
| Fullerton College | 321 E. Chapman Ave., Fullerton, CA 92632 | Nick Fuscardo | (714) 922-7401 |
| Fulton-Montgomery CC | 2805 State Hwy. 67, Johnstown, NY 12095 | Mike Mulligan | (518) 762-4651 |
| | | | |
| Gadsden State CC | PO Box 227, Gadsden, AL 35902 | Bill Lockridge | (256) 549-8200 |
| Galveston College | 4015 Avenue Q, Galveston, TX 77550 | Javier Solis | (409) 944-1315 |
| Garden City CC | 801 Campus Dr., Garden City, KS 67846 | Rick Sabath | (620) 276-9595 |
| Garrett College | 687 Mosser Rd., McHenry, MD 21541 | Eric Hallenbeck | (301) 387-3052 |
| Gateway CC | 108 N. 40th St., Phoenix, AZ 85034 | Victor Solis | (602) 286-8216 |
| Gateway CC/Tech College | 60 Sargent Dr., New Haven, CT 06511 | Lance Lusisnan | (203) 285-2213 |
| Gavilan College | 5055 Santa Teresa Blvd., Gilroy, CA 95020 | Neal Andrade | (408) 476-0684 |
| Genesee CC | 1 College Rd., Batavia, NY 14020 | Skip Sherman | (585) 345-6898 |
| Georgia Perimeter College | 3251 Panthersville Rd., Decatur, GA 30034 | Ted Wallen | (770) 551-3128 |
| Glen Oaks CC | 62249 Shimmel Rd., Centreville, MI 49032 | Junie Melendez | (888) 994-7818 |
| Glendale CC | 6000 W. Olive Ave., Glendale, AZ 85302 | David Grant | (623) 845-3046 |
| Glendale College | 1500 N. Verdugo Rd., Glendale, CA 91208 | Chris Cicuto | (818) 240-1000 |
| Globe Tech | 291 Broadway, New York, NY 10007 | Danny Ramirez | (212) 349-4330 |
| Gloucester County College | 1400 Tanyard Rd., Sewell, NJ 08080 | Rob Valli | (856) 415-2257 |
| Golden West College | 15744 Golden West St., Huntington Beach, CA 92647 | Roberto Villarreal | (714) 895-8260 |
| Gordon College | 419 College Dr., Barnesville, GA 30204 | Travis McClanahan | (770) 358-5061 |
| Grand Rapids CC | 143 Bostwick Ave. NE, Grand Rapids, MI 49503 | Mike Cupples | (616) 234-4270 |
| Grays Harbor College | 1620 Edward P. Smith Dr., Aberdeen, WA 98520 | Shon Schreiber | (360) 538-4062 |
| Grayson County College | 6101 Grayson Dr., Denison, TX 75020 | Dusty Hart | (903) 463-8753 |
| Green River CC | 12401 SE 320th St., Auburn, WA 98092 | Matt Acker | (253) 833-9111 |
| Grossmont College | 8800 Grossmont College Blvd., El Cajon, CA 92020 | Randy Abshier | (619) 644-7423 |
| Gulf Coast CC | 5230 W. Hwy. 98, Panama City, FL 32401 | Mike Kandler | (850) 872-3830 |

| | | | |
|---|---|---|---|
| Hagerstown CC | 11400 Robinwood Dr., Hagerstown, MD 21742 | Scott Jennings | (301) 790-2800 |
| Harford CC | 401 Thomas Run Rd., Bel Air, MD 21015 | Bill Greenwell | (410) 836-4321 |
| Harper College | 1200 W. Algonquin Rd., Palatine, IL 60067 | Vern Hasty | (847) 925-6969 |
| Hartnell CC | 156 Homestead Ave., Salinas, CA 93901 | Dan Teresa | (831) 755-6840 |
| Henry Ford CC | 5101 Evergreen Rd., Dearborn, MI 48128 | Jeff Child | (313) 845-9647 |
| Herkimer County CC | 100 Reservoir Rd., Herkimer, NY 13350 | Jason Rathbun | (315) 866-0300 |
| Hesston College | PO Box 3000, Box 3000, Hesston, KS 67062 | Art Mullet | (620) 327-8278 |
| Hibbing CC | 1515 E. 25th St., Hibbing, MN 55746 | Mike Turnbull | (218) 262-6749 |
| Highland CC | 2998 W. Pearl City Rd., Freeport, IL 61032 | Don Tresemer | (815) 599-3465 |
| Highland CC | 606 W. Main, Highland, KS 66035 | Rick Eberly | (785) 442-6070 |
| Hill College | PO Box 619, Hillsboro, TX 76645 | Brian Strickland | (254) 582-2555 |
| Hillsborough CC | 4001 W. Tampa Bay Blvd., Tampa, FL 33614 | Gary Calhoun | (813) 253-7446 |
| Hinds CC | PO Box 1100, Raymond, MS 39154 | Sam Temple | (601) 857-3362 |
| Hiwassee College | 225 Hiwassee College Dr., Madisonville, TN 37354 | Lance Knight | (423) 442-2001 |
| Holmes CC | PO Box 369, Goodman, MS 39079 | Kenny Dupont | (662) 472-9065 |
| Holyoke CC | 303 Homestead Ave., Holyoke, MA 01040 | J.C. Fernandes | (413) 552-2163 |
| Hostos CC | 500 Grand Concourse, Bronx, NY 10451 | Unavailable | (718) 518-6551 |
| Howard College | 1001 Birdwell Lane, Big Spring, TX 79720 | Britt Smith | (432) 264-5195 |
| Hudson Valley CC | 80 Vandenburg Ave., Troy, NY 12180 | Tom Reinisch | (518) 629-7328 |
| Hutchinson CC | 1300 N. Plum St., Hutchinson, KS 67501 | Kyle Crookes | (316) 665-3586 |
| | | | |
| Illinois Central College | One College Dr., East Peoria, IL 61635 | Brett Kelley | (309) 694-5429 |
| Illinois Valley CC | 815 N. Orlando Smith Rd., Oglesby, IL 61348 | Unavailable | (815) 224-0471 |
| Imperial Valley College | PO Box 158, Imperial, CA 92251 | Jim Mecate | (760) 355-6341 |
| Independence CC | 1057 W. College Ave., Independence, KS 67301 | Jon Olsen | (620) 332-5480 |
| Indian Hills CC | 721 N. 1st St., Centerville, IA 52544 | Cam Walker | (641) 856-2143 |
| Indian River CC | 3209 Virginia Ave., Fort Pierce, FL 34981 | Bob O'Brien | (772) 462-7760 |
| Iowa Central CC | 330 Avenue M, Fort Dodge, IA 50501 | Rick Pederson | (515) 576-7201 |
| Iowa Lakes CC | 300 S. 18th St., Estherville, IA 51334 | Jason Nell | (712) 362-7915 |
| Iowa Western CC | 2700 College Rd., Council Bluffs, IA 51503 | Marc Rardin | (712) 325-3402 |
| Irvine Valley College | 5500 Irvine Center Dr., Irvine, CA 92618 | Kent Madole | (949) 451-5763 |
| Itasca CC | 1851 E. Hwy. 169, Grand Rapids, MN 55744 | Justin Lamppa | (218) 327-4460 |
| Itawamba CC | 602 W. Hill St., Fulton, MS 38843 | Rick Collier | (662) 862-8123 |
| | | | |
| Jackson State CC | 2046 N. Parkway, Jackson, TN 38301 | Steve Cornelison | (731) 425-2649 |
| Jamestown CC | 525 Falconer St., Jamestown, NY 14701 | Kerry Kellogg | (716) 665-5220 |
| Jefferson College | 1000 Viking Dr., Hillsboro, MO 63050 | Dave Oster | (636) 789-3000 |
| Jefferson CC | 1220 Coffeen St., Watertown, NY 13601 | Paul Alteri | (315) 786-2248 |
| Jefferson Davis CC | PO Box 958, Brewton, AL 36427 | Darrell Blevins | (334) 809-1622 |
| Jefferson State CC | 2601 Carson Rd., Birmingham, AL 35215 | David Russo | (205) 856-7879 |
| John A. Logan College | 700 Logan College Rd., Carterville, IL 62918 | Jerry Halstead | (618) 985-2828 |
| John Wood CC | 1301 S. 48th St., Quincy, IL 62305 | Greg Wathen | (217) 224-6564 |
| Johnson County CC | 12345 College Blvd., Overland Park, KS 66210 | Kent Shelley | (913) 469-3820 |
| Joliet JC | 1215 Houbolt Rd., Joliet, IL 60431 | Wayne King | (815) 280-2210 |
| Jones County JC | 900 S. Court St., Ellisville, MS 39437 | Bobby Glaze | (601) 477-4088 |
| | | | |
| Kalamazoo Valley CC | PO Box 4070, Kalamazoo, MI 49003 | Bernie Vallier | (269) 488-4393 |
| Kankakee CC | PO Box 888, River Rd., Kankakee, IL 60901 | Todd Post | (815) 802-8602 |
| Kansas City Kansas CC | 7250 State Ave., Kansas City, KS 66112 | Steve Burleson | (913) 288-7150 |
| Kaskaskia CC | 27210 College Rd., Centralia, IL 62801 | Brad Tuttle | (618) 545-3146 |
| Kellogg CC | 450 North Ave., Battle Creek, MI 49017 | Russ Bortell | (269) 965-4151 |
| Kingsborough CC | 2001 Oriental Blvd., Brooklyn, NY 11235 | Jim Ryan | (718) 368-5737 |
| Kirkwood CC | 6301 Kirkwood Blvd. SW, Cedar Rapids, IA 52404 | John Lewis | (319) 398-5589 |
| Kishwaukee CC | 21193 Malta Rd., Malta, IL 60150 | Josh Pethoud | (815) 825-2086 |
| | | | |
| Labette CC | 200 S. 14th St., Parsons, KS 67357 | Aaron Keal | (620) 820-1017 |
| Lackawanna College | Athletic Department, Scranton, PA 18509 | Chris Pensak | (570) 961-0700 |
| Lake City CC | 149 SE Vocational Pl., Lake City, FL 32025 | Tom Clark | (386) 754-4363 |
| Lake County, College of | 19351 W. Washington St., Grayslake, IL 60030 | Cory Domel | (847) 543-2046 |
| Lake Land College | 5001 Lake Land Blvd., Mattoon, IL 61938 | Jim Jarrett | (217) 234-5296 |
| Lake Michigan College | 2755 E. Napier Ave., Benton Harbor, MI 49022 | Keith Schreiber | (616) 927-8165 |
| Lake Sumter CC | 9501 US Hwy. 441, Leesburg, FL 32788 | Mike Matulia | (352) 323-3643 |
| Lakeland CC | 7700 Clocktower Dr., Kirtland, OH 44094 | Howie Krause | (440) 525-7350 |
| Lamar CC | 2401 S. Main St., Lamar, CO 81052 | Scott Crampton | (719) 336-1681 |
| Lane CC | 4000 E. 30th Ave., Eugene, OR 97405 | Rob Strickland | (541) 463-5553 |
| Laney College | 900 Fallon St., Oakland, CA 94607 | Francisco Zapata | (510) 464-3476 |
| Lansing CC | PO Box 40010, Lansing, MI 48901 | Vaughn Vowels | (517) 483-1624 |
| Laredo CC | West End, Washington St., Laredo, TX 78040 | Chase Tidwell | (956) 721-5326 |
| Lassen College | PO Box 3000, Susanville, CA 96130 | John Bentley | (530) 251-8815 |
| Lawson State CC | 3060 Wilson Rd. SW, Birmingham, AL 35221 | Randle Jennings | (205) 929-2086 |
| Lenoir CC | PO Box 188, Kinston, NC 28502 | Stoney Wine | (252) 233-6818 |
| Lewis & Clark CC | 5800 Godfrey Rd., Godfrey, IL 62035 | Randy Martz | (618) 468-6000 |
| Lincoln College | 300 Keokuk St., Lincoln, IL 62656 | Tony Thomas | (217) 732-3155 |

| | | | |
|---|---|---|---|
| Lincoln Land CC | 5250 Shepherd Rd., Springfield, IL 62794 | Ron Riggle | (217) 786-2581 |
| Lincoln Trail College | 11220 State Hwy. 1, Robinson, IL 62454 | Mitch Hannahs | (618) 544-8657 |
| Linn-Benton CC | 6500 Pacific Blvd. SW, Albany, OR 97321 | Greg Hawk | (541) 917-4242 |
| Lon Morris College | 800 College Ave., Jacksonville, TX 75766 | Josh Stewart | (903) 589-4073 |
| Long Beach City College | 4901 E. Carson St., Long Beach, CA 90808 | Casey Crook | (562) 938-4242 |
| Longview CC | 500 Longview Rd., Lee's Summit, MO 64081 | Gary Harrmann | (816) 672-2440 |
| Los Angeles City College | 855 N. Vermont Ave., Los Angeles, CA 90029 | Melvin Aaron | (323) 953-4000 |
| Los Angeles Harbor College | 1111 Figueroa Pl., Wilmington, CA 90742 | Marco Alvillar | (310) 233-4140 |
| Los Angeles Mission College | 13356 Eldridge Ave., Sylmar, CA 91342 | Kent Cote | (818) 837-1201 |
| Los Angeles Pierce College | 6201 Winnetka Ave., Woodland Hills, CA 91371 | Bob Lofrano | (818) 710-2823 |
| Los Angeles Valley College | 5800 Fulton Ave., Van Nuys, CA 91491 | Dave Mallas | (818) 947-2509 |
| Los Medanos College | 2700 E. Leland Rd., Pittsburg, CA 94565 | Tony Dress | (925) 439-2185 |
| Louisburg College | 501 N. Main St., Louisburg, NC 27549 | Tommy Atkinson | (919) 497-3249 |
| Lower Columbia College | 1600 Maple St., Longview, WA 98632 | Kelly Smith | (360) 442-2471 |
| LSU-Eunice | PO Box 1129, Eunice, LA 70535 | Jeff Willis | (337) 550-1287 |
| Lurleen B. Wallace JC | PO Box 1418, Andalusia, AL 36420 | Steve Helms | (334) 222-6591 |
| Luzerne County CC | 1333 S. Prospect St., Nanticoke, PA 18634 | Ted Williams | (570) 740-0591 |
| | | | |
| Macomb CC | 14500 E. 12 Mile Rd., Warren, MI 48088 | Ken Vernier | (586) 445-7512 |
| Madison Area Tech | 3550 Anderson St., Madison, WI 53704 | Mike Davenport | (608) 246-6699 |
| Manatee CC | 5840 26th St. W, Bradenton, FL 34207 | Tim Hill | (941) 752-5575 |
| Manchester CC | Great Path MS No. 7, Manchester, CT 06045 | Chris Strahowski | (860) 512-2612 |
| Maple Woods CC | 2601 NE Barry Rd., Kansas City, MO 64156 | Marty Kilgore | (816) 437-3170 |
| Marin, College of | Athletic Dept., Kentfield, CA 94904 | Steve Berringer | (415) 485-9589 |
| Marshalltown CC | 3700 S. Center St., Marshalltown, IA 50158 | Kevin Benzing | (641) 752-7106 |
| Massachusetts Bay CC | 50 Oakland St., Wellesley Hills, MA 02481 | Ahleigh Davenport | (508) 270-4065 |
| Massasoit CC | 1 Massasoit Blvd., Brockton, MA 02302 | Tom Frizzell | (508) 588-9100 |
| McCook CC | 1205 E. 3rd St., McCook, NE 69001 | Jeremy Jorgensen | (308) 345-8144 |
| McHenry County College | 8900 U.S. Hwy. 14, Crystal Lake, IL 60012 | Kim Johnson | (815) 455-8580 |
| McLennan CC | 1400 College Dr., Waco, TX 76708 | Pete Mejia | (254) 299-8811 |
| Mendocino CC | 1000 Hensley Creek Rd, Ukiah, CA 95482 | Matt Gordon | (707) 468-3142 |
| Merced College | 3600 M St., Merced, CA 95348 | Chris Pedretti | (209) 384-6028 |
| Mercer County CC | PO Box B, Trenton, NJ 08690 | Matt Wolski | (609) 586-4800 |
| Mercyhurst-North East | 16 W. Division St., North East, PA 16428 | Ryan Smith | (814) 725-6390 |
| Meridian CC | 910 Hwy. 19 N., Meridian MS 39307 | Chris Rose | (601) 484-8699 |
| Mesa CC | 1833 W. Southern Ave., Mesa, AZ 85202 | Tony Cirelli | (480) 461-7561 |
| Mesabi Range College | 1001 W. Chestnut St., Virginia, MN 55792 | Brad Scott | (218) 749-2422 |
| Miami-Dade College | 11011 SW 104 St., Miami, FL 33176 | Steve Hertz | (305) 237-0730 |
| Miami U.-Middletown | 4200 E. University Blvd., Middletown, OH 45042 | Kenneth Prichard | (513) 727-3273 |
| Middle Georgia College | 1100 2nd St., Cochran, GA 31014 | Craig Young | (478) 934-3064 |
| Middlesex County College | 2600 Woodbridge Ave., Edison, NJ 08818 | Michael Lepore | (732) 906-2558 |
| Midland College | 3600 N. Garfield St., Midland, TX 79705 | Steve Ramharter | (432) 685-4581 |
| Miles CC | 2715 Dickinson St., Miles City, MT 59301 | Bob Bishop | (406) 874-6169 |
| Milwaukee Area Tech | 700 W. State St., Milwaukee, WI 53233 | Tony Goodenough | (414) 297-7872 |
| Mineral Area College | PO Box 1000., Park Hills, MO 63601 | Jim Gerwitz | (573) 431-4593 |
| Minn. State Comm & Tech | 1414 College Way, Fergus Falls, MN 56357 | Kent Bothwell | (218) 736-1618 |
| Minnesota West Comm. & Tech | 1450 College Way, Worthington, MN 56187 | Brian Iverson | (507) 372-3400 |
| Minot State U. | 105 Simrall Blvd., Bottineau, ND 58318 | Jason Harris | (701) 228-5474 |
| Mission College | 3000 Mission College Blvd., Santa Clara, CA 95054 | Todd Eagen | (408) 855-5366 |
| Mississippi Delta CC | PO Box 668, Moorhead, MS 38761 | Tony Hancock | (662) 246-6471 |
| Mississippi Gulf Coast JC | PO Box 548, Perkinston, MS 39573 | Cooper Farris | (601) 928-6224 |
| Modesto JC | 435 College Ave., Modesto, CA 95350 | Bo Aiello | (209) 575-6274 |
| Mohawk Valley CC | 1101 Sherman Dr., Utica, NY 13501 | Dave Warren | (315) 792-5570 |
| Monroe College | 2501 Jerome Ave., Bronx, NY 10468 | Juan Reyes | (718) 933-6700 |
| Monroe CC | 1000 E. Henrietta Rd., Rochester, NY 14623 | Skip Bailey | (585) 292-2088 |
| Monterey Peninsula College | 980 Fremont St., Monterey, CA 93940 | Dan Phillips | (831) 646-4223 |
| Montgomery College-Germantown | 20200 Observation Dr., Germantown, MD 20876 | Dan Rascher | (301) 353-7727 |
| Montgomery College-Rockville | 51 Mannakee St., Rockville, MD 20850 | Tom Shaffer | (301) 251-7587 |
| Moorpark College | 7075 Campus Rd., Moorpark, CA 93021 | Mario Porto | (805) 378-1537 |
| Moraine Valley CC | 10900 S. 88th Ave., Palos Hills, IL 60465 | Unavailable | (708) 974-5213 |
| Morris, County College of | 214 Center Grove Rd., Randolph, NJ 07869 | Ed Moskal | (973) 328-5252 |
| Morrisville State College | Student Activities Building, Morrisville, NY 13408 | Tim Byrnes | (315) 684-6072 |
| Morton College | 3801 S. Central Ave., Cicero, IL 60804 | Tony Hubbard | (708) 656-8000 |
| Motlow State CC | PO Box 8500, Lynchburg, TN 37352 | Don Rhoton | (931) 393-1614 |
| Mott CC | 1401 E. Court St., Flint, MI 48503 | Kevin Visser | (810) 762-0419 |
| Mount Hood CC | 26000 SE Stark St., Gresham, OR 97030 | Gabe Sandy | (503) 491-7352 |
| Mount San Antonio College | 1100 N. Grand Ave., Walnut, CA 91789 | Stacy Parker | (909) 594-5611 |
| Mount San Jacinto CC | 1499 N. State St., San Jacinto, CA 92583 | Steve Alonzo | (951) 487-6752 |
| Murray State College | 1 Murray Campus, Tishomingo, OK 73460 | Mike McBrayer | (580) 371-2371 |
| Muscatine CC | 152 Colorado St., Muscatine, IA 52761 | Rob Allison | (319) 288-6001 |
| Muskegon CC | 221 S. Quarterline Rd., Muskegon, MI 49442 | Cap Pohlman | (231) 777-0381 |

| | | | |
|---|---|---|---|
| Napa Valley College | 2277 Napa-Vallejo Hwy., Napa, CA 94558 | Bob Freschi | (707) 253-3232 |
| Nassau CC | 1 Education Dr., Garden City, NY 11530 | Larry Minor | (516) 572-7522 |
| Navarro College | 3200 W. 7th Ave., Corsicana, TX 75110 | Skip Johnson | (903) 875-7487 |
| Neosho County CC | 800 W. 14th St., Chanute, KS 66720 | Steve Murry | (620) 431-2820 |
| New Hampshire Tech | 31 College Dr., Concord, NH 03301 | Tom Neal | (603) 271-7127 |
| New Mexico JC | 5317 N. Lovington Hwy., Hobbs, NM 88240 | Ray Birmingham | (505) 392-5786 |
| New Mexico Military Inst. | 101 W. College Blvd., Roswell, NM 88201 | Marty Zeller | (505) 622-6250 |
| Niagara County CC | 3111 Saunders Settlement Rd., Sanborn, NY 14132 | Jerry Whitehead | (716) 614-6271 |
| North Arkansas College | 1515 Pioneer Dr., Harrison, AR 72601 | Phil Wilson | (870) 391-3287 |
| North Central Missouri College | 1301 Main St., Trenton, MO 64683 | James Arnold | (660) 359-3948 |
| North Central Texas College | 1525 W. California St., Gainesville, TX 76240 | Kevin Darwin | (940) 668-7731 |
| North Florida CC | 1000 Turner Davis Dr., Madison, FL 32340 | Steve Givens | (850) 973-1609 |
| North Iowa Area CC | 500 College Dr., Mason City, IA 50401 | Todd Rima | (641) 422-4281 |
| North Lake CC | 5001 N. MacArthur Blvd., Irving, TX 75038 | Steve Cummings | (972) 273-3518 |
| Northampton CC | 3835 Green Pond Rd., Bethlehem, PA 18020 | John Sweeney | (610) 861-5465 |
| Northeast Mississippi CC | 101 Cunningham Blvd., Booneville, MS 38829 | Ray Scott | (662) 720-7352 |
| Northeast Texas CC | PO Box 1307, Mount Pleasant, TX 75456 | Chris Smith | (903) 572-1911 |
| Northeastern JC | 100 College Dr., Sterling, CO 80751 | Bryan Shepherd | (970) 521-6641 |
| Northeastern Oklahoma A&M | 200 I Street NE, Miami, OK 74354 | Roger Ward | (918) 540-6323 |
| Northern Essex CC | 100 Elliott St., Haverhill, MA 01830 | Kerry Quinlan | (978) 556-3820 |
| Northern Oklahoma College | PO Box 310, Tonkawa, OK 74653 | Terry Ballard | (580) 628-6760 |
| Northern Oklahoma-Enid | 100 S. University Ave., Enid, OK 73701 | Raydon Leaton | (580) 548-2329 |
| Northland Comm. & Tech | 1101 Hwy. 1 E., Thief River Falls, MN 56701 | Steve Gust | (218) 681-0723 |
| Northwest Mississippi CC | 4975 Hwy. 51 N., Senatobia, MS 38668 | Mark Carson | (662) 562-3419 |
| Northwest Shoals CC | PO Box 2545, Muscle Shoals, AL 35662 | David Langston | (256) 331-5462 |
| | | | |
| Oakton CC | 1600 E. Golf Rd., Des Plaines, IL 60016 | Mike Pinto | (847) 635-1753 |
| Ocean County College | 1 College Dr., Toms River, NJ 08754 | Ernie Leta | (732) 255-0345 |
| Odessa College | 201 W. University Blvd., Odessa, TX 79764 | Brian Blessie | (432) 335-6574 |
| Ohlone College | 43600 Mission Blvd., Fremont, CA 94539 | Paul Moore | (510) 659-6056 |
| Okaloosa-Walton CC | 100 College Blvd., Niceville, FL 32578 | Keith Griffin | (850) 729-5379 |
| Olive-Harvey College | 10001 S. Woodlawn Ave., Chicago, IL 60628 | Norman Futrell | (773) 291-6279 |
| Olney Central College | 305 N. West Ave., Olney, IL 62450 | Dennis Conley | (618) 395-7777 |
| Olympic College | 1600 Chester Ave., Bremerton, WA 98337 | Michael Reese | (360) 475-7460 |
| Onondaga CC | 4941 Onondaga Rd., Syracuse, NY 13215 | Chris Cafalone | (315) 498-2492 |
| Orange Coast College | 2701 Fairview Rd., Costa Mesa, CA 92628 | John Altobelli | (714) 432-5892 |
| Orange County CC | 115 South St., Middletown, NY 10940 | Wayne Smith | (845) 341-4261 |
| Otero JC | 1802 Colorado Ave., La Junta, CO 81050 | Gary Addington | (719) 384-6833 |
| Owens CC | PO Box 10000, Toledo, OH 43699 | Bob Schultz | (419) 661-7974 |
| Oxnard College | 4000 S. Rose Rd., Oxnard, CA 93033 | John Larson | (805) 986-5800 |
| | | | |
| Palm Beach CC | 4200 S. Congress Ave., Lake Worth, FL 33461 | Alex Morales | (561) 439-8067 |
| Palomar College | 1140 Mission Rd., San Marcos, CA 92069 | Buck Taylor | (760) 744-1150 |
| Panola College | 1109 W. Panola St., Carthage, TX 75633 | Don Clinton | (903) 693-2062 |
| Paris JC | 2400 Clarksville St., Paris, TX 75460 | Deron Clark | (903) 782-0218 |
| Parkland College | 2400 W. Bradley Ave., Champaign, IL 61821 | Mitch Rosenthal | (217) 351-2409 |
| Pasadena City College | 1570 E. Colorado Blvd., Pasadena, CA 91106 | Evan O'Meara | (626) 585-7801 |
| Pasco-Hernando CC | 10230 Ridge Rd., New Port Richey, FL 34654 | Steve Winterling | (727) 816-3340 |
| Pearl River CC | PO Box 5440, Poplarville, MS 39470 | Jay Artigues | (601) 403-1175 |
| Penn State-Abington | 1600 Woodland Rd., Abington, PA 19001 | Dennis Weiner | (215) 881-7440 |
| Penn State-New Kensington | 3550 7th Street Rd., New Kensington, PA 15068 | Dave Montgomery | (724) 295-9544 |
| Penn State-Wilkes-Barre | PO Box PSU, Lehman, PA 18627 | Jack Monick | (570) 675-9262 |
| Penn State-Worthington | 120 Ridgeview Dr., Dunmore, PA 18512 | Jeff Mallas | (570) 963-2611 |
| Pennsylvania Tech | One College Ave., Williamsport, PA 17701 | Rees Daneker | (570) 327-4763 |
| Pensacola JC | 1000 College Blvd., Pensacola, FL 32504 | Bill Hamilton | (850) 484-1304 |
| Philadelphia, CC of | 1700 Spring Garden St., Philadelphia, PA 19130 | David Olmo | (215) 751-8966 |
| Phoenix College | 1202 W. Thomas Rd., Phoenix, AZ 85013 | Michael Rooney | (602) 285-7122 |
| Pierce College | 9401 Farwest Dr. SW, Lakewood, WA 98498 | Jason Picinich | (253) 964-6612 |
| Pima County CC | 4905 E. Broadway Blvd., B-215, Tucson, AZ 85709 | Edgar Soto | (520) 206-4985 |
| Pitt CC | Trailer 8, Greenville, NC 27835 | Tommy Eason | (252) 493-7633 |
| Polk CC | 999 Avenue H NE, Winter Haven, FL 33880 | Johnny Wiggs | (863) 297-1017 |
| Porterville College | 100 E. College Ave., Porterville, CA 93257 | Bret Davis | (559) 791-2335 |
| Potomac State College of W.V. | 101 Fort Ave., Keyser, WV 26726 | Doug Little | (304) 788-6879 |
| Prairie State College | 202 S. Halsted St., Chicago Heights, IL 60411 | Jeff Zurawicz | (708) 709-3950 |
| Pratt CC | 348 NE Hwy. 61, Pratt, KS 67124 | Jeff Brewer | (620) 450-2155 |
| Prince George's CC | 301 Largo Rd., Upper Marlboro, MD 20774 | James Williams | (301) 322-0066 |
| | | | |
| Queensborough CC | 222-05 56th Ave., Bayside, NY 11364 | Craig Everett | (718) 631-6322 |
| Quinsigamond CC | 670 W. Boylston St., Worcester, MA 01606 | Unavailable | (508) 854-4317 |
| | | | |
| Ranger College | 1100 College Circle, Ranger, TX 76470 | Robbie Harris | (254) 647-3234 |
| Raritan Valley CC | Rte. 28 & Lamington Rd., North Branch, NJ 08876 | George Repetz | (908) 526-1200 |
| Redlands CC | 1300 S. Country Club Rd., El Reno, OK 73036 | Matt Newgent | (405) 262-2552 |

| School | Address | Contact | Phone |
|---|---|---|---|
| Redwoods, College of the | 7351 Tompkins Hill Rd., Eureka, CA 95501 | Bob Brown | (707) 476-4239 |
| Reedley College | 995 N. Reed Ave., Reedley, CA 93654 | Jack Hacker | (559) 638-0303 |
| Rend Lake JC | 468 N. Ken Gray Pkwy., Ina, IL 62846 | Bob Simpson | (618) 437-5321 |
| Rhode Island, CC of | 400 East Ave. Warwick, RI 02886 | Ken Hopkins | (401) 825-2114 |
| Richland College | 12800 Abrams Rd., Dallas, TX 75243 | Joe Wharton | (972) 238-6261 |
| Ridgewater College | 2101 15th Ave. NW, Willmar, MN 56201 | Dwight Kotila | (320) 231-5124 |
| Rio Hondo College | 3600 Workman Mill Rd., Whittier, CA 90608 | Mike Salazar | (562) 692-0921 |
| Riverland CC | 1900 8th Ave. NW, Austin, MN 55912 | Scott Koenigs | (507) 433-0543 |
| Riverside CC | 4800 Magnolia Ave., Riverside, CA 92506 | Dennis Rogers | (909) 222-8333 |
| Roane State CC | 276 Patton Lane, Harriman, TN 37748 | Larry Works | (865) 882-4583 |
| Rochester Comm. &Tech College | 851 30th Ave. SE, Rochester, MN 55904 | Steve Hucke | (507) 285-7106 |
| Rock Valley College | 3301 N. Mulford Rd., Rockford, IL 61114 | Jeremy Warren | (815) 921-3802 |
| Rockingham CC | PO Box 38, Wentworth, NC 27375 | Scott Cates | (336) 342-4261 |
| Rockland CC | 145 College Rd., Suffern, NY 10901 | Joe Zeccardi | (845) 574-4452 |
| Rose State College | 6420 SE 15th St., Midwest City, OK 73110 | Lloyd Cummings | (405) 733-7350 |
| Roxbury CC | 1234 Columbus Ave., Roxbury Crossing, MA 02120 | Edsel Neal | (617) 541-2477 |
| | | | |
| Sacramento City College | 3835 Freeport Blvd., Sacramento, CA 95822 | Andy McKay | (916) 558-2684 |
| Saddleback CC | 28000 Marguerite Pkwy., Mission Viejo, CA 92692 | Jack Hodges | (949) 582-4642 |
| St. Catharine College | 2735 Bardstown Rd., St. Catharine, KY 40061 | Luther Bramblet | (859) 336-5082 |
| St. Charles CC | 4601 Mid Rivers Mall Dr., Cottleville, MO 63376 | Chris Gober | (636) 922-8211 |
| St. Clair County CC | PO Box 5015, Port Huron, MI 48061 | Rick Smith | (810) 989-5671 |
| St. Cloud Tech | 1540 Northway Dr., St. Cloud, MN 56303 | Mark Hollenhorst | (320) 308-5922 |
| St. Johns River CC | 5001 St. Johns Ave., Palatka, FL 32177 | Sam Rick | (904) 312-4162 |
| St. Louis CC-Florissant Valley | 3400 Pershall Rd., St. Louis, MO 63135 | Don Hillerman | (314) 513-4274 |
| St. Louis CC-Forest Park | 5600 Oakland Ave., St. Louis, MO 63110 | Royce Tippett | (314) 644-9688 |
| St. Louis CC-Meramec | 11333 Big Bend Blvd., St. Louis, MO 63122 | Tony Duttoli | (314) 984-7786 |
| St. Petersburg College | PO Box 13489, St. Petersburg, FL 33733 | Dave Pano | (727) 341-4777 |
| Salem CC | 460 Hollywood Ave., Carney's Point, NJ 08069 | Ron Palmer | (856) 351-2693 |
| Salt Lake CC | 4600 S. Redwood Rd., Salt Lake City, UT 84130 | David Nelson | (801) 957-4515 |
| San Bernardino Valley JC | 701 S. Mt. Vernon Ave., San Bernardino, CA 92403 | Bill Mierzwik | (909) 888-6511 |
| San Diego City College | 1313 12th Ave., San Diego, CA 92101 | Chris Brown | (619) 388-3705 |
| San Diego Mesa College | 7250 Mesa College Dr., San Diego, CA 92111 | Kevin Hazlett | (619) 388-5804 |
| San Francisco City College | 50 Phelan Ave., South Gym, San Francisco, CA 94112 | John Vanoncini | (415) 239-3811 |
| San Jacinto College-North | 5800 Uvalde Rd., Houston, TX 77049 | Tom Arrington | (281) 459-7673 |
| San Joaquin Delta College | 5151 Pacific Ave., Stockton, CA 95207 | Jim Yanko | (209) 954-5198 |
| San Jose City College | 2100 Moorpark Ave., San Jose, CA 95128 | Doug Robb | (408) 298-2181 |
| San Mateo, College of | 1700 W. Hillsdale Blvd., San Mateo, CA 94402 | Doug Williams | (650) 358-6875 |
| Santa Ana College | 1530 W. 17th St., Santa Ana, CA 92706 | Don Sneddon | (714) 564-6911 |
| Santa Barbara City College | 721 Cliff Dr., Santa Barbara, CA 93109 | Teddy Warrecker | (805) 965-0581 |
| Santa Fe CC | 3000 NW 83rd St., Gainesville, FL 32606 | Harry Tholen | (352) 395-5536 |
| Santa Rosa JC | 1501 Mendocino Ave., Santa Rosa, CA 95401 | Damon Neidlinger | (707) 527-4389 |
| Sauk Valley CC | 173 State Route 2, Dixon, IL 61021 | Al Ready | (815) 288-5511 |
| Schenectady County CC | 78 Washington Ave., Schenectady, NY 12305 | Tim Andi | (518) 381-1356 |
| Scottsdale CC | 9000 E. Chaparral Rd., Scottsdale, AZ 85256 | Alex Cherney | (480) 423-6000 |
| Seminole CC | 100 Weldon Blvd., Sanford, FL 32773 | Mike Nicholson | (407) 328-4722 |
| Seminole State College | PO Box 351, Seminole, OK 74818 | Eric Myers | (405) 382-9201 |
| Sequoias, College of the | 915 S. Mooney Blvd., Visalia, CA 93277 | Jody Allen | (559) 737-6196 |
| Seward County CC | PO Box 1137, Liberal, KS 67905 | Galen McSpadden | (620) 629-2730 |
| Shasta College | 11555 N. Old Oregon Trail, Redding, CA 96049 | Brad Rupert | (530) 225-4679 |
| Shawnee CC | 8364 College Rd., Ullin, IL 62992 | Greg Sheppard | (618) 634-3245 |
| Shelton State | 9500 Old Greensboro Rd., Tuscaloosa, AL 35405 | Bobby Sprowl | (205) 391-2918 |
| Shoreline CC | 16101 Greenwood Ave. N., Seattle, WA 98133 | Steve Seki | (206) 546-4740 |
| Sierra College | 5000 Rocklin Rd., Rocklin, CA 95677 | Rob Willson | (916) 781-0580 |
| Sinclair CC | 444 W. 3rd St., Dayton, OH 45402 | Mike Goldschmidt | (937) 512-2353 |
| Siskiyous, College of the | 800 College Ave., Weed, CA 96094 | James Frisbie | (530) 938-5231 |
| Skagit Valley College | 2405 E. College Way, Mount Vernon, WA 98273 | Kevin Matthews | (360) 416-7780 |
| Skyline College | 330 College Dr., San Bruno, CA 94066 | Dino Nomicos | (650) 738-4197 |
| Snead State CC | 220 N. Walnut St., Boaz, AL 35957 | Gerry Ledbetter | (256) 593-5120 |
| Solano CC | 4000 Suisun Valley Rd., Suisun, CA 94585 | Scott Stover | (707) 863-7822 |
| South Carolina-Salkehatchie | PO Box 617, Allendale, SC 29810 | Charles Dorman | (803) 584-3446 |
| South Florida CC | 600 W. College Dr., Avon Park, FL 33825 | Rick Hitt | (863) 784-7036 |
| South Georgia College | 100 W. College Park Dr., Douglas, GA 31533 | Scott Sims | (912) 389-4078 |
| South Mountain CC | 7050 S. 24th St., Phoenix, AZ 85042 | Todd Eastin | (602) 243-8257 |
| South Suburban College | 15800 S. State St., South Holland, IL 60473 | Steve Ruzich | (708) 596-2000 |
| Southeastern CC | 1500 W. Agency Rd., West Burlington, IA 52655 | Justin Schulte | (319) 752-2731 |
| Southeastern CC-Whiteville | PO Box 151, Whiteville, NC 28472 | Joey Autry | (910) 642-7141 |
| Southeastern Illinois College | 3575 College Rd., Harrisburg, IL 62946 | Paul McSpann | (618) 252-6376 |
| Southern Idaho, College of | 315 Falls Ave., Twin Falls, ID 83303 | Boomer Walker | (208) 733-9554 |
| Southern Maine CC | 2 Fort Rd., South Portland, ME 04106 | Philip Desjardins | (207) 839-6563 |
| Southern Maryland, Col of | PO Box 910, La Plata, MD 20646 | Joe Blandford | (301) 934-2251 |
| Southern Nevada, CC of | 700 College Dr., Henderson, NV 89015 | Tim Chambers | (702) 651-3008 |
| Southern Union State CC | PO Box 1000, Wadley, AL 36276 | Joe Jordan | (256) 395-2211 |

| | | | |
|---|---|---|---|
| Southwest Mississippi CC | 1156 College Dr., Summit, MS 39666 | Butch Holmes | (601) 276-3848 |
| Southwest Tennessee CC | PO Box 780, Memphis, TN 38101 | Johnny Ray | (901) 333-5143 |
| Southwestern CC | 1501 W. Townline Rd., Creston, IA 50801 | Andy Osborne | (641) 782-7081 |
| Southwestern College | 900 Otay Lakes Rd., Chula Vista, CA 92010 | Jerry Bartow | (619) 421-6700 |
| Southwestern Illinois College | 2500 Carlyle Ave., Belleville, IL 62221 | Neil Fiala | (618) 235-2700 |
| Southwestern Oregon CC | 1988 Newmark Ave., Coos Bay, OR 97420 | Corky Franklin | (541) 888-7348 |
| Spartanburg Methodist College | 1000 Powell Mill Rd., Spartanburg, SC 29301 | Tim Wallace | (864) 587-4237 |
| Spokane CC | N. 1810 Greene St., Spokane, WA 99217 | Dave Keller | (509) 533-3390 |
| Spoon River College | 23235 N. County Rd. 22, Canton, IL 61520 | Joe Moore | (309) 649-6303 |
| Springfield College | 1500 N. 5th St., Springfield, IL 62702 | Steve Torricelli | (217) 525-1420 |
| Springfield Tech CC | 1 Armory Sq., Springfield, MA 01105 | J.C. Fernandez | (413) 755-4069 |
| Suffolk County CC-Grant | 1001 Crooked Hill Rd., Brentwood, NY 11717 | Bobby Molinaro | (631) 851-6706 |
| Suffolk County CC-Selden | 533 College Rd., Selden, NY 11784 | Eric Brown | (631) 451-4881 |
| Sullivan County CC | 112 College Rd., Loch Sheldrake, NY 12759 | Michael Marra | (845) 434-5750 |
| SUNY Canton | 34 Cornell Dr., Canton, NY 13617 | Tim Mickle | (315) 386-7335 |
| SUNY Cobleskill | 107 Schenectady Ave., Cobleskill, NY 12043 | Unavailable | (518) 255-5127 |
| SUNY Morrisville | PO Box 901, Morrisville, NY 13408 | Tim Byrnes | (315) 684-6317 |
| Surry CC | 630 S. Main St., Dobson, NC 27017 | Mark Tucker | (336) 386-3238 |
| Sussex County CC | 1 College Hill Rd., Newton, NJ 07860 | Todd Poltersdorf | (973) 300-2252 |
| | | | |
| Tacoma CC | 6501 S. 19th St., Tacoma, WA 98466 | Donegal Fergus | (253) 566-5046 |
| Taft College | 29 Emmons Park Dr., Taft, CA 93268 | Vince Maiocco | (661) 763-7822 |
| Tallahassee CC | 444 Appleyard Dr., Tallahassee, FL 32304 | Mike McLeod | (850) 201-8066 |
| Temple College | 2600 S. 1st St., Temple, TX 76504 | Craig McMurtry | (254) 298-8524 |
| Texarkana College | 2500 N. Robison Rd., Texarkana, TX 75599 | James Mansinger | (903) 838-4541 |
| Texas-Brownsville, U. of | 80 Fort Brown, Brownsville, TX 78520 | Eliseo Herrera | (956) 544-8911 |
| Three Rivers CC | 2080 Three Rivers Blvd., Poplar Bluff, MO 63901 | Stacey Burkey | (573) 840-9611 |
| Treasure Valley CC | 650 College Blvd., Ontario, OR 97914 | Rick Baumann | (503) 881-8822 |
| Trinidad State JC | 600 Prospect St., Trinidad, CO 81082 | Scott Douglas | (719) 846-5510 |
| Triton College | 2000 5th Ave., River Grove, IL 60171 | Harry Torgerson | (708) 456-0300 |
| Truett McConnell College | 100 Alumni Dr., Cleveland, GA 30528 | Jim Waits | (706) 865-2136 |
| Tyler JC | PO Box 9020, Tyler, TX 75711 | Jon Groth | (903) 510-2320 |
| | | | |
| Ulster County CC | Cottekill Rd., Stone Ridge, NY 12484 | Ryan Snair | (845) 687-5277 |
| Union County College | 1033 Springfield Ave., Cranford, NJ 07016 | Mark Domashinski | (908) 709-7093 |
| | | | |
| Ventura College | 4667 Telegraph Rd., Ventura, CA 93003 | Don Adams | (805) 654-6400 |
| Vermilion CC | 1900 E. Camp St., Ely, MN 55731 | Ray Podominick | (218) 365-7276 |
| Vernon College | 4400 College Dr., Vernon, TX 76384 | Kevin Lallmann | (940) 552-6291 |
| Victor Valley CC | 18422 Bear Valley Rd., Victorville, CA 92392 | Sean Sers | (760) 245-4271 |
| Vincennes U. | 1002 N. 1st St., PE-19, Vincennes, IN 47591 | Jerry Blemker | (812) 888-4511 |
| Volunteer State CC | 1480 Nashville Pike, Gallatin, TN 37066 | Michael Crossland | (615) 230-3244 |
| | | | |
| Wabash Valley College | 2200 College Dr., Mount Carmel, IL 62863 | Rob Fournier | (618) 262-8641 |
| Walla Walla CC | 500 Tausick Way, Walla Walla, WA 99362 | Mike Cummins | (509) 527-4494 |
| Wallace CC-Dothan | 1141 Wallace Dr., Dothan, AL 36303 | Mackey Sasser | (334) 556-2216 |
| Wallace CC-Selma | 3000 Earl Goodwin Pkwy., Selma, AL 36702 | Lawrence Gullette | (334) 876-9292 |
| Wallace State CC-Hanceville | PO Box 2000, Hanceville, AL 35077 | Randy Putman | (256) 352-8247 |
| Walters State CC | 500 S. Davy Crockett Pkwy., Morristown, TN 37813 | Ken Campbell | (423) 585-2680 |
| Waubonsee College | Route 47 at Waubonsee Dr., Sugar Grove, IL 60554 | Dave Randall | (630) 466-2527 |
| Waukesha County Tech | 800 Main St., Pewaukee, WI 53072 | Ronnie Nedset | (262) 691-5545 |
| Wenatchee Valley CC | 1300 5th St., Wenatchee, WA 98801 | Bob Duda | (509) 682-6886 |
| Weatherford College | 225 College Park Dr., Weatherford, TX 76086 | Jeff Lightfoot | (817) 598-6256 |
| West Hills College | 300 Cherry Lane, Coalinga, CA 93210 | Archie Hodsdon | (559) 934-2000 |
| West Valley College | 14000 Fruitvale Rd., Saratoga, CA 95070 | Mike Perez | (408) 741-2176 |
| Westchester CC | 75 Grasslands Rd., Valhalla, NY 10595 | Larry Massaroni | (914) 606-7895 |
| Western Nebraska CC | 1601 E. 27th St., Scottsbluff, NE 69361 | Mike Jones | (308) 635-6798 |
| Western Nevada CC | 2201 W. College Pkwy., Carson City, NV 89703 | D.J. Whittemore | (775) 445-3271 |
| Western Oklahoma State College | 2801 N. Main St., Altus, OK 73521 | Kurt Russell | (580) 477-7800 |
| Western Texas College | 6200 S. College Ave., Snyder, TX 79549 | Billy Hefflinger | (915) 573-8511 |
| Western Wisconsin Tech | 304 Sixth St. N., La Crosse, WI 54602 | Zeb Allert | (608) 785-9442 |
| Westmoreland County CC | 400 Armbrust Rd., Youngwood, PA 15697 | Mike Draghi | (724) 925-4129 |
| Wharton County JC | 911 Boling Hwy., Wharton, TX 77488 | Bob Nottebart | (979) 532-6369 |
| Wilkes CC | PO Box 120, Wilkesboro, NC 28697 | Unavailable | (336) 838-6189 |
| Williamson Free School | 106 S. New Middletown Rd., Media, PA 19063 | Kevin Scott | (610) 566-1776 |
| Williston State College | 1410 University Ave., Williston, ND 58801 | Kelly Heller | (701) 744-4242 |
| | | | |
| Yakima Valley CC | 16th & W. Nob Hill Blvd., Yakima, WA 98902 | Ken Mortensen | (509) 574-4720 |
| Yavapai College | 1100 E. Sheldon St., Prescott, AZ 86301 | Sky Smeltzer | (928) 776-2235 |
| Young Harris College | PO Box 37, Young Harris, GA 30582 | Rick Robinson | (706) 379-4311 |
| Yuba CC | 2088 N. Beale Rd., Marysville, CA 95901 | Tim Gloyd | (530) 634-7725 |

# AMATEUR

# INTERNATIONAL

## INTERNATIONAL OLYMPIC COMMITTEE
**Mailing Address:** Chateau de Vidy, 1007 Lausanne, Switzerland. **Telephone:** (41-21) 621-6111. **FAX:** (41-21) 621-6216. **Website:** www.olympic.org.
**President:** Jacques Rogge. **Director, Communications:** Giselle Davies.
**Games of the XXIX Olympiad:** Aug. 8-24 at Beijing, China.

## U.S. OLYMPIC COMMITTEE
**Mailing Address:** One Olympic Plaza, Colorado Springs, CO 80909. **Telephone:** (719) 632-5551. **FAX:** (719) 866-4654. **Website:** www.usoc.org.
**Chief Executive Officer:** Jim Scherr. **Chief Communications Officer:** Darryl Seibel.

## INTERNATIONAL BASEBALL FEDERATION
**Mailing Address:** Avenue de Mon-Repos 24, Case Postale 6099, 1002 Lausanne 5, Switzerland **Telephone:** (41-21) 318-8240. **FAX:** (41-21) 318-8241. **E-Mail Address:** ibaf@baseball.ch. **Website:** www.baseball.ch.
**Year Founded:** 1938.
**Number of Affiliated National Federations:** 115.
**President:** Aldo Notari (Italy). **Secretary General:** Eduardo De Bello (Panama). **Treasurer:** Alexander Ratner (Russia). **First Vice President:** Tom C.H. Peng (Taiwan). **Second Vice President:** Rodolfo Puente (Cuba). **Third Vice President:** Miguel Pozueta (Spain). **Members, At Large:** Mark Alexander (South Africa), Petr Ditrich (Czech Republic), Paul Seiler (United States). **Ex Officio Member:** Jianguo Hu (China).
**Continental Vice Presidents:** Africa—Ishola Williams (Nigeria). America—Hector Pereyra (Dominican Republic). Asia—Nae-Heun Lee (Korea). Europe—Martin Miller (Germany). Oceania—John Ostermeyer (Australia).
**Executive Director:** Miquel Ortin. **Communications Manager:** Enzo Di Gesu.

### 2006 Events
| | |
|---|---|
| World Baseball Classic | Various sites, March 3-20 |
| Olympic Qualifier-Americas | Havana, Cuba; Aug. 21-Sept. 3 |
| World Junior Championship | Sancti Spiritus, Cuba, Sept. 17-27 |
| Intercontinental Cup | Taiwan, Nov. 9-19 |

## CONTINENTAL ASSOCIATIONS

### CONFEDERATION PAN AMERICANA DE BEISBOL (COPABE)
**Mailing Address:** Avenida Cerro Patacon, Kilometro 3, Estadio Nacional, Apartado 9664, Zona 4, Panama. **Telephone:** (507) 261-3654; (507) 261-1014. **FAX:** (507) 229-3914. **E-Mail Address:** copabe@sinfo.net.
**President:** Eduardo De Bello (Panama). **Secretary General:** Hector Pereyra (Dominican Republic).

#### 2006 Events
| | |
|---|---|
| COPABE AA Pan American Youth Championship | Barquisimeto, Venez., August |
| Olympic Qualifier-Americas | Havana, Cuba, Aug. 21-Sept. 3 |

### AFRICAN BASEBALL/SOFTBALL ASSOCIATION
**Mailing Address:** Paiko Road, Changaga, Minna, Niger State, PMB 150, Nigeria. **Telephone:** (234-66) 224-555. **FAX:** (234-66) 224-555. **E-Mail Address:** absasecretariat@yahoo.com.
**President:** Ishola Williams (Nigeria). **Executive Director:** Friday Ichide (Nigeria). **Secretary General:** Fridah Shiroya (Kenya).

### BASEBALL FEDERATION OF ASIA
**Mailing Address:** Mainichi Palaceside Bldg., 1-1-1, Hitotsubahi, Chiyoda-ku, Tokyo 100, Japan. **Telephone:** (81-3) 201-1155, (81-3) 213-6776. **FAX:** (81-3) 201-0707.
**President:** Eiichiro Yamamoto (Japan). **Secretary General:** Sang-Kyu Park (Korea).

### EUROPEAN BASEBALL CONFEDERATION
**Mailing Address:** Avenue de Mon-Repos 24, Case postale 6099, 1002 Lausanne, Switzerland. **Telephone:** (32-3) 219-0440. **FAX:** (32-3) 772 7727. **E-Mail Address:** info@baseballeurope.com. **Website:** baseballeurope.com.
**President:** Aldo Notari (Italy). **Secretary General:** Gaston Panaye (Belgium).

### BASEBALL CONFERERATION OF OCEANIA
**Mailing Address:** 48 Partridge Way, Mooroolbark, Victoria 3138, Australia. **Telephone:** (61-3) 9727-1779. **FAX:** (61-3) 9727-5959. **E-Mail Address:** bcosecgeneral@baseballoceania.com. **Website:** www.baseballoceania.com.
**President:** Mark Peters (Australia). **Secretary General:** Chet Gray (Australia).

## ORGANIZATIONS

### INTERNATIONAL GOODWILL SERIES, INC.
**Mailing Address:** P.O. Box 213, Santa Rosa, CA 95402. **Telephone:** (707) 975-7894. **FAX:** (707) 525-0214. **E-Mail Address:** rwilliams@goodwillseries.org. **Website:** www.goodwillseries.org.
**President, Goodwill Series, Inc.:** Bob Williams.
**16th International Friendship Series** (18 and Under): June 7-20 in Japan.

### INTERNATIONAL SPORTS GROUP
**Mailing Address:** 11430 Kestrel Rd., Klamath Falls, OR 97601. **Telephone:** (541) 882-4293. **E-Mail Address:** isg-baseball@yahoo.com. **Website:** www.isgbaseball.com.
**President:** Jim Jones. **Vice President:** Tom O'Connell. **Secretary/Treasurer:** Randy Town.

# NATIONAL

## USA BASEBALL

**Mailing Address, Corporate Headquarters:** P.O. Box 1131, Durham, NC 27702. **Office Address:** 403 Blackwell St., Durham, NC 27701 **Telephone:** (919) 474-8721. **FAX:** (919) 474-8822. **E-Mail Address:** info@usabaseball.com. **Website:** www.usabaseball.com.

**President:** Mike Gaski. **Secretary General:** Jack Kelly. **Vice President, Treasurer:** Abraham Key. **Vice President, Administration:** Jerry Kindall. **Vice President, Secretary:** Elliott Hopkins. **General Counsel:** Lindsay Burbage.

**Executive Director, Chief Executive Officer:** Paul Seiler. **Directors, National Teams:** Eric Campbell, Ray Darwin. **Assistant Director, National Teams:** Jeff Singer. **Director, Finance:** Miki Partridge. **Director, Marketing/Licensing:** David Perkins. **Director, Communications:** Dave Fanucchi.

**National Members:** Amateur Athletic Union (AAU), American Amateur Baseball Congress (AABC), American Baseball Coaches Association (ABCA), American Legion Baseball, Babe Ruth Baseball, Dixie Baseball, Little League Baseball, National Amateur Baseball Federation (NABF), National Association of Intercollegiate Athletics (NAIA), National Baseball Congress (NBC), National Collegiate Athletic Association (NCAA), National Federation of State High School Athletic Associations, National High School Baseball Coaches Association, National Junior College Athletic Association (NJCAA), Police Athletic League (PAL), PONY Baseball, T-Ball USA, United States Specialty Sports Association (USSSA), YMCAs of the USA.

### 2006 Events
#### Team USA—Professional Level

World Baseball Classic ................................................................................................ Various sites, March 3-20
2008 Olympics/COPABE Continental Qualifier ............................................................. Havana, Cuba, Aug. 21-Sept. 3

#### Team USA—College Level

National Team Trials ................................................................................................................ June, site unavailable
USA/Japan Collegiate Series ................................................................................................... July, sites unavailable
FISU World University Championship .......................................................................................... Havana, Cuba, Aug. 6-16

#### Team USA—Junior Level (18 and under)

Tournament of Stars ................................................................................................................. Joplin, MO, June 19-26
National Team Trials ............................................................................................................ September, site unavailable
Junior World Championships ............................................................................................ Sancti Spiritus, Cuba, Sept. 17-27

#### Team USA—Youth Level (16 and under)

Junior Olympic Championship—West ............................................................................ Peoria/Surprise, AZ, June 23-July 1
Junior Olympic Championship—East ................................................................................... Jupiter, FL, June 23-July 1
National Team Trials ................................................................................................................. August, site unavailable
COPABE AA Pan American Championship ...................................................................... Barquisimeto, Venezuela, August

## BASEBALL CANADA

**Mailing Address:** 2212 Gladwin Cres., Suite A7, Ottawa, Ontario K1B 5N1. **Telephone:** (613) 748-5606. **FAX:** (613) 748-5767. **E-Mail Address:** info@baseball.ca. **Website:** www.baseball.ca.

**Director General:** Jim Baba. **Head Coach/Director, National Teams:** Greg Hamilton. **Manager, Baseball Operations:** Andre Lachance. **Manager, Media/Public Relations:** Luc Hebert.

### 2006 Events

World Baseball Classic ................................................................................................ Various sites, March 3-20
Baseball Canada Cup (17 and under) ......................................................................... Medicine Hat, Alberta, Aug. 17-21
2008 Olympics/COPABE Continental Qualifier ............................................................. Havana, Cuba, Aug. 21-Sept. 3
Junior World Championship (18 and under) ............................................................. Sancti Spiritus, Cuba, Sept. 17-27

## NATIONAL BASEBALL CONGRESS

**Mailing Address:** P.O. Box 1420, Wichita, KS 67201. **Telephone:** (316) 267-3372. **FAX:** (316) 267-3382. **Year Founded:** 1931.

**General Manager:** Eric Edelstein. **Assistant GM:** Josh Robertson. **Tournament Director:** Jerry Taylor. **Sales Manager:** Justin Cole.

**2006 NBC World Series (Collegiate, ex-professional, unlimited age):** July 28-Aug. 12 at Wichita, KS (Lawrence Dumont Stadium).

## ATHLETES IN ACTION

**Mailing Address:** 651 Taylor Dr., Xenia, OH 45385. **Telephone:** (937) 352-1000. **FAX:** (937) 352-1245. **E-Mail Address:** baseball@aia.com. **Website:** www.aiabaseball.org.

**Director, AIA Baseball:** Jason Lester. **General Managers, AIA Teams:** Chris Beck (Alaska), Eddie Lang (Great Lakes), John McLaughlin (International), John Scholl (New York).

# SUMMER COLLEGE
## LEAGUES

### NATIONAL ALLIANCE OF COLLEGE SUMMER BASEBALL
**Telephone:** (704) 896-9100. **E-Mail Address:** jcarter@standpointtech.com.
**Executive Director:** Paul Galop (Cape Cod League). **Assistant Executive Directors:** Kim Lance (Great Lakes League), David Biery (Valley League). **Secretary:** Jeff Carter (Southern Collegiate League). **Treasurer:** Jim Phillips (Valley League).
**Member Leagues:** Atlantic Collegiate League, Cape Cod League, Central Illinois Collegiate League, Great Lakes League, New England Collegiate League, New York Collegiate League, Southern Collegiate League, Valley League.

### SUMMER COLLEGIATE BASEBALL ASSOCIATION
**Mailing Address:** 4900 Waters Edge Dr., Suite 201, Raleigh, NC 27606. **Telephone:** (919) 852-1960. **E-Mail Address:** info@summercollegiatebaseball.com. **Website:** www.summercollegiatebaseball.com.
**Affiliated Leagues:** Coastal Plain League, Northwoods League.

### ALASKA BASEBALL LEAGUE
**Mailing Address:** P.O. Box 240061, Anchorage, AK 99524. **Telephone/FAX:** (907) 283-6186.
**Year Founded:** 1974 (reunited, 1998).
**President:** Don Dennis (Alaska Goldpanners). **First Vice President/Secretary:** Mike Baxter (Peninsula Oilers). **VP, Marketing:** Lefty Van Brunt (Anchorage Glacier Pilots). **VP, Scheduling:** Chris Beck (AIA Alaska). **VP, Rules/Membership:** Pete Christopher (Mat-Su Miners). **VP, Umpiring:** Dennis Mattingly (Anchorage Bucs).
**Division Structure:** None.
**Regular Season:** 35 league games. **2006 Opening Date:** June 9. **Closing Date:** July 27.
**All-Star Game:** None.
**Playoff Format:** Season-ending tournament, Anchorage, July 28-31. League champion qualifies for National Baseball Congress World Series in Wichita, Kan.
**Roster Limit:** 22, plus exemption for Alaska residents.
**Player Eligibility Rule:** Players with college eligibility, except drafted seniors.

#### ALASKA GOLDPANNERS
**Mailing Address:** P.O. Box 71154, Fairbanks, AK 99707. **Telephone:** (907) 451-0095, (619) 561-4581. **FAX:** (907) 456-6429. **E-Mail Address:** addennis@cox.net. **Website:** www.goldpanners.com.
**General Manager:** Don Dennis. **Head Coach:** Ed Cheff (Lewis-Clark State, Idaho, College).

#### ANCHORAGE BUCS
**Mailing Address:** P.O. Box 240061, Anchorage, AK 99524. **Telephone:** (907) 561-2827. **FAX:** (907) 561-2920. **E-Mail Address:** admin@anchoragebucs.com. **Website:** www.anchoragebucs.com.
**General Manager:** Dennis Mattingly. **Head Coach:** Mike Garcia (Canada, Calif., JC).

#### ANCHORAGE GLACIER PILOTS
**Mailing Address:** 207 E. Northern Lights Blvd., Suite 105, Anchorage, AK 99503. **Telephone:** (907) 274-3627. **FAX:** (907) 274-3628. **E-Mail Address:** gpilots@alaska.net. **Website:** www.glacierpilots.com.
**General Manager:** Lefty Van Brunt. **Head Coach:** Chris Jones (Glendale, Calif., JC).

#### ATHLETES IN ACTION-ALASKA
**Mailing Address:** 651 Taylor Dr., Xenia, OH 45385. **Telephone:** (937) 352-1237. **FAX:** (937) 352-1245. **E-Mail Address:** chris.beck@aia.com. **Website:** www.aiabaseball.org.
**General Manager/Head Coach:** Chris Beck.

#### MAT-SU MINERS
**Mailing Address:** P.O. Box 2690, Palmer, AK 99645. **Telephone:** (907) 746-4914. **FAX:** (907) 746-5068. **E-Mail Address:** generalmanager@matsuminers.org. **Website:** www.matsuminers.org.
**General Manager:** Pete Christopher. **Head Coach:** Matt Dorey (Washington State U.).

#### PENINSULA OILERS
**Mailing Address:** 601 S. Main St., Kenai, AK 99611. **Telephone:** (907) 283-7133. **FAX:** (907) 283-3390. **E-Mail Address:** admin@oilersbaseball.com. **Website:** www.oilersbaseball.com.
**General Manager:** Mike Baxter. **Head Coach:** Thad Johnson (Riverside, Calif., CC).

### ATLANTIC COLLEGIATE LEAGUE
**Mailing Address:** 43-18 209 St., Bayside, NY 11361. **Telephone:** (917) 882-5240. **FAX:** (718) 225-5695. **E-Mail Address:** metronycadets@aol.cm. **Website:** www.acbl-online.com.
**Year Founded:** 1967.
**Commissioner:** Fred Cambria. **President:** Tom Bonekemper. **Secretary/Treasurer:** Melinda Lavanco.
**Division Structure:** Wolff—Jersey Pilots, Kutztown Rockies, Lehigh Valley Catz, Quakertown Blazers. Kaiser—Long Island Stars, Metro New York Cadets, New York Generals, Stamford Robins.
**Regular Season:** 40 games. **2006 Opening Date:** June 1. **Closing Date:** Aug. 15.
**All-Star Game:** July 17 at St. John's University.
**Playoff Format:** Top two teams in each division meet in best-of-3 semifinals. Winners meet in one-game championship.
**Roster Limit:** 25 (college-eligible players only).

#### JERSEY PILOTS
**Mailing Address:** 401 Timber Dr., Berkeley Heights, NJ 07922. **Telephone:** (908) 464-8042. **E-Mail Address:** jerseypilots1@aol.com.
**President/General Manager:** Ben Smookler. **Head Coach:** Ray Ciecisz.

#### KUTZTOWN ROCKIES
**Mailing Address:** 429 Baldy Rd., Kutztown, PA 19530. **Telephone:** (610) 683-5273. **E-Mail Address:** kutztownrockies@aol.com.
**President/General Manager:** Jon Yeakel. **Head Coach:** Rich DeLucia.

#### LEHIGH VALLEY CATZ
**Mailing Address:** 103 Logan Dr., Easton, PA 18045. **Telephone:** (610) 533-9349. **E-Mail Address:** valley-

catz@hotmail.com. **Website:** www.lvcatz.com.
**Owner/President:** Tommy Lisinicchia. **General Manager:** Pat O'Connell. **Head Coach:** Adrian Yaguez.

## LONG ISLAND STARS
**Mailing Address:** 46 Columbine Lane, Kings Park, NY 11754. **Telephone:** (917) 670-9862. **E-Mail Address:** longislandstars@aol.com.
**Owner/General Manager:** Tom Muratore. **Head Coach:** John Musmacker.

## METRO NEW YORK CADETS
**Mailing Address:** 220-55 46 Ave., Bayside, NY 11361. **Telephone:** (917) 882-5904. **FAX:** (718) 225-5695. **E-Mail Address:** metronycadets@aol.com.
**Owner:** Gus Antico. **General Manager:** Charles Papetti. **Head Coach:** Darren Gurney.

## NEW YORK GENERALS
**Mailing Address:** 123 Euclid Ave., Ardsley, NY 10502. **Telephone/FAX:** (914) 693-4542. **E-Mail Address:** apolloto@aol.com.
**Owner/General Manager:** Nick DiSciullo. **Head Coach:** Unavailable.

## QUAKERTOWN BLAZERS
**Mailing Address:** 510 Buttonwood St., Perkasie, PA 18944. **Telephone:** (215) 257-2645.
**General Manager:** Todd Zartman. **Head Coach:** Dennis Robison.

## STAMFORD ROBINS
**Mailing Address:** P.O. Box 113254, Stamford, CT 06911. **Telephone:** (212) 522-5543, (203) 981-7516. **E-Mail Address:** coachwolff@aol.com, michaelhalo3131@aol.com.
**General Managers:** Rick Wolff, Mike D'Angelo. **Head Coach:** Unavailable.

## CALIFORNIA COLLEGIATE LEAGUE
**Mailing Address:** 4299 Carpinteria Ave., Suite 201, Carpinteria, CA 93013. **Telephone:** (805) 684-0657. **FAX:** (805) 684-8596. **E-Mail Address:** calsummerball.com.
**Year Founded:** 1993.
**President:** Bill Pintard.
**Member Clubs:** California Oaks, Monterey Bay Sox, Salinas Packers, San Luis Obispo Blues, Santa Barbara Foresters, Santa Maria Indians, Surf City Hammerheads.
**Division Structure:** None.
**Regular Season:** 36 games. **2006 Opening Date:** June 1. **Closing Date:** July 31.
**Playoff Format:** League champion and runner-up advance to National Baseball Congress World Series in Wichita, Kan.
**Roster Limit:** 33.

## CAL RIPKEN SR. COLLEGIATE BASEBALL LEAGUE
**Mailing Address:** P.O. Box 22471, Baltimore, MD 21203. **Telephone:** (410) 588-9900. **E-Mail Address:** athompson@crscbl.org. **Website:** www.ripkensrcollege-baseball.org
**Year Founded:** 2005.
**Commissioner:** William Spencer. **Deputy Commissioner:** Robert Jursch. **Executive Director:** Alex Thompson.
**Division Structure:** None.
**Regular Season:** 40 games. **2006 Opening Date:** June 9. **Closing Date:** July 30.
**All-Star Game:** July 17, site unavailable.
**Playoff Format:** Double-elimination tournament, July 31-Aug. 4.

**Roster Limit:** 30 (college-eligible players 22 and under).

## BETHESDA BIG TRAIN
**Mailing Address:** P.O. Box 30306, Bethesda, MD 20824. **Telephone:** (301) 983-1006. **FAX:** (301) 652-0691. **E-Mail Address:** david@bigtrain.org. **Website:** www.bigtrain.org.
**President:** Bruce Adams. **General Manager:** David Ireland. **Head Coach:** Sal Colangelo.

## COLLEGE PARK BOMBERS
**Mailing Address:** 5033 56th Ave., Hyattsville, MD 20781. **Telephone:** (301) 674-7362. **FAX:** (301) 927-6997. **E-Mail Address:** bovello2@aol.com. **Website:** www.marylandbomberscp.com.
**President/General Manager/Head Coach:** Gene Bovello.

## MARYLAND REDBIRDS
**Mailing Address:** 10819 Sandringham Rd., Cockeysville, MD 21030. **Telephone:** (410) 823-3399, ext. 118. **FAX:** (410) 823-4144. **E-Mail Address:** redbird1@hotmail.com. **Website:** www.mdredbirds.com.
**General Manager/Manager:** Mark Russo. **Head Coach:** Pat Nagle.

## ROCKVILLE EXPRESS
**Mailing Address:** P.O. Box 10188, Rockville, MC 20849. **Telephone:** (301) 340-1697. **FAX:** (240) 465-0296. **E-Mail Address:** jhpmort@aol.com. **Website:** www.rockvilleexpress.org.
**President:** John Pflieger. **General Manager:** Jim Adams. **Head Coach:** Tom Shaffer.

## SILVER SPRING-TAKOMA THUNDERBOLTS
**Mailing Address:** 906 Glaizewood Ct., Takoma Park, MD 20912. **Telephone:** (301) 270-0598. **E-Mail Address:** EFSharp@juno.com. **Website:** www.tbolts.org
**President/General Manager:** Richard O'Connor. **Head Coach:** Bobby St. Pierre.

## YOUSE'S MARYLAND ORIOLES
**Mailing Address:** 6451 St. Phillips Rd., Linthicum, MD 21090. **Telephone:** (443) 690-6550. **E-Mail Address:** daalbany22@cablespeed.com.
**President:** Dave Caplan. **General Manager/Head Coach:** Dean Albany.

## CAPE COD LEAGUE
**Mailing Address:** P.O. Box 266, Harwich Port, MA 02646. **Telephone:** (508) 432-6909. **E-Mail Address:** info@capecodbaseball.org. **Website:** www.capecod-baseball.org.
**Year Founded:** 1885.
**Commissioner:** Paul Galop. **President:** Judy Walden Scarafile. **Senior Vice President:** Jim Higgins. **Vice Presidents:** Phil Edwards, Peter Ford. **Deputy Commissioner:** Richard Sullivan. **Deputy Commissioner/Director, Officiating:** Sol Yas. **Treasurer/Website Manager:** Steven Wilson. **Director, Public Relations/Broadcast Media:** John Garner. **Director, Communications:** Jim McGonigle. **Director, Publications:** Lou Barnicle.
**Division Structure:** East—Brewster, Chatham, Harwich, Orleans, Yarmouth-Dennis. West—Bourne, Cotuit, Falmouth, Hyannis, Wareham.
**Regular Season:** 44 games. **2006 Opening Date:** June 15. **Closing Date:** Aug. 6.
**All-Star Game:** July 29 at Yarmouth-Dennis.
**Playoff Format:** Top two teams in each division meet in best-of-3 semifinals. Winners meet in best-of-3 series for league championship.

Roster Limit: 23 (college-eligible players only)

## BOURNE BRAVES

**Mailing Address:** P.O. Box 895, Monument Beach, MA 02553. **Telephone:** (508) 759-7711, ext. 224. **FAX:** (508) 759-7208. **E-Mail Address:** mcarrier@upper-capetech.org. **Website:** www.bournebraves.org.
**President:** Thomas Fink. **General Manager:** Michael Carrier.
**Head Coach:** Harvey Shapiro.

## BREWSTER WHITE CAPS

**Mailing Address:** P.O. Box 2349, Brewster, MA 02631. **Telephone:** (617) 835-7130. **FAX:** (781) 934-0506. **E-Mail Addresses:** contact@brewsterwhitecaps.com, dpmfs@aol.com. **Website:** www. brewsterwhitecaps.com.
**President:** Hester Grue. **General Manager:** Dave Porter.
**Head Coach:** Bob Macaluso (Muhlenberg, Pa., College).

## CHATHAM A's

**Mailing Address:** P.O. Box 428, Chatham, MA 02633. **Telephone:** (508) 945-3841. **FAX:** (508) 945-4787. **E-Mail Address:** cthoms@verizon.net. **Website:** www.chathamas.com.
**President:** Peter Troy. **General Manager:** Charles Thoms.
**Head Coach:** John Schiffner (Plainville, Conn., HS).

## COTUIT KETTLEERS

**Mailing Address:** P.O. Box 411, Cotuit, MA 02635. **Telephone:** (508) 428-3358. **FAX:** (508) 420-5584. **E-Mail Address:** info@kettleers.org. **Website:** www.kettleers.org.
**President:** Martha Johnson. **General Manager:** Bruce Murphy.
**Head Coach:** Mike Roberts.

## FALMOUTH COMMODORES

**Mailing Address:** 33 Wintergreen Rd., Mashpee, MA 02649. **Telephone:** (508) 477-5724. **FAX:** (508) 862-6011. **E-Mail Address:** chuckhs@comcast.net. **Website:** www.falcommodores.org.
**President:** Gerry Reily. **General Manager:** Chuck Sturtevant. **Assistant GM:** Dan Dunn.
**Head Coach:** Jeff Trundy (The Gunnery School, Conn.).

## HARWICH MARINERS

**Mailing Address:** P.O. Box 201, Harwich Port, MA 02646. **Telephone:** (508) 432-2000. **FAX:** (508) 432-5357. **Website:** www.harwichmariners.org. **E-Mail Address:** mehendy@comcast.net.
**President:** Mary Henderson. **General Manager:** John Reid.
**Head Coach:** Steve Englert (Boston College).

## HYANNIS METS

**Mailing Address:** P.O. Box 852, Hyannis, MA 02601. **Telephone:** (508) 420-0962. **FAX:** (508) 428-8199. **E-Mail Address:** jhowitt932@comcast.net. **Website:** www.hyannismets.org.
**General Manager:** John Howitt.
**Head Coach:** Greg King (Thomas, Maine, College).

## ORLEANS CARDINALS

**Mailing Address:** P.O. Box 504, Orleans, MA 02653. **Telephone/FAX:** (508) 255-0793. **FAX:** (508) 255-2237. **Website:** www.orleanscardinals.com.
**President:** Bob Korn. **General Manager:** Sue Horton.
**Head Coach:** Kelly Nicholson (Loyola HS, Los Angeles).

## WAREHAM GATEMEN

**Mailing Address:** 71 Towhee Rd., Wareham, MA 02571. **Telephone:** (508) 295-3956. **FAX:** (508) 295-8821. **E-Mail Address:** wylde@comcast.net. **Website:** www.gatemen.org.
**President/General Manager:** John Wylde.
**Head Coach:** Cooper Farris (Mississippi Gulf Coast CC).

## YARMOUTH-DENNIS RED SOX

**Mailing Address:** P.O. Box 814, South Yarmouth, MA 02664. **Telephone:** (508) 394-9387. **FAX:** (508) 398-2239. **E-Mail Address:** jimmartin321@yahoo.com. **Website:** ydredsox.org.
**President:** Bob Mayo. **General Manager:** Jim Martin.
**Head Coach:** Scott Pickler (Cypress, Calif., CC).

## CENTRAL ILLINOIS COLLEGIATE LEAGUE

**Mailing Address:** 1137 Acacia Lane, Chatham, IL 62629. **Telephone:** (217) 483-5673. **FAX:** (217) 786-2788. **E-Mail Address:** commissioner@ciclbaseball.com **Website:** www.ciclbaseball.com.
**Year Founded:** 1963.
**Commissioner:** Ron Riggle. **President:** Duffy Bass. **Administrative Assistant:** Mike Woods.
**Division Structure:** None.
**Regular Season:** 44 games. **2006 Opening Date:** June 8. **Closing Date:** Aug. 13.
**All-Star Game:** July 12 at DuPage.
**Playoff Format:** Top four teams meet in best-of-3 series. Winners meet in best-of-3 series for league championship.
**Roster Limit:** 24 (college-eligible players only).

## DANVILLE DANS

**Mailing Address:** 138 E. Raymond, Danville, IL 61832. **Telephone:** (217) 446-5521. **FAX:** (217) 442-2137. **E-Mail Address:** jc@cooketech.net.
**General Manager:** Rick Kurth. **Assistant GM:** Jeanie Cooke. **Head Coach:** Jamie Sailors.

## DUBOIS COUNTY BOMBERS

**Mailing Address:** P.O. Box 332, Huntingburg, IN 47542. **Telephone:** (812) 683-3700. **E-Mail Address:** dcbombers@psci.net.
**General Manager:** John Bigness. **Head Coach:** John Fitzgerald.

## DUPAGE DRAGONS

**Mailing Address:** P.O. Box 3076, Lisle, IL 60532. **Telephone:** (630) 241-2255. **FAX:** (708) 784-1468. **E-Mail Address:** mike@madisongroupltd.com. **Website:** www.dupagedragons.com.
**General Manager:** Mike Thiessen. **Head Coach:** Mark Viramontes.

## GALESBURG PIONEERS

**Mailing Address:** P.O. Box 1387, Galesburg, IL 61402. **Telephone:** (309) 345-3629. **FAX:** (309) 343-2311. **E-Mail Address:** jeguiste@ci.galesburg.il.us.
**General Manager:** John Guiste. **Head Coach:** Jim Sammons.

## QUINCY GEMS

**Mailing Address:** 300 Civic Center Plaza, Quincy, IL 62301. **Telephone:** (217) 223-1000. **FAX:** (217) 223-1330. **E-Mail Address:** jjansen@quincygems.com. **Website:** www.quincygems.com.
**Executive Director:** Jeff Jansen. **Head Coach:** Luke Sabers.

## SPRINGFIELD RIFLES

**Mailing Address:** 5250 Shepherd Rd., Springfield, IL

62794. **Telephone:** (217) 415-5631. **FAX:** (217) 786-2788. **E-Mail Address:** sqular@aol.com.

**General Manager:** Larry Squires. **Head Coach:** Unavailable.

## TWIN CITY STARS

**Mailing Address:** 907 N. School St., Normal, IL 61761. **Telephone:** (309) 452-3317. **FAX:** (217) 452-0377. **E-Mail Address:** duffybass@aol.com.

**General Manager:** Duffy Bass. **Head Coach:** Josh Manning.

## CLARK GRIFFITH COLLEGIATE LEAGUE

**Mailing Address:** 10915 Howland Dr., Reston, VA 20191. **Telephone:** (703) 860-0946. **FAX:** (703) 860-0143. **E-Mail Address:** fannanfj@erols.com. **Website:** www.clarkgriffithbaseball.com.

**Year Founded:** 1945.

**Executive Vice President:** Frank Fannan. **Treasurer:** Tom Dellinger. **Media Director:** Ben Trittipoe. **VP/Rules Enforcement:** Byron Zeigler.

**Regular Season:** 40 games. **2006 Opening Date:** June 2. **Closing Date:** July 28.

**Playoff Format:** Top four teams meet in a double-elimination tournament.

**Roster Limit:** 25 (college-eligible players only).

### FAIRFAX NATIONALS

**Mailing Address:** 1844 Horseback Trail, Vienna, VA 22182. **Telephone:** (703) 201-3346. **E-Mail Address:** garyboss@gmail.com.

**President:** Gary Boss. **General Manager:** Jim Beck. **Head Coach:** Billy Emerson.

### FAUQUIER GATORS

**Mailing Address:** P.O. Box 740, Warrenton, VA 20186. **Telephone:** (540) 341-3454. **FAX:** (540) 347-5199. **E-Mail Address:** gators@fauquiergators.org. **Website:** www.fauquiergators.com.

**President:** Alison Athey. **General Manager:** Sam Johnson. **Head Coach:** Paul Koch.

### HERNDON BRAVES

**Mailing Address:** 1305 Kelly Court, Herndon, VA 20170. **Telephone:**
(703) 973-4444. **FAX:** (703) 783-1319. **E-Mail Address:** herndonbraves@cox.net. **Website:** www.herndonbraves.com.

**President:** Lisa Lombardozzi. **General Manager/Head Coach:** Greg Miller.

### RESTON HAWKS

**Mailing Address:** 10915 Howland Dr., Herndon, VA 20191. **Telephone:** (703) 860-0946. **FAX:** (703) 860-0143. **E-Mail Address:** fannanfj@erols.com.

**General Manager:** Frank Fannan. **Head Coach:** Kevin Kawecki.

### VIENNA SENATORS

**Mailing Address:** 2727 Hidden Rd., Vienna, VA 22180. **Telephone:** (703)
534-5081. **FAX:** (703) 534-5085. **E-Mail Address:** cburr17@hotmail.com. **Website:** www.senatorbaseball.org.

**President:** Bill McGillicuddy. **General Manager:** Bob Menefee. **Head Coach:** Chris Burr.

## COASTAL PLAIN LEAGUE

**Mailing Address:** 4900 Waters Edge Dr., Suite 201, Raleigh, NC 27606. **Telephone:** (919) 852-1960. **FAX:** (919) 852-1973. **Website:** www.coastalplain.com.

**Year Founded:** 1997.

**Chairman/Chief Executive Officer:** Jerry Petitt.

**President:** Pete Bock. **Director, Media Relations:** Justin Sellers. **Director, Administration:** Erin Callahan.

**Division Structure: North**—Edenton, Outer Banks, Peninsula, Petersburg, Wilson. **South**—Columbia, Fayetteville, Florence, New Bern, Wilmington. **West**—Asheboro, Gastonia, Martinsville, Spartanburg, Thomasville.

**Regular Season:** 56 games (split schedule). **2006 Opening Date:** May 31. **Closing Date:** Aug. 9.

**All-Star Game:** July 18 at Fayetteville.

**Playoff Format:** Eight-team modified double-elimination tournament, Aug. 11-13.

**Roster Limit:** 25 (college-eligible players only).

### ASHEBORO COPPERHEADS

**Mailing Address:** P.O. Box 4006, Asheboro, NC 27204. **Telephone:** (336) 460-7018. **FAX:** (336) 629-2651. **E-Mail Address:** info@teamcopperhead.com. **Website:** www.teamcopperhead.com.

**Owner:** Ronnie Pugh. **Co-General Managers:** Aaron Pugh, William Davis. **Head Coach:** Patrick Swift (Chowan, N.C., College).

### COLUMBIA BLOWFISH

**Mailing Address:** P.O. Box 1328, Columbia, SC 29202. **Telephone:** (803) 254-4029. **FAX:** (803) 254-4482. **E-Mail Address:** skip@blowfishbaseball.com. **Website:** www.blowfishbaseball.com.

**Owner:** HWS Baseball V (Michael Savit, Bill Shanahan). **General Manager:** Skip Anderson. **Head Coach:** Tim Medlin.

### EDENTON STEAMERS

**Mailing Address:** P.O. Box 86, Edenton, NC 27932. **Telephone:** (252) 482-4080. **FAX:** (252) 482-1717. **E-Mail Address:** edentonsteamers@hotmail.com. **Website:** www.edentonsteamers.com.

**Owner:** Edenton-Chowan Community Foundation, Inc. **General Manager:** George Mohr. **Head Coach:** David Scoggin (College of Charleston).

### FAYETTEVILLE SWAMPDOGS

**Mailing Address:** P.O. Box 64691, Fayetteville, NC 28306. **Telephone:** (910) 426-5900. **FAX:** (910) 426-3544. **E-Mail Address:** info@fayettevilleswampdogs.com. **Website:** www.fayettevilleswampdogs.com.

**Owner:** Lew Handelsman. **Head Coach/Director of Operations:** Darrell Handelsman.

### FLORENCE REDWOLVES

**Mailing Address:** P.O. Box 809, Florence, SC 29503. **Telephone:** (843) 629-0700. **FAX:** (843) 629-0703. **E-Mail Address:** Jamie@florenceredwolves.com. **Website:** www.florenceredwolves.com.

**President:** Kevin Barth. **General Manager:** Jamie Young. **Head Coach:** Sean Heffernan (Florence-Darlington Tech, S.C.).

### GASTONIA GRIZZLIES

**Mailing Address:** P.O. Box 177, Gastonia, NC 28053. **Telephone:** (704) 866-8622. **FAX:** (704) 864-6122. **E-Mail Address:** kevin@gastonia-grizzlies.com. **Website:** www.gastonia-grizzlies.com.

**President:** Ken Silver. **Chief Executive Officer:** Jack Thompson. **General Manager:** Kevin Ferris. **Head Coach:** Chris Wiley (Louisburg, N.C., JC).

### MARTINSVILLE MUSTANGS

**Mailing Address:** P.O. Box 1112, Martinsville, VA 24114. **Telephone:** (276) 632-9913. **FAX:** (276) 645-0404. **E-Mail Address:** mustangsgm28@aol.com. **Website:** www.martinsvillemustangs.com.

**General Manager:** Doug Gibson. **Head Coach:** Rob Watt (Mount Olive, N.C., College).

## NEW BERN RIVER RATS
**Mailing Address:** 1311 N. Craven St., New Bern, NC 28560. **Telephone:** (252) 675-5689. **FAX:** (252) 637-2721. **E-Mail Address:** newbernriverrats@yahoo.com. **Website:** www.newbernriverrats.com.
**President:** Sabrina Bengel. **Vice President:** Buddy Bengel. **General Manager:** Michael Weisbart. **Head Coach:** Darin Vaughan (Central Missouri State U.).

## OUTER BANKS DAREDEVILS
**Mailing Address:** P.O. Box 7596, Kill Devil Hills, NC 27948. **Telephone:** (252) 480-0903. **FAX:** (252) 473-5070. **E-Mail Address:** obxdaredevils@yahoo.com. **Website:** www.outerbanksdaredevils.com.
**Owner:** Marcus Felton. **General Manager:** Mike Stephens. **Head Coach:** Ted Tom (Indiana U.).

## PENINSULA PILOTS
**Mailing Address:** P.O. Box 7376, Hampton, VA 23666. **Telephone:** (757) 245-2222. **FAX:** (757) 245-8030. **E-Mail Address:** hank@peninsulapilots.com. **Website:** www.peninsulapilots.com.
**Owner:** Henry Morgan. **General Manager:** Hank Morgan. **Head Coach:** Matt Reid (UNC Asheville).

## PETERSBURG GENERALS
**Mailing Address:** 1981 Midway Ave., Petersburg, VA 23804. **Telephone:** (804) 722-0141. **FAX:** (804) 733-7370. **E-Mail Address:** pbgenerals@aol.com. **Website:** www.petersburgsports.com/generals.
**President:** Larry Toombs. **General Manager, Baseball Operations:** Jeremy Toombs. **General Manager, Team Operations:** Chris Gerrity. **Head Coach:** Bob Fenn (UNC Asheville).

## SPARTANBURG STINGERS
**Mailing Address:** P.O. Box 5493, Spartanburg, SC 29304. **Telephone:** (864) 591-2250. **FAX:** (864) 591-2131. **E-Mail Address:** kferris@spartanburgstingers.com. **Website:** www.spartanburgstingers.com.
**Owner:** Ken Silver. **Chief Operating Officer:** Jack Thompson. **General Manager:** James Wolfe. **Head Coach:** Matt Hayes (Limestone, S.C., College).

## THOMASVILLE HI-TOMS
**Mailing Address:** P.O. Box 3035, Thomasville, NC 27360. **Telephone:** (336) 472-8667. **FAX:** (336) 472-7198. **E-Mail Address:** info@hitoms.com. **Website:** www.hitoms.com
**President:** Greg Suire. **General Manager:** Jared Schjei. **Head Coach:** Alan Beck (Western Carolina U.).

## WILMINGTON SHARKS
**Mailing Address:** P.O. Box 15233, Wilmington, NC 28412. **Telephone:** (910) 343-5621. **FAX:** (910) 343-8932. **E-Mail Address:** info@wilmingtonsharks.com. **Website:** www.wilmingtonsharks.com.
**President:** Jim Morrison. **General Manager:** Amanda Yerdon. **Head Coach:** Andrew Wright (West Virginia U.).

## WILSON TOBS
**Mailing Address:** P.O. Box 633, Wilson, NC 27894. **Telephone:** (252) 291-8627. **FAX:** (252) 291-1224. **E-Mail Address:** wilsontobs@earthlink.net. **Website:** www.wilsontobs.com.
**President:** Greg Turnage. **General Manager:** Mike Edwards. **Head Coach:** Jeff Steele (Lubbock Christian U.).

## FLORIDA COLLEGIATE SUMMER LEAGUE
**Mailing Address:** 1778 N. Park Ave., Suite 201,

Maitland, FL 32751. **Telephone:** (321) 206-9174. **FAX:** (407) 628-8535. **E-Mail Address:** swhiting@floridaleague.com. **Website:** www.floridaleague.com.
**Year Founded:** 2004.
**President:** Sara Whiting. **Vice President:** Rob Sitz. **Treasurer:** Mike Whiting. **Business Operations:** Pepi Ribley. **Public Relations:** Mack Whiting.
**Division Structure: North**—Sanford, Altamonte Springs, Winter Park. **South**—Orlando Hammers, Orlando Shockers, Winter Pines.
**Regular Season:** 35 games. **2006 Opening Date:** June 8. **Closing Date:** July 29.
**All-Star Game:** July 16 at Sanford.
**Playoff Format:** Six-team, modified double-elimination tournament, July 31- Aug. 6.
**Roster Limit:** 25 (college-eligible players only).

## ALTAMONTE SPRINGS SNAPPERS
**Mailing Address:** 1778 N. Park Ave., Suite 201, Maitland, FL 32751. **Telephone:** (321) 206-9174. **E-Mail Address:** swhiting@floridaleague.com. **Website:** www.floridaleague.com/altamonte.html.
**Team President:** Sal Lombardo. **Head Coach:** Bryan Peters (Stetson U.)

## ORLANDO HAMMERS
**Mailing Address:** Athletes In Action, 651 Taylor Dr., Xenia, OH 45385. **Telephone:** (321) 206-9174. **E-Mail Address:** john.mclaughlin@aia.com. **Website:** www.floridaleague.com/hammers.html.
**Head Coach:** John McLaughlin.

## ORLANDO SHOCKERS
**Mailing Address:** 1778 N. Park Ave., Suite 201, Maitland, FL 32751. **Telephone:** (321) 206-9174. **E-Mail Address:** swhiting@floridaleague.com. **Website:** www.floridaleague.com/shockers.html.
**Team President:** Joe Russell. **Head Coach:** Chuck Stegall (Neosho County, Kan., CC).

## SANFORD RIVER RATS
**Mailing Address:** 1778 N. Park Ave., Suite 201, Maitland, FL 32751. **Telephone:** (321) 206-9174. **E-Mail Address:** swhiting@floridaleague.com. **Website:** www.floridaleague.com/sanford.html.
**Team President:** Dan Ping. **Head Coach:** Kenne Brown.

## WINTER PARK DIAMOND DAWGS
**Mailing Address:** 1778 N. Park Ave., Suite 201, Maitland, FL 32751. **Telephone:** (321) 206-9174. **E-Mail Address:** swhiting@floridaleague.com. **Website:** www.floridaleague.com/winterpark.html.
**Team President:** Ian Nathanson. **Head Coach:** Scott Makarewicz.

## WINTER PINES WART HOGS
**Mailing Address:** 1778 N. Park Ave., Suite 201, Maitland, FL 32751. **Telephone:** (321) 206-9174. **E-Mail Address:** swhiting@floridaleague.com. **Website:** www.floridaleague.com/winterpines.html.
**Team President:** Sean Connolly. **Head Coach:** Rich Wallace (U. of Central Florida).

## FLORIDA COLLEGIATE INSTRUCTIONAL LEAGUE
**Mailing Address:** IMG Academies/Bollettieri Campus, 5500 34th St. W., Bradenton, FL 34210. **Telephone:** (941) 727-0303. **FAX:** (941) 727-2962. **E-Mail Address:** tpluto@gte.net. **Website:** www.imgacademies.com.
**Year Founded:** 2001.
**President:** Tom Pluto. **Secretary:** Flody Suarez.

Regular Season: 36 games (split schedule). **2006 Opening Date:** June 11. **Closing Date:** July 31.

**All-Star Game:** July 9.

**Playoff Format:** One-game playoff between first- and second-half winners.

**Roster Limit:** Open (college-eligible players only).

## GREAT LAKES LEAGUE

**Mailing Address:** 133 W. Winter St., Delaware, OH 43015. **Telephone:** (740) 368-3527. **FAX:** (740) 368-3999. **E-Mail Address:** kalance@greatlakesleague.org. **Website:** www.greatlakesleague.org.

**Year Founded:** 1986.

**President, Commissioner:** Kim Lance.

**Division Structure:** None.

**Regular Season:** 40 games. **2006 Opening Date:** June 10. **Closing Date:** Aug. 5.

**All-Star Game:** July 16 at Athens, OH.

**Playoff Format:** Top eight teams meet in double-elimination tournament.

**Roster Limit:** 27 (college-eligible players only).

### CINCINNATI STEAM
**Mailing Address:** 2745 Anderson Ferry Rd., Cincinnati, OH 45238. **Telephone:** (513) 922-4272.

**General Manager:** Max McLeary. **Head Coach:** Jeremy Isom.

### COLUMBUS ALL-AMERICANS
**Mailing Address:** 50 West Broad St., Suite #700, Columbus, OH 43215. **Telephone:** (614) 620-1734.

**General Manager/Head Coach:** Brian Mannino.

### DELAWARE COWS
**Mailing Address:** 2379 Sherwood Rd., Bexley, OH 43209. **Telephone:** (614) 237-3837.

**General Manager:** Jay Sokol. **Head Coach:** Bruce Heine.

### GRAND LAKE MARINERS
**Mailing Address:** 717 W. Walnut St., Coldwater, OH 45828. **Telephone:** (419) 678-3607.

**General Manager:** Wayne Miller. **Head Coach:** Scott French.

### GRANVILLE SETTLERS
**Mailing Address:** Department of Physical Education, Denison University, Granville, OH 43023. **Telephone:** (740) 587-6714.

**General Manager:** Barry Craddock. **Head Coach:** Corey Stevens.

### LAKE ERIE MONARCHS
**Mailing Address:** 26670 Glenwood Rd., Bldg. #2, Perrysburg, OH 43551. **Telephone:** (734) 626-1166.

**General Manager:** Jim DeSana. **Head Coach:** Brian McGee.

### LIMA LOCOS
**Mailing Address:** 3588 South Conant Rd., Spencerville, OH 45887. **Telephone:** (419) 647-5242.

**General Manager:** Steve Meyer. **Head Coach:** Rob Livchak.

### SOUTHERN OHIO COPPERHEADS
**Mailing Address:** 32 Grand Park Blvd., Athens, OH 45701. **Telephone:** (740) 541-9284.

**General Manager:** David Palmer. **Head Coach:** Stas Swerdzewski.

### XENIA ATHLETES IN ACTION
**Mailing Address:** 651 Taylor Dr., Xenia, OH 45385. **Telephone:** (937) 352-1234

**General Manager:** Eddie Lang. **Head Coach:** Unavailable.

## JAYHAWK LEAGUE

**Mailing Address:** 5 Adams Place, Halstead, KS 67056. **Telephone:** (316) 755-2361. **FAX:** (316) 755-1285.

**Year Founded:** 1976.

**Commissioner:** Bob Considine. **President:** J.D. Schneider. **Vice President:** Curt Bieber. **Public Relations/Statistician:** Gary Karr. **Secretary:** Christi Billups.

**Regular Season:** 40 games. **2006 Opening Date:** June 10. **Closing Date:** July 29.

**Playoff Format:** Top two teams qualify for National Baseball Congress World Series in Wichita, Kan..

**Roster Limit:** 30 to begin season; 25 at midseason.

### EL DORADO BRONCOS
**Mailing Address:** 865 Fabrique, Wichita, KS 67218. **Telephone:** (316) 687-2309. **FAX:** (316) 942-2009. **Website:** www.eldoradobroncos.com.

**General Manager:** J.D. Schneider. **Head Coach:** J.R. DiMercurio.

### HAYS LARKS
**Mailing Address:** 1207 Felton Dr., Hays, KS 67601. **Telephone:** (785) 625-3486. **FAX:** (785) 625-8542. **E-Mail address:** cbieber@waffle-crete.com.

**General Manager:** Curt Bieber. **Head Coach:** Frank Leo.

### JOPLIN SLASHERS
**Mailing Address:** 807 2nd Ave., Monett, MO 65708. **Telephone:** (417) 235-3193.

**General Manager:** Scott Wright.

### LIBERAL BEEJAYS
**Mailing Address:** P.O. Box 793, Liberal, KS 67901. **Telephone:** (620) 624-1904. **FAX:** (620) 624-1906.

**General Manager:** Kim Snell.

### NEVADA GRIFFONS
**Mailing Address:** 200 S. Alma, Nevada, MO 64772. **Telephone:** (417) 667-8308. **FAX:** (417) 667-8108.

**General Manager:** Jason Meisenheimer.

### WICHITA TWINS
**Mailing Address:** 1245 N. Pine Grove, Wichita, KS 67212. **Telephone:** (316) 667-1104.

**General Manager:** Jeff Wells.

## MOUNTAIN COLLEGIATE BASEBALL LEAGUE

**E-Mail Address:** info@mcbl.net. **Website:** www.mcbl.net.

**Year Founded:** 2005.

**Directors:** Kurt Colicchio, Ron Kailey, Ray Klesh, Heidi Peterson.

**Director of Umpires:** Dewey Larson.

**Regular Season:** 48 games. **Opening Date:** June 2. **Closing Date:** Aug. 2.

**Playoff Format:** Top two teams meet in best-of-3 series.

**Roster limit:** 25 (college-eligible players only).

### CHEYENNE GRIZZLIES
**Telephone:** (307) 631-7337. **E-Mail Address:** rkaide@aol.com. **Website:** www.cheyennegrizzlies.com.

**Owner/General Manager:** Ron Kailey. **Head Coach:** Josh Schultz.

### FORT COLLINS FOXES
**Telephone:** (970) 225-9564. **E-Mail Address:** kcolicchio@msn.com. **Website:** www.fortcollinsfoxes.com.

**Owner/General Manager:** Kurt Colicchio. **Head Coach:** Paul Svagdis (Azusa Pacific, Calif., U.).

### GREELEY GRAYS
**Telephone:** (303) 870-2523. **E-Mail Address:** rklesh@earthlink.net. **Website:** www.greeleygrays.com.
**Owner/General Manager:** Ray Klesh. **Head Coach:** Sam Blackmon (U. of Dallas).

### LARAMIE COLTS
**Telephone:** (307) 742-2191. **E-Mail Address:** laramiecolts@aol.com. **Website:** www.laramiecolts.com.
**Owners:** Heidi Peterson, Matt Peterson. **General Manager:** Heidi Peterson. **Head Coach:** Kevin Moulder (Central Missouri State U.).

## NEW ENGLAND COLLEGIATE LEAGUE
**Mailing Address:** 515 Hawthorne Lane, Windsor, CT 06905. **Website:** www.necbl.com.
**Year Founded:** 1993.
**Commissioner/Acting President:** Kevin MacIlvane. **Executive Vice President:** Joel Cooney. **Deputy Commissioner:** Mario Tiani.
**Division Structure: North**—Concord, Holyoke, Keene, Lowell, Sanford, Montpelier. **South**—Danbury, Manchester, Newport, North Adams, Pittsfield, Torrington.
**Regular Season:** 42 games. **2006 Opening Date:** June 8. **Closing Date:** July 31.
**All-Star Game:** July 23 at Keene.
**Playoff Format:** Top four teams in each division meet in best-of-3 quarterfinals; winners meet in best-of-3 divisional championship. Winners meet in best-of-3 final for league championship.
**Roster Limit:** 25 (college-eligible players only).

### CONCORD QUARRY DOGS
**Mailing Address:** P.O. Box 2502, Concord, NH 03302.
**Telephone:** (603) 502-4713. **E-Mail Address:** info@quarrydogs.org. **Website:** www.q-dogs.org.
**President/General Manager:** Peter Dupuis. **Head Coach:** Tim Rice (U. of Washington).

### DANBURY WESTERNERS
**Mailing Address:** 5 Old Hayrake Rd., Danbury, CT 06811. **Telephone:** (203) 313-3024. **FAX:** (203) 792-6177. **Website:** www.danburywesterners.com. **E-Mail Address:** westerners1@aol.com.
**General Manager:** Terry Whalen. **Head Coach:** Unavailable.

### HOLYOKE GIANTS
**Mailing Address:** 6 Draper Rd., Wayland, MA 01778.
**Telephone:** (508) 358-5426. **Website:** www.holyokegiants.com.
**President/General Manager:** Philip Rosenfield. **Head Coach:** Joel Southern.

### KEENE SWAMP BATS
**Mailing Address:** 31 W. Surry Rd., Keene, NH 03431.
**Telephone:** (603) 357-2578. **FAX:** (603) 354-7842.
**General Manager:** Vicki Bacon. **Head Coach:** Mike Sweeney (U. of Massachusetts).

### LOWELL ALL-AMERICANS
**Mailing Address:** P.O. Box 2228, Lowell, MA 01851.
**Telephone:** (978) 454-5058. **FAX:** (978) 251-1211. **E-Mail Address:** info@millcityallamericans.com.
**General Manager:** Harry Ayotte. **Head Coach:** Ken Connerty.

### MANCHESTER SILKWORMS
**Mailing Address:** 16 West St., Manchester, CT 06040.
**Telephone:** (860) 559-3126. **FAX:** (860) 432-1665.

**Website:** www.manchestersilkworms.org.
**General Manager:** Ed Slegeski. **Head Coach:** Anthony DeCicco (U. of Vermont).

### NEWPORT GULLS
**Mailing Address:** P.O. Box 777, Newport, RI 02840.
**Telephone:** (401) 845-6832. **Website:** www.newport-gulls.com
**President/General Manager:** Chuck Paiva. **Assistant GM:** Chris Patsos. **Head Coach:** Tom Atkinson (Louisburg, N.C., JC).

### NORTH ADAMS STEEPLECATS
**Mailing Address:** P.O. Box 540, North Adams, MA 01247. **Telephone:** (413) 652-1031. **Website:** www.steeplecats.com
**General Manager:** Sean McGrath. **Head Coach:** Laz Gutierrez (Barry, Fla., U.).

### PITTSFIELD DUKES
**Mailing Address:** 75 S. Church St., Pittsfield, MA 01201. **Telephone:** (413) 447-3853. **Website:** www.pittsfielddukes.com.
**President:** Dan Duquette. **Chief Operating Officer:** Rick Murphy. **General Manager:** Kent Qualls. **Head Coach:** Unavailable.

### SANFORD MAINERS
**Mailing Address:** P.O. Box 26, Sanford, ME 04073.
**Telephone:** (207) 324-0010. **FAX:** (207) 324-2227.
**General Manager:** Neil Olson. **Head Coach:** Joe Brown (Cortland State, N.Y., U.).

### TORRINGTON TWISTERS
**Mailing Address:** 4 Blinkoff Ct., Torrington, CT 06790.
**Telephone/FAX:** (860) 482-0450.
**General Manager:** Kirk Fredriksson. **Head Coach:** Gregg Hunt.

### VERMONT MOUNTAINEERS
**Mailing Address:** P.O. Box 586, Montpelier, VT 05602.
**Telephone:** (802) 223-5224.
**General Manager:** Brian Gallagher. **Head Coach:** John Russo.

## NEW YORK COLLEGIATE LEAGUE
**Summer Address:** 28 Dunbridge Heights, Fairport, NY 14450. **Winter Address:** P.O. Box 2516, Tarpon Springs, FL 34688. **Telephone:** Florida—(585) 223-2328, New York—(727) 942-9120.
**Year Founded:** 1986.
**Commissioner:** Dave Chamberlain. **President/Publicity:** Brian Spagnola. **Vice Chairman:** Paul Welker. **Treasurer:** Dan Russo. **Secretary:** Ted Ford.
**Member Clubs:** Alfred A's, Alleghany County Nitros, Amsterdam Mohawks, Elmira Pioneers, Geneva Redwings, Genesee Valley River Bats, Glens Falls Golden Eagles, Hornell Dodgers, Little Falls, Rochester Royals, Saratoga Phillies, Watertown Wizards.
**Regular Season:** 44 games. **2006 Opening Date:** June 9. **Closing Date:** Aug. 6.
**All-Star Game:** July 6 at Watertown, N.Y.
**Playoff Format:** Top eight teams meet in best-of-3 series; winners meet in best-of-3 series. Winners meet in best-of-3 series for league championship.
**Roster Limit:** 25 (college-eligible players only).

## NORTHWOODS LEAGUE
**Office Address:** 2900 4th St. SW, Rochester, MN 55902. **Telephone:** (507) 536-4579. **FAX:** (507) 536-4579. **E-Mail Address:** nwl@chartermi.net. **Website:** www.northwoodsleague.com.
**Year Founded:** 1994.

**President:** Dick Radatz Jr. **Director, Operations:** Rick Lindau.

**Division Structure: North**—Alexandria, Brainerd, Duluth, Mankato, St. Cloud, Thunder Bay. **South**—Eau Claire, La Crosse, Madison, Rochester, Waterloo, Wisconsin.

**Regular Season:** 68 games (split schedule). **2006 Opening Date:** June 1. **Closing Date:** Aug. 19.

**All-Star Game:** July 12 at La Crosse.

**Playoff Format:** First-half and second-half division winners meet in best-of-3 series. Winners meet in best-of-3 series for league championship.

**Roster Limit:** 26 (college-eligible players only).

### ALEXANDRIA BEETLES

**Mailing Address:** 418 Third Ave. E., Alexandria, MN 56308. **Telephone:** (320) 763-8151. **FAX:** (320) 763-8152. **E-Mail Address:** beetles@alexandriabeetles.com. **Website:** www.alexandriabeetles.com.

**General Manager:** Ron Voz. **Head Coach:** Erik Maas (U. of North Alabama).

### BRAINERD BLUE THUNDER

**Mailing Address:** P.O. Box 1028, Brainerd, MN 56401. **Telephone:** (218) 828-2825. **FAX:** (218) 828-2825. **E-Mail Address:** pmarrplayball@yahoo.com. **Website:** www.brainerdbluethunder.com.

**General Manager:** Skip Marr. **Head Coach:** Jason Huskey (Hutchinson, Kan., CC).

### DULUTH HUSKIES

**Mailing Address:** 207 W. Superior St., Suite 206, Holiday Center Mall, Duluth, MN 55802. **Telephone:** (218) 786-9909. **FAX:** (218) 786-9001. **E-Mail Address:** huskies@duluthhuskies.com. **Website:** www.duluthhuskies.com.

**General Manager:** Craig Smith. **Head Coach:** Dave Parra.

### EAU CLAIRE EXPRESS

**Office Address:** 108 E. Grand Ave., Eau Claire, WI 54701. **Mailing Address:** P.O. Box 1111, Eau Claire, WI 54702. **Telephone:** (715) 839-7788. **FAX:** (715) 839-7676. **E-Mail Address:** info@eauclaireexpress.com. **Website:** www.eauclaireexpress.com.

**General Manager:** Jeff Jones. **Head Coach:** Dale Varsho.

### LA CROSSE LOGGERS

**Mailing Address:** 1223 Caledonia St., La Crosse, WI 54603. **Telephone:** (608) 796-9553. **FAX:** (608) 796-9032. **E-Mail Address:** info@lacrosseloggers.com. **Website:** www.lacrosseloggers.com.

**General Manager:** Chris Goodell. **Head Coach:** Rick Boyer.

### MADISON MALLARDS

**Mailing Address:** 2920 N. Sherman Ave., Madison, WI 53704. **Telephone:** (608) 246-4277. **FAX:** (608) 246-4163. **E-Mail Address:** vern@mallardsbaseball.com. **Website:** www.mallardsbaseball.com.

**General Manager:** Vern Stenman. **Head Coach:** C.J. Thieleke (Madison Area Tech, Wis., JC).

### MANKATO MOONDOGS

**Mailing Address:** 310 Belle Ave., Suite L-8, Mankato, MN 56001. **Telephone:** (507) 625-7047. **FAX:** (507) 625-7059. **E-Mail Address:** office@mankatomoondogs.com. **Website:** www.mankatomoondogs.com.

**General Manager:** Kyle Mrozek. **Head Coach:** Jason Nell (Iowa Lakes CC).

### ROCHESTER HONKERS

**Office Address:** Mayo Field, 403 E. Center St.,

Rochester, MN 55904. **Mailing Address:** P.O. Box 482, Rochester, MN 55903. **Telephone:** (507) 289-1170. **FAX:** (507) 289-1866. **E-Mail Address:** honkers@rochesterhonkers.com. **Website:** www.rochesterhonkers.com.

**General Manager:** Dan Litzinger. **Head Coach:** Greg Labbe (U. of North Florida).

### ST. CLOUD RIVER BATS

**Office Address:** Dick Putz Field, 5001 8th St. N., St. Cloud, MN 56303. **Mailing Address:** P.O. Box 5059, St. Cloud, MN 56302. **Telephone:** (320) 240-9798. **FAX:** (320) 255-5228. **E-Mail Address:** info@riverbats.com. **Website:** www.riverbats.com.

**General Manager:** Marc Jerzak. **Head Coach:** Tony Arnerich (Sonoma, Calif., State U.).

### THUNDER BAY BORDER CATS

**Office Address:** Port Arthur Stadium, 425 Winnipeg Ave., Thunder Bay, Ontario P7B 6P7. **Mailing Address:** P.O. Box 29105, Thunder Bay, Ontario P7B 6P9. **Telephone:** (807) 766-2287. **FAX:** (807) 345-8299. **E-Mail Address:** baseball@tbaytel.net. **Website:** www.bordercatsbaseball.com.

**General Manager:** Greg Balec. **Head Coach:** Brad Stromdahl (Central Michigan U.).

### WATERLOO BUCKS

**Office Address:** Riverfront Stadium, 850 Park Rd., Waterloo, IA 50703. **Mailing Address:** P.O. Box 4124, Waterloo, IA 50704. **Telephone:** (319) 232-0500. **FAX:** (319) 232-0700. **E-Mail Address:** waterloobucks@winning.com. **Website:** www.waterloobucks.com.

**General Manager:** Dan Corbin. **Head Coach:** Cory Allen (U. of Dayton).

### WISCONSIN WOODCHUCKS

**Office Address:** Athletic Park, 300 Third St., Wausau, WI 54402. **Mailing Address:** P.O. Box 6157, Wausau, WI 54402. **Telephone:** (715) 845-5055. **FAX:** (715) 845-5015. **E-Mail Address:** info@woodchucks.com. **Website:** www.woodchucks.com.

**General Manager:** Matt Brklacich. **Head Coach:** Joel Barta (Northland, Wis., College).

## PACIFIC INTERNATIONAL LEAGUE

**Mailing Address:** 4400 26th Ave. W., Seattle, WA 98199. **Telephone:** (206) 623-8844. **FAX:** (206) 623-8361. **E-Mail Address:** spotter@potterprinting.com. **Website:** www.pacificinternationalleague.com.

**Year Founded:** 1992

**President:** Steve Konek. **Commissioner:** Brian Gooch. **Secretary:** Steve Potter. **Treasurer:** Mark Dow.

**Member Clubs:** Everett (Wash.) Merchants, Langley (B.C.) Blaze, Northwest Javelinas (Portland, Ore.), Portland (Ore.) Kings, Portland (Ore.) Titans, Seaside (Ore.) Wildcats, Seattle Studs, Skagit Eagles (Mount Vernon, Wash.).

**Regular Season:** 28 league games. **2006 Opening Date:** June 1. **Closing Date:** July 31.

**Playoff Format:** Regular-season winner earns automatic berth in National Baseball Congress World Series in Wichita, Kan.

**Roster Limit:** 30; 25 eligible for games (players must be at least 18 years old).

## SOUTHERN COLLEGIATE BASEBALL LEAGUE

**Mailing Address:** 9300 Fairway Ridge Rd., Charlotte, NC 28277. **Telephone:** (704) 847-5075. **FAX:** (704) 847-1455. **E-Mail Address:** SCBLCommissioner@aol.com.

Website: www.scbl.org.
Year Founded: 1999.
Commissioner: Bill Capps. President: Jeff Carter.
Vice President: Brian Swords. Vice President, Marketing/Development: Wes Cook. Secretary: Larry Tremitiere. Treasurer: Steve Cunningham.
Division Structure: North--Davidson, Monroe, Morganton, Tennessee. South--Asheville, Carolina, Rock Hill, Spartanburg.
Regular Season: 44 games. 2006 Opening Date: May 30. Closing Date: July 30.
All Star Game: July 13 at Fort Mill, S.C.
Playoff Format: Top two teams from each division will play a double-elimination tournament for league championship.
Roster Limit: 30 (College-eligible players only).

### ASHEVILLE REDBIRDS
Mailing Address: P.O. Box 1515, Johnson City, TN 37605. Telephone: (423) 854-9282, (423) 914-0621. FAX: (423) 854-9594. E-Mail Address: EntSport@aol.com.
Owner/General Manager: Lyn Jeffers. Head Coach: Unavailable.

### CAROLINA CHAOS
Mailing Address: 142 Orchard Dr., Liberty, SC 29657. Telephone: (864) 843-3232, (864) 901-4331. E-mail Address: brian_swords@carolinachaos.com. Website: www.carolinachaos.com.
Owner/General Manager: Brian Swords. Associate Head Coach: Scott Whitlock.

### DAVIDSON COPPERHEADS
Mailing Address: P.O. Box 928, Cornelius, NC 28031. Telephone: (704) 892-1041, (704) 564-9211. E-Mail Address: jcarter@standpointtech.com. Website: www.Copperheadsports.org.
Owner: Carolina Copperhead Baseball, Inc. General Manager: Jeff Carter. Head Coach: David Darwin.

### MONROE CHANNELCATS
Mailing Address: 1409-B Babbage Lane, Indian Trail, NC 28079. Telephone: (704) 821-5610, (704) 207-6242. E-Mail Address: info@monroechannelcats.com.
Owner: Wesley Cook. General Manager: Tommy Greene. Head Coach: Jose Vazquez.

### MORGANTON AGGIES
Mailing Address: P.O. Box 3448, Morganton, NC 28680. Telephone: (828) 438-5351. FAX: (828) 438-5350. E-Mail Address: gwleonhardt@aol.com.
General Manager: Gary Leonhardt. Head Coach: Jason Burke.

### ROCK HILL SOX
Mailing Address: 1443 Wedgefield Dr., Rock Hill, SC 29732. Telephone: (803) 366-2207, (803) 517-6626. FAX: (803) 980-7438. E-Mail Address: Ltrem1214@cs.com.
Owner: Rock Hill Sox Baseball, Inc. General Manager: Larry Tremitiere. Head Coach: Ryan Quirello.

### SPARTANBURG CRICKETS
Mailing Address: P.O. Box 1429, Cowpens, SC 29330. Telephone: (864) 463-6667, (864) 266-3727. E-Mail Address: cricketsbb@bellsouth.net.
Owner/General Manager: Steve Cunningham. Head Coach: Mike Cunningham.

### TENNESSEE THUNDER
Mailing Address: P.O. Box 1515, Johnson City, TN 37605. Telephone: (423) 854-9282, (423) 914-0621. FAX: (423) 854-9594. E-Mail Address: EntSport@aol.com.
Owner/General Manager: Lyn Jeffers. Head Coach: Glenn Davis.

## TEXAS COLLEGIATE LEAGUE
Mailing Address: 512 Main St., Suite 1200, Fort Worth, TX 76102. Telephone: (817) 339-9367. FAX: (817) 339-9309. E-Mail Address: info@texascollegiate-league.com. Website: www.texascollegiateleague.com.
Year Founded: 2004.
Chairman/Chief Executive Officer: Gerald Haddock.
Commissioner/Chief Operating Officer: John Blake.
Vice President, Baseball Operations: Darren Hall.
Director, Sponsor/Team Services: Ginger Reed.
Supervisor, Umpires: John Ausmus.
Division Structure: Rogers Hornsby—Denton, Graham, Mineral Wells, Weatherford. Tris Speaker—Coppell, Duncanville, Euless, Highland Park, McKinney.
Regular Season: 48 games. 2006 Opening Date: June 6. Closing Date: Aug. 6.
All-Star Game: July 10 at Weatherford.
Playoff Format: Top two teams in each division meet in best-of-3 division series. Winners meet in best-of-3 series for league championship.
Roster Limit: 25 (College-eligible players only).

### COPPELL COPPERHEADS
Mailing Address: 509 W. Bethel Rd., Suite 100, Coppell, TX 75019. Telephone: (972) 745-2929. FAX: (972) 745-0063. E-Mail Address: info@tclcopper-heads.com. Website: www.tclcopperheads.com.
President: Steve Pratt. General Manager: John Marston. Head Coach: Skip Johnson (Navarro, Texas, JC).

### DENTON OUTLAWS
Mailing Address: 16250 Dallas Pkwy., Suite 102, Dallas, TX 75248. Telephone: (940) 250-1037. FAX: (972) 250-1343. Website: www.thedentonoutlaws.com.
Owners: Jim Leslie, Todd Van Poppel. General Manager: Candiss Caudle. Head Coach: Derek Matlock (Texas Christian U.).

### DUNCANVILLE DEPUTIES
Mailing Address: 407 N. Cedar Ridge, Suite 315, Duncanville, TX 75116. Telephone: (972) 296-9700. Website: www.duncanvilledeputies.com.
President: Chris Najork. General Manager: Jeff Najork. Head Coach: Kyle Houser (Klein Forest HS, Houston).

### EULESS LONESTARS
Mailing Address: 4709 Colleyville Blvd., P.O. Box 160, Colleyville, TX 76034. Telephone: (817) 577-4445. FAX: (817) 633-5729. E-Mail Address: info@tcllonestars.com. Website: www.tcllonestars.com.
Owner: Britt Britton. Owner/President: Stacey Hollinger. General Manager: Scott Livingstone. Head Coach: Rob Penders (U. of Texas).

### GRAHAM ROUGHNECKS
Mailing Address: 1346 Corvadura, Graham, TX 76450. Telephone: (940) 549-5700. FAX: (940) 549-2019. E-Mail Address: info@tclroughnecks.com. Website: www.tclroughnecks.com.
Owner: Frank Beaman. General Manager: Lisa McCool. Head Coach: Johnny Cardenas (Stephen F. Austin U.).

### HIGHLAND PARK BLUE SOX
Mailing Address: 2200 Ross Ave., Suite 2200, Dallas, TX 75201. Telephone: (214) 740-8278. FAX: (214) 768-3142. E-Mail Address: info@tclbluesox.com. Website:

www.tclbluesox.com.

**Managing Partner:** Paul Rogers. **General Manager:** Christi Baker. **Head Coach:** Unavailable.

## McKINNEY MARSHALS

**Mailing Address:** The Ballfields at Craig Ranch, 6151 Alma Rd., McKinney, TX 75070. **Telephone:** (972) 747-8248. **FAX:** (972) 747-9231. **E-Mail Address:** info@tclmarshals.com. **Website:** www.tclmarshals.com.

**Owner:** David Craig. **Owner/President:** Mike Henneman. **Executive Vice President/General Manager:** Ray Ricchi. **Head Coach:** Kyle Hope (Richardson, Texas, HS).

## MINERAL WELLS STEAM

**Mailing Address:** P.O. Box 606, Mineral Wells, TX 76068. **Telephone:** (940) 325-8500. **FAX:** (940) 328-0850. **E-Mail Address:** info@tclsteam.com. **Website:** www.tclsteam.com.

**Owner:** Athletes in Action. **General Manager:** Jason Lester. **Head Coach:** Mike Bard (Athletes in Action).

## WEATHERFORD WRANGLERS

**Mailing Address:** P.O. Box 2108, Weatherford, TX 76086. **Telephone:** (817) 771-8882. **FAX:** (817) 447-8637. **E-Mail Address:** info@tclwranglers.com. **Website:** www.tclwranglers.com.

**Managing Partner:** Lonna Leach. **Business Manager:** Misti Lightfoot. **Head Coach:** Jeff Lightfoot (Weatherford, Texas, JC).

## VALLEY LEAGUE

**Mailing Address:** 58 Bethel Green Rd., Staunton, VA 24401. **Telephone:** (540) 885-8901. **FAX:** (540) 885-2068. **E-Mail Addresses:** davidb@fisherautoparts.com, kevin.warner@emu.edu. **Website:** www.valleyleague-baseball.com.

**Year Founded:** 1961.

**President:** David Biery. **Executive Vice President:** Todd Thompson. **Sports Information Director:** Kevin Warner.

**Division Structure: North**—Front Royal, Haymarket, Luray, New Market, Winchester. **South**—Covington, Harrisonburg, Staunton, Waynesboro, Woodstock.

**Regular Season:** 42 games. **2006 Opening Date:** June 2. **Closing Date:** July 23.

**All-Star Game:** July 9 at Harrisonburg.

**Playoff Format:** Top four teams in each division meet in best-of-3 intra-divisional semifinal and final series. Winners meet in best-of-5 series for Jim Lineweaver Trophy.

**Roster Limit:** 28 (college eligible players only).

## COVINGTON LUMBERJACKS

**Mailing Address:** P.O. Box 171, Low Moor, VA 24457. **Telephone/FAX:** (540) 863-5225. **E-Mail Address:** rh@alcovamortage.com. **Website:** www.lumberjacks-baseball.com.

**Owners:** Clyde Helmintoller, Jason Helmintoller. **Head Coach:** Anthony Everman.

## FRONT ROYAL CARDINALS

**Mailing Address:** P.O. Box 995, Front Royal, VA 22630. **Telephone:** (540) 636-1882, (540) 671-9184. **FAX:** (540) 635-8746. **E-Mail Address:** frcardinals@adel-phia.net. **Website:** www.frcardinalbaseball.com.

**President:** Linda Keen. **Head Coach:** Mike Smith.

## HARRISONBURG TURKS

**Mailing Address:** 1489 S. Main St., Harrisonburg, VA 22801. **Telephone/FAX:** (540) 434-5919. **E-Mail Address:** turksbaseball@hotmail.com. **Website:** www.harrisonburgturks.com.

**General Manager/Head Coach:** Bob Wease. **Operations Manager:** Teresa Wease. **Public Relations:** Curt Dudley.

## HAYMARKET BATTLE CATS

**Mailing Address:** P.O. Box 95, Haymarket, VA 20168. **Telephone:** (703) 768-5588. **E-Mail Address:** haymkt-battlecats@aol.com. **Website:** www.haymarketbattle-cats.com.

**President/General Manager:** Pat Malone. **Assistant GM:** Scott Newell. **Head Coach:** Mark Keagle.

## LURAY WRANGLERS

**Mailing Address:** 1203 E. Main St., Luray, VA 22835. **Telephone:** (540) 743-3338. **E-Mail Addresses:** luray-wranglers@hotmail.com, gmoyer@shentel.net. **Website:** www.luraywranglers.com.

**President:** Bill Turner. **General Manager:** Greg Moyer. **Head Coach:** Mike Bocock.

## NEW MARKET REBELS

**Mailing Address:** P.O. Box 902, New Market, VA 22844. **Telephone:** (540) 740-4247, (540) 740-8569. **E-Mail Address:** nmrebels@shentel.net. **Website:** www.rebelsbaseball.biz.

**President/General Manager:** Bruce Alger. **Executive Vice President:** Jim Weissenborn. **Head Coach:** Blaine Brown (U. of Maryland).

## STAUNTON BRAVES

**Mailing Address:** 14 Shannon Place, Staunton, VA 24401. **Telephone/FAX:** (540) 886-0905. **E-Mail Address:** sbraves@hotmail.com. **Website:** www.stauntonbraves.com.

**General Manager:** Steve Cox. **Director, Operations:** Kay Snyder. **Head Coach:** Lance Mauck (Baltimore City CC).

## WAYNESBORO GENERALS

**Mailing Address:** P.O. Box 615, Waynesboro, VA 22980. **Telephone:** (540) 949-0370, (540) 942-2474. **FAX:** (540) 949-0653. **E-Mail Address:** jim_critzer@hot-mail.com. **Website:** www.waynesborogenerals.com.

**Owner:** Jim Critzer. **Head Coach:** Lawrence Nesselrodt.

## WINCHESTER ROYALS

**Mailing Address:** P.O. Box 2485, Winchester, VA 22604. **Telephone:** (540) 667-7677, (540) 662-1434. **FAX:** (540) 662-3299. **E-Mail Addresses:** va.naviga-tor@verizon.net, jimphill@shentel.net. **Website:** www.winchesterroyals.com.

**President:** Jim Shipp. **Vice President:** Jim Phillips. **Public Relations:** Bob Stoddard. **Baseball Operations:** Brian Burke. **Head Coach:** Kevin Anderson (Shenandoah, Va., U.)

## WOODSTOCK RIVER BANDITS

**Mailing Address:** 2115 Battlefield Run Ct., Richmond, VA 23231. **Telephone:** (804) 795-5128. **FAX:** (804) 226-8706. **E-Mail Address:** woodstockriverbandits@yahoo.com. **Website:** www.woodstockriverbandits.org.

**Owner/President:** Stu Richardson. **Vice President:** Glenn Berger. **General Manager:** Jerry Walters. **Assistant GM:** Harry Combs. **Head Coach:** Aaron Carroll (Chowan, N.C., College).

## WEST COAST COLLEGIATE LEAGUE

**Mailing Address:** 610 N. Mission St., Suite C-3, Wenatchee, WA 98801. **Telephone:** (509) 888-9378. **Website:** www.wccbl.com.

**Year Founded:** 2005.

**Commissioner:** Jim Dietz. **President:** Tony Larson. **Vice President:** Dan Segel.

**Division Structure:** None.

**Regular Season:** 42 league games. **2006 Opening Date:** June 15. **Closing Date:** Aug. 11.

**Playoff Format:** Top two teams meet in best-of-3 series.

**Roster Limit:** 25 (college-eligible players only).

## ALOHA KNIGHTS

**Mailing Address:** P.O. Box 40212, Portland, OR 97240. **Telephone:** (503) 219-9919. **E-Mail Address:** info@alohaknights.com. **Website:** www.alohaknights.com.

**President:** Dan Segel. **General Manager:** Brooke Knight. **Head Coach:** Dale Stebbins (Mt. Hood, Ore., CC).

## BELLINGHAM BELLS

**Mailing Address:** 1732 Iowa St., Bellingham, WA 98226. **Telephone:** (360) 527-1035. **E-Mail Address:** info@bellinghambells.com. **Website:** www.bellinghambells.com.

**President/General Manager:** Tony Larson. **Head Coach:** Kevin Frady (Phoenix, Ariz., JC).

## BEND ELKS

**Mailing Address:** P.O. Box 9009, Bend, OR 97708. **Telephone:** (541) 312-9259. **E-Mail Address:** richardsj@bendcable.com. **Website:** www.bendelks.com.

**Owner/General Manager:** Jim Richards. **Business Manager:** Elise Michaels. **Head Coach:** Nathan Pratt (Western Oregon U.).

## KELOWNA FALCONS

**Mailing Address:** 201-1014 Glenmore Dr., Kelowna, B.C., V1Y 4P2. **Telephone:** (250) 763-4100. **E-Mail Address:** kelownafalcons@aol.com. **Website:** www.kelownafalcons.com.

**Owner:** Dan Nonis. **General Manager:** Bill Featherstone. **Business Manager:** Mark Nonis. **Head Coach:** David Robb.

## KITSAP BLUE JACKETS

**Mailing Address:** P.O. Box 68, Silverdale, WA 98383. **Telephone:** (360) 692-5566. **E-Mail Address:** rick@tscnet.com. **Website:** www.kitsapbluejackets.com.

**Managing Partner/General Manager:** Rick Smith. **Business Manager:** Wynne Littman. **Head Coach:** Matt Acker (Green River, Wash., CC).

## MOSES LAKE PIRATES

**Mailing Address:** 831 E. Colonial Ave., Moses Lake, WA 98837. **Telephone:** (509) 750-1000. **E-Mail Address:** bkirwan@remax.net. **Website:** www.moseslakepirates.com.

**Owners:** Amy Kirwan, Brent Kirwan. **General Manager:** Brent Kirwan. **Head Coach:** Gabe Boruff (Wenatchee Valley, Wash., CC).

## SPOKANE RIVERHAWKS

**Mailing Address:** E. 303 Pacific, Spokane, WA 99202. **Telephone:** (509) 747-4991. **E-Mail Address:** mmccoy@spokaneriverhhawks.com. **Website:** www.spokaneriverhawks.com.

**Owner:** Bill Hogeboom. **General Manager/Head Coach:** Steve Hertz. **Business Manager:** Matt McCoy.

## WENATCHEE APPLESOX

**Mailing Address:** P.O. Box 5100, Wenatchee, WA 98807. **Telephone:** (509) 665-6900. **E-Mail Address:** sales@applesox.com. **Website:** www.applesox.com.

**Owner/General Manager:** Jim Corcoran. **Head Coach:** Ed Knaggs.

# HIGH SCHOOL/
# YOUTH

# HIGH SCHOOL
## BASEBALL

### NATIONAL FEDERATION OF STATE HIGH SCHOOL ASSOCIATIONS
**Mailing Address:** P.O. Box 690, Indianapolis, IN 46206. **Telephone:** (317) 972-6900. **FAX:** (317) 822-5700. **E-Mail Address:** baseball@nfhs.org. **Website:** www.nfhs.org.
**Executive Director:** Robert Kanaby. **Chief Operating Officer:** Bob Gardner. **Assistant Director/Baseball Rules Editor:** Elliot Hopkins. **Director, Publications/Communications:** Bruce Howard.

### NATIONAL HIGH SCHOOL BASEBALL COACHES ASSOCIATION
**Mailing Address:** P.O. Box 12843, Tempe, AZ 85284. **Telephone:** (602) 615-0571. **FAX:** (480) 838-7133. **E-Mail Address:** rdavini@cox.net. **Website:** www.baseballcoaches.org.
**Executive Director:** Ron Davini. **President:** Frank Carey (North Reading HS, Reading, MA). **First Vice President:** Craig Anderson (Pine Island HS, Zumbrota, MN). **Second Vice President:** Bill Seamon (Owensville, Mo., HS).
**2006 National Convention:** Nov. 30-Dec. 3 at St. Louis, Mo.

### GATORADE CIRCLE OF CHAMPIONS
(National High School Player of the Year Award)
**Mailing Address:** The Gatorade Company, 321 N. Clark St., Suite 24-3, Chicago, IL 60610. **Telephone:** (312) 821-1000. **Website:** www.gatorade.com.
**Mailing Address, Scholastic Coach and Athletic Director:** 557 Broadway, New York, NY 10012. **Telephone:** (212) 343-6131. **FAX:** (212) 343-6376. **E-Mail Address:** mwallace@scholastic.com. **Website:** coachad.com. **Publisher:** Bruce Weber. **Marketing Manager:** Mike Wallace.

## NATIONAL TOURNAMENTS

### In-Season
### BASEBALL AT THE BEACH
**Mailing Address:** P.O. Box 1717, Georgetown, SC 29442. **Telephone:** (843) 546-3020. **FAX:** (843) 527-1816. **E-Mail Address:** winyahchiropractic@sc.rr.com. **Website:** baseballatthebeach.com.
**Tournament Director:** Jim Owens.
**2006 Tournament:** Feb. 23-26 at Myrtle Beach, SC (Coastal Federal Stadium/Myrtle Beach High School, 8 teams).

### BATTLE AT THE RIDGE
**Mailing Address:** Southridge HS, 19355 SW 1114th Ave., Miami, FL 33157. **Telephone:** (305) 238-6110. **FAX:** (305) 253-4456. **E-Mail Address:** edoskow@miamisouthridge.com.
**Tournament Director:** Ed Doskow.
**2006 Tournament:** February 13-18 (8 teams).

### BLAZER SPORTCO SPRING BASH
**Mailing Address:** Durango HS, 7100 W. Dewey Dr., Las Vegas, NV 89113. **Telephone:** (702) 799-5850. **FAX:** (702) 799-1286. **E-Mail Address:** shknapp@interact.ccsd.net.
**Tournament Director:** Sam Knapp.
**2006 Tournament:** April 10-12 (36 teams).

### FIRST BANK CLASSIC
**Mailing Address:** 8708 Savannah Ave., Lubbock, TX 79424. **Telephone:** (806) 535-4505. **FAX:** (806) 794-5306. **E-Mail Address:** scottgwinn@cox.net.
**Tournament Director:** Scott Gwinn.
**2006 Tournament:** March 10-12 (16 teams).

### HORIZON CLEATS NATIONAL INVITATIONAL
**Mailing Address:** Horizon High School, 5653 Sandra Terrace, Scottsdale, AZ 85254. **Telephone:** (602) 867-9003.
**Tournament Director:** Eric Kibler.
**2006 Tournament:** March 27-31 (16 teams).

### INTERNATIONAL PAPER CLASSIC
**Mailing Address:** 4775 Johnson Rd., Georgetown, SC 29440. **Telephone:** (843) 527-9606. (843) 546-3807. **FAX:** (843) 546-8521. **Website:** www.ipclassic.com.

**Tournament Director:** Alicia Johnson.
**2006 Tournament:** March 2-5 (8 teams).

### LIONS INVITATIONAL
**Mailing Address:** 3502 Lark St., San Diego CA 92103. **Telephone:** (619) 602-8650. **FAX:** (619) 239-3539. **E-Mail Address:** peter.gallagher@sdcourt.ca.gov.
**Tournament Director:** Peter Gallagher.
**2006 Tournament:** April 10-14 (112 teams).

### MIDLAND TOURNAMENT OF CHAMPIONS
**Mailing Address:** Midland High School, 906 W. Illinois Ave., Midland, TX 79701. **Telephone:** (432) 689-1337. **FAX:** (432) 689-1335. **E-Mail Address:** barryrussell@esc18.net.
**Tournament Director:** Barry Russell.
**2006 Tournament:** March 2-4 (16 teams).

### PHIL NEVIN NATIONAL CLASSIC
**Mailing Address:** P.O. Box 338, Placentia, CA 92870. **Telephone:** (714) 993-2838. **FAX:** (714) 993-5350. **E-Mail Address:** placentiamustang@aol.com. **Website:** national-classic.com
**Tournament Director:** Todd Rogers.
**2006 Tournament:** April 16-20 at Cal State Fullerton (16 teams).

### USA CLASSIC
**Mailing Address:** 5900 Walnut Grove Rd., Memphis, TN 38120. **Telephone:** (901) 872-8326. **FAX:** (901) 681-9443. **Website:** www.usabaseballstadium.org.
**Tournament Organizers:** John Daigle, Buster Kelso.
**2006 Tournament:** April 5-8 at USA Baseball Stadium, Millington, TN (16 teams).

### WEST COAST CLASSIC
**Mailing Address:** 5000 Mitty Way, San Jose, CA 95129. **Telephone:** (408) 342-4273. **E-Mail Address:** hutton@mitty.com.
**Tournament Director:** Bill Hutton.
**2006 Tournament:** April 18-20 at Archbishop Mitty HS, San Jose, CA (16 teams).

## SUNBELT BASEBALL CLASSIC SERIES
**Mailing Address:** 505 North Blvd., Edmond, OK 73034. **Telephone:** (405) 348-3839. **FAX:** (405) 340-7538.
**Chairman:** John Schwartz.
**2006 Senior Series:** Norman, OK, June 19-24. (8 teams: Arizona, California, Florida, Georgia, Maryland, Ohio, Oklahoma, Texas).

**2006 Junior Series:** McAlester and Hartshorne, OK, June 9-14 (10 teams: Arizona, California, Canada, Georgia, Mississippi, Missouri, Oklahoma Blue, Oklahoma Gold, Tennessee, Texas).

**2006 Sophomore Series:** Edmond, OK, June 1-4 (4 teams: Oklahoma, Tennessee, Texas, Missouri).

# ALL-STAR GAMES

## AFLAC HIGH SCHOOL ALL-AMERICA CLASSIC
**Mailing Address:** 10 S. Adams St., Rockville, MD 20850. **Telephone:** (301) 762-7188. **FAX:** (301) 762-1491.
**Event Organizer:** Sports America, Inc. **President, Chief Executive Officer:** Robert Geoghan.
**2006 Game:** High School Class of 2007, East vs. West, San Diego, CA, Aug. 13.

## PLAYSTATION ALL-AMERICAN BASEBALL GAME
**Mailing Address:** 224 Stiger St., Hackettstown, NJ 07840. **Telephone:** (908) 684-5410. **FAX:** (908) 684-5415.
**Event Organizer:** SportsLink, Inc. **President, Chief Executive Officer:** Rich McGuinness.
**2006 Game:** High School Class of 2006, East vs. West, Albuquerque, NM, June 11.

# SHOWCASE
## EVENTS

## ALL-AMERICAN BASEBALL TALENT SHOWCASES
**Mailing Address:** 6 Bicentennial Ct., Erial, NJ 08081. **Telephone:** (856) 354-0201. **FAX:** (856) 354-0818. **E-Mail Address:** hitdoctor@thehitdoctor.com **Website:** thehitdoctor.com.
**National Director:** Joe Barth.

## AREA CODE GAMES
**Mailing Address:** 3954 Madison St., Torrance, CA, 90254. **Telephone:** (310) 791-1142 x 4424. **E-Mail Address:** andrew@studentsports.com. **Website:** www.areacodebaseball.org
**Event Organizer:** Andrew Drennen.
**2006 Area Code Games:** Aug. 5-10 at Long Beach, CA (Blair Field).

## ARIZONA FALL CLASSIC
**Mailing Address:** 6102 W. Maui Lane, Glendale, AZ 85306 **Telephone:** (602) 978-2929. **FAX:** (602) 439-4494. **E-Mail Address:** azbaseballted@msn.com. **Website:** www.azfallclassic.com.
**Directors:** Ted Heid, Tracy Heid.

### 2006 Events

| | |
|---|---|
| Four Corner Classic (Open, 16 & under, 14 & Under) | Peoria, AZ, June 2-4 |
| Senior Fall Classic (HS seniors) | Peoria, AZ, Oct. 12-15 |
| Junior Fall Classic (HS juniors/sophomores) | Peoria, AZ, Oct. 20-22 |
| Premier Baseball Classic (Open) | Peoria, AZ, Oct. 27-29 |
| Champions Classic (18 & Under, 16 & Under, 14 & Under) | Peoria, AZ, Nov. 3-5 |

## BASEBALL FACTORY
**Office Address:** 9176 Red Branch Rd., Suite M, Columbia, MD 21045. **Telephone:** (800) 641-4487, (410) 715-5080. **FAX:** (410) 715-1975. **E-Mail Address:** info@baseballfactory.com. **Website:** www.baseballfactory.com.
**Chief Executive Officer:** Steve Sclafani. **President:** Rob Naddelman. **Senior Vice President, Baseball Operations:** Steve Bernhardt.
**BATS Program:** Year-round, various locations.

## DOYLE BASEBALL SELECT SHOWCASES
**Mailing Address:** P.O. Box 9156, Winter Haven, FL 33883. **Telephone:** (863) 439-1000. **FAX:** (863) 439-7086. **E-Mail Address:** info@doylebaseball.com. **Website:** www.doylebaseball.com.
**President:** Denny Doyle. **Director, Satellite School:** Rick Siebert.

## IMPACT BASEBALL
**Mailing Address:** P.O. Box 47, Sedalia, NC 27342. **E-Mail Address:** andypartin@aol.com. **Website:** www.impact-baseball.com.
**Operator:** Andy Partin.
**2006 Showcases:** June 12-13 at Winston-Salem, NC (Wake Forest U.); June 19-20 at Norfolk, VA (Old Dominion U.); July 14-15 at Spartanburg, SC (Winthrop U.); Aug. 4-7 at Chapel Hill, NC (U. of North Carolina).

## EAST COAST PROFESSIONAL SHOWCASE
**Mailing Address:** 601 S. College Rd., Wilmington, NC 28403. **Telephone:** (910) 962-3570.
**Facility Directors:** Mark Scalf, Randy Hood, Scott Jackson.
**2006 Showcase:** Aug. 1-4 at Wilmington, NC (UNC Wilmington).

## MID-AMERICA FIVE STAR BASEBALL SHOWCASE

Mailing Address—Cincinnati: Champions Baseball Academy, 510 E. Business Way, Cincinnati, OH 45241. Telephone: (513) 247-9511. FAX: (513) 247-0040. Mailing Address—Louisville: Champions Baseball Academy, 10701 Plantside Dr., Louisville, KY 40299. Telephone: (502) 261-9200. FAX: (502) 261-9278. E-Mail Address: champ8@aol.com. Website: championsbaseball.com.

President: John Marshall.

2006 Showcases: July 9-11 at Louisville, KY (U. of Louisville); Aug. 7-9 at Cincinnati, OH (Midland Field).

## PACIFIC NORTHWEST CHAMPIONSHIP

Mailing Address: 42783 Deerborn Rd., Springfield, OR, 97478. Telephone: (541) 896-0841. E-Mail Address: mckay@baseballnorthwest.com. Tournament Organizer: Jeff McKay.

2006 Events: Aug. 15-18 at Portland, OR (PGE Park). Idaho Prospect Games: June 13-14 (Twin Falls, ID, HS) Oregon Prospect Games: June 19-20 at Corvallis, OR (Oregon State U.). Southwest Washington Prospect Games: June 21-22 at Portland, OR (U. of Portland). West Washington Prospect Games: Unavailable. East Washington Prospect Games: July 10-11 at Pullman, WA (Washington State U.).

## PERFECT GAME USA

Mailing Address: 1203 Rockford Road SW, Cedar Rapids, IA 52404. Telephone: (319) 298-2923, (800) 447-9362. FAX: (319) 298-2924. E-Mail Address: jerry@perfectgame.org. Website: www.perfectgameusa.com.

President, Director: Jerry Ford. Vice Presidents: Andy Ford, Jason Gerst, Tyson Kimm. International Director: Kentaro Yasutake.

National Showcase Director: Jim Arp. Scouting Directors: Blaine Clemmens, Kirk Gardner, Wes Penick, David Rawnsley (WWBA). National Tournament Director: Taylor McCollough. California Director: Mike Spiers. Florida Director: Ben Ford. Northeast Director/State Showcase National Director: Dan Kennedy. Southeast Director: Jeff Simpson. Arizona Supervisor: Dick Vaske. Florida Supervisor: Jim Grevel. Mit-Atlantic Supervisor: Bobby McKinney.

League Director: Steve James. Director, Instruction: Jim Van Scoyoc.

Director, BaseballWebTV.com: Rick Stephenson.

Public Relations Director: Andrea Bachman. Marketing/Sponsorship Director: Frank Fulton. Merchandise Director: Tom Jackson. Building Manager: Eric Johnson.

Business Manager: Don Walser. Office Managers: Betty Ford, Nancy Lain.

National Softball Director: Wendi Krejci.

### 2006 Events

Southern California Pre-High School Showcase: March 4-5 at Valencia, CA (College of the Canyons). San Diego Pre-High School Showcase: March 11-12 at San Diego (Westview HS, Los Angeles). Northern California Pre-High School Showcase: April 8-9 at Danville, CA (East Bay Athenia HS). Spring Top Prospect Showcase: April 22-23 at Cedar Rapids, IA. 15 and under Midwest Showcase: May 13-14 at Cedar Rapids, IA (Daniels Park). National Pre Draft Showcase: May 15 at Cedar Rapids, IA (Veterans Memorial Stadium). Sunshine East Showcase: June 10-11 at Fort Myers, FL (Red Sox complex). Sunshine South Showcase: June 10-11 at Austin, TX (Concordia College). Sunshine West Showcase: June 10-11 at San Diego (University of San Diego). Academic Showcase: June 12-13 at Fort Myers, FL (Terry Park). Unsigned Seniors Showcase: June 12-13 at Fort Myers, FL (Terry Park). National Showcase: June 16-18, site unavailable. Ohio Valley Top Prospect Showcase: June 23-24 at Dayton, OH (Wright State University). South Underclass Showcase: July 22-23 at Waco, TX (Baylor University). South Top Prospect Showcase: July 29-30 at Waco, TX (Baylor University). Atlantic Coast Top Prospect Showcase: Aug. 12-13 at Chapel Hill, NC (University of North Carolina). Northeast Underclass Showcase: Aug. 14-16 at Wareham, MA (Clem Spillane Field). Northeast Top Prospect Showcase: Aug. 18-20 at Wareham, MA (Clem Spillane Field). Atlantic Coast Underclass Showcase: Aug. 19-20 at Raleigh, NC (North Carolina State University). Northeast Top Prospect Games: Aug. 25 at Long Island, NY. California Showcase: Aug. 26-27, site unavailable. Mid-Atlantic Underclass Showcase: Sept. 2-3 at Bowling Green, VA. Southeast Underclass Showcase: Sept. 2-3 at Marietta, GA (East Cobb complex). Mid-Atlantic Top Prospect Showcase: Sept. 9-10 at Bowling Green, VA. Southeast Top Prospect Showcase: Sept. 9-10 at Marietta, GA (East Cobb complex). West Coast Top Prospect Showcase: Sept. 9-10 at Riverside, CA. Midwest Top Prospect Showcase: Sept. 30-Oct. 1 at Cedar Rapids, IA (Veterans Memorial Stadium). National Open Top Prospect Showcase: Sept-30-Oct. 1 at Fort Myers, FL (Terry Park). Hawaii High School Showcase: Dates unavailable at Hilo, HI. Northern California Underclass Showcase: Oct. 7-8 at Moraga, CA (St. Mary's College). Southern California Underclass Showcase: Oct. 7-8, site unavailable. California Uncommitted Showcase: Nov. 4-5 at Riverside, CA. Northern California Pre-High School Showcase: Nov. 18-19, site unavailable. Southern California Pre-High School Showcase: Nov. 18-19 at San Bernardino, CA (Arrowhead Credit Union Park). National Underclass Showcase: Dec. 28-30 at Fort Myers, FL (Terry Park, Red Sox complex).

### 2007 Events

World Showcase: Jan. 6-7 at Fort Myers, FL (Terry Park). Hawaii High School Prospect Camp: Jan. 6-7 at Honolulu, HI (University of Hawaii). Freshman National Showcase: Jan. 13-15 at South Orange County, CA. California Underclass Showcase: Jan. 20-21 at San Bernardino, CA (Arrowhead Credit Union Park). California All-Star Games: Jan. 27-28 at San Bernardino, CA (Arrowhead Credit Union Park). West Coast Pre-High School Showcase: Feb. 24-25 at San Bernardino, CA (Arrowhead Credit Union Park).

## SELECTFEST BASEBALL

Mailing Address: 60 Franklin Pl., Morris Plains, NJ 07950. Telephone: (973) 539-4781. E-Mail Address: selectfest@optonline.net.

Camp Directors: Brian Fleury, Bruce Shatel.

2006 Showcase: June 23-24 at Piscataway, NJ (Rutgers U.).

## TEAM ONE SHOWCASES
**Mailing Address:** P.O. Box 129, Hendersonville, NC 28793. **Telephone:** (800) 340-2360. **E-Mail Address:** roncox@teamonebaseball.com. **Website:** www.teamonebaseball.com.
**President, Team One Sports:** Jeff Spelman. **Directory, Player Development:** Ron Cox.
**2006 Team One National Showcase:** Date and site unavailable.
**2005 Regional Showcases:** West—June 20-22 at Tempe, AZ (Diablo Stadium); South—July 16-18 at Atlanta (Georgia Tech); Midwest—July 7-9 at Cincinnati, OH (U. of Cincinnati); East and Texas showcases on dates and sites to be announced.

## TPX TOP 96 BASEBALL SHOWCASES/CLINICS
**Mailing Address:** P.O. Box 5481, Wayland, MA 01778. **Telephone:** (508) 481-5939.
**E-Mail Address:** doug.henson@tpxtop96.net. **National Directors:** Doug Henson, Ken Hill.
**2006 Events:** June 2-3 at Carrolton, TX (Newman Smith HS). June 21- 22 at St. Louis, MO (St. Louis CC). June 24-25 at Boca Raton, FL (Lynn University). June 24-25 at Summit, MS (Southwest Mississippi CC). July 8-9 at Bronx, NY (Fordham University). July 11-12 at Oxford, OH (Miami University). July 14-15 at Oklahoma City, OK (Oklahoma City University). July 15-16 at Rocky Mount, NC (North Carolina Wesleyan College). July 15-16 at Houston, TX (Sam Houston State University). July 22-23 at Erie, PA (Mercyhurst College). July 22-23 at Spartanburg, SC (University of South Carolina-Upstate). July 24-25 at St. Boniface, MN (Crown College). July 29-30 at Sanford, FL (Municipal Stadium). Aug. 1-2 at Mishawaka (Bethel College). Aug. 5-6 at Hartford, CT (University of Hartford). Aug. 5-6 at Newport News, VA (Christopher Newport University). Aug.8-9 at Elgin, IL (Trout Park). Aug. 12-13 at Vacaville, CA (Travis Credit Union Park). Aug. 15-16 at Shippensburg, PA (Shippensburg University). Aug. 19-20 at Gambrills, MD (Arundel HS). Aug. 21-22 at Spring Arbor, MI (Spring Arbor University). Nov. 4-5 at Redlands, CA (University of Redlands).

## COLLEGE PROSPECT DEVELOPMENT CAMPS

### COLLEGE SELECT SHOWCASE
**Mailing Address:** P.O. Box 783, Manchester, CT 06040. **Telephone:** (800) 782-3672. **E-Mail Address:** TRhit@msn.com. **Website:** www.collegeselect.org.
**Consulting Director:** Tom Rizzi.
**2006 Showcases:** July 17-19 at Norwich, CT; Aug. 12-14 at Binghamton, NY; Aug. 16-19 at Warwick, RI.

### TOP 96 INVITATIONAL BASEBALL SHOWCASE
**Mailing Address:** 2 Hewes Circle, Peabody, MA 01960. **Telephone:** (978) 536-2022. **E-Mail Address:** dave.callum@top96.com.
**President:** Dave Callum.
**2006 Invitational Showcases:** Academic Invitational Baseball Showcase, June 17-18 at Hartford, CT (University of Hartford). New England Invitational Baseball Showcase, Aug. 11-12 at Lowell, MA (Alumni Field).

### TOP GUNS PROSPECT DEVELOPMENT CAMPS
**Mailing Address:** 7890 N. Franklin Rd., Suite 2, Coeur d'Alene, ID 83815. **Telephone/FAX:** (208) 762-1100. **E-Mail Address:** topgunsbss@hotmail.com. **Website:** www.topgunsbaseball.com.
**President:** Nick Rook. **National Director, Field Operations:** Gary Ward. **Assistant Directors:** Cody Rook, Jason Rook.
**2006 National Development Camps:** June 27-29 at Las Vegas, NV (U. of Nevada-Las Vegas). Nov. 24- 26 at Orlando, FL (U. of Central Florida); Nov. 24-26 at Las Vegas, NV (U. of Nevada-Las Vegas); Nov. 24-26 at Arlington, TX (U. of Texas-Arlington).

## SCOUTING SERVICES/High School, College

### BASEBALL FACTORY
**Office Address:** 9176 Red Branch Rd., Suite M, Columbia, MD 21045. **Telephone:** (800) 641-4487, (410) 715-5080. **FAX:** (410) 715-1975. **E-Mail Address:** info@baseballfactory.com. **Website:** www.baseballfactory.com.
**Chief Executive Officer:** Steve Sclafani. **President:** Rob Naddelman. **Senior Vice President, Baseball Operations:** Steve Bernhardt.

### PROSPECTS PLUS
(A Joint Venture of Baseball America and Perfect Game USA)
**Mailing Address:** Baseball America, P.O. Box 2089, Durham, NC 27702. **Telephone:** (800) 845-2726. **FAX:** (919) 682-2880. **E-Mail Addresses:** alanmatthews@baseballamerica.com; jerry@perfectgame.org. **Website:** www.baseballamerica.com; www.perfectgame.org
**Editors, Baseball America:** Alan Matthews, Allan Simpson. **Director, Perfect Game USA:** Jerry Ford.

### SKILLSHOW, INC.
**Mailing Address:** 290 King of Prussia Rd., Suite 102, Radnor, PA 19087. **Telephone:** (610) 687-9072. **FAX:** (610) 687-9629. **E-Mail Address:** info@skillshow.com. **Website:** www.skillshow.com.
**Chief Executive Officer:** Tom Koerick Jr. **President/Director, Sales:** Tom Koerick Sr.

### TEAM ONE
**Mailing Address:** P.O. Box 8843, Cincinnati, OH 45208. **Telephone:** (859) 466-8326. **E-Mail Address:** TeamOneBB@aol.com. **Website:** www.teamonebaseball.com.
**President, Team One Sports:** Jeff Spelman.

# YOUTH
## BASEBALL

### ALL AMERICAN AMATEUR BASEBALL ASSOCIATION (AAABA)

**Mailing Address:** 331 Parkway Dr., Zanesville, OH 43701. **Telephone:** (740) 453-8531. **FAX:** (740) 453-3978. **E-Mail Address:** clw@aol.com. **Website:** www.aaaba.us.
**Year Founded:** 1944.
**President:** George Arcurio. **Executive Director/Secretary:** Bob Wolfe.
**2006 National Tournament** (21 and under): Aug. 7-12 at Johnstown, PA (16 teams). **AAABA Regionals:** July 31-Aug. 3 at Altoona, PA, Schenectady, NY and Zanesville, OH.

### AMATEUR ATHLETIC UNION OF THE UNITED STATES, INC. (AAU)

**Mailing Address:** P.O. Box 22409, Lake Buena Vista, FL 32830. **Telephone:** (407) 934-7200. **FAX:** (407) 934-7242. **E-Mail Address:** jeremy@aausports.org. **Website:** www.aaubaseball.org.
**Year Founded:** 1982.
**Senior Sports Manager/Baseball:** Jeremy Bullock.

#### DIVISION I
#### Age Classifications, National Championships

| | |
|---|---|
| 8 and under (player pitch) | Memphis, TN, July 16-22 |
| 8 and under (coach pitch) | Concord, NC, July 16-22 |
| 9 and under | *Orlando, July 7-15 |
| 10 and under (46/60 foot) | Tampa, FL, July 14-22 |
| 10 and under (48/65 foot) | Charlotte, NC, July 16-22 |
| 11 and under (50/70 foot) | *Orlando, July 14-22 |
| 12 and under (50/70 foot) | Hampton Roads, VA, July 28-Aug. 5 |
| 13 and under (54/80 foot) | Louisville, KY., July 15-22 |
| 13 and under (60/90 foot) | Myrtle Beach, SC, July 14-22 |
| 14 and under (60/90 foot) | Sarasota, FL, July 21-29 |
| 15 and under | Kingsport, TN, July 14-21 |
| Junior Olympics (16 and under) | Hampton Roads, VA, July 28-Aug. 5 |
| 17 and under | Fort Myers, FL, July 11-17 |
| 18 and under/19 and under | *Orlando, July 7-15 |

#### DIVISION II
#### Age Classifications, National Championships

| | |
|---|---|
| 10 and under (46/60 foot) | Tampa, FL, July 14-22 |
| 10 and under (48/65 foot) | Charlotte, NC, July 16-22 |
| 11 and under (50/70 foot) | *Orlando, July 14-22 |
| 12 and under (50/70 foot) | Hampton Roads, VA, July 28-Aug. 5 |
| 13 and under (54/80 foot) | Louisville, KY, July 15-22 |
| 14 and under (60/90 foot) | *Orlando, July 21-29 |
| 15 and under | *Orlando, July 14-22 |
| 16 and under | *Orlando, July 14-22 |

#### Age Classifications, Regional National Championships
#### NORTHEAST

| | |
|---|---|
| 10 and under (46/60 foot) | Voorhees, NJ, Dates unavailable |
| 11 and under (50/70 foot) | Reading, PA, Dates unavailable |
| 12 and under (50/70 foot) | Salisbury, MD, Dates unavailable |
| 13 and under (60/90 foot) | Allentown, PA, Dates unavailable |

#### SOUTHEAST

| | |
|---|---|
| 10 and under (46/60 foot) | Tampa, FL, Dates unavailable |
| 10 and under (48/65 foot) | Charlotte, NC, Dates unavailable |
| 11 and under (50/70 foot) | *Orlando, Dates unavailable |
| 12 and under (50/70 foot) | Virginia Beach, VA, Dates unavailable |
| 13 and under (60/90 foot) | Myrtle Beach, SC, Dates unavailable |

#### CENTRAL

| | |
|---|---|
| 10 and under (48/65 foot) | Des Moines, IA, Dates unavailable |
| 11 and under (50/70 foot) | Burnsville/Lakeville, MN, Dates unavailable |
| 12 and under (50/70 foot) | Burnsville/Lakeville, MN, Dates unavailable |
| 13 and under (60/90 foot) | Des Moines, IA, Dates unavailable |

#### NORTHWEST

| | |
|---|---|
| 10 and under (46/60 foot) | Unavailable |
| 10 and under (48/65 foot) | Unavailable |
| 11 and under (50/70 foot) | Unavailable |
| 12 and under (50/70 foot) | Unavailable |
| 13 and under (60/90 foot) | Unavailable |

## SOUTHWEST

| | |
|---|---|
| 10 and under (48/65 foot) | Unavailable |
| 10 and under (46/60 foot) | Unavailable |
| 11 and under (50/70 foot) | Unavailable |
| 12 and under (50/70 foot) | Unavailable |
| 13 and under (54/80 foot) | Unavailable |

### Age Classifications, West Coast Nationals

| | |
|---|---|
| 10 and under | Portland, OR/Vancouver, WA, Sept. 1-5 |
| 11 and under | Portland, OR/Vancouver, WA, Sept. 1-5 |
| 12 and under | Portland, OR/Vancouver, WA, Sept. 1-5 |
| 13 and under | Portland, OR/Vancouver, WA, Sept. 1-5 |

### International Championships

| | |
|---|---|
| 10 and under (46/60 foot) | *Orlando, June 9-15 |
| 12 and under (50/70 foot) | *Orlando, June 9-15 |

### Wood Bat Nationals

| | |
|---|---|
| 8-18 and under | Winter Haven, FL, Dates unavailable |

### Winter Nationals

| | |
|---|---|
| 8-18 and under | Tampa, Dates unavailable |

*Disney's Wide World of Sports Complex, Lake Buena Vista.

## AMERICAN AMATEUR BASEBALL CONGRESS (AABC)

**National Headquarters:** 100 West Broadway, Farmington, NM 87401. **Telephone:** (505) 327-3120. **FAX:** (505) 327-3132. **E-Mail Address:** aabc@aabc.us. **Website:** www.aabc.us.
**Year Founded:** 1935.
**President:** Mike Dimond.

### Age Classifications, World Series

| | |
|---|---|
| Roberto Clemente (8 and under) | McDonough, GA, July 19-23 |
| Willie Mays (9) | Tulsa, OK, July 26-30 |
| Willie Mays (10 and under) | Catano, PR, July 26-31 |
| Pee Wee Reese (11) | Brooklyn, NY, July 26-30 |
| Pee Wee Reese (12 and under) | Toa Baja, PR, Aug. 2-6 |
| Sandy Koufax (13) | Battle Creek, MI, July 25-30 |
| Sandy Koufax (14 and under) | Douglasville, GA, July 26-30 |
| Mickey Mantle (15) | Owasso, OK, Aug. 1-6 |
| Mickey Mantle (16 and under) | McKinney, TX, Aug. 2-6 |
| Connie Mack (17) | Site and date unavailable |
| Connie Mack (18 and under) | Farmington, NM, Aug. 4-11 |
| Stan Musial (unlimited) | Huntsville, TX, Aug. 17-20 |

## AMERICAN AMATEUR YOUTH BASEBALL ALLIANCE

**Mailing Address:** 3851 Iris Lane, Bonne Terre, MO 63628. **Telephone:** (573) 518-0319. **FAX:** (314) 822-4974. **E-Mail Address:** clwjr28@aol.com. **Website:** www.aayba.com.
**President, Baseball Operations:** Carroll Wood.

### Age Classifications, Open World Series

| | |
|---|---|
| 10 and under | St. Louis, July 9-15 |
| 11 and under | St. Louis, July 9-15 |
| 12 and under | St. Louis, July 23-29 |
| 13 and under | St. Louis, July 23-29 |
| 14 and under | St. Louis, July 9-15 |

## AMERICAN LEGION BASEBALL

**National Headquarters:** American Legion Baseball, 700 N. Pennsylvania St., Indianapolis, IN 46204. **Telephone:** (317) 630-1213. **FAX:** (317) 630-1369. **E-Mail Address:** acy@legion.org. **Website:** www.baseball.legion.org.
**Year Founded:** 1925.
**Program Coordinator:** Jim Quinlan.
**2006 World Series** (19 and under): Aug. 18-22 at Veterans Memorial Stadium, Cedar Rapids, IA (8 teams). **Mailing Address:** P.O. Box 2001, Cedar Rapids, IA 52406. **Telephone:** (800) 860-3609. **E-Mail Address:** alws2006@ialegion.com. **Website:** www.alws2006.org.
**2006 Regional Tournaments** (Aug. 10-14, 8 teams): **Northeast**—Brockton, MA; **Mid-Atlantic**—Newburg, NY; **Southeast**—Deland, FL; **Mid-South**—Crowley, LA; **Great Lakes**—Evansville, IN; **Central Plains**—Aberdeen, SD; **Northwest**—Casper, WY; **Western**—Albuquerque, NM.

## BABE RUTH BASEBALL

**International Headquarters:** 1770 Brunswick Pike, P.O. Box 5000, Trenton, NJ 08638. **Telephone:** (609) 695-1434. **FAX:** (609) 695-2505. **Website:** www.baberuthleague.org.
**Year Founded:** 1951.
**President, Chief Executive Officer:** Steven Tellefsen.
**Executive Vice President/Chief Financial Officer:** Rosemary Schoellkopf. **Vice President, Operations/Marketing:** Joe Smiegocki. **Vice President/Commissioner:** Robert Faherty. **Commissioner:** Robert Connor. **Executive Director, Special Events:** David Froelich.

| | |
|---|---|
| 10 and under | Abbeville, LA, Aug. 5-12 |
| Cal Ripken (11-12) | Aberdeen, MD, Aug. 10-18 |
| 13 | Hamilton Township, NJ, Aug. 17-25 |
| 14 | Wilson, NC, Aug. 19-26 |
| 13-15 | Clifton Park, NY, Aug. 18-25 |
| 16 | Monticello, AR, Aug. 11-19 |
| 16-18 | Newark, OH, Aug. 11-18 |

## BASEBALL CHAMPIONSHIP SERIES
### (A Division of Perfect Game USA)

**Mailing Address:** 1203 Rockford Rd SW, Cedar Rapids, IA 52404 **Telephone:** (319) 298-2923 **Fax:** (319) 298-2924 **E-Mail Address:** aford@perfectgame.org. **Website:** www.perfectgamebcs.com.
**Year Founded:** 2005.
**President:** Andy Ford. **National Director:** Taylor McCollough

### Tournament Championship Events

| | |
|---|---|
| 12 and under | Clearwater, FL, June 24-28 |
| 13 and under | Jupiter, FL, July 25-30 |
| 14 and under | Jupiter, FL, July 11-16 |
| 15 and under | Jupiter, FL, July 25-30 |
| 16 and under | Jupiter, FL, July 11-16 |
| 17 and under | Jupiter, FL, July 18-23 |
| 18 and under | Atlanta, GA (Turner Field), July 18-21 |

### Tournament Championship Open Events

| | |
|---|---|
| 12 and under | Clearwater, FL, June 24-28 |
| 13 and under | Jupiter, FL, July 25-30 |
| 14 and under | Jupiter, FL, July 11-16 |
| 15 and under | Jupiter, FL, July 25-30 |
| 16 and under | Jupiter, FL, July 11-16 |
| 17 and under | Jupiter, FL, July 18-23 |
| 18 and under | Jupiter, FL, July 18-23 |

## CONTINENTAL AMATEUR BASEBALL ASSOCIATION (CABA)

**Mailing Address:** 1173 French Court, Maineville, Ohio 45039. **Telephone:** (513) 677-1580. **E-Mail Address:** lredwine@cababaseball.com. **Website:** www.cababaseball.com.
**Year Founded:** 1984.
**Commissioner:** John Mocny. **Executive Vice President:** Fran Pell. **Executive Director:** Larry Redwine.

### Age Classifications, Ultimate World Series

| | |
|---|---|
| 9 and under/11 and under/15 and under | Crystal Lake, IL, July 28-Aug. 6 |
| 10 and under | Lynwood, IL, July 24-31 |
| 12 and under | Cincinnati, July 21-30 |
| 13 and under | Marion, OH, July 21-30 |
| 14 and under (54/80 foot) | Painesville/Perry, OH, July 21-30 |
| 14 and under (60/90 foot) | Nashville, July 20-29 |
| 16 and under | Marietta, GA, July 29-Aug. 7 |
| High school age | Euclid, OH, July 21-30 |
| 18 and under | Homestead, FL, July 14-23 |
| 18 and under (wood bats) | Charleston, SC, July 28-Aug. 5 |
| College age (wood bats) | Elgin, IL, July 21-30 |

### Age Classifications, Quality World Series

| | |
|---|---|
| 12 and under | Painesville/Perry, OH, July 21-30 |
| 14 and under | Painesville/Perry, OH, July 21-30 |
| 13 and under | Tealtown, OH, July 29-Aug. 4 |
| 15 and under | Nashville, TN, July 28-Aug. 6 |

### Age Classifications, Open World Series

| | |
|---|---|
| 10 and under—Great Lakes | St. Clair Shores, MI, July 21-29 |
| 11 and under—Great Lakes | St. Clair Shores, MI, July 16-23 |
| 12 and under—Great Lakes | St. Clair Shores, MI, July 21-29 |
| 13 and under—Great Lakes | St. Clair Shores, MI, July 21-29 |
| 13 and under—Midwest | Lynwood, IL, July 24-31 |
| 13 and under—Northwest | Seattle, July 20-30 |
| 14 and under—Great Lakes | St. Clair Shores, MI, July 16-23 |
| 14 and under—Midwest | Lynwood, IL, July 24-31 |
| 14 and under—Nothwest | Seattle, July 20-30 |
| 15 and under—Great Lakes | St. Clair Shores, MI, July 21-29 |
| 16 and under—Northwest | Seattle, July 20-30 |
| 16 and under—Southeast | Marietta, GA, July 29-Aug. 7 |
| 18 and under—Great Lakes | St. Clair Shores, MI, July 16-23 |
| 18 and under—Northwest | Tacoma, WA, July 20-30 |

# DIXIE BASEBALL, INC.

**Mailing Address:** P.O. Box 877, Marshall, TX 75671. **Telephone:** (903) 927-2255. **FAX:** (903) 927-1846. **E-Mail Address:** dyb@dixie.org. **Website:** www.dixie.org.
**Year Founded:** 1955.
**Commissioner:** Wes Skelton. **Commissioner/Chief Executive Officer:** Sandy Jones, P.O. Box 8263, Dothan, AL 36304. Telephone: (334) 793-3331. **Office Manager:** Rhonda Skelton.

## Age Classifications, World Series

| | |
|---|---|
| Dixie Youth (9-10) | Goodlettsville, TN, Aug. 14-19 |
| Dixie Youth (12 and under, 46/60 foot) | Goodlettsville, TN, Aug. 14-19 |
| Dixie Youth O-Zone (12 and under, 50/70 foot) | Dothan, AL, Aug. 5-10 |
| Junior Dixie Boys (13) | Grand Prairie, TX, Aug. 5-10 |
| Dixie Boys (13-14) | Grand Prairie, TX, Aug. 5-10 |
| Dixie Pre-Majors (15-16) | Thomasville, AL, July 29-Aug. 4 |
| Dixie Majors (15-18) | North Charleston, SC, July 29-Aug. 4 |

# DIZZY DEAN BASEBALL, INC.

**Mailing Address:** P.O. Box 856, Hernando, MS 38632. **Telephone:** (662) 429-4365, (850) 455-8827. **E-Mail Address:** dizzydeanbaseball@yahoo.com. **Website:** www.dizzydeanbbinc.org.
**Year Founded:** 1962.
**Commissioner:** Danny Phillips. **Treasurer/Administrator:** D.B. Stewart.

## Age Classifications, World Series

| | |
|---|---|
| 6 and under | Rossville, GA, July 14-19 |
| 7 and under | Henry County, GA, July 14-19 |
| 8 and under | Southaven, MS, July 21-26 |
| 9 and under | Southaven, MS, July 21-26 |
| 10 and under | Moody, AL, July 14-19 |
| 11 and under | Henry County, GA, July 14-19 |
| 12 and under | Moody, AL, July 14-19 |
| 13 and under | Southaven, MS, July 21-26 |
| 14 and under | Southaven, MS, July 21-26 |
| Junior (15-16) | Southaven, MS, July 21-26 |
| Senior (17-18) | Southaven, MS, July 21-26 |
| High school | Starkville, MS, July 13-18 |

# HAP DUMONT YOUTH BASEBALL
### (A Division of the National Baseball Congress)

**Mailing Address:** P.O. Box 720120, Norman, OK 73070. **Telephone:** (405) 899-7689. **E-Mail Address:** steve-smith@hapdumontbaseball.com. **Website:** hapdumontbaseball.com.
**Year Founded:** 1974.
**National Tournament Coordinator:** Steve Smith.

## Age Classifications, World Series

| | |
|---|---|
| 8 and under | Wichita, KS, July 21-26 |
| 9 and under | Harrison, AR, July 21-26 |
| 10 and under | Kearney, MO, July 21-26 |
| 11 and under | Oklahoma City, July 21-26 |
| 12 and under | Simpsonville, SC, July 21-26 |
| 13 and under | Tunica, MS, July 21-26 |
| 14 and under | Pratt, KS, July 21-26 |
| 15 and under | Leesburg, FL, July 21-26 |
| 16 and under | Pittsburg, KS, July 21-26 |
| 17 and under | Topeka, KS, July 21-26 |
| 18 and under | Topeka, KS, July 21-26 |

# LITTLE LEAGUE BASEBALL, INC.

**International Headquarters:** P.O. Box 3485, Williamsport, PA 17701. **Telephone:** (570) 326-1921. **FAX:** (570) 326-1074. **Website:** www.littleleague.org.
**Year Founded:** 1939.
**Chairman:** Timothy Hughes.
**President/Chief Executive Officer:** Steve Keener. **Chief Financial Officer:** David Houseknecht. **Vice President, Operations/Secretary:** Joseph Losch. **Treasurer:** Melissa Singer. **Senior Communications Executive:** Lance Van Auken. **Director, League Development:** Dan Velte.

## Age Classifications, World Series

| | |
|---|---|
| Little League (11-12) | Williamsport, PA, Aug. 18-27 |
| Junior League (13-14) | Taylor, MI, Aug. 13-19 |
| Senior League (15-16) | Bangor, ME, Aug. 13-19 |
| Big League (17-18) | Easley, SC, July 29-Aug. 5 |

## NATIONAL AMATEUR BASEBALL FEDERATION (NABF)

**Mailing Address:** P.O. Box 705, Bowie, MD 20718. **Telephone:** (301) 464-5460. **FAX:** (301) 352-0214. **E-Mail Address:** nabf1914@aol.com. **Website:** www.nabf.com.
**Year Founded:** 1914.
**Executive Director:** Charles Blackburn. **Special Events Coordinator, NABF Classics:** Michael Felton.

### Age Classifications, World Series

| | |
|---|---|
| Freshman (12 and under) | Hopkinsville, KY, July 13-17 |
| Sophomore (14 and under) | Springboro, OH, July 19-23 |
| Junior (16 and under) | Northville, MI, July 27-31 |
| High School (17 and under) | Greensboro, NC, July 19-23 |
| Senior (18 and under) | Jackson, MS, Aug. 3-7 |
| College (22 and under) | Toledo, OH, Aug. 3-7 |
| Major (unlimited) | Louisville, KY, Aug. 17-21 |

### NABF Classics (Invitational)

| | |
|---|---|
| 9 and under | Southaven, MS, July 3-7 |
| 10 and under | Southaven, MS, July 3-7 |
| 11 and under | Southaven, MS, July 3-7 |
| 13 and under (54/80 foot) | Southaven, MS, July 3-7 |
| 13 and under (60/90 foot) | Southaven, MS, July 3-7 |
| 15 and under | Nashville, July 21-25 |

## NATIONAL ASSOCIATION OF POLICE ATHLETIC LEAGUES

**Mailing Address:** 658 W. Indiantown Road #201, Jupiter, FL 33458. **Telephone:** (561) 745-5535. **FAX:** (561) 745-3147. **E-Mail Address:** copnkid@nationalpal.org. **Website:** www.nationalpal.org.
**Year Founded:** 1914.
**Interim Executive Director:** Mike Dillhyon. **National Program Manager:** Eric Widness.

### Age Classifications, World Series

| | |
|---|---|
| 12 and under | Unavailable |

## PONY BASEBALL, INC.

**International Headquarters:** P.O. Box 225, Washington, PA 15301. **Telephone:** (724) 225-1060. **FAX:** (724) 225-9852. **E-Mail Address:** info@pony.org. **Website:** www.pony.org.
**Year Founded:** 1951.
**President:** Abraham Key. **Director, Baseball Operations:** Don Clawson.

### Age Classifications, World Series

| | |
|---|---|
| Shetland (5-6) | No National Tournament |
| Pinto (7-8) | No National Tournament |
| Mustang (9-10) | Irving, TX, Aug. 2-5 |
| Bronco (11-12) | Monterey, CA, Aug. 3-8 |
| Pony (13) | Chino Hills, CA, July 27-31 |
| Pony (13-14) | Washington, PA, Aug. 12-19 |
| Colt (15-16) | Lafayette, IN, Aug. 2-9 |
| Palomino (17-18) | Caguas, PR, Aug. 3-6 |

## REVIVING BASEBALL IN INNER CITIES (RBI)

**Mailing Address:** 245 Park Ave., New York, NY 10167. **Telephone:** (212) 931-7800. **FAX:** (212) 949-5695.
**Year Founded:** 1989.
**Founder:** John Young. **Vice President, Community Affairs:** Thomas Brasuell.

### Age Classifications, World Series

| | |
|---|---|
| Junior Boys (13-15) | Unavailable |
| Senior Boys (16-18) | Unavailable |

## SUPER SERIES BASEBALL OF AMERICA

**National Headquarters:** 4036 East Grandview St., Mesa, AZ 85205. **Telephone:** (480) 664-2998. **FAX:** (480) 664-2997. **E-Mail Address:** info@superseriesbaseball.com. **Website:** www.superseriesbaseball.com.
**President:** Mark Mathew.

### Age Classifications, National Championships
### NATIONAL DIVISION

| | |
|---|---|
| 8 and under | Cordova, TN, July 8-16 |
| 9 and under | Cordova, TN, July 8-16 |
| 10 and under | Broken Arrow, OK, July 8-16 |
| 11 and under | Cordova, TN, July 8-16 |
| 12 and under | Collierville, TN, July 15-23 |
| 13 and under | Cordova, TN, July 8-16 |
| 14 and under (54/80 foot) | Euless, TX, July 15-23 |
| 14 and under (60/90 foot) | Peoria, AZ, July 8-16 |
| 15 and under | Peoria, AZ, July 22-30 |
| 16 and under | Peoria, AZ, July 15-23 |
| 18 and under | Peoria, AZ, July 15-23 |

## AMERICAN DIVISION

| | |
|---|---|
| 8 and under (coach pitch) | DeSoto, TX, July 22-30 |
| 9 and under | McKinney, TX, July 8-16 |
| 10 and under | Broken Arrow, OK, July 8-16 |
| 11 and under | O'Fallon, MO, July 15-23 |
| 12 and under | Collierville, TN, July 15-23 |
| 13 and under | Tulsa, OK, July 15-23 |
| 14 and under (54/80 foot) | Liberty, MO, July 22-30 |
| 14 and under (60/90 foot) | Peoria, AZ, July 8-16 |

## MINORS DIVISION

| | |
|---|---|
| 8 and under (machine pitch) | Euless, TX, July 15-23 |
| 9 and under | Desoto, TX, July 22-30 |
| 10 and under | Broken Arrow, OK, July 8-16 |
| 11 and under | Sherwood, AR, July 22-30 |
| 12 and under | McKinney, TX, July 8-16 |
| 13 and under | McKinney, TX, July 8-16 |
| 14 and under (54/80 foot) | Liberty, MO, July 22-30 |

## T-BALL USA ASSOCIATION, INC.

**Office Address:** 2499 Main St., Stratford, CT 06615. **Telephone:** (203) 381-1449. **FAX:** (203) 381-1440. **E-Mail Address:** teeballusa@aol.com. **Website:** www.teeballusa.org.
**Year Founded:** 1993.
**President:** Bing Broido. **Executive Vice President:** Lois Richards.

## TRIPLE CROWN SPORTS

**Mailing Address:** 3930 Automation Way, Fort Collins, CO 80525. **Telephone:** (970) 223-6644. **FAX:** (970) 223-3636. **Websites:** www.triplecrownsports.com.
**Director, Baseball Operations:** Sean Hardy.

### Age Classifications, National Championships

| | |
|---|---|
| 10, 13, 15 World Series | Steamboat Springs, CO, July 18-23 |
| 8, 9, 12, 14 (60'6/90 foot) World Series | Steamboat Springs, CO, July 25-30 |
| 11, 13, 14 World Series | Steamboat Springs, CO, Aug. 1-6 |
| 13, 16, 18 Summer Nationals | Myrtle Beach, SC, July 24-29 |
| 8, 9, 10, 11, 12, 14, 15 Summer Nationals | Myrtle Beach, SC, July 27-30 |
| 8, 9, 11, 15, 16, 18 Fall Nationals | Henderson, NV, Sept. 15-17 |
| 10, 12, 13, 14 Fall Nationals | Henderson, NV, Sept. 22-24 |
| 12, 16, 18 Fall Nationals | St. Augustine, FL. Oct. 13-15 |
| 8, 10, 14, 15 Fall Nationals | St. Augustine, FL. Oct. 20-22 |
| 9, 11, 13 Fall Nationals | St. Augustine, FL, Oct. 27-29 |

## U.S. AMATEUR BASEBALL ASSOCIATION (USABA)

**Mailing Address:** 7101 Lake Ballinger Way, Edmonds, WA 98026. **Telephone/FAX:** (425) 776-7130. **E-Mail Address:** usaba@usaba.com. **Website:** www.usaba.com.
**Year Founded:** 1969.
**Executive Director:** Al Rutledge. **Secretary:** Roberta Engelhart.

### Age Classifications, World Series

| | |
|---|---|
| 10 and under | Unavailable |
| 11 and under | Unavailable |
| 12 and under | Site unavailable, Aug. 1-7 |
| 13 and under | Unavailable |
| 14 and under | Pasco, WA, July 28-Aug. 6 |
| 15 and under | Hoquiam, WA, July 29-Aug. 5 |
| 16 and under | Kennewick, WA, July 29-Aug. 5 |
| 18 and under | Sacramento, CA, Aug. 3-9 |

## U.S. AMATEUR BASEBALL FEDERATION (USABF)

**Mailing Address:** 911 Stonegate Court, Chula Vista, CA 91913. **Telephone:** (619) 934-2551. **FAX:** (619) 271-6659. **E-Mail Address:** usabf@cox.net. **Website:** www.usabf.com.
**Year Founded:** 1997.
**Senior Chief Executive Officer/President:** Tim Halbig.

### Age Classifications, World Series

| | |
|---|---|
| Junior World Series (10-, 11-, 12-, 13-year-old divisions) | San Diego, July 26-30 |
| Senior World Series (14-, 15-, 16-, 18-year-old divisions) | San Diego, Aug. 3-12 |
| Open World Series | San Diego, July 26-30 |

## UNITED STATES SPECIALTY SPORTS ASSOCIATION (USSSA)
**Vice President, Baseball:** Joey Odom, 614 South Lake Court Dr., Lake Charles, LA 70605. **Telephone:** (337) 562-1251. **E-Mail Address:** jodom@lausssabaseball.com.

**Executive Vice President:** Rick Fortuna, 6324 N. Chatham Ave., #136, Kansas City, MO 64151 **Telephone:** (816) 587-4545. **E-Mail Address:** rick@kcsports.org.

**Website:** www.usssabaseball.org.

**Year Founded:** 1965/Baseball 1996.

### Age Classifications, World Series
| | |
|---|---|
| 6 and under (tee)/7 and under (coach pitch) | Sulphur, LA, July 9-16 |
| 6 and under (tee)/7 and under (machine pitch) | Edmond, OK, July 10-16 |
| 6 and under (tee)/7 and under (machine pitch) | Charlotte, NC, July 17-23 |
| 8 and under (coach pitch) | Sulphur, LA, July 9-16 |
| 8 and under (machine pitch) | Edmond, OK, July 10-16 |
| 8 and under (machine pitch) | Thompson, GA, July 16-23 |
| 8 and under (machine pitch) | Charlotte, NC, July 17-23 |
| 8 and under—West | Chino Hills, CA, July 18-23 |
| 8 and under—East | Atlanta, July 9-16 |

### Age Classifications, Elite World Series
| | |
|---|---|
| 9 and under | St. Louis, July 16-23 |
| 10 and under | Southaven, MS, July 9-16 |
| 10 and under | Chino Hills, CA, July 18-23 |
| 11 and under | Overland Park, KS, July 9-16 |
| 12 and under | Hutchinson, KS, July 16-23 |
| 13 and under | Canton, MI, July 16-23 |
| 14 and under (54/80 foot) | Tulsa, OK, July 9-16 |
| 14 and under (60/90 foot) | Kingsport, TN, July 22-28 |
| 15 and under/Freshman | Kissimmee, FL, July 23-30 |
| 16 and under/Sophomore | Kissimmee, FL, July 16-23 |
| 17 and under/Junior | Edmond, OK, July 16-23 |
| 18 and under/Senior | Kissimmee, FL, July 16-23 |

### Age Classifications, Major World Series
| | |
|---|---|
| 10 and under | Kansas City, July 23-30 |
| 11 and under/12 and under—East | Statesboro, GA, July 23-30 |
| 11 and under/12 and under/13 and under/14 and under—West | Dallas, July 23-30 |
| 13 and under—East | Salisbury, MD, July 23-30 |
| 14 and under—East | State College, PA, July 23-30 |
| 15 and under/Freshman | Kissimmee, FL, July 23-30 |
| 16 and under/Sophomore | Kissimmee, FL, July 16-23 |
| 17 and under/Junior | Edmond, OK, July 16-23 |
| 18 and under/Senior | Kissimmee, FL, July 16-23 |

## USA JUNIOR OLYMPIC BASEBALL CHAMPIONSHIP
**Mailing Address:** USA Baseball, 403 Blackwell St., Durham, NC 27701. **Telephone:** (919) 474-8721. **FAX:** (919) 474-8822. **E-Mail Address:** jeffsinger@usabaseball.com. **Website:** www.usabaseball.com.

**Assistant Director, Baseball Operations:** Jeff Singer.

### Age Classifications, Championships
| | |
|---|---|
| 16 and under—West (72 teams) | Peoria/Surprise, AZ, June 23-July 1 |
| 16 and under—East (72 teams) | Jupiter, FL, June 23-July 1 |

## WORLD WOOD BAT ASSOCIATION
### (A Division of Perfect Game USA)
**Mailing Address:** 1203 Rockford Road SW, Cedar Rapids, IA 52404. **Telephone:** (319) 298-2923, (800) 447-9362. **FAX:** (319) 298-2924. **E-Mail Address:** Aford@worldwoodbat.com **Website:** www.worldwoodbat.com.

**Year Founded:** 1997.

**President:** Andy Ford. **National Director:** Taylor McCullough. **Scouting Director:** David Rawnsley.

### Age Classifications, National Championships
| | |
|---|---|
| 2009 graduates/15 and under | Marietta, GA, June 28-July 2 |
| 2008 graduates/16 and under—East | Marietta, GA, July 18-23 |
| 2008 graduates/16 and under—West | Riverside, CA, July 18-23 |
| 2008 graduates/16 and under—National | Marietta, GA, Aug. 6-8 |
| 2007 graduates/17 and under | Marietta, GA, July 3-9 |
| 2006 graduates/18 and under | Marietta, GA, July 10-16 |
| Fall Championship (underclassmen) | Fort Myers, FL, Oct. 6-9 |
| Fall Championship (high school) | Jupiter, FL, Oct. 26-30 |

## BASEBALL USA

**Mailing Address:** 2626 W. Sam Houston Pkwy. N., Houston, TX 77043. **Telephone:** (713) 690-5055. **FAX:** (713) 690-9448. **E-Mail Address:** info@baseballusa.com. **Website:** www.baseballusa.com.
**President:** Charlie Maiorana. **Tournament Director:** Steve Olson. **Building Manager, Accounting:** Ken Ahrens. **Director, Marketing/Development:** Christiana Yaya. **League Baseball:** Chip Naila. **Pro Shop Manager:** Don Lewis.
**Activities:** Camps, baseball/softball spring and fall leagues, instruction, indoor cage and field rentals, youth tournaments, World Series events, corporate days, summer college league, pro shop.

## CALIFORNIA COMPETITIVE YOUTH BASEBALL

**Mailing Address:** P.O. Box 338, Placentia, CA 92870. **Telephone:** (714) 993-2838. **FAX:** (714) 961-6078. **E-Mail Address:** ccybnet@aol.com.
**Tournament Director:** Todd Rogers.

## COCOA EXPO SPORTS CENTER

**Mailing Address:** 500 Friday Rd., Cocoa, FL 32926. **Telephone:** (321) 639-3976. **FAX:** (321) 639-0598. **E-Mail Address:** athleticdirector@cocoaexpo.com. **Website:** www.cocoaexpo.com.
**Athletic Director:** Jeff Biddle.
**Activities:** Spring training program, instructional camps, team training camps, youth tournaments.
**2006 Events/Tournaments (ages 10-18):** First Pitch Festival, May 12-14. Cocoa Expo Internationale, June 30-July 5. Cocoa Expo Summer Classic, Aug. 1-6. Labor Day Challenge, Sept. 1-4. Cocoa Expo Fall Classic, Oct. 13-15.

## COOPERSTOWN BASEBALL WORLD

**Mailing Address:** P.O. Box 398, Bergenfield, NJ 07621. **Telephone:** (888) 229-8750. **FAX:** (888) 229-8720. **E-Mail Address:** cbw@cooperstownbaseballworld.com.
**Complex Address:** Cooperstown Baseball World, SUNY-Oneonta, Ravine Parkway, Oneonta, NY 13820.
**President/Chairman:** Eddie Einhorn. **Vice President:** Debra Sirianni. **Senior Coordinator, Special Events:** Jennifer Einhorn.

## COOPERSTOWN DREAMS PARK

**Mailing Address:** 330 S. Main St. E. Fisher St., 3rd Floor, Salisbury, NC 28144. **Telephone:** (704) 630-0050. **FAX:** (704) 630-0737. **E-Mail Address:** info@cooperstowndreamspark.com. **Website:** www.cooperstowndreamspark.com.
**Complex Address:** 4450 State Highway 28, Cooperstown, NY 13807.
**Chief Executive Officer:** Lou Presutti. **Program Director:** Phil Kehr.
**2006 Invitational Tournaments** (80 teams per week): 10 and under—June 17-23; 12 and under—June 24-June 30, July 1-7, July 8-14, July 15-21, July 22-28, July 29-Aug. 4, Aug. 5-11, Aug. 12-18, Aug. 18-25.
**2006 National American Tournament of Champions:** 12 and under—Aug. 26-Sept. 1.

## DISNEY'S WIDE WORLD OF SPORTS

**Mailing Address:** P.O. Box 10000, Lake Buena Vista, FL 32830. **Telephone:** (407) 938-3802. **FAX:** (407) 938-3442. **E-Mail Address:** wdw.sports.baseball@disney.com. **Website:** www.disneyworldsports.com.
**Manager, Sports Events:** Kevin Reynolds. **Sports Manager:** Brian Fling. **Tournament Director:** Al Schlazer. **Sales Manager, Baseball:** Rick Morris. **Sports Sales Coordinator, Baseball:** Kirk Stanley.

## KC SPORTS TOURNAMENTS

**Mailing Address:** KC Sports, 6324 N. Chatham Ave., No. 136, Kansas City, MO 64151. **Telephone:** (816) 587-4545. **FAX:** (816) 587-4549. **E-Mail Addresses:** rick@kcsports.org, wally@kcsports.org, linda@kcsports.org. **Website:** www.kcsports.org.
**Activities:** Youth tournaments (ages 6-18).
**Tournament Organizers:** Rick Fortuna, Wally Fortuna.

## U.S. AMATEUR BASEBALL FEDERATION (USABF)

**Mailing Address:** 911 Stonegate Court, Chula Vista, CA 91913. **Telephone:** (619) 934-2551. **FAX:** (619) 271-6659. **E-Mail Address:** usabf@cox.net. **Website:** www.usabf.com.
**Senior Chief Executive Officer/President:** Tim Halbig.

# INSTRUCTIONAL SCHOOLS/PRIVATE CAMPS

## ACADEMY OF PRO PLAYERS

**Mailing Address:** 317 Midland Ave., Garfield, NJ 07026. **Telephone:** (973) 772-3355. **FAX:** (973) 772-4839. **Website:** www.academypro.com.
**Camp Director:** Lar Gilligan.

## ALDRETE BASEBALL ACADEMY

**Office Address:** P.O. Box 4048, Monterey, CA 93942. **Telephone:** (831) 884-0400. **FAX:** (831) 884-0800. **E-Mail Address:** aldretebaseball@aol.com. **Website:** www.aldretebaseball.com.
**Camp Director:** Rich Aldrete.

## ALL-STAR BASEBALL ACADEMY

**Mailing Addresses:** 650 Parkway Blvd., Broomall, PA 19008; 52 Penn Oaks Dr., West Chester, PA 19382. **Telephone:** (610) 355-2411, (610) 399-8050. **FAX:** (610) 355-2414. **E-Mail Address:** info@allstarbaseballacademy.com. **Website:** www.allstarbaseballacademy.com.
**Directors:** Mike Manning, Chris Madonna.

## AMERICAN BASEBALL FOUNDATION

**Mailing Address:** 2660 10th Ave. South, Suite 620. Birmingham, AL 35205. **Telephone:** (205) 558-4235. **FAX:** (205) 918-0800. **E-Mail Address:** abf@asmi.org. **Website:** www.americanbaseball.org.
**Executive Director:** David Osinski. **Chairman of the Board:** Dr. James Andrews.

## THE BASEBALL ACADEMY

**Mailing Address:** IMG Academies, 5500 34th St. W., Bradenton, FL 34210.
**Telephone:** (941) 727-0303. **FAX:** (941) 727-2962. **E-Mail Address:** kpoffenbarger@imgworld.com. **Website:** www.imgacademies.com.
**Camp Director, Baseball:** Ken Bolek.

## BUCKY DENT'S BASEBALL SCHOOL

**Mailing Address:** 490 Dotterel Rd., Delray Beach, FL 33444. **Telephone:** (561) 265-0280. **FAX:** (561) 278-6679. **E-Mail Address:** staff@dentbaseball.com. **Website:** www.dentbaseball.com.
**Vice President:** Larry Hoskin.

## DOYLE BASEBALL SCHOOL

**Mailing Address:** P.O. Box 9156, Winter Haven, FL 33883. **Telephone:** (863) 439-1000. **FAX:** (863) 439-7086. **E-Mail Address:** doyleinfo@doylebaseball.com. **Website:** www.doylebaseball.com.
**President:** Denny Doyle. **Chief Executive Officer:** Blake Doyle. **Director, Satellite School:** Rick Siebert.

## FROZEN ROPES TRAINING CENTERS

**Mailing Address:** 12 Elkay Dr., Chester, NY 10918. **Telephone:** (877) 846-5699. **FAX:** (845) 469-6742. **E-Mail Address:** specialevents@frozenropes.com. **Website:** www.frozenropes.com.
**Corporate Director:** Tony Abbatine. **Camp Director:** Dan Hummel.

## MARK CRESSE BASEBALL SCHOOL

**Mailing Address:** 1188 N. Grove St., Suite C, Anaheim, CA 92806. **Telephone:** (714) 892-6145. **FAX:** (714) 892-1881. **E-Mail Address:** info@markcresse.com. **Website:** www.markcresse.com.
**Owner/Founder:** Mark Cresse. **Executive Director:** Jeff Courvoisier.

## MICKEY OWEN BASEBALL SCHOOL

**Mailing Address:** P.O. Box 88, Miller, MO 65707. **Telephone:** (417) 882-2799, (417) 452-3211. **FAX:** (417) 889-6978. **E-Mail Address:** info@mickeyowen.com. **Website:** www.mickeyowen.com.
**President:** Ken Rizzo. **Camp Director:** Bobby Doe. **Clinician:** Joe Fowler. **Advisor:** Howie Bedell.

## NORTH CAROLINA BASEBALL ACADEMY

**Mailing Address:** 1137 Pleasant Ridge Rd., Greensboro, NC 27409. **Telephone:** (336) 931-1118. **E-Mail Address:** ncba@att.net. **Website:** www.ncbaseball.com.
**Owner/Director:** Scott Bankhead. **Assistant Director:** Matt Schirm. **Academy Director:** Tommy Jackson.

## PENNSYLVANIA DIAMOND BUCKS BASEBALL CAMP

**Mailing Address:** 2320 Whitetail Court, Hellertown, PA 18055. **Telephone:** (610) 838-1219, (610) 442-6998. **E-Mail Address:** jciganick@moravian.edu.
**Camp Director:** Chuck Ciganick.

## PERFECT GAME USA

**Mailing Address:** 1203 Rockford Rd. SW, Cedar Rapids, IA 52404. **Telephone:** (319) 298-2923. **FAX:** (319) 298-2924. **E-Mail Address:** staff@perfectgame.org. **Website:** www.perfectgame.org.
**President, Director:** Jerry Ford. **National Supervisor:** Andy Ford. **Director, Instruction:** Jim VanScoyac.

## PROFESSIONAL BASEBALL INSTRUCTION

**Mailing Address:** 107 Pleasant Ave., Upper Saddle River, NJ 07458. **Telephone:** (800) 282-4638 (NY/NJ), (877) 448-2220 (rest of U.S.). **FAX:** (201) 760-8820. **E-Mail Address:** info@baseballclinics.com. **Website:** www.baseballclinics.com.
**President:** Doug Cinnella.

## RIPKEN BASEBALL CAMPS

**Mailing Address:** 1427 Clarkview Rd., Suite 100, Baltimore, MD 21209. **Telephone:** (800) 486-0850. **Fax:** (410) 823-0850. **E-Mail Address:** information@ripken-baseball.com. **Website:** www.ripkenbaseball.com.
**Director, Operations:** Bill Ripken.

## SHO-ME BASEBALL CAMP

**Mailing Address:** P.O. Box 2270, Branson West, MO 65737. **Telephone:** (800) 993-2267, (417) 338-5838. **FAX:** (417) 338-2610. **E-Mail Address:** info@shome-baseball.com. **Website:** www.shomebaseball.com.
**Camp Director:** Christopher Schroeder. **Head of Instruction:** Dick Birmingham.

## SOUTHWEST PROFESSIONAL BASEBALL SCHOOL

**Mailing Address:** 462 S. Gilbert Rd., #599 Mesa, AZ 85204. **Telephone:** (888) 830-8031. **FAX:** (480) 830-7455. **E-Mail Address:** leonard@swpbs.com. **Website:** www.swpbs.com
**Camp Directors:** Leonard Garcia, Chris Gump.

## UTAH BASEBALL ACADEMY

**Mailing Address:** 389 West 10000 South, South Jordan, UT 84095. **Telephone:** (801) 561-1700. **FAX:** (801) 571-1762. **E-Mail Address:** info@utahbaseballacademy.com. **Website:** www.utahbaseballacademy.com.

## COLLEGE CAMPS

Almost all of the elite college baseball programs have summer/holiday instructional camps. Please consult the college section, Pages 305-325 for listings.

# SENIOR LEAGUES

## MEN'S SENIOR BASEBALL LEAGUE
(28 and Over, 38 and Over)

**Mailing Address:** One Huntington Quadrangle, Suite 3N07, Mellville, NY 11747. **Telephone:** (631) 753-6725. **FAX:** (631) 753-4031.
**President:** Steve Sigler. **Vice President:** Gary D'Ambrisi.
**E-Mail Address:** info@msblnational.com. **Website:** www.msblnational.com.
**2005 World Series:** Oct. 15-Nov. 4, Phoenix, AZ (28-plus, 38-plus, 48-plus, 58-plus, father/son divisions). **Fall Classic:** Nov. 2-11, St. Petersburg, FL (28-plus, 38-plus, 47-plus).

## MEN'S ADULT BASEBALL LEAGUE
(18 and Over)

**Mailing Address:** One Huntington Quadrangle, Suite 3N07, Mellville, NY 11747. **Telephone:** (631) 753-6725. **FAX:** (631) 753-4031.
**E-Mail Address:** info@msblnational.com. **Website:** www.msblnational.com.
**President:** Steve Sigler. **Vice President:** Gary D'Ambrisi.
**2005 World Series:** Oct. 18-22, Phoenix, AZ (four divisions). **Fall Classic:** Nov. 3-6, Clearwater, FL.

## NATIONAL ADULT BASEBALL ASSOCIATION
**Mailing Address:** 3609 S. Wadsworth Blvd., Suite 135, Lakewood, CO 80235. **Telephone:** (800) 621-6479. **FAX:** (303) 639-6605. **E-Mail:** nabanational@aol.com. **Website:** www.dugout.org.
**President:** Shane Fugita.
**2006 Events. Memorial Day Tournaments:** 18 and over, 30 and over, 40 and over, 50 and over—May 27-29, Las Vegas, NV; 18 and over, 28 and over, 38 and over, May 27-29, Atlantic City, NJ. **Hall of Fame Tournament:** 18 and over, 28 and over, July 1-4, Cooperstown, NY. **Mile High Classic:** 18 and over, 28 and over, 38 and over, July 1-3, Denver, CO. **NABA World Championship Series:** 18 and over, 28 and over, 38 and over, 48 and over, 57 and over, Oct. 3-14, Phoenix, AZ. **NABA Over 50 Baseball National Tournament:** 48 and over, 58 and over, Oct. 23-28, Las Vegas, NV.

## ROY HOBBS BASEBALL
Open (28-over), Veterans (38-over), Masters (48-over),
Legends (55-over), Classics (60-over), Women's open

**Mailing Address:** 2048 Akron Peninsula Rd., Akron, OH 44313. **Telephone:** (330) 923-3400. **FAX:** (330) 923-1967.
**E-Mail Address:** rhbb@royhobbs.com. **Website:** www.royhobbs.com.
**President:** Tom Giffen. **Vice President:** Ellen Giffen.
**2005 World Series** (all in Fort Myers, FL): Oct. 21-28—Open Division; Oct. 28-Nov. 4—Veterans Division; Oct. 25-29—Women's Division; Nov. 4-11—Masters Division; Nov. 10-15—Father-Son Division; Nov. 11-18—Legends Division, Classics Division, Seniors Division.

## AMATEUR ATHLETIC UNION WOMEN'S BASEBALL
Open Division (16 and over)

**Mailing Address:** 2048 Akron Peninsula Rd., Akron, OH 44313. **Telephone:** (330) 923-3400. **FAX:** (330) 923-1967.
**E-Mail Address:** uswb@royhobbs.com. **Website:** www.uswb.org.
**National Women's Baseball Chairman:** Tom Giffen. **Vice Chairman:** Chris Hill. **Youth Chairman:** John Kovach. **Committee Members:** Adriane Adler, Tina Beining, Cherie Leatherwood, Robin Wallace.
**2005 National Championship:** Nov. 4-8 at Fort Myers, FL.

# AGENT
DIRECTORY

# SERVICE
DIRECTORY

# INDEX

# **AGENT** D I R E C T O R Y

## Aces Inc.
Seth Levinson, Esq.
Sam Levinson
Keith Miller
Peter Pedalino, Esq.
Eric Amador
Michael Zimmerman
188 Montague Street
Brooklyn, NY 11201
718-237-2900
fax 718-522-3906
acesinc2@aol.com

## Advance Athletic Representation
Michael Moline
Mike Mosa
PO Box 2578
Agoura Hills, CA 91376
818-889-3933

## Barry Axelrod, APC
2236 Encinitas Blvd., Suite A
Encinitas, CA 92024
760-753-0088
fax 760-436-7399
baxy@pacbell.net

## Bouza, Klein & Goosenburg
Joseph Klein
950 S. Flower Street #100
Los Angeles, CA 90015
213-488-0675
fax 213-488-1316
jkleine@bkglaw.com

## David Abramson, Esq.
Verrill Dana, LLP
One Portland Square
Portland, ME 04112-0582
207-774-4000
fax 207-774-7499
dabramson@verilldana.com
dabramson@sportslaw.com

## Diamond Stars Sports Management
Lenard Sapp
5119 6th Avenue
Los Angeles, CA 90043
323-627-8882
fax 310-798-1019
diamondstarmgt@aol.com

## DRM Brothers Sports Management
William S. Rose
Brian Doyle
Todd Middlebrooks, Esq.
31 Compass Lane
Ft. Lauderdale, FL 33308
954-609-1505
fax 954-267-0336
www.drmsportsmgmt.com
ltdnyy@aol.com

## Focus Management
Frank A. Blandino
Jonathan J. DeSimone
204 Towne Centre Drive
Hillsborough, NJ 08844
908-281-0550
fax 908-281-0596
www.focusmanagementinc.com
fablaw@earthlink.net

## Garden City Sports Council Inc.
Glenn Kempa, CPA
David M. Namm, Esq. (Of Counsel)
PO Box 7477
Wantagh, NY 11793
516-318-1940
631-875-0166 Espanol
fax 516-935-6295
GCSCforMLB@aol.com

## Iglesias Sports Management
Juan C. Iglesias
Fernando Iglesias, Esq.
2655 LeJeune Rd., Suite 532
Coral Gables, FL 33134
305-446-9960
fax 305-446-9980
grndslm@aol.com

## Impact Sports
Mitch Frankel
Adriana Merigliano
12429 Ventura Court
Studio City, CA 91604
818-623-2800
fax 818-623 2810
admin@impactse.com

## Jet Sports Management
B.B. Abbott
Hank Sargent
3514 West Obispo Street
Tampa, FL 33629
813-902-9511
fax 813-902-0900
www.jetsportsmanagement.com
bbabbott@jetsportsmanagement.com
sarge@jetsportsmanagement.com

## KDN Sports
10801 National Blvd., Suite 525
Los Angeles, CA 90064
213-488-6430
Fax 213-488-6436

## King & King LLC
Stanley O. King
231 South Broad Street
Woodbury, NJ 08096
856-845-3001
fax 856-845-3079
stan@kingslaw.com

## McDowell And Associates
Jim McDowell
Craig Wallenbrock
10061 Riverside Drive #870
Toluca Lake, CA 91602
818-597-9948
fax 818-597-3212
jimmcdowell@sbcglobal.net

## Mighty Warriors of Rhode Island
Jose De La Rosa
Keila De La Rosa
2 Norwich Drive
Johnston, RI 02919
401-529-3969
fax 401-383-7335
dkdelarosa@aol.com

## Monaco Law Office
660 Newport Center Drive, Suite 400
Newport Beach, CA 92660
949-719-2669
fax 949-720-4111
randell@monacolawoffice.com

## Peter E. Greenberg & Associates, Ltd.
Peter E. Greenberg, Esq.
Edward L. Greenberg
Chris Leible
200 Madison Ave., Suite 2225
New York, NY 10016
212-334-6880
fax 212-334-6895

## Platinum Sports & Entertainment Management
Nick Brockmeyer, President
Bert Fulk
Kenneth Powell
123 N. 5th Street
St. Charles, MO 63301
636-946-0960
fax 636-946-0283
www.psemagents.com
nbrockmeyer@psemagents.com

## Pro Agents Inc.
David P. Pepe
Billy Martin Jr.
90 Woodbridge Center Drive
Woodbridge, NJ 07095
800-795-3454
fax 732-726-6688
pepeda@wilentz.com

## Professional Sports Management Group
Alan Meersand
2100 N. Sepulveda Blvd.
Manhattan Beach, CA 90266
310-546-3400
fax 310-546-4046
meersand@aol.com

You can also find this list at http://www.baseballamerica.com/today/booksupdate/2006directory.html.

973-825-7360

# DIRECTOR

Aces Inc.

Advance Athletic
Representation

Barry Axelrod, APC

Bouza, Klein & Goosenburg

David Abramson Es .

Diamond Stars Sports
Management

DRM Brothers Sports
Management

Focus Management

Garden City Sports Council Inc.

Iglesias Sports Mangement

Impact Sports

Jet Sports Management

KDN Sports

King & King LLC

McDowell And Associates

Mighty Warriors of Rhode Island

Monaco Law Office

Peter E. Greenberg &
Associates, Ltd.

Platinum Sports &
Entertainment Mangement

Pro Agents Inc.

Professional Sports
Management Group

**Professional Sports Planners**
Michael M. Walkins
J.D. Sanchez
3300 Irvine Ave., Suite 320
Newport Beach, CA 92660
949-752-1010
fax 949-835-7960
www.prosportsplanners.com
mwatkins@prosportsplanners.com

**Prospex Sports Management Inc.**
Edwin K. Setlik
Amber E. Simons
721 Enterprise Drive, Suite 201
Oak Brook, IL 60523
800-899-9159
fax 630-472-0562
ambersimons12@hotmail.com

**ProSport Management Inc.**
Jim Krivacs
1831 N. Belcher Rd., G-3
Clearwater, FL 33765
727-791-7556
fax 727-791-1489

**Pro Star Management Inc.**
Joe Bick
1600 Scripps Center, 312 Walnut St.
Cincinnati, OH 45202
513-762-7676
fax 513-721-4628
prostar@fuse.net

**Pro-Talent Inc.**
3753 North Western Ave.
Chicago, IL 60618
773-583-3411
fax 773-583-4277
protalentchicago@aol.com

**Reynolds Sports Management**
Larry Reynolds
Patrick Murphy
Matt Kinzer
3880 Lemon Street
Riverside, CA 92501
951-784-6333
fax 951-784-1451
reynoldssports@aol.com

**Riverfront Sports Management**
Brian M. Goldberg
4300 Carew Tower
441 Vine Street
Cincinnati, OH 45202
513-721-3111
fax 513-721-3077

**RMG Sports Management**
Robert Garber, Esq.
Brett Laurvick
Robert Lisanti
Matt Colleran
115 S. Vine St. 1E
Hinsdale, IL 60521
630-986-2500
fax 630-986-0171
www.rmgsports.com

**The Show**
Andrew Mongelluzzi, Esq.
P.O Box 2375
Palm Harbor, FL 34684
727-789-2109
fax 727-789-2586
www.theshow-baseball.com

**SKA Sports & Entertainment**
Steve Greenberg
Steve Goldstein
Jerry Bajek
499 North Canon Drive 4th Floor
Beverly Hills, CA 90210
310-551-0381
fax 310-551-0386
www.skasports.com
skasports@aol.com

**Sosnick Cobbe Sports**
Paul Cobbe
Matt Sosnick
1601 North California Blvd. Suite 150
Walnut Creek, CA 94596
650-697-7070
fax 650-697-7004
www.sosnickcobbesports.com
mattsoz@aol.com
paulcobbe@msn.com

**The Sparta Group Inc.**
Michael Nicotera
Gene Casaleggio
140 Littleton Road, Suite 100
Parsippany, NJ 07054
973-335-0550
fax 973-335-2148
frontdesk@thespartagroup.com

**Turner-Gary Sports Inc.**
Jim Turner
Rex Gary
101 S. Hanley Road, Suite 1065
St. Louis, MO 63105
314-863-6611
fax 314-863-6611

**West Coast Sports Management LLC**
Bill Shupper
Len Strelitz
Jim Lentine
369 South Fairoaks
Pasadena, CA 91105
626-844-1861
fax 626-844-1863
www.proballfirm.com
bills@proballfirm.com

# SERVICE DIRECTORY

## ACCESSORIES

**Great American Products**
1661 S. Seguin
New Braunfels, TX 78130
830-620-4400 (3023)
fax 830-620-8430
www.gap1.com
wally@gap1.com

**JKP Sports**
PO Box 3126
Tualatin, OR 97062
800-547-6843
fax 503-691-1100
www.jugsports.com

## ACCOUNTING

**Kempa and Company, CPAs, LLP**
300 Motor Parkway Suite 200
Hauppauge, NY 11788
800-477-5857
631-875-0166 Espanol
fax 516-935-6295
www.BaseballCPAs.com
glennkempa@aol.com

**Resnick Amsterdam Leshner P.C**
653 Skippack Pike Suite 300
Blue Bell, PA 19422
215-628-8080
fax 215-618-4752
www.baseballaccountants.com
sxr@ral-cpa.com

## APPAREL

**All-Pro Sports**
5341 Derry Ave.
Agoura Hills, CA 91301
818-707-3178
www.allprosportsshoes.com
allprosports@sbcglobal.net

**The College House**
1400 Chamberlayne Ave.
Richmond, VA 23222
800-888-7606
fax 804-643-4408
www.chsport.com
chouse601@aol.com

**Holloway Sportswear Inc.**
2633 Campbell Rd.
Sidney, OH 45365
937-497-7575
www.hollowayusa.com
cathy.billing@hollowayusa.com

**Minor Leagues, Major Dreams**
PO Box 6098
Anaheim, CA 92816
800-345-2421
fax 714-939-0655
www.minorleagues.com
mlmd@minorleagues.com

**Ropes Baseball Apparel**
Box 521
Southbury, CT 06488
203-267-1823
fax 203-267-1825
www.ropesbaseball.com
info@ropesbaseball.com

## ARTWORK

**Low and Inside, LLC**
2022 N. Ferry Street, Suite 3100
Minneapolis, MN 55303
763-797-0777
fax 763-767-5510
www.lowandinside.com
creative@lowandinside.com

## AUCTIONS

**Heritage Auction Galleries**
3500 Maple Avenue, 17th Floor
Dallas, TX 75219
800-872-6467
HeritageAuctions.com/Sports

See our ad
on Inside
Front Cover

## BACKPACKS

**Grand River Company**
16580 Harbor Blvd #C
Fountain Valley, CA 92708
714-839-8788
fax 714-839-9889
www.grandriverco.com
sales@grandriverco.com

## BACKSTOPS

**L.A Steelcraft Products**
PO Box 90365
Pasadena, CA 91109
626-798-7401/800-371-2438
fax 626-798-1482
www.lasteelcraft.com
info@lasteelcraft.com

## BAGS

**Gerry Cosby and Co. Inc.**
3 Pennslyvania Plaza
Madison Square Garden
New York, NY 10001
877-563-6464
fax 212-967-0876
www.cosbysports.com
gcsmsg@cosbysports.com

**The Paul Pryor Company**
12401 66th Street North
Largo, FL 33773
727-531-8400
fax 727-530-1255
www.paulpryorbags.com
pryorco@verizon.net

## BANNERS/FLAGS

**GCSC Inc.**
PO Box 7477
Wantagh, NY 11793
516-318-1940
631-875-0166 Espanol
fax 516-935-6295
GCSCforMLB@aol.com
www.gcscpromos.com

**Olympus Flag and Banner**
9000 W. Heather Ave.
Milwaukee, WI 53224
414-355-2010
fax 414-355-1931
www.olympus-flag.com
diane.potter@olympus-flag.com

## BASEBALLS

**Ampac Ent./All-Star**
PO Box 1356
Shirley, MA 01464
978-425-6266
fax 978-425-4068
www.all-starsports.com
jurga@all-starsports.com

**Diamond Sports**
11130 Warland Drive
Cypress, CA 90630
562-598-9717
562-598-0906
www.diamond-sports.com
info@diamond-sports.com

**JKP Sports**
PO Box 3126
Tualatin, OR 97062
800-547-6843
fax 503-691-1100
www.jugsports.com

**Markwort Sporting Goods Co.**
1101 Research Blvd.
St. Louis, MO 63132
314-652-3757
fax 314-652-6241
www.markwort.com
sales@markwort.com

## BASES

**Ampac Ent./All-Star**
PO Box 1356
Shirley, MA 01464
978-425-6266
978-425-4068
www.all-starsports.com
jurga@all-starsports.com

**L.A. Steelcraft Products**
PO Box 90365
Pasadena, CA 91109
626-798-7401/800-371-2438
fax 626-798-1482
www.lasteelcraft.com
info@lasteelcraft.com

## BASEBALL CARDS

**Grandstand Cards**
22647 Ventura Blvd. #192
Woodland Hills, CA 91364
818-992-5642
fax 818-348-9122
gsl@pacbell.net

## BATS

**Brett Bros. Sports International**
East 9514 Montgomery St. Blvd #25
Spokane, WA 99206
509-891-6435
fax 509-891-4155
www.brettbros.com
brettbats@aol.com

**BWP Bats**
80 Womel Dorf Lane
Brookville, PA 15825
814-849-0089
fax 814-849-4143
www.bwpbats.com
sales@bwpbats.com

**D-Bat Inc.**
17440 Dallas Parkway Suite 112
Dallas, TX 75282
888-398-3393
fax 972-398-1001
www.dbatinc.com
batsales@dbatinc.com

**Dinger Bats**
PO Box 88 109 Kimbro St.
Ridgway, IL
866-9-dinger
fax 618-272-7253
www.dingerbats.com
info@dingerbats.com

**Hoosier Bat Co.**
4511 Evans Ave.
Valparasio, IN 46383
800-228-3787
fax 219-465-0877
www.hoosierbat.com
baseball@netnitco.net

**Old Hickory Bat Company**
1735 Hwy 31W
Goodlettsville, TN 37072
866-Pro-Bats
fax 615-285-0512
www.oldhickorybats.com
mail@oldhickorybats.com

**The Original Maple Bat Company**
202 Rochester St.
Ottawa, ON K1R7M6
613-724-2421
613-725-3299
www.sambat.com
bats@sambat.com

**Zinger-X Bat Professional Bats**
939 W. Center A
Lindon, UT 84042
800-488-9722
www.zingerbats.com
contact@zingerbats.com

### BATTING CAGES

**C&H Baseball Inc.**
2215 60th Dr. East
Bradenton, FL 34203
941-727-1533
fax 941-727-0588
www.chbaseball.com
info@chbaseball.com

**JKP Sports**
PO Box 3126
Tualatin, OR 97062
800-547-6843
fax 503-691-1100
www.jugsports.com

**Lanier Batting Cages**
206 S. Three Notch
Andalusia, AL 36420
800-716-9189
334-222-3323
alaweb.com/~battingcages
battingcages@alaweb.com

**L.A. Steelcraft Products**
PO Box 90365
Pasadena, CA 91109
626-798-7401/800-371-2438
fax 626-798-1482
www.lasteelcraft.com
info@lasteelcraft.com

**Miller Net Company**
PO Box 18787
Memphis, TN 38181
901-744-3804
901-743-6580
www.millernets.com
miller@millernets.com

**National Batting Cages**
PO Box 250
Forest Grove, Oregon 97116-0250
800-547-8800
fax 503-3573727
www.nationalbattingcages.com
sales@nationalbattingcages.com

**Russell Batting Cages**
205 Malaga Ave.
Birmingham, AL 35216
205-870-1081
fax 205-870-1087
www.russellbattingcages.com

### BATTING GLOVES

**All-Pro Sports**
5341 Derry Ave.
Agoura Hills, CA 91301
818-707-3178
www.allprosportshoes.com
allprosports@sbcglobal.net

**National Sports Products**
3441 S. 11th Avenue
Eldridge, IA 52748
877-589-3342
fax 800-443-8907
www.nationalsportsproducts.com
sales@nationalsportsproducts.com

### BOOKS

**BaltimoreChop.com**
625 Washington Blvd.
Baltimore, MD 21230
888-543-CHOP
www.baltimorechop.com
sales@baltimorechop.com

### BUSINESS CONSULTING

**Action Sports America**
5263 Placentia Pkwy
Las Vegas, NV 89118
610-832-7500
fax 610-832-7500
240-220-8597
www.actionsportsamerica.com
fun@giantjersey.com

### CAMPS/SCHOOLS

**Mickey Owen Baseball School**
PO Box 4504
Springfield, MO 65808
417-882-2799
fax 417-889-6978
www.mickeyowen.com
info@mickeyowen.com

**Professional Baseball Instruction**
107 Pleasant Avenue
Upper Saddle, NJ 07458
877-448-2220
fax 941-752-8820
www.baseballclinics.com
info@baseballclinics.com

**The Baseball Academy**
5500 34th St. West
Bradenton, FL 34210
800-872-6425
fax 941-752-2531
www.imgacademies.com
netsales@imgworld.com

### CAPS/HEADWEAR

**Minor Leagues, Major Dreams**
PO Box 6098
Anaheim, CA 92816

800-345-2421
fax 714-939-0655
www.minorleagues.com
mlmd@minorleagues.com

### CASH REGISTER/POINT OF SALE

**Casio Inc.**
570 Mt. Pleasant Ave.
Dover, NJ 07801
973-361-5400
fax 973-537-8979
www.casio.com
lsampey@casio.com

### CHAMPIONSHIP RINGS

**Bailey Banks & Biddle Fine Jewelers**
19575 Biscayne Blvd. #799
Aventura, FL 33180
214-763-2489
fax 305-933-8745
Neil Meany, Program Coordinator
nmeany@zalescorp.com

### CLEATS/FOOTWEAR

**All-Pro Sports**
5341 Derry Ave.
Agoura Hills, CA 91301
818-707-3178
www.allprosportshoes.com
allprosports@sbcglobal.net

### CONCESSIONS

**Houston's Peanuts**
PO Box 160
Dublin, NC 28332
800-334-8383
fax 910-862-2136
www.houstonspeanuts.com
peanutprocessors@carolina.net

### CUP HOLDERS

**Caddy Products**
72-064 Adelaid Street
Thousand Palms, CA 92276
800-845-0591
Fax 760-343-7598
www.caddyproducts.com
sales@caddyproducts.com

*See our ad on Page 9*

### EDUCATION/PROFESSIONAL DEVELOPMENT

**IAAM (International Association of Assembly Managers)**
635 Fritz Dr.
Coppell, TX 75019
972-906-7441
fax 972-906-7418
www.IAAM.com
rick.fritsche@iaam.org

### ENTERTAINMENT

**Birdzerk!**
PO Box 36061
Louisville, KY 40233
800-219-0899
502-458-0867
www.birdzerk.com
johnny@birdzerk.com

**ElvisHimselvis (DCTB Productions)**
1918 Jeanette Lane #5
Springfield, IL 62702
888-784-5587
www.elvishimselvis.tripod.com
elvisdunham77@hotmail.com

**Gameopps.com**
P.O Box 770440
Lakewood, OH 44107
1-866-GAMEOPS
fax 978-418-0058
www.gameops.com
info@gameops.com

**Street Characters**
#2 2828 18 St. NE
Calgary, AB T2E 7B1
888-627-2687
fax 403-250-3846
www.mascots.com
sales@mascots.com

**ZOOperstars!**
PO Box 36061
Louisville, KY 40233
www.zooperstars.com
johnny@zooperstars.com

## FIELD CONSTRUCTION/ RENOVATION

**Alpine Services Inc.**
5313 Brookeville Road
Gaithersburg, MD 20882
301-963-8833
301-963-7901
www.alpineservices.com
asi@alpineservices.com

## FIELD COVERS/TARPS

**C&H Baseball Inc.**
2215 60th Dr. East
Bradenton, FL 34203
941-727-1533
fax 941-727-0588
www.chbaseball.com
info@chbaseball.com

**Covermaster Inc.**
100 Westmore Dr. 11-D
Rexdale, ON M9V5C3
800-387-5808
416-742-6837
www.covermaster.com
info@covermaster.com

**National Sports Products**
3441 S. 11th Avenue
Eldridge, IA 52748
877-589-3342
fax 800-443-8907
www.nationalsportsproducts.com
sales@nationalsportsproducts.com

**Reef Industries**
9209 Almeda Genoa
Houston, TX 77075
713-507-4251
fax 713-507-4295
www.reefindustries.com
ri@reefindustries.com

## FIELD WALL PADDING

**C&H Baseball Inc.**
2215 60th Dr. East
Bradenton, FL 34203
941-727-1533
fax 941-727-0588
www.chbaseball.com
info@chbaseball.com

**Covermaster Inc.**
100 Westmore Dr. 11-D
Rexdale, ON M9V5C3
800-387-5808
416-742-6837
www.covermaster.com
info@covermaster.com

**Fisher Athletic**
2060 Cauble Rd. PO Box 28145
Salisbury, NC 28145
800-438-6028
fax 800-272-4448
www.fisherathletic.com
customerservice@fisherathletic.com

**L.A. Steelcraft Products**
PO Box 90365
Pasadena, CA 91109
626-798-7401/800-371-2438
fax 626-798-1482
www.lasteelcraft.com
info@lasteelcraft.com

**Promats Inc.**
PO Box 508
Ft. Collins, CO 80522
800-678-6287
970-482-7740
www.promats.com
info@promats.com

## FIREWORKS

**Fireworks Productions Inc.**
PO Box 294
Maryland Line, MD 21105
800-765-2264
410-357-0187
www.fireworksproductionsinc.com
larry@fireworksproductions.com

**Pyrotecnico**
PO Box 149
New Castle, PA 16103
800-854-4705
724-652-1288
www.pyrotecnico.com
svitale@pyrotecnico.com

**Zambelli Fireworks Int'l**
PO Box 1463
New Castle, PA 16103
800-245-0397
724-658-8318
www.zambellifireworks.com
zambelli@zambellifireworks.com

## FOOD SERVICE

**Concession Solutions Inc.**
16022-26th Ave NE
Shoreline, WA 98155
206-440-9203
206-440-9213
www.concessionsolutions.com
theresa@concessionsolutions.com

## GRAPHIC DESIGN

**Low and Inside Inc.**
2022 N. Ferry Street, Suite 3100
Minneapolis, MN 55303
763-797-0777
763-767-5510
www.lowandinside.com
creative@lowandinside.com

## HIGH SCHOOL SHOWCASE EVENTS/SCOUTING SERVICES

**Baseball Factory**
9176 Red Branch Road, Suite M
Columbia, MD 21045
800-641-4487
410-715-1975
www.baseballfactory.com

## INSURANCE

**K&K Insurance**
PO Box 2338
Fort Wayne, IN 46801
www.kandkinsurance.com

*See our ad after Page 224*

**Marketing, Etc.**
3675 Crestwood Pkwy. Ste. 380
Duluth, GA 30096
770-924-7366
fax 770-921-2199
www.holeandoneetc.com
info@holeinoneetc.com

## INSURANCE, LIFE AND DISABILITY

**Mar uis Investor Strategies, LLC, Glenn Kempa, Licensed Broker**
300 Motor Parkway Ste. 200
Hauppauge, NY 11788
800-477-5857
631-875-0166 Espanol
fax 516-935-6295
glennkempa@aol.com

## INVENTORY

**Retail Pro-BHD Information Systems**
3205 Ramos Circle
Sacramento, CA 95827
800-377-7776
fax 916-368-1411
www.bighairydog.com
info@bighairydog.com

## LIGHTING

**Musco Lighting, LLC**
200 1st Ave West
Oskaloosa, IA 52577
641-673-0411
fax 641-673-4740
www.musco.com
rick.sneed@musco.com

## MASCOTS

**Olympus Flag and Banner**
9000 W. Heather Ave.
Milwaukee, WI 53224
www.olympus-flag.com
diane.potter@olympus-flag.com

## Scollon Productions Inc.
PO Box 486
White Rock, SC 29177
803-345-3922
fax 803-345-9313
www.scollon.com
rick@scollon.com

## Street Characters
#2 2828 18 St. NE
Calgary, AB T2E 7B1
888-627-2687
fax 403-250-3846
www.mascots.com
sales@mascots.com

## Action Sports Media
4380 SW Macadam Ave. Suite 540
Portland, OR 97239
503-963-3802
fax 503-963-3822
www.gameopscommander.com
johnjackson@actionsportsmedia.com

## BaltimoreChop.com
625 Washington Blvd.
Baltimore, MD 21230
888-543-CHOP
www.baltimorechop.com
sales@baltimorechop.com

## Sound and Video Creations
2820 Azalea Place
Nashville, TN 37204
615-460-7331
fax 615-460-7331
www.clickeffects.com
fran2nz@aol.com

See our ad
on Page 25

## C&H Baseball Inc.
2215 60th Dr. East
Bradenton, FL 34203
941-727-1533
fax 941-727-0588
www.chbaseball.com
info@chbaseball.com

## L.A. Steelcraft Products
PO Box 90365
Pasadena, CA 91109
626-798-7401/800-371-2438
fax 626-798-1482
www.lasteelcraft.com
info@lasteelcraft.com

## Miller Net Company
PO Box 18787
Memphis, TN 38181
901-744-3804
901-743-6580
www.millernets.com
miller@millernets.com

## GCSC Inc.
POBox 7477
Wantagh, NY 11793
516-318-1940
631 875-0166 Espanol
fax 516-935-6295
GCSCforMLB@aol.com
www.gcscpromos.com

## Rico Industries Inc./Tag Express
7000 N. Austin
Nile, IL 60714
800-423-5856
fax 312-427-0190
www.ricoinc.com
jimz@ricoinc.com

## Throwthecurve.com
107 Pleasant Avenue
Upper Saddle, NJ 07458
877-448-2220
fax 201-760-8820
www.throwthecurve.com
info@baseballclinics.com

## Bata
2910 Norman Strasse Unit 102
San Marcos, CA 92069
760-597-9501
fax 760-597-9502
www.batabaseball.com
batabaseball@sbcglobal.net

## JKP Sports
PO Box 3126
Tualatin, OR 97062
800-547-6843
fax 503-691-1100
www.jugsports.com

## Master Pitching Machines
4200 Northeast Birmingham Road
Kansas City, MO 64117
800-878-8228
www.masterpitch.com

## Miller Net Company
PO Box 18787
Memphis, TN 38181
901-744-3804
901-743-6580
www.millernets.com
miller@millernets.com

## Sports Tutor Inc.
3300 Winona Ave.
Burbank, CA 91504
818-972-2772
818-972-9651
www.sportsmachines.com
jmillerst2@yahoo.com

## All-Pro Sports
5341 Derry Ave.
Agoura Hills, CA 91301
818-707-3178
www.allprosportshoes.com
allprosports@sbcglobal.net

## Beam Clay
Kelsey Park
Great Meadows, NJ 07838
800-247-Beam
Fax 908-637-8421
www.beamclay.com
partec@goes.com

See our ad
on Page 392

## C&H Baseball Inc.
2215 60th Dr. East
Bradenton, FL 34203
941-727-1533
fax 941-727-0588
www.chbaseball.com
info@chbaseball.com

## Diamond Pro (Txi)
1341 West Mockingbird Lane
Dallas, TX 75247
800-228-2987
800-640-6735
www.diamondpro.com
diamondpro@txi.com

## L.A. Steelcraft Products
PO Box 90365
Pasadena, CA 91109
626-798-7401/800-371-2438
fax 626-798-1482
www.lasteelcraft.com
info@lasteelcraft.com

## Midwest Athletic Surfaces
1125 West State St.
Marshfield, WI 54449
715-384-7027
fax 715-384-7027
webpages.charter.net/warningtrack
warningtrack@charter.net

## National Sports Products
3441 S. 11th Avenue
Eldridge, IA 52748
877-589-3342
fax 800-443-8907
www.nationalsportsproducts.com
sales@nationalsportsproducts.com

## Pro's Choice
410 N. Michigan Suite 400
Chicago, IL 60611
800-648-1166
fax 312-321-9525
www.proschoice1.com
proschoice@oildri.com

## Promats Inc.
PO Box 508
Ft. Collins, CO 80522
800-678-6287
970-482-7740
ww.promats.com
info@promats.com

## Retail Pro-BHD Information Systems
3205 Ramos Circle
Sacramento, CA 95827
800-377-7776
fax 916-368-1411
www.bighairydog.com
info@bighairydog.com

## PRINTING

**Low and Inside Inc.**
2022 N. Ferry, Suite 3100
Minneapolis, MN 55303
763-797-0777
fax 763-767-5510
www.lowandinside.com
creative@lowandinside.com

## PROFESSIONAL SERVICES

**Alpine Services Inc.**
5313- Brookeville Road
Gaithersburg, MD 20882
301-963-8833
301-963-7901
www.alpineservices.com
asi@alpineservices.com

## PROMOTIONAL ITEMS

**Bannerol Innovations Inc.**
10 Cross Street
Norwalk, CT 06851
404-661-3737
fax 404-745-8766
www.bannerolinnovations.com
stephanie@bannerolinnovations.com

**Gameops.com**
PO Box 770440
Lakewood, OH 44107
1-866-GAMEOPS
fax 978-418-0058
www.gameops.com
info@gameops.com

**Grand River Company**
16580 Harbor Blvd #C
Fountain Valley, CA 92708
714-839-8788
fax 714-839-9889
www.grandriverco.com
sales@grandriverco.com

**O-2 Cool**
1415 N. Dayton St.
Chicago, IL 60622
312-951-6700
312-951-6707
www.o2-cool.com
sales@o2-cool.com

**Phoenix Sports Inc.**
301 Boren Ave. North
Seattle, WA 98109
800-776-9229
fax 800-776-4422
www.phoenixsportsinc.com
phoesports@aol.com

**Rico Industries Inc./Tag Express**
7000 N. Austin
Niles, IL 60714
800-423-5856
fax 312-427-0190
www.ricoinc.com
jimz@ricoinc.com

**Street Characters**
#2 2828 18 St. NE
Calgary, AB T2E 7B1
888-627-2687
fax 403-250-3846
www.mascots.com
sales@mascots.com

## PROTECTIVE EQUIPMENT

**Ampac Ent./All-Star**
PO Box 1356
Shirley, MA 01464
978-425-6266
fax 978-425-4068
www.all-starsports.com
jurga@all-starsports.com

## PUBLICATIONS

**Junior Baseball Magazine**
PO Box 9099
Canoga Park, CA 91309
818-710-1234
818-710-1877
www.juniorbaseball.com
publisher@juniorbaseball.com

## RADAR EQUIPMENT

**Applied Concepts/Stalker Radar**
2609Technology Drive
Plano, TX 74074-7467
800-Stalker
www.stalkerradar.com

See our ad on Page 19

**JKP Sports**
PO Box 3126
Tualatin, OR 97062
800-547-6843
fax 503-691-1100
www.jugsports.com

## SCOREBOARDS

**360 Architecture**
2020 Baltimore Ave, Suite 400
Kansas City, MO 64108
816-472-3240
fax 816-472-2100
www.360architects.com

**All-American Scoreboards**
401 S. Main St.
Pardeeville, WI 53954
800-356-8146
fax 608-429-9216
www.allamericanscoreboards.com
scoreboards@everbrite.com

## SCOREBOOKS

**BaltimoreChop.com**
625 Washington Blvd.
Baltimore, MD 21230
888-543-CHOP
www.baltimorechop.com
sales@baltimorechop.com

## SEATING

**L.A Steelcraft Products**
PO Box 90365
Pasadena, CA 91109
626-798-7401/800-371-2438
fax 626-798-1482
www.lasteelcraft.com
info@laststeelcraft.com

**Southern Bleacher Company**
PO Box One
Graham, TX 76450
800-433-0912
fax 940-549-1365
www.southernbleacher.com
info@southernbleacher.com

## Sturdisteel Company
PO Box 2655
Waco, TX 76702
800-433-3116
fax 254-666-4472
www.sturdisteel.com
rgroppe@sturdisteel.com

See our ad on Page 17

## SOFTWARE

**E Solutions**
400 North Tampa Street 16th Floor
Tampa, FL 33602
888-840-4999
fax 813-342-2123
www.esnet.com
mmorizio@esnet.com

See our ad after Page 32

**Retail Pro-BHD Information Systems**
3205 Ramos Circle
Sacramento, CA 95827
800-377-7776
fax 916-368-1411
www.bighairydog.com
info@bighairydog.com

## SOUVENIERS

**Grand River Company**
16580 Harbor Blvd #C
Fountain Valley, CA 92708
714-839-8788
fax 714-839-9889
www.grandriverco.com
sales@grandriverco.com

## SPONSORSHIP SOFTWARE

**Sponsorship PRO+**
1954 Airport Road Ste 207
Atlanta, GA 30341
678-720-0700
fax 678-720-0704
www.sponsorshippro.com
sales@sponsoshippro.com

## SPORTING GOODS

**All-Pro Sports**
5341 Derry Ave.
Agoura Hills, CA 91301
818-707-3178
www.allprosportshoes.com
allprosports@sbcglobal.net

**Frank's Sport Shop**
430 East Tremont Avenue
New York, New York 10457
718-299-9628
fax 718-583-1652
www.frankssportshop.com

See our ad after Page 128

**JugheadSports**
107 Pleasant Avenue
Upper Saddle, NJ 07458
877-448-2220
fax 201-760-8820
www.jugheadsports.com
info@baseballclinics.com

## SPORTS MEDICINE

**Cho-Pat**
PO Box 293
Hainesport, NJ 08036
800-221-2601
609-261-7593
www.cho-pat.com
sales@cho-pat.com

## STADIUM ARCHITECTS

**360 Architecture**
1801 McGee St. Suite 200
Kansas City, MO 64108
816-472-3360
fax 816-531-3388
www.360architects.com
clamberth@360architects.com

## STATISTICAL SERVICES

**Baseball Info Solutions**
528 North New Street
Bethlehem, PA 18018
610-814-0107
fax 610-814-0166
www.baseballinfosolutions.com
info@baseballinforsolutions.com

## TICKETS

**Etix.com**
5171 Glenwood Ave.
Raliegh, NC, 27612
919-782-5010
www.etix.com
steve@etix.com
ben@etix.com

**National Ticket Co.**
PO Box 547
Shamokin, PA 17872
800-829-0829
570-672-2999
www.nationalticket.com
ticket@nationalticket.com

**Ticketcraft**
1390 Jerusalem Ave.
Merrick, NY 11566
800-645-4944
fax 516-538-4860
www.ticketcraft.com
tickets@ticketcraft.com

## TICKETING SOLUTIONS

**TicketForce**
835 W. Warner Rd. Ste. 101-421
Gilbert, AZ 85233
480-726-2581
480-840-0459
www.ticketforce.com
sales@ticketforce.com

## TRAINING EQUIPMENT

**Fitter International-XCO Trainers**
3050, 2600 Portland Street SE
Calgary, AB T264M6
403-243-3860
fax 403-229-1230
www.fitter1.com
media@fitter1.com

**Jump Stretch**
1230 N. Meridian Rd.
Youngstown, OH 44509
800-344-3539
fax 330-793-8719
www.jumpstretch.com

**Sports Tutor Inc.**
3300 Winona Ave.
Burbank, CA 91504
818-972-2772
818-972-9651
www.sportsmachines.com
jmillerst2@yahoo.com

## TRAVEL

**Broach Baseball Tours**
5821 Fairview Rd, Suite 118
Charlotte, NC 28209
800-849-6345
704-365-3800
www.baseballtoursusa.com
info@broachsportstours.com

**Sports Travel and Tours**
PO Box 50, 60 Main Street
Hatfield, MA 01038
413-247-7678
fax 413-247-5700
www.sportstravelandtours.com
christine@sportstravelandtours.com

**Trailway Transportation Systems Inc.**
3554 Chain Bridge Rd-Suite 301
Fairfax, VA 22030
703-691-3052
fax 703-691-9047
www.trailways.com
bustrails@trailways.com

## TRAVEL, TEAM

**World Sports International Sports Tours**
PO Box 661624
Los Angeles, CA 90495
800-496-8687
fax 310-314-8872
www.worldsport-tours.com

## UNIFORMS

**AIS Custom Uniforms**
2202 Anderson Street
Vernon, CA 90058
323-582-3005
323-582-2831
www.aisuniforms.com
info@aisuniforms.com

**Ampac Ent./All-Star**
PO Star 1356
Shirley, MA 01464
978-425-6266
fax 978-425-4068
www.all-starsports.com
jurga@all-starsports.com

**OT Sports**
172 Boone Street
Burlington, NC 27215
800-988-6285
fax 336-227-3765
www.otsports.com
sales@otsports.com

## VIDEOS

**BaltimoreChop.com**
625 Washington Blvd.
Baltimore, MD 21230
888-543-CHOP
www.baltimorechop.com
sales@baltimorechop.com

## WASTE RECEPTACLES

**Witt Industries**
4454 Steel Place
Cincinnati, Ohio 45209
800-543-7417
fax 877-891-8200
www.witt.com
products@witt.com

## WIND SCREENS

**C&H Baseball Inc.**
2215 60th Dr. East
Bradenton, FL 34203
941-727-1533
fax 941-727-0588
www.chbaseball.com
info@chbaseball.com

**Covermaster Inc.**
100 Westmore Dr. 11-D
Rexdale, ON M9V5C3
800-387-5808
416-742-6837
www.covermaster.com
info@covermaster.com

**Miller Net Company**
PO Box 18787
Memphis, TN 38181
901-744-3804
fax 901-743-6580
www.millernets.com
miller@millernets.com

**National Sports Products**
3441 S. 11th Avenue
Eldridge, IA 52748
877-589-3342
fax 800-443-8907
www.nationalsportsproducts.com
sales@nationalsportsproducts.com

# 2006 DIRECTORY
## INDEX

| 136 | Charlotte | IL | 704-357-8071 | 704-329-2155 |
| 161 | Chattanooga | Southern | 423-267-2208 | 423-267-4258 |
| 182 | Clearwater | FSL | 727-712-4300 | 727-712-4498 |
| 189 | Clinton | Midwest | 563-242-0727 | 563-242-1433 |
| 144 | Colorado Springs | PCL | 719-597-1449 | 719-597-2491 |
| 196 | Columbus, GA | SAL | 706-571-8866 | 706-571-9984 |
| 137 | Columbus, OH | IL | 614-462-5250 | 614-462-3271 |
| 155 | Connecticut | Eastern | 860-887-7962 | 860-886-5996 |
| 166 | Corpus Christi | Texas | 361-561-4665 | 361-561-4666 |
| 216 | Danville | Appy | 434-797-3792 | 434-797-3799 |
| 189 | Dayton | Midwest | 937-228-2287 | 937-228-2284 |
| 182 | Daytona | FSL | 386-257-3172 | 386-257-3382 |
| 196 | Delmarva | SAL | 410-219-3112 | 410-219-9164 |
| 183 | Dunedin | FSL | 727-733-9302 | 727-734-7661 |
| 137 | Durham | IL | 919-687-6500 | 919-687-6560 |
| 216 | Elizabethton | Appy | 423-547-6440 | 423-547-6442 |
| 155 | Erie | Eastern | 814-456-1300 | 814-456-7520 |
| 210 | Eugene | Northwest | 541-342-5367 | 541-342-6089 |
| 210 | Everett | Northwest | 425-258-3673 | 425-258-3675 |
| 183 | Fort Myers | FSL | 239-768-4210 | 239-768-4211 |
| 190 | Fort Wayne | Midwest | 260-482-6400 | 260-471-4678 |
| 177 | Frederick | Carolina | 301-662-0013 | 301-662-0018 |
| 145 | Fresno | PCL | 559-320-4487 | 559-264-0795 |
| 167 | Frisco | Texas | 972-731-9200 | 972-731-7455 |
| 220 | Great Falls | Pioneer | 406-452-5311 | 406-454-0811 |
| 197 | Greensboro | SAL | 336-268-2255 | 336-273-7350 |
| 217 | Greeneville | Appy | 423-638-0411 | 423-638-9450 |
| 197 | Greenville | SAL | 864-422-1510 | 864-422-1435 |
| 198 | Hagerstown | SAL | 301-791-6266 | 301-791-6066 |
| 155 | Harrisburg | Eastern | 717-231-4444 | 717-231-4445 |
| 221 | Helena | Pioneer | 406-495-0500 | 406-495-0900 |
| 198 | Hickory | SAL | 828-322-3000 | 828-322-6137 |
| 171 | High Desert | Cal | 760-246-6287 | 760-246-3197 |
| 204 | Hudson Valley | NY-P | 845-838-0094 | 845-838-0014 |
| 161 | Huntsville | Southern | 256-882-2562 | 256-880-0801 |
| 221 | Idaho Falls | Pioneer | 208-522-8363 | 208-522-9858 |
| 138 | Indianapolis | IL | 317-269-3542 | 317-269-3541 |
| 171 | Inland Empire | Cal | 909-888-9922 | 909-888-5251 |
| 145 | Iowa | PCL | 515-243-6111 | 515-243-5152 |
| 162 | Jacksonville | Southern | 904-358-2846 | 904-358-2845 |
| 205 | Jamestown | NY-P | 716-664-0915 | 716-664-4175 |
| 217 | Johnson City | Appy | 423-461-4866 | 423-461-4864 |
| 184 | Jupiter | FSL | 561-775-1818 | 561-691-6886 |
| 190 | Kane County | Midwest | 630-232-8811 | 630-232-8815 |
| 198 | Kannapolis | SAL | 704-932-3267 | 704-938-7040 |
| 217 | Kingsport | Appy | 423-378-3744 | 423-392-8538 |
| 177 | Kinston | Carolina | 252-527-9111 | 252-527-0498 |
| 199 | Lake County | SAL | 440-975-8085 | 440-975-8958 |
| 172 | Lake Elsinore | Cal | 951-245-4487 | 951-245-0305 |
| 184 | Lakeland | FSL | 863-686-8075 | 863-688-9589 |
| 199 | Lakewood | SAL | 732-901-7000 | 732-901-3967 |
| 172 | Lancaster | Cal | 661-726-5400 | 661-726-5406 |
| 191 | Lansing | Midwest | 517-485-4500 | 517-485-4518 |
| 146 | Las Vegas | PCL | 702-386-7200 | 702-386-7214 |
| 200 | Lexington | SAL | 859-252-0747 | 859-252-0747 |
| 138 | Louisville | IL | 502-212-2287 | 502-515-2255 |
| 205 | Lowell | NY-P | 978-459-2255 | 978-459-1674 |
| 177 | Lynchburg | Carolina | 434-528-1144 | 434-846-0768 |
| 205 | Mahoning Valley | NY-P | 330-505-0000 | 330-505-9696 |
| 146 | Memphis | PCL | 901-721-6000 | 901-842-1222 |
| 167 | Midland | Texas | 432-520-2255 | 432-520-8326 |
| 162 | Mississippi | Southern | 601-932-8788 | 601-936-3567 |
| 222 | Missoula | Pioneer | 406-543-3300 | 406-543-9463 |
| 163 | Mobile | Southern | 251-479-2327 | 251-476-1147 |
| 173 | Modesto | Cal | 209-572-4487 | 209-572-4490 |
| 163 | Montgomery | Southern | 334-323-2255 | 334-323-2225 |
| 178 | Myrtle Beach | Carolina | 843-918-6002 | 843-918-6001 |
| 147 | Nashville | PCL | 615-242-4371 | 615-256-5684 |
| 156 | New Britain | Eastern | 860-224-8383 | 860-225-6267 |
| 156 | New Hampshire | Eastern | 603-641-2005 | 603-641-2055 |
| 147 | New Orleans | PCL | 504-734-5155 | 504-734-5118 |
| 139 | Norfolk | IL | 757-622-2222 | 757-624-9090 |
| 222 | Ogden | Pioneer | 801-393-2400 | 801-393-2473 |

| 148 | Oklahoma | PCL | 405-218-1000 | 405-218-1001 |
| 148 | Omaha | PCL | 402-734-2550 | 402-734-7166 |
| 206 | Oneonta | NY-P | 607-432-6326 | 607-432-1965 |
| 223 | Orem | Pioneer | 801-377-2255 | 801-377-2345 |
| 139 | Ottawa | IL | 613-747-5969 | 613-747-0003 |
| 185 | Palm Beach | FSL | 561-775-1818 | 561-691-6886 |
| 140 | Pawtucket | IL | 401-724-7300 | 401-724-2140 |
| 191 | Peoria | Midwest | 309-680-4000 | 309-680-4080 |
| 157 | Portland, ME | Eastern | 207-874-9300 | 207-780-0317 |
| 149 | Portland, OR | PCL | 503-553-5400 | 503-553-5405 |
| 178 | Potomac | Carolina | 703-590-2311 | 703-590-5716 |
| 218 | Princeton | Appy | 304-487-2000 | 304-487-8762 |
| 218 | Pulaski | Appy | 540-980-1070 | 540-980-1850 |
| 191 | Quad Cities | Midwest | 563-324-3000 | 563-324-3109 |
| 173 | Rancho Cucamonga | Cal | 909-481-5000 | 909-481-5005 |
| 157 | Reading | Eastern | 610-375-8469 | 610-373-5868 |
| 140 | Richmond | IL | 804-359-4444 | 804-359-0731 |
| 141 | Rochester | IL | 585-454-1001 | 585-454-1056 |
| 200 | Rome | SAL | 706-368-9388 | 706-368-6525 |
| 149 | Round Rock | PCL | 512-255-2255 | 512-255-1558 |
| 150 | Sacramento | PCL | 916-376-4700 | 916-376-4710 |
| 185 | St. Lucie | FSL | 772-871-2100 | 772-878-9802 |
| 179 | Salem | Carolina | 540-389-3333 | 540-389-9710 |
| 211 | Salem-Keizer | Northwest | 503-390-2225 | 503-390-2227 |
| 150 | Salt Lake | PCL | 801-325-2273 | 801-485-6818 |
| 168 | San Antonio | Texas | 210-675-7275 | 210-670-0001 |
| 174 | San Jose | Cal | 408-297-1435 | 408-297-1453 |
| 185 | Sarasota | FSL | 941-365-4460 | 941-365-4217 |
| 201 | Savannah | SAL | 912-351-9150 | 912-352-9722 |
| 141 | Scranton/Wilkes-Barre | IL | 570-969-2255 | 570-963-6564 |
| 192 | South Bend | Midwest | 574-235-9988 | 574-235-9950 |
| 192 | Southwest Michigan | Midwest | 269-660-2287 | 269-660-2288 |
| 211 | Spokane | Northwest | 509-535-2922 | 509-534-5368 |
| 168 | Springfield | Texas | 417-863-2143 | 417-863-0388 |
| 206 | State College | NY-P | 814-272-1711 | 814-272-1718 |
| 207 | Staten Island | NY-P | 718-720-9265 | 718-273-5763 |
| 174 | Stockton | Cal | 209-644-1900 | 209-644-1931 |
| 142 | Syracuse | IL | 315-474-7833 | 315-474-2658 |
| 151 | Tacoma | PCL | 253-752-7707 | 253-752-7135 |
| 186 | Tampa | FSL | 813-875-7753 | 813-673-3174 |
| 164 | Tennessee | Southern | 865-286-2300 | 865-523-9913 |
| 142 | Toledo | IL | 419-725-4367 | 419-725-4368 |
| 158 | Trenton | Eastern | 609-394-3300 | 609-394-9666 |
| 207 | Tri-City, NY | NY-P | 518-629-2287 | 518-629-2299 |
| 212 | Tri-City, WA | Northwest | 509-544-8789 | 509-547-9570 |
| 151 | Tucson | PCL | 520-434-1021 | 520-889-9477 |
| 169 | Tulsa | Texas | 918-744-5998 | 918-747-3267 |
| 212 | Vancouver | Northwest | 604-872-5232 | 604-872-1714 |
| 208 | Vermont | NY-P | 802-655-4200 | 802-655-5660 |
| 186 | Vero Beach | FSL | 772-569-4900 | 772-567-0819 |
| 175 | Visalia | Cal | 559-625-0480 | 559-739-7732 |
| 193 | West Michigan | Midwest | 616-784-4131 | 616-784-4911 |
| 164 | West Tenn | Southern | 731-988-5299 | 731-988-5246 |
| 201 | West Virginia | SAL | 304-344-2287 | 304-344-0083 |
| 169 | Wichita | Texas | 316-267-3372 | 316-267-3382 |
| 208 | Williamsport | NY-P | 570-326-3389 | 570-326-3494 |
| 179 | Wilmington | Carolina | 302-888-2015 | 302-888-2032 |
| 180 | Winston-Salem | Carolina | 336-759-2233 | 336-759-2042 |
| 193 | Wisconsin | Midwest | 920-733-4152 | 920-733-8032 |
| 213 | Yakima | Northwest | 509-457-5151 | 509-457-9909 |

*Phone and FAX numbers for minor league offices can be found on page 129.*

## INDEPENDENT LEAGUE TEAMS

| Page | Club | League | Phone | FAX |
| --- | --- | --- | --- | --- |
| 265 | Atlantic City | Atlantic | 609-344-8873 | 609-344-7010 |
| 265 | Bridgeport | Atlantic | 203-345-4800 | 203-345-4830 |
| 269 | Brockton | Can-Am | 508-559-7000 | 508-587-2802 |
| 281 | Calgary | Northern | 403-277-2255 | — |
| 265 | Camden | Atlantic | 856-963-2600 | 856-963-8534 |
| 278 | Chico | Golden | 530-345-3210 | — |
| 273 | Chillicothe | Frontier | 740-773-8326 | 740-773-8338 |
| 260 | Coastal Bend | American Assoc. | 361-387-8585 | 361-387-3535 |

| 281 | Edmonton | Northern | 780-423-2255 | 780-423-3112 |
|-----|----------|----------|--------------|--------------|
| 260 | El Paso | American Assoc. | 915-755-2000 | 915-757-0671 |
| 273 | Evansville | Frontier | 812-435-8686 | 812-435-8688 |
| 281 | Fargo-Moorhead | Northern | 701-235-6161 | 701-297-9247 |
| 273 | Florence | Frontier | 859-594-4487 | 859-647-4639 |
| 261 | Fort Worth | American Assoc. | 817-226-2287 | 817-534-4620 |
| 278 | Fullerton | Golden | 714-526-8326 | — |
| 282 | Gary Southshore | Northern | 219-882-2255 | 219-882-2259 |
| 274 | Gateway | Frontier | 618-337-3000 | 618-332-3625 |
| 282 | Joliet | Northern | 815-726-2255 | 815-726-9223 |
| 274 | Kalamazoo | Frontier | 269-388-8326 | 269-388-8333 |
| 282 | Kansas City | Northern | 913-328-2255 | 913-685-5652 |
| 266 | Lancaster | Atlantic | 717-509-4487 | 717-509-4456 |
| 261 | Lincoln | American Assoc. | 402-474-2255 | 402-474-2254 |
| 278 | Long Beach | Golden | 562-597-9787 | — |
| 266 | Long Island | Atlantic | 631-940-3825 | 631-940-3800 |
| 269 | Nashua | Can-Am | 603-883-2255 | 603-883-0880 |
| 269 | New Haven County | Can-Am | 203-777-5636 | 203-777-4369 |
| 270 | New Jersey | Can-Am | 973-746-7434 | 973-655-8021 |
| 267 | Newark | Atlantic | 973-848-1000 | 973-621-0095 |
| 270 | North Shore | Can-Am | 781-592-0007 | 781-592-0004 |
| 261 | Pensacola | American Assoc. | 850-934-8444 | 850-934-8744 |
| 270 | Quebec | Can-Am | 418-521-2255 | 418-521-2266 |
| 279 | Reno | Golden | 775-348-7769 | — |
| 274 | River City | Frontier | 636-240-2287 | 636-240-7313 |
| 274 | Rockford | Frontier | 815-964-2255 | 815-964-2462 |
| 262 | St. Joseph | American Assoc. | 816-279-6777 | 816-279-9025 |
| 262 | St. Paul | American Assoc. | 651-644-3517 | 651-644-1627 |
| 279 | San Diego | Golden | 619-282-4487 | — |
| 283 | Schaumburg | Northern | 877-891-2255 | 847-891-6441 |
| 262 | Shreveport | American Assoc. | 318-636-5555 | 318-636-5670 |
| 263 | Sioux City | American Assoc. | 712-277-9467 | 712-277-9406 |
| 263 | Sioux Falls | American Assoc. | 605-333-0179 | 605-333-0193 |
| 267 | Somerset | Atlantic | 908-252-0700 | 908-252-0776 |
| 271 | Sussex | Can-Am | 973-300-1000 | 508-300-9000 |
| 275 | Traverse City | Frontier | 231-943-0100 | 231-943-0900 |
| 275 | Washington | Frontier | 724-250-9555 | 724-250-2333 |
| 276 | Windy City | Frontier | 708-489-2255 | 708-489-2999 |
| 283 | Winnipeg | Northern | 204-982-2273 | 204-982-2274 |
| 271 | Worcester | Can-Am | 508-792-2288 | 508-592-0004 |
| 279 | Yuma | Golden | 928-257-4700 | — |

## OTHER ORGANIZATIONS

| Page | Organization | Phone | FAX |
|------|-------------|-------|-----|
| 118 | ABC Sports | 212-456-4878 | 212-456-2877 |
| 373 | Academy of Pro Players | 973-772-3355 | 973-772-4839 |
| 363 | AFLAC High School Classic | 301-762-7894 | 301-762-1491 |
| 348 | African Baseball/Softball Assoc. | 234-66-224-711 | 234-66-224-555 |
| 350 | Alaska Baseball League | 907-283-6186 | 907-274-3628 |
| 373 | Aldrete Baseball Academy | 831-884-0400 | 831-884-0800 |
| 366 | All-American Amateur Baseball Association | 740-453-8351 | 740-453-3978 |
| 363 | All-American Baseball Talent Showcases | 856-354-0201 | 856-354-0818 |
| 373 | All-Star Baseball Academy | 610-355-2411 | 610-355-2414 |
| 366 | Amateur Athletic Union | 407-934-7200 | 407-934-7242 |
| 375 | Amateur Athletic Union Women's Baseball | 330-923-3400 | 330-923-1967 |
| 367 | American Amateur Baseball Congress | 505-327-3120 | 505-327-3132 |
| 367 | American Amateur Youth Baseball Alliance | 573-518-0319 | 314-822-4974 |
| 300 | American Baseball Coaches Association | 989-775-3300 | 989-775-3600 |
| 367 | American Legion Baseball | 317-630-1213 | 317-630-1369 |
| 363 | Area Code Games | 856-354-0201 | 856-354-0818 |
| 363 | Arizona Fall Classic | 602-978-2929 | 602-439-4494 |
| 297 | Arizona Fall League | 480-496-6700 | 480-496-6384 |
| 119 | Associated Press | 212-621-1630 | 212-621-1639 |
| 127 | Association of Professional Baseball Players | 714-935-9993 | 714-935-0431 |
| 349 | Athletes In Action | 937-352-1000 | 937-352-1245 |
| 121 | Athlon Sports Baseball | 615-327-0747 | 615-327-1149 |
| 350 | Atlantic Collegiate League | 917-882-5240 | - |
| 367 | Babe Ruth Baseball | 609-695-1434 | 609-695-2505 |
| 125 | Babe Ruth Birthplace/Orioles Museum | 410-727-1539 | 410-727-1652 |
| 374 | The Baseball Academy | 941-727-0303 | 941-727-2962 |
| 121 | Baseball America | 919-682-9635 | 919-682-2880 |
| 127 | Baseball Assistance Team | 212-931-7822 | 212-949-5433 |
| 362 | Baseball At The Beach | 843-546-3020 | 843-527-1816 |

| 349 | Baseball Canada | 613-748-5606 | 613-748-5767 |
|-----|-----------------|--------------|--------------|
| 127 | Baseball Chapel | 609-391-6444 | — |
| 348 | Baseball Confederation of Oceania | 61-3-9727-1779 | 61-3-9727-5959 |
| 121 | Baseball Digest | 847-491-6440 | 847-491-6203 |
| 363 | Baseball Factory | 410-715-5080 | 410-715-1975 |
| 348 | Baseball Federation of Asia | 81-3-320-11155 | 81-3-320-10707 |
| 127 | Baseball Trade Show | 727-822-6937 | 727-825-3785 |
| 373 | Baseball USA | 713-690-5055 | 713-690-9448 |
| 120 | Baseball Writers Association of America | 718-767-2582 | 718-767-2583 |
| 362 | Battle at the Ridge | 843-546-3020 | 843-527-1816 |
| 122 | Beckett Media | 800-840-3137 | 972-991-8930 |
| 119 | Bloomberg Sports News | 609-750-4691 | 609-897-8397 |
| 373 | Bucky Dent Baseball School | 561-265-0280 | 561-278-6679 |
| 118 | CBS Sports | 212-975-5230 | 212-975-4063 |
| 348 | COPABE | 507-2361-5977 | 507-261-5215 |
| 351 | California Collegiate League | 805-684-0657 | 805-684-8596 |
| 299 | California CC Commision on Athletics | 916-444-1600 | 916-444-2616 |
| 373 | California Competitive Youth Baseball | 714-993-2838 | 714-961-6078 |
| 351 | Cal Ripken Sr. Collegiate Baseball League | — | — |
| 125 | Canadian Baseball Hall of Fame | 519-284-1838 | 519-284-1234 |
| 119 | Canadian Press | 416-364-0321 | 416-364-0207 |
| 351 | Cape Cod League | 508-432-6909 | — |
| 295 | Caribbean Baseball Confederation | 809-562-4737 | 809-565-4654 |
| 352 | Central Illinois Collegiate League | 217-483-5673 | 217-786-2788 |
| 290 | China Baseball Association | 86-10-8582-6002 | 86-10-8582-5994 |
| 291 | Chinese Professional Baseball League | 886-2-2577-6992 | 886-2-2577-2606 |
| 353 | Clark Griffith League | 703-860-0946 | 703-860-0143 |
| 353 | Coastal Plain League | 919-852-1960 | 919-852-1973 |
| 373 | Cocoa Expo Sports Center | 321-639-3976 | 321-639-0598 |
| 365 | College Select Baseball Showcase | 800-782-3672 | — |
| 121 | Collegiate Baseball | 520-623-4530 | 520-624-5501 |
| 368 | Continental Amateur Baseball Association | 740-382-4620 | — |
| 373 | Cooperstown Baseball World | 888-229-8750 | 888-229-8720 |
| 373 | Cooperstown Dreams Park | 704-630-0050 | 704-630-0737 |
| 373 | Disney's Wide World of Sports | 407-938-3802 | 407-938-3442 |
| 369 | Dixie Baseball, Inc. | 903-927-2255 | 903-927-1846 |
| 369 | Dizzy Dean Baseball | 662-429-4365 | — |
| 289 | Dominican Summer League | 809-532-3619 | — |
| 295 | Dominican Winter League | 809-567-6371 | 809-567-5720 |
| 128 | Donruss/Playoff Trading Cards | 817-983-0300 | 817-983-0400 |
| 363 | Doyle Baseball Select Showcases | 863-439-1000 | 863-439-7086 |
| 292 | Dutch Major League | 31-30-607-6070 | 31-30-294-3043 |
| 117 | ESPN/ESPN2-TV | 860-766-2000 | 860-766-2213 |
| 121 | ESPN The Magazine | 212-515-1000 | 212-515-1290 |
| 119 | ESPN Radio | 860-766-2000 | 860-589-5523 |
| 363 | East Coast Professional Baseball Showcase | 910-962-3570 | — |
| 117 | Elias Sports Bureau | 212-869-1530 | 212-354-0980 |
| 348 | European Baseball Confederation | 32-3-219-0440 | 32-3-772-7727 |
| 126 | Field of Dreams Movie Site | 888-875-8404 | 319-875-7253 |
| 362 | First Bank HS Classic | 806-535-4505 | 806-794-5306 |
| 354 | Florida Collegiate Instructional League | 941-727-0303 | 941-727-2962 |
| 354 | Florida Collegiate Summer League | 407-694-6511 | 407-628-8535 |
| 117 | FOX Sports | 212-556-2500 | 212-354-6902 |
| 118 | FOX Sports Net | 310-369-1000 | 310-969-6049 |
| 374 | Frozen Ropes Training Centers | 877-846-5699 | 845-469-6742 |
| 362 | Gatorade Circle of Champions | 312-821-3593 | — |
| 128 | Grandstand Cards | 818-992-5642 | 818-348-9122 |
| 354 | Great Lakes League | 740-368-3527 | 740-368-3999 |
| 369 | Hap Dumont Youth Baseball | 316-721-1779 | 316-721-8054 |
| 125 | Harry Wendelstedt Umpire School | 386-672-4879 | 386-672-3212 |
| 362 | Horizon Cleats National High School Invitational | 602-867-9003 | — |
| 363 | Impact Baseball Showcase | — | — |
| 124 | Inside Edge Scouting | 800-808-3343 | 508-526-6145 |
| 348 | International Baseball Federation | 41-21-318-8240 | 41-21-318-8241 |
| 348 | International Olympic Committee | 41-21-621-6111 | 41-21-621-6216 |
| 362 | International Paper Classic | 843-527-9606 | 843-546-3807 |
| 348 | International Sports Group | 925-798-4591 | 925-680-1182 |
| 292 | Italian Serie A/1 | 39-06-36858376 | 39-06-36858201 |
| 290 | Japan League | 03-3502-0022 | 03-3502-0140 |
| 355 | Jayhawk League | 316-755-2361 | 316-755-1285 |
| 125 | Jim Evans Academy of Professional Umpiring | 512-335-5959 | 512-335-5411 |
| 121 | Junior Baseball Magazine | 818-710-1234 | 818-710-1877 |
| 373 | KC Sports Tournaments | 816-587-4545 | 816-587-4549 |

| | | | |
|---|---|---|---|
| 291 | Korea Baseball Organization | 02-3460-4643 | 02-3460-4649 |
| 122 | Krause Publications | 715-445-4612 | 715-445-4087 |
| 126 | Legends of the Game Baseball Museum | 817-273-5600 | — |
| 369 | Little League Baseball, Inc. | 570-326-1921 | 570-326-1074 |
| 126 | Little League Baseball Museum | 570-326-3607 | 570-326-2267 |
| 362 | Lions High School Invitational | 619-602-8650 | 619-239-3539 |
| 126 | Louisville Slugger Museum | 502-588-7228 | 502-585-1179 |
| 117 | MLB Advanced Media (MLB.com) | 212-485-3444 | 212-485-3456 |
| 119 | MLB.com Radio | 212-485-3444 | 212-485-3456 |
| 33 | MLB Commissioner's Office | 212-931-7800 | — |
| 33 | MLB International | 212-931-7500 | 212-949-5795 |
| 127 | MLB Players Alumni Association | 719-477-1870 | 719-477-1875 |
| 124 | MLB Players Association | 212-826-0808 | 212-752-4378 |
| 33 | MLB Productions | 212-931-7777 | 212-931-7788 |
| 124 | Major League Scouting Bureau | 909-980-1881 | 909-980-7794 |
| 374 | Mark Cresse Baseball School | 714-892-6145 | 714-892-1881 |
| 375 | Men's Adult Baseball League | 631-753-6725 | 631-753-4031 |
| 375 | Men's Senior Baseball League | 631-753-6725 | 631-753-4031 |
| 288 | Mexican League | 555-557-1007 | 555-395-2454 |
| 295 | Mexican Pacific League | 667-761-25-70 | 667-761-25-71 |
| 374 | Mickey Owen Baseball School | 800-999-8369 | 417-889-6978 |
| 364 | Mid-America Five Star Showcase | 513-247-9511 | 513-247-0040 |
| 129 | Minor League Baseball | 727-822-6937 | 727-821-5819 |
| 127 | Minor League Baseball Alumni Association | 727-477-6937 | 727-825-3785 |
| 355 | Mountain Collegiate Baseball League | — | |
| 128 | Multi-Ad Sports | 800-348-6485 | 309-692-8378 |
| 299 | NAIA | 913-791-0044 | 913-791-9555 |
| 118 | NBC Sports | 212-664-2014 | 212-664-6365 |
| 299 | NCAA | 317-917-6857 | 317-917-6826 |
| 299 | NJCAA | 719-590-9788 | 719-590-7324 |
| 128 | National Adult Baseball Association | 800-621-6479 | 303-639-6605 |
| 350 | National Alliance of Collegiate Summer Baseball | 704-896-9100 | — |
| 369 | National Amateur Baseball Federation | 301-464-5460 | 301-352-0214 |
| 349 | National Baseball Congress | 316-267-3372 | 316-267-3382 |
| 126 | National Baseball Hall of Fame | 607-547-7200 | 607-547-2044 |
| 120 | National Collegiate Baseball Writers | 214-753-0102 | 214-753-0145 |
| 362 | National Federation of State High School Association | 317-972-6900 | 317-822-5700 |
| 362 | National High School Baseball Coaches Association | 602-615-0571 | 480-838-7133 |
| 126 | Negro Leagues Baseball Museum | 816-221-1920 | 816-221-8424 |
| 356 | New England Collegiate League | — | |
| 356 | New York Collegiate League | 585-223-2328 | — |
| 126 | Nolan Ryan Foundation and Exhibit Center | 281-388-1134 | 281-388-1135 |
| 374 | North Carolina Baseball Academy | 336-931-1118 | — |
| 356 | Northwoods League | 507-536-4579 | 507-289-1866 |
| 122 | Outside Pitch (Orioles) | 410-234-8888 | 410-234-1029 |
| 357 | Pacific International League | 206-623-8844 | 602-623-8361 |
| 364 | Pacific Northwest Championship | 253-536-8001 | — |
| 374 | Pennsylvania Diamond Bucks Camp | 610-838-1219 | — |
| 364 | Perfect Game USA | 800-447-9362 | 319-298-2924 |
| 370 | Police Athletic Leagues | 561-844-1823 | 561-863-6120 |
| 370 | PONY Baseball, Inc. | 724-225-1060 | 724-225-9852 |
| 125 | Professional Baseball Athletic Trainers Society | 404-875-4000 | 404-892-8560 |
| 128 | Professional Baseball Employment Opportunities | 866-937-7236 | 727-821-5819 |
| 374 | Professional Baseball Instruction | 877-448-2220 | 201-760-8820 |
| 124 | Professional Baseball Scouts Foundation | 310-858-1935 | 310-246-4862 |
| 125 | Professional Baseball Umpire Corp. | 727-822-6937 | 727-821-5819 |
| 125 | Prospects Plus/The Scouting Report | 800-845-2726 | 919-682-2880 |
| 296 | Puerto Rican League | 787-765-6285 | 787-767-3028 |
| 370 | RBI | 212-931-7897 | 212-949-5695 |
| 122 | Reds Report | 614-486-2202 | 614-486-3650 |
| 374 | Ripken Baseball Camps | 800-486-0850 | |
| 118 | Rogers SportsNet | 416-332-5600 | 416-332-5767 |
| 375 | Roy Hobbs Baseball | 330-923-3400 | 330-923-1967 |
| 127 | SABR | 216-575-0500 | 216-575-0502 |
| 124 | Scout of the Year Foundation | 561-798-5897 | 561-798-4644 |
| 364 | Selectfest Baseball | 973-539-4781 | — |
| 374 | Sho-Me Baseball Camp | 800-993-2267 | 417-338-5838 |
| 125 | Skillshow, Inc. | 610-687-9072 | 610-687-9629 |
| 357 | Southern Collegiate League | 704-847-5075 | 704-847-1455 |
| 374 | Southwest Professional Baseball School | 888-830-8031 | 480-830-7455 |
| 122 | The Sports Encyclopedia: Baseball | 212-764-5151 | — |
| 120 | The Sporting News | 314-997-7111 | 314-997-0765 |
| 121 | Sporting News Baseball Yearbook | 314-997-7111 | 314-997-0765 |

| | | | |
|---|---|---|---|
| 119 | Sporting News Radio Network | 847-509-1661 | 847-509-1677 |
| 119 | Sports Byline USA | 415-434-8300 | 415-391-2569 |
| 120 | SportsTicker | 201-309-1200 | 201-860-9742 |
| 120 | Sports Illustrated | 212-522-1212 | 212-522-4543 |
| 121 | Sports Illustrated for Kids | 212-522-1212 | 212-522-0120 |
| 118 | The Sports Network | 416-332-5000 | 416-332-7658 |
| 121 | Spring Training Baseball Yearbook | 919-967-2420 | 919-967-6294 |
| 117 | STATS, Inc. | 847-583-2100 | 847-470-9160 |
| 121 | Street and Smith's Baseball Yearbook | 704-973-1575 | 704-973-1576 |
| 350 | Summer Collegiate Baseball Association | 919-852-1960 | — |
| 363 | Sunbelt High School Baseball Classic Series | 405-348-3839 | 405-340-7538 |
| 370 | Super Series Baseball of America | 480-664-2998 | 480-664-2997 |
| 371 | T-Ball USA Association, Inc. | 203-381-1449 | 203-381-1440 |
| 118 | TBS | 404-827-1700 | 404-827-1593 |
| 365 | Team One Showcases | 859-466-8326 | — |
| 127 | Ted Williams Museum/Hitters Hall of Fame | 352-527-6566 | 352-527-4163 |
| 358 | Texas Collegiate League | 807-339-9367 | 817-339-9309 |
| 365 | Top 96 Showcase | 508-651-0165 | — |
| 365 | Top Guns Showcase | 208-762-1100 | — |
| 128 | Topps | 212-376-0300 | 212-376-0573 |
| 122 | Total Baseball | 416-466-0418 | 416-466-9530 |
| 370 | Triple Crown Sports | 970-223-6644 | 970-223-3636 |
| 128 | Upper Deck | 800-873-7332 | 760-929-6548 |
| 371 | US Amateur Baseball Association | 425-776-7130 | — |
| 371 | US Amateur Baseball Federation | 619-934-2551 | 619-271-6659 |
| 372 | US Specialty Sports Association | 816-587-4545 | 816-587-4549 |
| 349 | USA Baseball | 919-474-8721 | 919-474-8822 |
| 362 | USA HS Classic | 901-872-8326 | 901-681-9443 |
| 372 | USA Junior Olympic BB Championship | 919-474-8721 | 919-474-8822 |
| 372 | USSSA | 816-587-4545 | 816-587-4549 |
| 348 | US Olympic Committee | 719-866-4500 | 719-866-4654 |
| 120 | USA Today | 703-854-5954 | 703-854-2072 |
| 120 | USA Today Sports Weekly | 703-854-6319 | 703-854-2034 |
| 374 | Utah Baseball Academy | 801-561-1700 | 801-561-5965 |
| 359 | Valley League | 540-885-8901 | 540-885-2068 |
| 289 | Venezuelan Summer League | 58-241-824-0321 | 58-241-824-0705 |
| 296 | Venezuelan Winter League | 58-212-761-4932 | 58-212-761-7661 |
| 122 | Vine Line (Cubs) | 773-404-2827 | 773-404-4129 |
| 119 | WGN | 773-528-2311 | 773-528-6050 |
| 362 | West Coast Classic | 408-252-6670 | — |
| 359 | West Coast Collegiate League | 509-888-9378 | — |
| 125 | World Umpires Association | 920-969-1580 | 920-969-1892 |
| 372 | World Wood Bat Association | 319-298-2923 | 319-298-2924 |
| 119 | XM Satellite Radio | 202-380-4000 | 202-280-4500 |
| 122 | Yankees Magazine | 800-469-2657 | — |